The
Pub Guide
2010

AA Lifestyle Guides

13th edition September 2009.
© AA Media Limited 2009.

Please contact:
Advertising Sales Department: advertisingsales@theAA.com
Editorial Department: lifestyleguides@theAA.com

AA Media Limited would like to thank the following photographers, companies and picture libraries for their assistance in the preparation of this book.
Abbreviations for the picture credits are as follows: (t) top; (b) bottom; (l) left; (r) right; (c) centre; (AA) AA World Travel Library.
Front Cover: (t) Hind's Head Hotel, Bray photo by Ashley Palmer Watts; (bl) Royal Oak Inn; (br) The Bridge Inn & Restaurant, Barnard Castle;
Back Cover: (l) AA/C Sawyer; (c) The Horns, Crazies Hill; (r) AA/R Ireland.
Every effort has been made to trace the copyright holders, and we apologise in advance for any accidental errors. We would be happy to apply any corrections in the following edition of this publication.
Photographs in the gazetteer provided by the establishments.
Typeset/Repro: Keenes, Andover.
Printed in Italy by Printer Trento SRL, Trento
This directory is compiled by AA Lifestyle Guides; managed in the Librios Information Management System and generated by the AA establishment database system.
Pub descriptions have been contributed by the following team of writers: Phil Bryant, David Foster, David Halford, David Hancock, Julia Hynard and Jenny White.
Published by AA Publishing, a trading name of AA Media Limited, whose registered office is Fanum House, Basing View, Basingstoke RG21 4EA. Registered number 06112600.
A CIP catalogue for this book is available from the British Library.
ISBN: 978-0-7495-6282-3
A03989

Maps prepared by the Mapping Services Department of AA Publishing.

Maps © AA Media Limited 2009.

 This product includes mapping data licensed from Ordnance Survey® with the permission of the Controller of Her Majesty's Stationery Office. © Crown copyright 2009. All rights reserved. Licence number 100021153.

Information on National Parks in England provided by the Countryside Agency (Natural England).
Information on National Parks in Scotland provided by Scottish Natural Heritage.
Information on National Parks in Wales provided by The Countryside Council for Wales.

Contents

How to Use the Guide

1 LOCATION

Guide order Pubs are listed alphabetically by name (ignoring The) under their village or town. Towns and villages are listed alphabetically within their county (a county map appears at the back of the guide). The guide has entries for England, Channel Islands, Isle of Man, Scotland and Wales in that order. Some village pubs prefer to be initially located under the nearest town, in which case the village name is included in the address and directions.

Pick of the Pubs Around 750 of the best pubs in Britain have been selected by the editor and inspectors and these are highlighted. They have longer, more detailed descriptions and a tinted background. Around 220 of these have a full page entry and two photographs.

2 MAP REFERENCE

The map reference number denotes the map page number in the atlas section at the back of the book and (except for London maps) the National Grid reference. The London map references help locate their position on the Central and Greater London maps.

3 ESTABLISHMENT NAME AND SYMBOLS

See Key to symbols in the panel on page 5.

4 ADDRESS AND POSTCODE DETAILS

This gives the street name and the postcode, and if necessary the name of the village is included (see 1 above). This may be up to five miles from the named location.

☎ **Telephone number,** 🖶 **fax number, e-mail and websites:** Wherever possible we have included an e-mail address.

5 DIRECTIONS

Directions are given only when they have been supplied by the proprietor.

6 DESCRIPTION

Description of the pub and food.

7 OPEN

Indicates the hours and dates when the establishment is open and closed.

1

2

DENHAM	Map 06 TQ08

3

The Falcon Inn NEW ★★★★ INN ⊕ ♟

14

4

Village Rd UB9 5BE ☎ **01895 832125**
e–mail: falcon.inn@btconnect.com
dir: *Exit M40 junct 1, follow A40/Gerrards Cross signs. Approx 200yds turn right onto Old Mill Rd. Pass church on right, enter village. Pub opposite village green*

5

6

This traditional 16th-century inn, located opposite the green in beautiful Denham Village, is an ideal base for exploring Colne Valley Country Park. Expect excellent real ales and award-winning food. Lunch could include Spanish tortilla with mixed salad, or a home-made burger with fries; in the evening, perhaps ginger king prawns and scallops with aubergine caviar, rôsti potatoes, langoustine and herb oil, or rack of lamb with marinated courgettes, straw potatoes and red wine sauce. There are four comfortable en suite bedrooms if you would like to stay over.

7

Open 12-3 5-11 (summer Sat/Sun 12-11) **Bar Meals** L served all week 12-2.30 D served all week 6.30–9.30 (Sun 12-4) Av main course £9 **Restaurant** L served Mon-Sat 12-2.30 D served Mon-Sat 6.30-10 (Sun 12-4, 6.30-9.30) ⊕ FREE HOUSE ◀ Timothy Taylor Landlord, Bombardier, Youngs, Deuchars, Guest ale Ò Aspall ♟ 11

8

9

10

11

Facilities Children's menu Garden Parking **Rooms** 4

12

13

Notes ⊠

---

8 BAR MEALS

Indicates the times and days when proprietors tell us bar food can be ordered, and the average price of a main course as supplied by the proprietor. Please be aware that last orders could vary by up to 30 minutes.

9 RESTAURANT

Indicates the times and days when proprietors tell us food can be ordered from the restaurant. The average cost of a 3-course à la carte meal and a 3- or 4-course fixed-price menu are shown as supplied by the proprietor. Last orders may be approximately 30 minutes before the times stated.

10 ⊕ BREWERY AND COMPANY

This is the name of the Brewery to which the pub is tied, or the Company which owns it. A free house is where the pub is independently owned and run.

◀ **The beer tankard symbol** indicates the principal beers sold by the pub. Up to five cask or hand-pulled beers are listed. Many pubs have a much greater selection, with several guest beers each week.

ŏ **The apple symbol** indicates that real cider is available and listed.

♀ **The wine glass symbol** followed by a number indicates the number of wines sold by the glass.

11 FACILITIES

Indicates if a pub has a children's menu (which might mean children's portions), a garden, allows dogs on the premises, offers parking and has a children's play area. For further information please phone the pub.

12 ROOMS

Only accommodation that has been inspected is indicated. In the case of AA rated accommodation only, the number of en suite bedrooms is listed. Many pubs have rooms but we only indicate those that are AA rated.

13 NOTES

As so many establishments take one or more of the major credit cards we only indicate if a pub does not take cards.

14 AA STARS/DESIGNATORS

AA Stars (and designators as appropriate) are shown at the beginning of an entry. The AA, in partnership with the national tourist bodies (VisitBritain, VisitScotland and VisitWales) has introduced new Quality Standards for accommodation that is inspected. See pages 6-7 for details of AA ratings.

KEY TO SYMBOLS

◎	Rosettes – The AA's food award. Explanation on page 7
★★	Stars – Accommodation rating. Explanation on pages 6–7
⊕	Barrel – Name of Brewery, Company or Free House
◀	Tankard – Principal beers sold
ŏ	Apple – Real cider available
♀	Wine glass – Indicates that at least six wines are available by the glass. For the exact number of wines served this way, see notes at the bottom of each entry
NEW	Pubs appearing in the guide for the first time in 2010

AA Classifications and Awards

AA Classifications & Awards

Many of the pubs in this Guide offer accommodation. Where a Star rating appears next to an entry's name in the Guide, the establishment has been inspected by the AA under common Quality Standards agreed between the AA, VisitBritain, VisitScotland and VisitWales. These ratings are for the accommodation, and ensure that it meets the highest standards of cleanliness, with an emphasis on professionalism, proper booking procedures and prompt and efficient services. Some of the pubs in this Guide offer accommodation but do not belong to a rating scheme. In this case the accommodation is not included in their entry.

AA recognised establishments pay an annual fee that varies according to the classification and the number of bedrooms. The establishments receive an unannounced inspection from a qualified AA inspector who recommends the appropriate classification. Return visits confirm that standards are maintained; the classification is not transferable if an establishment changes hands.

The annual *AA Hotel Guide* and *AA Bed & Breakfast Guide* give further details of recognised establishments and the classification schemes. Details of AA recognised hotels, guest accommodation, restaurants and pubs are also available at **theAA.com,** along with a useful Route Planner.

AA Hotel Classification

Hotels are classified on a 5-point scale, with one star being the simplest, and five stars offering a luxurious service at the top of the range. The AA's top hotels in Britain and Ireland are identified by red stars. (★)

In addition to the main **Hotel** (HL) classification which applies to some pubs in this Guide, there are other categories of hotel applicable also to pubs, as follows:

Town House Hotel (TH) - A small, individual city or town centre property, which provides a high degree of personal service and privacy

Country House Hotel (CHH) - Quietly located in a rural area

Small Hotel (SHL) - Has fewer than 20 bedrooms and is owner managed

Metro Hotel (MET) - A hotel in an urban location that does not offer an evening meal

Budget Hotel (BUD) - These are usually purpose-built modern properties offering inexpensive accommodation. Often located near motorways and in town or city centres. **They are not awarded stars**

AA Guest Accommodation

Guest accommodation is also classified on a scale of one to five stars, with one being the most simple, and five being more luxurious. Yellow stars (★) indicate the very best B&Bs, Guest Houses, Farmhouses, Inns and Guest Accommodation in the 3, 4 and 5 star ratings. Stars have replaced the Diamond Classification for this type of accommodation, in accordance with Common Standards agreed between the AA and the UK tourist authorities of VisitEngland, VisitScotland and VisitWales. To differentiate them from Hotel Stars, they have been given a series of designators appropriate to the type of accommodation they offer, as follows:

Bed & Breakfast (B&B) – Accommodation provided in a private house, run by the owner and with no more than six paying guests

Guest House (GH) – Accommodation provided for more than six paying guests and run on a more commercial basis than a B&B. Usually more services, for example dinner, provided by staff as well as the owner

Farmhouse (FH) – B&B or guest house rooms provided on a working farm or smallholding

Restaurant with Rooms (RR) – Destination restaurant offering overnight accommodation. The restaurant is the main business and is open to non-residents. A high standard of food should be offered, at least five nights a week. A maximum of 12 bedrooms. Most Restaurants with Rooms have been awarded AA Rosettes for their food

Guest Accommodation (GA) – Any establishment which meets the entry requirements for the Scheme can choose this designator

Inn (INN) – Accommodation provided in a fully licensed establishment. The bar will be open to non-residents and provide food in the evenings
U A small number of pubs have this symbol because their Star classification was not confirmed at the time of going to press
A Refers to hotels rated by another organisation, eg VisitBritain.

Rosette Awards

Out of the thousands of restaurants in the British Isles, the AA identifies, with its Rosette Awards, around 2000 as the best. What to expect from restaurants with AA Rosette Awards is outlined here; for a more detailed explanation of Rosette criteria please see **theAA.com**

⍟ Excellent local restaurants serving food prepared with care, understanding and skill and using good quality ingredients.

⍟⍟ The best local restaurants, which consistently aim for and achieve higher standards and where a greater precision is apparent in the cooking. Obvious attention is paid to the selection of quality ingredients.

⍟⍟⍟ Outstanding restaurants that demand recognition well beyond their local area.

⍟⍟⍟⍟ Amongst the very best restaurants in the British Isles, where the cooking demands national recognition.

⍟⍟⍟⍟⍟ The finest restaurants in the British Isles, where the cooking stands comparison with the best in the world.

AA Pub of the Year

The AA Pub of the Year for England, Scotland and Wales have been selected with the help of our AA inspectors; we have chosen three very worthy winners for this prestigious annual award.

The winners stand out for being great all-round pubs or inns, combining a good pub atmosphere, a warm welcome from friendly, efficient hosts and staff, excellent food and well-kept beers.

ENGLAND

THE TROUT INN AT TADPOLE BRIDGE ★★★★ INN
FARINGDON, OXFORDSHIRE

Page 364

Sitting peacefully on the River Thames twenty minutes from Oxford is this historic, multi-award-winning free house with rooms. A destination in its own right, it offers log fires, cask ales, riverside garden and walks, berthing for six boats and a kitchen that makes expert use of the best local ingredients. Having run several fine-dining restaurants, owners Gareth and Helen wanted somewhere to raise their family, so the need for games, toys, space and a decent children's menu is understood. The two of them take food seriously, but not so much as to marginalise the drinker, as the locals coming in every night for the fine range of regional beers would undoubtedly affirm. From a sample menu come smoked eel salad with Noilly Prat jelly and shallot purée; followed by steamed beef and ale pudding or blue brie and sun-blushed tomato strudel. There are six luxury bedrooms available if you would like to stay over.

SCOTLAND

THE INN AT INVERBEG ★ ★ ★ ★ INN
LUSS, ARGYLL AND BUTE

Page 554

Situated just off the A82 and commanding stunning views across Loch Lomond and its surrounding hills, this is Scotland's first boutique inn. Dating from 1814, it has been remodelled and refurbished in contemporary style, yet retains its old-world charm and character – typically find roaring log fires fronted by swish leather and cow hide seating. At the Whisky Bar you have over 200 malts and real ales like Deuchars IPA to choose from and in Mr C's, the relaxed and informal dining room, you can tuck into fresh, sustainable fish caught off Scottish shores. Start with steamed mussels, Loch Fyne oysters or chilli-coated squid with garlic mayonnaise, move on to fishcakes with spinach and lemon hollandaise or simply grilled cod or haddock served with chips, or Buccleuch sirloin steak with herb butter. Comfortable, individually styled rooms are split between the inn and a sumptuous beach house beside the loch, the latter featuring wooden floors, hand-crafted furniture, crisp linen, and a hot tub.

WALES

THE QUEEN'S HEAD
LLANDUDNO JUNCTION, CONWY

Page 587

Just five minutes from the seaside at Llandudno, this charming free house is perfectly situated for country walks, cycling, or a day on the beach. Owners Rob and Sally Cureton have created one of North Wales' best-kept secrets: a smart country pub with creative, appealing menus, a good selection of wines and beers, and a team of attentive staff. The stylish patio is great for summer evenings, whilst on colder nights the relaxed atmosphere in the bar makes it just the place for a pre-dinner drink by the log fire. Creative chefs make good use of local produce, modern and traditional ideas and freshly prepared dishes. Varied menus range from light lunchtime bites such as warm brie and crispy bacon on ciabatta bread, with balsamic drizzle and vine tomatoes; to more substantial fare that reflects the inn's surroundings – try Welsh lamb shank with rosemary and redcurrant jus, or Conwy mussels with brown bread and butter. Leave room for the extravagant home-made desserts.

Welcome to the Guide

We aim to bring you the country's best pubs, selected for their atmosphere, great food and good beer. Ours is the only major pub guide to feature colour photographs, and to highlight the 'Pick of the Pubs', revealing Britain's finest hostelries. Updated every year, this edition includes lots of old favourites, as well as plenty of new destinations for eating and drinking, and great places to stay across Britain.

Who's in the Guide?

We make our selection by seeking out pubs that are worth making a detour - 'destination' pubs - with publicans exhibiting real enthusiasm for their trade and offering a good selection of well-kept drinks and good food. We also choose neighbourhood pubs supported by locals and attractive to passing motorists or walkers. Our selected pubs make no payment for their inclusion in our guide. They are included entirely at our discretion.

Tempting Food

We are looking for menus that show a commitment to home cooking, making good use of local produce wherever possible, and offering an appetising range of freshly-prepared dishes. Pubs presenting well-executed traditional dishes like ploughman's or pies, or those offering innovative bar or restaurant food, are all in the running. In keeping with recent trends in pub food, we are keen to include those where particular emphasis is placed on imaginative modern dishes. Occasionally we include pubs that serve no food, or just snacks, but are very special in other ways.

That Special Place

We look for pubs that offer something special: pubs where the time-honoured values of a convivial environment for conversation while supping or eating have not been forgotten. They may be attractive, interesting, unusual or in a

good location. Some may be very much a local pub or they may draw customers from further afield, while others may be included because they are in an exceptional place. Interesting towns and villages, eccentric or historic buildings, and rare settings can all be found within this guide.

Pick of the Pubs and Full Page Entries

Some of the pubs included in the guide are particularly special, and we have highlighted these as Pick of the Pubs. For 2010 around 750 pubs have been selected by the personal knowledge of our editorial team, our AA inspectors, and suggestions from our readers. These pubs have a coloured panel

and a more detailed description. From these, around 220 have chosen to enhance their entry in the 2010 Guide by purchasing two photographs as part of a full-page entry.

Smoking Regulations

A law banning smoking in public places came into force in July 2007. This covers all establishments in this guide. Some pubs provide a private area in, for example an outbuilding, for smokers. If the freedom to smoke is important to you, we recommend that you check with the pub when you book.

Tell us what you think

We welcome your feedback about the pubs included and about the guide itself. We are also delighted to receive suggestions about good pubs you have visited and loved. A Reader's Report form appears at the back of the book, so please write in or e-mail us at lifestyleguides@theAA.com to help us improve future editions. The pubs also feature on the AA website, **theAA.com**, along with our inspected restaurants, hotels and bed & breakfast accommodation.

Ye Olde Trip to Jerusalem

WHERE DO PUB NAMES COME FROM?

by **Norman Miller**

Ever since people began naming pubs back around the 12th century, debates over derivations could drive you to drink.

Take The Old Bull & Bush, a name made famous in the 1920s music-hall song by Florrie Forde with its "Down at the Old Bull & Bush" singalong chorus.

One side say it just joins two words with deep roots in the naming game: Bull indicating a place that was once a farmhouse, Bush as the English take on the vine leaves traditionally hung outside Roman drinking dens. Oh no, say others: the name is an English corruption of 'Boulogne Bouche' - the mouth of Boulogne being a reference to the city harbour where Henry VIII scored a victory over the French by way of distraction from his marital difficulties.

As far as the venerable Hampstead boozer celebrated in the song is concerned the first explanation looks sounder, since it sits on the site of a 17th century farmhouse that began selling ale in the 1720s before becoming a beacon for Cockneys on a day out to the Heath.

Similar arguments swirl round other names. To romantics, *Bag O'Nails* is a corruption of Bacchanals (a suitably boozy possibility, for sure) though others scoff at the idea and say it's just a reference to olde days when a lot of drinkers were workmen who needed bags of nails when not needing beer.

Or how about *Elephant & Castle*? Does it really refer to 'La Infante de Castile' - a nod to various Spanish princesses who played a part in English history, such as Catherine of Aragon or Maria, daughter of Philip III? Or is it inspired by a fabulous vision apparently spotted on London Bridge of an elephant with a castle on its back in the clouds (possibly after a few drinks)? More prosaically, it could have something to do with the elephant and castle on the arms of the Worshipful Company of Cutlers, a venerable London trading guild.

Another thorny thicket of derivations revolves around the various pubs called *The Case Is Altered*. Some credit the name to 19th century British soldiers returning from fighting in Spain with various misunderstood Spanish phrases - Casa Alta (high house), Casa Altera

("alternative/second house") or even a euphemism for a brothel (based on something like Casa Salterinas, a house of 'dancers').

More likely, though, it is just a legal reference, via a phrase coined by 16th century lawyer Edmund Plowden when new evidence arose in court. When Ben Jonson used it as the title for a 1590s comedy, perhaps pubs with a legal wrangle in their history were inspired to take it up. Though I'm not saying anything definite until I've spoken to a lawyer!

In the meantime, why would quite a few pubs call themselves *The Goat & Compass*? Rather than anything weird involving an animal with an interest in magnetic North, fans of English corruptions suggest it's a take on the phrase "God Encompasses" or "God encompasseth us" from a more religious era. Pah!, say the prosaic set. It's just another coat-of-arms reference, this time to the Worshipful Company of Cordwainers, who in olden days made shoes from goat skin.

Religious notions

Religion does, however, clearly underpin some other classic pub names. Some are linked to the Crusades, such as *Ye Olde Trip to Jerusalem*, a name most famously borne by a 12th century Nottingham inn popular with soldiers en route to the Holy Land. Other variations on this theme include *The Saracen's Head* and *Lamb & Flag* (the lamb represents Christ with the flag the sign of the Crusaders). Religious connections also survive in two names that might at first seem nautical - *The Ship* (symbolising the Ark) and *The Anchor* (the Christian faith) - hence also *The Hope & Anchor*. Add to those, *The Crossed Keys* - emblem of St. Peter.

Royalty links

Royalty has inspired several names. *The Red Lion* - second only to *The Crown* in the name stakes - refers to the gaudy big cat on various coats-of-arms, notably James I (VI of Scotland) whose red lion symbol was displayed on many buildings after he unified the thrones of England and Scotland in 1603.

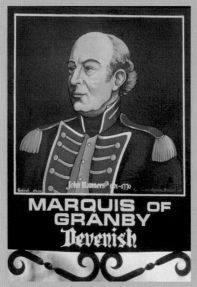

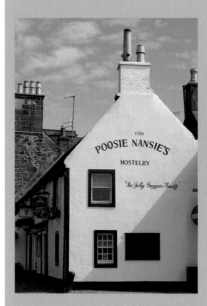

The *White Hart*, meanwhile, isn't a homage to an albino deer (hart is an old word for stag) but rather the heraldic emblem of Richard II, who in the 14th century ordered pubs and inns to show a suitable sign identifying themselves to the official Ale Taster (now there's a job!).

While you can see why currying favour with monarchs might influence a choice of name, why did so many boozers honour the *Marquis Of Granby*? Step forward John Manners, an 18th century general who before being ennobled acquired a legendary reputation for the welfare of his men that extended to providing funds for many ex-soldiers to establish taverns, which they naturally named after him.

George Orwell

What a socialist like George Orwell would have made of such a benevolent aristocrat we'll never know, but an idealised fictional pub described by Orwell in a 1946 essay has given its name to an increasing number of real-life boozers - *The Moon Under Water*.

In Orwell's dream pub, you'd find a beautiful Victorian interior with darts played in the public bar, a noise level undisturbed by any form of music, plus barmaids who knew regulars by name and took an interest in everyone who came in. It sold snacks including liver-sausage sandwiches and mussels (a favourite of Orwell's) as well as cheese and pickles, plus a good solid meat-and-two-veg lunch costing 3 shillings. Creamy stout was served, ideally in pewter pots, and a narrow passage led from the saloon bar into a pub garden. If only more real-life places were like that…

Unusual names

Many unusual pub names have derivations that are clearcut but still refreshingly whimsical. *The Flying Bedstead* in Nottinghamshire, for example, comes from the nickname of a prototype vertical take-off aircraft (now at the Science Museum in London), while *The Atmospheric Railway* near Exeter is another homage to unusual transport - this time, an experimental compressed

air railway system built in the area by Brunel in the 1830s.

Quirky names derived from real-life characters include *The Young Vanish* in Chesterfield (a racehorse) and *Poosie Nansie's* in Ayrshire, which refers to a female friend of Robert Burns. Huyton's *The Pipe & Gannex*, meanwhile, namechecks two items famously linked to their one-time local MP and later PM Harold Wilson.

The Bucket of Blood in Hayle doesn't refer to either the soup of the day or regular punch-ups but rather the days of Cornish smuggling when legend tells of blood drawn from the nearby well, followed by the discovery of a murdered revenue officer at the bottom.

Ancient trades have also provided inspiration - my favourite being *The Tappers Harker* in Long Eaton (Notts), which refers to an old railway job involving someone listening to the tone of a hammer being hit onto a railway carriage wheel to check its soundness. This job also inspired the naming of the fictional *Wheeltappers And Shunters*

social club in the 1970s TV show of the same name.

Animal rights folk needn't spill their pint over *The Blazing Donkey* in Ramsgate (either in anger or to put the flames out) - 'blazing' was simply Kentish dialect for 'braying'. Sticking with animals, the various pubs called *The Swan With Two Necks* refer not to a genetic monstrosity but marks put on the beaks of swans owned by the Worshipful Company of the Vintners (a right granted them by Elizabeth I) to distinguish them from those owned by the monarch - the 'nicks' on the beak becoming transposed into 'necks' by joke-loving (or illiterate) landlords.

The *Ashen Faggot* in Devon, meanwhile, isn't as saucy as it sounds. It's just another piece of country dialect referring to a bundle (faggot) of ash sticks used to light a fire in a traditional West Country ceremony marking the onset of the New Year.

How about the pubs going by the name *Antigallican*? This comes from the 18th century when opposition to all-things

French was deemed a patriotic duty and many pubs took the name - and though most changed it when relations improved, some survive.

Literature inspired the wonderfully-named *Balancing Eel* in South Shields, courtesy of a verse in *Alice In Wonderland* about being dexterous enough to balance an eel on the end of your nose - doubtless an especially difficult task after a couple of drinks.

A memorable name apparently inspired by a misheard instruction rather than a corruption is *The Same Yet* near Prestwich. Originally called *The Bulls Head*, rumour has it that the name got accidentally changed in the late 1800s when the person painting a new sign asked the busy landlord what to write, and received the Northern dialect reply "Same Yet"…

Let's finish with Pig & Whistle, because it's a name as evocative as its derivation is simple - just a corruption of the Anglo-Saxon phrase "piggin wassail" meaning "good health". Cheers!

HOW PUBS ARE SURVIVING

by **Phil Bryant**

One day last May, BBC Radio 2 presenter Jeremy Vine presented his programme from a popular Victorian pub in Cardiff. The Vulcan Hotel, built in 1853, and with an interior dating from 1914, had just become Cardiff CAMRA's Pub of the Year 2009.

Yet time was finally running out for the Vulcan and those hoping to save it from demolition to make way for a multi-storey car park.

In addition to the more than 5,000 people who signed an online petition, its destruction was also opposed by The National Trust, SAVE Britain's Heritage, The Victorian Society and the Cardiff Civic Society. In 'The Rough Pub Guide: A Celebration of the Great British Boozer', in which it was placed eighth out of 50, authors Paul Moody and Robin Turner wrote: "Without somewhere like this for future generations, people will think the only places we boozed in were Irish theme bars." (And what future for this Guide then!)

At the time of writing the Vulcan's fate remained unknown, but if it did disappear during the summer of 2009 it would have been far from alone. At that time, pubs were closing at a rate of 39 a week - that's almost six every day - compared to four a week in 2006.

Reasons for closures

The credit crunch is only one reason for so many closures in recent years. Their viability is being challenged from several directions - the smoking ban, cheap beer in supermarkets, the rise in property prices, changes in employment patterns, consumer preferences and the regulatory framework, and increases in excise duty.

In the 2008 Budget, the Government increased Beer Tax by 18 per cent and plans further increases of two per cent above the rate of inflation. In 2009, the Chancellor raised the price of a pint by 1p, thus reneging, said pub support groups, on a promise to introduce inflation-linked price increases. Between those two Budgets, more than 20,000 people lost their jobs and independent research consultancy Oxford Economics has forecast that a further 60,000 jobs are at risk if the Government's tax escalator plans go ahead.

In response, the British Beer & Pub Association (BBPA) has set up an 'Axe the Beer Tax, Save the Pub' campaign with the Campaign for Real Ale (CAMRA) to save pubs as a vital part of British life. "It now," says the association, "becomes a matter of the highest priority. We will be mobilising public, consumer, and industry support to force the Government to scrap the duty escalator as part of a co-ordinated plan to save the Great British Pub."

The day after Jeremy Vine pulled his first-ever pint, the House of Commons Business and Enterprise Select Committee demanded a shake-up of Britain's ailing pub industry. In its Seventh Report on Pub Companies (pubcos), it asked the Competition Commission to look into the 'tie' that requires an estimated 24,000 pub tenants to buy their beer supplies from their landlords, an arrangement that has also been blamed for tenants calling last orders.

Survival ventures

Thankfully, despite the carnage, thousands of pubs are meeting the threats to their viability with good marketing, ingenuity, common sense and recognition of their role at the centre of their communities.

But more than ever, pubs need support. Drop into a rural pub on a busy Sunday lunchtime (perhaps for your 'credit crunch lunch' of two roasts for £10) and you would be forgiven for thinking that all is well, but come back on, say, a Tuesday and it'll be a different story. Long gone are the local agricultural workers and skilled craftsmen who would have popped in daily for a pint and a pie, providing a predictable, if not necessarily lucrative, income stream.

CAMRA estimates that over a third of its branches have participated in pub campaigns, such as National Pubs Week, Community Pubs Week and now, its Save Our Pubs forum, which is designed for both members and non-members to share ideas, advice and comments on the best way of saving local pubs.

The organisation is also behind Local Pubs Week, a campaign with three main aims: to raise the profile and importance of pubs in the community; to encourage people of all ages and backgrounds to visit the pub more often than they currently do; and to encourage pubs to organise events during the week to entice more trade.

And last April, glasses were raised countrywide as thousands of pubs and pub-goers took part in Britain's first National Cask Ale Week, organised jointly by CAMRA, Cask Marque, brewers and pubcos to encourage people into pubs to

drink real ale. Activities included real ale trails, FemAle Day tastings and beer and food pairings. Another is planned for 2010.

As James Wilmore wrote in The Publican in August 2008: "A bar, a decent selection of drinks – handpulled ales are essential – a jolly publican and folk to chew the fat with is all you need. Except nowadays, regrettably, that's not enough. Yup, afraid so. To use a horrible marketing term, you need a bit of added value".

Added value is behind the survival, and revival, of plenty of pubs that can be regarded as beacons of hope. Some of the solutions – two for one deals, quizzes, karaoke nights - have become commonplace, but some are a little more enterprising. Around the country pubs are offering computer literacy courses, coffee mornings, book clubs, pharmacy collections, dry cleaning drop-off and collection, ATMs, crèche facilities, sales of farm produce, art and craft galleries and online deliveries. At least one has a betting shop, another a hairdressing salon, and there's even a report of another in which church services are held.

Pub is the hub

Behind at least 360 such ventures so far is Pub is the Hub, set up in 2001 by HRH The Prince of Wales, to encourage breweries, pub owners, licensees and local communities to work together to help retain and enhance rural pubs.

Its first ever project was in Blythburgh, Suffolk, where at the White Hart Inn villagers can now buy a pint of milk, drop off their dry cleaning and pick up a prescription, all in the shop within the pub. At Tirril, in Cumbria, Pub is the Hub worked closely with brewers Robinson's in a move that enables the Queens Head to sell postage stamps, fresh groceries and locally made gifts. Helping to attract

even more customers are an autumn beer and sausage festival, family-based Wii games in a back room, and a smoking shelter.

Claire Johnston, who took on the pub's tenancy in 2008, says: "With a small population, it may not have been viable for Tirril to support a shop until now. But, with the Queens Head diversifying to integrate a convenience store, the two businesses work very well together. For our local customers and the valuable tourist trade, the initiative should...secure the future of the pub."

Also in Cumbria is the picturesque village of Hesket Newmarket, where regulars of The Old Crown can sleep soundly in the knowledge that their favourite beers will always be waiting for them. That's because the pub and its associated micro-brewery are owned by a dedicated co-operative of more than one hundred local people and other supporters. Doubling too as the village library, it also stages quizzes, folk nights and tall story competitions.

When, in 2007, Prince Charles made his second visit to The Old Crown, he was able to see for himself that the co-operative sufficiently sound financially to meet the cost of a new kitchen and dining room.

Pub is the Hub's close links with the Post Office has resulted in a whole host of pubs, like the Queens Head, selling stamps and offering other Royal Mail facilities. At Osmaston, near Ashbourne, Derbyshire, the village post office was successfully relocated into a redundant outbuilding at the Shoulder of Mutton some years ago, then in November 2007 a shop selling milk, bread and other essentials was added, further strengthening this pub's role at the heart of community life.

Shipton Gorge is a small village three miles east of Bridport, Dorset, with a population of around 300 residents, made up mainly of older people and working families with children. There is a village hall and church, but no post office or local shop, and the local bus service is infrequent. In 2005, locals had contacted Pub is the Hub, not least to ensure that The New Inn, which at that time was closed, was not sold for property development. Following considerable fund-raising effort and a grant from DEFRA, a new six-year lease was agreed with a very supportive Palmers Brewery of Bridport.

The pub re-opened its doors in August 2006 with experienced landlords Gary Pellow and Sandra Tyson at the helm. The couple have quickly built up a reputation for good food and drink, have restored darts, cribbage and skittles, and hold regular coffee mornings. It is now very much a community meeting place and even provides a Meals on Legs service to octogenarian villagers. Says Gary: "We've now had people from other Dorset villages asking our advice on how they should go about doing something similar to save their pubs."

Other ideas

Further case studies are not hard to find. Take, for example, the Dyke's End at Reach in Cambridgeshire, which was given its memorable name (it was previously The Kings) in the 1990s by village shareholders after buying the freehold, rather than see their only pub close and revert to being a private dwelling.

The plan had always been to sell it once it was successfully up and running. Since 2003 it has been owned by Frank Feehan and Simon Owers, whose ambition has been "to create the sort of pub that we find hard to find in an industry now dominated by pub companies and greedy breweries". The Dyke's End is now at the heart of community life, as well as being the destination for people who travel considerable distances to enjoy a place Frank and Simon describe as "Undeniably quirky, and unashamedly out-of-step with the modern world."

At The Greys, a popular back-street pub in the Hanover district of Brighton, Chris Beaumont has introduced a strict "quality not quantity" entertainment policy. He books only well-known, named artists from as far away as Nashville, Chicago and Toronto, as well as from all over the UK. Even if his policy now means fewer gigs, he can at least be pretty sure of a full house.

Says Chris: "The main difficulty I have in keeping customers is competition from supermarkets and, believe it or not, the good weather! When the weather gets hotter, people are far more likely to buy beer from the supermarket and have a barbie in their gardens or on the beach." He's hoping a newly acquired small beer garden will help to combat that.

Regrettably, not all original ideas guarantee lasting success. In 2008, following an approach by the local primary school, The Blacksmith's Arms at Rothwell in the Lincolnshire Wolds went into school dinners as a sideline. With county council support and a grant from the East Midlands Development Corporation, the pub began supplying five local primary schools.

After salaries and food costs, the profit was small, but with rocketing electricity and gas bills, and trade down 10 per cent since the smoking ban, the extra income was a lifeline and helped to keep the pub open. Sadly, not for long, as by last spring it had ceased trading.

What do you want from your pub?

If you ask anybody what they want from their pub, the answer is likely to be somewhere with a friendly atmosphere, which they can visit in their walking boots or their business suit, and where they will always find a warm welcome, good home-prepared food, and a decent selection of real ales and wines. Furthermore, somewhere whose landlord or landlady understands how integral their pub is to the local community.

Thankfully, there are thousands of pubs that fulfil those requirements, which is why they're in this Guide. What they need now is you.

Local and Regional
BREWERIES

by Martyn Cornell

It's one of those paradoxes to be pondered over a pint that while beer sales across Britain are declining, and pubs are closing down everywhere, with around 40 a week calling "last orders" for the very last time, the choice for the discerning drinker is the best it has been for 60 or more years.

While traditional family-run breweries have continued closing with depressing regularity, their place has been taken by scores – hundreds – of new small brewers, making once-vanished historical beers such as porter and Imperial stout through to authentically made Continental-style lagers and wheat beers, including everything in between, from best bitter to dark mild, from brown ale to barley wine.

For the truth is that declining overall beer sales hide a renaissance in traditional British beer, as more than 500 small breweries, most founded in the past 15 to 20 years, bring back the local and the individual to the bartops of Britain's pubs. Sales of locally produced beers rose 10 per cent in 2008, while the wider beer market suffered an 8 per cent fall.

Britain's 30 or so surviving older-established family brewers are still able to show the newcomers how it's done: Palmer's of Bridport, in Dorset, for example, suppliers of beers such as the dark and delicious Tally Ho! to some of the country's prettiest pubs. Palmer's, the country's only thatched brewery, dates from 1794 and is run by the great-grandsons of the men who acquired the premises in 1896.

The South West Elsewhere in the South West, brews from the St Austell Brewery in Cornwall, founded by Walter Hicks in 1854, are available from the Isles of Scilly to Somerset. St Austell has also linked up with one of Cornwall's best-known celebrity chefs, Rick Stein, who now leases one of the brewery's pubs in his home village, St Merryn. Visitors to Cornwall should also not miss the Blue Anchor at Helston, Britain's oldest home-brew pub, where "bragget" – honey beer – is a summer speciality.

Devon has no family brewers left, but 30 small brewers supply thirsty

holidaymakers, meaning visitors are seldom far from a local brew – even on Dartmoor, where a brewery at Princetown makes Jail Ale.

Another family brewer producing unusual beers with a tie-up to a TV chef is Hall & Woodhouse of Blandford St Mary in Dorset. Among its brews is one called Stinger, made with "organic" stinging nettles (are there any other kind?) harvested on the farm run by Hugh Fearnley-Whittingstall. The company's "Badger" beers, which include one with a warning in its name, Tanglefoot, are available along the South Coast as far as Sussex.

Sussex Sussex itself still has a surviving family brewer, Harvey's of Lewes, so close to the River Ouse that the brewery occasionally suffers floods. The brewery is now run by the Jenner family, and if you take the brewery tour you may be lucky enough to be shown round by the highly knowledgeable Miles Jenner, Harvey's MD. It only has some 48 tied houses, but ten times that number of freetrade accounts, almost all concentrated in Sussex and Kent.

Kent Kent, of course, is famous for hops, the plant that gives beer its bitterness, and the beers of its one surviving family brewer, Shepherd Neame, are certainly hoppy, including Bishops Finger, named for a particular style of Kentish signpost. Kent has nine small local brewers, the best-known, perhaps, being Goacher's of Maidstone.

Essex and Suffolk Essex lost its last long-established family brewery in 2005, but 16 small brewers, including Crouch Vale, now nearly 30 years old, supplying the county's clapperboard pubs and waterside inns. In neighbouring Suffolk Adnam's still flies the flag of

Above: Everards Brewery, Leicestershire

independence under chairman Jonathan Adnam. Its justly famous beers now include a "carbon neutral" brew, East Green (named after one of the streets in its pretty seaside home, Southwold). Among Adnam's 15 smaller Suffolk rivals is Mauldon's of Sudbury, a revival from 1982 of an old-established business than closed in the 1960s.

Norfolk and Cambridgeshire
Norfolk, too, has no remaining old-established family brewers, but it does have around 30 recently established concerns to delight the palates of locals and visitors. They include the excellent Woodforde's at Woodbastwick, whose Wherry bitter is deservedly popular in around 600 outlets. There is also a small brewery on the Elvedon estate, the stately home owned by Lord Iveagh, head of the Guinness family.

Just across the county border in Wisbech, Cambridgeshire, the fifth-generation family owners of Elgood & Sons supply some 40 tied houses and free houses throughout East Anglia with beers including Black Dog, an award-winning, dark, liquorishy ale. Elgood's beers are not as well-known as they ought

to be, unlike its neighbour and rival in Wainfleet, Lincolnshire, Bateman's. The brewery is now run by the great-grandchildren of the founder, and its 67 tied houses are worth finding for the XXXB bitter alone.

The Midlands
Leicestershire also boasts a well-known family brewer, Everard's, whose 160 tenanted houses can be spotted across the Midlands. Nottinghamshire and Derbyshire have both lost their family brewers, but run to more than 30 newer concerns between them, including Springhead, near Newark, where all the beers have Civil War-themed names. Staffordshire is the home of Britain's brewing capital, Burton upon Trent, where the gypsum-impregnated well waters made terrific beers. There are still six brewers in the town: two national giants, and four new start-ups, including Burton Bridge, which suppliers 300 outlets.

The West Midlands used to be full of hundreds of small breweries and home-brew pubs, of which only a tiny handful survive today. Batham's of Delph, Brierly Hill, another family concern on its fifth generation of owners, is based behind the Vine pub and serves only 40 or so outlets

in total with just two beers, both excellent. Nearby in Woodsetton, Dudley, Holden's, which began in the 1920s, has 100 or so outlets for its beers. In Netherton a short distance away is the Olde Swan, a home-brew pub since Victorian times, apart from a short break in the 1990s.

The Welsh Marches have a host of little brewers now, although a couple have ancient roots: the Three Tuns at Bishop's Castle, another long-established home-brew establishment which now suppliers 125 outlets, and Worfield, at Madeley, Telford, which is based in the brewery attached to the next-door All Nations pub, like the Three Tuns one of only four home-brew pubs left in 1974.

Cotswolds
The pretty thatched pubs of the Cotswolds are still, many of them, supplied by the Hook Norton brewery, near Banbury, owned by the same family since 1849, while the tiny Donnington brewery, near Stow-on-the-Wold, has been making beer for the past 145 years. Another local family brewer is Arkell's of Swindon, while the region's many newer small brewers include Hopback of Salisbury and Uley and Wickwar in the villages of the same name.

Wales
In Wales only Brain's in Cardiff (sponsors of the Wales rugby team) and Felinfoel (pronounced vellinvoe-el) near Llanelli survive of the principality's former family breweries, though there are more than 30 newer operators, several named after vanished Welsh brewers, including Tomos Watkin in Swansea and Rhymney in Merthyr Tydfil. Others include Plassey in Wrexham, which was once an important brewing town, and Purple Moose at Porthmadog.

Merseyside and Manchester
On Merseyside the magnificent Robert Cain's brewery in Liverpool qualifies as a family operation, being run by the Dusanj brothers, who bought it in 2002: it has around 300 outlets for its beers, which include a fine example of a classic dark mild. Manchester, however, lines up four genuine old-established family operators, Robinson's of Stockport, Holt's of Cheetham, JW Lees in Middleton and Hyde's of Moss Side. With 20 other newer brewers as well, Greater Manchester is a magnet for beer tourists.

Lancashire
Lancashire had several surviving family brewers 30 years ago but is down to only one now, the 200-year-old Thwaite's brewery in Blackburn, a comparatively large concern with 400 tied houses. It also has a an old-established firm, Moorhouse's of Burnley, which began as a soft drinks manufacturer in 1865 and only began brewing in 1978, but which boasts more CAMRA and international awards for its beers than any other brewery of its size.

Yorkshire
Yorkshire, for all its size, has only a trio of family brewers, but they are all justly famous: Samuel Smith's in Tadcaster, Timothy Taylor's of Keighley, maker of what many believe to be the best beer in Britain, Landlord bitter; and Theakston's of Masham, which was brought back by the Theakston family in 2003 after 20 years under outside control. Masham also contains the Black Sheep brewery, owned by another member of the Theakston family, which also makes well-regarded ales.

The North
The four northernmost counties of England lack any old family brewers, but visitors to the high hills, moors and lakes of Cumbria and Northumberland, and the cities of Durham and Tyne and Wear, have more than 30 new small brewers to discover, including the award-winning Coniston, whose Bluebird bitter, named after Donald Campbell's record-breaking speedboat, is highly regarded.

Scotland
In Scotland the closest to a surviving family brewery is at Traquair House in Peeblesshire in the Borders, where the Maxwell Stuarts, owners of this stately home, revived brewing in the 18th century brewhouse in 1965. Another 40 or so small brewers have sprung up, however, including Williams Brothers of Alloa, maker of Heather Ale; Harviestoun in Clackmannanshire, who brew a cask-conditioned lager called Schiehallion; Brewdog, near Aberdeen, who make a strong stout aged in whisky barrels; and Britain's northernmost brewery, Valhalla, on Unst, in the Shetlands.

Make more of your money with the AA

- Attractive rates on savings accounts
- A range of fixed term and easy access accounts
- Joint and single account options

**To open a savings account and
start making more of your money call**

0845 603 6589* quoting ref AA Guides

See our full range of savings accounts at **theAA.com/savings**

Lines are open between 8am and 8pm, Monday to Saturday.

Savings

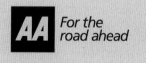 For the road ahead

Beer Festivals

Beer festivals, or their equivalent, are as old as the hills. The brewing of hops goes back to the beginning of human civilisation, and the combination of common crop and a fermenting process that results in alcoholic liquid has long been a cause of celebration. Beer festivals officially began in Germany with the first Munich Oktoberfest in 1810. Wherever in the world beer is brewed, today and for the last few millennia, admirers, enthusiasts, aficionados – call them what you will – have gathered together to sample and praise its unique properties. It happens throughout Europe, in Australia and New Zealand, and in America and Canada, and annual events are held in pubs all over Britain.

Beer festivals are often occasions for the whole family, when entertainment is laid on for children as well as adults. Summer is naturally a popular season for festivals, when the action can be taken outdoors. Other festivals are held in October, traditionally harvest time, but they can be at any time of the year. They can be large and well-advertised gatherings that attract a wide following for sometimes several days of unselfconscious consumption of unusual or award-winning ales; or they might be local but none the less enthusiastic get-togethers of neighbourhood or pub micro-breweries.

We list here a selection of pubs that appear in this guide, that hold usually annual beer festivals. *For up-to-date information, please check directly with the pub.* We would love to hear from our readers about their favourite beer festivals.

E-mail us at
lifestyleguides@theAA.com

The Stag & Huntsman, Hambleden, Buckinghamshire 01491 571227
A weekend beer festival is held in early September.

The White Horse, Hedgerley, Buckinghamshire 01753 643225
An annual beer festival is held at the end of May Bank Holiday.

The Crown Inn, Elton, Cambridgeshire 01832 280232
Annual treats include a May Day hog roast and a summer beer festival.

Bhurtpore Inn, Aston, Cheshire 01270 780917
Annual beer festival in November and early July. The summer festival is one of the largest in Cheshire with 120 beers.

The Smugglers Den Inn, Cubert, nr Newquay, Cornwall & Isles of Scilly 01637 830209
The impressive selection of real ales is at its best during the real ale and pie festival over the May Day weekend.

Queens Head Inn, Tirril, Cumbria 01768 863219
In August every year the Cumbrian beer and sausage festival is held here.

Wasdale Head Inn, Wasdale Head, Cumbria 019467 26229
Large numbers descend on this old drovers' inn to sample beers from the pub's micro-brewery at their annual beer festivals.

The Royal Hotel, Hayfield, Derbyshire 01663 741721
Annual beer festival held in the autumn.

Greyhound Inn, Corfe Castle, Dorset 01929 480205
A full diary of events features two annual beer festivals in May and August and a West Country sausage and cider festival in October half term.

Bankes Arms, Studland, Dorset 01929 450225
The annual beer festival held in August in its large garden showcases 60 real ales and live music.

The Hoop, Stock, Essex 01277 841137
The annual beer festival enjoys growing popularity, but the food is also a major draw.

Boat Inn, Ashleworth, Gloucestershire 01452 700272
Renowned for its real ales, it hosts a popular annual beer festival.

The Yew Tree, Clifford's Mesne, Gloucestershire 01531 820719
In May, the Yew Tree holds a beer, cider and local produce festival.

The White Horse, Petersfield, Hampshire 01420 588387
3-day festival in June. Bouncy castle, live music, barbecue plus lots more entertainment.

The Bowl Inn, Charing, Kent 01233 712256
The Bowl has been an alehouse since 1606, and was built as a farmhouse in 1512. Look out for the annual beer festival.

Chequers Inn, Smarden, Kent 01233 770217
The pub is much involved with the local community throughout the year, and hosts an annual beer festival in August, plus other events.

Eureka, Ormskirk, Lancashire 01695 570819
In August there's a beer festival with up to sixteen real ales on offer.

The Eagle and Child, Parbold, Lancashire 01257 462297
The pub maintains its traditional atmosphere and offers five regularly changing guest ales, real ciders and a beer festival every May.

Swan in the Rushes, Loughborough, Leicestershire 01509 217014
Two annual festivals second weekend November and last weekend May. Live music, 20 beers.

Cow and Plough, Oadby, Leicestershire
0116 272 0852
St Georges beer festival, 30 beers and 10 ciders, and live music.

Junction Tavern, London NW5
020 7485 9400
The pub has a beer festival 9-11 October 2009 and the last Bank Holiday in May.

White Horse, London SW6
020 7736 2115
The 2-day beer festival held annually in November with over 300 beers waiting to be sampled is a magnet for lovers of real ale and European beers. Begium beer festival August Bank Holiday, American beer festival Independence weekend, London Beer Festival in May.

The Hill House, Happisburgh, Norfolk
01692 650004
Look out for the Solstice beer festival in June for the chance to sample a wide range of real ales, ciders and perries.

The Stuart House Hotel, Kings Lynn, Norfolk 01553 772169
A programme of events includes an annual beer festival last weekend of July. Live music.

Angel Inn, Larling, Norfolk
01953 717963
This pub offers an annual beer festival in August.

White Hart, Fyfield, Oxfordshire
01865 390585
An annual beer festival is held during the May Day bank holiday, with hog roasts and at least 13 real ales.

The Grainstore Brewery, Oakham, Rutland 01572 770065
Attend the annual beer festival during the August Bank Holiday.

The Surrey Oaks, Newdigate, Surrey
01306 631200
Late May Bank Holiday and August Bank Holiday beer festivals. Live music, Rock and Roll, Blues and Jazz band.

Kings Arms, Fernhurst, West Sussex
01428 652005
A wisteria-clad barn is used for the pub's annual three-day beer festival at the end of August.

The Dog & Duck, Kingsfold, West Sussex 01306 627295
It hosts many events, including quizzes, darts evenings, a big beer festival and fundraising activities for St George's Hospital.

The Smoking Dog, Malmesbury, Wiltshire 01666 825823
A renowned beer and sausage festival over Whitsun weekend is the time to sample over 30 brews and 15 banger varieties.

The Bridge Inn, West Lavington, Wiltshire 01380 813213
Annual events are now a regular feature at The Bridge, from Harvest Supper in September to the Charity Beer Festival over the August Bank Holiday weekend.

Clytha Arms, Abergavenny, Monmouthshire, Wales 01873 840209
This former dower house is heavily involved with the Welsh Cider Festival in May and the Beer and Cheese Festival in August.

Lion Inn, Monmouthshire, Wales
01600 860322
There are plenty of activities to enjoy most nights, plus a summer and winter beer festival.

Kilverts Inn, Powys, Wales
01497 821042
At the bar there's an impressive selection of ales and ciders. There is an annual beer festival too.

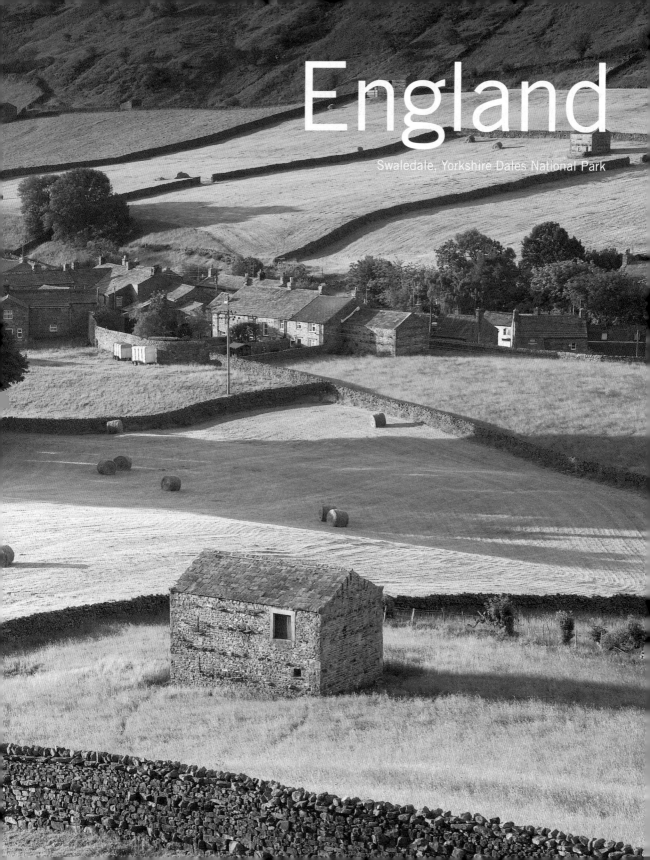

England

Swaledale, Yorkshire Dales National Park

BEDFORDSHIRE

BEDFORD   Map 12 TL04

PICK OF THE PUBS

The Knife & Cleaver Inn ♀

The Grove, Houghton Conquest MK45 3LA
☎ **01234 740387** 🗎 **01234 740900**
e-mail: info@theknifeandcleaver.com
dir: 11m from M1 junct 12/13. 5m S of Bedford. Off A6. In village opp church

Originally called the Butchers Arms, the pub was owned as part of the manor house properties by the Conquest family, who had the manor from the 13th century. Records date from 1796, but the building is thought to be older. It stands opposite the medieval church of All Saints, Bedfordshire's largest parish church. Historical features include the Jacobean oak panelling in the lounge bar, which came from Houghton House. Light meals and hand-drawn ales are served in the bar, where leather sofas and winter log fires bring welcome comfort. The seasonal menu in the conservatory restaurant is strong on fresh seafood, and also offers a varied choice of meat and vegetarian dishes, such as pan-fried lamb rump with apricots, couscous and Moroccan-style tagine sauce, or chargrilled aubergine tower with pesto dressing.

Open all wk 12-3 6-11 (Sun noon-10.30pm) **Bar Meals** L served all wk 12-2.30 D served all wk 7-9.30 Av main course £10 **Restaurant** L served all wk 12-2.30 D served all wk 7-9.30 Fixed menu price fr £14.50 Av 3 course à la carte fr £20 ⊕ FREE HOUSE ◀ Village Bike, Potton Brewery, Adnams Broadside. ♀ 20 **Facilities** Children's menu Family room Dogs allowed Garden Parking

The Three Tuns ♀

57 Main Rd, Biddenham MK40 4BD ☎ **01234 354847**
dir: On A428 from Bedford towards Northampton 1st left signed Biddenham. Into village, pub on left

A stone-built, thatched roof pub, The Three Tuns stands in the heart of the beautiful village of Biddenham. It has a large garden with a patio and decking, and a separate children's play area with swings and a climbing frame. The old morgue, situated between the two garden areas, is the oldest building in the village and is said to be haunted. Home-cooked dishes on the regularly-changing menus include pies, steaks, curries, fish, local sausages, burgers and vegetarian specialities; all washed down with award-winning Greene King beers.

Open all wk 12-3 6-11 (Sun 12-4 7-10.30; 12-11 in summer) **Bar Meals** L served all wk 12-2 D served Mon-Sat 6-9 **Restaurant** L served all wk 12-2 booking required D served Mon-Sat 6-9 booking required ⊕ GREENE KING ◀ Greene King IPA, Abbot Ale, guest ale, Guinness. ♀ 6 **Facilities** Children's menu Play area Family room Dogs allowed Garden Parking

BLETSOE   Map 11 TL05

PICK OF THE PUBS

The Falcon ♀

Rushden Rd MK44 1QN
☎ **01234 781222** 🗎 **01234 781222**
e-mail: thefalcona6@aol.com
dir: 9m from M1 junct 13, 3m from Bedford

The 17th-century Falcon stands in rolling downland, beside the River Great Ouse. Before becoming a coaching inn in 1727 it was a mill, and in 1859 Edward FitzGerald translated *The Rubaiyat of Omar Khayyam* here, describing The Falcon as 'The cleanest, the sweetest, the civilest, the quietest, the liveliest and the cheapest that was ever built'. Not one to prevaricate, then. Inside are an inglenook fireplace, beams galore, a splendidly oak-panelled restaurant and a secret tunnel to Bletsoe Castle. In winter, you can enjoy the crackling log fires and in summer there is a large riverside garden and marquee. Lunchtime favourites include piri piri squid; gnocchi with yam and spinach; pie of the day; soups and sandwiches. Dinner might starter with Glenfiddich chicken liver pâté, or asparagus Benedict, while typical mains are chargrilled 21-day sirloin steak; pan-fried lamb cutlets; lemon and thyme-roasted poussin; and seafood medley. As well as traditional roasts on Sunday lunch, why not ask about the fish of the day?

Open all wk ⊕ CHARLES WELLS ◀ Wells Bombardier, Wells Eagle, Red Stripe. ♀ 13 **Facilities** Garden Parking

BOLNHURST   Map 12 TL05

PICK OF THE PUBS

The Plough at Bolnhurst ◉ ♀

Kimbolton Rd MK44 2EX ☎ **01234 376274**
e-mail: theplough@bolnhurst.com
dir: On B660 N of Bedford

This beautiful building goes back to Tudor times, as plainly testified by low beams, an intriguing layout, few windows, and open fires. In the kitchen, which you can see from the bar and the restaurant, Martin Lee and his dedicated team prepare exciting English food with a strong Italian and French influence. Sourced from farms and estates around the country, the Plough's menu is as likely to include asparagus from nearby fields as beef from distant Aberdeenshire, simply because they're the best of their kind to be had. Menus change daily to reflect market availability, but tend to offer such treats as pan fried foie gras with shallot confit, crisp potato galette and sherry vinegar sauce; braised fillet of brill with spinach and tomato and coriander chowder; roast Suffolk pheasant with roast potatoes, Brussels tops, shallots and roast chestnuts. Follow with bread and butter pudding with orange marmalade ice cream. Extensive wine list and plenty of real ales to choose from.

Closed: 1 Jan, 2wks Jan, Mon **Bar Meals** L served Tue-Sun 12-2 booking required D served Tue-Sat 6.30-9.30 booking required Av main course £16 **Restaurant** L served Tue-Sun 12-2 booking required D served Tue-Sat 6.30-9.30 booking required Fixed menu price fr £17 Av 3 course à la carte fr £28.30 ⊕ FREE HOUSE ◀ Adnams Broadside, Nethergate Azzanewt, Batemans XB, Village Bike Potton, Fuller's London Pride. ♀ 12 **Facilities** Dogs allowed Garden Parking

BROOM   Map 12 TL14

The Cock

23 High St SG18 9NA
☎ **01767 314411** 🗎 **01767 314284**
dir: Off B658 SW of Biggleswade. 1m from A1

Unspoilt to this day with its intimate quarry-tiled rooms with latched doors and panelled walls, this 17th-century establishment is known as 'The Pub with no Bar'. Real ales are served straight from casks racked by the cellar steps. A straightforward pub grub menu includes jumbo cod, roast chicken, gammon steak, breaded lobster, and breast of Cajun chicken.

Open all wk 12-4 6-11 **Bar Meals** L served all wk 12-2.15 D served all wk 7-9 **Restaurant** L served all wk 12-2.15 D served all wk 7-9 ⊕ GREENE KING ◀ Greene King Abbot Ale, IPA, Ruddles County. **Facilities** Children's menu Play area Family room Dogs allowed Garden Parking

EATON BRAY   Map 11 SP92

The White Horse ♀

Market Square LU6 2DG
☎ **01525 220231** 🗎 **01525 222485**
e-mail: davidsparrow@onetel.net
web: www.the-whitehorse.co.uk
dir: A5 N of Dunstable onto A505, left in 1m, follow signs

For almost 20 years, David and Janet Sparrow have built their reputation on great home cooked food at this traditional 300-year-old village inn with its oak beams and horse brasses. There's a wide ranging menu including comfort food like beef in ale pie, plus daily specials that might include sea bass fillets in lemon butter; Horton's pork with apple sausages and bubble and squeak. It's worth booking for the restaurant, but the same menu is also available in the bar.

Open all wk Closed: Sun eve Jan-Mar **Bar Meals** L served all wk 12-2.15 D served all wk 7-9.30 booking required Av main course £9.50 **Restaurant** L served all wk 12-2.15 D served all wk 7-9.30 booking required Av 3 course à la carte fr £21.50 ⊞ PUNCH TAVERNS ◖ Greene King IPA, Shepherd Neame Spitfire. ♟ 8 **Facilities** Children's menu Play area Family room Garden Parking

HARROLD
Map 11 SP95

PICK OF THE PUBS

The Muntjac ♟

71 High St MK43 7BJ ☎ 01234 721500
e-mail: muntjacharrold@hotmail.co.uk

Located on the borders of three shires - Bedfordshire, Buckinghamshire and Northamptonshire - the Muntjac is a 17th-century coaching inn in a picturesque village. Head chef Gary Robbins creates a menu of contemporary dishes that reflect his desire to experiment with new ideas, flavours and presentation. He prefers to offer lighter, fish-based dishes in the summer, and the likes of casseroles in the winter. A bar menu includes pick-and-mix tapas-style snacks. On the lunch menu look for moules marinière with crusty ciabattas; chargrilled Cajun chicken with spicy potato wedges and sour cream; and toasted filled paninis. The main carte offers monkfish, bacon and pea casserole with basmati and wild rice; pan-fried pork fillet with roast apple and red cabbage coleslaw; and spiced butternut squash risotto with mascarpone. Desserts include the chef's trademark crème brûlée.

Open all wk ⊞ FREE HOUSE ◖ Black Sheep Best Bitter, John Smith's Extra Smooth, guest ales ♂ Stowford Press. ♟ 7 **Facilities** Garden Parking

KEYSOE
Map 12 TL06

The Chequers

Pertenhall Rd, Brook End MK44 2HR
☎ 01234 708678   📠 01234 708678
e-mail: chequers.keysoe@tesco.net
dir: *On B660, 7m N of Bedford. 3m S of Kimbolton*

This peaceful 15th-century country pub has been in the same safe hands for over 25 years. No games machines, pool tables or jukeboxes disturb the simple pleasures of well-kept ales and tasty home-made food. The menu offers pub stalwarts like home-made steak and ale pie; fried scampi and a variety of grilled steaks and a blackboard displays further choice plus the vegetarian options. For a lighter option try the home-made soup or chicken liver pâté.

Closed: Mon eve & Tue ⊞ FREE HOUSE ◖ Hook Norton Best, Fuller's London Pride. **Facilities** Play area Family room Garden Parking **Notes** ⊛

LINSLADE
Map 11 SP92

The Globe Inn ♟

Globe Ln, Old Linslade LU7 2TA
☎ 01525 373338   📠 01525 850551
e-mail: 6458@greeneking.co.uk

Originally a farmhouse and stables, this friendly waterside inn was converted to serve passing boat crews on the Grand Union Canal. Open fires and candles set the scene for winter evenings, whilst for warmer days there's a large garden and children's play area. Expect an appetising range of light bites and mixed smoked deli board for sharing, as well as hot dishes like pan-seared Barbary duck with dauphinoise potatoes; sweet potato, chick pea and spinach curry; and daily fresh fish specials.

Open all day all wk 11-11 **Bar Meals** Av main course £8.95 food served all day **Restaurant** Av 3 course à la carte fr £20 food served all day ⊞ GREENE KING ◖ Greene King Abbot Ale, Old Speckled Hen, IPA & Ruddles County Ale, Hook Norton. ♟ 16 **Facilities** Children's menu Play area Dogs allowed Garden Parking

MILTON BRYAN
Map 11 SP93

The Red Lion ♟

Toddington Rd, South End MK17 9HS ☎ 01525 210044
e-mail: paul@redlion-miltonbryan.co.uk
dir: *Telephone for directions*

Set in a pretty village near Woburn Abbey, this attractive brick-built pub is festooned with dazzling hanging baskets in the summer months. Comfortable, neatly maintained interior, with beams, rugs on wooden floors, and well-kept ales. Wide-ranging menu offering the likes of roast rump of lamb with potato purée, wilted spinach and ratatouille sauce; supreme of chicken stuffed with ricotta cheese, basil and Parma ham on wild rocket and roasted cherry tomato; and baked Cornish cod.

Open 12-3 6-11 (Sun 12-4) Closed: 25-26 Dec, 1 Jan, Sun eve & Mon eve in Winter **Bar Meals** L served Mon-Sat 12-2.30, Sun 12-3 D served Mon-Sat 7-9.30 ⊞ GREENE KING ◖ Greene King IPA, Old Speckled Hen, Abbot Ale, plus guest ales. ♟ 7 **Facilities** Garden Parking

NORTHILL
Map 12 TL14

The Crown ♟

2 Ickwell Rd SG18 9AA
☎ 01767 627337   📠 01767 627279
e-mail: info@thecrown-northill.com
dir: *Telephone for directions*

A delightful 16th-century pub with chocolate box setting between Northill church and the village duck pond. Its acre of garden includes a children's play area, and plenty of tables for alfresco eating. Inside, the unique copper-covered bar leads to an informal dining area, where the bar menu of pub favourites applies. The candlelit split-level restaurant boasts much locally sourced produce served in home-cooked dishes such as roasted lamb chump with port and rosemary jus; smoked hake fillets on tomato sauce; and pork tenderloin medallions wrapped in bacon.

Open all wk 11.30-3 6-11 (Sun 12-11 Summer Sat 11.30am-11pm) Closed: 25 Dec eve **Bar Meals** L served Mon-Sat 12-2.30, Sun 12-8 D served Mon-Sat 6.30-9.30, Sun all day Av main course £8.95 **Restaurant** L served Mon-Sat 12-2.30, Sun 12-8 booking required D served Mon-Sat 6.30-9.30, Sun all day booking required Av 3 course à la carte fr £23 ⊞ GREENE KING ◖ Greene King IPA, Abbot Ale, Old Speckled Hen, Olde Tripplus, Guest ales. ♟ 9 **Facilities** Children's menu Play area Dogs allowed Garden Parking

ODELL
Map 11 SP95

The Bell ♟

Horsefair Ln MK43 7AU ☎ 01234 720254
dir: *Telephone for directions*

A Grade II listed 16th-century thatched pub with a patio and aviary outside, situated next to a spacious garden leading down to the River Ouse. The lunch menu offers a wide choice of sandwiches, baguettes, filled jacket potatoes and light options also suitable for children. The main menu is also available at lunch or dinner, and features the likes of poached fillet of salmon with white wine sauce, home-made steak and Abbot pie, and mushroom Stroganoff.

Open all wk ⊞ GREENE KING ◖ Greene King IPA, Abbot Ale, Ruddles County, Seasonal ales. ♟ 6 **Facilities** Family room Garden Parking

OLD WARDEN
Map 12 TL14

PICK OF THE PUBS

Hare and Hounds ♟

See Pick of the Pubs on page 30

PICK OF THE PUBS

Hare & Hounds 🍷

OLD WARDEN Map 12 TL14

SG18 9HQ
☎ 01767 627225 📄 01767 627209
web: www.charleswells.co.uk
dir: *From Bedford turn right off A603 (or left from A600) to Old Warden. Also accessed from Biggleswade rdbt on A1*

At the heart of a prosperous, leafy village on the Shuttleworth estate, home to the famous collection of classic cars and vintage aeroplanes, this attractive, 200-year-old pub makes a good first impression. The inside doesn't disappoint either, you may be greeted by the warmth from the two log fires as you head either for the bar, or one of the three cosy-chic country dining rooms, which feature timbered walls, warm red and cream colours, fresh flowers and contemporary furnishings. Food is taken very seriously, the printed menu listing a well-balanced choice of rustic traditional dishes and more modern offerings, with every effort made to use local, even organic produce, including pork reared on the estate and herbs and vegetables from the kitchen garden, with fish delivered daily from Billingsgate Market, and bread and ice creams made on the premises. Typically, start with deep-fried whitebait with garlic mayonnaise, chicken liver pâté, or why not share a camembert, baked in the box and served with walnut toast and cranberry sauce. For main course, try the deep-fried haddock in beer batter with mushy peas, tartare sauce and hand-cut chips, or opt for mussels, tiger prawns and scallops cooked with green chilli, coriander and coconut sauce, local Gamlingay sausages with mash and red wine sauce, or braised wild rabbit in puff pastry with shallots, wholegrain mustard and tarragon sauce. Round off with tarte Tatin, caramelised lemon tart, warm Bakewell tart, or one of an interesting selection of cheeses, including cheeses from Neal's Yard Dairy, and Gubbeens from Co Cork. Thursday is fresh fish night. Wines from around the world include some from the local Warden Abbey vineyard and cracking beers come courtesy of Wells & Youngs Eagle and Bombardier. On warmer days, enjoy the super views from the garden and patio area.

Open Tue-Sun Closed: Mon (ex BH)
🍺 CHARLES WELLS 🍺 Wells Bombardier Premium & Eagle IPA, Adnams. 🍷 8
Facilities Garden Parking

SALFORD	Map 11 SP93

PICK OF THE PUBS

The Swan NEW ♀

2 Warendon Rd MK17 8BD ☎ 01908 281008
e-mail: swan@peachpubs.com
dir: *M1 junct 13, follow signs to Salford*

Not far from central Milton Keynes is this attractive village and the tile-hung, Edwardian Swan, which has earned a great local reputation in recent years. In the kitchen Neil Simons and his team take pride in using top ingredients from ethical British producers, not least to cut down on air freight, to produce starters of pheasant, apricot and smoked bacon terrine with Cumberland sauce; and Thai crab beignet with pickled ginger and chilli dressing. From the plentiful main courses come free-range coq au vin; sea bass with crunchy winter vegetable slaw; and leek, red onion, broccoli and blue cheese strudel with Meaux mustard sauce. Deli boards - mixed, charcuterie, cheese, antipasti, fish and Indian - are a house speciality. The kitchen will happily prepare children's versions of anything the grown-ups eat. A short, sensibly priced wine list changes frequently. On sunny days, check for a barbecue on the terrace.

Open all day all wk 11am-mdnt (Sun 12-10.30) Closed: 25 Dec **Bar Meals** Av main course £13 food served all day **Restaurant** food served all day ⊕ Peach Pubs ◀ IPA, Black Sheep, Guinness. ♀ 8 **Facilities** Children's menu Dogs allowed Garden Parking

SHEFFORD	Map 12 TL13

The Black Horse ♀

Ireland SG17 5QL ☎ 01462 811398 🖹 01462 817238
e-mail: countrytaverns@aol.com
dir: *From S: M1 junct 12, A5120 to Flitwick. Onto A507 by Redbourne School. Follow signs for A1, Shefford (cross A6). Left onto A600 towards Bedford*

This traditional pub is set in a lovely garden surrounded by peaceful countryside. The name of the tiny hamlet is thought to be derived from the Irish navvies who built the local railway line in the 1850s. The memorable menu draws a devoted following, with imaginative meals that might include leg of lamb roasted with garlic and thyme; locally farmed pork loin with prune and apple sauce; and fillet of sea bass with warm fennel and red onion salad. Westons Stowford Press cider is available, along with real ales like Village Bike.

Open all wk 12-3 6-12 (Sun noon-6pm) Closed: 25-26 Dec, 1 Jan **Bar Meals** L served Mon-Sat 12-2.30, Sun 12-5 D served Mon-Sat 6.30-10 **Restaurant** L served Mon-Sat 12-2.30, Sun 12-5 D served Mon-Sat 6.30-10 ◀ Greene King IPA, London Pride, Village Bike Ŏ Westons Stowford Press. ♀ 17 **Facilities** Children's menu Garden Parking

SOUTHILL	Map 12 TL14

The White Horse ♀

High St SG18 9LD ☎ 01462 813364
e-mail: paul.e.cluett@virgin.net
dir: *Telephone for directions*

A village pub with traditional values, happily accommodating the needs of children and those who like to sit outside on cool days (the patio has heaters). Locally renowned for its chargrilled steaks from the Duke of Buccleuch's Scottish estate. Other main courses include Cajun chicken; chargrilled pork loin steaks; Whitby Bay scampi; and stuffed breaded plaice. Enjoy Greene King beers, with London Pride up from Chiswick. Recent change of management.

Open all wk **Bar Meals** L served Mon-Fri 12-2.30, Sat-Sun 12-10 booking required D served Mon-Fri 6-10, Sat-Sun 12-10 booking required Av main course £7.50 **Restaurant** L served Mon-Fri 12-2.30, Sat-Sun 12-10 booking required D served Mon-Fri 6-10, Sat-Sun 12-10 booking required Fixed menu price fr £5.50 Av 3 course à la carte fr £15 ⊕ ENTERPRISE INNS ◀ Greene King IPA, London Pride, Speckled Hen, Flowers. ♀ 8 **Facilities** Children's menu Play area Dogs allowed Garden Parking

STANBRIDGE	Map 11 SP92

PICK OF THE PUBS

The Five Bells ♀

Station Rd, Stanbridge LU7 9JF ☎ 01525 210224
e-mail: fivebells@fullers.co.uk
dir: *Off A505 E of Leighton Buzzard*

A stylish and relaxing setting for a drink or a meal is offered by this white-painted 400-year-old village inn, which has been delightfully renovated and revived. The bar features lots of bare wood as well as comfortable armchairs and polished, rug-strewn floors. The modern decor extends to the bright, airy 75-cover dining room. There's also a spacious garden with patio and lawns. The inn offers bar meals, set menus and a carte choice for diners. The bar menu typically includes dishes such as smoked chicken, sun-dried tomato and pine nut salad; battered fish, chips and mushy peas; baked courgettes stuffed with goats' cheese and mint with a mixed salad; rib-eye steak with fries; and chicken, ham, leek and mushroom pie.

Open all wk ⊕ FULLERS BREWERY ◀ Greene King IPA, Timothy Taylor Landlord, London Pride. ♀ 8 **Facilities** Dogs allowed Garden Parking

SUTTON	Map 12 TL24

John O'Gaunt Inn ♀

30 High St SG19 2NE ☎ 01767 260377
dir: *Off B1040 between Biggleswade & Potton*

Situated in one of Bedfordshire's most picturesque villages, the John O'Gaunt is a traditional village inn

where a guest ale features alongside the regular beers supplied in rotation from various breweries. Piped music is notable by its absence, though you may be encouraged to join in the occasional informal folk music sessions. The pub offers a large garden, and welcoming winter fires. A wide choice of good food is available most lunchtimes and evenings.

Open all wk 12-3 7-11 (Fri 12-3 6-11, Sun 12-5 7-11) **Bar Meals** L served all wk 12.30-1.45 D served all wk 7-9 Av main course £8 ⊕ ADMIRAL TAVERNS ◀ Rotating - Woodforde's Wherry, Black Sheep, London Pride, Abbot Ale Ŏ Westons Old Rosie. ♀ 10 **Facilities** Dogs allowed Garden Parking **Notes** ⊕

TILSWORTH	Map 11 SP92

The Anchor Inn ♀

1 Dunstable Rd LU7 9PU
☎ 01525 210289 🖹 01525 211578
e-mail: tonyanchorinn@aol.com
dir: *Exit A5 at Tilsworth. In 1m pub on right at 3rd bend*

The only pub in a Saxon village, the Anchor dates from 1878. The restaurant is a recent addition to the side of the pub, and the whole building has been refurbished. The licensees pride themselves on their fresh food and well-kept beers and guest ales. An acre of garden includes patio seating for alfresco dining, an adventure playground and a barbecue. Recent change of hands.

Open all day all wk noon-11.30pm **Bar Meals** Av main course £5 food served all day **Restaurant** Fixed menu price fr £10 food served all day ⊕ GREENE KING ◀ Greene King IPA, Abbot Ale, Wadworth 6X, guest ales. ♀ 12 **Facilities** Children's menu Play area Family room Garden Parking

WOBURN	Map 11 SP93

The Birch at Woburn ♀

20 Newport Rd MK17 9HX
☎ 01525 861414 🖹 01525 861323
e-mail: ctaverns@aol.com
dir: *Telephone for directions*

A beautifully presented family-run establishment, The Birch is located opposite Woburn Championship Golf Course, close to Woburn Abbey and the Safari Park. It has built its reputation on the friendly service of freshly cooked food. A comprehensive menu offers a range of English and Continental dishes, and there is a griddle area where customers can make their selection from the array of fresh steaks and fish, which are then cooked to their preference by the chefs.

Open 12-3 6-12 Closed: Sun eve **Bar Meals** booking required Av main course £13.95 **Restaurant** booking required ⊕ FREE HOUSE ◀ London Pride, Adnams, Guinness. ♀ 6 **Facilities** Parking

BERKSHIRE

ALDERMASTON
Map 5 SU56

Hinds Head ☻

Wasing Ln RG7 4LX
☎ 0118 971 2194 📠 0118 97 14511
e-mail: hindshead@accommodating-inns.co.uk
dir: *M4 junct 12, A4 towards Newbury, left on A340 towards Basingstoke, 2m to village*

This 17th-century inn with its distinctive clock and bell tower still incorporates the village lock-up, which was last used in 1865. The former brew house behind the pub has been refurbished to create an additional dining area. Menu choices range from jacket potatoes and filled baguettes to whole baked sea bass; carbonara pasta; and cauliflower cheese.

Open all wk ⊕ FULLERS BREWERY ◀ Fullers HSB. ☻ 12 **Facilities** Family room Garden Parking

ALDWORTH
Map 5 SU57

PICK OF THE PUBS

The Bell Inn ☻

RG8 9SE ☎ 01635 578272
dir: *Just off B4009 (Newbury to Streatley road)*

One might be surprised to discover that an establishment without a restaurant can hold its own in a world of smart dining pubs and modish gastro-pubs. Well, be surprised. The Bell not only survives, it positively prospers and, to be fair, it does serve some food, if only hot, crusty, generously filled rolls. And since it is one of the few truly unspoiled country pubs left, and serves cracking pints of Arkell's, West Berkshire and guest real ales, this alimentary limitation has been no disadvantage. The Bell is old, very old, beginning life in 1340 as a five-bay cruck-built manor hall. It has reputedly been in the same family for 200 years: ask Mr Macaulay, the landlord - he's been here for more than thirty of them, and he has no plans to change it from the time warp it is. A 300-year-old, one-handed clock still stands in the taproom, and the rack for the spit-irons and clockwork roasting jack are still over the fireplace. Taller customers may bump their heads at the glass-panelled bar hatch.

Open Mon-Sat 11-3 6-11 (Sun 12-3, 7-10.30) Closed: 25 Dec, Mon (BH Mon lunch only) ⊕ FREE HOUSE ◀ Arkell's Kingsdown, 3B, West Berkshire Old Tyler & Maggs Magnificent Mild, guest ales. ☻ 6 **Facilities** Dogs allowed Garden Parking **Notes** ⊜

ASCOT
Map 6 SU96

The Thatched Tavern ☻

Cheapside Rd SL5 7QG
☎ 01344 620874 📠 01344 623043
dir: *Follow Ascot Racecourse signs. Through Ascot 1st left (Cheapside). 1.5m, pub on left*

Just a mile from the racecourse, a 17th-century building of original beams, flagstone floors and very low ceilings. In summer the sheltered garden makes a fine spot to enjoy real ales and varied choice of food. In the same safe hands for over ten years, the kitchen produces dishes like pan-fried chicken breast with cheddar mash, black pudding, Muscat and thyme sauce, seared calves' liver on bubble and squeak, and steak and kidney pudding with mustard mash.

Open all wk ⊕ FREE HOUSE ◀ Fuller's London Pride, IPA. ☻ 8 **Facilities** Garden Parking

ASHMORE GREEN
Map 5 SU56

The Sun in the Wood ☻

Stoney Ln RG18 9HF ☎ 01635 42377 📠 01635 528392.
e-mail: info@suninthewood.co.uk
dir: *From A34 at Robin Hood Rdbt left to Shaw, at mini-rdbt right then 7th left into Stoney Ln 1.5m, pub on left*

The name promises woodland beauty and the setting delivers it, yet the centre of Newbury is surprisingly close by. Expect stone floors and plenty of wood panelling within, and a country garden, decking terrace for alfresco dining and crazy golf outside. Sample a pint of Wadworth's or one of 16 wines by the glass, and enjoy food made using local ingredients at this award-winning country pub: perhaps crisp whitebait with home-made tartare sauce, then chicken breast with wild mushroom sauce.

Closed: Mon **Bar Meals** L served Tue-Sat 12-2, Sun 12-4 booking required D served Tue-Sat 6-9.30 booking required Av main course £10.95 **Restaurant** L served Tue-Sat 12-2, Sun 12-4 booking required D served Tue-Sat 6-9.30 booking required Av 3 course à la carte fr £19.95 ⊕ WADWORTH ◀ Wadworth 6X, Henrys Original IPA, Badger Tanglefoot Ö Westons Stowford Press. ☻ 16 **Facilities** Children's menu Play area Garden Parking

BOXFORD
Map 5 SU47

The Bell at Boxford 🅰 ★★★ INN ☻

Lambourn Rd RG20 8DD
☎ 01488 608721 📠 01488 658502
e-mail: paul@bellatboxford.com
dir: *A338 toward Wantage, right onto B4000, take 3rd left to Boxford*

Mock Tudor country pub at the heart of the glorious Lambourn Valley, noted for its pretty villages and sweeping Downland scenery. Cosy log fires add to the appeal in winter, and the patio is popular throughout the year with its array of flowers and outdoor heating, hog roasts, barbecues and parties.

Open all wk 11-3 6-11 (Sun noon-10.30) **Bar Meals** L served Mon-Sat 12-2, Sun 12-3 D served Mon-Sat 7-9.30, Sun 7-9 Av main course £8.95 **Restaurant** L served Mon-Sat 12-2, Sun 12-3 D served Mon-Sat 7-9.30, Sun 7-9 Av 3 course à la carte fr £28.50 ⊕ FREE HOUSE ◀ Interbrew Bass, Courage Best, Wadworth 6X, Henrys IPA. ☻ 60 **Facilities** Children's menu Dogs allowed Garden Parking **Rooms** 11

See advertisement under NEWBURY

BRAY
Map 6 SU97

PICK OF THE PUBS

The Hinds Head ☺☺☺ ☻

See Pick of the Pubs on opposite page

CHADDLEWORTH
Map 5 SU47

The Ibex ☻

Main St RG20 7ER ☎ 01488 638311 📠 01488 639458
e-mail: inn@the-ibex.co.uk
dir: *A338 towards Wantage, through Great Shefford then right, then 2nd left, pub on right in village*

Originally two cottages forming part of a 17th-century farm, this Grade II listed building was later used as a bakery and then an off-licence before eventually becoming a pub. In more recent years it was run by ex-jockey Colin Brown who partnered the legendary Desert Orchid for many years, and kept the cosy lounge bar with low ceilings and bench seats. Popular bar menu includes chicken and leek pie; beef and ale casserole; liver and onions; and halibut with red wine and wild mushrooms.

Open all wk 12-3 6-mdnt (Fri-Sun noon-mdnt) **Bar Meals** L served all wk 12-3 D served all wk 6-9 ⊕ GREENE KING ◀ Regularly changing guest ales Ö Stowford Press. ☻ 7 **Facilities** Family room Dogs allowed Garden Parking

PICK OF THE PUBS

The Hinds Head ❀❀ ⚲

High St SL6 2AB
☎ **01628 626151**   📄 **01628 623394**
e-mail: info@hindsheadhotel.co.uk
web: www.hindsheadhotel.co.uk
dir: *M4 junct 8/9 take exit to Maidenhead*
Central. Next rdbt take exit for Bray &
Windsor. After 0.5m take B3028 to Bray

Having dropped its 'hotel' suffix, the Hinds Head is now owned by internationally acclaimed chef (some say culinary alchemist) Heston Blumenthal, and business partner Jamie Lee. Not surprisingly, it has become a gastronomic destination, yet remains very much a village local. With origins in Tudor times, celebrated past patrons include Prince Philip, who held his stag night here in 1947, and Princess Margaret and Lord Snowdon, who celebrated their engagement here in 1963. Sturdy oak panelling and beams, leather chairs and real fires characterise the interior. On the ground floor is the two-AA Rosette main restaurant and a cosy bar area with comfortable seating

and small alcoves. Upstairs are two further dining areas, the Vicars Room, and the larger Royal Room. Blumenthal, who through working alongside the Tudor Kitchens at Hampton Court Palace is rediscovering the origins of British cuisine, has reintroduced dishes from a bygone era. His starters include pea and ham soup; soused herrings with beetroot and horseradish; and rabbit and bacon terrine with cucumber pickles. Among his typical main dishes are oxtail and kidney pudding; Lancashire hot pot; skate wing with capers, lemon and parsley; Gloucester Old Spot pork chop with mustard mash; and rump steak with bone-marrow sauce and triple-cooked chips. To follow come banana Eton Mess, the traditional pudding from Eton College tuck shop; poached pear in red wine and spices; the indubitably medieval quaking pudding (a cross between a custard tart without the pastry and a very light bread pudding); and British cheese with oatcakes and quince paste. In addition, a wide selection of specials is available Monday to Friday, while a separate lunchtime bar menu includes home-made Scotch quail egg; devils on horseback; and smoked salmon with cucumber and cream cheese. Guest ales and well-selected, widely sourced wines complete the picture.

Open all week Closed: 25-26 Dec **Bar Meals** L served all week 12-2.30 D served Mon-Sat 6.30-9.30 **Restaurant** L served all week 12-2.30 D served Mon-Sat 6.30-9.30 ⊞ FREE HOUSE ◀ Greene King IPA, Greene King Abbot Ale, Marlow Rebellion, Timothy Taylor Landlord, London Pride ⚬ Stowford Press. ⚲ 15 **Facilities** Children's menu Parking

CHIEVELEY
Map 5 SU47

The Crab at Chieveley ★★★★ GA ◉◉ ☷

North Heath, Wantage Rd RG20 8UE
☎ 01635 247550 📠 01635 247440
e-mail: info@crabatchieveley.com
dir: *M4 junct 13. 1.5m W of Chieveley on B4494*

Break that tedious M4 journey with a pit-stop at this old thatched dining pub, one of the best seafood restaurants in England. Specialising in mouth-watering fish dishes, with fresh deliveries daily, the Fish Bar offers, for example, hot Irish oysters with chorizo as a starter, and Cornish fish curry with coconut and cardamom-scented rice as a main. In the elegant, maritime-themed restaurant, try the unfishy salt marsh lamb confit accompanied by goats' cheese and shallot tart. There are 14 en suite rooms available.

Open all day all wk 11-11 **Bar Meals** L served all wk 12-2.30 D served all wk 7-9.30 ⊕ FREE HOUSE ◗ Fuller's London Pride, Spitfire. ☷ 16 **Facilities** Garden Parking **Rooms** 14

COOKHAM DEAN
Map 5 SU88

PICK OF THE PUBS

Chequers Brasserie ☷

Dean Ln SL6 9BQ ☎ 01628 481232 📠 01628 481237
e-mail: info@chequersbrasserie.co.uk
dir: *From A4094 in Cookham High St towards Marlow, over rail line. 1m on right*

Kenneth Grahame, who wrote *The Wind in the Willows*, spent his childhood in these parts. He'd surely have enjoyed this historic pub, tucked away between Marlow and Maidenhead in one of the prettiest villages in the Thames Valley. Striking Victorian and Edwardian villas around the green set the tone, whilst the surrounding wooded hills and dales have earned Cookham Dean a reputation as a centre for wonderful walks. Today, the Chequers offers carefully chosen wines and a good selection of real ales to accompany an Anglo-French menu, dedicated to the use of fresh, excellent produce. Sample the likes of rump of Buckinghamshire lamb with sautéed chorizo, fondant potato and ratatouille, fillet of black bream with marsh samphire, brown shrimp, dill beurre blanc and a bobbin of linguini. There is a good value lunch two-course menu and great Sunday roasts. Westons, Thatchers and Aspall ciders also available.

Open all day all wk 11-11 **Bar Meals** L served Mon-Sat 12-2.30, Sun 12-9.30 D served Mon-Thu 6.30-9.30, Fri-Sat 6.30-10, Sun 12-9.30 Av main course £12.50 **Restaurant** L served Mon-Sat 12-2.30, Sun 12-9.30 D served Mon-Thu 6.30-9.30, Fri-Sat 6.30-10, Sun 12-9.30 Fixed menu price fr £26.95 Av 3 course à la carte fr £18.95 ⊕ FREE HOUSE ◗ Guinness, Greene King IPA, Rebellion Marlow Brewery ◗ Stowford Press, Thatchers Cox, Aspall. ☷ 14 **Facilities** Children's menu Garden Parking

CRAZIES HILL
Map 5 SU78

PICK OF THE PUBS

The Horns ☷

RG10 8LY ☎ 0118 940 1416 📠 0118 940 4849
e-mail: reservations@thehornspub.com
dir: *Off A321 NE of Wargrave*

A Tudor hunting lodge to which a barn (now the Horns' dining area) was added 200 years ago. The restored building has three interconnecting terracotta-coloured oak beamed rooms full of old pine tables, stripped wooden floors, open fires and rugby memorabilia. The peaceful atmosphere, untroubled by music or electronic games, makes it a great place to enjoy a pint of ale or pie of the day. At the end of the 19th century there were only 15 houses in Crazies Hill, in which the Horns occupied a central position. Since then the hamlet has expanded rapidly and, incredibly, at one time supported six pubs. There are extensive and secluded garden with children's play area, and ample off-street parking. Look out for regular jazz and comedy nights.

Open all wk ⊕ BRAKSPEAR ◗ Brakspear Bitter. ☷ 6 **Facilities** Play area Family room Dogs allowed Garden Parking

CURRIDGE
Map 5 SU47

The Bunk Inn ☷

RG18 9DS ☎ 01635 200400 📠 01635 200336
e-mail: thebunkinn@btconnect.com
dir: *M4 junct 13, A34 N towards Oxford. Take 1st slip road then right for 1m. Right at T-junct, 1st right signed Curridge*

Owned by the Liquorish family since 1991, this village free house is renowned for its cuisine and friendly atmosphere. Stay in the log fire-warmed bar in winter or, in summer, head for the attractive garden and patio. The only question is, where to dine - stylish restaurant or lovely conservatory? All food is fresh, and wherever possible, seasonal and local. An impressive carte menu, plus specials that usually include fresh Brixham fish.

Open all day all wk 11am-11.30pm **Bar Meals** L served Mon-Fri 12-2.30, Sat 12-9.30, Sun 12-9 D served Mon-Fri 6-9.30, Sat 12-9.30, Sun 12-9 **Restaurant** L served Mon-Fri 12-2.30, Sat 12-9.30, Sun 12-9 D served Mon-Fri 6-9.30, Sat 12-9.30, Sun 12-9 ⊕ FREE HOUSE ◗ Fuller's London Pride, Good Old Boy ◗ Stowford Press. ☷ 9 **Facilities** Play area Dogs allowed Garden Parking

EAST GARSTON
Map 5 SU37

PICK OF THE PUBS

The Queen's Arms Country Inn

RG17 7ET ☎ 01488 648757 📠 01488 648642
e-mail: info@queensarmshotel.co.uk
dir: *M4 junct 14, 4m onto A338 to Great Shefford, then East Garston*

This 18th-century inn is pleasantly located in a small village in the Lambourn Valley, with its many racehorse training yards. It is also an excellent area for walking, being quite close to the Ridgeway. Now part of the small and select Miller's Collection of pubs, the Queen's Arms offers a warm welcome in stylishly traditional setting. The menu offers a good selection of traditional country food made from fresh local ingredients. On the main menu are dishes such as goats' cheese and black pudding salad; wild boar and leek sausages; lamb cutlets; and roast peppers stuffed with brie, mushrooms and red onion served with tagliatelle. The terrace and large garden are popular in the summer, when barbecues and hog roasts take place.

Open all wk **Bar Meals** L served all wk 12-2 D served all wk 7-9 Av main course £16 **Restaurant** L served all wk 12-2 D served all wk 7-9 Av 3 course à la carte fr £32 ⊕ MILLERS COLLECTION ◗ Guinness, 1664 Ringwood Best, Ringwood 49er, guest ale. **Facilities** Children's menu Dogs allowed Garden Parking

HERMITAGE
Map 5 SU57

The White Horse of Hermitage ☷

Newbury Rd RG18 9TB ☎ 01635 200325
e-mail: thewh@btconnect.com
web: www.thewhitehorseofhermitage.co.uk
dir: *5m from Newbury on B4009. Follow signs to Chieveley, right into Priors Court Rd, turn left at mini-rdbt, pub approx 1m*

The White Horse has achieved a solid reputation for its pub food, using the freshest and finest local produce to create a daily menu, including signature dishes such as BBQ babyback ribs. The interior bar and restaurant is contemporary in decor, and outside you choose between the Mediterranean-style patio or the large garden which is equipped with swings and a football area.

Open noon-3 5-11 Closed: Sun eve, Mon (ex BH) **Bar Meals** Av main course £10 food served all day **Restaurant** Av 3 course à la carte fr £15 food served all day ⊕ GREENE KING ◗ Abbot Ale, Greene King IPA, Guinness. ☷ 9 **Facilities** Children's menu Play area Dogs allowed Garden Parking

HUNGERFORD
Map 5 SU36

PICK OF THE PUBS

The Crown & Garter ★★★★ INN ☷

See Pick of the Pubs on opposite page

PICK OF THE PUBS

The Crown & Garter ★★★★ INN ♥

HUNGERFORD Map 5 SU36

Inkpen Common RG17 9QR
☎ **01488 668325**
e-mail: gill.hern@btopenworld.com
web: www.crownandgarter.com
dir: *From A4 to Kintbury & Inkpen. At village store left into Inkpen Rd, follow signs for Inkpen Common 2m*

A family-owned, personally run 17th-century inn in a really pretty part of Berkshire. James II allegedly used to stop off here on his way to visit one of his mistresses - perhaps he wasn't in such a hurry to see her. The inn's barn was used to lay out the bodies of two lovers hanged at nearby Combe Gibbet for killing the woman's husband. There have been four of these gruesome constructions: the original rotted away, its replacement was struck by lightning, the third lasted a hundred years or so until felled by a gale in 1949, and then there's the one you see today. The inn's ancient charm can best be seen in the bar area, where there's a huge inglenook fireplace and criss-crossing beams. You can eat here, in the restaurant, or outside in the enclosed beer garden or patio, choosing from a variety of dishes all freshly prepared on the premises from local produce. The daily changing menu might feature twice-baked smoked haddock and cheese soufflé; or chicken liver parfait with red onion marmalade to start. Among the main courses are likely to be seafood pie topped with cheesy potatoes; steak and kidney pie; or breast of chicken chasseur with sauté potatoes. Apple strudel with toffee ice cream or dark and white chocolate pots with orange sorbet might tempt you for dessert. Eight spacious en suite bedrooms have been built around a pretty cottage garden. Nearby Hungerford has some good antique shops, and Bath, Oxford and Winchester are less than an hour away. But why drive when the stunning countryside surrounding the inn is so perfect for walking, cycling, fishing, shooting or simply chilling out?

Open 12-3 5.30-11 (Sun 12-5 7-10.30, closed Mon & Tue lunch) **Bar Meals** L served Wed-Sat 12-2, Sun 12-2.30 D served Mon-Sat 6.30-9.30 **Restaurant** L served Wed-Sat 12-2, Sun 12-2.30 D served Mon-Sat 6.30-9.30 ⊕ FREE HOUSE ◼ Mr Chubbs, Good Old Boy, Guinness, Moonlight, Timothy Taylor Landlord. ♥ 9 **Facilities** Garden Parking Wi-fi **Rooms** 8

HUNGERFORD *continued*

PICK OF THE PUBS

The Swan Inn ★★★★ INN

Craven Rd, Lower Green, Inkpen RG17 9DX
☎ 01488 668326 📄 01488 668306
e-mail: enquiries@theswaninn-organics.co.uk
web: www.theswaninn-organics.co.uk
dir: *S down Hungerford High St (A338), under rail bridge, left to Hungerford Common. Right signed Inkpen (3m)*

Organic beef farmers Mary and Bernard Harris preside over this rambling 17th-century free house, which stands in fine walking country just below Combe Gibbet and Walbury Hill. In addition to ramblers, the pub is a magnet for cyclists, hang gliders, shooting parties and organic food enthusiasts. An attractive terraced garden sets the scene for alfresco summer dining, in contrast to the heavily beamed interior with its old photographic prints and open winter fires. Almost everything on the menu is prepared using their own fresh produce; meats are 100% organic and butchered on the premises, earning accreditation by the Soil Association. The bar menu offers traditional English favourites, while the Cygnet restaurant serves dishes like creamy mushroom and artichoke tart with pesto dressing; pan-fried breast of Barbary duck with bacon and mushroom sauce; and a full range of organic steaks. The vegetarian options are tempting. There's an organic farm shop to visit too, plus 10 spacious en suite bedrooms if you would like to stay over.

Open all wk 11-11 (Sun noon-10.30) Closed: 25-26 Dec **Bar Meals** L served all wk 12-2 D served all wk 7-9.30 Av main course £10 **Restaurant** L served Wed-Sun 12-2.30 booking required D served Wed-Sat 7-9.30 booking required Av 3 course à la carte fr £25 ⊕ FREE HOUSE ◀ Butts Traditional & Jester Bitter, Butts Blackguard, guest ales. **Facilities** Children's menu Play area Garden Parking **Rooms** 10

HURST   Map 5 SU77

The Green Man ☕

Hinton Rd RG10 0BP
☎ 0118 934 2599 📄 0118 934 2939
e-mail: simon@thegreenman.uk.com
dir: *Off A321, adjacent to Hurst Cricket Club*

The pub gained its first licence in 1602, and Brakspear purchased a 1,000 year lease on the building in 1646. The old black beams, low in places, are still to be seen and the building has been developed to include all the old features, while newer areas reflect a similar theme. Inside you'll find open fires, hand drawn beer and good food, from sandwiches to Sunday roasts. The garden, open to fields and woodland, includes a children's play area.

Open all wk 11-3 5.30-11 (Sun noon-10.30) **Bar Meals** food served all day **Restaurant** food served all day ⊕ BRAKSPEAR ◀ Brakspear Bitter, Hobgoblin, seasonal ales. ☕ 8 **Facilities** Children's menu Play area Garden Parking

---

KINTBURY   Map 5 SU36

PICK OF THE PUBS

The Dundas Arms ☕

53 Station Rd RG17 9UT
☎ 01488 658263 📄 01488 658568
e-mail: info@dundasarms.co.uk
dir: *M4 junct 13 take A34 to Newbury, then A4 to Hungerford, left to Kintbury. Pub 1m by canal & rail station*

Set in an Area of Outstanding Natural Beauty on the banks of the Kennet and Avon Canal, this free house has been welcoming travellers since the end of the 18th century. The pub has been in the same family for over 42 years, and proprietor David Dalzell-Piper has worked and cooked here throughout that time. Traditional beers like West Berkshire are served in the

---

convivial bar, whilst the simply styled restaurant is redolent of a French auberge. On warmer days, outdoor tables offer views of the narrow boats and wildlife on the canal. Meanwhile, a typical restaurant meal might start with crab au gratin or salad of fillet steak with beetroot, grapeseed and horseradish sauce, before moving on to pan-fried venison haunch steak with red wine and pepper sauce, spiced red cabbage; fried calves' liver with bacon, mash and onion; or baked Orkney salmon with fennel and saffron risotto.

Closed: 25 & 31 Dec, Sun eve **Bar Meals** L served Mon-Sat 12-2 D served Tue-Sat 7-9 Av main course £11.50 **Restaurant** L served Mon-Sat 12-2 D served Tue-Sat 7-9 booking required Av 3 course à la carte fr £23 ⊕ FREE HOUSE ◀ West Berkshire, Mr Chubbs Lunchtime Bitter, Adnams, West Berkshire Good Old Boy, Ramsbury Gold. ☕ 10 **Facilities** Children's menu Family room Parking

---

KNOWL HILL   Map 5 SU87

PICK OF THE PUBS

Bird In Hand Country Inn 🅐 ★★★ HL ☕

Bath Rd RG10 9UP
☎ 01628 826622 & 822781 📄 01628 826748
e-mail: sthebirdinhand@aol.com
web: www.birdinhand.co.uk
dir: *On A4, 5m W of Maidenhead, 7m E of Reading*

In the same family for three generations, the inn prides itself on providing personal service in a friendly atmosphere. Parts of the building date from the 14th century, and legend has it that in the late 1700s George III wet his regal whistle here while his horse was being re-shod at the forge next door. There is a wood-panelled Oak Lounge Bar serving a range of hand-pumped ales, and an attractive restaurant overlooking the courtyard and fountain. A buffet bar is available to diners from the main bar or restaurant, while dishes from the respective menus range from steak and kidney pudding with Guinness, to roast whole stuffed quail with apricot and thyme in an oyster mushroom and grape sauce. Monthly themed evenings feature cuisines from around the world.

Open all wk Mon-Sat 11am-11pm (Sun noon-10.30pm) **Bar Meals** food served all day ⊕ FREE HOUSE ◀ Guest ales. ☕ 12 **Facilities** Dogs allowed Garden Parking **Rooms** 15

LECKHAMPSTEAD   Map 5 SU47

PICK OF THE PUBS

The Stag ☕

See Pick of the Pubs on page 38

MAIDENHEAD   Map 6 SU88

The Belgian Arms ☕

Holyport SL6 2JR ☎ 01628 634468 📠 01628 777952
e-mail: enquiries@thamessideevents.com
dir: *In Holyport, 2m from Maidenhead, off Ascot road*

Originally known as The Eagle, the Prussian eagle inn sign attracted unwelcome attention during the First World War. As a result, the name was changed to reflect an area where the fiercest fighting was taking place. Things are more peaceful now, and details of local walks are listed outside the pub. The attractive menu includes snacks and light lunches, as well as hot dishes like sausages, mash and onion gravy, and spicy beanburger and chips.

Open all wk 12-3 5.30-11.30 (Fri-Sat 11-11.30 Sun noon-10.30) **Bar Meals** L served Mon-Sat 12-2.30, Sun 12-3.30 D served Mon-Sat 6-9.30 ⊕ BRAKSPEAR ◀ Brakspear Best, Brakspear Organic Gold. ☕ 8 **Facilities** Dogs allowed Garden Parking

The White Hart ☕

Moneyrow Green, Holyport SL6 2ND
☎ 01628 621460 📄 01628 621460
dir: *2m S from Maidenhead. M4 junct 8/9, follow Holyport signs then Moneyrow Green. Pub by petrol station*

A busy 19th-century coaching inn offering quality home-made food, with most vegetables and herbs used freshly picked from its own organic allotment. Typical mains are caramelised breast of duck; calves' liver and bacon; venison sausages; grilled fillet of plaice; and slow-roasted tomato tart with Somerset brie. The wood-panelled lounge bar is furnished with leather chesterfields and warmed by an open fire. There are large gardens to enjoy in summer and a boules pitch. Recent change of hands.

Open all day all wk 12-11.30 (Fri-Sat 12-1am, Sun 12-11) **Bar Meals** L served Tue-Sat 12.30-3, Sun 12-4 D served Tue-Sat 6-9 Av main course £7.50 ⊕ GREENE KING ◀ Guinness, IPA, Morland Original ♂ Stowford Press. ☕ 7 **Facilities** Children's menu Dogs allowed Garden Parking

NEWBURY   Map 5 SU46

PICK OF THE PUBS

The Yew Tree Inn ◉◉ ☕

See Pick of the Pubs on page 39

PALEY STREET   Map 5 SU87

PICK OF THE PUBS

The Royal Oak ◉◉ ☕

SL6 3JN ☎ 01628 620541
dir: *From Maidenhead take A330 towards Ascot for 2m, turn right onto B3024 signed White Waltham, 2nd pub on left*

Drop by for a drink and relax on one of the comfortable sofas at this traditional English dining pub, owned by Nick Parkinson, son of Sir Michael Parkinson. Fullers provide the reliable ales, but the wine list is undoubtedly the star of the drinks show; around 20 wines are served by the glass, and the main listings begin with a selection of over 20 champagnes. Meanwhile, head chef Dominic Chapman has a solid reputation in the kitchen, using the best seasonal produce to create outstandingly good British food. Choose from a small selection of bar snacks or sample the lunch and dinner menus, which might begin with smoked haddock soup or potted Devon crab with toast. Typical mains include peppered haunch of venison with creamed spinach, Old Spot belly pork with mushy peas and braised onions, or grilled lemon sole with wild mushrooms and watercress. A large beer garden completes the picture for alfresco dining in warmer weather.

Open 12-3 6-11 (Sun 12-4) Closed: 25 Dec & 1 Jan, Sun eve **Restaurant** L served Mon-Sat 12-3, Sun 12-4 booking required D served Mon-Thu 6.30-9.30, Fri-Sat 6.30-10 Av 3 course à la carte fr £35 ⊕ FULLERS ◀ Fuller's London Pride. ☕ 20 **Facilities** Children's menu Garden Parking

PICK OF THE PUBS

The Stag ♉

LECKHAMPSTEAD   Map 5 SU47

Shop Ln RG20 8QG ☎ 01488 638436
e-mail: enquiries@stagleckhampstead.co.uk
dir: *6m from Newbury on B4494*

To look at, the privately owned, white-painted Stag could only be a pub. It lies just off the village green in a sleepy downland village and close by are the Ridgeway long-distance path and Snelsmore Common, home to nightjar, woodlark and grazing Exmoor ponies. Needless to say, with such beautiful countryside all around, muddy wellies and wet dogs are expected - in fact, the latter are as genuinely welcome as their owners. During the winter months the wood-burning stove is always ready with its dancing flames. The bar and restaurant walls are painted in warm red, or left as bare brick, while old black and white photographs tell of village life many years ago. Surrounding farms and growers supply all produce, including venison, pheasant and fresh river trout. These fish often appear on the specials board, courtesy of a regular customer who barters them for a few glasses of Rioja, depending on their size. Aberdeen Angus beef from cattle raised next door may also feature as a special, and those lucky enough to find it there agree that its taste and texture are sublime. Other possibilities, depending on the prevailing menu, are Cornish mussels in cream, white wine and herbs; sword fish steak pan fried with lemon, sun-dried tomato and basil; noisettes of lamb with apricot, fig and date couscous; Mediterranean skewers of chicken with feta cheese, olives and pitta bread; and a daily vegetarian special. Home-made desserts include apricot bread and butter pudding with cream, and chocolate and Cointreau cheesecake. There are around 20 red and white wines, among them varieties from Australia, California and France. Compulsive workers can take advantage of a wireless internet connection, although in a pub like this it would have to be pretty urgent work.

Open 12-3, 6-11 **Bar Meals** L served all wk 12-2.30 D served all wk 6-9.30 Av main course 9 **Restaurant** L served all wk 12-2.30 D served all wk 6-9.30 Av 3 course à la carte fr £15 ⊕ FREE HOUSE ◀ Morlands Original ♉ 8 **Facilities** Children's menu Dogs allowed Garden Parking

PICK OF THE PUBS

The Yew Tree Inn ❀❀ 🍷

NEWBURY   Map 5 SU46

**Hollington Cross, Andover Rd,
Highclere RG20 9SE**
☎ **01635 253360**   🖷 **01635 255035**
e-mail: info@theyewtree.net
*dir: A34 toward Southampton, 2nd exit
bypass Highclere, onto A343 at rdbt, through
village, pub on right*

The former 16th-century coaching inn
stands just south of the village on the
A343 and is well placed following a visit
to nearby Highclere Castle. Owned and
sympathetically remodelled by the
celebrated chef-turned restaurateur,
Marco Pierre White, whose famed
perfectionism is evident throughout the
rambling building, from the immaculate
styling that blends original features of
old beams, tiled floors, and inglenooks
with huge smouldering logs, with the
refinement of crisp linen tablecloths,
sparkling glassware, and a
contemporary finish. Equally, he
performs a similar trick with the menu,
offering both traditional British food
and time-honoured classics from the
French culinary canon. The Anglo-French
cooking takes a brasserie approach,
with the menu split into sections like
hors d'oeuvres, fish and seafood, pies
and puddings and roasts and grills, and
delivers accomplished, well-presented
dishes that are driven by quality
ingredients. Kick off a memorable meal
with pea and ham soup; Morecambe Bay
potted shrimps; or calves' tongue with
celeriac remoulade, then move on to
braised oxtail and kidney pudding;
Marsh Benham lamb with dauphinoise;
chicken and morel pie; honey-roast pork
belly with apple sauce and roasting
juices; or rib-eye steak with béarnaise.
Tellingly, the desserts are described as
'puddings' and might include such
familiar comforts as rice pudding with
red fruit compôte and caramelised
apple pie. Good value fixed-price menus
are also a feature at lunchtime and on
Sundays. To drink, you'll find cracking
ales on handpump, including brews
from local Butt's and West Berkshire
breweries, Weston's cider, and an
excellent list of wines (10 available by
the glass).

Open all week **Bar Meals** L served all
week 12-3 D served all week 6-9 Av
main course £15 **Restaurant** L served
all week 12-3 D served all week 6-9
Fixed menu price fr £15.50 Av 3 course
à la carte fr £27 ⊕ FREE HOUSE
◀ Timothy Taylor, Adnams, Butt's
Barbus Barbus, Mr Chubbs 🍎 Westons
Old Rosie, Westons Bounds Brand. 🍷 10
Facilities Children's menu Dogs allowed
Garden Parking

READING
Map 5 SU77

The Crown ♈

Playhatch RG4 9QN
☎ 0118 947 2872 📠 0118 946 4586
e-mail: info@thecrown.co.uk
dir: *From Reading take A4155 towards Henley-on-Thames. At 1st rdbt take 1st exit, pub 400mtrs on left*

This charming 16th-century country inn with its lovely garden and excellent restaurant nestles between the Thames and the Chilterns, an Area of Outstanding Natural Beauty. Head Chef Nana Akuffo is behind the move to buy fresh local produce wherever possible. Dinner starters may include grilled Brixham sardine fillets, or Thai beef salad; main course examples are confit of duck en croûte, and slow-roasted Cornish lamb; typical desserts are hot sticky toffee pudding, and carpaccio of fresh pineapple.

Open all day all wk 10am-11.20pm (Fri-Sat 10am-12.20am) **Bar Meals** L served Mon-Sat 12-3, Sun 12-8 D served Mon-Thu 6-9.30, Fri-Sat 6-10, Sun 12-8 ⊕ BRAKSPEAR ◀ Brakspear Bitter, Brakspear Special, Brakspear Seasonal, Oxford Gold, Guinness. ♈12 **Facilities** Garden Parking

The Flowing Spring ♈

Henley Rd, Playhatch RG4 9RB ☎ 0118 969 9878
e-mail: flowingspring@aol.com
dir: *3m N of Reading*

A lovely country pub on the Henley road, much favoured by walkers and cyclists. It's family friendly too, with a menu for under-12s and a small play area in the large well-kept garden. Representative dishes on the combined bar/restaurant menu include chicken goujons with chips and salad; battered cod and chips; spotted dick; and sticky toffee pudding. Being a Fullers pub, Chiswick, London Pride and ESB are all well kept on tap.

Open all wk 11-11 **Bar Meals** L served all wk D served all wk Av main course £6.95 food served all day **Restaurant** L served all wk D served all wk Av 3 course à la carte fr £12 food served all day ⊕ FULLERS ◀ London Pride, ESB, Chiswick, HSB. ♈7 **Facilities** Children's menu Play area Family room Dogs allowed Garden Parking

The Shoulder of Mutton ♈

Playhatch RG4 9QU ☎ 0118 947 3908
e-mail: grnwillows@hotmail.com
dir: *From Reading follow signs to Caversham, then onto A4155 to Henley-on-Thames. At rdbt left to Binfield Heath, pub on left*

Just a stone's throw from both Reading and Henley, the Shoulder of Mutton has a stylish, contemporary atmosphere. The pub offers a varied menu; but, true to its name, mutton remains the speciality. It has featured on BBC1's *The One Show*, providing mutton pie for the presenters and guests. Other dishes might include a range of gourmet burgers, slow roasted half a duck with an orange and kumquat glaze; and the famous shoulder of mutton from Hampshire Down Cross slow roasted for 5 hours in rosemary, red capsicum, onions and red wine.

Closed: 26-30 Dec, 1 Jan, Sun pm ⊕ GREENE KING ◀ Greene King IPA, Old Speckled Hen. ♈7 **Facilities** Garden Parking

STANFORD DINGLEY
Map 5 SU57

The Old Boot Inn ♈

RG7 6LT ☎ 0118 974 4292 📠 0118 974 4292
dir: *M4 junct 12, A4/A340 to Pangbourne. 1st left to Bradfield. Through Bradfield, follow Stanford Dingley signs*

Set in the glorious Pang Valley, in a village of Outstanding Natural Beauty, the original 18th-century Old Boot has been extended to include a popular conservatory. Fresh seafood choices are announced daily, and include the likes of seabass, cod, scallops, haddock and swordfish. There is an excellent choice of real ales always available.

Open all wk **Bar Meals** L served all wk 12-2 D served all wk 7-9 **Restaurant** L served all wk 12-2 D served all wk 7-9 ⊕ FREE HOUSE ◀ Brakspear Bitter, Interbrew Bass, West Berkshire Dr Hexters, Archers Best, Thomas Hardy Royal Oak. ♈8 **Facilities** Play area Dogs allowed Garden Parking

SWALLOWFIELD
Map 5 SU76

PICK OF THE PUBS

The George & Dragon

Church Rd RG7 1TJ
☎ 0118 988 4432 📠 0118 988 6474
e-mail: nikita.staen@yahoo.co.uk
dir: *M4, junct 11, A33 towards Basingstoke. Left at Barge Lane to B3349 onto The Street, right onto Church Rd*

Don't judge a pub by its façade, at least not this one. It may look unassuming, but it has a smart, cosy interior with stripped low beams, terracotta-painted walls, log fires and rug-strewn floors, and it has earned quite a reputation for its food. Dining takes precedence over drinking, and booking for lunch or dinner would be prudent. Main courses include Caribbean jerk chicken with jollof rice and mojo salsa; fillet of sea bass with creamed spinach and aubergine ragoût; and wild mushroom and asparagus tagliatelle with gorgonzola cream. A typical specials board could offer a starter of smoked quail filled with winter fruits and nuts on poached apricots, followed by grilled cod with a smoked haddock, mussel and clam broth with champ mash.

Open all wk Closed: 25-26 Dec eve & 1 Jan eve **Bar Meals** L served Mon-Sat 12-2.30, Sun 12-3 D served Mon-Sat 7-9.30, Sun 7-9 **Restaurant** L served Mon-Sat 12-2.30, Sun 12-3 D served Mon-Sat 7-9.30, Sun 7-9 ⊕ FREE HOUSE ◀ Fuller's London Pride, Brakspears, Youngs. **Facilities** Dogs allowed Garden Parking

THATCHAM
Map 5 SU56

The Bladebone Inn

Chapel Row, Bucklebury RG7 6PD ☎ 0118 971 2326
e-mail: simon.kelly2@btconnect.com
dir: *2m NE of Thatcham, 5m from Newbury*

Above the entrance to this historic inn hangs a bladebone, which, according to legend, originally came from a mammoth that once stalked the Kennet valley. A more probable explanation is that it was used to indicate that whale oil was sold here for use in oil-burning lamps and probably of 17th-century origin. These days the Bladebone is a stylish dining venue with a mixture of English and Mediterranean influences.

Open all day all wk noon-11 (Sun noon-6) **Bar Meals** L served Mon-Fri 12-3, Sat 12-9.30, Sun 12-5 D served Mon-Fri 5.30-9.30, Sat 12-9.30 ◀ Good Old Boy. **Facilities** Dogs allowed Garden Parking

WALTHAM ST LAWRENCE
Map 5 SU87

The Bell ♈

The Street RG10 0JJ ☎ 0118 934 1788
e-mail: scott@thebellinn.biz
dir: *On B3024 E of Twyford. From A4 turn at Hare Hatch*

In 1608 this 14th-century building was given to the village; it now runs as a free house with the rent going towards village charities. The Bell is renowned for its ever-changing range of real ales selected from smaller micro-breweries all over the country. It also has a growing reputation for its food - perhaps sea bass with roasted new potatoes, sunblush tomatoes, rocket and endive salad; or roast beetroot and squash salad with goats' cheese dressing.

Open all wk 12-3 5-11 (Sat noon-11 Sun noon-10.30) **Bar Meals** L served Mon-Fri 12-2, Sat-Sun 12-3 D served all wk 7-9.30 ⊕ FREE HOUSE ◀ Waltham St Lawrence No.1 Ale, 4 Guest Ales ♒ 3 Guest Ciders. ♈7 **Facilities** Play area Dogs allowed Garden Parking

WARGRAVE
Map 5 SU77

St George and Dragon ♈

High St RG10 8HY ☎ 0118 9404474
dir: *3.5m from Henley on A321*

A friendly Thames-side pub, in one of the river's most scenic locations. Heaters on the outdoor decking make it possible to enjoy the view all year round, while inside are open kitchens, stone-fired ovens and log-burning fires. The menu offers the familiar - pizza, pasta and steaks - and the not so familiar, such as duck confit with pak choi, egg noodles, black bean and chilli sauce; and swordfish with Tuscan bean cassoulet and chorizo.

Open all day all wk noon-11 (Fri-Sat noon-mdnt Sun noon-10.30) **Bar Meals** food served all day ⊕ FREE HOUSE ◀ Loddon Hulabaloo, Timothy Taylor Landlord ♒ Aspalls. ♈14 **Facilities** Dogs allowed Garden Parking

WINKFIELD
Map 6 SU97

Rose & Crown ☆

Woodside, Windsor Forest SL4 2DP
☎ **01344 882051** 🖷 01344 885346
e-mail: info@roseandcrownascot.com
dir: *M3 junct 3 from Ascot Racecourse on A332 take 2nd
exit from Heatherwood Hosp rdbt, then 2nd left*

A 200-year-old traditional pub complete with old beams
and low ceilings. Hidden down a country lane, it has a
peaceful garden overlooking open fields where you can
see horses and llamas at pasture. A typical menu may
include pan-fried fillet steak with blue cheese gratin
potatoes, with seasonal vegetables and a bourguignon
sauce; pavé of halibut with rosemary sauté potatoes,
chargrilled asparagus and baby leeks, with horseradish
cream sauce; or asparagus tortellini with basil and
parmesan cheese.

Open all day all wk 11-11 (Sun noon-7) **Bar Meals** L
served Mon-Sat 12-2.15, Sun 12-3.15 D served Tue-Sat
7-9.15 ⊕ GREENE KING ◀ Morland Original, Greene
King IPA & guest ale. ☂ 9 **Facilities** Play area Garden
Parking

WINTERBOURNE
Map 5 SU47

The Winterbourne Arms ☆

RG20 8BB ☎ **01635 248200** 🖷 01635 248824
e-mail: winterbournearms@tiscali.co.uk
dir: *M4 junct 13 into Chieveley Services, follow
Donnington signs to Winterbourne sign. Turn right into
Arlington Ln, right at T-junct, left into Winterbourne*

A large 300-year-old free house once sheltered the village
shop and bakery - the remains of the bread oven survive
in the restaurant. In winter the interior is candle-lit with
a log fire, while the extensive gardens offer alfresco
dining in summer. Local game and daily fresh fish from
Brixham provide the basic ingredients for mainly British-
style dishes such as warm goats' cheese and red onion
tartlet; beer battered fillet of cod; and pan-fried supreme
of salmon with lobster bisque and prawn sauce.

Open all wk noon-3 6-11 (Sun noon-10.30) **Bar Meals** L
served all wk 12-2.30 D served all wk 6-10 Av main
course £10 food served all day **Restaurant** L served all
wk 12-2.30 D served all wk 6-10 Fixed menu price fr £10
Av 3 course à la carte fr £15.25 ⊕ FREE HOUSE
◀ Ramsbury Gold, Guinness, Fuller's London Pride. ☂ 20
Facilities Children's menu Dogs allowed Garden Parking

WORLD'S END
Map 5 SU47

The Langley Hall Inn ☆

RG20 8SA ☎ **01635 248332** 🖷 01635 248571
dir: *Exit M4 junct 13 north, take 1st slip road signed
Beedon & Chieveley. Left & immediately right, inn 1.5m
on left*

Friendly, family-run bar/restaurant with a reputation for
freshly prepared food, real ales and a good selection of
wines. Fresh fish dishes vary according to the daily catch
- maybe pan-fried crevettes, grilled Dover sole, salmon
fishcakes with spinach and parsley sauce, or roast cod
fillet with cheese and herb crust. Other favourites are
braised lamb, beef stir-fry, and Thai chicken curry.
Outside there is a large patio and garden, plus a
petanque court for fine weather use

Open all wk 12-3.30 5.30-11 (Sun 12-6) Closed: 26
Dec-2 Jan **Bar Meals** L served all wk 12-2.30 (Sun 12-4)
D served Mon-Sat 6.30-10 booking required **Restaurant** L
served all wk 12-2.30 (Sun 12-4) booking required D
served Mon-Sat 6.30-10 booking required ⊕ ENTERPRISE
INNS ◀ West Berkshire Brewery - Good Old Boy, Mr
Chubbs, Lunchtime Bitter, Deuchars IPA, London Pride,
Brakspears ♂ Stowford Press. ☂ 12 **Facilities** Children's
menu Dogs allowed Garden Parking

YATTENDON	Map 5 SU57

PICK OF THE PUBS

The Royal Oak Hotel ☻

The Square RG18 0UG
☎ 01635 201325 ▤ 01635 201926
e-mail: info@royaloakyattendon.com
web: www.royaloakyattendon.com
dir: *M4 junct 12, A4 to Newbury, right at 2nd rdbt to Pangbourne then 1st left. From junct 13, A34 N 1st left, right at T-junct. Left then 2nd right to Yattendon*

This quintessentially English country inn dates back to the 16th century, as the timber framework attests. The Oak – as it was formerly known – reputedly played host to Oliver Cromwell before the battle of Newbury, but today it's rarely interrupted by anything more than the clip-clop of passing horse-riders. The popular village bar serves West Berkshire Brewery's Good Old Boy, Mr Chubbs and a third real ale. The culinary emphasis is based on a brasserie-style menu and extensive wine list served in a choice of private or open dining rooms. A sample selection from the menu could be starters of Brixham crab chowder, or crisp confit of pork belly, black pudding and apple ravioli; main courses of line-caught halibut with braised oxtail and roasted salsify; or breast of guinea fowl stuffed with haggis. There are beautiful gardens to enjoy and a boules pitch.

Open all wk **Bar Meals** L served all wk 12-2.30 **Restaurant** L served all wk 12-2.30 D served all wk 7-9.30 Fixed menu price fr £15 Av 3 course à la carte fr £33 ⊕ FREE HOUSE ◖ West Berks, Good Old Boy, Mr Chubbs, 1 guest ale. ☻ 8 **Facilities** Garden Parking

See advert on page 41

BRISTOL	

BRISTOL	Map 4 ST57

Cornubia

142 Temple St BS1 6EN
☎ 0117 925 4415 ▤ 0117 929 1523
e-mail: thecornubia@hotmail.co.uk
dir: *Opposite Bristol Fire Station*

This characterful Georgian city-centre pub was originally built as two houses, and now owned by the Hidden Brewery company. Office workers love it, not just because of its convenience, but also for its choice of seven changing real ales, two draught ciders and a serious collection of malts and bottled beers. And then there's the food – pork and apple sausages and mash or home-made soups for example - chalked up on a blackboard. Cornubia, by the way, is the Latinised name for Cornwall.

Open all wk Closed: 25-26 Dec, 1 Jan **Bar Meals** L served Mon-Fri 12-2.30, Sun 2-6 D served Mon-Fri 5-9 Av main course £6 ⊕ HIDDEN PUB CO ◖ All Hidden Brewery ales, Erdinger Ö Cheddar Valley, Guest ciders. **Facilities** Dogs allowed Parking

The Hare on the Hill NEW

Dove St, Kingsdown BS2 8LX ☎ 0117 908 1982
e-mail: harehill@bathales.co.uk

If you can find it in the maze of streets that is Kingsdown, this is a gem – a small, street-corner local from the good old days. If all you want is a pint of one of Bath Ales award-winning brews, a real cider or a European-style beer, come here. All food (except fresh fish) is sourced from within a 40 mile radius. Typical are steak baguette; home-made quiche; five-bean chilli and rice; plus a roast on Sundays with live music in the evening.

Open 12-2.30 5-11 (Sat 12-11.30 Sun 12-11) **Bar Meals** L served Mon-Sat 12-2 (Sun 12-4) D served Mon-Sat 6-9

Highbury Vaults

164 St Michaels Hill, Cotham BS2 8DE
☎ 0117 973 3203
e-mail: highburyvaults@youngs.co.uk
dir: *Take A38 to Cotham from inner ring dual carriageway*

Once a turnpike station, this 1840s pub has retained much of its Victorian atmosphere. In days when hangings took place on nearby St Michael's Hill, many victims partook of their last meal in the vaults. Today, it's a business crowd by day and students at night feasting on chilli, meat and vegetable curries, casseroles, pasta dishes, and jacket potatoes. No fried foods, no music or fruit machines, but a popular heated garden terrace.

Open all day all wk noon-mdnt (Sun 12-11) **Bar Meals** L served Mon-Fri 12-2, Sat 12-2.30, Sun 12-3 D served Mon-Fri 5.30-8.30 Av main price £4.95 ⊕ YOUNG & CO BREWERY PLC ◖ Bath Ales Gem, St Austells Tribute, Brains SA, Young's Special & Bitter, Wells Bombardier, Guest ales rotating Ö Addlestones. **Facilities** Garden **Notes** ⊗

Robin Hood's Retreat ☻

197 Gloucester Rd BS7 8BG ☎ 0117 924 8639
e-mail: info@robinhoodsretreat.gmail.com
web: www.robinhoodsretreat.co.uk
dir: *At main rdbt at Broad Mead take Gloucester Rd exit, St Pauls. Road leads into Gloucester Rd (A38)*

In the heart of Bristol this Victorian red-brick pub is popular with real ale lovers, who usually have eight to choose from. These days there's also a choice of real ciders. The interior has been superbly refurbished, keeping original features and adding to the richly coloured wood panelling and furniture. There's plenty of attention to detail in the food too, which is all prepared on the premises. Favourites are slow-cooked British dishes with a French accent, and several seafood options such as devilled crab.

Open all wk noon-11 (Sat 9-mdnt) Closed: 25 Dec **Bar Meals** Av main course £13 **Restaurant** L served all wk D served all wk Fixed menu price fr £14.50 ⊕ ENTERPRISE INNS ◖ Doom Bar, Eden, Tribute, Tanglefoot Ö Stowford Press, Weston's Organic, Addlestones. ☻ 7 **Facilities** Garden

BUCKINGHAMSHIRE	

AMERSHAM	Map 6 SU99

Hit or Miss Inn ☻

Penn Street Village HP7 0PX
☎ 01494 713109 ▤ 01494 718010
e-mail: hit@ourpubs.co.uk
dir: *M25 junct 18, A404 (Amersham to High Wycombe road) to Amersham. Past crematorium on right, 2nd left into Whielden Ln (signed Winchmore Hill). 1.25m, pub on right*

Michael and Mary Macken welcome you to their 18th-century cottage-style dining pub with its fires and old world beams. The Hit or Miss overlooks the cricket ground from which the pub takes its name, and there's a beautiful country garden with lawn, patio and picnic tables for warmer days. Home-cooked dishes range from tempting well-filled sandwiches and baked potatoes to maple syrup and mustard marinated salmon fillet, venison pie with raspberry jus, or a selection of steaks. There are daily specials and Sunday roasts, too.

Open all day all wk 11-11 (Sun 12-10.30) **Bar Meals** L served Mon-Sat 12-2.30, Sun 12-8 D served Mon-Sat 6.30-9.30, Sun 12-8 **Restaurant** L served Mon-Sat 12-2.30, Sun 12-8 D served Mon-Sat 6.30-9.30, Sun 12-8 ⊕ HALL & WOODHOUSE ◖ Badger Best, Tanglefoot, Sussex, Hopping Hare Ö Stowford Press. ☻ 12 **Facilities** Children's menu Dogs allowed Garden Parking

PICK OF THE PUBS

The Royal Standard of England ⚑

Brindle Ln, Forty Green HP9 1XT ☎ 01494 673382
e-mail: theoldestpub@btinternet.com
dir: *A40 to Beaconsfield, right at church rdbt onto B474 towards Penn, left onto Forty Green Rd, 1m*

Situated in the beautiful Chilterns village of Forty Green, this welcoming country inn traces its roots to Saxon times. During the Civil War the pub was a mustering place for Royalists, and the ancient building is said to be haunted by the ghost of a 12 year-old drummer boy. Today, good hearty food is served amid the striking stained glass windows, beams and flagstone floors, whilst in winter the building is warmed by a large inglenook fireplace. Seasonal wild game is a regular feature on the specials board, supported by an extensive bill of fare. Start, perhaps, with a pork terrine before moving on to main course dishes such as mutton shepherd's pie; seasonal vegetable risotto; or Buckinghamshire bacon badger suet roll. The pub boasts a wide choice of interesting ales and real ciders, with many popular wines served by the glass.

Open all day all wk 11-11 **Bar Meals** Av main course £12 food served all day **Restaurant** food served all day ⊕ FREE HOUSE ◀ Marston's Pedigree, Brakspear Bitter, Rebellion IPA, Theakston Old Peculier, Guest Ales Ò Westons Stowford Press, Old Rosie Scrumpy. ⚑ 12 **Facilities** Children's menu Family room Dogs allowed Garden Parking

The Lions of Bledlow ⚑

Church End HP27 9PE
☎ 01844 343345 📄 01844 343345
dir: *M40 junct 6, B4009 to Princes Risborough, through Chinnor into Bledlow*

This traditional free house is located at the foot of the Chilterns, just above a private railway line where steam trains run between Chinnor and Horsenden. It has a low-beamed bar and log fire, and in summer seating in the spacious garden overflows onto the village green. The menu, written on boards, might offer liver and bacon with bubble and squeak; spinach and potato cakes with chilli sauce and salad; and salmon fillet with honey mustard dressing.

Open all wk 11.30-3 6-11 (Sat 11.30-11 Sun noon-11) **Bar Meals** L served Mon-Sat 12-2.30, Sun 12-4 D served Mon-Sat 6.30-9.30 ⊕ FREE HOUSE ◀ Wadworth 6X, Guest ales Ò Stowford Press. ⚑ 10 **Facilities** Family room Dogs allowed Garden Parking

PICK OF THE PUBS

The Crooked Billet ◉ ⚑

2 Westbrook End, Newton Longville MK17 0DF
☎ 01908 373936
e-mail: john@thebillet.co.uk
dir: *M1 junct 13, follow signs to Buckingham. 6m, signed at Buttledump rdbt to Newton Longville*

Built as a farmhouse in about 1665, the Crooked Billet was first licensed in the early 1700s. A brew house was added during the 19th century in response to growing demand. Nevertheless, farming continued into the early 20th century; pigs and hens were kept in a barn, whilst apples were harvested from the orchards. Today, the pub retains much of its traditional charm, with original oak beams, open log fires and a large garden. But the top attraction is the food and wine from husband-and-wife team John and Emma Gilchrist. Emma's regularly-changing menus are based on the finest, freshest ingredients from a multitude of small specialist food producers and suppliers. The emphasis is on taste, combined with modern presentation. Lunchtime in the relaxed bar area brings sandwiches, salads, and pastas, together with traditional pub dishes. Typical choices on the evening menu are cream of white bean soup, followed by pan-fried trout fillet, green beans and buttered Jersey Royals; or chicken Kiev with roasted wild garlic butter and soft herb gnocchi.

Open noon-2.30 5-11 (Sun noon-4) Closed: Mon L **Bar Meals** L served Tue-Sat 12-2, Sun 12-4 D served Mon-Sat 7-9.30 Av main course £12.50 **Restaurant** L served Tue-Sat 12-2, Sun 12-4 D served Mon-Sat 7-9.30 booking required Fixed menu price fr £12 Av 3 course à la carte fr £24 ⊕ GREENE KING ◀ Old Speckled Hen, Badger Tanglefoot, Hobgoblin, Ruddles County. ⚑ 300 **Facilities** Children's menu Garden Parking

PICK OF THE PUBS

The Royal Oak ⚑

See Pick of the Pubs on page 44

The Pheasant Inn ⚑

Windmill St HP18 9TG ☎ 01844 239370
e-mail: info@thepheasant.co.uk
dir: *In village centre, by windmill*

Set on the edge of Brill Common, the large garden and veranda at this 17th-century beamed inn make the most of its fine hilltop position, with stunning views over seven counties. The popular menu offers a selection of locally produced steaks; duck breast with blueberry juniper sauce; braised lamb shank with sweet potato and Stilton mash; and red mullet in rich saffron mussel stew. Roald Dahl and JRR Tolkien were both frequent visitors, and the annual Brill Music Festival is on the first Saturday of July.

Open all day all wk 11-11 (Fri-Sun 11am-mdnt) **Bar Meals** L served all wk 12-2 D served all wk 6.30-9 **Restaurant** L served all wk 12-2 D served all wk 6.30-9 ◀ Triple B, Courage Best Ò Thatchers. ⚑ 9 **Facilities** Children's menu Garden Parking

The Red Lion ⚑

27 Church St HP18 9RT ☎ 01844 238339
e-mail: lyngarh@aol.com
dir: *Off B4011 (Thame to Bicester road)*

The Red Lion dates back to the early 17th century and was originally five separate buildings. Plenty of walking and cycling routes converge upon the village, which is overlooked by a famous windmill. Simple, traditional menus change regularly and may feature pork medallions; beer-battered cod; or lamb shank braised in red wine. In summer the secluded garden is home to fierce competitions of Aunt Sally - a local form of skittles.

Open all day all wk noon-11.30 **Bar Meals** L served all wk 12-2.30 D served Mon-Sat 6.30-9.30 ⊕ GREENE KING ◀ Greene King IPA, Old Trip, Fireside, Old Speckled Hen. ⚑ 7 **Facilities** Dogs allowed Garden

The Old Thatched Inn ⚑

Main St, Adstock MK18 2JN
☎ 01296 712584 📄 01296 715375
e-mail: manager@theoldthatchedinn.co.uk
web: www.theoldthatchedinn.co.uk
dir: *Telephone for directions*

Listed in 1645, this lovely old thatched and beamed inn still boasts the traditional beams and inglenook fireplace.

continued on page 46

PICK OF THE PUBS

The Royal Oak 🍷

BOVINGDON GREEN　　　Map 5 SU88

Frieth Rd SL7 2JF
☎ **01628 488611**　📄 **01628 478680**
e-mail: info@royaloakmarlow.co.uk
web: www.royaloakmarlow.co.uk
dir: *From Marlow, take A4155. In 300yds right signed Bovingdon Green. In 0.75m pub on left*

With red kites thriving following their reintroduction to the Chilterns, you can reasonably expect to see them soaring above this delightful whitewashed village pub just out of Marlow. It is set amid its own spacious surroundings, which include a sunny terrace, pétanque piste and herb garden, while inside you'll find a cosy interior with a wood-burning stove, rich fabrics, a rose-red dining room and lustrous dark floorboards. The imaginative British food on the menu makes good use of fresh local produce, and an exclusively European wine list includes a white from Hertfordshire, at the other end of the Chilterns. Among the menu's 'small plate' selection you might find crispy salt and pepper baby squid on saffron-soused vegetables, with chilli and honey yoghurt; devilled lamb's kidneys on eggy bread brioche with crispy pancetta; and bubble and squeak with oak-smoked bacon, poached egg and hollandaise sauce. Main meals include classic fish pie with buttered Chantenay carrots; slow-cooked Amersham pork belly on champ with black pudding and cider cream sauce; and crispy herb polenta cake with sautéed wild mushrooms, glazed goat's cheese and balsamic roast beetroot. Sunday roasts are also popular. Among the decent selection of puddings are vanilla bean crème brûlée with lemon thyme shortbread; and spiced apple and blackberry crumble. Try one of the several pudding wines - the one from Worcestershire, maybe. The beers come from the Rebellion Brewery in Marlow Bottom and Wychwood in Witney, both not far away. Free WiFi is available if you're planning a working lunch or dinner.

Open 11-11 (Sun 12-10.30) Closed: 26 Dec **Bar Meals** L served Mon-Fri 12-2.30, Sat 12-3, Sun 12-4 D served Sun-Thu 6.30-9.30, Fri-Sat 6.30-10 **Restaurant** L served Mon-Fri 12-2.30, Sat 12-3, Sun 12-4 D served Sun-Thu 6.30-9.30, Fri-Sat 6.30-10 🌐 SALISBURY PUBS LTD 🍺 Brakspears, Marlow Rebellion IPA, Wychwood Hobgoblin. 🍷 19 **Facilities** Children's menu Dogs allowed Garden Parking

PICK OF THE PUBS

The Ivy House ♀

CHALFONT ST GILES   Map 6 SU99

London Rd HP8 4RS
☎ **01494 872184** 📄 **01494 872870**
e-mail: ivyhouse@fullers.co.uk
dir: *On A413 2m S of Amersham & 1.5m N of Chalfont St Giles*

Set close to John Milton's cottage in Chalfont St Giles, this beautiful 250-year-old brick and flint coaching inn enjoys amazing views of the Chiltern Hills. The pub is handy for local country walks as well as several nearby golf courses, and is well-known for its friendly welcome, great food and extensive wine list. Open fires, comfy armchairs, old beams and brasses all give the place a cosy, warm and welcoming atmosphere. Naturally there's the odd ghost story to be told, and whisky lovers will appreciate the range of over 30 malts, including some of the landlord's favourite rarities.

Meals are served in the bar, the former coach house and the restaurant, and in fine weather there's also the option of alfresco dining in the garden. The fresh seasonal menu features daily blackboard specials, with the emphasis on quality local produce, fresh fish, and salads. Lunchtime brings a selection of sandwiches and filled baked potatoes; the Ivy House ploughman's with Stilton, Cheddar and ham; as well as hot dishes like chilli con carne; and hand-carved ham, eggs and French fries. More formal dining might begin with starters like stuffed field mushroom with goats' cheese and walnut; lamb and kiwi brochettes; or mussels in a cream, white wine and leek sauce. Moving on, you could choose from marinated pork steak with wild mushroom risotto, root vegetable crisps and baby spinach; Shropshire fidget pie with mash and broccoli; Toulouse cassoulet with chunky white bread; or multi award-winning speciality sausages of the day served with bubble and squeak. Desserts include traditional baked apple with cinnamon and raisins; and chocolate fudge fondue.

Open all week **Bar Meals** L served Mon-Fri 12-3, Sat-Sun all day D served Mon-Fri 6-10, Sat-Sun all day **Restaurant** L served Mon-Fri 12-3, Sat-Sun all day D served Mon-Fri 6-10, Sat-Sun all day ⊕ FULLERS SMITH & TURNER ◀ Fuller's London Pride, Chiswick, Guest Ale. ♀ 10 **Facilities** Children's menu Dogs allowed Garden Parking

BUCKINGHAM *continued*

The spacious interior consists of a formal conservatory and a bar with comfy furniture and a welcoming atmosphere. Fresh fish is a speciality, try grilled turbot with tiger prawn ravioli for a typical example, and there are always two additional fish specials on a Friday. Meat options might include roast duck breast with celeriac purée, braised chicory and griottes cherry sauce.

Open all wk noon-11 (Mon-Tue 12-2.30 6-11 Sun noon-10.30) **Bar Meals** L served Mon-Fri 12-2.30, Sat 12-3, Sun 12-8 D served Mon-Sat 6-9.30 ⊕ FREE HOUSE ◄ Hook Norton Best, Timothy Taylors, Doom Bar, Old Speckled Hen. ♀ 10 **Facilities** Dogs allowed Garden Parking

---

The Wheatsheaf ♀

Main St, Maids Moreton MK18 1QR
☎ 01280 815433   📄 01280 814631
dir: *M1 junct 13, (or M40 junct 9, A34 to Bicester) A421 to Buckingham, then A413 to Maids Moreton*

This traditional, thatched village inn has been a pub since 1750, and offers an appetising à la carte menu in the spacious conservatory overlooking the secluded beer garden. Eating options include baked cod and prawns in cream; roast aubergine stuffed with ratatouille; and home-made Thai chicken curry. Real ales and snacks can also be enjoyed in the bar, with its cosy inglenook fireplaces. Children will be delighted with the outdoor play equipment.

Open all wk **Bar Meals** L served all wk 12-2.15 D served Tue-Sat 6.45-9.30 **Restaurant** L served all wk 12-2.15 D served Tue-Sat 6.45-9.30 ⊕ FREE HOUSE ◄ John Smiths, Side Pocket For A Toad, Reverend James, Pitstop. ♀ 10 **Facilities** Children's menu Play area Family room Dogs allowed Garden Parking

---

CHALFONT ST GILES   Map 6 SU99

PICK OF THE PUBS

The Ivy House ♀

See Pick of the Pubs on page 45

The White Hart ♀

Three Households HP8 4LP
☎ 01494 872441   📄 01494 876375
e-mail: enquiries@thewhitehartstgiles.co.uk
dir: *Off A413 (Denham to Amersham road)*

Oak and brown leather furniture and a refurbished bar characterise the quiet, relaxed atmosphere of this prettily-located 100-year-old inn, giving it a welcoming, contemporary feel. The menu offers the likes of loin of pork en croute, carpet bag fillet steak, supreme of chicken, lamb shank, and calves' liver. Fish dishes include baked sea bass with vegetables and Thai fish sauce, and seared blue-fin tuna.

Open all wk 11-3.30 5-11.15 (Sun noon-3.30 5-10.30) **Bar Meals** L served Mon-Sat 12-2.30, Sun 12-2.30 D served Mon-Sat 6.30-9.30 ⊕ GREENE KING ◄ Greene King Morland Original, Abbot Ale, Rev. James. ♀ 12 **Facilities** Garden Parking

---

CHALFONT ST PETER   Map 6 TQ09

PICK OF THE PUBS

The Greyhound Inn ♀

SL9 9RA ☎ 01753 883404   📄 01753 891627
e-mail: reception@thegreyhoundinn.net
dir: *M40 junct 1/M25 junct 16, follow signs for Gerrards Cross, then Chalfont St Peter*

The 14th-century Greyhound has a macabre place in English history. Not only are its grounds believed to be where the last man hanged for stealing sheep was executed, but a former patron was Sir George Jeffreys, known as the Hanging Judge for his harsh sentencing policy during the Monmouth Rebellion. While still a local magistrate he held court in a room above the restaurant, mention of which brings us neatly to the food here. The cooking style is essentially classic British with a modern twist, producing starters such as moules marinière, shallots, parsley, white wine and cream; chargrilled chicken Caesar salad; and avocado, orange and prawn salad with Marie Rose sauce. From a well balanced list of main courses choose from deep-fried haddock in beer batter; whole baked sea bass; pan-fried calf's liver; home-made shepherd's pie; or leg of duck confit, among many others.

Open all wk Mon-Wed 6.30am-10.30pm (Thu 6.30am-11.30pm, Fri-Sat 6.30am-1am, Sun 8.30am-10.30pm) Closed: 1 Jan **Bar Meals** food served all day ⊕ ENTERPRISE INNS ◄ London Pride. ♀ 12 **Facilities** Dogs allowed Garden Parking

---

CHEDDINGTON   Map 11 SP91

The Old Swan ♀

58 High St LU7 0RQ ☎ 01296 668226   📄 01296 663811
e-mail: geoffrsmith@btconnect.com
dir: *From Tring towards Marsworth take B489, 0.5m. Left towards Cooks Wharf onto Cheddington, pub on left*

Formed out of three cottages in the 15th century, this delightful thatched pub is known not only for its real ales and traditional charm but also for its ghosts. A man in 18th-century dress reputedly tries to kiss ladies in the restaurant area! Food ranges from roasted half pheasant with black cherry and port sauce; sea bass fillets with pine nuts and baby spinach; to five bean, vegetable and tomato hotpot. Outside there's a large garden with a children's play area. A great choice of real ales and Westons Stowford Press cider is available.

Open all wk Mon-Fri 12-3, 5-11 (Sat-Sun 11-11) **Bar Meals** L served Mon-Thu 12-2, Fri-Sat 12-2.30, Sun 12-4 D served Mon-Thu 6-9, Fri-Sat 6-9.30 Av main course £10 **Restaurant** L served Mon-Thu 12-2, Fri-Sat 12-2.30, Sun 12-4 D served Mon-Thu 6-9, Fri-Sat 6-9.30

⊕ PUNCH TAVERNS ◄ Courage Best, St Austell Tribute, Everard's Tiger, Shepherd Neame Spitfire, Adnams Broadside ♂ Stowford Press. ♀ 12 **Facilities** Children's menu Play area Dogs allowed Garden Parking

---

CHENIES   Map 6 TQ09

PICK OF THE PUBS

The Red Lion ♀

See Pick of the Pubs on opposite page

CHESHAM   Map 6 SP90

The Black Horse Inn ♀

Chesham Vale HP5 3NS ☎ 01494 784656
e-mail: mgoodchild@btconnect.com
dir: *A41 from Berkhamsted, A416 through Ashley Green, 0.75m before Chesham right to Vale Rd, at bottom of Mashleigh Hill, 1m, inn on left*

Set in some beautiful valley countryside, this 500-year-old pub is ideal for enjoying a cosy, traditional environment without electronic games or music. During the winter there are roaring log fires to take the chill off those who may spot one of the resident ghosts. An ever-changing menu includes an extensive range of snacks, while the main menu may feature steak and Stallion Ale pie, trout and almonds, various home-made pies, steaks and gammon, stuffed plaice, or salmon supreme.

Open all wk 11-3 5.30-11 (Sun noon-3 7-11) **Bar Meals** L served all wk 12-2.30 D served Mon-Sat 6.30-9.30, Sun 7-9 ⊕ PUNCH TAVERNS ◄ Adnams Bitter, Speckled Hen, Wadworth 6X, Guest ale ♂ Stowford Press. ♀ 10 **Facilities** Dogs allowed Garden Parking

---

The Swan ♀

Ley Hill HP5 1UT ☎ 01494 783075
e-mail: swanleyhill@btconnect.com
dir: *1.5m E of Chesham by golf course*

Once three cottages, the first built around 1520, qualifying it as one of Buckinghamshire's oldest pubs. Condemned prisoners, heading for nearby gallows, would drink 'a last and final ale' here. During the Second World War, Clark Gable, James Stewart and Glenn Miller frequently drank here after cycling from Bovingdon airbase. Menus change several times monthly, and a blackboard features daily specials. Corn-fed chicken and home honey-roasted ham pie, and venison wrapped in smoked pancetta with confit new potatoes are typical dinner choices.

Open all wk 12-3 5.30-11 (Sun 12-10.30) **Bar Meals** L served all wk 12-2.30 D served Tue-Sat 7-9 **Restaurant** L served Tue-Sun 12-2.30 D served Tue-Sat 7-9 booking required ⊕ PUNCH RETAIL ◄ Adnams Bitter, Fuller's London Pride, Timothy Taylor Landlord, Brakspears, guest ales. ♀ 8 **Facilities** Children's menu Garden Parking

---

PICK OF THE PUBS

The Red Lion ♈

CHENIES   Map 6 TQ09

WD3 6ED

☎ 01923 282722   📄 01923 283797

dir: *Between Rickmansworth & Amersham on A404, follow signs for Chenies & Latimer*

With over 20 years' experience behind them, Mike and Heather Norris firmly believe the 17th-century Red Lion's popularity stems from being a pub that serves good food, not a restaurant that serves beer. You'll find the unassuming, white-painted pub in the Chess Valley, just up the lane from Chenies Manor in the picture-book village, replete with a pretty green and an ancient parish church. Expect a plain, simply-furnished main bar, a charming, snug dining area housed in the original cottage to the rear with a tiled floor, old inglenook and rustic furniture, a new restaurant, and Mike talking passionately about his real

ales. Lion's Pride, brewed by Rebellion in Marlow, is available here and here alone; other local beers come from Vale Brewery in Haddenham. Heather cooks everything, including fresh daily pastas; bangers with bubble-and-squeak; big chunks of oven-baked leg of lamb (much like Greek kleftiko); roast pork belly on leek and potato mash; game pie; fishcakes with horseradish and beetroot dip; Orkneys rump steak; curries; poached haddock with peppered red wine sauce; and sausage, apple and cheddar pie. Speaking of pies, brace yourself for the famous lamb version, which a visiting American serviceman once declared beat a rival pub's pies hands down. Ever since, its entry on the menu has acquired an additional adjective every time it is rewritten. Today, therefore, it reads (take a deep breath) 'The awesome, internationally acclaimed, world-renowned, aesthetically and palatably pleasing, not knowingly genetically modified, hand-crafted, well-balanced, famous, original Chenies lamb pie'. Outside, on the pub's sunny side, is a small seating area.

Open all week Closed: 25 Dec **Restaurant** booking required 🍺 FREE HOUSE 🛢 Wadworth 6X, Rebellion's, Lion's Pride, Vale Best, plus guest ales. ♈ 10 **Facilities** Dogs allowed Garden Parking

CHOLESBURY
Map 6 SP90

PICK OF THE PUBS

The Full Moon ☻

Hawridge Common HP5 2UH
☎ 01494 758959 📄 07092 875764
e-mail: annie@alberto1142.freeserve.co.uk
dir: *At Tring on A41 follow signs for Wiggington & Cholesbury. On Cholesbury Common pub by windmill*

When this 17th-century former coaching inn was first built the local Chiltern Hills were overrun with alehouses. These days, only three remain. Fortunately, the Full Moon, which graduated from The Half Moon in 1812, is something of an ideal country pub, complete with beams, flagstones, winter fires and a windmill-backed setting. Comprehensive menus cover a range of possibilities, from baguettes and jacket potatoes to more adventurous fare. Smoked fish platter, Barnsley lamb chops and Szechuan sirloin stir-fry give an indication of the choice. If you like your desserts there is a good variety, from cold mixed berry soufflé to hot sticky toffee pudding with sticky toffee sauce and custard. In 1907, the landlord was fined for permitting drunkenness on the premises: these days the clientele is much better behaved when it comes to the eclectic selection of real ales.

Open all day all wk 12-11 (Sun 12-10.30) Closed: 25 Dec **Bar Meals** L served all wk 12-2 D served Mon-Sat 6.30-9, Sun 6-8 **Restaurant** L served all wk 12-2 D served Mon-Sat 6.30-9, Sun 6-8 ⊕ ADMIRAL TAVERNS ◀ Interbrew Bass & Adnams, Fuller's London Pride, Timothy Taylor Landlord, and guest ales. ☻ 7 **Facilities** Dogs allowed Garden Parking

CUDDINGTON
Map 5 SP71

PICK OF THE PUBS

The Crown ☻

See Pick of the Pubs on opposite page

DENHAM
Map 6 TQ08

The Falcon Inn ★★★★ INN ☻

Village Rd UB9 5BE ☎ 01895 832125
e-mail: mail@falcondenham.com
dir: *M40 junct 1, follow A40/Gerrards Cross signs. Approx 200yds turn right onto Old Mill Rd. Pass church on right, enter village. Pub opposite village green*

This traditional, historic 16th-century inn, located opposite the green in beautiful Denham Village, is an ideal base for exploring Colne Valley Country Park. Very little alteration has taken place and it retains its old world charm. Expect excellent real ales and great food, particularly fish. A sample menu includes lake-caught wild trout fillet with sauce Albert, rib-eye steak on Cajun dusted potato wedges, pan-fried sea bass on braised fennel and crushed potatoes, Thai chicken curry, or steak and kidney pie. Beamed en suite bedrooms with original features are also available.

Open all wk 11-3 5-11 (Fri-Sun all day) **Bar Meals** L served all wk 12-2.30 D served all wk 5-9.30 Av main course £9 **Restaurant** L served all wk 12-2.30 D served all wk 5-9.30 Av 3 course à la carte fr £19 ◀ Timothy Taylor Landlord, Bombardier, Archers, Brakspear & Guest Ale ♂ Stowford Press. ☻ 11 **Facilities** Children's menu Dogs allowed Garden **Rooms** 4

PICK OF THE PUBS

The Swan Inn ☻

See Pick of the Pubs on page 50

DORNEY
Map 6 SU97

The Palmer Arms ☻

Village Rd SL4 6QW ☎ 01628 666612
e-mail: chrys@thepalmerarms.co.uk
dir: *From A4 take B3026, over M4 to Dorney*

The Palmer Arms, dating from the 15th century, is well-located in the beautiful conservation village of Dorney. Its owners are passionate about providing high standards of food and service, and like to think of their cooking as 'English with a twist'. Seasonal game dishes are always available, and fish is well represented on the menu. It is open every day of the year for lunch, afternoon tea, dinner and all-day coffee.

Open all day all wk 11am-11.30pm (Sun 11-9) **Bar Meals** L served all wk 11-9 D served all wk 11-9 food served all day ⊕ GREENE KING ◀ Greene King Abbot Ale, IPA, Guinness. ☻ 18 **Facilities** Garden Parking

FARNHAM COMMON
Map 6 SU98

The Foresters ☻

The Broadway SL2 3QQ
☎ 01753 643340 📄 01753 647524
e-mail: barforesters@aol.com
dir: *Telephone for directions*

There's a great atmosphere at the Foresters, a pub dating back to the 1930s and built to replace a Victorian building. It's conveniently situated for discovering the delights of Burnham Beeches containing the world's largest collection of ancient beech. The quality daily menu might include fillet of brill colbert with parsley potatoes; pork loin steak with bubble and squeak and shallot and mustard sauce; and escalopes of veal with fondant potato and Irish cabbage.

Open all wk ⊕ PUNCH TAVERNS ◀ Fuller's London Pride, Draught Bass & guest ale. ☻ 10 **Facilities** Dogs allowed Garden Parking

FARNHAM ROYAL
Map 6 SU98

The Emperor ☻

Blackpond Ln SL2 3EG ☎ 01753 643006
e-mail: manager@theemperorfarnhamroyal.com
dir: *Telephone for directions*

This old inn has a wealth of polished wood floors and original beams running through its bar, conservatory and refurbished barn. A log fire burns in winter, and tables outside beckon on summer days. British food based on fresh seasonal fare is the overriding emphasis on the menus. You may find potted Aylesbury duck with baby leaf salad to start, followed by canon of Welsh lamb with dauphinoise potatoes, and fresh fruit meringue to finish.

Open all day all wk 11-late **Bar Meals** L served Mon-Thu 12-3, Fri-Sat 12-10, Sun 12-8 D served Mon-Thu 6-10, Fri-Sat 12-10, Sun 12-8 ⊕ OPENING COUNTY LEISURE ◀ London Pride, Timothy Taylor Landlord. ☻ 8 **Facilities** Dogs allowed Garden Parking

PICK OF THE PUBS

The Crown ♟

CUDDINGTON   Map 5 SP71

Spurt St HP18 0BB ☎ **01844 292222**
e-mail: david@anniebaileys.com
web: www.thecrowncuddington.co.uk
dir: *Off A418 between Aylesbury & Thame*

Fans of the popular TV series *Midsomer Murders* may recognise The Crown, as it has been used several times as a location. The inhabitants of the fictional county of Midsomer are, according to a fans' website, 'wealthy, amoral and snobbish eccentrics, often obsessed with the fairly small lives they lead in these isolated communities'. Well, whatever the inhabitants of the very real county of Buckinghamshire might be labelled, one thing's for certain - they know a good pub when they see one, because this delightful, Grade II listed, thatched and whitewashed enterprise

has made a name for itself as a great place to dine. The choice is either in one of the several low-beamed dining areas filled with charming prints and the glow of evening candlelight, or outside on the small patio, weather permitting. Fullers and Adnams are on tap in the bar, and an extensive wine list suggests the perfect match for every dish on the regularly changing menus. Among the starters to try are marinated sardines with coriander and spring onion pesto; crayfish and rocket salad; and hoi sin duck and bacon salad. Seafood dishes are a major attraction, and usually include seafood pie; smoked haddock with grilled Welsh rarebit, tomato salad and chips; and scallops with pancetta, salad leaves and truffle vinaigrette. Other typical main courses include gnocchi and spinach bake with gorgonzola; medallions of pork with mushroom and paprika sauce, chorizo and boulangère potatoes; and rib-eye steak with pink peppercorn and brandy sauce. A changing selection of desserts is chalked up on a blackboard. Sandwiches and 'small plates' are also available.

Open all week **Bar Meals** L served all week 12-2.15 D served Mon-Sat 6.30-9.15 Av main course £11 **Restaurant** L served all week 12-2.15 D served Mon-Sat 6.30-9.15 Fixed menu price fr £12.50 Av 3 course à la carte fr £22 ⊕ FULLERS BREWERY ◀ Fuller's London Pride, Adnams, Guinness. ♟ 9 **Facilities** Children's menu Garden Parking

PICK OF THE PUBS

The Swan Inn ♀

Village Rd UB9 5BH
☎ 01895 832085 📠 01895 835516
e-mail: info@swaninndenham.co.uk
web: www.swaninndenham.co.uk
dir: *From A40 take A412. In 200yds follow Denham Village sign on right. Through village, over bridge, last pub on left*

The Swan is the embodiment of the traditional country inn - a double fronted Georgian property swathed in wisteria and set in the beautiful village of Denham. Though the location is wonderfully secluded, it is not too far from the bright lights by a choice of nearby motorways. The interior is cosily welcoming with a large log fire and a collection of pictures picked up at local auctions, while outside there is a sunny terrace and large gardens. A private dining room is also available for family occasions or business meetings. Though The Swan is still very much a pub, the quality of the food is a great attraction to customers. Fresh, seasonal produce underpins a menu that re-invigorates some old favourites and makes the most of market availability with a daily-changing specials board. For a starter or light meal look to the 'small plates' section of the menu, with the likes steamed Scottish mussels with shallots, parsley, white wine and cream; warm Marlow rabbit terrine with sauerkraut. Among the main meals you'll find plenty of variety from braised Stockings Farm lamb shoulder shepherd's pie with smoked potato mash to beetroot-cured roast Scottish organic salmon on creamed saffron curly kale with lemon thyme dressing. An interesting option is also provided for vegetarians, starting with maybe a caramelised red onion tarte Tatin with Rowan Tree goats' cheese, or hand-made gnocchi with wild mushrooms, baby spinach, Oxford Blue and toasted pine nuts.

Open 11-11 (Sun 12-10.30) Closed: 26 Dec **Bar Meals** L served Mon-Fri 12-2.30, Sat 12-3, Sun 12-4 D served Sun-Thu 6.30-9.30, Fri-Sat 6.30-10 **Restaurant** L served Mon-Fri 12-2.30, Sat 12-3, Sun 12-4 D served Sun-Thu 6.30-9.30, Fri-Sat 6.30-10 ⊕ SALISBURY PUBS LTD 🍺 Wadworth 6X, Courage Best, Marlow Rebellion IPA. ♀ 19 **Facilities** Children's menu Dogs allowed Garden Parking

PICK OF THE PUBS

The Nag's Head ★★★★ INN ❀ ☙

GREAT MISSENDEN   Map 6 SP80

London Rd HP16 0DG
☎ 01494 862200   📠 01494 862685
e-mail: goodfood@nagsheadbucks.com
web: www.nagsheadbucks.com
dir: *1m from Great Missenden on London Rd. From A413 (Amersham to Aylesbury) turn left signed Chiltern Hospital. After 500mtrs pub on corner of Nags Head Ln & London Rd*

This charming free house was built in the 15th century as three small cottages for the local craftsmen who produced chair spindles and other furniture components. The parts were collected from the many similar 'bodger cottages' in the area, and were taken to London for assembly into finished pieces of furniture. Capitalising on their unique position on the London Road, the cottages were later converted into a coaching inn, offering rest and refreshment to weary horses and travellers. More recently the Nags Head has welcomed numerous Prime

Ministers and heads of state on their journey to Chequers, and it was a favourite of the late Harold Wilson. Now in the hands of the Michaels family, the Nag's Head has been earning a solid local reputation following extensive restoration in 2008. Original features including the low oak beams and inglenook fireplace have been carefully retained as a backdrop for the stylish new bar and beautifully refurbished en suite bedrooms. The dining room is decorated with limited edition prints by local children's author the late Roald Dahl, who was once a regular. Food is a passion here, and chef Alan Bell sources the finest ingredients from local suppliers wherever possible. The varied menus offer starters like salmon and fresh tarragon rillette, and Swiss cheese ravioli with Julienne vegetables. Main courses range from slow-cooked lamb shank to steamed salmon and lemon sole with queen scallops, and red pepper and saffron risotto. Leave room for a tempting pudding; typical choices include lemon tarte with white peach and redcurrant ice cream or layered chocolate trio. In summer, customers can relax over a drink or a meal whilst gazing out over the Chiltern Hills from the pub's lovely informal garden.

Open all day noon-11.30 (closed Sun eve) **Bar Meals** L served Mon-Sat 12-2.30, Sun 12-3.30 D served Mon-Sat 6.30-9.30 Av main course £14.95 **Restaurant** L served Mon-Sat 12-2.30, Sun 12-3.30 D served Mon-Sat 6.30-9.30 Av 3 course à la carte fr £30 ◀ London Pride, Black Sheep, Old Speckled Hen, Jack O'Legs, Rebellion. ☙ 14 **Facilities** Children's menu Dogs allowed Garden Parking **Rooms** 5

FORD — Map 5 SP70

PICK OF THE PUBS

The Dinton Hermit ★★★ INN ☻

Water Ln HP17 8XH
☎ 01296 747473 📠 01296 748819
e-mail: relax@dintonhermit.co.uk
dir: *Off A418 between Aylesbury & Thame*

Deep in the Vale of Aylesbury, this traditional stone-built inn is a comfortable and friendly place to pop in for a quick drink in front of the open fire. You'll find guest beers and locally brewed ales at the bar, as well as a wide selection of wines. In summer, the large garden is just the place to enjoy the sunshine in the peace and quiet of the Buckinghamshire countryside. Both the restaurant and the bar menus offer a range of quality dishes, with locally sourced ingredients wherever possible. Menus change with the seasons, but might include cod cheek and saffron stew; pea and mushroom risotto with a fine leaf salad; or Welsh lamb shank with glazed root vegetables. And, if you can't bear to leave, just book into one of the 13 contemporary and newly-refurbished bedrooms.

Open all day all wk 10am-11pm (Sun noon-10.30pm) Closed: 25-26 Dec & 1 Jan **Bar Meals** Av main course £10 food served all day **Restaurant** Fixed menu price fr £15.50 Av 3 course à la carte fr £20 food served all day ⊕ FREE HOUSE ◀ Adnams Bitter, 6X Brakspears, London Pride, Batemans XB. ☻ 13 **Facilities** Children's menu Dogs allowed Garden Parking **Rooms** 13

FRIETH — Map 5 SU79

The Prince Albert ☻

RG9 6PY ☎ 01494 881683
dir: *4m N of Marlow. Follow Frieth road from Marlow. Straight across at x-rds on Fingest road. Pub 200yds on left*

Set in the Chilterns, close to Hambledon and Marlow, this traditional country pub prides itself on old world values. There are no televisions, juke boxes or games - just good conversation and a welcoming atmosphere. Warm open fires enhance the mood in winter. Expect baguettes, jacket potatoes and ploughman's lunches among the lunchtime light bites, while the evening menu typically offers jumbo battered cod, chilli con carne, lamb shank, and home-made steak and kidney pie.

Open all day all wk 11-11 (Sun noon-10.30pm) **Bar Meals** L served Mon-Sat 12.15-2.30, Sun 12.30-3 D served Fri-Sat 7.30-9.30 ⊕ BRAKSPEAR ◀ Brakspear Bitter, Brakspear seasonal ales. ☻ 9 **Facilities** Children's menu Dogs allowed Garden Parking

The Yew Tree

RG9 6PJ ☎ 01494 882330 📠 01494 883497
e-mail: infos@theyewtreerestaurant.com
dir: *From M40 towards Stokenchurch, through Cadmore End, Lane End right to Frieth*

Deep in the Chiltern Hills, the 16th-century, red-brick Yew Tree manages to be both traditional rustic country pub and contemporary restaurant, its unexpected pale beams contributing to the effect. Bar meals are available, although you may prefer the dining room where main courses include crispy-skinned sea bass with stir-fried vegetables and honey and soy glaze; and lamb shank, dauphinoise potatoes and garlic and thyme jus. A paddock with three llamas adjoins the substantial rear garden.

Open 11-3 6-11, Sun 11-5 Closed: Sun eve, Mon **Bar Meals** L served Tue-Sat 11-2.30, Sun 11-5 D served Tue-Sat 6-10.30 ⊕ FREE HOUSE ◀ Fuller's Honeydew, Rebellion, IPA, Smuggler, Guinness, guest ale. **Facilities** Play area Dogs allowed Garden Parking

GREAT HAMPDEN — Map 5 SP80

The Hampden Arms ☻

HP16 9RQ ☎ 01494 488255 📠 01494 488094
dir: *From M40 junct 4 take A4010, turn right before Princes Risborough. Great Hampden signed*

Whether you're celebrating a special occasion or just want a quiet pint of real ale, you'll find a warm and friendly welcome at this mock Tudor pub restaurant in the heart of the beautifully wooded Hampden Estate. The menu features such dishes as game pie set on a rich port sauce; baked halibut steak with a watercress, mussel and cream sauce; and roasted vegetables set on a rocket and parmesan salad. Lighter snacks are available, and there is a good choice of hot puddings.

Open all wk noon-3 6-mdnt **Bar Meals** L served Mon-Sat 12-2, Sun 12-3 D served Mon-Sat 6-9.30 Sun 7-9.30 ⊕ FREE HOUSE ◀ Adnams Bitter, Guest ales. ☻ 7 **Facilities** Family room Dogs allowed Garden Parking

GREAT MISSENDEN — Map 6 SP80

PICK OF THE PUBS

The Nags Head ★★★★ INN ◉ ☻

See Pick of the Pubs on page 51

PICK OF THE PUBS

The Polecat Inn ☻

170 Wycombe Rd, Prestwood HP16 0HJ
☎ 01494 862253 📠 01494 868393
e-mail: polecatinn@btinternet.com
dir: *On A4128 between Great Missenden & High Wycombe*

John Gamble bought the closed and dilapidated Polecat some 19 years ago, renovating and extending it to create an attractive free house, while retaining many original features. The inn dates back to the 17th century and part of its great attraction is its beautiful three-acre garden, set amidst rolling Chilterns countryside. Small low-beamed rooms radiate from the central bar, providing a great choice for sitting and relaxing over a pint or a plate of freshly cooked food. Dishes are prepared from local ingredients, including herbs from the garden. There is a lunchtime snack menu (sandwiches, warm baguettes, jacket and ploughman's) and a regular menu supplemented by a daily blackboard selection. Daily specials include Stilton soufflé, red onion marmalade and Melba toast; and venison paupiettes with wild boar, juniper and apple stuffing and Calvados sauce.

Open 11-2.30 6-11 (Sun noon-3) Closed: 25-26 Dec, 1 Jan, Sun eve **Bar Meals** L served all wk 12-2 booking required D served Mon-Sat 6.30-9 booking required Av main course £11 **Restaurant** Av 3 course à la carte fr £19.50 ⊕ FREE HOUSE ◀ Marston's Pedigree, Morland, Old Speckled Hen, Interbrew Flowers IPA & Brakspears Bitter. ☻ 16 **Facilities** Play area Family room Garden Parking

PICK OF THE PUBS

The Rising Sun ☻

See Pick of the Pubs on opposite page

HADDENHAM — Map 5 SP70

PICK OF THE PUBS

The Green Dragon ◉◉ ☻

See Pick of the Pubs on page 54

PICK OF THE PUBS

The Rising Sun ♒

GREAT MISSENDEN Map 6 SP80

Little Hampden HP16 9PS
☎ 01494 488393 & 488360
📄 01494 488788
e-mail: sunrising@rising-sun.demon.co.uk
web: www.rising-sun.demon.co.uk
dir: *From A413, N of Gt Missenden, take Rignall Rd on left signed Princes Risborough 2.5m. Turn right signed 'Little Hampden only'*

You'll find this 250-year-old inn tucked away in the Chiltern Hills, close to the Ridgeway, down a single track, no-through road, surrounded by beech woods and glorious scenery. It is just three miles from the Prime Minister's country retreat at Chequers and was once frequented by Harold Wilson and Ted Heath. The original clientele were more likely to be farm labourers or bodgers who worked in the local beech woods. A network of footpaths begins just outside the front door, so it's a perfect base for country walks. An attractive new feature is the landscaped garden area with comfortable armchair seating and tables for outside wining and dining in beautiful surroundings. There's some good seafood, like fresh mussels with a creamy saffron sauce; pan-fried curried prawns on mango and orange salad; baked red snapper Catalan style with tomatoes, anchovies, olives and capers; and charcoal grilled tuna steak with chilli tomato mayonnaise. Otherwise look out for roast Deben duck with black cherry and red wine sauce; steak and kidney pie; smoked chicken, sausage and bacon pie; and for something lighter, toasted panini baguette with various fillings; chicken saté with basmati rice and salad; Woodman's lunch - soup, warm roll and butter, four cheeses, mixed pickles and salad; wild mixed mushroom puff pastry basket with a creamy Stilton sauce. Make sure you save room for tempting desserts such as bitter sweet flummery with raspberries; 'More than just' chocolate mousse, and plum and ginger pancake with custard.

Open Tue-Sat 11-3, 6.30-10 (Sun 12-3) Closed: Sun eve & Mon **Bar Meals** L served Tue-Sun 12-2 D served Tue-Sat 7-9 Av main course 9.95 **Restaurant** L served Tue-Sun 12-2 D served Tue-Sat 7-9 Fixed menu price fr £20 Av 3 course à la carte fr £21 ⊕ FREE HOUSE
◀ Adnams, Spitfire, Marstons Pedigree, Brakspear Special, Exmoor Gold, Old Speckled Hen. ♒ 10 **Facilities** Children's menu Dogs allowed Garden Parking

PICK OF THE PUBS

The Green Dragon ❀❀ ♟

HADDENHAM　　　　　Map 5 SP70

8 Churchway HP17 8AA
☎ 01844 291403
e-mail: enquiries@greendragon.co.uk
web: www.greendragon.co.uk
dir: *SW from Aylesbury on A418 (Oxford road) pass Stone, Upton & Dinton. In 7m left signed Haddenham. Pub approx 1m*

Popular with TV and film crews, Haddenham is a picturesque village with this 18th century pub at the heart of the old part, close to the green and the 12th-century church. Pub records date back to 1754 and it was once a manorial courthouse. The Green Dragon re-opened its doors in July 2008 as a classic country pub providing a welcome for locals and visitors with Sharp's Doom Bar, Timothy Taylor Landlord and a guest ale on hand-pumps. Inside, stone and wooden floors contrast with modern decor and leather sofas in the single, large bar/dining area which is dominated by a bar accessible on three sides. The focus is on good, fresh food, and locally sourced produce is used to great effect on the monthly-changing menus and daily chalkboards. Fresh fish comes from Cornwall daily. When popping in for lunch one could expect a selection of doorstop sandwiches and baguettes served with twice-cooked, chunky chips and salad; ham, eggs and chips or a home-made burger with chips and Green Dragon relish. Available at lunch and dinner are starters such as warm pork and black pudding terrine or crispy squid with chilli, lime and coriander. Main courses take in venison and wild mushroom suet pudding with curly kale; shepherd's pie made with braised, pressed shoulder of Welsh lamb; pan-roasted skate wing with fennel and cucumber salad and wilted wild garlic; and 28-day aged rib-eye steak with all the trimmings. Don't miss the puddings — perhaps apple, raisin and cinnamon crumble with home-made ice creams, or mandarin soufflé with glazed mandarin cream and dark chocolate sorbet. Great value set lunch and evening menus are available early week. The garden offers two large areas of lawn and an enclosed gravelled area which offers some shade.

Open noon-11 (Sun noon-10.30pm)
Closed: 26 Dec **Bar Meals** L served all week 12-2.30 D served all week 6.30-9.30 Av main course £12.95
Restaurant L served all week 12-2.30 D served all week 6.30-9.30
🍺 ENTERPRISE 🍺 Sharps Doom Bar, Timothy Taylor Landlord, Guest Ale 🍏 Westons Stowford Press.
Facilities Children's menu Dogs allowed Garden Parking

HAMBLEDEN · Map 5 SU78

The Stag & Huntsman Inn

RG9 6RP ☎ **01491 571227** 📄 **01491 413810**
e-mail: andy@stagandhuntsman.com
dir: *5m from Henley-on-Thames on A4155 toward Marlow, left at Mill End towards Hambleden*

Close to the glorious beech-clad Chilterns, this 400-year-old brick and flint village pub has featured in countless films and television series. Ever-changing guest ales are served in the public bar, larger lounge bar and cosy snug. Food is available in the bars as well as the dining room, from an extensive menu of home-made dishes prepared with local seasonal produce. Hambleden estate game features in the season. A weekend beer festival is held in early September.

Open all wk 11-2.30 (Sat-Sun 11-3), 6-11 (Sun 7-10.30), 25 Dec 12-1 Closed: 25-26 Dec & 1 Jan evenings **Bar Meals** L served all wk 12-2 D served Mon-Sat 7-9.30 ⊕ FREE HOUSE ◀ Rebellion IPA, Wadworth 6X, guest ales. **Facilities** Children's menu Garden Parking

HEDGERLEY · Map 6 SU98

The White Horse 🍷

SL2 3UY ☎ **01753 643225**
dir: *Telephone for directions*

The original part of the pub is 500 years old, and over 1000 beers take their turn at the pumps during each year. At least seven real ales are always available, served by gravity. An annual beer festival is held at the end of May bank holiday. Home-made food ranges from a salad bar with pies, quiches, sandwiches and ploughman's through to curries, chilli, pasta dishes, pies and steaks.

Open all wk 11-2.30 5-11 (Sat 11-11, Sun 11-10.30) **Bar Meals** L served Mon-Fri 12-2, Sat-Sun 12-2.30 ⊕ FREE HOUSE ◀ Regularly changing ♂ Regularly changing. 🍷 10 **Facilities** Children's menu Family room Dogs allowed Garden Parking

KINGSWOOD · Map 11 SP61

Crooked Billet 🍷

Ham Green HP18 0QJ
☎ **01296 770239** 📄 **01296 770094**
dir: *On A41 between Aylesbury & Bicester*

Located in peaceful Buckinghamshire countryside, this 200-year-old pub offers an extensive and tempting choice of food. Starters may include port and stilton rarebit with date and walnut bread, and tomato Cumberland sauce, or salad of queenie scallops with smoked salmon. Among the main courses can be found pasta alla Fiorentina smothered in cream cheeses and spinach; roasted sea bass fillet with shrimp velouté and parsley mash; or gratin of fine herb gnocchi with chard, turnips and carrots.

Open all day all wk **Bar Meals** L served all wk 6.30am-11 breakfast, 12-3 lunch D served all wk 6-10 ⊕ FREE HOUSE ◀ Hook Norton, Guinness, Tetley's. 🍷 15 **Facilities** Play area Garden Parking

LONG CRENDON · Map 5 SP60

PICK OF THE PUBS

The Angel Inn ◎ 🍷

47 Bicester Rd HP18 9EE
☎ **01844 208268** 📄 **01844 202497**
e-mail: angelrestaurant@aol.com
dir: *M40 junct 7, A418 to Thame, B4011 to Long Crendon. Inn on B4011*

Wattle-and-daub walls and inglenook fireplaces attest to the age of this former coaching inn, located in the pretty village of Long Crendon. Original materials and classic decorations have been used throughout. There is a warm bar area with leather settees, and a bright conservatory and outside patio area, which come into their own in summer. Real ales are served, along with cocktails, champagne and wine by the glass, but food is the main focus here. At lunch, choose between tempting sandwiches with hot or cold fillings, and the more substantial fare on offer, typically rump of English lamb on chargrilled vegetables, fillet of John Dory on pea bonne femme in surf clam and saffron sauce, or poached smoked haddock on leek and mustard mash. Vegetarian options, like sesame tempura vegetables with ginger noodles and wasabi, can be taken as a starter or main course.

Open all wk **Bar Meals** L served all wk 12-3 D served all wk 7-10 Av main course £14.95 **Restaurant** L served all wk 12-3 D served all wk 7-10 Fixed menu price fr £19.95 Av 3 course à la carte fr £24.95 ⊕ FREE HOUSE ◀ Oxford Blue, IPA, Brakspear. 🍷 11 **Facilities** Children's menu Garden Parking

MARLOW · Map 5 SU88

PICK OF THE PUBS

The Hand and Flowers NEW ◎◎◎ 🍷

126 West St SL7 2BP
☎ **01628 482277** 📄 **01628 401913**
e-mail: theoffice@thehandandflowers.co.uk
web: www.thehandandflowers.co.uk
dir: *M4 junct 9, A404 N into Marlow, A4155 towards Henley-on-Thames. Pub on outskirts on right*

Dedicated chef Tom Kerridge took pub cooking to a new level when he bought the lease to this unassuming Greene King pub in 2005. Despite gaining three AA rosettes in the first year, the pub remains a relaxed and unpretentious place, with beams, timbers, open fires and small bar area serving decent Abbot Ale and a short bar menu – fish and chips, rare roast beef and horseradish sandwich with chips. Tom's cooking is intelligently straightforward and elegant, with simplicity, flavour and skill top of his agenda, and the style is modern Anglo-French built around top-notch produce. From the tiny kitchen and served at plain, solid-wood tables in the dining area come terrine of Old Spot pork and bacon with hot pickled pineapple; slow-cooked Oxford beef with bone marrow bread pudding; sea bream with braised Puy lentils, mussels and parsley; Valrhona chocolate tart with malted milk ice cream, and rhubarb crumble soufflé with stem ginger anglaise. A class act in a refreshingly informal pub.

Open 12-2.30 6.30-9.30 (Sun 12-3.30) Closed: 24-26 Dec, 31 Dec L, 1 Jan D, Sun eve **Bar Meals** L served Mon-Sat 12-2.30 booking required D served Mon-Sat 6.30-9.30 booking required Av main course £9.80 **Restaurant** L served all wk 12-2.30 booking required D served all wk 6.30-9.30 booking required Av 3 course à la carte fr £35 ⊕ Greene King ◀ Abbot Ale, IPA. 🍷 10 **Facilities** Children's menu Garden Parking

MARLOW *continued*

The Kings Head

Church Rd, Little Marlow SL7 3RZ
☎ 01628 484407 01628 484407
dir: *M40 junct 4 take A4040 S, then A4155 towards Bourne End. Pub 0.5m on right*

Together with the Old Forge, this flower-adorned, 17th-century pub forms part of an attractive group of buildings a few minutes' walk from the Thames Footpath. It has an open-plan but cosy interior with original beams and open fires. In addition to sandwiches and jacket potatoes, the menu offers quite a range of more substantial meals, including salmon fillet hollandaise; mixed fish salad; lamb shank with rich minty gravy; pheasant casserole; and stir-fry duck with plum sauce.

Open all day all wk 11-11 **Bar Meals** L served Mon-Sat 12-2.15, Sun 12-7 booking required D served all wk booking required **Restaurant** L served Mon-Sat 12-2.15, Sun 12-7 booking required ENTERPRISE INNS Fuller's London Pride, Timothy Taylor Landlord, Adnam Broadside, St Austell Tribute Westons Stowford Press. 9 **Facilities** Children's menu Garden Parking

MARLOW BOTTOM — Map 5 SU88

Pegasus NEW

☎ 01628 484926
e-mail: pegasusmarlow@hotmail.co.uk
dir: *3m outside Marlow town centre, follow signs to Marlow Bottom*

New chef-landlord Oliver Reichhold snapped up the former TJ O'Reilly's pub late in 2008 and has breathed new life into the building, restoring its old name and offering quality, affordable modern pub food. The short, innovative menu may feature John Dory with cucumber and black pudding to start, followed by pork belly with lentil casserole and apple gravy; local Dexter beef fillet with red wine butter; or brill with red wine risotto and oxtail sauce, with Bakewell tart with coffee ice cream to finish. Wash down with a pint of Marlow Rebellion or one of eight wines by the glass.

Open 12-3 5.30-11.30 (Sun 12-5) Closed: Mon **Bar Meals** L served Tue-Sun 12-2.30 D served Tue-Sun 6-9 Av main course £8 **Restaurant** L served Tue-Sun 12-2.30 booking required D served Tue-Sun 6.30-10 booking required Fixed menu price fr £15 Av 3 course à la carte fr £25 FREE HOUSE Rebellion IPA, London Pride, Greene King. 8 **Facilities** Children's menu Garden Parking

MENTMORE — Map 11 SP91

PICK OF THE PUBS

Il Maschio@ The Stag

The Green LU7 0QF
☎ 01296 668423 01296 660264
e-mail: info@ilmaschio.com
dir: *Telephone for directions*

The imposing Stag stands in a picture-postcard village with a lovely summer garden, overlooking Mentmore Towers, a huge Elizabethan-style stately home built in 1855 for Baron Amschel de Rothschild. In this idyllic setting there is a wealth of fresh resources, and head chef and co-owner Mani Rebelo has tapped into the local Chiltern farming community and suppliers for his raw materials. The cooking is a distinctive fusion of British and Mediterranean cuisine. From the seasonally-changing lunch menu you can enjoy freshly made pizzas, pasta gamberetti (prawns, garlic, white wine and cream), and decent salads, perhaps mixed seafood marinated in oil, lemon, garlic and parsley. Evening additions may include venison steak, tuna cooked in lemon juice, olive oil and fresh thyme, seafood mixed grill, and free-range chicken breast with mushroom, brandy and cream sauce. Check out the cocktail bar for some exotic flavoured infusions in the form of martinis, daiquiris and margaritas.

Open all wk **Bar Meals** food served all day CHARLES WELLS Youngs Bitter, Guinness, Bombardier. 8 **Facilities** Children's menu Dogs allowed Garden Parking

MILTON KEYNES — Map 11 SP83

The Swan Inn NEW

Broughton Rd, Milton Keynes Village MK10 9AH
☎ 01908 665240 01908 395091
e-mail: info@theswan-mkvillage.co.uk
dir: *M1 junct 14 towards Milton Keynes. Pub off V11 or H7*

Lots of pubs claim to source their menu ingredients locally, but not many take home-grown vegetables as currency. This one does. Its 13th-century thatch shelters a cosy yet stylish interior, with log fires, flagstone floors, a snug, and a spacious garden at the back. From his open plan kitchen, Toni the Italian chef dispenses a simple yet creative menu that changes monthly with the seasons. Crusty ciabatta sandwiches, daily pies and pasta dishes; and pub classics like hand-made lamb and coriander burgers, and salmon and spring onion fishcakes, are fine examples of the fare.

Open all day all wk 11-11 (Fri-Sat 11-mdnt, Sun noon-10.30) Closed: 25-26 Dec, 1 Jan (morning) **Bar Meals** L served Mon-Sat 12-9.30, Sun 12-6 D served Mon-Sat 12-9.30, Sun 12-6 Av main course £9.50 food served all day **Restaurant** L served Mon-Sat 12-3, Sun 12-6 booking required D served Mon-Sat 6-9.30 booking required Av 3 course à la carte fr £22 Adnams, Old Speckled Hen. 6 **Facilities** Children's menu Dogs allowed Garden Parking

MOULSOE — Map 11 SP94

The Carrington Arms

Cranfield Rd MK16 0HB
☎ 01908 218050 01908 217850
e-mail: carringtonarms@aol.com
dir: *M1 junct 14, A509 to Newport Pagnell 100yds, turn right signed Moulsoe & Cranfield. Pub on right*

This Grade II listed building is surrounded by farm land in a conservation area. Customers can 'create' their own menu from the meat and seafood counter, which the chef then cooks in full view of his expectant diners. Aberdeen beef, monkfish, tiger prawns, Colchester oysters are all on offer, along with unusual meats like ostrich, crocodile and kangaroo, plus vegetarian dishes and chef's specials. Friday night is fish night and lobster is available for pre-order.

Open all wk noon-3 5.30-11 (Sat noon-3 5.30-mdnt, Sun noon-3 7-10.30) **Bar Meals** L served Mon-Sat 12-2.30, Sun 12-3 D served Mon-Sat 6-10, Sun 7-9.30 FREE HOUSE Morland Old Speckled Hen, Greene King IPA, London Pride, Guest ales. 10 **Facilities** Garden Parking

OVING — Map 11 SP72

The Black Boy

Church Ln HP22 4HN
☎ 01296 641258 01296 641271
e-mail: theblackboyoving@aol.com
dir: *4.6m N of Aylesbury*

Oliver Cromwell and his soldiers camped in the Black Boy's huge garden after sacking nearby Bolebec Castle during the Civil War. Today, the 16th-century pub is a rural oasis, with spectacular views over the Vale of Aylesbury to Stowe School and beyond. Choices in the dining room include Scottish salmon with new potatoes and seasonal greens; local lamb shank with minted gravy and root vegetables; and a vegetarian cheese and onion filo parcel.

Open noon-3 6-11 (Sun noon-4.30) Closed: 25 Dec **Bar Meals** L served Mon-Sat 12-2, Sun 12-2.30 D served Mon-Sat 6-9 FREE HOUSE Brakspear, Rebellion, Youngs Bitter, Batemans Bitter, Guest ales Aspalls. 10 **Facilities** Dogs allowed Garden Parking

PENN — Map 6 SU99

PICK OF THE PUBS

The Old Queens Head

See Pick of the Pubs on opposite page

PICK OF THE PUBS

The Old Queens Head

PENN

Hammersley Ln, Tylers Green HP10 8EY
☎ **01494 813371** 📄 **01494 816145**
e-mail: info@oldqueensheadpenn.co.uk
web: www.oldqueensheadpenn.co.uk
dir: *B474 (Penn road) through Beaconsfield New Town towards Penn, approx 3m left into School Rd, left in 500yds into Hammersley Ln. Pub on corner opp church*

In 1666, local builders made good use of the plentiful supplies of local timber to build the barn that, with several additions, today houses the dining room of this charming old pub. Communications being what they were, they were probably totally unaware that 30 miles away the Great Fire was destroying the City of London's countless wooden houses. But the fact that, with its cosy corners, real fires and frequent changes in floor level, the restaurant is still standing perhaps serves to vindicate their choice of

material. The owners have clearly spent many hours at local auctions finding lovely old furniture and pictures in keeping with the age of the pub, whose warm heritage colours harmonise well with the dark floorboards, flagstones, rugs and classic fabrics. A sunny terrace overlooks the village church of St Margaret's and there's a large garden in which to eat and drink. The highly versatile kitchen is responsible for a modern British menu offering a good choice, with starters such as seared local pigeon breast on caramelised red onion tarte Tatin with beetroot marmalade; and crispy smoked haddock fishcake with saffron mayonnaise and slow-roast tomato relish. You might then find yourself torn between pan-fried duck breast on confit duck hash with purple sprouting broccoli and Madeira jus; grilled sea bass fillet on chorizo, mussel, squid, chilli and tomato stew; and roast leek, spring onion and thyme gnocchi with creamy Barkham blue cheese sauce. Puddings include steamed apple and sherried raisin roly-poly with cinnamon ice cream; and Marsala roast figs with honey and lavender ice cream. Free WiFi is useful for those business lunches where yesterday's sales figures are suddenly needed.

Open 11-11 (Sun 12-10.30) Closed: 26 Dec **Bar Meals** L served all week 12-2.30, Sat 12-3, Sun 12-4 D served all week 6.30-9.30, Fri & Sat 6.30-10 **Restaurant** L served all week 12-2.30, Sat 12-3, Sun 12-4 D served all week 6.30-9.30, Fri & Sat 6.30-10
🍺 SALISBURY PUBS LTD 🍺 Ruddles County, Greene King IPA, Guinness. 🍷 19 **Facilities** Children's menu Dogs allowed Garden Parking

PRESTON BISSETT Map 11 SP62

The White Hart NEW ♀

Pound Ln MK18 4LX ☎ 01280 847969
dir: *2.5m from A421*

Seek out this pretty thatched free house in the winter months for traditional game dishes from the local shoots. The Grade II listed building dates from 1545 and lies amid the rolling hills of rural Buckinghamshire. There's a good selection of wines and local real ales, and a small select menu that changes with the seasons; expect classic dishes like steak and ale pie, and slow-cooked belly of pork. There's a nice, secluded garden, too.

Open 12-2.30 6-11 (Sat-Sun noon-11pm) Closed: Mon **Bar Meals** L served Tue-Sun 12-2.30 D served Tue-Sun 6-11 Av main course £9.50 **Restaurant** L served Tue-Sun 12-2.30 booking required D served Tue-Sun 6-10 booking required Av 3 course à la carte fr £20 ◀ Hooky Best Bitter, Old Hooky, Timothy Taylor Landlord, Rev James, Tribute. ♀ 6 **Facilities** Children's menu Dogs allowed Garden Parking

RADNAGE Map 5 SU79

The Three Horseshoes Inn ♀

Horseshoe Rd, Bennett End HP14 4EB ☎ 01494 483273
e-mail: threehorseshoes@btconnect.com
dir: *M40 junct 5 Stokenchurch to High Wycombe, turn left Radnage 1.8m, left & follow road*

Dating from 1748, this delightful little inn is tucked away down a leafy lane. Stone floors, original beams, a bread oven and an open fire are among the features. The modern English and European menu changes daily, and award-winning chef/owner Simon Cranshaw uses as much local produce as possible. Enjoy a Rebellion Ale at the bar, or wander outside in the lovely gardens. Dame Judy Dench and Sir Derek Jacobi have been spotted here.

Open 12-3 6-11 (Sun 12-4) Closed: Mon **Bar Meals** L served Wed-Sun 12-2.30 D served Tue-Sat 6-9.30 Av main course £9.50 **Restaurant** L served Wed-Sun 12-2.30 D served Tue-Sat 6-9.30 Fixed menu price fr £25 Av 3 course à la carte fr £28.50 ⊕ FREE HOUSE ◀ Rebellion beers. ♀ 10 **Facilities** Children's menu Dogs allowed Garden Parking

SKIRMETT Map 5 SU79

The Frog ♀

RG9 6TG ☎ 01491 638996 📄 01491 638045
e-mail: thefrogatskirmett@gmail.com
web: www.thefrogatskirmett.co.uk
dir: *Turn off A4155 at Mill End, pub in 3m*

This privately owned pub and restaurant is tucked away in the beautiful Hambleden valley. The simple set menu offers great value for money with options like salad of gravadlax, followed by roast loin of pork, and sticky toffee pudding to finish. The carte offers a range of starters like soup, garlic bread or bruschetta; followed by mains like pan-seared salmon with curried lentils and coriander cream sauce.

Open 11.30-3 6-11 Closed: Sun eve (Oct-Apr) **Bar Meals** L served all wk 12-2.30 D served all wk 6.30-9.30 ⊕ FREE HOUSE ◀ Adnams Best, Hook Norton, Rebellion, Fuller's London Pride, IPA, Guest Ale ♂ Thatchers Dry. ♀ 14 **Facilities** Family room Dogs allowed Garden Parking

TURVILLE Map 5 SU79

PICK OF THE PUBS

The Bull & Butcher ♀

RG9 6QU ☎ 01491 638283 📄 01491 638836
e-mail: info@thebullandbutcher.com
dir: *M40 junct 5 follow Ibstone signs. Right at T-junct. Pub 0.25m on left*

You'll probably recognise the Bull & Butcher, even if you've never been there before. For Turville, with its delightful 16th-century pub and 10th-century church, has won celebrity status in numerous film and television productions: *Midsomer Murders, The Vicar of Dibley, Goodbye Mr Tom,* and *Chitty Chitty Bang Bang.* After an exhilarating walk amid the glorious Chilterns scenery, drop down from the windmill on Turville Hill and unwind with a pint from a fantastic choice of real ales in the Well Bar or Windmill Lounge with their natural oak beams and open fires. There's also a function room ideal for leisure and corporate occasions, and a large garden and patio area. Menu choices begin with starters that include a platter of cured meats with olives and bread, whilst main course dishes range from cod, chips and mushy peas or pan-fried duck with rice and stir-fried vegetables to roasted vegetable cannelloni with spinach.

Open all day all wk 11-11 (Sun noon-10.30pm) **Bar Meals** L served Mon-Fri 12-2.30, Sat-Sun 12-4 booking required D served Mon-Fri 6.30-9.30, Sat 6-9.30, Sun 7-9 booking required Av main course £12 **Restaurant** L served Mon-Fri 12-2.30, Sat-Sun 12-4 booking required D served Mon-Fri 6.30-9.30, Sat 6-9.30, Sun 7-9 booking required Av 3 course à la carte fr £22.50 ⊕ BRAKSPEAR ◀ Brakspear Bitter, Hooky Dark, Oxford Gold, Brewers selections. ♀ 36 **Facilities** Children's menu Dogs allowed Garden Parking

WEST WYCOMBE Map 5 SU89

PICK OF THE PUBS

The George and Dragon Hotel ♀

High St HP14 3AB
☎ 01494 464414 📄 01494 462432
e-mail: sue.raines@btconnect.com
dir: *On A40*

A traditional coaching inn with 14th-century origins inn, in a National Trust village. It was once the haunt of highwaymen stalking travellers between London and Oxford and, indeed, one unfortunate guest robbed and murdered here is rumoured still to haunt its corridors. The hotel is reached through a cobbled archway and comprises a delightful jumble of whitewashed, timber-framed buildings. The 'English-at-heart' carte menu offers an extensive selection of freshly-prepared dishes, including game from the local estate; spatchcock lemon chicken; beef Wellington with red wine and mushroom sauce; bean and wild mushroom goulash; salmon in pastry, served with crème fraîche; chargrilled steaks; and lentil and cider loaf with tomato and basil sauce. Home-made desserts include classic spotted dick, allegedly destined to become extinct according to a 2008 survey. Visitors to the area will enjoy exploring West Wycombe Caves, and the stately houses at Cliveden and Hughenden Manor.

Open all wk ⊕ ENTERPRISE INNS ◀ Courage Best, Wells Bombardier, Timothy Taylor Landlord. ♀ 7 **Facilities** Play area Family room Dogs allowed Garden Parking

WHEELEREND COMMON Map 5 SU89

The Chequers ♀

Bullocks Farm Ln HP14 3NH ☎ 01494 883070
dir: *4m N of Marlow*

This picturesque 17th-century inn, with its roaring winter fires and two attractive beer gardens, is ideally located for walkers on the edge of Wheelerend Common. A solid choice of mouth-watering sandwiches and bar meals supplements the main menu, which features plenty of fresh fish and local estate game. Warm pigeon and apple salad; venison pie with red wine and juniper; and roast salmon on crushed potato tartare are typical choices.

Open 12-3 6-11 (Sun 12-3 7-10.30) Closed: Mon L **Bar Meals** L served Tue-Sat 12-2, Sun 12-3.30 D served Tue-Sat 6.30-9 **Restaurant** L served Tue-Sat 12-2, Sun 12-3.30 D served Tue-Sat 6.30-9 ⊕ FULLER SMITH TURNER PLC ▪ Fuller's ESB, London Pride, Guest ale. ☂ 7 **Facilities** Dogs allowed Garden Parking

WHITELEAF — Map 5 SP80

Red Lion

Upper Icknield Way HP27 0LL
☎ 01844 344476 ▤ 01844 344476
e-mail: tim_hibbert@hotmail.co.uk
dir: *A4010 through Princes Risborough, turn right into The Holloway, at T-junct turn right, pub on left*

Family-owned 17th-century traditional country inn in the heart of the Chilterns, surrounded by National Trust land and situated close to the Ridgeway national trail. There are plenty of good local walks with wonderful views. A cosy fire in winter and a secluded summer beer garden add to the appeal. Hearty pub fare is served in the bar area and includes rib-eye steak, sausage and mash, vegetarian lasagne, haddock and chips, warm baguettes and jacket potatoes. You can also dine in the recently built restaurant.

Open all wk **Bar Meals** L served all wk 12-2 D served Mon-Sat 7-9 booking required Av main course £8.50 **Restaurant** L served all wk 12-2 booking required D served Mon-Sat 7-9 booking required Fixed menu price fr £9.50 ⊕ FREE HOUSE ▪ Brakspear Bitter, Hook Norton, Tribute, Guinness. **Facilities** Children's menu Family room Dogs allowed Garden Parking

WOOBURN COMMON — Map 6 SU98

PICK OF THE PUBS

Chequers Inn ★★★ HL ⊚ ☂

Kiln Ln HP10 0JQ ☎ 01628 529575 ▤ 01628 850124
e-mail: info@chequers-inn.com
dir: *M40 junct 2, A40 through Beaconsfield Old Town towards High Wycombe. 2m from town left into Broad Ln. Inn 2.5m*

Oak posts and beams, flagstone floors and a wonderful open fireplace blackened by a million blazing logs: this 17th-century inn is an absolute charmer. It has been owned and run by the same family for 35 years, ensuring a friendly, relaxed and welcoming atmosphere. Overlooking open Chiltern Hills countryside, its interior includes an attractively decorated restaurant, but an alternative dining option is the extensive lunch and dinner bar menu backed by a large selection of beers, guest ales and wines; the same menu is served in the contemporary lounge. The restaurant is as ideal for a quick business lunch as for a long romantic dinner. Fresh, predominantly local ingredients are used in dishes such as slow-cooked Oxfordshire pork belly with cauliflower purée, black pudding and caramelised apple sauce; pan-fried fillet of brill with samphire, boulangère potatoes and a light

chicken and tomato jus; and chocolate torte with orange sorbet. Outside is a large garden area where barbecues are held in summer.

Open all day all wk noon-mdnt **Bar Meals** L served Mon-Fri 12-2.30, Sat 12-10, Sun 12-9.30 D served Mon-Thu 6-9.30, Fri 6-10, Sat 12-10, Sun 12-9.30 Av main course £10.95 **Restaurant** L served all wk 12-2.30 booking required D served all wk 7-9.30 booking required Fixed menu price fr £13.95 Av 3 course à la carte fr £29.95 ⊕ FREE HOUSE ▪ IPA, Rebellion Smuggler, Old Speckled Hen. ☂ 12 **Facilities** Children's menu Garden Parking **Rooms** 17

CAMBRIDGESHIRE

BABRAHAM — Map 12 TL55

PICK OF THE PUBS

The George Inn at Babraham ⊚

High St CB2 4AG ☎ 01223 833800 ▤ 01223 833800
e-mail: stevelythall@btinternet.com
dir: *In High St, just off A11/A505 & A1307*

An 18th-century coaching inn once renowned for the Whitsun and May Day revels hosted here. Set in the heart of rural Cambridgeshire, it was devastated by fire in 2004 but new kitchens and three restaurant areas have restored this village dining pub to its former glory. At the bar, Greene King's reliable beers include Old Speckled Hen, while the food operation continues to maintain 'a passion for detail'. For lunch you could snack on roasted cashews, marinated olives, toasted herb and garlic croutons, and sun-blushed tomatoes; alternatively a freshly baked ciabatta with poached salmon and baby prawns might suffice. Favourites from the bar menu include beer-battered fresh cod fillet, and home-made lasagne with garlic bread. A full à la carte choice could include seared queen scallops to start, Suffolk rack of lamb with herb and Stilton crust, and brandy snap basket filled with exotic fruit salad. Roasts on Sunday include Norfolk turkey, and all are served with fresh market vegetables.

Open all wk noon-3 6-11 **Bar Meals** L served all wk 12-3 D served all wk 6-9.30 Av main course £9 **Restaurant** L served all wk 12-3 D served all wk 6-9.30 Fixed menu price fr £7.95 Av 3 course à la carte fr £25 ⊕ GREENE KING ▪ Old Speckled Hen, Greene King IPA, Abbot Ale. **Facilities** Children's menu Dogs allowed Garden Parking

BARRINGTON — Map 12 TL34

The Royal Oak ☂

31 West Green CB22 7RZ
☎ 01223 870791 ▤ 01223 870791
e-mail: info@royaloak.uk.net
dir: *From Barton off M11, S of Cambridge*

One of the oldest thatched pubs in England, this rambling, timbered 13th-century building overlooks one of the largest village greens in England. It's only six miles from Cambridge, three miles from the M11 and a mile from Shepreth Station. A wide range of fish dishes includes scallops, trout, scampi, tuna, swordfish, tiger prawns, squid and other seasonal offerings. There is also a carvery on Sunday which could be accompanied by a pint of IPA Potton Brewery or Young's Bitter.

Open all wk noon-2.30 6-11 (Sun 12-3 6.30-10.30) **Restaurant** L served noon-2, Sun noon-2.30 booking required D served 6.30-9.30, Sun 7-9 booking required ⊕ FREE HOUSE ▪ IPA Potton Brewery, Adnams, Young's Bitter, Morland Original. ☂ 6 **Facilities** Children's menu Garden Parking

BROUGHTON — Map 12 TL27

PICK OF THE PUBS

The Crown ☂

See Pick of the Pubs on page 60

CAMBRIDGE — Map 12 TL45

PICK OF THE PUBS

The Anchor ☂

Silver St CB3 9EL
☎ 01223 353554 ▤ 01223 327275
e-mail: 7614@greeneking.co.uk
dir: *Telephone for directions*

Situated at the end of the medieval lane that borders Queens' College in the heart of the University city, this attractive waterside pub appeals to students and visitors alike. Hard by the bridge over the River Cam, in fine weather the riverside patio is an ideal spot for enjoying one of a range of good ales including guest beers while watching the activities on the water. The more adventurous can hire a punt for a leisurely trip to Grantchester (of Rupert Brooke and Jeffrey Archer fame), and on return sample a choice of hearty meals from a range that includes lasagne, home-made pie, and roast beef.

Open all wk Mon-Fri 11am-11pm (Fri-Sat 11am-12.30am, Sun 11am-10.30pm) Closed: 25 Dec ⊕ GREENE KING ▪ Greene King, IPA, Abbot Ale. ☂ 12

PICK OF THE PUBS

The Crown ♀

BROUGHTON   Map 12 TL27

Bridge Rd PE28 3AY ☎ 01487 824428
e-mail: info@thecrowninnrestaurant.co.uk
dir: *Just off A141 between Huntingdon & Warboys, by church in village centre*

Quality, flavour and the freshest seasonal food are the hallmarks of this picturesque 18th-century free house, just across the road from the church. The village itself dates back to Saxon times, and an old insurance policy shows that in 1857 The Crown also incorporated a saddler's shop, thatched stables and piggeries. When the pub closed in 2000, the villagers rallied round and raised enough money buy and renovate it, later running it as a village-owned tenancy until chef David Anderson and his team took over in 2008. Today, The Crown lies at the heart

of a thriving local community; it's popular with walkers and visitors alike, and the extensive rear garden is perfect for leisurely summer afternoons. Whether you pop in for a coffee, a quick pint or a lovingly prepared meal, you're sure to find a warm welcome. At the bar, choose real ales from Adnams, Elgoods and other local breweries; there's a different guest ale every week, and you'll also find Aspalls ciders. The restaurant combines a traditional pub interior with touches of contemporary design, and this is the place to sample good, honest British food with a French and Italian twist. Begin, perhaps, with roast parsnip soup with aged balsamic vinegar; Bottisham smoked duck salad; or carrot and coriander roulade. Moving on to the main course, the choices might include four-hour roast pork belly; fish pie with mashed potato; or braised fennel and goat's cheese tart. Round off with apple and sultana crumble, pear and almond frangipane tart, or decadent chocolate Nemesis.

Open 11.30-3 6.30-11 (Sun 11.30-6) Closed: 1-11 Jan, Mon-Tue **Bar Meals** L served Wed-Sun 12-2.30 D served Wed-Sun 7-10 Av main course £13 **Restaurant** L served Wed-Sun 12-2.30 D served Wed-Sun 7-10 Fixed menu price fr £11.50 ⊕ FREE HOUSE ◀ Adnams Broadside, Elgoods Black Dog, Greene King IPA, City of Cambridge Hobson Choice, Potton Brewery Shambles ◐ Aspalls. ♀ 10 **Facilities** Children's menu Dogs allowed Garden Parking

CAMBRIDGE *continued*

Cambridge Blue ☻

85 Gwydir St CB1 2LG ☎ 01223 471680
dir: *City centre*

A friendly 1860s backstreet pub with an unexpected garden. Inside are two real fires and lots of memorabilia. The tap room has seven handpumps, but there are always at least 12 real ales to choose from, such as Bishop's Farewell and Nethergate Dewdrop (the pub used to be called the Dew Drop Inn, a Victorian pun). Good value pub grub made on the premises ranges from ciabattas and jackets to curries, pies, chilli con carne and sticky toffee pudding.

Open all wk noon-2.30 5-11 (Thu-Sat noon-11 Sun noon-10.30) **Bar Meals** L served Mon-Fri 12-2, Sat-Sun 12-4 D served all wk 6-9 Av main course £7 ⊕ FREE HOUSE ◀ Woodforde's Wherry, Oakham Bishops Farewell, guest ales. ☻ 8 **Facilities** Children's menu Family room Dogs allowed Garden

Free Press ☻

Prospect Row CB1 1DU ☎ 01223 368337
e-mail: craig.bickley@ntlworld.com
dir: *Telephone for directions*

Students, academics, locals and visitors rub shoulders in this atmospheric and picturesque back-street pub near the city centre. It has open fires and a beautiful walled garden - but no music, mobile phones or gaming machines. Punters are attracted by first-rate real ales and nourishing home-made food such as chilli with garlic bread; goat's cheese salad; filled toasted ciabattas; venison sausages; salmon filled with couscous and vegetables; and fresh pasta.

Open all wk noon-2.30 6-11 (Fri noon-2.30 4.30-11, Sat noon-11, Sun noon-3 7-10.30) Closed: 25-26 Dec, 1 Jan ⊕ GREENE KING ◀ Greene King IPA, Abbot Ale, Dark Mild, guest ales. ☻ 10 **Facilities** Children's menu Dogs allowed Garden

DUXFORD	Map 12 TL44

The John Barleycorn

3 Moorfield Rd CB2 4PP
☎ 01223 832699 🖳 01223 832699
e-mail: info@johnbarleycorn.co.uk
dir: *Turn off A505 into Duxford*

Traditional thatched and beamed English country pub situated close to Cambridge. Originally built as a coaching house in 1660, it was renamed once or twice, until 1858 when the current name was attached. The same menu is served throughout and ranges from a cheese sandwich to tournedos Rossini. Typical dishes are large leg of lamb in mint gravy, and chicken breast with garlic and herbs.

Open all wk **Bar Meals** L served all wk D served all wk ⊕ GREENE KING ◀ Greene King IPA, Abbot Ale, Old Speckled Hen, Ruddles Best & County. ☻ 6 **Facilities** Dogs allowed Garden Parking

ELSWORTH	Map 12 TL36

The George & Dragon ☻

41 Boxworth Rd CB3 8JQ
☎ 01954 267236 🖳 01954 267080
e-mail: www.georgeanddragon-elsworth.co.uk
dir: *SE of A14 between Cambridge & Huntingdon*

Set in a pretty village just outside Cambridge, this pub offers a wide range of satisfying food to locals and visitors alike. Look out for halibut mornay, steak and kidney pie, and fresh cod, haddock or plaice from Lowestoft. For a lighter meal, ploughman's lunches and sandwiches are available. There are special menus for occasions such as Valentine candlelit dinner and Mother's Day. Friday night is Aberdeen Angus steak night.

Open all wk 11-2.30 6-11 **Bar Meals** L served all wk 11-2.30 D served all wk 6-11 Av main course £11.50 **Restaurant** L served all wk 11-2.30 D served all wk 6-11 Fixed menu price fr £10.50 Av 3 course à la carte fr £16 ⊕ FREE HOUSE ◀ Greene King IPA, Ruddles County, Greene King Old Speckled Hen. ☻ 8 **Facilities** Children's menu Garden Parking

ELTON	Map 12 TL09

PICK OF THE PUBS

The Black Horse ☻

14 Overend PE8 6RU
☎ 01832 280240 & 280875 🖳 01832 280875
e-mail: blackhorseelton@btconnect.com
dir: *Off A605 (Peterborough to Northampton road)*

Antique furnishings and open log fires crank up the old world charm in this 17th-century inn, while the delightful one-acre rear garden overlooks Elton's famous church and rolling open countryside. The real ales include Everards Tiger, seasonal Nethergate brews, and Barnwell Bitter, which is brewed locally. The superb selection of food ranges from bar snacks to a full à la carte. Among the 'snacks' are sandwiches, filled baguettes jacket potatoes, a home-made pie of the day, and seasonal salads. Or you might start with Portobello mushrooms topped with bacon and cheese gratin; or freshly dressed crab with brown bread and salad. Typical main courses include guinea fowl stuffed with black pudding and chorizo sausage,

wrapped in Parma ham and served with a rich red wine jus; fillet of sea bass with braised pak choi, pesto and sun-blushed tomatoes; and bangers and mash.

Open all day noon-11.30pm Closed: Sun eve ⊕ FREE HOUSE ◀ Bass, Everards Tiger, Nethergate, Barnwell Bitter. ☻ 14 **Facilities** Play area Family room Dogs allowed Garden Parking

The Crown Inn ★★★★★ INN ☻

8 Duck St PE8 6RQ ☎ 01832 280232
e-mail: inncrown@googlemail.com
dir: *A1(M) junct 17, W on A605 signed Oundle/Northampton. In 3.5m right to Elton, 0.9m left signed Nassington. Inn 0.3m on right*

Almost hidden by a towering chestnut tree, The Crown is a beautiful, 17th-century thatched building opposite the village green. Chef/owner Marcus Lamb places great emphasis on the food, using local supplies for everything from sandwiches to salmon and prawn ravioli in a Thai broth followed by pork loin layered with mushroom, leek and Stilton, and served with mashed potato and a mustard sauce. Annual treats include a May Day hog roast and a summer beer festival. There are five en suite bedrooms, each with its own individual appeal.

Open all wk noon-11 (Mon 5-11 (BH noon-11)) Closed: 1-7 Jan (Restaurant) **Bar Meals** L served Tue-Sun 12-2 D served Tue-Sat 6.30-8.45 Av main course £13.95 **Restaurant** L served Tue-Sun 12-2 booking required D served Tue-Sat 6.30-8.45 booking required Fixed menu price fr £12 Av 3 course à la carte fr £32 ⊕ FREE HOUSE ◀ Golden Crown Bitter, Greene King IPA, Adnams, Jeffrey Hudson Bitter, Black Sheep. ☻ 10 **Facilities** Children's menu Dogs allowed Garden Parking **Rooms** 5

ELY	Map 12 TL58

PICK OF THE PUBS

The Anchor Inn ★★★★ RR ☻

See Pick of the Pubs on page 62

PICK OF THE PUBS

The Anchor Inn ★★★★ RR 🌹 🍷

Map 12 TL58

Sutton Gault CB6 2BD
☎ 01353 778537 📄 01353 776180
e-mail: anchorinn@popmail.bta.com
web: www.anchorsuttongault.co.uk
dir: *From A14, B1050 to Earith, take B1381 to Sutton. Sutton Gault on left*

Gault, as in the hamlet's name, is the type of thick clay used for the banks of the rivers and dykes that criss-cross the billiard-table-flat fen country. Today it is rich agricultural land, but in the mid-17th century these fens were lawless and malaria-ridden until, in 1630, the Earl of Bedford commissioned Dutch engineer Cornelius Vermuyden to drain them. The Old and New Bedford Rivers are his legacy, and the Anchor was built to provide shelter for the Scottish prisoners of war who built them. It's been an inn, today a family-run free house, ever since. Scrubbed pine tables on gently undulating floors, old prints, evening candle glow and winter log fires

help to engender its timeless charm and character. The core of its monthly menus, for which it continues to win wide recognition, is traditional British in the best sense, using local produce wherever possible, including daily deliveries of fresh seafood, such as hand-dressed Cromer crab and Brancaster oysters and mussels, and game from the market. Spring specialities may be samphire and new season's lamb; in summer there'll be asparagus, Bottisham smoked hams, and fresh strawberries; while in the winter look out for pheasant, pigeon, and wild duck from the marshes. The house speciality is grilled dates wrapped in bacon in a mild grain mustard cream sauce. A typical three-course meal (taken on the riverside terrace, maybe) would be Bottisham 'hot-smoked' eel and smoked salmon on herb blinis with pea shoots and horseradish cream; pan-fried breast of Gressingham duck on potato rösti and pak choi with stem ginger and lemongrass sauce; and warm chocolate and pecan brownie with vanilla ice cream. The Sunday lunch menu always includes roast beef, along with another roast, fresh fish and vegetarian dishes. Some of the suites and rooms overlook the river.

Open all wk 12-2.30, 7-10.30 (Sat 12-3, 6.30-11) **Bar Meals** Av main course £13 **Restaurant** L served Mon-Sat 12-2, Sun 12-2.30 booking required D served Mon-Fri 7-9, Sat 6.30-9.30, Sun 6.30-8.30 booking required Fixed menu price fr £11.95 Av 3 course à la carte fr £25 ⊕ FREE HOUSE ◄■ Pegasus. 🍷 12 **Facilities** Children's menu Garden Parking **Rooms** 4

FEN DITTON — Map 12 TL46

PICK OF THE PUBS

Ancient Shepherds ☕

High St CB5 8ST ☎ 01223 293280 📠 01223 293280
e-mail: ancientshepherds@hotmail.co.uk
dir: *From A14 take B1047 signed Cambridge/Airport*

Named after the ancient order of Shepherders who used to meet here, this heavily-beamed pub and restaurant was built originally as three cottages in 1540. The two bars, a lounge and a dining room all boast inglenook fireplaces. Located three miles from Cambridge in the riverside village of Fen Ditton, it provides a welcome escape for those who like to enjoy their refreshments without the addition of music, darts or pool. Among the fish dishes on the menu are fillet of sea bass on a bed of creamed leeks and home-made fishcakes. Meat eaters are equally well catered for with perhaps half a casseroled guinea fowl in Burgundy with roast vegetables, Barnsley lamb chops, and pork loin steaks in cream and mustard sauce to choose from.

Open noon-2.30 6-11 Closed: 25-26 Dec, Mon eve & Sun eve **Bar Meals** L served all wk 12-2.30 Av main course £7.95 **Restaurant** L served all wk 12-2.30 D served Tue-Sat 6.30-9 booking required Av 3 course à la carte fr £22 ⊕ PUNCH TAVERNS ◀ Adnams Bitter, Greene King IPA. ☕ 8 **Facilities** Children's menu Dogs allowed Garden Parking

FENSTANTON — Map 12 TL36

King William IV ☕

High St PE28 9JF ☎ 01480 462467 📠 01480 468526
e-mail: mail@kingwilliampub.co.uk
dir: *Off A14 junct 27 between Cambridge & Huntingdon*

Three 17th-century cottages make up this rambling old inn, set beside the clock tower in the heart of the village.

Inside are low beams, a lively bar and the appropriately named Garden Room. Food ranges from bar food such as sausages and mash or beer battered fish and chips through to an evening meal of pan-fried Mediterranean prawns with red onion marmalade and Melba toast followed by roasted roulade of chicken with creamed leeks.

Open all wk ⊕ GREENE KING ◀ Greene King Abbot Ale & IPA, guest ales. ☕ 9 **Facilities** Dogs allowed Garden Parking

FORDHAM — Map 12 TL67

PICK OF THE PUBS

White Pheasant ☕

CB7 5LQ ☎ 01638 720414
e-mail: chef@whitepheasant.com
web: www.whitepheasant.com
dir: *From Newmarket A142 to Ely, approx 5m to Fordham. Pub on left in village*

This 18th-century building stands in a fenland village between Ely and Newmarket. In recent years its considerable appeal has been subtly enhanced by improvements that preserve its period charm. You can enjoy the locally brewed ale, a glass of wine or home-made lemonade or strawberryade while perusing the menus. Food is taken seriously here: the kitchen offers globally-influenced, traditional British dishes ranging from light bites to full à la carte meals. Prime produce is used from local suppliers and all the meat is free range. Lighter meals might include the lunchtime deli board; a salad of confit duck with orange and spring onion; or a Scottish smoked salmon croque monsieur. A choice of 'old favourites' includes Suffolk ham with fried free-range eggs and chips, while an evening meal could start with home-made local game pâté with cranberry and caper relish, followed by slow-roasted belly of free-range Suffolk pork with black pudding. Fish and game are often found on the specials board. The pub also offers hog and spit roast catering.

Open all wk noon-3 6-11 (Sun 7-9.30) Closed: 26-29 Dec, 1 Jan **Bar Meals** L served Mon-Sat 12-2.30 booking required Av main course £14 **Restaurant** L served Mon-Sun 12-2.30 booking required D served Mon-Sat 6-9.30, Sun 7-9 booking required Av 3 course à la carte fr £27 ⊕ FREE HOUSE ◀ Rusty Bucket, Woodforde's Wherry, Nethergate ♂ Aspalls. ☕ 14 **Facilities** Children's menu Garden Parking

See advert on this page

FOWLMERE — Map 12 TL44

The Chequers ☺

High St SG8 7SR ☎ 01763 208369 📄 01763 208944
e-mail: info@thechequersfowlmere.co.uk
dir: From M11, A505, 2nd right to Fowlmere. 8m S of
Cambridge, 4m E of Royston

The pub dates from the 16th century, and was visited by
Samuel Pepys in 1660, but the pub's sign - blue and red
chequers - honours the British and American squadrons
based nearby during World War II. These days the
Chequers is known for its imaginative cooking served in
the galleried restaurant, bar or attractive garden.
Specials include pan-fried Barbary duck breast
marinated in ginger and soy, featherblade of beef braised
in a Portobello mushroom red wine, or sautéed chicken
breast with olive oil mashed potato.

Open all wk 12-3 6-11 Closed: 25-26 Dec eve & 1 Jan eve
Bar Meals L served Mon-Fri 12-2, Sat 12-2.30, Sun 12-3
D served Mon-Sat 7-9.30 Av main course £15
Restaurant L served Mon-Fri 12-2, Sat 12-2.30, Sun 12-3
D served Mon-Sat 7-9.30, Sun 7-9 Av 3 course à la carte
fr £30 ⊕ FREE HOUSE ◀ Adnams, Cottage, Buntingford,
Archers, Sharps. ☺ 20 Facilities Garden Parking

GRANTCHESTER — Map 12 TL45

The Rupert Brooke ☺

2 Broadway CB3 9NQ
☎ 01223 840295 📄 01223 841251
e-mail: info@therupertbrooke.com
dir: M11 junct 12, follow Grantchester signs

Only five minutes from the centre of Cambridge and the
M11, yet set in an idyllic location overlooking the
meadows close to the River Cam, sits the Rupert Brooke,
named after the WWI poet. Inside, you'll find timber
beams and winter log fires, with relaxing sofas and tub
chairs. Using local, seasonal produce and with regularly
changing menus, watch the chefs at work in the theatre-
style kitchen, creating their range of modern British
dishes - winter squash and sage risotto; Grasmere Farm
sausages with creamy mash are typical choices. The pub
provides newspapers and Wi-fi.

Open all wk 11.30-11 (Fri-Sat 11.30-mdnt) Bar Meals L
served Mon-Sat 12-3 D served Mon-Fri 6-9.30 Av main
course £11 Restaurant L served Mon-Sat 12-3 (Sun 12-6
(8 May-Sep)) booking required D served Mon-Sat 6-9.30
booking required Av 3 course à la carte fr £25
⊕ ENTERPRISE INNS ◀ Harveys Sussex Best, Woodforde's
Wherry, London Pride, Timothy Taylor Landlord ⦿ Westons
Stowford Press. ☺ 12 Facilities Children's menu Family
room Garden Parking

GREAT CHISHILL — Map 12 TL43

The Pheasant ☺

24 Heydon Rd SG8 8SR ☎ 01763 838535
dir: Off B1039 between Royston & Saffron Walden

Stunning views and roaring log fires characterise this
traditional, beamed village free house, where
Nethergates, Woodforde's Wherry and Greene King ales
are some of the choices. There are no gaming machines
or piped music to disturb the friendly, sociable bar, and
children under 14 are not allowed in. In summer, bird
song holds sway in the idyllic pub garden. Freshly-made
sandwiches come complete with chips and salad garnish
or there is a deal to include home-made soup as well,
whilst home-made dishes like slow roast belly pork;
grilled haddock and crayfish; and confit of duck leg cater
for larger appetites.

Open all wk noon-3 6-11 (all day Sat-Sun) Bar Meals L
served all wk 12-2 D served all wk 6-9.30 Av main course
£14 Restaurant L served all wk 12-2 D served all wk
6-9.30 Av 3 course à la carte fr £25 ⊕ FREE HOUSE
◀ Nethergates, Greene King IPA, London Pride,
Woodforde's Wherry, Oakham JHB ⦿ Stowford Press. ☺ 10
Facilities Dogs allowed Garden Parking

HEMINGFORD GREY — Map 12 TL27

The Cock Pub and Restaurant ☺

47 High St PE28 9BJ
☎ 01480 463609 📄 01480 461747
e-mail: cock@cambscuisine.com
dir: 2m S of Huntingdon and 1m E of A14

There's been a spring in the step of this village pub since
Oliver Thain and Richard Bradley arrived a few years ago;
it has had a recent refurbishment too. Transforming it
into an dining pub, they've retained traditional values,
with well kept real ales, log fires blazing when the
weather demands and a delightful garden in summer,
and a welcome for walkers, children and dogs. In the
wooden-floored restaurant fresh fish, including seared
sea bream and mushroom sauce, and chef's various
home-made sausages, may prove irresistible. Gluten-free
dishes offered.

Open all wk 11.30-3 6-11 Restaurant L served all wk
12-2.30 D served all wk 6.15-9.30 Fixed menu price fr
£11 Av 3 course à la carte fr £20 ⊕ FREE HOUSE
◀ Golden Jackal, Wolf Brewery, Victoria Bitter,
Buntingford Highwayman IPA, seasonal ale from
Nethergate. ☺ 13 Facilities Children's menu Dogs allowed
Garden Parking

HILDERSHAM — Map 12 TL54

The Pear Tree ☺

High St CB21 6BU ☎ 01223 891680
e-mail: peartreeinn@btconnect.com
dir: 5m E of Cambridge, take A1307 to Haverhill, turn left
to Hildersham

Popular with walkers and locals alike, the Pear Tree is
every inch the traditional village pub, set opposite the
village green with beams and a stone floor inside and a
country garden outside. It has a well-deserved local
reputation for its home-cooked food including a range of
freshly prepared pies served with seasonal vegetables
and desserts like apple and fruit crumbles. New owner.

Open 6.30-11 (Fri 6-11, Sun 11.30-2.30 6.30-10.30)
Closed: Tue Bar Meals L served Sun 12-2.30 D served all
wk 6.30-9.30 ⊕ FREE HOUSE ◀ Greene King IPA , Abbot
Ale. ☺ 12 Facilities Dogs allowed Garden Parking

HILTON — Map 12 TL26

The Prince of Wales ★★★ INN ☺

Potton Rd PE28 9NG ☎ 01480 830257
e-mail: simon@hiltonpow.co.uk
dir: On B1040 between A14 & A428 S of St Ives

The Prince of Wales is a traditional, 1830s-built, two-bar
village inn with four comfortable bedrooms. Food options
range from bar snacks to full meals, among which are
grills, fish, curries brought in from a local Indian
restaurant, and daily specials, such as lamb hotpot.
Home-made puddings include crème brûlée and sherry
trifle. The village's 400-year-old grass maze was where
locals used to escape the devil.

Open 12-2.30 6-11 Closed: Mon L Bar Meals L served all
wk 12-2 D served all wk 7-9 ⊕ FREE HOUSE ◀ Adnams,
Timothy Taylor Landlord, Smoothflow, Worthingtons, guest
ales. ☺ 9 Facilities Garden Parking Rooms 4

HINXTON   Map 12 TL44

The Red Lion ★★★★ INN ◉ ♀

32 High St CB10 1QY
☎ 01799 530601   🖹 01799 531201
e-mail: info@redlionhinxton.co.uk
dir: *1m from M11 junct 9*

The Red Lion has been in Hinxton, a conservation village, since the 16th century. The bar is in the oldest part, while the spacious oak-built extension is the dining room. Pub policy is always to use fresh local produce where possible to create imaginative dishes such as Poché-grillé pheasant breast wrapped in streaky bacon; or pork belly confit with sage dauphinoise potato, fine beans and apple jus. Enjoy your visit with a pint of Rusty Bucket, Village Bike or Aspall cider, or stay over and explore the area.

Open all wk 11-3 6-11 **Bar Meals** L served Mon-Thu 12-2, Fri-Sun 12-2.30 D served Sun-Thu 7-9, Fri-Sat 7-9.30 Av main course £11 **Restaurant** L served Mon-Thu 12-2, Fri-Sun 12-2.30 D served Sun-Thu 7-9, Fri-Sat 7-9.30 Av 3 course à la carte fr £22 ⊕ FREE HOUSE ◀ Adnams, Greene King IPA, Woodforde's Wherry, Rusty Bucket, Village Bike, guest ales ♂ Aspall. ♀ 12 **Facilities** Children's menu Dogs allowed Garden Parking **Rooms** 8

HOLYWELL   Map 12 TL37

The Old Ferryboat Inn Ⓐ ★★ HL ♀

Back Ln PE27 4TG ☎ 01480 463227   🖹 01480 463245
e-mail: 8638@greeneking.co.uk
dir: *From Cambridge on A14 right onto A1096, then right onto A1123, right to Holywell*

Renowned as England's oldest inn, built some time in the 11th century, but with a hostelry history that goes back to the 6th. In a tranquil setting beside the Great Ouse river, The Old Ferryboat has immaculately maintained thatch, white stone walls, cosy interior and bags of charm and character. A pleasant atmosphere - despite the resident ghost of a lovelorn teenager - in which to enjoy grilled bacon and warm poached egg salad; British beef and Ruddles ale pie, mash, seasonal vegetables and onion gravy; or sweet potato, chick pea and spinach curry. There are seven en suite bedrooms available.

Open all wk 11-11 (Sun noon-10.30) **Bar Meals** food served all day **Restaurant** food served all day ⊕ OLD ENGLISH INNS & HOTELS ◀ Greene King Abbot Ale/IPA, guest ales. ♀ 18 **Facilities** Children's menu Garden Parking **Rooms** 7

HORNINGSEA   Map 12 TL46

The Crown & Punchbowl NEW

CB5 9JG ☎ 01223 860643   🖹 01223 441814
e-mail: info@thecrownandpunchbowl.co.uk
dir: *Please telephone for directions*

Soft colours and wooden floors create a warm and cosy atmosphere beneath the tiled roof of this whitewashed free house, just ten minutes from Cambridge city centre. The large restaurant caters equally for business lunches and those with more time to relax; expect roast guinea fowl with braised lentils; stuffed field mushroom with goats' cheese, spinach and beans; and home-made pie with seasonal vegetables. Fresh fish and home-made sausages also feature on the chalkboard menus.

Open noon-2.30 6.30-9 Closed: Sun eve & BH eve **Bar Meals** Av main course £12.95 **Restaurant** L served all wk 12-2.30 booking required D served Mon-Sat 6.30-9 booking required Fixed menu price fr £11.95 Av 3 course à la carte fr £19.95 ⊕ FREE HOUSE ◀ Hobson's Choice. **Facilities** Children's menu Garden Parking

HUNTINGDON   Map 12 TL27

The Three Horseshoes ★★★★ INN ♀

Moat Ln, Abbots Ripton PE28 2PA
☎ 01487 773440   🖹 01487 773440
e-mail: abbotsripton@aol.com

Dating back to 1654 and retaining many original features, the picturesque Three Horseshoes once had the lowest ceiling of any pub in the county. Stepping inside today, customers are greeted by three bar areas, a restaurant and a range of hand pumped Adnams real ales; there's accommodation too. Typical food includes Sunday roasts like rib of beef with Yorkshire pudding; roast loin of pork with crackling and apple sauce; and grilled tuna steak.

Closed: Mon ◀ Adnams Bitter, Adnams Broadside, Oakhams JHB. ♀ 12 **Facilities** Family room Garden Parking **Rooms** 6

KEYSTON   Map 11 TL07

PICK OF THE PUBS

Pheasant Inn ◉ ♀

See Pick of the Pubs on page 66

KIMBOLTON   Map 12 TL16

The New Sun Inn ♀

20-22 High St PE28 0HA
☎ 01480 860052   🖹 01480 869353
e-mail: newsunninn@btinternet.com
dir: *From A1 N take B645 for 7m. From A1 S take B661 for 7m. From A14 take B660 for 5m*

An impressive array of flowers greets visitors to this 16th-century inn near Kimbolton Castle. As well as being a real ale pub, it offers a good choice of wines by the glass. Dishes from the restaurant menu include king prawns in hot garlic and ginger oil, or whole baked camembert to start, then venison sausages with grain mustard mash or home-made steak and kidney pudding as mains. Lighter meals, such as jacket potatoes or sandwiches are also available.

Open all wk 11.30-2.30 6-11 (Sun all day) **Bar Meals** L served all wk 12-2.15 D served Tue-Sat 7.30-9.30 **Restaurant** L served all wk 12-2.15 D served Tue-Sat 7.30-9.30 ⊕ CHARLES WELLS ◀ Wells Bombardier & Eagle IPA, Greene King Old Speckled Hen, Guest Ale. ♀ 12 **Facilities** Dogs allowed Garden

LITTLE WILBRAHAM   Map 12 TL55

Hole in the Wall ◉ ♀

2 High St CB1 5JY ☎ 01223 812282
e-mail: jenniferleeton@btconnect.com
dir: *Telephone for directions*

People say local farm workers had to collect their beer through a hole in the wall back when only the gentry were admitted. Today the pub welcomes all comers for a pint of Nelson's Revenge or Stowford Press cider. Midday and evening menus differ, but both are based on seasonal local produce: pan-fried free-range chicken livers on toast make a flavoursome lunch, while dinner could comprise free-range crisp-fried pork belly, Cajun-spiced Cornish monkfish with saffron mash, and toffee and banana strudel.

Open 11.30-3 6.30-11 Closed: 2 wks Jan, 25 Dec, Mon (ex BH L), Sun eve **Bar Meals** L served Tue-Sun 12-2 booking required D served Tue-Sat 7-9 booking required Av main course £12 **Restaurant** L served Tue-Sun 12-2 booking required D served Tue-Sat 7-9 booking required Av 3 course à la carte fr £24 ⊕ FREE HOUSE ◀ Woodforde's Wherry, Cambridge Bitter, Sparta, Nelsons Revenge ♂ Stowford Press. ♀ 9 **Facilities** Dogs allowed Garden Parking

PICK OF THE PUBS

Pheasant Inn 🌹 ▽

KEYSTON Map 11 TL07

Village Loop Rd PE28 ORE
☎ **01832 710241** 📄 **01832 710340**
e-mail: info@thepheasant-keyston.co.uk
dir: *0.5m off A14, clearly signed, 10m W of Huntingdon, 14m E of Kettering*

A 15th-century, thatched English inn, set in a sleepy farming village. Its traditional and unspoilt bar is full of oak beams and simple wooden furniture, and is warmed by large open fires. Three distinct dining areas are all comfortable, intimate and relaxed. Three is also how many Suffolk real ales on offer, alongside an acclaimed wine list. In charge of this very popular pub are Jay and Taffeta Scrimshaw, he having previously run the White Swan off London's Fleet Street, she Itsu, a busy Japanese restaurant in Chelsea. Keyston is undoubtedly calmer than London, but the metropolitan efficiency shines through. In fine weather you can enjoy the garden at the rear of the pub, or sit on one of the benches out front. Expect good things of the restaurant – it has an AA Rosette - where the cooking style owes much to the South of France, as well as to the best seasonal produce from mostly local suppliers within a 10-mile radius. Menus change daily, offering starters of snails in garlic butter; potato, spring onion and chive soup with poached egg; fish goujons with tartare sauce, lemon and deep-fried parsley; or lamb pie with piccalilli and watercress. Among typical mains are coq au vin with confit garlic mashed potato and cavolo nero; steak and ale suet pudding with green peppercorn sauce, new potatoes and Italian chicory; crisp nut-roast with caramelised artichokes, balsamic shallots, watercress, home-made soft cheese and lentil vinaigrette; and crisp grey mullet with bourride sauce, tapenade potatoes, brown shrimps and mussels. Puddings include chocolate Pithiviers with thyme ice cream; and banana sticky toffee pudding with butterscotch sauce and Jersey cream.

Open all day Closed: Sun eve, Mon (ex BH) **Bar Meals** L served Mon-Sat 12-2.30 booking required D served Mon-Sat 6.30-9.30 booking required Av main course £14 **Restaurant** L served all wk 12-2.30 booking required D served all wk 6.30-9.30 booking required Fixed menu price fr £15 ⊕ THE PHEASANT KEYSTON LTD ◀ Adnams, Village Bike Potton Brewery, Augustinian Nethergate Brewery. ▽ 16 **Facilities** Children's menu Dogs allowed Garden Parking

MADINGLEY   Map 12 TL36

PICK OF THE PUBS

The Three Horseshoes ◉ ▼

High St CB3 8AB ☎ 01954 210221 📠 **01954 212043**
e-mail: thethreehorseshoes@huntsbridge.co.uk
dir: M11 junct 13, 1.5m from A14

This picturesque thatched inn enjoys a charming location; its large garden extends towards meadowland and the local cricket pitch. Inside is a small, bustling bar and a pretty conservatory restaurant. Chef-Patron Richard Stokes is a local from the fens who has eaten his way around the world, and his success can be gauged by the long queues for tables. Richard's own style is a modern take on Italian cuisine, characterised by seasonal and imaginative dishes with intense flavours. After antipasti, you could try risotto di pesce or aqua cotta (a 'boiled water' classic Italian soup), followed by line-caught grey mullet with Casteluccio lentils, Italian sea kale, slow cooked fennel and salsa verde; or pot-roasted free-range organic chicken stuffed with garlic, thyme, butter and lemon, potato purée, cavolo nero and chicken liver crostino. Desserts might include lemon tart with Seville orange and Campari sorbet. Prior booking is advisable.

Open all wk 11.30-3 6-11 (Sun 6-9.30) **Bar Meals** L served Mon-Fri 12-2, Sat-Sun 12-2.30 D served all wk 6.30-9.30 Av main course £15 **Restaurant** L served all wk 12-2.30 D served Mon-Sat 6.30-9.30 Fixed price fr £20 Av 3 course à la carte fr £30 ⊕ FREE HOUSE ◖ Adnams Bitter, Hook Norton Old Hooky, Smile's Best, Cambridge Hobsons Choice, guest ales. ▼ 20 **Facilities** Children's menu Garden Parking

MILTON   Map 12 TL46

Waggon & Horses

39 High St CB24 6DF ☎ 01223 860313
e-mail: winningtons.waggon@ntlworld.com
dir: A14/A10 junct. Past Tesco, through village, approx 1m set back on left

Elgood Brewery's most southerly house, the pub is an imposing mock-Tudor building famed for its large collection of hats. Real cider is also served, from local producer Cassels. A challenging quiz is set on Wednesday nights and baltis are the speciality on Thursdays. All meals are good value and the chilli is particularly recommended. Bar billiards is popular inside, and outside there is a large child-safe garden with a slide and swings, and a pétanque terrain.

Open all wk noon-2.30 5-11 (Fri 5-mdnt, Sat noon-3 6-11.30, Sun noon-3 7.30-10.30) **Bar Meals** L served all wk 12-2 D served all wk 7-9 Av main course £5 ⊕ ELGOOD & SONS LTD ◖ Elgoods Cambridge Bitter, Black Dog Mild, Golden Newt, seasonal and guest ales ♻ Cassells. **Facilities** Children's menu Dogs allowed Garden Parking

NEWTON   Map 12 TL44

The Queen's Head ▼

Fowlmere Rd CB22 7PG ☎ 01223 870436
dir: 6m S of Cambridge on B1368, 1.5m off A10 at Harston, 4m from A505

Best described as 'quintessentially English', this 17th-century village pub has been run by the same family since 1962. They continue to steadfastly ban fruit machines and piped music from the two small bars. Lunches are limited to home-made soup, Aga-baked potatoes, and sandwiches. In the evening it's just soup and cold platters. There's no specials board since, as the landlord says, 'We have no specialist'! There is a green opposite where customers can eat and drink.

Open all wk 11.30-2.30 6-11 (Sun noon-2.30 7-10.30) Closed: 25-26 Dec **Bar Meals** L served all wk 12-2.15 D served all wk 7-9.30 ⊕ FREE HOUSE ◖ Adnams Southwold, Broadside, Fisherman, Bitter, Regatta ♻ Crones. ▼ 8 **Facilities** Family room Dogs allowed Parking **Notes** ⊛

PETERBOROUGH   Map 12 TL19

The Brewery Tap ▼

80 Westgate PE1 2AA
☎ 01733 358500 📠 **01733 310022**
e-mail: brewerytap@hotmail.com
dir: Opposite bus station

This is the home of multi-award-winning Oakham Ales, moved here from their home in Rutland when Peterborough's spacious old labour exchange opened its doors as the Brewery Tap in 1998. Visitors to this striking pub can see the day-to-day running of the brewery through a glass wall spanning half the length of the bar. As if the appeal of the beer range were not enough, Thai chefs beaver away producing delicious snacks, soups, salads, stir-fries and curries. Look out for live music nights.

Open all day all wk noon-11pm (Fri-Sat noon-mdnt) Closed: 25-26 Dec, 1 Jan **Bar Meals** L served Sun-Thu 12-2.30, Fri-Sat 12-10.30 D served Sun-Thu 6-9.30, Fri-Sat 12-10.30 **Restaurant** L served Sun-Thu 12-2.30, Fri-Sat 12-10.30 D served Sun-Thu 6-9.30, Fri-Sat 12-10.30 ⊕ FREE HOUSE ◖ Oakham Inferno, Jeffery Hudson Bitter, Bishops Farewell, White Dwarf Elgoods Black Dog, 7 guest ales ♻ Westons 1st Quality. ▼ 7 **Facilities** Dogs allowed

Charters Bar & East Restaurant ▼

Upper Deck, Town Bridge PE1 1FP
☎ 01733 315700 & 315702 (bkgs) 📠 **01733 315700**
e-mail: manager@charters-bar.co.uk
dir: A1/A47 towards Wisbech, 2m for city centre & town bridge (River Nene). Barge moored at Town Bridge, west side

Moored in the heart of Peterborough on the River Nene, this 176-foot converted barge promises 'brews, blues and fine views'. It motored from Holland across the North Sea in 1991, and is now a haven for real ale lovers. Twelve hand pumps dispense a continually changing repertoire of brews, while Friday and Saturday nights bring live blues music. The East part of the name applies to the oriental restaurant on the upper deck.

Open all day all wk noon-11pm (Fri-Sat noon-2am) Closed: 25-26 Dec, 1 Jan **Bar Meals** L served all wk 12-2.30 Av main course £5.95 **Restaurant** L served Mon-Sat 12-2.30, Sun 12-3.30 D served all wk 5.30-10.30 booking required Fixed menu price fr £8.95 Av 3 course à la carte fr £18 ⊕ FREE HOUSE ◖ Oakham JHB, Oakham Bishops Farewell, Crouchvale Brewers Gold, Abbeydale Absolution, ♻ Westons Old Rosie, Westons Traditional Draught Scrumpy. ▼ 6 **Facilities** Dogs allowed Garden Parking

REACH   Map 12 TL56

Dyke's End ▼

CB25 0JD ☎ 01638 743816
dir: Telephone for directions

In 1996/7 villagers saved this pub from closure and ran it as a co-operative until 2003, when it was bought by Frank Feehan, who has further refurbished and extended it. Frank's additions include the Devil's Dyke microbrewery, which produces four real ales, including a strong mild. The pub's local reputation for the quality of its food means restaurant booking is strongly advised, particularly at weekends. A fenced front garden overlooks the village green.

Open Mon-Fri 12-2.30 6-11 (Sat-Sun noon-11) Closed: Mon L **Bar Meals** L served all wk 12-2 D served all wk 7-9 ⊕ FREE HOUSE ◖ Devil's Dyke microbrewery beer, Woodforde's Wherry, Adnams Bitter ♻ Aspalls, Old Rosie. ▼ 8 **Facilities** Play area Family room Dogs allowed Garden Parking

SPALDWICK — Map 12 TL17

PICK OF THE PUBS

The George Inn ?

High St PE28 0TD ☎ **01480 890293** 🖹 **01480 896847**
e-mail: info@georgeofspaldwick.co.uk
*dir: 6m W of Huntingdon on A14, junct 18 towards
Spaldwick/Stow Longa*

Refurbished to create a pleasing blend of traditional
and modern, this fine old building retains historic
features such as original beams and fireplaces. It
started life as a large private residence belonging to
the Dartington family, and became a coaching inn in
1679. Today it remains a serene presence beside the
manor house, overlooking the village green. The bar is
relaxing with its comfortable leather sofas, while the
restaurant, set in a beautifully converted barn, offers a
pleasing selection of traditional British and
Mediterranean-influenced dishes. Typical choices
include a starter of crispy duck salad with spicy
chorizo, bacon lardons, croutons and plum dressing,
followed by wood pigeon breasts with herb dumplings,
mash, red cabbage and a chocolate red wine sauce.
Finish with apple crumble tart or a delightful selection
of cheeses. A good choice of wines is available by the
glass, and there are plenty of well-kept real ales.

Open all day all wk noon-11.30pm Closed: 1 Jan **Bar
Meals** L served all wk 12-2.30 D served all wk 6-9.30
Restaurant L served all wk 12-2.30 D served all wk
6-9.30 ⊕ PUNCH TAVERNS ◀ Adnams Broadside,
Greene King IPA, Youngs Special. ? 25
Facilities Children's menu Garden Parking

STAPLEFORD — Map 12 TL45

The Rose at Stapleford NEW ?

81 London Rd CB22 5DE ☎ **01223 843349**
e-mail: paulnbeer@aol.com

Having made a success of the George and Dragon at
Elsworth (see entry), Paul and Karen Beer are weaving
their magic at the Rose, a traditional village pub close to
Cambridge and Duxford Imperial War Museum. Expect a
comfortably refurbished interior, replete with low beams
and inglenook fireplaces, and extensive menus that draw
on local Suffolk produce, particularly meat with fish from
Lowestoft. Typical dishes take in calves' liver and bacon
with onion gravy, fish pie, and local farm-reared steaks
with pepper sauce.

Open 12-2.30 6-11 Closed: Sun eve **Bar Meals** L served
all wk 12-2.30 D served all wk 6-9.30 Av main course £12
food served all day **Restaurant** L served all wk 12-2.30 D
served all wk 6-9.30 Fixed menu price fr £11 Av 3 course
à la carte fr £20 food served all day ⊕ Enterprise ◀ IPA,
Tribute, Guest Ale. ? 9 **Facilities** Children's menu Dogs
allowed Garden Parking

STILTON — Map 12 TL18

PICK OF THE PUBS

The Bell Inn Hotel ★★★ HL ◉ ?

Great North Rd PE7 3RA
☎ **01733 241066** 🖹 **01733 245173**
e-mail: reception@thebellstilton.co.uk
*dir: From A1(M) junct 16 follow signs for Stilton. Hotel
on main road in village centre*

Steeped in history and reputedly the oldest coaching
inn on the Great North Road, the Bell's impressive
16th-century stone façade hides a fine interior that
boasts original features, including a grand stone
fireplace in the Village Bar. In its time the inn has
hosted highwayman Dick Turpin, Lord Byron and, more
recently, Clark Gable and Joe Louis, who were stationed
nearby in World War II. The Bell is also famous for
Stilton cheese, which was first served here in the early
1700s. Imaginative modern British dishes are served in
the atmospheric, galleried restaurant, the set menu
offering pumpkin, Stilton and rosemary soup,
chargrilled lamb with pea and mint purée and
redcurrant jus, and prune and Armagnac tart. Tuck into
pasta with crab and chorizo or steak and kidney suet
pudding in the more informal bistro. Note the
magnificent inn sign, it's a replica of the original
weighing two and three quarter tonnes.

Open all wk noon-2.30 6-11 (Sat-Sun noon-3 Sun
7-11) Closed: 25 Dec **Bar Meals** L served all wk
12-2.30 D served all wk 6-9.30 Av main course £13
Restaurant L served Sun-Fri 12-2 booking required D
served Mon-Sat 7-9.30 booking required Fixed menu
price fr £29.95 Av 3 course à la carte fr £18.95 ⊕ FREE
HOUSE ◀ Greene King Abbot Ale, Oakham JHB, Fuller's
London Pride, Greene King IPA, Brewers Gold. ? 8
Facilities Children's menu Garden Parking **Rooms** 22

STRETHAM — Map 12 TL57

The Lazy Otter

Cambridge Rd CB6 3LU
☎ **01353 649780** 🖹 **01353 649314**
e-mail: restaurant@lazy-otter.com
dir: Telephone for directions

Just off the A10 between Ely and Cambridge, the Lazy
Otter stands overlooking the marina beside the River
Great Ouse. There's been a pub on this site since the 18th
century, but the old building was redeveloped in 1986.
Today, the large beer garden and riverside restaurant are

popular summer attractions. Lunchtime brings baguettes,
sandwiches and jacket potatoes, whilst main course
choices include ham and eggs; baked cod au gratin; and
home-made spinach lasagne. Enjoy your meal with a pint
of Lazy Otter best bitter or Pickled Pig cider.

Open all day all wk 11-11 (Sun noon-10.30pm) **Bar
Meals** L served Mon-Sat 12-2, Sun 12-7 booking required
D served Mon-Sat 6.30-9, Sun 12-7 booking required Av
main course £8.50 **Restaurant** L served Mon-Sat 12-2,
Sun 12-7 booking required D served Mon-Sat 6.30-9, Sun
12-7 booking required ⊕ FREE HOUSE ◀ Greene King,
IPA, Guest ales ♻ Pickled Pig. **Facilities** Children's menu
Play area Garden Parking

CHESHIRE

ALDFORD — Map 15 SJ45

PICK OF THE PUBS

The Grosvenor Arms ?

Chester Rd CH3 6HJ
☎ **01244 620228** 🖹 **01244 620247**
e-mail: grosvenor.arms@brunningandprice.co.uk
dir: On B5130 S of Chester

Described by its owners as a 'large, rather austere
Victorian governess of a building which looks a little
ungainly from the road side', the Grosvenor was the
work of a locally infamous mid-Victorian architect who,
in the name of progress, destroyed many fine medieval
buildings in and around Chester. It is endearing
nonetheless, and viewed from the garden it's 'a delight
of higgledy-piggledy rooflines and soft, warm Cheshire
brick'. The spacious, open-plan interior includes an airy
conservatory and a panelled, book-filled library. On the
bistro-style menu are a range of sandwiches and
unusual starters such as oxtail potato cake with
poached egg, and seared squid with lightly spiced
couscous. Main courses range from country vegetable
and lentil cottage pie, to 8oz steakburger topped with
smoked bacon and mozzarella. Sandwiches and light
bites are also available. Desserts include the sticky
toffee pudding with butterscotch sauce, and lemon and
lavender pannacotta with blackcurrant sorbet. An
outside terrace leads into a small but pleasing garden
which, in turn, takes you out to the village green.

Open all wk **Bar Meals** food served all day ⊕ FREE
HOUSE ◀ Weetwood-Eastgate, Caledonian Deuchars
IPA, Phoenix Arizona, Thwaites Original, Oakham
JHB. ? 20 **Facilities** Dogs allowed Garden Parking

ASTON — Map 15 SJ64

PICK OF THE PUBS

The Bhurtpore Inn ?

See Pick of the Pubs on opposite page

PICK OF THE PUBS

The Bhurtpore Inn ♀

ASTON
Map 15 SJ64

Wrenbury Rd CW5 8DQ
☎ **01270 780917**
e-mail: simonbhurtpore@yahoo.co.uk
dir: *Just off A530 between Nantwich & Whitchurch. Turn towards Wrenbury at x-rds in village*

When, in 1991, Simon and Nicky George were pub-hunting they came across the boarded-up, stripped-out Bhurtpore. Despite its condition, it ticked just about every box on their lengthy checklist. They were not the first Georges to have their names over the door of this traditional village pub; in 1849 James George leased it from the local Combermere estate, and in 1895

Philip George bought it from them, selling it six years later to a Crewe brewery. Although a pub since at least 1778, it was the 1826 Siege of Bhurtpore in India, where Lord Combermere had distinguished himself, that inspired its name. In the bar, eleven, ever-changing real ales are always available (a total of 728 different ones passed through in 2008!), mostly from local micro-breweries, as are real ciders, Continental draught beers and around 150 of the world's bottled beers. The pub has been short-listed four times for the 'National Whisky Pub of the Year' award, and it has a menu of soft drinks as long as your arm. The set menus are complemented by daily specials that include chicken breast marinated in lemon and paprika; salmon and smoked haddock fishcakes; lamb burger flavoured with coriander, cumin, garlic and green chillies; grilled duck breast with red wine and blackberry sauce; sautéed pheasant breast with smoked

bacon, chestnuts, sprouts and cream; and goats' cheese pastry tartlet with red onion chutney, sunblush tomatoes and basil sauce. A selection of curries and balti dishes may be found on the blackboard. The pub is home to an enthusiastic cricket team, while the first Thursday evening of each month sees the arrival of a cavalcade of venerable cars and other vehicles. Behind the pub is a lawn with countryside views.

Open 12-2.30 6.30-11.30 (Fri-Sat 12-12, Sun 12-11) Closed: 25-26 Dec, 1 Jan **Meals** L served Mon-Fri 12-2 D served Mon-Fri 6.30-9.30, Sat 12-9.30, Sun 12-9 ⊕ FREE HOUSE ◼ Salopian Golden Thread, Abbeydale Absolution, Weetwood Oasthouse Gold, Copper Dragon Golden Pippin, Townhouse Audley Gold. ♀ 11 **Facilities** Dogs allowed Garden Parking

BOLLINGTON
Map 16 SJ97

The Church House Inn ★★★ INN ♥

Church St SK10 5PY
☎ 01625 574014 📠 01625 562026
e-mail: info@thechurchhouseinn-bollington.co.uk
dir: *From A34 take A538 towards Macclesfield. Through Prestbury, then follow Bollington signs*

Exposed beams, log fires and agricultural decorations lend a homely feel to this stone-built village free house, which hit the headlines when it was bought by a group of local residents. The varied menu includes home-made soup, the inn's own sausages and pies, and other traditional British favourites. Vegetarian options feature on the daily specials board. The pub also has a small enclosed beer garden.

Open all wk 12-3 5.30-11 (Sun 12-10.30) **Bar Meals** L served Mon-Sat 12-2, Sun 12-8 D served Mon-Sat 6-9.30, Sun 12-8 ⊕ FREE HOUSE ◀ Greene King IPA, Timothy Taylor Golden Best, Jennings Cocker Hoop. ♥ 18 **Facilities** Parking **Rooms** 5

BUNBURY
Map 15 SJ55

PICK OF THE PUBS

The Dysart Arms ♥

Bowes Gate Rd CW6 9PH
☎ 01829 260183 📠 01829 261286
e-mail: dysart.arms@brunningandprice.co.uk
dir: *Between A49 & A51, by Shropshire Union Canals*

Built as a farmhouse in the mid-18th century, and licensed since the late 1800s, this is a quintessentially English village pub, right down to its pretty garden with views of two castles and the parish church next door. Around its central bar are several airy rooms with solid wood furnishings, bare floors, open fires and a couple of large bookcases. There is a great choice of real beers including Phoenix Struggling Monkey. Home-grown herbs are used in a please-all menu, which opens with starters such as pigeon and smoked bacon pasty with pear chutney; smoked salmon with pickled cucumber and granary bread; and chicken liver pâté with pear chutney. Among the main courses are steak, kidney and ale pie; pan-fried lamb rump on celeriac rösti; and grilled trout fillets with smoked bacon, cabbage and new potato cake. Decadent desserts might include chocolate bread and butter pudding with fresh cream; and a warm waffle with honeycomb ice cream and butterscotch sauce.

Open all day all wk 11.30-11 (Sun noon-10.30) **Bar Meals** L served all wk D served all wk food served all day **Restaurant** L served all wk D served all wk food served all day ⊕ FREE HOUSE ◀ Phoenix Struggling Monkey, Weetwood Eastgate, Thwaites Bitter, Coach House Honey Pot, Sharp's Doom Bar. ♥ 17 **Facilities** Dogs allowed Garden Parking

BURLEYDAM
Map 15 SJ64

The Combermere Arms ♥

SY13 4AT ☎ 01948 871223 📠 01948 661371
e-mail: combermere.arms@brunningandprice.co.uk
dir: *From Whitchurch take A525 towards Nantwich, at Newcastle/Audlem/Woore sign, turn right at junct. Pub 100yds on right*

Popular with local shoots, walkers and town folk alike, this busy 17th-century inn retains great character and warmth. Three roaring fires complement the wealth of oak, pictures and old furniture. Dishes range from light bites and sandwiches to shin of beef and Weetwood ale pie or pot-roasted Combermere Abbey pheasant; and puddings like steamed blackcurrant roly poly with custard. There is a great choice of real ales and ciders, and a very impressive cheese list.

Open all wk 11.30-11 **Bar Meals** Av main course £10 food served all day **Restaurant** food served all day ⊕ FREE HOUSE ◀ Woodlands Oak Beauty, Weetwood Cheshire Cat, Thornbridge Jaipur Monsoon, St Austells Tribute, Storm Hurricane Hubert ♂ Weston Stowford Press, Thatchers Gold, Inch's Stonehouse. ♥ 15 **Facilities** Children's menu Dogs allowed Garden Parking

BURWARDSLEY
Map 15 SJ55

PICK OF THE PUBS

The Pheasant Inn ★★★★ INN ♥

See Pick of the Pubs on opposite page

CHESTER
Map 15 SJ46

PICK OF THE PUBS

Albion Inn

See Pick of the Pubs on page 72

Old Harkers Arms ♥

1 Russell St CH1 5AL
☎ 01244 344525 📠 01244 344812
e-mail: harkers.arms@brunningandprice.co.uk
dir: *Follow steps down from City Road onto canal path*

A buzzy meeting place with the feel of a gentlemen's club, this former Victorian chandler's warehouse on the Shropshire Union Canal is one of Chester's more unusual pubs. The bar offers over 100 malt whiskies, 20 wines by the glass, and hand pumps dispensing four regular and six guest ales mostly from local micro-breweries. The daily-changing menu runs from light dishes such as breaded tiger prawns with pineapple salsa, through to main courses of braised lamb shoulder or Gloucester Old Spot sausages.

Open all wk 11.30-11 (Sun noon-10.30) Closed: 25 Dec **Bar Meals** Av main course £11.25, a la carte fr £21.45 food served all day ⊕ BRUNNING & PRICE ◀ Weetwood Cheshire Cat, Flowers Original, Wapping Bitter, Titanic Stout, Spitting Feathers ♂ Westons Organic, Scrumpy, Old Rosie. ♥ 20 **Facilities** Dogs allowed

CHOLMONDELEY
Map 15 SJ55

PICK OF THE PUBS

The Cholmondeley Arms ♥

SY14 8HN ☎ 01829 720300 📠 01829 720123
e-mail: guy@cholmondeleyarms.co.uk
dir: *On A49, between Whitchurch & Tarporley*

Formerly the village school, this elegant pub had been closed for six years when in 1988 the current owners embarked on its conversion. It is located in quiet Cheshire countryside adjoining the parks and gardens of historic Cholmondeley Castle, home to Lord and Lady Cholmondeley, and is also close to the Sandstone Trail, the Shropshire Union Canal, Beeston Castle and historic Chester. All food is freshly prepared, using local produce wherever possible, and is offered from a daily changing menu. You might start with crispy black pudding, stilton pannacotta, or a Mediterranean platter comprising Manchengo cheese, prosciutto, olives, sun-blushed tomatoes, anchovies and warm bread. Main courses range from beer battered haddock or hot Madras beef curry to pan-fried gurnard fillet with sautéed samphire grass and steamed mussels. There is also an extensive choice of home-made puddings. The pub has its own permanent collection of original art with a sporting theme.

Open all wk 10-3.30 6-11 (Sat-Sun 10-11) Closed: 25 Dec **Bar Meals** L served Mon-Fri 12-2.30, Sat-Sun 12-10 D served Mon-Fri 6-10, Sat-Sun 12-10 Av main course £10 ⊕ FREE HOUSE ◀ Weetwood Eastgate Ale, Salopian Gold, Woodlands Light Oak, Cumberland Ale. ♥ 11 **Facilities** Children's menu Dogs allowed Garden Parking

PICK OF THE PUBS

The Pheasant Inn ★★★★ INN ♀

BURWARDSLEY Map 15 SJ55

CH3 9PF
☎ 01829 770434 📄 01829 771097
e-mail: info@thepheasantinn.co.uk
dir: *A41 (Chester to Whitchurch), after 4m
left to Burwardsley. Follow 'Cheshire
Workshops' signs*

Tucked away in a peaceful corner of
rural Cheshire, this 300-year-old half-
timbered former farmhouse is just
quarter of an hour's drive from historic
Chester. Standing way up in the
Peckforton Hills, the views from the
terrace are magnificent. Since it became
an alehouse in the mid-17th century,
only five families have been licensees,
today's incumbents being the Nelsons,
who came here in 2004. Four real ales
are always on tap in the wooden-floored
bar, where hefty beams support the
storey above; drinks are also to be
enjoyed in the stone-flagged
conservatory and flower-filled courtyard.
The wholesome food is good, the service
friendly and relaxed; children are
welcome during the day but, sorry, not
in the evenings. The three-section menu
breaks down into light-bites, deli-
boards and sandwiches for those who
want to make a quick pit-stop; a
selection for those who fancy eating
gastro-pub style; and principally British
and European main courses for those
who want something more substantial.
Among these are fresh Menai mussels in
white wine cream sauce; home-made
chilli con carne with crème fraîche and
flavoured rice; pan-fried fillet of brill
with caponata and olive-crushed new
potatoes; fine tomato and red onion tart
with baked goat's cheese, balsamic and
red pepper dressing; duo of belly pork
and fillet with fondant potato, braised
red cabbage and wholegrain mustard
sauce; and home-made fish pie, topped
with creamed mash and melted cheddar
cheese. Puddings follow traditional lines
with warm chocolate fudge cake and
vanilla ice cream; and homemade apple
and blackberry crumble with custard.
There's also a selection of ice creams
made by Gog's Cheshire Farm just down
the road. If the thought of driving home
threatens to spoil your evening, why not
stay in one of the en suite country-style
bedrooms.

Open all week **Bar Meals** L served all
week (no food Mon 3-6) D served all
week (no food Mon 3-6) Av main course
£11.50 **Restaurant** L served all week (no
food Mon 3-6) D served all week (no
food Mon 3-6) Av 3 course à la carte fr
£21.50 ⊕ NELSON NORTH WEST
◀ Weetwood Old Dog, Eastgate, Best,
guest Bitter ♂ Stowford Press. ♀ 8
Facilities Children's menu Dogs allowed
Garden Parking **Rooms** 12

PICK OF THE PUBS

Albion Inn

CHESTER Map 15 SJ46

Park St CH1 1RN ☎ **01244 340345**
e-mail: christina.mercer@tesco.net
web: www.albioninnchester.co.uk
dir: *In city centre adjacent to Citywalls & Newgate*

Michael Mercer has run Chester's last Victorian corner pub, which stands in the shadow of the city's Roman wall, for over 37 years and has created and captured the essence of the Great War (1914-18). The home fires still burn on winter nights at this living memorial, with its splendid cast-iron fireplaces and original three-room layout, now filled with sepia photographs and prints on flocked wallpaper, leather sofas and artefacts and enamelled advertisements from the World War I period. The lounge wallpaper was designed on the first day of the Great War and other objects of interest include a 1928 Steck Duo Art

player piano, which still performs on occasions. 'Trench rations' are locally and regionally sourced wherever possible. Expect Penrith Cumberland sausages; a classic fish pie topped with mash and parmesan; McSween's haggis (traditional and vegetarian); lambs' liver, bacon and onions with a rich cider gravy; boiled gammon and pease pudding served with parsley sauce; McConickies corned beef hash with pickled red cabbage. The house speciality is filled Staffordshire oatcakes - the oatcakes are collected from Burslem in Staffordshire each week. Fillings include West Country brie, bacon and chutney; black pudding, bacon and cheese; and ham, leek and Cheddar, among many others. Desserts include a creamy coconut pudding with caramelised oranges and treacle tart with crème fraiche. Alternatively, finish with English cheese served with fruitcake, in true northern style. A selection of club and doorstep sandwiches is also available. There are four cask ales on tap, a good range of malts and a decent list of New World wines. Please note that this is a grown-ups only pub.

Open 12-3, Tue-Fri 5-11, Sat 6-11, Sun 7-10.30, Mon 5.30-11 Closed: 25-26 Dec, 1-2 Jan **Bar Meals** L served all week 12-2 D served Mon-Sat 5-8 Av main course £9.70 **Restaurant** L served all week 12-2 D served Mon-Sat 5-8 ⊕ PUNCH TAVERNS ◼ Black Sheep, Batemans, Deuchars, Adnams, Guest ales ♻ Westons Organic Bottled Cider. **Facilities** Dogs allowed **Notes** ⊗

CONGLETON   Map 16 SJ86

The Plough At Eaton ★★★★ INN ¶

Macclesfield Rd, Eaton CW12 2NH
☎ 01260 280207   🖹 01260 298458
e-mail: theploughinn@hotmail.co.uk
web: www.theploughinnateaton.co.uk
dir: *On A536 (Congleton to Macclesfield road)*

Like a giant jigsaw puzzle, an ancient Welsh barn was transported here in hundreds of pieces to become a marvellously atmospheric restaurant adjoining this Elizabethan inn. From the specials menu come poached fresh salmon and prawn salad; chicken Madras with rice; and lamb Henry with mash. The carte offers lightly grilled turbot with lemon butter, and fillet steak cooked at the table. Apple crumble and custard and chocolate fudge cake are typical desserts. There are 17 modern annexe en suite bedrooms available, and gardens with sitting areas.

Open all day all wk 11am-mdnt **Bar Meals** L served Mon-Sat 12-2.30, Sun 12-8 D served Mon-Sat 6-9.30, Sun 12-8 **Restaurant** L served Mon-Sat 12-2.30, Sun 12-8 D served Mon-Sat 6-9.30, Sun 12-8 ⊕ FREE HOUSE ◀ Boddingtons, Hydes, Moore Houses, Storm Brew, Guest ales. ¶ 10 **Facilities** Dogs allowed Garden Parking **Rooms** 17

HANDLEY   Map 15 SJ45

The Calveley Arms ¶

Whitchurch Rd CH3 9DT
☎ 01829 770619   🖹 01829 770901
e-mail: calveleyarms@btconnect.com
dir: *5m S of Chester, signed from A41. Follow signs for Handley & Aldersey Green Golf Course*

Built as a coaching in the early 17th century, the smart black-and-white pub stands opposite the church with views of the distant Welsh hills. Chock full of old timbers, jugs, pots, pictures, prints and ornaments, the rambling bars provide an atmospheric setting in which to sample some good pub food. From salads and sandwiches, the menu extends to seasonal game, quality steaks, lamb cutlets, lobster, and roast rib of beef on Sundays.

Open all wk noon-3 6-11 (Sun 7-11) **Bar Meals** food served all day **Restaurant** food served all day ⊕ ENTERPRISE INNS ◀ Castle Eden Ale, Marston's Pedigree, Black Bull, Bombardier. ¶ 10 **Facilities** Dogs allowed Garden Parking

HAUGHTON MOSS   Map 15 SJ55

The Nags Head ¶

Long Ln CW6 9RN ☎ 01829 260265   🖹 01829 261364
e-mail: roryk1@btinternet.com
dir: *Turn off A49 S of Tarporley at Beeston/Haughton sign into Long Ln, continue for 1.75m*

Set amid beautiful Cheshire countryside, this 16th-century black and white building, once a smithy, is every inch the friendly, traditional pub. Inside are low ceilings, crooked beams, exposed brickwork and real fires. Outside, there are spacious gardens and a bowling green. The extensive menu might offer moules marinière or stilton and Guinness pâté to start, followed by steak and chips or fajitas. An impressive choice of home-made desserts could include syrup and pear sponge or triple chocolate roulade.

Open all day all wk 11-mdnt **Bar Meals** L served all wk 12-10 D served all wk 12-10 Av main course £10 food served all day **Restaurant** L served all wk 12-10 D served all wk 12-10 Fixed menu price fr £8.85 Av 3 course à la carte fr £20 food served all day ⊕ FREE HOUSE ◀ Flowers IPA, Sharps Doom Bar, guest ales. ¶ 14 **Facilities** Children's menu Play area Dogs allowed Garden Parking

HUXLEY   Map 15 SJ56

Stuart's Table at the Farmer's Arms ¶

Huxley Ln CH3 9BG ☎ 01829 781342   🖹 01829 781794
e-mail: stuart@stuartstable.com
dir: *Telephone for directions*

Reputedly a hospital during the civil war, the Farmers Arms was first recorded as a pub in 1802. It has grown into an inviting country pub and restaurant specialising in quality British steaks, served with an appealing range of sauces and accompaniments. Other choices include lunchtime tapas and sandwiches, and meals such as game terrine with parsley and shallot sauce and crab apple jelly followed by slow-roasted belly pork with chorizo and white bean cassoulet.

Open all wk noon-3 5-11 (Fri-Sat noon-mdnt, Sun noon-10.30, Mon 5-11) **Bar Meals** L served Tue-Sat 12-2 **Restaurant** L served Tue-Sat 12-2, Sun 12-4 D served Tue-Thu 6.30-9, Fri-Sat 6.30-9.30 Fixed menu price fr £16.95 Av 3 course à la carte fr £20 ⊕ ADMIRAL TAVERNS ◀ Black Sheep, Adnams, guest ale. ¶ 30 **Facilities** Children's menu Garden Parking

KNUTSFORD   Map 15 SJ77

PICK OF THE PUBS

The Dog Inn ★★★★ INN ¶

Well Bank Ln, Over Peover WA16 8UP
☎ 01625 861421   🖹 01625 864800
e-mail: thedog-inn@paddockinns.fsnet.co.uk
web: www.doginn-overpeover.co.uk
dir: *S from Knutsford take A50. Turn into Stocks Ln at The Whipping Stocks pub. 2m*

In the summer colourful flowerbeds, tubs and hanging baskets create quite a setting for the timbered Dog Inn, which has served ale to locals and travellers since the turn of the 19th century. In its time it has been a row of cottages, a grocer's, a shoemaker's and a farm, but now faithful regulars and visitors come for its range of cask ales from small regional breweries, large array of malt whiskies, and classic English menu prepared from ingredients sourced largely from within a six-mile radius. Starters include sticky chilli prawns; and Bury black pudding stack with bacon, while typical among the main courses are baked salmon fillet; half-roasted crispy duck; steak and ale pie; and stuffed Staffordshire oatcakes. Ever popular desserts include strawberry Pavlova, and Bramley apple pie. Stay overnight in one of the six comfortable and well-equipped en suite bedrooms and visit a nearby National Trust property.

Open all wk ⊕ FREE HOUSE ◀ Hydes Traditional Bitter, Weetwood Best, Skipton Brewery, Moorhouses. ¶ 8 **Facilities** Dogs allowed Garden Parking **Rooms** 6

LACH DENNIS Map 15 SJ77

The Duke of Portland ☼

Penny's Ln CW9 7SY ☎ 01606 46264
e-mail: info@dukeofportland.com
web: www.dukeofportland.com
dir: M6 junct 19, A556 towards Northwich. Left onto B5082 to Lach Dennis

Expect to eat well at this independent family-run pub set in the heart of the glorious Cheshire plain. The sunny, landscaped garden complements the attractively refurbished building, and the owners have a genuine commitment to local producers, many of whom have never supplied other commercial customers. Why not try the antipasti – an ideal way to share, start or nibble while enjoying a drink. Other dishes include seared chicken breast and fresh tomato purée with crushed new season potatoes or The Dukes legendary fish and chips.

Open all wk Restaurant Fixed menu price fr £9.95 Av 3 course à la carte fr £10.95 food served all day
◄ Thwaites Bomber, Marstons Pedigree, Banks Original, Sneck Lifter. ☼ 7 Facilities Children's menu Garden Parking

LITTLE NESTON Map 15 SJ27

The Old Harp

19 Quay Side CH64 0TB
☎ 0151 336 6980 ▤ 0151 336 6980
e-mail: jonesalbert@sky.com
dir: From Neston town centre, at 2nd mini-rdbt, turn right onto Marshlands Rd. At bottom turn left, 200yds ahead

Migrant Welsh coalminers named this isolated pub overlooking the Dee marshes after it had been converted from two old cottages in 1780. Although renovated over the years, it remains a simple two-roomed pub, the public bar on the left, the lounge on the right, with quarry-tiled floors and low beams. In the old days, the miners used one room, their managers the other. Bar lunches only, and a good range of real ales.

Open all day all wk 12-12 Bar Meals L served Mon-Fri 12-2 ⊕ ADMIRAL TAVERNS ◄ Joseph Holts, Titanic Iceberg, Timothy Taylor Landlord, Guest ales.
Facilities Family room Dogs allowed Garden Parking
Notes ⊛

LOWER WHITLEY Map 15 SJ67

PICK OF THE PUBS

Chetwode Arms ☼

Street Ln WA4 4EN
☎ 01925 730203 ▤ 01925 730870
e-mail: info@chetwodearms.com
dir: On A49, 2m S from M56 junct 10, 6m S of Warrington

Adorned with window boxes and built from Cheshire brick, this 400-year-old former coaching inn is a welcoming sight in the heart of this small village. It is said that a tunnel leads from the pub to the vicarage, and then on to St Luke's church, which is believed to be the oldest brick-built church in England. The inn's interior is as cosy and rambling as you could wish for: a tap room welcomes walkers and their dogs; the bar room is tiny but nonetheless warmed by an open log fire; and leading off the bar is a warren of small, intimate dining rooms and passageways. From the main dining room you can step onto a terrace overlooking the pub's own crown bowling green. There, with the wall heated gently by the sun, you can while away an evening very comfortably. The pub's owners are English and Austrian, so expect a continental touch to the cooking. Look out for the 'hot rock' dishes – steak and fish cooked on a hot stone.

Open all wk ⊕ PUNCH TAVERNS ◄ Marston's Pedigree, Banks Original, Adnams Broad, Jennings Cumberland, guest ale. ☼ 12 Facilities Play area Dogs allowed Garden Parking

MACCLESFIELD Map 16 SJ97

The Windmill Inn ☼

Holehouse Ln, Whitely Green, Adlington SK10 5SJ
☎ 01625 574222
e-mail: mail@thewindmill.info
dir: Between Macclesfield & Poynton. Follow brown tourist signs on main road. Pub in 1.5m

Just two minutes walk from the Macclesfield Canal and close to the Middlewood Way, this former farmhouse is an ideal place to start or end a country stroll. It has an extensive landscaped garden, complete with children's maze, while the interior is made cosy with a real fire and sofas. The menu runs from tempting sandwiches and light lunches, like potted Goosnargh duck with spiced plum relish and toasted sourdough, to full meals such as smoked haddock and leek tart with hollandaise sauce followed by braised steak and onions with horseradish mash and roast parsnips.

Open all wk noon-3 5-11 (Fri-Sat noon-11, Sun noon-10.30) Bar Meals L served Mon-Fri 12-2.30, Sat-Sun 12-4 booking required D served Mon-Fri 5.30-9.30, Sat 12-9.30, Sun 12-8 booking required Av main course £10.95 Restaurant L served Mon-Fri 12-2.30, Sat 12-9, Sun 12-8 booking required D served Mon-Fri 5.30-9.30, Sat 12-9.30, Sun 12-8 booking required ⊕ Mitchels & Butler - Moyo Ltd ◄ Black Sheep, Old Speckled Hen, Wadworth 6X, guest ale. ☼ 14 Facilities Children's menu Dogs allowed Garden Parking

MARTON Map 16 SJ86

PICK OF THE PUBS

The Davenport Arms ☼

See Pick of the Pubs on opposite page

MOULDSWORTH Map 15 SJ57

PICK OF THE PUBS

The Goshawk ☼

Station Rd CH3 8AJ
☎ 01928 740900 ▤ 01928 740965
dir: A51 from Chester onto A54. Left onto B5393 towards Frodsham. Enter Mouldsworth, pub on left opposite rail station

A welcoming pub with log fires and stripped pine floors, The Goshawk is conveniently located opposite the railway station in Mouldsworth, one stop from Chester on the Manchester to Stockport line. Close by are the Delamere Forest and Country Park, and the Mouldsworth Motor Museum. The menu has something for everyone, with light snacks of Bury black pudding with chicken and beetroot, or eggs Benedict, and shellfish starters like potted shrimps or seared scallops. There is a good choice of salads, and more substantial fare, with up to 12 fish dishes, steaks from the chargrill, and vegetarian options such as stuffed roasted red peppers. House favourites are lobster thermidor and steak and kidney pudding made with Timothy Taylor's Ale, while alternatives include braised lamb shank with dauphinoise potatoes and honey roast chantenay carrots, or halibut topped with pesto and crab crust served with couscous, chickpeas and Thai asparagus.

Open all wk noon-11 (Sun noon-10.30) Closed: 25 Dec & 1 Jan Bar Meals food served all day Restaurant food served all day ◄ Timothy Taylor Landlord, Greene King IPA, Deuchars, Old Speckled Hen. ☼ 14 Facilities Children's menu Play area Family room Garden Parking

PICK OF THE PUBS

The Davenport Arms ♟

MARTON   Map 16 SJ86

Congleton Rd SK11 9HF
☎ **01260 224269**   📠 **01260 224565**
e-mail: enquiries@thedavenportarms.co.uk
web: www.thedavenportarms.co.uk
dir: *3m from Congleton off A34*

As hereditary royal foresters, the Davenports once wielded considerable power, including the right to try, convict and hang highwaymen. Trials took place upstairs in this 18th-century pub, then a farmhouse, the miscreants being hanged from a gibbet that is thought to have been attached to a farm building opposite. In the village is the somewhat battered Marton Oak, which the Ancient Tree forum reckons is at least 1200 years old and probably the oldest tree in England. Amazingly, it still produces acorns. Cushioned settles and leather armchairs by a log fire characterise the traditional bar, while in the middle of the restaurant is a well, now purely decorative. With Theakston Yorkshire Bitter and Courage Directors being

regulars, there are always two guest ales on the pumps. All food - and this includes chutneys, sauces and desserts - is freshly made on the premises from local suppliers. In addition to speciality baguettes, lunchtime temptations include starters of home-made fishcake with citrus mayonnaise and sweet chilli dip; and Bury black pudding on sweet potato rösti with shallot purée and green peppercorn sauce; then for a main course you might try Cajun salmon fillets with mango and plum, red onion and sweet chilli salsa; home-baked ham, free-range eggs and chips; or chicken, broccoli and bacon tagliatelle. In similar vein, the dinner menu offers tiger prawn with sweet and spicy ginger and chilli marinade, and mango salad; and goat's cheese parcels with cranberry compote as starters; followed by breast of local pheasant in red wine sauce with braised red cabbage; lamb Henry with root vegetable and rosemary jus, carrot and swede mash and mange tout; and fillets of sea bream with citrus couscous and Pernod cream sauce. The menu is updated on a seasonal basis. The lovely beer garden contains a discreet children's play area. You might wish to know that the annual Marton Show once entered the Guinness Book of Records for displaying the world's largest gooseberry.

Open noon-3 6-mdnt (Fri-Sun noon-mdnt) Closed: Mon L (ex BH) **Bar Meals** L served Tue-Sat 12-2.30, Sun 12-3 D served Tue-Sat 6-9, Sun 6-8.30 Av main course £8.95 **Restaurant** L served Tue-Sat 12-2.30, Sun 12-3 D served Tue-Sat 6-9, Sun 6-8.30 Av 3 course à la carte fr £22 ⊕ FREE HOUSE ◀ Copper Dragon, Storm Brewing, Directors, Weetwood, Theakstons. ♟ 9 **Facilities** Children's menu Play area Garden Parking

NANTWICH
Map 15 SJ65

The Thatch Inn ♀

Wrexham Rd, Faddiley CW5 8JE ☎ 01270 524223
dir: *Follow signs for Wrexham from Nantwich, inn 4m from Nantwich*

The black-and-white Thatch Inn is believed to be the oldest as well as one of the prettiest pubs in south Cheshire. It has a three quarter acre garden, and inside you'll find oak beams, and open fires in winter. The menu is divided between options from the grill; traditional favourites (pies, roasts and casseroles); tastes from afar (nachos, lasagne, curry); and fish, summer salads, light bites and a children's menu. Speciality coffees are a feature.

Open Mon-Tue 6-11, Wed-Thu 12-3 6-11, Fri-Sat 12-11, Sun 12-10.30 Closed: Mon L & Tue L **Bar Meals** L served Wed-Thu 12-3, Fri-Sat 12-9, Sun 12-8.30 D served Mon-Thu 6-9, Fri-Sat 12-9, Sun 12-8.30 ⊕ ENTERPRISE INNS ◖ Timothy Taylor Landlord, Weetwoods. ♀ 24 **Facilities** Play area Family room Garden Parking

PARKGATE
Map 15 SJ27

The Boat House NEW ♀

1 The Parade CH64 6RN
☎ 0151 336 4187 ▤ 01928 740965
dir: *On B5135, 3m from Heswall*

Situated beside the RSPB's Parkgate Reserve, with magnificent views across the Dee estuary to Wales, this striking black-and-white timbered building is a haven for bird-watchers and food lovers. Eat in the airy dining room looking out across salt marshes, or in the cosy, modernised bars. The extensive menu favours fresh fish and seafood, perhaps halibut with crab and a pesto crust or a bowls of mussels with chips. Alternatives include steak and kidney pie and braised lamb shank. Look out for the flooding, about four times a year, where the water laps right up to the walls of the pub!

Open all wk 11.30-11 (Sun noon-10.30) **Bar Meals** L served all wk 12-5 D served Mon-Sat 5-9.30, Sun 5-9 **Restaurant** L served all wk 12-5 D served Mon-Sat 5-9.30, Sun 5-9 ⊕ FREE HOUSE ◖ Theakstons, John Smiths, Greene King IPA, Timothy Taylor Landlord, Old Speckled Hen. ♀ 17 **Facilities** Family room Garden Parking

PLUMLEY
Map 15 SJ77

The Golden Pheasant Hotel ♀

Plumley Moor Rd WA16 9RX
☎ 01565 722261 ▤ 01565 723804
dir: *M6 junct 19, A556 signed Chester. 2m, left at Plumley/Peover signs. Through Plumley, pub 1m opp rail station*

Set in the beautiful Cheshire countryside, The Golden Pheasant is convenient for Chester and Manchester, with trains from the station opposite hourly. This 200-year-old, traditional wayside inn is privately owned and proud of its real ales, extensive wine list and home-cooked, locally sourced food served in the dining room and lounge bar areas. Expect roaring log fires, comfy sitting areas, alfresco dining, a children's play area and a locals' bar with a darts board.

Open all day all wk 11-11 (Sun noon-10.30) **Bar Meals** Av main course £10.95 food served all day **Restaurant** Fixed menu price fr £15.95 Av 3 course à la carte fr £21.95 food served all day ⊕ J W LEES ◖ J W Lees Bitter, John Willies Bitter, Guinness. ♀ 12 **Facilities** Children's menu Play area Garden Parking

---

The Smoker ♀

WA16 0TY ☎ 01565 722338 ▤ 01565 722093
e-mail: smoker@plumley.fsword.co.uk
dir: *From M6 junct 19 take A556 W. Pub 1.75m on left*

This 400-year-old thatched coaching inn is actually named after a white racehorse bred by the Prince Regent, although recent legislation has prompted the addition of a covered smokers' courtyard complete with heating and seating. The pub's striking wood-panelled interior of three connecting rooms provides a traditional welcoming atmosphere, with log fires, beams and copper kettles. The menu has an appealing and lengthy array of starters; main courses include Barnsley chop; deep-fried haddock; and lamb Henry.

Open all wk 10-3 6-11 (Sun 10am-10.30pm) **Bar Meals** L served Mon-Fri 10-2.30, Sun 10-9 D served Mon-Fri 6-9.30, Sun 10-9 Av main course £10 **Restaurant** L served Mon-Fri 10-2.30, Sun 10-9 booking required D served Mon-Fri 6-9.30, Sun 10-9 booking required Av 3 course à la carte fr £18.50 ⊕ FREDERIC ROBINSON ◖ Robinson's Best, Double Hop, Robinsons Smooth. ♀ 10 **Facilities** Children's menu Play area Garden Parking

SHOCKLACH
Map 15 SJ44

The Bull ♀

Worthenbury Rd SY14 7BL ☎ 01829 250239
e-mail: info@thebullshocklach.com
dir: *12m S of Chester, 3m W of Malpas*

Recently completely refurbished, this village pub retains its old beams, cosy rooms and log fire but has a new bar, distinctive furniture and attractive stone and wood flooring. The menu is locally sourced and dishes, such as belly pork, steak pie and fish and chips, are freshly made. Look out for daily specials and Fish Friday options. Five local ales are served along with a 60-bin wine list and a malt whisky collection approaching 35.

Open all wk noon-3 6-11 (Sun 10-8) **Bar Meals** L served Mon-Sat 12-2.30, Sun 10-8 booking required D served Mon-Thu 6-9.30, Fri-Sat 6-10, Sun 10-8 booking required Av main course £10 **Restaurant** L served Mon-Sat 12-2.30, Sun 10-8 booking required D served Mon-Thu 6-9.30, Fri-Sat 6-10, Sun 10-8 booking required Av 3 course à la carte fr £22 ⊕ Admiral Taverns ◖ Stonehouse Station Bitter, Guinness, guest ales. ♀ 10 **Facilities** Children's menu Garden Parking

SWETTENHAM
Map 15 SJ86

PICK OF THE PUBS

The Swettenham Arms ♀

Swettenham Ln CW12 2LF
☎ 01477 571284 ▤ 01477 571284
e-mail: info@swettenhamarms.co.uk
dir: *M6 junct 18 to Holmes Chapel, then A535 towards Jodrell Bank. 3m right (Forty Acre Lane) to Swettenham*

Winter in this delightful 600-year-old pub means log fires and mulled wine; summer means abundant lavender and sunflowers in the meadow; in autumn there are the arboretum and nature reserve. And spring? Well, everywhere's lovely in spring, so just enjoy the high standards of food and service, which of course are year-round attributes. The pub was once a nunnery, linked to the village church by an underground passage where corpses 'rested' before burial. So, expect ghost stories: indeed, in 2005, after seeing an apparition in the fireplace, a lady customer sought urgent counselling from the vicar. Begin your meal with smoked halibut salad and quenelles of mascarpone; then 21-day roast Cheshire beef and Yorkshire pudding, or one of Chef's signature dishes: supreme of chicken, brie and spring onion in filo pastry, and white wine and basil cream sauce, perhaps. Vegetarians have a good choice.

Open all wk noon-3.30 6-11 (Sat-Sun noon-11) **Bar Meals** L served Mon-Sat 12-2.30, Sun 12-9.30 booking required D served Mon-Sat 6.30-9.30, Sun 12-9.30 booking required Av main course £10 **Restaurant** L served Mon-Sat 12-2.30, Sun 12-9.30 booking required D served Mon-Sat 6.30-9.30, Sun 12-9.30 booking required Av 3 course à la carte fr £20 ⊕ FREE HOUSE ◖ Landlord, Hydes, Beartown, Pride of Pendle, guest ales ♂ Addlestones. ♀ 8 **Facilities** Children's menu Garden Parking

TARPORLEY
Map 15 SJ56

Alvanley Arms Inn ★★★★ INN ♀

Forest Rd, Cotebrook CW6 9DS ☎ 01829 760200
e-mail: info@alvanleyarms.co.uk
dir: *On A49, 1.5m N of Tarporley*

A charming 16th-century, family-run coaching inn with shire horse-themed décor: rosettes, harnesses and horseshoes decorate the walls, linking the inn to the landlords' Cotebrook Shire Horse Centre next door. Hand-pulled ales in the oak-beamed bar complement a range of freshly prepared dishes, based on ingredients from local family businesses. Dishes range from traditional steak and ale pie or gammon steak with egg and chips to oriental duck pancakes or Thai fish goujons.

Open all wk noon-3 5.30-11.30 (Sat-Sun noon-11) **Bar Meals** L served Mon-Sat 12-2, Sun 12-9 D served Mon-Sat 6-9, Sun 12-9 **Restaurant** L served Mon-Sat 12-2, Sun 12-9 D served Mon-Sat 6-9, Sun 12-9 booking required ⊕ FREDERIC ROBINSON ◖ Robinsons Best & guest ales. ♀ 12 **Facilities** Children's menu Dogs allowed Garden Parking **Rooms** 7

PICK OF THE PUBS

The Boot Inn ♛

Boothsdale, Willington CW6 0NH ☎ 01829 751375
dir: *Off A54 Kelsall by-pass or off A51(Chester-Nantwich), follow signs to Willington*

Originally a row of red brick and sandstone cottages, this charming building became a small beer house before evolving into the inviting pub and restaurant it is today. Quarry tiled floors, old beams and open fires enhance the welcome. The kitchen uses local suppliers wherever possible. Dishes might include oak-smoked salmon with sour cream, herb dressing and salad, or spicy crab fishcakes to start, followed by baked Spanish omelette with salad and beetroot relish; Moroccan spiced chicken with couscous and minted cucumber yogurt; fisherman's pie; or natural smoked haddock with a mustard stout rarebit topping and cherry tomato chutney. For something lighter try salad platters, sandwiches, fresh baguettes and hot paninis. A booklet of circular walks is available at the pub. It includes an account of the pub's long history; among the interesting tales is the fact that a previous landlord was the father of current James Bond 007 Daniel Craig.

Open all day all wk 11am-11pm Closed: 25 Dec **Bar Meals** L served Mon-Thu 12-2.30, Fri-Sun, BH 11-11 D served Mon-Thu 6-9.30, Fri-Sun, BH 11-11 ⊕ FREE HOUSE ◀ Weetwood, Bass, Tetleys, Greene King IPA. ♛ 10 **Facilities** Family room Garden Parking

---

TUSHINGHAM CUM GRINDLEY   Map 15 SJ54

PICK OF THE PUBS

Blue Bell Inn

SY13 4QS ☎ 01948 662172 📄 01948 662172
dir: *A41, 4m N of Whitchurch, signed Bell O' the Hill*

In what must be a unique tale from the annals of pub-haunting, this inn reputedly has a ghost duck, whose spirit is sealed in a bottle buried in the bottom step of the cellar. Believe that or not, the Blue Bell remains a charming and characterful pub. A lovely black-and-white building that oozes character with its abundance of beams, open fires and horse brasses, its oldest part dates to approximately 1550, and the main building was completed in 1667. It has all the features you'd

expect of a timber-framed building of this date, including one of the largest working chimneys in Cheshire and a priest hole. Curios that have been discovered from within the wall structure are on show in the pub. A menu of hearty, home-cooked pub food includes curries, steak and chips, and chilli with garlic bread. Drink options include well-kept ales, Cheddar Valley cider and a selection of wines.

Open noon-3 6-11.30 Closed: (Mon ex BH) **Bar Meals** L served Tue-Sun 12-2 D served Tue-Sun 6-9 Av main course £6 **Restaurant** L served Tue-Sun 12-2 D served Tue-Sun 6-9 booking required Av 3 course à la carte fr £9 ⊕ FREE HOUSE ◀ Carling, Shropshire Gold, Oakham JHB, guest ales. **Facilities** Family room Dogs allowed Garden Parking

---

WARMINGHAM   Map 15 SJ76

The Bear's Paw

School Ln CW11 3QN ☎ 01270 526317
e-mail: info@thebearspaw.co.uk
web: www.thebearspaw.co.uk
dir: *M6 junct 18, A54, A533 towards Sandbach. Follow signs for village*

Delightful country house hotel conveniently situated within easy reach of many Cheshire towns and some of the county's prettiest countryside. Wide-ranging menus offer an extensive selection of starters, including chicken liver pâté, smoked haddock fish cake, and bacon and black pudding salad, followed by breast of chicken stuffed with spinach and brie, and red mullet on a crab mash. Beef lasagne, cod supreme and Cumberland sausage are other options.

Open all day all wk noon-11 **Bar Meals** L served Mon 12-3, Tue-Thu 12-9.30, Fri-Sat 12-10, Sun 12-8 D served Mon 6-9.30, Tue-Thu 12-9.30, Fri-Sat 12-10, Sun 12-8 ⊕ FREE HOUSE **Facilities** Garden Parking

---

WRENBURY   Map 15 SJ54

The Dusty Miller ♛

CW5 8HG ☎ 01270 780537
dir: *Telephone for details*

A beautifully converted 16th-century mill building beside the Shropshire Union Canal. A black and white lift bridge, designed by Thomas Telford, completes the picture postcard setting. The menu, which tends to rely on ingredients from the region, offers light bites including filled rolls and a cheese platter alongside the more substantial baked hake with buttery mash and a white wine and parsley sauce, and home-made Aberdeen Angus burger with pear and apple chutney.

Open 12-3 6.30-11 Closed: Mon in winter **Bar Meals** L served all wk 12-2 D served all wk 6.30-9.30 ⊕ ROBINSONS ◀ Robinson's Unicorn, Double Hop, Old Tom, Hatters Mild, Hartleys XB ♨ Stowford Press, Westons Traditional Scrumpy. ♛ 12 **Facilities** Dogs allowed Garden Parking

---

WYBUNBURY   Map 15 SJ64

The Swan ♛

Main Rd CW5 7NA ☎ 01270 841280 📄 01270 841200
e-mail: jacqueline.harris7@btinternet.com
dir: *M6 junct 16 towards Chester & Nantwich. Turn left at lights in Wybunbury*

The Swan, a pub since 1580, is situated in the village centre next to the church. All the food is freshly prepared on the premises and includes pork and liver pâté with apple and cider brandy chutney; root vegetable casserole with cheddar cheese mash; Thai green curry; and beer battered haddock and handcut chips. Light bites feature spicy chicken tortilla wrap and penne pasta with roasted Tuscan vegetables. Sit in the garden overlooking the famous leaning church tower.

Open all wk noon-mdnt, (Mon 5-mdnt) **Restaurant** L served Tue-Sat 12-2, Sun 12-5.30 booking required D served all wk 6.30-9.30 booking required ⊕ ROBINSONS ◀ Unicorn, Cumbria Way, guest ales ♨ Stowford Press. ♛ 9 **Facilities** Dogs allowed Garden Parking

CORNWALL & ISLES OF SCILLY

BLISLAND   Map 2 SX17

The Blisland Inn

PL30 4JF ☎ 01208 850739
dir: *5m from Bodmin towards Launceston. 2.5m off A30 signed Blisland. On village green*

An award-winning inn in a very picturesque village on the edge of Bodmin Moor. The superb parish church was a favourite of John Betjeman who wrote about it extensively. Most of the traditional pub fare is home cooked, including a variety of puddings. Leek and mushroom bake is a perennial favourite, while lasagne, sausage and mash, and traditional farmhouse ham, egg and chips are also popular.

Open all wk ◀ Guest ales. **Facilities** Family room Dogs allowed Garden

BODINNICK   Map 2 SX15

Old Ferry Inn ♥

PL23 1LX ☎ 01726 870237 📄 01726 870116
e-mail: royce972@aol.com
dir: *A38 towards Dobwalls, left onto A390. After 3m left onto B3359 then right to Bodinnick/Polruan for 5m*

This friendly, family-run free house stands just 50 yards from the scenic River Fowey, where the car ferry still makes regular crossings to Fowey itself. Inside the 400-year-old building, old photographs and nautical bric-a-brac set the scene for sampling Sharp's Bitter and an extensive bar menu. Choices range from snacks to home-cooked food like steak and ale pie, curries, vegetarian and fish dishes.

Old Ferry Inn

Open all day all wk 11-11 (summer), noon-10 (winter) Closed: 25 Dec **Bar Meals** L served all wk 12-3 (summer), 12-2.30 (winter) D served all wk 6-9 (summer), 6.30-8.30 (winter) Av main course £8.50 **Restaurant** D served all wk 7-8.30 booking required Av 3 course à la carte fr £20 ⊕ FREE HOUSE ◀ Sharp's Bitter, Guinness Ò Stowford Press. ♥ 6 **Facilities** Children's menu Family room Dogs allowed Garden Parking

BOLVENTOR   Map 2 SX17

Jamaica Inn ♥

PL15 7TS ☎ 01566 86250 📄 01566 86177
e-mail: enquiry@jamaicainn.co.uk
dir: *Follow A30 from Exeter. 10m after Launceston take Bolventor road, follow signs*

The setting for Daphne du Maurier's famous novel, this 18th-century inn stands high on Bodmin Moor. Its Smugglers Museum houses fascinating artefacts, while the Daphne du Maurier room honours the great writer. The place is big on atmosphere, with a cobbled courtyard, beamed ceilings and roaring fires. Lunches range from hot ciabattas to grills; the evening menu served from 3pm could start with warm melted goats' cheese bruschetta, and follow with barbecued pork ribs or poached fillet of Port Isaac salmon.

Open all day all wk 9am-11pm **Bar Meals** L served all wk Av main course £9 food served all day ⊕ FREE HOUSE ◀ Doom Bar, Tribute, Jamaica Inn Ale. ♥ 8 **Facilities** Children's menu Play area Dogs allowed Garden Parking

BOSCASTLE   Map 2 SX09

PICK OF THE PUBS

The Wellington Hotel ★★ HL ◉ ♥

The Harbour PL35 0AQ
☎ 01840 250202 📄 01840 250621
e-mail: info@boscastle-wellington.com
dir: *A30/A395 at Davidstowe follow Boscastle signs. B3266 to village. Right into Old Rd*

This listed 16th-century coaching inn nestles on one of England's most stunning coastlines at the end of a glorious wooded valley where the rivers Jordan and Valency meet. It retains much of its original charm, including beamed ceilings and real log fires. The cosy atmosphere makes it easy to believe - as the locals do - that many ghostly guests and staff still linger. With a minstrels' gallery, the traditional beamed bar provides a good selection of Cornish ales, malt whiskies, bar

continued on page 80

PICK OF THE PUBS

Cadgwith Cove Inn

CADGWITH Map 2 SW71

TR12 7JX
☎ 01326 290513 📄 01326 291018
e-mail:
enquiries@cadgwithcoveinn.com
web: www.cadgwithcoveinn.com
dir: *10m from Helston on main Lizard road*

An unspoilt fishing hamlet of thatched cottages on the rugged Lizard coastline is the appealing setting for this 300-year-old pub, formerly the haunt of smugglers and now popular with coast path walkers and local fishermen. In summer, ramblers mingle with tourists and locals on the sunny front patio, which affords views across the old pilchard cellar to the peaceful cove. The atmospheric, simply furnished bars are adorned with relics that record a rich seafaring history, and it's easy to imagine that the ghosts of smugglers still gather within these cosy walls. The pub offers a warm welcome and authentic local colour – come on a Friday night and relax with pint of Sharp's Doom Bar and listening to sea shanties sung by the Cadgwith Singers late into the night. On Tuesday nights the inn hosts a thriving folk club when guests are invited to join in or just sit back and enjoy the music. On any night of the week you might find yourself swapping tales with one of the fishermen whose catches feature on the popular menus – their colourful boats rest on the shingle a few steps down the lane from the pub. As may be expected, these are positively laden with seafood – lobster and crab of course, but also grilled red mullet or bass, moules marinière, the special Cadgwith fish casserole, and traditional fish and chips. Meat eaters and vegetarians are also well provided for, with ingredients coming from local butchers and surrounding farms. Meals can be served in the garden in clement weather, and the large terrace is also an ideal spot during the summer gig races, or for one of the regular seafood barbecues prepared by local fishermen.

Open all week **Restaurant** ⊕ PUNCH TAVERNS ◖ Interbrew Flowers IPA, Sharp's, Abbot Ale, guest ales.
Facilities Family room Dogs allowed Garden Parking

BOSCASTLE *continued*

snacks and meals from a pub menu using the same kitchen as the smart Waterloo restaurant - the focus of more serious dining. Food here could include monkfish pavé with pickled red cabbage, crispy angel hair and beet dressing, followed by seared fillet steak with a veal shin burger, caraway dauphinoise, onion confit, beetroot purée and marrow. Finish with excellent cheeses, or perhaps deep-fried strawberries in black pepper batter with five berry sorbet and berry salad.

Open all day all wk 11am-11pm (Sun noon-10pm) **Bar Meals** L served Mon-Fri 12-3, Sat-Sun 12-9 D served Mon-Fri 6-10, Sat-Sun 12-9 **Restaurant** L served Mon-Fri 12-3, Sat-Sun 12-9 D served Mon-Fri 6-10, Sat-Sun 12-9 ⊕ FREE HOUSE ◀ St Austell HSD, St Austell Tribute, Skinners Ales-Spriggan, Betty Stoggs. ♥ 8 **Facilities** Dogs allowed Garden Parking **Rooms** 15

CADGWITH Map 2 SW71

PICK OF THE PUBS

Cadgwith Cove Inn

See Pick of the Pubs on page 79

CALLINGTON Map 3 SX36

The Coachmakers Arms ♥

6 Newport Square PL17 7AS
☎ 01579 382567 🖺 01579 384679
dir: Between Plymouth & Launceston on A388

Traditional stone-built pub on the A388 between Plymouth and Launceston. Clocks, plates, pictures of local scenes, old cars and antique trade advertisements contribute to the atmosphere, as do the fish tank and aviary. There's plenty of choice on the menu, from chargrilled steaks, steak and kidney pie or hot-pot, to oven-baked plaice, vegetable balti or salads. Regulars range from the local football team to the pensioners dining club. On Wednesday there's a charity quiz night, and Thursday is steak night.

Open all day all wk **Bar Meals** L served all wk 12-2 D served all wk 7-9.30 Av main course £5 **Restaurant** L served all wk 12-2 D served all wk 7-9.30 Av 3 course à la carte fr £15 ⊕ ENTERPRISE INNS ◀ Sharp's Doom Bar, Worthing Best Bitter, Bass. ♥ 7 **Facilities** Children's menu Dogs allowed Parking

Manor House Inn ♥

Rilla Mill PL17 7NT ☎ 01579 362354
dir: 5m from Callington, just off B3257

Set by the River Lynher, once a granary for the mill next door, Manor House is a traditional pub that offers real ales and ciders, and a reasonably-priced selection of home-made food. Careful attention is paid to sourcing quality local ingredients, including fresh fish. Typical choices include steak and ale pie, battered haddock and

chips, chicken chasseur, and curry of the week. Lighter options include club sandwich, tuna melt, toasted sandwiches and salads.

Closed: Mon **Bar Meals** L served Tue-Sun 11.30-2 D served Tue-Sun 6-9 Av main course £5 **Restaurant** L served Tue-Sun 11.30-2 D served Tue-Sun 6-9 Av 3 course à la carte £18 ⊕ FREE HOUSE ◀ Sharp's Own & Special, Doom Bar, Betty Stogs ☼ Thatchers Gold, Westons Scrumpy, Cornish Rattler. ♥ 8 **Facilities** Children's menu Dogs allowed Garden Parking

CONSTANTINE Map 2 SW72

PICK OF THE PUBS

Trengilly Wartha Inn ★★★ INN ◉ ♥

See Pick of the Pubs on opposite page

CUBERT Map 2 SW75

The Smugglers' Den Inn ♥

Trebellan TR8 5PY ☎ 01637 830209 🖺 01637 830580
e-mail: info@thesmugglersden.co.uk
web: www.thesmugglersden.co.uk
dir: From Newquay take B3075 to Cubert x-rds, then right, then left signed Trebellan, 0.5m

Set in a valley leading to the coast, this thatched 16th-century pub comprises a long bar, family room, children's play area, courtyards and huge beer garden. The no-nonsense, modern menu might offer houmous and flatbread with rocket and sun-blushed tomatoes at lunch, or tempura king prawns followed by Falmouth Bay moules marinière in the evening. The impressive selection of real ales is at its best during the real ale and pie festival over the May Day weekend.

Open all day all wk 11-3 6-11 (Sat-Sun 11-3 6-mdnt, summer open all day) Closed: Jan-Mar closed Mon-Tue L **Bar Meals** L served all wk 12-2.30 (winter 12-2) D served all wk 6-9.30 (winter Sun-Thu 6-9, Fri-Sat 6-9.30) **Restaurant** L served all wk 12-2.30 (winter 12-2) booking required D served all wk 6-9.30 (winter Sun-Thu 6-9, Fri-Sat 6-9.30) booking required ⊕ FREE HOUSE ◀ Skinner's Smugglers Ale, Sharp's Doom Bar, St Austell Tribute, Rotating Guest Ales ☼ Healey's Cornish Rattler. ♥ 12 **Facilities** Children's menu Play area Family room Dogs allowed Garden Parking

See advert on page 78

DULOE Map 2 SX25

Ye Olde Plough House Inn ♥

PL14 4PN ☎ 01503 262050 🖺 01503 264089
dir: A38 to Dobwalls, take turn signed Looe

The pub is an 18th-century building set in the heart of the Cornish countryside, just three miles from the coast at Looe. Inside there are slate floors, wood-burning stoves, settles and old pews, and outside a fenced, grassy garden. Fresh fish is offered from the daily specials board, supplementing main menu choices such as braised lamb shank, roast duck and homity pie. In the evening you can cook your own steak on a preheated grillstone.

Open all wk Closed: 25-26 Dec ⊕ FREE HOUSE ◀ Sharp's Doom Bar, Butcombe Bitter, Worthington. ♥ 9 **Facilities** Dogs allowed Garden Parking

DUNMERE Map 2 SX06

The Borough Arms

PL31 2RD ☎ 01208 73118
dir: From A30 take A389 to Wadebridge, pub approx 1m from Bodmin

Built in the 1850s for train crews taking china clay from the moors down to the port at Padstow, but it seems much older. Walkers, cyclists and horseriders drop in for refreshment as they follow the disused railway line, now the 17-mile Camel Trail. The menus offer steak and ale pie, Spanish chicken, fish and chips, tender meats from the carvery, and snacks. Specials, mostly home made, are on the chalkboards.

Open all wk ⊕ SPIRIT GROUP ◀ Sharp's Bitter, Skinner's, John Smith's Smooth. **Facilities** Play area Family room Dogs allowed Garden Parking

FEOCK Map 2 SW83

The Punch Bowl & Ladle ♥

Penelewey TR3 6QY
☎ 01872 862237 🖺 01872 870401
dir: Off Truro to Falmouth road, after Shell garage at 'Playing Place' rdbt follow signs for King Harry Ferry to right. 0.5m, pub on right

This ancient and fascinating thatched building comprises three cob-built 17th-century farm workers' cottages and a former customhouse. There are delightful rural views

continued on page 82

PICK OF THE PUBS

Trengilly Wartha Inn ★★★ INN ❀ ☉ ☻

CONSTANTINE   Map 2 SW72

Nancenoy TR11 5RP
☎ 01326 340332   🖨 01326 340332
e-mail: reception@trengilly.co.uk
dir: *Follow signs to Nancenoy, left towards Gweek until 1st sign for inn, left & left again at next sign, continue to inn*

This unusually named inn is situated in the hamlet of Nancenoy, in an Area of Outstanding Natural Beauty, about a mile from the village of Constantine. The name is actually Cornish and means a settlement above the trees, in this case the wooded valley of Polpenwith Creek, an offshoot of the lovely Helford River. The six acres of gardens and meadows that surround the inn include a vine-shaded pergola just perfect for summer dining. There's a small bistro on one side of the inn, and plenty more space for eating in the informal bar area, where a conservatory extension houses the family room. Talented chefs prepare everything from scratch using the best locally produced meats, game, fish and shellfish from local waters. The bar menu offers pub favourites like beef stroganoff, steak, and wholetail scampi, as well as less traditional choices such as courgette and rosemary pancakes stuffed with Cornish feta, cashew nuts, spinach and smoked cherry tomatoes; chicken breast with chilli and cranberry butter with creamed Savoy cabbage and crispy pancetta; and warm fillet of lightly smoked, locally caught pollack with herb butter. The bistro always has a good seafood selection, but watch out, because in summer the day's boatload of fresh fish can sell out fast. Fresh home-made steak and kidney puddings are sold through the winter on Wednesday nights. Since it's a free house, there's a good selection of unusual real ales, over 40 malt whiskies and 150 wines, with 15 available by the glass.

Open 11-3, 6-12 **Bar Meals** L served all wk 12-2.15 D served all wk 6.30-9.30 Av main course £10 **Restaurant** L served all wk 12-2.15 D served all wk 6.30-12 Av 3 course à la carte fr £20 ⊕ FREE HOUSE ◀ Skinners Cornish Knocker, Betty Stogs, Sharp's Doom Bar, Sharp's Edenale, Guest Ales ♉ Cornish Rattler, Thatchers Gold. ☙ 15
Facilities Children's menu Play area Family room Dogs allowed Garden Parking

FEOCK *continued*

from the inn's patio, and in warmer weather you can enjoy a drink in the walled garden. The menu uses 99 per cent Cornish goods, and choices include fish pie; local mussels in Cornish cider; Malaysian chicken; and venison steak in chocolate sauce. There is live music monthly, and regular food theme nights.

Open all day all wk 11.30am-11pm (Fri 11.30am-mdnt, Sun noon-10.30) **Bar Meals** L served all wk 12-5 Av main course £9 food served all day **Restaurant** L served all wk 12-2.30 D served all wk 6-8.30 booking required Av 3 course à la carte fr £17 ⊕ St Austell Brewery ◀ Tribute, Tinners, Proper Job, Cornish Cream. ♚ 8
Facilities Children's menu Dogs allowed Garden Parking

FOWEY   Map 2 SX15

The Ship Inn

Trafalgar Square PL23 1AZ ☎ 01726 832230
e-mail: shipinnfowey@hotmail.com
dir: *From A30 take B3269 & A390*

One of Fowey's oldest buildings, The Ship was built in 1570 by John Rashleigh, who sailed to the Americas with Walter Raleigh. Given Fowey's riverside position, assume a good choice of fish, including River Fowey mussels, pan-fried scallops with mushrooms and bacon, and Ship Inn fish pie. Other options include beef and Guinness pie or local butcher's sausages and mash. St Austell ales, real fires and a long tradition of genial hospitality add the final touches.

Open all day all wk 11am-mdnt (Fri-Sat 11am-1am) **Bar Meals** L served Mon-Sat 12-2.30, Sun 12-4 D served Mon-Sat 6-9 Av main course £10 **Restaurant** L served Mon-Sat 12-2.30 (summer only), Sun 12-4 D served Mon-Sat 6-9, (Sun 6-9 summer only) Fixed menu price fr £12.50 ⊕ ST AUSTELL BREWERY ◀ St Austell Tinners Ale, Tribute, Proper Job ♡ Cornish Rattler.
Facilities Children's menu Family room Dogs allowed

GOLDSITHNEY   Map 2 SW53

The Trevelyan Arms ♚

Fore St TR20 9JU ☎ 01736 710453
e-mail: mikehitchens@hotmail.com
web: www.trevelyanarms.com
dir: *5m from Penzance. A394 signed to Goldsithney*

The former manor house for Lord Trevelyan, this 17th-century property stands at the centre of the picturesque village just a mile from the sea. It has also been a

coaching inn and a bank/post office in its time, but these days is very much the traditional family-run Cornish pub. Food is fresh and locally sourced, offering good value for money. Typical dishes are T-bone steaks, home-made pies and curries, pasta dishes and local fish.

Open all wk 4-mdnt (Sat-Sun noon-mdnt) **Bar Meals** L served Sun D served all wk 6-9 **Restaurant** L served Sun D served all wk 6-9 ⊕ PUNCH TAVERNS ◀ Morland Speckled Hen, Guinness, St Austell Tribute. ♚ 12
Facilities Dogs allowed Garden

GUNNISLAKE   Map 3 SX47

The Rising Sun Inn

Calstock Rd PL18 9BX ☎ 01822 832201
dir: *From Tavistock take A390 to Gunnislake, pub through village 0.25m on left. Left at lights, 0.25m on right*

A traditional two-roomed picture postcard pub set in award winning terraced gardens overlooking the beautiful Tamar Valley. Great walks start and finish at the Rising Sun, which is understandably popular with hikers and cyclists, locals and visitors. Enjoy a pint of real ales like Cornish Coaster or Betty Stogs and local real cider.

Open all wk ⊕ FREE HOUSE ◀ Spitfire, Otter, Sharp's Cornish Coaster, Skinner's Betty Stogs Bitter, Timothy Taylor Landlord. **Facilities** Dogs allowed Garden Parking **Notes** ⊛

GUNWALLOE   Map 2 SW62

PICK OF THE PUBS

The Halzephron Inn ♚

TR12 7QB ☎ 01326 240406 ▤ 01326 241442
e-mail: halzephroninn@gunwalloe1.fsnet.co.uk
dir: *3m S of Helston on A3083, right to Gunwalloe, through village. Inn on left*

The name of this ancient inn derives from Als Yfferin, old Cornish for 'cliffs of hell', an appropriate description of its situation on this hazardous stretch of coastline. Once a haunt of smugglers, the pub stands just 300 yards from the famous South Cornwall footpath and is the only pub on the stretch between Mullion and Porthleven. Originally called The Ship, it changed its name in the late 1950s when it regained its licence after 50 'dry' years. Today it offers a warm welcome, a wide selection of ales including Organic Halzephron Gold and whiskies, and meals prepared from fresh local produce. Lunch brings a choice of platters accompanied by home-made granary or white

rolls, plus specials such as seafood chowder. The evening menu shifts comfortably from the classic (beef bourguignon) to the modern: perhaps whole roast partridge en croûte; or roast saddle of rabbit wrapped in prosciutto filled with mushroom and herb duxelle. There is an excellent Junior Menu available.

Open all wk Closed: 25 Dec **Bar Meals** L served all wk 12-2 D served all wk 7-9 **Restaurant** L served all wk 12-2 D served all wk 7-9 ⊕ FREE HOUSE ◀ Sharp's Own, Doom Bar & Special, St Austell Tribute, Organic Halzephron Gold ♡ Cornish Rattler. ♚ 8
Facilities Children's menu Family room Garden Parking

GWEEK   Map 2 SW72

The Gweek Inn

TR12 6TU ☎ 01326 221502 ▤ 01326 221164
e-mail: steve.gilks@btinternet.com
dir: *2m E of Helston near Seal Sanctuary*

The lovely location of this traditional family-run village pub at the mouth of the pretty Helford River makes booking a table a wise precaution. It is known for value-for-money food, typically steak, kidney and ale pie; tagliatelle con pollo; filled jacket potatoes; and a range of salads. The chalkboard lists locally caught seafood.

Open all day all wk 11.30-closing **Bar Meals** L served all wk 12-2 D served all wk 6-9 **Restaurant** L served all wk 12-2 D served all wk 6-9 ⊕ PUNCH TAVERNS ◀ Sharp's Doom Bar, Sharps Own, Sharps Special, Skinners Betty Stogs, Guest ale. **Facilities** Play area Dogs allowed Garden Parking

KINGSAND   Map 3 SX45

The Halfway House Inn ♚

Fore St PL10 1NA ☎ 01752 822279 ▤ 01752 823146
e-mail: info@halfwayinn.biz
dir: *From Torpoint Ferry or Tamar Bridge follow signs to Mount Edgcumbe*

Set among the narrow lanes and colour-washed houses of a quaint fishing village, this family-run inn has been licensed since 1850, and has a pleasant stone-walled bar with low-beamed ceilings and a large central fireplace. Locally caught seafood is a feature of the small restaurant, including crab cocktail; sautéed scallops with white wine, cream and parsley sauce; whole sea bass with toasted almonds; and baked monkfish with Mediterranean vegetables. For the lunchtime visitor there's a good selection of bar snacks.

Open all wk ⊕ FREE HOUSE ◀ Sharp's Doom Bar & Own, Marstons Pedigree, Guinness, John Smith's Smooth. ♚ 10
Facilities Dogs allowed

PICK OF THE PUBS

The Crown Inn ★★★ INN ♉

LANLIVERY Map 2 SX05

PL30 5BT
☎ **01208 872707**
e-mail: thecrown@wagtailinns.com
dir: *Signed from A390. Follow brown sign about 1.5m W of Lostwithiel*

This ancient pub has been extensively, but sympathetically, restored. The work uncovered a huge, deep well under the porch, which is now covered by glass enabling you to peer down as you walk over it. The pub was built in the 12th century to house the stonemasons constructing the next-door church of St Brevita, past which runs Saints' Way, the old coast-to-coast path linking Padstow and Fowey. Needless to say, with such a history, everything about this charming pub oozes tradition - its thick stone walls, granite and slate floors, low beams, open fireplaces, and large, unusual bread oven. Fowey harbour is only a few miles away, so expect the menu to offer fresh crab, scallops, mackerel and much more. Other local produce also features strongly, including meats from a butcher's in Par, fruit and vegetables from Bodmin and dairy products from Lostwithiel. A typical meal might begin with an appetiser of marinated olives and ciabatta bread, then a starter of locally smoked duck, Cornish charcuterie, or pan-seared scallops. Main courses include slow roasted belly pork; fresh Cornish crab gratin; and wild mushroom risotto. Have a fresh Fowey crab sandwich at lunchtime, or a Cornish brie, bacon and watercress ciabatta; or just a proper Cornish pasty. The beers come from Sharps in Rock and Skinners of Truro, while a reasonably priced wine list offers seven wines by the glass. The pretty front garden is a lovely spot to enjoy a summer evening, perhaps with a glass of Pimms. Five of the bed and breakfast rooms are in an annexe.

Open all day all year **Meals** 12-2.30 6.30-9 12-9 Etr-mid-Sep Av main course £10 ⊞ FREE HOUSE ◖ Sharp's Doom Bar, Skinners Betty Stogs, Skinners Cornish Knocker, Edenale. ♉ 7 **Facilities** Children's menu Dogs allowed Garden Parking **Rooms** 9

LAMORNA — Map 2 SW42

Lamorna Wink

TR19 6XH ☎ 01736 731566
dir: *4m on B3315 towards Land's End, then 0.5m to turn on left*

This oddly-named pub was one of the original Kiddleywinks, a product of the 1830 Beer Act that enabled any householder to buy a liquor licence. Popular with walkers and not far from the Merry Maidens standing stones, the Wink provides a selection of local beers and a simple menu that includes sandwiches, jacket potatoes and fresh local crab. The management have been at the Wink for over thirty years, and pride themselves on providing diners with as much local produce as possible.

Open all wk ⊕ FREE HOUSE ◀ Sharp's Doom Bar, Skinners, Cornish Ale, Heligan Honey. **Facilities** Family room Dogs allowed Garden Parking **Notes** ⊜

LANLIVERY — Map 2 SX05

PICK OF THE PUBS

The Crown Inn INN ☗

See Pick of the Pubs on page 83

LOSTWITHIEL — Map 2 SX15

The Royal Oak ☗

Duke St PL22 0AG
☎ 01208 872552 ◻ & 872922 ▤ 01208 872922
e-mail: stay@royaloaklostwithiel.co.uk
dir: *A30 from Exeter to Bodmin then onto Lostwithiel. Or A38 from Plymouth towards Bodmin then left onto A390 to Lostwithiel*

There is believed to be a secret tunnel connecting this 12th-century inn to Restormel Castle a short way up the River Fowey. The tunnel was some kind of escape route, perhaps for smugglers. Though there is a strong emphasis on the restaurant side of the business, The Royal Oak also has a stone-flagged public bar, cosy and welcoming with a log fire, and separate lounge bar, both serving real ales like Betty Stogs and Sharp's Doom Bar. Quality Cornish produce is used wherever possible in a menu of largely traditional fare, with dishes such as deep-fried haddock with hand-cut chips, pea purée and tartare sauce, and slow-cooked belly pork with black

pudding and Bramley apple sauce. Vegetarian options are also available, like baked aubergine herb salad with wild Cornish Yarg and basil dressing.

Open all day all wk 11-mdnt **Bar Meals** L served all wk 12-3 D served all wk 6-9 **Restaurant** L served all wk 12-3 D served all wk 6-9 ⊕ PUNCH TAVERNS ◀ Interbrew Bass, Fuller's London Pride, Sharp's Doom Bar. ☗ 8 **Facilities** Family room Dogs allowed Garden Parking

LUDGVAN — Map 2 SW53

White Hart ☗

Churchtown TR20 8EY ☎ 01736 740574
dir: *From A30 take B3309 at Crowlas*

Built somewhere between 1280 and 1320, the White Hart retains the peaceful atmosphere of a bygone era and offers splendid views across St Michael's Mount and Bay. Although there has been a recent change of hands, things haven't changed that much. Real ales are still sold from the back of the bar, and the food is still as popular as ever. Mr and Mrs Gibbard, the new owners, also run the Turk's Head in Penzance.

Open all wk **Bar Meals** L served all wk 12-2.30 booking required D served all wk 6-9.30 booking required Av main course £7 **Restaurant** L served all wk 12-2.30 booking required D served all wk 6-9.30 ⊕ PUNCH TAVERNS ◀ Sharp's Doom Bar, Flowers IPA, Betty Stogs, Abbots. ☗ 12 **Facilities** Children's menu Dogs allowed Garden Parking

MALPAS — Map 2 SW84

The Heron Inn

Trenhaile Ter TR1 1SL
☎ 01872 272773 ▤ 01872 272773
e-mail: theheron@hotmail.co.uk
dir: *From Trafalgar rdbt in Truro exit towards BBC Radio Cornwall, & pub sign. Follow Malpas Rd for 2m into village. Pub on left*

Two miles from Truro's city centre, the pub enjoys panoramic River Fal views from its large terrace. The building may be old but its interior is light and airy, echoing the colours of the river. Local produce is used in traditional home-made dishes such as local roast ham, fried egg and chips; beef lasagne with garlic bread; and a pan-fried trio of Cornish fish. Open all day through the summer months.

Open all wk 11-3 6-11 (all day Fri-Sat (Sun till 10.30) summer all day every day) **Bar Meals** Av main course £9 **Restaurant** L served all wk 12-2 booking required D served Mon-Sat 6.30-9, Sun 7-9 booking required ⊕ ST AUSTELL BREWERY ◀ Tribute, IPA, Black Prince Ở Cornish Rattler. **Facilities** Children's menu Garden Parking

MANACCAN — Map 2 SW72

The New Inn ☗

TR12 6HA ☎ 01326 231323
e-mail: penny@stmartin.wanadoo.co.uk
dir: *7m from Helston*

This thatched village pub, deep in Daphne du Maurier country, dates back to Cromwellian times, although obviously Cromwell forbade his men to drink here. Attractions include the homely bars and a large, natural garden full of flowers. At lunchtime you might try a locally made pasty or moules marinière, and in the evening perhaps sea bass and chive fishcakes with tomato coulis and sautéed vegetables, or slow-roasted lamb shank with red wine and redcurrant gravy.

Open all wk 12-3 6-11 (Sat-Sun all day in summer) **Bar Meals** L served Mon-Sat 12-2.30, Sun 12-2 D served Mon-Sat 6-9.30, Sun 7-9 **Restaurant** L served all wk D served all wk ⊕ PUNCH TAVERNS ◀ Flowers IPA, Sharp's Doom Bar. ☗ 10 **Facilities** Play area Dogs allowed Garden Parking

MARAZION — Map 2 SW53

PICK OF THE PUBS

Godolphin Arms ★★★★ INN

TR17 0EN ☎ 01736 710202 ▤ 01736 710171
e-mail: enquiries@godolphinarms.co.uk
dir: *From A30 just outside Penzance follow Marazion signs. Pub 1st large building on right in Marazion, opposite St Michael's Mount*

Locations don't come much more spectacular than this: the Godolphin Arms stands atop a sea wall directly opposite St Michael's Mount, and has superb views across the bay. It's so close that the sea splashes at the windows in the winter, and you can watch the movement of seals, dolphins, ferries, and fishing boats returning to Newlyn with their daily catch. From the traditional bar and beer terrace to the more homely restaurant and most of the stylishly-decorated bedrooms, the Mount is clearly visible. Seafood figures prominently in the restaurant: the specials blackboard lists daily choices such as lemon sole pan fried in butter and capers; moules; scallops; or seafood tagliatelle. Aside from the view, the highlight of any stay is breakfast, which includes everything from a full English breakfast to kippers on toast.

Open all day all wk 11am-mdnt (Sun noon-mdnt) **Bar Meals** L served all wk 8am-9pm D served all wk 8am-9pm food served all day **Restaurant** L served all wk 8am-9pm D served all wk 8am-9pm food served all day ⊕ FREE HOUSE ◀ Sharp's Doom Bar & Special, St Austell Tribute, Tetley's Smooth ⊙ Cornish Rattler. **Facilities** Dogs allowed Garden Parking **Rooms** 10

| MEVAGISSEY | Map 2 SX04 |

The Ship Inn ★★★ INN ♀

Fore St PL26 6UQ ☎ 01726 843324 ▤ 01726 844368
e-mail: shipinnian@hotmail.co.uk
dir: 7m S of St Austell

The inn stands just a few yards from Mevagissey's picturesque fishing harbour, so the choice of fish and seafood dishes comes as no surprise: moules marinière, beer-battered cod, and oven-baked fillet of haddock topped with prawns and Cornish Tiskey cheese and served with a lemon and dill sauce. Other options take in baguettes, burgers, jacket potatoes, steaks, and trio of Cornish sausages served with creamy mash and rich red onion gravy.

Open all wk **Bar Meals** L served all wk 12-6 D served all wk 6-9 food served all day ⊕ ST AUSTELL BREWERY ◀ St Austell Ales. ♀ 8 **Facilities** Children's menu Family room Dogs allowed **Rooms** 5

| MITCHELL | Map 2 SW85 |

PICK OF THE PUBS

The Plume of Feathers ★★★★ INN ♀

TR8 5AX ☎ 01872 510387 ▤ 01637 839401
e-mail: enquiries@theplume.info
dir: Exit A30 to Mitchell/Newquay

Over the years, this 16th century building has welcomed various historical figures - John Wesley preached Methodism from the pillared entrance, and Sir Walter Raleigh used to live locally. The present owners have established it as a successful destination pub restaurant; the imaginative kitchen has an excellent reputation for its food, based on a fusion of modern European and classical British dishes, with an emphasis on fresh fish and the best Cornish ingredients. Lunch brings starters such as home-made fishcake with sweet chilli and mixed leaves followed by a home-made beef burger with home-made relish and fries or venison stew with creamed potato and Savoy cabbage. Dinner could start with smoked mackerel fillet with houmous and toasted crostini followed by confit of Cornish duck leg with Toulouse sausage, tomato and mixed bean cassoulet. Finish with baked cheesecake of the day with clotted cream.

Open all day all wk 9am-11/mdnt (25 Dec 11-5) **Bar Meals** Av main course £10 food served all day **Restaurant** Av 3 course à la carte fr £22 food served all day ⊕ FREE HOUSE ◀ Doom Bar, John Smiths Smooth, Betty Stogs. ♀ 7 **Facilities** Children's menu Play area Dogs allowed Garden Parking **Rooms** 7

| MORWENSTOW | Map 2 SS21 |

PICK OF THE PUBS

The Bush Inn ♀

EX23 9SR ☎ 01288 331242
web: www.bushinn-morwenstow.co.uk
dir: Exit A39, 3m N of Kilkhampton, 2nd right into village of Shop. 1.5m to Crosstown. Inn on village green

The Bush is a 13th-century pub set in an isolated cliff-top hamlet, close to a dramatic stretch of the north Cornish coast, so was understandably popular with 18th-century smugglers. The historic interior features stone-flagged floors, old stone fireplaces and a 'leper's squint', a tiny window through which the needy grabbed food scraps. It's very different today. Meals are freshly prepared from fresh local produce, including beef from the inn's own farm, and lamb, pork, salad and vegetables from others nearby. Local shoots provide all the game and seafood comes from home waters. Dishes might include Thai scallop salad to start, with mains such as tarragon stuffed chicken breast wrapped in Parma ham with Jerusalem artichoke purée, sautéed potatoes, spinach and red wine sauce; or whole roast John Dory with new potatoes, caper and parsley brown butter. Finish with rich chocolate cake, or apple and cherry crumble with clotted cream.

Open all day all wk 11am-12.30am **Bar Meals** L served all wk D served all wk Av main course £10 food served all day **Restaurant** L served all wk D served all wk ⊕ FREE HOUSE ◀ St Austell HSD, Sharp's Doom Bar, Skinners Betty Stogs, St Austell Tribute ⊙ Thatchers. ♀ 8 **Facilities** Play area Dogs allowed Garden Parking

---

| MYLOR BRIDGE | Map 2 SW83 |

PICK OF THE PUBS

The Pandora Inn ♀

Restronguet Creek TR11 5ST
☎ 01326 372678 ▤ 01326 378958
dir: From Truro/Falmouth follow A39, left at Carclew, follow signs to pub

Rather romantically, you can reach this thatched, white-painted inn by foot, bicycle and boat. It has a breathtaking location, set right on the banks of the Restronguet Creek, with panoramic views across the water. There's seating right outside, and also at the end of the pontoon, where up to twenty boats can moor at high tide. The inn itself dates back in part to the 13th century, and its flagstone floors, low-beamed ceilings and thatched roof suggest little can have changed since. The name stems from the good ship Pandora, sent to Tahiti to capture the Bounty mutineers. Sadly, it was wrecked and the captain court-martialled. Forced into early retirement, he bought the inn. Call in for a casual lunch: perhaps smoked mackerel fillets with creamed horseradish. In the evening make a meal of grilled sea bass with spinach risotto; or home-made Cornish crab cakes in saffron dressing.

Open all day all wk 10.30am-11pm ⊕ ST AUSTELL BREWERY ◀ St Austell Tinners Ale, HSD, Bass, Tribute, Tetley's. ♀ 12 **Facilities** Dogs allowed Garden Parking

---

| NEWQUAY | Map 2 SW86 |

The Lewinnick Lodge Bar & Restaurant NEW ♀

Pentire Headland TR7 1NX
☎ 01637 878117 ▤ 01637 870130
e-mail: ask@lewinnick-lodge.info
dir: From Newquay take Pentire Rd 0.5m, pub on right

Originally built as a small stone cottage in the late 18th century, the Lodge enjoys stunning views of Cornwall's Atlantic coast. One of only two properties on the rugged Pentire Headland, the pub has established a great reputation, built up by the current owners over the last 20 years, with locals and visitors alike. Menu choices include fishcakes with sweet chilli, mixed leaves and fries; steak with braised shallots and slow-roasted vine tomatoes; and roasted red pepper, ricotta and spinach linguine with walnut dressing.

continued

NEWQUAY *continued*

Open all day all wk **Bar Meals** Av main course £5 food served all day **Restaurant** Fixed menu price fr £12 Av 3 course à la carte fr £18 food served all day ⊕ FREE HOUSE ◀ Sharp's Doom Bar, Skinner's Betty Stogs. ♟ 10 **Facilities** Children's menu Dogs allowed Garden Parking

---

PENZANCE Map 2 SW43

Dolphin Tavern

Quay St TR18 4BD ☎ 01736 364106
e-mail: dolphin@tiscali.co.uk

A 600-year-old harbourside pub overlooking Mounts Bay and St Michael's Mount. In this building, apparently, Sir Walter Raleigh first smoked tobacco on English soil and, the following century, Judge Jeffreys held court. Haunted by not one but several ghosts. A good choice of seafish is among the options on the menu.

Open all day all wk **Bar Meals** food served all day ⊕ ST AUSTELL BREWERY ◀ St Austell HSD, Tinners Tribute. **Facilities** Family room Dogs allowed Garden

The Turks Head Inn ♟

Chapel St TR18 4AF
☎ 01736 363093 📄 01736 360215
e-mail: turkshead@gibbards9476.fsworld.co.uk
dir: *Telephone for directions*

Dating from around 1233, making it Penzance's oldest pub, it was the first in the country to be given the Turks Head name. Sadly, a Spanish raiding party destroyed much of the original building in the 16th century, but an old smugglers' tunnel leading directly to the harbour and priest holes still exist. Typically available are fresh seafood choices like crab, ray wing, gurnard and tandoori monkfish, along with others such as pan-fried venison, chicken stir-fry, pork tenderloin, steaks, mixed grill and salads. A sunny flower-filled garden lies at the rear.

Open all wk **Bar Meals** L served all wk 12-2.30 booking required D served all wk 6-9.30 booking required Av main course £8 **Restaurant** L served all wk 12-2.30 booking required D served all wk 6-9.30 booking required ⊕ PUNCH TAVERNS ◀ Betty Stogs, 6X, Sharp's Doom Bar, Guest ale. ♟ 14 **Facilities** Family room Dogs allowed Garden

---

PERRANUTHNOE Map 2 SW52

The Victoria Inn ★★★ INN ⊛ ♟

TR20 9NP ☎ 01736 710309
e-mail: enquiries@victoriainn-penzance.co.uk
dir: *Off A394 (Penzance to Helston road), signed Perranuthnoe*

Reputedly Cornwall's oldest inn, the Victoria dates from the 12th century. Set within sight of the sea, it's popular with walkers and has a restful, Mediterranean-style garden. Food is taken seriously here, not least local fish and seafood offered on a daily board of specials. Using the best of local ingredients, typical dishes are goats'

cheese and sweet pepper fondue; roasted pork belly with champ, black pudding and apple and bay sauce; and poached pear with caramel sauce, shortbread and ginger ice cream. If you want to stay, there are two individually-decorated, en suite bedrooms.

Open 12-2 6.30-11 Closed: 25-26 Dec, 1 Jan, 1st wk Jan, Sun eve & Mon (off season) **Bar Meals** L served all wk 12-2 booking required D served all wk 6.30-11 booking required Av main course £14 **Restaurant** L served all wk 12-2 booking required D served all wk 6.30-11 booking required Av 3 course à la carte fr £19.85 ◀ Doom Bar, Tribute. ♟ 6 **Facilities** Children's menu Dogs allowed Garden Parking **Rooms** 2

POLKERRIS Map 2 SX05

The Rashleigh Inn ♟

PL24 2TL ☎ 01726 813991 📄 01726 815619
e-mail: jonspode@aol.com
web: www.rashleighinnpolkerris.co.uk
dir: *Off A3082 outside Fowey*

This 300-year-old, stone-built building on the beach - once a boathouse and coastguard station - became the village pub in 1915 when the previous one was swept away during a storm. There are panoramic views across St Austell Bay from the multi-level heated and panelled terrace. Excellent real ale selection, with two real ciders and local organic soft drinks are on offer. And superb food too, using the best of locally sourced ingredients (suppliers listed on the menu): Fowey river mussels, kiln smoked trout and mackerel; Cornish beef and lamb too – lamb steak with port and redcurrant glaze.

Open all day all wk **Bar Meals** L served all wk 12-5 D served all wk 6-9 Av main course £8.95 food served all day **Restaurant** L served all wk 12-2 booking required D served all wk 6-9 booking required Av 3 course à la carte fr £20 ⊕ FREE HOUSE ◀ Sharp's Doom Bar, Cotleigh Tawny, Blue Anchor Spingo, Timothy Taylor Landlord, Rashleigh Bitter Ő Stowford Press, Addlestones. ♟ 8 **Facilities** Dogs allowed Garden Parking

---

POLPERRO Map 2 SX25

Old Mill House Inn

Mill Hill PL13 2RP ☎ 01503 272362
e-mail: enquiries@oldmillhouseinn.co.uk
dir: *Telephone for directions*

In the heart of historic Polperro, this 16th-century inn has been extensively refurbished. Here you can sample well-kept local ales and 'scrumpy' cider beside a log fire in the bar, or sit out over lunch in the riverside garden during fine weather. Local ingredients, with an emphasis on freshly caught fish, are the foundation of dishes on the restaurant menu. Traditional roasts are served on Sundays.

Open all day all wk 10am-12.30am (Sun 10am-11.30pm) **Bar Meals** L served all wk 10-2.30 D served all wk 5.30-9 ⊕ FREE HOUSE ◀ Skinners, Skinners Mill House Ale, Sharps, Guest Ales Ő Stowford Press. **Facilities** Dogs allowed Garden Parking

---

PORT GAVERNE Map 2 SX08

PICK OF THE PUBS

Port Gaverne Hotel ★★ HL ♟

PL29 3SQ ☎ 01208 880244 📄 01208 880151
web: www.chycor.co.uk/hotels/port-gaverne
dir: *Signed from B3314, S of Delabole via B3267 on E of Port Isaac*

Just up the lane from a secluded cove is this delightful 17th-century inn. In this once thriving port, women unloaded coal and general merchandise from ships then loaded them up again with slate from the great Delabole quarry until, in 1893, the coming of the railway put paid to the port's prosperity. A meandering building with plenty of period detail, the hotel has long association with fishing and smuggling. As you might expect, locally supplied produce includes plenty of fresh fish, and it appears on all the menus. For example, along with a selection of ploughman's, you might fancy a half pint of prawns at lunchtime, or a seafood pie. At dinner expect starters like tomato, red onion and Cornish goats' cheese salad; crab soup; or lobster and monkfish Thermidor; and mains of sautéed trio of Cornish fish on vegetable rösti; pan-fried John Dory with olive oil mash; or chargrilled sirloin steak au poivre. Walkers from the Heritage Coast Path can pause for a pint in the comfortable, picture-adorned bar or in the small beer garden.

Open all day all wk **Bar Meals** L served all wk 12-2.30 D served all wk 6-9 Av main course £9 **Restaurant** D served all wk 7-9 Av 3 course à la carte fr £27 ⊕ FREE HOUSE ◀ Sharp's Doom Bar, Bass, St Austell Tribute. ♟ 9 **Facilities** Children's menu Dogs allowed Garden Parking **Rooms** 14

PORTHLEVEN   Map 2 SW62

The Ship Inn

TR13 9JS ☎ 01326 564204 📄 **01326 564204**
e-mail: cjoakden@yahoo.co.uk
dir: *From Helston follow signs to Porthleven, 2.5m. On entering village continue to harbour. Take W road by side of harbour to inn*

Dating from the 17th century, this smugglers' inn is actually built into the cliffs, and is approached by a flight of stone steps. During the winter two log fires warm the interior, while the flames of a third flicker in the separate Smithy children's room. Expect a good selection of locally caught fish and seafood, such as crab and prawn mornay, or the smoked fish platter, all smoked in Cornwall. The pub has declared itself a 'chip-free zone'.

Open all day all wk 11.30am-11.30pm (Sun noon-10.30) **Bar Meals** L served all wk 12-2 D served all wk 6.30-9 ⊕ FREE HOUSE ◀ Courage Best, Sharp's Doom Bar & Special, guest ales. **Facilities** Children's menu Family room Dogs allowed Garden

PORTREATH   Map 2 SW64

Basset Arms

Tregea Ter TR16 4NG ☎ 01209 842077
e-mail: bassettarms@btconnect.com
dir: *From Redruth take B3300 to Portreath. Pub on left near seafront*

Tin-mining and shipwreck paraphernalia adorn the low-beamed interior of this early 19th-century Cornish stone cottage, built as a pub to serve harbour workers. At one time it served as a mortuary for ill-fated seafarers, so there are plenty of ghost stories! The menu makes the most of local seafood, such as mussels and fries, and home-made fish pie, but also provides a wide selection of alternatives, including half chicken in barbecue sauce; 12oz gammon steak; curry of the day; and salads including crab, when available.

Open all day all wk 11am-11pm (Fri-Sat 11am-mdnt, Sun 11-10.30) **Bar Meals** L served all wk 12-2 D served all wk 6-9 Av main course £9.50 **Restaurant** L served all wk 12-2 D served all wk 6-9 Av 3 course à la carte fr £18 ⊕ FREE HOUSE ◀ Sharp's Doom Bar, Courage, John Smith's Smooth. **Facilities** Children's menu Play area Dogs allowed Garden Parking

RUAN LANIHORNE   Map 2 SW84

The Kings Head ♥

TR2 5NX ☎ 01872 501263
e-mail: contact@kings-head-roseland.co.uk
dir: *3m from Tregony Bridge on A3078*

Expect a warm welcome at this traditional country pub set deep in the Roseland countryside. Roaring winter fires, beamed ceilings and mulled wine contrast with summer days relaxing on the terrace with a jug of Pimms, a pint of Betty Stogs or Press Gang Cornish cider. Whatever the time of year, the chef responds with

seasonal dishes using the best of local produce, ranging from ploughman's lunches to wiener schnitzel with celeriac and potato mash. Look out for the signature dish, too - slow-roasted Ruan duckling with a warm pepper sauce.

Open 12-2.30 6-11 Closed: Sun eve, Mon (Nov-Etr) **Restaurant** L served all wk 12.30-2 booking required D served all wk 6.30-9 booking required ⊕ FREE HOUSE ◀ Skinners Kings Ruan, Cornish Knocker, Betty Stogs Ö Skinners Press Gang. ♥ 7 **Facilities** Dogs allowed Garden Parking

ST AGNES   Map 3 SW75

Driftwood Spars ★★★★ GA ♥

Trevaunance Cove TR5 0RT
☎ 01872 552428 📄 **01872 553701**
e-mail: driftwoodspars@hotmail.com
dir: *A30 onto B3285, through St Agnes, down steep hill, left at Peterville Inn, onto road signed Trevaunance Cove*

Just off the South West Coastal Path, and a short walk from the beach, this family-run pub with rooms, restaurant, beer gardens and micro-brewery, is housed in a 300-year-old tin miners' store, chandlery and sail loft, complete with its own smugglers' tunnel. The name comes from the huge beams that were originally spars from a shipwrecked boat. Eight hand-pulled real ales are served alongside 50 malts, 10 rums, a 40-bin wine list and a home-brewed alcoholic ginger beer. Daily changing specials supplement the seasonal menu and seafood figures strongly. There is live music at weekends.

Open all day all wk 11-11 (Fri-Sat 11-1am, 25 Dec 11am-2pm) **Bar Meals** L served all wk 12-2.30 Av main course £9.50 **Restaurant** L served Sun 12-2.30 booking required D served all wk 7-9, (winter Thu-Sat 7-9) booking required Av 3 course à la carte fr £25 ⊕ FREE HOUSE ◀ Tinners, Blue Hills Bitter, Tribute, Betty Stogs, Doom Bar Ö Cornish Rattler, Addlestones. ♥ 10 **Facilities** Children's menu Dogs allowed Garden Parking Rooms 15

ST AGNES (ISLES OF SCILLY)   Map 2 SV80

Turks Head

TR22 0PL ☎ 01720 422434
dir: *By boat or helicopter to St Mary's & boat on to St Agnes*

Named after the 16th-century Turkish pirates who arrived from the Barbary Coast, the Turks Head is Britain's most southwesterly inn. Noted for its atmosphere and superb location overlooking the island quay, this former coastguard boathouse is packed with fascinating model ships and maritime photographs. Lunchtime brings soup, salads and open rolls, while evening dishes might include blackened swordfish steak in Cajun spices, or sirloin steak with all the trimmings.

Open all wk Closed: Nov-Feb ⊕ FREE HOUSE ◀ Skinners Betty Stogs, Sharp's Doom Bar, Ales of Scilly, Scuppered, Turks Ale. **Facilities** Dogs allowed Garden

ST BREWARD   Map 2 SX07

The Old Inn & Restaurant ♥

Churchtown, Bodmin Moor PL30 4PP
☎ 01208 850711 📄 **01208 851671**
e-mail: theoldinn@macace.net
dir: *A30 to Bodmin. 16m, right just after Temple, follow signs to St Breward. B3266 (Bodmin to Camelford road) turn to St Breward, follow brown signs*

Located high up on Bodmin Moor, one of Cornwall's oldest inns is now owned and run by local man Darren Wills, the latest licensee in its 1,000-year history. The solid granite pub has slate flagstone floors and two huge granite fireplaces with real fires in winter. It is well-known throughout this glorious area for its wholesome home-cooked food, frequented by many regulars who are drawn by its Moorland Grills and Sunday roasts. Check out the local Cornish wines as well. There is also a large beer garden with a children's pet corner.

Open all day all wk 11-11 **Bar Meals** L served Sun-Fri 11-2, Sat 11-9 D served Sun-Fri 6-9, Sat 11-9 Av main course £8.95 **Restaurant** L served Mon-Fri 11-2, Sat-Sun 11-9 booking required D served Mon-Fri 6-9, Sat-Sun 11-9 booking required Av 3 course à la carte fr £19 ⊕ FREE HOUSE ◀ Sharp's Doom Bar & Special, guest ales. ♥ 20 **Facilities** Children's menu Family room Dogs allowed Garden Parking

ST EWE
Map 2 SW94

The Crown Inn ♟

PL26 6EY ☎ 01726 843322 📠 01726 844720
e-mail: linda@thecrowninn737.fsnet.co.uk
dir: *From St Austell take B3273. At Tregiskey x-rds turn right. St Ewe signed on right*

Hanging baskets add plenty of brightness and colour to this delightful 16th-century inn, just a mile from the famous 'Lost gardens of Heligan', which Crown chef John Nelson co-founded and helped to restore. Well-kept St Austell ales complement an extensive menu and daily specials. Expect cod in beer batter, local steaks, rack of lamb, and liver and bacon among other favourites. Try a glass of Polmassick wine from the vineyard only half a mile away.

Open all wk ⊕ ST AUSTELL BREWERY ◀ Tribute, Hicks Special, Tinners, guest ale. ♟ 8 Facilities Play area Family room Dogs allowed Garden Parking

ST IVES
Map 2 SW54

The Watermill ♟

Lelant Downs TR27 6LQ ☎ 01736 757912
e-mail: watermill@btconnect.com
dir: *Exit A30 at junct for St Ives/A3074, turn left at 2nd mini rdbt*

Built in the 1700s to mill grain for the local estate, the watermill was converted into a pub/restaurant in the 1970s. Old mill machinery is still in place and the iron waterwheel still turns, gravity fed by the mill stream. It is a family friendly establishment, with extensive gardens and fantastic views up the valley towards Trencrom Hill. Bar meals are served, and there is a separate restaurant where steaks and fish (sea bass, sardines and mackerel perhaps) are specialities. Cornish Rattler cider is served along with a range of real ales including Betty Stogs.

Open all day all wk noon–11 Bar Meals L served all wk 12-2.30 D served all wk 6-9 Av main course £7.50 Restaurant D served all wk 6-9 booking required Av 3 course à la carte fr £15 ⊕ FREE HOUSE ◀ Sharp's Doom Bar, Skinners Betty Stogs, Guest Ales Ô Cornish Rattler. ♟ 6 Facilities Play area Dogs allowed Garden Parking

ST JUST (NEAR LAND'S END)
Map 2 SW33

PICK OF THE PUBS

Star Inn

TR19 7LL ☎ 01736 788767
dir: *Telephone for directions*

Plenty of tin mining and fishing stories are told at this traditional Cornish pub, located in the town of St Just, near Lands End. It dates back a few centuries, and was reputedly built to house workmen constructing the 15th-century church. John Wesley is believed to have been among the Star's more illustrious guests over the years, but these days the pub is most likely to be recognised for having featured in several television and film productions. A choice of local beers is served, but there is no food. Monday night is folk night, and there's live music on Thursdays and Saturdays, too, in a whole range of styles.

Open all day all wk 11am-12.30am ⊕ ST AUSTELL BREWERY ◀ St Austell HSD, Tinners Ale, Tribute, Dartmoor Ô Cornish Rattler. Facilities Family room Dogs allowed Garden Notes ⊗

The Wellington NEW ★★ INN

Market Square TR19 7HD
☎ 01736 787319 📠 01736 787906
e-mail: wellingtonhotel@msn.com
dir: *Take A30 to Penzance, then A3071 W of Penzance to St Just*

Standing in the market square of an historic mining town, this family-run inn makes an ideal base for exploring the spectacular beaches and countryside of West Penwith. Low ceilings, Cornish stonework and a secluded walled garden help to evoke the atmosphere of old Cornwall. The blackboard menu features fresh crab, local fish and daily home-cooked specials: Stilton and vegetable crumble; smoked mackerel salad; country ham, eggs and chips; and a prize-winning ploughman's are typical selections.

Open all day all wk Bar Meals L served all wk 12-2 D served all wk 6-9 (winter 6-8.30) Av main course £8 Restaurant D served all wk 6-9 (summer) ⊕ ST AUSTELL BREWERY ◀ St Austell Tinners, St Austell Tribute, HSD Ô Cornish Rattler. Facilities Children's menu Play area Dogs allowed Garden Rooms 11

ST MAWES
Map 2 SW83

PICK OF THE PUBS

The Victory Inn ♟

Victory Hill TR2 5PQ
☎ 01326 270324 📠 01326 270238
e-mail: contact@victory-inn.co.uk
dir: *Take A3078 to St Mawes. Pub up Victory Steps adjacent to harbour*

A friendly fishermen's local, close to St Mawes Harbour on the Roseland Peninsula, The Victory is named after Nelson's flagship. It is a traditional pub with a modern approach to food, which is served at lunchtime and dinnertime seven days a week. The warm welcome from Phil and Debbie Heslip embraces one and all, including children who are provided with paper, crayons and their own menu, while dogs are given treats. The first-floor Seaview Restaurant connects to a recently completed outside terrace, which looks across the rooftops to the harbour. Not surprisingly, the freshest of local seafood is high on the list of ingredients - all supplied from Cornwall - and the choice of fish and shellfish changes almost daily. Favourite dishes include crab risotto, beer battered cod with hand-cut chips, and the range of curries and casseroles.

Open all day all wk 11am-mdnt Bar Meals L served all wk 12-3 D served all wk 6-9.30 booking required Av main course £8.95 Restaurant L served all wk 12-3 D served all wk 6-9.15 booking required Fixed menu price fr £10.95 Av 3 course à la carte fr £16.95 ⊕ PUNCH TAVERNS ◀ Sharp's, Bass, Wadworth 6X, Adnams Broadside, Brains Reverend James, Otter Ale Ô Addlestones. ♟ 8 Facilities Children's menu Dogs allowed Garden

ST MAWGAN — Map 2 SW86

PICK OF THE PUBS

The Falcon Inn ★★★★ INN ♚

TR8 4EP ☎ **01637 860225** 📠 **01637 860884**
e-mail: info@thefalcon-stmawgan.co.uk
dir: *From A30 (8m W of Bodmin) follow signs to Newquay/St Mawgan Airport. After 2m right into village, pub at bottom of hill*

Nestling in the sheltered Vale of Lanherne conservation area is the wisteria-covered Falcon with large attractive garden, a lovely magnolia tree and cobbled courtyard. The interior is cosy and relaxed, with flagstone floors and log fires in winter; two en suite letting rooms make the inn a handy overnight stop before catching a plane from Newquay. Beers from St Austell Brewery are augmented by Scrumpy and Rattler ciders; half a dozen wines available by the glass complete the range of refreshments. At lunchtime you'll find home-made soup, sandwiches, jacket potatoes, and main courses such as chicken and mushroom pie. Weather permitting, summer barbecues are planned for the garden. An à la carte evening menu is served in the more formal restaurant. Dishes may feature starters of antipasto misto or roast vegetable bruschetta. Main courses always include fresh fish options such as red mullet, hake or trout, and vegetarians are well catered for.

Open all wk 11-3 6-11 (Jul-Aug open all day) Closed: 25 Dec (open 12-2) **Bar Meals** L served all wk 12-2 D served all wk 6-9 **Restaurant** L served all wk 12-2 D served all wk 6-9 ⊕ ST AUSTELL BREWERY ◀ St Austell HSD, Tinners Ale, Tribute ⊘ Cornish Rattler. ♚ 7 **Facilities** Children's menu Dogs allowed Garden Parking **Rooms** 2

ST MERRYN — Map 2 SW87

PICK OF THE PUBS

The Cornish Arms NEW ♚

PL28 8ND ☎ **01841 520288** 📠 **01841 521496**
e-mail: cornisharms@rickstein.com
dir: *From Padstow follow signs for St Merryn then Churchtown*

Rick Stein and his ex-wife Jill liked their local pub so much that, like the man in a famous Remington razor ad on TV, they bought it. Actually, they're tenants, but that spoils the story. Initially, the locals were concerned they were going to turn it into a gastro-pub, but that was never their intention. Head chef Julian Lloyd's no-nonsense British pub menu lists goujons of lemon sole with salad and tartare sauce; pan-fried polenta with field mushroom, rocket and aïoli; Tywardreath pork and garlic sausages, mash and onion gravy; and hot and spicy Goan chicken curry with steamed rice. As happy St Austell Brewery tenants, they serve Tribute, Tinners, HSD and Proper Job cask ales, while Rick has developed a couple of recipes to go with their bottled beer, Clouded Yellow, as an alternative to his own Chalky's Bark and Chalky's Bite, named after his much-missed rough-haired Jack Russell.

Open all day all wk (25 Dec open 2hrs only) **Bar Meals** L served all wk 12-3 D served all wk 6-10 Av main course £9.60 ⊕ ST AUSTELL BREWERY ◀ St Austell Tribute, Proper Job, Tinners, Sharp's Chalky's Bite ⊘ Cornish Rattler. ♚ 11 **Facilities** Children's menu Dogs allowed Garden Parking

ST NEOT — Map 2 SX16

The London Inn ♚

PL14 6NG ☎ **01579 320263** 📠 **01579 321642**
e-mail: ho@ccinns.com

Dating back to the 18th century, this pub was the first coaching inn on the route from Penzance to London. The bar and dining areas have old beamed ceilings and polished flagstone floors. Seafood platter, salmon, and halibut are among the fish dishes, while other main courses include lamb shank in a spiced port sauce. Lighter fare ranges from ciabatta bread with a variety of fillings, including roast beef, chicken, bacon and cheese, to a choice of ploughman's lunches.

Open all wk ⊕ COAST & COUNTRY INNS ◀ Doom Bar, Courage Best, John Smiths & guest ales. ♚ 16 **Facilities** Dogs allowed Parking

SALTASH — Map 3 SX45

The Crooked Inn ★★★ GA

Stoketon Cottage, Trematon PL12 4RZ
☎ **01752 848177** 📠 **01752 843203**
e-mail: info@crooked-inn.co.uk
dir: *Telephone for directions*

Overlooking the lush Lyher Valley, a family-run inn that once housed staff from Stoketon Manor, whose ruins lie the other side of the courtyard. Traditional, home-made dishes include pie, pasta or curry of the day; battered fresh cod; breaded wholetail scampi; and 'generous, hefty, ample or copious' steaks. Boards list lunchtime, evening and vegetarian specials and there's a special Little Horrors menu. The children's playground has friendly animals, swings, slides, a trampoline and a treehouse. Spacious bedrooms are well equipped.

Open all wk Closed: 25 Dec ⊕ FREE HOUSE ◀ Hicks Special Draught, Sharp's Own Ale, Skinner's Cornish Knocker Ale. **Facilities** Play area Dogs allowed Garden Parking **Rooms** 18

SENNEN — Map 2 SW32

The Old Success Inn

Sennen Cove TR19 7DG
☎ **01736 871232** 📠 **01736 871457**
e-mail: oldsuccess@sennencove.fsbusiness.co.uk
dir: *Telephone for directions*

Once the haunt of smugglers and now a focal point for the Sennen Lifeboat crew, this 17th-century inn enjoys a glorious location overlooking Cape Cornwall. Its name comes from the days when fishermen gathered here to count their catch and share out their 'successes'. Fresh local seafood is to the fore, and favourites include cod in Doom Bar batter, steaks, chilli, and vegetable lasagne. Live music every Saturday night in the bar.

Open all wk ⊕ FREE HOUSE ◀ Doom Bar, Skinners, Heligan Honey, Headlaunch Special. **Facilities** Dogs allowed Garden Parking

TINTAGEL — Map 2 SX08

The Port William ♚

Trebarwith Strand PL34 0HB
☎ **01840 770230** 📠 **01840 770936**
e-mail: theportwilliam@btinternet.com
dir: *Off B3263 between Camelford & Tintagel, pub signed*

Occupying one of the best locations in Cornwall, this former harbourmaster's house lies directly on the coastal path, 50 yards from the sea. There is an entrance to a smugglers' tunnel at the rear of the ladies' toilet! Focus on the daily-changing specials board for such dishes as artichoke and roast pepper salad, warm smoked trout platter, and spinach ricotta tortelloni.

Open all wk ⊕ FREE HOUSE ◀ St Austell Tinners Ale & Hicks, Interbrew Bass. ♚ 8 **Facilities** Family room Dogs allowed Garden Parking

PICK OF THE PUBS

Edgcumbe Arms ☕

Cremyll PL10 1HX
☎ 01752 822294 📄 01752 822014
dir: *Telephone for directions*

The inn dates from the 15th century and is located right on the Tamar estuary, next to the National Trust Park, close to the foot ferry from Plymouth. Views from the bow window seats and waterside terrace are glorious, taking in Drakes Island, the Royal William Yard and the marina. Real ales from St Austell like Cornish Cream, Tribute HS, and Tinners, and quality home-cooked food are served in a series of rooms, which are full of character with American oak panelling and stone flagged floors. A good choice of bar snacks is also offered. The inn has a first floor function room with sea views, and a courtyard garden; it also holds a civil wedding licence.

Open all day all wk 11am-11pm **Bar Meals** L served Mon-Fri 12-6, Sat-Sun 12-9 D served Mon-Fri 6-9, Sat-Sun 12-9 ⊕ ST AUSTELL BREWERY ◀ St Austell HSD, Tribute HS, IPA, guest ales. ☕ 10 **Facilities** Dogs allowed Garden Parking

PICK OF THE PUBS

The Mill House Inn ☕

See Pick of the Pubs on opposite page

PICK OF THE PUBS

The Springer Spaniel ☕

See Pick of the Pubs on page 92

Eliot Arms (Square & Compass) ☕

PL15 7EU ☎ 01566 772051
dir: *From Launceston take A30 towards Bodmin. Then follow brown signs to Tregadillett*

The extraordinary décor in this charming creeper-clad coaching inn includes Masonic regalia, horse brasses and 54 clocks. It was believed to have been a Masonic lodge for Napoleonic prisoners, and even has its own friendly ghost! Customers can enjoy real fires in winter and lovely hanging baskets in summer. Food is served in the bar or bright and airy restaurant and includes home-made soup, pie and curry of the day; steak and chips; chargrills; and home-made vegetarian dishes such as spinach and mushroom lasagne or spicy vegetable curry.

Open all day all wk 11.30-11 (Fri-Sat 11.30am-mdnt, Sun noon-10.30) **Bar Meals** L served all wk 12-2 booking required D served all wk 6-9 booking required Av main course £8.95 **Restaurant** L served all wk 12-2 booking required D served all wk 6-9 booking required ⊕ FREE HOUSE ◀ Sharp's Doom Bar, Courage Best. ☕ 9 **Facilities** Children's menu Family room Dogs allowed Parking

PICK OF THE PUBS

The New Inn ★★★★ INN ⊛ ☕

New Grimsby TR24 0QQ
☎ 01720 422844 📄 01720 423200
e-mail: newinn@tresco.co.uk
dir: *By New Grimsby Quay*

Tresco is one of five inhabited islands in the Scillies, 29 miles south west of Land's End. The New Inn is the only pub remaining out of thirteen and, as you might expect, the sea has always been a big influence - even its signboard was salvaged from a wreck. The Main Bar is famous for its Cornish and Scillonian ales, plus Cornish Rattler cider. On the lunchtime menu some starters, such as salmon fishcakes and grilled goats' cheese, double up as mains, while locally caught fish and seafood appear on the specials board. For evening dining, there's a choice - the quiet restaurant, the livelier Driftwood Bar, the Pavillion, or simply alfresco. The dinner menu offers, for example, confit duck leg; pan-fried calves' liver; and even a chateaubriand for two is complemented by daily specials. On Sundays there's a traditional roast. Many of the double rooms have ocean views.

Open all wk all day (Apr-Oct) phone for winter opening **Bar Meals** L served all wk 12-2.30 D served all wk 6-9 Av main course £12.50 **Restaurant** D served all wk 6-9 booking required ⊕ FREE HOUSE ◀ Skinner's Betty Stogs Bitter, Tresco Tipple, Ales of Scilly Scuppered & Firebrand, St Austell IPA Ŏ Cornish Rattler. ☕ 12 **Facilities** Garden Rooms 16

Old Ale House ☕

7 Quay St TR1 2HD ☎ 01872 271122 📄 01872 271817
e-mail: old.ale.house@btconnect.com
dir: *In town centre*

Olde-worlde establishment with a large selection of real ales on display, as well as more than twenty flavours of fruit wine. Lots of attractions, including live music and various quiz and games nights. Food includes 'huge hands of hot bread', oven-baked jacket potatoes, ploughman's lunches and daily specials. Vegetable stir fry, five spice chicken and sizzling beef feature among the sizzling skillets.

Open all wk Closed: 25 Dec, 1 Jan ⊕ ENTERPRISE INNS ◀ Skinners Kiddlywink, Shepherd Neame Spitfire, Courage Bass, Greene King Abbot Ale, Fuller's London Pride. ☕ 9

The Wig & Pen Inn

Frances St TR1 3DP
☎ 01872 273028 📄 01872 277351
dir: *City centre near Law Courts, 10 mins from railway station*

A listed city centre pub originally known as the Star, that became the Wig & Pen when the county court moved to Truro. There is a ghost called Claire who lives in the cellar, but she is friendly! The choice of food includes such home-made dishes as steak and ale pie, curry, casseroles, steaks and vegetarian dishes, and a range of fish options such as sea bass, John Dory, mullet or monkfish.

Open all wk ⊕ ST AUSTELL BREWERY ◀ St Austell, Tribute, IPA, HSD, guest ales. **Facilities** Dogs allowed Garden

The Royal Inn ★★★★ INN ☕

66 Eastcliffe Rd PL24 2AJ
☎ 01726 815601 📄 01726 816415
e-mail: info@royal-inn.co.uk
dir: *A3082 Par, follow brown tourist signs for 'Newquay Branch line' or railway station. Pub opp rail station*

Travellers and employees of the Great Western Railway once frequented this 19th-century inn, which was named after a visit by King Edward VII to a local copper mine. These days it's much extended and smartly refurbished, with food and drink offerings that support Cornwall's micro-breweries and food producers. The open-plan bar with large log fire is a great place for, say, simple trio of local pork sausages and mash, while the restaurant and conservatory might offer creamy mushroom and tarragon chicken. There are 15 bedrooms available.

Open all day all wk 11.30am-11pm (Sun 12-10.30) **Bar Meals** L served all wk 12-2 D served Mon-Sat 6.30-9, Sun 7-9 **Restaurant** L served all wk 12-2 D served Mon-Sat 6.30-9, Sun 7-9 booking required ⊕ FREE HOUSE ◀ Sharp's Doom Bar & Special Ale, Wells Bombardier, Shepherd Neame Spitfire, Cotleigh Barn Owl Ŏ Cornish Rattler. ☕ 11 **Facilities** Children's menu Dogs allowed Garden Parking Rooms 15

The New Inn ☕

TR2 5QA ☎ 01872 501362 📄 01872 501078
e-mail: jack@newinn-veryan.fsnet.co.uk
dir: *From St Austell take A390 towards Truro, in 2m left to Tregony. Through Tregony, follow signs to Veryan*

Based in a pair of 16th-century cottages, this unspoilt pub is found in the centre of a pretty village on the Roseland Peninsula. It has a single bar, open fires and a beamed ceiling, and the emphasis is on good ales and home cooking. Simple, satisfying dishes abound, with seafood featuring heavily: expect pan-fried bass fillet and Dover sole grilled on the bone, plus jumbo rump steak or a special like Louisiana jambalaya.

Open all wk ⊕ ST AUSTELL BREWERY ◀ St Austell HSD, Dartmoor Ale & Tribute. ☕ 8 **Facilities** Garden

PICK OF THE PUBS

The Mill House Inn ♥

TREBARWITH   Map 2 SX08

PL34 0HD
☎ 01840 770200   📄 01840 770647
e-mail:
management@themillhouseinn.co.uk
web: www.themillhouseinn.co.uk
dir: *From Tintagel take B3263 S, right after Trewarmett to Trebarwith Strand. Pub 0.5m on right*

Originally known as Treknow Mill, the building dates from 1760 and was still working in the late 1930s. It then became successively a private house, a guest house and finally, in 1960, a public house. Set in seven acres of wooded gardens on the north Cornish coast, this beautifully atmospheric stone building has log fires in the residents' lounge and Delabole slate-floored bar, where wooden tables and chapel chairs give off a relaxed, family-friendly feel. Lunches, evening drinks and barbecues can be enjoyed outside on the attractive split-level terraces, while dinner in the restaurant over the millstream is a particular treat. Sharp's Doom Bar and other local ales and an unusual and creative wine list complement the regularly changing lunch menus, all featuring the best local fresh fish, meat and other produce. At lunchtime, traditional pub favourites, such as sausages and mash, or battered haddock and chips, appear alongside less 'comfort foody' dishes, such as Tuscan bean cassoulet with dressed leaves, Parmesan and ciabatta. In the restaurant, a typical meal might be lobster and sea trout terrine with light herb salad and asparagus cream; then honey-glazed Tintagel duck breast with fondant potatoes and roasted carrot and maple purée; and to finish chocolate and orange cheesecake with mint ice cream. Live music is popular on either Friday or Saturday nights every week. Dotted around the surrounding area are surfing beaches and numerous tourist attractions, including Tintagel Castle, which the legendary King Arthur had the decency and foresight to build in the very next valley.

Open all week 11-11 (Fri-Sat 11am-mdnt) (Sun noon-10.30) Closed: 25 Dec **Bar Meals** L served Mon-Sat 12-2.30, Sun 12-3 D served all week 6.30-8.30 **Restaurant** D served all week 6.30-9 ⊕ FREE HOUSE 🛢 Sharp's Doom Bar, Red Stripe, Skinners Cornish Knocker ♂ Inch's Stonehouse, Stowford Press. ♥ 7 **Facilities** Children's menu Play area Family room Dogs allowed Garden Parking

PICK OF THE PUBS

The Springer Spaniel ♟

TREBURLEY Map 3 SX37

PL15 9NS ☎ 01579 370424
e-mail: enquiries@thespringerspaniel.org.uk
web: www.thespringerspaniel.org.uk
dir: *On A388 halfway between Launceston & Callington*

Reputedly a pub for the last 200 years, with old creeper-clad walls concealing a cosy bar with high-backed wooden settles, farmhouse-style chairs, and a wood-burning stove. The atmosphere is friendly, and there's bound to be a local willing to reveal an interesting nugget or two about the area. This is a pub that seeks to bring the best that a traditional Cornish hostelry can offer - delectable ales, delicious food, fine wines and tip-top service. You can bring your dog, join in with the chat or read the papers, or cast an eye over the many books in the snug. Children are always welcome, and will have fun with the 'Little Jack Russell' menu which serves up chicken goujons; sausages, chips and beans; and fresh penne bolognaise. The restaurant is full of plants and flowers, with flickering candles in the evenings adding to the romantic atmosphere. In summer the small and sheltered garden is a great place to relax and enjoy the sunshine with a pint of Skinners. The fully stocked bar also includes other award-winning local brews and guest ales, as well as a wine list designed to suit the food on offer, and an eclectic range of spirits and liqueurs. Food is a big draw here, with daily-changing blackboards displaying the best of fresh and seasonal produce. Imaginative menus feature fresh fish and seafood from Cornish waters, meat and game from local farmers and estates, with organic beef and lamb from the pub owner's own farm. Seared scallops are always a wonderful summer treat, while dishes of rabbit, venison and boar represent 'wild food' at its best. Try a ciabatta filled with meltingly tender steak, or an organic beefburger and Springer chips.

Open noon-2.30 6-10.30 **Bar Meals** L served all wk 12-1.45 D served all wk 6.15-8.45 Av main course £8.95 **Restaurant** L served all wk 12-1.45 D served all wk 6.15-8.45 Av 3 course à la carte fr £22 ⊕ FREE HOUSE ◗ Sharp's Doom Bar, Skinner's Betty Stogs, St Austell Tribute, guest ale ♂ Rattler, Cornish Orchard's Black & Gold. ♟ 7 **Facilities** Children's menu Family room Dogs allowed Garden Parking

WADEBRIDGE
Map 2 SW97

The Quarryman Inn

Edmonton PL27 7JA ☎ **01208 816444**
dir: *Off A39 opposite Royal Cornwall Showground*

Close to the famous Camel Trail, this friendly 18th-century free house has evolved from a courtyard of cottages once home to slate workers from the nearby quarry. Several bow windows, one of which features a stained-glass quarryman panel, add character to this unusual inn. Expect the likes of creamy garlic mushrooms and slow-braised leg of moorland lamb; puddings are on the blackboard. The first Tuesday night of the month features curries made to authentic recipes.

Open all day all wk noon–11pm **Bar Meals** L served all wk 12-2.30 booking required D served all wk 6-9 booking required ⊕ FREE HOUSE ◖ Sharp's, Skinners, Timothy Taylor Landlord, guest ales. **Facilities** Children's menu Dogs allowed Garden Parking

Swan ☻

9 Molesworth St PL27 7DD
☎ **01208 812526** 📠 **01208 812526**
e-mail: reservations@smallandfriendly.co.uk
dir: *In centre of Wadebridge on corner of Molesworth St & The Platt*

A town centre hotel that is family friendly, it was originally called the Commercial Hotel, and sits alongside the Camel Trail. Typical pub food includes doorstep sandwiches and baguettes, light snacks like cheesy chips, salads, chargrill dishes, full Cornish breakfast and main courses like Tribute beer-battered cod, or curry of the day. Children's dishes include chicken nuggets made of 100% chicken breast; pizza or pork sausage.

Open all wk ⊕ ST AUSTELL BREWERY ◖ HSD, Tribute, Guinness. ☻ 13 **Facilities** Family room Dogs allowed Garden

WIDEMOUTH BAY
Map 2 SS20

Bay View Inn ☻

EX23 0AW ☎ **01288 361273** 📠 **01288 361145**
e-mail: thebayviewinn@aol.com
dir: *On Marine Drive adjacent to beach in Widemouth Bay*

As its name implies, this pub has wonderful views of the rolling Atlantic from its restaurant and the large raised decking area outside. About a hundred years old, it was a guest house for many years before becoming an inn in the 1960s. The menu makes excellent use of Cornish produce, including fresh fish (perhaps in Betty Stogs beer batter) and signature dish of fillet steak with spinach, porcini mushroom pâté, pancetta and a red wine reduction.

Open all day all wk **Bar Meals** L served Mon-Sat 12-2.30, Sun 12-8 D served Mon-Sat 6-9, Sun 12-8 food served all day **Restaurant** L served Mon-Sat 12-2.30, Sun 12-8 D served Mon-Sat 6-9, Sun 12-8 ⊕ FREE HOUSE ◖ Sharp's Doom Bar & Own, Skinner's Betty Stogs. ☻ 17 **Facilities** Children's menu Play area Dogs allowed Garden Parking

ZENNOR
Map 2 SW43

PICK OF THE PUBS

The Gurnards Head ★★★ INN ⊛⊛ ☻

Treen TR26 3DE ☎ **01736 796928**
e-mail: enquiries@gurnardshead.co.uk
dir: *5m from Penzance. 5m from St Ives on B3306*

An imposing, colour-washed building dominating the coast above Gurnard's Head, this restaurant and pub with rooms is just the place to stay on a windswept night, when Cornwall is at its most brutal. When the weather's good (which it often is) the coastal path and rugged Penwith Moors walks are fantastic. The bar has old tables and chairs, rugs on a stone floor, log fires, and loads of books; the snug leads to the simply furnished, candlelit restaurant. Here, venison carpaccio with horseradish, beetroot and spring cream; and brill, fennel and tomato stew are typical starters, while frequently appearing as main courses are stuffed pork loin with sage gnocchi, carrots and purple sprouting broccoli; mackerel with chorizo, Puy lentils and rocket; and butternut squash with spinach, sage and walnut risotto. Skinner's Press Gang cider accompanies the same brewery's Betty Stogs and Ginger Tosser real ales at the bar.

Open all wk Closed: 24-25 Dec, 4 days mid Jan **Bar Meals** L served all wk 12.30-2.30 booking required D served all wk 6.30-9.30 booking required Av main course £11.50 **Restaurant** L served all wk 12.30-2.30 booking required D served all wk 6.30-9.30 booking required Av 3 course à la carte fr £19.50 ⊕ FREE HOUSE ◖ Betty Stogs, Tribute, Ginger Tosser ☻ Skinner's Press Gang. ☻ 8 **Facilities** Children's menu Dogs allowed Garden Parking **Rooms** 7

The Tinners Arms ☻

TR26 3BY ☎ **01736 796927**
e-mail: tinners@tinnersarms.com
dir: *Take B3306 from St Ives towards St Just. Zennor approx 5m*

The only pub in the village, this 13th-century, granite-built free house is close to the South West coastal path and is particularly popular with walkers. It has changed very little over the years, with its stone floors and low ceilings. The main bar has open fires at both ends and outside there is a large terrace with sea views. A sample menu features sirloin steak, chicken pie, slow-cooked duck leg, and butternut squash risotto. For a lighter bite enjoy a fresh Newlyn crab sandwich.

Open all wk **Bar Meals** L served all wk 12-2 D served all wk 6.30-9 ⊕ FREE HOUSE ◖ Zennor Mermaid, Tinners Ale, Sharps Own ☻ Burrow Hill. ☻ 12 **Facilities** Children's menu Family room Dogs allowed Garden Parking

CUMBRIA

AMBLESIDE
Map 18 NY30

PICK OF THE PUBS

Drunken Duck
Inn ★★★★★ INN ⊛⊛ ☻

See Pick of the Pubs on page 94

Wateredge Inn ★★★★ INN ☻

Waterhead Bay LA22 0EP
☎ **015394 32332** 📠 **015394 31878**
e-mail: stay@wateredgeinn.co.uk
dir: *M6 junct 36, A591 to Ambleside, 5m from Windermere station*

The inn's name sums up its idyllic position on the banks of Lake Windermere, with Ambleside just a short stroll away. Run by the same family for over 25 years, the inn was originally developed from two 17th-century fishermen's cottages. Real ales and 14 wines by the glass can be sipped whilst appreciating the spectacular views from the heated lakeside patio. On the bar and bistro menu, choose from classic pub fare augmented by some gastro dishes. There are pretty, spacious bedrooms available.

Open all wk ⊕ FREE HOUSE ◖ Black Sheep, Coniston Bluebird, Colly Wobbles, Tag Lag, Cat Nap. ☻ 13 **Facilities** Dogs allowed Garden Parking **Rooms** 22

PICK OF THE PUBS

Drunken Duck Inn ★★★★★ INN ◉◉ ♍

AMBLESIDE   Map 18 NY30

Barngates LA22 0NG
☎ **015394 36347** 📠 **015394 36781**
e-mail: info@drunkenduckinn.co.uk
web: www.drunkenduckinn.co.uk
dir: *From Kendal on A591 to Ambleside, then follow Hawkshead sign. In 2.5m inn sign on right, 1m up hill*

There are fabulous views towards Lake Windermere from this 17th-century inn which stands in splendid isolation in glorious Lakeland countryside between Ambleside and Hawkshead, just a short drive from the local beauty spot of Tarn Hows. In the same ownership for over three decades and constantly evolving with modern-day expectations, the traditional whitewashed inn continues to offer good service, excellent food and drink, comfortable accommodation, and a friendly, relaxed atmosphere. The amusing name stems from a flock of comatose ducks found by a former landlady. Thinking of her guests' stomachs, she began to pluck them for the pot, unaware that they were not dead but merely legless from drinking beer that had leaked into their feed. No such risk today - the adjoining Barngates Brewery takes good care of its award-winning real ales, which are served in the oak-floored and beamed bar, with open fire, numerous pictures, leather club chairs and beautiful Brathay Black slate bar top from the local quarry. Excellent locally sourced food is served in three informal restaurant areas, from lunchtime dishes like braised beef and dumplings; lamb hotpot with pickled red cabbage; confit duck leg with bean casserole; and rare roast beef and horseradish sandwiches (walkers can take these away), to more imaginative evening meals like roast partridge with spiced cabbage and pan jus, duck breast with confit garlic risotto and duck jus, and roast halibut with red wine reduction. Desserts are equally tempting: steamed marmalade sponge pudding with clotted cream and vanilla sauce. Each of the seventeen bedrooms comes complete with antique furniture, prints and designer fabrics. After an invigorating walk there's nothing better than relaxing on the front verandah with a pint of Cracker Ale and soaking up at view to Lake Windermere.

Open all week Closed: 25 Dec **Bar Meals** L served all week 12-4 Av main course £20 **Restaurant** D served all week 6-9.30 Av 3 course à la carte fr £40 ⊕ FREE HOUSE ◂ Barngates Cracker Ale, Chesters Strong & Ugly, Tag Lag, Catnap, Mothbag, 1 guest ale. ♍ 20 **Facilities** Children's menu Garden Parking **Rooms** 17

The Royal Oak ♥

Bongate CA16 6UN ☎ 017683 51463 📠 017683 52300
e-mail: jan@royaloakappleby.co.uk
dir: M6 junct 38 take B6260 to Appleby-in-Westmorland

An inn with a long and venerable history, with parts dating back to 1100 and the rest to the 17th century. Today, a classic dog-friendly tap-room with blackened beams, an oak-panelled lounge with open fire, and a comfortable restaurant have been sympathetically modernised to serve real ales and fresh local food at reasonable prices. Settle down with a bowl of appetising olives while choosing from home-made soups, pastas, curries and blackboard specials. Excellent Sunday roasts and children's menu.

Open all wk ⊕ FREE HOUSE ◀ Hawkshead, Black Sheep, Timothy Taylor. ♥ 8 **Facilities** Dogs allowed Garden Parking

PICK OF THE PUBS

Tufton Arms Hotel ♥

Market Square CA16 6XA
☎ 017683 51593 📠 017683 52761
e-mail: info@tuftonarmshotel.co.uk
dir: In town centre

Appleby-in-Westmorland is a medieval market town nestling in the heart of a valley so magically unspoilt that the only possible name for it is Eden. The Milsom family have lovingly restored the Tufton Arms to its former Victorian splendour with rich drapes, period paintings and antique furniture. The elegant conservatory restaurant overlooks a cobbled mews courtyard; light and airy in the daytime, this room takes on an attractive glow in the evening when the curtains are closed and the lighting is low. Chef David Milsom and his kitchen team have won many accolades for their superb food, which comprises a selection of delicious dishes made from the finest and freshest local ingredients. Typical starters include creamy garlic mushrooms or a platter of oak-smoked salmon. Move on to roast rack of Eden Valley lamb; loin of pork chop; or baked cod steak. Round off with home-made lemon cheesecake or brandy snap basket filled with chocolate mousse.

Open all day all wk 7am-11pm Closed: 25-26 Dec **Bar Meals** L served all wk 12-2 D served all wk 6.30-9 **Restaurant** L served all wk 12-2 D served all wk 6.30-9 ⊕ FREE HOUSE ◀ Tufton Arms Ale, Flowers IPA, Tennants. ♥ 15 **Facilities** Children's menu Dogs allowed Parking

The Dukes Head Inn ★★★ INN ♥

Front St CA4 9PB ☎ 016974 72226
e-mail: info@dukeshead-hotel.co.uk
dir: 9m from Penrith, 10m from Carlisle between junct 41 & 42 of M6

Originally a farm, this pub was licensed during the construction of the Settle to Carlisle railway. Set in the pretty red sandstone village of Armathwaite, it has been proudly run by the Lynch family for over 21 years. The River Eden runs through the village and provides wonderful walks along its banks and up into the woods beyond. Re-fuel with hot steak sandwich or a starter of home-made salmon and haddock fishcake followed by venison, pheasant and rabbit hotpot with home-pickled cabbage. Look out for the many special events and offers. There are five comfortable bedrooms available.

Open all wk 11.30-11.30 Closed: 25 Dec **Bar Meals** L served Mon-Sat 12-2, Sun 12-2.30 D served all wk 6.30-9 **Restaurant** L served Mon-Sat 12-2, Sun 12-2.30 D served all wk 6.30-9 ⊕ PUNCH TAVERNS ◀ Jennings Cumberland Ale, Black Sheep Bitter, Deuchars IPA, Black Cat Mild ♂ Aspall's Premier Cru, Westons, Thatchers. ♥ 6 **Facilities** Children's menu Dogs allowed Garden Parking **Rooms** 5

Mardale Inn

CA10 2RQ ☎ 01931 713244
e-mail: info@mardaleinn.co.uk
dir: Telephone for directions

A whitewashed, early 18th-century inn situated in one of the most rural parts of the Lake District, perfect for walking, biking and fishing. The interior is a refreshing mix of rural beams and rustic furniture and more modern colours and design. A sample dinner menu may include lamb burger, aubergine stuffed with goats' cheese, or trio of local sausage with creamy chive mash. Dogs are welcome in all public areas, and fans of cult movie, Withnail and I, will find plenty of the film's locations in the area.

Open all wk 11-11 **Bar Meals** Av main course £9.50 food served all day ⊕ FREE HOUSE ◀ Coniston Bluebird, Timothy Taylors Landlord, Hesket Newmarket Scafell Blonde, Dent Aviator. **Facilities** Children's menu Dogs allowed Parking

The Barbon Inn ♥

LA6 2LJ ☎ 015242 76233 📠 051242 76574
e-mail: info@barbon-inn.co.uk
dir: 3.5m N of Kirkby Lonsdale on A683

A 17th-century coaching inn with oak beams and open fires, the Barbon is situated in a quiet village between the lakes and dales. Pockmarks in a settle tell of a 19th-century shooting, and there's also a tale of a hanged highwayman. A good choice of wines and real ales is offered alongside dishes like Morecambe Bay potted shrimps and roast fillet of pork with Marsala sauce and apricot compote. Special diets are happily catered for.

Open all wk Closed: 25 Dec ⊕ FREE HOUSE ◀ Theakston, Barngates Westmorland Gold, Speckled Hen, York Brewery, Dent, Tirril. ♥ 20 **Facilities** Dogs allowed Garden Parking

PICK OF THE PUBS

The Pheasant ★★★ HL ⚬ ♥

See Pick of the Pubs on page 96

PICK OF THE PUBS

The Wheatsheaf at Beetham ♥

LA7 7AL ☎ 015395 62123 📠 015395 64840
e-mail: info@wheatsheafbeetham.com
dir: On A6 5m N of junct 35

This 16th-century former coaching inn, now a freehouse, stands in the village centre, close to the little River Bela. Fallow deer wander neighbouring fields, and thousands of pheasants are reared locally every year. A small bar services the dining areas, all decorated with fresh flowers and illuminated with candles in the evening. Well-behaved children may eat from their own menu in a small upstairs room before 7pm. As far as possible, seasonal menus use the freshest and finest local produce. Lunchtime light meals include hot and cold sandwiches, salads such as warm black pudding and smoked bacon, and larger plates of Cumberland sausage and mash or steak and ale pie. Sample dishes from the carte include Forest of Bowland ham hock terrine to start, Fleetwood fisherman's pie to follow, and Sandra's sticky toffee pudding to finish. The reasonably priced wine list mixes classic European with New World offerings, and a dozen are served by the glass.

Open all day all wk noon-11pm Closed: 25 Dec **Bar Meals** L served Mon-Sat 12-9, Sun 12-8.30 D served Mon-Sat 12-9, Sun 12-8.30 food served all day ⊕ FREE HOUSE ◀ Jennings Cumberland Ale, Yates. ♥ 12 **Facilities** Garden Parking

PICK OF THE PUBS

The Pheasant ★★★ HL ❀ ♜

BASSENTHWAITE Map 18 NY23

CA13 9YE
☎ 017687 76234 🖷 017687 76002
e-mail: info@the-pheasant.co.uk
web: www.the-pheasant.co.uk
dir: *A66 to Cockermouth, 8m N of Keswick on left*

First a farmhouse, then a coaching inn, this Lake District favourite surrounded by lovely gardens dates back some 500 years. Today it enjoys an international reputation as a traditional Cumbrian hostelry with all the benefits of a comfortable modern hotel. You sense the history the moment you walk through the door - huntsman John Peel, his 'coat so gay' immortalised in song, was a regular (actually, his coat was probably grey, the colour of local Herdwick sheep wool), and the Cumbrian painter Edward H Thompson, who died in 1949, bartered his works for beer in the pub. Two of his originals hang in the bar, a richly inviting area with polished parquet flooring, panelled walls and oak settles. Cast your eyes over the extensive selection of malt whiskies. The high standard of food is well known within a wide catchment area, and meals are served in the attractive beamed dining room, bar and lounges overlooking the gardens. Light lunches include open sandwiches, ploughman's, seafood platters and cottage pie, while a three-course dinner could feature spiced fillet of monkfish with chorizo chips, apple and citrus salad and tarragon oil; followed by seared rack of Lakeland lamb with compote of tomato, aubergine and olives, parsley potato and fresh mint oil; and finally, baked egg custard with nutmeg ice cream and fresh strawberries. Treat the family to afternoon tea with home-made scones and rum butter. A private dining room is available for small parties, and there are individually decorated bedrooms with attractive fabrics, fine antique pieces and impressive en suite bathrooms.

Open all week Closed: 25 Dec ⊕ FREE HOUSE ◀ Theakston Best, Interbrew Bass, Jennings Cumberland Ale. ♜ 12 **Facilities** Dogs allowed Garden Parking **Rooms** 15

BLENCOGO
Map 18 NY14

The New Inn ⬤

CA7 0BZ ☎ 016973 61091 📄 016973 61091
dir: *From Carlisle take A596 towards Wigton, then B5302 towards Silloth. After 4m Blencogo signed on left*

This late Victorian sandstone pub has superb views of the north Cumbrian fells and Solway Plain. It is located in a farming hamlet, and the impressive menu makes good use of produce from the region - perhaps chargrilled tenderloin of pork topped with apricot and herb crust; fresh salmon served with hollandaise sauce and asparagus; or yellow-fin tuna with mild curried mango and Armagnac sauce. A selection of malt whiskies is kept.

Closed: 1st 2wks Jan, Mon-Wed **Bar Meals** Av main course £15 **Restaurant** L served Sun 12-2 booking required D served Thu-Sun 6.30-9 booking required Fixed menu price fr £18.50 Av 3 course à la carte fr £26 ⊕ FREE HOUSE ◂ Yates, Carlisle State Bitter, Hesket Newmarket, Black Sheep. ⬤ 10 **Facilities** Children's menu Garden Parking

BOOT
Map 18 NY10

PICK OF THE PUBS

The Boot Inn
See Pick of the Pubs on page 98

PICK OF THE PUBS

Brook House Inn ★★★★ INN ⬤
See Pick of the Pubs on page 99

BORROWDALE
Map 18 NY21

The Langstrath Country Inn ⬤

CA12 5XG ☎ 017687 77239
e-mail: info@thelangstrath.com
dir: *B5289 past Grange, through Rosthwaite, left to Stonethwaite. Inn on left after 1m*

Refurbishments over the years at this 16th-century, family-run inn, include the addition of a restaurant with spectacular views up the Langstrath valley. A meal here could start with Cumbrian cheese soufflé or smoked Borrowdale trout and avocado salad; continue with Goosnargh chicken breast on olive oil mash or Cumbrian sirloin steak; and wind up with some delicious sticky toffee pudding. The bar offers decent ales and an extensive wine list. Set on the coast-to-coast and Cumbrian Way walks, this is an ideal spot for hikers.

Open noon-10.30 Closed: Dec-Jan, Mon **Bar Meals** L served Tue-Sun 12-2.30 D served Tue-Sun 6-9 Av main course £12 **Restaurant** L served Tue-Sun 12-2.30 D served Tue-Sun 6-9 Av 3 course à la carte fr £21 ⊕ FREE HOUSE ◂ Jennings Bitter, Black Sheep, Hawkshead Bitter, Cocker Hoop ○ Thatchers Gold. ⬤ 8 **Facilities** Children's menu Garden Parking

BOUTH
Map 18 SD38

The White Hart Inn ⬤

LA12 8JB ☎ 01229 861229 📄 01229 861836
e-mail: nigelwhitehart@aol.com
dir: *1.5m from A590. 10m from M6 junct 36*

Bouth today reposes quietly in the Lake District National Park, although once it housed an occasionally noisy gunpowder factory. When this closed in 1928 villagers turned to woodland industries and farm labouring instead, and some of their tools now adorn this 17th-century coaching inn. Ever-changing specials are served in the upstairs restaurant that looks out over woods, fields and fells, or the horseshoe-shaped bar.

Open all day all wk noon-11 (Sun noon-10.30) **Bar Meals** L served Mon-Fri 12-2 booking required D served all wk 6-8.45 booking required **Restaurant** L served Mon-Fri 12-2 booking required D served all wk 6-8.45 booking required ⊕ FREE HOUSE ◂ Black Sheep Best, Jennings Cumberland Ale, Coniston Bluebird, Ulverston. ⬤ 7 **Facilities** Children's menu Dogs allowed Garden Parking

BOWLAND BRIDGE
Map 18 SD48

PICK OF THE PUBS

Hare & Hounds Country Inn ⬤

LA11 6NN ☎ 015395 68333 📄 015395 68777
dir: *M6 onto A591, left after 3m onto A590, right after 3m onto A5074, after 4m sharp left & next left after 1m*

This 17th-century coaching inn is set in the pretty little hamlet of Bowland Bridge, not far from Bowness. A traditional country pub atmosphere is fostered by the flagstone floors, exposed oak beams, ancient pews warmed by open fires, and cosy niches. The bar menu offers local Cumberland sausage with egg and chips; toasted muffin with smoked haddock; confit of duck; and king prawns in filo pastry. The seasonal main menu could offer asparagus and saffron risotto; and smoked salmon and prawn roulade as starters, followed by butternut squash, spinach and mozzarella strudel; fresh cod in batter with home-made chips; or steak and ale pie. There is also a specials board with fresh fish and game always available. A safe garden with play area and swings for the children makes this pub particularly family friendly, and there are gorgeous views all round, especially of Cartmel Fell.

Open all day all wk 11am-11pm **Bar Meals** L served 12-9 D served 12-9 food served all day ⊕ JENNINGS ◂ Jennings, Marstons Pedigree, Cumberland Ale, guest beers. ⬤ 10 **Facilities** Play area Family room Garden Parking

BRAITHWAITE
Map 18 NY22

Coledale Inn

CA12 5TN ☎ 017687 78272 📄 017687 78272
e-mail: info@coledale-inn.co.uk
dir: *M6 junct 50, A66 towards Cockermouth for 18m. Turn to Braithwaite then towards Whinlatter Pass. Follow sign on left, over bridge to Inn*

Set in a peaceful spot above Braithwaite village, this inn is ideal for exploring the footpaths that begin nearby. The building started life as a woollen mill in the 1820s, and is full of attractive Victorian prints, furnishings and antiques. Home-made meals, such as Cumberland sausage with mash or home-made steak and kidney pie, are backed by an impressive wine list. Don't expect an explanation of the strange-shaped tree in the garden, because no-one knows.

Open all day all wk 11-11 **Bar Meals** L served all wk 12-2 D served all wk 6-9 Av main course £8.95 ⊕ FREE HOUSE ◂ Yates, Theakstons, Jennings Best, John Smiths. **Facilities** Children's menu Play area Dogs allowed Garden Parking

The Royal Oak ★★★★ INN ⬤

CA12 5SY ☎ 017687 78533 📄 017687 78533
e-mail: tpfranks@hotmail.com
dir: *Exit M6 junct 40, A66 to Keswick, 20m. Bypass Keswick & Portinscale juncts, take next left, pub in village centre*

The Royal Oak is set in the centre of Braithwaite village in a walkers' paradise surrounded by high fells and beautiful scenery. The interior is all oak beams and log fires, and the menu offers hearty pub food in the bar area or restaurant, served alongside local ales, such as Jennings Lakeland or Cocker Hoop. Visitors can extend the experience by staying over in the comfortable en suite bedrooms, some with four-poster beds.

Open all wk **Bar Meals** L served all wk 12-2 D served all wk 6-9 Av main course £9 **Restaurant** L served all wk 12-2 D served all wk 6-9 ⊕ MARSTONS ◂ Jennings Lakeland Ale, Cumberland Ale, Cocker Hoop, Sneck Lifter. ⬤ 8 **Facilities** Children's menu Dogs allowed Garden Parking **Rooms** 10

PICK OF THE PUBS

The Boot Inn

BOOT Map 18 NY10

CA19 1TG
☎ 019467 23224 📠 019467 23337
e-mail: enquiries@bootinn.co.uk
web: www.bootinn.co.uk
dir: *From A595 follow signs for Eskdale then Boot*

The Boot takes its name from the pretty pink granite village in which it sits, which also boasts England's oldest working watermill. But the name becomes especially apt when you consider the glorious green and russet peaks that rise up on every side. This is some of England's finest walking country, and the award-winning, delightfully traditional Boot Inn sits slap bang in the middle of it. A beck wends its way through the valley, crossed by a 17th-century packhorse bridge. Scafell Pike (England's highest mountain) and Wastwater (England's deepest lake) are within rambling distance and, naturally enough, the pub attracts many cold and hungry climbers. Fortunately there's a roaring fire on cooler days, and plenty of hearty home-made dishes to restore them. The beamed Burnmoor Room restaurant dates back to 1578, but there's also a modern conservatory with spectacular views and an eating area in the bar by the fire. A fourth option is the beer garden, which has two children's play areas, where you can enjoy a pint of Dizzy Blonde or Dark Hatters. Tempting sandwiches, jacket potatoes and ploughman's platters (ham or cheese) on the lunch menu are supported by hearty options such as Cumberland sausage with home-made chips or great home-made pies. Local produce is taken seriously here, with lamb, beef, eggs, cheese and sausages all coming from nearby suppliers. In the evening the range broadens with starters of mozzarella and tomatoes or prawn cocktail; main courses such as home-made curry or gammon, chips and peas; and traditional puddings like fruit crumble or sticky toffee pudding. Children can opt for small versions of several dishes from the main menu, or for the likes of local sausages and chips. Dogs under control are welcome. Landlords Lesley and Francis Dantinnes have left, but their successors Lesley's son Sean King and his partner Caroline Friel are determined to maintain standards.

Open all week Closed: 25 Dec **Bar Meals** Av main course 7.95 **Restaurant** D served all wk 6-8.30 ⊕ ROBINSONS ◀ Double Hop, Unicorn, Dizzy Blonde, Dark Hatters ♻ Westons Stowford Press Organic. **Facilities** Children's menu Play area Family room Dogs allowed Garden Parking

PICK OF THE PUBS

Brook House Inn ★★★★ INN 🍷

BOOT   Map 18 NY10

CA19 1TG
☎ 019467 23288   📄 019467 23160
e-mail: stay@brookhouseinn.co.uk
dir: *M6 junct 36, A590 follow Barrow signs. A5092, then A595. Past Broughton-in-Furness then right at lights to Ulpha. Cross river, next left signed Eskdale, & on to Boot. (NB not all routes to Boot are suitable in bad weather conditions)*

The La'al Ratty steam railway terminates at Dalegarth station, just 200 metres from Brook House, and frequently disgorges visitors to this popular Eskdale inn. Run by two generations of the Thornley family, the business has grown enormously since they took over, attracting a wide-ranging clientele. Its position is superb, with glorious views and fabulous walking country all around, so the provision of a small drying room for wet walkers is greatly appreciated, as is accommodation for several bikes. Between three and seven real ales are

kept, including Hawkshead Bitter and Jennings Cumberland, and an amazing collection of 170 malt whiskies. Home-made food prepared from locally supplied fresh produce is available in the restaurant, bar and snug all day. These quality ingredients include fell-bred lamb, Cumberland cheeses, free-range eggs and home-smoked chicken, fish, cheese and garlic. Home-made chutney, biscuits, sauces and stocks are also a feature, not to mention the award-winning bread, which is used for the freshly prepared daytime sandwiches. There are two delightful dining rooms, the Scafell Restaurant and The Grainstore, with exposed granite walls, which is ideal for family parties. The dinner menu is the same throughout the inn, offering an evening of fine dining on fresh Islay scallops; brill with saffron sauce; sea bass with roasted red pepper and vine tomato salsa; local organic steaks; trio of lamb chops with Madeira and mushroom sauce; and Moroccan vegetable and bean casserole. Home-made desserts include meringues, 'real' cheese cake, and caramelised lemon tart with lime syrup. The tastefully furnished en suite bedrooms all have views of the surrounding fells.

Open all week Closed: 25 Dec **Restaurant** L served by arrangement D served 6-8.30 ⊕ FREE HOUSE ◀ Timothy Taylor Landlord, Hawkshead Bitter, Jennings Cumberland, Yates, guests ○ Westons Old Rosie, Westons Perry. 🍷 10 **Facilities** Garden Parking **Rooms** 7 (incl 2 fmly rms)

BRAMPTON
Map 21 NY56

Blacksmiths Arms ★★★★ INN ☕

Talkin Village CA8 1LE
☎ 016977 3452 📠 016977 3396
e-mail: blacksmithsarmstalkin@yahoo.co.uk
dir: *From M6 take A69 E, after 7m straight over rdbt, follow signs to Talkin Tarn then Talkin Village*

This attractive family-run village inn stands in some of northern Cumbria's most scenic countryside; the Borders, Hadrian's Wall and the Lakes are all close by. The original smithy, dating from 1700, remains part of inn along with the bar, restaurant and accommodation. Enjoy the warm hospitality and a pint of ale from Brampton Brewery, while choosing from the menus that range from bar snacks to full a la carte offerings. Dishes typically include lasagne, assorted pies, Cumberland sausages, and fresh local trout.

Open all wk noon-3 6-mdnt **Bar Meals** L served all wk 12-2 D served all wk 6-9 Av main course £9.95 **Restaurant** L served all wk 12-2 D served all wk 6-9 Av 3 course à la carte fr £15.95 ⊕ FREE HOUSE ◀ Yates, Brampton, Black Sheep. ☕ 20 **Facilities** Children's menu Garden Parking **Rooms** 8

BROUGHTON-IN-FURNESS
Map 18 SD28

PICK OF THE PUBS

Blacksmiths Arms ☕

See Pick of the Pubs on opposite page

The Old Kings Head NEW ★★★★ INN

Church St LA20 6HJ ☎ 01229 716293
e-mail: russell@clar7jw.freeserve.co.uk
dir: *Telephone for directions*

With a history spanning 400 years, the spick-and-span former coaching inn is one of the oldest buildings in the town. Perfectly located for exploring the southern Lakes, the pub offers comfortable en suite rooms and freshly prepared food using local ingredients. Look to the chalkboard for daily fish specials, perhaps hot potted prawns, and whole bass with lemon and lime cream, or tuck into winter lamb casserole, rack of lamb, or a classic steak and ale pie.

Open all wk noon-3 5-mdnt **Bar Meals** L served all wk 12-2 booking required D served all wk 5-9 booking required **Restaurant** L served all wk 12-2 booking

required D served all wk 5-9 booking required ⊕ ENTERPRISE INNS ◀ Beckstones, Black Sheep, IPA, Black Dog. **Facilities** Children's menu Play area Garden Parking **Rooms** 6

BUTTERMERE
Map 18 NY11

Bridge Hotel ★★★ CHH ☕

CA13 9UZ ☎ 017687 70252 📠 017687 70215
e-mail: enquiries@bridge-hotel.com
web: www.bridge-hotel.com
dir: *Take B5289 from Keswick*

An 18th-century former coaching inn set between Buttermere and Crummock Water in an outstandingly beautiful area, surrounded by the Buttermere Fells. There are wonderful walks right from the front door. Good food and real ales are served in the character bars (Cumberland sausage, rainbow trout or Scottish salmon), and a four-course dinner in the dining room - including, perhaps, roast Lakeland lamb with Cumberland sauce and crispy leeks, or venison braised with mushrooms and Old Peculier jus.

Open all day all wk 10.30am-11.30pm **Bar Meals** food served all day **Restaurant** D served all wk 6-8.30 Av 3 course à la carte fr £31.50 ⊕ FREE HOUSE ◀ Theakston's Old Peculier, Black Sheep Best, Buttermere Bitter, Boddingtons, Hawkshead Gold. ☕ 12 **Facilities** Children's menu Garden Parking **Rooms** 21

CALDBECK
Map 18 NY34

Oddfellows Arms

CA7 8EA ☎ 016974 78227 📠 016974 78056
dir: *Telephone for directions*

This 17th-century former coaching inn is set in a scenic conservation village in the northern fells. Popular with coast-to-coast cyclists and walkers on the Cumbrian Way, the Oddfellows serves Jennings Bitter and Cumberland Ale. Lunchtime snacks include jacket potatoes, sandwiches, or hot beef in a roll, whilst specials and vegetarian blackboards supplement the regular menu. Expect bacon chops with stilton; sirloin steaks; and local trout fillets. There's a daily curry, too.

Open all day all wk **Bar Meals** L served all wk 12-2 D served all wk 6.15-8.30 Av main course £8.50 **Restaurant** L served all wk 12-1.30 booking required D served all wk 6.15-8.30 booking required Av 3 course à la carte fr £15 ⊕ MARSTONS ◀ Jennings Bitter, Cumberland Ale. **Facilities** Children's menu Dogs allowed Garden Parking

CARTMEL
Map 18 SD37

PICK OF THE PUBS

The Cavendish Arms ☕

See Pick of the Pubs on page 102

COCKERMOUTH
Map 18 NY13

The Trout Hotel ★★★ HL ☕

Crown St CA13 0EJ ☎ 01900 823591 📠 01900 827514
e-mail: enquiries@trouthotel.co.uk

Overlooking the River Derwent, the Trout's well-appointed rooms make a good base for horse riding, cycling, fell walking, climbing and fishing trips. The patio of the Terrace Bar and Bistro, with its large heated parasols, offers al fresco dining any time of the year, while the Derwent Restaurant, dominated by a classic fireplace and ornate mirrored sideboard, offers daily changing menus featuring the best local produce, such as pheasant and pigeon breast, grilled sea bass, and mushroom risotto.

Open all wk ⊕ FREE HOUSE ◀ Jennings Cumberland Ale, Theakston Bitter, John Smiths, Marston's Pedigree, Courage Directors. ☕ 24 **Facilities** Garden Parking **Rooms** 49

CONISTON
Map 18 SD39

PICK OF THE PUBS

The Black Bull Inn & Hotel ☕

1 Yewdale Rd LA21 8DU
☎ 015394 41335 & 41668 📠 015394 41168
e-mail: i.s.bradley@btinternet.com
dir: *M6 junct 36, A590. 23m from Kendal via Windermere & Ambleside*

A cosy refuge in the heart of the Lake District, this 400-year-old coaching inn has been run by the same family for nearly 30 years. Set at the foot of the Old Man of Coniston mountain and adjacent to Coniston Water, it has welcomed some famous faces over the years, from Coleridge and Turner to Anthony Hopkins. Back in the 1990s the owners' son started a micro-brewery behind the inn, which has gone from strength to strength; the award-winning real ales are not only sold behind the bar, but shipped out to 30 neighbouring hostelries. There is also a good range of real ciders available. For hungry ramblers calling in at lunchtime, there is an excellent and unfussy range of snacks including toasted sandwiches, soups and jacket potatoes. Alternatively, the restaurant menu runs from hearty winter warmers such as a bowl of home-made chilli through to a salad of local Esthwaite trout fillets - perfect on a summer's day.

Open all wk Closed: 25 Dec **Bar Meals** food served all day **Restaurant** D served all wk 6-9 booking required ⊕ FREE HOUSE ◀ Coniston Bluebird, Old Man Ale, Opium, Blacksmith, XB, Oatmeal Stout. ☕ 10 **Facilities** Children's menu Family room Dogs allowed Garden Parking

PICK OF THE PUBS

Blacksmiths Arms ♟

BROUGHTON-IN-FURNESS Map 18 SD28

Broughton Mills LA20 6AX
☎ **01229 716824**
e-mail: blacksmithsarms@aol.com
web: www.theblacksmithsarms.com
dir: *A593 from Broughton-in-Furness towards Coniston, in 1.5m left signed Broughton Mills, pub 1m on left*

Set in a secluded South Lakeland valley, this quaint whitewashed cottage dates back to 1577 and was originally a farmhouse called Broadstones. It was an ale-house serving beer to travellers and local farmers from the kitchen and in 1748 it was recorded as being an inn, working farm with 34 acres and a blacksmiths. The original four-room interior has been beautifully preserved and oozes charm and character, each with glowing winter log fires, with one in the old farmhouse range, oak-panelled corridors, worn slate floors sourced from local quarries, and low beams. Gaslights in the dining room and bar still work when the electricity fails and, in time-honoured fashion, there are classic pub games like dominoes, cribbage and board games to while away a few hours with a cracking pint of local ale – Jennings Cumberland, Dent Aviator and Hawkshead Bitter are tapped from the cask. Michael and Sophie Lane took over in 2004 and love it here, and it shows, so expect a warm welcome, which extends to children and dogs. Interesting, freshly cooked food makes good use of local produce from quality Cumbrian suppliers. You will often find Herdwick lamb, which is reared in the Lickle Valley, on the menu, along with traditional steak pie in suet pastry made from local beef. Dishes might include Morecambe Bay potted shrimps; Cajun chicken salad; a choice of sandwiches or baguettes or a ploughman's at lunch. The dinner menu offers main courses like oven-baked Cumberland sausage served with creamy chive mash and red onion gravy; pheasant wrapped in pancetta with parsnip mash; or deep-fried cod or haddock with Cumberland beer batter, chips and mushy peas. There's a sheltered, flower-filled front patio garden for summer alfresco eating and drinking. Miles of glorious walks radiate from the front door.

Open all week Closed: 25 Dec
Restaurant ⊕ FREE HOUSE 🛢 Jennings Cumberland Ale, Dent Aviator, Barngates Tag Lag, Moorhouses Pride of Pendle, Hawkshead Bitter. ♟ 7
Facilities Dogs allowed Garden Parking

PICK OF THE PUBS

The Cavendish Arms ♀

CARTMEL   Map 18 SD37

LA11 6QA
☎ **015395 36240**   📄 **015395 35082**
e-mail: food@thecavendisharms.co.uk
dir: *M6 junct 36, A590 signed Barrow-in-Furness. Cartmel signed. In village take 1st right*

Situated within the village walls, this 450-year-old coaching inn is Cartmel's longest-surviving hostelry. Many traces of its history remain, from the mounting block outside the main door to the bar itself, which used to be the stables. Oak beams, uneven floors and an open fire create a traditional, cosy atmosphere, and outside a stream flows past a tree-lined garden. The food, from the lunchtime sandwiches to the cheeses served at the end of dinner, owes much to its local origins (and, of course, to the skilled kitchen team). The sandwiches include egg and fresh watercress; topside of beef with sliced red onion; and roast ham with orange and thyme marmalade; all use locally-baked bread and come with a portion of chips. Other lunch options include Morecambe Bay shrimps with herb butter; toasted brie and bacon ciabatta; and Mediterranean vegetable and goats' cheese crostini. Enjoy your meal with a pint of traditional beer or ale. In the evening might begin your meal with locally smoked duck breast and raspberry vinaigrette, or tiger prawn piri-piri with garlic and chilli oil. Then move on to Cumbrian rib-eye steak with field mushrooms, beef tomato and French onion rings; supreme of guinea fowl with braised fennel and orange; pan-fried fillet of hake with lemon and chive sauce; or oven-baked sweet potato with curried vegetables. Desserts include rhubarb crumble, pecan pie and various Lakeland ice creams. The owners have teamed up with a local company that offers carriage tours of the village. This popular area is ideal for walking, horse riding, visiting Cartmel races, Lake Windermere and car museum.

Open all week ⊕ FREE HOUSE ◖ Greene King IPA, Cumberland, Bombardier, Theakstons. ♀ 8 **Facilities** Dogs allowed Garden Parking

CONISTON *continued*

PICK OF THE PUBS

Sun Hotel & 16th Century Inn ⚑

LA21 8HQ ☎ 015394 41248 📄 015394 41219
e-mail: thesun@hotelconiston.com
dir: *From M6 junct 36, A591, beyond Kendal &
Windermere, then A598 from Ambleside to Coniston.
Pub signed from bridge in village*

A 16th-century inn with a 10-room hotel attached, this
was Donald Campbell's base during his final water
speed record attempt. Coniston Bluebird is one of the
ales behind the bar, along with guest ales like Black
Cat, Black Sheep Special and Speckled Hen. The menu
offers seafood paella; pan-roasted pheasant with baby
spinach ragout; and Hungarian goulash with
dumplings. Outside is a large quiet garden with
benches, and the conservatory offers exceptional views
that can be enjoyed whatever the weather.

Open all day all wk 11am-mdnt **Bar Meals** L served all
wk 12-3 D served all wk 6-9 ⊕ FREE HOUSE
◀ Coniston Bluebird, Hawkshead, Copper Dragon, 4
guest ales. ⚑ 7 **Facilities** Play area Family room Dogs
allowed Garden Parking

CROOK   Map 18 SD49

The Sun Inn ⚑

LA8 8LA ☎ 01539 821351 📄 01539 821351
dir: *Off B5284*

A welcoming inn which has grown from a row of cottages
built in 1711, when beer was served to travellers from a
front room. The same pleasure is dispensed today by the
winter fires or on the summer terrace. The bar and
regular menus feature steak and mushroom pie, beer
battered cod and chips, curries, steaks, salads and
vegetarian dishes. Enjoy dining in the restaurant for that
special occasion. The seasonal menus use locally sourced
produce.

Open all wk **Bar Meals** L served Mon-Fri 12-2.30, Sat-
Sun 12-10.30 D served Mon-Fri 6-9, Sat-Sun 12-10.30
Restaurant L served Mon-Fri 12-2.30, Sat-Sun 12-10.30
D served Mon-Fri 6-9, Sat-Sun 12-10.30 booking
required ⊕ Scottish & Newcastle ◀ Theakston, John
Smiths's, Courage Directors, Coniston Bluebird,
Hawkeshead. ⚑ 14 **Facilities** Children's menu Dogs
allowed Garden Parking

CROSTHWAITE   Map 18 SD49

PICK OF THE PUBS

The Punch Bowl
Inn   INN ☒ ⚑

LA8 8HR ☎ 015395 68237 📄 015395 68875
e-mail: info@the-punchbowl.co.uk
dir: *M6 junct 36, A590 towards Barrow, A5074 & follow
signs for Crosthwaite. Pub by church on left*

Located in the stunning Lyth Valley beside the ancient
parish church, this classy inn operates as a bar
serving locally brewed Barngates beers, an elegant
restaurant noted for using local seasonal ingredients,
as well as swish, boutique-style rooms, and the village
post office. Although stylishly remodelled with a
contemporary feel, it retains bags of character. Witness
oak beams, roaring log fires and gleaming wooden
floors here, and elegant dining rooms with white linen
and colourful local artwork. The menu is served
throughout the bar and restaurant and champions
local suppliers, many of them organic. Start with ham
hock terrine with piccalilli, follow with battered hake
with chips and mushy peas, or confit pork belly with
sage and apple sauce, and finish with Valrhona
chocolate tart with beer ice cream. Good lunchtime
snacks take in roast beef and horseradish sandwiches.
Beautiful rooms boast flat-screen TVs, Roberts Revival
radios and a freestanding roll-top bath. Great walks
from the front door.

Open all wk noon-mdnt **Bar Meals** Av main course £12
food served all day **Restaurant** Av 3 course à la carte
fr £25.30 food served all day ⊕ FREE HOUSE ◀ Tag
Lag, Cat Nap, Erdinger, Westmorland Gold, Coniston
Bluebird, Hawkshead Gold ♻ Thatchers Gold. ⚑ 16
Facilities Children's menu Dogs allowed Garden
Parking **Rooms** 9

ELTERWATER   Map 18 NY30

PICK OF THE PUBS

The Britannia Inn

LA22 9HP ☎ 015394 37210 📄 015396 78075
e-mail: info@britinn.co.uk
dir: *Inn in village centre*

Situated in the very heart of Beatrix Potter country, The
Britannia Inn was built over 400 years ago - the
quintessential Lakeland inn. The Britannia really
comes to life in summer when colourful hanging
baskets dazzle the eye and the garden fills up with
customers (and occasionally Morris dancers). In colder
weather, the thick stone walls, log fires and beamed
ceilings come into their own, and at any time the inn
offers a big selection of real ales and a wide choice of
fresh home-cooked food. Informal bar lunches might
take in Cumberland sausage and mash, or home-made
steak and ale pie. In the evening, start with oak-
smoked salmon and prawn platter perhaps, followed by
local fillets of trout, or red pesto and sweet pepper tart.

Open all day all wk 10am-11pm **Bar Meals** L served
12-9.30 D served 12-9.30 food served all day ⊕ FREE
HOUSE ◀ Jennings Bitter, Coniston Bluebird, Thwaites
Wainwright. **Facilities** Dogs allowed Garden Parking

ENNERDALE BRIDGE   Map 18 NY01

PICK OF THE PUBS

The Shepherd's Arms Hotel

See Pick of the Pubs on page 104

ESKDALE GREEN   Map 18 NY10

PICK OF THE PUBS

Bower House Inn ★★ HL

CA19 1TD ☎ 019467 23244 📄 019467 23308
e-mail: info@bowerhouseinn.co.uk
dir: *4m off A595, 0.5m W of Eskdale Green*

Despite its out-of-the-way location, in gloriously
unspoilt Eskdale overlooking Muncaster Fell, the
traditional appeal of this 17th-century inn finds favour
with an eclectic clientele, from walkers and tourists to
business folk and wedding parties. Headquarters of the
village cricket team (the pitch is next door), the bar
has a distinctly clubby feel, with oak beams, ticking
clocks, crackling log fires and local Coniston,
Hawkshead and Jennings ales on tap, and opens out on
to an enchanting, enclosed garden. The rambling
restaurant is a charming room with candlelit tables,
exposed stone, log fires and equestrian pictures
creating a welcoming, traditional setting for some
hearty, imaginative food. Try Morecambe Bay potted
shrimps or smoked Herdwick lamb with minted apple
chutney for starters, followed by beef fillet cooked in
red wine; roast venison with juniper berry sauce; local
wild duck and trout; or poached salmon with white
wine and cucumber sauce. Cosy bedrooms are divided
between the main building and the more modern
converted stables and garden cottages.

Open all day all wk 11-11 **Bar Meals** L served all wk D
served all wk Av main course £10.50 food served all
day **Restaurant** D served 7-9 Av 3 course à la carte fr
£22 ⊕ FREE HOUSE ◀ Theakston Bitter, Jennings
Bitter, Coniston Bluebird, Hawkshead Bitter, Dent Ales.
Facilities Children's menu Dogs allowed Garden
Parking **Rooms** 29

PICK OF THE PUBS

The Shepherd's Arms Hotel

ENNERDALE BRIDGE Map 18 NY01

CA23 3AR
☎ 01946 861249 📠 01946 861249
e-mail: shepherdsarms@btconnect.com
web: www.shepherdsarmshotel.co.uk
dir: *A66 to Cockermouth (25m), A5086 to Egremont (5m) then follow sign to Ennerdale*

Located on one of the most beautiful stretches of Wainwright's Coast to Coast footpath, this informal free house is a favourite with walkers. Bike hire and pony trekking can also be arranged for an enjoyable alternative day out. During their ownership, Val and Steve Madden have created an unusual combination of country house hotel and wayside inn. The bar has a long serving counter, a long case clock and wood-burning stove below a large beam hung with copper and brass pieces. The carpeted main area has an open log fire and comfortable seating, and is a venue for local musicians; it opens into a small conservatory with pub tables and an additional outdoor sitting area. Shepherd's Arms own brew heads a list of beers that includes Jennings Bitter and a regular guest ale. A nicely varied menu is served throughout, with plenty of choice for vegetarians, as well as daily specials and à la carte options in the dining room. Using locally sourced produce where possible, dinner might begin with fresh home-made soup, or deep-fried brie with a hot redcurrant sauce, before moving on to nut and mushroom fettuccine; breaded haddock with lemon; Herdwick lamb half shoulder slow cooked in a mint and garlic jus; grilled swordfish; or local sirloin steak with brandy and black pepper sauce. After finishing, perhaps, with raspberry meringue or apple and blackberry crumble, diners can relax in the comfortable lounge.

Open all week **Bar Meals** L served all week 12-2 D served all week 6-9 Av main course £8 ⊕ FREE HOUSE 🍺 Jennings Bitter, Cumberland, Guest Ales. **Facilities** Children's menu Dogs allowed Garden Parking

King George IV Inn

CA19 1TS ☎ 019467 23262
e-mail: info@kinggeorge-eskdale.co.uk
dir: *From Broughton-in-Furness, over Ulpha Fell towards Eskdale*

What we see today is a 17th-century coaching inn, although Roman origins are likely. It lies in one of Lakeland's finest hidden valleys, close to the narrow gauge Ravenglass & Eskdale steam railway, known affectionately as La'al Ratty. Inside are open fires, oak beams, low ceilings, flagged floors and antiques. Dishes include home-made steak and ale, curry, pan-fried liver and onions, ostrich fillet, and salmon in Martini, orange and ginger sauce. Vegetarian dishes and a children's menus, pizzas and sandwiches are also served.

Open all wk ⊕ FREE HOUSE ◀ Coniston Bluebird, Black Sheep Special, Jennings Cumberland Ales, Jennings Sneck Lifter, guest ales. **Facilities** Dogs allowed Garden Parking

FAUGH   Map 18 NY55

The String of Horses Inn NEW ⚠ ★★★ INN ▼

CA8 9EG ☎ 01228 670297
e-mail: info@stringofhorses.com
dir: *M6 at junct 43 towards Newcastle on A69. Turn right at lights, after village for 1m turn left into Faugh the Inn is on the left*

A former 17th-century pack-horse inn tucked away in a sleepy village close to Talkin Tarn, this traditional Lakeland inn oozes old world charm. The bar and restaurant have oak beams, roaring log fires, wood panelling and oak settles, and you'll find a good range of pub food on offer, from chicken liver pâté with Cumberland sauce to lamb shoulder with mint gravy, and a classic sticky toffee pudding. Well-appointed rooms make for a comfortable base for exploring the North Lakes.

Open 6pm-mdnt (Sun noon-3 7-11) Closed: Mon **Bar Meals** L served Sun 12-2 D served Tue-Sun 6-8.45 Av main course £7.95 **Restaurant** D served Tue-Sun 6-8.45 ⊕ FREE HOUSE ◀ Brampton Bitter, Theakston Best, John Smiths, Guinness. ▼ 8 **Facilities** Children's menu Parking **Rooms** 11

GARRIGILL   Map 18 NY74

The George & Dragon Inn ▼

CA9 3DS ☎ 01434 381293   ▤ 01434 382839
e-mail: info@garrigill-pub.co.uk
dir: *Telephone for details*

Once serving the local zinc and lead mining communities, this 17th-century coaching inn is popular with walkers who enjoy log fires that stave off that brisk North Pennine weather. Look on the menu to find local Cumberland sausage, steak and ale pie, gammon steak, battered cod or Whitby scampi. There are plenty of Yorkshire puddings, jacket potatoes or sandwiches for a lighter meal.

Open Thu-Fri 5-11 (Sat 11-11, Sun noon-11) Closed: Mon-Wed ⊕ FREE HOUSE ◀ Black Sheep Bitter, Bombardier, guest ales. ▼ 9 **Facilities** Dogs allowed

GRASMERE   Map 18 NY30

The Travellers Rest Inn ▼

Keswick Rd LA22 9RR
☎ 015394 35604   ▤ 017687 72309
e-mail: stay@lakedistrictinns.co.uk
dir: *From M6 take A591 to Grasmere, pub 0.5m N of Grasmere*

Located on the edge of picturesque Grasmere and handy for touring and exploring the ever-beautiful Lake District, the Travellers Rest has been a pub for more than 500 years. Inside, a roaring log fire complements the welcoming atmosphere of the beamed and inglenooked bar area. An extensive menu of traditional home-cooked fare is offered, ranging from Westmorland terrine and eggs Benedict, to wild mushroom gratin and rump of Lakeland lamb.

Open all day all wk **Bar Meals** food served all day ⊕ FREE HOUSE ◀ Jennings Bitter & Cocker Hoop, Cumberland Ale, Sneck Lifter, guest ales. ▼ 10 **Facilities** Children's menu Family room Dogs allowed Garden Parking

GREAT LANGDALE   Map 18 NY20

The New Dungeon Ghyll Hotel ★★ HL ▼

LA22 9JY ☎ 015394 37213   ▤ 015394 37666
e-mail: enquiries@dungeon-ghyll.com
dir: *From M6 into Kendal then A591 into Ambleside onto A593 to B5343, hotel 6m on right*

Traditional Cumberland stone hotel dating back to medieval times, and full of character and charm. The hotel stands in its own lawned grounds in a spectacular position beneath the Langdale Pikes and Pavey Ark. Local specialities, expertly cooked, are served in the smart dining room. A sample dinner menu offers pan-fried venison steak on a parsnip rösti with blood orange sauce; griddled grey mullet with stir-fried vegetables and a sweet chilli sauce, venison casserole; or spinach and ricotta cannelloni.

Open all wk ⊕ FREE HOUSE ◀ Thwaites Bitter, Smooth, Thoroughbred. ▼ 7 **Facilities** Family room Dogs allowed Garden Parking **Rooms** 20

GREAT SALKELD   Map 18 NY53

PICK OF THE PUBS

The Highland Drove Inn and Kyloes Restaurant ▼

See Pick of the Pubs on page 106

HAWKSHEAD   Map 18 SD39

Kings Arms ★★★ INN

The Square LA22 0NZ
☎ 015394 36372   ▤ 015394 36006
e-mail: info@kingsarmshawkshead.co.uk
dir: *M6 junct 36, A590 to Newby Bridge, right at 1st junct past rdbt, over bridge, 8m to Hawkshead*

Overlooking the picturesque square at the heart of this virtually unchanged Elizabethan Lakeland village, made famous by Beatrix Potter who lived nearby, this 16th-century inn throngs in summer. In colder weather, bag a table by the fire in the traditional carpeted bar, quaff a pint of Hawkshead bitter and tuck into lunchtime rolls (bacon and brie with cranberry sauce), or for dinner try lamb Henry (slow braised shoulder with red wine and rosemary gravy, or chargrilled rib-eye steak with peppercorn sauce. Look out for the carved figure of a king in the bar.

Open all day all wk 11am-mdnt **Bar Meals** L served all wk 12-2.30 D served all wk 6-9.30 Av main course £8.50 **Restaurant** L served all wk 12-2.30 booking required D served all wk 6-9.30 booking required Fixed menu price fr £11.50 ⊕ FREE HOUSE ◀ Tetley Bitter, Black Sheep Best, Hawkshead Gold, Hawkshead Bitter, Coniston Bluebird, guest ales. **Facilities** Children's menu Dogs allowed Garden **Rooms** 8

PICK OF THE PUBS

The Highland Drove Inn and Kyloes Restaurant ♀

GREAT SALKELD   Map 18 NY53

CA11 9NA
☎ 01768 898349   📄 01768 898708
e-mail:
highlanddroveinn@btinternet.com
dir: *Exit M6 junct 40, take A66 E'bound then A686 to Alston. After 4m, left onto B6412 for Great Salkeld & Lazonby*

Donald and Paul Newton's 300-year-old country inn nestles by the church in a picturesque village deep in the lovely Eden Valley. It stands on an old drove road and Kyloes were the original Highland cattle that were bred in the Western Isles and then driven over the short channels of water to the mainland. Looking more like an old farmhouse, the pub is a great all-round inn, the area's social hub with a well-deserved reputation for high quality food and conviviality. Inside, there's an attractive brick and timber bar, old tables and settles in the main bar area, and a lounge with log fire, dark wood furniture and tartan fabrics. Kyloes Restaurant is upstairs and has a unique hunting lodge feel, with a verandah and lovely country views. Menus list traditional local dishes, alongside daily specials reflecting the availability of local game and fish, and meat from herds reared and matured in Cumbria. Expect to find sea bass, brill or wild salmon sharing the menu with innovative chicken dishes, succulent steaks, and even mallard. Typical meals might be rabbit and bacon pie baked in a double crust with cider and cream; honeyed duck breast with black pudding; pan-fried plaice fillet with spiced melon and lime butter; vegetarian mezze of Mediterranean appetisers; then pannacotta and stewed rhubarb. The area's many attractions include Hadrian's Wall. Despite the excellence of the food, the Highland Drove is still a pub where locals come to enjoy the wide range of cask-conditioned real ales, plenty of other beers and ciders, and a good selection of wines.

Open noon-2 6-late (Closed Mon L)
Bar Meals L served Tue-Sun 12-2
D served all wk 6-9 **Restaurant** L served Tue-Sun 12-2 D served all wk 6-9
⊕ FREE HOUSE 🛢 Theakston Black Bull, John Smiths Cask, John Smiths Smooth, Theakstons Best, Theakstons Mild & guest ale. ♀ 25 **Facilities** Children's menu Dogs allowed Garden Parking

HAWKSHEAD *continued*

PICK OF THE PUBS

Queens Head Hotel ★★ HL 🍴 ☕

See Pick of the Pubs on page 108

The Sun Inn ★★★★ INN

Main St LA22 0NT ☎ 015394 36236
e-mail: rooms@suninn.co.uk
dir: *N on M6 junct 36, A591 to Ambleside, B5286 to Hawkshead. S on M6 junct 40, A66 to Keswick, A591 to Ambleside, B5286 to Hawkshead*

The Sun is a listed 17th-century coaching inn at the heart of the charming village where Wordsworth went to school. Inside are two resident ghosts - a giggling girl and a drunken landlord - and outside is a paved terrace with seating. The wood-panelled bar has low, oak-beamed ceilings, and hill walkers and others will enjoy the log fires, real ales and locally-sourced food. There are 8 attractive bedrooms, some with four-posters.

Open all day all wk 11am-11pm (Sun noon-10.30pm) **Bar Meals** L served all wk 12-3 D served all wk 6-9 ⊕ FREE HOUSE ◀ Jennings, Timothy Taylor Landlord, Hawkshead Bitter, Cocker Hoop, plus two guest ales.
Facilities Garden **Rooms** 8

HESKET NEWMARKET   Map 18 NY33

The Old Crown ☕

CA7 8JG ☎ 016974 78288
e-mail: malcolm.hawksworth@yahoo.co.uk
dir: *From M6 take B5305, left after 6m towards Hesket Newmarket*

Regulars here can sleep soundly, in the knowledge that their favourite beers will always be waiting for them. That's because the pub and its associated micro-brewery, which stands at the rear, are owned by a dedicated co-operative of local people. Real ales aside, traditional home-cooked food includes steak in Hesket Newmarket ale; breaded haddock with chips and peas; lamb and vegetarian curries; and Normandy-style chicken with bacon and mushrooms in a cream and cider sauce.

Closed: Mon-Thu pm ⊕ FREE HOUSE ◀ Doris, Skiddaw, Blencathra, Helvellyn Gold, Catbells, Great Cockup. ☕ 11
Facilities Family room Dogs allowed Garden

HEVERSHAM   Map 18 SD48

Blue Bell Hotel

Princes Way LA7 7EE
☎ 015395 62018   📠 015395 62455
e-mail: stay@bluebellhotel.co.uk
dir: *On A6 between Kendal & Milnthorpe*

Originally a vicarage for the old village, this hotel dates back as far as 1460. Heversham is an ideal base for touring the scenic Lake District and Yorkshire Dales, but pleasant country scenery can also be viewed from the hotel's well-equipped bedrooms. The charming lounge bar, with its old beams, is the perfect place to relax with a drink or enjoy one of the meals available on the menu, including potted shrimps, sirloin steak, Cumbrian game pie and Isle of Man crab.

Open all wk ⊕ SAMUEL SMITH ◀ Samuel Smith Old Brewery Bitter. ☕ 6 **Facilities** Family room Dogs allowed Garden Parking

KENDAL   Map 18 SD59

Gateway Inn ☕

Crook Rd LA8 8LX ☎ 01539 724187   📠 01539 720581
dir: *From M6 junct 36 take A590/A591, follow signs for Windermere, pub on left after 9m*

Located within the Lake District National Park, this Victorian country inn offers delightful views, attractive gardens and welcoming log fires. A good range of appetising dishes includes chicken casserole with red wine and herb dumplings, grilled fillets of sea bass with ratatouille and mussels, and roasted butternut squash filled with leeks and stilton. Traditional English favourites of liver and onions or rabbit pie are also a feature.

Open all wk ⊕ DANIEL THWAITES PLC ◀ Thwaites Bitter, Thwaites Smooth & Cask Ales. ☕ 11 **Facilities** Play area Dogs allowed Garden Parking

KESWICK   Map 18 NY22

The Farmers ☕

Portinscale CA12 5RN ☎ 01768 773442
e-mail: grew2157@tiscali.co.uk
dir: *Exit M6 junct 40 (Penrith) onto A66, pass Keswick B5289 junct, turn left to Portinscale*

Set in a small village a mile from bustling Keswick, this historic village pub has traditional decor and long-standing ties with the local hunt. Expect good quality, well-kept ales, a friendly welcome and traditional home-cooked food. Typical offerings include home-made lasagne; fish and chips; home-made steak and ale pie; and sweet and sour chicken in batter. Leave room for dessert, perhaps a chocolate brownie or home-made strawberry pie.

Open all wk noon-11pm (winter Mon-Fri 3-11 Sat-Sun noon-11) **Bar Meals** L served all wk 12-3 (winter Sat-Sun 12-3) D served Mon-Sat 5-9, Sun 6-9 Av main course £7.95 **Restaurant** Fixed menu price fr £12.95 ◀ Jennings Bitter, Jennings Cumberland Ale, guest ale. ☕ 6 **Facilities** Children's menu Dogs allowed Garden

PICK OF THE PUBS

The Horse & Farrier Inn ☕

See Pick of the Pubs on page 109

PICK OF THE PUBS

The Kings Head ☕

See Pick of the Pubs on page 110

The Swinside Inn

Newlands Valley CA12 5UE ☎ 017687 78253
e-mail: info@theswinsideinn.com
dir: *1m from A66, signed for Newlands/Swinside*

Situated in the quiet Newlands Valley, the Swinside Inn is a listed building dating back to about 1642. From the pub there are superb views of Causey Pike and Cat Bells - among other landmarks. Nearby is the market town of Keswick, a good base for visiting the area's many attractions. Inside are two bars, traditional open fires and oak-beamed ceilings. From Easter to late October food is served all day. Extensive bar menu may offer lamb Henry, Cumberland sausage, Swinside chicken, and fresh, grilled Borrowdale trout. Friday fish night specials.

Open all wk ⊕ SCOTTISH & NEWCASTLE ◀ Jennings Cumberland Ale, John Smith's Smooth, Deuchars, Caledonian IPA, guest ales. **Facilities** Dogs allowed Garden Parking

PICK OF THE PUBS

Queens Head Hotel ★★ HL 🌹 🍷

HAWKSHEAD   Map 18 SD39

Main St LA22 0NS
☎ 015394 36271   📄 015394 36722
e-mail:
enquiries@queensheadhotel.co.uk
web: www.queensheadhotel.co.uk
dir: *M6 junct 36, A590 to Newby Bridge, 1st right, 8m to Hawkshead*

This charming hotel has been part of Hawkshead since the 16th century. This is the picturesque village where William Wordsworth attended grammar school. Later, in the early 20th century, the writer and illustrator Beatrix Potter lived just up the road. Her husband was the local solicitor and his old offices, now the Beatrix Potter Gallery, are full of her illustrations. Behind the Queen's Head's flower-bedecked exterior you'll find low oak-beamed ceilings, wood-panelled walls, an original slate floor and a welcoming fire. Among the pictures and plates on display is the curious Girt Clog, a 20-inch-long shoe made for an elephantitis sufferer in the 1820s. An extensive wine list and a selection of real ales is offered, plus a full à la carte menu and an ever-changing specials board. Dishes draw from the wealth of quality produce on the doorstep: trout from Esthwaite Water, pheasant from Graythwaite, traditionally cured hams and Cumberland sausage from Waberthwaite, and slow-maturing Herdwick lamb. For lunch try sandwiches, salads or light bites such as a steamed, naturally-smoked haddock fillet with mixed leaves or chicken liver pâté with orange and tequila served with toasted brioche. Heartier lunch options include a 'pot of fish' in a lemon and parsley cream sauce; or Thai curry with saffron rice. An evening meal might open with game and wild mushroom terrine with juniper berry oil, brioche toast with pear and date chutney, followed by venison casserole; Fellside lamb cutlets; or pan-fried West Coast sea bass fillet. Vegetarians might like to choose roasted butternut squash risotto or baby spinach and leek bake. The surrounding area is a haven for walkers, and Esthwaite Water is a stone's throw away. For those wishing to stay, the hotel has 13 very attractive en suite rooms.

Open 11-11.45 (Sun 12-11.45) **Bar Meals** L served all wk 12-2.30 D served all wk 6.15-9.30 (Sun 12-5 6.15-9.30) Av main course £12.95 **Restaurant** L served all wk 12-2.30 D served all wk 6.15-9.30 🍺 FREDERIC ROBINSON 🍺 Hartleys Cumbria Way, Double Hop, Guest Ale. 🍷 11 **Facilities** Children's menu Family room Garden **Rooms** 13

PICK OF THE PUBS

The Horse & Farrier Inn ♀

KESWICK   Map 18 NY22

Threlkeld Village CA12 4SQ
☎ **017687 79688**   📠 **017687 79823**
e-mail: info@horseandfarrier.com
web: www.horseandfarrier.com
dir: *M6 junct 40 follow Keswick (A66) signs,
after 12m turn right signed Threlkeld. Pub in
village centre*

The Horse & Farrier stands in the picturesque hamlet of Threlkeld at the foot of 868-metre Blencathra, with views of Skiddaw to the west and Helvellyn to the south. Fell walkers like to make the most of this stunning location with a beer in the garden - a case of up hill and down ale, perhaps. Within its thick, whitewashed stone walls you'll find slate-flagged floors, beamed ceilings and all the essential features of an inn built over 300 years ago. Hunting prints decorate the traditional bars, warmed by crackling log fires in winter. The inn has an excellent local reputation for good food, from hearty Lakeland breakfasts to home-cooked lunches and dinners served in either the bar, or the charming period restaurant. The chefs make full use of local, seasonal produce when preparing their varied menus. Lunchtime brings a range of open sandwiches and baguettes, as well as hot pub favourites like deep fried breaded Whitby scampi; steak and kidney pie with ale gravy; and bean and celery chilli with salad and pilau rice. A more formal dinner might begin with seared smoked salmon escalope with asparagus and lemon oil; or duck liver and brandy pâté with fresh beetroot chutney. Then, turn your attention to pan-roasted stuffed chicken breast with tomato and herb risotto; steamed sea bass on tagliatelle verdi; or pan-fried fillet steak with shallot and port wine sauce. A range of premium Swiss ice creams characterises the dessert menu – choices range from pink grapefruit and orange sorbet to chocolate mint parfait. There's an extensive wine list, too.

Open all day all wk 7.30am-mdnt
Bar Meals food served all day
Restaurant food served all day
🍺 JENNINGS BROTHERS PLC 🛢 Jennings Bitter, Cocker Hoop, Sneck Lifter, Cumberland Ale & guest ale. ♀ 9
Facilities Children's menu Family room Dogs allowed Garden Parking

PICK OF THE PUBS

The Kings Head ♇

KESWICK Map 18 NY22

Thirlspot CA12 4TN
☎ **017687 72393** 🖨 **017687 72309**
e-mail: stay@lakedistrictinns.co.uk
web: www.lakedistrictinns.co.uk
dir: *From M6 take A66 to Keswick then A591, pub 4m S of Keswick*

Stunning Lakeland scenery surrounds this 17th-century former coaching inn, which is spectacularly located at the foot of Helvellyn and boasts sublime views across pasture towards St Johns in the Vale and the peaks of Blencathra and Skiddaw. On warm days and in summer, the garden is the best place to enjoy a meal or drink. Inside, old beams and inglenook fireplaces are traditional features of the bar, while a separate games room offers pool, snooker and darts. Popular real ales include beers from the Jennings brewery in nearby

Cockermouth, and there is a fine selection of wines and malt whiskies. In the elegant restaurant you can linger over a four-course seasonal menu of traditional English dishes and local specialities, perhaps choosing between spicy citrus-crusted pork roast and oven-baked sea bass, which might be preceded by filo wrapped prawns, or mushroom and thyme soup, and followed by home-made lemon and lime tartlet. On the bar menu you'll find Cumberland chargrill; beef stroganoff; wild mushroom gratin; Borrowdale trout stuffed with prawns; and local Waberthwaite sausages; and there are sandwiches, cold platters and salads. A steak menu is offered during the week and a choice of roasts is available on Sunday lunchtimes – booking advisable. There are also facilities for functions and wedding receptions at this perfect Lakeland retreat. Don't miss the new Lakeland Store at the inn, a deli-cum-farm shop where you can take home goodies from local producers – Hawkshead Relish Company, Romney's Fudge, Strawberry Bank liqueurs – and locally made pottery and crafts.

Open all week 🛢 FREE HOUSE
🍺 Jennings Bitter, Cumberland Ale, Sneck Lifter, Cocker Hoop & guest ales.
♇ 10 **Facilities** Family room Dogs allowed Garden Parking

KIRKBY LONSDALE
Map 18 SD67

PICK OF THE PUBS

The Pheasant Inn ♛

Casterton LA6 2RX
☎ 01524 271230 📠 01524 274267
e-mail: info@pheasantinn.co.uk
dir: *M6 junct 36, A65 for 7m, left onto A683 at Devils Bridge, 1m to Casterton centre*

A whitewashed 18th-century coaching inn, The Pheasant nestles beneath the fells in the quiet hamlet of Casterton, just a mile from the market town of Kirkby Lonsdale in the beautiful Lune Valley. The Dixon family and staff ensure a warm welcome and food is served daily in both the restaurant and bar, where beams, panelling and open fireplaces add to the relaxing atmosphere. An extensive choice of dishes is prepared from local ingredients, including steaks, fresh salmon and the likes of roast topside of beef with Yorkshire pudding and gravy; chef's seafood mixed grill cooked in lemon butter; and spinach, feta cheese and mushroom strudel with crisp salad and salsa sauce. There is also a daily changing selection of specials that makes the most of the markets and the seasons. In fine weather you can sit outside on the patio or lawn and enjoy a pint of real ale and the lovely views of the fells.

Open all wk noon-3 6-11 Closed: 2 wks mid Jan **Bar Meals** L served all wk 12-2 D served all wk 6-9 **Restaurant** L served all wk 12-2 booking required D served all wk 6-9 booking required Av 3 course à la carte fr £18.50 ⊕ FREE HOUSE ◀ Theakston Best & Cool Cask, Black Sheep Best, Dent Aviator, Timothy Taylor Landlord, John Smiths. ♛ 7 **Facilities** Garden Parking

PICK OF THE PUBS

The Sun Inn ★★★★★ INN ⊛ ♛

Market St LA6 2AU
☎ 015242 71965 📠 015242 72485
e-mail: email@sun-inn.info
dir: *From M6 junct 36 take A65 for Kirkby Lonsdale. In 5m left signed Kirkby Lonsdale. At next T-junct turn left. Right at bottom of hill*

Natural stone and oak floors, log fires and window seats create a relaxed atmosphere at this welcoming 17th century inn, just a few minutes' walk from Ruskin's View, famously painted by Turner. In the bar, which is rumoured to have a resident ghost, you'll find a selection of cask ales from Jennings, Timothy Taylor, Hawkshead and Marstons. Lunchtime choices include sandwiches and light bites, as well as main course dishes like rare breed beef cheeseburger with watercress salad; fish goujons with herb mayonnaise; and a locally-made charcuterie platter. The restaurant menu changes regularly to include options such as mushroom suet pudding with baby root vegetables; and Gloucester Old Spot pork belly with bubble and squeak. Eleven deluxe bed and breakfast rooms blend modern comforts with character and charm, making the Sun an ideal base from which to explore the Lake District and Yorkshire Dales.

Open all day all wk 10am-11pm **Bar Meals** L served Tue-Sun 12-2.30 D served all wk 7-9 Av main course £7.95 **Restaurant** L served Tue-Sun 12-2.30 D served all wk 7-9 Av 3 course à la carte fr £20 ⊕ FREE HOUSE ◀ Jennings Cumberland Ale, Timothy Taylor Landlord, guest ales. ♛ 7 **Facilities** Children's menu Dogs allowed **Rooms** 11

The Whoop Hall ★★ HL ♛

Skipton Rd LA6 2HP
☎ 015242 71284 📠 015242 72154
e-mail: info@whoophall.co.uk
dir: *From M6 junct 36 take A65. Pub 1m SE of Kirkby Lonsdale*

This 16th-century converted coaching inn was once the kennels for local foxhounds. In an imaginatively converted barn you can relax and enjoy Yorkshire ales and a good range of dishes based on local produce. Oven baked fillet of sea bass with tagliatelle verde and tiger prawns, and stir-fried honey roast duck with vegetables and water chestnuts are among the popular favourites. The bar offers traditional hand-pulled ales and roaring log fires, while outside is a terrace and children's area.

Open all wk ⊕ FREE HOUSE ◀ Black Sheep, Greene King IPA, Tetley Smooth. ♛ 14 **Facilities** Play area Family room Dogs allowed Garden Parking **Rooms** 24

LITTLE LANGDALE
Map 18 NY30

PICK OF THE PUBS

Three Shires Inn ★★★★ INN

LA22 9NZ ☎ 015394 37215 📠 015394 37127
e-mail: enquiry@threeshiresinn.co.uk
web: www.threeshiresinn.co.uk
dir: *Turn off A593, 2.3m from Ambleside at 2nd junct signed 'The Langdales'. 1st left 0.5m. Inn in 1m*

The traditional Cumbrian slate and stone inn was built in 1872 and enjoys a stunning location in the beautiful Little Langdale valley. Just as it did in the late 19th century, it provides a much-needed resting place and watering hole for travellers on the journey over the high passes of Hardknott and Wrynose, and is the perfect pit-stop for lunch on walks in the Langdale and Skelwith area. Named after its situation near the meeting point of three county shires - Westmorland, Cumberland and Lancashire – it has been personally run by the Stephenson family since 1983. The bars boasting bare beams and slate walls are warmed in winter by cosy log fires, while on fine summer days, locals, walkers and tourists head for the picnic tables by a lakeland stream in the landscaped garden – the fell views are magnificent. Refreshments include tip-top Cumbrian ales from Jennings, Hawkshead and Coniston breweries. Food is locally sourced and very popular, with evening booking advisable. Light lunches start with tempting sandwiches, baguettes, soups and the perfect walkers' lunch, a ham and cheese ploughman's or hot food such as Angus steak burger and beef and ale pie. Hearty evening choices take in marinated rump of Lakeland lamb with garlic and herb mash and port and redcurrant sauce, and rib-eye steak with all the trimmings. The inn offers ten prettily furnished bedrooms with lovely views of the valley.

Open all wk 11-3 6-10.30 Dec-Jan, 11-10.30 Feb-Nov (Fri-Sat 11-11) Closed: 25 Dec **Bar Meals** L served all wk 12-2 (ex 24 Dec) D served all wk 6-8.45 (ex mid wk Dec-Jan) booking required Av main course £12.95 **Restaurant** D served all wk 6-8.45 (ex mid wk Dec-Jan) booking required Fixed menu price fr £18.95 Av 3 course à la carte fr £18 ⊕ FREE HOUSE ◀ Jennings Best & Cumberland, Coniston Old Man, Hawkshead Bitter, Blacksheep Bitters. **Facilities** Children's menu Garden Parking **Rooms** 10

LOWESWATER — Map 18 NY12

PICK OF THE PUBS

Kirkstile Inn ★★★★ INN ♛

See Pick of the Pubs on opposite page

MUNGRISDALE — Map 18 NY33

The Mill Inn ★★★ INN ♛

CA11 0XR ☎ 017687 79632 🖹 017687 79981
e-mail: enquiries@the-millinn.co.uk
dir: *From Penrith A66 to Keswick, after 10m right to Mungrisdale, pub 2m on left*

Set in a peaceful village, this 16th-century coaching inn is handy for spectacular fell walks. Charles Dickens and John Peel once stayed here. The inn has an annual pie festival which raises money for charity with its huge selection of pies. At lunchtime, hungry walkers could tuck into local Cumberland sausages or home-made fishcakes. Evening specials always include tempting pies with fillings such as local lamb and apricot; steak with roasted onions; and spiced chicken.

Open all wk **Bar Meals** L served all wk 12-2 booking required D served all wk 6-8.30 booking required **Restaurant** L served all wk 12-2 booking required D served all wk 6-8.30 booking required ⊕ ROBINSONS ◄ Robinsons ale, Hartleys XB. ♈ 7 **Facilities** Dogs allowed Garden Parking **Rooms** 6

NEAR SAWREY — Map 18 SD39

Tower Bank Arms ♛

LA22 0LF ☎ 015394 36334
e-mail: enquiries@towerbankarms.com
dir: *On B5285 SW of Windermere.1.5m from Hawkshead. 2m from Windemere via ferry*

This 17th-century Lakeland inn was immortalised in Beatrix Potter's *Tales of Jemima Puddleduck*. The author's former home, Hilltop, now a National Trust property, is just behind the pub. Food based on local produce is served in the bar or restaurant, and children are made welcome. Typical menu starts with plate of smoked salmon and crayfish tails or flat field mushroom topped with local blue cheese, continues with breast of Barbary duck with sweet plum and ginger sauce or Cumbrian beef and ale stew, and winds up with bread and butter pudding. There is also an excellent cheese slate.

Open all day Etr-Oct **Bar Meals** L served all wk 12-2 D served Mon-Sat 6-9, Sun & BH 6-8 (Mon-Thu in winter) Av main course £9.50 **Restaurant** D served Mon-Sat 6-9, Sun & BH 6-8 (Mon-Thu in winter) Av 3 course à la carte fr £18.45 ⊕ FREE HOUSE ◄ Barngates Tag Lag, Hawkshead Bitter, Brodies Prime, Keswick, Ulverston. ♈ 7 **Facilities** Children's menu Dogs allowed Garden Parking

NETHER WASDALE — Map 18 NY10

The Screes Inn

CA20 1ET ☎ 019467 26262 🖹 019467 26262
e-mail: info@thescreesinnwasdale.com
dir: *A595 to Gosforth, in 3m turn right signed Nether Wasdale. In village on left*

This friendly family-run pub is situated in the picturesque village of Nether Wasdale and makes an excellent base for walking, mountain biking or diving in this lovely area, particularly Scawfell. It dates back 300 years and offers a log fire, real ales and large selection of malt whiskies. There is a good choice of sandwiches at lunchtime, and other dishes include lasagne, roast leg of lamb off the bone, vegetarian chilli, chick pea and sweet potato curry, or goats' cheese strudel filled with roast parsnips, celeriac, leek and apple.

Open all day all wk 11-11 (Sun 11-10.30) Closed: 25 Dec, 1 Jan **Bar Meals** L served all wk 12-3 D served all wk 6-9 Av main course £9 **Restaurant** L served all wk 12-3 D served all wk 6-9 ⊕ FREE HOUSE ◄ Yates Bitter, Derwent, Black Sheep. **Facilities** Children's menu Dogs allowed Garden Parking

OUTGATE — Map 18 SD39

Outgate Inn ♛

LA22 0NQ ☎ 015394 36413
e-mail: outgate@outgate.wanadoo.co.uk
dir: *Exit M6 junct 36, by-passing Kendal, A591 towards Ambleside. At Clappersgate take B5285 to Hawkshead then Outgate 3m*

Once a mineral water manufacturer, and now part of Robinson's and Hartley's Brewery, whose ales are served in the bar. During the winter there's a real fire, while summer warmth should be available in the secluded beer garden. Daily specials supplement grilled local gammon with free range egg and pineapple, pan-fried rib-eye steak, Cumberland sausage and mash, and lightly grilled fillet of lemon sole. Popular for live jazz on Fridays from March to October.

Open all wk all day Mar-Nov **Bar Meals** L served all wk 12-2 D served all wk 6-9 **Restaurant** L served all wk 12-2 D served all wk 6-9 ⊕ FREDERIC ROBINSON ◄ Hartleys XB, Old Stockport Bitter, Robinsons Smooth. ♈ 10 **Facilities** Children's menu Dogs allowed Garden Parking

RAVENSTONEDALE — Map 18 NY70

PICK OF THE PUBS

The Black Swan ★★★★ INN ♛

CA17 4NG ☎ 015396 23204
e-mail: enquiries@blackswanhotel.com
dir: *M6 junct 38 take A685 E towards Brough*

A grand, family-run Victorian inn in a peaceful conservation village in the upper Eden Valley. Its lovely riverside garden is home to red squirrels, which will let you share their space to relax after you've walked the Howgill Fells, explored the Lakes or toured the Yorkshire Dales. Local ales are served in the bar, while in the beautifully decorated dining rooms main meals include award-winning local sausage casseroled with red wine, mushrooms and shallots; whole horseshoe of local gammon served with grilled tomato, mushrooms, chips and egg or pineapple; aromatic Mughlai chicken or vegetable curry with almonds, sultanas, basmati rice and coriander; fresh cod or haddock in Black Sheep beer batter with mushy or garden peas and chips; and vegetable and lentil shepherd's pie with goats' cheese mash. In 2009 the Black Swan earned an AA Breakfast and Dinner award for its food and use of freshly prepared local ingredients (There is menu sourcing information about all their suppliers.) There are individually-styled bedrooms available.

Open all wk 8.30am-11.30pm **Bar Meals** L served all wk 12-2 D served all wk 6-9 Av main course £8.95 **Restaurant** L served all wk 12-2 booking required D served all wk 6-9 ⊕ FREE HOUSE ◄ Black Sheep, John Smith's, Dent, Tirril Brewery, Hawkshead Brewery ☼ Thatchers. ♈ 7 **Facilities** Children's menu Dogs allowed Garden Parking **Rooms** 10

PICK OF THE PUBS

The Fat Lamb Country Inn ★★ HL

See Pick of the Pubs on page 114

PICK OF THE PUBS

Kirkstile Inn ★★★★ INN ♓

LOWESWATER   Map 18 NY12

CA13 0RU
☎ **01900 85219** 📠 **01900 85239**
e-mail: info@kirkstile.com
dir: *From A66 Keswick take Whinlatter Pass at Braithwaite. Take B5292, at T-junct left onto B5289. 3m to Loweswater. From Cockermouth B5289 to Lorton, past Low Lorton, 3m to Loweswater. At red phone box left, 200yds*

Standing in the shadow of Melbreak, the Kirkstile Inn has offered shelter and hospitality amidst the stunning Cumbrian fells for some four hundred years. Located between Loweswater and Crummock Water, the inn makes an ideal base for walking, climbing, boating and fishing. Of course, you may simply prefer relaxing over a beer from one of the local breweries. If you're a fan of real ale, be sure to try something from the Loweswater Brewery, which is attached to the inn: maybe Melbreak

Bitter, Yates Bitter, or Loweswater Gold at the bar. Alternatively, Stowford Press is on offer for cider drinkers. The dining room dates back to 1549 and is the oldest part of the inn, facing south down to the Buttermere Valley. Here the food matches the quality of the views, with plenty of choice from both the regular menus and the daily changing blackboard specials. Expect a choice of baguettes, sandwiches and jacket potatoes at lunchtime, as well as a range of hot dishes like pan-fried chicken with salad and wild rice; Cumberland tattie pot; and cream cheese tart with salad and new potatoes. The evening menu might begin with black pudding in beer batter with a red wine sauce; or smoked chicken salad with olive dressing. Move on, perhaps, to roasted hake fillet with sweet potato; goat's cheese, spinach and roasted vegetable lasagne; or slow-cooked Lakeland lamb shoulder with rosemary mash. Dessert options include Cumberland rum Nicky, pecan pie, and chocolate marquise. The friendly atmosphere extends through to the accommodation, comprising seven en suite rooms and a family suite. Two private lounges ensure that guests enjoy total relaxation.

Open all week Closed: 25 Dec **Bar Meals** L served all week 12-3 D served all week 6-9 Av main course £10.25 **Restaurant** D served all week 6-9 Av 3 course à la carte fr £21 ⊕ FREE HOUSE
◀ Loweswater Gold, Yates Bitter, Melbreak, Grasmoor Ale ♂ Stowford Press. ♓ 10 **Facilities** Children's menu Family room Dogs allowed Garden Parking **Rooms** 8

PICK OF THE PUBS

The Fat Lamb Country Inn ★★ HL

RAVENSTONEDALE   Map 18 NY70

Crossbank CA17 4LL
☎ **015396 23242**   📄 **015396 23285**
e-mail: enquires@fatlamb.co.uk
web: www.fatlamb.co.uk
dir: *On A683 between Sedbergh & Kirkby Stephen*

Modern amenities blend with old fashioned hospitality at this 350 year-old free house. The former coaching inn is solidly built of local stone, and stands in open countryside between the Lake District and the Yorkshire Dales National Parks. An open fire on the traditional Yorkshire range warms the bar in winter; this is the oldest part of the building, and was converted from the former kitchen and living area. Here, visitors and locals can mingle without the distraction of a pool table or electronic entertainment to intrude on

their conversation. Snacks and meals are served here and in the relaxed restaurant, which is decorated with old prints and plates. The table d'hôte menu might feature dishes such as local lamb cutlets in mint jus; pan-fried tuna steak with black olive and red onion dressing; or roast guinea fowl with caramelised onion and apple sauce – but, whatever you choose, it will have been prepared on site using the best available local ingredients. All the bedrooms have en suite bathrooms and tea and coffee making facilities. The inn stands in informal gardens with a patio and picnic tables – and you might also like to visit the adjoining nature reserve. It was founded by the present landlord Paul Bonsall in 1989, following concerns that the land might fall into the hands of a shooting syndicate. After buying the site at auction, he enlisted help from the Countryside Commission and many others to create this unique wildlife haven. Now, visitors are welcome to wander round the reserve and admire the magnificent views.

Open all week **Bar Meals** L served all week 12-2 D served all week 6-9 Av main course £9.60 **Restaurant** L served all week 12-2 D served all week 6-9 Fixed menu price fr £22 Av 3 course à la carte fr £12.50 ⊕ FREE HOUSE ◀ Black Sheep Bitter. **Facilities** Children's menu Play area Dogs allowed Garden Parking **Rooms** 12

SEDBERGH — Map 18 SD69

The Dalesman Country Inn ♈

Main St LA10 5BN ☎ 015396 21183 ▤ 015396 21311
e-mail: info@thedalesman.co.uk
dir: *M6 junct 37, follow signs to Sedbergh, 1st pub in town on left*

Restored 16th-century coaching inn, noted for its dazzling floral displays and handy for a choice of glorious walks along the River Dee or up to the Howgill Fells. The menu changes every fortnight, and among the main courses are trio of chargrilled lamb chops, wild salmon fillet, home-made mushroom stroganoff, fresh swordfish nicoise, and organic chicken breast. Popular patio and garden, and a good wine selection.

Open all wk ⊕ FREE HOUSE ◀ Carlsberg-Tetley, Theakston Best Bitter, Black Sheep. ♈ 9 **Facilities** Family room Garden Parking

TIRRIL — Map 18 NY52

PICK OF THE PUBS

Queen's Head Inn ♈

CA10 2JF ☎ 01768 863219
e-mail: bookings@queensheadinn.co.uk
dir: *A66 towards Penrith then A6 S towards Shap. In Eamont Bridge turn right just after Crown Hotel. Tirril in 1m on B5320*

Situated on the edge of the Lake District National Park, this traditional English country inn dates from 1719 and is chock-full of beams, flagstones and memorabilia as you would expect from an old inn. While enjoying a pint of Unicorn, Cumbrian Way and Dizzy Blonde in the bar, look for the Wordsworth Indenture, signed by the great poet himself, his brother, Christopher, and local wheelwright John Bewsher, to whom the Wordsworths sold the pub in 1836. You can eat in the bar or restaurant, and a meal might include bacon and black pudding salad; oven-baked chicken stuffed with Blengdale Blue and spinach; and chocolate and orange tart. In August every year the Cumbrian beer and sausage festival is held here. The village shop is located at the back of the inn.

Open all day all wk noon-11pm Sun-Thu, noon-mdnt Fri-Sat **Bar Meals** L served all wk 12-8.30 Mar-Oct, 12-2.30 Nov-Feb D served all wk 12-8.30 Mar-Oct, 5.30-8.30 Nov-Feb Av main course £9.95 **Restaurant** L served all wk 12-8.30 Mar-Oct, 12-2.30 Nov-Feb D served all wk 12-8.30 Mar-Oct, 5.30-8.30 Nov-Feb Fixed menu price fr £8.95 Av 3 course à la carte fr £17.95 ⊕ ROBINSONS ◀ Unicorn, Cumbria Way, Dizzy Blonde. ♈ 10 **Facilities** Children's menu Dogs allowed Parking

TROUTBECK — Map 18 NY40

PICK OF THE PUBS

Queens Head ★★★★ INN ♈

Townhead LA23 1PW
☎ 015394 32174 ▤ 015394 31938
e-mail: feast@queensheadhotel.com
dir: *M6 junct 36, A590/591, W towards Windermere, right at mini-rdbt onto A592 signed Penrith/Ullswater. Pub 2m on left*

The lovely undulating valley of Troutbeck, with its maze of footpaths and felltop views, is a magnet for ramblers. True to its roots, this smart 17th-century coaching inn offers sustenance and comfortable accommodation to the weary and footsore. The bar is perhaps its most remarkable feature, carved from a four-poster bed that once resided in Appleby Castle. Nooks and crannies, low beams stuffed with old pennies by farmers on their way home from market, and a log fire throughout the year complete the heart-warming picture. Robinson's Brewery furnishes the likes of Cumbria Way, Old Tom and Dizzy Blonde at the pumps, while the chef's reputation for accomplished cooking is well established. The menu proffers hearty fare – from tempting baguettes filled with warm Cumberland sausage, caramelised onion and English mustard mayonnaise, to pan-roasted chicken supreme with bubble and squeak. In addition a three-course set menu, with meat, fish and vegetarian options at each course, is always available.

Open all day all wk **Bar Meals** food served all day **Restaurant** booking required food served all day ⊕ FREDERIC ROBINSON ◀ Hartleys XB, Cumbria Way, Double Hop, Old Tom, Dizzy Blonde. ♈ 8 **Facilities** Children's menu Dogs allowed Parking **Rooms** 15

ULVERSTON — Map 18 SD27

Farmers Arms ♈

Market Place LA12 7BA
☎ 01229 584469 ▤ 01229 582188
dir: *In town centre*

A warm welcome is extended at this lively 16th-century inn located at the centre of the attractive, historic market town. The visitor will find a comfortable and relaxing beamed front bar with an open fire in winter. Landlord Roger Chattaway takes pride in serving quality food; his

---

Sunday lunches are famous locally, and at other times there's a varied and tempting specials menu, and lunchtime choice of hot and cold sandwiches, baguettes or ciabatta, and various salads.

Open all wk ⊕ FREE HOUSE ◀ Hawkshead Best Bitter, John Smiths. ♈ 12 **Facilities** Children's menu Garden

WASDALE HEAD — Map 18 NY10

Wasdale Head Inn ♈

CA20 1EX ☎ 019467 26229 & 26333 ▤ 019467 26334
e-mail: wasdaleheadinn@msn.com
dir: *From A595 follow Wasdale signs. Inn at head of valley*

Famous historic mountain inn dramatically situated at the foot of England's highest mountains and beside her deepest lake. The oak-panelled walls are hung with photographs reflecting a passion for climbing. Exclusive real ales are brewed in the pub's own micro brewery and celebrated by annual beer festivals. Abraham's Restaurant offers dishes like roast lamb chump on braised Canadian lentils served with a honey and redcurrant sauce, or seared venison steak on maris piper mash and juniper berry sauce.

Open all day all wk 11-11 (Sun noon-10.30) **Bar Meals** L served all wk 12-9 D served all wk 12-9 Av main course £9.50 food served all day **Restaurant** D served all wk 7-8 booking required Fixed menu price fr £28 ⊕ FREE HOUSE ◀ Great Gable, Wasd Ale, Burnmoor, Yewbarrow, Illgill, Liar. ♈ 15 **Facilities** Children's menu Dogs allowed Garden Parking

WATERMILLOCK — Map 18 NY42

PICK OF THE PUBS

Brackenrigg Inn ★★★ INN ♈

See Pick of the Pubs on page 116

WHITEHAVEN — Map 18 NX91

The Waterfront ♈

West Strand CA28 7LR ☎ 01946 691130
dir: *M6 junct 40, A66 towards Workington. Take A595 towards Whitehaven then A5094. Pub in town centre on harbourside*

Set on Whitehaven's historic harbourside, once the third busiest port in the country. The Waterfront serves both food and drink outside in summer, where unrivalled views across the Solway can be enjoyed. There's a contemporary feel to the interior, and the friendly, knowledgeable staff are eager to make you feel at home. Modern and traditional dishes are locally sourced - the evening menu is particularly strong on chargrilled steaks with a choice of sauces.

Open all wk **Bar Meals** L served all wk 12-2 D served all wk 6-9 **Restaurant** L served all wk 12-2 D served all wk 6-9 ⊕ PUBLIC ANA LTD ◀ Guest ales. ♈ 16

PICK OF THE PUBS

Brackenrigg Inn ★★★ INN ♥

WATERMILLOCK   Map 18 NY42

CA11 0LP
☎ **017684 86206**   📄 **017684 86945**
e-mail: reception@brackenrigginn.co.uk
dir: *M6 junct 40 take A66 signed Keswick. Then A592 signed Ullswater. Right at lake. Inn 6m from M6 & Penrith*

The breathtaking views across Lake Ullswater and its surrounding fells are beyond compare from the elevated terrace and fine gardens at this traditional 18th-century coaching inn. An appealing, homely feel is retained inside the long, white-washed inn, thanks in part to the attractive panelled bar, with its welcoming atmosphere, glowing winter fires, polished board floor, and views over the surrounding countryside. There's a good choice of real ales, such as Coniston Bluebird, Jennings Cumberland and Copper Dragon 1816, and the wine list is well balanced and full of interest, with helpful suggestions on food and wine pairing and a choice of 12 by the glass. Fresh local produce is to the fore on the comprehensive all-day menu. Typical choices include starters of pan-fried chicken liver and bacon salad with red wine and balsamic dressing; ham hock terrine wrapped in Cumbrian air-dried ham with home-made piccalilli, and deep-fried calamari with tartare sauce. Follow, perhaps, with braised lamb shank with colcannon mash and pan gravy, fish pie, Ullswater beef with hand-cut chips and all the trimmings, and Cumberland sausage with mustard mash and red onion gravy. If time is short, try one of the excellent sandwiches (crab and spring onion crème fraîche). If you can't tear yourselves away from the peace and beauty of the place, there are smart bedrooms, some housed in the newly refurbished Stables Cottages, where a good night's sleep and a traditional Cumbrian breakfast are guaranteed. This is a superb base for exploring the delights of the North Lakes - walking, climbing, watersports, golf, or touring by car.

Open noon-11 (Nov-Mar closed Mon-Fri 3-5) **Bar Meals** L served all week 12-5 D served all week 5-9 **Restaurant** L served all week 12-2.30 D served all week 6-9 Av 3 course à la carte fr £28 ⊕ FREE HOUSE ◀ Jennings Cumberland, Coniston Bluebird, Copper Dragon, Tirril Brewery, Old Faithful, Guinness. ♥ 12 **Facilities** Dogs allowed Garden Parking **Rooms** 17

WINDERMERE — Map 18 SD49

The Angel Inn 🍷

Helm Rd LA23 3BU ☎ 015394 44080 📠 015394 46003
e-mail: rooms@the-angelinn.com
dir: From Rayrigg Rd (parallel to lake) into Crag Brow, then right into Helm Rd

City chic style is offered at this sophisticated gastro-pub in a great location five minutes' from Lake Windermere in the centre of Bowness-on-Windermere. Local ales vie with international beers at the bar, and good food based on local produce is available throughout the day from a choice of menus: breakfast/brunch; sandwiches and light lunches; starters, nibbles and salads; main courses - braised Cumbrian farmed pork belly with parmentier potatoes, carrot purée and black pudding - desserts and a children's menu. In warmer weather head for the garden terrace where there are great views.

Open all day all wk 9am-11pm Closed: 25 Dec Bar Meals L served all wk 11.30-4 D served all wk 5-9 Restaurant L served all wk 11.30-4 D served all wk 5-9 ⊕ FREE HOUSE ◀ Coniston Bluebird Bitter, Hawkshead Bitter. 🍷 12 Facilities Children's menu Garden Parking

Eagle & Child Inn ★★★ INN 🍷

Kendal Rd, Staveley LA8 9LP ☎ 01539 821320
e-mail: info@eaglechildinn.co.uk
web: www.eaglechildinn.co.uk
dir: M6 junct 36, A590 towards Kendal then A591 towards Windermere. Staveley approx 2m

The rivers Kent and Gowan meet at the gardens of this friendly inn, and it's surrounded by miles of excellent walking, cycling and fishing country. Several pubs in Britain share the same name, which refers to a legend of a baby found in an eagle's nest. Dishes include Fleetwood mussels in tomato, garlic and white wine sauce, local rump steak braised with onions; and roast cod loin in anchovy and parsley butter. There is comfortable accommodation available.

Open all wk 11am-11pm Bar Meals L served Mon-Fri 12-2.30, Sat-Sun 12-3 D served Mon-Fri 6-8.45, ◀ Black Sheep Best Bitter, Coniston, Hawkshead Bitter, Dent Ales, Yates Bitter, Tirril Brewery Ŏ Westons. 🍷 10
Facilities Children's menu Dogs allowed Garden Parking Rooms 5

WORKINGTON — Map 18 NY02

The Old Ginn House

Great Clifton CA14 1TS
☎ 01900 64616 📠 01900 873384
e-mail: enquiries@oldginnhouse.co.uk
dir: Just off A66, 3m from Workington & 4m from Cockermouth

The inn was converted from a 17th-century farmstead. The Ginn Room was where farm horses were harnessed to a grindstone to crush crops. Today the unique rounded room is the main bar offering warm hospitality and a well stocked bar; there is also a cosy lounge. The butter yellows, bright check curtains and terracotta tiles of the dining areas exude a warm Mediterranean glow. A menu of the usual bar food is supplemented by larger dishes such as a Ginn House steak, which is stuffed with ham and onion and topped with stilton or cheddar.

Open all day all wk 11am-mdnt Closed: 24-26 Dec, 1 Jan Bar Meals L served all wk 12-2 D served all wk 6-9.30 Av main course £8 Restaurant L served all wk 12-2 D served all wk 6-9.30 Av 3 course à la carte fr £16 ⊕ FREE HOUSE ◀ Jennings Bitter, John Smiths Bitter.
Facilities Children's menu Garden Parking

YANWATH — Map 18 NY52

PICK OF THE PUBS

The Yanwath Gate Inn 🍷

CA10 2LF ☎ 01768 862386
e-mail: enquiries@yanwathgate.com
dir: Telephone for directions

The Yanwath Gate Inn has been offering hospitality in the North Lakes since 1683. Today the ethos of owner Matt Edwards is to offer good quality informal dining based on produce which is usually local and organic if possible. While choosing from the regularly changing seasonal menu, enjoy a pint of Doris' 90th Birthday Ale or one of the other Cumbrian ales on offer. Fish is delivered fresh every morning so there are always half a dozen fish and seafood specials on the carte menu. A typical dinner choice could be white bean and garlic soup; or wood pigeon and chestnut salad; followed by smoked venison loin; or gilthead bream; then sticky date pudding to finish. A cosy reading area in the bar ensures a relaxed mood for diners who can choose to eat here by the log fire or at a table in one of the two dining rooms.

Open all day all wk noon-11pm Bar Meals L served all wk 12-2.30 booking required D served all wk 6-9 booking required Av main course £10 Restaurant L served all wk 12-2.30 booking required D served all wk 6-9 booking required Av 3 course à la carte fr £30 ⊕ FREE HOUSE ◀ Hesket Newmarket Doris's 90th Birthday Ale, Tirril, Keswick, Paulaner Hefeweizen, De Koninck. 🍷 12 Facilities Children's menu Dogs allowed Garden Parking

DERBYSHIRE

ASHBOURNE — Map 10 SK14

Barley Mow Inn

Kirk Ireton DE6 3JP ☎ 01335 370306
dir: Telephone for directions

On the edge of the Peak District National Park, this imposing 17th-century inn has remained largely unchanged over the years. Close to Carsington Water, ideal for sailing, fishing and bird watching. There are also good walking opportunities on nearby marked paths. Ales from the cask and traditional cider; fresh granary rolls at lunchtime and evening meals for residents only.

Open all wk noon-2 7-11 (Sun noon-2 7-10.30) Closed: 25 Dec, 1 Jan ⊕ FREE HOUSE ◀ Changing micro breweries. Facilities Dogs allowed Garden Parking

Dog & Partridge Country Inn 🍷

Swinscoe DE6 2HS ☎ 01335 343183 📠 01335 342742
e-mail: info@dogandpartridge.co.uk
dir: From Ashbourne take A52 to Leek. 3m, pub on left in Swinscoe

This country free house was extended in 1966 to accommodate the Brazilian World Cup football team, who practised in a nearby field. Nowadays the pub scores highly for its extensive menus, offering a good selection of grills, fish, poultry and vegetarian dishes. Start, perhaps, with seafood pancake, followed by pan-fried liver with apple and cranberry; or local trout with a creamy stilton sauce. To finish, there's a wide choice of sweets, ice creams and cheeses.

Open all wk ⊕ FREE HOUSE ◀ Greene King Old Speckled Hen & Ruddles County, Hartington Best, Wells Bombardier, Courage Directors. 🍷 6 Facilities Play area Family room Dogs allowed Garden Parking

BAKEWELL — Map 16 SK26

PICK OF THE PUBS

The Bull's Head

Church St, Ashford-in-the-Water DE45 1QB
☎ **01629 812931**
e-mail: bullshead.ashford@virgin.net
dir: *Off A6, 2m N of Bakewell, 5m from Chatsworth Estate*

A family affair for several generations, the Bull's Head has seen the London and Manchester coaches come and go, though the village's famous well dressing is still a sight to enjoy. Everything about this cosy pub is smartly turned out, from the roses climbing round the door to the shiny brassware in the bar where you may choose between a pint of Robinson's Old Stockport, Unicorn or Double Hop. The interior is unpretentious, with dark wooden beams, open brick fires and comfy banquettes. There is no restaurant as such; dishes from a frequently changing menu are cooked to order and served in the small lounge bar. Lunchtime sees a range of sandwiches on offer, or delicious home-made soups such as tomato and lovage; or yellow split pea. Steak and Old Stockport ale pie served with braised red cabbage and dripping-roasted potatoes is a popular main course choice, with blueberry crumble pie and vanilla ice cream to finish.

Open all wk 11-3 (summer) noon-3 (winter) 6-11 (Sun noon-3 7-10.30) **Bar Meals** L served all wk 12-2 D served Mon-Sat (ex Thu in winter) 6.30-9, Sun 7-9 ⊕ ROBINSONS ◀ Old Stockport, Unicorn, Double Hop. **Facilities** Children's menu Family room Dogs allowed Garden Parking

PICK OF THE PUBS

The Monsal Head Hotel ★★ HL ◉ ♥

See Pick of the Pubs on opposite page

BAMFORD — Map 16 SK28

PICK OF THE PUBS

Yorkshire Bridge Inn ★★★★ INN ♥

See Pick of the Pubs on page120

BARLOW — Map 16 SK37

The Trout at Barlow

33 Valley Rd S18 7SL
☎ 0114 289 0893   📠 0114 289 0893
e-mail: mikenorie@btconnect.com
dir: *From Chesterfield follow the Newbold Rd B619 for 4.5m*

This country pub, a few miles outside Chesterfield at the start of the Peak District, has recently changed hands. It is strong on food and jazz, with Jazz Club every Saturday

night and Jazz Dining the first Monday of the month. There is also a quiz on a Wednesday night. A weekly-changing choice of two real ales is offered and freshly prepared, home-cooked food. All special occasions are catered for, such as weddings and parties.

Open all wk 12-3 6-11 (Sun noon-9.30) **Bar Meals** booking required Av main course £10.95 **Restaurant** L served Mon-Sat 12-2, Sun 12-4 booking required D served Mon-Sat 6-9 booking required ⊕ MARSTON'S ◀ Marston's Pedigree, Mansfield Smooth, Marston's Finest Creamy, Guest. **Facilities** Children's menu Garden Parking

BARROW UPON TRENT — Map 11 SK32

Ragley Boat Stop NEW ♥

Deepdale Ln, Off Sinfin Ln DE73 1HH ☎ **01332 703919**
e-mail: ragley@king-henry-taverns.co.uk
dir: *Please telephone for directions*

When King Henry's Taverns bought this canalside pub, its outbuildings were in a dangerous condition, there was no sewerage, and three acres of overgrown garden sloped down to the waterside. But now it offers pub grub to satisfy the appetites of boaters hungry after hours sitting motionless at the tiller. Traditional favourites include bangers and mash; fisherman's pie; and for the truly ravenous a Mighty Man mixed grill. Pan-fried swordfish and steaks in different guises, such as fillet steak fajitas, are other tempting choices.

Open all day all wk noon-11 **Bar Meals** Av main course £3 food served all day **Restaurant** food served all day ⊕ KING HENRY TAVERNS ◀ Greene King IPA, Marstons Pedigree, Guinness. ♥ 15 **Facilities** Children's menu Play area Family room Garden Parking

BASLOW — Map 16 SK27

Rowley's ◉◉ ♥

Church Ln DE45 1RY
☎ 01246 583880   📠 01246 583818
e-mail: info@rowleysrestaurant.co.uk
dir: *A619/A623 signed Chatsworth. Baslow on edge of Chatsworth Estate*

While the emphasis here is on classy eating, Rowley's honours its roots as a village pub (formerly The Prince of Wales): drinkers are still welcome in the stone-flagged bar with its open fire. Serving a mix of modern and traditional British food using fresh local produce, typical dishes include clam and mussel risotto followed by pork osso buco with cider fondant potatoes, spring cabbage, glazed baby onions and pork jus. Outside is a terrace with lovely church views - ideal for enjoying a pint of local cask ale.

Open 11-3 5.30-mdnt, Sat 11-mdnt Closed: 1st wk Jan, Sun eve **Bar Meals** L served Mon-Fri 12-2, Sat 12-2.30, Sun 12-3 D served Mon-Thu 5.30-7.30 **Restaurant** L served Mon-Fri 12-2, Sat 12-2.30, Sun 12-3 D served Mon-Thu 5.30-9, Fri-Sat 6-10 ⊕ FREE HOUSE ◀ Thornbridge, Black Sheep Best Bitter Ö Aspalls. ♥ 9 **Facilities** Children's menu Parking

BIRCHOVER — Map 16 SK26

PICK OF THE PUBS

The Druid Inn ♥

Main St DE4 2BL ☎ **01629 650302**
e-mail: thedruidinn@hotmail.co.uk
dir: *From A6 between Matlock & Bakewell take B5056 signed Ashbourne. Approx 2m left to Birchover*

This family-run free house was built in 1607, and retains its original tiled floor and real log fires. Choose between a leisurely lunch and a pint of Druid Ale in the bar and snug, or go for a more formal experience in the upper or lower restaurant. On bright, sunny days, the outside terrace presents a further option, with views over the surrounding Derbyshire countryside. The same menu is served throughout, offering a selection of light bites; classic or hot sandwiches; and full meals. Starters such as honey-roasted belly pork with hoi sin sauce, spring onion and cucumber salad herald main course dishes like penne pasta with peas, pesto and Parmesan; Druid game pie with garlic mash; and grilled pollack with tomato and grain mustard herb crust. The pub is especially popular on summer weekends, when many visitors walk up to the moors behind the inn.

Open 11-3 6-11 (Sat 11am-mdnt) Closed: Sun eve **Bar Meals** L served Mon-Sat 12-2.30, Sun 12-3 booking required D served Mon-Thu 6-9, Fri-Sat 6-9.30 booking required **Restaurant** L served Mon-Sat 12-2.30, Sun 12-3 booking required D served Mon-Thu 6-9, Fri-Sat 6-9.30 booking required ⊕ FREE HOUSE ◀ Druid Bitter, Guest ale. ♥ 12 **Facilities** Children's menu Garden Parking

The Red Lion

Main St DE4 2BN ☎ **01629 650363**
e-mail: matteo@frau36.fsnet.co.uk
dir: *5.5m from Matlock, off A6 onto B5056*

Druids practised their magic amidst Rowter Rocks, a 70-yard-long pile of gritstone with fine views of the wooded hillside and valley below. Originally a farmhouse, the Red Lion was built in 1680, and gained its first licence in 1722. Its old well, now glass-covered, still remains in the Tap Room. The exposed stone walls, scrubbed oak tables and quarry tiled floor add to the cosy and welcoming atmosphere. Expect reasonably priced home-cooked food made with local ingredients, with dishes ranging from a simple sandwich to a rustic Sardinian dish from co-owner Matteo's homeland.

Open 12-2.30 7-11.30 (Sat & BH Mons noon-mdnt) Closed: Mon in winter **Bar Meals** L served Tue-Sun 12-2 D served Tue-Sun 7-9 Av main course £8 **Restaurant** L served Tue-Sun 12-2 D served Tue-Sun 7-9 Fixed menu price fr £11.95 Av 3 course à la carte fr £8 ⊕ FREE HOUSE ◀ Boddingtons, Nine Ladies, Black Sheep, Ichinusa (Sardinian), Peakstone's Rock Brewery Bitters. **Facilities** Children's menu Dogs allowed Garden Parking

PICK OF THE PUBS

The Monsal Head Hotel ★★ HL ❀ ♀

BAKEWELL   Map 16 SK26

Monsal Head DE45 1NL
☎ 01629 640250 📠 01629 640815
e-mail: enquiries@monsalhead.com
dir: *A6 from Bakewell towards Buxton. 1.5m
to Ashford. Follow Monsal Head signs, B6465
for 1m*

Built in the 19th century as the Bull's
Head, this distinctive balconied free
house was later rebuilt as the Railway
Hotel. Set in the heart of the Peak
District National Park just three miles
from Bakewell, the hotel enjoys lovely
views over Monsal Dale. There are seven
en suite bedrooms, and the complex is
ideally located for touring and walking;
Chatsworth House and Haddon Hall are
a ten-minute drive away. The hotel's
real ale pub, the Stables, reflects its
earlier role as the home of railway
horses which collected passengers from

Monsal Dale station. Today, this
delightful venue features original
flagstone floors and seating in the
former horse stalls, with horse tack on
the walls and a hay rack at the back of
the bar. You'll find welcoming winter
fires, and a range of cask ales that
includes Theakstones and Lloyds
Monsal. Lagers, wheat beers and wines
by the bottle or glass are also on offer.
Food is served all day in the bar and
Longstone restaurant, or in fine weather
you may prefer to eat in the large
enclosed garden. There's a full range of
snacks, sandwiches and jacket
potatoes, as well as a children's menu.
Typical choices from the main menu
might start with chestnut and sweet
potato risotto cakes; or duck and
pistachio galantine with tomato and
pepper chutney. Main course options
include seared venison medallions with
red cabbage and mashed potato;
crusted roast salmon tournedos; and
pan-fried wild mushrooms with cream
and Stilton sauce. There are daily
choices of brûlée or fruit crumble to
round things off, or you might prefer a
sorbet or sticky toffee pudding.

Open 8am-11pm **Bar Meals** L served
Mon-Sat 12-9.30, Sun 12-9 D served
Mon-Sat 12-9.30, Sun 12-9 Av main
course £12 **Restaurant** L served Mon-
Sat 12-9.30, Sun 12-9 D served Mon-
Sat 12-9.30, Sun 12-9 Av 3 course à la
carte fr £25 🛢 FREE HOUSE
🍺 Theakstons, Bradfield ales, Lloyds
Monsal, Thornbridge ales, Abbeydale.
♀ 17 **Facilities** Children's menu Dogs
allowed Garden Parking **Rooms** 7

PICK OF THE PUBS

Yorkshire Bridge Inn ★★★★INN ♀

BAMFORD Map 16 SK28

Ashopton Rd S33 0AZ
☎ 01433 651361 📄 01433 651361
e-mail: info@yorkshire-bridge.co.uk
web: www.yorkshire-bridge.co.uk
dir: *A57 from M1, left onto A6013, pub 1m on right*

The old packhorse bridge that crosses the River Derwent here on Derbyshire's border with Yorkshire gives this early 19th-century inn its name. It is surrounded by wonderful Peak District walking country, while a short stroll away are the Ladybower and other Derwent Valley reservoirs, famed for the RAF's Dambuster training runs in 1943.

These reservoirs caused heated controversy when they were created in the first half of the 20th century, but have long-since matured into beautiful attractions in their own right. The inn's beamed and chintz-curtained bars are cosy and welcoming in winter, although in warmer weather you might want to be in the stone-built conservatory, outside in the courtyard, or in the spacious beer garden. Good quality, freshly made pub food is prepared to order using local produce; the standard menu, complemented by daily specials, lists submarines, toasted sandwiches and filled jacket potatoes (lunchtime only), plus grills and other hot dishes which are available throughout the day. Starters include garlic mushrooms (with or without Stilton); large Yorkshire pudding with creamy onion sauce and gravy; and homemade soup with French bread and croutons. Among the main courses are chicken tikka masala; rosemary and garlic lamb steaks; home-

made steak and kidney pie; fish of the day; and sweet potato and leek crumble. There's also a good choice of salads and grilled steaks. For dessert, you could try English treacle and orange tart, or a home-made crumble. The en suite bedrooms, including one with a four-poster, make a good base for touring the nearby attractions of Chatsworth, Dovedale and Bakewell.

Open all wk 11am-11pm **Bar Meals** L served Mon-Sat 12-2, Sun 12-8.30 D served Mon-Thu 6-9, Fri-Sat 6-9.30, Sun 12-8.30 🛢 FREE HOUSE ◀ Bakewell Best, Pale Rider, Golden Pippen, Copper Dragon Scotts 1816. ♀ 13
Facilities Children's menu Garden Parking **Rooms** 14

BIRCH VALE — Map 16 SK08

PICK OF THE PUBS

The Waltzing Weasel Inn ★★★ INN ♥

New Mills Rd SK22 1BT
☎ 01663 743402 📄 01663 743402
e-mail: w-weasel@zen.co.uk
dir: *Village at junct of A6015 & A624, halfway between Glossop & Chapel-en-le-Firth*

Dramatic views of Kinder Scout set this 400-year-old quintessentially English inn apart from the crowd. Situated beside the Sett Valley trail, it is an ideal spot for walkers. The bar is warmed by a real fire and furnished with country antiques, while the restaurant has more of those wonderful views from its mullioned windows. There are no games machines or piped music; just the occasional live jazz session. The pub is a popular dining venue, and deservedly so; menus draw on excellent local produce, including beef (in everything from lasagne to cottage pie); Hartington chicken, which might be stuffed with mushrooms, pan fried and served with a Stilton and white wine sauce; and game, which appears in home-made kinder pie with lamb, orange and red wine. Be sure to try some of the Weasel's own sausages - Harvey Bangers. There are eight en suite bedrooms available, some with fine rural views.

Open all wk ⊕ FREE HOUSE ◀ Marston's Best & Pedigree, Jennings Sneck Lifter, Greene King IPA, Old Speckled Hen. ♥ 10 **Facilities** Garden Parking **Rooms** 8

BRADWELL — Map 16 SK18

The Old Bowling Green Inn ♥

Smalldale S33 9JQ ☎ 01433 620450
dir: *Off A6187 onto B6049 towards Bradwell*

A 16th-century coaching inn with impressive views over glorious countryside. Traditional country cooking and good value daily specials supplemented by weekly changing ales produce grilled goats' cheese with sun-dried tomatoes and caramelised onions; chicken breast in mushroom, white wine and mustard grain cream sauce; sea bass fillets on celeriac mash, and meat and potato pie. Bakewell tart and apple crumble feature among a range of tempting home-made puddings.

Open all day all wk noon-mdnt **Bar Meals** L served Mon-Sat 12-2.30, Sun 12.30-4 D served Mon-Sat 6-9 **Restaurant** L served Mon-Sat 12-2.30, Sun 12.30-4 D served Mon-Sat 6-9 ⊕ ENTERPRISE INNS ◀ Stones, Tetleys, Theakstons, Copper Dragon, Black Sheep, guest ales. ♥ 8 **Facilities** Play area Garden Parking

BRASSINGTON — Map 16 SK25

PICK OF THE PUBS

Ye Olde Gate Inne

Well St DE4 4HJ ☎ 01629 540448 📄 01629 540448
e-mail: theoldgateinn@supanet.com
dir: *2m from Carsington Water off A5023 between Wirksworth & Ashbourne*

Built in 1616 out of local stone and timbers allegedly salvaged from the wrecked Armada fleet, this venerable inn stands beside an old London to Manchester turnpike in the heart of Brassington, a hill village on the southern edge of the Peak District. Oak beams, black cast iron log burner, an antique clock, charmingly worn quarry-tiled floors and a delightful mishmash of polished furniture give the inn plenty of character. Hand-pumped Marston's Pedigree Bitter takes pride of place behind the bar, alongside guest ales such as Jennings Cumberland. The menu offers firm lunchtime favourites, such as home-roasted ham, egg and home-made chips; and Cumberland sausages with creamed mash and onion gravy. In the evening, start with crevettes cooked in garlic butter and choose from the likes of roast pheasant breast wrapped in bacon with a port sauce, or pan-fried fillet of beef served with an oxtail broth.

Closed: Mon (ex BH), Tue L **Bar Meals** L served Wed-Sat 12-2, Sun 12-2.30 D served Tue-Sat 6.30-8.45 Av main course £9 ⊕ MARSTON'S ◀ Marston's Pedigree, Jennings Cumberland, guest ales. **Facilities** Children's menu Family room Dogs allowed Garden Parking

CASTLETON — Map 16 SK18

The Peaks Inn ♥

How Ln S33 8WJ ☎ 01433 620247 📄 01433 623590
e-mail: info@peaks-inn.co.uk
dir: *On A625 in town centre*

An attractive, stone-built village pub standing below the ruins of Peveril Castle, after which Castleton is named. The bar is warm and welcoming, with leather armchairs for weary walkers, and open log fires for their wet socks. The menu offers old favourites of steak and ale pie, bangers and mash; ham, egg and chips; beer battered cod; and a range of steaks.

Open all wk ⊕ PUNCH TAVERNS ◀ Black Sheep, Deuchars IPA, Tetley Smooth, 1 guest on rotation. ♥ 9 **Facilities** Dogs allowed Garden Parking

Ye Olde Nag's Head

Cross St S33 8WH
☎ 01433 620248 & 620443 📄 01433 621501
e-mail: info@yeoldenagshead.co.uk
web: www.yeoldenagshead.co.uk
dir: *A625 from Sheffield, W through Hope Valley, through Hathersage & Hope. Pub on main road*

A grey-stone, traditional 17th-century inn situated in the heart of the Peak District National Park, close to Chatsworth House, Haddon Hall and miles of wonderful walks. Walkers are welcome to seek refreshment in the cosy bars, warmed by open fires and kitted out with antiques, and where you'll find three ales on handpump and a good choice of pub food, including the all-day giant Derbyshire breakfast, sausages and mash, liver and onions and steak and ale pie.

Open all day all wk **Bar Meals** food served all day **Restaurant** food served all day ⊕ FREE HOUSE ◀ Black Sheep, Guinness. **Facilities** Children's menu Dogs allowed Parking

CHESTERFIELD — Map 16 SK37

PICK OF THE PUBS

Red Lion Pub & Bistro NEW ♥

Darley Rd, Stone Edge S45 0LW
☎ 01246 566142 📄 01246 591040
e-mail: ewen@redlionpubandbistro.com
dir: *Telephone for directions*

Located on the edge of the Peak District, the Red Lion is rumoured to stand at the very centre of Great Britain. Despite its wooden beams and stone walls, this stylish tree house is an effortless blend of old and new, with discreet lighting and comfy leather armchairs that place the spacious interiors firmly in the 21st century. Ian Daisley's striking black and white photographs decorate the walls, whilst local jazz bands liven the bar on Thursdays evenings. Home-grown salads and fresh, seasonal produce feature on the menus, and the chefs make everything from chutneys to black pudding. Typical choices might start with chicken liver parfait, followed by pan-seared duck breast, or one of the daily fish specials. Leave space for desserts like chocolate delice and toffee apple crumble with crème Anglais. Meals are served in the bar and bistro, or beneath white umbrellas in the large garden.

continued

CHESTERFIELD *continued*

Open all day all wk **Bar Meals** Av main course £16 food served all day **Restaurant** Av 3 course à la carte fr £35 food served all day ⊕ FREE HOUSE ◄ Timothy Taylor Landlord. ☺ 8 **Facilities** Children's menu Garden Parking

DERBY	Map 11 SK33

The Alexandra Hotel ☺

203 Siddals Rd DE1 2QE ☎ 01332 293993
dir: *Telephone for directions 150yds from railway station*

This two-roomed hotel is filled with railway memorabilia. It is noted for its real ale (11 hand pumps and 450 different brews on tap each year), range of malt whiskies, real ciders, and friendly atmosphere. A typical menu offers chilli con carne; liver and bacon; home-baked ham with free range egg and chips; filled Yorkshire puddings; ploughman's lunches; and freshly-made filled hot and cold cobs. Recent change of landlord.

Open all day all wk 11-11 (Sun 12-3 7-10) Closed: 25 Dec **Bar Meals** L served Thu-Sat 12-2.30 ⊕ TYNEMILL LTD ◄ Castle Rock, Elsie Mo, Harvest Pale ♂ Old Rosie, Stowford Press. ☺ 6 **Facilities** Dogs allowed Garden Parking **Notes** ⊠

DOE LEA	Map 16 SK46

Hardwick Inn ☺

Hardwick Park S44 5QJ
☎ 01246 850245   📄 01246 856365
e-mail: batty@hardwickinn.co.uk
web: www.hardwickinn.co.uk
dir: *M1 junct 29 take A6175. 0.5m left (signed Stainsby/ Hardwick Hall). After Stainsby, 2m, left at staggered junct. Follow brown tourist signs*

Built from locally quarried sandstone, this 15th-century inn stands by the south gate of the National Trust's Hardwick Hall, and has been run by three generations of the same family. The historic atmosphere has been retained, particularly when the coal fires are lit in winter. On the menu are local estate lamb dishes, (roast, grilled steak, and shepherd's pie); local game and ale casserole, and home-made vegetarian dishes including balti with rice and naan bread.

Open all wk **Bar Meals** food served all day **Restaurant** L served Tue-Sat 12-2, Sun 12-1 & 4-5.30 booking required D served Tue-Sat 7-8.30 booking required ⊕ FREE HOUSE ◄ Theakston Old Peculier & XB, Greene King Old Speckled Hen, Black Sheep, Bombardier. ☺ 24 **Facilities** Play area Family room Garden Parking

EYAM	Map 16 SK27

Miners Arms

Water Ln S32 5RG ☎ 01433 630853
dir: *Off B6521, 5m N of Bakewell*

This welcoming 17th-century inn and restaurant in the famous plague village of Eyam gets its name from the local lead mines of Roman times. Fish features strongly on the menu, with the likes of seafood pie, tuna steak on a bed of ratatouille, and grilled salmon fillet with a herb crust and sweet chilli sauce. Wash it all down with a pint of Theakston's Best, or Old Peculier.

Open all wk Closed: 26 Dec eve ◄ Worthington's Creamflow, Theakstons Best Pedigree, John Smiths, Old Peculier. **Facilities** Dogs allowed Garden Parking

FENNY BENTLEY	Map 16 SK14

PICK OF THE PUBS

Bentley Brook Inn ★★★ INN ☺

See Pick of the Pubs on opposite page

The Coach and Horses Inn ☺

DE6 1LB ☎ 01335 350246
e-mail: coachandhorses2@btconnect.com
dir: *On A515 (Ashbourne to Buxton road), 2.5m from Ashbourne*

A cosy refuge in any weather, this family-run, 17th-century coaching inn stands on the edge of the Peak District National Park. Besides the beautiful location, its charms include stripped wood furniture and low beams. Expect real ales and good home cooking along the lines of honey-roasted duck breast with a port and berry sauce; or whole roasted trout stuffed with pearl barley, wild mushrooms and parsley and finished with lemon butter.

Open all day all wk 11-11 (Sun 12-10.30) **Bar Meals** Av main course £9.50 food served all day **Restaurant** food served all day ⊕ FREE HOUSE ◄ Marston's Pedigree, Timothy Taylor Landlord, Black Sheep Best, Oakham JHB, Peak Ales Swift Nick. ☺ 6 **Facilities** Family room Garden Parking

FOOLOW	Map 16 SK17

The Bulls Head Inn NEW ★★★★ INN

S32 5QR ☎ 01433 630873   📄 01433 631738
e-mail: wilbnd@aol.com
dir: *Just off A623, N of Stoney Middleton*

Open fires, oak beams, flagstone floors, great views and good food are among the attractions at his 19th-century former coaching inn, tucked away in a conservation village high up in the Peak District. A welcome pit-stop for walkers and visitors for lunchtime sandwiches, minted lamb casserole, beef Wellington with red wine gravy, and roast sea bass with fennel, washed down with a pint of Black Sheep. Bedrooms are comfortable and well equipped.

Open 12-3 6.30-11 (all day Sun) Closed: Mon (ex BH) **Bar Meals** L served Tue-Sun 12-2 D served Tue-Sun 6.30-9 **Restaurant** L served Tue-Sun 12-2 D served Tue-Sun 6.30-9 ⊕ FREE HOUSE ◄ Black Sheep, Peak Ales, Adnams, Tetley. **Facilities** Children's menu Dogs allowed Parking **Rooms** 3

FROGGATT	Map 16 SK27

PICK OF THE PUBS

The Chequers Inn ★★★★ INN ⊛ ☺

Froggatt Edge S32 3ZJ
☎ 01433 630231   📄 01433 631072
e-mail: info@chequers-froggatt.com
dir: *On A625, 0.5m N of Calver*

Originally four stone-built 18th-century cottages, the Chequers stands above Calver on the steep banks of Froggatt Edge; its westward panorama of the Peak District National Park reached by a steep, wild woodland footpath from the elevated secret garden. The civilised interior of wooden floors, Windsor chairs, antique furnishings, blazing log fires is perfect for a contemplative pint of Kelham Island Easy Rider or your choice from an innovative modern European menu (with some British favourites). The food is prepared from locally sourced produce, ranging from sandwiches and salads through to starters as varied as grilled sardines with caper oil, and pork belly with saffron and red pepper potatoes. Mains take in smoked haddock and parsley fishcake; roast duck breast with pumpkin mash; and pan-fried calves' liver with mash, pancetta and fruit chutney. Finish with Bakewell pudding and custard. There are five en suite bedrooms available.

Open all wk 12-2 6-9.30 (Sat 12-9.30, Sun 12-9) Closed: 25 Dec **Bar Meals** L served Mon-Fri 12-2, Sat-Sun 12-6 D served Mon-Sat 6-9.30, Sun 6-9 Av main course £15 ⊕ FREE HOUSE ◄ Greene King IPA, Black Sheep, Kelham Island Easy Rider. ☺ 9 **Facilities** Children's menu Garden Parking **Rooms** 5

PICK OF THE PUBS

Bentley Brook Inn ★★★ INN ♟

FENNY BENTLEY　　　　Map 16 SK14

DE6 1LF
☎ 01335 350278　📠 01335 350422
e-mail: all@bentleybrookinn.co.uk
web: www.bentleybrookinn.co.uk

Completely refurbished but still full of traditional charm and atmosphere, this lovely building began life as a medieval farmhouse made from wattle and daub. Its near neighbour was the manor house, whose fortifications included five square towers - you can see the only remaining one from the inn's car park. The farmhouse was twice extended in the 1800s and, on the second occasion, re-roofed with slate. Between the World Wars, two elderly ladies lived here in considerable style, attended to by five servants, a gardener, an under-gardener and a coachman. The house became a restaurant in 1954, and a full drinks licence was granted in the 1970s. The inn serves a selection of real ales, some brewed by the local Leatherbritches brewery. Both the bar and the restaurant, which overlooks the terrace and garden, serve everything from sandwiches to substantial home-cooked dishes. Lunch might include black pudding and bacon tarlet with mustard sauce, followed by pork and leek sausages and mash, or chicken breast in a pesto sauce served on a bed of tagliatelle. The menus are changed with the seasons and in response to the usually plentiful supply of local game. Home-made desserts include sticky toffee pudding with butterscotch sauce and ice cream, and fresh fruit Pavlova with fruit coulis. Traditional English Sunday lunch is served as a three-course, three-roast carvery, and during the summer the barbecue in the garden is fired up. In the winter, snuggle up by the central open log fire and play dominoes, cards or chess - just ask at the bar. There are 11 en suite bedrooms available.

Open all week **Bar Meals** L served all wk 12-9 (Oct-Mar 12-3) D served all wk 12-9 (Oct-Mar 6-9) **Restaurant** L served all wk 12-9 (Oct-Mar 12-3) D served all wk 12-9 (Oct-Mar 6-9)
🍺 Leatherbritches Bespoke, Leatherbritches Hairy Helmet, Goldings, Marstons Pedigree. ♟ 7
Facilities Children's menu Play area Dogs allowed Garden Parking **Rooms** 11

GREAT HUCKLOW — Map 16 SK17

The Queen Anne Inn ★★★ INN ☂

SK17 8RF ☎ 01298 871246 ▤ 01298 873504
e-mail: angelaryan100@aol.com
dir: *A623 onto B6049, turn off at Anchor pub towards Bradwell, 2nd right to Great Hucklow*

A warm welcome awaits at this traditional country free house with its log fires, good food, and an ever-changing range of cask ales. The inn dates from 1621; a licence has been held for over 300 years, and the names of all the landlords are known. Stunning open views can be enjoyed from the sheltered south-facing garden. Specialities include lamb and beef from neighbouring farms, making Sunday lunch a particular favourite among the locals. Expect mains like halibut with creamy leeks and Gressingham duck breast with orange, sherry and pomegranate. There is also a wide choice of vegetarian dishes and a children's menu too.

Open noon-2.30 5-11 (Fri-Sun noon-11) Closed: Mon **Bar Meals** L served Tue-Sun 12-2 D served Tue-Thu 6-8.30 (Fri-Sat 6-9, Sun 6-8) Av main course £8.95 **Restaurant** L served Tue-Sun 12-2 D served Tue-Thu 6-8.30 (Fri-Sat 6-9, Sun 6-8) ⊕ FREE HOUSE ◀ Adnams Bitter, Shaws, Storm Brewery, Kelham Island, Phoenix Brewery. ☂ 10 **Facilities** Children's menu Garden Parking **Rooms** 2

GRINDLEFORD — Map 16 SK27

PICK OF THE PUBS

The Maynard ★★★ HL ◉◉

Main Rd S32 2HE ☎ 01433 630321 ▤ 01433 630445
e-mail: info@themaynard.co.uk
dir: *From M1 junct 30 take A619 into Chesterfield, then onto Baslow. A623 to Calver, right into Grindleford*

This fine stone-built inn stands grandly in immaculately kept grounds overlooking the Derwent Valley, in the heart of the Peak District National Park. You may eat in either the Longshore Bar or in the Padley Restaurant, with its large windows facing the gardens. Choose the bar, and the menu may well offer seared breast of chicken with mushroom risotto and balsamic oil; Moroccan-spiced braised lamb with couscous; or grilled sea bass on champ with tomato and olive salsa. Opt for the restaurant and discover other possibilities, such as eggs Benedict with chive oil, or smoked haddock fishcake as starters; main courses of fillet of beef with fondant potato, wild mushrooms and caramelised red wine onion; pan-fried calf's liver with olive oil mash, onion fritters and grilled pancetta; and pan-seared red mullet with shellfish paella and lobster oil. For dessert, try sticky toffee parkin pudding with stem ginger ice cream.

Open all day all wk noon-9 **Bar Meals** L served Sun-Fri 12-2 D served Sat 7-9 ⊕ FREE HOUSE ◀ Abbey Dale Moonshine, Bakewell Bitter. **Facilities** Dogs allowed Garden Parking **Rooms** 10

HARTSHORNE — Map 10 SK32

The Mill Wheel ★★★★ INN ☂

Ticknall Rd DE11 7AS
☎ 01283 550335 ▤ 01283 552833
e-mail: info@themillwheel.co.uk
dir: *A511 from Burton-on-Trent towards Leicester. Left at island signed A514/Derby. Pub a short distance*

This old building's huge mill wheel has survived for some 250 years. In 1945 a dispute over water rights cut off the supply and the site became derelict. Since being restored in 1987, the wheel has been slowly turning once again, and is very much the focus of attention in the bar and restaurant. Here dishes such as pan-fried Cornish mackerel with tapenade bruschetta are served, followed perhaps by roast loin of lamb with dauphinoise potatoes. If you want to stay over, there are modern bedrooms available.

Open all wk **Bar Meals** food served all day **Restaurant** L served 12-2.30 (Sun 12-8.30) D served 6-9.15 Mon-Thu (6-9.30 Fri-Sat, 12-8.30 Sun) ⊕ FREE HOUSE ◀ Abbot Ale, Oakham Ale, Summer Lightning, Bass, Pedigree. ☂ 8 **Facilities** Children's menu Garden Parking **Rooms** 4

HASSOP — Map 16 SK27

Eyre Arms ☂

DE45 1NS ☎ 01629 640390
e-mail: nick@eyrearms.com
dir: *On B6001 N of Bakewell*

Formerly a farmstead and 17th-century coaching inn, this traditional free house stands in one of the most beautiful parts of rural Derbyshire. Oak settles, low ceilings and cheery log fires create a cosy atmosphere, while the secluded garden overlooks the rolling Peak District countryside with its lovely local walks. Typical dishes include local venison pie; Grand Marnier duckling; and local trout baked with butter and almonds. Enjoy your meal with a pint of Black Sheep Special or Stowford Press cider.

Open all wk 11-3 6.30-11 Closed: 25 Dec **Bar Meals** L served all wk 12-2 D served all wk 6.30-9 ⊕ FREE HOUSE ◀ Marston's Pedigree, Black Sheep Special, Bakewell Best Bitter ♺ Westons Stowford Press. ☂ 9 **Facilities** Garden Parking

HATHERSAGE — Map 16 SK28

Millstone Inn ★★★★ INN ☂

Sheffield Rd S32 1DA
☎ 01433 650258 ▤ 01433 650276
e-mail: jerry@millstone.co.uk
dir: *Telephone for directions*

Striking views over the picturesque Hope Valley are afforded from this former coaching inn, set amid the beauty of the Peak District yet convenient for the city of Sheffield. The atmospheric bar serves six traditional cask ales all year round and the menu offers a good choice of dishes prepared from local produce, including a popular Sunday carvery of freshly roasted joints. A range of accommodation is available from single to family rooms.

Open all day all wk 11.30am-11pm **Bar Meals** L served all wk 12-9 booking required Av main course £9 food served all day ⊕ FREE HOUSE ◀ Timothy Taylor Landlord, Black Sheep, guest ales. ☂ 16 **Facilities** Children's menu Dogs allowed Garden Parking **Rooms** 8

PICK OF THE PUBS

The Plough Inn — INN ◉☂

Leadmill Bridge S32 1BA
☎ 01433 650319 & 650180 ▤ 01433 651049
e-mail: sales@theploughinn-hathersage.com
dir: *M1 junct 29, take A617W, A619, A623, then B6001 N to Hathersage*

This 17th-century free house stands in nine acres of its own grounds on the banks of the River Derwent. London Pride, Black Sheep and Old Speckled Hen accompany bar meals such as smoked salmon and crème fraîche tartlet with mixed leaves and new potatoes. Restaurant diners can look forward to pan-roast sea trout with mint gnocchi; wild mushroom and pearl barley risotto; and roast Owen Taylor beef with shallots, bacon, mushrooms and horseradish mash. With five tastefully decorated en suite bedrooms housed in the main building and across the cobbled courtyard in September Cottage, the Plough makes an ideal base for exploring the surrounding Peak District countryside. Nearby attractions include Chatsworth House, Haddon Hall and the Blue John Mine. The sheltered garden is a delight in summer, and a pretty array of flower-filled baskets adorns the inn's external walls.

Open all wk Closed: 25 Dec **Bar Meals** L served all wk 12-2.30 D served all wk 6.30-9.30 booking required **Restaurant** L served all wk 12-2.30 booking required D served all wk 6.30-9.30 booking required Fixed menu price fr £17.95 Av 3 course à la carte fr £20.05 ⊕ FREE HOUSE ◢ London Pride, Old Speckled Hen, Black Sheep, Youngs Bitter, Bombardier. ⊥ 14 **Facilities** Garden Parking **Rooms** 5

The Scotsmans Pack Country Inn NEW ★★★★ INN ⊥

School Ln S32 1BZ ☎ 01433 650253 📄 01433 650712
web: www.scotsmanspack.com
dir: *Hathersage is on A625 8m from Sheffield*

This historic inn in the beautiful Hope Valley is located on one of the old packhorse trails used by Scottish 'packmen' or travelling drapers. Just a short walk away from Hathersage church and Little John's Grave, the inn is ideally placed for walking and touring the Peak District, with five individually designed en suite bedrooms. Hearty pub dishes include braised steak in red wine sauce, home-made lasagne and salad, and lamb's liver and bacon with onion gravy. Wash you meal down with a great choice of real ales.

Open all day all wk 11-3 6-mdnt (all day Fri-Sun) **Bar Meals** L served Mon-Fri 12-2 booking required D served Mon-Fri 6-9, Sat-Sun 12-9 booking required ⊕ MARSTONS PLC ◢ Jennings Cumberland, Pedigree, Mansfield Bitter. ⊥ 7 **Facilities** Children's menu Family room Garden Parking **Rooms** 5

The Royal Hotel ⊥

Market St SK22 2EP ☎ 01663 742721
e-mail: enquiries@theroyalhayfield.co.uk
web: www.theroyalhayfield.co.uk
dir: *Off A624*

A fine-looking, mid-18th-century building in a High Peak village. The oak-panelled Windsor Bar has log fires, and serves bar snacks and selected dishes, while the dining room offers a traditional menu from which you might select spinach and mushroom pancake, followed by rack of lamb (served pink) with rich port jus; or grilled plaice with cream and prawn sauce. Then chef's hot pudding and custard to finish. Kinder Scout looks impressive from the patio.

Open all day all wk 12-11 **Bar Meals** L served Mon-Fri 12-2.30, Sat 12-9, Sun 12-6 D served Mon-Fri 6-9, Sat 12-9, Sun 12-6 ⊕ FREE HOUSE ◢ Hydes, Guest Ales ○ Stowford Press. ⊥ 8 **Facilities** Family room Garden Parking

---

The Red Lion Inn ⊥

Main St DE6 1PR ☎ 01335 370396 📄 01335 370396
e-mail: redlion@w3z.co.uk
web: www.redlionhognaston.co.uk
dir: *From Ashbourne take B5035 towards Wirksworth. Approx 5m follow Carsington Water signs. Turn right to Hognaston*

Set on the edge of the Peak District National Park just a short walk from beautiful Carsington Water, this 17th-century inn has a wealth of original features including beamed ceilings, open fireplaces and church pew seating. Its past includes a visit from John Kennedy Jr and his wife; modern-day visitors can enjoy food made with excellent local produce: perhaps Derbyshire steak and ale pie or pan-fried liver and onions with red wine gravy, plus roast pheasant or game pie when in season.

Open all wk 12-3 6-11 **Bar Meals** L served all wk 12-2.30 D served all wk 6.30-9 Av main course £9.95 **Restaurant** L served all wk 12-2.30 D served all wk 6.30-9 Av 3 course à la carte fr £24.50 ⊕ FREE HOUSE ◢ Marston's Pedigree, Guinness, Guest ales. ⊥ 9 **Facilities** Children's menu Garden Parking

Cheshire Cheese Inn ⊥

Edale Rd S33 6ZF ☎ 01433 620381 📄 01433 620411
e-mail: tcheese@gmail.com
dir: *On A6187 between Sheffield & Chapel-en-le-Frith*

Located on the old trans-Pennine salt route in the heart of the Peak District, this 16th-century inn owes its name to the tradition of accepting cheese as payment for lodgings. It has a reputation for good home-made food and hand-pulled beer served in a relaxed atmosphere with open fires. There is a choice of light bites and main meals, ranging from toasted sandwiches or jacket potatoes to a mixed grill or roasted lamb shank.

Open all wk ⊕ FREE HOUSE ◢ Slaters Toptotty, Wentworthy Pale Ale, Black Sheep Best, Hartington Bitter, Wards Bitter. ⊥ 13 **Facilities** Dogs allowed Garden Parking

Red Lion Inn ⊥

SK17 8QU ☎ 01298 871458 📄 01298 871458
e-mail: theredlionlitton@yahoo.co.uk
dir: *Just off A623 (Chesterfield to Stockport road), 1m E of Tideswell*

The Red Lion is a beautiful, traditional pub on the village green, very much at the heart of the local community. With its wood fires, selection of real ales and friendly atmosphere, it's a favourite with walkers and holiday-makers too. The menu offers hearty pub food at reasonable prices, such as haddock goujons to start, lambs' liver and bacon with horseradish mash to follow, and treacle sponge pudding with custard to round things off.

Open all wk ⊕ FREE HOUSE ◢ Barnsley Bitter, Timothy Taylor, Thornbridge Hall, Kelham Island, Whim Ales, Pale Rider, Hartingdon Bitter, Jaipuff. ⊥ 9 **Facilities** Dogs allowed Garden

LONGSHAW — Map 16 SK27

Fox House BUD ♥

Hathersage Rd S11 7TY ☎ 01433 630374
dir: From Sheffield follow A625 towards Castleton

A delightfully original 17th-century coaching inn and, at 1,132 feet above sea level, one of the highest pubs in Britain. The Longshaw dog trials originated here, after an argument between farmers and shepherds as to who owned the best dog. A simple menu lists sandwiches, starters, Sunday roasts, and mains like chicken and ham pie, ground Scottish beefsteak burger, spicy prawn pasta, and lamb cutlets.

Open all wk **Restaurant** L served all wk 12-5 D served Mon-Sat 12-10, Sun 12-9.30 ⊕ VINTAGE INNS ◀ Guest ales ♂ Aspall. ♥ 20 **Facilities** Garden Parking **Rooms** 10

MATLOCK — Map 16 SK35

The Red Lion ★★★★ INN

65 Matlock Green DE4 3BT ☎ 01629 584888
dir: From Chesterfield, A632 into Matlock, on right just before junct with A615

This friendly, family-run free house makes a good base for exploring local attractions like Chatsworth House, Carsington Water and Dovedale. Spectacular walks in the local countryside help to work up an appetite for bar lunches, steaks and a wide selection of home-cooked meals. In the winter months, open fires burn in the lounge and games room, and there's a boules area in the garden for warmer days. There are 6 comfortable bedrooms.

Open all wk **Bar Meals** L served Tue-Fri 12-2, Sun 12-2.30 booking required **Restaurant** D served Tue-Thu 7-9, Fri-Sat 7-9.30 booking required ⊕ FREE HOUSE ◀ Courage Directors, John Smiths & Theakstons Bitter, Peak Ales, guest ales. **Facilities** Garden Parking **Rooms** 6

MELBOURNE — Map 11 SK32

The Melbourne Arms ★★★ INN ♥

92 Ashby Rd DE73 8ES
☎ 01332 864949 & 863990 ▤ 01332 865525
e-mail: info@melbournearms.co.uk

This restaurant on the village outskirts was tastefully converted from an 18th-century pub about 13 years ago. There are two bars, a coffee lounge and the restaurant itself, traditionally decorated, - no, not red flock wallpaper - where an extensive menu of authentic Indian dishes is offered. With a range of English dishes and a children's menu too, there's no reason why the whole family can't find plenty to enjoy. You can stay over in one of the modern bedrooms.

Open all day all wk 11.30am-11.30pm **Bar Meals** Av main course £6.99 food served all day **Restaurant** Fixed menu price fr £12.99 Av 3 course à la carte fr £19 food served all day ⊕ FREE HOUSE ◀ Pedigree, Tetley's Smooth, Guinness. ♥ 12 **Facilities** Children's menu Play area Family room Garden Parking **Rooms** 7

MILLTOWN — Map 16 SK36

The Nettle Inn ♥

S45 0ES ☎ 01246 590462

A 16th-century hostelry on the edge of the Peak District, this inn has all the traditional charm you could wish for, from flower-filled hanging baskets to log fires and a stone-flagged taproom floor. Expect well-kept ales and impressive home-made food (including breads, pickles and sauces), using the best of seasonal, local produce. Typical dishes are locally made chorizo with pancetta, quail egg and salad; and pollack with broad bean and mint risotto and breaded deep-fried tripe. Look out for the special event evenings.

Open all wk Sat-Sun all day **Bar Meals** Av main course £6.75 food served all day **Restaurant** Av 3 course à la carte fr £25 food served all day ⊕ FREE HOUSE ◀ Bradfield Farmers Best Bitter, Bradfield Farmers Blonde, Hardy & Hansons, Olde Trip, Bradfield Belgian Blue, Bradfield Farmers Brown Cow. ♥ 9 **Facilities** Children's menu Dogs allowed Garden Parking

RIPLEY — Map 16 SK35

The Moss Cottage Hotel

Nottingham Rd DE5 3JT ☎ 01773 742555
e-mail: doug-ashley@hotmail.co.uk
dir: Telephone for directions

This red-brick free house specialises in carvery dishes, with four roast joints each day. Expect popular menu choices like prawn cocktail or mushroom dippers; ham, egg and chips; liver and onions; or battered haddock. Hot puddings include rhubarb crumble and chocolate fudge cake. Wash down your meal with a pint of Old Tripp.

Open 12-3 5-11 (Sun 5-8) Closed: Sun eve Mon L **Bar Meals** L served Tue-Sun 12-2 D served Mon-Sat 6-8 Av main course £8 **Restaurant** L served Tue-Sun 12-2 D served Mon-Sat 6-8 ⊕ FREE HOUSE ◀ Old Tripp, Guinness, Guest ale ♂ Old Rosie Scrumpy. **Facilities** Children's menu Parking

ROWSLEY — Map 16 SK26

The Grouse & Claret ★★★★ INN ♥

Station Rd DE4 2EB ☎ 01629 733233 ▤ 01629 735194
dir: On A6 between Matlock & Bakewell

A popular venue for local anglers, this pub takes its name from a fishing fly. It is also handy for touring the Peak District or visiting the stately homes of Haddon Hall and Chatsworth House. A meal from the cosmopolitan menu might include crispy duck salad with hoi sin sauce, and chicken and seafood paella or, for the more traditionally minded, prawn cocktail followed by steak and ale pie. Food served all day and accommodation is available.

Open all wk ⊕ WOLVERHAMPTON & DUDLEY BREWERIES PLC ◀ Marston's Pedigree, Mansfield, Bank's Bitter. ♥ 12 **Facilities** Play area Garden Parking **Rooms** 8

SHARDLOW — Map 11 SK43

The Old Crown Inn

Cavendish Bridge DE72 2HL ☎ 01332 792392
e-mail: the.oldcrowninn@btconnect.com
dir: M1 junct 24 take A6 towards Derby. Left before river, bridge into Shardlow

A family-friendly pub on the south side of the River Trent, where up to seven guest ales are served. It was built as a coaching inn during the 17th century, and retains its warm and atmospheric interior. Several hundred water jugs hang from the ceilings, while the walls display an abundance of brewery and railway memorabilia. Traditional food is lovingly prepared by the landlady, including sandwiches, jackets, omelettes, ham and eggs, and Cumberland sausages.

Open all day all wk 11am-mdnt (Fri-Sat 11am-1am) **Bar Meals** L served Mon-Fri 12-2, Sat 12-8, Sun 12-3 served Mon-Fri 5-8, Sat 12-8 Av main course £6.50 **Restaurant** L served Mon-Fri 12-2, Sat 12-8, Sun 12-3 D served Mon-Fri 5-8, Sat 12-8 Fixed menu price fr £9.25 (Sun L only) ⊕ MARSTONS ◀ Marston's Pedigree, Jennings Cocker Hoop, Guest ales. **Facilities** Children's menu Play area Dogs allowed Garden Parking

TIDESWELL — Map 16 SK17

The George Hotel ♥

Commercial Rd SK17 8NU
☎ 01298 871382 ▤ 01298 871382
e-mail: georgehoteltideswell@yahoo.co.uk
dir: A619 to Baslow, A623 towards Chapel-en-le-Frith, 0.25m

A 17th-century coaching inn in a quiet village conveniently placed for exploring the National Park and visiting Buxton, Chatsworth and the historic plague village of Eyam. Quality home-cooked food includes venison cooked in red wine sauce, roast pheasant with bacon, potatoes and mushrooms, seafood crumble, and whole rainbow trout with almonds.

Open all wk ⊕ HARDY & HANSONS PLC ◀ Kimberley Cool, Olde Trip Bitter, Best Bitter. ♥ 12 **Facilities** Dogs allowed Garden Parking

Three Stags' Heads

Wardlow Mires SK17 8RW ☎ 01298 872268
dir: At junct of A623 (Baslow to Stockport road) & B6465

Grade II listed 17th-century former farmhouse, designated by English Heritage as one of over 200 heritage pubs throughout the UK. It is located in the limestone uplands of the northern Peak District, and is now combined with a pottery workshop. Well-kept real ales and hearty home-cooked food for ramblers, cyclists and locals includes chicken and spinach curry; pork, leek and stilton pie, and game in season. No children under eight.

Open noon-mdnt (Fri 7-mdnt) Closed: Mon-Thu (ex BH) **Bar Meals** L served Sat-Sun 12.30-3 D served Fri-Sun 7.30-9.30 ⊕ FREE HOUSE ◀ Abbeydale Matins, Absolution, Black Lurcher & Brimstone Bitter. **Facilities** Dogs allowed Parking **Notes** ⊗

WESSINGTON   Map 16 SK35

The Three Horseshoes

The Green DE55 6DQ ☎ 01773 834854
dir: *A615 towards Matlock, 3m after Alfreton, 5m before Matlock*

A century ago horses were still being traded over the bar at this late-17th-century former coaching inn and associated blacksmith's forge, to both of which activities it no doubt owes its name. For a true taste of the Peak District try Derbyshire chicken with black pudding and apple; or braised lamb shank with celeriac purée. Several local walks start or end at the pub - why not order a picnic, or a hamper for refreshment?

Closed: Mon (winter) ◀ Guinness, Hardys & Hansons Olde Trip, guest ale. **Facilities** Play area Dogs allowed Garden Parking

DEVON

ASHBURTON   Map 3 SX77

The Rising Sun ★★★★ INN ⬤

Woodland TQ13 7JT ☎ 01364 652544
e-mail: admin@therisingsunwoodland.co.uk
dir: *From A38 E of Ashburton take lane signed Woodland/ Denbury. Pub on left, approx 1.5m*

A former drovers' inn, largely rebuilt following a fire in 1989, The Rising Sun is set in beautiful Devon countryside, convenient for Exeter, Plymouth and Torbay. Regularly changing real ales are served. Owner Paul is the chef and is dedicated to using local and seasonal produce on his menus. There's a good choice of fish from Brixham – baked Brixham sea bass - and excellent West Country cheeses; children's menu too. As well as dishes like roasted rack of Woodland lamb or belly of Tamworth pork, the pub is well known for its home-made pies (available to take home). There are five en suite bedrooms available.

Open all wk noon-3 6-11 (Sun noon-3 6.30-11, all day mid Jul-mid Sep) Closed: 25 Dec **Bar Meals** Av main course £8.50 food served all day **Restaurant** Av 3 course à la carte fr £17 food served all day ⊕ FREE HOUSE ◀ Princetown Jail Ale, IPA, Teignworthy Reel Ale, guest ales ⬥ Thatchers. ⬤ 10 **Facilities** Children's menu Play area Family room Dogs allowed Garden Parking **Rooms** 5

AVONWICK   Map 3 SX75

The Avon Inn ⬤

TQ10 9NB ☎ 01364 73475
e-mail: dfreresmith@yahoo.co.uk
dir: *Telephone for directions*

There's a change of ownership at this handsome whitewashed free house, just off the busy Exeter to Plymouth trunk road. The focus is on great home-cooked food using fresh local produce, with fruit and vegetables from the owners own allotment. Warm and cosy in winter, the large beer garden is perfect for the warmer weather with its three areas – lawn and flowers, new family area and a secluded section that goes down to the river Avon. Look out for barbecues at weekends.

Open all day all wk 10.30am-11.30pm (Sun 10.30am-11pm) **Bar Meals** Av main course £7 food served all day **Restaurant** Av 3 course à la carte fr £20 food served all day ⊕ FREE HOUSE ◀ Otter Bitter, Otter Bright, Blackawton 44 Special, Guinness ⬥ Thatchers Gold. ⬤ 6 **Facilities** Children's menu Play area Dogs allowed Garden Parking

PICK OF THE PUBS

The Turtley Corn Mill   INN ⬤

TQ10 9ES ☎ 01364 646100 ▤ 01364 646101
e-mail: mill@avonwick.net
dir: *Please teleohone for directions*

Milling apart, this sprawling old building has witnessed a number of activities, including chicken hatching, before its transformation to a pub in the 1970s. The idyllic six-acre site is bordered by a river and includes a lake with its own small island. Completely renovated five years ago, the interior is light and fresh with oak and slate floors, bookcases, old furniture and pictures galore of the chicken hatchery. There are no fruit machines, pool tables or music, but plenty of newspapers and books to browse through while supping an agreeable pint of Tamar Ale, Tribute or Dartmoor IPA. Daily changing menus, based extensively on local produce, feature starters such as spiced goats' cheese and pear tartlet; main courses of warm salad of Cornish scallops with sautéed potatoes and crispy bacon; and 'the most sublime Rocombe organic Devon ice creams'. Some desserts can be boxed to take home if you are too full, with clotted cream substituted for ice cream for obvious reasons. If you would like to stay over there are four comfortable bedrooms.

Open all wk Closed: 25 Dec **Bar Meals** Av main course £13.45 food served all day **Restaurant** food served all day ⊕ FREE HOUSE ◀ Tamar Ale, Jail Ale, Tribute, Dartmoor IPA, guest ales ⬥ Thatchers. ⬤ 9 **Facilities** Children's menu Dogs allowed Garden Parking **Rooms** 4

AXMOUTH   Map 4 SY29

PICK OF THE PUBS

The Harbour Inn

Church St EX12 4AF ☎ 01297 20371
e-mail: theharbourinn@live.co.uk
dir: *Main street opposite church, 1m from Seaton*

The River Axe meanders through its valley into Lyme Bay, but just before they meet is Axmouth harbour, which accounted for one sixth of Devon's trade during the 16th century. This cosy, oak-beamed, harbourside inn was built four centuries earlier, however. Gary and Graciela Tubb have maintained three principles - local ingredients bought from small family businesses, nothing frozen, and everything home made. A bar and bistro menu offers scampi and chips, lasagne, sausages or faggots with mash and gravy, jacket potatoes, baguettes and sandwiches. From a daily updated blackboard menu, you might want to consider pork tenderloin with prunes and bacon; swordfish steak with niçoise salad; or tagliatelle, wild mushrooms and spicy tomato sauce. The Harbour makes a great stop if you are walking the South West Coast Path between Lyme Regis and Seaton.

Open all wk **Bar Meals** L served 12-2 D served 6.30-9 (Sun 7-9) **Restaurant** L served 12-2 D served 6.30-9 (Sun 7-9) ⊕ HALL & WOODHOUSE ◀ Badger 1st Gold, Tanglefoot, Sussex ⬥ Stowford Press, Applewood. **Facilities** Children's menu Play area Dogs allowed Garden Parking

The Ship Inn ⬤

EX12 4AF ☎ 01297 21838
dir: *1m S of A3052 between Lyme & Sidmouth. Signed to Seaton at Boshill Cross*

There are long views over the Axe estuary from the beer garden of this creeper-clad family-run inn. It was built soon after the original Ship burnt down on Christmas Day 1879, and is able to trace its landlords back to 1769; the current ones have been there for over 40 years. Well kept real ales complement an extensive menu including daily blackboard specials where local fish and game feature, cooked with home-grown herbs.

Open all day all wk 11am-11pm **Bar Meals** L served all wk 12-2.30 booking required D served all wk 6-9 booking required **Restaurant** L served all wk 12-2.30 booking required D served all wk 6-9 booking required ⊕ PUNCH TAVERNS ◀ Otter Bitter, Guinness, 6X ⬥ Stowford Press. ⬤ 10 **Facilities** Children's menu Play area Family room Dogs allowed Garden Parking

BARBROOK — Map 3 SS74

The Beggars Roost

EX35 6LD ☎ 01598 752404
e-mail: info@beggarsroost.co.uk
dir: *A39, 1m from Lynton*

Originally a manor farmhouse with attached cow barn, the buildings were converted into a hotel in the 1970s with the barn becoming the Beggars Roost. The long, low bar has tables around a warm log-burner; the restaurant on the floor above extends up into the beamed apex and is popular for parties. The pub menu offers a great range of reasonably priced favourites such as casseroles, terrines and ploughman's, while the restaurant focuses on more sophisticated fare.

Open noon-2.30 6-close **Closed:** Mon (Nov-Feb) **Bar Meals** L served all wk 12-2.30 D served all wk 6-9 **Restaurant** L served all wk 12-2.30 D served all wk 6-9 ⊕ FREE HOUSE ◀ Exmoor Ale, Cotleigh Barn Owl, Exmoor Silver Stallion, Cotleigh Tawny Ö Thatchers. **Facilities** Children's menu Dogs allowed Garden Parking

BEER — Map 4 SY28

Anchor Inn ☻

Fore St EX12 3ET ☎ 01297 20386 ▤ 01297 24474
e-mail: 6403@greeneking.co.uk
dir: *A3052 towards Lyme Regis. At Hangmans Stone take B3174 into Beer. Pub on seafront*

Fish caught by local boats feature strongly on the menu at this pretty colour-washed hotel, which overlooks the sea in the picture-perfect Devon village of Beer. Dine on beer-battered cod and chips; local crab with salad; smoked haddock on Cheddar cheese mash with a mustard cream sauce; or chicken breast stuffed with brie, wrapped in bacon and served with a cranberry and red wine sauce.

Open all day all wk 8am-11pm **Bar Meals** L served Mon-Fri 11-2.30, Sat-Sun 11-4 D served Sun-Thu 6-9, Fri-Sat 6-9.30 **Restaurant** L served Mon-Fri 12-2.30, Sat-Sun 12-3 D served Sun-Thu 6-9, Fri-Sat 6-9.30 ⊕ GREENE KING ◀ Otter Ale, Greene King IPA, Abbot Ale. ☻ 14 **Facilities** Children's menu Garden

BERE FERRERS — Map 3 SX46

Olde Plough Inn

PL20 7JL ☎ 01822 840358
e-mail: info@oldeploughinn.co.uk
dir: *A390 from Tavistock*

Originally three cottages, dating from the 16th century, this inn has bags of character, with its old timbers and flagstones, which on closer inspection are revealed to be headstones. To the rear is a fine patio overlooking the River Tavey, and there are lovely walks in the Bere Valley on the doorstep. The area is ideal for birdwatchers. Dishes on offer range through fresh fish, crab, local pies, curries and stir-fries.

Open all wk 11-3 6-11 (Sat end May-end Aug 11-11 Sun noon-11) **Closed:** 1st wk Jan **Bar Meals** L served all wk 12-2.30 D served all wk 6.30-9.30 **Restaurant** L served all wk 12-2.30 D served all wk 6.30-9.30 ⊕ FREE HOUSE ◀ Sharp's Doom Bar & Own, guest ale Ö Winkleigh. **Facilities** Family room Dogs allowed Garden

BICKLEIGH — Map 3 SS90

Fisherman's Cot ☻

EX16 8RW ☎ 01884 855237 ▤ 01884 855241
e-mail: fishermanscot.bickleigh@marstons.co.uk
dir: *Telephone for directions*

Well-appointed thatched inn by Bickleigh Bridge over the River Exe with food all day and large beer garden, just a short drive from Tiverton and Exmoor. The Waterside Bar is the place for snacks and afternoon tea, while the restaurant incorporates a carvery and à la carte menus. Sunday lunch is served, and champagne and smoked salmon breakfast is optional.

Open all day all wk 11am-11pm (Sun noon-10.30pm) **Bar Meals** L served all wk 12-9 booking required D served all wk 12-9 booking required food served all day **Restaurant** L served all wk 12-9 booking required D served all wk 12-9 booking required food served all day ⊕ ELDRIDGE POPE ☻ 8 **Facilities** Children's menu Garden Parking

BIGBURY-ON-SEA — Map 3 SX64

Pilchard Inn ☻

Burgh Island TQ7 4BG
☎ 01548 810514 ▤ 01548 810243
e-mail: reception@burghisland.com
dir: *From A38 turn off to Modbury then follow signs to Bigbury & Burgh Island*

A small 14th-century smugglers' inn located on a tiny island off the Devon coast; access is either on foot at low tide or by hydraulic sea tractor when the tide is high.

Pilchard Inn

Bigbury-on-Sea, Devon, TQ7 4BG

The Pilchard Inn is a genuine smugglers' pub, established 1336. Owned by Burgh Island Hotel, The Pilchard serves fine wines, local draught beers and regional ciders. Food is freshly prepared by the Hotel's kitchen: bar food during the day, popular curry buffets on Fridays and evening meals on Thursdays and Saturdays. Two cosy bars, an open fire and endless sea views.

Tel: 01548 810514

Soup, baguettes and bar snacks are on offer at lunchtime, while evening meals served on Fridays (curry club night) and Saturdays (smart seafood buffet) must be reserved. Teignworthy and St Austell ales sit alongside Heron Valley and Thatcher's Gold ciders in the bar.

Open all day all wk 11-11 (Sun 11-10.30) **Bar Meals** Av main course £5 food served all day **Restaurant** D served Fri-Sat 7-9 booking required Fixed menu price fr £18.75 ⊕ FREE HOUSE ◀ Teignworthy, St Austell ◔ Thatchers Gold. ♟ 13 **Facilities** Play area Family room Dogs allowed Garden

See advert on opposite page

BRAMPFORD SPEKE   Map 3 SX99

The Lazy Toad Inn NEW ♟

EX5 5DP ☎ 01392 841591   📄 01392 841591
e-mail: thelazytoadinn@btinternet.com
dir: *From Exeter take A377 towards Crediton 1.5m, right signed Brampford Speke*

Substantial renovation at this Grade II listed 19th-century free house has created a series of cosy, beamed rooms in which to enjoy good food, real ales and traditional ciders. Winter fires and a new walled beer garden mark the passage of the seasons, whilst home-grown herbs complement meat and fish cured in the pub's own smokery. Menu choices might include steamed port and pigeon pudding; or Gloucester Old Spot sausages with bubble and squeak. There is a great selection of real ales and ciders to choose from.

Open 11.30-2.30 6-11 (Sun 12-3) Closed: 2 wks Jan, Sun eve & Mon **Bar Meals** L served Tue-Sun 12-2 booking required D served Tue-Sat 6-9 booking required Av main course £11.50 **Restaurant** Av 3 course à la carte fr £24 ⊕ FREE HOUSE ◀ St Austell Tribute, Exmoor Fox, Otter Ale & Bitter, Exe Valley Exeter Old ◔ Sandford Devon Red, Traditional Farmhouse, Old Kirton. ♟ 12 **Facilities** Children's menu Family room Dogs allowed Garden Parking

---

BRANSCOMBE   Map 4 SY18

PICK OF THE PUBS

The Masons Arms ★★ HL ⊚ ♟

See Pick of the Pubs on page 130

BRAUNTON   Map 3 SS43

The Williams Arms

Wrafton EX33 2DE ☎ 01271 812360   📄 01271 816595
e-mail: info@williamsarms.co.uk
dir: *On A361 between Barnstaple & Braunton*

Spacious thatched pub dating back to the 16th century, and adjacent to the popular Tarka Trail, named after the much-loved otter created by author Henry Williamson. The restaurant has a carvery serving fresh locally-sourced meat and various vegetable dishes. Breakfast all day.

Open all day all wk 8.45am-11pm **Bar Meals** food served all day **Restaurant** food served all day ⊕ FREE HOUSE ◀ Guinness, Creamflow, Doom Bar ◔ Thatchers. **Facilities** Play area Garden Parking

---

BRENDON   Map 3 SS74

Rockford Inn

EX35 6PT ☎ 01598 741214
e-mail: enquiries@therockfordinn.com
dir: *A39 through Minehead follow signs to Lynmouth. Turn left off A39 to Brendon approx 5m before Lynmouth*

Standing right on the water's edge overlooking the River Lyn, this traditional 17th-century free house is popular with fisherman (fishing permits available in the pub) and handy for several Exmoor walking routes. Thatchers ciders complement local ales served straight from the cask, and there's a choice of good home-made pub meals with an international twist. Eat in the garden in fine weather, or come indoors to the open fire and wood burning stoves when the nights draw in.

Open noon-11 (Mon 6-11) Closed: Mon L **Bar Meals** L served Tue-Sun 12-4 D served all wk 6-9 **Restaurant** L served Tue-Sun 12-4 D served all wk 6-9 booking required ⊕ FREE HOUSE ◀ Barn Owl, Tribute, Cotleigh 25, Exmoor, Cavalier ◔ Thatchers. **Facilities** Children's menu Dogs allowed Garden Parking

---

BROADHEMPSTON   Map 3 SX86

The Monks Retreat Inn

The Square TQ9 6BN ☎ 01803 812203
dir: *Exit Newton Abbot to Totnes road at Ipplepen, follow signs for Broadhempston for 3.5m*

Apparently a friendly ghost inhabits this inn - certainly it's the sort of place you'd want to linger in: the building (listed as of outstanding architectural interest) is full of fascinating features, including a panelled oak screen typical of ancient Devon houses. Sit by one of the cosy log fires and enjoy a pint of Otter Bitter or Jail Ale.

Closed: Mon **Bar Meals** L served Tue-Sun 12-1.45 D served Tue-Sun 6.30-9 **Restaurant** L served Tue-Sun 12-1.45 booking required D served Tue-Sun 6.30-9 booking required ⊕ ENTERPRISE INNS ◀ Jail Ale, Otter Bitter. **Facilities** Dogs allowed

---

BUCKFASTLEIGH   Map 3 SX76

Dartbridge Inn ⓐ ★★★ INN ♟

Totnes Rd TQ11 0JR
☎ 01364 642214   📄 01364 643839
e-mail: dartbridge.buckfastleigh@oldenglishinns.co.uk
dir: *From Exeter A38, take 1st Buckfastleigh turn, then right to Totnes. Inn on left*

Standing close to the River Dart, this 19th-century building was originally a simple dwelling, then a teashop before becoming a pub. Well known for its eye-catching floral displays, inside are open fires and oak beams. The lunch/bar menu includes slow-cooked Welsh lamb, and spinach and ricotta girasole, while dinner mains are typically baked rainbow trout with pan-fried tiger prawns, gammon and other steaks, sausages and mash, and chicken Caesar salad.

Open all wk ⊕ OLD ENGLISH INNS & HOTELS ◀ Scottish Courage, Abbot Ale, IPA, Otter Ale. ♟ 12 **Facilities** Parking **Rooms** 10

BUCKLAND MONACHORUM   Map 3 SX46

Drake Manor Inn ♟

The Village PL20 7NA
☎ 01822 853892   📄 01822 853892
e-mail: drakemanor@drakemanorinn.co.uk
web: www.drakemanorinn.co.uk
dir: *Off A386 near Yelverton*

Originally built in the 12th century and rebuilt in the 16th century, the pub housed masons constructing the church next door. Mandy, the licensee, has been in residence for 20 years and prides herself on running a proper pub with a locals' bar where friends gather to chat and drink fine ales and whisky. Food is locally sourced and daily specials reflect seasonal variations and availability. The sunny cottage garden is popular in fine weather.

Open all wk 11.30-2.30 (Sat 11.30-3) 6.30-11 (Fri-Sat 6.30-11.30) (Sun noon-11) **Bar Meals** L served all wk 12-2 D served Mon-Sat 7-10, Sun 7-9.30 Av main course £8.50 **Restaurant** L served all wk 12-2 D served Mon-Sat 7-10, Sun 7-9.30 ⊕ PUNCH TAVERNS ◀ John Smiths & Courage Best, Greene King Abbot Ale, Sharp's Doom Bar. ♟ 9 **Facilities** Family room Dogs allowed Garden Parking

PICK OF THE PUBS

The Masons Arms ★★ HL 🏵 ♉

EX12 3DJ
☎ 01297 680300 📠 01297 680500
e-mail: reception@masonsarms.co.uk
dir: *Turn off A3052 towards Branscombe, down hill, hotel at bottom of hill*

Just thinking about the great age of the creeper-clad Masons Arms can stop you in your tracks. It actually dates back to 1360, when it was just a simple cider house measuring a mere 8ft x 4ft, squeezed into the middle of a row of cottages. Today that row of cottages is an independent, family-run pub and hotel offering accommodation that includes cottage rooms and suites set in their own peaceful gardens with views across the valley and out to sea. Once the haunt of smugglers, the Masons Arms has a bar that can hardly have changed in 200 years, with stone walls, ancient ships' beams, slate floors, and

a splendid open fireplace used for spit-roasts, including Sunday lunchtimes. Five real ales are always available, including several that are locally brewed. Food is a serious business here and the restaurant maintains a standard of cooking worthy of its AA Rosette. Where possible all ingredients are grown, reared or caught locally, none perhaps more so than the lobster and crab landed on Branscombe beach, a ten-minute stroll away. There is a choice of dining experiences: in the bar, or in the waiter-serviced restaurant. The former can keep you happy with an extensive menu of sandwiches, paninis and ploughman's, starters like roasted pepper and tomato soup, and steamed West Country mussels, and main courses such as confit of aromatic duck leg; seared loin of tuna with stir fry vegetables; and chicken rogan josh curry. In the restaurant the menu typically offers Dartmouth Freedom smoked salmon with cucumber and dill pickle; pork tenderloin, crispy black pudding, cider jus, and Branscombe apple compote; white chocolate pannacotta with West Country dark chocolate ice cream.

Open Mon-Fri 11-3 6-11 (Sat 11-11, Sun 12-10.30) **Bar Meals** L served Mon-Fri 12-2, Sat-Sun 12-2.15 D served all wk 7-9 Av main course £12
Restaurant D served all wk 7-9 Fixed menu price fr £29.95 ⊞ FREE HOUSE
🍺 Otter Ale, Masons Ale, Tribute, Branoc & guest ales. ♉ 14
Facilities Children's menu Dogs allowed Garden Parking **Rooms** 21

BUTTERLEIGH — Map 3 SS90

The Butterleigh Inn ♥

EX15 1PN ☎ 01884 855407 📠 01884 855600
e-mail: enquiries@thebutterleighinn.com
dir: *3m from M5 junct 28 turn right by Manor Hotel in Cullompton. Follow Butterleigh signs*

After a recent change in ownership, this 400-year-old traditional free house remains a friendly local. There's a mass of local memorabilia throughout the pub, and customers can choose from a selection of real ales including O'Hanlon's Yellow Hammer, and ciders including Sam's Medium from Winkleigh Cider. On fine days, the garden with its huge flowering cherry tree is very popular. Booking is recommended for the restaurant, where home-made dishes and daily specials are always available.

Open all wk **Bar Meals** L served Mon-Sat 12-2 D served Mon-Sat 7-9 **Restaurant** L served Mon-Sat 12-2 D served Mon-Sat 7-9 ⊕ FREE HOUSE ◀ Cotleigh Tawny Ale, Yellow Hammer, guest ale. ♥ 7 **Facilities** Dogs allowed Garden Parking

CHAGFORD — Map 3 SX78

PICK OF THE PUBS

The Sandy Park Inn ♥

TQ13 8JW ☎ 01647 433267
e-mail: sandyparkinn@aol.com
dir: *From A30 exit at Whiddon Down, turn left towards Moretonhampstead. Inn 5m from Whiddon Down*

Everything about the thatched Sandy Park is just as it should be. Dogs are frequently to be found slumped in front of the fire, horse-brasses and sporting prints adorn the walls, and the beamed bar attracts locals and tourists alike, all happily setting the world to rights with the help of an eclectic wine list and good range of traditional local ales, including Otter Ale, St Austell Tribute and Sharp's Doom Bar. The candlelit restaurant is equally appealing, offering a brasserie-style menu that changes daily to make the most of local produce. Starters might include deep-fried brie with redcurrant jelly, or smoked mackerel, to be followed by venison casserole, roast cod, or spinach and mushroom pie - the perfect fare after a day spent stomping on the moors.

Open all day all wk noon-11pm **Bar Meals** L served all wk 12-2.30 D served all wk 6-9 ⊕ FREE HOUSE ◀ Otter Ale, O'Hanlons, St Austell Tribute ♂ Thatchers. ♥ 14 **Facilities** Family room Dogs allowed Garden Parking

Three Crowns Hotel ★★ SHL

High St TQ13 8AJ
☎ 01647 433444 & 433441 📠 01647 433117
e-mail: threecrowns@msn.com
dir: *Telephone for directions*

An impressive, 13th-century, granite-built inn with a wealth of historical associations to investigate. Take young poet and Cavalier Sydney Godolphin, for example, who was shot in the hotel doorway in 1643 and who continues to 'appear', making him the hotel's oldest resident. Period features include mullioned windows, sturdy oak beams and a massive open fireplace. Among chef's specialities are sautéed fillet of pork with mango salsa; roasted breast of duck with plum sauce; and lemon sole poached in white wine with mixed seafood sauce.

Open all day all wk 8am-mdnt **Bar Meals** L served all wk 12-2.30 booking required D served all wk 6-9 booking required **Restaurant** L served all wk 12-2.30 booking required D served all wk 6-9 booking required ⊕ FREE HOUSE ◀ Bass, Whitbread, Jail Ales, Guest ales ♂ Thatchers Gold. **Facilities** Children's menu Dogs allowed Parking **Rooms** 17

CHARDSTOCK — Map 4 ST30

The George Inn

EX13 7BX ☎ 01460 220241
e-mail: info@george-inn.co.uk
dir: *A358 from Taunton through Chard towards Axminster, left at Tytherleigh. Signed from A358*

Graffiti from 1648 can be seen in the snug of this 700-year-old pub, which was once a parish house. A friendly parson named Copeland haunts the cellar, while cheerful locals who've been drinking in the George for the past 40 years preside over 'Compost Corner'. Hearty dishes include feta, spinach and mozzarella pie; pan-fried lambs' liver or beer battered cod.

Open all wk **Bar Meals** L served all wk 12-2 D served all wk 6.30-9.30 Av main course £9 **Restaurant** L served all wk 12-2 D served all wk 6.30-9.30 Av 3 course à la carte fr £15 ⊕ FREE HOUSE ◀ Ruddles County Bitter, Branoc, guest ale ♂ Stowford Press. **Facilities** Children's menu Dogs allowed Garden Parking

CHERITON BISHOP — Map 3 SX79

PICK OF THE PUBS

The Old Thatch Inn ♥

EX6 6HJ ☎ 01647 24204
e-mail: mail@theoldthatchinn.f9.co.uk
dir: *0.5m off A30, 7m SW of Exeter*

This charming 16th-century free house sits within the Dartmoor National Park, just half a mile off the main A30. It's a popular halfway house for travellers on their way to and from Cornwall, and once welcomed stagecoaches on the London to Penzance road. For a time during its long history, the inn passed into private hands and then became a tea room, before its licence was renewed in the early 1970s. A major refurbishment during the winter of 2006, following a fire, has preserved the period appeal. Owners David and Serena London pride themselves on their high standards. All the food is prepared using fresh ingredients from the southwest, with seafood featuring strongly. Dishes change every day depending on supplies; examples include grilled whole sardines with garlic herb butter; pan-seared breast of duck with dauphinoise potatoes; or baked fillet of sea bass with a crayfish tail, lemon and thyme risotto. Look out for the speciality pumpkin and sunflower seed mini loaf sandwich filled with a variety of choices such as Somerset brie, smoked chicken and redcurrant sauce.

Open all wk 11.30-3 6-11 Closed: 25-26 Dec, Sun eve **Bar Meals** L served all wk 12-2.30 D served Mon-Sat 6.30-9 Av main course £12 **Restaurant** L served all wk 12-2.30 D served Mon-Sat 6.30-9 Av 3 course à la carte fr £22.50 ⊕ FREE HOUSE ◀ Otter Ale, Port Stout, O'Hanlon's Royal Oak, Skinners Betty Stogs, Yellowhammer ♂ Thatchers Scrumpy Jack. ♥ 9 **Facilities** Children's menu Family room Dogs allowed Garden Parking

CLAYHIDON — Map 4 ST11

PICK OF THE PUBS

The Merry Harriers ₹

Forches Corner EX15 3TR
☎ 01823 421270 📠 01823 421270
e-mail: peter.gatling@btinternet.com
dir: *Wellington A38, turn onto Ford Street (marked by brown tourist sign). At top of hill turn left, 1.5m on right*

The Merry Harriers is a 15th-century inn that stands high on the Blackdown Hills, with plenty of space for a large beer garden and a five-lane skittle alley, one of the longest in the county. Inside the characterful bar are beamed ceilings, a cosy inglenook and attractive dining areas. Peter and Angela Gatling have worked tirelessly to build the local drinks trade while expanding the food operation. More than 90 per cent of kitchen ingredients are from the surrounding hills, or further afield in the West Country. The regularly changing menus offer a wide choice, including Somerset pork chop with apple sauce; pan-fried Somerset lamb's liver and bacon; grilled fillets of Combe St Nicholas rainbow trout; smoked North Petherton duck breast served on a mixed leaf and pomegranate salad; or West Country chicken korma. Children can select from a menu that contains kiddie curry, mad cow (steak and kidney) pie, and whizzers (organic pork and apple sausages) and chips.

Open noon-3 6.30-11 Closed: Sun eve & Mon **Bar Meals** L served Tue-Sat 12-2, Sun 12-2.15 booking required D served Tue-Sat 6.30-9 booking required Av main course £9 food served all day **Restaurant** L served Tue-Sat 12-2, Sun 12-2.15 booking required D served Tue-Sat 6.30-9 booking required food served all day ⊕ FREE HOUSE ◀ Otter Head, Cotleigh Harrier, Exmoor Gold, St Austell Tinners, ♂ Thatchers Gold. ₹ 14 **Facilities** Children's menu Play area Family room Dogs allowed Garden Parking

CLEARBROOK — Map 3 SX56

The Skylark Inn

PL20 6JD ☎ 01822 853258
e-mail: skylvic@btinternet.com
dir: *5m N of Plymouth on A386 towards Tavistock. Take 2nd right signed Clearbrook*

The beamed bar with its large fireplace and wood-burning stove characterises this attractive village inn. Although only ten minutes from Plymouth, the Skylark is set in the Dartmoor National Park and the area is ideal for cyclists and walkers. Good wholesome food is served from an extensive menu that features rainbow trout with new potatoes and salad; vegetable stew with dumplings; and a range of shortcrust pastry pies.

Open all wk 11.30-3 6-11.30 **Bar Meals** L served all wk 12-2 booking required D served all wk 6.30-9 booking required Av main course £9.70 **Restaurant** L served all wk 12-2 booking required D served all wk 6.30-9 booking

required ⊕ UNIQUE PUB CO LTD ◀ Otter Ale, St Austell Tribute, Dartmoor Best Bitter. **Facilities** Play area Family room Dogs allowed Garden Parking

CLOVELLY — Map 3 SS32

PICK OF THE PUBS

Red Lion Hotel ★★ HL

The Quay EX39 5TF
☎ 01237 431237 📠 01237 431044
e-mail: redlion@clovelly.co.uk
dir: *From Bideford rdbt, follow A39 to Bude for 10m. At Clovelly Cross rdbt turn right, follow past Clovelly Visitor Centre entrance, bear to left. Hotel at bottom of hill*

Clovelly, the famously unspoilt 'village like a waterfall', descends down broad steps to a 14th-century harbour and this charming hostelry is located right on the quay. Guests staying in the whimsically decorated bedrooms can fall asleep to the sound of waves lapping the shingle and wake to the cries of gulls squabbling for scraps. Seafood, unsurprisingly, is a priority on the modern French-influenced menu, which could offer grilled Cornish oysters with champagne sabayon, or home-made wild rabbit terrine with red onion marmalade to start, followed by chargrilled turbot steak; cod fillet in tempura batter with minted pea purée, or pan-seared tuna steak with grilled foie gras and shallots. Desserts are equally artful: frozen mango parfait with grapefruit confit and black peppercorn meringue sounds especially intriguing. Daytime visitors can tuck into a locally-made Cornish pasty, or a plate of cod and chips.

Open all wk **Bar Meals** L served all wk 12-2.30 D served all week 6-8.30 Av main course £6.95 **Restaurant** D served all wk 7-9 booking required Fixed menu price fr £29.50 Av 3 course à la carte fr £29.50 ⊕ FREE HOUSE ◀ Doom Bar, Old Appledore, Guinness, Clovelly Cobbler ♂ Thatchers. **Facilities** Family room Parking **Rooms** 11

CLYST HYDON — Map 3 ST00

PICK OF THE PUBS

The Five Bells Inn ₹

EX15 2NT ☎ 01884 277288
e-mail: info@fivebellsclysthydon.co.uk
dir: *B3181 towards Cullompton, right at Hele Cross towards Clyst Hydon. 2m turn right, then sharp right at left bend at village sign*

Originally a 16th-century thatched farmhouse, this attractive country pub in rolling east Devon countryside started serving ale about a hundred years ago, and takes its name from the five bells hanging in the village church tower. It's gone from strength to strength in recent years, thanks to its family-friendly owners and a focus on real ales, good food and cheerful hospitality. The well-maintained garden is a delight in summer, with twenty tables enjoying lovely

views, and a children's play area. The interior boasts two wood fires, numerous prints and watercolours, and brass and copper artefacts. Excellent real ales are augmented by draught lagers, cider and bottled beers. When it comes to food, why not start with bacon and garlic mushroom tart, or crab cakes with sweet chilli dip. Then indulge in a West Country steak served with mushrooms, peas and chips; or a slowly cooked duck leg on a bed of colcannon with orange and spring onion.

Open 11.30am-3 6.30-11pm Closed: 25 Dec, Mon L **Bar Meals** L served Tue-Sun 11.30-2 D served all wk 6.30-9 ⊕ FREE HOUSE ◀ Cotleigh Tawny Ale, Otter Bitter, O'Hanlon's. ₹ 8 **Facilities** Play area Family room Garden Parking

COCKWOOD — Map 3 SX98

PICK OF THE PUBS

The Anchor Inn ₹

EX6 8RA ☎ 01626 890203 📠 01626 890355
dir: *Off A379 between Dawlish & Starcross*

Overlooking a small landlocked harbour on the River Exe, this former Seamen's Mission has been a haven to sailors and smugglers for centuries. In summer customers spill out onto the veranda and harbour wall, while real fires and low beams make the interior cosy in winter. Nautical bric-a-brac abounds, with lights inside divers' helmets, ropes and pulleys, binnacles, and a wall displaying over 200 cast ship badges. A recent extension has taken over the old village hall, so now a further 90 customers can be comfortably seated while choosing between nearly 30 different ways to eat mussels. If mussels don't appeal, there are scallops, oysters, crab, lobster, whole grilled plaice, Cockwood mackerel smokies with lumberjack chips. If meat is preferred, look to the range of Devon pies and sausages, or your favourite cut - it's almost certainly on the truly comprehensive menu.

Open all wk 11-11 (Sun noon-10.30, 25 Dec 12-2) **Bar Meals** Av main course £8.95 food served all day **Restaurant** L served all wk 12-2.15 D served all wk 6.30-10 booking required Av 3 course à la carte fr £30 ⊕ HEAVITREE ◀ Interbrew Bass, Timothy Taylor Landlord, Fuller's London Pride, Otter Ale, Abbot, Adnams Broadside. ₹ 10 **Facilities** Children's menu Dogs allowed Garden Parking

COLEFORD — Map 3 SS70

PICK OF THE PUBS

The New Inn ★★★★ INN ₹

See Pick of the Pubs on opposite page

PICK OF THE PUBS

The New Inn ★★★★ INN 🍷

EX17 5BZ
☎ **01363 84242** 📠 **01363 85044**
e-mail: enquiries@thenewinncoleford.
co.uk
dir: *From Exeter take A377, 1.5m after
Crediton turn left for Coleford, continue for
1.5m*

A pretty, 13th-century cob and thatch
inn set beside the babbling River Cole in
a sleepy conservation village, deep in
the heart of unspoilt countryside. George
and Carole Cowie took over this Devon
gem in 2008, having fallen for the
obvious charms of this historic building,
and plan on-going improvements.
'Captain', the chatty resident parrot,
who came as part of the fixtures and
fittings, welcomes folk into the rambling
interior, with the ancient, slate-floored
bar, replete with a time-worn feel, old
carved chests, polished brass and
roaring log fires, blending effortlessly
with the dining room extension into the
old barns: warm red carpets, fresh white
walls, original oak beams, simple
wooden furniture and cushioned settles,
antique prints and assorted bric-a-brac.
Bar food is reliable and home cooked,
relying on fresh local ingredients:
Brixham fish, Devon cheeses and
produce sourced from surrounding
farms and villages. The menu takes in
lunchtime sandwiches and ploughman's
platters to posh bangers and mash,
posh pies and a pint, and home-made
soups. For something more substantial,
tuck into venison and red wine pie,
fruity lamb tagine, whole plaice with
herb butter, or goats' cheese, spinach
and tomato pancake served with salad
and chips. Leave room for an indulgent
pudding, perhaps almond macaroons
with clotted cream and chocolate sauce,
a selection of local farm-made ice
creams, or a plate of West Country
cheeses. To drink, you'll find Sam's
heady farm cider and local Otter and
Exmoor ales on tap, and ten wines by
the glass. Comfortable and peaceful
overnight accommodation is guaranteed
in the six, well-appointed en suite
bedrooms. Make the most of the idyllic,
willow-fringed riverside garden, perfect
for summer alfresco dining and the hog
roasts at the end of each summer
month.

Open 12-3 6-11 (Sun 7-10.30 winter)
Closed: 25-26 Dec **Bar Meals** L served
all wk 12-2 D served all wk 7-9.30 Av
main course £7.50 **Restaurant** L served
all wk 12-2 D served all wk 7-9.30 Av 3
course à la carte fr £20 🍺 FREE
HOUSE 🛢 Doom Bar, Otter Ale, Exmoor
Ale, Spitfire, Rev James Ŏ Thatchers,
Winkleigh Sam's. 🍷 10
Facilities Children's menu Dogs allowed
Garden Parking **Rooms** 6

COLYFORD   Map 4 SY29

The Wheelwright Inn NEW ♟

Swanhill Rd EX24 6QQ ☎ 01297 552585
dir: *Please telephone for directions*

This pretty thatched inn has earned a reputation for outstanding food and service since Gary and Toni Valentine took over in 2007. The 17th-century pub has undergone substantial refurbishment, but the low beams, wooden floors and log fire ensure that it retains its authentic country feel. Expect a varied contemporary menu, including well-filled sandwiches on locally baked bread; local pork cutlet with creamy potato and swede mash; and moules marinière with crusty bread.

Open all day all wk **Bar Meals** food served all day **Restaurant** food served all day ⊕ HALL & WOODHOUSE ◀ Badger First Gold, Tanglefoot, Hopping Hare, Guinness ♂ Stowford Press. ♟ 8 **Facilities** Children's menu Family room Dogs allowed Garden Parking

CORNWORTHY   Map 3 SX85

Hunters Lodge Inn ♟

TQ9 7ES ☎ 01803 732204
dir: *Off A381, S of Totnes*

Built in 1740, this country local is at the hub of village life, sponsoring a football team, charity events and a dog show (it's a dog friendly pub). There's even a Christmas party for children. Other notable features are the real log fire and resident ghost. An extensive menu offers dishes from the sea (sesame battered Brixham cod fillet), and from the land (gammon steak, Cornworthy hens' eggs) as well as a selection of pasta dishes (spaghetti carbonara).

Open all wk 11.30am-2.30 6.30-close (Closed Mon L) **Bar Meals** L served Tue-Sun 11.30-2 booking required D served all wk 6.30-9 booking required **Restaurant** L served Tue-Sun 11.30-2 booking required D served all wk 6.30-9 booking required ⊕ FREE HOUSE ◀ Teignworthy Reel Ale, Sharp's Doom bar, Guest ales. ♟ 14 **Facilities** Children's menu Play area Dogs allowed Garden Parking

CULMSTOCK   Map 3 ST11

Culm Valley Inn ♟

EX15 3JJ ☎ 01884 840354 ▤ 01884 841659
e-mail: culmvalleyinn@btinternet.com
dir: *2m from A38, 3m from Wellington*

A former station hotel in which the owners exposed a long-hidden bar during a renovation re-creating a 'between the wars' look. The ever-changing blackboard menu displays a lengthy list of home-made dishes, mostly using locally-grown or raised ingredients, including chicken breast with a cider brandy sauce. Fish and shellfish mostly from South Devon or Cornwall, including shellfish platters and Portuguese fish stew. Several real ales straight from the cask.

Open all wk noon-3 7-11pm (Fri-Sat noon-11pm Sun noon-10.30pm Open all day in summer) Closed: 25 Dec eve **Bar Meals** L served all wk 12-2 D served Mon-Sat 7-9 **Restaurant** L served all wk 12-2 D served Mon-Sat 7-9 ⊕ FREE HOUSE ◀ O'Hanlons Firefly, Branscombe Branoc. ♟ 50 **Facilities** Children's menu Dogs allowed Garden Parking **Notes** ⊛

DALWOOD   Map 4 ST20

PICK OF THE PUBS

The Tuckers Arms ♟

EX13 7EG ☎ 01404 881342 ▤ 01404 881138
e-mail: davidbeck@tuckersarms.freeserve.co.uk
dir: *Off A35 between Honiton & Axminster*

A centuries-old Devon longhouse which enjoys a pretty setting between two ridges of the Blackdown Hills; it was built to accommodate artisans who were constructing the church across the way. The interior is everything you would expect of a traditional, thatched inn – inglenook fireplaces, low beams and flagstone floors. Today it's a popular and hospitable village inn proffering good quality sustenance for modern travellers. The pub specialises in fresh fish and game, supplemented by great home-made desserts. A dozen starters may include home-made beef and butterbean soup, or kidneys in red wine. Main course fresh fish dishes (the pub is only 15 minutes from Lyme Regis) usually find crab, lobster, lemon sole, halibut, and cod among the options. Game and specialities could include confit of duck 'du chef'; rack of lamb with shallots, fresh basil and garlic; and venison escalope pan-fried in butter. Alternatively rib-eye, sirloin, rump and fillet steaks can all be cooked on the grill to your liking.

Open all wk ⊕ FREE HOUSE ◀ Otter Bitter, Courage Best, Old Speckled Hen. ♟ 8 **Facilities** Garden Parking

DARTMOUTH   Map 3 SX85

PICK OF THE PUBS

Royal Castle Hotel ★★★ HL ♟

11 The Quay TQ6 9PS
☎ 01803 833033 ▤ 01803 835445
e-mail: becca@royalcastle.co.uk
dir: *In town centre, overlooking inner harbour*

Visitors often don't realise just how old this building is; it dates from the 1630s when two merchants built their neighbouring quayside houses in commanding positions on the Dart estuary. A century later, one had become The New Inn and by 1782 it had been combined with its neighbour to become The Castle Inn. Further rebuilds incorporated the battlemented turrets and cornice that gave it an appearance worthy of its name. The Nu restaurant occupies a large first floor room with a bay window and river views, and bar food is served in both the Galleon and Harbour Bars. In the former you can still have your meat roasted on the Lydstone Range, forged in Dartmouth over 300 years ago. Dishes range from slow-cooked Devon lamb shank in red wine and pearl barley, and trio of local pork sausages, to catch of the day on the specials board and river Exe mussels steamed in creamy white wine and garlic. Tudor fireplaces, spiral staircases and priest holes are other intriguing features, along with many fine antique pieces, including four-poster and brass beds still used in the hotel's bedrooms.

Open all day all wk 8am-11.30pm **Bar Meals** Av main course £9.95 food served all day **Restaurant** L served all wk 12-2 D served all wk 6-9 Fixed menu price fr £12.50 Av 3 course à la carte fr £25 ⊕ FREE HOUSE ◀ Jail Ale, Bays Gold, Doom Bar ♂ Thatchers Gold. ♟ 24 **Facilities** Children's menu Family room Dogs allowed Parking **Rooms** 25

DENBURY · Map 3 SX86

The Union Inn ♥

Denbury Green TQ12 6DQ
☎ **01803 812595** 📄 **01803 814206**
e-mail: unioninn@hotmail.co.uk
dir: *2m form Newton Abbot, signed Denbury*

The Union Inn is at least 400 years old and counting. Inside are the original stone walls that once rang to the hammers of the blacksmiths and cartwrights who worked here many moons ago. Choose freshly prepared, mouthwatering starters such as moules marinière or smoked chicken in mango vinaigrette, and follow with slow-roasted shoulder of lamb with mint garlic and redcurrant jelly, or a rib-eye steak on a bed of haggis with stilton and whisky sauce. The guest ale is changed on a keg-by-keg basis.

Open all wk noon-3 6-11.30 (Fri-Sat noon-mdnt)
Bar Meals L served all wk 12-2 D served all wk 6-9
Restaurant L served all wk 12-2 D served all wk 6-9 ⊕ ENTERPRISE INNS 🍺 Otter, London Pride, guest ale. ♀ 9 **Facilities** Children's menu Dogs allowed Garden Parking

DITTISHAM · Map 3 SX85

PICK OF THE PUBS

The Ferry Boat ♥

Manor St TQ6 0EX ☎ **01803 722368**
dir: *Telephone for directions*

Set right at the water's edge with a pontoon outside its front door, this riverside inn (the only one on the River Dart) dates back 300 years. There are tables at the front with views across the river to Greenway House and Gardens, a National Trust property that was once Agatha Christie's home. The pub has plenty of marine connections, being just a few miles upriver from the Royal Naval College in Dartmouth. The pontoon outside guarantees popularity with the boating fraternity, but the pub is also a favourite of walkers and families. In the winter months, open log fires crackle in the grates, making it a snug place to go for a pint of Adnams Broadside. Home-cooked food, made from fresh local produce, is served lunchtimes and evenings, and the bar is well-stocked with everything from ales to fine wines.

Open all day all wk 11am-mdnt **Bar Meals** L served all wk 12-2 D served all wk 7-9 ⊕ PUNCH TAVERNS 🍺 Youngs, Adnams, St Austell Tribute, Proper Job IPA, Sharp's Doom Bar. ♀ 9 **Facilities** Family room Dogs allowed

DODDISCOMBSLEIGH · Map 3 SX88

PICK OF THE PUBS

The Nobody Inn ★★★★ INN ♥

See Pick of the Pubs on page 136

DOLTON · Map 3 SS51

Rams Head Inn ♥

South St EX19 8QS ☎ **01805 804255** 📄 **01805 804509**
e-mail: ramsheadinn@btopenworld.com
dir: *8m from Torrington on A3124*

Travelling through the rolling mid-Devon countryside and in need of refreshment, then head for Dolton and this character free house. Dating from the 15th century, original features abound throughout the bar and restaurant, from huge old fireplaces with bread ovens and pot stands to oak beams. Expect cask ales on tap, traditional lunchtime bar food and an extensive evening menu listing locally sourced beef and fish dishes. Ideal location for touring, fishing, golf and shooting.

Open all wk 10-3 5-11 (Fri-Sat noon-mdnt Sun noon-4 6-11) **Bar Meals** L served Mon-Sat 12-2.30 **Restaurant** L served all wk 12-2.30 booking required ⊕ FREE HOUSE 🍺 Flowers IPA Cask, Trophy, Sharps Own. ♀ 8 **Facilities** Dogs allowed Garden Parking

DREWSTEIGNTON · Map 3 SX79

PICK OF THE PUBS

The Drewe Arms ♥

The Square EX6 6QN
☎ **01647 281224** 📄 **01647 281179**
e-mail: mail@thedrewearms.co.uk
dir: *W of Exeter on A30 for 12m. Left at Woodleigh junct follow signs for 3m to Drewsteignton*

Tucked away in a sleepy village square close to the National Trust's Castle Drogo, this quintessentially English thatched inn is an ideal place for refreshments after a country walk in the surrounding Dartmoor National Park. Built in 1646, the inn was originally known as the Druid Arms but in the 1920s the Drewe family, for whom Castle Drogo was built, persuaded the brewery to change the pub's name. Their family coat of arms is still on the sign. Traditional ales are drawn direct from the cask, housed in the original 'tap bar' and served through a hatchway into the snug. The Card Room has a log fire for cold winter days, and in summer you can relax in the attractive gardens or enjoy a game of boules. Expect half crispy roast duck, local butcher's sausages, braised lamb shank, Mediterranean chicken bake, and Thai-style red snapper, as well as sandwiches and ploughman's lunches.

Open all day all wk 11am-mdnt (winter 11-3 6-mdnt)
Bar Meals L served all wk 12-10 (winter 12-2.30, 6-9.30) D served all wk 12-10 (winter 12-2.30, 6-9.30) food served all day ⊕ ENTERPRISE INNS 🍺 Otter Ale, Tribute, Tanglefoot, Druid's. ♀ 6 **Facilities** Dogs allowed Garden Parking

EAST ALLINGTON · Map 3 SX74

Fortescue Arms ♥

TQ9 7RA ☎ **01548 521215**
e-mail: info@fortescuearms.co.uk
dir: *Please telephone for directions*

A charming old country inn, the Fortescue Arms is set in the village of East Allington some four miles from Kingsbridge. Landlords, Austrian chef proprietor Werner Rott and business partner Tom Kendrick, promise real ale, fine wines, good food and a welcoming atmosphere by an open fire. Typical dishes include potted crab sealed with garlic herb butter; local lamb loin on sweet potato cake with rosemary sauce; and warm apfelstrudel with crème patissiere.

Closed: Mon lunch ⊕ FREE HOUSE 🍺 Butcombe Bitter, Dartmoor IPA, Guinness, Guest ales. ♀ 9 **Facilities** Family room Dogs allowed Garden Parking

EXETER · Map 3 SX99

Red Lion Inn ♥

Broadclyst EX5 3EL ☎ **01392 461271**
dir: *On B3181 (Exeter to Cullompton)*

A 16th-century inn set at the heart of a delightful National Trust village, next to the church. Typical examples of the restaurant menu include monkfish medallions with bacon and tomato jus; seafood gratin; pan-fried pigeon; roast pheasant with redcurrant and red onion jus; and a range of steaks. In the bar expect ham, egg and chips; venison sausages with colcannon; and Thai curry.

Open all wk 11-3.30 5.30-11.30 (Sat-Sun 11-11.30) **Bar Meals** L served all wk 12-2.30 D served all wk 6-9.30 Av main course £5 **Restaurant** L served all wk 12-2.30 D served all wk 6-9.30 Av 3 course à la carte fr £24 ⊕ FREE HOUSE 🍺 Bass, Fuller's London Pride, O'Hanlons Local Blakelys Red, Old Speckled Hen. ♀ 7 **Facilities** Garden Parking

PICK OF THE PUBS

The Nobody Inn ★★★★ INN

DODDISCOMBSLEIGH Map 3 SX88

EX6 7PS
01647 252394 01647 252978
e-mail: info@nobodyinn.co.uk
dir: *3m SW of Exeter Racecourse (A38)*

Low ceilings, blackened beams, an inglenook fireplace and antique furniture all contribute to the timeless atmosphere of this late 16th-century inn, set in a pretty cottage garden in rolling countryside between the Haldon Hills and the Teign Valley. For many years it served as the village's unofficial church house and meeting place, becoming a de facto inn along the way, before being officially licensed as the New Inn in 1838. In 1952, following the innkeeper's death, his body was accidentally left in the mortuary while the funeral took place around an empty coffin - thus 'no body' – and the pub's name was changed. Its new owners – only the fifth since 1838 - have undertaken a major investment programme (in the restaurant and five guest bedrooms, for example) but have sensibly bypassed the bar, which retains its traditional ambience, and continues to amaze customers with the breadth of refreshments on offer: real ales from Branscombe, over 200 wines, and around 240 whiskies. Imaginative bar meals are served every lunchtime and evening from a regularly changing menu. The pub is also famous for its range of local cheeses - there are usually over fifteen varieties – and fresh fish is delivered daily from Brixham. Dinner might begin with ratatouille on wilted spinach with Parmesan shavings; continue with roast loin of cod with crispy cured ham, saffron sauce and roast cherry tomatoes; or breast of duck with a Kirsch sauce; and finish with steamed orange sponge pudding with orange and Cointreau sauce and marmalade ice cream. A small bar shop sells some of the items you are likely to have enjoyed in the pub. Five attractive bedrooms are available.

Open all wk 11-11 (Sun 12-10.30) Closed: 25-26 & 31 Dec, 1 Jan **Bar Meals** L served Mon-Sat 12-2, Sun 12-3 D served Mon-Thu 6.30-9, Fri-Sat 6.30-9.30, Sun 7-9 Av main course £8 **Restaurant** D served Mon-Thu 6.30-9, Fri-Sat 6.30-9.30, Sun 7-9 (Jan-Mar Thu-Sat only) Av 3 course £23 FREE HOUSE Branscombe Nobody's Bitter, Exe Valley Ales, Sharp's Doom Bar Brimblecombes Local Cider, Westons Stowford Press. 20 **Facilities** Dogs allowed Garden Parking **Rooms** 5

EXETER *continued*

The Twisted Oak ♀

Little John's Cross Hill EX2 9RG ☎ 01392 273666
e-mail: info@twistedoakpub.com
dir: *A30 to Okehampton, follow signs for pub*

Set in a beautiful part of Ide just outside Exeter, this large pub has been turned into a quality, food-driven venue in the last few years. There is a choice of dining areas - an informal place where you can relax on the leather sofas and eat; a separate lounge bar restaurant; and a more formal conservatory area, which is adult only in the evenings. During the summer months the huge garden provides seating and a children's play area.

Open all wk 11am-3 5-11pm (Fri-Sun 11am-mdnt) **Bar Meals** L served Mon-Thu 12-2.30, Fri-Sun all day D served Mon-Thu 6-9, Fri-Sun all day **Restaurant** L served Mon-Thu 12-2.30, Fri-Sun all day D served Mon-Thu 6-9, Fri-Sun all day ◀ Sharp's Doom Bar, Exmoor Ale. ♀ 7 **Facilities** Children's menu Play area Family room Dogs allowed Garden Parking

---

EXMINSTER   Map 3 SX98

Swans Nest ♀

Station Rd EX6 8DZ ☎ 01392 832371
web: www.swans-nest.co.uk
dir: *From M5 junct 30 follow A379 (Dawlish road)*

A much extended pub in a pleasant rural location whose facilities, unusually, extend to a ballroom, dance floor and stage. The carvery is a popular option for diners, with a choice of meats served with freshly prepared vegetables, though the salad bar is a tempting alternative, with over 39 items, including quiches, pies and home-smoked chicken. A carte of home-cooked fare includes grilled lamb steak, Devon pork chop, and five-bean vegetable curry.

Open all wk 11-2.30 6-11 (Sun 12-3 6-11) **Bar Meals** D served Sun-Fri 6-9, Sat 6-9.30 ⊕ FREE HOUSE ◀ Otter Ale, Guest Ales ♂ Stowford Press. ♀ 8 **Facilities** Play area Family room Garden Parking

---

EXTON   Map 3 SX98

PICK OF THE PUBS

The Puffing Billy ♀

Station Rd EX3 0PR
☎ 01392 877888   🖹 01392 876232
dir: *A376 signed Exmouth, through Ebford. Follow signs for Puffing Billy, turn right into Exton*

Named for its proximity to the Exeter-Exmouth branch line, the 16th-century Puffing Billy enjoys views of the Exe estuary. Diners can see the serious approach to food expressed pictorially in the original artwork on display. Enjoy mackerel rillette with marinated aubergine, pink fir potato and tapenade salad; caramelised scallops with truffled baby leek terrine; confit duck leg and fennel risotto; twice-baked Cornish Blue soufflé with walnuts and French bean salad; slow honey-roasted pork belly with creamed potato and pine nut salad; and Crediton duckling with fondant potato, turnip, apples and fig jus. Rhubarb crumble soufflé with ginger ice cream is a typical dessert.

Open all wk noon-3 6-11 Closed: selected days over Xmas **Bar Meals** L served Mon-Sat 12-2 Av main course £11.50 **Restaurant** L served Mon-Sat 12-2 (Sun 12-2.30) booking required D served Mon-Sat 6.30-9.30 (Sun 6-9) booking required Av 3 course à la carte fr £22 ⊕ FREE HOUSE ◀ Otter, Bays. ♀ 12 **Facilities** Children's menu Garden Parking

---

HARBERTON   Map 3 SX75

The Church House Inn ♀

TQ9 7SF ☎ 01803 863707
dir: *From Totnes take A381 S. Turn right for Harberton, pub by church in village centre*

Built to house masons working on the church next door (around 1100), the inn has some fascinating historic features, including a Tudor window frame and latticed window with 13th-century glass; there's even a resident ghost. The extensive menu is supplemented by daily specials and a traditional roast on Sundays. There's plenty of seafood/fish, and a family room is provided.

Open all wk noon-3 6-11pm **Bar Meals** L served all wk 12-2 D served all wk 6.30-9 **Restaurant** L served all wk 12-2 D served all wk 6.30-9 ⊕ FREE HOUSE ◀ Skinners, Dartmoor IPA, Dartmoor Jail Ale, Guest ales. ♀ 8 **Facilities** Children's menu Family room Dogs allowed

---

HAYTOR VALE   Map 3 SX77

PICK OF THE PUBS

The Rock Inn ★★ HL ◉ ♀

TQ13 9XP ☎ 01364 661305   🖹 01364 661242
e-mail: inn@rock-inn.co.uk
dir: *A38 from Exeter, at Drum Bridges rdbt take A382 for Bovey Tracey, 1st exit at 2nd rdbt (B3387), 3m left to Haytor Vale*

The Rock is an 18th-century former coaching inn located just inside Dartmoor National Park below Haytor Rocks, with wonderful walks straight from the front door. The old stables recall the pub's strategic position on the road between Widecombe-in-the-Moor and Newton Abbot, and modern-day travellers will find nine comfortable en suite bedrooms, all named after Grand National winners. Open fires, antique tables and sturdy furnishings lend a traditional feel, but the cooking style is unashamedly modern British, using excellent produce in nicely presented dishes. Food is served in both the bar and cosy dining rooms, and you might try rump of Devon lamb with mustard and herb crumb set on roasted vegetables bound in tomato and basil, or pan-fried halibut with asparagus, new potatoes and hollandaise sauce. Devon cheese is a particular feature, alongside wine from the Sharpham Vineyard in Totnes and local ales, including Dartmoor Best.

Open all wk 11-11 (Sun noon-10.30) Closed: 25-26 Dec **Meals** L served all wk 12-2 booking required D served all wk 7-9 booking required ⊕ FREE HOUSE ◀ Old Speckled Hen, St Austell Dartmoor Best. ♀ 6 **Facilities** Family room Garden Parking **Rooms** 9

HOLSWORTHY Map 3 SS30

The Bickford Arms ★★★★ INN

Brandis Corner EX22 7XY
☎ 01409 221318 📠 01409 220085
e-mail: info@bickfordarms.com
dir: On A3072, 4m from Holsworthy towards Hatherleigh

This pub stood on the Holsworthy to Hatherleigh road for 300 years before it was gutted by fire in 2003. Although totally rebuilt by the current owners, it retains much period charm, with beams, a welcoming bar and two fireplaces. The bar and restaurant menu offers food prepared with locally-sourced ingredients - perhaps free-range Devon duck breast with redcurrant and red wine sauce or home-made steak and ale pie. There are five attractive en suite bedrooms available.

Open all wk 11-11 (11-3 5.30-11 winter) Closed: 25-26 Dec Bar Meals L served all wk 12-2 D served all wk 6-9 Av main course £9 ⊕ FREE HOUSE ◀ Skinners Betty Stogs, Lazy Daze, Tribute. Facilities Children's menu Garden Parking Rooms 5

HONITON Map 4 ST10

PICK OF THE PUBS

The Holt NEW ◉ ♀

See Pick of the Pubs on opposite page

The Otter Inn

Weston EX14 3NZ ☎ 01404 42594
dir: Just off A30 W of Honiton

On the banks of the idyllic River Otter, this ancient 14th-century inn is set in over two acres of grounds and was once a cider house. Enjoy one of the traditional real ales, try your hand at Scrabble, dominoes or cards, or peruse the inn's extensive book collection. A wide-ranging menu caters for all tastes and includes fresh fish, game, steak, vegetarian dishes, bar meals and Sunday lunch.

Open all wk ⊕ FREE HOUSE ◀ Otter Ale, London Pride, guest ales. Facilities Family room Dogs allowed Garden Parking

HORNDON Map 3 SX58

The Elephant's Nest Inn

PL19 9NQ ☎ 01822 810273 📠 01822 810273
e-mail: info@theelephantsnest.co.uk
dir: Off A386 N of Tavistock

The pub got its unique name in the 1950s when a regular made a humorous remark about the then rather portly landlord. An isolated inn on the flanks of Dartmoor National Park reached via narrow lanes from Mary Tavy, the 16th-century building retains its real fires, slate floors and low beamed ceilings decorated with elephant memorabilia. Meals include lunchtime baguettes, interesting vegetarian options and a good seafood selection - smoked haddock chowder, for example.

Open all wk ⊕ FREE HOUSE ◀ Palmers IPA, Copper, Otter Bright, Sail Ale, guest ales. Facilities Family room Dogs allowed Garden Parking

HORNS CROSS Map 3 SS32

PICK OF THE PUBS

The Hoops Inn & Country Hotel ★★★ HL ◉ ♀

Clovelly EX39 5DL
☎ 01237 451222 📠 01237 451247
e-mail: sales@hoopsinn.co.uk
web: www.hoopsinn.co.uk
dir: On A39 between Bideford & Clovelly

Having made their way along tortuous footpaths to evade the revenue men, smugglers would share out their spoils in this thatched, cob-walled, 13th-century inn. Set in 16 acres of gardens and meadows on the rugged Atlantic coast, it offers charm galore. Menus are based on the freshest produce Devon can offer, including herbs, fruit and vegetables from the garden, and a wide choice of wines by the glass from more than 20 bins. Guests may choose to eat in the bar, morning room or restaurant, where oak-panelled walls, period furniture and tables set with crisp white napkins create just the right level of formality. Seasonal menus focus on local producers and suppliers, and house specialities include terrine of Devon game with home-made piccalilli, and Exmoor venison with griottine cherry sauce.

Open all day all wk 7am-11pm (Sun 8.30am-10.30pm) Bar Meals L served all wk 12-6 D served all wk 6-9 Av main course £13.50 food served all day Restaurant D served all wk 7-9 booking required Fixed menu price fr £20 Av 3 course à la carte fr £27.50 ⊕ FREE HOUSE ◀ Hoops Old Ale & Best, Golden Pig, Doom Bar ♂ Thatchers Gold, Winkleigh. ♀ 20 Facilities Children's menu Play area Family room Dogs allowed Garden Parking Rooms 13

HORSEBRIDGE Map 3 SX47

The Royal Inn ♀

PL19 8PJ ☎ 01822 870214
e-mail: paul@royalinn.co.uk
dir: S of B3362 (Launceston-Tavistock road)

The pub, with a façade enlivened by superb pointed arched windows, was once a nunnery. Standing near a bridge built over the Tamar in 1437 by Benedictine monks, it was the Packhorse Inn until Charles I pitched up one day - his seal is in the doorstep. Beef for the steaks, casseroles and stews, and the pheasant and venison on the specials board are all locally supplied. Chilli cheese tortillas are much appreciated; so is the absence of noisy machines.

Open all wk noon-3 6.30-11pm Bar Meals L served all wk 12-2 booking required D served all wk 6.30-9 booking required Restaurant L served all wk 12-2 booking required D served all wk 6.30-9 booking required ⊕ FREE HOUSE ◀ Eastreet, Bass, Skinners, St Austell Proper Job. ♀ 6 Facilities Children's menu Dogs allowed Garden Parking

ILFRACOMBE Map 3 SS54

The George & Dragon ♀

5 Fore St EX34 9ED ☎ 01271 863851
e-mail: linda.quinn5@btinternet.com
dir: Telephone for directions

The oldest pub in town, The George & Dragon dates from 1360 and is reputedly haunted. The food is of the simple, no-nonsense variety - typical examples include home-cooked boozy beef; chicken curry; mixed grills; fiery chicken with sweet and sour vegetables; and home-cooked crab from the harbour when available. No fruit machines or pool table, but if you are lucky there will be a little home-produced background music.

Open all wk 10am-mdnt (Sun noon-mdnt) Bar Meals L served all wk 12-3 D served all wk 6.30-9 Restaurant L served all wk 12-3 D served all wk 6.30-9 ⊕ PUNCH TAVERNS ◀ Brakspear, Spitfire, Betty Stogs, Courage Directors. ♀ 7 Facilities Children's menu Dogs allowed Notes ◉

PICK OF THE PUBS

The Holt NEW

HONITON Map 4 ST10

178 High St EX14 1LA ☎ 01404 47707
e-mail: enquiries@theholt-honiton.com
web: www.theholt-honiton.com

A friendly, modern pub-cum-wine bar, run for the last four years or so by the McCaig brothers, Angus and Joe. Downstairs are the bar, with sofas and tables, and an open-plan kitchen providing plenty of activity and buzz; in the candlelit dining area upstairs tables look down on the bar below, so you can still feel totally involved. Meals are impressive without being showy (if that isn't a contradiction) and make the most of locally sourced food, including meats, poultry, fish and cheeses from the Holt's own smokery. The frequently changing menu is supplemented by daily specials and tapas, both at lunchtimes and in the evenings. A typical starter would be ham hock terrine, pea bubble and squeak, and deep-fried quail's egg; followed by main courses such as grilled bream with olive-crushed potatoes, crab and coriander cream sauce; pan-fried venison, juniper berry sauce, deep-fried dauphinoise potatoes and chocolate oil; or spinach and Parmesan tart with fresh herb pesto. For pudding, try the delicious but rarely found atholl brose parfait, spiced syrup and home-made biscuits; or passionfruit and ginger crème brûlée. Wednesday's comfort food menu features merguez sausages, home-made fish pie, local game casserole and chilli con carne. Real ale aficionados will delight in the knowledge that the Otter Brewery at nearby Luppitt owns the pub and therefore supplies its four beers; there are some local real ciders too. Flavoured vodkas - caramel, cherry and apple - sold under the Bernard and Kitty's brand are also produced in-house. Ask for a Traffic Light, so named because of the three vodkas' different colours.

Open 11-3 5.30-mdnt Closed: 25, 26 Dec & 1 Jan, Sun & Mon **Bar Meals** L served all week 12-2 D served all week 7-9.30 Av main course £8 **Restaurant** L served all week 12-2 D served all week 7-9.30 Av 3 course à la carte fr £23 ◖ Otter Bitter, Otter Ale, Otter Bright ♂ Aspall. ♟ 9
Facilities Children's menu Dogs allowed

KINGSBRIDGE — Map 3 SX74

The Crabshell Inn

Embankment Rd TQ7 1JZ
☎ 01548 852345 📄 01548 852262
dir: *A38 towards Plymouth, follow signs for Kingsbridge*

A traditional sailors' watering hole on the Kingsbridge estuary quayside (arrive by boat and you may moor free). As you would expect, the views from the outside tables and from the first-floor Waters Edge Restaurant are wonderful. The extensive menu and specials board range through grills, pies, pasta, jacket potatoes, salads and sandwiches, but the house speciality is fresh fish, with dishes such as monkfish provençale, and scallop and smoked bacon gratin.

Open all wk ⊕ FREE HOUSE ◀ Bass Bitter, Crabshell Bitter, Old Speckled Hen, Worthington Cream Flow. **Facilities** Play area Family room Dogs allowed Garden Parking

KINGSKERSWELL — Map 3 SX86

Barn Owl Inn ♟

Aller Mills TQ12 5AN ☎ 01803 872130
e-mail: barnowl.allermills@hall-woodhouse.co.uk
dir: *Telephone for directions*

Handy for Dartmoor and the English Riviera towns, this recently renovated and beautifully restored, 16th-century former farmhouse has many charming features, including flagged floors, a black-leaded range, and oak beams in a high-vaulted converted barn with a minstrels' gallery. Lunchtime snacks include toasties, wraps and baguettes, while the main menu features lots of traditional pub favourites all washed down with a pint of Tanglefoot or Badgers First Gold.

Open all wk noon-11 (Sun noon-10.30) **Bar Meals** Av main course £5 food served all day **Restaurant** food served all day ⊕ WOODHOUSE INNS ◀ Tanglefoot, Badger First Gold. ♟ 24 **Facilities** Children's menu Dogs allowed Garden Parking

PICK OF THE PUBS

Bickley Mill Inn ♟

TQ12 5LN ☎ 01803 873201
e-mail: info@bickleymill.co.uk
dir: *From Newton Abbot on A380 towards Torquay. Right at Barn Owl Inn, follow brown tourist signs*

The inn is a family-owned free house occupying a former flour mill, which dates from the 13th century. The beautifully refurbished property blends old and new in a fresh contemporary style and comprises an attractive bar, restaurant and rooms. It is located in the wooded Stoneycombe Valley, within convenient reach of Torquay, Newton Abbot and Totnes. An 18th-century former barn, the Millers Room, has been transformed into a function room catering for groups of 25 to 125 guests. Dishes are freshly prepared using quality produce from the southwest. Fish from Brixham is a feature of the daily specials, along with regulars like fresh haddock and crab fishcakes with home-made piccalilli, or garlic-crusted pollack fillet with roast cherry tomatoes and sweet pepper coulis. Other options include steak, onion and bacon pudding with roast garlic mash and interesting vegetarian options such as spinach, apricot, tomato and almond curry, with herb roti bread, steamed rice, carrot and ginger relish.

Open all wk Closed: 27-28 Dec & 1 Jan **Bar Meals** L served Mon-Sat 12-2 (Sun 12-2.30) D served Mon-Sat 6.30-9.15 (Sun 6-8.30) **Restaurant** L served Mon-Sat 12-2 (Sun 12-2.30) D served all wk 6.30-9.15 booking required ⊕ FREE HOUSE ◀ Otter Ale, Boddingtons, Teignworthy. ♟ 8 **Facilities** Dogs allowed Garden Parking

KING'S NYMPTON — Map 3 SS61

The Grove Inn ♟

EX37 9ST ☎ 01769 580406
e-mail: info@thegroveinn.co.uk
dir: *2.5m from A377 (Exeter to Barnstaple road)*

A true taste of Devon is offered at this 17th-century thatched inn, set in a beautiful conservation village. Real ales, real ciders and Devon wines are on offer, by an open fire in winter. Working closely with local farmers and producers, the food is sourced as close to home as possible. Look out for dishes such as roast rib of Lakeland Farm beef with Exmoor Ale Yorkshire pudding, breast of Devon chicken stuffed with mozzarella, sage and Parma ham, or Devon fish pie.

Open noon-3 6-11 (BH noon-3) Closed: Mon L ex BH **Bar Meals** L served Tue-Sat 12-2 **Restaurant** L served Tue-Sun 12-2 booking required D served Tue-Sat 7-9 booking required food served all day ⊕ FREE HOUSE ◀ Exmoor Ale, Otter Ale, Bath Gem Ale, Sharps Doom Bar, Teignworthy Springtide Ò Winkleigh. ♟ 7 **Facilities** Children's menu Dogs allowed Garden

KINGSTON — Map 3 SX64

The Dolphin Inn

TQ7 4QE ☎ 01548 810314 📄 01548 810314
e-mail: info@dolphininn.eclipse.co.uk
web: www.dolphin-inn.co.uk
dir: *From A379 (Plymouth to Kingsbridge road) take B3233 for Bigbury-on-Sea. Follow brown inn signs*

The Dolphin is just a mile from the beaches of the South Hams and the beautiful Erme Estuary, ideal for walkers, golfers and surfers. The inn dates from the 16th century and was originally built as cottages for stone masons working on the village church next door. All the food is home made and the menu includes pies, crab bake, lobster bisque, lamb stew, and stuffed chicken breast. Specials provide daily fish and game dishes.

Open noon-3 6-11 (Sun 7-10.30) Closed: Sun eve winter **Bar Meals** L served Mon-Fri 12-2 (Sat-Sun 12-2.30) D served all wk 6-9 (closed Sun & Mon eve winter) Av main course £8.95 **Restaurant** L served Mon-Fri 12-2 (Sat-Sun 12-2.30) D served all wk 6-9 (closed Sun & Mon winter) ⊕ PUNCH TAVERNS ◀ Teignworthy Spring Tide, Courage Best, Sharp's Doom Bar, Otter. **Facilities** Children's menu Play area Family room Dogs allowed Garden Parking

KINGSWEAR — Map 3 SX85

The Ship Inn ♟

Higher St TQ6 0AG ☎ 01803 752348
e-mail: theshipinnkingswear.co.uk
dir: *Telephone for directions*

Historic village pub overlooking the scenic River Dart towards Dartmouth and Dittisham. Located in one of South Devon's most picturesque corners, this tall, character inn is very much a village local with a friendly, welcoming atmosphere inside. Well-prepared fresh food is the hallmark of the menu. Sandwiches, baguettes and pies are available in the bar, while the restaurant menu offers crispy duck with stir-fried vegetables on egg noodles, or oven-baked cod with lemon and lime crust.

Open all day all wk noon-12pm (winter noon-3 6-mdnt) **Bar Meals** L served all wk 12-3 (winter hrs vary) booking required D served all wk 6.30-9.30 (winter hrs vary) booking required **Restaurant** L served all wk 12-3 (winter hrs vary) booking required D served all wk 6.30-9.30 (winter hrs vary) booking required ⊕ Free House ◀ Greene King IPA, Otter, Adnams, Timothy Taylor, Otter Bright Ò Aspall. ♟ 12 **Facilities** Family room Dogs allowed Garden

LEWDOWN — Map 3 SX48

PICK OF THE PUBS

The Harris Arms ♀

Portgate EX20 4PZ
☎ 01566 783331 📄 01566 783359
e-mail: whiteman@powernet.co.uk
dir: *From A30 take Lifton turn, halfway between Lifton & Lewdown in hamlet of Portgate*

A 16th-century inn with wonderful views to Brent Tor, this establishment lives up to its promotional strapline: 'Eat Real Food and Drink Real Wine'. Located on the old A30 close to the boundary between Devon and Cornwall, it's an accessible spot for honest food with substance and style, plus real ales and excellent wines. Owners Rowena and Andy Whiteman have previously run vineyards in France and New Zealand, so their wine list is both eclectic and extensive. The pub's excellent reputation, which reaches far beyond the local area, is built on exact cooking and locally-sourced ingredients. Example starters are fillets of warm home-smoked Cornish mackerel with horseradish cream; and grilled local goats' cheese on toasted baguette with mixed leaves, walnuts and pesto. Main courses might include slow-roasted confit of Devon pork belly with braised cabbage, potato and black pudding croquette, and sage and apple jus; and pub classics such as home-cooked ham with eggs and chips.

Closed: Mon & Sun eve **Bar Meals** L served Tue-Sun 12-2 booking required D served Tue-Sat 6.30-9 booking required Av main course £8.95 **Restaurant** L served Tue-Sun 12-2 booking required D served Tue-Sat 6.30-9 booking required Fixed menu price fr £13.95 Av 3 course à la carte fr £22.50 ⊕ FREE HOUSE ◄ Sharp's Doom Bar, Guinness Extra Cold, guest ales. ♀ 18 **Facilities** Children's menu Dogs allowed Garden Parking

LIFTON — Map 3 SX38

PICK OF THE PUBS

The Arundell Arms ★★★ HL ◉◉ ♀

See Pick of the Pubs on page 142

LITTLEHEMPSTON — Map 3 SX86

Tally Ho Inn ♀

TQ9 6NF ☎ 01803 862316 📄 01803 862316
e-mail: tally.ho.inn@btconnect.com
dir: *Off A38 at Buckfastleigh. A381 between Newton Abbot & Totnes*

A traditional, family-owned 14th-century thatched inn in a pretty village, with inglenook fireplaces and a flower-filled patio. Local suppliers are the mainstay of seasonal menus offering roasted lamb rump with herb crust; steak and kidney pie; smoked haddock with asparagus and poached egg; Moroccan lamb tagine flavoured with apricots and honey; or roasted pork tenderloin with an orange glaze and a lemon and parsley risotto. Real ales come from Devon breweries.

Open all wk noon-3 6.30-11 Closed: 25 Dec **Bar Meals** L served all wk 12-2 booking required D served all wk 6.30-9 booking required Av main course £5.95 **Restaurant** Av 3 course à la carte fr £20 ⊕ FREE HOUSE ◄ Exmoor Ale, Teignworthy Brewery Ales, Guinness, guest ales ♂ Thatchers Gold. ♀ 7 **Facilities** Dogs allowed Garden Parking

LUTON (NEAR CHUDLEIGH) — Map 3 SX97

The Elizabethan Inn ♀

Fore St TQ13 0BL ☎ 01626 775425 📄 01626 775151
e-mail: elizabethaninn@btconnect.com
dir: *Between Chudleigh & Teignmouth*

Known locally as the Lizzie, this cosy 16th-century free house boasts a pretty beer garden that makes a great destination on a fine summer's day. Sausages are home made and bacon is home cured, while local produce features strongly on the daily specials board. The extensive bar menu features a choice of omelettes, risottos and warm salads. Other dishes include West Country haddock in beer batter, red Thai curry, chilli con carne, or one of the risottos. A log fire burns in the bar on cold winter days where you can enjoy a pint from the great selection of real ales and ciders.

Open all wk Closed: 25-26 Dec, 1 Jan **Bar Meals** L served Mon-Sat 12-2 (Sun 12-2.30) booking required D served all wk 6-9.30 booking required Av main course £7 **Restaurant** L served Mon-Sat 12-2 (Sun 12-2.30) booking required D served all wk 6-9.30 booking required Fixed menu price fr £13.50 Av 3 course à la carte fr £22.50 ⊕ FREE HOUSE ◄ London Pride, Teignworthy Reel Ale, Otter Ale, O'Hanlon's Yellowhammer, Dartmoor IPA ♂ Stowford Press. ♀ 8 **Facilities** Dogs allowed Garden Parking

LYDFORD — Map 3 SX58

PICK OF THE PUBS

Dartmoor Inn ◉◉ ♀

EX20 4AY ☎ 01822 820221 📄 01822 820494
e-mail: info@dartmoorinn.co.uk
dir: *On A386 S of Okehampton*

Owners Karen and Philip Burgess have made their mark at this distinctive free house, which Charles Kingsley almost certainly described in his novel *Westward Ho!* The stylish, restrained décor extends through the cosy dining rooms and small bar, where an easy dining menu features dishes like bacon and egg salad with mustard dressing; and goats' cheese omelette with red onion. After your meal, you can even browse for beautiful accessories and home ware in the inn's own boutique.

Open all day noon-2.30 6.30-11pm Closed: Mon L **Bar Meals** L served Tue-Sun 12-2.15 D served all wk 6.30-9.15 ⊕ FREE HOUSE ◄ Otter Ale, Tribute. ♀ 6 **Facilities** Dogs allowed Garden Parking

LYMPSTONE — Map 3 SX98

The Globe Inn ♀

The Strand EX8 5EY ☎ 01395 263166
dir: *Telephone for directions*

Set in the estuary village of Lympstone, this traditional beamed inn has a good local reputation for seafood. The separate restaurant area serves as a coffee bar during the day. Look out for bass fillets with plum sauce; monkfish kebabs; seafood platter; and seafood grill. Weekend music and quiz nights are a feature.

Open all wk 10am-3 5.30-mdnt (Sun all day) **Bar Meals** L served all wk 10-2 booking required D served all wk 6.30-9.30 booking required **Restaurant** L served all wk 10-2 booking required D served all wk 6.30-9.30 booking required ⊕ HEAVITREE ◄ London Pride, Otter, Bass ♂ Aspall. ♀ 10 **Facilities** Children's menu Dogs allowed

PICK OF THE PUBS

The Arundell Arms ★★★ HL ◉◉ ♢

LIFTON   Map 3 SX38

PL16 0AA
☎ 01566 784666   📠 01566 784494
e-mail: reservations@arundellarms.com
web: www.arundellarms.com
dir: *1m off A30 dual carriageway, 3m E of Launceston*

Set in a valley of five rivers, close to the uplands of Dartmoor, Anne Voss-Bark's upmarket, creeper-clad old Devon inn is a favourite destination for those who enjoy the country pursuits of shooting, riding, walking and in particular fishing – the River Tamar flows past the bottom of the garden and guests have 20 miles of fishing rights along its length. Run by the same family for over forty years, it is one of England's premier fishing hotels, and the 18th-century inn is named after William Arundell, who took over the 'best and most respectable inn in the village' in 1815. The description is still apt. Today, it exudes warmth and a truly

civilised air pervades the smart interior – not only in the 'locals' bar, with its babble of conversation and simple food at lunchtime, but also in the smarter dining bar which has two AA rosettes for its food. You can choose to eat sandwiches (roast Devon beef with horseradish), or select from the starters and light snacks menu. Here you're likely to find tomato and red pepper soup, or a smooth chicken liver pâté with red onion marmalade for starters; and main courses like braised oxtail with roast vegetables; and spiced venison burgers with dressed leaves and chips. Three-course table d'hôte and à la carte menus are served in the elegant restaurant; typical dishes include asparagus with chervil hollandaise, casserole of John Dory, sea trout, scallops and sole, and hot chocolate pudding with whipped rum cream. There are 21 individually designed en suite bedrooms, and thoughtful touches are provided like home-made chocolates for after-dinner guests in the sitting room. From here you can see one of England's few remaining cockpits, now the hotel's fishing tackle room, set in the terraced garden where swifts and swallows soar overhead in the evening sunshine.

Open 12-3 6-11 **Bar Meals** L served all week 12-2.30 D served all week 6-9.30 Av main course £12 **Restaurant** L served all week 12-2.30 D served all week 6-9.30 Fixed menu price fr £30 ⊕ FREE HOUSE ◀ Tribute, Guest Ales ♻ Thatchers, Cornish Rattler. ♟ 9 **Facilities** Children's menu Dogs allowed Garden Parking **Rooms** 21

LYNMOUTH · Map 3 SS74

PICK OF THE PUBS

Rising Sun Hotel ★★ HL ♀

Harbourside EX35 6EG
☎ 01598 753223 📄 01598 753480
e-mail: reception@risingsunlynmouth.co.uk
dir: From M5 junct 25 follow Minehead signs. A39 to Lynmouth

Overlooking Lynmouth's tiny harbour and bay is the Rising Sun, a 14th-century thatched smugglers' inn. In turn, overlooking them all, are Countisbury Cliffs, the highest in England. The building's long history is evident from the uneven oak floors, crooked ceilings and thick walls. Literary associations are plentiful: R D Blackmore wrote some of his wild Exmoor romance, *Lorna Doone*, here; the poet Shelley is believed to have honeymooned in the garden cottage, and Coleridge stayed too. Immediately behind rises Exmoor Forest and National Park, home to red deer, wild ponies and birds of prey. With sea and moor so close, game and seafood are in plentiful supply, and pheasant, venison, hare, wild boar, monkfish, crab or scallops, for example, will appear variously as starter or main course dishes. At night the oak-panelled, candlelit dining room is an example of romantic British inn-keeping at its best.

Open all day all wk 11am-11pm (Sun noon-10.30pm) Closed: 25 Dec **Bar Meals** L served all wk 12-2.30 D served all wk 6.30-9 ⊕ FREE HOUSE ◖ Exmoor Gold, Fox, Tetley ♂ Thatchers Gold. ♀ 6 **Facilities** Dogs allowed Garden **Rooms** 14

LYNTON · Map 3 SS74

The Bridge Inn

Lynbridge Hill EX35 6NR
☎ 01598 753425 📄 01598 753225
dir: Turn off A39 at Barbrook onto B3234. In 1m pub on right just beyond Sunny Lyn camp site

Attractive 17th-century riverside inn overlooked by National Trust woodlands. In the cellars the remains of 12th-century salmon fishermen's cottages are still visible, and the unusually shaped windows at the front originally belonged to Charles I's hunting lodge at Coombe House, salvaged following flood damage in the 1680s. The 1952 Lynmouth Flood destroyed the Lyn Bridge and car park, but most of the pub survived intact.

Closed: Mon & Tue-Thu L Jan-Feb ⊕ FREE HOUSE ◖ St. Austell Tribute, Sharp's Doom Bar, Exmoor Fox. **Facilities** Dogs allowed Garden Parking

MARLDON · Map 3 SX86

The Church House Inn ♀

Village Rd TQ3 1SL ☎ 01803 558279 📄 01803 664865
dir: Take Torquay ring road, follow signs to Marldon & Totnes, follow brown signs to pub

An ancient inn with a contemporary feel located between Torbay and the market town of Newton Abbott. The building dates from around 1400, when it was a hostel for the builders of the adjoining village church, but it was rebuilt in 1750 incorporating beautiful Georgian windows. Typical evening menus include honey roast duck breast with a mixed berry sauce, slow-cooked shoulder of lamb in Moroccan spiced sultana and almond sauce, or fillet of salmon with a spring onion, mussel and white wine sauce.

Open all wk 11.30-2.30 5-11 (Fri-Sat 5-11.30 Sun 12-3 5.30-10.30) **Bar Meals** L served all wk 12-2 D served all wk 6.30-9.30 Av main course £13.50 **Restaurant** L served all wk 12-2 D served all wk 6.30-9.30 Av 3 course à la carte fr £26.30 ⊕ FREE HOUSE ◖ Dartmoor Best, Bass, Old Speckled Hen, Greene King IPA, London Pride. ♀ 10 **Facilities** Children's menu Dogs allowed Garden Parking

MEAVY · Map 3 SX56

The Royal Oak Inn ♀

PL20 6PJ ☎ 01822 852944
e-mail: sjearp@aol.com
dir: B3212 from Yelverton to Princetown. Right at Dousland to Meavy, past school. Pub opposite village green

Flagstone floors, oak beams and a welcoming open fire set the scene at this traditional 15th-century free house. Standing by the village green and close to the shores of Burrator reservoir on the edge of Dartmoor, the inn is popular with cyclists and walkers – 'muddy boots and muddy paws are always welcome'. Local cask ales, ciders and fine wines accompany the carefully sourced ingredients in a menu ranging from lunchtime baguettes and jackets to steak and Jail Ale pie; and monkfish and salmon kebabs.

Open all wk 11-3 6-11 (Sat-Sun & May-Oct all day) **Bar Meals** L served Mon-Fri 12-2.30, Sat-Sun 12-3 D served all wk 6-9 Av main course £5 **Restaurant** L served Mon-Fri 12-2.30, Sat-Sun 12-3 D served all wk 6-9 Fixed menu price fr £8 ⊕ FREE HOUSE ◖ Dartmoor Jail Ale, Dartmoor IPA, St Austell Tribute, Royal Oak, Guest ♂ Westons Scrumpy, Old Rosie, Thatchers Gold. ♀ 12 **Facilities** Children's menu Dogs allowed Garden

MODBURY · Map 3 SX65

California Country Inn

California Cross PL21 0SG
☎ 01548 821449 📄 01548 821566
e-mail: california@bellinns.entadsl.com
web: www.californiacountryinn.co.uk
dir: Telephone for details

Oak beams and exposed stonework are features of this whitewashed 14th-century free house. Brass, copper and old photographs decorate the interior, and there's a landscaped garden for summer use. Menus are created from only locally supplied produce, with prime meats from the chargrill, and dishes ranging from lasagne and beer-battered cod in the bar to roast monk fish with Yealm mussels, or loin of Plympton venison in the restaurant.

Open all day all wk 11-11 **Bar Meals** L served Mon-Sat 12-2, Sun 12-8 D served Mon-Sat 6-9, Sun 12-8 Av main course £9 **Restaurant** L served Sun 12-2 D served Wed-Sun 6-9 booking required Av 3 course à la carte fr £20 ⊕ FREE HOUSE ◖ Guinness, Abbot Ale, London Pride, Doom Bar. **Facilities** Children's menu Family room Dogs allowed Garden Parking

MOLLAND — Map 3 SS82

The London Inn

EX36 3NG ☎ **01769 550269**
dir: *Telephone for directions*

New owners at this 15th-century inn passionately believe that Exmoor needs to retain at least one of its traditional pubs. The London has many historic features and remains a centre for the shooting and hunting crowd. Home-made locally sourced food and ale straight from the cask are served, and the latest venture is a micro-brewery. Typical dishes include wood pigeon salad, venison sausages with bubble and squeak and gravy, and jam roly poly.

Open 12-3 6.30-11.30 (Sun 12-5) Closed: Sun eve **Bar Meals** L served Mon-Sat 12-2, Sun 12-3 D served Mon-Sat 7-9 Av main course £7 **Restaurant** L served Mon-Sat 12-2, Sun 12-3 booking required D served Mon-Sat 7-9 booking required ⊕ FREE HOUSE ◀ Exmoor Ale, Cotleigh Tawny Bitter ♂ Winkleigh Cider. **Facilities** Children's menu Family room Dogs allowed Garden Parking **Notes** ⊛

MORETONHAMPSTEAD — Map 3 SX78

The White Hart Hotel ★★★ HL ⊛ ♀

The Square TQ13 8NF
☎ **01647 441340** 🖹 **01647 441341**
e-mail: enquiries@Whitehartdartmoor.co.uk
dir: *From A30 at Whiddon Down take A382 for Chagford & Moretonhampstead. Pub in village centre. Parking in 20yds*

Set in the heart of Dartmoor, this Grade II listed building dates from 1639 and has a recently refurbished bar, lounge and brasserie restaurant area for informal dining and drinking. Locally brewed ales are served alongside locally sourced food and dishes include rump of Dartmoor lamb with mini moussaka and feta cheese, and steamed stone bass with scallop and mushroom fricassee. Customers can also call in for morning coffee or afternoon tea.

Open all day all wk 11-11 **Bar Meals** L served all wk 12-2.30 D served all wk 6-9.30 Av main course £7.95 **Restaurant** L served all wk 12-2.30 booking required D served all wk 6-9.30 booking required Fixed menu price fr £15.95 Av 3 course à la carte fr £25 ⊕ HART INNS LTD ◀ St Austell Tribute, Otter, Doom Bar ♂ Thatchers. ♀ 18 **Facilities** Children's menu Dogs allowed Garden **Rooms** 28

NEWTON ABBOT — Map 3 SX87

The Wild Goose Inn ♀

Combeinteignhead TQ12 4RA ☎ **01626 872241**
dir: *From A380 at Newton Abbot rdbt take B3195 (Shaldon road), signed Milber, 2.5m into village, right at sign*

Standing in the heart of the village at the head of a long valley, the pub was first licensed as the Country House Inn in 1840. Renamed in the 1960s when nearby geese began intimidating the pub's customers, this charming free house boasts a sunny garden sheltered by the adjacent 14th-century church tower. Behind the bar, cider from Thatchers, Wiscombe and MillTop join West Country ales like Otter, Sharp's, Skinner's and Exe Valley.

Open all wk **Bar Meals** L served all wk 12-2 D served all wk 7-9.30 booking required Av main course £6.50 **Restaurant** L served all wk 12-2 D served all wk 7-9.30 booking required Fixed menu price fr £6.50 ⊕ FREE HOUSE ◀ Otter Ale, Cotleigh, Sharp's Bitter, Skinner's Bitter, Teignworthy, Branscombe, Exe Valley ♂ Thatchers. ♀ 16 **Facilities** Children's menu Dogs allowed Garden Parking

NEWTON ST CYRES — Map 3 SX89

The Beer Engine ♀

EX5 5AX ☎ **01392 851282** 🖹 **01392 851876**
e-mail: info@thebeerengine.co.uk
dir: *From Exeter take A377 towards Crediton. Signed from A377 towards Sweetham. Pub opp rail station in village*

Originally opened as a railway hotel in 1852, this pretty, whitewashed free house is now acknowledged as one of Devon's leading micro-breweries. Engine ales with names like Piston bitter and Sleeper Heavy evoke the pub's antecedents, whilst cider drinkers can wash down their ploughman's with Dragon Tears or Stowford Press. With local suppliers listed, expect a wide choice of vegetarian and fresh fish dishes, as well as braised lamb shank, breaded veal escalope, and pan-fried venison sausages on bubble and squeak.

Open all day all wk 11am-11pm (Sun noon-10.30) **Bar Meals** L served all wk 12-2 D served Tue-Sat 6.30-9.15, Sun-Mon 6.30-8.30 Av main course £9 **Restaurant** L served all wk 12-2 booking required D served Tue-Sat 6.30-9.15, Sun-Mon 6.30-8.30 booking required ⊕ FREE HOUSE ◀ Engine Ales: Piston Bitter, Rail Ale, Sleeper Heavy ♂ Stowford Press. ♀ 7 **Facilities** Children's menu Dogs allowed Garden Parking

NORTH BOVEY — Map 3 SX78

PICK OF THE PUBS

The Ring of Bells Inn ♀

TQ13 8RB ☎ **01647 440375** 🖹 **01647 440746**
e-mail: info@ringofbellsinn.com
dir: *1.5m from Moretonhampstead off B3212. 7m S of Whiddon Down junct on A30*

The Ring of Bells is one of Dartmoor's most historic inns, an attractive thatched property located just off the village green. It was built in the 13th century as lodgings for the stonemasons who were working on the construction of the nearby church, and remains very much at the heart of the village's social life. Visitors too are attracted by the good Devon pub food and West Country ales, and there is certainly plenty to do and see in the area, particularly walking, cycling, fishing, riding and bird watching. The short daily menus are full of interesting options – to start perhaps Jerusalem artichoke soup; or a warm salad of goats' cheese, parmesan and olive oil. The main courses could feature loin of venison with celeriac and braised lentils; or grilled fillet of brill with asparagus and roast lobster sauce. Leave a little room for crème brûlée with figs or a home-made crumble.

Open all day all wk Closed: 25 Dec **Bar Meals** L served all wk all day Etr-Oct, all wk 12-2.30 Nov-Etr D served all wk all day Etr-Oct, all wk 6.30-9.30 Nov-Etr Av main course £10 **Restaurant** D served all wk 6.30-9.30 booking required ⊕ FREE HOUSE ◀ Otter Ale, St Austell Tribute, Sharps Doom Bar. ♀ 12 **Facilities** Children's menu Family room Dogs allowed Garden

NOSS MAYO — Map 3 SX54

PICK OF THE PUBS

The Ship Inn ♀

See Pick of the Pubs on opposite page

PICK OF THE PUBS

The Ship Inn ♉

NOSS MAYO   Map 3 SX54

PL8 1EW
☎ **01752 872387**   📄 **01752 873294**
e-mail: ship@nossmayo.com
web: www.nossmayo.com
dir: *5m S of Yealmpton on River Yealm estuary*

Reclaimed English oak and local stone characterise this beautifully renovated 16th-century free house. Huddled on Noss Mayo's tidal waterfront on the south bank of the stunning Yealm estuary, the style is simple and properly pub-like. The deceptively spacious building remains cosy thanks to the wooden floors, old bookcases, log fires and dozens of local pictures. Beers from nearby Summerskill's are supported by Butcombe Blonde, as well as a selection from Princetown Breweries. The inn's superb location makes it an especially popular port of call for sailing enthusiasts, who can tie up their boats right outside; walkers, too, throng the bar, and dogs are allowed downstairs. The ever-changing menu of home-made dishes is served from midday until 9:30pm, and majors on local produce, notably fish. Mature Devon Cheddar, Cornish Yarg and local Devon ham are amongst the choices with your ploughman's lunch, whilst alternatives include filled baguettes and hot dishes such as sausages and mash with onion gravy, and breaded scampi with fries and salad. For the hearty three-course appetite, classic starters like grilled goats' cheese on mixed salad, and traditional crayfish cocktail with Marie rose sauce, could be followed by pan-fried duck breast on potato rosti; Devon rib eye steak with peppercorn sauce; or seared sea bass fillet on stir-fried vegetables with noodles and hoi sin sauce. Round off with crème brûlée; bread and butter pudding with custard; or sticky toffee pudding with butterscotch sauce and vanilla ice cream. As well as an interesting and reasonably priced global wine choice, a decent list of malts, liqueurs and hot drinks completes the menu, which you can study at leisure while enjoying the great views from the waterside garden.

Open all week **Bar Meals** Av main course £12 **Restaurant** Av 3 course à la carte fr £23 ⊕ FREE HOUSE ◀ Tamar, Jail Ale, Butcombe Blonde, Dartmoor IPA. ♉ 10 **Facilities** Children's menu Dogs allowed Garden Parking

PICK OF THE PUBS

The Fox & Goose ♟

PARRACOMBE Map 3 SS64

EX31 4PE
☎ 01598 763239 📄 01598 763621
web: www.foxandgoose-parracombe.co.uk
dir: *1m from A39 between Blackmoor Gate (2m) & Lynton (6m). Signed to Parracombe. Fox & Goose sign on approach*

It's hard to believe that this striking building in this sleepy Exmoor village was once a couple of tiny thatched cottages serving the local farming community. It was changed beyond recognition when it was enlarged to compete with nearby hotels after the narrow gauge Lynton and Barnstaple Railway linked Parracombe with the outside world in 1898. Then, in 1925, the village's narrow street was sidelined by an early bypass, which may have contributed to the closure of the railway just ten years later. Through all this, the village has remained unspoilt and the pub continues to thrive, drawing locals and visitors for local Cotleigh and

Exmoor ales, and good home-made food listed on changing blackboard menus, which can be enjoyed in the homely bar and restaurant, adorned with farm memorabilia and old village photographs, or in the paved courtyard garden overlooking the river. Menus may champion meat and seasonal game from surrounding farms and estates, but fish dominates proceedings, all landed locally along the North Devon coast; lobster, for example, is caught off Lundy Island, or there could be pan-fried skate wing with brown shrimps and capers, halibut with creamed leeks, lemon sole fillets with creamy French peas, and a traditional bouillabaisse, a fish stew made with a selection from the day's catch. Meat-lovers will not be disappointed with slow-braised shoulder of lamb cooked in red wine and served with roasted root vegetables and creamy mash. Starters take in smoked mackerel and horseradish pâté and Taw mussels cooked with shallots, white wine and cream, while indulgent puddings may include hot chocolate brownie and a traditional rice pudding served with home-made jam. The cheese board offers local cheeses like Cornish Yarg wrapped in nettles. Don't miss the Sunday roast lunches.

Open all week **Bar Meals** L served 12-2 D served 6-9 (Sun 7-9) Av main course £12.95 **Restaurant** L served 12-2 D served 6-9 (Sun 7-9) ⊕ FREE HOUSE ◀ Cotleigh Barn Owl, Dartmoor Best, Exmoor Fox, Guinness Ö Winkleigh. ♟ 10 **Facilities** Children's menu Dogs allowed Garden Parking

OTTERY ST MARY — Map 3 SY19

The Talaton Inn

Talaton EX5 2RQ ☎ 01404 822214 📄 01404 822214
dir: Telephone for directions

Timber-framed, well-maintained 16th-century inn, run by a brother and sister partnership. The set menu might include crispy bacon, chicken and brie Caesar salad, braised lamb steak with rosemary, red wine and chive sauce, with Eton mess to finish. At Sunday lunchtimes, as well as the popular roast, there is also a pie and vegetarian choice. Good selection of real ales and malts, and a fine collection of bar games. There are also themed food nights on the last Thursday of each month – Indian, Spanish, Chinese etc.

Open all wk 12-3 7-11 **Bar Meals** L served all wk 12-2 D served Tue-Sat 7-9 Av main course £8.95 **Restaurant** L served all wk 12-2 D served Tue-Sat 7-9 booking required ⊕ FREE HOUSE ◀ Otter, Fuller's London Pride, O'Hanlon's, Badger Tanglefoot, Seasonal Brew. **Facilities** Dogs allowed Parking

PARRACOMBE — Map 3 SS64

PICK OF THE PUBS

The Fox & Goose ♀

See Pick of the Pubs on opposite page

RATTERY — Map 3 SX76

Church House Inn ♀

TQ10 9LD ☎ 01364 642220 📄 01364 642220
e-mail: ray12@onetel.com
dir: 1m from A38 Exeter to Plymouth Rd & 0.75m from A385 Totnes to South Brent Rd

This venerable inn dates from 1028 and its interior burgeons with brasses, bare beams, large fireplaces and other historic features. Some customers encounter the wandering spirit of a monk; fortunately he seems to be friendly. In the characterful dining room, the menu offers fresh fish of all kinds (snowcrab cocktail; lemon sole), as well as home-made moussaka, game pie and chilli, and lighter options such as salads or toasted sandwiches, plus and vegetarian balti and stroganoff.

Open all wk 11-2.30 6-11 (Sun noon-3 6-10.30) **Bar Meals** L served Mon-Sat 11.30-2, Sun 12-2 booking required D served all wk 6.30-9 booking required **Restaurant** L served Mon-Sat 11.30-2, Sun 12-2 booking required D served all wk 6.30-9 booking required ⊕ FREE HOUSE ◀ Princetown IPA, Princetown Jail Ale, Butcombe Best Bitter, Otter Ale. ♀ 8 **Facilities** Children's menu Dogs allowed Garden Parking

ROCKBEARE — Map 3 SY09

PICK OF THE PUBS

Jack in the Green Inn ◉◉ ♀

See Pick of the Pubs on page 148

SALCOMBE — Map 3 SX73

PICK OF THE PUBS

The Victoria Inn ♀

Fore St TQ8 8BU ☎ 01548 842604 📄 01548 844201
e-mail: info@victoriainn-salcombe.co.uk
dir: In town centre, overlooking estuary

From the first floor restaurant there are stunning views of the pretty harbour and the fishing boats bringing in the catch for the kitchen. Deciding which fresh fish dish to choose could be difficult: perhaps a chowder starter of handpicked Salcombe white crabmeat, prawns and other shellfish, white wine, fresh dill and Devon double cream. A main dish of slowly roasted half shoulder of new season Devon lamb encrusted with garlic and fresh herbs and served with a redcurrant and fresh mint sauce, served over a wholegrain mustard mash, could follow. Desserts include home-made apple and blackberry crumble and custard, and Devon ice creams and cheeses.

Open all day all wk 11.30am-11pm (Fri-Sat 11.30am-11.30pm) Closed: 25 Dec pm **Bar Meals** L served all wk 12-2.30 D served all wk 6-9 ⊕ ST AUSTELL BREWERY ◀ St Austell Tribute, Black Prince, Proper Job IPA. ♀ 12 **Facilities** Play area Dogs allowed Garden

---

SHEEPWASH — Map 3 SS40

Half Moon Inn

EX21 5NE ☎ 01409 231376 📄 01409 231673
e-mail: info@halfmoonsheepwash.co.uk
web: www.halfmoonsheepwash.co.uk
dir: From M5 take A30 to Okehampton then A386, at Hatherleigh, left onto A3072, after 4m right for Sheepwash

A very popular venue for anglers, this white-painted inn overlooking the village square in a remote Devon village is a Grade II listed building with fishing rights for ten miles of the River Torridge. Inside you'll find slate floors and a huge inglenook fireplace where a log fire burns in cooler weather. Bar snacks are available at lunchtime and a set menu of traditional English fare at dinner.

Open all wk 11-3 6-11.30 ⊕ FREE HOUSE ◀ Greene King Ruddles Best Bitter, St Austell Tribute, Bombardier ♂ Thatchers Gold. **Facilities** Dogs allowed Parking

SIDMOUTH — Map 3 SY18

PICK OF THE PUBS

The Blue Ball NEW   INN ♀

See Pick of the Pubs on page 149

PICK OF THE PUBS

Dukes ★★★★ INN ♀

See Pick of the Pubs on page 150

SLAPTON — Map 3 SX84

PICK OF THE PUBS

The Tower Inn ♀

See Pick of the Pubs on page 151

PICK OF THE PUBS

Jack in the Green Inn ❀❀ ♉

ROCKBEARE Map 3 SY09

London Rd EX5 2EE
☎ **01404 822240** 📄 **01404 823445**
e-mail: info@jackinthegreen.uk.com
web: www.jackinthegreen.uk.com
dir: *From M5 take old A30 towards Honiton,
signed Rockbeare*

Running this old freehouse is a 'well-travelled, rosy-cheeked rugby aficionado' – that's owner Paul Parnell's description. He's been here quite a few years, but his centuries-old inn comprehensively outdoes him, while its name goes back to pagan times when a 'green man' was associated with spring fertility celebrations. Today, wood-burning stoves and leather armchairs create a cosy, welcoming interior, with a bar serving Otter, Yellow Hammer and Cotleigh Tawny, which should satisfy real ale lovers. Overall, though, the inn is best known as a dining destination, Paul's simple philosophy being to serve the best of Devon's produce in stylish surroundings; the success of his kitchen team's modern British culinary achievements has been recognised with two AA Rosettes. Even the humble ploughman's is given the VIP treatment, and the more traditional dishes may also genuinely surprise. Bangers and mash, for example, comprises a quartet of local sausages with pumpkin purée, parsnip crisps and fresh, seasonal vegetables, while fish and chips 'is a million miles from the modern day travesty', with pollack (or is it colin these days?), home-made chips, salad 'with a bite' and tartare sauce. Freshly cut gerberas and roses, and Simon Drew prints decorate the Devon Restaurant, where a typical three-course meal from the Totally Devon menu might be grilled breast of wood-pigeon with creamed cabbage, smoked sausage and Puy lentils; followed by Aberdeen Angus rump steak with chunky chips and peppercorn sauce; and finally, lavender crème brûlée. For something different again, try a tasting menu featuring air-dried beef with Bordinski rye bread and celeriac rémoulade; seared sesame tuna with avocado and lime purée; rack of Whimple lamb with honey-roast garlic purée and basil mash; and passion fruit mousse with coconut sorbet. The wine list offers over 100 bins, each selected for character and excellent value.

Open 11-3 5.30-11 (Sun 12-11) Closed: 25 Dec-5 Jan **Meals** L served Mon-Sat 12-2 D served 6-9.30 (Sun 12-9) ⊕ FREE HOUSE ◂ Cotleigh Tawny Ale, Thomas Hardy Hardy Country, Otter Ale, Royal Oak, Branscombe Vale JIG, Yellowhammer. ♉ 12 **Facilities** Family room Parking

PICK OF THE PUBS

The Blue Ball NEW ★★★★ INN ♟

Stevens Cross, Sidford EX10 9QL
☎ **01395 514062** 📠 **01395 519584**
e-mail: rogernewton@blueballinn.net
web: www.blueballinn.net
dir: M5 junct 30 exit to A3052. Through Sidford towards Lyme Regis, on left after village, approx 13m

The Newton family has run this marvellous 14th-century thatched, cob-and-flint pub since 1912. Completely destroyed by fire in March 2006, Roger and Linda Newton painstakingly rebuilt this famous Devon landmark to its former glory, even sourcing old furniture, pictures and memorabilia, re-opening the doors in September 2007. In addition to re-capturing the unique atmosphere of the original inn, they have added nine contemporary-styled bedrooms, including a ground floor disabled room, and a function room with full conference facilities. The new-look inn is a hugely attractive, lovingly maintained building, festooned with colourful hanging baskets in summer, and cosy in winter within the rambling carpeted bars. Arrive early to bag one of the fireside seats (there are three log fires) and peruse the extensive menus, which begin at 8am with a tempting breakfast choice – smoked salmon and scrambled eggs, warm croissants and coffee. Classic pub favourites feature on the main menu, from fishcakes with tartare sauce and deep-fried whitebait for starters, to steak and kidney pudding; battered cod and chips; rib-eye steak with peppercorn sauce and all the trimmings, and various jacket potatoes with fillings; salads; and a good choice of sandwiches. Typical puddings include chocolate and walnut sponge pudding and range of Salcombe ice creams. To drink, try a pint of Otter Bitter or one of ten wines served by the glass, which are best enjoyed in the newly landscaped garden or on the sun-trap terrace. Its location, within easy reach of the M5, A303 and Exeter, and just minutes from the stunning Devon coastline and excellent walks make the Blue Ball an ideal base for exploring Devon, or as a stopover en route to the far west.

Open all week Closed: 25 Dec eve **Bar Meals** L served all week 12-3 D served all week 6-9 Av main course £9.50 **Restaurant** L served all week 12-3 D served all week 6-9 ⊞ PUNCH TAVERNS ◼ Otter Bitter, Tribute, John Smiths, Guest Ale ♂ Stowford Press. ♟ 10 **Facilities** Children's menu Play area Family room Dogs allowed Garden Parking **Rooms** 9

PICK OF THE PUBS

Dukes ★★★★ INN ♟

The Esplanade EX10 8AR
☎ **01395 513320** 📄 **01395 519318**
e-mail: dukes@hotels-sidmouth.co.uk
dir: *M5 junct 30 onto A3052, take 1st exit to Sidmouth on right then left onto Esplanade*

Situated at the heart of Sidmouth town centre on the Regency Esplanade, Dukes might be a contemporary inn, but its values are traditional. The interior is stylish and lively, with a relaxed Continental feel in the bar and public areas. In fine weather the patio garden overlooking the sea is the perfect place to soak up the sun with a mid-morning Italian freshly ground coffee and home-baked pastry, a pint of Branscombe's or Princetown's real ale, or one of the

dozen or so wines served by the glass. Varied menu choices include traditional English-style favourites and a specials board that offers a variety of fresh fish from Brixham and Lyme Bay, and prime meats from West Country farms. Lunch options include sautéed mackerel; sausage, mash and onion gravy; and fresh-baked quiche of the day, while main courses at dinner include honey-baked gammon; pan-fried skate wing with Mediterranean-style ratatouille; home-made lamb and mint burger; and fresh pappardelle pasta. If you just want a snack, possibilities range from a wide choice of stone-baked pizzas and thick-cut sandwiches made with local bread, to loaded nachos and home-made jacket wedges. Sundays mean traditional roasts – topside of West Country beef, leg of lamb, loin of pork and nut roast. In the afternoon some might feel like a Devon cream tea. Newly refurbished bed and breakfast accommodation is available, with most rooms overlooking the bay. All are en suite and come with free Wi-Fi.

Open all week **Bar Meals** L served Sun-Thu 12-9, Fri-Sat 12-9.30 D served Sun-Thu 12-9, Fri-Sat 12-9.30 Av main course £12 **Restaurant** L served Sun-Thu 12-9, Fri-Sat 12-9.30 D served Sun-Thu 12-9, Fri-Sat 12-9.30 Fixed menu price fr £15 Av 3 course à la carte fr £18 ⊕ FREE HOUSE ◀ Branscombe Vale Branoc & Summa That, O'Hanlon's Firefly, Princetown Jail Ale, Otter Ale. ♟ 16 **Facilities** Children's menu Play area Dogs allowed Garden Parking **Rooms** 13

PICK OF THE PUBS

The Tower Inn ♍

SLAPTON   Map 3 SX84

Church Rd TQ7 2PN ☎ 01548 580216
e-mail: towerinn@slapton.org
web: www.thetowerinn.com
dir: *Off A379 S of Dartmouth, turn left at Slapton Sands*

Only a short stroll from Slapton Sands and the Slapton Ley Nature Reserve is the Tower Inn. Dating from the 14th century, the inn owes its name to a ruined tower, all that remains of the Collegiate Chantry of St Mary, that overlooks the award-winning walled garden. The inn was probably built in 1347 as the chantry's guesthouse, from where alms and hospitality would have been dispensed. Approaching it by a narrow lane, you enter through a rustic porch to find a fascinating series of low-ceilinged, interconnecting rooms with stone walls and fireplaces, beams, pillars and pews. These in turn are decorated with plants, a giant cartwheel, brasses, pictures and violins. An excellent range of beers, including Butcombe and Otter, is augmented by local cider. Menus are based on fresh, locally produced ingredients wherever possible including fish freshly caught in nearby Start Bay. The dinner menu includes dishes such as pan-seared seabass, served with pea shoots and saffron sauce; local Start Bay hand-dived scallops with mussels and a lemon dressing, or belly of local pork with colcannon and home-made cider apple sauce. The menu is augmented by daily specials, while the lunch menu offers lighter fare such as a range of fresh sandwiches, home-made pâté and the famous Tower burger.

Open all week Closed: Mon winter **Bar Meals** L served all week 12-2 D served all week 7-9 (Spring-Autumn no food Sun eve or Mon) **Restaurant** L served all week 12-2 D served all week 7-9 (Summer 6-9) ⊕ FREE HOUSE ◖ Butcombe Bitter, Otter Bitter, Otter Ale, Tribute, guest ales. ♂ Addlestones, Cheddar Valley, Coltscombe Court Farmhouse ♍ 8 **Facilities** Family room Dogs allowed Garden Parking

SOURTON   Map 3 SX59

The Highwayman Inn

EX20 4HN ☎ 01837 861243 📠 01837 861196
e-mail: info@thehighwaymaninn.net
dir: *On A386 (Okehampton to Tavistock road). Exit A30
towards Tavistock. Pub 4m from Okehampton, 12m from
Tavistock*

A fascinating old inn full of eccentric furniture, unusual
architectural designs, and strange bric-a-brac. Since
1959 the vision of Welshman John 'Buster' Jones, and
now run by his daughter Sally, it is made from parts of
sailing ships, wood hauled from Dartmoor's bogs, and
Gothic church arches. Popular with holidaymakers and
international tourists, the menu consists of light snacks
including pasties, platters and organic nibbles. In the
garden, the kids will enjoy Mother Hubbard's Shoe, and
the Pumpkin House.

Open 11.30-2 6-11 (Sun 12-2 7-10.30) Closed: 25-28
Dec ⊕ FREE HOUSE ◀ St Austell Duchy. **Facilities** Play
area Dogs allowed Garden Parking

SOUTH POOL   Map 3 SX74

The Millbrook Inn ☘

TQ7 2RW ☎ 01548 531581
e-mail: info@millbrookinnsouthpool.co.uk
dir: *Take A379 from Kingsbridge to Frogmore then E for
2m to South Pool*

This quaint 16th-century village pub is cosy and unspoilt
inside, with open fires, fresh flowers, cushioned
wheelback chairs, and beams adorned with old banknotes
and clay pipes. Set at the head of the creek, its summer
barbecues attract small boats from Salcombe and
Kingsbridge. Fish is a speciality, and there's a peaceful
sunny rear terrace overlooking a stream with ducks. At
least two real ales always kept.

Open all wk 12-11 (Sun 12-10.30) **Bar Meals** L served all
wk 12-2 D served Mon-Sat 7-9 ⊕ FREE HOUSE ◀ Otter
Ale, Redrock Ở Thatchers Heritage. ☘ 10 **Facilities** Dogs
allowed Garden

SOUTH ZEAL   Map 3 SX69

Oxenham Arms ☘

EX20 2JT ☎ 01837 840244 📠 01837 840791
e-mail: relax@theoxenhamarms.co.uk
dir: *Just off A30 4m E of Okehampton, in village centre*

Probably built by monks in the 12th century, this inn on
the edge of Dartmoor is one of the oldest in England. First
licensed in 1477, the pub retains a historical feel with
beams, flagstone floors, blazing fires and a prehistoric
monolith – archaeologists believe the monks just built
around it. Burgoynes restaurant serves an eclectic
seasonal menu based on fine local produce. Expect the
likes of a choice of home-made pâtés, followed by coq au
vin, Cornish crab salad, and The Oxenham chicken curry.

Open all wk 10.30-3.30 5-11 **Bar Meals** L served all wk
11.30-3 D served all wk 6-9.30 Av main course £11
Restaurant L served all wk 11.30-3 D served all wk
6-9.30 Av 3 course à la carte fr £17 ⊕ FREE HOUSE
◀ Sharp's Doom Bar, Otter, guest. ☘ 8
Facilities Children's menu Dogs allowed Garden Parking

SPREYTON   Map 3 SX69

The Tom Cobley Tavern ☘

EX17 5AL ☎ 01647 231314
dir: *From A30 at Whiddon Down take A3124 N. Take 1st
right after services then 1st right over bridge.*

From this pub, one day in 1802, a certain Thomas Cobley
and his companions set forth for Widecombe Fair, an
event immortalised in song. Today, this traditional village
local offers a selection of bar snacks, lighter fare and
home-made main meals, including pies, salads, duck
and fish dishes, as well as a good vegetarian selection.
Finish off with one of the great ice creams or sorbets. The
bar offers up to 20 beers at one time, and has picked up
plenty of real ale awards. There is a pretty garden to enjoy
in the warmer months.

Open 12-3 6-11 (Sun 12-4 7-11 Mon 6.30-11 Fri-Sat
6-1am) Closed: Mon L **Bar Meals** L served Tue-Sat 12-3 D
served Sun-Thu 7-10 Av main course £6 food served all
day **Restaurant** L served all wk 12-3 booking required D
served all wk 7-10 Fixed menu price fr £10 food served all
day ⊕ FREE HOUSE ◀ Cotleigh Tawny Ale, Doom Bar,
Tribute, Otter Ale, Proper Job, Ở Winkleigh Cider, Stowford
Press. ☘ 7 **Facilities** Children's menu Dogs allowed
Garden Parking

STOCKLAND   Map 4 ST20

PICK OF THE PUBS

The Kings Arms Inn ☘

EX14 9BS ☎ 01404 881361 📠 01404 881387
e-mail: info@thekingsarmsinn.org.uk
dir: *Off A30 to Chard, 6m NE of Honiton*

A traditional 16th-century thatched, whitewashed
former coaching inn tucked away in the Blackdown
Hills. After passing through the impressive flagstone
entrance, you'll encounter two interesting features - a
medieval oak screen and an original bread oven. Locals
and visitors in the bar will, as likely as not, share a
fondness for Otter and Exmoor real ales. Pub food here
uses local suppliers and might include ham, egg and
chips; filled jacket potatoes with salad; local pork
sausages and mash; and chef's own recipe
beefburgers. The restaurant offers other choices:
pigeon breasts, ostrich fillets and gravadlax from the
blackboards, and from the carte menu rare fillet steak
with Roquefort cheese; poached salmon with Cajun
seasoning; king prawn Thermidor; and vegetarian
options. At lunchtime filled ciabattas are served with
chips and salad; soups are home made, and there's
usually a curry. Look out for the lively annual Stockland
Fair.

Open all wk 11.30-3 6-11 (Sun 12-3 6.30-10.30) **Bar
Meals** L served Mon-Sat 12-2 **Restaurant** L served all
wk 12-2 booking required D served all wk 6.30-9
booking required ⊕ FREE HOUSE ◀ Otter Ale, Exmoor
Ale Ở Thatchers. ☘ 15 **Facilities** Children's menu Dogs
allowed Garden Parking

STOKE FLEMING   Map 3 SX84

The Green Dragon Inn ☘

Church Rd TQ6 0PX ☎ 01803 770238 📠 01803 770238
e-mail: pcrowther@btconnect.com
dir: *Off A379 (Dartmouth to Kingsbridge coast road)
opposite church*

A smuggler's tunnel is said to link this 12th-century inn
to the beach at nearby Blackpool Sands. The pub, if not
the tunnel, was built by masons labouring on the nearby
church, and was first recorded as purveying ales in 1607.
Lunchtime snacks include baguettes, pies and trio of
West Country Smokehouse fish, while the evening menu
offers salmon fishcakes with herb butter sauce; honeyed
lamb casserole; game pie or West Country rump steak.
There's also a great pie and children's choice menu.

Open all wk **Bar Meals** L served all wk 12-2 D served all
wk 6.30-8.30 Av main course £9 ⊕ HEAVITREE ◀ Otter,
Flowers IPA, 6X, Otter Head Ở Aspalls. ☘ 10
Facilities Play area Dogs allowed Garden Parking

STRETE — Map 3 SX84

PICK OF THE PUBS

Kings Arms ◉ ♀

Dartmouth Rd TQ6 0RW
☎ 01803 770377 📄 01803 771008
e-mail: kingsarms_devon_fish@hotmail.com
dir: On A379 (Dartmouth-Kingsbridge road), 5m from Dartmouth

You can't miss this striking, 18th-century pub, with its unique cast-iron balcony, as it stands smack beside the coast road and the South West coast path passes the front door. Pop in for a pint of Otter Ale, bag a seat by the fire in the traditional, terracotta-walled bar, or head up the few steps into the light and airy contemporary-styled restaurant, replete with modern artwork and stunning views across Start Bay. Chef Rob Dawson's motto is 'keep it fresh, keep it simple' and on his daily lunch and dinner menus you'll find wonderfully fresh seafood, simply prepared with some modern twists, including crab, lobster and fish from a local boat (the boat trawls exclusively for the pub once a week). At lunch, tuck into delicious fish soup with saffron and rouille, a plate of smoked sprats, or smoked haddock and rocket fishcake with wholegrain mustard sauce. Evening choices extend to cod with local clams, peas and asparagus, red gurnard with scallion mash and roasted red pepper cream, and sirloin steak with Café de Paris butter. In summer, head for the flower-filled garden and dine alfresco overlooking the bay.

Open 11.30-3 6-11 (Sat-Sun 11.30-11) Bar Meals L served Mon-Fri 12-2, Sat-Sun 11.30-11 booking required D served Mon-Fri 6.30-9, Sat-Sun 11.30-11 booking required Av main course £12 Restaurant L served Tue-Fri 12-2, Sat-Sun 11.30-11 booking required D served Tue-Fri 6.30-9, Sat Sun 11.30-11 booking required Av 3 course à la carte fr £24 ⊕ HEAVITREE ◀ Otter Ale, Adnams Bitter, Guinness Ŏ Aspalls. ♀ 15 Facilities Children's menu Dogs allowed Garden Parking

THURLESTONE — Map 3 SX64

The Village Inn ♀

TQ7 3NN ☎ 01548 563525 📄 01548 561069
e-mail: enquiries@thurlestone.co.uk
dir: Take A379 from Plymouth towards Kingsbridge, at Bantham rdbt straight over onto B3197, then right into a lane signed Thurlestone, 2.5m

Built in the 16th century as a farmhouse, this old pub prides itself on good service, well-kept ales and decent food. Like the nearby Thurlestone Hotel, it has been owned by the Grose family for over a century. Seafood is a speciality, with Salcombe crabmeat, River Exe mussels and other local fish and shellfish to choose from on the seasonal menus. Other possibilities are Cajun roasted chicken breast, sirloin and rump steaks, and beef burgers.

Open all wk 11.30-3 6-11.30 (Sun 12-3 6.30-10.30) Bar Meals D served Mon-Sun 12-2, Mon-Sat 7-9 ⊕ FREE HOUSE ◀ Palmers IPA, Interbrew Bass, Sharp's Doom Bar, guest ale. ♀ 10 Facilities Family room Dogs allowed Garden Parking

TIPTON ST JOHN — Map 3 SY09

PICK OF THE PUBS

The Golden Lion Inn ♀

EX10 0AA ☎ 01404 812881
e-mail: info@goldenliontipton.co.uk

Francois (Franky) and Michelle Teissier are in their seventh year in this inviting village pub. Charmingly eclectic décor includes Art Deco prints jostling for space with Tiffany lamps and paintings by Devon artists. A combination of rustic Mediterranean and British traditional cooking produces dishes, usually titled in French, such as pork tenderloin with apples and calvados; breast of duck with a mixed peppercorn sauce; and sea bass with tomato and pesto. Blackboard specials feature fresh fish and seafood

landed at nearby Sidmouth, such as sea bass stuffed with cream cheese and sage; monkfish kebabs; and lobster in garlic butter. Other specials might be haunch of venison with chocolate sauce, and braised oxtail. Vegetarians have plenty of choice, from vegetable lasagne to butter bean cassoulet. The lunch menu is simpler, with a good selection of sandwiches, ploughman's and regular pub grub. In winter the pub is closed on Sunday evenings.

Open 12-2.30 6-11 Closed: (Sun eve Sep-Mar) Bar Meals L served all wk 12-2 D served Mon-Sat 6.30-8.30 booking required Restaurant L served Sun Mar-Sep 7-8.30 ⊕ HEAVITREE ◀ Otter Ale, Bass, Otter Bitter. ♀ 10 Facilities Garden Parking

TOPSHAM — Map 3 SX98

PICK OF THE PUBS

Bridge Inn

Bridge Hill EX3 0QQ ☎ 01392 873862
e-mail: su3264@eclipse.co.uk
dir: M5 junct 30 follow Sidmouth signs, in approx 400yds right at rdbt onto A376 towards Exmouth. In 1.8m cross mini-rdbt. Right at next mini rdbt to Topsham. 1.2m, cross River Clyst. Inn on right

There's been a building on this site since 1083 and a pub since 1512. Four generations of the same family have run the Bridge since great grandfather moved in during 1897, and it remains eccentrically and gloriously old fashioned. It has been described as a museum with beer, with its vernacular architecture - a mix of stone and cob - small rooms, open fires, an 18th-century malting kiln and an old malt house used for parties or overflow custom. Back in 1998 it became the only pub in England to have been officially visited by Queen Elizabeth II. This is a drinking pub with all real ales from independent breweries only, naturally cellared and served straight from the cask. There are also a few wines, including two from a local organic vineyard. Traditional bar food includes ploughman's, pasties, sandwiches and soup, all made with local ingredients. No lagers, no chips and definitely no mobile phones.

Open all wk Bar Meals L served all wk 12-2 Av main course £6.50 ⊕ FREE HOUSE ◀ Branscombe Vale-Branoc, Adnams Broadside, Exe Valley, O'Hanlons, Blackawton, Teignworthy. Facilities Dogs allowed Garden Parking Notes ☺

TOPSHAM *continued*

The Lighter Inn ▮

The Quay EX3 0HZ ☎ 01392 875439 📠 **01392 876013**
e-mail: lighterinn.topsham@hall-woodhouse.co.uk
dir: *Telephone for directions*

The imposing 17th-century customs house on Topsham Quay has been transformed into a popular waterside inn. A strong nautical atmosphere is reinforced with pictures, ship's instruments and oars beneath the pub's wooden ceilings, and the attractive quayside sitting area is popular in summer. Dishes may include whole sea bass or plaice, steaks, curries and salads, or steak, ale and mushroom pie.

Open all wk 11-11 (Sun noon-10.30) **Bar Meals** L served Mon-Sat 12-2.30, Sun 12-3 D served Mon-Sat 6.30-9 ⊕ HALL & WOODHOUSE ◀ Badger Best, Badger Tanglefoot, Sussex, Hopping Hare. ▮ 12 **Facilities** Family room Dogs allowed Parking

---

TORCROSS   Map 3 SX84

Start Bay Inn ▮

TQ7 2TQ ☎ 01548 580553 📠 **01548 581285**
e-mail: clair@startbayinn.co.uk
dir: *Between Dartmouth & Kingsbridge on A379*

Formerly the Fisherman's Arms, this 14th-century inn remains popular with local fishermen working off the adjacent beach. They deliver fresh-caught fish to the kitchen, and the retired landlord still dives for scallops for his daughters to serve at the inn. Look for locally-sourced ingredients such as steaks, Devon ham, and Hannaford's beefburgers; other menu choices range from sandwiches and jacket potatoes to vegetarian options like spinach and mascarpone lasagne.

Open all day all wk 11.30am-11.30pm **Bar Meals** L served all wk 11.30-2.15 D served all wk 6-9.30 winter, 6-10 summer Av main course £7 ⊕ HEAVITREE ◀ Interbrew Flowers Original & Bass, Otter Ale. ▮ 8 **Facilities** Family room Garden Parking

---

TOTNES   Map 3 SX86

PICK OF THE PUBS

The Durant Arms   INN ▮

See Pick of the Pubs on opposite page

Royal Seven Stars Hotel ▮

The Plains TQ9 5DD ☎ 01803 862125
e-mail: enquiry@royalsevenstars.co.uk
dir: *From A382 signed Totnes, left at 'Dartington' rdbt. Through lights towards town centre, through next rdbt, pass Morrisons car park on left. 200yds on right*

A Grade II listed pub dating from 1640 in the heart of Totnes. The traditional saloon bar with open fire serves Jail Ale and Doom Bar among others, with home-cooked bar meals available all day. Bar 7's more contemporary atmosphere, with slate floors and black leather sofas, is the setting for Mediterranean-inspired snacks, fruit smoothies, speciality coffees and a selection of cakes. The restaurant, called TQ9 after its town centre location, serves good local produce– including a Sunday carvery – in a relaxed, stylish environment.

Open all day all wk **Bar Meals** Av main course £8 food served all day **Restaurant** L served Sun 12-2.30 booking required D served all wk 6.30-9.30 booking required Av 3 course à la carte fr £20 ⊕ FREE HOUSE ◀ Jail Ale, Doom Bar, Bays Gold, Courage Best. ▮ 20 **Facilities** Children's menu Family room Dogs allowed Parking

---

Rumour ▮

30 High St TQ9 5RY ☎ 01803 864682 📠 **01803 732065**
dir: *On main street up hill above arch on left. 5 min walk from rail station, follow signs for Totnes castle/ town centre*

After a chequered history as a milk bar, restaurant and wine bar, this 17th-century building was named after a Fleetwood Mac album in the mid-1970s. Now comprehensively refurbished, including innovative heating and plumbing systems which reduce the pub's environmental footprint. Hospitable staff aim to provide the best drinking and dining experience possible. Try River Exe moules marinière, lamb shank braised in red wine, and chocolate parfait with griottine cherries.

Open all wk **Bar Meals** L served Mon-Sat 12-3 D served all wk 6-10 booking required **Restaurant** L served Mon-Sat 12-3 D served all wk 6-10 booking required ⊕ FREE HOUSE ◀ Erdinger, Abbots Ale, guest ales. ▮ 15 **Facilities** Children's menu

---

Steam Packet Inn ★★★★ INN ▮

St Peter's Quay TQ9 5EW
☎ 01803 863880 📠 **01803 862754**
e-mail: steampacket@buccaneer.co.uk
dir: *Exit A38 towards Plymouth, 18m. A384 to Totnes 6m. Left at mini-rdbt, pass Morrisons on left, over mini-rdbt, 400yds on left*

The inn's sign depicts the Amelia, a steam packet ship that regularly called here with passengers, parcels and mail before the days of modern road and rail transport. These days the building is a welcoming riverside pub with great views, particularly from the conservatory restaurant, and plenty of waterside seating for sunny days. Typical dishes from the menu include fresh Brixham sea bass fillet; haddock in 'jail ale' batter; roasted pork

---

cutlet with carrot and swede purée; and creamy pumpkin and goats' cheese gnocchi. Good local cheese selection.

Steam Packet Inn

Open all day all wk **Bar Meals** L served Mon-Fri 12-2.30, Sat 12-3, Sun 12-4 D served Mon-Sat 6-9.30, Sun 6-9 **Restaurant** L served Mon-Fri 12-2.30, Sat 12-3, Sun 12-4 D served Mon-Sat 6-9.30, Sun 6-9 ⊕ BUCCANEER HOLDINGS LTD ◀ Courage Best, Otter Bright, Jail Ale, Guest ale Ö Stowford Press. ▮ 8 **Facilities** Children's menu Dogs allowed Garden Parking **Rooms** 4

PICK OF THE PUBS

The White Hart ▮

Dartington Hall TQ9 6EL
☎ 01803 847111 📠 **01803 847107**
e-mail: bookings@dartingtonhall.com
dir: *From A38 take Totnes turn onto A384*

Surrounded by landscaped gardens, ancient deer park and woodland, the White Hart bar and restaurant occupies what were originally the kitchens of the magnificent 14th-century Dartington Hall. Inside you'll find a stylish dining venue with flagstone floors, limed oak settles, roughcast walls and a welcoming wood fire burning merrily in the grate. Enjoy the range of West Country ales, or choose from an accessible wine list that classifies bottles by taste. The daily-changing menu uses local and organic produce where possible to create dishes based on seasonal availability. You could start with grilled Capricorn goats' cheese served on a beetroot and walnut salad with balsamic dressing. Follow with a Dartington beef burger topped with melted Cheddar and caramelised onions; or Devon lamb casseroled in the Moroccan style. And finish with white chocolate Amaretti and apricot tart with clotted cream; or three local cheeses served with savoury biscuits, chutney and celery.

Open all day all wk 11-11 (Sun noon-10.30) Closed: 24-29 Dec **Bar Meals** L served all wk 12-2 booking required D served all wk 6-9 booking required **Restaurant** L served all wk 12-2 booking required D served all wk 6-9 booking required ⊕ FREE HOUSE ◀ Otter Brewery Ale & Bitter. ▮ 8 **Facilities** Garden Parking

PICK OF THE PUBS

The Durant Arms ★★★★ INN 🍷

TOTNES Map 3 SX86

Ashprington TQ9 7UP ☎ 01803 732240
web: www.durantarms.co.uk
dir: *Exit A38 at Totnes junct, to Dartington &
Totnes, at 1st lights right for Kingsbridge on
A381, in 1m left for Ashprington*

Locally renowned as a dining pub, the delightful Durant Arms is situated in the picturesque village of Ashprington, just outside the Elizabethan town of Totnes in the heart of the South Hams. Proprietors Graham and Eileen Ellis are proud to uphold British values of hospitality at the award-winning 18th-century hostelry. It was originally the counting house for the neighbouring 500-acre Sharpham Estate. For some years it was The Ashprington Inn, a smaller establishment than the Durant, which has expanded into an adjoining property. The small bar is fitted out in a traditional style, with work by local artists on display alongside horse-brasses, ferns and cheerful red velvet curtains. All dishes at the Durant are cooked to order, with a wide variety of meat, fish and fresh steamed vegetables, all sourced locally wherever possible. Local fish and seafood figure strongly in dishes such as Dartmouth smoked salmon with black pepper; or shell-on whole prawns with garlic dip, to start, and main courses of sea bass fillet on roasted vegetables with pepper sauce; or fillets of lemon sole roulade. Alternatives might be devilled kidneys with brandy and cream; and roast half pheasant with port wine sauce. Desserts range from chocolate fondant with clotted cream to treacle sponge pudding with vanilla ice cream. Award-winning, hand-made English cheeses from nearby Sharpham's organic dairy are another speciality of the house, and wines from the Sharpham vineyard - red, white and rosé - are offered on the wine list. The little courtyard to the rear provides a cosy spot to linger over a summer meal, and eight comfortably furnished and attractively decorated en suite bedrooms complete the package.

Open all week **Bar Meals** L served all week 12-2 D served all week 7-9.15 **Restaurant** L served all week 12-2 D served all week 7-9.15 ⊕ FREE HOUSE ◖ Dartmoor Bitter, Tetley, Tribute. 🍷 8 **Facilities** Children's menu Family room Dogs allowed Garden Parking **Rooms** 8

TRUSHAM — Map 3 SX88

PICK OF THE PUBS

Cridford Inn NEW ☘

See Pick of the Pubs on opposite page

TUCKENHAY — Map 3 SX85

The Maltsters Arms ☘

TQ9 7EQ ☎ 01803 732350 ≜ 01803 732823
e-mail: pub@tuckenhay.demon.co.uk
dir: *A381 from Totnes towards Kingsbridge. 1m, at hill top turn left, follow signs to Tuckenhay, 3m*

Accessible only along high-banked lanes, or by boat either side of high tide, this old stone country inn on Bow Creek off the River Dart was once owned by TV chef, Keith Floyd. The daily changing menu may feature pan-fried skate wing, beef and bell pepper balti, mushroom tortelloni, stone bass fillet and salmon in white wine sauce, or T-bone steak with mushroom and tarragon sauce. Famous for summer barbecues and occasional music events.

Open all day all wk 11-11 (25 Dec 12-2) **Bar Meals** L served all wk 12-3 D served all wk 7-9.30 Av main course £11 food served all day **Restaurant** L served all wk 12-3 booking required D served all wk 7-9.30 booking required Av 3 course à la carte fr £20 ⊕ FREE HOUSE
◀ Princetown Dartmoor IPA, Young's Special, Teignworthy Maltsters Ale, Sharps Doom Bar, Skinners Betty Stoggs
♻ Westons Perry. ☘ 18 **Facilities** Children's menu Family room Dogs allowed Garden Parking

TYTHERLEIGH — Map 4 ST30

Tytherleigh Arms Hotel

EX13 7BE
☎ 01460 220400 & 220214 ≜ 01460 220814
e-mail: tytherleigharms@aol.com
dir: *Equidistant from Chard & Axminster on A358*

Beamed ceilings and huge roaring fires are notable features of this family-run, 16th-century former coaching inn. It is a food-led establishment, situated on the Devon, Somerset and Dorset borders. Great pride is taken in sourcing local ingredients, and fish dishes are a speciality with fish landed locally – perhaps Lyme Bay scallops, crème fraîche and sweet chilli sauce. Other fresh home-cooked dishes might include liver and bacon, mash with onion gravy; and pork tenderloin with black pudding and wholegrain mustard sauce. To finish perhaps try Barbara's lemon posset or Tom's banoffee pie and delicious cheesecakes.

Open all wk 11-2.30 6.30-11 (Sun eve in winter) **Bar Meals** L served all wk 11-2.30 booking required D served all wk 6.30-9 booking required Av main course £9.95 **Restaurant** L served all wk 11-2.30 booking required D served all wk 6.30-9 booking required ⊕ FREE HOUSE
◀ Butcombe Bitter, Otter, Murphy's, Boddingtons
♻ Ashton Press. **Facilities** Children's menu Garden Parking

UMBERLEIGH — Map 3 SS62

PICK OF THE PUBS

The Rising Sun Inn ☘

EX37 9DU ☎ 01769 560447 ≜ 01769 560764
dir: *On A377 (Exeter-Barnstaple road) at junct with B3227*

Idyllically set beside the River Taw and with a very strong fly fishing tradition, the Rising Sun dates back in part to the 13th century. The traditional flagstone bar is strewn with fishing memorabilia, comfortable chairs and daily papers and magazines for a very relaxing visit. Outside is a sunny raised terrace with beautiful rural views of the valley, and the riverside walk is equally enjoyable before or after a meal. This inn is an excellent base for the touring motorist with several National Trust properties nearby. A choice of à la carte restaurant or regularly updated bar menus feature the best of West Country produce, with seasonal delights like seafood from the North Devon coast, salmon and sea trout from the Taw, game from Exmoor, and local cheeses. The daily changing specials board is often the best place to start looking. There's also a carvery every Sunday.

Open all wk 11.30am-3 6-11pm (Sat 11.30am-11pm Sun noon-11pm) **Bar Meals** L served Mon-Fri 12-2.30, Sat-Sun 12-3 D served all wk 6-9 ⊕ FREE HOUSE
◀ Cotleigh Barn Owl, Guinness, St Austell Tribute, Exmoor Fox ♻ Thatchers Gold. ☘ 9 **Facilities** Dogs allowed Garden Parking

WIDECOMBE IN THE MOOR — Map 3 SX77

The Old Inn ☘

TQ13 7TA ☎ 01364 621207 ≜ 01364 621407
e-mail: oldinn.wid@virgin.net
dir: *Telephone for directions*

Set in the heart of Dartmoor, this 600 year-old inn is a pub for all seasons. Sit outside or ask for a local walk guide in summer, or enjoy the five log fires when the weather turns cold. The wide selection of freshly prepared dishes ranges from traditional classics to Mediterranean cuisine. Lunchtime brings soups, potato wedges, filled baguettes, plus mezze and larder boards to share, whilst grilled vegetable linguine; smoked haddock 'Benedict'; and slow roast BBQ pork ribs cater for larger appetites.

Open all day all wk **Bar Meals** food served all day **Restaurant** food served all day ⊕ HALL & WOODHOUSE
◀ Badger, Guest ales. ☘ 12 **Facilities** Family room Dogs allowed Garden Parking

WINKLEIGH — Map 3 SS60

PICK OF THE PUBS

The Duke of York ☘

Iddesleigh EX19 8BG
☎ 01837 810253 ≜ 01837 810253
dir: *Telephone for directions*

The atmosphere of this venerable thatched inn is blissfully unsullied by juke box, fruit machine or karaoke. Set deep in rural mid-Devon, it was originally three cottages housing craftsmen who were rebuilding the parish church; local records accurately date this work to 1387. All the timeless features of a classic country pub remain - heavy old beams, scrubbed tables, farmhouse chairs and a huge inglenook fireplace with winter fires. Popular with all, it offers decent real ales (Cotleigh Tawny, for example) and hearty home cooking, with everything freshly prepared using local produce such as meat reared on nearby farms. Examples of bar meals taken from the large blackboard menu include rainbow trout, liver and bacon, and casseroles. From the dining room menu could come Dartmouth smokehouse salmon followed by pork loin with port and tarragon sauce, then a choice of more than a dozen classic home-made desserts.

Open all day all wk 11am-11pm **Bar Meals** L served all wk 11-10 D served all wk 11-10 food served all day ⊕ FREE HOUSE ◀ Adnams Broadside, Cotleigh Tawny, guest ales ♻ Winkleigh. ☘ 10 **Facilities** Dogs allowed Garden

The Kings Arms ☘

Fore St EX19 8HQ ☎ 01837 83384 ≜ 01834 83055
e-mail: kingsarmswinkleigh@googlemail.com
dir: *Village signed from B3220 (Crediton to Torrington road)*

Scrubbed pine tables and traditional wooden settles set the scene at this ancient thatched country inn in Winkleigh's central square. Wood-burning stoves keep the beamed bar and dining rooms warm in chilly weather, and traditional pub games are encouraged. Generous servings of freshly-made food include sandwiches and hot snacks, as well as steak and kidney parcel, loin of lamb with rosemary and redcurrant sauce, and Lucy's fish pie. Booking is recommended at weekends.

Open all day all wk 11-11 (Sun noon-10.30)
Bar Meals food served all day **Restaurant** food served all day ⊕ ENTERPRISE INNS ◀ Butcombe Bitter, Sharp's Doom Bar, Cornish Coaster ♻ Winkleigh Cider. ☘ 9 **Facilities** Children's menu Dogs allowed Garden

PICK OF THE PUBS

Cridford Inn NEW 🍷

TRUSHAM

TQ13 0NR
☎ **01626 853694**
e-mail: reservations@vanillapod-
cridfordinn.com
web: www.cridfordinn.co.uk
dir: *A38 take junct for Teign Valley, turn
right follow signs Trusham for 4m*

A thatched former longhouse with
origins in the mid-9th century, but
rebuilt in the late 11th, which means
that the rough stone walls, the
fireplaces in the bar and mosaic floor in
the Vanilla Pod restaurant, plus the
stained glass window in the bar, have
all been here for a long, long time. The
window, in fact, is probably the earliest

surviving domestic example in Britain.
The floors and ceilings also date from
this time, the marks of the masons still
visible on the beams in the traditional
bar. Sadly not on view, though, is the
fine smoke-blackened timber roof. The
inn was at one time a nunnery, which
explains the presence of one of the
ghosts – a nun – but not that of the
other, a cavalier (or maybe it does!). In
the bar (Doom Bar and Otter real ales)
the menu changes seasonally, although
there are daily specials. Here you can try
smoked Dartmouth salmon; game pie,
containing braised wild boar, venison,
pheasant and rabbit; baked field
mushrooms with smoked applewood and
herb crust; steak and kidney pie; honey-
baked West Country ham and eggs;
seafood mornay; or one of a selection of
chargrills. A three-course dinner from
the monthly-changing restaurant menu
might feature pan-fried red mullet with
red wine, beetroot, creamed leeks and
crispy bacon; followed by roasted guinea
fowl; and hand-made Belgian chocolate
pudding. Most of the vegetarian options
are on a separate board. Outside is a
terrace from which the rose-covered
longhouse looks wonderful.
Accommodation includes self-catering
holiday cottages.

Open all week 11-3 6-11 (Sat 11-11
Sun noon-10.30) **Bar Meals** L served all
week 12-2 D served all week 7-9.30 Av
main course £8.95 **Restaurant** L served
Sun 12-1.30 D served Mon-Sat 7-9.30
Fixed menu price fr £21.95 Av 3 course
à la carte fr £23.45 ⊕ FREE HOUSE
🍺 Doom Bar, Otter Ale 🍏 Thatchers. 🍷 8
Facilities Children's menu Family room
Garden Parking

PICK OF THE PUBS

The Digger's Rest 🍷

WOODBURY SALTERTON   Map 3 SY08

EX5 1PQ
☎ 01395 232375   📠 01395 232711
e-mail: bar@diggersrest.co.uk
dir: *2.5m from A3052. Signed from Westpoint*

A picturesque, 500-year-old country inn with thick, stone and cob walls and heavy beams under a thatched roof. It was originally a cider house, but the choice in today's bar is much wider, with a changing guest ale list that might include Tribute and Doom Bar from Cornwall and Wild Cat from Exmoor, as well as constants from the Otter Brewery up the road. The interior features West Country art, antique furniture and a skittle alley. The patio garden provides seating for up to 40 people and is the perfect setting for outdoor drinking and dining, especially at night when it is attractively illuminated. Simple, freshly cooked food is prepared from English produce, including fish from Brixham and Looe, 21-day West Country beef, and East Devon pork. The kitchen is committed to supporting good animal husbandry and buys organic where possible. Bar meals of herb-crusted cod fishcake, and Kenniford Farm finest pork sausages are supplemented by grills, salads, baguettes and ciabattas. Taken from daily changing blackboards are starters of pigeon breast with sweetened chicory and ruby chard garnish; and seared scallops with mango and redcurrant salsa, while among the main courses are slow-roasted lamb shank with rosemary mash and vegetables; Thai green chicken curry with green beans and jasmine rice; Digger's fish pie; and gilt-head bream stuffed with prawns, smoked salmon and fennel. Desserts not to be missed include treacle sponge with ice cream; lemon polenta cake; and sticky toffee pudding. Wines from Italy, Lebanon, South African and Argentina are among those listed.

Open all week 11-3 6-11 (all day Sat-Sun and in summer)
Restaurant 🌐 FREE HOUSE 🍺 Otter Bitter, Otter Ale, Exmoor Ales. 🍷 13
Facilities Garden Parking

WOODBURY SALTERTON   Map 3 SY08

PICK OF THE PUBS

The Digger's Rest ♀

See Pick of the Pubs on opposite page

YEALMPTON   Map 3 SX55

PICK OF THE PUBS

Rose & Crown ♀

Market St PL8 2EB
☎ **01752 880223** 📠 **01752 881058**
e-mail: info@theroseandcrown.co.uk

From the classic brown and cream décor to the comfy leather sofas and open fire, the interior of this stylish bar restaurant reflects a perfect balance between contemporary and traditional features. The head chef regularly changes his tempting à la carte and set menus, and sources his ingredients locally wherever possible. Many dishes are traditional classics with an extra touch of class, whilst others feature a Pacific Rim twist with exotic Indonesian and Malaysian flavours. 'Lite bites' are served in the sunken lounge, whilst the restaurant menu might include options like pan-seared pork with mustard potatoes and roasted carrots; wild sea bass on mussel chowder with chargrilled new potatoes; or courgette cannelloni with Parmesan and rocket. Look out for the newly landscaped terraced garden - the perfect place to enjoy a hot summer's afternoon.

Open all wk **Bar Meals** L served all wk 12-2.30 D served all wk 6.30-9.30 Av main course £11 **Restaurant** L served all wk 12-2.30 booking required D served all wk 6.30-9.30 booking required Fixed menu price fr £9.95 Av 3 course à la carte fr £24 ⊕ INNTRA WEST LTD ◧ Doom Bar, London Pride, Courage Best, IPA Greene King, Otter, Tribute. ♀ 8 **Facilities** Children's menu Family room Dogs allowed Garden Parking

---

DORSET

ABBOTSBURY   Map 4 SY58

Ilchester Arms ♀

9 Market St DT3 4JR
☎ **01305 871243** 📠 **01305 871225**
dir: *Telephone for directions*

Rambling 16th-century coaching inn set in the heart of one of Dorset's most picturesque villages. Abbotsbury is home to many crafts including woodwork and pottery. A good area for walkers, and handy for the Tropical Gardens and Swannery.

Open all wk ◧ Fuller's HSB, Courage Best, Tribute, Speckled Hen, Abbot. ♀ 12 **Facilities** Dogs allowed Garden Parking

---

BLANDFORD FORUM   Map 4 ST80

The Anvil Inn ★★★★ INN ♀

Salisbury Rd, Pimperne DT11 8UQ
☎ **01258 453431** 📠 **01258 480182**
e-mail: theanvil.inn@btconnect.com

A thatched roof, crooked beams and a cavernous fireplace are just a few of the rustic charms of this family-run 16th-century inn located in the pretty village of Pimperne, two miles from Blandford Forum. The two bars offer light bites, while the charming beamed restaurant with log fire offers a full menu. There are 12 en suite bedrooms available.

Open all wk **Bar Meals** food served all day **Restaurant** food served all day ⊕ FREE HOUSE ◧ Guinness, London Pride, IPA, Copper Ale. ♀ 6 **Facilities** Dogs allowed Garden Parking **Rooms** 12

Crown Hotel ★★★ HL ♀

West St DT11 7AJ ☎ **01258 456626** 📠 **01258 451084**
e-mail: crownhotel.blandford@hall-woodhouse.co.uk
web: www.innforanight.co.uk/The_Crown_Hotel_Think.asp
dir: *M27 junct 1 W onto A31 to A350 junct, right to Blandford Forum. 100mtrs from town bridge*

An 18th-century coaching inn which replaces an original inn destroyed by fire in 1731. Standing on the banks of the River Stour, the Crown has plenty of period atmosphere, and a separate restaurant. Begin a meal, perhaps, with cod and parsley fishcake with sweet chilli sauce, follow it with rosemary-crusted lamb cutlets with redcurrant scented gravy; or gammon steak with grilled pineapple, chips and peas. An extensive bar menu includes sandwiches and light bites.

Open all wk 10am-11.30pm (Sun 12-10.30) **Bar Meals** L served Mon-Sat 12-2, Sun 12-8 D served Mon-Sat 6-9, Sun 12-8 ⊕ HALL & WOODHOUSE ◧ Badger Tanglefoot, Badger 1st Gold. ♀ 20 **Facilities** Dogs allowed Garden Parking **Rooms** 32

BOURTON — Map 4 ST73

The White Lion Inn

High St SP8 5AT ☎ 01747 840866
e-mail: office@whitelionbourton.co.uk
dir: Off A303, opposite B3092 to Gillingham

Dating from 1723, the White Lion is a beautiful, stone-built, creeper clad Dorset inn. The bar is cosy, with beams, flagstones and an open fire, and serves a range of real beers and ciders. Imaginative menus draw on the wealth of quality local produce. Dishes range from home-made burger with Montgomery Cheddar, chutney, salad and chips in the bar, to pork belly slowly braised in Calvados, Cheddar Valley cider and thyme in the restaurant.

Open all wk noon-3 5-11 **Bar Meals** L served Mon-Sat 12-2.30, Sun 12-3.30 D served all wk 6-9 Av main course £9 **Restaurant** L served Mon-Sat 12-2.30, Sun 12-3.30 D served all wk 6-9 ⊕ ADMIRAL TAVERNS ◀ Fuller's London Pride, Greene King IPA, guest ale ♂ Thatchers. **Facilities** Children's menu Dogs allowed Garden Parking

See advert on this page

BRIDPORT — Map 4 SY49

The George Hotel ♥

4 South St DT6 3NQ ☎ 01308 423187
dir: In town centre, 1.5m from West Bay

Handsome Georgian town house, with a Victorian-style bar and a mellow atmosphere, which bustles all day, and offers a traditional English breakfast, decent morning coffee and a good menu featuring fresh local plaice, natural smoked haddock, avocado and bacon salad, and the famous rabbit and bacon pie. Everything is home cooked using local produce.

Open all wk 10am-11.30pm (Fri-Sat 10am-12.30am Sun noon-10.30) **Bar Meals** L served all wk 12-2.30 D served Tue-Sat 6-9.30 ⊕ PALMERS ◀ Palmers - IPA, Copper & 200, Tally Ho. ♥ 6 **Facilities** Family room Dogs allowed

PICK OF THE PUBS

Shave Cross Inn — INN ♥

See Pick of the Pubs on opposite page

The West Bay ♥

Station Rd, West Bay DT6 4EW
☎ 01308 422157 📄 01308 459717
e-mail: info@thewestbay.co.uk
dir: From A35 (Bridport by-pass) take B3157 (2nd exit) towards West Bay. After mini-rdbt 1st left (Station Road). Pub on left

Built in 1739, this traditional bar/restaurant lies at the foot of East Cliff, part of the impressive World Heritage Jurassic Coast. Specialities are fish and seafood: West Bay velvet crab soup; and Lyme Bay hot crab pâté on toasted sourdough are starter examples, which could be followed by lemon sole with brown shrimps and caper butter; or roast huss with surf clams and sea beet.

Palmers Brewery in Bridport furnishes the real ales, or you can ring the changes with a pint of Thatcher's Gold cider.

Open noon-3 6-11 Closed: Sun eve & winter Mon L **Bar Meals** L served all wk 12-2 (Tue-Sun 12-2 winter) D served Mon-Sat 6.30-9 (Tue-Sat 6.30-9 winter) Av main course £14.50 **Restaurant** L served all wk 12-2 (Tue-Sun 12-2 winter) booking required D served Mon-Sat 6.30-9 (Tue-Sat 6.30-9 winter) booking required Fixed menu price fr £15 Av 3 course à la carte fr £26.50 ⊕ PALMERS ◀ Palmers IPA, Palmers Copper, Palmers 200, Guinness, Tally Ho! ♂ Thatcher's Gold. ♥ 9 **Facilities** Children's menu Dogs allowed Garden Parking

BUCKHORN WESTON — Map 4 ST72

PICK OF THE PUBS

Stapleton Arms ♥

Church Hill SP8 5HS ☎ 01963 370396
e-mail: relax@thestapletonarms.com
dir: 3.5m from Wincanton in village centre

A stylish but unstuffy pub in a pretty village, with a spacious bar, elegant dining room and secluded garden. Hand-pumped ales, draught farm ciders, organic fruit juices and wines from new, old and emerging wine regions accompany simple, innovative food based on quality produce from small local suppliers. For starters try winter vegetable and thyme soup with a hunk of freshly delivered bread; or pan-fried scallops with celeriac purée, crispy Parma ham and toasted fennel seeds. Main courses include slow-roasted belly pork with apple mash and a cider sauce; and ruby red beetroot and fresh horseradish risotto. Fish caught off Dorset's south coast is delivered daily, and the award-winning menus continue to broaden – most recently with products from a smokery near Bath. You can even decide on your Sunday joint and the pub will prepare and cook it for you. Typical desserts are

continued on page 162

PICK OF THE PUBS

Shave Cross Inn ★★★★★ INN ♟

Shave Cross, Marshwood Vale DT6 6HW
☎ 01308 868358 📠 01308 867064
e-mail: roy.warburton@virgin.net
web: www.theshavecrossinn.co.uk
dir: *From Bridport take B3162. In 2m left signed 'Broadoak/Shave Cross', then Marshwood*

Delightfully situated off the beaten track down tortuous narrow lanes deep in the beautiful Marshwood Vale, five miles from Bridport, this charming, 14th-century thatched cob-and-flint inn could well be the inn that time forgot. It was once a busy resting place for 13th-century pilgrims on their way to the church of St Candida and St Cross in nearby Whitchurch Canonicorum, as well as monastic visitors, who frequently had their tonsures trimmed while staying, hence the pub's name. The classic main bar oozes character, with an ancient flagstone floor, oak beams, rustic furnishings, and a vast inglenook fireplace with a crackling winter log fire. Here you can quaff local beers from Quay Brewery in Weymouth and Devon's Branscombe Vale. Owners Roy and Mel Warburton spent a long time in Tobago, before returning to their roots in 2003 to revive the fortunes of this Dorset treasure. They brought with them their head chef, who is responsible for the authentically Caribbean touches to the menu. Typical examples include a salad of jerk chicken with plantain and crispy bacon with aioli, and spinach, coconut and crab soup for starter, while spicy main courses may take in Louisiana blackened chicken with cream and pepper sauce, Creole whole sea bass, and Jamaican jerk pork tenderloin with pineapple compôte and fried plantain. Fans of traditional British food won't be disappointed though: there are plenty of other options, especially at lunchtime, with battered haddock, rump steak, cheese ploughman's and fresh crab sandwiches on the menu. New-build bedrooms next door are luxuriously kitted out. The flower-filled sun-trap garden is a delight in summer, and through the oldest thatched skittle alley in the country, kids will find their play area. The inn maintains the traditions of Morris dancing, folk singing, and ashen-faggot burning on Twelfth Night.

Open 11-3 6-11.30 Closed: Mon (ex BHs) **Bar Meals** L served Tue-Sun 12-2.30 D served Tue-Sun 6-7 Av main course £10.95 **Restaurant** L served Tue-Sun 12-2.30 D served Tue-Sun 6-9 (closed Sun eve winter) Fixed menu price fr £32.50 ⊕ FREE HOUSE ◀ Local guest ales, Branoc (Branscombe Valley), Quay Brewery Weymouth ☼ Old Rosie, Thatchers, Stowford Press. ♟ 8 **Facilities** Play area Dogs allowed Garden Parking **Rooms** 7

BUCKHORN WESTON *continued*

gooey chocolate pudding with chocolate ice cream; and classic crème brûlée with a tuile biscuit. Alternatively the cheeseboard offers a selection of local cheeses including Somerset brie, Dorset blue vinney and Double Gloucester with chives.

Open all wk 11-3 6-11 (Sun noon-10.30) **Bar Meals** L served all wk 12-3 D served all wk 6-10 Av main course £12 **Restaurant** L served all wk 12-3 booking required D served all wk 6-10 booking required Av 3 course à la carte fr £23 ⊕ FREE HOUSE ◀ Butcombe, Hidden Brewery, Moor's Revival Ō Thatchers Cheddar Valley, Butcombe's Ashton Press, Orchard Pig. ♥ 12 **Facilities** Children's menu Dogs allowed Garden Parking

---

BUCKLAND NEWTON   Map 4 ST60

Gaggle of Geese NEW ♥

DT2 7BS ☎ 01300 345249
e-mail: gaggle@gaggleofgeese.co.uk
dir: *On B3143 N of Dorchester*

Mark and Emily Hammick have breathed new life into this now thriving community local since taking over in 2008. Fresh flowers and fat candles top scrubbed tables in the spruced-up bar, where you can sup West Country ales and local ciders, and tuck into some cracking pub food. Prepared from local seasonal produce, including meat from Mark's family farm, dishes include pork terrine with apple chutney, roasted butternut squash risotto, and rib-eye steak and peppercorn sauce. Well worth the diversion off the A352 south of Sherborne. In May and September, poultry auctions are held for charity.

Open all wk 11.30-3 6 11.30 (Sun 11.30-11.30, Sat 11.30-11.30 in summer) Closed: 1 wk Jan, 25 Dec **Bar Meals** L served Mon-Sat 12-2, Sun 12-3 booking required D served Sun-Thu 7-9, Fri-Sat 7-9.30 booking required Av main course £10 **Restaurant** L served Mon-Sat 12-2, Sun 12-3 booking required D served Sun-Thu 7-9, Fri-Sat 7-9.30 booking required Av 3 course à la carte fr £25 ⊕ FREE HOUSE ◀ Ringwood, Proper Job, Tribute, Butcombe Bitter, Hop Back Summer Lightning Ō Thatchers Gold, Lulworth Skipper, Bridge Farm Traditional. ♥ 10 **Facilities** Children's menu Play area Dogs allowed Garden Parking

---

BURTON BRADSTOCK   Map 4 SY48

PICK OF THE PUBS

The Anchor Inn ♥

High St DT6 4QF ☎ 01308 897228
e-mail: info@dorset-seafood-restaurant.co.uk
dir: *2m SE of Bridport on B3157 in centre of Burton Bradstock*

A 300-year-old coaching inn, the Anchor is located just inland from a stretch of the Jurassic Coast World Heritage Site, near Chesil Beach. As you might expect from its name, the pub is full of marine memorabilia: fishing nets hang from ceilings, and old fishing tools and arty things made by the chef-proprietor from shellfish adorn the walls. Seafood is a speciality, and there is an extensive selection of main fish courses on the menu, plus 'catch of the day' specials. The bouillabaisse is a substantial version of the celebrated French dish, including a wide variety of local fish and shellfish in a creamy lobster, white wine and brandy jus, served with a hot baguette. Dorset scallops, dived for around West Bay, are seared in butter and served in their shells with a creamy bacon and mushroom sauce, on a bed of savoury rice garnished with salad and prawns.

Open all wk Closed: 1 Jan **Bar Meals** L served all wk 12-2 booking required D served all wk 6-9.30 booking required food served all day **Restaurant** L served all wk 12-2 booking required D served all wk 6-9.30 booking required food served all day ⊕ PUNCH TAVERNS ◀ Otter Bitter, Tribute, Theakston Best Bitter, John Smith's Ō Thatchers. ♥ 10 **Facilities** Children's menu Dogs allowed Parking

---

CATTISTOCK   Map 4 SY59

Fox & Hounds Inn

Duck St DT2 0JH ☎ 01300 320444 ▤ 01300 320444
e-mail: lizflight@yahoo.co.uk
web: www.foxandhoundsinn.com
dir: *On A37, between Dorchester & Yeovil, follow signs to Cattistock*

This attractive 16th-century inn is set in the beautiful village of Cattistock. Original features include beams, open fires in winter and huge inglenooks, one with an original bread oven. It is a fascinating building, full of curiosities, such as the hidden cupboard reached by a staircase that winds around the chimney in one of the loft areas. Traditional home-made meals include locally made faggots; mushroom stroganoff; steak and kidney pudding; and Dorset apple cake. A superb garden is available in the summer. Recent change of ownership.

Open noon-2.30 7-11 (Thu-Sat 12-2.30 6-11) Closed: Mon L **Bar Meals** L served Tue-Sun 12-2 D served Tue-Sat 7-11 booking required Av main course £8.95 **Restaurant** L served Tue-Sun 12-2 D served Tue-Sat 7-11 booking required ⊕ PALMERS ◀ Palmers IPA, Copper Ale, Palmers 200, Dorset Gold Ō Thatchers Traditional. **Facilities** Children's menu Play area Dogs allowed Garden Parking

---

CHEDINGTON   Map 4 ST40

Winyards Gap Inn NEW ♥

Chedington Ln DT8 3HY ☎ 01935 891244
e-mail: enquiries@winyardsgap.com
web: www.winyardsgap.com
dir: *5m S of Crewkerne on A356*

An ancient inn tucked under an ancient earthwork on the edge of the Dorset Down, with a stunning view towards the Quantock Hills that inspired Thomas Hardy's poem 'At Winyard's Gap'. Savour the view from the beamed bar or

the terraced garden with a pint of Exmoor Ale and a decent meal – scallops with lemon butter sauce, lamb steak with redcurrant jus, Eton mess, or a traditional bar meal, perhaps, ham, egg and chips or a smoked salmon sandwich.

Open all wk 11.30-3 6-11 (Sat-Sun 11.30-11) Closed: 25 Dec **Bar Meals** L served Mon-Sat 12-2 D served all wk 6-9 Av main course £12 **Restaurant** L served all wk 12-2 booking required D served all wk 6-9 booking required Av 3 course à la carte fr £22 ⊕ FREE HOUSE ◀ Doom Bar, Exmoor Ale, Otter Ale ♂ Thatchers Gold. ♀ 8 **Facilities** Children's menu Dogs allowed Garden Parking

CHIDEOCK   Map 4 SY49

The Anchor Inn ♀

Seatown DT6 6JU ☎ **01297 489215**
dir: *On A35 turn S in Chideock opp church & follow single track rd for 0.75m to beach*

Originally a smugglers' haunt, The Anchor has an incredible setting in a little cove surrounded by National Trust land, beneath Golden Cap. The large sun terrace and cliff-side beer garden overlooking the beach make it a premier destination for throngs of holidaymakers in the summer, while on winter weekdays it is blissfully quiet. The wide-ranging menu starts with snacks and light lunches - three types of ploughman's and a range of sandwiches might take your fancy. For something more substantial you could try freshly caught seafood - crab salad, for example.

Open all wk 11.30am-10.30pm **Bar Meals** L served all wk 12-9 D served all wk 12-9 ⊕ PALMERS ◀ Palmers 200 Premium Ale, IPA, Copper Ale ♂ Thatchers Tradition, Thatchers Pear. ♀ 8 **Facilities** Family room Dogs allowed Garden Parking

CHRISTCHURCH   Map 5 SZ19

Fishermans Haunt ♀

Salisbury Rd, Winkton BH23 7AS
☎ **01202 477283** 🖹 **01202 478883**
e-mail: fishermanshaunt@fullers.co.uk
dir: *2.5m N on B3347 (Christchurch to Ringwood road)*

Dating from 1673, this inn overlooks the River Avon and is a popular place for walkers, and anglers visiting some of the local fisheries. The area is also well endowed with golf courses. The menu offers a daily fish selection, usually including trout and whole plaice, and staples such as steak and kidney pie, battered cod, and mixed grill along with sandwiches and baked potatoes. There's a more extensive carte menu in the restaurant.

Open all wk 11-11 (Fri 11am-mdnt, Sun 11.30-10.30) **Bar Meals** food served all day ⊕ FULLERS BREWERY ◀ Seafairers ale, HSB, London Pride, Fullers ESB. ♀ 7 **Facilities** Family room Dogs allowed Garden Parking

The Ship In Distress ⊛

66 Stanpit BH23 3NA
☎ **01202 485123** 🖹 **01202 483997**
e-mail: enquiries@theshipindistress.com
dir: *Telephone for directions*

Once a haunt of famous Christchurch smugglers, this 300-year-old pub featured in a recent documentary film about the history of smuggling. It is located close to Mudeford Quay and has an award-winning seafood restaurant. Typical dishes are moules marinière, and baked fillet of turbot with shallots, wild mushrooms and sunblush tomatoes. Fresh daily desserts include assiette of Belgian chocolate, and Cointreau orange mascarpone cheesecake with confit orange.

Open all day all wk 11am-mdnt (Sun 11-11) **Bar Meals** L served Mon-Fri 12-2, Sat- Sun 12-2.30 D served Sun-Thu 6.30-9, Fri-Sun 6.30-9.30 ⊕ PUNCH TAVERNS ◀ Ringwood Best, Fortyniner, Adnams Broadside, Guest Ales. **Facilities** Dogs allowed Garden Parking

CHURCH KNOWLE   Map 4 SY98

The New Inn ♀

BH20 5NQ ☎ **01929 480357** 🖹 **01929 480357**
e-mail: new_inn@hotmail.co.uk
dir: *From Wareham take A351 towards Swanage. At Corfe Castle turn right for Church Knowle. Pub in village centre*

Set in a picturesque village overlooking the Purbeck Hills, the Estop family has been running this quaint 16th century stone and thatched country inn for 23 years, with son Matthew as chef and daughter Alison as chef and front of house. Fresh fish is the speciality of the house, including haddock in beer batter, crab, lobster, moules marinière, black bream, plaice and fruits de mer. Menus also offer home-made British traditional favourites such as roasts and interesting daily specials. Vegetarian dishes and meals for allergy sufferers are cooked to order.

Open 11-3 6-11 Closed: Mon eve Jan & Feb **Bar Meals** L served all wk 12-2.15 booking required D served all wk 6-9.15 booking required **Restaurant** L served all wk 12-2.15 booking required D served all wk 6-9.15 booking required ⊕ PUNCH TAVERNS ◀ Wadworth 6X, Old Speckled Hen, Interbrew Flowers Original ♂ Old Rosie, Stowford Press. ♀ 8 **Facilities** Family room Garden Parking

CORFE CASTLE   Map 4 SY98

The Greyhound Inn ♀

The Square BH20 5EZ
☎ **01929 480205** 🖹 **01929 480205**
e-mail: eat@greyhoundcorfe.co.uk
dir: *W from Bournemouth, take A35 to Dorchester, after 5m left onto A351, 10m to Corfe Castle*

A classic coaching inn, set beneath the ruins of Corfe Castle, the Greyhound has a large beer garden with views of Swanage Steam Railway. A full diary of events features two annual beer festivals in May and August and a West Country sausage and cider festival in October half term. The convivial atmosphere embraces families, cyclists and walkers enjoying local food and ale, including winter game and summer shellfish from Swanage, Weymouth or Lulworth.

Open all wk 11-11 **Bar Meals** L served all wk 11-3 D served all wk 6-9 Av main course £10.75 ⊕ ENTERPRISE INNS ◀ Fuller's London Pride, Timothy Taylor Landlord, Black Sheep, Ringwood Best, Purbeck Brewery Fossil Fuel, Marston's Pedigree ♂ Westons Organic, Stowford Press. ♀ 6 **Facilities** Children's menu Play area Family room Dogs allowed Garden

CORFE MULLEN   Map 4 SY99

The Coventry Arms ⊛ ♀

Mill St BH21 3RH ☎ **01258 857284**
e-mail: info@coventryarms.co.uk
dir: *On A31 (Wimborne-Dorchester road)*

Built in the 13th-century, this friendly pub was once a watermill with its own island. Beer is served direct from the cask, while an annual spring seafood festival attracts many visitors. The inn specialises in fish and game from local estates, and most of the produce is sourced from within the area. Expect such creative dishes as open ravioli of monkfish medallions and mussels; or pan-seared Sika deer's liver with smoked bacon. There's a lovely garden to enjoy in warmer weather.

Open all wk 8am-3 5.30-11 (Sat-Sun 8-3 7-11) **Bar Meals** L served Mon-Fri 8-11, 12-2.30, Sat-Sun 9-11, 12-9.30 D served Mon-Fri 6-9.30, Sat-Sun 12-9.30 ⊕ FREE HOUSE ◀ Timothy Taylor Landlord, Guest Ales ♂ Stowford Press. ♀ 17 **Facilities** Dogs allowed Garden Parking

EAST CHALDON   Map 4 SY78

The Sailors Return

DT2 8DN ☎ **01305 853847** 🖹 **01305 851677**
dir: *1m S of A352 between Dorchester & Wool*

A splendid 18th-century thatched country pub in the village of East Chaldon (or Chaldon Herring - take your pick), tucked away in rolling downland near Lulworth Cove. Seafood includes whole local plaice, scallop and mussel Stroganoff, and wok-fried king prawns. Alternatives include half a big duck, local faggots, whole

continued

EAST CHALDON *continued*

gammon hock, and vegetarian dishes. Choose from the blackboard in the beamed and flagstoned bar and eat inside or in a grassy area outside.

Open all wk ⊕ FREE HOUSE ◄ Ringwood Best, Hampshire Strongs Best Bitter, Badger Tanglefoot. **Facilities** Play area Family room Garden Parking

EAST MORDEN — Map 4 SY99

PICK OF THE PUBS

The Cock & Bottle ♀

BH20 7DL ☎ 01929 459238
dir: *From A35 W of Poole turn right B3075, pub 0.5m on left*

Originally a cob-walled Dorset longhouse, dating back some 400 years, the pub acquired a brick skin around 1800, and remained thatched until 1966. The original interiors are comfortably rustic with quaint, low-beamed ceilings, attractive paintings and lots of nooks and crannies around the log fires. Additional to the lively locals' bar are a lounge bar and modern rear restaurant extension. Lovely pastoral views over farmland include the pub's paddock, where vintage car and motorcycle meetings are occasionally hosted during the summer. The experienced chef serves up an appealing mix of traditional and inventive cooking, with wholesome bar and light lunch menus supporting a varied daily carte. Dishes might include fresh dressed local crab to start, followed by loin of venison with wild mushroom ragout, and rum and raisin white chocolate tart to finish. A children's choice is also available.

Open all wk 11.30-2.30 6-11 (Sun noon-3 7-10.30) **Bar Meals** L served all wk 12-2 D served Mon-Sat 6-9 (Sun 7-9) **Restaurant** L served all wk 12-2 booking required D served Mon-Sat 6-9 (Sun 7-9) booking required ⊕ HALL & WOODHOUSE ◄ Badger Dorset Best, Tanglefoot & Sussex. ♀6 **Facilities** Children's menu Dogs allowed Garden Parking

EVERSHOT — Map 4 ST50

PICK OF THE PUBS

The Acorn Inn ★★★★ INN ◉ ♀

DT2 0JW ☎ 01935 83228 🖹 01935 83707
e-mail: stay@acorn-inn.co.uk
web: www.acorn-inn.co.uk
dir: *A303 to Yeovil, Dorchester Rd, on A37 right to Evershot*

Immortalised as the Sow and Acorn in Thomas Hardy's *Tess of the D'Urbervilles*, this 16th-century free house stands in an Area of Outstanding Natural Beauty, with walking, fishing, shooting and riding all nearby. The two oak-panelled bars are warmed by log fires, blazing in carved hamstone fireplaces. The skittle alley used to be the stables, and it's rumoured that the residents' sitting room was once used as Judge Jeffreys' court room. Most of the food is locally sourced, and the interesting menus might include starters such as chicken, wild mushroom and herb terrine. Typical main course choices include roasted butternut squash, Parmesan, cherry tomato and pine nut tagliatelle; sea bass on herb crushed new potatoes with basil pesto; and West Country sausages with grain mustard mash and rosemary jus. Finish with raspberry and Amaretto crème brulée; or creamed mango fool with sesame tuile biscuit and blackberries. Several of the bedrooms have four-poster beds.

Open all day all wk 11-11 **Bar Meals** L served all wk 12-2 D served all wk 7-9 **Restaurant** L served all wk 12-2 booking required D served all wk 7-9 booking required ⊕ FREE HOUSE ◄ Draymens, guest ale Ö Thatchers Gold, Thatchers Scrumpy. ♀7 **Facilities** Children's menu Family room Dogs allowed Garden Parking **Rooms** 10

FARNHAM — Map 4 ST91

PICK OF THE PUBS

The Museum Inn ◉ ♀

DT11 8DE ☎ 01825 516261 🖹 01825 516988
e-mail: enquiries@museuminn.co.uk
dir: *From Salisbury take A354 to Blandford Forum, 12m. Farnham signed on right. Pub in village centre*

The part-thatched Museum owes its name and present existence to the 17th-century archaeologist General Pitt-Rivers, who took over the Gypsy School nearby to house one of his museums. Beautifully refurbished, the inn retains many original features throughout its civilised beamed rooms, from the stone flagged floors and inglenook fireplace to a traditional bread oven. The same attention to detail is evident in the accomplished kitchen, where a commitment to sourcing local produce reared in traditional ways results in well prepared and presented modern British dishes. Try mussel broth with lemongrass, ginger and coriander, or smoked haddock leek fishcake with lightly curried beurre blanc, followed by confit duck leg with spring onion mash, or whole plaice with mussel and parsley. For dessert, perhaps iced nougat parfait with star anise roasted plum, or treacle tart with blackcurrant coulis. The cooking is back up by an excellent list of wines (13 by the glass) and hand-pulled ales include local Ringwood Old Thumper.

Open all wk noon-3 6-11 **Bar Meals** L served 12-2 D served 7-9 Av main course £17 **Restaurant** L served Sun 12-2.30 booking required D served Fri-Sat 7-9 booking required Av 3 course à la carte fr £32 ⊕ FREE HOUSE ◄ Ringwood Old Thumper, Timothy Taylor, Jimmy Riddle, Sunchaser Ö Stowford Press, Westons Organic. ♀13 **Facilities** Children's menu Dogs allowed Garden Parking

GILLINGHAM — Map 4 ST82

The Kings Arms Inn ♀

East Stour Common SP8 5NB ☎ 01747 838325
e-mail: nrosscampbell@aol.com
dir: *4m W of Shaftesbury on A30*

A family-run, 200-year-old free house, this village inn makes a great base for exploring Dorset's countryside and coast. There is a public bar with a log fire, the Mallard and Garden Room and an enclosed acre of attractive beer garden. The menus offer an extensive choice of restaurant fare and traditional pub grub. Popular choices include chicken breast stuffed with haggis on black pudding mash in a Drambuie sauce, or steak and kidney pudding with red onion marmalade. A separate menu is available for children and there is an eat lunch for a fiver deal.

Open all wk **Bar Meals** L served Mon-Sat 12-2.30, Sun 12-9.15 booking required D served Mon-Sat 5.30-9.15, Sun 12-9.15 booking required **Bar Meals** L served Mon-Sat 12-2.30, Sun 12-9.15 booking required D served Mon-Sat 5.30-9.15, Sun 12-9.15 booking required ⊕ FREE HOUSE ◀ London Pride, Copper Ale, Tribute, Wadworth 6X. ♀ 8 **Facilities** Children's menu Family room Dogs allowed Garden Parking

GUSSAGE ALL SAINTS   Map 4 SU01

The Drovers Inn ♀

BH21 5ET ☎ 01258 840084
e-mail: info@thedroversinn.biz
dir: A31 Ashley Heath rdbt, right onto B3081

Rural 16th-century pub with a fine terrace and wonderful views from the garden. Popular with walkers, its refurbished interior retains plenty of traditional appeal with flagstone floors and oak furniture. Ales include Ringwood's seasonal ales and guest beers. The menu features home-cooked pub favourites: fresh cod in home-made beer batter, curry, steak and kidney pie, and steak and chips.

Open all wk 12-3 6-12 (Sat-Sun 11am-mdnt) Closed: 26 Dec **Bar Meals** L served Mon-Sat 12-2 Sun 12-3 D served Mon-Fri 6-9 Sat 6-9.30 ⊕ RINGWOOD ◀ Ringwood Best, Old Thumper, Ringwood seasonal ales, Fortyniner, guest ales Ŏ Thatchers Gold. ♀ 10 **Facilities** Dogs allowed Garden Parking

KING'S STAG   Map 4 ST71

The Greenman ♀

DT10 2AY ☎ 01258 817338   ▤ 01258 818358
dir: E of Sherborne on A3030

Legend has it that King's Stag in the Blackmore Vale owes its name to Henry III's favourite white hart, hunted down and killed by a local nobleman. Built around 1775 and full of oak beams, the pub has five separate dining areas where you can order anything from a snack to a banquet. The Sunday carvery offers a choice of five meats and eight vegetables - booking is essential. Children will enjoy the play area.

Open all wk 11-3 5.30-11 **Bar Meals** L served all wk 12-2 D served all wk 6-9 Av main course £8 **Restaurant** L served all wk 12-2 D served all wk 6-9 Fixed menu price fr £8 Av 3 course à la carte fr £19.95 ⊕ ENTERPRISE INNS ◀ Exmoor, Spitfire, HBC, London Pride, Old Speckled Hen. ♀ 9 **Facilities** Play area Family room Dogs allowed Garden Parking

LODERS   Map 4 SY49

Loders Arms

DT6 3SA ☎ 01308 422431
e-mail: janelegg@aol.com
dir: Off A3066, 2m NE of Bridport

Unassuming stone-built local tucked away in a pretty thatched village close to the Dorset coast. Arrive early to bag a seat in the long cosy bar or the homely dining

room. A selection of mains includes scallops in Pernod and cream; fusilli with roasted vegetables, feta and pesto; wild boar sausages; and rack of lamb studded with garlic. There's a lovely garden with views of Boarsbarrow Hill, and a skittle alley that doubles as a function room.

Open all wk ⊕ PALMERS ◀ Palmers Copper, Palmers IPA, Palmers 200. **Facilities** Dogs allowed Garden Parking

LOWER ANSTY   Map 4 ST70

The Fox Inn ★★★★ INN ♀

DT2 7PN ☎ 01258 880328   ▤ 01258 881440
e-mail: fox@anstyfoxinn.co.uk
dir: A35 from Dorchester towards Poole for 4m, exit signed Piddlehinton/Athelhampton House, left to Cheselbourne, then right. Pub in village opposite post office

Looking more like a grand rectory than a pub, the 250-year-old Fox was built for brewer Charles Hall, later to co-found Blandford's Hall & Woodhouse brewery, whose Badger beers are, naturally enough, served in the bar. Typical main courses are pot-roasted half duck with cherry compote and red wine jus; sautéed tiger prawn in sweet pepper and tomato sauce; and grilled fillet steak glazed with Dorset Blue Vinny cheese and herb mash. Recent change of landlord. There is an extensive garden and patio area, plus eleven en suite bedrooms.

Open all wk 11-11 **Bar Meals** L served all wk 12-2.30 D served all wk 6.30-9 Av main course £7.25 **Restaurant** L served all wk 12-2.30 D served all wk 6.30-9 Av 3 course à la carte fr £21 ⊕ HALL & WOODHOUSE ◀ Badger Tanglefoot, Badger Best, Badger Smooth, seasonal guest ale. ♀ 11 **Facilities** Children's menu Dogs allowed Garden Parking **Rooms** 11

LYME REGIS   Map 4 SY39

Pilot Boat Inn ♀

Bridge St DT7 3QA ☎ 01297 443157
dir: Telephone for directions

Old smuggling and sea rescue tales are associated with this busy town centre pub, close to the sea front. However its biggest claim to fame is as the birthplace of the original Lassie, Hollywood's favourite collie. A good range of food offers sandwiches, salads and cold platters, Dorset chicken with cider sauce, local crab, real scampi and chips, and other fresh fish as available. There's also a good vegetarian choice, and a vegan three-bean casserole.

Open all wk 11-11 Closed: 25 Dec **Bar Meals** food served all day **Restaurant** food served all day ⊕ PALMERS ◀ Palmers Dorset Gold, IPA, 200, Bridport Bitter. ♀ 8 **Facilities** Dogs allowed Garden

MARSHWOOD   Map 4 SY39

PICK OF THE PUBS

The Bottle Inn ♀

DT6 5QJ ☎ 01297 678254   ▤ 01297 678739
e-mail: thebottleinn@msn.com
dir: On B3165 (Crewkerne to Lyme Regis road) 5m from the Hunters Lodge

The thatched Bottle Inn was first mentioned as an ale house back in the 17th century, and was the first pub in the area during the 18th century to serve bottled beer rather than beer from the jug - hence the name. Standing beside the B3165 on the edge of the glorious Marshwood Vale, its rustic interior has simple wooden settles, scrubbed tables and a blazing fire. Now under new management the pub's lunch menu keeps it simple with jacket potatoes, grilled paninis, burgers like wild boar and apple, ploughman's, baguettes, lite bites (perhaps crab cakes; pâté; or deep fried brie) plus haddock and chips; chilli; and gammon steak. At dinner the choices could be smoked duck with raspberry coulis or king prawns in garlic and cream, followed by traditional suet steak and kidney pudding or supreme of chicken stuffed with smoked salmon with whisky and mustard cream sauce. The pub is home to the annual World Stinging-Nettle Eating Championships. Look out for live music evenings, and remember Tuesday night is steak night and Thursday night is curry night.

Open all wk noon-3 6-11 **Bar Meals** L served all wk 12-2 booking required Av main course £8 **Restaurant** L served all wk 12-2 booking required D served all wk 6-9 booking required Fixed menu price fr £9.50 ⊕ FREE HOUSE ◀ Otter Ale, Otter Bitter, Stargazer, guest ale Ŏ Stowford Press, Thatchers Gold. ♀ 7 **Facilities** Children's menu Play area Family room Garden Parking

MILTON ABBAS   Map 4 ST80

The Hambro Arms ♀

DT11 0BP ☎ 01258 880233
e-mail: info@hambroarms.co.uk
dir: A354 (Dorchester to Blandford road), turn off at Royal Oak

This 18th-century thatched pub, now owned by a partnership of villagers, is set in the midst of a picturesque village of thatched, whitewashed cottages, believed to be the first planned settlement in England. The owners' aim is to provide a traditional country pub atmosphere with exceptional food, most of it locally sourced, whether you're looking for a lunchtime snack or fine dining experience. Regular gourmet and oriental evenings are featured.

Open all wk 11-3 6-11 (Sat-Sun 11-11) **Bar Meals** L served all wk 12-2.30 D served Sun-Thu 6.30-9, Fri-Sat 6.30-9.30 Av main course £8.95 **Restaurant** L served all wk 12-2.30 D served Sun-Thu 6.30-9, Fri-Sat 6.30-9.30 Fixed menu price fr £11.95 ⊕ FREE HOUSE ◀ Ringwood, Piddle Ales, Durdle Door Ŏ Stowford Press. ♀ 8 **Facilities** Children's menu Garden Parking

MOTCOMBE — Map 4 ST82

The Coppleridge Inn ▲ ★★★ INN ♥

SP7 9HW ☎ 01747 851980 📄 01747 851858
e-mail: thecoppleridgeinn@btinternet.com
web: www.coppleridge.com
dir: Take A350 towards Warminster for 1.5m, turn left at brown tourist sign. Follow signs to inn

Previously a dairy farm, this 18th-century building retains plenty of traditional features, including flagstone floors and log fires. Run by the Goodinge family for nearly 20 years, it offers a good range of real ales and a daily-changing menu of sophisticated pub food, ranging from roasted lamb rump on sweet potato mash with sage jus to grilled lemon sole with dill velouté. For sunny days there is a large garden and terrace with Blackmore Vale views, a secure children's playground and 10 bedrooms if you would like to stay over.

Open all wk 11-3 5-11 (Sat 11am-mdnt Sun noon-11) Bar Meals L served all wk 12-2.30 D served all wk 6-9 Av main course £11.50 Restaurant L served all wk 12-2.30 D served all wk 6-9 Av 3 course à la carte fr £22 ⊕ FREE HOUSE ◀ Butcombe Bitter, Greene King IPA, Wadworth 6X, Fuller's London Pride, Sharp's Doom Bar. ♥ 10 Facilities Children's menu Play area Family room Dogs allowed Garden Parking Rooms 10

NETTLECOMBE — Map 4 SY59

Marquis of Lorne ♥

DT6 3SY ☎ 01308 485236
e-mail: enquiries@marquisoflorne.com
dir: From A3066 (Bridport-Beaminster road) approx 1.5m N of Bridport follow Loders & Mangerton Mill signs. At junct left past Mangerton Mill, through West Milton. 1m to T-junct, straight over. Pub up hill, approx 300yds on left

A 16th-century farmhouse converted into a pub in 1871, when the Marquis himself named it to prove land ownership. Membership of the Campaign for Real Food means that much local produce is used. Daily menus offer such dishes as pigeon breast with juniper and red wine sauce, home-made curry, fresh cod fillet, and mushroom and pepper stroganoff. Desserts might be rum and chocolate truffle terrine or twice baked cheesecake. Superb gardens with beautiful views.

Open all wk 12-2.30 6-11 Closed: 25 Dec Bar Meals L served all wk 12-2 D served all wk 6-9 ⊕ PALMERS ◀ Palmers Copper, IPA, 200 Premium Ale. ♥ 8 Facilities Play area Dogs allowed Garden Parking

NORTH WOOTTON — Map 4 ST61

The Three Elms ♥

DT9 5JW ☎ 01935 812881
e-mail: mark@threeelms.co.uk
dir: From Sherborne take A352 towards Dorchester then A3030. Pub 1m on right

Recently re-opened under new management, The Three Elms has been refurbished but retains its original features, including beams and a log fire. Just outside Sherborne on the edge of the beautiful Blackmore Vale, the inn has a large beer garden with fabulous views. Freshly cooked British classics are served at candlelit tables, including Sunday roasts and regularly-changing blackboard specials. Typical dishes are roast leg of free-range lamb, beer-battered pollock with hand-cut chips, and local pork sausages with mash and caramelised onion jus.

Open all wk 11-2.30 6.30-11 (Sun noon-3 7-10.30) Closed: 25-26 Dec Bar Meals L served Mon-Sat 12-2, Sun 12-2.30 booking required D served Mon-Sat 6.30-9.30, Sun 7-9 booking required Restaurant L served Mon-Sat 12-2, Sun 12-2.30 booking required D served Mon-Sat 6.30-9.30, Sun 7-9 booking required ⊕ FREE HOUSE ◀ Butcombe Bitter ○ Thatchers Burrow Hill. ♥ 10 Facilities Children's menu Dogs allowed Garden Parking

OSMINGTON MILLS — Map 4 SY78

The Smugglers Inn ♥

DT3 6HF ☎ 01305 833125
e-mail: smugglers.weymouth@hall-woodhouse.co.uk
dir: 7m E of Weymouth towards Wareham, pub signed

Set on the cliffs at Osmington Mills with the South Coast Footpath running through the garden, the inn has beautiful views across Weymouth Bay. In the late 18th century (the inn dates back to the 13th century) it was the base of infamous smuggler Pierre La Tour who fell in love with the publican's daughter, Arabella Carless, who was shot dead while helping him to escape during a raid. Things are quieter now and you can enjoy a pint of Tanglefoot or one of the guest ales like Pickled Partridge. On the menu typical dishes are chicken and bacon salad, chargrilled rump steak, and Sussex smokey (fish pie).

Open all wk 11-11 (Sun noon-10.30) Bar Meals L served all wk 12-9.30 D served all wk 12-9.30 Av main course £9 food served all day Restaurant L served all wk 12-9.30 D served all wk 12-9.30 food served all day ⊕ HALL & WOODHOUSE ◀ Badger, Tanglefoot, guest ale. ♥ 12 Facilities Children's menu Play area Dogs allowed Garden Parking

PIDDLEHINTON — Map 4 SY79

The Thimble Inn

DT2 7TD ☎ 01300 348270
e-mail: thimbleinn@googlemail.com
dir: A35 W'bound, right onto B3143, Piddlehinton in 4m

Friendly village local with open fires, traditional pub games and good food cooked to order. The pub stands in a pretty valley on the banks of the River Piddle, and the riverside patio is popular in summer. The extensive menu ranges from sandwiches and jacket potatoes to fish choices like poached halibut on leek and white sauce; and grilled trout with almonds.

Open all wk 11.30-2.30 6-11 Closed: 25 Dec Bar Meals L served all wk 11.30-2 booking required D served all wk 6.30-9 booking required Restaurant L served all wk 11.30-2 booking required D served all wk 6.30-9 booking required ⊕ FREE HOUSE ◀ Ringwood Best, Palmer Copper Ale & Palmer IPA, Ringwood Old Thumper, Summer Lightning ○ Thatchers Gold, Thatchers Dry. Facilities Children's menu Dogs allowed Garden Parking

PIDDLETRENTHIDE — Map 4 SY79

PICK OF THE PUBS

The European Inn NEW ♥

See Pick of the Pubs on opposite page

The Piddle Inn ★★★★ INN ♥

DT2 7QF ☎ 01300 348468 📄 01300 348102
e-mail: piddleinn@aol.com
dir: 7m N of Dorchester on B3143, in village centre

In the heart of rolling Dorset downland, tucked away in the unspoilt Piddle Valley north of Dorchester, with the River Piddle flowing through the garden, this welcoming 18th-century pub is a popular village local and dining venue. Come for Ringwood Best straight from the cask and a good range of home-cooked food in the comfortably refurbished bars. Expect local cheese ploughman's, steak and ale pie, rack of lamb with rosemary jus, and fish of the day. There are 3 en suite bedrooms available.

Closed: Mon lunch ⊕ FREE HOUSE ◀ Greene King IPA, Ringwood Best, Ringwood 49er. ♥ 8 Facilities Dogs allowed Garden Parking Rooms 3

PICK OF THE PUBS

The European Inn NEW ♀

PIDDLETRENTHIDE   Map 4 SY79

DT2 7QT ☎ 01300 348308
e-mail: info@european-inn.co.uk
web: www.european-inn.co.uk
dir: *5m N of Dorchester on B3143*

You would be forgiven for thinking the name dates from recent times, but no, it dates from as long ago as 1860, when the landlord, a soldier, returned from fighting in the Crimean War. Mark and Emily Hammick bought the inn in 2007 and embarked on a major refurbishment programme, importing many of the pictures and furniture from their own home. Whether you want a pint of Palmer's Copper Ale and a packet of Jack & Ollie's crisps at the bar, or a three-course dinner with fine wine, the aim is to please everybody. It is self-evident therefore that foodwise, the Hammick ethos is to provide good pub grub, with produce as fresh, seasonal and local and possible. The menus are indisputably British, with starters of warm salad of pigeon breasts, bacon and black pudding; salt cod fritters with watercress and garlic mayo; and game terrine with toast and 'gaggle' chutney. To follow might come Sydling Brook organic pork three ways; line-caught fillet of wild Cornish sea bass with sautéed potatoes, curly kale and baked lemon dressing; or pumpkin risotto with sage butter, rocket, Parmesan and balsamic vinegar. Puddings originate this side of the Channel too, as testified by rice pudding with home-made damson jam; Piddlehinton apple crumble and custard; and Craig's Farm ice creams. Wines are a different matter, with most produced in France, Italy, Spain and the New World (although one of the whites does come from Dorset).

Closed: Xmas-New Year & last 2 weeks Jan, Sun eve & Mon **Bar Meals** L served all week 12-2 D served Mon-Sat 7-9 Av main course £12 **Restaurant** L served all week 12-2 D served Mon-Sat 7-9 Av 3 course à la carte fr £23 ◀ Palmers Copper, St Austell Tribute, Yeovil Stargazer, Sharps Doom Bar, Otter Bright. ♀ 9 **Facilities** Children's menu Dogs allowed Garden Parking

PIDDLETRENTHIDE *continued*

The Poachers Inn ★★★★ INN ⚑

DT2 7QX ☎ 01300 348358 📄 01300 348153
e-mail: info@ thepoachersinn.co.uk
dir: *6m N from Dorchester on B3143. At church end of village*

This family-run inn beside the River Piddle continues to provide real ales, good food, fires and traditional pub games right in the heart of Thomas Hardy country. There's an extensive menu, supported by daily specials that may include home-made spaghetti Bolognese, seafood salad with lemon and dill, or pork and leek sausages with mustard mash. Leave room for traditional red and blackcurrant crumble! AA-rated accommodation is on offer if you want to prolong the pleasure.

Open all day all wk 8am–mdnt **Bar Meals** food served all day **Restaurant** food served all day ⊕ FREE HOUSE ◀ Wadworth 6X, Palmers Copper Ale, Guinness, Hopback, John Smiths ♂ Thatchers Gold. ⚑ 6 **Facilities** Children's menu Dogs allowed Garden Parking **Rooms** 21

PLUSH   Map 4 ST70

The Brace of Pheasants ⚑

DT2 7RQ ☎ 01300 348357 📄 01300 348959
e-mail: information@braceofpheasants.co.uk
web: www.braceofpheasants.co.uk
dir: *A35 onto B3143, 5m to Piddletrenthide, then right to Mappowder & Plush*

Tucked away in a fold of the hills in the heart of Hardy's beloved county is this pretty 16th-century thatched village inn. With a welcoming open fire, oak beams and fresh flowers, it's an ideal place to start or end a walk. A lunch menu might offer crab, cheddar and saffron cream tarts; while for dinner pan-fried strips of chicken breast with chorizo, lime juice, cream and basmati rice could be an option.

Open noon–3 7–11 Closed: 25 Dec, Mon (ex BH) Sun eve **Bar Meals** L served Tue-Sun 12-2.30 D served Tue-Sat 7-9.30 **Restaurant** L served Tue-Sun 12-2.30 D served Tue-Sat 7-9.30 ⊕ FREE HOUSE ◀ Ringwood Best, Dorset Brewing Co, Palmers, Dorset Piddle. ⚑ 16 **Facilities** Dogs allowed Garden Parking

POOLE   Map 4 SZ09

The Guildhall Tavern ⚑

15 Market St BH15 1NB
☎ 01202 671717 📄 01202 242346
e-mail: sewerynsevfred@aol.com
dir: *2 mins from Quay*

Originally a cider house, this pub stands in the heart of Poole's Old Town, just two minutes from the historic quay. Beautifully fresh fish and seafood dominate the bilingual menus, which reflect the owners' Gallic roots. Moules marinière followed by pan-fried skate wing with butter jus and fresh caper berries are typical offerings, but meat eaters should be satisfied with the likes of pan-fried Scotch beef with Roquefort blue cheese sauce. French themed evenings are held every month.

Closed: 1st 2wks Nov, Mon **Bar Meals** L served Tue-Sun 12-2.30 Av main course £17 **Restaurant** L served Tue-Sun 12-2.30 D served Tue-Sun 6-10 Fixed menu price fr £14.25 Av 3 course à la carte fr £30 ⊕ PUNCH TAVERNS ◀ Ringwood Best. ⚑ 7 **Facilities** Children's menu Dogs allowed Parking

The Rising Sun NEW ⚑

3 Dear Hay Ln BH15 1NZ ☎ 01202 771246
e-mail: paul@risingsunpoole.co.uk
dir: *7m from Wimborne B3073, A349 take A350 signed Poole/Channel Ferries*

A warm and relaxing atmosphere greets friends, family and business folk at this 18th-century listed gastro-pub just off the High Street in Poole. Salads, inventive sandwiches and hot dishes, including mussels, are the lunchtime staples, with daily blackboard specials reflecting the pub's coastal setting. Evening diners might expect poached seafood puff pastry pie with new potatoes; oven roasted halibut with chorizo dauphinoise; or root vegetable and Parmesan crumble. Round off, perhaps, with lemon posset and poached figs.

Open all day 11-11 Closed: Sun eve **Bar Meals** L served Mon-Sat 12-2.30, Sun 12-5 D served Mon-Sat 6-9.30 Av main course £9.50 **Restaurant** L served Mon-Sat 12-2.30, Sun 12-5 booking required D served Mon-Sat 6-10 booking required Av 3 course à la carte fr £20 ⊕ ENTERPRISE ◀ Amstel, Ringwood Best Bitter ♂ Thatchers Gold. ⚑ 10 **Facilities** Garden Parking

POWERSTOCK   Map 4 SY59

PICK OF THE PUBS

Three Horseshoes Inn ⚑

DT6 3TF ☎ 01308 485328 📄 01308 485229
e-mail: info@threehorseshoesinn.com
dir: *3m from Bridport off A3066 (Beaminster road)*

Popularly known as the 'Shoes', this pretty, rural Victorian inn is surrounded by some of Dorset's finest scenery. In the restaurant, fresh local produce is used wherever possible; even the herbs, for example, are picked each day from the garden. Light lunches are available, with the main carte coming into play in the evening. From this choose starters of grilled goats' cheese salad with orange and pinenut dressing; seared scallops with orange and fennel broth, or deep-fried prawns with chilli. Main courses include Powerstock organic lamb noisettes with roasted pepper and almond dressing; braised rabbit, wild mushroom and green peppercorn sauce; pan-fried pigeon breasts with bourguignon sauce; Dorset crab mornay; and honey-and soy-roasted red snapper fillet with saffron potatoes, courgettes and mixed leaves. Desserts - all home made - include lime and ginger cheesecake, and strawberry and basil crème brûlée.

Open all wk 11-3 6.30-11.30 (Sun noon-4 7-10.30pm) **Bar Meals** L served Mon-Sat 12-2.30, Sun 12-3 D served Mon-Sat 7-9, Sun 7-8.30 ⊕ PALMERS ◀ Palmer's IPA, Copper Ale ♂ Thatchers Gold. ⚑ 7 **Facilities** Play area Family room Dogs allowed Garden Parking

PUNCKNOWLE   Map 4 SY58

The Crown Inn ⚑

Church St DT2 9BN ☎ 01308 897711
e-mail: crownpuncknowle@btinternet.com
dir: *From A35, into Bridevally, through Litton Cheney. From B3157, inland at Swyre*

There's a traditional atmosphere within the rambling, low-beamed bars at this picturesque 16th-century thatched inn, which was once the haunt of smugglers on their way from nearby Chesil Beach to visit prosperous customers in Bath. Food ranges from light snacks and sandwiches to home-made dishes like lamb chops with mint sauce; mushroom and nut pasta with French bread; and tuna steak with basil and tomato sauce. Recent change of hands.

Open 12-3 6-11 Closed: Sun eve **Bar Meals** L served all wk 12-2 D served Mon-Sat 6-9 Av main course £8 **Restaurant** L served all wk 12-2 D served Mon-Sat 6-9 Av 3 course à la carte fr £18 ⊕ PALMERS ◀ Palmers IPA, 200 Premium Ale, Copper, Tally Ho! ♂ Thatchers Gold. ♈10 **Facilities** Children's menu Family room Dogs allowed Garden Parking

SHERBORNE — Map 4 ST61

The Digby Tap

Cooks Ln DT9 3NS ☎ 01935 813148 📳 01935 816768
dir: Telephone for directions

Old-fashioned town pub with stone-flagged floors, old beams and a wide-ranging choice of real ale. A hearty menu of pub grub includes lasagne, steak and kidney pie, rump steak, gammon steak, and plaice or cod. The pub was used as a location for the 1990 TV drama *A Murder of Quality*, that starred Denholm Elliot and Glenda Jackson. Scenes from the film can be seen on the pub walls.

Open all day all wk 11-11 (Sun noon-11) **Bar Meals** L served Mon-Sat 12-1.45 ⊕ FREE HOUSE ◀ Otter Bitter, Sharp's Cornish Coaster, St Austell Tinners ♂ Thatchers Gold. **Facilities** Family room Dogs allowed **Notes** ⊛

Queen's Head

High St, Milborne Port DT9 5DQ ☎ 01963 250314
e-mail: info@queenshead.co.uk
dir: On A30, 2.5m W of Sherborne towards Sailsbury

Milborne Port has no facilities for shipping, the suffix being Old English for 'borough', a status it acquired in 1249. The building came much later, in Elizabethan times, although no mention is made of it as a hostelry until 1738. Charming and friendly bars, restaurant, beer garden and skittle alley combine to make it a popular free house in these parts.

Open all wk 11-2.30 5.30-11.30 (Fri-Sat 11am-mdnt) **Bar Meals** L served all wk 12-2.30 booking required D served all wk 5.30-9.30 booking required Av main course £7.50 **Restaurant** L served all wk 12-2.30 booking required D served all wk 5.30-9.30 booking required ⊕ FNTERPRISE INNS ◀ Butcombe Bitters, Fuller's London Pride, Hopback Summer Lightning. **Facilities** Children's menu Dogs allowed Garden Parking

Skippers Inn ♈

Horsecastles DT9 3HE ☎ 01935 812753
e-mail: chrisfrowde@tiscali.co.uk
dir: From Yeovil A30 to Sherborne

'You don't need a newspaper in Skippers, read the walls'. So says the proprietor about his end-of-terrace converted cider house, and Sherborne's self-styled premier fish restaurant. The crammed blackboard menu has everything from game, duck, chicken and venison to steaks, sandwiches, soup, and around 12 fresh fish dishes. On Sunday there are three roasts to choose from.

Open all wk 11-2.30 6-11 (Sun 12-2 7-10.30) Closed: 25 Dec **Bar Meals** L served all wk 12-2 D served Mon-Sat 6.30-9, Sun 7-9 ⊕ WADWORTH ◀ Wadworth 6X, Henrys IPA, Guest ales ♂ Stowford Press. ♈8 **Facilities** Garden Parking

SHROTON OR IWERNE COURTNEY — Map 4 ST81

PICK OF THE PUBS

The Cricketers

DT11 8QD ☎ 01258 860421 📳 01258 861800
e-mail: cricketers@heartstoneinns.co.uk
dir: 7m S of Shaftesbury on A350, turn right after Iwerne Minster. 5m N of Blandford Forum on A360, past Stourpaine, in 2m left into Shroton. Pub in village centre

The Cricketers nestles under Hambledon Hill, which is renowned for its Iron Age hill forts. A classically English pub, built at the turn of the 20th century, which guarantees a warm welcome. The open plan interior comprises a main bar, comfy bars and pleasant eating areas - all light and airy rooms leading to the restaurant at the rear. This in turn overlooks a lovely garden, well stocked with trees and flowers. Inside, the cricket theme is taken up in the collection of sports memorabilia on display, and during the summer months the local cricket team really does frequent the establishment. The pub is

also popular with hikers, lured from the Wessex Way, which runs conveniently through the garden. Expect a menu which contains freshly prepared local favourites and a fine selection of specials, with perhaps locally shot venison and pheasant, and fish direct from the Cornish coast. Themed nights and regular events put the Cricketers firmly at the heart of the community.

Open all wk 11-3 6-11 (Sat-Sun 11-11 summer only) **Bar Meals** L served all wk 12-2.30 booking required D served Mon-Sat 6-9.30 booking required Av main course £9.95 **Restaurant** L served all wk 12-2.30 booking required D served Mon-Sat 6-9.30 booking required ⊕ FREE HOUSE ◀ Tribute Cornish Ale, Ringwood Best, Butcombe, Piddle Ale ♂ Stowford Press. **Facilities** Children's menu Garden Parking

STOKE ABBOTT — Map 4 ST40

The New Inn

DT8 3JW ☎ 01308 868333
dir: 1.5m from Beaminster

A welcoming 17th-century farmhouse turned village inn, with thatched roof, log fires and a beautiful garden. It offers three real ales, and an extensive menu of light meals such as grilled black pudding with caramelised apples, and cold smoked duck breast with plum chutney, plus a good choice of baguettes, sandwiches and vegetarian dishes. Specials might include pork schnitzel with sweet chili dip, scallops wrapped in bacon, and beef and mushroom pie.

Closed: Mon ⊕ PALMERS ◀ Palmers IPA & 200 Premium Ale, Tally Ho, Copper IPA. **Facilities** Dogs allowed Garden Parking

STRATTON — Map 4 SY69

Saxon Arms ♈

DT2 9WG ☎ 01305 260020
e-mail: rodsaxonlamont1@yahoo.co.uk
dir: 3m NW of Dorchester on A37, pub at back of village green between church & new village hall

With its solid oak beams, log-burning stove and flagstone floors, this pretty thatched free house stands overlooking the village green. Popular with fishermen and cycling clubs, the pub is also handy for riverside walks. Stowford Press cider offers a fresh alternative to the regularly changing selection of beers, whilst menu choices include Dorset ham, egg and chips; smoked haddock and spring onion fishcake; and warm spinach and feta cheese pie.

Open all wk 11-3 5.30-late (Sat-Sun 11am-late) **Bar Meals** L served Mon-Sat 11-2.15, Sun 12-9 booking required D served Mon-Sat 6-9.15, Sun 12-9 booking required Av main course £8.95 **Restaurant** L served Mon-Sat 11-2.15, Sun 12-9 booking required D served Mon-Sat 6-9.15, Sun 12-9 booking required Av 3 course à la carte fr £15 ⊕ FREE HOUSE ◀ Fuller's London Pride, Palmers IPA, Ringwood, Timothy Taylor, Butcombe, Abbot, Ruddles ♂ Stowford Press. ♈15 **Facilities** Children's menu Dogs allowed Garden Parking

STUDLAND · Map 5 SZ08

The Bankes Arms Hotel

Watery Ln BH19 3AU
☎ 01929 450225 📄 01929 450307
web: www.bankesarms.com
dir: *B3369 from Poole, across on Sandbanks chain ferry, or A35 from Poole, A351 then B3351*

Close to sweeping Studland Bay, across which can be seen the prime real estate enclave of Sandbanks, is this part 15th-century, creeper-clad inn, once a smugglers' dive. It specialises in fresh fish and seafood, but also offers game casserole, lamb noisettes in mint, honey and orange sauce, and spicy pork in chilli, coriander and caper sauce. The annual beer festival held in its large garden showcases 60 real ales, music, Morris dancing and stone carving.

Open all day all wk 11-11 Closed: 25 Dec **Bar Meals** L served Mon-Fri 12-3, Sat 12-9.30, Sun 12-9 (Summer & BH 12-9.30) D served Mon-Fri 6-9, Sat 12-9.30, Sun 12-9 (Summer & BH 12-9.30) ⊕ FREE HOUSE ◀ Isle of Purbeck Fossil Fuel, Studland Bay Wrecked, Solar Power, IPA Ö Westons. **Facilities** Dogs allowed Garden Parking

SYDLING ST NICHOLAS · Map 4 SY69

The Greyhound Inn ★★★★ INN ☗

DT2 9PD ☎ 01300 341303
e-mail: info@thegreyhounddorset.co.uk
dir: *Off A37 (Yeovil to Dorchester road), turn off at Cerne Abbas/Sydling St Nicholas*

A 17th-century inn with a walled garden, The Greyhound is set in a picturesque village complete with stream. Food is served in the bar or cosy restaurant, ranging from snacks to the full dining experience. Local seafood is a speciality, with dishes such as pan-fried monkfish with chorizo, fresh basil, cherry tomatoes and sherry, and there is a good choice of meat and game. Stylish and well-equipped accommodation is available, including ground floor rooms.

Open all wk 11-2.30 6-11 Closed: Sun eve **Bar Meals** L served all wk 12-2 booking required D served Mon-Sat 6-9 booking required **Restaurant** L served all wk 12-2 booking required D served Mon-Sat 6-9 booking required ⊕ FREE HOUSE ◀ Palmer IPA, Wadworth 6X, St Austell Tinners, Old Speckled Hen, Spitfire Ö Thatchers Gold. ☗ 7 **Facilities** Children's menu Play area Dogs allowed Garden Parking **Rooms** 6

TARRANT MONKTON · Map 4 ST90

PICK OF THE PUBS

The Langton Arms ★★★★ INN ◉ ☗

DT11 8RX ☎ 01258 830225 📄 01258 830053
e-mail: info@thelangtonarms.co.uk
dir: *A31 from Ringwood, or A357 from Shaftesbury, or A35 from Bournemouth*

Occupying a peaceful spot close to the village church, this attractive 17th-century thatched inn serves real ales from four pumps, including the house beer, Hidden Pint, which comes from the Hidden Brewery at Dinton, near Salisbury. The Stables restaurant and conservatory offers the sort of fulfilling meal that on a weekday might comprise marinated crispy beef from the Tarrant Valley, followed by real ale battered haddock, and then home-made mango, pineapple and passion fruit parfait. Or at lunchtime on Sunday, the same degree of satisfaction could well be derived from home-cured gravadlax; roast loin of pork and caramelised onion gravy; and a selection of West Country cheeses with biscuits, celery, grapes and chutney. A comprehensive menu is also available in both bars. Guest rooms are built in rustic brick around an attractive courtyard.

Open all day all wk **Bar Meals** L served Mon-Fri 12-2.30, Sat-Sun all day D served Mon-Thu 6-9.30, Fri 6-10, Sat-Sun all day **Restaurant** L served Mon-Fri 12-2.30, Sat-Sun all day D served Mon-Thu 6-9.30, Fri 6-10, Sat-Sun all day ⊕ FREE HOUSE ◀ Guest ales (all local). ☗ 7 **Facilities** Children's menu Play area Family room Dogs allowed Garden Parking **Rooms** 6

TRENT · Map 4 ST51

PICK OF THE PUBS

Rose & Crown Trent ☗

See Pick of the Pubs on opposite page

WEST BEXINGTON · Map 4 SY58

The Manor Hotel ★★ HL ☗

DT2 9DF ☎ 01308 897616 📄 01308 897704
e-mail: themanorhotel@btconnect.com
dir: *On B3157, 5m E of Bridport*

Overlooking the Jurassic Coast's most famous feature, Chesil Beach, parts of this ancient manor house date from the 11th century. It offers an inviting mix of flagstones, Jacobean oak panelling, roaring fires, comfortable en suite rooms, and a cosy cellar bar serving Dorset beer and organic cider. Locally sourced dishes include grilled John Dory; Peggy's Gloucester Old Spot sausages; butternut squash risotto; and, in season, jugged hare. Muddy boots, dogs or children won't raise any eyebrows.

Open all day all wk 11.30am-11pm **Bar Meals** L served all wk 12-2 D served all wk 6.30-9 ⊕ FREE HOUSE ◀ Butcombe Gold, Piddle Brewery Ö Ashton Press. ☗ 7 **Facilities** Play area Family room Dogs allowed Garden Parking **Rooms** 13

WEST LULWORTH · Map 4 SY88

The Castle Inn ☗

Main Rd BH20 5RN ☎ 01929 400311 📄 01929 400415
e-mail: office@lulworthinn.com
dir: *Follow village signs from A352 (Dorchester to Wareham road). Inn on right on B3070 through West Lulworth. Car park opposite*

In a delightful setting near Lulworth Cove, this family-run thatched village inn lies close to plenty of good walks. The friendly bars offer a traditional atmosphere in which to enjoy a pint of well-kept Isle of Purbeck. Outside, you'll find large tiered gardens packed with plants, and in summer there's a giant outdoor chess set. The wide-ranging menu includes chicken stroganoff, seafood stew, sirloin steak grill, and tuna steak. There's also a good vegetarian choice.

Open all wk Closed: 25 Dec **Bar Meals** L served all wk 12-2 D served all wk 7-10 Av main course £8.50 ⊕ FREE HOUSE ◀ John Smiths, Sharps, Isle of Purbeck, Piddle Ales, Palmers. ☗ 8 **Facilities** Children's menu Dogs allowed Garden Parking

WEYMOUTH · Map 4 SY67

The Old Ship Inn ☗

7 The Ridgeway DT3 5QQ
☎ 01305 812522 📄 01305 816533
dir: *3m from Weymouth town centre, at bottom of The Ridgeway*

Copper pans, old clocks and a beamed open fire create just the right atmosphere at this historic pub, while outside the terrace offers views over Weymouth. Thomas Hardy refers to it in his novels *Under the Greenwood Tree* and *The Trumpet Major*. A good range of jacket potatoes, baguettes and salads is supplemented by traditional pub favourites, and there are fish dishes among the daily specials.

Open all wk ⊕ PUNCH TAVERNS ◀ Greene King, Old Speckled Hen, Ringwood Best, guest ales. ☗ 7 **Facilities** Dogs allowed Garden Parking

PICK OF THE PUBS

Rose & Crown Trent 🍷

TRENT   Map 4 ST51

DT9 4SL
☎ 01935 850776   📠 01935 850776
e-mail: hkirkie@hotmail.com
web: www.roseandcrowntrent.com
dir: *Just off A30 between Sherborne & Yeovil*

You'll find this thatched, ivy-clad inn tucked away in the conservation village of Trent, opposite St Andrew's church. The original building was actually created in the 14th century to house workers erecting the church spire opposite. The present structure was completed in the 18th century, and in the years that followed it served as a farmhouse and an inn. Although recently refurbished, the pub's interior speaks eloquently of its past; the Trent Barrow Room, with a massive open fire, plenty of seating, old bottles and books, is the perfect place to retire once the drinks have been bought. Generations of farmers have beaten a path to this pub for a pint of ale or cider; these days, ales such as Wadworth's Bishop's Tipple and cider from Westons and Thatchers Gold ensure that the line of tradition is unbroken. Although new to the trade, owners Heather Kirk and Stuart Malcom have quickly established a menu of impressive home-cooked food made using a delightful array of regional ingredients, from village eggs to local cheeses. The light bites and lunch menu brings ploughman's lunches with home-made bread, and platters of tapas to share, as well as more substantial offerings such as a salmon, crab and coriander fishcake with sweet chilli dressing, followed by roast corn-fed chicken breast with black pudding and a tarragon cream sauce with sautéed potatoes and seasonal vegetables. In the evening, dinner might comprise grilled goats' cheese bruschetta with a beetroot and pear dressing followed by rump of lamb with a herb crust, crushed new potatoes and a redcurrant and port sauce. Traditional puddings include Bramley apple and sultana crumble with vanilla custard; and warm sticky toffee pudding with clotted cream ice cream and butterscotch sauce.

Open 12-3 6-11 (Sat-Sun 12-11) Closed: Mon **Bar Meals** L served Tue-Sun 12-3 D served Tue-Sat 6-9 Av main course £8.95 **Restaurant** L served Tue-Sun 12-3 D served Tue-Sat 6-9 Fixed menu price fr £12.95 Av 3 course à la carte fr £26.95 ⊕ WADWORTH ⬤ 6X, Henry's IPA, Horizon, Bishops Tipple, guest ale Ö Stowford Press, Thatchers Gold. ♇ 8 **Facilities** Children's menu Family room Dogs allowed Garden Parking

WINTERBORNE ZELSTON   Map 4 SY89

Botany Bay Inne ♀

DT11 9ET ☎ 01929 459227
dir: *A31 between Bere Regis & Wimborne Minster*

An obvious question: how did the pub get its name? Built in the 1920s as The General Allenby, it was changed about 17 years ago in belated recognition of prisoners from Dorchester jail who were required to spend a night nearby before transportation to Australia. Since no such fate awaits anyone these days, meals to enjoy at leisure include bacon-wrapped chicken breast; steak and kidney pudding; roasted Mediterranean vegetable Wellington; and fish catch of the day. Real ales are locally brewed.

Open all day all wk 10-3 6-11.30 **Bar Meals** L served all wk (breakfast)10-12 (lunch)12-2.15 D served all wk 6.30-9.30 ◀ Badger First Gold, Tanglefoot, Badger Smooth, Guest Ales. ♀7 **Facilities** Family room Dogs allowed Garden

WORTH MATRAVERS   Map 4 SY97

PICK OF THE PUBS

The Square and Compass NEW

BH19 3LF ☎ 01929 439229
dir: *Between Corfe Castle and Swanage. From B3069 follow signs for Worth Matravers*

Overlooking the English Channel, an unspoilt, stone-built pub, which has been run by the Newman family since 1907. Its simple interior – there is no bar, just a serving hatch – can have seen few radical changes in that time. Stone flags on the floor come from local quarries, there's a wood-burner in the tap-room, an open fire in the oak-panelled larger room, a museum of local artefacts (some dating from Roman times) and a collection of fossils from the nearby Jurassic Coast. Award-winning Wessex and West Country beers come straight from the barrel, and real ciders include Hecks and one home-pressed by landlord Charlie Newman. Any one of these will perfectly accompany a traditional hot pasty or pie, being the only food options. Live music is played in the evenings throughout the year. Take a walk along the South West Coastal Path to Tilly Whim Caves and Lulworth Cove.

Open all wk 12-3 6-11 (12-11 in summer) **Bar Meals** L served all wk D served all wk food served all day ⊕ FREE HOUSE ◀ Palmer's Copper Ale & Dorset Gold, RCH Pitchfork, Hop Back Summer Lightning Ⓞ Hecks Farmhouse, Single Variety. **Facilities** Dogs allowed Garden **Notes** ☺

CO DURHAM

AYCLIFFE   Map 19 NZ22

The County ♀

13 The Green, Aycliffe Village DL5 6LX
☎ 01325 312273 ▤ 01325 312273
e-mail: colettefarrell@btinternet.com
dir: *Off A167 into Aycliffe Village. Off Junct 59 A1(M)*

Quietly positioned overlooking the village green, the award-winning County can be found in Aycliffe village some four miles north of Darlington. A selection of good real ales is backed by half a dozen wines served by the glass. Using the best of local ingredients, especially top quality fish and game, the bistro-type daily specials board adds variety to the menu. Pub under new ownership.

Open all wk 12-3 6-11 Closed: 25 Dec, 1 Jan **Bar Meals** L served Mon-Sat 12-2, Sun 12-2.30 D served all wk 6-9 Av main course £8.95 **Restaurant** L served Mon-Sat 12-2, Sun 12-2.30 D served all wk 6-9 Av 3 course à la carte fr £22 ⊕ FREE HOUSE ◀ Jennings Cumberland Ale, Castle Eden. ♀7 **Facilities** Children's menu Parking

BARNARD CASTLE   Map 19 NZ01

PICK OF THE PUBS

The Bridge Inn & Restaurant NEW

See Pick of the Pubs on opposite page

PICK OF THE PUBS

The Morritt Arms Hotel ★★★ HL ♀

Greta Bridge DL12 9SE
☎ 01833 627232 ▤ 01833 627392
e-mail: relax@themorritt.co.uk
dir: *At Scotch Corner take A66 towards Penrith, after 9m turn at Greta Bridge. Hotel over bridge on left*

Situated in rural Teesdale, The Morritt Arms has been an inn for two centuries. Full of character, the bar, with its interesting Dickensian mural, is very much focused on food. Here the carte offers starters of pressed ham, black pudding, Wensleydale cheese and home-made chutney; chilli and garlic tiger prawns with soft egg noodles, spring onions and coriander; British beef carpaccio with garlic dressing; wild mushrooms on toast with poached Neasham egg, truffle and tarragon dressing. Main courses include slow roasted belly pork with bubble and squeak, roasted roots and mustard jus; pan-fried trout, saffron and pea risotto, parsley oil; Teesdale lamb rack, leek and mustard mash, parsnips and redcurrant jus; and Mediterranean vegetables, sun blushed tomatoes, goats' cheese and tomato sauce. You can also dine in the oak-panelled hotel restaurant, Pallatt's bistro, or the landscaped gardens. There are 27 individually styled en suite bedrooms available.

Open all day all wk 7am-11pm **Bar Meals** food served all day **Restaurant** L served all wk 12-3 D served all wk 7-9.30 ⊕ FREE HOUSE ◀ John Smith's, Timothy Taylor Landlord, Black Sheep Best. ♀20 **Facilities** Children's menu Play area Family room Dogs allowed Garden Parking **Rooms** 27

COTHERSTONE   Map 19 NZ01

The Fox and Hounds ♀

DL12 9PF ☎ 01833 650241
e-mail: foxenquiries@tiscali.co.uk
dir: *4m W of Barnard Castle. From A66 onto B6277, signed*

This delightful 18th-century coaching inn in the heart of Teesdale is a perfect holiday base. Both the restaurant and the heavily beamed bar boast welcoming winter fires in original fireplaces. Fresh local ingredients are the foundation of home-made food such as a warm salad of Wensleydale cheese, bacon, cranberries and apple; steak, black pudding and Black Sheep ale pie; or pan-fried crown of Holwick pheasant on bubble and squeak mash with rich gravy.

Open all wk 12-2.30 6.30-11 (Sun 6.30-10.30) Closed: 25-26 Dec **Bar Meals** L served all wk 12-2 D served all wk 6.30-9 **Restaurant** D served all wk 6.30-9 ⊕ FREE HOUSE ◀ Black Sheep Best, Village Brewer Bull Bitter, Black Sheep Ale, Daleside Special, Yorkshire Terrier. ♀10 **Facilities** Children's menu Garden Parking

DURHAM   Map 19 NZ24

Victoria Inn

86 Hallgarth St DH1 3AS ☎ 0191 386 5269
dir: *In city centre*

Just five minutes from the cathedral, and carefully nurtured by the Webster family since 1975, this unique listed inn has scarcely changed since it was built in 1899. Small rooms warmed by coal fires include the unusual off-sales booth and tiny snug, where a portrait of Queen Victoria still hangs above the upright piano. You'll find a few simple snacks to tickle the taste buds, but it's the well-kept local ales, single malts, and over 40 Irish whiskeys that are the main attraction.

Open all wk ⊕ FREE HOUSE ◀ Wylam Gold Tankard, Durham Magus, Big Lamp Bitter, Jarrow Bitter, Mordue ales. **Facilities** Family room Dogs allowed Parking

PICK OF THE PUBS

The Bridge Inn & Restaurant NEW

BARNARD CASTLE   Map 19 NZ01

Whorlton Village DL12 8XD
☎ 01833 627341   🖷 01833 627995
e-mail: info@thebridgeinnrestaurant.co.uk
web: www.thebridgeinnrestaurant.co.uk

It was a bold move that brought chef/ patron Paul O'Hara to this quaint village near Barnard Castle, after six years in charge of the kitchen at Durham's renowned Bistro 21. "It's a big change for people here," he said. "My idea is to fuse together the creativity and excitement of the city, with great local produce that's freshly available right here on my doorstep." No longer, then, do the good people of Teesdale have to travel miles to experience the taste and sophistication of city dining. Paul and his family (wife Naomi, children Thomas and Sophie, and half a dozen free range hens) are now slowly transforming The

Bridge, offering a couple of good real ales, an extensive wine list and a wide choice of food. In either the restaurant or outside, start with smoked eel fillet with roast beetroot and horseradish cream; or roast wood-pigeon breasts, and then try to decide between champagne risotto with wild mushrooms and Parmesan crisp; salmon and cod fishcakes; fillet and slow-cooked beef with shallots and two celeries; pot-roast pheasant with bacon, chestnuts and Brussels sprouts, or something from the vegetarian menu. Blackboards display specials such as poached fillet of wild sea bass, monkfish tails and scallops with spring onion risotto. To finish, perhaps profiteroles; apple and cinnamon crumble; creamed rice pudding; dark chocolate soufflé with boozy cherries and pistachio ice cream; or sticky toffee pudding with butterscotch sauce. A lunchtime Dine with Wine deal offers two courses for £11.50, or three for £14. Dinner Dine with Wine offers two courses for £14 and three for £16.50. There are also similar offers for Sunday Supper.

Open 12-2 6.30-11 Closed: 24 Dec eve, 25 & 26 Dec, Mon & Tue **Meals** L served Wed-Sun 12-2 D served Wed-Sat 6.30-11 (Sun 5.30-10) Fixed menu price fr £14 Av 3 course à la carte fr £26 ⬛ Timothy Taylor Landlord, Theakstons Black Bull. **Facilities** Children's menu Dogs allowed Garden Parking

FIR TREE
Map 19 NZ13

Duke of York Inn

DL15 8DG ☎ 01388 767429 📠 01388 767429
e-mail: duke.of.york@live.co.uk
dir: On A68, 12m W of Durham. From Durham take A690
W. Left onto A68 to Fir Tree

Recently refurbished inside and out to a high standard,
keeping the traditional country feel with contemporary
touches. A former drovers' and coaching inn dating from
1749, it stands on the tourist route (A68) to Scotland.
Typical dishes include steak and ale pie; and chicken
with pepper sauce, plus choices from the carvery and
grill.

Open all day all wk **Bar Meals** Av main course £6.95 food
served all day **Restaurant** Fixed menu price fr £9.95 Av 3
course à la carte fr £15.95 food served all day
🍺 CAMERONS BREWERY 🍺 Camerons Smooth,
Strongarm, Castle Eden Ale, Guinness. **Facilities** Garden
Parking

HUTTON MAGNA
Map 19 NZ11

PICK OF THE PUBS

The Oak Tree Inn 🍷

DL11 7HH ☎ 01833 627371
dir: From A1 at Scotch Corner take A66. 6.5m, right for
Hutton Magna

Expect a warm welcome at this whitewashed, part
18th-century free house run by Alastair and Claire
Ross. Alastair previously spent 14 years in London
working at The Savoy, Leith's and, more recently, a
private members' club on the Strand. Meals in the
simply furnished dining room are based around the
finest local ingredients, and dishes change daily
depending on what is available. The fish choices, in
particular, rely on what comes in on the boats. The
cooking style combines classic techniques and
occasional modern flavours: you could start with
butternut squash soup, hand-rolled linguine with
smoked haddock or seared duck breast salad. Typical
mains include royal sea bream fillets with Shetland
mussels; sea bass with crab and spinach cannelloni; or
haunch of local venison with mashed swede, roasted
ceps and venison sausage. As well as fine real ales,
extensive wine list, list of 20 whiskies, and menu of
bottled beers available.

Open 6-11 (Sun 5.30-10.30) Closed: Xmas & New Year,
Mon **Restaurant** D served Tue-Sun 6-9 booking
required Av 3 course à la carte fr £29.50 🍺 FREE
HOUSE 🍺 Wells Bombardier, Timothy Taylor Landlord,
Black Sheep Best. 🍷 8 **Facilities** Dogs allowed Parking

MIDDLESTONE
Map 19 NZ23

Ship Inn 🍷

Low Rd DL14 8AB ☎ 01388 810904
e-mail: tony.theshipinn@googlemail.com
dir: On B6287 (Kirk Merrington to Coundon road)

Beer drinkers will appreciate the string of real ale-related
accolades received by this family-run pub on the village
green. In the last five years regulars could have sampled
well over 800 different beers. Home-cooked food is served
in the bar and restaurant, using beef, pork and lamb
reared locally. The Ship has three unique attributes – it is
23 miles from the sea, 550 feet above sea level and the
cellar is 9 feet above the bar! The rooftop patio has
spectacular views over the Tees Valley and Cleveland
Hills.

Open all wk 4-11 Mon-Thu (Fri-Sun noon-11) **Bar Meals** L
served Fri-Sun 12-2 D served all wk 6-9 Av main course
£4.95 🍺 FREE HOUSE 🍺 6 guest ales. 🍷 13
Facilities Children's menu Play area Family room Dogs
allowed Parking

MIDDLETON-IN-TEESDALE
Map 18 NY92

The Teesdale Hotel ★★ HL

Market Square DL12 0QG
☎ 01833 640264 📠 01833 640651
e-mail: enquiries@teesdalehotel.com
dir: Telephone for directions

Just off the Pennine Way, this tastefully modernised,
family-run former coaching inn enjoys some of Britain's
loveliest scenery. It has a striking 18th-century stone
exterior and archway, while the interior is warm and
friendly, with well-furnished bedrooms and an open fire in
the bar. All food is home-made using local produce. A
typical meal might include black pudding with a spicy
plum sauce followed by steak and ale pie with chips and
mushy peas.

Open all day all wk **Bar Meals** L served all wk 12.30-2.30
D served all wk 7-9 Av main course £6.50 **Restaurant** D
served all wk 7-9 Fixed menu price fr £8.50 Av 3 course à
la carte fr £16.50 🍺 FREE HOUSE 🍺 Guinness, Tetley
Smooth, Black Sheep Best Bitter. **Facilities** Children's
menu Dogs allowed Parking **Rooms** 14

NEWTON AYCLIFFE
Map 19 NZ22

Blacksmiths Arms 🍷

Preston le Skerne, (off Ricknall Lane) DL5 6JH
☎ 01325 314873

A former smithy dating from the 1700s, and still relatively
isolated in its farmland setting. Enjoying an excellent
reputation locally as a good dining pub, it offers starters
of hot smoked mackerel and potato salad; cod and prawn
brandade; chicken fillet goujons; and potted mushrooms.
Requiring their own page on the menu are fish dishes
such as grilled halibut steak with risotto, and gingered
salmon. Chef's specialities include Gressingham duck
breast, and pork au poivre.

Closed: 1 Jan, Mon 🍺 FREE HOUSE 🍺 Ever changing
selection of real ales. 🍷 10 **Facilities** Children's menu
Play area Garden Parking

ROMALDKIRK
Map 19 NY92

PICK OF THE PUBS

Rose & Crown ★★ HL 🍷

See Pick of the Pubs on opposite page

SEDGEFIELD
Map 19 NZ32

Dun Cow Inn 🍷

43 Front St TS21 3AT
☎ 01740 620894 📠 01740 622163
e-mail: dunn_cow@btconnect.com
dir: At junct of A177 & A689. Inn in village centre

An interesting array of bric-a-brac can be viewed inside
this splendid old village inn, which has many flower
baskets bedecking its exterior in summer. Typical
offerings include Angus sirloin steaks, locally-made
sausages, spring lamb cutlets, fresh Shetland mussels,
and mushroom stroganoff. Pudding choices often include
gooseberry crumble and chocolate fudge cake with
butterscotch sauce.

Open all wk 11am-3pm, 6pm-mdnt **Bar Meals** L served
Mon-Sat 12-2, Sun 12-8 D served Mon-Sat 6.30-9.30,
Sun 12-8 **Restaurant** L served Mon-Sat 12-2, Sun 12-8
booking required D served Mon-Sat 6.30-9.30, Sun 12-8
booking required 🍺 FREE HOUSE 🍺 Theakston Best
Bitter, John Smiths Smooth, Black Sheeps Bitter, Guest
ales. 🍷 8 **Facilities** Children's menu Parking

TRIMDON
Map 19 NZ33

The Bird in Hand

Salters Ln TS29 6JQ ☎ 01429 880391
dir: Telephone for directions

Village pub nine miles west of Hartlepool with fine views
over surrounding countryside from an elevated position.
There's a cosy bar and games room, stocking a good
choice of cask ales and guest beers, a spacious lounge
and large conservatory restaurant. Traditional Sunday
lunch goes down well, as does breaded plaice and other
favourites. In summer you can sit outside in the garden,
which has a roofed over area for climbing plants.

Open all wk **Facilities** Family room Dogs allowed Garden
Parking

PICK OF THE PUBS

Rose & Crown ★★ HL  🌹🌹 🍷

ROMALDKIRK   Map 19 NY92

DL12 9EB
☎ 01833 650213   📠 01833 650828
e-mail: hotel@rose-and-crown.co.uk
dir: *6m NW from Barnard Castle on B6277*

Enjoying a picture-postcard setting in the heart of a pretty Teesdale village, on the green next to the Saxon church, and opposite the ancient stocks and water pump, this splendid, ivy-clad 18th-century inn is one of the great all-rounders, boasting a cosy pub with excellent bar food, a smart restaurant and stylish bedrooms. Step inside and you'll be met by warm smiles and the scent of fresh flowers. Polished panelling, old beams, crackling fires, gleaming copper and brass artefacts, and creaking stairs add to the rustic charm. The brasserie has deep red walls decorated with large pictures of aloof French waiters. In the restaurant, there's more oak panelling, crisp white tablecloths, sparkling silver and soft lights - the perfect setting for a romantic supper. Lunch in the bar from the daily-changing menu could start with leek, bacon and black pudding risotto or baked goat's cheese soufflé with chive cream. Expect main courses like crispy duck leg with beetroot compôte and port wine jus, and pan-fried pigeon with Puy lentils, pancetta and Madeira sauce. Desserts follow traditional lines, with the likes of hot ginger flapjack cake with vanilla ice cream. There are sandwiches and ploughman's and good children's meals, perhaps bangers, beans and chips, scrambled eggs on toast, or smoked Scotch salmon for the more sophisticated. Dinner in the restaurant is a fixed-price four-course affair and might offer seared scallops with leek risotto; courgette and sweet pear soup; chargrilled rib-eye steak with garlic mushrooms; and hot sticky walnut tart. Wash down with one of a raft of wines served by the glass. If staying the night, twelve beautifully furnished en suite bedrooms are equipped with Bose music systems. It's the perfect base for exploring stunning Teesdale.

Open 11-11 Closed: 23-27 Dec
Bar Meals L served all week 12-1.30 D served all week 6.30-9.30 Av main course £14 **Restaurant** L served Sun 12-1.30 D served all week 7.30-8.45 Fixed menu price fr £30 ⊕ FREE HOUSE 🍺 Theakston Best, Black Sheep Best. 🍷 14 **Facilities** Dogs allowed Parking **Rooms** 12

ESSEX

ARKESDEN — Map 12 TL43

PICK OF THE PUBS

Axe & Compasses ♀

See Pick of the Pubs on opposite page

AYTHORPE RODING — Map 6 TL51

Axe & Compasses ♀

CM6 1PP ☎ 01279 876648
e-mail: shunt36@msn.com
dir: *From A120 take junct for Dunmow*

Husband and wife team David and Sheila Hunt bought this weatherboarded 17th-century pub after it had stood empty for over two years; it reopened in 2007. In the bar, ales from small regional brewers such as Nethergate Old Growler and Saffron Walden Gold are backed by Weston's ciders. David, a skilled self-taught chef, loves to offer old favourites such as trio of pork (fillet, belly and banger) with parsnip purée and bubble and squeak; and rice pudding with raspberry jam.

Open all wk 11am-11.30pm (Sun noon-11) **Bar Meals** L served all wk 12-10 Av main course £5.50 food served all day **Restaurant** L served all wk 12-2.30 booking required D served Mon-Sat 6-10, Sun 12-8 booking required Av 3 course à la carte fr £19.95 ⊕ FREE HOUSE ◀ Brentwood Best, Nethergate Old Growler, Crouch Vale Brewers Gold, Woodforde's Wherry, Saffron Walden Gold Ö Westons Old Rosie, Weston's Scrumpy. ♀ 11 **Facilities** Dogs allowed Garden Parking

BLACKMORE — Map 6 TL60

PICK OF THE PUBS

The Leather Bottle ♀

The Green CM4 0RL ☎ 01277 821891
e-mail: leatherbottle@tiscali.co.uk
dir: *M25 junct 8 onto A1023, left onto A128, 5m. Left onto Blackmore Rd, 2m. Left towards Blackmore, 2m. Right then 1st left*

According to local legend, Henry VIII used to stable his horses here when he came to visit his mistress. There has been a pub on the site for over 400 years, but the original building burned down in 1954 and was rebuilt in 1956. The present day pub is a family-run affair with

James and Gwen Wallace at the helm and their daughter Sarah in charge of the restaurant. The bar is a cosy, inviting place to savour real ales, while the restaurant is smart, with modern furnishings. There's also an airy conservatory which opens onto the spacious enclosed garden. Food options include a very reasonably priced lunchtime menu, which might include seafood chowder followed by sausages and mash. Typical evening dishes are pan-fried lambs' kidneys with toasted pine nuts and balsamic syrup, followed by a pork chop with roasted root vegetables, topped with apple and date chutney.

Open all wk **Bar Meals** L served all wk 12-2 D served all wk 7-9 Av main course £10.95 **Restaurant** L served all wk 12-2 D served all wk 7-9 Fixed menu price fr £9.95 Av 3 course à la carte fr £22 ⊕ FREE HOUSE ◀ Adnams Best, Adnams Broadside, Deuchars IPA, Woodforde's Wherry, Cottage Cactus Jack. ♀ 8 **Facilities** Garden

BRAINTREE — Map 7 TL72

PICK OF THE PUBS

The Green Dragon at Young's End ♀

Upper London Rd, Young's End CM77 8QN
☎ 01245 361030 📠 01245 362575
e-mail: info@thegreendragonyoungsend.co.uk
dir: *At Braintree bypass take A131 S towards Chelmsford, exit at Young's End on Great Leighs bypass*

The Green Dragon provides a comfortable venue for good drinking and dining, with winter fires creating a cosy atmosphere in the friendly bars, which are smartly decked in contemporary designs and lots of original exposed beams and stylish furnishings. The spacious restaurant maintains the rustic theme with bare brick walls and wonderful old beams. Outside there's a large garden and heated patio area. The bar menu offers the likes of beer-battered cod and chips, Essex bangers and mash, omelettes, jackets and sandwiches, while the restaurant goes in for dishes like chicken breast stuffed with brie and bacon, steak and ale pie, or halibut with mussels and tagliatelle of leek. There is also the option of private dining in the Hayloft Restaurant.

Open all wk **Bar Meals** L served Mon-Sat 12-3, Sun all day D served Mon-Sat 6-9, Sun all day Av main course £7.50 **Restaurant** L served Mon-Sat 12-3, Sun all day booking required D served Mon-Sat 6-9, Sun all day booking required Av 3 course à la carte fr £9.95 ⊕ GREENE KING ◀ Greene King IPA , Abbot Ale. ♀ 10 **Facilities** Children's menu Garden Parking

BURNHAM-ON-CROUCH — Map 7 TQ99

Ye Olde White Harte Hotel

The Quay CM0 8AS ☎ 01621 782106 📠 01621 782106
dir: *Along high street, right before clocktower, right into car park*

Directly overlooking the River Crouch, the hotel dates from the 17th century and retains many original features, including exposed beams. It also has its own private jetty. The food is mainly English-style with such dishes as roast leg of English lamb, local roast Dengie chicken and seasoning, and grilled fillet of plaice and lemon. There is also a range of bar snacks including toasted and plain sandwiches, jacket potatoes, and soup.

Open all wk ⊕ FREE HOUSE ◀ Adnams Bitter, Crouch Vale Best. **Facilities** Dogs allowed Parking

CASTLE HEDINGHAM — Map 13 TL73

The Bell Inn ♀

Saint James St CO9 3EJ ☎ 01787 460350
e-mail: bell-castle@hotmail.co.uk
web: www.hedinghambell.co.uk
dir: *On A1124 N of Halstead, right to Castle Hedingham*

Run by the same family for over 40 years, this unspoilt pub began life in the 15th century as a coaching inn. Today it oozes traditional charm, from log fires in winter to a huge orchard garden and vine-covered patio for summer lounging. Food from quality local suppliers is home cooked and largely traditional, although the Turkish chef offers interesting specials such as grilled lamb meatballs. Fish is hand-picked from Billingsgate or delivered fresh from Colchester. Summer and winter beer festivals are a feature.

Open all wk 11.45-3 6-11 (Fri-Sat noon-mdnt Sun noon-11) Closed: 25 Dec eve **Bar Meals** L served Mon-Fri 12-2, Sat-Sun 12-2.30 D served Sun-Mon 7-9, Tue-Sat 7-9.30 Av main course £8.50 ⊕ GRAYS ◀ Maldon Gold Mighty Oak, Adnams Bitter, Mighty Oak IPA, guest ale Ö Stowford Press. ♀ 8 **Facilities** Children's menu Play area Family room Dogs allowed Garden Parking

PICK OF THE PUBS

Axe & Compasses 🍷

ARKESDEN
Map 12 TL43

High St CB11 4EX
☎ 01799 550272 📄 01799 550906
dir: *From Buntingford take B1038 towards Newport. Then left for Arkesden*

Always known as the 'Axe' in the local vernacular, this old pub stands in the centre of a pretty village through which runs Wicken Water, a gentle stream spanned by footbridges leading to picture-postcard white, cream and pink-washed thatched cottages. The main section of the building, itself also thatched, which dates from 1650, is now the comfortable lounge containing easy chairs and settees, antique furniture and clocks, horse brasses and maybe the warming glow of an open fire. The part to the right is the public bar, built in the early 19th century as stabling, a function it performed until the 1920s. Meals in here range from sandwiches to monkfish with roasted red pepper sauce or pork loin with Stilton. In the cosy, softly lit restaurant area, which seats 50 on various levels, agricultural implements adorn the old beams. Here, the menu offers a good selection of starters, including fillet of plaice with mushrooms or deep fried brie wedges with a redcurrant and port coulis. There's a good choice of main courses too, examples being breadcrumbed tenderloin of pork, finished with ham and cheese with whole grain mustard sauce; or supreme of chicken Kiev with mushroom duxelle. Vegetarians may choose spinach and potato cakes, on a tomato and basil sauce; or farfalle pasta with mushrooms, courgette, white wine and cream. Round off with popular desserts from the trolley such as trifle of the day, or summer pudding. House wines are modestly priced. On a fine day many drinkers and diners head for the patio.

Open noon-2.30 6-11 (Sun noon-3 7-10.30) **Bar Meals** L served all wk 12-2 D served all wk 6.45-9.30 Av main course £15 **Restaurant** L served all wk 12-2 D served all wk 6.45-9.30 Fixed menu price fr £19 Av 3 course à la carte fr £28 ⊕ GREENE KING ◧ Greene King IPA, Abbot Ale, Old Speckled Hen. 🍷 14 **Facilities** Garden Parking

CHAPPEL — Map 13 TL82

The Swan Inn ♀

CO6 2DD ☎ 01787 222353 🖹 01787 220012
e-mail: theswan@cipubs.com
web: www.theswaninnchappel.co.uk
dir: *Pub visible just off A1124 (Colchester to Halstead road), from Colchester 1st left after viaduct*

This rambling low-beamed free house stands in the shadow of a magnificent Victorian railway viaduct, and boasts a charming riverside garden with overflowing flower tubs. Fresh meat arrives daily from Smithfield, and fish from Billingsgate. Typically the seafood may include crispy sole fillets, deep-fried monkfish or poached skate, while the grill comes into its own with prime steaks, platters of surf'n'turf, English pork chops and calves' liver and bacon. There are daily vegetarian specials, and home-made desserts too.

Open all wk 11-3 6-11 (Sat 11-11 Sun noon-10.30) **Bar Meals** L served Mon-Sat 12-2.30, Sun 12-8 D served Mon-Sat 6-9.30, Sun 12-8 ⊕ FREE HOUSE ◀ Adnam Bitter, Broadside, Guest Ale ♂ Aspalls. ♀ 6 **Facilities** Play area Dogs allowed Garden Parking

CHELMSFORD — Map 6 TL70

The Alma ♀

37 Arbour Ln CM1 7RG ☎ 01245 256783
e-mail: alma@cipubs.com
dir: *Telephone for directions*

Named after the bloodiest battle of the Crimean war, The Alma was built in the late 19th century as an alehouse for soldiers recovering in the neighbouring hospital. The present owners have refurbished the pub to give it a contemporary edge, and the menu follows suit with a stylish mix of traditional and modern dishes - perhaps monkfish with Parma ham, a crab cake and asparagus tips; or parsnip tart with pumpkin risotto.

Open all day all wk 11-11 (Fri-Sat 11-mdnt, Sun noon-10.30) Closed: 25 Dec pm **Bar Meals** L served Mon-Sat 12-2.30, Sun 12-8 D served Mon-Sat 6-9.30, Sun 12-8 ⊕ FREE HOUSE ◀ Adnams ♂ Aspalls. ♀ 11 **Facilities** Garden Parking

CLAVERING — Map 12 TL43

PICK OF THE PUBS

The Cricketers ♀

CB11 4QT ☎ 01799 550442 🖹 01799 550882
e-mail: info@thecricketers.co.uk
dir: *From M11 junct 10, A505 E. Then A1301, B1383. At Newport take B1038*

With landlords called Sally and Trevor Oliver, it might come as no surprise to learn that this newly refurbished, 16th-century village pub is where celebrity chef Jamie first learnt to devil a kidney. Its proximity to the cricket pitch long ago suggested that appropriate memorabilia should decorate the beamed, log fire-warmed bar and restaurant, both of which offer seasonally changing menus and daily specials. Head chef, Justin Greig, is passionate about using excellent produce. Typical are meat and vegetarian antipasti; braised rabbit with home-made gnocchi and mixed wild mushrooms; pavé of Scottish salmon on crab spaghetti; sautéed calf's liver and bacon with Szechuan spiced potatoes; and spinach and feta filo pastry pie, while there's always plenty of fish, and a roast every Sunday. The celebrity chef himself supplies the vegetables, herbs and leaves from his certified organic garden nearby. The children's menu steers clear of the 'dreaded nuggets'.

Open all day all wk Closed: 25-26 Dec **Bar Meals** L served all wk 12-2 booking required D served all wk 6.30-9.30 booking required Av main course £13 **Restaurant** L served all wk 12-2 booking required D served all wk 6.30-9.30 booking required Av 3 course à la carte fr £29.50 ⊕ FREE HOUSE ◀ Adnams Bitter, Tetley Bitter, Greene King IPA, Adnams Broadside, Woodforde's Wherry, Nog ♂ Aspall. ♀ 10 **Facilities** Children's menu Play area Family room Garden Parking

COLCHESTER — Map 13 TL92

The Rose & Crown Hotel ★★★ HL ⊛⊛ ♀

East St CO1 2TZ ☎ 01206 866677 🖹 01206 866616
e-mail: info@rose-and-crown.com
dir: *From M25 junct 28 take A12 N. Follow Colchester signs*

The Rose & Crown is a beautiful timber-framed building dating from the 14th century, believed to be the oldest hotel in the oldest town in England, just a few minutes' from Colchester Castle. The Tudor bar with its roaring fire is a great place to relax with a drink. Food is served in the Oak Room, the main restaurant awarded two AA rosettes, or the Tudor Room brasserie, an informal alternative serving classic bar food.

Open all wk **Bar Meals** L served all wk 12-2.30 D served all wk 6.30-9.30 Av main course £10 ⊕ FREE HOUSE ◀ Tetley's Bitter, Rose & Crown Bitter, Adnams Broadside. ♀ 7 **Facilities** Children's menu Family room Parking **Rooms** 38

DEDHAM — Map 13 TM03

Marlborough Head Inn ♀

Mill Ln CO7 6DH ☎ 01206 323250
e-mail: jen.pearmain@tiscali.co.uk
dir: *E of A12, N of Colchester*

Tucked away in glorious Constable Country, a 16th-century building that was once a clearing-house for local wool merchants. In 1660, after a slump in trade, it became an inn. Today it is as perfect for a pint, sofa and newspaper as it is for a good home-cooked family meal. Traditional favourites such as steak, Guinness and mushroom pie; and lamb shank with red wine and rosemary appear on the menu, plus fish is given centre stage on Fridays.

Open all wk 11.30-11 **Bar Meals** Av main course £8.95 food served all day **Restaurant** food served all day ⊕ PUNCH ◀ Adnams Southwold, Greene King IPA ♂ Aspall. ♀ 8 **Facilities** Children's menu Family room Dogs allowed Garden Parking

PICK OF THE PUBS

The Sun Inn INN ⊛ ♀

High St CO7 6DF ☎ 01206 323351
e-mail: office@thesuninndedham.com
dir: *From A12 follow signs to Dedham for 1.5m, pub on High Street*

Owner Piers Baker has transformed the Sun from a run-down village boozer to an inn of fine repute. With open fires, oak beams, a sun-trap terrace and walled garden, you'll find character everywhere you look. Here, a quiet pint goes hand in hand with robust food and drink; there's a decent selection of real ales and a respectable wine list, with up to twenty wines available by the glass. Locally sourced seasonal ingredients drive the menu of modern British dishes: expect roast partridge with pear, braised lentils and baked radicchio; baked organic salmon with chickpeas, Swiss chard, chilli and mint; and molten chocolate baby cake with cream. If you can't quite tear yourself away, the Sun boasts five en suite guest rooms with large comfy beds, crisp linen, character furniture, great showers and lazy continental breakfasts.

Open all day all wk 11am-11pm Closed: 25-27 Dec **Bar Meals** L served Mon-Thu 12-2.30, Fri-Sun 12-3 D served Sun-Thu 6.30-9.30, Fri-Sat 6.30-10 ⊕ FREE HOUSE ◀ Brewer's Gold Crouch Vale, Adnam's Broadside, 2 guest ales ♂ Aspall. ♀ 20 **Facilities** Family room Dogs allowed Garden Parking **Rooms** 5

EARLS COLNE
Map 13 TL82

PICK OF THE PUBS

The Carved Angel ☻

Upper Holt St CO6 2PG
☎ 01787 222330 🖨 01787 220013
e-mail: info@carvedangel.com
dir: A120 onto B1024 to Coggeshall, right at junct with A1124, pub 300yds on right

Once a haven for monks and nuns escaping persecution by Henry VIII, this 15th-century village inn is now a popular gastropub with a stylish bar and restaurant. Traditional ales from Adnams and Greene King are offered alongside continental beers and a global wine list. Frequently changing menus are created from fresh seasonal ingredients, with the aim of offering a high standard of food but in a relaxed setting at reasonable prices. The kitchen turns out well-crafted dishes such as prawn tails fried in tempura with home-made tartare sauce; confit of duck with caramelised apple and a burgundy and sage reduction; and iced rhubarb parfait with a winter berries compote. The lunch special menu is particularly good value. Special events are held on a regular basis, for Mothering Sunday, Valentine's Day and so on.

Open all wk Closed: 26 Dec, 1 Jan ⊕ FREE HOUSE ◀ Greene King IPA, Adnams Bitter. ☻ 14 **Facilities** Garden Parking

ELSENHAM
Map 12 TL52

The Crown

The Cross, High St CM22 6DG ☎ 01279 812827
e-mail: enquiries@thecrownelsenham.co.uk
dir: M11 junct 8 towards Takeley. Left at lights

A pub for 200 years, with oak beams, open fireplaces and Essex pargetting at the front. The menu, which has a large selection of fresh fish, might offer baked trout with toasted almonds, steak and kidney pie, Crown mixed grill with onion rings, a choice of steaks cooked to order, or breast of duck with peppercorn sauce. There's a good choice of vegetarian choices as well, plus lighter bites and jacket potatoes.

Open all day all wk noon-mdnt **Bar Meals** L served Mon-Fri 12-2.30, Sat 12-9.30, Sun 12-8 D served Mon-Fri 6-9.30, Sat 12-9.30, Sun 12-8 ⊕ PUNCH RETAIL ◀ IPA, Guinness, Guest Ale. **Facilities** Dogs allowed Garden Parking

FAIRSTEAD
Map 7 TL71

The Square and Compasses NEW ☻

Fuller St CM3 2BB ☎ 01245 361477 🖨 01245 361548
e-mail: info@thesquareandcompasses.co.uk
web: www.thesquareandcompasses.co.uk
dir: A131 Chelmsford to Braintree. Take Great Leighs exit, enter village turn right into Boreham rd. Turn left signed Fuller St & Terling. Pub on left as you enter hamlet

Brought back to life following a two-year closure, this lovingly restored 17th-century pub stands in a sleepy hamlet and is worth seeking out for local micro-brewery ales – try a pint of Stokers Ale – and hearty pub food cooked from local seasonal produce. Eat in the main bar, adorned with old farming tools, or at old oak tables by the fire in the dining room. Choose a classic chicken and leek pie or follow chilli and lime squid with pheasant and rabbit casserole, and chocolate cheesecake.

Open all wk 11.30-3 6-11 (Sat-Sun noon-11) **Bar Meals** L served Mon-Fri 12-2, Sat 12-2.30, Sun 12-4 D served Tue-Sat 6.30-9.30 booking required Av main course £10 **Restaurant** L served Tue-Fri 12-2, Sat 12-2.30, Sun 12-4 D served Tue-Sat 6.30-9.30 booking required Av 3 course à la carte fr £22 ⊕ FREE HOUSE ◀ Stokers Ales, Oscar Wilde, Mighty Oak, Suffolk County, Nethergate, Hophead Dark Star ○ Stowford Press, Thatchers. ☻ 14 **Facilities** Children's menu Dogs allowed Garden Parking

FEERING
Map 7 TL82

The Sun Inn ☻

Feering Hill CO5 9NH
☎ 01376 570442 🖨 01376 570442
e-mail: andy.howard@virgin.net
dir: On A12 between Colchester & Witham. Village 1m

Real ale and real food are at the heart of this pretty, timbered pub that dates from 1525. There's a large garden for the summer months, while winter warmth comes from two inglenook fireplaces. There are no TVs or games machines; instead the customers create the atmosphere. Food-wise, expect simple, seasonal dishes; perhaps tempura-battered prawns followed by fresh fish in a Spitfire ale batter with chips, peas and home-made tartare sauce, with plum crumble for pudding.

Open all wk **Bar Meals** L served Mon-Sat 12-2.30, Sun 12-9 D served Mon-Sat 6-9.30, Sun 12-9 Av main course £8 **Restaurant** L served Mon-Sat 12-2.30, Sun 12-9 D served Mon-Sat 6-9.30, Sun 12-9 ⊕ SHEPHERD NEAME ◀ Master Brew, Spitfire, Bishops Finger, seasonal ale. ☻ 8 **Facilities** Children's menu Dogs allowed Garden Parking

FELSTED
Map 6 TL62

PICK OF THE PUBS

The Swan at Felsted ☻

See Pick of the Pubs on page 180

FINGRINGHOE
Map 7 TM02

The Whalebone ☻

Chapel Rd CO5 7BG ☎ 01206 729307
e-mail: vicki@thewhaleboneinn.co.uk
dir: Telephone for directions

This Grade II listed 18th-century free house has panoramic views of the Roman river valley. The Whalebone has wooden floors, aubergine walls, unique artwork and sculptures, and roman blinds. The unusual name comes from bones, once fastened above the door of the pub, which came from a locally beached whale. Another unusual feature is the oak tree nearby, thought to be the largest in Essex. Legend has it that the tree grew from an acorn in the mouth of a pirate executed and buried there some centuries ago. No acorns on the menu though, just hearty home-made dishes like roasted poussin with ricotta, gorgonzola and mortadella; chargrilled sirloin steak and chips; roast belly of Suffolk pork; and roasted sea bass with vermouth braised fennel.

Open all wk noon-3 5.30-11 (Sat noon-11 Sun noon-10.30) **Bar Meals** L served Mon-Sat 12-2.30, Sun 12-3 (winter) 12-8 (summer) D served Mon-Thu 6.30-9, Fri-Sat 6.30-9.30, Sun 12-8 (summer) ⊕ FREE HOUSE ◀ 4 Guest Ales ○ Aspalls. ☻ 7 **Facilities** Dogs allowed Garden Parking

GOSFIELD
Map 13 TL72

The Green Man ☻

The Street CO9 1TP ☎ 01787 472746
dir: Take A131 N from Braintree then A1017 to village

A pink-washed medley of buildings housing a smart village dining pub, where Cumberland sausage, cottage pie, haddock fillet and spinach and ricotta cannelloni feature among good value lunch and dinner possibilities. Additional choices in the evening include a full rack of ribs with honey or mustard sauce, mushrooms, onion rings and chips; rump, rib-eye and fillet steaks; and chicken supreme.

Open noon-3.30 6-10 (Fri noon-3.30 6-11, Sat noon-3.30 6-mdnt, Sun noon-5) Closed: Sun & Mon eves **Bar Meals** L served Mon-Sat 12-2.30, Sun 12-4 D served Tue-Sat 6-9.30 ⊕ GREENE KING ◀ Greene King IPA. ☻ 6 **Facilities** Garden Parking

PICK OF THE PUBS

The Swan at Felsted ♀

FELSTED   Map 6 TL62

Station Rd CM6 3DG
☎ **01371 820245**   📠 **01371 821393**
e-mail: info@theswanatfelsted.co.uk
web: www.theswanatfelsted.co.uk
dir: *Exit M11 junct 8 onto A120 signed Felsted. Pub in village centre*

Venture through the door of this rather unprepossessing red brick-and-timber building and be pleasantly surprised. Rebuilt after a disastrous fire in the early 1900s and formally the village bank, then a run-down boozer, it was rescued and stylishly refurbished by

Jono and Jane Clarke in 2002. Today it's very much a gastro-pub, with polished wood floors, leather sofas, chunky furnishings and colourful modern art, and successfully balances being a traditional pub and a quality restaurant. The atmosphere is friendly and informal and locals beat a path to the door for cracking Greene King ales and imaginative menus that champion locally sourced produce. Menus are sensibly short, the pubby lunch choice taking in honey roast ham, egg and hand-cut chips, macaroni cheese with tomato and herb crust, and beer-battered fish and chips. Cooking moves up a gear in the evening, with pan-seared scallops with cauliflower purée and lamb rump with Puy lentils and winter vegetables to choose from. Worth noting as Stansted Airport is just 10 minutes away.

Open noon-3 5-11 (Sun noon-6) **Bar Meals** L served Mon-Sat 12-2.30, Sun 12-4 D served Mon-Sat 6-9.30 **Restaurant** L served Mon-Sat 12-2.30, Sun 12-4 D served Mon-Sat 6-9.30 ⊕ GREENE KING ◀ IPA, Prospect, Guinness & guest ale ♂ Stowford Press. ♀ 9 **Facilities** Children's menu Dogs allowed Garden Parking

GREAT BRAXTED
Map 7 TL81

The Ducane ♟

The Village CM8 3EJ
☎ 01621 891697 📠 01621 890009
e-mail: eat@theducane.co.uk
dir: *Great Braxted signed between Witham & Kelvedon on A12*

Walkers and cyclists mingle with the locals at this friendly pub, built in 1935 at the heart of this leafy village. Chef/patron Jonathan Brown has cooked to the highest standards for over 25 years. His aim, together with sous-chef Louise Partis, is to source the very best of local seasonal produce, prepare hearty plates of quality food, and look after customers with attentive service. Adnams Bitter, Maldon Gold and Farmers Ales are among the draught beers on offer.

Closed: Mon **Bar Meals** L served Tue-Sun 12-2.30 booking required D served Tue-Sat 7-9.30 booking required Av main course £8.50 **Restaurant** L served Tue-Sun 12-2.30 booking required D served Tue-Sat 7-9.30 booking required Fixed menu price fr £12.95 Av 3 course à la carte fr £18.50 ⊕ FREE HOUSE ◀ Adnams Bitter, Bass Bitter, Maldon Gold, Farmers Ales. ♟ 8
Facilities Dogs allowed Garden Parking

GREAT YELDHAM
Map 13 TL73

The White Hart ★★★★ RR ⊛ ♟

Poole St CO9 4HJ ☎ 01787 237250 📠 01787 238044
e-mail: mjwmason@yahoo.co.uk
dir: *On A1017 between Haverhill & Halstead*

Highwaymen were once locked up in a small prison under the stairs of this impressive, 500-year-old, timber-framed inn. An express lunch menu offers Adnams beer-battered cod; pork and leek sausages; and Mr Wu's chicken curry. Those with more time to spare might opt for local Auberie Estate fillet of venison; Colne Valley rack of lamb; or baked monkfish.

Open all wk ⊕ FREE HOUSE ◀ Adnams Bitter, Black Sheep, Adnams Broadside. ♟ 7 **Facilities** Play area Garden Parking **Rooms** 11

HORNDON ON THE HILL
Map 6 TQ68

PICK OF THE PUBS

Bell Inn & Hill House ♟

See Pick of the Pubs on page 182

INGATESTONE
Map 6 TQ69

The Red Lion ♟

Margaretting CM4 0EQ ☎ 01277 352184
e-mail: shunt36@msn.com
dir: *3m from Chelmsford town centre off A12*

The 17th-century Red Lion is what most would describe as a quintessential English pub. The bar area is decorated in warm shades of burgundy and aubergine, the restaurant in light coffee and cream. Seasonal menu highlights include steamed mussels; chicken, leek and mushroom pie; and calf's liver, smoked bacon and bubble and squeak at lunch, and deep-fried Lowestoft cod; chargrilled rib-eye steak; and butternut squash, broad bean and mushroom risotto at dinner.

Open all wk 11am-3 5.30-11pm (Sat-Sun 11am-11pm) **Bar Meals** L served Mon-Fri 12-2.30, Sat 12-9.30, Sun 12-8 D served Mon-Fri 5.30-9.30, Sat 12-9.30, Sun 12-8 ⊕ GREENE KING ◀ Greene King IPA, 2 guest ales. ♟ 11 **Facilities** Play area Dogs allowed Garden Parking

LANGHAM
Map 13 TM03

The Shepherd and Dog ♟

Moor Rd CO4 5NR ☎ 01206 272711 📠 01206 273136
dir: *A12 from Colchester towards Ipswich, take 1st left signed Langham*

Situated on the Suffolk/Essex border, in Constable country, this 1928 freehouse has the classic styling of an English country pub. Widely renowned for its food, the Shepherd and Dog serves an extensive variety of meat, fish and poultry dishes, plus a vegetarian selection and a children's menu.

Open all wk ⊕ FREE HOUSE ◀ Greene King IPA, Abbot Ale, guest ales. ♟ 6 **Facilities** Dogs allowed Garden Parking

LITTLE CANFIELD
Map 6 TL52

The Lion & Lamb ♟

CM6 1SR ☎ 01279 870257 📠 01279 870423
e-mail: info@lionandlamb.co.uk
dir: *M11 junct 8, B1256 towards Takeley & Little Canfield*

A favourite for business or leisure, this traditional country pub restaurant is handy for Stansted airport and the M11. Inside you'll find oak beams, winter log fires, and an extensive food selection. From the bar menu choose sandwiches, steak and ale pie, Lion & Lamb beef burger, lasagne or sausage and mash. In the restaurant sample vegetable moussaka of red lentils and aubergine, Thai red beef curry, or a kangaroo fillet from the grill!

Open all wk 11-11 **Bar Meals** Av main course £9 food served all day **Restaurant** Av 3 course à la carte fr £25 food served all day ⊕ GREENE KING ◀ Old Speckled Hen, Greene King IPA, Old Bob, guest ales. ♟ 10 **Facilities** Children's menu Play area Garden Parking

See Advert on page 183

LITTLE DUNMOW
Map 6 TL62

Flitch of Bacon

The Street CM6 3HT
☎ 01371 820323 📠 01371 820338
dir: *B1256 to Braintree for 10m, turn off at Little Dunmow, 0.5m pub on right*

A 15th-century country inn whose name refers to the ancient gift of half a salted pig, or 'flitch', to couples who have been married for a year and a day, and 'who have not had a cross word'.

Closed: Mon lunch ⊕ FREE HOUSE ◀ Fuller's London Pride, Greene King IPA. **Facilities** Family room Dogs allowed Garden Parking

PICK OF THE PUBS

Bell Inn & Hill House ♟

HORNDON ON THE HILL　Map 6 TQ68

High Rd SS17 8LD
☎ **01375 642463**　📄 **01375 361611**
e-mail: info@bell-inn.co.uk
dir: *M25 junct 30/31 signed Thurrock*

The Bell is a 15th-century coaching inn, as the archway through to the courtyard testifies. From the first-floor gallery that runs above the courtyard, luggage would once have been transferred to and from the top of the London stagecoaches. Once you are inside, look for the original king post that supports the inn's ancient roof timbers. An unusual tradition taking place at the Bell every year requires the oldest willing villager to hang a hot cross bun from a beam in the saloon bar, a custom that dates back about 100 years when the pub once happened to change hands on a Good Friday. Two bars serve a selection of regularly changing real ales, including Crouch Vale Brewers

Gold from Chelmsford. From the extensive wine list, plenty can be served by the glass; you may also purchase a bottle at the 'off-sales' price. The bar menu offers lunchtime sandwiches and light meals such as pan-fried fishcakes with poached egg and hollandaise; and braised lamb's liver with mustard mash and red wine sauce. From the daily-changing restaurant menu, built around the freshest produce, you might start with Loch Fyne smoked salmon with scrambled egg and cheddar rarebit; pan-fried snails with Café de Paris butter in puff pastry; or cream of parsnip soup with croutons. For your main course, options might include roast duck with balsamic roast fig and cranberry compote; pan-fried scallops with mushy peas and oyster dressing; or wild mushroom ravioli with sauté of wild mushroom and Parmesan. Stylish desserts could prove somewhat tempting: try Bramley apple, sultana and cinnamon filo millefeuille with caramel ice cream; or caramelised pannacotta with rhubarb compote, ginger ice cream and lemon shortbread. Accommodation is also available in Hill House, almost next door to the Bell.

Open all week Closed: 25-26 Dec
Bar Meals L served all week 12-1.45 D served all week 6.30-9.45 Av main course £15.95 **Restaurant** L served Mon-Sat 12-1.45, Sun 2-2.30 D served all week 6.30-9.45 Av 3 course à la carte fr £23 ⊕ FREE HOUSE ◀ Greene King IPA, Interbrew Bass, Crouchvale Brewers Gold, Ruddles County, Spitfire. ♟ 16 **Facilities** Children's menu Dogs allowed Garden Parking

MANNINGTREE
Map 13 TM13

PICK OF THE PUBS

The Mistley Thorn ◉◉ ♟

High St, Mistley CO11 1HE ☎ **01206 392821**
📠 **01206 390122**
e-mail: info@mistleythorn.com
dir: From Ipswich A12 junct 31 onto B1070, follow signs to East Bergholt, Manningtree & Mistley. From Colchester A120 towards Harwich. Left at Horsley Cross. Mistley in 3m

Built as a coaching inn around 1723, this historic free house overlooking the two-mile wide River Stour estuary, offers award-winning dining and accommodation in tastefully designed surroundings. Stylewise, the interior is a touch New England, with terracotta-tiled floors, exposed beams and high-quality furnishings. American-born executive chef Sherri

Singleton, who also runs the Mistley Kitchen cookery school, develops accomplished menus using abundant quantities of the best local produce – world-famous rock oysters from Mersea Island; lobsters from Harwich; Suffolk beef and lamb; and salad leaves and herbs grown by a certified-organic smallholder. Among the line-up worthy of the pub's two AA Rosettes are crayfish ceviche; smoked haddock chowder; chicken liver and smoked bacon rosemary skewer with balsamic onions and toast; roasted duck breast with spring onion potato cake, braised red cabbage and cherry jus; chargrilled rib-eye with tempura onion rings, grilled cherry tomatoes and garlic field mushrooms; and aubergine rollatini with ricotta, Parmesan and pesto.

Open all wk 12-2.30 6.30-9 (Sat-Sun all day) **Bar Meals** L served Mon-Fri 12-2.30, Sat-Sun all day D served Mon-Fri 6.30-9, Sat 6.30-9.30 Av main course £12 **Restaurant** L served Mon-Fri 12-2.30, Sat-Sun all day D served Mon-Fri 6.30-9, Sat 6.30-9.30 Fixed menu price fr £10.95 Av 3 course à la carte fr £21 ⊕ FREE HOUSE ◀ Adnams. ♟ 17 **Facilities** Children's menu Dogs allowed Parking

NORTH FAMBRIDGE
Map 7 TQ89

The Ferry Boat Inn

Ferry Ln CM3 6LR ☎ **01621 740208**
e-mail: sylviaferryboat@aol.com
dir: From Chelmsford take A130 S then A132 to South Woodham Ferrers, then B1012. right to village

Owned by the same family for 26 years, this 500-year-old traditional weatherboard inn has beams, log fires and a resident ghost. It is tucked away at the end of a lovely village on the River Crouch, next to the marina, and was once a centre for smugglers. These days it is understandably popular with the sailing fraternity. In addition to the extensive menu and chef's specials, dishes might include minted lamb chop, grilled sea bass, chicken korma or beef chilli.

Open all wk 11.30-3 6.30-11 (Sun 12-4 6.30-10.30 & all day in summer) **Bar Meals** food served all day **Restaurant** food served all day ⊕ FREE HOUSE ◀ Greene King IPA, Abbot Ale, Morland. **Facilities** Children's menu Family room Dogs allowed Garden Parking

PATTISWICK — Map 13 TL82

PICK OF THE PUBS

The Compasses at Pattiswick ♥

See Pick of the Pubs on opposite page

PELDON — Map 7 TL91

The Peldon Rose ♥

Colchester Rd CO5 7QJ
☎ 01206 735248 📄 01206 736303
e-mail: enquiries@thepeldonrose.co.uk
dir: *On B1025 Mersea Rd, just before causeway*

Locally famous as an old smugglers' inn, the Peldon Rose simply exudes character. Winter log fires burn in the bar, with its original beams and leaded windows. An airy conservatory leads out to the garden, which is ideal for summer dining. Fresh local ingredients including Mersea island fish and oysters feature on the menu; other dishes include lamb and vegetable casserole with herb dumplings; and field mushrooms with spinach, pine nut and Stilton stuffing.

Open all wk Closed: 25 Dec ◀ Adnams Broadside, Adnams bitter, IPA, local guest bitter. ♥ 26
Facilities Garden Parking

RADWINTER — Map 12 TL63

The Plough Inn

CB10 2TL ☎ 01799 599222
dir: *4m E of Saffron Walden, at junct of B2153 & B2154*

An Essex woodboard exterior, old beams, open fires and a thatched roof characterise this listed inn, once frequented by farm workers. Food is served in the 50-seat restaurant, making the Plough more a destination gastropub than a purely local village inn, without losing too much of the village pub feel. A typical menu includes the likes of smoked haddock parcels, lamb noisettes, partridge, duck breast, and a variety of home-made pies. Friday night is fish night.

Open all wk ⊕ FREE HOUSE ◀ Adnams Best, IPA, Woodforde's Wherry, Archers, guest. **Facilities** Dogs allowed Garden Parking

SHALFORD — Map 12 TL72

The George Inn

The Street CM7 5HH
☎ 01371 850207 📄 01371 851355
e-mail: info@thegeorgeshalford.com
dir: *5m Braintree*

A hundred years ago there were five pubs in Shalford, but the George Inn, which dates back some 500 years, is the only one now. It's a traditional village pub, with oak beams and open fires, surrounded by lovely countryside. Shalford Brewery ales are available in the bar, and menu is written up on the blackboard daily, including steaks, chicken breast specialities and popular Oriental and Indian dishes. Fish goes down well too, particularly battered plaice, cod mornay, and salmon en croute.

Open all wk **Bar Meals** L served Mon-Sat 12-2.30 **Restaurant** L served Sun 12-3 D served Mon-Sat 6-9 ⊕ FREE HOUSE ◀ Woodforde's Wherry, Adnams Bitter, Shalford. **Facilities** Garden Parking

STANSTED AIRPORT

See Little Canfield

STOCK — Map 6 TQ69

The Hoop ♥

21 High St CM4 9BD ☎ 01277 841137
e-mail: thehoopstock@yahoo.co.uk
dir: *On B1007 between Chelmsford & Billericay*

This 15th-century free house on Stock's village green is every inch the traditional pub. Expect a warm welcome, real ales and a pleasing lack of music or fruit machines. The annual beer festival enjoys growing popularity, but the food is also a major draw. In keeping with the gorgeously traditional interior, a meal might include potted shrimps with brown bread; calves' liver with bacon, mash and onion rings; and bread and butter pudding for dessert.

Open all wk 11-11 (Sun 12-10.30) **Bar Meals** L served Mon-Sat 12-2.30, Sun 12-5 D served Mon-Sat 6-9 Av main course £9 **Restaurant** L served Tue-Fri 12-2.30, Sun 12-5 booking required D served Tue-Sat 6-9 booking required Av 3 course à la carte fr £25 ⊕ FREE HOUSE ◀ Adnams Bitter, 4 guest ales Ö Westons, Thatchers. ♥ 10 **Facilities** Children's menu Dogs allowed Garden

WICKHAM BISHOPS — Map 7 TL81

The Mitre

2 The Street CM8 3NN
☎ 01621 891378 📄 01621 894932
dir: *Off B1018 at Witham exit A12. Right at Jack & Jenny pub. Right at end of road. 1st left & follow road over bridge. 2nd pub on left*

Originally the Carpenter's Arms, this friendly pub changed its name in the mid-1890s, presumably to reflect the one-time possession of the village by the Bishops of London. The pub's regular range of meat choices includes mixed grills, pies and curries, steaks, and dishes featuring duck, pork, lamb and chicken. Fish is strongly represented by dishes based on haddock, cod, trout, sea bass, swordfish, plaice, Dover sole, red mullet and sea halibut to name a few.

Open all wk ⊕ GREENE KING ◀ Greene King IPA, Greene King Abbot, Fireside, Ruddles, Old Bob. **Facilities** Play area Dogs allowed Garden Parking

WOODHAM MORTIMER — Map 7 TL80

Hurdle Makers Arms ♥

Post Office Rd CM9 6ST
☎ 01245 225169 📄 01245 225169
e-mail: gary@hurdlemakersarms.co.uk
dir: *From Chelmsford A414 to Maldon/Danbury. 4.5m, through Danbury into Woodham Mortimer. Over 1st rdbt, 1st left, pub on left. Behind golf driving range*

A Grade II listed building dating back 400 years, the Hurdle Makers Arms has been a pub since 1837. Right at the heart of village life, it has live music, quiz nights and regular themed food evenings. Real ale lovers who like to discover new ales will be delighted by the wide range of micro-brewery products on offer. There are even guest ciders. Home-made pub food is served seven days a week, and in summer there are weekend barbecues in the large beer garden.

Open all wk all day summer (winter Mon-Thu noon-3 5.30-11 Fri-Sat all day Sun 12-9) **Bar Meals** L served Mon-Fri 12-3, Sat 12-9.30, Sun 12-8 D served Mon-Fri 6-9.30, Sat 12-9.30, Sun 12-8 **Restaurant** L served Mon-Fri 12-3, Sat 12-9.30, Sun 12-8 D served Mon-Fri 6-9.30, Sat 12-9.30, Sun 12-8 ⊕ GRAY & SONS ◀ Abbot, Mighty Oak, Crouch Vale, Farmers ales, Guest ales Ö Old Rosie. ♥ 8 **Facilities** Children's menu Play area Garden Parking

PICK OF THE PUBS

The Compasses at Pattiswick 🍷

Compasses Rd CM77 8BG
☎ 01376 561322　📠 01376 564343
e-mail:
info@thecompassesatpattiswick.co.uk
web:
www.thecompassesatpattiswick.co.uk
dir: *From Braintree take A120 E towards Colchester. After Bradwell 1st left to Pattiswick*

Hidden away in beautiful countryside were once two estate workers' cottages. Today they are an award-winning dining pub, whose owners' passion for good food translates into straightforward but superbly cooked dishes, jam-packed with local produce. At lunchtime try potted shrimps; local pork pie with home-made piccalilli; grilled plaice fillets with scallop butter and cavolo nero; or a daily special. The dinner menu is studded with dishes like sweet potato and parsnip curry with braised rice and raita; rib-eye steak with sautéed mushrooms and peppercorn butter; roasted sea bass fillets with anchovy mash and chive clotted cream; and blackboard specials, such as Cajun-crusted sea trout with ginger and garlic-roasted peppers. The desserts list favours the classics — apple and rhubarb crumble with vanilla ice cream; and spotted dick with home-made custard. Wines are selected for simplicity and clarity of flavour from both New and Old World producers. A roaring log fire make a welcoming sight in winter after a local walk, while in summer the large garden is inviting.

Open 11-3 5.30-11 (Sat 5.30-mdnt, Sun noon-4.30, Sun eve in summer) **Bar Meals** L served all wk 12-3 D served Mon-Thu 6-9.30, Fri-Sat 6-9.45 **Restaurant** L served Mon-Sat 12-3, Sun 12-4.30 D served Mon-Thu 6-9.30, Fri-Sat 6-9.45 ⊕ FREE HOUSE
🛢 Woodforde's Wherry, Adnam's, Adnam's Broadside, St Austell Tribute, Hoegaarden 🍎 Aspalls. 🍷 12
Facilities Children's menu Play area Dogs allowed Garden Parking

GLOUCESTERSHIRE

ALDERTON   Map 10 SP03

The Gardeners Arms NEW ♀

Beckford Rd GL20 8NL ☎ 01242 620257
e-mail: gardeners1@btconnect.com
dir: *Please telephone for directions*

This family-run, 16th-century thatched free house is in a quiet Cotswolds village. You can play boules in the large beer garden, and shove ha'penny or other traditional bar games in the stone-walled bar. Seasonal local produce and daily fresh fish underpin simple dishes such as home-made beef lasagne; tiger prawn Thai green curry; liver, bacon and onions; broccoli and cauliflower cheese gratin; and Mediterranean vegetable Wellington. Monthly-changing specials include slow-braised Cotswold lamb shoulder; and pan-fried halibut steak. Two beer festivals are held, one in May and the other at Christmas.

Open all wk 10-2 5-10 (Sun all day, Fri till mdnt) **Bar Meals** L served all wk 12-2 D served all wk 5.30-9 Av main course £4.50 **Restaurant** L served Mon-Sat 12-2, Sun all day booking required D served all wk 5.30-9.30 booking required Fixed menu price fr £10 Av 3 course à la carte fr £15 ⊕ FREE HOUSE ◀ Doom Bar, Butcombe Best, Courage Best, Local Guest Ales ♻ Westons GWR. ♀ 8 **Facilities** Children's menu Dogs allowed Garden Parking

ALMONDSBURY   Map 4 ST68

The Bowl ♀

16 Church Rd BS32 4DT
☎ 01454 612757   ▤ 01454 619910
e-mail: bowlinn@sabrain.com
dir: *M5 junct 16 towards Thornbury. 3rd left onto Over Ln, 1st right onto Sundays Hill, next right onto Church Rd*

Originally built to house monks building the village church, The Bowl became an inn in 1550. Its name derives from the shape of the valley around the nearby Severn Estuary, which can be seen from the inn. Brains ales are on offer, and food can be eaten in the bar or the restaurant, which may offer roasted free range chicken breast, Vichycoisse and crisp pancetta; hand-made cheddar, garlic and mushroom ravioli; or pan-fried sea bass with courgette spaghetti. Recent change of landlord.

Open all wk 12-3 5-11 (Sat noon-11 Sun noon-10.30) **Bar Meals** L served Mon-Fri 12-2.30, Sat 12-10, Sun 12-8 D served Mon-Fri 6-10 Av main course £9 **Restaurant** L served Sun 12-2 booking required D served Mon-Sat 6-9 booking required Av 3 course à la carte fr £28 ⊕ BRAINS BREWERY S.A.BRAIN & CO LTD ◀ Butcombe, Tribute ♻ Stowford Press. ♀ 9 **Facilities** Children's menu Parking

ANDOVERSFORD   Map 10 SP01

PICK OF THE PUBS

The Kilkeney Inn ♀

See Pick of the Pubs on opposite page

The Royal Oak Inn ♀

Old Gloucester Rd GL54 4HR ☎ 01242 820335
e-mail: royal.oak1@unicombox.co.uk
dir: *200mtrs from A40, 4m E of Cheltenham*

The 17th-century Royal Oak stands on the banks of the River Coln, one of a small chain of popular food-centred pubs in the area. Originally a coaching inn, its main dining room, galleried on two levels, occupies the converted former stables. Four real ales and three varieties of draught cider are part of the allure here, and there is a good selection of coffees.

Open all wk ⊕ FREE HOUSE ◀ Stanway Ales, Doom Bar, Otter Ale, Broadside. ♀ 9 **Facilities** Dogs allowed Garden Parking

ARLINGHAM   Map 4 SO71

PICK OF THE PUBS

The Old Passage Inn ★★★★ RR ⊚⊚ ♀

Passage Rd GL2 7JR
☎ 01452 740547   ▤ 01452 741871
e-mail: oldpassage@ukonline.co.uk
dir: *5m from A38 adjacent M5 junct 13*

In a tranquil location on the banks of the tidal River Severn, surrounded by fields and wonderful views, this ancient inn was once a ferry station for services crossing the river. Although it's more restaurant-with-rooms than a pub, expect an informal atmosphere in the open and airy dining room, and a relaxed approach in summer when the riverside terrace throngs at lunchtimes. First-class seafood cookery is the real draw, the almost exclusively fish and shellfish menu attracting lovers of seafood. There are oysters and lobsters from the fish tank served in classic combinations with some contemporary twists. Start, perhaps, potted shrimps, fish soup with saffron mayonnaise, or simple smoked salmon with capers and lemon dressing. Fruits de mer are served hot or cold, with other fish dishes including wild sea bass with saffron and vanilla sauce, and fish stew. Non-fish

alternatives may include chargrilled sirloin steak and roast partridge. There are three modern en suite bedrooms here.

Open noon-2.30 7-9 Closed: 25 Dec, Sun eve & Mon **Bar Meals** Av main course £17.50 **Restaurant** L served Tue-Sat 12-2.30, Sun 12-3 booking required D served Tue-Sat 6-9 booking required Fixed menu price fr £15 Av 3 course à la carte fr £80 ⊕ FREE HOUSE ◀ Wickwar ♻ Westons Organic. ♀ 14 **Facilities** Children's menu Dogs allowed Garden Parking **Rooms** 3

ASHLEWORTH   Map 10 SO82

Boat Inn ♀

The Quay GL19 4HZ ☎ 01452 700272   ▤ 01452 700272
e-mail: elisabeth_nicholls@yahoo.co.uk
dir: *Turn off A417 between Gloucester & Ledbury at Hartpury follow signs for Ashleworth Quay*

This picturesque pub on the banks of the Severn has been in the same family for over 400 years, and has changed very little in that time. Renowned for its real ales, it hosts a popular annual beer festival but is also worth visiting for its eight different ciders from local cider house, Westons. Traditionally filled rolls, perhaps with home-made tomato chutney, form the hub of the simple but delicious food offering, available only at lunchtimes.

Closed: Mon & Wed L **Bar Meals** L served Tue, Thu-Sun 12-2 ⊕ FREE HOUSE ◀ Wye Valley, Church End, Arkells, RCH Pitchfork ♻ Westons Stowford Press, Westons Old Rosie Scrumpy, Westons Stowford Export. ♀ 6 **Facilities** Garden Parking **Notes** ⊛

PICK OF THE PUBS

The Queens Arms ♀

The Village GL19 4HT ☎ 01452 700395
dir: *From Gloucester N on A417 for 5m. At Hartpury, opp Royal Exchange turn right at Broad St to Ashleworth. Pub 100yds past village green*

Outside this 16th-century inn the front garden features two beautifully clipped, 200-year-old yew trees, while a flagstoned patio at the rear is decorated with white cast-iron garden furniture, flower tubs and hanging baskets. The interior was given a makeover by the Victorians; thankfully the original beams and iron fireplaces were untouched, now complemented by comfy armchairs and antiques. The summer floods in

continued on page 188

PICK OF THE PUBS

The Kilkeney Inn ♀

ANDOVERSFORD   Map 10 SP01

Kilkeney GL54 4LN
☎ 01242 820341   📄 01242 820133
dir: *On A436 1m W of Andoversford*

A visit to this charming country dining pub on the main road outside Andoversford is well worth the drive out from Cheltenham. With rolling landscapes stretching away on all sides, it's very much a desirable place to eat. But the aim of hosts Kevin and Michele is to mix traditional values with a certain sophistication and style, so beer drinkers are more than welcome and will find real ales served in good condition. The best views of the Cotswolds are from the front of the pub. The mature garden at the rear has bench seating; the expanse of greenery was originally six individual plots belonging to a terrace of mid-19th century stone cottages. Inside, fresh flowers, polished quarry floor tiles and twinkling lights illuminating the impressive wine display create a relaxing ambience. A wood-burning stove warms the beamed bar whenever there's a nip in the air, and the colourful seating and pastel walls make it welcoming and cosy. The Conservatory restaurant has a light airy feel with wicker tables and chairs, and striking prints adorn the walls. On suitable summer days the doors open on to the heated garden patio, ideal for a romantic alfresco meal. Lunches include 'lite' bites; starters; and main courses like gammon, egg and chips, or beef bourguignon with creamy mash. The dinner menu has starters for every taste; a special treat is the platter of smoked salmon, lightly grilled with pickled raspberries, roasted beetroot and blinis. Main courses too range from home-made beef, onion and mushroom pie with stilton, to a pork loin steak topped with thyme, apple and sage stuffing on creamy mash. Desserts, all crafted in the kitchen, could include rum and raisin cheesecake; apple and rhubarb crumble; and passion fruit and orange crème brûlée.

Open 11.30-3 5.30-11 Sun 11.30-11
Meals L served Mon-Sat 12-2 (Sun 12-3) D served all week 6.30-9 ⊕ FREE HOUSE ◀ Bombardier, Youngs Best Bitter, St Austells Tribute. ♀ 9
Facilities Garden Parking

ASHLEWORTH *continued*

2007 necessitated a change of carpet, but Tony and Gillian Burreddu have now celebrated more than ten happy years here. The bar stocks a good range of real ales and over a dozen wines served by the glass. The restaurant, which is really two intimate rooms, tempts with blackboards full of ideas: starters like king scallops with risotto or baked field mushrooms with goats' cheese; mains like salmon fillet supreme on green tagliatelle with asparagus and white wine cream sauce or roasted local partridge with juniper and red wine sauce; and desserts such as Cape brandy pudding or pecan nut and maple syrup pie.

Open noon-3 7-11 Closed: 25-26 Dec & 1 Jan, Sun eve (ex BH wknds) **Bar Meals** L served all wk 12-2 booking required D served Mon-Sat 7-9 booking required Av main course £12 **Restaurant** L served all wk 12-2 booking required D served Mon-Sat 7-9 booking required Av 3 course à la carte fr £20 ⊕ FREE HOUSE ◀ Timothy Taylor Landlord, Donnington BB, S A Brain & Company Rev James, Shepherd Neame Spitfire, Tetley Bitter. ♀ 14 **Facilities** Garden Parking

---

AWRE   Map 4 SO70

PICK OF THE PUBS

The Red Hart Inn at Awre ♀

GL14 1EW ☎ 01594 510220
dir: *E of A48 between Gloucester & Chepstow, access is from Blakeney or Newnham villages*

The history of this cosy traditional free house goes back to 1483, when it was built to house the workmen who were renovating the nearby 10th-century church. The charming interior includes all the hoped-for historic features such as flagstone floors, stone fireplaces, lots of exposed beams, and an original working well, which is now attractively illuminated. It's the kind of atmospheric place where one quick post-walk pint of Wye Valley Butty Bach could turn into a lengthy sojourn, probably involving a meal. Close to the beautiful River Severn, the setting is ideal for serious hikers, or for those simply seeking a relaxing, attractive place to walk off dinner – there's even a map by the front door for inspiration.

Closed: 23 Jan-5 Feb, Mon (winter) ⊕ FREE HOUSE ◀ Wye Valley Butty Bach, guest ales, Whttingtons, Archers, Freeminer, Wickwar. ♀ 11 **Facilities** Dogs allowed Garden Parking

---

BARNSLEY   Map 5 SP00

PICK OF THE PUBS

The Village Pub ◉◉ ♀

GL7 5EF ☎ 01285 740421   ▤ 01285 740925
e-mail: reservations@thevillagepub.co.uk
dir: *On B4425 4m NE of Cirencester*

Unique in preserving its unusual name, this 'Village Pub' is not your average local. Set in a charming Cotswold village, this enduringly popular pub-restaurant has been beautifully refurbished, yet retains its polished flagstones, oak floorboards, exposed timbers and open fireplaces. Expect a civilised atmosphere in the five rambling dining rooms, which sport an eclectic mix of furniture, rug-strewn floors, warm terracotta walls and crackling log fires. Innovative modern British pub food draws a discerning dining crowd, the daily menus featuring quality local ingredients, including traceable or organic meats, and fresh seasonal fish. Starters may take in potted rabbit with celeriac and mustard, and fresh asparagus with parmesan hollandaise, with main dishes ranging from John Dory with braised octopus, and roast cod with Niçoise salad, to lambs' sweetbreads with wild mushroom risotto cake. Typical desserts are rum baba with zabaglione ice cream, and chocolate and espresso tart.

Open all wk 11-3 6-11 (Fri-Sun 11am-11pm) **Bar Meals** L served all wk 12-2.30 D served Sun-Thu 7-9.30, Fri-Sat 7-10 Av main course £13 **Restaurant** Av 3 course à la carte fr £22 ⊕ FREE HOUSE ◀ Hook Norton Bitter, Wadworth 6X, Cotswold Premium. ♀ 12 **Facilities** Dogs allowed Garden Parking

---

BERKELEY   Map 4 ST69

The Malt House ★★★ INN ♀

Marybrook St GL13 9BA
☎ 01453 511177   ▤ 01453 810257
e-mail: the-malthouse@btconnect.com
web: www.themalthouse.uk.com
dir: *M5 junct 13/14, A38 towards Bristol. Pub on main road towards Sharpness*

Within walking distance of Berkeley Castle and its deer park, this family-run free house is also handy for the Edward Jenner museum, dedicated to the life of the founding father of immunology. Inside the heavily beamed pub you'll find a varied selection of lunchtime bar food, as well as weekly home-made specials. Pub

favourites like steak and ale pie rub shoulders with vegetarian stuffed peppers; and grilled halibut, butter and lime.

Open all wk 4-11 (Fri-Sat noon-mdnt Sun noon-4) **Bar Meals** L served Fri-Sun 12-2 D served Mon-Sat 6-9 **Restaurant** L served Fri-Sun 12-2 D served Mon-Sat 6-9 ⊕ FREE HOUSE ◀ Old Speckled Hen, Theakstons Best ♂ Stowford Press, Thatchers Gold. ♀ 6 **Facilities** Children's menu Garden Parking **Rooms** 10

BIBURY   Map 5 SP10

Catherine Wheel

Arlington GL7 5ND ☎ 01285 740250
dir: *Telephone for directions*

This low-beamed 15th-century pub is situated in a Cotswold village, which was described by William Morris as 'the most beautiful in England'. Inside is an original ship's timber beam, as well as various prints and photographs of Old Bibury, and blazing log fires in winter. Traditional pub food includes fresh Bibury trout, salmon and prawns, and tuna steak. Alongside a range of real ales, look out for Weston's Stowford Press, a traditional English cider.

Open all day all wk 10am-11pm (Mon-Fri 3-6 closed during winter) **Bar Meals** L served all wk 12-2.30 D served all wk 6-9.30 Av main course £10 **Restaurant** L served all wk 12-2.30 D served all wk 6-9.30 Av 3 course à la carte fr £20 ⊕ BARNSLEY HOUSE LTD ◀ Hook Norton, Sharps Doom Bar ♂ Westons Stowford Press. **Facilities** Children's menu Dogs allowed Garden Parking

---

BIRDLIP   Map 10 SO91

The Golden Heart ♀

Nettleton Bottom GL4 8LA
☎ 01242 870261   ▤ 01242 870599
e-mail: cathstevensgh@aol.com
dir: *On A417 Gloucester to Cirencester. 8m from Cheltenham. Pub at base of dip in Nettleton Bottom*

This centuries-old Cotswold stone inn has glorious views from its terraced gardens. It probably started life as a drovers' inn, and retains plenty of original features. Excellent local ales and traditional ciders are the focus of the bar, while the extensive menus show an equal commitment to local produce, particularly prize-winning meat from livestock markets and shows. On the other hand, it also makes room for exotic meats including a low fat ostrich casserole or a crocodile, zebra and rattlesnake mixed grill.

Open all wk 11-3 5.30-11 (Fri-Sun open all day) Closed: 25 Dec **Bar Meals** L served Mon-Sat 12-3, Sun all day D served Mon-Sat 6-10, Sun all day Av main course £11.25 **Restaurant** L served Mon-Sat 12-3, Sun all day D served Mon-Sat 12-3, Sun all day ⊕ FREE HOUSE ◀ Otter Bitter, Wickwar, Cotswolds Way, Wye Valley, Otter, Gold Festival ♂ Westons, Henney, Thatchers. ♀ 10 **Facilities** Children's menu Family room Dogs allowed Garden Parking

BLEDINGTON — Map 10 SP22

PICK OF THE PUBS

The Kings Head Inn ★★★★ INN ⊛ ☕

See Pick of the Pubs on page 190

BOURTON-ON-THE-HILL — Map 10 SP13

PICK OF THE PUBS

Horse and Groom ☕

GL56 9AQ ☎ 01386 700413 🖹 01386 700413
e-mail: greenstocks@horseandgroom.info
dir: *2m W of Moreton-in-Marsh on A44*

Owned and run by the Greenstock brothers, this is a honey-coloured Grade II listed Georgian building with a contemporary feel combined with original period features. This is a serious dining pub, as well as a friendly place for the locals to drink. The bar offers a selection of local favourites and guest ales, whilst the blackboard menu of regularly changing dishes provides plenty of appeal for even the most regular diners. With committed local suppliers backed up by the pub's own vegetable patch, the Horse and Groom's kitchen has plenty of good produce to work with. A typical menu might feature fragrant Thai broth of diver-caught scallops, prawns and steamed mussels; pan-roast stuffed duck breast with braised red cabbage and Madeira jus; or grilled organic salmon fillet with braised herb lentils and bacon. Leave room for puddings like apple and blueberry flapjack crumble or pear and almond tart. In summer, the mature garden offers panoramic hilltop views.

Open 11-3 6-11 Closed: 25 Dec, Sun eve **Bar Meals** L served all wk 12-2 booking required D served Mon-Sat 7-9 booking required **Restaurant** L served all wk 12-2 booking required D served Mon-Sat 7-9 booking required ⊕ FREE HOUSE ◀ Hook Norton Hooky, Dorothy Goodbody-Wye Valley, Pure UBU, Goffs Jouster, Cotswold Wheat ♻ Westons Stowford Press. ☕ 14 **Facilities** Children's menu Garden Parking

CHARLTON KINGS — Map 10 SO92

PICK OF THE PUBS

The Reservoir NEW ☕

See Pick of the Pubs on page 191

CHEDWORTH — Map 5 SP01

Hare & Hounds ☕

Foss Cross GL54 4NN ☎ 01285 720288
e-mail: stay@hareandhoundsinn.com
dir: *On A429 (Fosse Way), 6m from Cirencester*

A 14th-century inn with various interconnecting dining areas often described as a rabbit warren. Open fires, beams and stone and polished wood floors add to the charm. It's ideally placed for touring the Cotswolds or attending Cheltenham race meetings. There's a daily changing blackboard, along with a menu typically listing breast of Gressingham duck; baked fillet of cod; and Burmese vegetable tofu curry.

Open all wk 11-3 (Sat 6-close Sun 7- close) **Bar Meals** L served all wk 12-2.30 booking required D served Mon-Sat 6.30-9.30, Sun 7-9 booking required **Restaurant** L served all wk 12-2.30 booking required D served Mon-Sat 6.30-9.30, Sun 7-9 booking required ⊕ ARKELLS ◀ Arkells 2B, 3B, Moonlight ♻ Stowford Press. ☕ 10 **Facilities** Children's menu Family room Dogs allowed Garden Parking

PICK OF THE PUBS

Seven Tuns ☕

Queen St GL54 4AE
☎ 01285 720242 🖹 01285 720933
e-mail: theseventuns@clara.co.uk
dir: *Exit A429, turn off at junct to Chedworth. Approx halfway between Northleach & Cirencester, follow signs to pub*

Directly opposite this creeper-covered, unmistakably Cotswold inn, are a waterwheel, a spring and a raised terrace for summer dining. The pub dates back to the 17th century, and the name derives from the seven chimney pots that deck the roof. The lunch menu offers nothing too heavy - sandwiches, ploughman's, jacket potatoes and appealing Mediterranean dishes like croque monsieur, tagliatelle bolognese or minted lamb

kebabs. In the evening, try chorizo, new potato and goats' cheese salad; Mexican spiced chicken supreme with avocado and tomato salsa; or home-made sage, redcurrant and beef burgers. In the beer garden there's a revolving South African barbecue and a renovated skittle alley. Live music evenings held.

Open all wk noon-3 6-11 (Sat noon-mdnt Sun noon-10.30pm) **Bar Meals** L served Mon-Fri 12-2.30, Sat-Sun 12-3 D served Mon-Fri 6-9.30, Sat 6.30-9.30, Sun 6.30-9 ⊕ YOUNG ◀ Young's Bitter, Winter Warmer, Waggledance, Bombardier, Deuchars. ☕ 12 **Facilities** Family room Dogs allowed Garden Parking

CHIPPING CAMPDEN — Map 10 SP13

The Bakers Arms ☕

Broad Campden GL55 6UR ☎ 01386 840515
dir: *1m from Chipping Campden*

There is a friendly family atmosphere at this country Cotswold inn, where you can expect to find exposed stone walls, beams and an inglenook fireplace. A choice of four to five real ales is offered alongside reasonably priced meals. Choose from sandwiches, warm baguettes and filled giant Yorkshire puddings, or dishes such as mariner's pie, Thai red vegetable curry, and liver, bacon and onions with rich gravy.

Open all wk 11.30-2.30 4.45-11 (Fri-Sun 11.30-11 Apr-Oct all wk 11.30-11) Closed: 25 Dec **Bar Meals** L served Mon-Fri 12-2, Sat 12-2.30, Sun 12-6 D served Mon-Sat 6-9 Av main course £7.50 **Restaurant** L served Mon-Fri 12-2, Sat 12-2.30, Sun 12-6 D served Mon-Sat 6-9 ⊕ FREE HOUSE ◀ Stanway Bitter, Bombardier, Donnington BB. ☕ 6 **Facilities** Children's menu Play area Garden Parking **Notes** ⊛

PICK OF THE PUBS

Eight Bells ☕

Church St GL55 6JG
☎ 01386 840371 🖹 01386 841669
e-mail: neilhargreaves@bellinn.fsnet.co.uk
dir: *8m from Stratford-upon-Avon, M40 Junct 15*

A lovely old inn, located just off the High Street of this popular Cotswold destination, the Eight Bells was built in the 14th century to house stonemasons working on the nearby church and to store the eight church bells. A cobbled entranceway leads into two atmospheric bars, which retain the original oak beams, open fireplaces and a priest's hole. In summer, the exterior

continued on page 192

PICK OF THE PUBS

The Kings Head Inn ★★★★ INN ✿ ♇

BLEDINGTON   Map 10 SP22

The Green OX7 6XQ
☎ 01608 658365   📠 01608 658902
e-mail: info@kingsheadinn.net
dir: *On B4450 4m from Stow-on-the-Wold*

A more delightful spot would surely be hard to find: facing the village green with its brook and border-patrolling ducks, this is surely the quintessential Cotswold pub. Stone-built and dating back to the 16th-century, the former cider house stands on the Gloucester border and is the perfect country retreat. Much of the original structure has survived, leaving sturdy beams, low ceilings, flagstone floors, exposed stone walls, and big open fireplaces - all of which have been preserved and enhanced by more recent additions. Archie and Nicola Orr-Ewing have worked hard to earn an excellent reputation for their Cotswold treasure - one built on well-kept real ales, an extensive wine list and wonderful fresh produce in the kitchen. Ingredients are locally sourced and organic as far as possible, with beef (hung for 21 days) from the Archie's uncle's farm and fish delivered fresh from Grimsby. In the bar, Hook Norton Best is a mainstay, alongside guest ales from local micro-breweries, organic cider, local lagers, over 25 malt whiskies, and 8 wines by the glass. The lunch menu includes salads and sandwiches alongside the likes of kiln-roasted salmon fishcake with caper and chive mayonnaise, and local venison with Savoy cabbage, bubble-and-squeak and redcurrant jus. For dinner, you could try potted shrimps with lemon butter, or plum tomato, basil and mozzarella bruschetta for starters, followed by crayfish and rocket linguini, steak, ale and root vegetable pie, and chargrilled beef fillet with salad and chips. Round off with a home-made pudding, perhaps chocolate caramel brownie with vanilla ice cream, or lemon meringue tartlet, or a plate of English cheeses. Comfort, charm and style also sum up the twelve elegant bedrooms, which are split between the pub and a converted barn.

Open all week Closed: 24-25 Dec
Restaurant ⊕ FREE HOUSE 🛢 Hook Norton Bitter, Doom Bar, Vale Pale Ale, Wye Valley & Brakspear. ♇ 8
Facilities Garden Parking **Rooms** 12

PICK OF THE PUBS

The Reservoir NEW ♉

CHARLTON KINGS

London Rd GL54 4HG ☎ 01242 529671
e-mail: susan@thereservoirinn.co.uk
dir: *On A40, 5m E of Cheltenham*

Andy and Susan Proctor took over this friendly pub a few miles out of Cheltenham in March 2008, following three years at The Hinds Head, Heston Blumenthal's pub in Bray. The surroundings here are beautiful - opposite is the reason for the pub's name, Dowdeswell Reservoir - while the atmosphere inside is by any measure relaxing. Since it's a Greene King pub, expect IPA, Abbot and Morland Original in the spacious, log-burning-stove-warmed bar. The daily-changing menus are subtitled 'A Celebration of British Food' and use fresh, seasonal and

locally sourced ingredients in a range broad enough to satisfy everyone from Cotswold Way walkers looking for a ploughman's and a pint, to weekend diners with hearts set on locally shot game, washed down with a jolly decent wine. Behind all these classic dishes is business partner Martin Blunos, a regular guest TV chef who cooked for the Queen during her Jubilee celebrations. Using fresh, seasonal and locally sourced ingredients, he produces Cotswold ham, eggs and triple-cooked chips; Old Spot sausages, mash and onion gravy; chunky fish stew with garlic mayonnaise; Angus rump steak with shallot and peppercorn butter; and creamed pearl barley with roasted butternut squash. Desserts continue the British classics theme with spotted dick and custard pudding; warm fig and almond tart; and winter fruit mess. And if it's just a bar snack you want, the choice runs from a mug of soup to beer-battered fish with mushy peas and triple-cooked chips. A covered patio and large beer garden are ideal for those alfresco drinks and meals.

Open 11-3 5-11 (Fri-Sun open all day) Closed: 26 Dec, Mon **Bar Meals** Av main course £8 **Restaurant** L served Tue-Sat 12-2.30, Sun 12-8 D served Tue-Sat 5.30-9.30 Fixed menu price fr £10 Av 3 course à la carte fr £22 ⊕ Greene King ◼ IPA, Abbot, Morland Original Ŏ Stowford Press. ♉ 9
Facilities Children's menu Dogs allowed Garden Parking

CHIPPING CAMPDEN *continued*

is hung with flower baskets, and guests spill out into the enclosed courtyard or the beautiful terraced garden that overlooks the almshouses and church. Freshly prepared local food is offered in the bar or the modern dining room. Lunchtime sandwiches on freshly baked ciabatta bread are available Monday to Saturday, and dishes range through home-made soup, bruschetta, traditional fish and chips, monkfish tail wrapped in Parma ham, and Mr Lashford's sausage of the day. Home-made desserts take in hot ginger sponge or poached pear in a brandy-snap basket. There is a tempting children's menu available.

Open all day all wk noon–11 (Sun noon–10.30) Closed: 25 Dec **Bar Meals** L served Mon-Thu 12-2, Fri-Sun 12-2.30 D served Mon-Thu 6.30-9, Fri-Sat 6.30-9.30, Sun 6.30-8.45 **Restaurant** L served Mon-Thu 12-2, Fri-Sun 12-2.30 D served Mon-Thu 6.30-9, Fri-Sat 6.30-9.30, Sun 6.30-8.45 ⊕ FREE HOUSE ◖ Hook Norton Best & guest ales, Goff's Jouster, Marston Pedigree, Purity UBU ♂ Old Rosie. ♀ 8 **Facilities** Children's menu Family room Dogs allowed Garden

---

The Kings ★ ★ ★ ★ RR ◉

The Square GL55 6AW
☎ 01386 840256 📠 01386 841598
e-mail: info@kingscampden.co.uk

Set in the square of a pretty Cotswold town, this smart 17th-century inn has an air of relaxed elegance. There are plenty of snacks, but the full menu offers some imaginative delights: tournedos Rossini with home-made chicken liver pâté in a rich Madeira wine sauce; dressed crab with shell on prawns; or a gateaux of herb polenta cakes, mozzarella and plum tomatoes. Seafish comes fresh from Brixham daily. Have a look at the specials board for more choices, and take in some lovely artwork by a local painter. Bedrooms offer ample comfort with period features.

Open all wk Closed: 25 Dec ⊕ FREE HOUSE ◖ Hook Norton Best. **Facilities** Dogs allowed Garden Parking **Rooms** 19

PICK OF THE PUBS

Noel Arms Hotel ★ ★ ★ HL ♀

High St GL55 6AT ☎ **01386 840317** 📠 01386 841136
e-mail: reception@noelarmshotel.com
dir: *On High St, opposite Town Hall*

Charles II stayed in this 16th-century coaching inn, built like so much round here of golden Cotswold stone. It was through the carriage arch that packhorse trains used to carry bales of wool, the source of the town's prosperity, to Bristol and Southampton. Absorb the hotel's atmosphere in front of the log fire in Dover's Bar; read the papers over coffee in the conservatory; sleep in a four-poster made in 1657; and enjoy the very best food from the lush Cotswolds. The bar offers a good choice, from toasted ciabattas, sandwiches and soups, to main meals such as Thai green chicken curry with steamed rice and prawn crackers; and butter bean and roast pepper tagine with minted couscous. An evening meal might involve pan-fried sweetbreads on apple mash with vanilla vinaigrette; chargrilled tuna steak with sun-blushed tomato risotto and olive tapenade; and mango parfait with passion-fruit mousse and lime tuiles.

Open all day all wk 11am–11pm **Bar Meals** L served all wk 12-7 D served all wk 12-7 food served all day ⊕ FREE HOUSE ◖ Hook Norton Best Bitter, Guinness ♂ Westons Stowford Press. ♀ 10 **Facilities** Dogs allowed Garden Parking **Rooms** 26

The Volunteer Inn ♀

Lower High St GL55 6DY ☎ **01386 840688**
e-mail: mark_gibbo@yahoo.co.uk
dir: *From Shipston on Stour take B4035 to Chipping Campden*

A 300-year-old inn where, in the mid-19th-century, the able-bodied used to sign up for the militia. Ramblers can set off from here to walk the Cotswold Way. Food options are provided by the Pan-Asian Maharaja restaurant which serves food in the evenings.

Open all wk **Restaurant** D served all wk 5-10.30 booking required ⊕ FREE HOUSE ◖ Hook Norton, Hobgoblin. ♀ 12 **Facilities** Play area Family room Dogs allowed Garden

---

PICK OF THE PUBS

The Crown of Crucis ★ ★ ★ HL ♀

Ampney Crucis GL7 5RS
☎ **01285 851806** 📠 01285 851735
e-mail: reception@thecrownofcrucis.co.uk
dir: *On A417 to Lechlade, 2m E of Cirencester*

This 16th-century inn stands beside the Ampney brook in picturesque Ampney Crucis at the gateway to the Cotswolds. The name 'Crucis' refers to the Latin cross in the nearby churchyard. The inn itself retains its historical charm while feeling comfortably up-to-date. It overlooks the village cricket green, and on summer days the evocative sound of willow on leather and the quiet stream meandering past the lawns conspire to create a perfect picture of quintessential England. With its traditional beams, log fires and warm, friendly atmosphere, the bar has been recently restored. Bar food is served all day, along with a range of daily specials. The busy bar offers a large selection of draught and real ales and ten wines by the glass. The restaurant menu offers starters of carpaccio of beef with roast aubergines; and chicken skewers with lime and coriander marinade, followed perhaps by breast of guinea fowl and confit leg wrapped in pancetta with a celery and cranberry sauce.

Open all day all wk Closed: 25 Dec **Bar Meals** Av main course £9 food served all day **Restaurant** L served all wk 12-2.30 booking required D served all wk 7-9.30 booking required Av 3 course à la carte fr £25 ⊕ FREE HOUSE ◖ Doom Bar, Archers Village, John Smiths. ♀ 10 **Facilities** Children's menu Dogs allowed Garden Parking **Rooms** 25

PICK OF THE PUBS

The Yew Tree ♀

See Pick of the Pubs on opposite page

PICK OF THE PUBS

The Tunnel House Inn

See Pick of the Pubs on page 194

PICK OF THE PUBS

The Yew Tree ♆

CLIFFORD'S MESNE   Map 10 SO72

Clifford's Mesne GL18 1JS
☎ 01531 820719 📠 01531 820912
e-mail: cass@yewtreeinn.com
dir: *From Newent High Street follow signs to Clifford's Mesne. Pub at far end of village on road to Glasshouse*

Although it might stretch your map-reader's skills, it is well worth the effort finding The Yew Tree, a welcoming halt on the slopes of the National Trust's May Hill, Gloucestershire's highest point. Horses and sheep graze wild on its slopes, and from its 971ft summit you can, weather conditions permitting, see the bluish outlines of the Welsh Mountains and the Malvern Hills, as well as the River Severn - across seven counties, in fact. Many centuries ago the building was a cider press, and probably a lot less pretty than it is now. The interior features quarry-tiled floors, pleasant furnishings, winter log fires

and a good choice of real ales (Wye Valley, Cotswold Spring) and varieties of local artisan cider and perry are offered, while all the wines are imported by the inn and sold in its own wine shop. Free-range chickens provide eggs for the kitchen and many of the herbs, salad leaves, vegetables and fruit are home grown. While you peruse the seasonal menu, nibble on olives, pistachio nuts, or breadsticks with sun-dried tomato and cream cheese. Dishes are freshly prepared, and starters could include gravadlax with dill dressing; and chargrilled courgette and sun-dried tomato risotto. Daily specials complement old favourites such as slow-roasted belly of Old Spot pork with caramelised celeriac, and the pub's trademark rabbit and bacon pudding. Other main courses include seared duck breast with blackberry and shallot compote; line-caught fish with chunky tartare dressing; and mushroom, spinach and mascarpone roulade. There's a selection of local farmhouse cheeses too. Special events are a regular feature with monthly quiz and supper nights through the winter and occasional performances by guest musicians. In May, the Yew Tree holds a beer, cider and local produce festival.

Closed: Mon, Tue L, Sun eve **Bar Meals** L served Wed-Sat 12-2 D served Tue-Sat 6-9 Av main course £12 **Restaurant** L served Sun 12-4 Av 3 course à la carte fr £20 ⊕ FREE HOUSE ◀ Wye Valley HPA, CSB Glory, guests ♂ Stowford Press, Old Rosie. ♆ 16
Facilities Children's menu Play area Dogs allowed Garden Parking

PICK OF THE PUBS

The Tunnel House Inn

COATES　　　　　　Map 4 SO90

GL7 6PW
☎ 01285 770280　📄 01285 700040
e-mail: bookings@tunnelhouse.com
web: www.tunnelhouse.com
dir: *From Cirencester on A433 towards Tetbury, in 2m turn right towards Coates, follow brown signs to Canal Tunnel & Inn*

Lying between the Cotswold villages of Coates and Tarlton, the Tunnel House enjoys a glorious rural location down the bumpy track leading to the mouth of the two-mile long Sapperton Tunnel on the Thames and Severn Canal. Once providing accommodation for the 'navvies' building the canal, it is not far from the source of the Thames. In appropriate weather the garden is an ideal place for relaxing with a pint of Uley Bitter or Black Rat cider, and enjoying the views across the fields, while in the winter months three log fires warm the welcoming bar, where

oddities include an upside-down table on the ceiling. You may dine on simple, home-made cooking in the restaurant area or relax in the comfortable seating in the bar. Eat lightly at lunchtime with a bacon and brie sandwich or a ploughman's, or choose from the monthly changing menu, typically featuring good home-prepared dishes such as beer-battered cod and chips with salad; honey-roasted Wiltshire ham, eggs and chips; and rump steak with Café de Paris butter and rocket. Dinner, from a separate menu, could include chicken liver parfait, Melba toast and red onion confit; then braised lamb shank in Madeira sauce with boulangère potatoes and vegetables; blackened fillet of mackerel with roasted winter vegetables and horseradish cream; or wild mushroom, chilli, pine nut and cream cheese tagliatelle; with treacle tart and vanilla ice cream to follow. Children will probably opt for the usual favourites of sausage and mash with gravy; mini beefburger with cheese and bacon; fish and chips; or chicken goujons. A kiddie's play area and spectacular walks in the surrounding countryside add to the pub's popularity.

Open all week Closed: 25 Dec **Bar Meals** L served all week 12-2.15 D served all week 6.45-9.15 Av main course £10 **Restaurant** L served all week 12-2.15 D served all week 6.45-9.15 Fixed menu price fr £10 Av 3 course à la carte fr £22 ⊕ FREE HOUSE ◼ Uley Old Spot, Uley Bitter, Wye Valley Bitter, Hook Norton, Budding, Butcombe ♻ Cornish Rattler, Black Rat, Westons Organic. **Facilities** Children's menu Play area Family room Dogs allowed Garden Parking

COLESBOURNE | Map 10 SP01

PICK OF THE PUBS

The Colesbourne Inn ⚑

GL53 9NP ☎ **01242 870376**
e-mail: info@thecolesbourneinn.co.uk
dir: *Midway between Cirencester & Cheltenham on
A435*

A handsome 17th-century stone pub on the
Colesbourne estate at the heart of the Cotswolds. Set
between the historic towns of Cheltenham and
Cirencester, it is ideal for exploring the villages and
gentle, very English countryside of Gloucestershire.
Nearby is the source of the River Thames, which can be
reached on foot along delightful field and meadow
paths. Dating back to 1827 and set in two acres of
grounds, the Colesbourne Inn has been sympathetically
restored over the years. Among the distinguishing
features are a host of beams, roaring log fires, four
separate dining areas, and a superb terrace and
garden with stunning rural views. There is even a side
entrance from the bar originally used as a chamber for
smoking ham. Food is all important at the Colesbourne
Inn, and fresh local produce is used wherever possible;
there is an appetising range of light bites.

Open all wk noon-3 6-11 (Sat noon-11 Sun noon-10)
⊕ WADWORTH ◀ Wadworth 6X, Henrys IPA, Bishops
Tipple, Summersault ♂ Stowford Press. ⚑ 20
Facilities Play area Dogs allowed Garden Parking

COLN ST ALDWYNS | Map 5 SP10

The New Inn At Coln ★★ HL ⊛⊛ ⚑

GL7 5AN ☎ **01285 750651** 🖹 **01285 750657**
e-mail: info@thenewinnatcoln.co.uk
web: www.new-inn.co.uk
dir: *Between Bibury (B4425) & Fairford (A417), 8m E of
Cirencester*

A beautiful old building, stylishly renovated, the inn lies
at the heart of this Cotswold village community. Eat in
the bar or the award-winning restaurant, which has two
AA rosettes, or take a seat on the south-facing terrace or
meadow-side garden. Easy-eating food is offered at
lunchtime, while in the evening there might be toasted
fishcakes with citrus salad, prime rib-eye steaks, or
gilthead bream with tartare sauce. AA red-star
accommodation is available in luxuriously equipped
rooms, full character.

Open all wk **Bar Meals** L served all wk 12.30-3 D served
all wk 7-9 Av main course £9.50 **Restaurant** L served all
wk 12.30-3 D served all wk 7-9 Fixed menu price fr £25
Av 3 course à la carte fr £25 ⊕ FREE HOUSE ◀ Hook
Norton Best Bitter, Wadworth 6X, Donningtons BB. ⚑ 12
Facilities Play area Dogs allowed Garden Parking
Rooms 13

COWLEY | Map 10 SO91

PICK OF THE PUBS

The Green Dragon Inn ★★★★ INN ⚑

See Pick of the Pubs on page 196

CRANHAM | Map 10 SO81

The Black Horse Inn ⚑

GL4 8HP ☎ **01452 812217**
dir: *A46 towards Stroud, follow signs for Cranham*

Set in a small village surrounded by woodland and
commons, a mile from the Cotswold Way and Prinknash
Abbey, this is a traditional inn with two open fires and
two dining rooms upstairs. On the menu you'll find all
sorts of pies, as well as chops, gammon, salads,
casseroles and a variety of fish dishes including grilled
salmon, and trout with garlic and herb butter. There's
quite a bit of Morris dancing throughout the season, with
the sloping garden offering lovely views across the valley.

Open 12-2.30 6.30-11 (Sun 12-3.30 6.30-11) Closed: 25
Dec, Mon **Bar Meals** L served Tue-Sat 12-2, Sun 12-2.30
D served Tue-Sun 6.45-9 **Restaurant** L served Tue-Sat 12-2,
Sun 12-2.30 booking required D served Sat-Sun 6.45-9
booking required ⊕ FREE HOUSE ◀ Wickwar Brand Oak,
Archers, Golden Train & Village, Hancocks HB & guest
ales, Cats Whiskers, Gem, Bath Ales, Butcombe, Stroud
Brewery Buddings ♂ Thatchers Gold, Stowford
Press. ⚑ 16 **Facilities** Garden Parking

EBRINGTON | Map 10 SP14

PICK OF THE PUBS

The Ebrington Arms ★★★★ INN ⊛ ⚑

GL55 6NH ☎ **01386 593223**
e-mail: info@theebringtonarms.co.uk
dir: *Chipping Campden on B4035 towards Shipston on
Stour. Left to Ebrington signed after 0.5m, by village
green*

Ideally located for the Cotswold Way, this hidden gem
stands in an Area of Outstanding Natural Beauty just
two miles from Chipping Campden. Every inch a proper
pub, it dates from 1640 and retains its original
flagstones and beams, as well as the log burning
inglenook fireplaces that used to cook the village's
bread. It's the hub of community life, with locals
chatting over the merits of three award-winning real
ales and two ciders. As for the food, chef James Nixon's
talents are recognised with an AA rosette. He is a great
believer in low food miles and freshly harvested

organic produce when available. A meal could include
clam, chilli and coriander chowder followed by stuffed
belly pork with cabbage, bubble and squeak and cider
cream, and a pudding of warm chocolate and date
brownie with butterscotch sauce and clotted cream.
Music, games and quiz nights, and occasional themed
food evenings are held. If you would like to stay, there
are luxurious en suite bedrooms available.

The Ebrington Arms

Open noon-3 6-close (Fri-Sun all day summer) Closed:
Mon (ex BH) **Bar Meals** L served Tue-Sat 12-2.30, Sun
12-3.30 D served Tue-Thu 6.30-9, Fri-Sat 6.30-9.30 Av
main course £11.50 **Restaurant** L served Tue-Sat
12-2.30, Sun 12-3.30 booking required D served Tue-
Thu 6.30-9, Fri-Sat 6.30-9.30 booking required ⊕ FREE
HOUSE ◀ Goffs Brewery, Jouster, Tom Long Stroud. ⚑ 8
Facilities Children's menu Dogs allowed Garden
Parking **Rooms** 3

FORD | Map 10 SP02

PICK OF THE PUBS

The Plough Inn ★★★★ INN ⚑

GL54 5RU ☎ **01386 584215** 🖹 **01386 584042**
e-mail: info@theploughinnatford.co.uk
dir: *4m from Stow-on-the-Wold on B4077 towards
Tewkesbury*

Cheltenham racecourse is but a short drive from this
16th-century inn, and the famous Jackdaws Castle
racing stables are just across the street. Trainers,
jockeys and stable hands are always in the bar, which
features an award that recognises the pub's love of all
things racing. So committed is landlord Craig Brown
that he rode as a novice at Aintree on Grand National
day in April 2009. It's a traditional English pub, with
flagstone floors and log fires, sturdy pine furnishings
and remnants of the stocks that once held convicted
sheep-stealers. Meals chosen from lunch, dinner and

continued on page 197

PICK OF THE PUBS

The Green Dragon Inn ★★★★ INN ♓

COWLEY Map 10 SO91

Cockleford GL53 9NW
☎ 01242 870271 📄 01242 870171
e-mail: green-dragon@buccaneer.co.uk
web: www.green-dragon-inn.co.uk
dir: *Telephone for directions*

This handsome stone-built inn, dating from the 17th century, is situated in the Cotswold hamlet of Cockleford. The fittings and furniture are the work of Robert Thompson, the 'Mouse Man of Kilburn' (that's Kilburn, North Yorkshire, not London), so-called for his trademark mouse, after whom the popular Mouse Bar, with its stone-flagged floors, beamed ceilings and crackling log fires, is named. Here and in the Lower Bar freshly prepared traditional and modern 'pub food with a difference' is served from a weekly menu that includes sandwiches at lunchtime and children's favourites. A good choice of starters/light meals include warm pigeon breast and smoked bacon salad; cullen skink, a rich tasty soup of smoked haddock, potatoes and leeks; and chargrilled gammon steak with free-range fried egg. Typical main meals include game casserole with winter roots and marjoram savoury cobbler; pan-fried salmon fillet with a saffron risotto flavoured with crayfish tails and crab; and steak and kidney suet pudding with minted mushy peas. Vegetarians might opt for puff pastry tartlet filled with sunblush tomatoes, olives and rocket on a mizuna and Parmesan salad. Another important feature is the choice of real ales, with Hook Norton, Butcombe and a monthly guest. The Function Room can be turned into a skittle alley, where teams have been playing since the early 1900s. The bar here opens out on to a spacious patio area overlooking a lake, making it a lovely place for a meal. Comfortable bedrooms are individually furnished to a high standard, all with their own en suite bathroom.

Open all week **Bar Meals** L served Mon-Fri 12-2.15, Sat 12-2.30, Sun 12-3 D served all week 6-8.30 Av main course £13.50 **Restaurant** L served Mon-Fri 12-2.15, Sat 12-2.30, Sun 12-3 D served all week 6-8.30 ⊕ Buccaneer ◀ Hook Norton, Directors, Butcombe, guest ale ♻ Stowford Press. ♓ 9 **Facilities** Children's menu Dogs allowed Garden Parking **Rooms** 9

FORD *continued*

Sunday menus are cooked to order from local produce and usually include Gloucester Old Spot sausages with buttered mash and rich onion gravy; smoked haddock and spring onion fishcakes with poached free-range egg; and chicken Kiev with chips and garden peas. Visitors stay in en suite bedrooms in the former stable block.

Open all wk Closed: 25 Dec **Bar Meals** L served Mon-Fri 10-2, Sat-Sun all day D served Mon-Fri 6-9, Sat-Sun all day food served all day **Restaurant** L served Mon-Fri 10-2, Sat-Sun all day D served Mon-Fri 6-9, Sat-Sun all day food served all day ⊕ DONNINGTON ◀ Donnington BB, SBA & XXX (summer only) ♻ Stowfords. ☙ 7 **Facilities** Play area Garden Parking **Rooms** 3

FOSSEBRIDGE Map 5 SP01

PICK OF THE PUBS

The Inn at Fossebridge ★★★★ INN ☙

GL54 3JS ☎ 01285 720721 📠 01285 720793
e-mail: info@fossebridgeinn.co.uk
dir: *From M4 junct 15, A419 towards Cirencester, then A429 towards Stow. Pub approx 7m on left*

Set in extensive grounds with a lake, this imposing, family-run, 18th-century free house was once a coaching inn on the ancient Fosseway. Then it was known as Lord Chedworth's Arms, whose name is commemorated by the wonderful old bar. Exposed beams, stone walls, flagstone floors and open fires provide the setting for the varied bar food and restaurant menus, with snacks ranging from sandwiches, baguettes and jacket potatoes, to light meals and ever-changing specials such as steak and ale pie; and pan-fried sardines with chunky tomato sauce. Turn to the main menu for additional choices: starters of Thai fishcake on pak choi with chilli and lime dressing; duck pancake rolls with cucumber and plum sauce; and smooth game terrine, while main courses could include baked fillet of cod; wild mushroom and butternut squash risotto; and signature dish roasted best end of Cotswold lamb with herb crust. The bedrooms have all been refurbished in the Georgian style.

Open all day all wk noon-mdnt (Sun noon-11.30) **Bar Meals** L served all wk 12-3 D served Mon-Sat 6.30-10, Sun 6.30-9.30 Av main course £7.50 **Restaurant** L served all wk 12-3 booking required D served Mon-Sat 6.30-10, Sun 6.30-9.30 booking required ⊕ FREE HOUSE ◀ Tribute, Proper Job ♻ Stowford Press. ☙ 8 **Facilities** Children's menu Dogs allowed Garden Parking **Rooms** 8

FRAMPTON MANSELL Map 4 SO90

PICK OF THE PUBS

The Crown Inn ★★★★ INN ☙

GL6 8JG ☎ 01285 760601
e-mail: enquiries@thecrowninn-cotswolds.co.uk
dir: *A419 halfway between Cirencester & Stroud*

Overlooking the wooded Golden Valley in the heart of unspoilt Frampton Mansell, stands this 17th-century free house. Once a simple cider house, and now in the fresh hands of Simon Baker, it is the perfect village pub. The interior is full of old world charm, with honey-coloured stone walls, beams and open fireplaces where log fires are lit in winter. There is also plenty of seating in the large garden for the warmer months. Gloucestershire beers, such as Stroud Organic and Laurie Lee's Bitter, are usually showcased alongside others from the region, and a good choice of wines by the glass is served in the restaurant and three inviting bars. Fresh local food with lots of seasonal specials includes chicken, mushroom and leek pie; baby vegetable and lentil stew; slow-cooked lamb shank with chorizo cassoulet; and fish, chips and mushy peas.

Open all day all wk noon-11 **Bar Meals** L served Mon-Sat 12-2.30, Sun 12-8.30 booking required D served Mon-Sat 6-9.30, Sun 12-8.30 booking required Av main course £9 ⊕ FREE HOUSE ◀ Butcombe Bitter, Laurie Lee's Bitter. ☙ 12 **Facilities** Children's menu Dogs allowed Garden Parking **Rooms** 12

GLOUCESTER Map 10 SO81

Queens Head ☙

Tewkesbury Rd, Longford GL2 9EJ
☎ 01452 301882 📠 01452 524368
e-mail: queenshead@aol.com
dir: *On A38 (Tewkesbury to Gloucester road) in Longford*

This 250 year-old pub/restaurant is just out of town but there's no missing it in summer when it is festooned with hanging baskets. Inside, there's a lovely old flagstone-floored locals' bar which proffers a great range of real ales, while two dining areas tempt with comprehensive menus. These may include bison steak with red wine and shallot sauce, pan-fried marlin steak on wilted spinach, or the pub's signature dish, Longford lamb - a kilo joint slowly cooked in mint gravy until it falls off the bone.

Open all wk 11-3 5.30-11 **Bar Meals** L served all wk 12-2 D served all wk 6.30-9.30 Av main course £10 **Restaurant** D served all wk 6.30-9.30 ⊕ FREE HOUSE ◀ Butty Bach, Dursley Steam, Otter, Butcombe ♻ Ashton Press, Stowford Press. ☙ 8 **Facilities** Parking

---

GREAT BARRINGTON Map 10 SP21

PICK OF THE PUBS

The Fox ☙

OX18 4TB ☎ 01451 844385
e-mail: info@foxinnbarrington.com
dir: *3m W on A40 from Burford, turn N signed The Barringtons, pub approx 0.5m on right*

Picturesque 16th-century pub with a delightful patio and large beer garden overlooking the River Windrush - on warm days a perfect summer watering hole and very popular with those attending Cheltenham racecourse. Built of mellow Cotswold stone and characterised by low ceilings and log fires, the inn offers a range of well-kept Donnington beers and a choice of food using the best of local produce. In the Riverview Restaurant expect dishes like beef in ale pie; local pigeon breasts casseroled with button mushrooms; chicken piri-piri; Thai tuna steak; and spinach, leek and chestnut pie.

Open all day all wk 11-11 **Bar Meals** L served Mon-Fri 12-2.30, Sat-Sun 12-9.30 D served Mon-Fri 6.30-9.30, Sat-Sun 12-9.30 Av main course £9.95 **Restaurant** L served Mon-Fri 12-2.30, Sat-Sun 12-9.30 D served Mon-Fri 6.30-9.30, Sat-Sun 12-9.30 ⊕ DONNINGTON ◀ Donnington BB, SBA. ☙ 7 **Facilities** Children's menu Dogs allowed Garden Parking

---

GREET Map 10 SP03

The Harvest Home ☙

Evesham Rd GL54 5BH
☎ 01242 602430 📠 01242 602094
e-mail: harvesthome07@btinternet.com
dir: *M5 junct 9 take A435 towards Evesham, then B4077 & B4078 towards Winchcombe, 200yds from station*

Set in the beautiful Cotswold countryside, this traditional country inn draws steam train enthusiasts aplenty, as a restored stretch of the Great Western Railway runs past the end of the garden. Built around 1903 for railway workers, the pub is handy for Cheltenham Racecourse and Sudeley Castle. Expect a good range of snacks and mains, including locally-reared beef and tempting seafood dishes.

Open all wk 12-3 6-11 (Sun 12-10.30) **Bar Meals** L served all wk 12-3 D served all wk 6.30-9 **Restaurant** L served all wk 12-3 D served all wk 6.30-9 ⊕ ENTERPRISE INNS ◀ Goffs Jouster, Timothy Taylor Landlord, Courage Directors ♻ Stowford Press. ☙ 11 **Facilities** Children's menu Dogs allowed Garden Parking

The Hollow Bottom ☻

GL54 5UX ☎ 01451 850392 ▤ 01451 850945
e-mail: hello@hollowbottom.com
dir: Telephone for directions

There's a horse-racing theme at this 18th-century
Cotswold free house, often frequented by the Cheltenham
racing fraternity. Its nooks and crannies lend themselves
to an intimate drink or meal, and there's also a separate
dining room, plus outside tables for fine weather.
Specials include prawn cocktail on seasonal leaves with
a spicy tomato sauce; grilled salmon; breast of pan-fried
chicken with stilton, olive oil, tomato and spring onion;
and home-made raspberry cheesecake to finish.

Open all wk ⊕ FREE HOUSE ◪ Hollow Bottom Best Bitter,
Goff's Jouster, Timothy Taylor Landlord, Fuller's London
Pride, Caledonian IPA. ☻ 7 **Facilities** Dogs allowed Garden
Parking

The Bull Inn ☻

SN14 8HG ☎ 0117 937 2332
e-mail: diserwhite@aol.com
web: www.thebullathinton.co.uk
dir: From M4 junct 18, A46 to Bath 1m, turn right 1m,
down hill. Pub on right

Since it was built in the 17th century, The Bull has been
an inn, a farm and a dairy, and following some of that
tradition the owners now rear their own pigs for the
restaurant table. Inside it retains two inglenook fireplaces
and original flagstone flooring, while outside there's a
front-facing terrace and a large rear garden with a
children's play area. Food served draws on locally
supplied produce and home-grown fruit and vegetables.
Look out for Royal Gloucester steak and ale pie with
horseradish pastry; and deep fried cod in soda and lime
batter.

Open noon-3 6-11.30 (Sat-Sun & BH open all day)
Closed: Mon L (ex BH) **Bar Meals** L served Tue-Sat 12-2,
Sun 12-3.30 D served Mon-Thu 6-9, Fri-Sat 6-9.30 Av
main course £12 **Restaurant** L served Tue-Sat 12-2, Sun
12-3.30 booking required D served Mon-Thu 6-9, Fri-Sat
6-9.30 booking required ⊕ WADWORTH ◪ Wadworth 6X &
Henrys IPA, Wadworth Bishops Tipple, Wadworth
Summersault, guest ale. ☻ 12 **Facilities** Children's menu
Play area Dogs allowed Garden Parking

The Trout Inn ☻

St Johns Bridge GL7 3HA
☎ 01367 252313 ▤ 01367 252313
e-mail: chefpjw@aol.com
dir: A40 onto A361 then A417. From M4 junct 15, A419,
then A361 & A417 to Lechlade

In 1220, when workmen constructed a new bridge over
the Thames, they built an almshouse to live in. In 1472 it
became an inn, which it has been ever since. The bar, all
flagstone floors and beams, overflows into the old
boathouse. Appetising snacks, and dishes like rich lamb
and vegetable hotpot; locally made faggots; and
tempura-battered hake fillets are favourites. The large
garden often pulsates with tractor and steam events, and
jazz and folk festivals.

Open all wk 10-3 6-11 (summer all wk 10am-11pm)
Closed: 25 Dec **Bar Meals** L served all wk 12-2 D served
all wk 7-10 **Restaurant** L served all wk 12-2 D served all
wk 7-10 ◪ Courage Best, Doom Bar, Cornish Coaster,
guest ales. ☻ 15 **Facilities** Play area Family room Dogs
allowed Garden Parking

White Hart ☻

BS35 1NR ☎ 01454 412275
e-mail: whitehart@youngs.co.uk
dir: M48 junct 1 towards Chepstow left on rdbt, follow for
3m, 1st left to Littleton-on-Severn

A traditional English country pub dating back to the
1680s. It was originally a farmhouse, from which
flagstone floors and other features of the old building,
including two large inglenook fireplaces, survive. Food
ranges from home-cooked pub classics, such as beef and
ale winter stew with herb dumpling and vegetables, to
modern Anglo-French dishes that usually feature among
the specials. After all-day sun in the front garden, watch
it set over the Severn estuary.

Open all day all wk 12-11 **Bar Meals** L served Mon-Fri
12-2, Sat 12-9.30, Sun12-8 D served Mon-Fri 6-9, Sat
12-9.30, Sun 12-8 ⊕ YOUNGS ◪ Youngs Bitter, Youngs
Special, St Austell Tribute, Bath Ales Gem ♂ Thatchers
Heritage. ☻ 18 **Facilities** Family room Dogs allowed
Garden Parking

The Hobnails Inn ☻

GL20 8NQ ☎ 01242 620237 ▤ 01242 620458
dir: M5 junct 9, A46 towards Evesham then B4077 to
Stow-on-the-Wold. Inn 1.5m on left

Established in 1473, the Hobnails is one of the oldest
inns in the county. Inside you'll find winter log fires, and
you can tuck yourself into a private corner, or relax with a
pint of ale on one of the leather sofas. A good range of
bar snacks is supplemented by a lunchtime carvery and a
fresh fish range. Outside is a lovely large garden for
warmer days with views over surrounding countryside.

Open all wk ⊕ ENTERPRISE INNS ◪ London Pride, Flowers
IPA, Hook Norton Best, Deuchars IPA, Tetleys. ☻ 6
Facilities Dogs allowed Garden Parking

The Glasshouse Inn ☻

May Hill GL17 0NN ☎ 01452 830529
dir: Village off A40 between Gloucester & Ross-on-Wye

The Glasshouse is unique and its popularity confirms the
need for traditional pubs with no gimmicks. The inn dates
back to 1450 and gets its name from Dutch glassmakers
who settled locally in the 16th century. It is located in a
wonderful rural setting with a country garden outside and
a tranquil and dignified interior. Home-cooked dishes
include authentic Thai choices.

Closed: Sun eve **Bar Meals** L served all wk 12-2 booking
required D served Mon-Sat 6.30-9 ⊕ FREE HOUSE
◪ Butcombe, Spitfire, Black Sheep, London Pride, Greene
King ♂ Stowford Press. ☻ 6 **Facilities** Garden Parking

The Farmers Arms ☻

Ledbury Rd GL19 4DR ☎ 01452 780307
e-mail: danieljrpardoe@googlemail.com
dir: From Tewkesbury take A38 towards Gloucester/
Ledbury. 2m, right at lights onto B4213 (signed Ledbury).
1.5m, pub on left

A popular, 16th-century, timber-framed pub on the
village fringe and close to the River Severn. Low beams,
an open fire, regular guest ales and an extensive menu
are to be found within. Home-made dishes using locally
sourced produce include steak and kidney pie; honey
roast ham with free range eggs and chips; and luxury fish
pie.

Open all wk 11-3 6-12 (Sat-Sun & summer 11-mdnt) **Bar
Meals** L served all wk 12-2 D served all wk 6-9.30
Restaurant L served all wk 12-2 D served all wk
6-9.30 ⊕ WADWORTH ◪ Wadworth 6X, Henry's Original
IPA ♂ Stowford Press, Thatchers Gold. ☻ 10
Facilities Children's menu Play area Dogs allowed Garden
Parking

PICK OF THE PUBS

The Fox ☻

See Pick of the Pubs on opposite page

PICK OF THE PUBS

The Fox ♀

LOWER ODDINGTON   Map 10 SP22

GL56 0UR
☎ **01451 870555 & 870666**
🖷 **01451 870666**
e-mail: info@foxinn.net
web: www.foxinn.net
dir: *A436 from Stow-on-the-Wold then right to Lower Oddington*

Set in a quintessential Cotswold village close to Stow-on-the-Wold, this stone-built and creeper-clad free house dates back to the 17th century. Fresh flowers and antique furniture complete the period feel in the bar, with its polished flagstone floors, beams and log fires. Meanwhile, diners in the Red Room can admire a fine collection of drawings, water colours and oil paintings. The Fox's reputation for good food and wine at reasonable prices draws people in to enjoy the atmosphere of a traditional

English pub. Chefs Ray Pearce and James Cathcart create regularly changing menus, and the daily specials take full advantage of seasonal local produce and freshly-caught Cornish fish. Starters like chicken liver pâté with cornichons and French bread, and roasted butternut squash risotto herald main course options that include grilled sirloin steak with mustard and herb butter; individually baked beefsteak and kidney pie; and lamb chump with flageolet beans and red wine sauce. Desserts such as orange and apricot brioche bread and butter pudding, and apple and blackberry crumble with custard provide a satisfying conclusion, or you might try the selection of three cheeses with fig chutney. In summer, there's a heated terrace for alfresco dining, as well as a pretty, traditional cottage garden. The inn has three double bedrooms, two of which are en suite, whilst the third has a private shower room. Don't miss the medieval church wall paintings in Lower Oddington village, which is ideally situated for discovering the delights of the surrounding Cotswolds and visiting Shakespeare's Stratford-upon-Avon or Oxford's dreaming spires.

Open all week Closed: 25 Dec **Bar Meals** L served Mon-Sat 12-2, Sun 12-4 D served Mon-Sat 6.30-10, Sun 7-9.30 Av main course £12.50 **Restaurant** L served Mon-Sat 12-2, Sun 12-4 D served Mon-Sat 6.30-10, Sun 7-9.30 Av 3 course à la carte fr £20 ⊕ FREE HOUSE ◀ Hook Norton Best, Abbot Ale, Ruddles County, Wickwar's Old Bob, Purity UBU. ♀ 12 **Facilities** Children's menu Dogs allowed Garden Parking

LYDNEY   Map 4 SO60

The George Inn ▼

St Briavels GL15 6TA ☎ 01594 530228
dir: *Telephone for directions*

In a quiet village high above the Wye Valley and close to
the Forest of Dean, this pretty white-washed pub
overlooks a moody 12th-century castle ruin. The interior
includes an 8th-century Celtic coffin lid set into one of
the walls. The pub is famous for braised shoulder of lamb
and Moroccan lamb, along with popular dishes such as
traditional steak and kidney, and beef and Guinness pies.

Open all wk 12-3 6.30-11 **Bar Meals** L served all wk
12-2.30 D served all wk 6.30-9 ⊕ WADWORTH ◀ 6X, IPA,
JCB Ö Stowford Press. ▼ 10 **Facilities** Dogs allowed
Garden Parking

MARSHFIELD   Map 4 ST77

The Catherine Wheel

39 High St SN14 8LR ☎ 01225 892220
e-mail: bookings@thecatherinewheel.co.uk
dir: *Between Bath, Bristol & Chippenham on A420. 5m
from M4 junct 18*

Simple, stylish decor complements the clean lines of this
impressive, mainly 17th-century inn on the edge of the
Cotswolds, with its exposed brickwork and large open
fireplaces. Menus are also simple and well presented,
with favourites at lunchtime including jacket potatoes
and ploughman's. In the evening look forward to smoked
mackerel and crab fishcakes, followed by one of the
specials such as venison and pheasant stew. A small but
sunny patio is a lovely spot for a summertime pint brewed
by nearby Cotswold and Bath-based breweries.

Open all wk noon-3 6-11 (Sun noon-11) **Bar Meals** L
served Mon-Sat 12-2, Sun 12-3 booking required D served
Mon-Sat 7-10 booking required **Restaurant** L served Mon-
Sat 12-2, Sun 12-3 booking required D served Mon-Sat
7-10 booking required ⊕ FREE HOUSE ◀ Courage Best,
guest ales Ö Stowford Press. **Facilities** Children's menu
Dogs allowed Garden Parking

The Lord Nelson Inn ★★★ INN ▼

1 & 2 High St SN14 8LP ☎ 01225 891820
e-mail: thelordnelsoninn.@btinternet.com
dir: *On A420 between Bristol & Chippenham. M4 Junct
19 Bath then travel along A46 towards railway stations,
Bath & Chippenham.*

Located in a village at the edge of the Cotswolds, this
17th-century coaching inn is family run and has a good
reputation for its home-made food and quality cask ales.
There is a spacious bar, candlelit restaurant, log fires in
winter and a patio for summer use. Dishes range from
home-made burger with hand cut chips, to collops of
monkfish with saffron and red pepper dressing, and
timbale of white and wild rice. There are three en suite
bedrooms available.

Open all day all wk noon-11 (Fri-Sun all day) **Bar Meals** L
served Mon-Sat 12-2, Sun 12-3 D served Mon-Sat 6.30-9,
Sun 6-8 booking required Av main course £10.95
Restaurant L served Mon-Sat 12-2, Sun 12-3 D served
Mon-Sat 6.30-9, Sun 6-8 booking required Av 3 course à
la carte fr £14.95 ⊕ ENTERPRISE INNS ◀ Courage Best,
Bath Gem, 6X Ö Stowford Press. ▼ 12
Facilities Children's menu Play area Dogs allowed Garden
Rooms 3

MEYSEY HAMPTON   Map 5 SP10

The Masons Arms ▼

28 High St GL7 5JT ☎ 01285 850164 📠 01285 850164
dir: *6m E of Cirencester off A417, beside village green*

New landlords have taken over this 17th-century stone
pub beside the green in a charming village on the
southern edge of the Cotswolds near Cirencester. The hub
of the community, expect to find a log fire in the big
inglenook, straightforward pub food, and local Hooky and
changing guest ales on tap in the convivial beamed bar.
Worth noting if visiting the Cotswold Water Park nearby.

Open all wk **Bar Meals** L served all wk 12-3 D served all
wk 3-6 **Restaurant** L served all wk 12-3 D served all wk
3-6 ⊕ FREE HOUSE ◀ Hook Norton Best, Butcombes,
Theakstons, guest ales. ▼ 14 **Facilities** Children's menu
Play area Dogs allowed Garden Parking

MINCHINHAMPTON   Map 4 SO80

The Old Lodge ▼

Minchinhampton Common GL6 9AQ
☎ 01453 832047 📠 01453 834033
e-mail: old-lodge@food-club.com
dir: *Telephone for details*

A 400-year-old Cotswold inn, high on Minchinhampton
Common, where cattle range free and from where you can
see Wales. The stylish restaurant, adorned with paintings
and sculptures, has floor-to-ceiling windows that look
directly onto the common. Typically on the menu are roast
monkfish tail with curried parsnip purée and mussel
broth; braised shank of lamb with dauphinoise potato,
french beans and paprika sauce; and porcini mushroom
risotto with shaved Parmesan.

Open all day all wk 11-11 (Sun 11-10.30) Closed: 25 Dec
Bar Meals L served Mon-Fri 12-3, Sat 12-10, Sun 12-9.30
D served Mon-Fri 6-10, Sat 12-10, Sun 12-9.30
Restaurant L served Mon-Fri 12-3, Sat 12-10, Sun
12-9.30 D served Mon-Fri 6-10, Sat 12-10, Sun
12-9.30 ◀ Stroud Budding, Tom Long, Otter Bitter
Ö Stowford Press. ▼ 10 **Facilities** Children's menu Dogs
allowed Garden

PICK OF THE PUBS

The Weighbridge Inn ▼

See Pick of the Pubs on opposite page

NAILSWORTH   Map 4 ST89

PICK OF THE PUBS

The Britannia ▼

Cossack Square GL6 0DG ☎ 01453 832501
e-mail: pheasantpluckers2003@yahoo.co.uk
dir: *From A46 S'bound right at town centre rdbt. 1st
left. Pub directly ahead*

This stone-built 17th-century former manor house
occupies a delightful position on the south side of
Nailsworth's Cossack Square. The interior is bright and
uncluttered with low ceilings, cosy fires and a blue
slate floor. Outside you'll find a pretty garden with
plenty of tables, chairs and parasols for sunny days.
Whether inside or out, a pint of well-kept ale is sure to
go down well. The brasserie-style menu offers an
interesting blend of modern British and continental
food, with ingredients bought from local suppliers and
from Smithfield Market. You can go lightly with just a
starter from a tapas-style list that includes houmous,
deep-fried brie and moules marinière; or plunge into
hearty classics such as steak and ale pie or ham, egg
and chips. Other options include stone-baked pizzas
and impressive meat-free options such as butternut
squash and chilli risotto. Great wines, too.

Open all wk Closed: 25 Dec ⊕ FREE HOUSE ▼ 10
Facilities Dogs allowed Garden Parking

PICK OF THE PUBS

Egypt Mill ★★ HL ▼

GL6 0AE ☎ 01453 833449 📠 01453 839919
e-mail: reception@egyptmill.com
dir: *M4 junct 18, A46 N to Stroud. M5 junct 13, A46 to
Nailsworth*

Situated in the charming Cotswold town of Nailsworth,
this converted corn mill contains many features of
great character, including the original millstones and
lifting equipment. The ground floor bar and bistro enjoy
a picturesque setting, and its views over the pretty
water gardens complete the scene. There is a choice of
eating in the bistro or restaurant, and in both there is a
good selection of wines by the glass. For those who like
to savour an aperitif before dining, try the large Egypt
Mill Lounge. Tempting starters might offer ham hock
and pea risotto; smoked salmon and avocado parcels;
and salmon and lobster sausages. Main courses

continued on page 202

PICK OF THE PUBS

The Weighbridge Inn ♀

MINCHINHAMPTON
Map 4 SO80

GL6 9AL
☎ **01453 832520** 📠 **01453 835903**
e-mail: enquiries@2in1pub.co.uk
dir: *Between Nailsworth & Avening on B4014*

The 17th-century free house stands on the original London to Bristol packhorse trail, now a footpath and bridleway, ideal for exploring the South Cotswolds on foot. At one time the innkeeper also looked after the weighbridge, which served the local woollen mills; these included the long defunct Longfords Mill, memorabilia from which is displayed around the inn, alongside rural artefacts and rustic furnishings. Behind the scenes there has been careful renovation, but original features of the bars and the restaurant in the upstairs raftered hayloft, with its massive roof beams reaching almost to

the floor, remain untouched. The drinking areas are just as cosy for pints of Uley Old Spot and heady Westons cider while, outside, the patios and sheltered landscaped garden offer good views of the Cotswolds. Owner Howard Parker feels that in an ever-changing world some things should remain the same. The customers agree and find comfort in the familiar surroundings, to which some have been accustomed for over 60 years. The inn prides itself on the quality of its food, all cooked from scratch. The famous '2 in 1' pies, served straight from the oven on a wooden board, have been made here for 30 years, comprising the filling of your choice (such as pork, bacon and celery, or salmon in a creamy sauce) topped with home-made cauliflower cheese and a pastry lid. Also popular are the Sunday roasts and the daily specials that supplement the regular menu, which itself changes every five weeks and may list moules marinière, corned beef hash, salmon fishcakes with parsley and chive sauce, and almond and pear tart with amaretto custard. The future for the inn is really more of the same: great food, great service and great company.

Open noon-11 (Sun noon-10.30) Closed: 25 Dec & 10 days Jan **Bar Meals** L served all week 12-9.30 D served all week 12-9.30 Av main course £10 **Restaurant** L served all week 12-9.30 D served all week 12-9.30 ⊕ FREE HOUSE 🛢 Wadworth 6X, Uley Old Spot, Laurie Lee Ö Wicked Witch, Westons Bounds Brand. ♀ 16 **Facilities** Children's menu Family room Dogs allowed Garden Parking

NAILSWORTH *continued*

include the likes of saddle of lamb Greek style; calves' liver and bacon; breast of duck with apple and blackberry risotto; and Brixham fish and potato pie.

Open all day all wk 11am-11pm **Bar Meals** L served Mon-Fri 12-2, Sat 12-2.30, Sun 12-6 D served Mon-Thu 6-9.30, Fri-Sat 6-9.45, Sun 6.30-9 ⊕ FREE HOUSE ♻ Stowford Press. ♈ 10 **Facilities** Garden Parking **Rooms** 28

PICK OF THE PUBS

Tipputs Inn ♈

Bath Rd GL6 0QE ☎ 01453 832466 ▤ 01453 832010
e-mail: pheasantpluckers2003@yahoo.co.uk
dir: A46, 0.5m S of Nailsworth

Mellow Cotswold stone and stripped floorboards blend nicely with modern, clean-lined furniture in this impeccably decorated 17th-century pub-restaurant. A giant candelabra adds a touch of grandeur. Located in the heart of the Cotswolds, the Tipputs Inn is owned by Nick Beardsley and Christophe Coquoin. They started out as chefs together more than 12 years ago, but admit to spending less time in the kitchen these days now that they have to create menus for this and their other Gloucestershire food pubs, plus they select and import some ingredients and wines direct from France. There are dishes for every eventuality, starting with tapas-style appetisers and extending through starters such as pan-fried haloumi or spicy prawn cocktail to pub classics (fish and chips; home-made burger and chips) and classy options such as confit duck leg with black pudding, mashed potato and seasonal vegetables or cherry tomato, basil and ricotta risotto. Classic desserts include Eton mess and vanilla crème brûlée.

Open all wk Closed: 25 Dec ⊕ FREE HOUSE ♦ Greene King IPA, Abbot Ale, Stroud Brewery. ♈ 12 **Facilities** Dogs allowed Garden Parking

NAUNTON | Map 10 SP12

The Black Horse

GL54 3AD ☎ 01451 850565
dir: Telephone for directions

Renowned for its home-cooked food and Donnington real ales, this friendly inn enjoys a typical Cotswold village setting beloved of ramblers and locals alike. The Black Horse provides a traditional English menu featuring liver and bacon, cottage pie, and broccoli and cheese bake.

Open all wk 11-3 6-11 (Fri-Sat 11-11, Sun 12-11) **Bar Meals** L served Mon-Fri 12-2.30, Sat-Sun 12-3 D served Tue-Fri 6.30-9, Sat 6-9 **Restaurant** L served Mon-Fri 12-2.30, Sat-Sun 12-3 D served Tue-Fri 6.30-9, Sat 6-9 ⊕ DONNINGTON ♦ Donnington BB, SBA ♻ Stowford Press. **Facilities** Dogs allowed Garden Parking

NEWLAND | Map 4 SO50

PICK OF THE PUBS

The Ostrich Inn

GL16 8NP ☎ 01594 833260 ▤ 01594 833260
e-mail: kathryn@theostrichinn.com
dir: Follow Monmouth signs from Chepstow (A466), Newland signed from Redbrook

A 13th-century inn situated in a pretty village on the western edge of the Forest of Dean and adjoining the Wye Valley, both Areas of Outstanding Natural Beauty. To this day it still retains many of its ancient features, including a priest hole. With wooden beams and a welcoming log fire in the large lounge bar throughout the winter, visitors can enjoy a relaxed and friendly setting for a wide selection of cask-conditioned beers and good food. Diners are served in the small, intimate restaurant, the larger lounge bar, the garden and the patio. In the bar expect simpler dishes, such as salmon spinach fishcakes; steak and ale pie; and penne pasta. The monthly changing menu in the restaurant offers more sophistication in the form of slow-roasted spiced belly pork with pak choi; and supreme of Nile perch from Lake Victoria with black tiger prawns and chive cream sauce. No one will frown at your muddy boots.

Open all wk ⊕ FREE HOUSE ♦ Timothy Taylor Landlord, Butty Bach, Pigs Ear, Old Hooky, Adnams. **Facilities** Dogs allowed Garden

NORTH CERNEY | Map 5 SP00

Bathurst Arms ♈

GL7 7BZ ☎ 01285 831281
e-mail: james@bathurstarms.com
dir: 5m N of Cirencester on A435

A rambling, creeper-covered building on the Earl of Bathurst's estate, with gardens stretching to the banks of the River Churn, this is a cracking 17th-century inn in an enviably romantic location. The stone-flagged bar exudes character with beams and log fires, and draws walkers and locals in for pints of Hooky and decent pub food prepared from locally sourced ingredients. Bag a settle in the bar or walk through wine room to the restaurant, replete with open kitchen, and tuck into crab ravioli, pork belly and chorizo cassoulet, beer-battered pollack, and vanilla cheesecake.

Open all wk noon-3 6-11 (Sun noon-11) **Bar Meals** L served all wk 12-2 D served all wk 6-9 Av main course £12 **Restaurant** L served all wk 12-2 D served all wk 6-9 Fixed menu price fr £12 Av 3 course à la carte fr £25 ⊕ FREE HOUSE ♦ Cotswold Way, Tournament, Festival Gold ♻ Stowford Press. ♈ 60 **Facilities** Children's menu Dogs allowed Garden Parking

NORTHLEACH | Map 10 SP11

PICK OF THE PUBS

The Puesdown Inn ★★★★ INN ◉◉ ♈

Compton Abdale GL54 4DN
☎ 01451 860262 ▤ 01451 861262
e-mail: inn4food@btopenworld.com
dir: On A40 between Oxford & Cheltenham, 3m W of Northleach

Said to date from 1236, this refurbished coaching inn is set on the old Salt Way between Burford and Cheltenham. Inside, you'll find cosy sofas, log fires and warm, rich colours on the walls, providing a welcome refuge from the winter weather. For the inn is set 800 feet above sea level, and its unique name - an anagram for 'snowed up' - derives from an old English expression meaning 'windy ridge'. Guests were marooned here in 1947 during the worst blizzard of the century, but the spooky tales of the poacher who died on the doorstep with an arrow in his back date from much longer ago. The restaurant has earned two AA Rosettes for dishes such as roast local partridge with rosti potato and glazed apples; sea bass fillet with parsley potatoes and green beans; and organic pork loin with parsnip purée.

Closed: Sun eve **Bar Meals** L served Mon-Sat 12-3 D served Tue-Sat 6-10.30 Av main course £7.50 **Restaurant** L served all wk 12-3 booking required D served Tue-Sat 6-10.30 booking required Fixed menu price fr £10 Av 3 course à la carte fr £22.50 ⊕ FREE HOUSE ♦ Hook Norton Best Bitter, Hooky Dark, Old Hooky, Haymaker, Twelve Days. ♈ 15 **Facilities** Children's menu Dogs allowed Garden Parking **Rooms** 3

OAKRIDGE | Map 4 SO90

The Butcher's Arms

GL6 7NZ ☎ 01285 760371
e-mail: jemorgan@vwclub.net
dir: From Stroud A419, left for Eastcombe & Bisley signs. Just before Bisley right to Oakridge, follow brown signs for pub

Traditional Cotswold country pub with stone walls, beams and log fires in the renowned Golden Valley. Once a slaughterhouse and butchers shop. A full and varied restaurant menu offers steak, fish and chicken dishes, while the bar menu ranges from ploughman's lunches to home-cooked daily specials.

Open all wk 12-3 6-11 (Summer Fri-Sun noon-11) Closed: 1 Jan **Bar Meals** L served Tue-Sun 12-2 D served Tue-Sat 6-9 ⊕ WADWORTHS ♦ Henrys IPA, 6X, JCB, ♻ Stowford Press. **Facilities** Family room Dogs allowed Garden Parking

OLDBURY-ON-SEVERN — Map 4 ST69

The Anchor Inn ☻

Church Rd BS35 1QA ☎ 01454 413331
e-mail: info@anchorinnoldbury.co.uk
dir: *From N A38 towards Bristol, 1.5m then right, village signed. From S A38 through Thornbury*

Parts of this Cotswold stone pub, formerly a mill, date from 1540. The large garden by a stream has plenty of seats for summer dining, and a popular boules piste. Bar snacks include filled ciabattas, crayfish mayonnaise, and home-baked ham with eggs. Crispy roast belly of pork, Oldbury sausages and mash, jalfrezi chicken curry, Devon crab and scallop gratin and smoked haddock and salmon pie feature on the main menu.

Open all day all wk Sat-Sun **Bar Meals** L served Mon-Fri 12-2, Sat 12-2.30, Sun 12-3 D served Sat-Sun 6-9 Av main course £9.95 food served all day **Restaurant** L served Mon-Fri 12-2, Sat 12-2.30, Sun 12-3 booking required D served Sat-Sun 6-9 booking required Av 3 course à la carte fr £17 food served all day ⊕ FREE HOUSE ◀ Interbrew Bass, Theakston Old Peculier, Butcombe Best, Otter Bitter ◯ Ashton Press, Stowford Press. ☻ 12 **Facilities** Children's menu Dogs allowed Garden Parking

PAINSWICK — Map 4 SO80

PICK OF THE PUBS

The Falcon Inn ☻

New St GL6 6UN ☎ 01452 814222 📄 01452 813377
e-mail: enquiries@falconinn-cotswolds.co.uk
dir: *On A46 in centre of Painswick*

Boasting the world's oldest known bowling green in its grounds, the Falcon dates from 1554 and stands at the heart of a conservation village. For three centuries it was a courthouse, but today its friendly service extends to a drying room for walkers' gear. A sampling of dishes from the menu includes whole trout and almonds; gammon and egg; sirloin steak; chilli crust beef fillet; duck leg confit on a bed of sherry and Puy lentils with Madeira sauce; penne pasta arrabiatta; stuffed pork loin with apricot and pistachios; steamed seabass fillet with scallop mousseline; and minted lamb chop with fennel, asparagus and Jerusalem artichoke garnish.

Open all day all wk 10am-11pm **Bar Meals** L served all wk 12-3 D served all wk 7-9.30 ⊕ ENTERPRISE ◀ Otters Ale ◯ Stowford Press. ☻ 10 **Facilities** Dogs allowed Garden Parking

PAXFORD — Map 10 SP13

PICK OF THE PUBS

The Churchill Arms ☻ ☻

See Pick of the Pubs on page 204

POULTON — Map 5 SP00

PICK OF THE PUBS

The Falcon Inn ☻

London Rd GL7 5HN ☎ 01285 850844
e-mail: inn4food@btopenworld.com
dir: *From Cirencester E on A417 towards Fairford*

At the heart of the Cotswold village of Poulton, the Falcon has been transformed from a straightforward village local into a stylish and sophisticated gastro-pub which has become popular with drinkers and diners from far and wide. For beer drinkers this is a real ale paradise, with up to half a dozen breweries represented behind the colourful handles; the choice continues with many wines available by the glass. Diners too have decisions to make. Especially good value is the fixed-price two-course or three-course lunch menu, which offers choices of two starters and two main courses: pea and tomato risotto or leek and rocket soup followed by chargrilled sardines, new potatoes and salad, or pot roasted shoulder of lamb with winter vegetables. Desserts are along the lines of glazed rice pudding or lemon tart. Loin of Prinknash Abbey organic pork with pommes Anna and parsnip purée, and supreme of Great Farm guinea fowl with blackberry sauce are fine examples dinner main courses.

Closed: Sun eve & Mon **Bar Meals** L served Tue-Sat 12-3 D served Tue-Sat 6-10 Av main course £7 **Restaurant** L served Tue-Sun 12-3 booking required D served Tue-Sat 6-10 booking required Fixed menu price fr £10 Av 3 course à la carte fr £18.50 ⊕ ENTERPRISE INNS ◀ Hook Norton Best Bitter. ☻ 9 **Facilities** Children's menu Dogs allowed Garden Parking

SAPPERTON — Map 4 SO90

PICK OF THE PUBS

The Bell at Sapperton ☻

See Pick of the Pubs on page 205

SHEEPSCOMBE — Map 4 SO81

PICK OF THE PUBS

The Butchers Arms ☻

GL6 7RH ☎ 01452 812113 📄 01452 814358
e-mail: mark@butchers-arms.co.uk
dir: *1.5m S of A46 (Cheltenham to Stroud road), N of Painswick*

Set on the sunny side of Sheepscombe valley, this award-winning pub has a garden terrace with lovely views of beech-wooded slopes on all sides. Deer hunted by Henry VIII in his royal park used to hang in the bar - hence the pub's name. The area attracts many walkers, riders and tourists, all made welcome by hosts Mark and Sharon and their young team. A delightful range of hand-pulled real ales is offered in the bar, alongside a good selection of real ciders. The menus (a full menu is available at lunchtime and in the evening) include dishes made from produce raised in fields within sight of the pub. Light meals and salads are augmented by traditional favourites such as home-made cottage pie, chef's turkey curry, tomato and mushroom risotto, beer-battered fish and chips, and grilled steaks. Specials may include sea bass, scallops, pork belly, or local shoot pheasant. The 'Young Person's Menu' keeps children happy, or an adult-sized main course can be divided in two. An ever-changing specials board above the fireplace completes the choice and may include Pyll House Farm Barnsley lamb chop with grain mustard mash and redcurrant jus.

Open all wk 11.30-2.30 6.30-11 (Sat 11.30-11.30 Sun noon-10.30) **Bar Meals** L served all wk 12-2.30 booking required D served Mon-Sat 6.30-9.30, Sun 6.30-9 booking required Av main course £9.50 **Restaurant** L served all wk 12-2.30 booking required D served Mon-Sat 6.30-9.30, Sun 6.30-9 booking required Av 3 course à la carte fr £17.50 ⊕ FREE HOUSE ◀ Otter Bitter, Goffs Jouster, Butcombe Gold, St Austell Tribute ◯ Westons Stowford Press, Westons Bottled Ciders. ☻ 10 **Facilities** Children's menu Dogs allowed Garden Parking

PICK OF THE PUBS

The Churchill Arms 🏵 🍷

PAXFORD   Map 10 SP13

GL55 6XH
☎ **01386 594000** 📠 **01386 594005**
e-mail: info@thechurchillarms.com
web: www.thechurchillarms.com
dir: *2m E of Chipping Campden, 4m N of Moreton-in-Marsh*

The unpretentious, mellow-stone 17th-century pub enjoys an enchanting location, with glorious views over a stone chapel and rolling hills and looks no different in appearance to any other Cotswold village local. In January 2009, two locals, Sheridan Mather and Richard Shore, took over the pub with the intent of maintaining the relaxed and informal atmosphere and a quality food offering, recently taking on chef William Guthrie who headed up the brigade at the 5-star Jesmonds Hotel near Swindon. Expect innovative modern pub food that makes sound use of quality local suppliers, the short, interesting menu evolving with the seasons. For starters, try, perhaps, potato and roast garlic soup with confit chicken; salmon and spring onion fishcakes with saffron mayonnaise; and seared scallops with fennel purée and curry oil, then follow with pan-fried cod with spinach, beetroot and orange butter; breast of Cotswold White chicken with chive mash and morel jus; and braised shoulder of Lighthorne lamb with pea purée and broad bean sauce. Leave room for sticky toffee pudding; raspberry parfait with dark chocolate mousse and fresh raspberries, or plum and almond cream tart with vanilla ice cream. The Churchill draws an eclectic mix of customers, from drinkers, well-informed foodies and muddy walkers (the starting point of the Cotswold Way is a short stroll away), and this laid-back local offers Hooky and Arkells ales on tap and an impressive list of wines. The setting for savouring the imaginative food and tip-top ales is suitably cosy with a rustic interior - expect wooden floors, stone walls adorned with simple prints, a motley mix of furnishings, an inglenook fireplace with a wood-burning stove that blasts out heat in the winter, and a corner reserved for local drinkers.

Open all week ⊕ FREE HOUSE ◀ Hook Norton Bitter, Arkells, Moonlight. 🍷 10 **Facilities** Garden

PICK OF THE PUBS

The Bell at Sapperton ♟

SAPPERTON   Map 4 SO90

GL7 6LE
☎ 01285 760298   📠 01285 760761
e-mail:
thebell@sapperton66.freeserve.co.uk
dir: *From A419 halfway between Cirencester & Stroud follow signs for Sapperton. Pub in village centre near church*

Built of Cotswold stone, the Bell is close to the source of the River Thames at the not too surprisingly named Thames Head. Regular diners come to this stylish, contemporary pub for the quality and range of produce, much of which is bred or grown locally, and above all the consistency of the cooking. The owners, Paul Davidson and Pat LeJeune, who transformed the building after buying it in 1999, regularly review their suppliers and always give small businesses an opportunity to join the roster. If you just want a drink, there are plenty of wines

by the glass, or locally brewed real ales such as Uley Old Spot and Cotswold Way; these and others are a real passion of Paul's and he keeps them in tip-top condition. The daily changing lunchtime menu will always feature light and inexpensive ideas, such as pan-fried hare loin, and globe artichoke risotto with aged Parmesan. The evening menu offers a more structured selection, with choices like slow-braised veal cheeks with capers and tomatoes; line-caught sea bass fillet on red wine risotto; and home-made burger of Copsegrove Farm Welsh Black beef with dill pickles and bacon and cheese topping. Or you might see a dish featuring truffles unearthed by villager Ed's labrador, which with breathtaking originality he has named, er, Truffle. Another local, Adrian, supplies pigeon breasts and basketsful of the freshest woodland mushrooms. Although Sapperton is very much inland, the Bell has a reputation for excellent fish and seafood, including wild salmon, Cornish lobsters, Scottish langoustine and scallops, brill and wild turbot. Check the chalkboards for what's in on the day.

Open 11-2.30 6.30-11 (Sun 12-10.30)
Bar Meals L served all wk 12-2.15 D served all wk 7-9.15 Av main course £15 **Restaurant** Av 3 course à la carte fr £27.50 ⊕ FREE HOUSE 🛢 Uley Old Spot, Bath Ales, Butcombe Best, Cotswold Way ♻ Ashton Press. ♟ 20
Facilities Dogs allowed Garden Parking

SOMERFORD KEYNES — Map 4 SU09

The Bakers Arms ⛫

GL7 6DN ☎ 01285 861298

dir: Exit A419 signed Cotswold Water Park. Cross B4696, 1m, follow signs for Keynes Park & Somerford Keynes

A beautiful chocolate box pub built from Cotswold stone, with low-beamed ceilings and inglenook fireplaces. Dating from the 15th century, the building was formerly the village bakery and stands in mature gardens ideal for al fresco dining. Discreet children's play areas and heated terraces add to its broad appeal. Somerford Keynes is in the Cotswold Water Park, and the man-made beach of Keynes Park is within easy walking distance, while the nearby Thames Path and Cotswold Way make the pub popular with walkers.

Open all day all wk 11-11 (Sun 12-10.30) **Bar Meals** L served Mon-Fri 12-2.30, Sat-Sun 12-9 D served Mon-Fri 6-9, Sat-Sun 12-9 **Restaurant** L served Mon-Fri 12-2.30, Sat-Sun 12-9 D served Mon-Fri 6-9, Sat-Sun 12-9 ⊕ ENTERPRISE INNS ◀ Courage Best, Butcombe Bitter, Stroud Budding. ⛫ 8 **Facilities** Children's menu Play area Family room Dogs allowed Garden Parking

SOUTHROP — Map 5 SP10

PICK OF THE PUBS

The Swan at Southrop ◉◉ ⛫

GL7 3NU ☎ 01367 850205 📠 01367 850517
e-mail: info@theswanatsouthrop.co.uk
dir: Off A361 between Lechlade & Burford

The early 17th-century, creeper-clad Swan is a classic Cotswold inn on the village green. Sebastian and Lana Snow, both protegés of Antony Worrall-Thompson, relaunched it in September 2008. They are relocating his young family down to Southrop where they will be running The Swan with a new dynamic team. The interior - bar, snug and restaurant - is surprisingly light and airy for such an historic building, but homely too, especially when the log fire is ablaze. The menu line-up comprises carte, fixed-price, bar and weekend roast, with the former offering starters of salad of figs with Colston Basset Blue cheese, pine-nuts and apples; open ravioli of crab, salt cod, chilli and coconut; and carpaccio of veal with tonnato dressing, capers and basil. Mains include Southrop lamb rump with pea, mint, bacon and wood sorrel fricassée; wild sea bream fillet with pea purée, girolle mushrooms, spinach and pecorino; and chartreuse of Hatherop partridge with Savoy cabbage, cotechino sausage and lentils. Real ales are from Hook Norton, Wadworth and Wickwar.

Open all wk **Bar Meals** L served all wk 12-3 D served all wk 6-10.30 Av main course £8 **Restaurant** L served all wk 12-3 booking required D served all wk 6-10.30 booking required Av 3 course à la carte fr £25 ⊕ FREE HOUSE ◀ Hook Norton, Wadworth 6X, Cotswold Way, guest ale. ⛫ 10 **Facilities** Children's menu Dogs allowed

STONEHOUSE — Map 4 SO80

The George Inn

Peter St, Frocester GL10 3TQ
☎ 01453 822302 📠 01453 791612
e-mail: info@georgeinn.co.uk
dir: M5 junct 13, onto A419 at 1st rdbt 3rd exit signed Eastington, left at next rdbt signed Frocester. Approx 2m on right in village

An award-winning 18th-century coaching inn, unspoiled by juke box or fruit machine. Instead, crackling log fires and a sunny courtyard garden give the place all-year-round appeal. The Cotswold Way and a network of leafy paths and lanes are on the doorstep. Expect a warm welcome, a selection of real ales including three local brews, and good home-cooked food from nearby suppliers. Tuck in to half a roast chicken, or Frocester Fayre faggots with mash, peas and gravy.

Open all day all wk 7.30am-mdnt **Bar Meals** food served all day **Restaurant** food served all day ⊕ FROCESTER BEER CO LTD ◀ Deuchars IPA, Blacksheep, 3 guest ales. **Facilities** Children's menu Play area Family room Dogs allowed Garden Parking

STOW-ON-THE-WOLD — Map 10 SP12

PICK OF THE PUBS

The Eagle and Child ★★★ HL ◉◉ ⛫

GL54 1HY ☎ 01451 830670 📠 01451 870048
e-mail: stay@theroyalisthotel.com
dir: From Moreton-in-Marsh rail station take A429 Fosseway to Stow-on-the-Wold. At 2nd lights left onto Sheep St, A436. Establishment 100yds on left

Reputed the oldest inn in England, dating back to 947 AD and once a hospice to shelter lepers, the Eagle and Child is part of the Royalist Hotel. The social hub of the hotel and village, serving local ales on handpump, it also delivers pub food that manages to be both rustic and accomplished. Informality and flexibility go hand-in-hand with flagstone floors, oak beams and rustic tables; the light-flooded conservatory offering a striking contrast to the character, low-ceilinged dining room. Expect range of pub classics, from Old Spot sausages with leek mash, caramelised onions and red wine sauce to steak and Guinness pie with garlic mash, and more innovative food like seafood and charcuterie deli plates, wild mushroom, Parmesan and tarragon risotto, and braised duck leg with redcurrant and butterbean stew. Bedrooms successfully blend contemporary and tradition for maximum stylish impact.

Open all wk ⊕ FREE HOUSE ◀ Hook Norton, London Pride, Goffs, Donnington. ⛫ 8 **Facilities** Dogs allowed Garden Parking **Rooms** 14

The Unicorn ⛫

Sheep St GL54 1HQ ☎ 01451 830257 📠 01451 831090
e-mail: reception@birchhotels.co.uk

Attractive hotel of honey-coloured limestone, hand-cut roof tiles and abundantly flowering window boxes, set in the heart of Stow-on-the-Wold. The interior is stylishly presented with Jacobean pieces, antique artefacts and open log fires. Light meals are served in the bar (sandwiches and salads, plus beef and Guinness stew, and beer-battered fish and chips), and a dinner menu of modern British dishes is available in the elegant Georgian setting of the restaurant.

Open all wk ⛫ 6 **Facilities** Dogs allowed Garden Parking

STROUD — Map 4 SO80

PICK OF THE PUBS

Bear of Rodborough Hotel ★★★ HL ⛫

See Pick of the Pubs on opposite page

The Ram Inn

South Woodchester GL5 5EL
☎ 01453 873329 📠 01453 873329
e-mail: raminnwoodchester@hotmail.co.uk
dir: A46 from Stroud to Nailsworth, right after 2m into South Woodchester, follow brown tourist signs

From the plentiful seating on terrace of the 17th-century Cotswold stone Ram Inn, there are splendid views over five valleys, although proximity to the huge fireplace may prove more appealing in winter. Rib-eye steak, at least two fish dishes, home-made lasagne and Sunday roasts can be expected, washed down by regularly changing real ales such as Uley Old Spot, Stroud Budding and Stroud Organic. The Stroud Morris Men regularly perform.

Open all day all wk 11-11 **Bar Meals** L served all wk 12-2 D served all wk 6-9 Av main course £7.50 **Restaurant** L served all wk 12-2 D served all wk 6-9 ⊕ FREE HOUSE ◀ Uley Old Spot, Stroud Budding, Butcombe Bitter, Guests. **Facilities** Children's menu Family room Dogs allowed Garden Parking

PICK OF THE PUBS

Bear of Rodborough Hotel ★★★ HL 🍷

Rodborough Common GL5 5DE
☎ **01453 878522** 📄 **01453 872523**
e-mail: info@bearofrodborough.co.uk
web: www.cotswold-inns-hotels.co.uk/
bear
dir: *From M5 junct 13 follow signs for*
Stonehouse then Rodborough

Built in the 17th century, this former
Cotswolds alehouse stands 600 ft above
sea level, surrounded by 300 acres of
National Trust land. Its name comes
from the bear-baiting that used to take
place nearby. The hotel is worth seeking
out for all sorts of reasons: comfortable
accommodation, open log fires, stone
walls, solid wooden floors and an
interesting beam over the front doors
reading 'Through this wide opening gate
none come too early, none return too
late', reputedly carved by louche
sculptor and typographer, Eric Gill. A
running bear design is incorporated into
the ceiling beams in the elegant Box
Tree restaurant and Tower Room, while
additional character may be contributed
by a resident ghost whose unknown
identity is often discussed late at night
in the Grizzly Bar (say it right and it
sounds distinctly hillbilly) over pints of
Gloucestershire brews from Uley and
Wickwar. The restaurant offers a
contemporary British menu, so one
might start with traditional Welsh
rarebit; or salad of smoked Bibury trout
and smoked eel with avocado and lime
vinaigrette; continue with caramelised
loin of Gloucester Old Spot pork in
Parma ham; pan-fried calf's liver and
bacon; Uley beer-battered cod and
chips; or courgette pancakes with
Exmoor Blue cheese sauce; and finish
with a dessert from the daily specials,
such as warm local apple and
blackberry crumble and clotted cream.
There are two wine lists, one containing
a short, modestly priced selection, the
other running to the full 60 bins.
Outside is a croquet lawn created in the
1920s by a former resident called
Edmunds, a partner in a well-known
firm of proud Stroud nurserymen.

Open all week ⊕ FREE HOUSE 🛢 Uley
Bitter, Bob from Wickwar Brewery,
Stroud, Wadworth, guest ale. 🍷 6
Facilities Play area Dogs allowed
Garden Parking **Rooms** 46

STROUD *continued*

PICK OF THE PUBS

Rose & Crown Inn ▼

The Cross, Nympsfield GL10 3TU ☎ **01453 860240**
e-mail: acneave@btinternet.com
dir: *M5 junct 13 off B4066, SW of Stroud*

An imposing, 400-year-old coaching inn of honey-coloured local stone in the heart of the village close to the Cotswold Way and therefore a popular stop for walkers and cyclists. It could well be the highest pub in the Cotswolds, but whether it is or not is irrelevant as the views over the Severn are stunning anyway. Inside, the inn's character is preserved with natural stone, wood panelling, a lovely open fire and some local real ales. In the galleried restaurant, main courses include faggots cooked in onion gravy, enchiladas, and salmon en croûte. Just as satisfying might be Eastern Promise, a baked baguette filled with roast duck, spring onion, cucumber and hoi sin sauce. The kids will enjoy the playground area, which has a swing, slides and a climbing bridge.

Open all day all wk noon-mdnt **Bar Meals** L served all wk 12-3 D served all wk 6-9 ⊕ FREE HOUSE ◀ Uley, Pigs Ear, Butcombe Bitter ♂ Thatchers Stowford Press, Black Rat. ♥ 7 **Facilities** Play area Dogs allowed Garden Parking

The Woolpack Inn ▼

Slad Rd, Slad GL6 7QA
☎ **01452 813429** 📄 **01452 813429**
e-mail: info@thewoolpackinn-slad.com
dir: *2m from Stroud, 8m from Gloucester*

The Woolpack is a friendly local, situated in the beautiful Slad Valley close to the Cotswold Way, an area immortalised by Laurie Lee in his book *Cider with Rosie*. Indeed, the author was a regular at the pub. Not surprisingly, the place is popular with walkers. Walking boots and wellies aren't frowned upon here, and children and dogs are made welcome. Honest, straightforward food is freshly prepared from the best local produce, all washed down with a pint of Uley bitter.

Open all day all wk noon-mdnt (Sun noon-11pm) **Bar Meals** L served Mon-Sat 12-2, Sun 12-3.30 booking required D served Tue-Sat 6.30-9 booking required Av main course £11.50 **Restaurant** L served Mon-Sat 12-2, Sun 12-3.30 booking required D served Tue-Sat 6.30-9 booking required Av 3 course à la carte fr £18 ⊕ FREE HOUSE ◀ Uley Pig's Ear, Old Spot, Uley Bitter, guest ale ♂ Old Rosie, Stowfords Press. ♥ 8
Facilities Children's menu Family room Dogs allowed Garden Parking

TETBURY — Map 4 ST89

PICK OF THE PUBS

Gumstool Inn ▼

Calcot Manor GL8 8YJ
☎ **01666 890391** 📄 **01666 890394**
e-mail: reception@calcotmanor.co.uk
dir: *3m W of Tetbury*

The traditional country inn, Gumstool, is part of Calcot Manor Hotel, set in 220 acres of Cotswold countryside. The hotel is a successful conversion of a 14th-century stone farmhouse built by Cistercian monks, set around a flower-filled courtyard. The food at the inn is top notch gastro-pub quality. Monthly menus offer a good choice, with typical starters of crisp goats' cheese parcel, roasted beetroot salad; or Cajun spiced calamari salad with chilli jam. Starters or a larger portion for a light main course include warm Cornish crab and leek tart with rocket and frisée salad; crispy Asian duck noodle salad with Thai dressing; and grilled haloumi cheese, polenta and wood-roasted Mediterranean vegetables. Among the mains might be roasted pheasant with bacon, bread sauce and potato gratin; Moroccan spiced lamb tagine with lemon, rose harissa and coriander; or roasted halibut, curried mussels and leeks. As a free house, Gumstool stocks a good selection of some unusual real ales.

Open all wk 11.30-2.30 5.30-11 **Bar Meals** L served all wk 11.30-2 booking required D served all wk 7-9.30 booking required Av main course £8 **Restaurant** L served all wk 12-2 booking required D served all wk 7-9.30 booking required Av 3 course à la carte fr £35 ⊕ FREE HOUSE ◀ Atlantics Sharp's IPA, Matthews Bob Wool, Wickwar Cotswold Way, Butcombe Blonde. ♥ 12 **Facilities** Children's menu Play area Family room Garden Parking

PICK OF THE PUBS

The Priory Inn ★★★ SHL ▼

London Rd GL8 8JJ
☎ **01666 502251** 📄 **01666 503534**
e-mail: info@theprioryinn.co.uk
dir: *M4 junct 17, A429 towards Cirencester. Left onto B4014 to Tetbury. Over mini-rdbt onto Long St, pub 100yds after corner on right*

Thriving gastro-pub, hotel and coffee bar at the centre of Tetbury life. The aim is to provide excellent value modern rustic cuisine with a minimum of food miles.

Monthly newsletters keep customers informed of the local suppliers who have provided their supper. Children are especially welcome, with a specialised menu of home-made dishes and junior cocktails, plus the opportunity to decorate a personalised wood-fired pizza. Adults are equally coddled with a lunch menu that might include a sandwich of pickled cherry tomato and Godsell's Three Virgins cheese; or fresh sardines, tomato and oregano on toasted home-made bread. The evening meal could begin with devilled lambs' kidneys, and continue with melted Cotswold blue brie over mushrooms with a Jerusalem artichoke gratin. Try a scoop of Westonbirt ice cream with the warm chocolate fondant for dessert. Live music every Sunday evening.

Open all wk ⊕ FREE HOUSE ◀ Uley Bitter, Cotswold Premium Lager, Archers Ale ♂ Stowford Press ♥ 10 **Facilities** Play area Family room Garden Parking **Rooms** 14

PICK OF THE PUBS

The Trouble House ◉◉ ▼

Cirencester Rd GL8 8SG ☎ **01666 502206**
e-mail: info@thetroublehouse.co.uk
dir: *On A433 between Tetbury & Cirencester*

The aptly named Trouble House has something of a chequered past. It was the scene of agricultural riots and civil war conflicts and, it's claimed, two former landlords were driven to suicide. Today, there's a much warmer welcome from husband and wife team Martin and Neringa Caws — and original features like ancient beams, fireplaces and a charmingly crooked ceiling all add to the pub's very English allure. The Trouble House has an enviable reputation for food; bread is baked daily with organic flour from nearby Shipton Mill, whilst many other local ingredients appear on the menu. Begin, perhaps, with grilled sea scallops and apple purée; or warm beetroot tart, caramelised onion and goats' cheese. Main course dishes include slow-cooked Gloucestershire Old Spot pork belly with fondant potato; and Cornish lobster risotto with peas, tomato and tarragon. Praline parfait with raspberries; and coffee crème brûlée are typical desserts.

Open 11.30-3 7-11 Closed: 25-26 Dec, Sun eve, Mon **Bar Meals** L served Tue-Fri 12-2 booking required Av main course £10.50 **Restaurant** L served Tue-Sun 12-2 booking required D served Tue-Sat 7-9.30 booking required Av 3 course à la carte fr £25.50 ⊕ WADWORTH ◀ Wadworth 6X, Henrys IPA ♂ Stowford Press. ♥ 12 **Facilities** Children's menu Dogs allowed Garden Parking

TEWKESBURY Map 10 SO83

The Fleet Inn ⚐

Twyning GL20 6FL ☎ 01684 274310
e-mail: enquiries@fleet-inn.co.uk
dir: *M5 junct 8, M50 junct, 3m from Tewkesbury A38*

The gardens of this idyllic 15th-century pub run right down to the banks of the River Avon. The traditional bars and themed areas provide a wide range of dishes. Produce is locally sourced, and might include steak and kidney parcels; pheasant breast on colcannon mash; or half shoulder of lamb in mint and rosemary gravy. There's a boules court to keep the teenagers happy, and a pets' corner for the little ones.

Open all wk ⊕ ENTERPRISE INNS ◀ Bombardier, Banks, Cat's Whiskers. ⚐ 10 **Facilities** Play area Garden Parking

TODENHAM Map 10 SP23

PICK OF THE PUBS

The Farriers Arms ⚐

Main St GL56 9PF
☎ 01608 650901 📄 01608 650403
e-mail: info@farriersarms.com
dir: *Right to Todenham at N end of Moreton-in-Marsh. 2.5m from Shipston on Stour*

A traditional Cotswold pub built as a church house in 1650, later becoming an ironworks, before acquiring a beer licence in 1840. It has all the features you'd associate with a country pub: polished flagstone floors, exposed stone walls, wooden beams and a large inglenook fireplace. Outside, a suntrap patio garden offers views of the church. The bar and restaurant menu changes daily to offer a good range of freshly prepared dishes using local produce. Starters range from home-made chicken liver parfait to duo of Todenham sausages with grain mustard sauce, while typical main courses include braised steak and Hook Norton ale pie with puff pastry; cod in beer batter with chips and mushy peas; and roast vegetables and goat's cheese cannelloni. In the Aunt Sally season maybe have a game yourself, or just watch 'the professionals' as they compete against other local league players in this traditional pub throwing game.

Open all wk noon-3 6-11 (Sun noon-3 6.30-11) **Bar Meals** L served Mon-Sat 12-2, Sun 12-2.30 D served Mon-Sat 6-9, Sun 6.30-9 ⊕ FREE HOUSE ◀ Hook Norton Best, Wye Valley Butty Bach, Black Sheep, Pigbrook ⚲ Stowford Press. ⚐ 11 **Facilities** Family room Dogs allowed Garden Parking

TORMARTON Map 4 ST77

Best Western Compass Inn ⚐

GL9 1JB ☎ 01454 218242 📄 01454 218741
e-mail: info@compass-inn.co.uk
web: www.compass-inn.co.uk
dir: *From M4 junct 18 take A46 N towards Stroud. After 200mtrs 1st right towards Tormarton. Inn in 300mtrs*

A charming 18th-century inn, set in six acres of grounds in the heart of the Gloucestershire countryside, right on the Cotswold Way. Its extensive facilities include an orangery, and space for functions. Light bites and more filling meals can be taken in the bar, while the restaurant offers the likes of chicken liver pâté with brioche, followed by roasted pork fillet with sage mash, caramelised apple and grain mustard sauce.

Open all day all wk 7am-11pm (Sat-Sun 8am-11pm) Closed: 25-26 Dec **Bar Meals** Av main course £9 food served all day **Restaurant** Av 3 course à la carte fr £20 food served all day ⊕ FREE HOUSE ◀ Interbrew Bass, Butcombe Gold, Butcombe ⚲ Ashton Press. ⚐ 9 **Facilities** Children's menu Dogs allowed Garden Parking

UPPER ODDINGTON Map 10 SP22

PICK OF THE PUBS

The Horse and Groom Inn ⚐

GL56 0XH ☎ 01451 830584
e-mail: info@horseandgroom.uk.com
dir: *1.5m S of Stow-on-the-Wold, just off A436*

A 16th-century stone-built inn, the Horse & Groom is located in a Cotswold conservation village just a mile and a half from Stow-on-the-Wold. It is immaculately kept, with pale polished flagstone floors, beams, stripped stone walls and log fires in the inglenook. In fine weather you can enjoy the terrace and gardens, with grape vines bounded by dry stone walls. A great selection of cask ales is offered from local breweries and the wine list, including 25 available by the glass, is ever growing. Menus comprise regional food sourced from as close to the kitchen door as possible. Bread, for example, is made daily from Cotswold Flour Millers flour. Dishes might include pan-fried breast of Adlestrop pheasant with thyme and garlic roasted sweet potatoes and orange glazed chicory, or hand-cut, finest 21-day aged Hereford beef steaks served with a choice of sauces. Fish is featured on the daily blackboard menu.

Open all wk noon-3 5.30-11 (Sun 6.30-10.30) **Bar Meals** L served all wk 12-2 D served Mon-Sat 6.30-9, Sun 7-9 **Restaurant** L served all wk 12-2 D served Mon-Sat 6.30-9, Sun 7-9 ⊕ FREE HOUSE ◀ Wye Valley Butty Bach, Wye Valley Best, Hereford Pale Ale, Wickwar Bob Cotswold Premium Lager. ⚐ 25 **Facilities** Children's menu Play area Garden Parking

WINCHCOMBE Map 10 SP02

The White Hart Inn and Restaurant ⚐

High St GL54 5LJ ☎ 01242 602359 📄 01242 602703
e-mail: info@wineandsausage.com
dir: *In centre of Winchcombe on B4632*

In a pretty small town on the Cotswold Way, close to Sudeley Castle and glorious rolling countryside, this smart 16th-century inn provides welcome refreshment to walkers and tourists. Quaff a pint of Uley Bitter in traditional pubby front bar, with its wood floor, scrubbed old tables and cricketing memorabilia, and tuck into simple and unpretentious British food sourced from local farmers and suppliers. Typical dishes include ham hock terrine with piccalilli, beef Wellington, dressed crab, and rhubarb fool. Don't miss the wine shop next to the bar!

Open all day all wk 10am-11pm (Fri-Sat 10am-mdnt Sun 10am-10.30pm) **Bar Meals** L served all wk 12-3 D served all wk 6-9.30 ◀ Uley Old Spot, Whittingtons Cats Whiskers, Greene King IPA, Wadworth 6X, Old Speckled Hen, Butcombe, Otter, Jouster ⚲ Stowford Press. ⚐ 8 **Facilities** Dogs allowed Garden Parking

WITHINGTON Map 10 SP01

The Mill Inn

GL54 4BE ☎ 01242 890204 📄 01242 890195
dir: *3m from A40 between Cheltenham & Oxford*

Until 1914 the innkeeper also had to find time to grind corn in this 450-year-old inn on the banks of the River Coln. Inside are stone-flagged floors, oak panelling and log fires, while outside is a peaceful lawned garden with 40 tables. Lunch or dinner is selected from a wide selection of light meals and more substantial main courses, including blackened Cajun chicken, steak and ale pie, Barnsley chop, and Quorn and vegetable chilli.

Open all wk ⊕ SAMUEL SMITH ◀ Samuel Smith Old Brewery Bitter, Samuel Smith Sovereign, Alpine Lager, Pure Brew Lager, Extra Stout. **Facilities** Family room Dogs allowed Garden Parking

WOODCHESTER — Map 4 SO80

PICK OF THE PUBS

The Old Fleece ♥

Bath Rd, Rooksmoor GL5 5NB ☎ **01453 872582**
e-mail: pheasantpluckers2003@yahoo.co.uk
dir: *2m S of Stroud on A46*

Set amid beautiful countryside with miles of footpaths to explore, this delightful coaching inn was built in the 18th century from Cotswold stone and has a traditional stone roof. From the Old Fleece, you can walk to Rodborough, Minchinhampton and Selsley Commons, or go one step further and connect eventually with the scenic Cotswold Way long distance trail. The beautifully refurbished interior includes wooden floors, wood panelling and exposed stone, and the bar serves well kept Greene King Abbot Ale and Otter Bitter. Predominantly French chefs offer a comprehensive menu of British and continental dishes, ranging from classics such as Old Spot sausage and mash with onion gravy to the likes of confit duck leg with hoi sin noodles, whole sea bream with braised fennel, or pork loin steak with apple and Calvados purée.

Open all day all wk 11-11 Closed: 25 Dec **Bar Meals** L served all wk 11-2.45 D served all wk 5.30-10 **Restaurant** L served all wk 11-2.45 D served all wk 5.30-10 ⊕ PHEASANT PLUCKERS LTD ◀ Bass, Greene King Abbot Ale, Otter Bitter. ♥ 12 **Facilities** Children's menu Dogs allowed Garden Parking

GREATER MANCHESTER

ALTRINCHAM — Map 15 SJ78

PICK OF THE PUBS

The Victoria ♥

See Pick of the Pubs on opposite page

CHEADLE HULME — Map 16 SJ88

The Church Inn ♥

Ravenoak Rd SK8 7EG
☎ **0161 485 1897** 📠 **0161 485 1698**
e-mail: church_inn@yahoo.co.uk
dir: *3m from Stockport*

Cheadle Hulme's oldest hostelry, The Church Inn is family-run and-family friendly. It boasts welcoming log fires in winter and a furnished front patio for warmer days. Open all day, every day for drinks, its resident ales are Hatters and Unicorn from Robinsons. Food is also taken seriously; expect tried and tested favourites including pepper steak and tandoori chicken alongside daily specials such as ham hock with bubble and squeak.

Open all wk 11-11 (Sun noon-10.30) **Bar Meals** L served Mon-Sat 11.30-2.30, Sun 12-7.30 D served Mon-Sat 5.30-9.30, Sun 12-7.30 Av main course £9 **Restaurant** L served Mon-Sat 11.30-2.30, Sun 12-7.30 D served Mon-Sat 5.30-9.30, Sun 12-7.30 Fixed menu price fr £11.95 Av 3 course à la carte fr £12 ⊕ ROBINSONS ◀ Robinsons Best Bitter, Hatters Mild, Robinsons Old Stockport, guest ales. ♥ 18 **Facilities** Garden Parking

DENSHAW — Map 16 SD91

The Rams Head Inn ♥

OL3 5UN ☎ **01457 874802** 📠 **01457 820978**
e-mail: ramsheaddenshaw@aol.com
dir: *From M62 junct 22, 2m towards Oldham*

From its position 1212 feet above sea level, this 400-year-old country inn offers panoramic views over Saddleworth. Log fires and collections of memorabilia are features of the interior, where blackboard menus list everything available and food is cooked to order. Seafood figures strongly, with dishes such as crayfish tails with ginger crème fraîche, and monkfish wrapped in Parma ham. Another attraction is The Pantry (open 9am-8pm Tue-Sat, 11am-8pm Sun and BH Mon) at The Rams Head, a farm shop, deli, bakery, tearooms and patisserie.

Open noon-2.30 6-11 Closed: 25 Dec, Mon (ex BH) **Bar Meals** Av main course £10.95 **Restaurant** Fixed menu price fr £12.95 Av 3 course à la carte fr £20 food served all day ⊕ FREE HOUSE ◀ Carlsberg-Tetley Bitter, Timothy Taylor Landlord, Black Sheep Bitter, Copper Dragon. ♥ 8 **Facilities** Children's menu Parking

DIDSBURY — Map 16 SJ89

PICK OF THE PUBS

The Metropolitan ♥

2 Lapwing Ln M20 2WS
☎ **0161 438 2332** 📠 **0161 282 6544**
e-mail: info@the-metropolitan.co.uk
dir: *M60 junct 5, A5103, right onto Barlow Moor Rd, left onto Burton Rd. Pub at x-rds. Right onto Lapwing Ln for car park*

Originally a hotel for passengers riding the old Midland Railway into Manchester, the 'Met' still punches above its weight architecturally, but then that's how Victorian railway companies liked to gain a competitive edge over their rivals. Look in particular at the decorative flooring tiling, the ornate windows the impressive roof timbers and the delicate plasterwork. During the latter part of the 20th century the building became very run down, until in 1997 it was given a sympathetic renovation, reopening as a gastro-pub. Now one of several eating and drinking places in this buzzy southern city suburb, its huge, airy interior is well filled with antique tables and chairs, which suit the mainly young, cosmopolitan clientele. Food ranges from starters and light bites (smoked haddock fishcake; home-made soup) to main courses such as Ribble Valley Gloucester Old Spot sausages with onion mash or home-made chicken and ham pie with rustic fries. There's also always a good selection from the grill.

Open all day all wk 11.30-mdnt (Sun noon-11) Closed: 25 Dec **Bar Meals** Mon-Sat 12-7, Sun 12-6 **Restaurant** Mon-Thu 12-9.30, Fri-Sat 12-10, Sun 12-9 ◀ Timothy Taylor Landlord, Deuchars IPA, Guinness ♂ Westons. ♥ 20 **Facilities** Garden Parking

PICK OF THE PUBS

The Victoria ♥

ALTRINCHAM
Map 15 SJ78

Stamford St WA14 1EX
☎ **0161 613 1855**
e-mail: the.victoria@yahoo.co.uk
dir: *From rail station, cross main road, turn right. 2nd left onto Stamford St*

Tucked away behind the main shopping street, the beautifully restored Victoria has a new life as a stylish, food-led tavern. On one side is a wood-panelled dining area, set with linens and tableware, on the other a more casual bar area, with lots of wood, slate and exposed brickwork. All food is sourced locally and freshly prepared, and appears on six- to eight-weekly seasonal menus as modern British dishes. This approach leads to starters such as Morecambe Bay brown shrimp and battered prawn cocktail; Bury black

pudding Scotch egg topped with locally smoked bacon; Blackstick Blue cheese and broad bean rice pudding. Any of these could be followed by a main course such as naturally-raised Cumbrian pink veal and mushroom steamed pudding; pan-fried calf's liver with sweet red onion and sage faggots; chicken hotpot on a bed of braised root vegetables topped with Cheshire rarebit potatoes; or roasted monkfish on a bed of pease pudding. On Sundays a traditional roast rib of beef (hung for four weeks) is available. And are the puddings given a modern makeover too? Judge for yourself – there's chocolate and cherry sundae; baked apple and honey roly poly; and Bakewell tart, for instance. There are also lunchtime sandwiches, ploughman's, omelettes, battered butties, and light meals, such as pigeon pasty, and smoked mackerel salad. The wine list features more than 30 carefully chosen bins, and there are several hand-pulled real ales. For drivers, the Victoria has a temperance bar offering locally produced old favourites like dandelion and burdock and sarsaparilla.

Open noon-11 (Sun 12-6) Closed: 26 Dec & 1 Jan **Bar Meals** L served Mon-Sat 12-3 D served Mon-Sat 5.30-9 Av main course £7.95 **Restaurant** L served Mon-Sat 12-3 (Sun 12-4) D served Mon-Sat 5.30-9 Fixed menu price fr £12.95 Av 3 course à la carte fr £25 ◄ Old Speckled Hen, Jennings Cumberland, Flowers IPA ♂ Westons Organic. ♥ 9 **Facilities** Children's menu

The White House ⬚

Blackstone Edge, Halifax Rd OL15 0LG
☎ 01706 378456
dir: *On A58, 8m from Rochdale, 9m from Halifax*

A coaching house built in 1671, standing 1,300 feet above sea level on the Pennine Way, with panoramic views of the moors and Hollingworth Lake far below. Not surprising, then, that it attracts walkers and cyclists who rest up and sup on Theakstons and regular guest ales. A simple menu of pub grub ranges from sandwiches and starters like garlic and herb mushrooms, to grills, curries, chillis and traditional plates of home-made steak and kidney pie.

Open all wk Closed: 25 Dec **Bar Meals** L served all wk 12-2 D served all wk 6-9 Av main course £6.50 **Restaurant** L served all wk 12-2 D served all wk 6.30-9.30 ⊕ FREE HOUSE ◀ Timothy Taylor Landlord, Theakstons Bitter, Exmoor Gold, Blacksheep, Phoenix. ⬚ 6 **Facilities** Parking

Dukes 92

14 Castle St, Castlefield M3 4LZ
☎ 0161 839 8646   📄 0161 832 3595
e-mail: info@dukes92.com
dir: *In Castleford town centre, off Deansgate*

Beautifully-restored 19th-century stable building with a vast patio beside the 92nd lock of the Duke of Bridgewater canal, opened in 1762. The interior is full of surprises, with minimalist decor downstairs and an upper gallery displaying local artistic talent. A new grill restaurant supplements a lunchtime bar menu and evening pizza choices, as well as the renowned cheese and pâté counter with its huge range of British and continental cheeses, salad selection, and choice of platters for sharing.

Open all wk Closed: 25-26 Dec, 1 Jan ⊕ FREE HOUSE ◀ Interbrew Boddingtons Bitter, Boddingtons. **Facilities** Garden Parking

Marble Arch

73 Rochdale Rd M4 4HY
☎ 0161 832 5914   📄 0161 819 2694
dir: *In city centre (northern quarter of Manchester)*

A listed building with a strikingly original interior, the Marble Arch is a fine example of Manchester's Victorian heritage. It's also home to the award-winning organic Marble Brewery, with six regular and eight seasonal house beers. Snacks and more substantial meals are served in the bar - the pies are deservedly popular. Sample the likes of steak and Marble ale pie; black pudding and potato salad; and pot-roast chicken in Marble ginger beer.

Open all wk Closed: 25-26 Dec ⊕ FREE HOUSE ◀ GSB, Marble Best, Ginger Marble, Lagonda.

The Queen's Arms

6 Honey St, Cheetham M8 8RG ☎ 0161 835 3899
dir: *Telephone for directions*

The Queen's is part of a loose grouping of real ale pubs in Manchester's Northern Quarter. The original tiled frontage shows that it was once allied to the long-vanished Empress Brewery. Its clientele spans the socio-economic spectrum from 'suits' to bikers to pensioners, all seemingly happy with the heavy rock on the jukebox. Food is available, but it's the brewed, distilled and fermented products that attract, including an impressive 'menu' of bottled lagers, fruit beers, vodkas and wines.

Open all wk ◀ Timothy Taylor Landlord, Phoenix Bantam, guest ales. **Facilities** Play area Dogs allowed Garden **Notes** ☻

The Moorfield Arms ★★★★ INN ⬚

Shiloh Rd SK6 5NE
☎ 0161 427 1580   📄 0161 427 1582
e-mail: info@moorfieldarms.co.uk
dir: *From Marple station down Brabyns Brow to lights. Right into Town St. 3m, left into Shiloh Rd. 0.5m, pub on left*

This pub enjoys picturesque views of Kinder and the surrounding Pennine hills from its elevated position on the edge of the moors. The building dates from 1640 and retains plenty of old world charm and atmosphere, including a log fire. Comfortable, tastefully furnished accommodation in a barn conversation makes it an ideal base for outdoor activities. The menu includes hot sandwiches, lunchtime snacks, an extensive selection from the grill, and signature dishes such as steak and ale pie or lamb Henry.

Open all wk **Bar Meals** L served Mon-Sat 12-2, Sun 12-9 D served all wk 6-9.30 Av main course £10 **Restaurant** L served all wk 12-2 D served all wk 6-9.30 Fixed menu price fr £7 Av 3 course à la carte fr £20 ⊕ FREE HOUSE ◀ Pedigree Bitter, Guinness, Marsden, guest ales. ⬚ 16 **Facilities** Garden Parking **Rooms** 4

The Oddfellows Arms ⬚

73 Moor End Rd SK6 5PT ☎ 0161 449 7826
dir: *Telephone for details*

A friendly welcome can be expected in this c1650 building, which has had a liquor licence since 1805. It changed its name from 'The Angel Inn' in 1860 to accommodate the Oddfellows Society, a forerunner of the Trades Unions. There are always plenty of real ales to choose from. Recent change of hands.

Open all wk 4-late (Thu-Fri 12-late Sat 11-late Sun 11-6) Closed: 25-26 Dec, 31 Dec-1 Jan **Bar Meals** L served Thu-Fri 12-6, Sat-Sun 11-6 D served Thu-Fri 12-6, Sat-Sun 11-6 **Restaurant** L served Thu-Fri 12-2.30, Sun 12-5 booking required D served Wed-Sat 5.30-9 booking required ⊕ ENTERPRISE INNS PLC ◀ Adnams Southwold, Marston's Pedigree, Bitter, Fennicks Arizona, guest. ⬚ 8 **Facilities** Children's menu Dogs allowed Garden Parking

The Roebuck Inn ⬚

Strinesdale OL4 3RB
☎ 0161 624 7819   📄 0161 633 6210
e-mail: sehowarth1@hotmail.com
dir: *From Oldham Humps Bridge take Huddersfield Rd, right at 2nd lights onto Ripponden Rd, after 1m right at lights onto Turfpit Ln, follow for 1m*

Historic inn located on the edge of Saddleworth Moor in the rugged Pennines, 1,000 feet above sea level. Part of the pub was once used as a Sunday school, while the upstairs lounge served as a morgue. This may explain the presence of the ghost of a girl who drowned in the local reservoir. The menu offers an extensive choice from vegetarian dishes and steaks to fish dishes; from the fish board perhaps smoked haddock with poached egg and hollandaise sauce.

Open all wk **Bar Meals** food served all day **Restaurant** food served all day ⊕ FREE HOUSE ◀ Tetleys, guest ale. ⬚ 8 **Facilities** Play area Dogs allowed Garden Parking

The White Hart Inn ⊚⊚ ⬚

Stockport Rd, Lydgate OL4 4JJ
☎ 01457 872566   📄 01457 875190
e-mail: bookings@thewhitehart.co.uk
dir: *From Manchester A62 to Oldham. Right onto bypass, A669 through Lees. In 500yds past Grotton, at brow of hill turn right onto A6050*

An attractive 18th-century coaching inn, the White Hart is renowned for its award-winning restaurant, and the fact that the characters Compo, Clegg and Cyril from *Last of the Summer Wine* were based on former regulars here. Over the years the inn has served as a brewery, kennels, prison, school and weaver's cottage, before returning at last to its original purpose as a hostelry. A variety of eating areas includes the brasserie, a contemporary restaurant, the intimate library and the newer Oak Room. The pub menu offers plenty of choice, including six options for children and some classic local dishes. In the restaurant expect the likes of roast dorade fillet with cockle linguini, dill and fennel purée and vanilla nage, or Goosnargh duck breast with confit leg and Puy lentils, blackcurrants and carrot fondant. Beer comes from local breweries and there's an extensive wine list.

Open all day all wk **Bar Meals** L served Mon-Sat 12-2.30, Sun 1-7 booking required D served all wk 6-9.30 booking required Av main course £12 **Restaurant** L served Sun 12-3 booking required D served Mon-Sat 6-9.30 booking required Fixed menu price fr £19.95 Av 3 course à la carte fr £19.95 ⊕ FREE HOUSE ◀ Timothy Taylor Landlord, J W Lees Bitter, Carlsberg-Tetley Bitter, Copper Dragon, Golden Best. ⬚ 16 **Facilities** Children's menu Dogs allowed Garden Parking

STALYBRIDGE
Map 16 SJ99

The Royal Oak

364 Huddersfield Rd, Millbrook SK15 3EP
☎ 0161 338 7118
dir: From Stalybridge turn onto Huddersfield rd, pub located on the right next to Country Park

This family-run pub, once a coroner's evidence room, was later owned by the late Jackie Blanchflower of Manchester United, who took it on in the 1960s, and rumour has it that the players used to drink here. It stands next to a country park, which is great for walks before or after eating. The food is Italian influenced, and everything is freshly prepared and cooked to order. The wine list is short but well chosen.

Open Wed-Fri 5.30-11 (Tue 6-9 only by prior reservation, Sat 4.30-11, Sun noon-10.30) Closed: 1 Jan, Mon **Bar Meals** D served Tue 6-9, Wed-Fri 5.30-9, Sat 4.30-9, Sun 12-7 Av main course £7 **Restaurant** D served Tue 6-9, Wed-Fri 5.30-9, Sat 4.30-9, Sun 12-7 Fixed menu price fr £10.50 ⊕ ENTERPRISE INNS ◄ Boddingtons, John Smiths. **Facilities** Children's menu Garden Parking

Stalybridge Station Buffet Bar ☻

The Railway Station, Rassbottom St SK15 1RF
☎ 0161 303 0007
dir: Telephone for directions

Unique Victorian railway station refreshment rooms dating from 1885 and including original bar fittings, open fire and a conservatory. Decorated throughout with railway memorabilia, much donated by the regulars. There's always a wide choice of real ales (up to 20 guests a week, as well as a draught cider), and the bar hosts regular beer festivals and folk nights. Expect the pub's famous black pudding and black peas, pasta bake, pies, liver and onions, and sausage and mash on the bar menu.

Open all wk 11-11 (Sun noon-10.30) **Bar Meals** Av main course £5 food served all day ⊕ FREE HOUSE ◄ Boddingtons, Flowers IPA. ☻ 6 **Facilities** Dogs allowed Garden Parking **Notes** ⊜

STOCKPORT
Map 16 SJ89

The Arden Arms ☻

23 Millgate SK1 2LX ☎ 0161 480 2185
e-mail: steve@ardenarms.com
dir: M60 junct 27 to town centre. Across mini-rdbt, at lights turn left. Pub on right of next rdbt behind Asda

Last modernised in 1908, this Victorian coaching inn close to Stockport's historic market place ranks high among the country's timeless gems. Come to see the classic unspoilt layout, the original tiled floors and panelling, and order pint of Robinson's from the traditional curved bar, quaffing it by the coal fire in the tiny snug bar. Quality lunches include hot sandwiches, tempting ciabattas, gammon, egg and chips or grilled halloumi and vegetable kebabs, and banana and toffee pudding. There's a sheltered courtyard for summer drinking.

Open all wk noon-11.45 Closed: 25-26 Dec, 1 Jan **Bar Meals** L served Mon-Fri 12-2.30, Sat-Sun 12-4 Av main course £8.95 ⊕ ROBINSONS ◄ Unicorn Bitter, Hatters Mild, Robin Bitter, Double Hop, seasonal ales. ☻ 8 **Facilities** Children's menu Dogs allowed Garden **Notes** ⊜

The Nursery Inn ☻

Green Ln, Heaton Norris SK4 2NA
☎ 0161 432 2044   📠 0161 442 1857
e-mail: nurseryinn@hydesbrewery.com
dir: Green Ln off Heaton Moor Rd. Pass rugby club on Green Ln, at end on right. Little cobbled road, pub 100yds on right

Set in a conservation area complete with bowling green, the Nursery was originally the main headquarters of Stockport County Football Club, with players changing in what is now the pub's interior, and the pitch at the rear. Dating back to 1939, the pub's wood panelling in the lounge/dining room and other original features reflect that period. With Hydes beers on offer, food is available at lunchtime only - jacket potatoes, sandwiches and baguettes in the bar, and smoked haddock and tuna steak in the restaurant.

Open all wk **Bar Meals** L served Tue-Sun 12-2.30 Av main course £6.50 **Restaurant** L served Tue-Sun 12-2.30 ⊕ HYDES BREWERY ◄ Hydes Bitter, Hydes Jekylls Gold, Hydes Seasonal Ales, Hydes Smooth. ☻ 7 **Facilities** Children's menu Dogs allowed Garden Parking **Notes** ⊜

HAMPSHIRE

ALTON
Map 5 SU73

PICK OF THE PUBS

The Anchor Inn NEW ⊛⊛ ☻

Lower Froyle GU34 4NA
☎ 01420 23261   📠 01420 520467
e-mail: info@anchorinnatlowerfroyle.co.uk
dir: A31 signed Bentley, follow brown tourist signs to Anchor Inn

The boarded and tile-hung Anchor Inn has been sympathetically remodelled to create a classic gastro-pub with bags of atmosphere and appeal. The cosy snug and saloon bar are decked out with open fires, wooden floors and lots of original features, whilst period furnishings and old prints hint at a bygone era. In the informal dining room, candlesticks and polished wooden tables combine with the painted wall panelling to create a dark, romantic interior. The accomplished seasonal menu is driven by fresh local produce, blending modern presentation with simplicity and clear flavours. Typical menu choices might start with chicken liver and foie gras parfait with red onion marmalade, before moving on to halibut and Jerusalem artichoke risotto, or Donald Russell rib-eye steak with béarnaise sauce and hand-cut chips. The dessert selection includes buttermilk pannacotta with poached Yorkshire rhubarb, and treacle tart with clotted cream.

Open all day all wk **Bar Meals** L served all wk 12-2 D served all wk 7-9 Av main course £9 **Restaurant** L served all wk 12-2 booking required D served Mon-Sat 7-9 booking required Av 3 course à la carte fr £35 ⊕ THE MILLERS COLLECTION ◄ Ringwood Best, Ringwood 49er, guest ales Ö Thatchers. ☻ 9 **Facilities** Children's menu Dogs allowed Garden Parking

ANDOVER
Map 5 SU34

Wyke Down Country Pub & Restaurant ☻

Wyke Down, Picket Piece SP11 6LX
☎ 01264 352048   📠 01264 324661
e-mail: info@wykedown.co.uk
dir: 3m from Andover town centre/A303. Follow signs for Wyke Down Caravan Park

Combining a pub/restaurant with a caravan park and golf driving range, this establishment is a diversified farm on the outskirts of Andover. It still raises beef cattle, but the pub started in a barn 25 years ago and the restaurant was built 11 years ago. Dishes range from lasagne, curry and Cajun chicken supreme on the bar menu to restaurant fare such as maple roasted pork chop, nut loaf, or steaks from the griddle.

Open all wk noon-3 6-11 Closed: 25 Dec-2 Jan **Bar Meals** L served all wk 12-2 booking required D served all wk 6-9 booking required **Restaurant** L served all wk 12-2 booking required D served all wk 6-9 booking required ⊕ FREE HOUSE ◄ Guinness, Timothy Taylor, real ale. ☻ 6 **Facilities** Children's menu Play area Garden Parking

AXFORD
Map 5 SU64

PICK OF THE PUBS

The Crown at Axford ☻

RG25 2DZ ☎ 01256 389492
e-mail: crownaxford@yahoo.co.uk
dir: From Basingstoke take A339 towards Alton. Under M3 bridge, turn next right onto B3046 towards New Alresford. Axford in approx 5m

The Crown is a small country inn set at the northern edge of the pretty Candover Valley. Here you can enjoy your choice from a selection of real ales and wines, with some bread and olives to keep you going, and order dishes like pork, beer and watercress sausages. The food is all home cooked from local produce wherever possible, including fish, game, and veggie dishes from the board. Organic specials are a feature.

Open all wk noon-3 6-11 (Sun noon-4 7-10.30) **Bar Meals** L served all wk 12-2 D served all wk 6-9 ⊕ FREE HOUSE ◄ Triple FFF, guest ales Ö Stowford Press. ☻ 7 **Facilities** Dogs allowed Garden Parking

BASINGSTOKE — Map 5 SU65

Hoddington Arms ♀

Upton Grey RG25 2RL
☎ 01256 862371 📠 01256 862371
e-mail: monca777@aol.com
dir: *Telephone for directions*

The McCutcheon family and their dog Foxo run this charming 250-year-old village pub, popularly known as the Hodd, where a log fire burns, cask ales and Somerset ciders are served. Fresh-cooked food is displayed on a blackboard where you might choose a delicious home-made pie; oven-roasted salmon on a bed of strawberries; Slovak pork goulash; chargrilled vegetables with rich tomato provençale and rice; or a special, such as beef Madras. The enclosed garden features an adventure playground.

Open all wk noon-3 6-mdnt **Bar Meals** L served all wk 12-2 D served Mon-Sat 6.30-9 Av main course £9 **Restaurant** L served all wk 12-2 D served Mon-Sat 6.30-9 Av 3 course à la carte fr £10 ⊕ GREENE KING ◀ Greene King IPA, Old Speckled Hen, Ruddles Best ♂ Thatchers Gold, Thatchers Katy, Thatchers Pear. ♀ 7 **Facilities** Play area Family room Dogs allowed Garden Parking

BAUGHURST — Map 5 SU56

PICK OF THE PUBS

The Wellington Arms ◉◉ ♀

Baughurst Rd RG26 5LP ☎ 0118 982 0110
e-mail: info@thewellingtonarms.com
web: www.thewellingtonarms.com
dir: *M4 junct 12 follow Newbury signs on A4. At rdbt left signed Aldermaston. Through Aldermaston. Up hill, at next rdbt 2nd exit, left at T-junct, pub 1m on left*

Blackboard menus and Edwardian furniture set the scene at this tiny whitewashed pub. Fields and woodland surround the large lawned garden, an ideal setting for the free-range chickens whose eggs are used in the kitchen. There are beehives too; herbs are grown just outside the kitchen door, the bread is baked by a craft baker, and nearby Henwood Farm delivers fresh organic vegetables and salads every day. The impressive menus show attention to detail – and so must you; check the food service times and book in advance to sample the mouth-watering fare. Starters might include local rabbit and free-range pork terrine with apple chutney and hot toast, followed by main course options such as roast rack of English lamb with fennel gratin and oven-dried tomatoes, or seared

Brixham turbot on sautéed marsh samphire. Leave space for dessert; steamed apple and syrup sponge with custard is a typical choice.

Closed: Mon, Sun eve, Tue L **Bar Meals** Av main course £15 **Restaurant** L served Wed-Sun 12-2.30 booking required D served Tue-Sat 6.30-9.30 booking required Fixed menu price fr £15 Av 3 course à la carte fr £28 ⊕ PUNCH TAVERNS ◀ Wadworth 6X. ♀ 12 **Facilities** Children's menu Dogs allowed Garden Parking

BEAUWORTH — Map 5 SU52

The Milburys ♀

SO24 0PB ☎ 01962 771248 📠 01962 7771910
e-mail: info@themilburys.co.uk
dir: *A272 towards Petersfield, after 6m turn right for Beauworth*

A rustic hill-top pub dating from the 17th century and named after the Bronze Age barrow nearby. It is noted for its massive, 250-year-old treadmill that used to draw water from the 300ft well in the bar, and for the far-reaching views across Hampshire that can be savoured from the lofty garden. The African Oasis restaurant has a distinctly South African flavour.

Open all wk ⊕ FREE HOUSE ◀ Theakstons Old Peculier, Triple FFF Altons Pride, Deuchars, guest ale. ♀ 8 **Facilities** Dogs allowed Garden Parking

BENTLEY — Map 5 SU74

The Bull Inn ♀

GU10 5JH ☎ 01420 22156 📠 01420 520772
dir: *2m from Farnham on A31 towards Winchester*

15th-century beamed coaching inn in a Hampshire village made famous by a reality TV show called *The Village*. Inside are open log fires, two separate bars and a restaurant. Extensive selection of pub food complemented by braised shank of lamb with sweet potato mash and rosemary sauce; pan-fried fillet of salmon with a lemon and chive butter; and roasted hock of ham with swede and potato purée.

Open all day all wk 10.30am-mdnt (Sun 12.30-10.30) **Bar Meals** L served Mon-Sat 12-2.30, Sun 12-8.30 D served Mon-Sat 6.30-9.30, Sun 12-8.30 ◀ Courage Best, Ringwood Best, Young's Bitter, Timothy Taylor Landlord ♂ Thatchers Pear. ♀ 8 **Facilities** Dogs allowed Garden Parking

BENTWORTH — Map 5 SU64

PICK OF THE PUBS

The Sun Inn ♀

See Pick of the Pubs on opposite page

BOLDRE — Map 5 SZ39

The Hobler Inn ♀

Southampton Rd, Battramsley SO41 8PT
☎ 01590 623944
e-mail: hedi@alcatraz.co.uk
dir: *2m from Brockenhurst, towards Lymington on main road*

On the main road between Brockenhurst and Lymington, with a large grassed area and trestle tables ideal for families visiting the New Forest. It's more London wine bar than local, but still serves a well-kept pint of Ringwood. Hot lunchtime snacks like Welsh rarebit or Boston baked beans on toast are good value. Mains include a variation on the classic shepherd's pie but with added Nepalese spices.

Open all wk ◀ Ringwood, Ringwood Best, Timothy Taylor. ♀ 10 **Facilities** Garden Parking

PICK OF THE PUBS

The Red Lion ♀

Rope Hill SO41 8NE
☎ 01590 673177 📠 01590 674036
dir: *1m from Lymington off A337. From M27 junct 1 through Lyndhurst & Brockenhurst towards Lymington, follow signs for Boldre*

A proper New Forest pub, The Red Lion has a mention in the Domesday Book, although today's inn dates from the 15th century, when it was created from a stable and two cottages. Inside you'll find a rambling series of beamed rooms packed with rural memorabilia. Menus offer traditional, home-made dishes featuring local venison and fish from local catches; the inn is proud to hold the New Forest Marque for use and promotion of food produced in the New Forest area. Pie and Pudding evenings are very popular – a choice of six or seven home-made pies and a home-made pudding for £10. Another innovation is to eat at a patio hot table, where you cook your choice of meat, fish or game on a central hotplate.

continued on page 216

PICK OF THE PUBS

The Sun Inn ♀

BENTWORTH | Map 5 SU64

Sun Hill GU34 5JT ☎ 01420 562338
dir: *Telephone for directions*

This delightful flower-decked pub is either the first building you pass as you enter Bentworth from the Basingstoke-Alton road, or the last one out, depending on which way you are travelling, and it always seems to come as a surprise. Originally two cottages, it now has three interconnecting rooms, each with its own log fire and brick and wood floors. The bar is the middle room, right in front of the door. Pews, settles, scrubbed pine tables with lit candles in the evening add to the homely atmosphere. Food is hearty and traditional, with beef Stroganoff; minted lamb; a range of meat and vegetarian curries; liver and bacon; cheesy haddock bake; filled Yorkshire puddings; braised steak in red wine and mushroom sauce; and Mediterranean lamb. Game in season includes venison, cooked in Guinness with pickled walnuts, and pheasant. Everything, from the soup to the dessert, is home made. A thriving free house, it offers several hand-pumped real ales, including Cheriton Pots, Ringwood Best and Old Thumper, both from Hampshire breweries, and Fuller's London Pride. There is much to see and do in the area: Gilbert White's House and the Oates Museum in Selborne are not far away, and neither are Jane Austen's House at Chawton, nor the Watercress Line at Alresford. Also within easy reach is Basing House in Old Basing, on the outskirts of Basingstoke, where important Civil War sieges and bombardments brought about the ruin of the house, though parts of it are being restored.

Open all week ⊕ FREE HOUSE
◀ Cheriton Pots Ale, Ringwood Best & Old Thumper, Brakspear Bitter, Fuller's London Pride. **Facilities** Family room Dogs allowed Garden Parking

BOLDRE *continued*

Typical dishes are trio of Sway Butcher's Red Lion sausages; foresters chicken; Ringwood ale battered fish, and crab and spring onion fishcakes.

Open all wk 11-3 5.30-11 (Sun noon-4 6-10.30) **Bar Meals** L served Mon-Sat 12-2.30, Sun 12-3.30 D served Mon-Sat 6-9.30, Sun 6-9 Av main course £6 **Restaurant** L served Mon-Sat 12-2.30, Sun 12-3.30 D served Mon-Sat 6-9.30, Sun 6-9 Av 3 course à la carte fr £18 ⊕ FREE HOUSE ◀ Ringwood Best, Ringwood Fortyniner, Marstons Pedigree, Guinness, guest ales. ♀ 18 **Facilities** Children's menu Dogs allowed Garden Parking

See Advert under Lymington

BRAMDEAN | Map 5 SU62

The Fox Inn ♀

SO24 0LP ☎ 01962 771363
e-mail: thefoxinn@bramdean.net
dir: *A272 between Winchester & Petersfield*

The crest fixed to the exterior of this 400-year-old pub commemorates the day when the Prince of Wales (later King George IV) stopped by for refreshments. Situated in the beautiful Meon Valley surrounded by copper beech trees, The Fox serves locally sourced food including a good blackboard selection of fresh fish dishes - perhaps supreme of halibut with lime and chilli butter. Other typical choices include pork fillet with stilton and brandy sauce.

Open 11-3 6.30-11 Closed: Sun eve **Bar Meals** L served all wk 12-2 D served Mon-Sat 7-9 ⊕ GREENE KING ◀ IPA Smooth, Morlands Original. ♀ 7 **Facilities** Dogs allowed Garden Parking

---

BRANSGORE | Map 5 SZ19

PICK OF THE PUBS

The Three Tuns
Country Inn NEW ◉◉ ♀

Ringwood Rd BH23 8JH ☎ 01425 672232
e-mail: threetunsinn@btconnect.com
dir: *1.5m from A35 Walkford junct. 3m from Christchurch & 1m from Hinton Admiral railway station*

This award-winning, 17th-century inn is one of the few in the New Forest remaining under thatch. It offers five distinct public areas: a comfortable Lounge Bar, with no music, TV screens or games, and in winter a log fire; an oak-beamed Snug Bar, again with a log fire, and biscuits and water for dogs; a large terrace with its water feature; a south-facing garden, surrounded by fields, trees and ponies, and not a bouncy castle in sight, but space galore (on sunny days, out comes the barbecue); and finally, the restaurant. Here you'll find how fresh produce and seasonings from around the world are fused into classic dishes and seasonal specials, recognised for their quality by two AA

Rosettes. Expect venison bourguignonne, bacon and glazed onions; roasted halibut, polenta and artichoke, salsify, olives and squid fricassée; and wild mushroom risotto with truffle oil, Parmesan, rocket and tomato.

Open all day all wk 11.30-11 (Sun 12-10.30) **Bar Meals** L served Mon-Fri 12-2.15, Sat-Sun 12-9.15 booking required D served Mon-Fri 6.30-9.15, Sat-Sun 12-9.15 booking required Av main course £12 **Restaurant** L served Mon-Fri 12-2.15, Sat-Sun 12-9.15 booking required D served Mon-Fri 6.30-9.15, Sat-Sun 12-9.15 booking required Av 3 course à la carte fr £20 ⊕ ENTERPRISE INNS ◀ Hop Back Summer Lightning, Ringwood Best Bitter, Fortyniner, Marstons Porter, Timothy Taylor ♂ Thatchers Gold, New Forest Traditional Farmhouse. ♀ 11 **Facilities** Children's menu Dogs allowed Garden Parking

---

BUCKLERS HARD | Map 5 SU40

The Master Builders House
Hotel ★★★ HL ◉ ♀

SO42 7XB ☎ 01590 616253 📄 01590 616297
e-mail: enquiries@themasterbuilders.co.uk
dir: *From M27 junct 2 follow signs to Beaulieu. Left onto B3056. Left to Bucklers Hard. Hotel 2m on left*

Once home to master shipbuilder Henry Adams, this idyllic 18th-century inn is situated on the banks of the River Beaulieu, in the historic ship-building village of Bucklers Hard. Ducks, boats and river walks are all on the doorstep. Bar food includes grilled Lymington mackerel, tomato and red onion salad; Old Spot sausages, creamed potato and roast onions; and linguine with New Forest mushrooms, garlic and parsley, alongside a choice of real ales, particularly Ringwood, decent wines and Stowford Press cider.

Open all day all wk 11-11 (Sun 11-10.30) **Bar Meals** Av main course £9.50 food served all day **Restaurant** L served Mon-Sat 12-2.30, Sun 12-3 booking required D served all wk 7-9.30 booking required Fixed menu price fr £15 Av 3 course à la carte fr £25 ⊕ HILLBROOKE HOTELS ◀ Ringwood Best, Ringwood Thumper ♂ Stowford Press. ♀ 8 **Facilities** Children's menu Dogs allowed Garden Parking **Rooms** 25

BURGHCLERE | Map 5 SU46

PICK OF THE PUBS

Carnarvon Arms ♀

See Pick of the Pubs on opposite page

BURLEY | Map 5 SU20

The Burley Inn ♀

BH24 4AB ☎ 01425 403448
e-mail: info@theburleyinn.co.uk
dir: *4m from Ringwood*

Before it became a pub, this spacious Edwardian building was where the local doctor practised, the waiting room now being the bar and dining areas. The menu offers a broad choice, including pie of the day; beef bourguignon; salmon in white wine and chive sauce; and lasagne and vegetable tagine. The inn stands in the heart of the New Forest, so take care when driving as ponies, donkeys and cattle freely roam the local roads.

Open all wk ⊕ FREE HOUSE ◀ Ringwood Best, Ringwood Old Thumper. ♀ 11 **Facilities** Dogs allowed Garden Parking

---

CADNAM | Map 5 SU31

Sir John Barleycorn ♀

Old Romsey Rd SO40 2NP ☎ 023 8081 2236
e-mail: hedi@alcatraz.co.uk
dir: *From Southampton M27 junct 1 into Cadnam*

Reputedly the oldest inn in the New Forest, this friendly establishment is formed from three 12th-century cottages, one of which was once home to the charcoal burner who discovered the body of King William Rufus. A thorough menu covers all the options from quick snacks and sandwiches to toad-in-the-hole; chicken, leek and bacon pie; and Thai chicken curry. The name derives from a folksong celebrating the transformation of barley to beer.

Open all day all wk 9am-11pm (Sat-Sun 11-11) **Bar Meals** L served all wk 12-9.30 D served all wk 12-9.30 food served all day ⊕ ALCATRAZ PUB COMPANY LTD ◀ Ringwood, Ringwood 49er ♂ Stowford Press. ♀ 10 **Facilities** Garden Parking

---

CHALTON | Map 5 SU71

PICK OF THE PUBS

The Red Lion ♀

PO8 0BG ☎ 023 9259 2246 📄 023 9259 6915
e-mail: redlionchalton@fullers.co.uk
dir: *Just off A3 between Horndean & Petersfield. Follow signs for Chalton*

Believed to be Hampshire's oldest pub, The Red Lion was built in 1147 as a workshop and residence for the craftsmen working on St Michael's church across the road. By 1460 it had become a hostel for church dignitaries, and was later extended to accommodate coachmen on their regular journey from London to Portsmouth. Constructed from wood, white daub and thatch, the ancient building blends effortlessly into the hills and trees of the South Downs, and original features inside include an inglenook fireplace. There are spectacular views from the large garden and

continued on page 218

PICK OF THE PUBS

Carnarvon Arms 🍷

BURGHCLERE   Map 5 SU46

Winchester Rd RG20 9LE
☎ **01635 278222** 📠 **01635 278444**
e-mail: info@carnarvonarms.com
web: www.carnarvonarms.com
dir: *M4 junct 13, A34 S to Winchester. Exit A34 at Tothill Services, follow Highclere Castle signs. Pub on right*

The Carnarvon Arms is a modern country inn offering good food, good beer and sensible prices. The word 'modern' needs putting into context, however, because it was actually built in the mid-1800s as a coaching inn providing a stop-off for travellers to nearby Highclere Castle, the family seat of the Earls of Carnarvon. It was the 5th Earl who famously opened Tutankhamun's tomb in 1922, dying the following year and triggering suggestions of a Mummy's Curse. He is buried on nearby Beacon Hill, an ancient hill fort – quite appropriate for an archaeologist. The warm and friendly bar, decorated in fresh natural colours and furnished with rich leather upholstery, offers a menu of sandwiches, salads, pan-fried liver and bacon with mash and shallot sauce; and tomato and basil shepherd's pie topped with butternut squash and Parmesan. In the stunning dining room, with its high vaulted ceiling, the Egyptian-inspired wall carvings pay homage to those remarkable excavations in the Valley of the Kings. Modern British food, with a strong emphasis on fresh seasonal ingredients at sensible prices, is head chef Justin Brown's objective. From the carte come starters of pan-fried scallops with buttered samphire and herb fish cream; and risotto of leeks, Oxford Blue cheese and toasted walnuts. Among the main courses are pan-roasted, corn-fed chicken breast with bubble and squeak, asparagus and coarse-grain mustard; fillet of John Dory with sautéed potato, bacon and spinach and dill fish cream; and pan-roasted rump of pork with Jersey Royals, baby leeks and herb red wine sauce. Puddings include traditional tarts and crumbles, in addition to contemporary favourites such as trio of chocolate desserts - mousse, brûlée and fondant. An excellent cheeseboard is served with pressed fruits. Vegetarian and set-price lunch menus are also available.

Open all week **Bar Meals** L served all week 12-2.30 D served all week 6.30-9.30 **Restaurant** L served all week 12-2.30 D served all week 6.30-9.30 🛢 MERCHANT INNS LTD 🍺 Guinness, guest ales. 🍷 15 **Facilities** Children's menu Dogs allowed Garden Parking

CHALTON *continued*

modern dining room. The pub has a good reputation locally for the quality of its food. You can choose from the daily changing menu of freshly cooked dishes, which relies heavily on locally sourced produce, or the popular snack menu of traditional pub fare, all washed down with a pint of real ale or cider.

Open all day all wk 11.30-11 (Sun 11.45-10.30) **Bar Meals** food served all day **Restaurant** food served all day ⊕ FULLER, SMITH & TURNER PLC ◀ Fuller's, HSB, London Pride, Discovery, ESB, seasonal ales ⌂ Heart of Hampshire, Boxing Dog, Sweet Russett. ♀ 20 **Facilities** Children's menu Family room Dogs allowed Garden Parking

---

CHARTER ALLEY — Map 5 SU55

The White Hart Inn ♀

White Hart Ln RG26 5QA
☎ 01256 850048 📄 01256 850524
e-mail: enquiries@whitehartcharteralley.com
dir: *From M3 junct 6 take A339 towards Newbury. Turn right to Ramsdell. Right at church, then 1st left into White Hart Lane*

On the outskirts of the village overlooking open farmland and woods, this pub draws everyone from cyclists and walkers to real ale enthusiasts. Dating from 1818, it originally refreshed local woodsmen and coach drivers visiting the farrier next door. Today's more modern menu is likely to include confit of duck leg with orange and tarragon sauce; venison steak with red wine and redcurrant sauce; or vegetarian stir-fry. Look to the blackboard for specials and fish dishes.

Open all wk noon-2.30 7-11 (Sun 7-10.30) Closed: 25-26 Dec, 1 Jan **Bar Meals** L served all wk 12-2 D served Tue-Sat 7-9 Av main course £10 **Restaurant** L served Tue-Sun 12-2 booking required D served Tue-Sat 7-9 booking required ⊕ FREE HOUSE ◀ West Berkshire Mild, Palmers IPA, Triple FFF Alton Pride, Stonehenge Great Bustard, Loddon Ferryman's Gold. ♀ 7 **Facilities** Children's menu Family room Dogs allowed Garden Parking

---

CHAWTON — Map 5 SU73

The Greyfriar ♀

Winchester Rd GU34 1SB
☎ 01420 83841 📄 01420 83841
e-mail: peter@thegreyfriar.co.uk
dir: *Just off A31 near Alton. Access to Chawton via A31/A32 junct. Follow Jane Austen's House signs*

A terrace of 16th-century cottages opposite Jane Austen's house, which was divided into a 'beer shop' and grocery in the 1860s. Proper pub status followed with a licence granted to the Chawton Arms; for reasons unknown it became the Greyfriar in 1894. Today it's a family-run and friendly place to enjoy Fullers beers and quality food from a varied and imaginative menu. Expect the likes of sautéed fresh asparagus, Scottish scallops grilled in the shell, and main courses that include fresh lamb reared in the village.

Open all day all wk noon-11 (Sun noon-10.30) **Bar Meals** L served Mon-Sat 12-2.30, Sun 12-3 D served Mon-Sat 7-9.30, Sun 6.30-8 ◀ Fuller's London Pride, ESB, Seasonal ales. ♀ 6 **Facilities** Play area Dogs allowed Garden Parking

---

CHERITON — Map 5 SU52

PICK OF THE PUBS

The Flower Pots Inn

SO24 0QQ ☎ 01962 771318 📄 01962 771318
dir: *A272 towards Petersfield, left onto B3046, pub 0.75m on right*

This friendly red brick village pub was built as a farmhouse in the 1840s by the head gardener of nearby Avington Park. There are two bars: the rustic, pine-furnished public bar and the cosy saloon with its comfy sofa, both with welcoming open fires in winter. A large, safe garden, with a covered patio area, allows young ones to let off steam (under 12s are not permitted in the bar). Simple home-made food is the order of the day: expect toasted sandwiches, jacket potatoes and tasty hotpots - perhaps beef bourguignon, spicy mixed bean, or lamb and apricot - served with a choice of crusty bread, basmati rice, garlic bread or jacket potato. There are also ploughman's (with cheese, ham or beef), and giant baps filled with a choice of beef, pork steak and onions, bacon and mushroom, cheese, or Coronation chicken. Be sure to try the award-winning beers like Pots Ale or Goodens Gold, brewed in the micro-brewery across the car park.

Open all wk noon-2.30 6-11 (Sun noon-3 7-10.30) **Bar Meals** L served all wk 12-2 D served Mon-Sat 7-9 Av main course £7 ⊕ FREE HOUSE ◀ Flower Pots Bitter, Goodens Gold ⌂ Westons Old Rosie. **Facilities** Dogs allowed Garden Parking **Notes** ⊛

CHILWORTH — Map 5 SU41

Chilworth Arms ♀

Chilworth Rd SO16 7JZ ☎ 023 8076 6247
dir: *3m N of Southampton on A27 (Romsey road)*

Formerly known as the Clump Inn, this gastro-pub is warmed by log fires and furnished with leather sofas. There's a great mix of freshly prepared dishes, from simple pizzas to well-aged steaks, fresh fish and traditional pub classics, many with a hint of Italian about them. Regularly changing real ales vie for popularity with continental beers, fine wines and fresh juices. Eat in the spacious dining area, or out on the covered patio.

Open all day all wk 11-10.30 (Sun noon-8.30) **Bar Meals** L served Mon-Sat 12-2.30, Sun 12-8.30 D served Mon-Sat 6-9.30, Sun 12-8.30 ⊕ FREE HOUSE ◀ Timothy Taylor Landlord. ♀ 15 **Facilities** Garden Parking

---

CRAWLEY — Map 5 SU43

The Fox and Hounds ♀

SO21 2PR ☎ 01962 776006 📄 01962 776006
e-mail: liamlewisairey@aol.com
dir: *A34 onto A272 then 1st right into Crawley*

Just north west of Winchester, at the heart of a peaceful Hampshire village, this mock Tudor traditional inn enjoys a burgeoning reputation for simple well-cooked food. Restored to former glories, it features beamed rooms warmed by log fires that create a welcoming, lived-in atmosphere. Typical dishes are roast beetroot salad with goats' cheese; smokey chicken with bacon leek and cream sauce; home-made beef lasagne; and sticky toffee pudding.

Open all wk 11-3 6-mdnt **Bar Meals** L served all wk 12-2 booking required **Restaurant** L served all wk 12-2 booking required D served all wk 6.30-9.30 booking required ⊕ ENTERPRISE INN ◀ Wadworth 6X, Ringwood Best, Ringwood 49, Bombardier. ♀ 36 **Facilities** Children's menu Play area Garden Parking

---

CRONDALL — Map 5 SU74

PICK OF THE PUBS

The Hampshire Arms ♀

Pankridge St GU10 5QU ☎ 01252 850418
e-mail: info@thehampshireatcrondall.co.uk
dir: *From M3 junct 5 take A287 S towards Farnham. Follow signs to Crondall on right*

The Hampshire Arms bar is light and elegant, as are the two main dining areas and intimate alcoves. Throughout the public rooms open fires, exposed beams and candlelight combine to create a delightfully welcoming atmosphere. The building dates from the 18th century and began as two cottages, but over the years it has also been a courthouse, a post office and a bakery. Outside there is a large landscaped garden with a patio area. For a leisurely lunch you could try chef's special chicken liver parfait with red onion marmalade, freshly made brioche and sultanas soaked in jasmine tea, as a starter. Smoked salmon and haddock fishcakes with buttered spinach and French butter sauce are an established favourite, as is the classic dessert, French lemon tart, served with chocolate chip shortbread. The mid-week fixed-price menu offers value for money with seared scallops with apple and ginger purée and soft herb salad; and roast rump of lamb with three mustards, wilted greens and lamb reduction.

Open all day noon-11pm (Fri-Sat noon-mdnt Sun noon-10.30pm) Closed: Mon **Bar Meals** L served Mon-Sat 12-2.30, Sun 12-6.30 D served Mon-Sat 6.30-9.30, Sun 12-6.30 ⊕ GREENE KING ◀ Greene King IPA, guest ales. ♀ 10 **Facilities** Dogs allowed Garden Parking

DAMERHAM — Map 5 SU11

The Compasses Inn ♀

SP6 3HQ ☎ 01725 518231 📠 01725 518880
e-mail: linda@compassesinn.co.uk
web: www.compassesinn.uk.com
dir: From Fordingbridge (A338) follow signs for
Sandleheath/Damerham. Signed from B3078

The Compasses is a perfect example of the traditional
family-run country free house. Set next to the village
green, it is an ideal spot for a tranquil summer pint or a
winter warmer round the welcoming open fires. The ales
are augmented by over 100 malt whiskies and a good
selection of wines. Freshly prepared food is served in the
bar, dining room or garden: it ranges from a simple
home-baked bread ploughman's to pan-fried sea bass
with prawns.

Open all wk 11-3 6-11 (Sat-Sun all day) **Bar Meals** L
served all wk 12-3 D served all wk 6.30-9.30
⊕ ENTERPRISE INNS ◖ Ringwood Best, Hop Back
Summer Lightning, Courage Best, Ringwood 49er, Guest
Ale. ♀ 8 **Facilities** Children's menu Dogs allowed Garden
Parking

DOWNTON — Map 5 SZ29

The Royal Oak ♀

Christchurch Rd SO41 0LA ☎ 01590 642297
e-mail: royaloak@alcatraz.co.uk
dir: On A337 between Lymington & Christchurch

Two miles south of the New Forest and just one mile from
the beach at Lymington, this renovated pub is renowned
for its food. Snack on a traditional ploughman's platter or
daytime sandwiches such as warm chicken, chorizo and
rocket or brie and bacon. Main meals include salmon fish
cakes with tomato and chilli jam; sirloin steak with
peppercorn sauce; and gourmet burgers.

Open all day all wk 11-11.30 **Bar Meals** food served all
day **Restaurant** Fixed menu price fr £9.95 Av 3 course à
la carte fr £19 food served all day ⊕ ENTERPRISE
INNS ◖ Ringwood Best Bitter, Fuller's London Pride,
HSB. ♀ 15 **Facilities** Children's menu Garden Parking

DROXFORD — Map 5 SU61

PICK OF THE PUBS

The Bakers Arms NEW ◉ ♀

High St SO32 3PA ☎ 01489 877533
e-mail: enquiries@thebakersarmsdroxford.com
dir: 10m E of Winchester on A32 between Fareham
& Alton. 7m SW of Petersfield. 10m inland from
Portsmouth

This unpretentious, white-painted pub and restaurant
could teach many pubs that never feature in this guide
a thing or two. It has been opened up inside, but it still
oozes country charm and character, the staff are
smiley, and the locals clearly love it. Over the big log
fire a blackboard menu lists the simple, well cooked
and locally sourced food, while in the bar customers
make short work of its barrels of Wallops Wood from
the village's own Bowman Brewery. Mostly classic
British cuisine includes pea and ham soup; potted
mackerel with toast and piccalilli; gratinated
Hampshire pike quenelles; grilled chicken breast with
rösti potato and wild mushroom sauce; crispy duck leg
with chorizo, sautéed potatoes and thyme gravy;
roasted polenta with blue cheese and field mushrooms;
and orechiette pasta with lamb ragout. Every village
should have a local like this.

Open 11.45-3 6-11 (Sun 12-3) Closed: Sun eve & Mon
Bar Meals L served Tue-Sun 12-2 booking required D
served Tue-Sun 7-9 booking required Av main course
£12.95 **Restaurant** L served Tue-Sun 12-2 booking
required D served Tue-Sun 7-9 booking required
◖ Bowman Swift one, Bowman Wallops Wood
Ŏ Stowford Press. ♀ 7 **Facilities** Children's menu
Dogs allowed Garden Parking

DUMMER — Map 5 SU54

The Queen Inn ♀

Down St RG25 2AD ☎ 01256 397367 📠 01256 397601
e-mail: richardmoore49@btinternet.com
dir: M3 junct 7, follow Dummer signs

You can dine by candlelight from the restaurant menu at
this 16th-century village pub with low beams and huge
open log fire. Alternatively you'll find lunchtime savouries
like Welsh or Scottish rarebits alongside the sandwiches
and jackets. A bar menu offers everything from starters
and healthy options to flame grills, house favourites, and
specials like chargrilled half chicken piri piri and beef
bourguignon. Beers include guest ales, and the wine list
is commendably unpretentious.

Open all wk **Bar Meals** L served all wk 12-2.30 D served
all wk 6.30-9.30 **Restaurant** L served all wk 12-2.30
booking required D served all wk 6.30-9.30 booking
required ⊕ ENTERPRISE INNS ◖ Courage Best & John
Smiths, Fuller's London Pride, Old Speckled Hen, guest
ales. ♀ 10 **Facilities** Garden Parking

EAST END — Map 5 SZ39

PICK OF THE PUBS

The East End Arms

Main Rd SO41 5SY
☎ 01590 626223 📠 01590 626223
e-mail: manager@eastendarms.co.uk
dir: From Lymington towards Beaulieu (past Isle of
Wight ferry), 3m to East End

Close to Beaulieu and historic Buckler's Hard, this New
Forest inn, owned by John Illsley, the bass player of Dire
Straits, combines the authenticity of a proper local
with a good reputation as a gastro-pub. Ringwood ales
are drawn straight from the wood in The Foresters Bar,
where stone floors and open fires create a homely,
traditional feel. The atmospheric lounge bar, with its
sofas and winter fires, is a comfortable setting for a
meal from the daily-changing, brasserie-style menu.
Locally sourced fish/seafood make a strong showing in
dishes such as grilled Porbeagle shark loin with
cucumber and dill salad, or seared hand-dived
scallops with Chinese stir-fried vegetables. An
alternative might be pan-fried pigeon breasts with
blue cheese and walnut salad, or roast chicken breast
stuffed with buffalo mozzarella and Parma ham. The
pub is well worth the drive down country lanes or a
short diversion from the nearby Solent Way long
distance footpath.

Open all wk **Restaurant** L served all wk 12-2.30
booking required D served Mon-Sat 7-9.30 booking
required ⊕ FREE HOUSE ◖ Ringwood Best, Archers,
Fortyniner. **Facilities** Dogs allowed Garden Parking

EAST MEON — Map 5 SU62

Ye Olde George Inn ♀

Church St GU32 1NH
☎ 01730 823481 📠 01730 823759
dir: S of A272 (Winchester/Petersfield). 1.5m from
Petersfield turn left opposite church

This 15th-century inn is located in a lovely old village on
the River Meon, close to a magnificent Norman church.
Its open fires, heavy beams and rustic artefacts create an
ideal setting for a good choice of real ales and freshly
prepared food in the bar or restaurant. Fish features
strongly with dishes of baked sea bass with samphire
and balsamic olive dressing, or poached halibut with
mussel sauce.

Open all wk ⊕ HALL & WOODHOUSE ◖ Badger Best,
Tanglefoot, King & Barnes Sussex. ♀ 8 **Facilities** Dogs
allowed Garden Parking

EASTON   Map 5 SU53

PICK OF THE PUBS

The Chestnut Horse ♈

SO21 1EG ☎ 01962 779257 📠 01962 779037
dir: *From M3 junct 9 take A33 towards Basingstoke, then B3047. Take 2nd right, then 1st left*

This 16th-century pub is located in the pretty Itchen Valley village of Easton and there are some good walks directly from the door. Old tankards and teapots hang from the low-beamed ceilings in the two bar areas, where a large open fire is the central focus through the winter months. The romantic candlelit restaurants are equally inviting: plates adorn the light, panelled Green Room, and there's a wood-burning stove in the darker low-beamed Red Room. A good-value set price menu is offered Monday to Saturday lunchtime (12-2pm) or Monday to Thursday early evening (6-7.30pm). This might include fish and chips, local pheasant casserole or chilli con carne. Typical main menu dishes are baked trout fillet with chestnut and herb crust, or slow braised shoulder of lamb with butternut mash. A vegetarian alternative could be tagliatelle with Alresford watercress and gruyère cheese sauce.

Open all wk noon-3.30 5.30-11 (Sun eve closed winter) **Bar Meals** L served all wk 12-2.30 booking required D served Mon-Sat 6-9.30 booking required Av main course £12 **Restaurant** L served all wk 12-2 booking required D served Mon-Sat 6-9.30 booking required Fixed menu price fr £12 Av 3 course à la carte fr £24 ⊕ HALL & WOODHOUSE ◀ Chestnut Horse Special, Badger First Gold, Tanglefoot ♂ Stowford Press. ♈ 9 **Facilities** Children's menu Dogs allowed Garden Parking

The Cricketers Inn ★★★ INN ♈

SO21 1EJ ☎ 01962 779353 📠 01962 779010
e-mail: cricketersinn@btconnect.com
dir: *M3 junct 9, A33 towards Basingstoke, right at Kingsworthy onto B3047. In 0.75m turn right. Pub signed*

Standing on a corner in the heart of a popular village, this 1904 pub is a real local, with a single L-shaped bar and cricketing memorabilia on the walls. Look out for crusty doorstep sandwiches and open toasties, in addition to filled Yorkshires and specials of ribs, sweet and sour chicken and cottage pie. Accommodation is available.

Open all wk **Bar Meals** L served Mon-Sat 12-2.30, Sun 12-4 D served Mon-Sat 6-9 **Restaurant** L served Mon-Sat 12-2.30, Sun 12-4 D served Mon-Sat 6-9 ⊕ MARSTONS ◀ Ringwood, guest ales. ♈ 8 **Facilities** Dogs allowed Garden Parking **Rooms** 3

EAST TYTHERLEY   Map 5 SU22

PICK OF THE PUBS

The Star Inn
Tytherley ★★★★ INN ☺☺ ♈

SO51 0LW ☎ 01794 340225
e-mail: info@starinn.co.uk
dir: *5m N of Romsey off A3057, left for Dunbridge on B3084. Left for Awbridge & Kents Oak. Through Lockerley then 1m*

The 16th-century Star Inn stands overlooking the village cricket green in the smallest village in the Test Valley. You'll find Hidden Brewery beers and other guest ales behind the bar, plus an extensive international wine list. Dine where you like, in the bar, at dark-wood tables in the main dining room, or outside on the patio in summer, where you can also play king-sized chess. Lunchtime brings a variety of platters (fish, Barkham Blue, or Winchester farmhouse cheese), sandwiches (perhaps smoked salmon, crème fraîche and dill, or Cumberland sausage with caramelised onion), and a good value two-course menu (stir-fried tiger prawns with chorizo and gremolata, and roast chicken supreme). The evening menu might offer crab soufflé with watercress and saffron cream, and braised belly pork with sage polenta and celeriac purée. There's a good choice at Sunday lunch, too, including traditional roasts. Children of well behaved parents are welcome.

Open 11-2.30 6-10 Closed: Sun eve & Mon (ex BH) **Bar Meals** L served Tue-Sun 12-2 booking required D served Tue-Fri 7-9 booking required Av main course £8.50 **Restaurant** L served Tue-Sun 12-2 booking required D served Tue-Sat 7-9 booking required Av 3 course à la carte fr £20 ⊕ FREE HOUSE ◀ Hidden Quest, Hidden Pint, guest ales ♂ Thatchers Gold. ♈ 8 **Facilities** Children's menu Dogs allowed Garden Parking **Rooms** 3

EMSWORTH   Map 5 SU70

The Sussex Brewery ♈

36 Main Rd PO10 8AU
☎ 01243 371533 📠 01243 379684
e-mail: info@sussexbrewery.com
dir: *On A259 (coast road), between Havant & Chichester*

The Sussex Brewery is set in the picturesque village of Emsworth, renowned for its annual food festival in September. This 17th-century pub upholds traditional values with its sawdust covered floors, real ales and open fires, and the two dining rooms that have recently been refurbished. The menu includes a large variety of sausages, from beef and Guinness to tomato and garlic (there's a good choice for vegetarians too). Breakfast and light lunch menus are also available.

Open all wk 7am-mdnt **Bar Meals** L served all wk 12-2.30 D served all wk 6.30-9.30 **Restaurant** L served all wk 12-2.30 booking required D served all wk 6.30-9.30 booking required ⊕ YOUNG & CO BREWERY PLC ◀ Youngs Special, Youngs Ordinary, Waggle Dance, Bombardier Tribute. ♈ 12 **Facilities** Children's menu Dogs allowed Garden Parking

EVERSLEY   Map 5 SU76

The Golden Pot ♈

Reading Rd RG27 0NB ☎ 0118 973 2104
e-mail: jcalder@goldenpot.co.uk
web: www.golden-pot.co.uk
dir: *Between Reading & Camberley on B3272 approx 0.25m from Eversley cricket ground*

Dating back to the 1700s, this well-established hostelry has recently converted to a free house. Expect three pumps rotating ales by Andwell Brewing Company, Loddon Brewery and Hogs Back among others. A warming fire connects the bar and restaurant, while the Snug and Vineyard are comfortable outside areas surrounded by colourful tubs and hanging baskets for summer relaxation. All food is home-made, offering traditional and modern choices, and prepared on the premises; children are not only welcome but also specially catered for.

Open all wk 11.30-3 5.30-10.30 Closed: 25-26 & 31 Dec, 1 Jan, (Sun eve) **Bar Meals** L served all wk 12-2.45 booking required D served Mon-Sat 6-9 booking required **Restaurant** L served all wk 12-2.45 booking required D served Mon-Sat 6-9 booking required ⊕ FREE HOUSE ◀ Andwell Brewery, Loddon Brewery, West Berkshire, Hogs Back Brewery, Shepherd Neame. ♈ 8 **Facilities** Children's menu Dogs allowed Garden Parking

EXTON   Map 5 SU62

The Shoe Inn NEW ♈

Shoe Ln SO32 3NT ☎ 01489 877526
dir: *Exton is on A32 between Fareham & Alton*

In the heart of the Meon Valley, this popular village pub owes much of its success to the food on offer. And that in turn is due to extensive use by the kitchen of local ingredients, including from an ever-expanding herb garden that produces organic vegetables, salad leaves and fruit nourished by compost and manure from the local stud farm. The bar offers well-kept hand-pumped Wadworth ales, a selection of lagers, ciders and soft drinks, along with an extensive list of wines and

Champagnes served by the glass or bottle. You can enjoy a light meal from the Cobbler's menu, or from a seasonal menu, home-made faggots; slow-cooked leg of Hampshire pork; fillet of organic sea trout; Mediterranean cassoulet; or rigatone with roasted vegetables. Eat inside or in the garden overlooking Old Winchester Hill, while watching the river drift by, with ducks swimming, fish feeding and dragon-flies presumably flying.

Open 11-3 6-11 Closed: 25 Dec, Mon eve **Bar Meals** L served all wk 12-2 **Restaurant** L served all wk 12-2 D served Tue-Sun 6-9 ⊕ WADWORTH ◀ Wadworth 6X, IPA ♂ Stowford Press. ♀ 18 **Facilities** Children's menu Dogs allowed Garden Parking

FORDINGBRIDGE   Map 5 SU11

The Augustus John ♀

116 Station Rd SP6 1DG ☎ 01425 652098
e-mail: enquiries@augustusjohn.com
dir: *12m S of Salisbury on A338 towards Ringwood*

In keeping with its name, this pub and restaurant has a collection of paintings by Augustus John, who lived in the village. Set on the edge of the New Forest, it's a friendly, welcoming refuge offering a good selection of drinks including Ringwood Best Bitter and Wychwood cider. The extensive menu includes Thai food, fresh fish and hearty meals such as creamy garlic mushrooms followed by roast lamb with a red wine sauce.

Open all wk 10.30-3 5-11.30 (wknds open until 1.30am) **Bar Meals** Av main course £5 food served all day **Restaurant** Fixed menu price fr £8.95 Av 3 course à la carte fr £22 food served all day ⊕ MARSTONS ◀ Ringwood Best, Pedigree, Porter, Fortyniner ♂ Wychwood. ♀ 8 **Facilities** Children's menu Dogs allowed Garden Parking

FRITHAM   Map 5 SU21

The Royal Oak ♀

SO43 7HJ ☎ 023 8081 2606 📄 023 8081 4066
e-mail: royaloakfritham@btopenworld.com
dir: *M27 junct 1, B3078 signed Fordingbridge. 2m, then left at x-rds signed Ocknell & Fritham. Then follow signs to Fritham*

A small traditional thatched pub dating from the 15th century, deep in the New Forest. Walkers, cyclists and horse-riders delight in the large garden overlooking the forest and the pub's own farm. Unaltered for 100 years and with no jukebox or fruit machine, the three small bars focus on serving good real ales and simple plates of local food: quiches, sausages, pork pies and sausage rolls are all home made using the farm's pigs; chicken breasts are cured and smoked in apple wood, also by the pub.

Open all wk ⊕ FREE HOUSE ◀ Ringwood Best & Fortyniner, Hop Back Summer Lightning, Palmers Dorset Gold, Bowman Ales Swift One. ♀ 12 **Facilities** Dogs allowed Garden **Notes** ☺

GOSPORT   Map 5 SZ69

The Seahorse ♀

Broadsands Dr PO12 2TJ ☎ 023 9251 2910
e-mail: simonl29@aol.com
dir: *A32 onto Military Rd, 2nd exit rdbt onto Gomer Ln, 0.5m on left*

Much more than just a local pub, the refurbished Seahorse includes Leonard's restaurant, as well as a large bar with terrace. This is a family-run business, where head chef Simon Leonard uses locally sourced ingredients to create a wide range of traditional and speciality dishes. Typical choices include boiled ham, duck egg and hand-cut chips; mutton suet pudding; and chargrilled steak with wild mushrooms.

Open all day all wk 11-11 Closed: 25 Dec **Bar Meals** L served all wk 12-2.30 D served Sun-Thu 6-8.45, Fri-Sat 6-9.45 (no food Mon eve) ⊕ ENTERPRISE INNS ◀ London Pride, Worthington. ♀ 8 **Facilities** Children's menu Dogs allowed Garden Parking

HAMBLEDON   Map 5 SU61

The Vine at Hambledon ♀

West St PO7 4RW ☎ 023 9263 2419
e-mail: landlord@vinepub.com
dir: *Just off B2150 between Droxford (A32) & Waterlooville (A3)*

A cosy little pub with a welcoming atmosphere, tucked away in the main street of the pretty village of Hambledon. Over the past few years Tom and Vicki Faulkner have made an impression with their modern menus built around traditional British cooking. Look out for starters like scallops wrapped in Parma ham with a truffle scented green bean salad, and mains such as pan-fried fillet of turbot with braised butterbean and chorizo ragout.

Open all wk ⊕ WOLVERHAMPTON & DUDLEY BREWERIES PLC ◀ Ringwood Best, Jennings Cockerhoop, Ringwood 49er, "Vine" House Bitter ♂ Thatchers. ♀ 11 **Facilities** Dogs allowed Garden

HAMBLE-LE-RICE   Map 5 SU40

PICK OF THE PUBS

The Bugle ♀

See Pick of the Pubs on page 222

HANNINGTON   Map 5 SU55

PICK OF THE PUBS

The Vine at Hannington ♀

See Pick of the Pubs on page 223

HAVANT   Map 5 SU70

The Royal Oak ♀

19 Langstone High St, Langstone PO9 1RY
☎ 023 9248 3125
e-mail: 7955@greeneking.co.uk
dir: *Telephone for directions*

Occupying an outstanding position overlooking Langstone Harbour, this historic 16th-century pub is noted for its rustic, unspoilt interior. Flagstone floors, exposed beams and winter fires contrast with the waterfront benches and secluded rear garden for alfresco summer drinking. Light lunches such as rich tomato soup or chicken Caesar salad support a dinner menu that includes slow-cooked Welsh lamb; baked salmon fillet; and British ham hock glazed with honey mustard.

Open all day all wk 11-11 **Bar Meals** L served all wk 12-9 D served all wk 12-9s food served all day ⊕ GREENE KING ◀ Greene King IPA, Ruddles County, Ruddles Best, Abbot Ale, Speckled Hen. ♀ 16 **Facilities** Family room Dogs allowed Garden

HIGHCLERE   Map 5 SU45

The Furze Bush Inn NEW ♀

Hatt Common, East Woodhay RG20 0NQ
☎ 01635 253228 📄 01635 254883
e-mail: info@furzebushinn.co.uk
web: www.furzebushinn.co.uk
dir: *Please telephone for directions*

Handy for Highclere Castle, the M4, Newbury Races and hiking the Berkshire Downs, the Furze Bush lies tucked down lanes in a glorious rural location. Expect a peaceful
continued on page 224

PICK OF THE PUBS

The Bugle ♀

HAMBLE-LE-RICE Map 5 SU40

High St SO31 4HA
☎ **023 8045 3000** 📠 **023 8045 3051**
e-mail: manager@buglehamble.co.uk
dir: *M27 junct 8, follow signs to Hamble. In village centre turn right at mini-rdbt into one-way cobbled street, pub at end*

There is an interesting story to this Grade II listed waterside pub, which sparked a successful rescue campaign by villagers when housing developers threatened to demolish the site. Much to the relief of loyal locals, The Bugle was subsequently bought by local independent operators and lovingly refurbished in close consultation with English Heritage, using traditional methods and materials. Features include exposed beams and brickwork, an oak bar and a wood burning stove, plus a heated terrace perfect for alfresco dining with lovely views over the River Hamble. Rotating ales brewed in the region make an ideal partner for appetising pub food. A selection of doorstep sandwiches includes roast beef and horseradish, smoked salmon and cucumber, and mature cheddar and pickle. Dishes range through Welsh rarebit, home-made burgers, quiche and salad, risotto as a starter or main course, and fish cake with poached egg and beurre blanc. In addition, daily specials might include deep-fried squid with chilli dip and roast rump of lamb with Greek salad. Finish with chocolate tart, bread and butter pudding, or classic crème brûlée. The wine list is concise but offers good scope nonetheless, with several bottles priced under the £20 mark and eight served by the glass. For private dining, there is the Captain's Table upstairs, available to book for dinner parties and special occasions. Regular events at The Bugle include the wine club, a two course meal with four tasting wines with information imparted by an expert wine guru. Quiz and curry night and live music nights are also firm favourites.

Open all week 12-2.30 6-9.30 Mon-Thu (Fri 12-3 6-10, Sat 12-10, Sun 12-9) ⬛ Rotating locally brewed ales, Courage Best. ♀ 8

PICK OF THE PUBS

The Vine at Hannington ♀

HANNINGTON   Map 5 SU55

RG26 5TX
☎ **01635 298525**   📠 **01635 298027**
e-mail: info@thevineathannington.co.uk
web: www.thevineathannington.co.uk
dir: *Hannington signed from A339 between Basingstoke & Newbury*

A traditional village pub high up on the beautiful Hampshire Downs, with views across the countryside from its sheltered garden and attractive conservatory. It was originally the Wellington Arms, since the land once belonged to the Iron Duke, then it became the Shepherd's Crook and Shears until 1960, when it was renamed after the local Vine and Craven Hunt. Visitors can be assured of friendly service and good home-made pub food, many of the herbs, salad leaves and vegetables used coming from the pub garden. Seasonal menus of home-cooked, affordable dishes, including daily specials, might suggest starting with local watercress and spinach soup with focaccia bread; chicken liver parfait with spicy fruit chutney and toasted bread; or maybe a share of a generous plate of antipasti. Then follows a selection of mains, among which you'll find home-baked ham with egg and chips; chicken curry with rice, poppadom and mango chutney; free-range Hampshire pork loin with cider and apple sauce and stuffing; herb-crusted salmon fillet with red pepper sauce; and spinach and Parmesan risotto. Turn your attention to the specials board for local venison pie with juniper, orange and honey; grilled skate wing with black butter and capers; or king prawns in garlic butter and tomato and onion salad. Should you just want a bar snack, there are ploughman's and sandwiches, or you could again consider the antipasti. The compact wine list should satisfy most tastes. The garden behind the Vine is large, but a cosy wood-burner might make staying inside preferable when the sun isn't shining. There are plenty of excellent countryside walks and cycle routes nearby, including the Wayfarers Walk, which runs from Emsworth to Inkpen Beacon.

Open 12-3 6-11 (Sat-Sun all day)
Closed: 25 Dec, Sun eve & Mon in Winter
Bar Meals L served Mon-Fri 12-2, Sat-Sun 12-2.30 D served all week 6-9 Av main course £9 **Restaurant** L served Mon-Fri 12-2, Sat-Sun 12-2.30 D served all week 6-9 Av 3 course à la carte fr £20 ◖ Black Sheep, Bombardier. ♀ 10
Facilities Children's menu Play area Family room Dogs allowed Garden Parking

HIGHCLERE *continued*

night in one of the ten, well-appointed bedrooms, and a good range of pub food. In the bar, order favourites like chicken pie and ham, egg and chips, or book a restaurant table for game casserole, neck of lamb and rosemary sauce, and treacle tart and custard. There is a large front beer garden.

Open all day all wk **Bar Meals** L served Mon-Fri 12-2.30, Sat-Sun & BH all day D served Mon-Sat 6-10, Sun 6-9 Av main course £10 **Restaurant** L served Mon-Fri 12-2.30, Sat-Sun & BH 12-6 booking required D served Mon-Sat 6-10, Sun 6-9 booking required Fixed menu price fr £15 Av 3 course à la carte fr £22 ⊕ FREE HOUSE ◀ Flowers IPA, guest ale. ⏱ 8 **Facilities** Children's menu Play area Dogs allowed Garden Parking **Rooms** 10

HOOK   Map 5 SU75

Crooked Billet ⏱

London Rd RG27 9EH
☎ 01256 762118 📠 01256 761011
e-mail: richardbarwise@aol.com
web: www.thecrookedbillethook.co.uk
dir: *From M3 take Hook ring road. At 3rd rdbt turn right onto A30 towards London, pub on left 0.5m by river*

The present pub dates back to 1935, though there has been a hostelry on this site since the 1600s. Food to suit all appetites includes half shoulder of lamb in mint gravy; Billet toad in the hole with mash and onion gravy; home-made steak and kidney pie; fresh cod fillets in beer batter; and a range of ploughman's with hot French bread. Guest ales are a speciality, over 750 served to date.

Open all wk **Bar Meals** L served Mon-Sat 12-2.30, Sun 12-3 booking required D served Mon-Fri 6.30-9.30, Sat-Sun 6.30-10 booking required **Restaurant** L served 10 ⊕ FREE HOUSE ◀ Courage Best, Andwells Brewery, guest. ⏱ 8 **Facilities** Play area Dogs allowed Garden Parking

The Hogget NEW ⏱

London Rd, Hook Common RG27 9JJ ☎ 01256 763009
e-mail: home@hogget.co.uk
dir: *M3 junct 5 0.5m. Located on the A30 between Hook and Basingstoke*

Following a major refurbishment in 2008, The Hogget has quickly established a local reputation for good food and wine in a relaxed setting. Beers from Ringwood, Jennings and Marston's support a sensible wine list, with plenty of choice by the glass. Local ingredients from named suppliers are the foundation of freshly-cooked dishes like sausages with colcannon and onion gravy; poached smoked haddock on mustard mash; and roast butternut squash with wild mushrooms and sautéed leeks.

Open all wk noon-3 6-11 (Fri 5-11 Sun 7-11) Closed: 25 Dec **Bar Meals** L served all wk 12-2 booking required D served all wk 6.30-9 booking required Av main course £8.50 **Restaurant** L served all wk 12-2 booking required D served all wk 6.30-9 booking required Av 3 course à la carte fr £25 ⊕ MARSTONS PUB COMPANY ◀ Ringwood Best, Ringwood 49er, Jennings Sneck Lifter, Marstons Oyster Stout ♂ Thatchers Gold. ⏱ 14 **Facilities** Children's menu Dogs allowed Garden Parking

HORSEBRIDGE   Map 5 SU33

John O'Gaunt Inn ⏱

SO20 6PU ☎ 01794 388394
e-mail: keithnigeldavid@hotmail.com
dir: *A3057 (Stockbridge to Romsey road). Horsebridge 4m from Stockbridge, turn right at brown information board*

Walkers from the nearby Test Way, fishermen from the River Test and the winter shooting fraternity all frequent this small country inn, six miles north of Romsey. It provides a great atmosphere for well-kept ales and generously priced food. The menu showcases fresh local produce, with dishes such as homemade steak and kidney pudding, liver and bacon, followed by a good selection of puddings. A traditional roast at Sunday lunchtime too.

Open 11-3 6-11 (Sat 11-11 Sun noon-10) Closed: Mon L **Bar Meals** L served Tue-Fri 12-2.30, Sat 12-3, Sun 12-4 D served Tue-Sat 6-9 ⊕ FREE HOUSE ◀ Ringwood Best Bitter, Ringwood Fortyniner, Palmers IPA ♂ Thatchers. ⏱ 8 **Facilities** Dogs allowed Garden Parking

HURSLEY   Map 5 SU42

The Dolphin Inn NEW ⏱

SO21 2JY ☎ 01962 775209
e-mail: mandy@dolphininn.demon.co.uk
web: www.dolphinhursley.co.uk
dir: *Please telephone for directions*

Reputedly built from the timbers of an early HMS Dolphin, hence the pub name, the roadside village inn dates from the 16th century and was once a thriving coaching inn. Follow a stroll through nearby Farley Mount Country Park with a traditional pub lunch in the mature garden or in the beamed bars – ham, egg and chips, steak and Guinness pie, sausage and onion baguette, or a healthy tuna Niçoise. Look out for the local butcher's meat draw in Fridays nights.

Open all wk Mon-Thu 11-3 6-11 (Fri-Sat 11-11 Sun 12-10.30) **Bar Meals** L served Mon-Thu 12-2, Fri-Sat 12-2.30, Sun 12-8.30 booking required D served Mon-Thu 6-9, Fri-Sat 6.30-9.30, Sun 12-8.30 booking required Av main course £8 **Restaurant** Fixed menu price fr £15 ⊕ ENTERPRISE ◀ Ringwood, Summer Lightning, HBB, HSB ♂ Thatchers dry, Thatchers Premium. ⏱ 23 **Facilities** Children's menu Play area Family room Dogs allowed Garden Parking

IBSLEY   Map 5 SU10

Old Beams Inn ⏱

Salisbury Rd BH24 3PP
☎ 01425 473387 📠 01202 743080
e-mail: hedi@alcatraz.co.uk
dir: *On A338 between Ringwood & Salisbury*

Old Beams is a beautiful 14th-century thatched and timber-framed village inn located at the heart of the New Forest with views of countryside and ponies. It has a beer garden with a decked area and patio, and a cosy old world interior revitalised by a recent refurbishment. Pub food favourites based on local and New Forest produce dominate the menu, and on Friday night (fish night) there's a large selection.

Open all wk 11-11.30 **Bar Meals** Av main course £10 food served all day **Restaurant** Fixed menu price fr £11.95 food served all day ◀ IPA, Speckled Hen. ⏱ 10 **Facilities** Children's menu Garden Parking

ITCHEN ABBAS — Map 5 SU53

The Trout ♟

Main Rd SO21 1BQ ☎ 01962 779537 📄 **01962 791046**
dir: *M3 junct 9, A34, right onto A33, follow signs to Itchen Abbas, pub 2m on left*

A 19th-century coaching inn located in the Itchen Valley close to the river itself. Originally called The Plough, it is said to have been the location that inspired Charles Kingsley to write *The Water Babies*. Freshly cooked, locally sourced produce is served in the bar and restaurant: trout, of course, perhaps pan fried, home-made fishcakes, and a lunchtime selection that includes baguettes, wraps, foccacias and salads.

Open all wk Closed: 26 Dec & 1 Jan ⊕ GREENE KING ◄ Greene King IPA, Morland Speckled Hen. ♟ 9 **Facilities** Play area Dogs allowed Garden Parking

LINWOOD — Map 5 SU10

PICK OF THE PUBS

The High Corner Inn ♟

See Pick of the Pubs on page 226

LITTLETON — Map 5 SU43

PICK OF THE PUBS

The Running Horse ★★★★ INN ◉ ♟

See Pick of the Pubs on page 227

LONGPARISH — Map 5 SU44

PICK OF THE PUBS

The Plough Inn ♟

See Pick of the Pubs on page 228

LOWER WIELD — Map 5 SU64

PICK OF THE PUBS

The Yew Tree ♟

SO24 9RX ☎ 01256 389224 📄 **01256 389224**
dir: *Take A339 from Basingstoke towards Alton. Turn right for Lower Wield*

Ale was first served in this free house in 1845 but the nearby yew tree that gives the pub its name is 650 years old. In winter a crackling log fire burns in the bar, but as the days lengthen attention turns to the adjacent cricket ground. In fact, the Yew Tree's association with England's favourite summer sport has been immortalised in Elizabeth Gibson's book *Cricket and Ale*. Events are held throughout the year, including quiz nights, a sports day, and a cricket match followed by an Aussie barbecue. The pub has a reputation for both good fun and good food, with dishes ranging from the hearty, such as sausages of the week with mustard mash and onion gravy, to the exotic, like Malaysian chicken curry with citrus-infused rice. The resident Cheriton Pots ale is backed up by a selection of guest beers from up to 15 local breweries, plus a good wine list with 13 available by the glass.

Closed: 1st 2wks Jan, Mon **Bar Meals** L served Tue-Sun 12-2 D served Tue-Sat 6.30-9, Sun 6.30-8.30 Av main course £11 **Restaurant** L served Tue-Sun 12-2 D served Tue-Sat 6.30-9, Sun 6.30-8.30 ⊕ FREE HOUSE ◄ Cheriton Pots, Hidden Pint, Triple FFF Moondance, Hogs Back TEA, Itchen Valley Hampshire Rose. ♟ 13 **Facilities** Dogs allowed Garden Parking

LYMINGTON — Map 5 SZ39

The Kings Arms ♟

Saint Thomas St SO41 9NB ☎ 01590 672594
dir: *Approach Lymington from N on A337, left onto Saint Thomas St. Pub 50yds on right*

King Charles I is reputed to have patronised this historic coaching inn, which these days enjoys an enviable reputation for its cask ales, housed on 150-year-old stillages. Local Ringwood ales as well as national brews are served. It is a real community pub, with a dartboard and Sky TV, and the open brick fireplaces are used in winter.

Open all wk ⊕ WHITBREAD ◄ Weekly rotating guest ales. ♟ 6 **Facilities** Garden **Notes** ◉

Mayflower Inn ♟

Kings Saltern Rd SO41 3QD
☎ 01590 672160 📄 **01590 679180**
e-mail: info@themayflower.uk.com
dir: *A337 towards New Milton, left at rdbt by White Hart, left to Rookes Ln, right at mini-rdbt, pub 0.75m*

A favourite with yachtsmen and dog walkers, this solidly built mock-Tudor inn overlooks the Lymington River, with glorious views to the Isle of Wight. There's a magnificent garden with glorious sun terraces, a purpose-built play area for children and an on-going summer barbecue in fine weather. Light bites and big bowl salads are backed up with heartier choices like traditional lamb and rosemary hotpot, pan-fried liver and bacon, and beer battered fish of the day.

Open all day all wk **Bar Meals** Av main course £8.50 food served all day **Restaurant** food served all day ⊕ ENTERPRISE INNS ◄ Ringwood Best, Fuller's London Pride, 6X, Goddards Fuggle Dee Dum. ♟ 8 **Facilities** Children's menu Play area Dogs allowed Garden Parking

PICK OF THE PUBS

The High Corner Inn ♀

BH24 3QY ☎ **01425 473973**
e-mail: highcorner@wadworth.co.uk
dir: *From A338 (Ringwood to Salisbury road) follow brown tourist signs into forest. Pass Red Shoot Inn, after 1m turn down gravel track at Green High Corner Inn*

Lost down a quarter-mile gravel track a mile from the village of Linwood, off the narrow lane linking Lyndhurst and the A338 near Ringwood, this much extended and modernised, early 18th-century inn is set in seven beautiful acres of woodland deep in the heart of the New Forest. The cluster of rambling buildings began life as a farm in the early 1700s and the old stables have over time been connected to the main inn to create family and function rooms, the latter proving very popular for weddings in this gloriously peaceful forest location. A quiet hideaway in winter, mobbed in summer, it is a popular retreat for families with its numerous bar-free rooms, an outdoor adventure playground and miles of wildlife-rich forest and heathland walks and cycle trails. The beamy bars, replete with roaring winter log fires and the full range of Wadworth ales on tap, and the lovely forest garden are very agreeable settings for sampling an extensive range of home-cooked meals and bar snacks; daily specials are shown on chalkboards and a carvery is available on Sunday. Rest and refuel during or following a forest ramble with a refreshing pint of 6X and a bowl of home-made soup and a plate of sandwiches or a ploughman's lunch, best enjoyed on the flower-filled terrace or in the garden with its forest views, or tuck into something more substantial from the traditional pub menu, perhaps home-made game terrine; hunter's chicken; beer battered cod; steak and kidney pie; gammon, egg and chips; decent steak with all the trimmings; or the High Corner hot pot. Leave room for a nursery-style pudding, perhaps a traditional crumble. Dogs and horses are welcome.

Open all day all wk 11am-3 6-11pm (3-6 winter) **Bar Meals** L served all wk 12-2.30 D served all wk 6-9 **Restaurant** L served all wk 12-2.30 D served all wk 6-9 ⊕ WADWORTH ◀ Wadworth 6X, Horizon, IPA, Red Shoot New Forest Gold, Toms Tipple ⚬ Westons, Thatchers Gold. ♀ 14 **Facilities** Children's menu Play area Dogs allowed Garden Parking

PICK OF THE PUBS

The Running Horse ★★★★ INN

LITTLETON Map 5 SU43

88 Main Rd SO22 6QS
☎ 01962 880218 📠 01962 886596
e-mail: runninghorseinn@btconnect.com
web: www.runninghorseinn.co.uk
dir: *3m from Winchester, signed from Stockbridge Rd*

Situated on the western outskirts of Winchester, this pretty rural gastro-pub offers a special blend of atmosphere, food and luxurious accommodation. The bar is a successful marriage of the traditional and the modern, with stripped wooden floor, leather tub chairs around an original fireplace, and white walls. But the focus here is undoubtedly on good eating, and the chefs' sourcing of seasonal produce of impeccable freshness helped the Running Horse to gain an AA Rosette for the quality of its modern international cuisine. Choose between dining outside on the front or rear terrace, casually in the bar, or more formally in the stylish restaurant. Dinner might begin with tomato and grilled cheese millefeuilles, or oriental crab and salmon fishcakes. Main courses include pan-fried fillet of sea bass with creamed leeks; steak and Winchester ale shortcrust pie; and crispy shoulder of lamb with dauphinoise potatoes. Vegetarians are well served too, a typical choice being tempura mozzarella with rocket and sun-blushed tomato. Locally brewed beers, including Flowerpots from nearby Cheriton, and a comprehensive wine list complete the package. The garden behind the Running Horse and the patio to the front are large and peaceful. The rear garden is particularly good for children as it is a safe distance from the road and there's a huge expanse of grass for them to run on while you enjoy a quiet drink on the verandah. Elegant en suite rooms to the rear of the building overlook the garden and the terrace.

Open all week **Bar Meals** L served all week 12-2 D served all week 6-9.30 **Restaurant** L served all week 12-2 D served all week 6-9.30 FREE HOUSE Ringwood Best, Flowerpots. 10 **Facilities** Children's menu Dogs allowed Garden Parking **Rooms** 9

PICK OF THE PUBS

The Plough Inn 🍷

LONGPARISH   Map 5 SU44

SP11 6PB ☎ 01264 720358
e-mail: eat@theploughinn.info
web: www.theploughinn.info
dir: *From M3 junct 8 take A303 towards Andover. In approx 6m take B3048 towards Longparish*

According to parish records, this charming old inn dates from 1721, although it has undoubtedly seen some changes in the intervening years as it looks at first glance like an early 1900s building. A convenient mile from the A303 and only minutes from Andover, it stands so close to the Test Way that the path cuts right through the inn's car-park. The Test itself, one of southern England's finest trout rivers, is not far away and a familiar sight is the web-footed residents of Longparish (so named because it is) waddling over to share whatever titbits might be going begging. The interior was sympathetically renovated in late 2006, the resulting pleasing colour scheme creating a warm, comfortable atmosphere, with flagstone and oak floors complemented by leather chairs, subtle soft furnishings and open log fires. Sandwiches, ciabattas, baguettes and toasted snacks (black pudding, watercress and poached egg, and wild mushroom, pecorino and rocket, for example) are available at lunchtime and early evening, as are chicken and ham pie with market vegetables; Calabrian lasagne; and home-made beefburger with smoked cheese. Main course dishes are no less appetising: slow-cooked lamb with chickpeas, cumin, spinach, roasted baby aubergine, and chilli and coriander salsa; Italian sausages with green lentils and oven-roast tomatoes; and free-range chicken and ham pie with triple-cooked chips and salad are typical. Leave room for desserts like passion fruit crème brûlée, or treacle sponge and custard. The wine list isn't long, but there's enough choice for most tastes.

Closed: 25 Dec, Sun eve ⊕ ENTERPRISE INNS ◼ Ringwood, Fuller's London Pride, Wadworth 6x, HSB, Otter. 🍷 10 **Facilities** Dogs allowed Garden Parking

LYNDHURST · Map 5 SU30

New Forest Inn ♀

Emery Down SO43 7DY ☎ 023 8028 4690
e-mail: info@thenewforestinn.co.uk
dir: *M21 junct 1 follow signs for A35/Lyndhurst. In Lyndhurst follow signs for Christchurch, turn right at Swan Inn towards Emery Down*

The inn, which prides itself on its friendliness, is located in the heart of the New Forest, with ponies constantly trying to get in the front door. The pub has its own local walk and dogs are made welcome. Inside you'll find oak beams and floors and two open fires in feature fireplaces. Outside there's a lovely garden for summer use. Home-cooked food includes local game, locally sourced meat and vegetarian options.

Open all day all wk **Bar Meals** Av main course £8 food served all day **Restaurant** food served all day ⊕ ENTERPRISE INNS ◀ Ringwood Best, Ringwood 49, guest ales ♂ Stowford Press. ♀ 8 **Facilities** Children's menu Dogs allowed Garden Parking

The Oak Inn ♀

Pinkney Ln, Bank SO43 7FE
☎ 023 8028 2350 ▤ 023 8028 4601
e-mail: oakinn@fullers.co.uk
dir: *From Lyndhurst signed A35 to Christchurch, follow A35 1m, turn left at Bank sign*

Ponies, pigs and deer graze outside this former ciderhouse. Behind the bay windows are a traditional woodburner, antique pine and an extensive collection of bric-a-brac. There is also a large beer garden for those fine summer days. A wide selection of fresh seafood, including Selsey crab gratin, and seared tuna steak, features among an interesting choice of dishes, including the local wild boar sausages and daily pies.

Open all wk **Bar Meals** L served all wk 12-2.30 booking required D served Mon-Sat 6-9.30, Sun 5-9 booking required **Restaurant** L served all wk 12-2.30 booking required D served Mon-Sat 6-9.30, Sun 5-9 booking required ⊕ FULLERS BREWERY ◀ Ringwood Best, Hop Back Summer Lightening, London Pride, Fuller's HSB. ♀ 9 **Facilities** Children's menu Dogs allowed Garden Parking

The Trusty Servant

Minstead SO43 7FY ☎ 023 8081 2137
dir: *Telephone for directions*

Popular New Forest pub overlooking the village green and retaining many Victorian features. The famous sign is taken from a 16th-century Winchester scholar's painting portraying the qualities of an ideal college servant. The menu prides itself on its real food, good value and generous portions. You might sample snacks, home-made pies, steaks from the grill, venison or tenderloin of pork. There's also a good choice of vegetarian dishes, such as sizzling Thai vegetable stir-fry.

Open all wk ⊕ ENTERPRISE INNS ◀ Ringwood Best, Fuller's London Pride, Wadworth 6X, Timothy Taylor Landlord. **Facilities** Family room Dogs allowed Garden Parking

MAPLEDURWELL · Map 5 SU65

The Gamekeepers ♀

Tunworth Rd RG25 2LU
☎ 01256 322038 ▤ 01256 322038
e-mail: costellophil@hotmail.co.uk
dir: *M3 junct 6, take A30 towards Hook. Turn right after The Hatch pub. The Gamekeepers signed*

A 19th-century pub/restaurant with an indoor well, the Gamekeepers has a very rural location with a large secluded garden. Relax on a leather settee with a pint of Fursty Ferret or Stinger and enjoy the cosy atmosphere of low beams and flagstone floors. An impressive range of game and seafood (Dover sole, John Dory, monkfish) is offered, with dishes like oven-baked salmon topped with fontina cheese and wrapped in Parma ham, or chargrilled beef fillet on dauphinoise potatoes with blue cheese and pink peppercorn butter.

Open all day all wk **Bar Meals** Av main course £9 food served all day **Restaurant** Av 3 course à la carte fr £30 food served all day ⊕ HALL & WOODHOUSE ◀ Badgers First Gold, Tanglefoot, Sussex Best, Fursty Ferret, Stinger. ♀ 12 **Facilities** Children's menu Dogs allowed Garden Parking

MICHELDEVER · Map 5 SU53

Half Moon & Spread Eagle ♀

Winchester Rd SO21 3DG
☎ 01962 774339 ▤ 01962 774339
e-mail: debbiethickett@hotmail.co.uk
dir: *From Winchester take A33 towards Basingstoke. In 5m turn left after small car garage. Pub 0.5m on right*

Old drovers' inn located in the heart of a pretty thatched and timbered Hampshire village, overlooking the cricket green. The pub, comprising three neatly furnished interconnecting rooms, has a real local feel, and a few years back reverted to its old name having been the Dever Arms for eight years. An extensive menu ranges through Sunday roasts, Moon burgers, honeyed salmon supreme with lime courgettes, fresh battered cod, and half shoulder of minted lamb.

Open all wk ⊕ GREENE KING ◀ Greene King IPA, Abbot Ale, guest ales. ♀ 9 **Facilities** Play area Dogs allowed Garden Parking

MORTIMER WEST END · Map 5 SU66

The Red Lion ♀

Church Rd RG7 2HU
☎ 0118 970 0169 ▤ 0118 970 1729
dir: *Telephone for directions*

Original oak beams and an inglenook fireplace are the mark of this traditional pub, which dates back to 1650. Quality food and a range of real ales are served, with dishes to suit all tastes. Where possible produce is locally sourced, including free-range chicken and eggs, and English beef hung for 21 days. Home-made pies are a speciality - seafood, venison, wild boar, and steak with house ale - and there's a daily changing specials board.

Open all wk ⊕ HALL & WOODHOUSE ◀ Tanglefoot, Badger First Gold, Guinness. ♀ 10 **Facilities** Play area Family room Dogs allowed Garden Parking

NEW ALRESFORD · Map 5 SU53

The Woolpack Inn NEW ♀

Totford, Nr Northington SO24 9TJ
☎ 0845 293 8066 ▤ 0845 293 8055
e-mail: info@thewoolpackinn.co.uk
dir: *M3 south towards A27, take A339 to Alton and first right to B3046 Candovers & Alresford*

Approach this old drovers' inn at night and just as you prepare to descend a steep hill you'll see its welcoming lights down below. The inn changed hands in 2008 and the new owners have really smartened it up, creating a sense of calm modernity while still retaining a traditional feel. Its new seasonal menus offers, in the traditional bar area, bacon butty on farmhouse bread, and Heineken-battered fish and chips; and in the dining room, warm smoked trout and crispy bacon salad; pot-roast Candover Park partridge; and pan-roasted salmon with bacon, pea and potato broth.

Open 11.30am-3 6-close (Sat open all day) Closed: Sun eve in winter **Bar Meals** L served all wk 11.30-3 D served Mon-Sat 6-close Av main course £9.50 **Restaurant** L served all wk 11.30-3 D served Mon-Sat 6-close Av 3 course à la carte fr £20 ⊕ FREE HOUSE ◀ Palmers IPA, Palmers Copper, Moondance Triple FFF ♂ Thatchers Gold. ♀ 9 **Facilities** Children's menu Play area Dogs allowed Garden Parking

NORTH WALTHAM — Map 5 SU54

PICK OF THE PUBS

The Fox ☻

RG25 2BE ☎ 01256 397288
e-mail: info@thefox.org
dir: *From M3 junct 7 take A30 towards Winchester. Village signed on right. Take 2nd signed road*

A peaceful village pub down a quiet country lane enjoying splendid views across fields and farmland - an ideal stop off the M3 just south of Basingstoke. Built as three farm cottages in 1624, the Fox can offer families three large level gardens, one of which is a dedicated children's play area, and superb flower borders and hanging baskets in summer. The husband and wife team of Rob and Izzy MacKenzie split their responsibilities between bar and kitchen. Amidst over a thousand miniatures on show, Rob ensures that the beers are kept in top condition, while Izzy produces mouthwatering traditional dishes using seasonal produce; she prepares everything by hand from the mayonnaise upwards. A dedicated bar menu proffers the likes of ham, double egg and chips; and cottage pie. The monthly-changing restaurant choice may include Hampshire venison; trio of seafood (crevette, marlin and tuna); Barbary duck breast; and slow roasted pork belly with grain mustard mash.

Open all day all wk 11-11 **Bar Meals** L served all wk 12-2.30 D served all wk 6-9.30 **Restaurant** L served all wk 12-2.30 booking required D served all wk 6-9.30 booking required ⊕ PUNCH TAVERNS ◀ Ringwood Best Bitter, Adnams Broadside, Brakspear, guest ale ♨ Aspall. ☻ 17 **Facilities** Children's menu Play area Dogs allowed Garden Parking

See advert on this page

OLD BASING — Map 5 SU65

The Millstone ☻

Bartons Ln RG24 8AE ☎ 01256 331153
e-mail: millstone@wadworth.co.uk
dir: *From M3 junct 6 follow brown signs to Basing House*

Basingstoke is just a stone's throw away, which makes this attractive old building's rural location, beside the River Loddon, all the more delightfully surprising. Nearby are the extensive ruins of Old Basing House, one of Britain's most famous Civil War sites. Typical main dishes might include battered or grilled cod; creamy vegetable korma; and spinach, mushroom and brie filo parcel. Snacks include baguettes, bocottas and ciabattas, jacket potatoes and ploughman's.

Open all day all wk 11.30-11 **Bar Meals** L served Mon-Sat 12-2.30, Sun 12-6 D served Mon-Thu 6-9, Fri-Sat 6-9.30 ⊕ WADWORTH ◀ Wadworth 6X, Wadworth JCB, Henrys Smooth, Henrys IPA. ☻ 9 **Facilities** Dogs allowed Garden Parking

OVINGTON — Map 5 SU53

PICK OF THE PUBS

The Bush ☻

See Pick of the Pubs on opposite page

PETERSFIELD — Map 5 SU72

The Good Intent ☻

40-46 College St GU31 4AF
☎ 01730 263838 ▤ 01730 302239
e-mail: dianne@goodintentpetersfield.co.uk
dir: *Telephone for directions*

Candlelit tables, open fires and well-kept ales characterise this 16th-century pub, and in summer, flower tubs and hanging baskets festoon the front patio. Regular gourmet evenings are held and there is live music on Sunday evenings. Sausages are a speciality (up to 12 varieties) alongside a daily pie and the likes of seafood chowder and Thai fish curry. As members of the Campaign For Real Food they have well-established links with the local junior school.

Open all wk 11-3 5.30-11 (Sun 12-3 7-11) **Bar Meals** L served all wk 12-2.30 D served Sun-Mon 7-9, Tue-Sat 6.30-9.30 food served all day ⊕ FULLERS BREWERY ◀ Fuller's HSB, London Pride, Guest Ales. ☻ 6 **Facilities** Dogs allowed Garden Parking

---

PICK OF THE PUBS

The Bush ♗

OVINGTON Map 5 SU53

SO24 0RE
☎ **01962 732764** 📠 **01962 735130**
e-mail: thebushinn@wadworth.co.uk
web: www.wadworth.co.uk
dir: *A31 from Winchester, E to Alton & Farnham, approx 6m turn left off dual carriageway to Ovington. 0.5m to pub*

"Hard to find – worth the finding". That's what it says on the business cards of this one-time refreshment stop on the Pilgrim's Way between Winchester and Canterbury. And indeed it is. Tucked away just off a meandering lane and overhung by trees, the rose-covered building is a vision of a bygone age, so don't expect a jukebox, fruit machine or pool table. While the outside is painted white, the interior is softly lit and atmospheric; there's a central wooden bar, high-backed seats and pews and stuffed animals on the wall. In the winter you can warm up in front of the log fire, while in the summer, the garden is perfect for spreading out with the family. A gentle riverside stroll along the neighbouring River Itchen will set you up for a leisurely drink or lingering meal. The regularly-changing menu is based on the freshest food the owners, Nick and Cathy Young, can source, including local farm cheeses, meats from Wiltshire, Hampshire and Scotland, and fish from the Dorset and Cornish coasts. Choices range from sandwiches, ploughman's lunches and other bar snacks, through to satisfying meals such as sautéed lamb's kidneys in Madeira, mushroom and pancetta cream sauce on toasted brioche; followed by Loch Fyne smoked haddock risotto, poached egg, parsley oil and Parmesan; and roast leg of Wiltshire Downs spring lamb with garlic, mint and rosemary and white wine gravy. Finish with Eton mess or rhubarb crumble. You will certainly find a wine to suit your palate, including from among the dozen or so served by the glass. Real ales keep their end up too, with Wadworth 6X and guest ales. Traditional afternoon tea is available on Fridays and every weekend throughout the year.

Open all week **Bar Meals** Av main course £11 🍺 WADWORTH 🍺 Wadworth 6X, IPA, Farmers Glory, JCB, Summersault, Old Timer, guest ales. 🍷 12 **Facilities** Family room Dogs allowed Garden Parking

PETERSFIELD *continued*

PICK OF THE PUBS

The Trooper Inn ☺

Alton Rd, Froxfield GU32 1BD
☎ 01730 827293 📠 01730 827103
e-mail: info@trooperinn.com
dir: From A3 take A272 Winchester exit towards Petersfield (NB do not take A272 to Petersfield). 1st exit at mini-rdbt for Steep. 3m, pub on right

Located at one of the highest points in Hampshire, The Trooper is an isolated free house on the downs west of Petersfield, with the stunning countryside of Ashford Hangers Nature Reserve right on the doorstep. The building dates from the 17th century and has had a chequered history, it is said that it was used as a recruiting centre at the outset of the First World War. With its pine furnished interior, log fires warm the bar in winter, and in addition to the dining areas adjoining the bar there is a charming restaurant with wooden settles and a vaulted ceiling. Menus offer country cooking prepared from quality ingredients, including fresh fish and game, much of it from local suppliers and producers. Half shoulder of lamb is a house speciality, and Tuesday is pie and pudding evening with a special meal deal.

Open noon-3 6-11 Closed: 25-26 Dec & 1 Jan, Sun eve **Bar Meals** L served Tue-Sun 12-2 booking required D served Mon-Sat 6-9.30 booking required Av main course £10 **Restaurant** L served Tue-Sun 12-2 booking required D served Mon-Sat 6-9.30 booking required Fixed menu price fr £14 Av 3 course à la carte fr £25 ⊕ FREE HOUSE ◀ Ringwood Best, Ballards, local guest ales. ☻ 50 **Facilities** Dogs allowed Garden Parking

The White Horse Inn ☺

Priors Dean GU32 1DA
☎ 01420 588387 📠 01420 588387
dir: A3/A272 to Winchester/Petersfield. In Petersfield left to Steep, 5m then right at small x-rds to East Tisted, take 2nd drive on right

Also known as the 'Pub With No Name' as it has no sign, this splendid 17th-century farmhouse was originally used as a forge for passing coaches. The blacksmith sold beer to the travellers while their horses were attended to. Restaurant dishes include carrot and cashew nut roast, and Gressingham duck breast with fondant potato and spiced grape chutney. Special fresh fish dishes are available on Fridays and Saturdays.

Open all wk ⊕ FULLERS BREWERY ◀ No Name Best, No Name Strong, Butser Bitter, Ringwood 49er, Sharps Doom Bar, Discovery. ☻ 7 **Facilities** Family room Dogs allowed Garden Parking

---

PILLEY Map 5 SZ39

The Fleur de Lys ☺

Pilley St SO41 5QG ☎ 01590 672158
e-mail: hrh7@btinternet.com
dir: From Lymington A337 to Brockenhurst. Cross Ampress Park rdbt, right to Boldre. At end of Boldre Ln turn right. Pub 0.5m

Dating from 1014, parts of the building pre-date the forest which surrounds it; as the Fleur de Lys, it has been serving ales since 1498. Today this traditional thatched inn exudes centuries of character, warmed by an open fire and two wood burning stoves; outside is a large landscaped garden with wooden tables and chairs. The emphasis here is on fine dining, with a concise menu which may feature pan-fried rabbit loin; marinated saddle of New Forest venison; and chocolate and marshmallow soufflé.

Open 11-3 6-11 (Sun noon-4) Closed: Sun eve, Mon all day **Bar Meals** L served Tue-Sat 12-2.30, Sun 12-3 D served Tue-Sat 6.30-9.30 ⊕ ENTERPRISE INNS ◀ Ringwood Best, Guest ales ☉ Stowford Press. ☻ 10 **Facilities** Family room Dogs allowed Garden Parking

---

PORTSMOUTH & SOUTHSEA Map 5 SZ69

The Wine Vaults ☺

43-47 Albert Rd, Southsea PO5 2SF ☎ 023 9286 4712
e-mail: wine.vaults@fullers.co.uk
dir: Telephone for directions

Originally several Victorian shops, now converted into a Victorian-style alehouse with wooden floors, panelled walls, and seating from old churches and schools. Partly due to the absence of a jukebox or fruit machine, the atmosphere is relaxed, and there is a good range of real ales and good-value food. A typical menu includes beef stroganoff, Tuscan vegetable bean stew, grilled gammon steak, salads, sandwiches, and Mexican specialities.

Open all day all wk noon-11 (Fri-Sat noon-mdnt Sun noon-10.30) **Bar Meals** food served all day ⊕ FULLERS ◀ Fuller's London Pride, Discovery, Fuller's ESB, Fuller's HSB, Guest ales. ☻ 20 **Facilities** Family room Dogs allowed Garden

---

ROCKBOURNE Map 5 SU11

PICK OF THE PUBS

The Rose & Thistle ☺

SP6 3NL ☎ 01725 518236
e-mail: enquiries@roseandthistle.co.uk
web: www.roseandthistle.co.uk
dir: Follow Rockbourne signs from A354 (Salisbury to Blandford Forum road), or from A338 at Fordingbridge follow signs to Rockbourne

This is a picture postcard pub if ever there was one, with a stunning rose arch, flowers around the door and a delightful village setting. The low-beamed bar and dining area are furnished with country house fabrics, polished oak tables and chairs, cushioned settles and

---

carved benches, and homely touches include floral arrangements and a scatter of magazines. Open fires make this a cosy retreat in cold weather, whilst the summer sun encourages visitors to sit in the neat cottage garden. Lunchtime favourites are listed as steak and kidney pudding; scrambled egg with smoked salmon; or mixed mushroom stroganoff. In the evening look out for rack of lamb with champ; pesto cous cous with roasted vegetables; or a variety of fish specials on the blackboard. Recent change of landlord.

The Rose & Thistle

Open all wk **Bar Meals** L served all wk 12-2.30 booking required D served Mon-Sat 7-9.30 booking required Av main course £10 **Restaurant** L served all wk 12-2.30 booking required D served Mon-Sat 7-9.30 booking required ⊕ FREE HOUSE ◀ Fuller's London Pride, Palmers Copper Ale, Timothy Taylor Landlord. ☻ 12 **Facilities** Children's menu Dogs allowed Garden Parking

---

ROCKFORD Map 5 SU10

The Alice Lisle ☺

Rockford Green BH24 3NA ☎ 01425 474700
e-mail: alicelisle@fullers.co.uk

Well-known New Forest pub with landscaped gardens overlooking a lake, popular with walkers and visitors to the region. It was named after the widow of one of Cromwell's supporters who gave shelter to two fugitives from the Battle of Sedgemoor. Choose from a varied menu which might include salmon and crab cakes, honey minted lamb shoulder, liver and bacon, and Mexican enchilada. There's a good range of starters and children's dishes.

Open all day all wk 10am-11pm **Bar Meals** L served Mon-Fri 12-2.30, Sat 12-9, Sun 12-8 D served Mon-Fri 6-9, Sat 12-9, Sun 12-8 ⊕ FULLERS BREWERY ◀ HSB, London Pride, Discovery. ☻ 7 **Facilities** Play area Family room Dogs allowed Garden Parking

ROMSEY
Map 5 SU32

PICK OF THE PUBS

The Dukes Head ⏣

Greatbridge Rd SO51 0HB ☎ 01794 514450
dir: *Telephone for directions*

A long, whitewashed, 400-year-old pub a little way out of Romsey, and little more than a hefty cast from the Test, England's leading trout river. There are large gardens at the front and rear, while inside are the main bar, the snug and four other rooms, all themed. Andy Cottingham and Suzie Russell have made their mark by shifting the balance of the menu more firmly towards fish and seafood. This means you can reliably expect dishes featuring turbot, halibut, oysters, mussels and scallops, and much more, but if you don't want fish there'll almost certainly be a succulent fillet steak, duck breast or local game, such as venison. Food is largely locally sourced, seasonally influenced as far as possible, and freshly prepared. Andy is an acknowledged wine expert and is proud of his well-balanced wine list. Go on a Sunday for wonderful live jazz, most likely outside in the summer, and on a Tuesday night for blues and folk.

Open all wk ⏣ FREE HOUSE ◀ Fuller's London Pride, Ringwood Best Bitter, 49ers, Summer Lightning, John Smith's, Guinness. ⏣ 8 **Facilities** Dogs allowed Garden Parking

The Three Tuns ⏣

58 Middlebridge St SO51 8HL ☎ 01794 512639
e-mail: guru.palmer@yahoo.co.uk
dir: *Romsey bypass, 0.5m from main entrance of Broadlands Estate*

Centrally located in the abbey town, the 400-year-old Three Tuns is just a short walk from the front gates of Broadlands, country seat of Earl Mountbatten. In the last couple of years new owners Hannah and David have sought out local suppliers, aiming at a gastro-pub style operation. Typical dishes are braised shoulder of Romsey lamb, and Swish and Chips (plaice, haddock, king prawn and scallop in beer batter with real tartare and pea purée).

Open all day Closed: Mon L **Bar Meals** L served Tue-Sat 12-3, Sun 12-9 D served all wk 6.30-10.30 Av main course £7 **Restaurant** L served Tue-Sat 12-3, Sun 12-9 booking required D served all wk 6.30-10 booking required Av 3 course à la carte fr £25 ⏣ SWISH CATERING LTD ◀ Ringwood Best, Ringwood 49ers, Sharpe's Doom Bar, Hobgoblin ♂ Old Rosie. ⏣ 8 **Facilities** Children's menu Dogs allowed Garden Parking

ROWLAND'S CASTLE
Map 5 SU71

The Castle Inn ⏣

1 Finchdean Rd PO9 6DA
☎ 023 9241 2494   ▤ 023 9241 2494
e-mail: rogerburrell@btconnect.com
dir: *N of Havant take B2149 to Rowland's Castle. Pass green, under rail bridge, pub 1st on left opposite Stansted Park*

A Victorian building directly opposite Stansted Park, part of the Forest of Bere. Richard the Lionheart supposedly hunted here, and the house and grounds are open to the public for part of the year. Traditional atmosphere is boosted by wooden floors and fires in both bars. Menu options include pies, lasagne, curry, steaks, local sausages, and chilli.

Open all day all wk **Bar Meals** L served Mon-Sat 12-2.30, Sun 12-3 D served Mon-Sat 6-9 Av main course £7.50 **Restaurant** L served Mon-Sat 12-2.30, Sun 12-3 D served Mon-Sat 6-9 Av 3 course à la carte fr £16 ⏣ FULLERS BREWERY ◀ Fuller's Butser, HSB, London Pride, guest ales. ⏣ 8 **Facilities** Dogs allowed Garden Parking

The Fountain Inn

34 The Green PO9 6AB
☎ 023 9241 2291   ▤ 023 9241 2291
e-mail: fountaininn@amserve.com
dir: *Telephone for directions*

Set by the village green in pretty Rowlands Castle, The Fountain is a lovingly refurbished Georgian inn complete with resident ghost. Food is served in Sienna's bistro, where dishes include hand rolled, stone baked pizzas, pasta dishes, and specials like flame-grilled chicken and Serrano ham salad, and crusted fillet steak with a roasted vegetable chutney.

Open all wk ⏣ FREE HOUSE ◀ Ruddles IPA, Abbot, Ruddles Cask. **Facilities** Play area Dogs allowed Garden Parking

ST MARY BOURNE
Map 5 SU45

The Bourne Valley Inn ⏣

SP11 6BT ☎ 01264 738361   ▤ 01264 738126
dir: *Telephone for directions*

Located in the charming Bourne valley, this popular traditional inn is the ideal setting for conferences, exhibitions, weddings and other notable occasions. The riverside garden abounds with wildlife, and children can happily let off steam in the special play area. Typical menu includes deep fried brie or a cocktail of prawns, followed by rack of lamb with a redcurrant and port sauce, salmon and prawn tagliatelle, steak and mushroom pie, crispy haddock and chips and warm duck salad.

Open all wk ⏣ FREE HOUSE ◀ guest ales. ⏣ 8 **Facilities** Play area Dogs allowed Garden Parking

SELBORNE
Map 5 SU73

The Selborne Arms ⏣

High St GU34 3JR ☎ 01420 511247   ▤ 01420 511754
e-mail: info@selbornearms.co.uk
web: www.selbornearms.co.uk
dir: *From A3 follow B3006, pub on left in village centre*

Real fires and a warm welcome make this traditional pub a safe bet for a leisurely drink; but try, if you can, to fit in a meal. Chef and co-owner Nick Carter showcases the best local food and drink - perhaps home-made pâté of Bowtell's pork with aromatic spices and Mr Whitehead's cider served with home-made apple and cider bread; or pan-fried saddle of Blackmoor venison on spiced braised red cabbage with a quince game sauce.

Open all wk 11-3 6-11 (Sat-Sun 11-11) **Bar Meals** L served all wk 12-2 D served Mon-Sat 7-9, Sun 7-8.30 ◀ Courage Best, Ringwood 49er, local guest ales ♂ Thatchers. ⏣ 10 **Facilities** Play area Garden Parking

SILCHESTER
Map 5 SU66

Calleva Arms ⏣

Little London Rd, The Common RG7 2PH
☎ 0118 970 0305
dir: *A340 from Basingstoke, signed Silchester. M4 junct 11, 20 mins signed Mortimer then Silchester*

Standing opposite the village green, the pub is popular with walkers, cyclists, and visitors to the nearby Roman town of Calleva Atrebatum with the remains of its town walls and amphitheatre. A pleasant, airy conservatory added to the 19th-century building overlooks a large enclosed garden. Lunchtime favourites include steaks, bangers and mash and special salads. A typical dinner selection could start with Thai spiced crab cakes with mango salsa or Indian, nacho or antipasti sharing platters; followed by aromatic half duck with hoi sin sauce; and chef's fruit crumble served with custard.

continued

SILCHESTER *continued*

Open all wk 11-3 5.30-11.30 (Sat 11-11.30 Sun noon-11) **Bar Meals** L served all week 12-2 D served all wk 6.30-9 **Restaurant** L served all wk 12-2 booking required D served all wk 6.30-9 booking required ⊕ FULLER, SMITH & TURNER ⬛ London Pride, HSB, Guinness, Butser Bitter. ▼ 8 **Facilities** Children's menu Dogs allowed Garden Parking

---

SOUTHAMPTON Map 5 SU41

The White Star Tavern & Dining Rooms ★★★★ INN ⊛ ▼

28 Oxford St SO14 3DJ
☎ 023 8082 1990 📄 023 8090 4982
e-mail: reservations@whitestartavern.co.uk
dir: *M3 junct 13, take A33 to Southampton, towards Ocean Village & Marina*

This former seafarers' hotel has been stylishly renovated to create an attractive venue incorporating a good blend of old and new. The all-day menu includes light bites like chicken liver and foie gras parfait; pub classics such as beer-battered haddock and chips; main dishes of pan-fried brisket of beef; and desserts such as roasted pear and almond tart. On sunny days you can take a pavement table and watch the world go by on Southampton's restaurant row. There are 13 smart bedrooms available.

Open all day all wk 7am-11pm (Fri 7am-mdnt, Sat 9am-mdnt, Sun 9am-10.30pm) Closed: 25 Dec **Bar Meals** L served Mon-Thu 7-2.30, Fri 7-3, Sat 9-3, Sun 9-4 D served Mon-Thu 6-9, Fri 6-10, Sat 6-9, Sun 6-9.30 ⊕ ENTERPRISE INNS ⬛ London Pride, Ringwood. ▼ 8 **Rooms** 13

SOUTHSEA

See Portsmouth & Southsea

SPARSHOLT Map 5 SU43

PICK OF THE PUBS

The Plough Inn ▼

See Pick of the Pubs on opposite page

STEEP Map 5 SU72

PICK OF THE PUBS

Harrow Inn ▼

GU32 2DA ☎ 01730 262685
dir: *Off A3 to A272, left through Sheet, take road opposite church (School Lane) then over A3 by-pass bridge*

A 16th-century, tile-hung gem that has changed little over the years. The McCutcheon family has run it since 1929; sisters Claire and Nisa, both born and brought up here, are now the third generation with their names over the door. Tucked away off the road, it comprises two tiny bars - the 'public' is Tudor, with beams, tiled floor, inglenook fireplace, scrubbed tables, wooden benches, tree-trunk stools and a 'library'; the saloon (or Smoking Room, as it is still called) is Victorian. Beers are dispensed from barrels, there is no till and the toilets are across the road. Food is in keeping: ham and pea soup; hot scotch eggs (some days); Cheddar ploughman's; and various quiches. The garden has a dozen tables surrounded by country-cottage flowers and fruit trees. Quiz nights raise huge sums for charity, for which Claire's partner Tony grows and sells flowers outside, so far raising £30,000.

Open all wk Closed: Sun eve in winter **Bar Meals** L served all wk 12-2 D served all wk 7-9 Av main course £8.50 ⊕ FREE HOUSE ⬛ Ringwood Best, Oakleaf Bitter, Hop Back GFB, Bowman Ales, Suthwyk Bloomfields Bitter. ▼ 6 **Facilities** Dogs allowed Garden Parking **Notes** ⊛

STOCKBRIDGE Map 5 SU33

Mayfly ▼

Testcombe SO20 6AZ ☎ 01264 860283
dir: *Between A303 & A30, on A3057*

Idyllically situated right on the banks of the swiftly flowing River Test, this beamed old farmhouse has a traditional bar, a bright conservatory and a splendid riverside terrace. Unrivalled tranquil river views, complete with ducks and swans, make the Mayfly a popular drinking spot so arrive early on warm summer days to sup a pint of Adnams Broadside on a waterside bench. All-day bar food includes fisherman's pie, rib-eye steak, herb-crusted pork fillet with mustard jus, and lasagne with garlic bread.

Open all day all wk 10am-11pm **Bar Meals** L served all wk 11.30-9 D served al wk 11.30-9 food served all day ⊕ FREE HOUSE ⬛ Wadworth 6X, Adnams Broadside, Adnams Best, guest ales Ö Aspall. ▼ 20 **Facilities** Family room Dogs allowed Garden Parking

---

PICK OF THE PUBS

The Peat Spade ⊛ ▼

Longstock SO20 6DR ☎ 01264 810612
e-mail: info@peatspadeinn.co.uk
dir: *Telephone for directions*

Unusual paned windows overlook the peaceful village lane and idyllic heavily thatched cottages at this striking, redbrick and gabled Victorian pub, which stands tucked away in the heart of the Test Valley, only 100 yards from the famous trout stream. Former Hotel du Vin chefs Lucy Townsend and Andrew Clark have created a classy country inn, one where you will find a relaxed atmosphere in the cosy fishing and shooting themed bar and dining room, and a simple, daily-changing menu listing classic English food. Using locally-sourced produce, including allotment fruit and vegetables and game from the Leckford Estate, the choice may take in devilled whitebait with tartare sauce for starters, with main dishes ranging from rump steak with garlic butter to roast halibut with squid ink risotto and sweet fennel. For pudding, try the Cambridge burnt cream or the lemon meringue pie. To drink, there's Ringwood Fortyniner on tap and a choice of 10 wines by the glass – quaff them on the super summer terrace.

Open all day all wk Closed: 25-26 Dec **Bar Meals** L served all wk 12-2 booking required D served all wk 7-9 booking required Av main course £15.50 **Restaurant** L served all wk 12-2 booking required D served all wk 7-9 booking required Av 3 course à la carte fr £35 ⊕ FREE HOUSE ⬛ Ringwood Best, Ringwood 49er, guest ales. ▼ 10 **Facilities** Children's menu Dogs allowed Garden Parking

---

PICK OF THE PUBS

The Three Cups Inn NEW ★★★ INN ▼

See Pick of the Pubs on page 236

STRATFIELD TURGIS Map 5 SU65

The Wellington Arms ▼

RG27 0AS ☎ 01256 882214 📄 01256 882934
e-mail: wellington.arms@hall-woodhouse.co.uk
dir: *On A33 between Basingstoke & Reading*

Looking at this Grade II listed hotel today, it is hard to believe it was originally a farmhouse. The Wellington Arms is an ideal base for visiting the nearby Stratfield Saye estate, formerly the home of the Duke of Wellington. Well-kept real ales complement a good selection of eating options, including liver and bacon served with bubble and squeak; steak and kidney pudding; fanned avocado, cherry, tomato and bacon salad; and smoked salmon and prawn platter.

Open all day all wk noon-11 (Sun noon-10.30) **Bar Meals** food served all day ⊕ HALL & WOODHOUSE ⬛ Badger 1st Gold, Seasonal Ales. ▼ 12 **Facilities** Dogs allowed Garden Parking

PICK OF THE PUBS

The Plough Inn 🍷

SPARSHOLT   Map 5 SU43

Main Rd SO21 2NW
☎ **01962 776353** 📄 **01962 776400**
dir: *From Winchester take B3049 (A272) W, left to Sparsholt, Inn 1m*

A delightful flower- and shrub-filled garden complete with a play fort and donkeys is a popular summer feature at this much-extended 200-year-old cottage, located on the edge of the village in beautiful countryside. Worth noting if you are visiting nearby Winchester or following a walk in Farley Mount Country Park, just a mile away. Inside, the main bar and dining areas blend together very harmoniously,

helped by judicious use of farmhouse-style pine tables, a mix of wooden and upholstered seats, collections of agricultural implements, stone jars, wooden wine box end-panels and dried hops. The dining tables to the left of the entrance have a view across open fields to wooded downland, and it's at this end you'll find a blackboard menu offering lighter dishes exemplified by salmon and crab fishcakes with saffron sauce; lambs' liver and bacon with mash and onion gravy; beef, ale and mushroom pie; and whole baked camembert with garlic and rosemary. The menu board at the right-hand end of the bar offers more adventurous meals – perhaps venison steak with celeriac mash and roasted beetroot; roast pork belly with bubble-and-squeak, five spice and sultana gravy; chicken breast with black pudding and apple and bacon and bean jus; and a bowl of moules marinière served with crusty bread. Lunchtime regulars know

that 'doorstep' is the most apt description for the great sandwiches, perhaps crab and mayonnaise, or beef and horseradish. Puddings include rich chocolate tart with clotted cream, and banana pannacotta with chocolate sauce. Wadworth supplies the tip-top real ales and there's a good wine selection. Booking is definitely advised for any meal.

Open all week Closed: 25 Dec
Restaurant ⊕ WADWORTH 🛢 Wadworth Henry's IPA, 6X, Old Timer & JCB. 🍷 14
Facilities Play area Family room Dogs allowed Garden Parking

PICK OF THE PUBS

The Three Cups NEW ★★★ INN ♟

STOCKBRIDGE   Map 5 SU33

High St SO20 6HB ☎ **01264 810527**
e-mail: manager@the3cups.co.uk
web: www.the3cups.co.uk
dir: *M3 junct 8, A303 towards Andover. Left onto A3057 to Stockbridge*

There are many reasons to visit Stockbridge, and this 15th-century, timber-framed building at the western end of its unusually wide main street is one. The pub's name derives from an Old English phrase for a meeting of three rivers, although the only river here is the Test, famous for its trout, which splits into several streams through the village. Lucia Foster, the present owner, has been here for just over 30 years and it would be hard to find what, if any, material changes she has made that would surprise a visitor returning after

three decades. The interior is predictably low-beamed, with some floors of stone, some of wood, with high-backed chairs and hand-crafted tables arranged throughout a series of snug rooms. The single, most appealing bar, serves Ringwood, Itchen Valley's Fagin's and two guest ales. Modern European and traditional selections on the four menus, including a daily changing blackboard, blend Hampshire's freshest local ingredients to create an excellent choice. Typically, you might well find warm goat's cheese on toast and salad; and seafood cassoulet as starters, with main courses of caramelised shoulder of pork and mangetout; poached chunky sea bass with mousseline of celeriac and citrus shallot sauce; and vegetarian moussaka. Desserts include chocolate and cardamom brownie with home-made blueberry ripple ice cream; and vanilla macaroon with raspberry mousse. A lovely riverside terrace overlooks a rose-filled garden, where you can dine alfresco while trying to spot a wild brown trout in the river. Accommodation suites provide Egyptian cotton sheets and real ground coffee.

Open 10am-10.30pm **Bar Meals** L served all week 12-2.30 D served all week 6-9.30 Av main course £10 **Restaurant** L served all week 12-2.30 D served all week 6-9.30 Fixed menu price fr £12.95 Av 3 course à la carte fr £20 ◧ Fagin's Itchen Valley, Ringwood, Flowerpots, Guest Ales Ö Stowford Press. ♟ 10 **Facilities** Children's menu Dogs allowed Garden Parking **Rooms** 8

TANGLEY
Map 5 SU35

The Fox Inn ?

SP11 0RU ☎ 01264 730276 🖹 01264 730478
e-mail: info@foxinntangley.co.uk
dir: *A343, 4m from Andover*

The 300-year-old brick and flint cottage that has been the Fox since 1830 stands on a small crossroads, miles, it seems, from anywhere. The blackboard menu offers reliably good lunchtime snacks and imaginative evening dishes. Enjoy a pint of London Pride or Ramsbury in the tiny, friendly bar, and perhaps moules marinière or sea bass fillets in the unpretentious restaurant.

Open all day all wk noon-11 (Sun noon-10.30) Closed: 25 Dec, 1 Jan **Bar Meals** L served all wk 12-2.30 booking required D served all wk 6-10 booking required Av main course £12 **Restaurant** L served all wk 12-2.30 booking required D served all wk 6-10 booking required Av 3 course à la carte fr £22 ⊕ FREE HOUSE ◀ London Pride, Adnams. ♀ 12 **Facilities** Dogs allowed Garden Parking

TICHBORNE
Map 5 SU53

PICK OF THE PUBS

The Tichborne Arms ?

SO24 0NA ☎ 01962 733760 🖹 01962 733760
e-mail: tichbornearms@xln.co.uk
dir: *Off A31 towards Alresford, after 200yds right at Tichborne sign*

A picturesque thatched free house in the heart of the Itchen valley. Three pubs have been built on this site, the first in 1429, but each has been destroyed by fire; the present red-brick building was erected in 1939. An interesting history is attached to this idyllic rural hamlet, which was dramatised in a feature film *The Tichborne Claimant*; it told the story of a butcher's boy from Australia who impersonated the son of Lady Tichborne (with her support) to claim the family title and estates. The pub interior displays an eclectic mix of artefacts, from stuffed animals and antiques to a chiming grandfather clock. A glowing wood-burning stove matches the warmth of the welcome from Patrick and Nicky Roper, who serve a range of real ales at the bar including Hopback, Palmers and Bowman; Mr Whitehead's Cirrus Minor cider is pulled straight from the barrel. A large, well-stocked garden is ideal for summer eating and drinking.

Open 11.30-3 6-11.30 Closed: Sun eve **Bar Meals** L served all wk 11.30-2 D served all wk 6.30-9 ⊕ FREE HOUSE ◀ Hopback Brewery, Palmers, Bowman, Sharps Downton. ♀ 9 **Facilities** Children's menu Dogs allowed Garden Parking

UPPER FROYLE
Map 5 SU74

The Hen & Chicken Inn ?

GU34 4JH ☎ 01420 22115
e-mail: bookings@henandchicken.co.uk
dir: *2m from Alton, on A31 next to petrol station*

Highwayman Dick Turpin is said to have hidden upstairs in this 18th-century coaching inn. Today it retains a traditional atmosphere thanks to large open fires, wood panelling and beams - but the post boxes above the inglenook remain empty. Food ranges from snacks to meals such as home-made linguine niçoise with a poached quail egg, followed by pan-fried calves' liver with bubble and squeak and red wine sauce; and then spotted dick with custard.

Open all wk 11.45-3 5.30-close (Sat-Sun all day) **Bar Meals** L served Mon-Sat 12-2.30, Sun 12-7 booking required D served Mon-Thu 6-9, Fri-Sat 6-9.30, Sun 12-7 booking required **Restaurant** L served Mon-Sat 12-2.30, Sun 12-7 booking required D served Mon-Thu 6-9, Fri-Sat 6-9.30, Sun 12-7 booking required ⊕ HALL & WOODHOUSE ◀ Badger Best, Tanglefoot, King, Barnes Sussex Ale Ö Stowford Press. ♀ 8 **Facilities** Children's menu Play area Dogs allowed Garden Parking

WARSASH
Map 5 SU40

The Jolly Farmer Country Inn ?

29 Fleet End Rd SO31 9JH
☎ 01489 572500 🖹 01489 885847
e-mail: mail@thejollyfarmeruk.com
dir: *Exit M27 junct 9 towards A27 Fareham, right onto Warsash Rd. Follow for 2m, left onto Fleet End Rd*

Multi-coloured classic cars are lined up outside this friendly pub close to the Hamble River, and boasting its own golf society and cricket team. The bars are furnished in a rustic style with farming equipment on the walls and ceilings. There's also a patio and a purpose-built children's play area. Grills, including succulent steaks, 8oz gammon steaks, and house specialities such as shank of lamb, chicken stroganoff, and locally caught seafood characterise the dishes.

Open all day all wk 11am-11pm **Bar Meals** L served Mon-Sat 12-2.30 (Sun all day) D served Mon-Sat 6-10 (Sun all day) **Restaurant** L served all wk 12-2.30 D served all wk 6-10 ⊕ WHITBREAD ◀ Fuller's London Pride & HSB, Interbrew Flowers IPA. ♀ 6 **Facilities** Play area Family room Dogs allowed Garden Parking

WELL
Map 5 SU74

The Chequers Inn ?

RG29 1TL ☎ 01256 862605 🖹 01256 861116
e-mail: roybwells@aol.com
dir: *From Odiham High St turn right into Long Ln, follow for 3m, left at T-junct, pub 0.25m on top of hill*

Set deep in the heart of the Hampshire countryside, in the village of Well near Odiham, this 15th-century pub is full of charm and old world character, with a rustic, low-beamed bar, log fires, scrubbed tables and vine-covered front terrace. The menu offers good pub food such as steak and Tanglefoot pie, fishcakes, slow whole roast pheasant; and the chef's ultimate beefburger, served with home-made chips, new potatoes or creamy mash.

Open all wk noon-3 6-11pm (Sat noon-11pm Sun noon-10.30pm) **Bar Meals** L served Mon-Thu 12-2, Fri-Sat 12-9.30, Sun 12-8 D served Mon-Thu 6.30-9, Fri-Sat 12-9.30, Sun 12-8 **Restaurant** L served Mon-Thu 12-2, Fri-Sat 12-9.30, Sun 12-8 D served Mon-Thu 6.30-9, Fri-Sat 12-9.30, Sun 12-8 ⊕ HALL & WOODHOUSE ◀ Badger First Gold, Tanglefoot, Seasonal Ales, Guinness Ö Stowford Press. ♀ 8 **Facilities** Family room Dogs allowed Garden Parking

WHERWELL
Map 5 SU34

The White Lion ?

Fullerton Rd SP11 7JF ☎ 01264 860317
dir: *M3 junct 8, A303, then B3048 to Wherwell; or A3057 (S of Andover), B3420 to Wherwell*

The White Lion is a well-known historic pub in the heart of the Test Valley, where Adrian and Patti have been welcoming their customers for over 20 years. Parts of the building date back to before the Civil War, during which one of Cromwell's cannon balls supposedly fell down the chimney and is on display today. Enjoy a pint of Ringwood Best while reflecting upon other historical features, such as the bricked-up windows which resulted from the Window Tax introduced in 1696. Food consists of traditional favourites and a seasonal specials board.

Open all wk 11-2.30 6-10.30 (Thu-Sat 6-11 Sun noon-3) Closed: 25 Dec **Bar Meals** L served all wk 12-2 D served Mon-Sat 7-9 Av main course £10.50 **Restaurant** L served all wk 12-2 D served Mon-Sat 7-9 Av 3 course à la carte fr £21 ⊕ PUNCH TAVERNS ◀ Ringwood Best Bitter, John Smiths Smooth. ♀ 12 **Facilities** Children's menu Dogs allowed Garden Parking

WHITCHURCH
Map 5 SU44

Watership Down Inn ?

Freefolk Priors RG28 7NJ ☎ 01256 892254
dir: *On B3400 between Basingstoke & Andover*

Enjoy an exhilarating walk on Watership Down before relaxing with a pint of well-kept local ale at this homely 19th-century inn named after Richard Adams' classic tale of rabbit life. The menu choices range from sandwiches, jacket potatoes, salads and ploughman's through to liver and bacon casserole, sausage and mash, mushroom stroganoff, Somerset chicken, and braised lamb shank in a red wine gravy. Just don't expect any rabbit dishes!

Open all wk ⊕ FREE HOUSE ◀ Oakleaf Bitter, Butts Barbus Barbus, Triple FFF, Pressed Rat & Warthog, Hogs Back TEA, Stonehenge Danish Dynamite. ♀ 8 **Facilities** Play area Garden Parking

PICK OF THE PUBS

The Wykeham Arms ♟

WINCHESTER   **Map 5 SU42**

75 Kingsgate St SO23 9PE
☎ **01962 853834**   📄 **01962 854411**
e-mail: wykehamarms@
accommodating-inns.co.uk
web: www.fullershotels.com/
rte.asp?id=129
dir: *Near Winchester College & Winchester
Cathedral*

A map-reader in the party would be an asset in finding the 270-year-old Wyk, even though it's only a spit from the High Street through the cathedral precincts. Standing on the corner of two narrow streets, the Wyk's internal layout invites you to take one of two routes – straight on into the main bar, or left into a smaller one, both hugely convivial and warmed by open log fires. Beyond each one are several tucked-away dining areas, although you may also eat in the bars themselves at one of the old Winchester College desks, placed inkwell to inkwell. You may eat sausages, which you can buy singly, at the bar, and peanuts and crisps but, be prepared, these are decanted into wooden bowls, so if there are some out already, don't assume they are on the house! Photographs, paintings and miscellaneous ephemera fill most walls, and pewter tankards, walking canes and heaven knows what else hang from the ceilings. A good selection of wines is kept, with up to 20 by the glass chalked on a blackboard. For a lunchtime snack, the sandwiches - smoked salmon and cream cheese, for example - are good, as is Wyk pie; gravadlax; and pea pâté. The daily-changing menu offers dishes such as pork tenderloin; new season rack of lamb; fillet of salmon; and mushroom tagliatelle. Outside is a patio, a remnant of what until last year was a garden, now sacrificed to the needs of the internal combustion engine. But fair enough, street parking can be pretty difficult round here, so one can understand the dilemma.

Open 11-11 (Sun 11-10.30) Closed: 25 Dec **Bar Meals** L served Mon-Sat 12-2.30 Av main course £9 **Restaurant** L served all week 12-2.30 D served all week 6.30-9 Av 3 course à la carte fr £25 ⊕ Fullers ◀ Butser Bitter, HSB, London Pride, Chiswick, guest ales. ♟ 18 **Facilities** Dogs allowed Garden Parking

WICKHAM
Map 5 SU51

Greens Restaurant & Pub ♟

The Square PO17 5JQ ☎ 01329 833197
e-mail: DuckworthGreens@aol.com
dir: 2m from M27, on corner of historic Wickham Square. 3m from Fareham

The enduring popularity of Greens, on a corner of Wickham's picturesque square, is entirely down to the standards set by Frank and Carol Duckworth, who have run it for 25 years. Drinkers will find award-winning real ales from nearby Droxford, while front-of-house staff are trained in guest care ensure a warm and welcoming reception for diners. Modern European cooking may offer Rosary goats' cheese salad with walnut and raspberry dressing; braised beef with red wine and chorizo with basil mash; and spiced apricot bread and butter pudding.

Open 10-3 6-11 (Sun & BH noon-4) Closed: Sun eve & Mon **Bar Meals** L served Tue-Sat 12-2.30, Sun 12-3 booking required D served Tue-Sat 6.30-9.30 booking required **Restaurant** L served Tue-Sat 12-2.30, Sun 12-3 booking required D served Tue-Sat 6.30-9.30 booking required Fixed menu price fr £9.95 Av 3 course à la carte fr £20 ⊕ FREE HOUSE ◄ Hopback Summer Lightning, Youngs Special, Guinness, Timothy Taylor, Local ales. ♟ 10 **Facilities** Children's menu Garden Parking

WINCHESTER
Map 5 SU42

The Bell Inn NEW ♟

83 St Cross Rd SO23 9RE ☎ 01962 865284
e-mail: the_bellinn@btconnect.com
dir: M3 junct 11, follow B rd into Winchester for approx 1m. Pub on right

Edge of town local that's worth noting as it stands close to the 12th-century St Cross Hospital, with its fine Norman church, and glorious walks through the River Itchen water meadows to Winchester College and the city centre. Very much a community local, with Greene King ales and good-value food served in the main bar and the pine-furnished lounge, plus a warm welcome to families and dogs. Head for the sunny walled garden on warm summer days.

Open all day all wk 11-11 (Fri-Sat 11am-mdnt Sun noon-10.30) **Bar Meals** L served all wk 12-2 booking required D served all wk 6.30-9 booking required Av main course £8 ⊕ GREENE KING ◄ IPA, 2 guest ales Ō Stowford Press. ♟ 8 **Facilities** Children's menu Play area Dogs allowed Garden Parking

The Westgate Inn ★★★ INN ♟

2 Romsey Rd SO23 8TP
☎ 01962 820222 📄 01962 820222
e-mail: wghguy@yahoo.co.uk
dir: Pub on corner Romsey Rd & Upper High St, opposite Great Hall & Medieval West Gate

A quirky building at the top end of Winchester's main shopping street, opposite the medieval West Gate and historic Great Hall, the Westgate Inn has been trading since the 1850s. Home-cooked meals are served in the bar, including satisfying hot pot dishes, steaks from Hampshire grass-fed herds, fish and chips and snacks and sharer platters including oriental, Indian, vegetarian and meat lovers. Also on the premises is the Tiffin Club restaurant, serving Epicurean Indian food. Accommodation is provided in eight bedrooms named after famous people associated with Winchester.

Open all day all wk noon-11.30 **Bar Meals** Av main course £7 ⊕ MARSTONS ◄ Jennings Cumberland, Banks Original, Marstons Burton Bitter, guest ales Ō Thatchers Gold, Wychwood Green Goblin. ♟ 7 **Facilities** Dogs allowed **Rooms** 8

PICK OF THE PUBS

The Wykeham Arms ♟

See Pick of the Pubs on opposite page

HEREFORDSHIRE

ASTON CREWS
Map 10 SO62

PICK OF THE PUBS

The Penny Farthing Inn ♟

HR9 7LW ☎ 01989 750366 📄 01989 750366
e-mail: info@pennyfarthinginn.co.uk
dir: 5m E of Ross-on-Wye

This whitewashed 17th-century blacksmith's shop and coaching inn is located high above the River Wye valley. From its large, sloping garden you can take in views of the Malvern Hills, the Black Hills and the Forest of Dean. Inside are lots of nooks and crannies with oak beams, antiques, saddlery and cheerful log fires. At least two real ales and local cider are guaranteed to be on tap, and the wine list focuses on lesser known wineries to bring quality at a reasonable price. The same objective applies to the menu, which capitalises on the wealth of local vegetable and fruit growers' produce, and some of the best meat in the country. The lunchtime bar menu ranges from sandwiches, baguettes and jacket potatoes, to the pub's pie of the week, and chef's home-made curry. Main courses in the restaurant are likely to feature local lamb and renowned Hereford beef.

Open 12-3 6-11 Closed: Mon in winter **Bar Meals** food served all day **Restaurant** food served all day ◄ John Smith's, Black Sheep, Spitfire Ō Westons Stowford Press. ♟ 7 **Facilities** Children's menu Dogs allowed Garden Parking

AYMESTREY
Map 9 SO46

PICK OF THE PUBS

The Riverside Inn ♟

See Pick of the Pubs on page 240

BODENHAM
Map 10 SO55

England's Gate Inn ♟

HR1 3HU ☎ 01568 797286 📄 01568 797768
dir: Hereford A49, turn onto A417 at Bosey Dinmore hill, 2.5m on right

A pretty black and white coaching inn dating from around 1540, with atmospheric beamed bars and blazing log fires in winter. A picturesque garden attracts a good summer following, and so does the food. The menu features such dishes as pan-fried lamb steak with apricot and onion marmalade, roasted breast of duck with parsnip mash and spinach, and wild rice cakes with peppers on a chilli and tomato salsa.

Open all wk ⊕ FREE HOUSE ◄ Wye Valley Bitter, Butty Bach, Shropshire Lad, guest ales. ♟ 7 **Facilities** Dogs allowed Garden Parking

CANON PYON
Map 9 SO44

The Nags Head Inn

HR4 8NY ☎ 01432 830252
dir: Telephone for directions

More than four hundred years old, with flagstone floors, open fires and exposed beams to prove it. A comprehensive menu might entice you into starting with slices of smoked salmon drizzled with brandy, lemon and cracked pepper, then to follow with medallions of lamb in a sticky Cumberland sauce, breast of Gressingham duck in a rich morello cherry sauce, or butterflied sea bass on sautéed strips of carrot and chopped coriander. Vegetarian options include stuffed peppers and tagliatelle. Curry nights and Sunday carvery. The large garden features a children's adventure playground.

Open all wk Mon-Thu 3-12.30 (Fri-Sun 3-mdnt) **Bar Meals** L served Mon-Fri 4-7, Sat-Sun 12-7 D served Mon-Fri 4-7, Sat-Sun 12-7 **Restaurant** L served Mon-Fri 4-7, Sat-Sun 12-7 D served Mon-Fri 4-7, Sat-Sun 12-7 ⊕ FREE HOUSE ◄ Fuller's London Pride, Boddingtons, Flowers, Nags Ale Ō Stowford Press. **Facilities** Children's menu Play area Dogs allowed Garden Parking

PICK OF THE PUBS

The Riverside Inn ♈

AYMESTREY   Map 9 SO46

HR6 9ST
☎ 01568 708440   📄 01568 709058
e-mail: theriverside@btconnect.com
dir: *On A4110, 18m N of Hereford*

A handsome half-timbered 16th-century inn on the banks of the River Lugg, overlooking an old stone bridge, peaceful woodland and lush meadows. It's a popular pit-stop for walkers hiking the Mortimer Way as the pub stands at the halfway point, and numerous circular walks start from the front door (guidebooks on sale at the bar). Mortimer Way walking packages are offered, with transportation to and from start/finish points included in the room price. Anglers are also drawn to inn as it offers a mile of private fishing for brown trout and grayling. The interior, with its wood panelling, low beams and log fires, engenders a relaxed atmosphere reflecting 300 years of hospitality. Owner Richard Gresko has a very focused approach to food, and locally grown and reared produce is used as much as possible in his kitchen. Visitors are welcome to take a stroll round the pub's extensive vegetable, herb and fruit gardens. Real ales and ciders are locally sourced, including Wye Valley Butty Bach and Brook Farm cider made in the next village, and the menu combines modern and traditional English cooking. Typical starters may include Lugg trout gravadlax with beetroot and horseradish relish, and Hereford Hop and smoked haddock soufflé with a creamy mustard sauce. Main dishes range from traditional favourites like lambs' liver and bacon with shallot gravy, and beer-battered cod with home-made chips, to more adventurous specials like braised rare breed shin of beef and oxtail stew, cooked in local ale with wild mushrooms; organic belly pork cooked in local cider served with garden rhubarb and apple sauce; rack of Welsh lamb with pea purée and mint jus, and wild sea bass with creamy mushroom sauce.

As befits a Herefordshire location, locally bred fillet and sirloin of beef always feature, but so too do vegetarian dishes such as Moroccan spiced filo tart (squash, nuts, spinach and spices), lunchtime baguettes, and a good choice of home-made puddings. Gluten and dairy free diets catered for.

Open 11-3 6-11 (Sun 12-3 6-10.30) Closed: 26 Dec & 1 Jan, Mon lunch, Sun eve in winter **Bar Meals** L served Tue-Sun 12-2 D served Mon-Sat 7-9 Av main course £9.95 **Restaurant** L served Tue-Sun 12-2 D served Mon-Sat 7-9 Av 3 course à la carte fr £21 ⊕ FREE HOUSE ◀ Wye Valley Bitter & Butty Bach, Hobsons Best Bitter, Spinning Dog, Owd Bull ☉ Brooke Farm Medium Dry, Westons Stowford Press. ♈ 7 **Facilities** Children's menu Dogs allowed Garden Parking

CRASWALL
Map 9 SO23

The Bulls Head

HR2 0PN ☎ 01981 510616
e-mail: info@thebullsheadcraswall.co.uk
dir: From A465 turn at Pandy. Village in 11m

This old drovers inn, located in remote countryside six miles south of Hay-on-Wye, is not easy to find but well worth the effort. It is popular with walkers and riders, who tie their horses at the rail outside. Real ales and ciders are served through the hole in the wall bar, and there are log fires in winter. Traditional dishes include beef pie and Herefordshire steaks, while others might be home-cured bresaola, roast partridge, or mixed game pie.

Open 12-3 6-11 (Sat-Sun 12-11) Closed: check winter opening with pub **Bar Meals** L served all wk 12-2 booking required D served all wk 6.30-9 booking required Av main course £10.95 **Restaurant** L served all wk 12-2 booking required D served all wk 6.30-9 booking required Av 3 course à la carte fr £25 ⊕ FREE HOUSE ◀ Butty Bach, Wye Valley Organic Bitter ♂ Gwatkin's Farmhouse & Norman, Westons Old Rosie Scrumpy. **Facilities** Dogs allowed Garden

DORSTONE
Map 9 SO34

PICK OF THE PUBS

The Pandy Inn

HR3 6AN ☎ 01981 550273 📄 01981 550277
e-mail: magdalena@pandyinn.wanadoo.co.uk
dir: Off B4348 W of Hereford

The Pandy is one of the oldest inns in the country and has a fascinating history. One of the four Norman knights who killed Thomas à Becket in Canterbury Cathedral in 1170, Richard de Brito, built a chapel at Dorstone as an act of atonement after 15 years in the Holy Land. He also built the Pandy to house the workers, subsequently adapting it to become an inn. Later, during the Civil War in the 17th century, Oliver Cromwell is known to have taken refuge here. The ancient hostelry is located opposite the village green and part of it retains its original flagstone floors and beams. The large garden, which offers 19 tables and a children's playground, has views of Dorstone Hill. Food is freshly prepared daily and the seasonal menu includes Pandy pies and home-made puddings. Farmhouse ciders are served alongside local cask ales.

Closed: Mon Oct-Jun ⊕ FREE HOUSE ◀ Wye Valley Bitter & Butty Bach. **Facilities** Play area Dogs allowed Garden Parking

FOWNHOPE
Map 10 SO53

The Green Man Inn ☂

HR1 4PE ☎ 01432 860243 📄 01432 860920
e-mail: greenman.hereford@thespiritgroup.com
dir: From M50 junct 4 take A449 then B4224 towards Hereford to Fownhope

This white-painted 15th-century coaching inn has a host of beams inside and out. Set in an attractive garden close to the River Wye, it's an ideal base for walking, touring and salmon fishing. The extensive menu has something for everyone, with a range of chunky sandwiches, jacket potatoes, burgers and ciabatta melts. Then there are hand-made pies, gourmet grills, and main course favourites like sausages and mash. All this, and sticky puddings too!

Open all day all wk 11am-11pm (Sun noon-10.30pm) **Bar Meals** L served Mon-Thu 12-3, Fri-Sun 12-9 D served Mon-Thu 6-9, Fri-Sun 12-9 **Restaurant** L served Mon-Thu 12-3, Fri-Sun 12-9 D served Mon-Thu 6-9, Fri-Sun 12-9 ⊕ SPIRIT GROUP ◀ John Smith's Smooth, Bombardier, Adnams ♂ Stowford Press. ☂ 8 **Facilities** Garden Parking

HAMPTON BISHOP
Map 10 SO53

The Bunch of Carrots ☂

HR1 4JR ☎ 01432 870237 📄 01432 870237
e-mail: bunchofcarrots@buccaneer.co.uk
dir: From Hereford take A4103, A438, then B4224

The name has nothing to do with crunchy orange vegetables - it comes from a rock formation in the River Wye, which runs alongside this friendly pub. Inside, expect real fires, old beams and flagstones. There is an extensive menu plus a daily specials board, a carvery, salad buffet, and simple bar snacks. Real ale aficionados should certainly sample the local organic beer, or enjoy a pint of Wye Valley Bitter or Black Bull, plus Westons real cider is available.

Open all wk **Bar Meals** L served Mon-Fri 12-2.30, Sat-Sun all day D served Mon-Fri 5.30-9, Sat-Sun all day **Restaurant** L served Mon-Fri 12-2.30, Sat-Sun all day booking required D served Mon-Fri 5.30-9, Sat-Sun all day booking required ⊕ FREE HOUSE ◀ Directors, Wye Valley Bitter, Black Bull Bitter, Organic Bitter ♂ Westons Stowford Press. ☂ 11 **Facilities** Children's menu Play area Dogs allowed Garden Parking

HEREFORD
Map 10 SO53

The Crown & Anchor ☂

Cotts Ln, Lugwardine HR1 4AB
☎ 01432 851303 📄 01432 851637
dir: 2m from Hereford on A438. Left into Lugwardine down Cotts Lane

Old Herefordshire-style black-and-white pub with quarry tile floors and a large log fire, just up from the bridge over the River Lugg. Among the many interesting specials you might find fillets of Torbay sole with mussels and white wine; mushrooms in filo pastry with wild mushroom and marsala sauce; seafood tagliolini; supreme of chicken stuffed with wild mushrooms and chestnuts with cranberry and white wine sauce; or Brother Geoffrey's pork sausages with juniper and red wine sauce and mash. A long lunchtime sandwich list is available.

Open all wk Closed: 25 Dec ⊕ ENTERPRISE INNS ◀ Worthington Bitter, Timothy Taylor Landlord, Marstons Pedigree, Butcombe Ale, Ruddells. ☂ 8 **Facilities** Dogs allowed Garden Parking

KIMBOLTON
Map 10 SO56

PICK OF THE PUBS

Stockton Cross Inn ☂

HR6 0HD ☎ 01568 612509
e-mail: info@stocktoncrossinn.co.uk
dir: On A4112, 0.5m off A49, between Leominster & Ludlow

A drovers' inn dating from the 16th century, the Stockton Cross Inn stands beside a crossroads where witches, rounded up from the surrounding villages such as Ludlow, were allegedly hanged. This grisly past is at odds with the peace and beauty of the setting, which includes a pretty country garden with umbrellas and trees for shade. The building itself is regularly photographed by tourists and featured on calendars and chocolate boxes. Landlord Mike Bentley tends a range of ales which include Wye Valley Butty Bach and HPA, Hobson's Town Crier and Tetleys Smooth Flow. Children are welcome and enjoy their own menu. A popular traditional Sunday roast and an appealing list of pub favourites (gammon steak with egg, plum tomato, field mushroom and home-made chips, for example) keep hungry customers coming – all meals are prepared on the premises using organic produce wherever possible.

Closed: Sun & Mon eve **Bar Meals** L served Tue-Sun 12-2 D served Tue-Sun 7-9 Av main course £10 **Restaurant** L served Tue-Sun 12-2 D served Tue-Sun 7-9 ⊕ FREE HOUSE ◀ Wye Valley Butty Bach & HPA, Hobson's Town Crier, Flowers Best Bitter, Murphys, Tetley's Smooth Flow, guest ales. ☂ 6 **Facilities** Children's menu Garden Parking

KINGTON   Map 9 SO25

PICK OF THE PUBS

The Stagg Inn and Restaurant ◉◉ ☂

Titley HR5 3RL ☎ 01544 230221 📠 **01544 231390**
e-mail: reservations@thestagg.co.uk
dir: Between Kington & Presteigne on B4355

Rather ordinary looking from the outside and comfortably rustic within, The Stagg stands amid unspoilt Welsh border country. Farmhouse tables and crackling log fires make for a relaxed atmosphere in the homely bar, where local farmers gather for pints of Hobson's and Ralph's Radnorshire cider, and the rambling dining rooms beyond. Local boy and Roux-trained chef Steve Reynolds has a passion for local produce and delves deep into treasure trove of quality raw ingredients on his doorstep and uses herbs, vegetables and soft fruit from the pub garden. His assured modern approach to cooking allows key flavours to shine through in such robust, earthy dishes as a starter of pigeon breast with herb risotto and thyme jus, and main dishes like braised belly of home-reared middle white pork with haricot beans, or saddle of venison with beetroot dauphinoise. Lunch and bar snacks take in a superb three-cheese ploughman's (from the fabulous 20-strong cheeseboard), and home-made faggots with mash and onion gravy.

Closed: Sun eve & Mon **Bar Meals** L served Tue-Sat 12-2 D served Tue-Thu 6.30-9 Av main course £9.90 **Restaurant** L served Tue-Sun 12-2 booking required D served Tue-Sat 6.30-9 booking required ⊕ FREE HOUSE 🍺 Hobsons-Town Crier, Old Henry & Best Bitter, Brains Rev James, Timothy Taylor Landlord, Ludlow Best Ö Dunkertons Black Fox, Ralph's Welsh Cider. ☗ 10 **Facilities** Children's menu Dogs allowed Garden Parking

LEDBURY   Map 10 SO73

The Farmers Arms ☂

Horse Rd, Wellington Heath HR8 1LS ☎ 01531 632010
dir: Through Ledbury, pass rail station, right into Wellington Heath, 1st right for pub

Handy for the breathtaking high ground of the Malvern Hills and the seductive charms of Ross and the Wye Valley, this refurbished country inn retains lots of character and charm. In addition to the changes inside there is an outdoor decked seating area with a large heated canopy perfect for alfresco eating. The bar menu includes lots of pub favourites - ploughman's, local sausages of the week, fish and chips, steak and ale pudding plus a choice of grills.

Open all wk ⊕ ENTERPRISE INNS 🍺 guest ales. ☗ 8 **Facilities** Play area Dogs allowed Garden Parking

The Talbot ☂

14 New St HR8 2DX ☎ 01531 632963 📠 **01531 633796**
e-mail: talbot.ledbury@wadworth.co.uk
dir: Follow Ledbury signs, turn into Bye St, 2nd left into Woodley Rd, over bridge to junct, left into New St. Pub on right

It's easy to step back in time with a visit to this late 16th-century black-and-white coaching inn. Dating from 1596, the oak-panelled dining room (appropriately called Panels), with fine carved overmantle, still displays musket-shot holes after a skirmish between Roundheads and Cavaliers. Choose from a good selection of local ales, and menus with starters of whitebait or duck and orange pâté, and main dishes of local faggots and onion gravy, or pan-fried lambs' liver.

Open all wk ⊕ WADWORTH 🍺 Wadworth 6X & Henrys Original IPA, Wye Valley Butty Bach, Wadworth guest ales, Henry's Smooth. ☗ 15 **Facilities** Parking

The Trumpet Inn ☂

Trumpet HR8 2RA ☎ 01531 670277
dir: 4m from Ledbury, at junct of A438 & A417

This traditional black and white free house dates back to the late 14th century. The former coaching inn and post house takes its name from the days when mail coaches blew their horns on approaching the crossroads. The cosy bars feature a wealth of exposed beams, with open fireplaces and a separate dining area. Light sandwich lunches and salad platters complement main dishes like salmon fishcakes; kleftiko; or vegetable stroganoff.

Open all wk ⊕ FREE HOUSE 🍺 Wadworth 6X, Henrys IPA, Old Father Time. ☗ 6 **Facilities** Dogs allowed Garden Parking

LEOMINSTER   Map 10 SO45

The Grape Vaults ☂

Broad St HR4 8BS ☎ 01568 611404
e-mail: jusaxon@tiscali.co.uk
dir: Telephone for directions

An unspoilt pub with a small, homely bar complete with real fire - in fact it's so authentic that it's Grade II listed, even down to the fixed seating. Real ale is a popular feature, and includes microbrewery products. The good food includes turkey and ham pie, bubble and squeak with bacon and egg, steak and ale pie, and various fresh fish dishes using cod, plaice, salmon and whitebait. No music, gaming machines, or alcopops!

Open all day all wk 11-11 **Bar Meals** L served all wk 12-2 D served Mon-Sat 5.30-9 ⊕ PUNCH TAVERNS 🍺 Banks Bitter, Pedigree, Original, guest ales. ☗ 6 **Facilities** Dogs allowed **Notes** ⊜

The Royal Oak Hotel

South St HR6 8JA ☎ 01568 612610 📠 **01568 612710**
e-mail: reservations@theroyaloakhotel.net
dir: Town centre, near A44/A49 junct

Coaching inn dating from around 1733, with log fires, antiques and a minstrels' gallery in the original ballroom. The pub was once part of a now blocked-off tunnel system that linked the Leominster Priory with other buildings in the town. Good choice of wines by the glass and major ales, and a hearty menu offering traditional British food with a modern twist.

Open all wk ⊕ FREE HOUSE 🍺 Shepherd Neame Spitfire, Wye Valley Butty Bach. **Facilities** Dogs allowed Garden Parking

LITTLE COWARNE   Map 10 SO65

The Three Horseshoes Inn ☂

HR7 4RQ ☎ 01885 400276 📠 **01885 400276**
e-mail: janetwhittall@threehorseshoes.co.uk
dir: Off A456 (Hereford/Bromyard). At Stokes Cross follow Little Cowarne/Pencombe signs

They no longer shoe horses at the blacksmith next door, but this old ale house's long drinking pedigree - 200 years and counting - looks secure. The hop-bedecked bar serves real ales and cider from nearby orchards, while meals made extensively from fresh local ingredients can be enjoyed in the restaurant or garden room. Prawn and haddock smokies to start, fillet of pork with crispy belly to follow, and a home-made ice cream are typical choices.

Open 11-3 6.30-mdnt (Sun noon-4 7-mdnt) Closed: 25-26 Dec, 1 Jan & Sun eve Winter, Sun eve in Winter **Bar Meals** food served all day **Restaurant** food served all day ⊕ FREE HOUSE 🍺 Greene King Old Speckled Hen, Wye Valley Bitter, Ruddles Best Ö Stowford Press. ☗ 12 **Facilities** Family room Garden Parking

MADLEY   Map 9 SO43

The Comet Inn ☂

Stoney St HR2 9NJ ☎ 01981 250600
e-mail: thecometinn-madley@hotmail.co.uk
dir: 6m from Hereford on B4352

Originally three cottages, this black and white 19th-century inn occupies a prominent corner position and is set in two and a half acres. Inside it retains many original features and a roaring open fire. Expect simple, hearty pub food ranging from baguettes and jacket potatoes to comforting options such as steak and ale pie, shank of lamb, grilled gammon, chicken curry, cod in crispy batter, mushroom stroganoff, and a variety of steaks.

Open all wk 12-3 6-11 (Fri-Sun all day) **Bar Meals** Av main course £4.95 food served all day **Restaurant** Fixed menu price fr £9.95 food served all day ⊕ FREE HOUSE 🍺 Wye Valley Bitter Ö Stowford Press. ☗ 6 **Facilities** Children's menu Play area Garden Parking

MICHAELCHURCH ESCLEY Map 9 SO33

The Bridge Inn ☕

HR2 0JW ☎ **01981 510646** 📠 **01981 510646**
e-mail: nickmaddy@aol.com
dir: From Hereford A465 towards Abergavenny, then
B4348 towards Peterchurch. Left at Vowchurch to village

By Escley Brook, at the foot of the Black Mountains and
close to Offa's Dyke, there are 14th-century parts to this
oak-beamed family pub: the dining room overlooks the
garden, abundant with rose and begonias, and the river -
an ideal area for walkers and nature lovers. On rainy days
guests may prefer the games room. Speciality dishes
include steak and kidney with crispy dumplings.

Open all wk ⊕ FREE HOUSE ◀ Wye Valley ales, John
Smiths, Bridge Bitter. ☕ 20 **Facilities** Play area Dogs
allowed Garden Parking

MUCH MARCLE Map 10 SO63

The Slip Tavern ☕

Watery Ln HR8 2NG
☎ **01531 660246** 📠 **01531 660700**
e-mail: thesliptavern@aol.com
dir: Follow signs off A449 at Much Marcle junction

Curiously named after a 1575 landslip which buried the
local church, this country pub is delightfully surrounded
by cider apple orchards. An attractive conservatory
overlooks the award-winning garden, where summer
dining is popular, and there's also a cosy bar. It's next to
Westons Cider Mill, and cider is a favourite in the bar.

Open all wk Closed: Mon lunch ⊕ FREE HOUSE ◀ John
Smiths, Tetleys Smooth Flow, guest ales. ☕ 8
Facilities Play area Garden Parking

ORLETON Map 9 SO46

The Boot Inn

SY8 4HN ☎ **01568 780228** 📠 **01568 780228**
e-mail: traceytheboot65@live.co.uk
web: www.thebootinnorleton.co.uk
dir: Follow A49 S from Ludlow (approx 7m) to B4362
(Woofferton), 1.5m off B4362 turn left. Inn in village
centre

A black and white half timbered village inn, The Boot
dates from the 16th century, and in winter a blazing fire
in the inglenook warms the bar. You will be welcomed
with excellent service, a good quality English menu with
locally sourced produce and a fine range of cask ales. The
wine list has been chosen to compliment the menu and to
suit all pockets. Recent change of ownership.

Open all wk 12-3 5-11 (Sat-Sun noon-11) **Bar Meals** L
served all wk 12-3 D served all wk 6-9 Av main course
£10 **Restaurant** L served all wk 12-3 D served all wk
6-9 ⊕ VILLAGE GREEN INNS LTD ◀ Hobsons Best, Local
Real Ales, Woods, Wye Valley ♂ Stowford Press.
Facilities Children's menu Play area Dogs allowed
Garden Parking

PEMBRIDGE Map 9 SO35

New Inn

Market Square HR6 9DZ
☎ 01544 388427 📠 01544 388427
dir: From M5 junct 7 take A44 W through Leominster
towards Llandrindod Wells

Worn flagstone floors and open fires characterise this
unspoilt black and white timbered free house. Formerly a
courthouse and jail, the building dates from the early
14th century. In summer, customers spill out into the
pub's outdoor seating area in the Old Market Square. It
attracts locals and summer tourists alike with dishes of
lamb and vegetable hotpot; cream cheese and spinach
lasagne; and trout fillets in lemon butter.

Open all wk ⊕ FREE HOUSE ◀ Fuller's London Pride,
Three Tuns from Bishops Castle, Black Sheep Best,
Timothy Taylor, Ludow Brewery, Hobsons.
Facilities Family room Garden Parking

ROSS-ON-WYE Map 10 SO52

The Moody Cow

Upton Bishop HR9 7TT ☎ 01989 780470
e-mail: info@themoodycow.biz
dir: A449 take the Newent turn then carry on for 1m into
Upton Bishop. M50 take Newent exit then left at the
junction. After 1.5m the pub is straight ahead.

The pub's name causes endless speculation – it was
once called the Wellington. But chef/proprietor Jonathan
Rix certainly knows his onions, having previously worked
in several establishments recognised for their culinary
prowess. He serves local ales such as Wye Valley and
Spinning Dog, as well as Weston's ciders, and sources
much of his produce from within 20 miles. Menus cover
light lunches, pub classics and dinner options such as
carpaccio of swordfish with avocado salsa; and roast
breast and confit leg of Madgetts farm duck with apricot
and thyme jus. There is a separate vegetarian menu.

Open 11-3.30 6-11 (Sun 6-10.30) Closed: Mon **Bar
Meals** L served Tue-Sun 11.30-2.30 D served Tue-Sat
6.30-10 Av main course £13 **Restaurant** L served Tue-
Sun 11.30-2.30 D served Tue-Sat 6.30-10 booking
required Fixed menu price fr £14 Av 3 course à la carte fr
£24.50 ⊕ ENTERPRISE ◀ Wye Valley Bitter, Butty Bach,
Spitfire ♂ Stowford Press, Westons Organic.
Facilities Children's menu Garden Parking

ST OWENS CROSS Map 10 SO52

PICK OF THE PUBS

The New Inn NEW ☕

See Pick of the Pubs on page 244

SELLACK Map 10 SO52

PICK OF THE PUBS

The Lough Pool Inn at Sellack ⊚⊚ ☕

HR9 6LX ☎ **01989 730236** 📠 **01981 570322**
e-mail: david@loughpool.co.uk
dir: 4m NW from Ross-on-Wye, 2m off A49 (Hereford
road). Follow signs for Sellack

This black and white half-timbered pub takes its name
(pronounced 'luff pool') from the old English or Gaelic
for an enclosed piece of land with water. It is indeed
idyllically situated beside the eponymous pool. Based
on a 16th-century blacksmith's cottage, it has all the
character you'd expect from such a venerable building.
David and Jan Birch are passionate about the superb
produce on their doorstep, a passion shared by their
award-winning chef, who cooks up meals such as
smoked duck breast with beetroot and avocado salad
followed by pan-fried rump of Herefordshire beef with
rocket, garlic mushrooms and hand-cut chips. Bar
meals include Cornish crab linguine; and bacon and
brie ciabatta. For refreshment, real ales are backed by
local ciders, perry, expertly chosen wines and varieties
of pure apple juice from local orchards. Outside, the
peaceful garden leads to lovely walks on the new
Herefordshire Trail to the River Wye.

Open 11.30-3 6-11 Closed: 25 Dec, Mon & Sun eve in
winter ex BH **Bar Meals** L served all wk 12-2 D served
all wk 7-9 **Restaurant** L served all wk 12-2 D served all
wk 7-9 ⊕ FREE HOUSE ◀ Wye Valley, Butcombe Bitter,
Butty Bach, guest ales ♂ Westons Stowford Press,
Dunkertons. ☕ 10 **Facilities** Family room Dogs allowed
Garden Parking

SHOBDON Map 9 SO46

The Bateman Arms ★★★★ INN

HR6 9LX ☎ **01568 708374**
e-mail: diana@batemanarms.co.uk
dir: On B4362 off A4110 NW of Leominster

An 18th-century three-storey coaching inn of striking
appearance, with old cobbled paving lining its street
frontage. The only pub in the village of Shobdon, there's
character inside too; in the bar you can sit beneath
ancient oak beams on 300-year-old wooden settles and
enjoy a light meal, or head for the restaurant and its
menu based on locally-sourced produce. Enjoy gammon
steak, chips and peas or seafood fishcakes with green

continued on page 245

PICK OF THE PUBS

The New Inn NEW ♀

ST OWENS CROSS   Map 10 SO52

HR2 8LQ
☎ **01989 730274** 🖷 **01989 730557**
e-mail: info@newinn.biz
web: www.newinn.biz
dir: *Off A4137 W of Ross-on-Wye*

This delightful, multi-award-winning 16th-century inn has been under the caring eye of Nigel and Tee Maud since February 2006. They have lavished care and attention on every aspect of the place, extending the kitchen, re-designing the garden to offer excellent alfresco dining, and totally refurbishing the bar, lounge and bedrooms. The spacious beer garden overlooks rolling Herefordshire countryside, with views stretching to the Black Mountains in the distance. Family-friendly outdoor games include giant versions of Jenga and Connect Four. Thankfully the interior refurbishments have preserved characterful features such as exposed beams and woodwork, creating a cosy

and traditional backdrop for a drink, a quick snack or a leisurely meal. Among the changing selection of ales you might find Wychwood's Hobgoblin, Marstons Burton Bitter, and Jennings Redbreast. At the helm in the kitchen is award-winning chef Tee, whose cooking is recognised with a plaque from the Hairy Bikers. Her ever-changing menus reveal a keen sense of the seasons and a commitment to sourcing excellent local ingredients. Typical starters such as deep-fried brie with cranberry sauce or creamy garlic mushrooms on toasted baguette might be followed by steak, ale and mushroom pie made with Herefordshire beef; oven-baked chicken breast with Hereford Hop and leek sauce; or shank of local lamb with red wine sauce and champ. Impressive vegetarian dishes could include sweet and sour mixed bean hot pot, while an irresistible list of traditional puddings takes in fruit crumble with granola topping and home-made ice cream; Bakewell tart; and local perry jelly with home-made elderflower ice cream. Ross on Wye is just four miles away, and the surrounding area includes countless other attractions such as Symonds Yat rock, Goodrich Castle and Hereford Cathedral, all of which are within easy reach.

Open all day all week 11-11 **Bar Meals** L served all wk from 12 D served all wk from 12 Av main course £8.75 food served all day **Restaurant** L served all wk from 12 D served all wk from 12 Av 3 course à la carte fr £20 food served all day ⊞ MARSTONS ♀ 8
Facilities Children's menu Play area Dogs allowed Garden Parking

SHOBDON *continued*

salad and new potatoes; desserts are all home made. There is also a games room, large beer garden, and nine comfortable en suite bedrooms.

Open all day all wk noon-11 (Sat 11am-mdnt) **Bar Meals** food served all day **Restaurant** L served all wk 12-2 D served Mon-Sat 7-9 ⊕ FREE HOUSE ◆ Butty Bach, Hobgoblin, Mansfield Bitter. **Facilities** Children's menu Garden Parking **Rooms** 9

SYMONDS YAT (EAST) Map 10 SO51

PICK OF THE PUBS

The Saracens Head Inn ★★★★ INN ♥

See Pick of the Pubs on page 246

TILLINGTON Map 9 SO44

The Bell

HR4 8LE ☎ 01432 760395 ▤ 01432 760580
e-mail: beltill@aol.com
dir: *NE Hereford, on road to Weobley via Burghill*

Run by the same family since 1988, The Bell offers something for everybody, with quiet gardens, a formal dining area and a traditional public bar complete with oak parquet flooring, an open fire and a dart board. The varied menus cover all dining requirements, from bar snacks to more elaborate meals: smoked salmon terrine, followed by roast Madgett's Farm duck breast, or venison, wild boar and pheasant casserole, perhaps.

Open all wk **Bar Meals** L served all wk 12-3 D served Mon-Sat 6-9.30 Av main course £11 **Restaurant** L served all wk 12-3 D served Mon-Sat 6-9.30 Fixed menu price fr £15 Av 3 course à la carte fr £15 ◆ London Pride, Hereford Bitter, other local ales. **Facilities** Play area Dogs allowed Garden Parking

ULLINGSWICK Map 10 SO54

PICK OF THE PUBS

Three Crowns Inn ◉ ♥

HR1 3JQ ☎ 01432 820279 ▤ 08700 515338
e-mail: info@threecrownsinn.com
dir: *From Burley Gate rdbt take A465 toward Bromyard, after 2m left to Ullingswick, left after 0.5m, pub 0.5m on right*

An unspoilt country pub in deepest rural Herefordshire, where food sources are so local that their distance away is measured in fields rather than miles. A hand-written sign offering to buy surplus fruit and veg gives locals a gentle reminder, as they sup their favourite real ale at the bar. Parterres in the garden grow varieties of produce that are not easy, or even possible, to buy commercially. Among them is a pea whose provenance can be traced back to a phial found by Lord Carnarvon in Tutankhamun's tomb. The daily-changing menus are refreshingly brief and uncomplicated; half a dozen options within each course are all priced the same - so eating to a budget is easily accomplished. A typical selection could be fish soup with rouille and croutons, followed by poached knuckle of Shropshire veal, or fish such as grilled Cornish gurnard. Puddings include chocolate truffle torte.

Closed: 25-26 Dec, 1 Jan, Mon ⊕ FREE HOUSE ◆ Hobsons Best, Wye Valley Butty Bach & Dorothy Goodbody's, guest ales. ♥ 9 **Facilities** Dogs allowed Garden Parking

WALFORD Map 10 SO52

PICK OF THE PUBS

The Mill Race ♥

HR9 5QS ☎ 01989 562891
e-mail: enquiries@millrace.info
dir: *From Ross-on-Wye take B4234 to Walford. Pub 3m on right after village hall*

There's a great mix of old and new in this comfortable, contemporary village pub. In winter there's a roaring fire, while in summer the patio doors are flung open into the external dining area, from where Goodrich Castle is visible across the fields. The bar serves local ales, including Roaring Meg, named after a cannon used by the Parliamentarians to regain the castle during the Civil War. The pub has its own 1000-acre farm, rearing free-range cattle, rare-breed pigs, poultry and game. Dishes on the menu change weekly, often to feature cottage pie; beer-battered coley and chips; Madgetts Farm chicken breast with potato rösti, chestnut mushrooms and sage sauce; oxtail faggots with crushed root vegetables and red wine sauce; and

continued on page 247

PICK OF THE PUBS

The Saracens Head Inn ★★★★ INN 🍷

SYMONDS YAT (EAST) Map 10 SO51

HR9 6JL
☎ 01600 890435 📠 01600 890034
e-mail:
contact@saracensheadinn.co.uk
web: www.saracensheadinn.co.uk
dir: *From Ross-on-Wye take A40 to Monmouth. In 4m take Symonds Yat East turn. 1st right before bridge. Right in 0.5m. Right in 1m*

Once a cider mill, the Saracens Head lies on the east bank of the River Wye where it flows into a steep wooded gorge. This is the yat, the local name for a gate or pass, while Robert Symonds was a Sheriff of Herefordshire in the 17th century. The inn's own ferry across the river to Symonds Yat West is hand operated, just as it has been for the past 200 years. You can eat in the lounge, dining room, flag-floored bar, or on one of the two sunny riverside terraces. Regularly changing menus and daily specials boards offer both traditional – moules marinière, for example - and modern, such as gnocchi in sun-dried tomato and pesto cream; or chicken and wild mushroom terrine with apple jelly and port reduction. Main courses might be rump of rump of Welsh Mountain lamb with dauphinoise potatoes; autumnal seafood casserole, rouille crouton, aioli and crusty bread; roasted butternut squash, goats' cheese and pine nut risotto cake; breast of local pheasant with game sausage black pudding and smoked bacon potato cake. The inn is situated in an Area of Outstanding Natural Beauty on the edge of the Royal Forest of Dean, so a stay in one of the ten en suite bedrooms is a must for exploring the unspoiled local countryside. Activities available nearby include walking, cycling, mountain biking, canoeing, kayaking, climbing, abseiling, potholing and, free to residents, fishing.

Open 11-11 Closed: 25 Dec **Bar Meals** L served all wk 12-2.30 D served all wk 6.30-9 Av main course £11 **Restaurant** L served all wk 12-2.30 D served all wk 6.30-9 Fixed menu price fr £28 Av 3 course à la carte fr £25 ⊕ FREE HOUSE ◀ Theakstons Old Peculier, Old Speckled Hen, Wye Valley Hereford Pale Ale, Wye Valley Butty Bach, Buttcombe Bitter Ö Westons Organic, Stowford Press, Lyne Down's Roaring Meg. 🍷 7 **Facilities** Children's menu Dogs allowed Garden Parking **Rooms** 10

WALFORD *continued*

mushroom Stroganoff. Afterwards, should, inexplicably, neither apple and cinnamon crumble nor sticky toffee pudding appeal, there's a good farmhouse cheese selection. The wine list includes a Welsh Seyval Blanc.

Open all wk 11-3 5-11 (Sat-Sun all day) **Bar Meals** L served Mon-Fri 12-2, Sat-Sun 12-2.30 booking required D served Mon-Sat 6-9.30, Sun 6-9 booking required Av main course £8 **Restaurant** L served Mon-Fri 12-2, Sat-Sun 12-2.30 booking required D served Mon-Sat 6-9.30, Sun 6-9 booking required Fixed menu price fr £8 Av 3 course à la carte fr £23 ⊕ FREE HOUSE ◀ Wye Valley Bitter, Guest Ales, Guinness ᵇ Westons, Stowford Press, Roaring Meg. ♀ 9 **Facilities** Children's menu Garden Parking

See advert on page 245

WALTERSTONE
Map 9 SO32

Carpenters Arms ♀

HR2 0DX ☎ 01873 890353
dir: *Off A465 between Hereford & Abergavenny at Pandy*

There's plenty of character in this 300-year-old free house located on the edge of the Black Mountains where the owner, Mrs Watkins, was born. Here you'll find beams, antique settles and a leaded range with open fires that burn all winter. Popular food options include beef and Guinness pie; beef lasagne; and thick lamb cutlets. Ask about the vegetarian selection, and large choice of home-made desserts.

Open all day all wk noon-11pm Closed: 25 Dec **Bar Meals** food served all day ⊕ FREE HOUSE ◀ Wadworth 6X, Breconshire Golden Valley & Rambler's Ruin. ♀ 6 **Facilities** Play area Family room Garden Parking **Notes** ☺

WELLINGTON
Map 10 SO44

The Wellington ♀

HR4 8AT ☎ 01432 830367
e-mail: thewellington@hotmail.com
dir: *Off A49 into village centre. Pub 0.25m on left*

Owners Ross and Philippa Williams came from London to create one of Herefordshire's finest gastro-pubs. They've done well, with Ross quickly becoming an award-winning champion of food prepared from local, seasonal produce. Start with Parma ham and porcini mushroom lasagne, followed by slow-roasted belly and pan-fried tenderloin of Welsh white pork with cider sauce and mustard mash, and then lemon semifreddo with home-made orange shortbread. Sunday lunch could include roast leg of local venison.

Open 12-3 6-11 Closed: Mon L, Sun eve in winter **Bar Meals** L served Tue-Sun 12-2 D served all wk 7-9 Av main course £8.50 **Restaurant** L served Tue-Sun 12-2 D served all wk 7-9 Av 3 course à la carte fr £25 ⊕ FREE HOUSE ◀ Hobsons, Wye Valley Butty Bach, Wye Valley HPA, Guest ales ᵇ Westons Scrumpy. ♀ 8 **Facilities** Children's menu Play area Dogs allowed Garden Parking

---

WEOBLEY
Map 9 SO45

PICK OF THE PUBS

The Salutation Inn ♀

Market Pitch HR4 8SJ
☎ 01544 318443 ▤ 01544 318405
dir: *A44, then A4112, 8m from Leominster*

A black and white timber-framed pub dating back more than 500 years and situated in a corner of the country renowned for its hops, cattle and apple orchards. The inn, sympathetically converted from an old ale house and adjoining cottage, is the perfect base for exploring the lovely Welsh Marches and enjoying a host of leisure activities, including fishing, horse riding, golf, walking, and clay shooting. The book capital of Hay-on-Wye and the cathedral city of Hereford are close by. The inn's restaurant offers a range of award-winning dishes created with the use of locally sourced ingredients. Chef's specials are also served in the traditional lounge bar with its welcoming atmosphere and cosy inglenook fireplace. Starters include confit of duck and pan-seared Cornish scallops, while main courses range from roast rump of Welsh lamb, and oven-baked fillet of salmon, to whole roast breast of chicken, and medley of sea bass and oysters.

Open all day all wk noon-11 (Sun noon-10.30) **Bar Meals** L served all wk 12-3 D served all wk 6-9 **Restaurant** L served Sun 12-3 ⊕ ENTERPRISE INNS ◀ Betty Stogs, Courage Directors Best ᵇ Stowford Press. ♀ 6 **Facilities** Dogs allowed Garden Parking

---

WHITNEY-ON-WYE
Map 9 SO24

PICK OF THE PUBS

Rhydspence Inn ★★★★ INN

HR3 6EU ☎ 01497 831262 ▤ 01497 831751
e-mail: info@rhydspence-inn.co.uk
dir: *N side of A438, 1m W of Whitney-on-Wye*

This charming inn dates from 1380 and was extended in the 17th and 20th centuries. It was most likely built to provide comfort for travellers and pilgrims from Abbey Cwmhir to Hereford Cathedral, but it later became a watering hole for drovers taking cattle, sheep and geese to market in London. These days the pub is rather more elegant, with a cosy bar and spacious dining room giving way to stunning views over the Wye Valley. Food options range from deep-fried cod in lemon batter and French fries or braised shank of lamb from the bar bites and brasserie selection, to main menu dishes such as peppered venison with fricassee of mushrooms and port and redcurrant reduction or pan-fried sea bass with tempura courgettes and lemon aïoli. There is also a good choice of steaks from the grill. The friendly ghost of a former landlady is said to frequent the inn, though only when young children are staying.

Open all wk 11-2.30 7-11 **Bar Meals** L served all wk 11-2 D served all wk 7-9 Av main course £9 **Restaurant** L served all wk 11-2 booking required D served all wk 7-9 booking required Av 3 course à la carte fr £25 ⊕ FREE HOUSE ◀ Robinsons Best, Interbrew Bass. **Facilities** Children's menu Family room Garden Parking **Rooms** 7

WOOLHOPE
Map 10 SO63

The Crown Inn ♀

HR1 4QP ☎ 01432 860468 ▤ 01432 860770
e-mail: menu@crowninnwoolhope.co.uk
dir: *B4224 to Mordiford, left after Moon Inn. Pub in village centre*

Every cider and perry producer in Herefordshire is represented at this real, old fashioned free house, and over 100 types of real ale are served over the course of the year. Good quality local ingredients – wet and dry – are to the fore, with lunchtime baguettes and pub favourites such as chilli, Hereford beef burger, or cider braised ham with chunky chips. There is also an outdoor bar with a heated smoking area and beautiful views.

Open all wk 12-2.30 6.30-11 (Sat-Sun all day) **Bar Meals** L served all wk 12-2 D served all wk 6.30-9 Av main course £10 **Restaurant** L served all wk 12-2 D served all wk 6.30-9 Fixed menu price fr £18 Av 3 course à la carte fr £18 ⊕ FREE HOUSE ◀ Wye Valley Best, Black Sheep, guest ales ᵇ Westons Stowford Press. ♀ 6 **Facilities** Children's menu Garden Parking

HERTFORDSHIRE

ALDBURY Map 6 SP91

The Greyhound Inn ¶

19 Stocks Rd HP23 5RT
☎ 01442 851228 📠 01442 851495
e-mail: greyhound@aldbury.wanadoo.co.uk
dir: Telephone for directions

Nestled in picturesque Aldbury close to the National Trust's renowned Ashridge Estate, this pub is ideal for walks. It faces the village duck pond and ancient stocks. Log fires warm the bar in winter, whilst summer brings the option of an alfresco lunch. Food is available all day, from lunchtime potted ham hock with piccalilli and toast through to evening meals such as twice baked cheese soufflé followed by roast cinnamon-coated pork fillet with black pudding and apple mash. There is an afternoon menu plus cakes and afternoon tea.

Open all day all wk 11.30-11 (Sun noon-10.30) Closed: 25 Dec **Bar Meals** Av main course £9.50 food served all day **Restaurant** Av 3 course à la carte fr £20 food served all day ⊕ HALL & WOODHOUSE ◀ Badger Best, Tanglefoot, King & Barnes Sussex. ¶ 10 **Facilities** Family room Dogs allowed Garden Parking

PICK OF THE PUBS

The Valiant Trooper ¶

Trooper Rd HP23 5RW
☎ 01442 851203 📠 01442 851071
e-mail: info@thevalianttrooper.co.uk
dir: A41 at Tring junct, follow rail station signs 0.5m, at village green turn right, 200yds on left

Now run by husband and wife team Beej and Beth Parmar, this country pub and restaurant is set in a pretty village at the foot of the Chiltern Hills. The pub's deeds date back to 1752, when it was The Royal Oak, though it was originally a group of 17th-century cottages. It became The Trooper Alehouse in 1803, allegedly because the Duke of Wellington discussed tactics here with his troops. The large beer garden now has a wooden adventure trail, and children are handsomely catered for with their own healthy home-cooked menu. Dogs are also welcome in the bar or garden. The emphasis is on quality local produce in a menu of British classics. Snacks take in tempting sandwiches, cured meat or seafood platters, and savouries such as Welsh rarebit on toast. Typical main courses are pie of the day, five-bean chilli; and marinated chicken breast with white wine, garlic and spinach creamed tagliatelle.

Open all day all wk 11.30am-11pm (Sun noon-10.30) **Bar Meals** Av main course £9.50 food served all day **Restaurant** Fixed menu price fr £13.50 Av 3 course à la carte fr £19 food served all day ⊕ FREE HOUSE ◀ Fuller's London Pride, Tring Jack O'Legs, 2 Guest ales. ¶ 8 **Facilities** Children's menu Play area Family room Dogs allowed Garden Parking

ARDELEY Map 12 TL32

The Rabbit's Foot

SG2 7AH ☎ 01438 861350 📠 01438 861350
e-mail: info@therabbitsfoot.co.uk
dir: Follow B1037 6m from Stevenage, 2m from Walkern

Formerly known as The Jolly Waggoner, this 500-year-old village pub has recently changed hands. Three real ales are served along with guest beers, and fresh local ingredients are used in the seasonal menus — venison stew with caramelised shallots. Families are welcome and the children's menu has a simple, freshly prepared theme. The pub is also dog friendly, so you can enjoy a meal in the bar with your best friend! There's a large garden to enjoy in summer and open fires in winter.

Open 12-3 6-11 Closed: Mon, Tue **Bar Meals** L served Wed-Sun 12-3 D served Wed-Sat 6-9 **Restaurant** L served Wed-Sun 12-3 booking required D served Wed-Sat 6-9 booking required ⊕ ADMIRAL ◀ Greene King IPA, 2 Guest ales. **Facilities** Children's menu Dogs allowed Garden Parking

ASHWELL Map 12 TL23

The Three Tuns ¶

High St SG7 5NL ☎ 01462 742107 📠 01462 743662
e-mail: claire@tuns.co.uk
dir: Telephone for directions

The building, dating from 1806, replaces an earlier one first recorded as a public house in 1700. Original features survive in the two bars and large dining room, probably once a smokehouse, judging by the rows of old hanging hooks. Traditional pub food and an à la carte menu are on offer. The menu might offer steak and kidney pie; Spanish pork casserole and a selection of steaks with interesting sauces.

Open all day all wk 11am-11.30pm (Fri-Sat 11am-12.30am) **Bar Meals** L served Mon-Fri 12-2.30, Sat-Sun all day booking required D served Mon-Fri 6.30-9.30, Sat-Sun all day booking required Av main course £18 **Restaurant** L served Mon-Fri 12-2.30, Sat-Sun all day booking required D served Mon-Fri 6.30-9.30, Sat-Sun all day booking required Av 3 course à la carte fr £20 ⊕ GREENE KING ◀ Greene King IPA, Abbot, Guest. ¶ 12 **Facilities** Children's menu Play area Family room Dogs allowed Garden Parking

BARLEY Map 12 TL43

The Fox & Hounds ¶

High St SG8 8HU ☎ 01763 848459 📠 01763 849080
e-mail: info@foxandhoundsbarley.co.uk
dir: A505 onto B1368 at Flint Cross, pub 4m

Set in a pretty village, this former 17th-century hunting lodge is notable for its pub sign which extends across the lane. It has real fires, a warm welcome and an attractive garden. A typical menu includes wild mushroom risotto, beef burger with chunky-cut chips, Irish stew, and beer-battered fish and chips. Opening in 2009, the Saffron Deli and Farm Shop.

Open 10-3 6-late (Sat 10am-late, Sun 10-6) Closed: Mon **Bar Meals** L served Tue-Fri 12-3, Sat 12-late, Sun 12-5.30 booking required D served Tue-Sun 6-10 booking required Av main course £8.95 food served all day **Restaurant** L served Tue-Fri 12-3, Sat 12-4, Sun 12-5 booking required D served Tue-Sun 6-10 booking required Av 3 course à la carte fr £20 food served all day ⊕ SAFFRON LEISURE ◀ Adnams Best, Flowers IPA, Woodforde's Wherry. ¶ 12 **Facilities** Children's menu Play area Garden Parking

BUNTINGFORD Map 12 TL32

The Sword Inn Hand ★★★★ INN ¶

Westmill SG9 9LQ ☎ 01763 271356
e-mail: welcome@theswordinnhand.co.uk
dir: Off A10 1.5m S of Buntingford

Midway between London and Cambridge in the lovely award-winning village of Westmill, and welcoming travellers since the 14th century - you can't miss the oak beams, flag floor and open fireplace. It styles itself a 'real English', family-run pub offering a large selection of snacks, specials, beers and wines. Fresh produce is delivered daily to create herb-crushed rack of lamb, sea bass fillet with stir-fry vegetables, escalope of veal with melted brie or Chef's cod and chips. There are four ground floor bedrooms available.

Open all wk 12-3 5-11 (Sun Sep-Apr 12-7, May-Aug 12-10) **Bar Meals** L served Mon-Sat 12-2.30, Sun 12-4 D served Mon-Sat 6.30-9.30 **Restaurant** L served Mon-Sat 12-2.30, Sun 12-4 D served Mon-Sat 6.30-9.30 ⊕ FREE HOUSE ◀ Greene King IPA, Young's Bitter, Timothy Taylor Landlord, Guest ales ♻ Aspalls. ¶ 8 **Facilities** Children's menu Play area Dogs allowed Garden Parking **Rooms** 4

COTTERED — Map 12 TL32

The Bull at Cottered ♀

Cottered SG9 9QP ☎ **01763 281243**
e-mail: cordell39@btinternet.com
dir: On A507 in Cottered between Buntingford & Baldock

Low-beamed ceilings, antique furniture, cosy fires and pub games typify this traditional village local. The setting is picturesque, and a well-tended garden offers an alternative dining venue in summer. The menu presents a classy and comprehensive carte of all home-made brasserie-style food, ranging from home-made beef burgers with tempting toppings to a smoked salmon and prawn parcel followed by fillet of chicken cooked in a cream, wine and garlic sauce. There are live music and dinner nights, plus relaxing Sunday evening bar nights with reduced price dishes.

Open all wk 11.30-3 6.30-11 (Sun 12-10.30) **Bar Meals** L served Mon-Sat 12-2, Sun 12-4 D served Mon-Sat 6.30-9.30, Sun 6-9 Av main course £8 **Restaurant** L served Mon-Sat 12-2, Sun 12-4 D served Mon-Sat 6.30-9.30, Sun 6-9 booking required Fixed menu price fr £20 Av 3 course à la carte fr £26 ⊕ GREENE KING ◄ Greene King IPA, Abbot Ale. ♀ 7 **Facilities** Garden Parking

FLAUNDEN — Map 6 TL00

PICK OF THE PUBS

The Bricklayers Arms ♀

See Pick of the Pubs on page 250

HEMEL HEMPSTEAD — Map 6 TL00

PICK OF THE PUBS

Alford Arms ♀

See Pick of the Pubs on page 251

HEXTON — Map 12 TL13

The Raven ♀

SG5 3JB ☎ **01582 881209** 📄 01582 881610
e-mail: jack@ravenathexton.f9.co.uk
dir: 5m W of Hitchin. 5m N of Luton, just outside Barton-le-Clay

This neat 1920s pub is named after Ravensburgh Castle in the neighbouring hills. It has comfortable bars and a large garden with a terrace and play area. Snacks include ploughman's and salad platters, plus tortilla wraps, filled baguettes and jacket potatoes. The main menu offers lots of steak options, and dishes like smoky American chicken, whole rack of barbecue ribs, Thai red vegetable curry and an all-day breakfast.

Open all wk **Bar Meals** L served 12-2.15 (Fri-Sun all day) D served 6-9 (Fri-Sun all day) Av main course £9 **Restaurant** L served 12-2.15 (Fri-Sun all day) D served 6-9 (Fri-Sun all day) Av 3 course à la carte fr £15 ⊕ ENTERPRISE INNS ◄ Greene King, Old Speckled Hen, Fuller's London Pride, Greene King IPA. ♀ 24 **Facilities** Children's menu Play area Garden Parking

HINXWORTH — Map 12 TL24

Three Horseshoes

High St SG7 5HQ ☎ **01462 742280**
dir: E of A1 between Biggleswade & Baldock

Thatched 18th-century country pub with a dining extension into the garden. Parts of the building date back 500 years, and the walls are adorned with pictures and photos of the village's history. Samples from a typical menu include chicken of the wood, lamb cutlets with champ, rainbow trout with almonds, sea bass provençale, steak and Guinness pie, bacon and cheese pasta bake, and roasted Tuscan red peppers.

Open all wk ⊕ GREENE KING ◄ Greene King IPA, Abbot Ale, guest ales. **Facilities** Garden Parking

HITCHIN — Map 12 TL12

The Greyhound ★★★ INN ♀

London Rd, St Ippolyts SG4 7NL ☎ **01462 440989**
e-mail: greyhound@freenet.co.uk
web: www.thegreyhoundpubhotel.co.uk
dir: 1.5m S of Hitchin on B656

There has been a pub on the site for 300 years although the current building dates from 1900. The Greyhound was rescued from dereliction by the present owner who previously worked for the London Fire Brigade. It is now a popular, family-run hostelry surrounded by pleasant countryside and open farmland, yet handy for the M1 and Luton Airport. The shotguns over the bars are said to have been owned by notorious poacher twins who used each other as an alibi. The food is unpretentious, generous and competitively priced. There are five cheerfully coloured en suite bedrooms available.

Open all wk 7am-2.30 5-11 (Sun 7am-8pm) **Bar Meals** L served Mon-Sat 7-2, Sun 7am-8pm D served Mon-Sat 5-9, Sun 7am-8pm Av main course £9 **Restaurant** L served Mon-Sat 7-2, Sun 7am-8pm D served Mon-Sat 5-9, Sun 7am-8pm Av 3 course à la carte fr £18.75 ⊕ FREE HOUSE ◄ Adnams, guest. ♀ 8 **Facilities** Children's menu Dogs allowed Parking **Rooms** 5

HUNSDON — Map 6 TL41

PICK OF THE PUBS

The Fox and Hounds ♀

2 High St SG12 8NH
☎ **01279 843999** 📄 01279 841092
e-mail: info@foxandhounds-hunsdon.co.uk
web: www.foxandhounds-hunsdon.co.uk
dir: From A414 between Ware & Harlow take B180 in Stanstead Abbotts N to Hunsdon

Nestled in a sleepy village in the heart of the Hertfordshire countryside, this pub has a warm, welcoming atmosphere and a large pretty garden, with a heated covered terrace. The bar is stocked with a fine array of locally brewed real ales, and meals can be taken in the bar and the lounge, and in the more formal dining room with its chandelier and period furniture on Friday evenings and weekends. Expect serious, inspired cooking that combines classics with modern touches. Lunch could begin with mussels, cider, leeks and cream; or sautéed squid, chorizo and butter beans, followed by roast skate wing, lentils and salsa verde; or perhaps calves' liver persillade and duck fat potato cake. For dinner, perhaps try smoked eel, crispy Parma ham and potato pancake; or rabbit rillettes, pickles and toast, followed by Black Angus côte de boeuf, fat chips and sauce bearnaise; or fillet of wild line caught sea bass with purple sprouting broccoli and anchovy and chilli dressing. Roast black figs, honey and mascarpone is an elegant way to round matters off.

Open noon-4 6-11 Closed: Sun, Mon eve **Bar Meals** L served Tue-Sun 12-3 D served Tue-Sat 6.30-9.30 Av main course £15 **Restaurant** L served Sun 12-3 booking required D served Fri-Sat 7-9.30 booking required Fixed menu price fr £12.50 Av 3 course à la carte fr £26 ⊕ FREE HOUSE ◄ Adnams Bitter, Adnams Broadside, Guinness ♂ Aspall. ♀ 10 **Facilities** Children's menu Play area Dogs allowed Garden Parking

PICK OF THE PUBS

The Bricklayers Arms ♀

FLAUNDEN Map 6 TL00

Hogpits Bottom HP3 0PH
☎ 01442 833322 📠 01442 834841
e-mail: goodfood@bricklayersarms.com
web: www.bricklayersarms.com
dir: *M25 junct 18 onto A404 (Amersham road). Right at Chenies for Flaunden*

In 1722, this attractive pub and restaurant was an ordinary pair of brick and flint cottages, one belonging to a butcher, the other to a blacksmith. In 1832 Benskin's brewery converted one of them into an alehouse, which it remained until the 1960s, when it was joined by its neighbour. A more recent, sympathetic conversion of the outbuilding and barn resulted in today's popular restaurant. Tucked away in deepest Hertfordshire, it has featured in many fictional film and TV programmes, and is a favourite with locals, walkers, horse-riders and, well, just about everyone. One reason for its success is an ivy-covered façade that gives way to an immaculate interior, complete with low beams, exposed brickwork, candlelight and open fires. Another is a happy marriage between traditional English and French fusion cooking. The Gallic influence comes from acclaimed head chef, Claude Paillet, and his team who use fresh organic produce from local suppliers to create seasonal lunch and dinner menus, plus daily specials. Among many choices of starter are mushroom feuilleté and creamy brandy sauce; or poached eggs on garlic croutons with a red wine reduction, smoked bacon, onions and mushrooms. To follow might come quail stuffed with mushrooms and a balsamic sauce; fillet of Scotch beef with a choice of freshly prepared sauces; or pan-fried sea bass with smoked paprika and scallop cream sauce. But don't stop there, as the Bricklayers is also held in high esteem for its pudding menu, on which you're likely to find crêpe filled with Cointreau-flavoured mascarpone and citrus fruits; and lemon tart with pannacotta and raspberry ice cream. Choose one of the 120 wines from all corners of the world and, in the summer, enjoy it with your lunch in the terraced garden.

Open all week 12-11.30 (25 Dec 12-3) **Bar Meals** L served Mon-Sat 12-2.30, Sun 12-3.30 D served Mon-Sat 6.30-9.30, Sun 6.30-8.30 Av main course £13 **Restaurant** L served Mon-Sat 12-2.30, Sun 12-3.30 D served Mon-Sat 6.30-9.30, Sun 6.30-8.30 Av 3 course à la carte fr £28 ⊕ FREE HOUSE ◖ Old Speckled Hen, Greene King IPA, London Pride, Jack O'Legs (Tring Brewery), Rebellion. ♀ 12 **Facilities** Children's menu Dogs allowed Garden Parking

PICK OF THE PUBS

Alford Arms

HEMEL HEMPSTEAD Map 6 TL00

Frithsden HP1 3DD
☎ 01442 864480 **01422 876893**
e-mail: info@alfordarmsfrithsden.co.uk
web: www.alfordarmsfrithsden.co.uk
dir: *From Hemel Hempstead on A4146 take 2nd left at Water End. In 1m left at T-junct, right after 0.75m. Pub 100yds on right*

An attractive Victorian pub, the Alford Arms is set in the hamlet of Frithsden surrounded by National Trust woodland. The pretty garden overlooks the village green, and historic Ashridge Forest is close by - the perfect place to walk off your meal. Cross the threshold and you'll immediately pick up on the warm and lively atmosphere, derived in part from the buzz of conversation and the background jazz music, and partly from the rich colours and eclectic mixture of furniture and pictures in the dining room and bar. The staff are renowned for their good humour and trouble is taken to ensure an enjoyable experience for customers; and, if you can't make it back to the office, free Wi-fi is available. The seasonal menu balances innovative dishes with more traditional fare, and everything is prepared from fresh local produce whenever possible. There's a great choice of light dishes or 'small plates', from rustic breads with roast garlic, balsamic and olive oil, to roast local wood pigeon breast on baked apple tarte Tatin; or potted organic Scottish salmon with sour dough toast. Main meals with a similarly imaginative approach include baked Chiltern lamb and rabbit shepherd's pie; Ashridge Estate venison steak and kidney pudding; and beer battered haddock with hand-cut chips. Puddings have an interesting tweak too, such as warm fig chocolate brownie with crème fraîche ice cream; or vanilla and ginger cheesecake. The British cheese plate is a tempting alternative to finish, with Alford oatcakes, sticky malt loaf and fig jam.

Open 11-11 (Sun 12-10.30) Closed: 26 Dec **Bar Meals** L served Mon-Fri 12-2.30, Sat 12-3, Sun 12-4 D served Mon-Thu 6.30-9.30, Fri-Sat 6.30-10, Sun 7-9.30 **Restaurant** L served Mon-Fri 12-2.30, Sat 12-3, Sun 12-4 D served Mon-Thu 6.30-9.30, Fri-Sat 6.30-10, Sun 7-9.30 SALISBURY PUBS LTD Marstons Pedigree, Brakspear, Flowers Original, Marlow Rebellion IPA. 19 **Facilities** Children's menu Dogs allowed Garden Parking

LITTLE HADHAM — Map 6 TL42

The Nags Head ♈

The Ford SG11 2AX ☎ 01279 771555 ▤ 01279 771555
e-mail: paul.arkell@virgin.net
dir: *M11 junct 8 take A120 towards Puckeridge & A10. Left at lights in Little Hadnam. Pub 1m on right*

Formerly a coaching inn, this 16th-century pub has also been a brewery, a bakery and Home Guard arsenal in its time. The 1960s folk-rock group Fairport Convention once performed in concert opposite and the pub ran dry! Open brickwork and an old bakery oven are among the features at this village inn. An extensive menu offers everything from braised lamb joint and roast spiced duck breast to pasta carbonara and mixed grill. Plenty of starters available and more than 20 fish choices.

Open all wk **Bar Meals** L served Mon-Sat 12-2, Sun 12-3 D served Mon-Sat 6-9, Sun 7-9 Av main course £10 **Restaurant** L served Mon-Sat 12-2, Sun 12-3 booking required D served Mon-Sat 6-9, Sun 7-9 booking required ⊕ GREENE KING ◐ Greene King Abbot Ale, IPA, Old Speckled Hen & Ruddles County Ale, Marstons Pedigree. ♈ 6 **Facilities** Children's menu Garden

OLD KNEBWORTH — Map 6 TL22

The Lytton Arms ♈

Park Ln SG3 6QB ☎ 01438 812312 ▤ 01438 817298
e-mail: thelyttonarms@btinternet.com
dir: *From A1(M) take A602. At Knebworth turn right at rail station. Follow Codicote signs. Pub 1.5m on right*

The pub was designed around 1877 by Lord Lytton's brother-in-law, who happened to be the architect Sir Edwin Lutyens. It replaced the previous inn, now a residence next door. Also next door, but in a much grander way, is the Lytton estate, the family home for centuries. On the simple but wide-ranging menu are Mrs O'Keefe's flavoured sausages; chicken or vegetable balti; honey-roast ham; chargrilled lamb's liver and bacon; and fisherman's pie.

Open all wk ⊕ FREE HOUSE ◐ Fuller's London Pride, Adnams Best Bitter, Broadside, Woodforde's Wherry, Deuchars IPA. ♈ 30 **Facilities** Dogs allowed Garden Parking

POTTERS CROUCH — Map 6 TL10

The Hollybush ♈

AL2 3NN ☎ 01727 851792 ▤ 01727 851792
e-mail: info@thehollybushpub.co.uk
dir: *Ragged Hall Ln off A405 or Bedmond Ln off A4147*

Run by the same family for over 30 years, The Hollybush is a picturesque country pub with a quaint, white-painted exterior, attractively furnished interior and a large enclosed garden. An antique dresser, a large fireplace and various prints and paintings help to create a delightfully welcoming atmosphere. Traditional pub fare is offered: ploughman's, burgers, jacket potatoes, salads, platters and toasted sandwiches, along with an evening

menu including beef and stilton pie, pork casserole, or cod and pancetta fishcakes. The pub is close to St Albans with its Roman ruins and good local walks.

Open all wk noon-2.30 6-11 (Sun 7-10) **Bar Meals** L served all wk 12-2 D served Wed-Sat 6-9 ⊕ FULLER SMITH TURNER PLC ◐ Fuller's Chiswick Bitter, Fuller's London Pride, ESB, seasonal ales. ♈ 7 **Facilities** Garden Parking

RICKMANSWORTH — Map 6 TQ09

The Rose and Crown ♈

Harefield Rd WD3 1PP ☎ 01923 897680
e-mail: roseandcrown@morethanjustapub.com
web: www.morethanjustapub.co.uk/theroseandcrown
dir: *M25 junct 17/18, follow Northwood signs. Past Tesco, pub 1.5m on right*

With the restaurant, conservatory and garden newly renovated, this 16th-century former farmhouse hosts events ranging from wine tastings to a monthly farmers' market. Inside the wisteria-clad building, you'll find low-beamed ceilings and real fires, while the large garden looks out across the lovely Colne Valley. There's a strong emphasis on home-cooked food, sometimes with a fusion twist, supplied locally wherever possible. Look out for escalope of British veal in a white wine and mushroom cream; pan-seared calves' liver with bubble and squeak; and rosemary braised lamb shank, champ and vegetables.

Open all day all wk 11am-11.30pm **Bar Meals** Av main course £11 food served all day **Restaurant** Fixed menu price fr £10 Av 3 course à la carte fr £21 food served all day ⊕ MORE THAN JUST A PUB CO LTD ◐ London Pride, Deuchars IPA, Timothy Taylor Landlord Ö Addlestones. ♈ 12 **Facilities** Children's menu Play area Dogs allowed Garden Parking

ROYSTON — Map 12 TL34

PICK OF THE PUBS

The Cabinet Free House and Restaurant ♈

See Pick of the Pubs on opposite page

ST ALBANS — Map 6 TL10

Rose & Crown ♈

10 Saint Michael St AL3 4SG
☎ 01727 851903 ▤ 01727 761775
e-mail: ruth.courtney@ntlworld.com
dir: *Telephone for details*

Traditional 16th-century pub situated in a beautiful part of St Michael's 'village', opposite the entrance to Verulanium Park and the Roman Museum. It has a classic beamed bar with a huge inglenook, open fire in winter and a lovely walled garden. The pub offers a distinctive range of American deli-style sandwiches, which are served with potato salad, kettle crisps and pickled cucumber. There is traditional folk music on Thursday nights, live music on Monday nights.

Open all day all wk 11.30-3 5.30-11 (Sat 11.30-11.30) **Bar Meals** L served Mon-Sat 12-2.30, Sun 12-5 D served Mon-Sat 6-9 ⊕ PUNCH TAVERNS ◐ Adnams Bitter, Tetley Bitter, Fuller's London Pride, Courage Directors, guest ales. ♈ 20 **Facilities** Children's menu Dogs allowed Garden Parking

STAPLEFORD — Map 6 TL31

Papillon Woodhall Arms ★★★ INN ♈

17 High Rd SG14 3NW
☎ 01992 535123 ▤ 01992 587030
e-mail: info@papillon-woodhallarms.com
dir: *On A119, between A602 & Hertford*

A pink-washed, twin-gabled building behind a neat white picket fence, this is the latest Papillon restaurant; it was preceded by two others in Hertfordshire. The bar serves well-kept ales in a welcoming atmosphere, plus an eclectic mix of snacks or pub lunches. Restaurant food includes plentiful fish dishes (perhaps fresh halibut with tomato and thermidor sauces) while others might include venison with a cinnamon black cherry sauce. Accommodation is available in ten en suite bedrooms.

Open all wk **Bar Meals** L served all wk 12-2 D served Sun-Fri 6.30-10 **Restaurant** L served all wk 12-2 booking required D served all wk 6.30-10 booking required ⊕ FREE HOUSE ◐ Greene King IPA, Archers, Cottage, Nethergate, Youngs Special. ♈ 10 **Facilities** Family room Garden Parking **Rooms** 10

PICK OF THE PUBS

The Cabinet Free House & Restaurant ♀

ROYSTON   Map 12 TL34

High St, Reed SG8 8AH
☎ **01763 848366**
e-mail: thecabinet@btconnect.com
dir: *2m S of Royston, just off A10*

The Cabinet is a 16th-century country inn and restaurant located in the little village of Reed just off the A10 London to Cambridge road, within easy striking distance of the capital. It's situated on a chalk ridge at almost the highest point in Hertfordshire, with the Roman highway Ermine Street passing just to the west. There has been a settlement here for many centuries - the community is mentioned in the Domesday Book of 1086. Now in the capable hands of Tracey Hale and Angus Martin, the refurbished inn has a cosy and comfortable interior with low beamed ceilings and an open fire. The lovely surroundings lend themselves to special occasions, particularly weddings, and the premises are licensed for civil ceremonies. As well as a great selection of real ales, the menu is an eclectic mix, based on personal taste and sound cooking techniques rather than a particular type of cuisine. Food is prepared from the best local produce, but draws inspiration from around the world to offer an interesting variety of dishes including traditional favourites. The restaurant and snug lunchtime offerings range from soup of the day or macaroni cheese, to toad-in-the-hole with scallion mash, or pea and gorgonzola risotto. Comfort desserts include rice pudding with home-made jam, and Eton mess. Evening suppers are equally appealing while moving up a gear or two in complexity: a typical choice could start with "Crayfish Bloody Mary" or bouillabaisse of red mullet; continue with daube of venison with dumplings, roasted beetroot and mustard mash or lobster and chicken casserole; and round off with chocolate torte with walnut meringue. Mind the resident ghost - an old gentleman in a dark coat.

Open 12-3 6-11 (Sat-Sun 12-11) Closed: 1 Jan, Mon L **Bar Meals** L served Tue-Sun 12-3 D served Tue-Sat 6-9 Av main course £10 **Restaurant** L served Tue-Sun 12-3 D served Tue-Sat 6-9 Fixed menu price fr £10-25 Av 3 course à la carte fr £25 ⊕ FREE HOUSE ◀ Woodforde's Wherry, Adnams, Old Speckled Hen, Nelson's Revenge, Timothy Taylor, Augustinian ♂ Aspall. ♀ 12 **Facilities** Children's menu Family room Dogs allowed Garden Parking

PICK OF THE PUBS

The Fox ◉ 🍷

WILLIAN   Map 12 TL23

Baldock Ln SG6 2AE
☎ **01462 480233** 📠 **01462 676966**
e-mail: restaurant@foxatwillian.co.uk
dir: *A1(M) junct 9 towards Letchworth, 1st left to Willian, 0.5m on left*

Around 250 years old, the Fox stands opposite the village pond and right next door to the church. It has answered to several names over the years, being the Orange Tree from c1750, then until 1870 the Dinsdale Arms (after the family who owned the village), when it became for a while the Willian Arms. In 1907, after its first incarnation as The Fox, the People's Refreshment House Association, whose aim was to bring respectability to public houses, took it over. Six years ago businessman Cliff Nye (who also has two hostelries in Norfolk) immaculately restyled it to create a modern, laid-back bar with

eating areas, local artists' work on display, and a glazed restaurant atrium. Outside are a Spanish-style courtyard and two beer gardens. The range of real ales includes Woodforde's Wherry, Adnams Bitter, Fullers London Pride plus a weekly changing guest ale; Staropramen, Leffe and Aspall's Cyder are on tap, and over a dozen wines may be drunk by the glass. Young and friendly staff serve food from the daily-changing, one-AA Rosette menu, which includes fish and shellfish brought in from north Norfolk - Brancaster Staithe oysters grilled in Parmesan cream, for example. A typical dinner menu offers starters of Moroccan spiced chickpea, carrot and coriander cake with apricot relish; and tempura tiger prawns, herb salad, sweet chilli and soy dip. It continues with main courses such as braised beef ballottine and chargrilled sirloin steak with dauphinoise potato and carrot purée; and pan-seared scallops, celeriac and pinenut risotto and Parma ham crisp. Finally, desserts are typified by star anise spiced pear tart Tatin; and banana and dark rum parfait.

Open Mon-Thu noon-11 (Fri-Sat noon-mdnt, Sun noon-10.30) **Bar Meals** L served Mon-Sat 12-2 Av main course £9 **Restaurant** L served Mon-Sat 12-2, Sun 12-2.45 D served Mon-Sat 6.45-9.15 Av 3 course à la carte fr £27 ⊕ FREE HOUSE ◖ Adnam Bitter, Woodforde's Wherry, Fuller's London Pride, Weekly changing guest ales Ŏ Aspall Cyder. 🍷 15 **Facilities** Dogs allowed Garden Parking

TEWIN · Map 6 TL21

The Plume of Feathers ♈

Upper Green Rd AL6 0LX ☎ 01438 717265
dir: *E from A1(M) junct 6 towards WGC, follow B1000 towards Hertford. Tewin signed on left*

Built in 1596, this historic inn, firstly an Elizabethan hunting lodge and later the haunt of highwaymen, boasts several ghosts including a 'lady in grey'. Interesting menus change daily, and include a tapas bar from noon till close. Other options available are Moroccan spiced baby shark with king prawns and couscous, honey-roast duck with sweet potato wontons, or slow-roasted belly pork with bacon and cabbage. Be sure to book in advance.

Open all day all wk 9am-11pm (Fri-Sat 9am-mdnt) **Bar Meals** L served Mon-Thu 12-2.30, Fri-Sat 12-9.30, Sun 12-8 D served Mon-Thu 6-9.30, Fri-Sat 12-9.30, Sun 12-8 **Restaurant** L served Mon-Thu 12-2.30, Fri-Sat 12-9.30, Sun 12-8 D served Mon-Thu 6-9.30, Fri-Sat 12-9.30, Sun 12-8 ⊕ GREENE KING ◀ IPA, Abbot Ales, Guest. ₹ 30 **Facilities** Dogs allowed Garden Parking

WALKERN · Map 12 TL22

The White Lion ♈

31 The High St SG2 7PA ☎ 01438 861251
e-mail: info@whitelionwalkern.co.uk
dir: *B1037 from Stevenage*

In rolling chalk downland, Walkern manages to keep a respectable distance from nearby Stevenage, Britain's first 'new town'. The bar in this 16th-century pub has oak beams, an inglenook, leather sofas, newspapers and a computer for those who still need to surf the net over a pint of Greene King or cup of hot chocolate. The informal restaurant offers a traditional pub menu, with ham, egg and chips, fillet of beef stroganoff, and succulent steaks.

Open noon-3 4.30-11 (Mon 4.30-11 Sat-Sun noon-mdnt) Closed: Mon L **Bar Meals** L served Tue-Fri 12-2.30, Sat-Sun 12-3 D served Tue-Sat 6-9 ⊕ GREENE KING ◀ Greene King IPA, Abbot Ale, Guinness. ₹ 8 **Facilities** Play area Dogs allowed Garden Parking

WELWYN · Map 6 TL21

The White Hart NEW ♈

2 Prospect Place AL6 9EN
☎ 01438 715353 📄 01438 714448
e-mail: bookings@thewhitehartotel.net
dir: *Just off junct 6 of A1(M) on corner of Prospect Place (just past fire station) and top of High Street/London Rd*

The former 17th-century coaching inn on the old Great North Road was revamped in 2005, creating an elegant town centre inn with a contemporary feel – wood floors, heritage colours, leather chairs, period fireplaces, and bold artwork. In keeping, menus are modern and innovative, utilising local market and farm produce. Follow sardines with pesto and rocket, with venison on pea mash with port and juniper sauce, and lemon tart

with raspberry coulis. Classic pub dishes are served in the bar.

Open all day all wk 7am-mdnt (Sun 9am-10.30pm) **Bar Meals** L served Mon-Sat 12-2.30 D served Mon-Sat 6.30-9.30 Av main course £13.50 **Restaurant** L served all wk 12-2.30 booking required D served Mon-Sat 6.30-9.30 booking required Fixed menu price fr £9.99 Av 3 course à la carte fr £19.95 ⊕ PUNCH TAVERNS ◀ Flowers IPA, Fullers London Pride, Adnams Bitter ♉ Stowford Press. ₹ 6 **Facilities** Children's menu Parking

WESTON · Map 12 TL23

The Rising Sun ♈

21 Halls Green SG4 7DR
☎ 01462 790487 📄 01462 790846
e-mail: therisingsun@hotmail.co.uk
dir: *A1(M) junct 9 take A6141 towards Baldock. Then right towards Graveley. 1st left in 100yds*

Set in picturesque Hertfordshire countryside, the Rising Sun offers a regularly changing menu. Starters include stilton mushrooms, and salmon fishcakes with dill sauce. Main courses include chargrilled steaks, salmon with dill and mustard sauce, or smoked fish crumble. A huge choice of sweets, and blackboard specials change daily. The owners say that their pub may be hard to find on your first visit, but that it's well worth the trouble.

⊕ MCMULLEN & SONS LTD ◀ McMullen Original AK Ale, Macs Country Best. ₹ 6 **Facilities** Play area Dogs allowed Garden Parking

WILLIAN · Map 12 TL23

PICK OF THE PUBS

The Fox ◉ ♈

See Pick of the Pubs on opposite page

KENT

BIDDENDEN · Map 7 TQ83

PICK OF THE PUBS

The Three Chimneys ♈

Biddenden Rd TN27 8LW ☎ 01580 291472
dir: *From A262 midway between Biddenden & Sissinghurst, follow Frittenden signs. (Pub seen from main road). Pub immediately on left in hamlet of Three Chimneys*

A 15th-century Wealden treasure that has every natural advantage of being a classic country pub, its original, small-roomed layout and old-fashioned furnishings remain delightfully intact. There are old settles, low beams, wood-panelled walls, worn brick floors, crackling log fires, soft evening candlelight, absence of music and electronic games – glorious. Modern-day demand for dining space has seen the addition of the rear Garden Room and a tasteful new conservatory,

and drinkers and diners spill out onto the secluded heated side patio and vast shrub-filled garden, which are perfect for summer eating. Food is bang up-to-date and listed on daily-changing chalkboards. Tuck into a hearty ploughman's lunch, red lentil and tomato soup or potted shrimps, or something more substantial, perhaps roast cod on wilted spinach with chive velouté or local pork sausages with mash and port and red wine gravy. If you have room for a pudding, try the rhubarb and apple crumble. Adnams and Shepherd Neame ales and the heady Biddenden cider are tapped direct from cask.

Open all wk 11.30-3 5.30-11 (Sat-Sun 11.30-4, 5.30-11) Closed: 25 Dec **Bar Meals** L served all wk 12-2.30 booking required D served all wk 6.30-9.30 booking required **Restaurant** L served all wk 12-2.30 booking required D served all wk 6.30-9.30 booking required ⊕ FREE HOUSE ◀ Adnams, Harveys Old, Special ♉ Biddenden. ₹ 10 **Facilities** Children's menu Dogs allowed Garden Parking

BODSHAM GREEN · Map 7 TR14

PICK OF THE PUBS

Froggies At The Timber Batts

School Ln TN25 5JQ
☎ 01233 750237 📄 01233 750176
e-mail: joel@thetimberbatts.co.uk
dir: *4m E of Wye*

A venerable building dating to the 15th century, and a pub since 1747 after housing hop-growers who brewed for their own consumption. Named after a nearby wood yard, Froggies was added when French chef Joël Gross took it over in 2002. No surprise then that the wine list and dishes based on locally sourced produce are classically French. Seared scallops with lardons, and pan-fried duck foie gras with apricots are typical starters. Main courses encompass game from local shoots: roasted partridge with olives; pheasant poached in cider; and pan-fried venison saddle. A seafood platter can be provided with 48 hours notice. Desserts may include classic crème brûlée, and crêpes Suzette. Or you could just enjoy a real ale in one of the beamed bars where log fires crackle in winter. A monthly evening of magic, a charity weekend in June, a firework display on Bastille Day, and countryside views from the garden are all added bonuses.

Open all wk 12-3 6.30-close Closed: 24 Dec-2 Jan **Bar Meals** L served all wk 12-2.30 D served all wk 7-9.30 **Restaurant** L served all wk 12-2.30 D served all wk 7-9.30 ⊕ FREE HOUSE ◀ Adnams, London Pride, Woodforde's Wherry. **Facilities** Dogs allowed Garden Parking

BOSSINGHAM Map 7 TR14

The Hop Pocket

The Street CT4 6DY ☎ **01227 709866** 🖹 **01227 709866**
dir: *Telephone for directions*

Birds of prey and an animal corner for children are among the more unusual attractions at this family pub in the heart of Kent. Canterbury is only five miles away and the county's delightfully scenic coast and countryside are within easy reach. Menu may include fish pie, supreme of chicken, spicy salmon, Cajun beef, chilli nachos and fish platter. There is also an extensive range of sandwiches and omelettes. Recent change of landlord.

Open all wk 11-3 6-mdnt (Sun noon-3 7-11) **Bar Meals** L served all wk 12-2.30 D served Mon-Sat 7-9.30 **Restaurant** L served all wk 12-2.30 D served Mon-Sat 7-9.30 ⊕ FREE HOUSE ◀ London Pride, Master Brew, Wadworth 6X, Spitfire. **Facilities** Children's menu Dogs allowed Garden Parking

BOUGHTON MONCHELSEA Map 7 TQ75

PICK OF THE PUBS

The Mulberry Tree NEW ◎◎

Hermitage Ln ME17 4DA ☎ **01622 749082** & **714058**
e-mail: info@themulberrytreekent.co.uk
dir: *M20 to junct 8. B2163 towards Coxheath, left after Ralphs Garden Centre into Wierton Rd, over x-rds, 1st left down East Hall Hill.*

In beautiful Kent countryside, this contemporary country bar and restaurant attracts people from a wide catchment area, simply because it is relaxed, informal and eminently capable of providing very good food. The Mulberry Tree is a member of Produced in Kent, from whose suppliers the kitchen sources the seasonal, free-range and organic produce it needs for its two-AA Rosette-awarded, modern British and European cuisine. From the skilled hands of head chef Alan Irwin and his team come meals such as raviolo of scallop with roasted native lobster; slow-roast belly of Kentish pork, boulangère potato and hispi cabbage; and gratin of spiced tangerines and Cox's apples with white chocolate cheesecake. An extensive wine list offers many New World wines from smaller, including several English, vineyards. Outside, a sunny terrace overlooks the garden, both areas being ideal for alfresco dining.

Open noon-3 6.30-11 (Sun noon-4) Closed: Sun eve, Mon **Bar Meals** L served Tue-Sat 12-2 (Sun 12-2.30) booking required D served Tue-Thu 6.30-9, Fri-Sat 6.30-9.30 Av main course £12.95 **Restaurant** L served Tue-Sat 12-2 (Sun 12-2.30) booking required D served Tue- Thu 6.30-9, Fri-Sat 6.30-9.30 Fixed menu price fr £12.95 Av 3 course à la carte fr £25 ⊕ FREE HOUSE ◀ Harveys, Goacher's. **Facilities** Children's menu Garden Parking

BRABOURNE Map 7 TR14

The Five Bells ♥

The Street TN25 5LP
☎ **01303 813334** 🖹 **01303 814667**
dir: *5m E of Ashford*

A 16th-century free house pub surrounded by rolling hills and orchards and the perfect pit stop for walkers and cyclists. Originally a poor house, the old stocks are located across the road, while inside are whitewashed walls and a huge inglenook fireplace. An extensive menu and a range of popular daily specials include traditional steak and kidney pie; liver and bacon with sage and onion gravy; and fillet of salmon with creamed leeks and smoked salmon mash.

Open all wk ⊕ FREE HOUSE ◀ Shepherd Neame Master Brew, London Pride, Greene King IPA, Adnams. ♥ 12 **Facilities** Play area Dogs allowed Garden Parking

BROOKLAND Map 7 TQ92

PICK OF THE PUBS

The Royal Oak ♥

High St TN29 9QR ☎ **01797 344215**
e-mail: dzrj@btinternet.com
dir: *A259, 5m E of Rye. In village by church*

This smart marshland pub began life as a house in 1570. A succession of parish clerks and sextons lived here until 1736 when it started to function as a pub – a role it has amply fulfilled every since. These days its uncluttered interior is a pleasing combination of original features and modern furnishings. The menus cater for everything from speedy lunchtime dining to leisurely three-course meals. Regularly changing dishes draw on local, seasonal produce. Simple options are filled baguettes; beer-battered local white fish with mushy peas and home-made tartare sauce; and home-cooked honey-roasted ham with local free-range eggs and chips. At the other end of the scale, there are meals such as Thai fish cakes, followed by spiced slow-roasted belly pork with seasonal vegetables and mashed potato, with treacle tart for dessert. A well-kept and tranquil garden borders the churchyard of St Augustine, one of only four in England with a separate bell tower.

Open 12-3 6-11 Closed: Sun eve & Mon eve **Bar Meals** L served all wk 12-2 D served all wk 6.30-9 **Restaurant** L served all wk 12-2 D served all wk 6.30-9 ⊕ ENTERPRISE INNS ◀ Harvey's Best Bitter, Adnams Best Bitter, guest ale ♂ Westons Stowford Press. ♥ 8 **Facilities** Dogs allowed Garden Parking

PICK OF THE PUBS

Woolpack Inn

See Pick of the Pubs on opposite page

BURHAM Map 6 TQ76

The Golden Eagle

80 Church St ME1 3SD ☎ **01634 668975**
e-mail: kathymay@btconnect.com
web: www.thegoldeneagle.org
dir: *S from M2 junct 3 or N from M20 junct 6 on A229, signs to Burham*

Built around 1850, this popular free house has every appearance of a traditional English inn, set on the North Downs with fine views of the Medway Valley. What sets it apart is its 30-year history of serving oriental food. The chef's specialities are spare ribs, mee goreng, king prawn sambal, wortip crispy chicken, and sweet and sour crispy pork. Chocolate fudge cake and apple crumble are among the puddings. Vegetarians are well catered for.

Open all wk Closed: 25-26 Dec **Bar Meals** L served all wk 12-2 D served all wk 7-9.30 Av main course £8.50 **Restaurant** L served all wk 12-2 D served all wk 7-9.30 Fixed menu price fr £8.50 ⊕ FREE HOUSE ◀ Wadworth 6X, Boddingtons. **Facilities** Parking

CANTERBURY Map 7 TR15

The Chapter Arms ♥

New Town St, Chartham Hatch CT4 7LT
☎ **01227 738340**
e-mail: david.durell@vmicombox.co.uk
dir: *3m from Canterbury. Off A28 in Chartham Hatch or A2 at Upper Harbledown*

Situated on the North Downs Way, this charming and picturesque free house is set in over an acre of gardens overlooking apple orchards and oast houses. It was once three cottages owned by Canterbury Cathedral's Dean and Chapter - hence the name. Any day's menu might offer Kentish lamb crusted with garlic and thyme, Thai salmon fishcakes, or steak and kidney pie. Live Sixties music and jazz evenings are popular. Suitable for marquee weddings.

Open all wk Closed: 25 Dec eve **Bar Meals** L served all wk 12-2.30 D served Mon-Sat 6.30-9 booking required Av main course £8.95 **Restaurant** L served all wk 12-2.30 D served Mon-Sat 6.30-9 booking required Av 3 course à la carte fr £25 ⊕ FREE HOUSE ◀ Shepherd Neame Master Brew, Adnams, Harveys, Youngs, Wells Bombardier, guest ales. ♥ 10 **Facilities** Children's menu Play area Dogs allowed Garden Parking

PICK OF THE PUBS

Woolpack Inn

BROOKLAND Map 7 TQ92

Beacon Ln TN29 9TJ ☎ 01797 344321
web: www.thewoolpackbrookland.co.uk
dir: *1.5m past Brookland towards Rye on A259*

Built in the 15th century when smuggling was rife in these parts, it's rumoured that at one time the Woolpack had a secret tunnel used by smugglers to escape from the Excise men. The old spinning wheel mounted on the bar ceiling was used to divide up their contraband; but, nowadays, the pub is ideally situated for those who wish to explore this unique and beautiful area of Kent. There are many walks in the area to study nature at close quarters, go fishing, or just to stop and let the world go by. Surrounded by the dykes and reed beds of Romney Marsh, the place oozes charm and character. Open beams and an inglenook fireplace add to the atmosphere, and landlord Barry Morgan and his staff extend a warm welcome to all. The chef makes extensive use of fresh produce including fish from the local fishermen. The menu offers a wide variety of home-made meals, whilst dishes on the specials board make the most of seasonal produce. Lunchtime brings ploughman's, sandwiches and filled jacket potatoes, and there are hog roasts and barbecues in the pub garden on summer evenings. On the main menu, expect pub favourites like ham, egg, chips and peas, or home-made chilli and rice. There are also game and vegetarian dishes like braised rabbit with shallots and wholegrain mustard in a cider and cream sauce, or mushroom, cranberry and Brie Wellington. Finish with the likes of honey and cinnamon pudding, steamed spotted Dick, or bitter chocolate and orange sponge. Home-made meals are listed on the children's menu.

Open all week **Meals** L served Mon-Fri 12-2.30, Sat-Sun 12-9 D served Mon-Fri 6-9, Sat-Sun 12-9 Av main course £8 ⊕ SHEPHERD NEAME ◖ Shepherd Neame Spitfire Premium Ale, Master Brew Bitter. **Facilities** Play area Family room Dogs allowed Garden Parking

CANTERBURY *continued*

PICK OF THE PUBS

The Dove Inn ⊛ ♀

Plum Pudding Ln, Dargate ME13 9HB
☎ 01227 751360 🖹 01227 751360
e-mail: pipmacgrew@hotmail.com
dir: *5m NW of Canterbury, A299 Thanet Way, turn off at Lychgate service station*

The Dove is a splendid vine-covered Victorian country pub, tucked away in a sleepy hamlet between Faversham and Whitstable, surrounded by orchards and farmland. It has established a reputation for well-kept Shepherd Neame ales and good food based on locally sourced ingredients. The interior is simple and relaxed with stripped wooden floors and scrubbed tables. Outside is a large formal garden where, appropriately, a dovecote and doves present an agreeably scenic backdrop for an alfresco meal or quiet pint. The menu succeeds in offering something for everyone, including light lunches, snacks and restaurant quality food. The chef has a talent for producing country cooking with a strong French influence. Local gamekeepers provide much of the meat and game, and fresh fish features prominently. Both children and dogs are made welcome.

Open noon-3 6-mdnt (Fri noon-mdnt Sun noon-9 (Apr-Oct) noon-4 (Nov-Mar)) Closed: Mon **Bar Meals** L served Tue-Sat 12-2.30 D served Tue-Thu 6.30-9 Av main course £10 **Restaurant** L served Tue-Sun 12-2.30 booking required D served Tue-Sat 7-9 booking required Av 3 course à la carte fr £25 ⊕ SHEPHERD NEAME ◀ Shepherd Neame Master Brew, Spitfire, seasonal ale. ♀ 8 **Facilities** Children's menu Dogs allowed Garden Parking

PICK OF THE PUBS

The Granville ♀

Street End, Lower Hardres CT4 7AL
☎ 01227 700402 🖹 01227 700925
dir: *On B2068, 2m from Canterbury towards Hythe*

Named after the Tudor warship, the Granville is a handsome solid building firmly anchored in the ancient village of Lower Hardres, just a five-minute drive from Canterbury city centre. With ample parking, a patio and large beer garden at the rear where summer barbecues take place, this Shepherd Neame pub is an ideal family venue, and dogs too are made welcome. Nevertheless this is not a place for pub grub. The short but lively menu is designed for sophisticated tastebuds, offering for starters the likes of rock oysters with shallot vinegar, smoked local wigeon (a small wild duck) with mustard fruits, and antipasti. Main courses always comprise three meat and three fish dishes: slow-roast Waterham Farm chicken with truffle cream sauce, and Dungeness brill fillet braised in Macvin and morels are two examples. There is no children's menu as such, but portions from the main menu can be served where appropriate.

Open all wk noon-3 5.30-11 Closed: 25-26 Dec **Bar Meals** L served Tue-Sat 12-2 D served Tue-Sun 7-9 Av main course £13.95 **Restaurant** L served Tue-Sun 12-2 booking required D served Tue-Sat 7-9 booking required Av 3 course à la carte fr £27 ⊕ SHEPHERD NEAME ◀ Master Brew, seasonal ale. ♀ 6 **Facilities** Dogs allowed Garden Parking

PICK OF THE PUBS

The Red Lion ♀

High St, Stodmarsh CT3 4BA
☎ 01227 721339 🖹 01227 721339
e-mail: tiptop-redlion@hotmail.com
dir: *From Canterbury take A257 towards Sandwich, left into Stodmarsh road and continue to the hamlet of Stodmarsh*

Built in 1475 and burnt to the ground in 1720, The Red Lion was subsequently rebuilt and remains much the same to this day. Set in a tiny hamlet, it is surrounded by reed beds, which are home to marsh harriers, bearded tits and bitterns. The pub's interior, warmed by two large log fires, is adorned with traditional hop garlands, curios, antiques and a collection of international menus. Outside, there is an extensive garden with an antique forge, which doubles as a barbecue in the summer. The menu majors on produce from local allotments and changes every 10 days. A typical starter is baby carrot and honey roasted parsnip soup and main courses feature game in season, maybe half a pheasant or partridge. A pint of Old Speckled Hen by the fire is a favourite, but alternatives include spicy mulled local cider or, in summer, a colourful fruit-laden Pimms.

Open all wk 10.30am-11pm (Sun 10.30-4.30) Closed: Sun eve **Bar Meals** L served all wk 12-2.30 booking required D served Mon-Sat 7-9.30 booking required Av main course £12.50 **Restaurant** L served all wk 12-2.30 booking required D served Mon-Sat 7-9.30 booking required Fixed menu price fr £22 Av 3 course à la carte fr £36 ⊕ FREE HOUSE ◀ Greene King IPA, Ruddles County, Speckled Hen. ♀ 7 **Facilities** Play area Family room Dogs allowed Garden Parking

The White Horse Inn ♀

53 High St, Bridge CT4 5LA
☎ 01227 832814 🖹 01227 832814
dir: *3m S of Canterbury, just off A2*

This medieval and Tudor building was originally a staging post close to a ford on the main Dover to Canterbury road, and still provides a stirling service to modern travellers. An enormous log fire burning in the beamed bar during the winter months provides a guaranteed warm welcome, whilst the extensive garden is popular for al fresco dining on warmer days. Fullers and Shepherd Neame are amongst the real ales served in the bar, with up to ten wines available by the glass. You'll find a strong emphasis on food, with seasonal dishes created from the best local ingredients. Choose between the relaxed

blackboard bar menu, and more formal dining in the restaurant.

Closed: 25 Dec, 1 Jan, Sun eve ◀ Shepherd Neame Masterbrew, Greene King Abbot Ale, Fuller's London Pride, Greene King IPA, Gadds No. 5. ♀ 10 **Facilities** Garden Parking

CHARING Map 7 TQ94

The Bowl Inn ♀

Egg Hill Rd TN27 0HG
☎ 01233 712256 🖹 01233 714705
e-mail: info@bowl-inn.co.uk
dir: *M20 junct 8/9, A20 to Charing, then A252 towards Canterbury. Left at top of Charing Hill down Bowl Rd, 1.25m*

Standing on top of the North Downs, The Bowl has been an alehouse since 1606, and was built as a farmhouse in 1512. Alan and Sue Paine have been here since 1992, and run a relaxed and welcoming hostelry. The small but varied menu of mostly traditional country pub snacks includes Kent-cured ham, English cheddar ploughman's, and hot bacon and sausage sandwiches. Relax in front of the huge old inglenook fireplace or play pool on an unusual rotating hexagonal table. Even in summer, if necessary, the south-facing sun terrace is covered and heated. Look out for the annual beer festival.

Open all wk Mon-Sat noon-mdnt Sun noon-11 (Mon-Thu 4-11 Fri-Sun noon-mdnt winter) **Bar Meals** food served all day ⊕ FREE HOUSE ◀ Fuller's London Pride, Adnams Southwold, Harveys Sussex Best, Whitstable IPA, Youngs Best. ♀ 8 **Facilities** Dogs allowed Garden Parking

CHIDDINGSTONE Map 6 TQ54

PICK OF THE PUBS

Castle Inn ♀

See Pick of the Pubs on opposite page

CHILHAM Map 7 TR05

PICK OF THE PUBS

The White Horse ♀

The Square CT4 8BY ☎ 01227 730355
dir: *Take A28 from Canterbury then A252, in 1m turn left*

One of the most photographed pubs in Britain, The White Horse stands next to St Mary's church facing onto the 15th-century village square, where the May Fair is an annual event. The pub offers a traditional atmosphere and modern cooking from a monthly-changing menu based on fresh local produce. Dishes include fillet steak poached in red wine, and cod and smoked haddock fishcakes served with a sweet chilli sauce.

Open all day all wk noon-close **Bar Meals** L served Mon-Sat 12-2.30, Sun 12-4 D served Mon-Sat 6.30-9.30 ⊕ FREE HOUSE ◀ Masterbrew, Guest. ♀ 6 **Facilities** Dogs allowed Garden

PICK OF THE PUBS

Castle Inn ♀

CHIDDINGSTONE   Map 6 TQ54

TN8 7AH
☎ **01892 870247** 📠 **01892 871420**
e-mail: info@castleinn.co.uk
dir: *1.5m S of B2027 between Tonbridge & Edenbridge*

Located at the end of a unique, unspoilt row of Tudor timbered houses opposite the parish church, this historic, tiled-hung building dates from 1420 and boasts leaded casement windows and projecting upper gables. Like the rest of the village street, the pub is owned by the National Trust, hence why this handsome building has starred in films as diverse as *Elizabeth R, Room with a View, The Life of Hogarth* and *The*

Wicked Lady. The interior is equally atmospheric, remaining delightfully unchanged within its two traditional bars, with heavy beams, quarry-tiled floors, an old brick fireplace, and rustic wall benches in the classic public bar. For an alfresco drink, head for the vine-hung courtyard, or cross the bridge to the lawn and its beautifully tended flowerbeds. You can sample Larkins Traditional and Larkins Porter, brewed just up the road at Larkins Farm or delve into the 100-bin lists of wine, while whisky lovers can, preferably over time, work their way through 30 malts from Aberlour to Tomintoul. The bar menu offers soup with ciabatta bread; beef or smoked salmon sandwiches; ploughman's lunches and a range of hot dishes that includes pie and mash; chilli con carne with rice; and a pasta dish, perhaps penne with pesto and parmesan. The more adventurous restaurant menu starts with smoked Loch Fyne salmon; deep fried brie with

mixed leaves and cranberry sauce; or garlic mushrooms. Main course options include lamb cutlets with wild berry sauce; pork loin on sage and onion rösti with cider sauce; and salmon and smoked haddock fishcakes with wholegrain mustard sauce. Round things off with bread-and-butter pudding; sticky brownies with toffee sauce; or a plate of British and local cheeses.

Open 11-11 Sun 12-10.30
Restaurant ⊕ FREE HOUSE 🛢 Larkins Traditional, Harveys Sussex, Young's Ordinary, Larkins Porter. ♀ 10
Facilities Dogs allowed Garden

CHILLENDEN — Map 7 TR25

PICK OF THE PUBS

Griffins Head ♀

See Pick of the Pubs on opposite page

DARTFORD — Map 6 TQ57

The Rising Sun Inn ★★★ INN ♀

Fawkham Green, Fawkham DA3 8NL
☎ 01474 872291 📠 01474 872779
dir: *0.5m from Brands Hatch Racing Circuit & 5m from Dartford*

A pub since 1702, The Rising Sun stands on the green in a picturesque village not far from Brands Hatch. Inside you will find a bar full of character complete with inglenook log fire and a cosy restaurant. Starters include crispy soy duck; Stilton and bacon field mushrooms; and tempura tiger prawns. Follow with pork loin with honey and herb crust, or sea bass fillets with mango and garlic beurre. There is also a patio for alfresco dining in warmer weather, plus comfortable en suite bedrooms.

Open all wk **Bar Meals** food served all day **Restaurant** L served all wk 12-3 D served all wk 6.30-9.30 ⊕ FREE HOUSE ◀ Courage Best, Courage Directors, London Pride, Timothy Taylor Landlord, Harveys, Dartford Wobbler. ♀ 7
Facilities Children's menu Garden Parking **Rooms** 5

DEAL — Map 7 TR35

The King's Head

9 Beach St CT14 7AH
☎ 01304 368194 📠 01304 364182
e-mail: booking@kingsheaddeal.co.uk
dir: *A249 from Dover to Deal, on seafront*

A 250-year-old public house, The King's Head stands overlooking the sea only a minute's walk from the town centre. It has been established for over 28 years under the same ownership and is particularly well known for the annual display of flowers that adorns the building. Hand-pulled bitter and bar meals are served, including steaks, sandwiches and seafood, plus a daily-changing specials board.

Open all day all wk **Bar Meals** L served all wk 11.30-2.30 (11.30-9 Jul & Aug) D served all wk 6-9 (11.30-9 Jul & Aug) Av main course £7.95 ⊕ FREE HOUSE ◀ Shepherd Neame Master Brew, Spitfire, Fuller's London Pride.
Facilities Dogs allowed Garden

DOVER — Map 7 TR34

The Clyffe Hotel ♀

High St, St Margaret's at Cliffe CT15 6AT
☎ 01304 852400 📠 01304 851880
dir: *3m NE of Dover*

Quaint Kentish clapperboard building dating back to the late 16th century. In its time it has been a shoemaker's and an academy for young gentlemen. Just a stone's throw from the Saxon Shore Way and the renowned White Cliffs of Dover. The main bar and neatly furnished lounge lead out into the delightful walled rose garden. Seared fillet of tuna and lightly steamed halibut are among the seafood specialities; other options include pan-fried chicken breast and pasta dishes.

Open all wk ⊕ FREE HOUSE ◀ Interbrew Bass, Boddingtons, Fuller's London Pride. ♀ 30 **Facilities** Play area Dogs allowed Garden Parking

---

FAVERSHAM — Map 7 TR06

Shipwright's Arms ♀

Hollowshore ME13 7TU ☎ 01795 590088
dir: *A2 through Ospringe then right at rdbt. Right at T-junct then left opposite Davington School, follow signs*

Step back in time to this remote pub on the Swale marshes which is well over 300 years old, and once a favourite with sailors and fishermen waiting to dock in Faversham. The pub still draws its water from a well. Examine the maritime artefacts in the many nooks and crannies, while downing a Kent-brewed cask ale. Home cooked food includes locally caught fish in season, and English pies and puddings during the winter, where four open fires keep things cosy.

Closed: Mon (Oct-Mar) **Bar Meals** L served Tue-Sat 11-2.30, Sun 12-2.30 D served Tue-Sat 7-9 **Restaurant** L served Tue-Sat 11-2.30, Sun 12-2.30 D served Tue-Sat 7-9 ⊕ FREE HOUSE ◀ Local ales. ♀ 6
Facilities Children's menu Family room Dogs allowed Garden Parking

---

FOLKESTONE — Map 7 TR23

The Lighthouse Inn ♀

Old Dover Rd, Capel le Ferne CT18 7HT
☎ 01303 223300 📠 01303 842270
e-mail: james@thelighthouseinn.net
dir: *M20 junct 13 follow signs for Capel le Ferne*

There are sweeping Channel views from this pub on the edge of Dover's famous White Cliffs. The Lighthouse began as an ale house in 1840, later becoming, successively, a billiard hall, convalescent home, psychiatric hospital and country club while, more recently still, Channel Tunnel builders headquartered here. Expect decent home-made food along the lines of traditional prawn cocktail followed by local sausages with mash and onion jus, Channel fisherman's pie or classic ham, egg and chips.

Open all day all wk 11-11 **Bar Meals** Av main course £12.50 food served all day **Restaurant** Fixed menu price fr £14 Av 3 course à la carte fr £25 food served all day ⊕ FREE HOUSE ◀ IPA, 6X, Adnams. ♀ 14
Facilities Children's menu Play area Family room Dogs allowed Garden Parking

---

FORDCOMBE — Map 6 TQ54

Chafford Arms ♀

TN3 0SA ☎ 01892 740267 📠 01892 740703
e-mail: chaffordarms@btconnect.com
dir: *On B2188 (off A264) between Tunbridge Wells, East Grinstead & Penshurst*

A lovely mid-19th-century tile-hung village pub, with a working red telephone kiosk in the car park and a large garden with great views across the weald. Larkins and Harveys ales are stocked at the bar, and the menu offers a great range of traditional pub food. While mum and dad choose between chicken, ham and leek pie or a crock of chilli con carne, the children can pick their favourites from the likes of golden whale with chips, or crispy chicken teddies and salad.

Open all day all wk 11am-mdnt **Bar Meals** L served 12-9 (Sun 12-4) D served 12-9 (Sun 12-4) Av main course £9 food served all day **Restaurant** L served 12-9 (Sun 12-4) D served 12-9 (Sun 12-4) food served all day ⊕ ENTERPRISE INNS ◀ Larkins Bitter, Harvey's Best. ♀ 9
Facilities Children's menu Dogs allowed Garden Parking

GOODNESTONE — Map 7 TR25

The Fitzwalter Arms ♀

The Street CT3 1PJ ☎ 01304 840303
e-mail: thefitzwalter arms@gmail.com
dir: *Signed from B2046 & A2*

The 'Fitz', hostelry to the Fitzwalter Estate, has been a pub since 1702. Quintessentially English, it is a place of conviviality and conversation. Jane Austen was a frequent visitor to nearby Goodnestone Park after her brother, Edward, married into the family. On the menu, home cured ham with figs and parmesan; roast partridge with bread sauce and bacon; baked line-caught cod fillet, fishcake and old-fashioned egg sauce; treacle tart and custard.

Open all wk noon-3 6-11 (Fri-Sun noon-11) **Closed:** 25 Dec, 1 Jan **Restaurant** L served Mon & Wed-Sun 12-2 booking required D served Mon & Wed-Sat 7-9 booking required Fixed menu price fr £12.50 Av 3 course à la carte fr £20 ⊕ SHEPHERD NEAME ◀ Master Brew, Spitfire. ♀ 12
Facilities Children's menu Dogs allowed Garden

PICK OF THE PUBS

Griffins Head ♓

CHILLENDEN Map 7 TR25

CT3 1PS
☎ 01304 840325 📄 01304 841290
dir: *A2 from Canterbury towards Dover, then B2046. Village on right*

An architectural gem of a building nestling in a tiny farming hamlet amid rolling open countryside south-east of Canterbury. Dating from 1286, the Griffin's Head is a fine black-and-white half-timbered Wealden hall house that was originally built as a farmhouse to serve the local estate. Ale and cider were always brewed on the premises for the workers but it was only granted an ale licence in 1743 so the rector could hold tithe suppers in the building. The present Tudor structure is built around the original wattle and daub walls, remains of which can be viewed in one of the three delightfully unspoilt rooms, which also feature flagstone floors, exposed brick walls and beams and a tasteful mix of furnishings, from old scrubbed pine tables and chairs to church pews. Fine Shepherd Neame ales and home-made food have helped this old inn to make its mark with visitors as well as locals, among them Kent's cricketing fraternity. The menu is typically English, and specialises in game from local estates in season, and locally caught fish where possible. Typical dishes include lamb stew, braised steak, onions and mash, mussels marinière, prawn chowder, warm salads with steak and roasted vegetable or sautéed prawns and squid, and traditional pub dishes like cottage pie and ham, egg and chips. Desserts include apple crumble, raspberry almond torte, or home-made ice creams like passionfruit, ginger, or raspberry and strawberry. Rambling roses and clematis fill the attractive garden, the setting for popular summer weekend barbecues. A vintage car club meets here on the first Sunday of every month.

Open all day, Closed Sun pm
Restaurant L served 12-2 D served 7-9
⊕ SHEPHERD NEAME ◖ Shepherd Neame. ♓ 10 **Facilities** Garden Parking

GOUDHURST | Map 6 TQ73

Green Cross Inn

TN17 1HA ☎ 01580 211200 📄 01580 212905
dir: *A21 from Tonbridge towards Hastings turn left onto A262 towards Ashford. 2m, Goudhurst on right*

A food orientated pub in an unspoiled corner of Kent, originally built to serve the Paddock Wood-Goudhurst railway line, which closed in 1968. The dining room is prettily decorated with fresh flowers. The pub specialises in fresh seafood including oysters, crab, mussels, smoked eel – the list goes on. Main courses in the bar range from home-made steak, kidney and mushroom pie with shortcrust pastry, to calves' liver and bacon Lyonnaise.

Open all wk noon-3 6-11 Closed: Sun eve **Bar Meals** L served all wk 12-2.30 booking required D served Mon-Sat 7-9.45 booking required Av main course £13.50 **Restaurant** L served all wk 12-2.30 booking required D served Mon-Sat 7-9.45 booking required Av 3 course à la carte fr £30 ⊕ FREE HOUSE ◀ Harvey's Sussex Best Bitter, Guinness Ö Biddenden. **Facilities** Children's menu Garden Parking

PICK OF THE PUBS

The Star & Eagle ★★★★ INN ♥

High St TN17 1AL ☎ 01580 211512 📄 01580 212444
e-mail: starandeagle@btconnect.com
dir: *Just off A21 towards Hastings. Take A262 into Goudhurst. Pub at top of hill next to church*

A commanding position at 400 feet above sea level gives the 14th-century Star & Eagle outstanding views of the orchards and hop fields that helped earn Kent the accolade 'Garden of England'. The vaulted stonework suggests that this rambling, big-beamed building may once have been a monastery, and the tunnel from the cellars probably surfaces underneath the neighbouring parish church. These days, it's a place to unwind and enjoy fine traditional and continental food, prepared under the guidance of Spanish chef/proprietor Enrique Martinez. A typical bar meal might be field mushrooms stuffed with bacon and stilton; and cod, salmon and smoked haddock fish pie. From the restaurant menu might come soupe de poisson laced with brandy and cream; and Scottish rope mussels with chilli. Follow with pot-roast shoulder of lamb baked Spanish style; or sautéed calves' livers. Comfortable bedrooms are available.

Open all wk 11-11 (Sun 12-3 6.30-10.30) **Bar Meals** L served all wk 12-2.30 D served all wk 7-9.30 Av main course £15 **Restaurant** L served all wk 12-2.30 D served all wk 7-9.30 Fixed menu price fr £24 Av 3 course à la carte fr £30 ⊕ FREE HOUSE ◀ Adnams Bitter, Harvey's, Grasshopper. ♥ 24 **Facilities** Children's menu Family room Garden Parking **Rooms** 10

GRAVESEND | Map 6 TQ67

The Cock Inn

Henley St, Luddesdowne DA13 0XB
☎ 01474 814208 📄 01474 812850
e-mail: andrew.r.turner@btinternet.com
dir: *Telephone for directions*

Seven hand pumps deliver a wonderful array of well-kept real beers at this traditional English alehouse in the beautiful Luddesdowne Valley. Wood burning stoves in the two bars with exposed beams set the warm ambience, with not a fruit machine, jukebox or television in sight. Orders for excellent home-made food (steak and ale pie, scampi, pork in apple and cider sauce) are taken at the bar; there is no dedicated restaurant, so table reservations cannot be made. No children under 18.

Open all day all wk noon-11 (Sun noon-10.30) **Bar Meals** L served all wk 12-3 D served Mon-Sat 6-9 ⊕ FREE HOUSE ◀ Adnams Southwold, Adnams Broadside, Shepherd Neame Master Brew, Goacher's Real Mild Ale, Woodforde's Wherry. **Facilities** Dogs allowed Garden Parking

HARRIETSHAM | Map 7 TQ85

The Pepper Box Inn ♥

MF17 1LP ☎ 01622 842558 📄 01622 844218
dir: *From A20 in Harrietsham take Fairbourne Heath turn. 2m to x-rds, straight over, 200yds, pub on left*

A delightful 15th-century country pub enjoys far-reaching views over the Weald of Kent from its terrace, high up on the Greensand Ridge. The pub takes its name from an early type of pistol, a replica of which hangs behind the bar. Using the best of local seasonal produce, typical dishes might include rack of pork with apples and cider, chargrilled lamb fillet with beetroot and crème fraiche, and fillet of sea trout.

Open all wk 11-3 6.30-11 **Bar Meals** L served all wk 12-2.15 D served Tue-Sat 7-9.45, Sun 12-3 Av main course £11 **Restaurant** L served Tue-Sat 12-2 D served Tue-Sat 7-9.45 ⊕ SHEPHERD NEAME ◀ Shepherd Neame Master Brew, Spitfire, seasonal ales. ♥ 6 **Facilities** Dogs allowed Garden Parking

HAWKHURST | Map 7 TQ73

PICK OF THE PUBS

The Great House ♥

Gills Green TN18 5EJ
☎ 01580 753119 📄 01622 851881
e-mail: enquiries@thegreathouse.net
dir: *Just off A229 between Cranbrook & Hawkhurst*

The Great House is a wonderfully atmospheric 16th-century free house with a warm and comfortable ambience. There are three dining areas to choose from, and the Orangery which opens onto a Mediterranean-style terrace overlooking a pretty garden. The food is fresh and seasonal, and all meat is sourced from a local organic farm. Dishes range from favourites from the bar menu and might include Park Farm Cumberland sausages and mash, liver and bacon, or one of various ploughman's. Alongside the deli board selection (cheese, fish, antipasti, charcuterie), there are starters of grilled goats' cheese with sesame crust and sweet chilli dressing, or Nicoise-style fish soup with potato aioli, which may be followed by slow-cooked lamb shank with olive mash; sweet and sour pumpkin risotto; or roast breast of Norfolk chicken with haricot beans and bacon ragout. Imaginative desserts might take in Bailey's chocolate parfait with cherry sauce, or Kentish apple and cinnamon crumble. Part of the pub has been transformed into a deli/farmers' market.

Open all wk noon-11 **Bar Meals** L served Mon-Fri 12-3, Sat 12-10, Sun 12-8 D served Mon-Fri 6.30-9.30, Sat 12-10, Sun 12-8 Av main course £11 **Restaurant** L served Mon-Fri 12-3, Sat 12-10, Sun 12-8 D served Mon-Fri 6.30-9.30, Sat 12-10, Sun 12-8 Fixed menu price fr £11 Av 3 course à la carte fr £22 ⊕ FREE HOUSE ◀ Harvey's, Guinness, Youngs. ♥ 13 **Facilities** Children's menu Garden Parking

HEVER | Map 6 TQ44

The Wheatsheaf

Hever Rd, Bough Beech TN8 7NU ☎ 01732 700254
dir: *M25 & A21 take exit for Hever Castle & follow signs. 1m past Castle on right*

Originally built as a hunting lodge for Henry V, this splendid creeper-clad inn has some stunning original features, including a crown post revealed during renovation in 1997. Timbered ceilings and massive Tudor fireplaces set off various curios, such as the mounted jaw

of a man-eating shark, and a collection of musical instruments. Food served all day encompasses light lunches from Monday to Saturday; the daily board menu may include houmous with olives and pitta bread followed by lightly spiced pork casserole. Real ales include Harvey's Sussex best and interesting ciders like Kentish Biddenden cider served by handpump.

Open all wk 11am-11.30pm **Bar Meals** Av main course £10 food served all day **Restaurant** Av 3 course à la carte fr £19 ⊕ FREE HOUSE ◀ Harveys Sussex Bitter, Grasshopper ♻ Biddenden, Westons Stowford Press. **Facilities** Dogs allowed Garden Parking

HODSOLL STREET   Map 6 TQ66

The Green Man

TN15 7LE ☎ 01732 823575
e-mail: the.greenman@btinternet.com
dir: *On North Downs between Brands Hatch & Gravesend on A227*

Set in the picturesque village of Hodsoll Street on the North Downs, this 300-year-old, family-run pub is loved for its decent food and real ales. Food is prepared to order using fresh local produce, and includes a wide variety of fish (especially on Wednesday, which is fish night). Curry takes centre stage on Thursday nights, while Tuesday night is steak and rib night. Live music features every second Thursday of each month.

Open all wk **Bar Meals** L served Mon-Fri 12-2, Sat-Sun 12-3 D served Mon-Sat 6.30-9.30, Sun 6.30-9 **Restaurant** L served Mon-Fri 12-2, Sat-Sun 12-3 D served Mon-Sat 6.30-9.30, Sun 6.30-9 ⊕ HAYWOOD PUB COMPANY LTD ◀ Timothy Taylor Landlord, Harvey's, Old Speckled Hen, guest ale. **Facilities** Children's menu Play area Dogs allowed Garden Parking

IDEN GREEN   Map 6 TQ73

The Peacock ☕

Goudhurst Rd TN17 2PB ☎ 01580 211233
dir: *A21 from Tunbridge Wells to Hastings, onto A262, pub 1.5m past Goudhurst*

A Grade II listed building dating from the 17th century with low beams, an inglenook fireplace, old oak doors, real ales on tap, and a wide range of traditional pub food. A large enclosed garden with fruit trees and picnic tables on one side of the building is popular in summer, and there's also a patio.

Open all wk 12-11 (Sun 12-6) **Bar Meals** L served Mon-Fri & Sun 12-2.30, Sat all day D served Mon-Fri 6-8.45, Sat all day **Restaurant** L served Mon-Fri & Sun 12-2.30, Sat all day D served Mon-Fri 6-8.45, Sat all day ⊕ SHEPHERD NEAME ◀ Shepherd Neame Master Brew, Spitfire, seasonal ales. ☕ 12 **Facilities** Children's menu Family room Dogs allowed Garden Parking

IGHTHAM   Map 6 TQ55

PICK OF THE PUBS

The Harrow Inn ☕

Common Rd TN15 9EB ☎ 01732 885912
dir: *1.5m from Borough Green on A25 to Sevenoaks, signed Ightham Common, turn left into Common Rd. Inn 0.25m on left*

Within easy reach of both M20 and M26 motorways, yet tucked away down country lanes close to the National Trust's Knole Park and Ightham Mote, this Virginia creeper-hung stone inn dates back to the 17th century and beyond. The bar area comprises two rooms with a great brick fireplace, open to both sides and piled high with blazing logs; meanwhile the restaurant boasts a vine-clad conservatory that opens to a terrace that's ideal for summer dining. Menus vary with the seasons, and seafood is a particular speciality: fish aficionados can enjoy dishes such as crab and ginger spring roll; swordfish with Cajun spice and salsa; or pan-fried fillets of sea bass with lobster cream and spinach. Other main courses have included Bishop's Finger (one of Shepherd Neame's fine beers) baked sausage with gammon, fennel, red onions and garlic; and tagliatelle with a wild mushroom, fresh herb, lemongrass and chilli ragoût. Children are welcome but it's a more grown up affair on Friday and Saturday evenings (no young children and babies).

Open noon-3 6-11 Closed: 26 Dec, 1 Jan, Sun eve & Mon **Bar Meals** L served Tue-Sun 12-2 D served Tue-Sat 6-9 Av main course £13.50 **Restaurant** L served Tue-Sun 12-2 booking required D served Tue-Sat 6-9 booking required Av 3 course à la carte fr £30 ⊕ FREE HOUSE ◀ Greene King Abbot Ale, IPA. ☕ 8 **Facilities** Family room Garden Parking

IVY HATCH   Map 6 TQ55

PICK OF THE PUBS

The Plough at Ivy Hatch ☕

See Pick of the Pubs on page 264

LAMBERHURST   Map 6 TQ63

The Swan at the Vineyard ☕

The Down TN3 8EU ☎ 01892 890170
dir: *Telephone for directions*

Outside the Swan, which dates from the 1700s, is a beautiful floral display; inside there are open fireplaces and leather couches, and as many as three ghosts. There are two dining areas, one traditional, the other a 'cellar restaurant', with high-back leather chairs and an art gallery. A comprehensive menu features coq au vin; coconut and galangal Thai risotto with tiger prawns; and spinach and chanterelle lasagne. Try one of the award-winning English wines.

Open all wk ◀ Harveys Best, Adnams Broadside, Bombardier, Adnams Regatta, guest ales. ☕ 11 **Facilities** Play area Dogs allowed Garden Parking

LEIGH   Map 6 TQ54

The Greyhound Charcott ☕

Charcott TN11 8LG ☎ 01892 870275
e-mail: ghatcharcott@aol.com
dir: *From Tonbridge take B245 N towards Hildenborough. Left onto Leigh road, right onto Stocks Green road. Through Leigh, right then left at T-junct, right into Charcott (Camp Hill)*

This cosy pub has been welcoming locals and visitors for around 120 years. Tony French, who took over four years ago, has maintained the traditional atmosphere in which music, pool table and fruit machine have no place. Winter brings log fires, while in summer you can enjoy the garden. Meals could include home-made pork and brandy terrine with apple chutney, followed by pan-fried medallions of local venison saddle with redcurrant sauce. Enjoy your meal with a good selection of well-kept ales.

Open all wk noon-3 5.30-11 (Sat-Sun all day) **Bar Meals** L served Mon-Sat 12-2, Sun 12-3 D served Mon-Sat 6.30-9.30 Av main course £10 **Restaurant** L served Mon-Sat 12-2, Sun 12-3 D served Mon-Sat 6.30.9.30 Fixed menu price fr £18 Av 3 course à la carte fr £25 ⊕ ENTERPRISE INNS ◀ Harvey's, Timothy Taylor, Westerham British Bulldog. ☕ 8 **Facilities** Dogs allowed Garden Parking

LINTON   Map 7 TQ75

The Bull Inn ☕

Linton Hill ME17 4AW ☎ 01622 743612
dir: *S of Maidstone on A229 (Hastings road)*

A traditional 17th-century coaching inn in the heart of the Weald with stunning views from the glorious garden, and a large inglenook fireplace and wealth of beams inside. An inviting bar menu includes lasagne, spinach and ricotta tortellini, cod and chips, and bubble and squeak, as well as sandwiches, baguettes, and ploughman's. From the restaurant menu comes pan-fried venison steak wrapped in pancetta, served on sautéed oyster mushrooms.

Open all day all wk 11am-11.30pm (Sun noon-10.30pm) **Bar Meals** L served Mon-Fri 12-2.30, Sat-Sun 12-9 D served Mon-Fri 6-9, Sat-Sun 12-9 ⊕ SHEPHERD NEAME ◀ Shepherd Neame Master Brew, Kent's Best. ☕ 7 **Facilities** Dogs allowed Garden Parking

PICK OF THE PUBS

The Plough at Ivy Hatch ♀

IVY HATCH   Map 6 TQ55

High Cross Rd TN15 ONL
☎ **01732 810100**
e-mail: theploughpubco@tiscali.co.uk
dir: *Off A25 between Borough Green & Sevenoaks, follow signs to Ightham Mote*

Set deep in Kent countryside, and just a quarter of a mile from the National Trust's 14th-century Ightham Mote, the 17th-century Plough is the perfect spot for a lingering lunch or supper. Now the last bastion of a once-thriving community, it fulfils an integral part of village life, even more so since refurbishment provided smart oak flooring and a new seating area around the fireplace. Plans to establish a kitchen garden within the grounds will complement the locally sourced produce that's already used, including a wide

selection of seafood from the south coast and seasonal game from local shoots. Starters might include lentil and lovage soup; and fruits de mer, consisting of langoustines, crevettes, North Atlantic prawns and Colchester rock oysters. To follow, stay with the fish, perhaps, with Isle of Shuna (Argyll & Bute) mussels in white wine and cream sauce with hand-cut chips; or tackle a Sussex rib-eye steak with caramelised banana shallots and peppercorn sauce; or, for vegetarians, wild mushroom pie with new potatoes, green beans and cep sauce. Desserts include a range of ice creams; lemon tart with mascarpone; and crème brûlée. Lunch on Sunday need not be limited to roasts, but roasts there are, namely rump of beef, leg of lamb, loin of pork and haunch of venison. The compact wine list takes a broad view of the world from France to New Zealand one way, and to Chile and California the other. There's a terrace and garden ideal for alfresco dining. If you go on one of the many good walks in the area, don't worry about how muddy your boots are when you squelch to the pub.

Open all week 12-3 6-11 (Sat 12-11 Sun 10-6) **Bar Meals** L served Mon-Sat 12-2.45, Sun 12-6 D served Mon-Sat 6-9.30 Av main course £10 **Restaurant** L served Mon-Sat 12-2.45, Sun 12-6 D served Mon-Sat 6-9.30 Fixed menu price fr £15 Av 3 course à la carte fr £19.50 ⊕ FREE HOUSE ◼ Harveys Best & Seasonal ales & Westerham Finchcocks Ŏ Stowford Press. ♀ 8 **Facilities** Children's menu Garden Parking

LITTLEBOURNE — Map 7 TR25

King William IV

4 High St CT3 1UN ☎ 01227 721244 📠 01227 721244
e-mail: sam@bowwindow.co.uk
dir: From A2 follow signs to Howletts Zoo. After zoo & at end of road, pub straight ahead

Located just outside the city of Canterbury, the King William IV overlooks the village green and is well placed for Sandwich and Herne Bay. With open log fires and exposed oak beams, this friendly inn is a good place for visitors and locals.

Open all wk ⊕ FREE HOUSE ◀ John Smith's, Sussex Harveys. Facilities Parking

MAIDSTONE — Map 7 TQ75

The Black Horse Inn ★★★★ INN ♥

Pilgrims Way, Thurnham ME14 3LD
☎ 01622 737185 📠 01622 739170
e-mail: info@wellieboot.net
dir: M20 junct 7, A249, right into Detling. Opposite Cock Horse Pub turn onto Pilgrims Way

Tucked beneath the steep face of the North Downs on the Pilgrims Way, this homely and welcoming free house has oak beams, exposed brickwork and an open log fire in winter. The building is thought to have been a forge before its conversion to an inn during the middle years of the 18th century. The bar and restaurant menus range from traditional favourites like honey and mustard roasted ham on bubble and squeak to grilled fillet of sea bass with Mediterranean vegetables. Local ales and Biddenden cider is available. There are stylish bed and breakfast rooms available.

Open all day all wk 11-11 Bar Meals Av main course £8.95 food served all day Restaurant Fixed menu price fr £8.95 Av 3 course à la carte fr £11.95 food served all day ⊕ FREE HOUSE ◀ Kents Best, London Pride, Greene King IPA, Black Sheep, Late Red Ď Biddendens. ♥ 30 Facilities Children's menu Dogs allowed Garden Parking Rooms 30

MARKBEECH — Map 6 TQ44

The Kentish Horse

Cow Ln TN8 5NT ☎ 01342 850493
dir: 3m from Edenbridge & 7m from Tunbridge Wells

Surrounded by Kent countryside, this pub is popular with ramblers, cyclists and families. The inn dates from 1340 and is said to have a smuggling history; it also boasts a curious street-bridging Kentish sign. The menu is cooked simply from fresh ingredients, and can be served anywhere in the pub or garden. Harvey's Larkins and regular guest ales available.

Open all day all wk Bar Meals L served Mon-Sat 12-2.30, Sun 12-3.30 D served Mon-Sat 7-9.30 ⊕ FREE HOUSE ◀ Harvey's Larkins, guest ales. Facilities Play area Dogs allowed Garden Parking

NEWNHAM — Map 7 TQ95

The George Inn ♥

44 The Street ME9 0LL
☎ 01795 890237 📠 01795 890726
dir: 4m from Faversham

The George is an attractive country inn with a large beer garden. Despite the passing of the centuries, the inn retains much of its historic character with beams, polished wooden floors, inglenook fireplaces and candlelit tables. Food is served in the bar and 50-seater restaurant. Bar snacks range from sandwiches to sausage and mash, while main meals could include pan-fried fillet of red snapper with crushed potatoes, baby fennel, fresh scampi and rosemary butter; or peppered duck breast with celeriac mash and cherry and port sauce. Regular events include live jazz, quizzes and murder mystery evenings.

Open all wk 11-3 6.30-11 (Sun noon-4 7-10.30) Bar Meals L served all wk 12-2.30 booking required D served all wk 7-9.30 booking required Av main course £10 Restaurant L served all wk 12-2.30 booking required D served all wk 7-9.30 booking required Av 3 course à la carte fr £20 ⊕ SHEPHERD NEAME ◀ Shepherd Neame Master Brew, Spitfire, Bishops Finger, Kent Best, seasonal ale. ♥ 8 Facilities Children's menu Garden Parking

PENSHURST — Map 6 TQ54

PICK OF THE PUBS

The Bottle House Inn ♥

See Pick of the Pubs on page 266

The Leicester Arms

High St TN11 8BT ☎ 01892 870551
dir: From Tunbridge Wells take A26 towards Tonbridge. Left onto B21765 towards Penshurst

A large and picturesque country inn at the centre of a picturesque village, the Leicester Arms stands in its own pretty gardens looking out over the River Medway. It was once part of the Penshurst Place estate. The wood-panelled dining room is worth a visit for the views over the weald and river alone. Dishes range from traditional pub food in the bar to the likes of pressed pork belly with crackling, chicken curry, or Moroccan vegetable tagine from the carte menu.

The Leicester Arms

Open all wk 11am-mdnt Bar Meals Av main course £10 food served all day Restaurant Av 3 course à la carte fr £19 ⊕ ENTERPRISE INNS ◀ Harvey's Sussex Bitter, Shepherd Neame Master Brew, Sharp's Doom Bar. Facilities Children's menu Dogs allowed Garden Parking

PICK OF THE PUBS

The Spotted Dog ♥

Smarts Hill TN11 8EE
☎ 01892 870253 📠 01892 870107
e-mail: info@spotteddogpub.co.uk
dir: Off B2188 between Penshurst & Fordcombe

Deep in the Kent countryside, this 16th-century white weather-boarded free house enjoys fine views over the Weald from the rear terrace. The rambling interior with its tiled and oak floors, low beams and three open fireplaces creates a welcoming atmosphere for both locals and visitors alike. But don't expect fast food or a huge menu, because everything here is freshly prepared to order, using traceable local produce wherever possible. Starters like rare roasted venison salad with red wine vinaigrette set the stage for main course choices that might include mushroom stroganoff with rice; calves' liver and bacon with creamy mash, vegetables and rich gravy; or grilled whole sea bass, lemon hollandaise sauce, new potatoes and vegetables. If you fancy re-creating some of those dishes at home, then help is at hand; just pop into the adjacent Spotted Dog Farm Shop for a comprehensive range of produce from local suppliers.

Open all wk noon-3 6-11 (Sun noon-10.30) Bar Meals L served Mon-Sat 12-2.30 D served Mon-Sat 6-9 Restaurant L served Mon-Sat 12-2.30, Sun 12-5 D served Mon-Fri 6-9, Sat 6-9.30 ⊕ FREE HOUSE ◀ Sharp's Doom Bar, Larkins Traditional, guest ale Ď Chiddingstone. ♥ 20 Facilities Children's menu Dogs allowed Garden Parking

PICK OF THE PUBS

The Bottle House Inn 🍷

PENSHURST Map 6 TQ54

Coldharbour Rd TN11 8ET
☎ 01892 870306 📄 01892 871094
e-mail:
info@thebottlehouseinnpenshurst.co.uk
web:
www.thebottlehouseinnpenshurst.co.uk
dir: *From Tunbridge Wells take A264 W, then B2188 N. After Fordcombe left towards Edenbridge & Hever. Pub 500yds after staggered x-rds*

A well-regarded dining pub, The Bottle House was built as a farmhouse in 1492, and later divided into two properties. Thomas Scraggs, 'a common beer seller of Speldhurst', leased one of them in 1806 and obtained a licence to sell ales and ciders. It was registered as an alehouse at each subsequent change of hands, at a time when hop-growing was the major local industry. During the 19th century it also housed a shop, a farrier and a cobbler, and there was a skittle alley at the back. The pub was said to be the originator of the ploughman's lunch, made with bread from the old bakery next door and cheese donated by Canadian soldiers billeted nearby. The building was completely refurbished in 1938 and granted a full licence; it was reputedly named after all the old bottles discovered during these works. Today, low beams and a copper-topped counter give the bar a warm, welcoming atmosphere. Choose from the range of Harveys and Larkins hand-pumped beers and eight wines by the glass before settling at a bench seat on the patio or in the garden. The menu has something for everyone, starting with grilled green lip mussels stuffed with Welsh rarebit, duck liver and orange parfait with toasted brioche, or deep-fried sesame coated brie and breaded mozzarella with plum and apple chutney. Lighter meals and shares are also available and may include smoked fish platter, ploughmans' or linguini in creamy basil pesto sauce. Moving on to main courses, diners may enjoy trio of Kentish sausages with mustard mash; oven-roasted skate wing with cracked black pepper crust; braised lamb shank with mint and rosemary gravy; or red snapper fillet with soy, ginger, chilli and spring onion dressing. Ploughman's and ciabattas are also served.

Open 11-11 (Sun 11-10.30) Closed: 25 Dec **Meals** 12-10 (Sun 12-9) FREE HOUSE Larkins Ale, Harveys Sussex Best Bitter. 🍷 8 **Facilities** Children's menu Dogs allowed Garden Parking

PLUCKLEY
Map 7 TQ94

PICK OF THE PUBS

The Dering Arms ♟

See Pick of the Pubs on page 268

See Pick of the Pubs on page 268

The Mundy Bois ♟

Mundy Bois TN27 0ST
☎ 01233 840048 📠 01233 840193
e-mail: helen@mundybois.com
dir: *From A20 at Charing exit towards Pluckley. Right into Pinnock at bottom of Pluckley Hill. Next right into Mundy Bois Rd. 1m left*

An ale house since 1780 and formerly named the Rose and Crown, this creeper-clad pub is on the outskirts of Pluckley, considered to be the most haunted place in England. A blackboard menu features frequently changing dishes created from local produce where possible, and a nearby farm specializing in rare breeds — rare breed Welsh pork chops on mustard mash with caramelised apples and cider sauce. A patio dining area allows alfresco eating, and the garden has an adventure playground.

Open all wk Bar Meals L served all wk 12-2 D served all wk 6.30-9 Restaurant L served all wk 12-2 D served all wk 6.30-9 ⊕ FREE HOUSE ◀ Master Brew, Youngs. ♟ 8 Facilities Children's menu Play area Dogs allowed Garden Parking

ST MARGARET'S AT CLIFFE
Map 7 TR34

PICK OF THE PUBS

The Coastguard

St Margaret's Bay CT15 6DY ☎ 01304 853176
e-mail: thecoastguard@talk21.com
dir: *2m off A258 between Dover & Deal, follow St Margaret's at Cliffe signs. Through village towards sea*

The Coastguard is set in one of the most delightful spots on the Kentish coast, St Margaret's Bay, with its breathtaking white cliffs and beach walks. The pub stands only a stone's throw from the water's edge and

has spectacular views out to sea. It is renowned for its food and hospitality, and everything is freshly made on the premises, including the breads and sauces, using local produce whenever possible. The menu changes daily, even during service, depending on the weather and what is available, and features award-winning fish dishes, beef from a local farm and 'garden of Kent' fresh salad. The cheeseboard is highly regarded and has attracted many accolades. The regular selection of traditional British beers and cask ales is supplemented by guest ales, and there are some rare single malts including some from defunct distilleries.

Open all day all wk 11-11 (Sun 11-10.30) Bar Meals L served all wk 12.30-2.45 D served all wk 6.30-8.45 food served all day Restaurant L served all wk 12.30-2.45 D served all wk 6.30-8.45 ⊕ FREE HOUSE ◀ Gadds of Ramsgate, Hop Daemon, Adnams, Caledonian, Isle of Arran. Facilities Children's menu Play area Dogs allowed Garden Parking

SANDWICH
Map 7 TR35

George & Dragon Inn ♟

Fisher St CT13 9EJ ☎ 01304 613106
e-mail: enquiries@georgeanddragon-sandwich.co.uk
dir: *Between Dover & Canterbury*

The George and Dragon has seen and undergone many changes since it was built in 1446, but from the day it was first licensed in 1615, the house has never closed. This friendly, family-owned pub serves a full selection of draught beers, wines and spirits, alongside a modern British menu, using fresh, seasonal produce (rib-eye steak; cod wrapped in Parma ham; braised shoulder of lamb with olive mash). Enjoy your meal by the log fire inside, or outside in the courtyard garden.

Open all wk 11-3 6-11 (Sat 11-11 Sun 11-10.30 summer, 11-6 winter) Bar Meals L served all wk 12-3 booking required D served all wk 6-9 booking required Av main course £10.50 Restaurant L served all wk 12-3 booking required D served all wk 6-9 booking required Av 3 course à la carte fr £19.27 ⊕ ENTERPRISE INNS ◀ Shepherd Neame Master Brew, Youngs Special, Harvey's Sussex Best, Adnams Broadside, Sharp's Doom Bar. ♟ 10 Facilities Dogs allowed Garden

SELLING
Map 7 TR05

The Rose and Crown

Perry Wood ME13 9RY ☎ 01227 752214
e-mail: perrywoodrose@btinternet.co.uk
dir: *From A28 right at Badgers Hill, left at end. 1st left signed Perry Wood. Pub at top*

Set amidst 150 acres of woodland in the middle of an Area of Outstanding Natural Beauty, this 16th-century pub's beamed interior is decorated with hop garlands, corn dollies, horse brasses and brass cask taps. The perfumed summer garden includes a children's play area and bat and trap pitch. Expect a choice of four real ales including a guest, and a menu high in comfort factor. The ploughman's is served with huffkin, a bread made with

eggs, milk and ground paragon wheat - a little like brioche but less sweet. A game menu is available in season.

Open all wk noon-3 6.30-11 Closed: 25-26 Dec eve, 1 Jan eve, Mon eve Bar Meals L served all wk 12-2 D served Tue-Sun 7-9 Restaurant L served all wk 12-2 D served Tue-Sun 7-9 ⊕ FREE HOUSE ◀ Adnams Southwold, Harvey's Sussex Best Bitter, guest ale. Facilities Children's menu Play area Dogs allowed Garden Parking

SMARDEN
Map 7 TQ84

The Bell ♟

Bell Ln TN27 8PW ☎ 01233 770283
e-mail: thesmardenbell@btconnect.com
dir: *Telephone for directions*

Built in the year 1536, the Bell was originally a farm building on a large estate. It was used as a blacksmiths forge right up until 1907, but it had also been an alehouse since 1630. A typical menu includes seared king scallops with spinach and a crab sauce, chargrilled chicken breast with Mozzarella, basil and wild mushroom sauce, gammon steak with beetroot mash and parsley sauce, and tournedos of monkfish Rossini.

Open all day all wk noon-11 Bar Meals L served all wk 12-2.30 D served Mon-Sat 6.30-9.30, Sun 6.30-8.30 Restaurant L served all wk 12-2.30 D served Mon-Sat 6.30-9.30, Sun 6.30-8.30 ⊕ SHEPHERD NEAME ◀ Shepherd Neame Master Brew, Spitfire, seasonal ales. ♟ 15 Facilities Dogs allowed Garden Parking

PICK OF THE PUBS

The Chequers Inn

The Street TN27 8QA
☎ 01233 770217 📠 01233 770623
e-mail: spaldings@thechequerssmarden.com
dir: *Through Leeds village, left to Sutton Valence/ Headcorn then left for Smarden. Pub in village centre*

A ghost is said to haunt the Chequers — an atmospheric 14th-century inn with clapboard façade in the centre of one of Kent's prettiest villages. The inn has its own beautiful landscaped garden with large duck pond and attractive south-facing courtyard. Real ales by Harveys and Adnams are served in the low beamed bars. Food ranges from traditional to modern, with something for every taste and appetite including further options on the specials board. The bar menu tempts with sausages and mash or home-made spaghetti bolognaise, while main courses may include steak and ale pie; chicken chasseur; or roasted cod rarebit. Fish specials change daily according to the season, and Sundays offer a popular choice of two roasts and a reduced à la carte menu. The pub is much involved with the local community throughout the year, and hosts an annual beer festival in August, plus other events.

Open all wk Bar Meals L served all wk 12-3 D served all wk 6-9 Restaurant L served all wk 12-3 D served all wk 6-9 ⊕ FREE HOUSE ◀ Harvey's, IPA, Adnams. Facilities Children's menu Dogs allowed Garden Parking

PICK OF THE PUBS

The Dering Arms 🍷

PLUCKLEY Map 7 TQ94

Station Rd TN27 0RR
☎ 01233 840371 📄 01233 840498
e-mail: jim@deringarms.com
web: www.deringarms.com
dir: *M20 junct 8, A20 to Ashford. Right onto B2077 at Charing to Pluckley*

Pluckley's residents cherish its claim to fame as the most haunted village in England; they're also proud of its starring role in the 1990s TV series, *The Darling Buds of May.* The village was for centuries the home of the Dering family and community legend has it that the first baronet, Sir Edward Dering, escaped from the Roundheads through a narrow, round-topped window at the manor. The Victorians, in a flurry of romanticism, added rounded 'Dering windows' to the family's houses, including their 1840s hunting lodge, a smaller version of the main house, which is now the Dering Arms. It has two simply furnished traditional bars with mounted stags' heads and fishing rods, roaring fires in winter, an intimate restaurant, and a family room with a baby grand piano (there to be played). Chef/patron James Buss has managed this distinctive inn with passion and flair since 1984. He does the main cooking himself, preparing every meal to order using only the finest, freshest produce. The extensive daily menus reflect his love of fresh fish and seafood, such as starters of Sussex mackerel smokies and grilled Irish oysters with chorizo. Appearing as main course options might be confit of duck with bubble and squeak potato cake and wild mushroom sauce; pan-fried tuna steak with garlic and lemon butter; and grilled skate wing with capers and beurre noisettes. Do check the blackboards for specials, as well. Jim's Seafood Special, a traditional fruits de mer for a minimum of two people, costs £30 a head and requires 24 hours' notice. Desserts range from oranges in caramel with Grand Marnier, to prunes marinated in Cointreau. Black tie gourmet evenings, featuring seven courses of unusual and intriguing dishes, are held throughout the winter, and classic car meetings are held every second Sunday of the month.

Open Tue-Sun 11.30-3.30 6-11 (ex Sun eve) Closed: 26-29 Dec & Mon **Bar Meals** L served Tue-Sun 12-2 D served Tue-Sat 7-9.30 Av main course £17 **Restaurant** L served Tue-Sun 12-2 D served Tue-Sat 7-9.30 Av 3 course à la carte fr £32 FREE HOUSE Goacher's Dering Ale, Maidstone Dark, Gold Star, Old Ale. 🍷 7 **Facilities** Children's menu Family room Dogs allowed Garden Parking

SPELDHURST
Map 6 TQ54

PICK OF THE PUBS

George & Dragon 🍷

Speldhurst Hill TN3 0NN
☎ 01892 863125 📠 01892 863216
e-mail: julian@speldhurst.com
dir: *Telephone for directions*

Built around 1500, the George and Dragon is a venerable timber-clad village hostelry. Some say its origins are earlier, when Speldhurst would have seen archers departing for the Battle of Agincourt. At the beginning of the 17th century the curative powers of the village's iron-rich waters were discovered, which put nearby Tunbridge Wells on the map. Today's customers enjoy a modern gastro-pub, where refreshments include a range of local organic fruit juices. The menu offers half a dozen eclectic choices at each stage: you could start with parsnip and coriander soup with parsnip crisps and follow with Ashdown Forest venison stew, sautéed potatoes and wilted greens; roast guinea fowl with chilli and tarragon butter; or fillet of wild sea bass with brown shrimp and caper butter. Food can be served in the two gardens - one a modern layout with bay trees and herbs, the other a Mediterranean garden with 200-year-old olive tree.

Open all wk **Bar Meals** L served all wk 12-2.45 D served Mon-Sat 7-9.45 Av main course £9 **Restaurant** L served Sat-Sun 12-3 booking required D served Fri-Sun 7-10 booking required Av 3 course à la carte fr £25 ⊕ FREE HOUSE ◀ Harvey's Best, Sussex Pale, Larkins, Porter. 🍷 10 **Facilities** Children's menu Family room Dogs allowed Garden Parking

TENTERDEN
Map 7 TQ83

White Lion Inn 🍷

57 High St TN30 6BD
☎ 01580 765077 📠 01580 764157
e-mail: whitelion.tenterden@marstons.co.uk
dir: *On A28 (Ashford to Hastings road)*

A 16th-century coaching inn on a tree-lined street of this old Cinque Port, with many original features retained. The area is known for its cricket connections, and the first recorded county match between Kent and London was played here in 1719. The menu offers plenty of choice, from calves' liver and bacon, shoulder of lamb, and Cumberland cottage pie to tuna pasta bake and various ploughman's.

Open all wk 10am-11pm (wknds 10am-mdnt) **Bar Meals** food served all day **Restaurant** food served all day ⊕ MARSTONS ◀ Marstons Pedigree, Cumberland. 🍷 10 **Facilities** Children's menu Garden Parking

TONBRIDGE

See Penshurst

TUNBRIDGE WELLS (ROYAL)
Map 6 TQ53

PICK OF THE PUBS

The Beacon ★★★★ INN 🍷

See Pick of the Pubs on page 270

The Crown Inn 🍷

The Green, Groombridge TN3 9QH ☎ 01892 864742
e-mail: crowngroombridge@aol.com
dir: *Take A264 W of Tunbridge Wells, then B2110 S*

Dating back to 1585, this charming free house was a favourite haunt for Keira Knightley and the cast of *Pride and Prejudice* during filming at Groombridge Place a few years ago. Sir Arthur Conan Doyle was a frequent visitor while staying at Groombridge Place situated opposite. Also a haunt for smugglers once, low beams and an inglenook fireplace are the setting for some great food. Expect dishes such as traditional French cassoulet, home-made steakburger with applewood cheese and bacon, and favourites like Cumberland sausage with bubble and squeak and onion gravy.

Open all wk 11-3 6-11 (Sat 11-11 Sun noon-10.30 Sun noon-5 winter) **Bar Meals** L served Mon-Fri 12-2.30, Sat-Sun 12-3 D served Mon-Thu 6.30-9, Fri-Sat 6.30-9.30 Av main course £9.50 **Restaurant** L served Mon-Fri 12-2.30, Sat-Sun 12-3 booking required D served Mon-Thu 6.30-9, Fri-Sat 6.30-9.30 booking required Av 3 course à la carte fr £19.50 ⊕ FREE HOUSE ◀ Harvey's IPA, Larkins, IPA Ŏ Stowford Press. 🍷 8 **Facilities** Play area Dogs allowed Garden Parking

PICK OF THE PUBS

The Hare on Langton Green 🍷

Langton Rd, Langton Green TN3 0JA
☎ 01892 862419 📠 01892 861275
e-mail: hare@brunningandprice.co.uk
dir: *From Tunbridge Wells follow A264 towards East Grinstead. Village on A264*

There has been an inn on this site since the 16th century, though the previous version was partially destroyed in a fire in 1900. What remained was too dilapidated to restore, and the present Victorian-Tudor model was built a year later. In a spooky twist, a woman holding a child is said to haunt the main staircase and cellar, though what era she dates back to nobody can say. On the comfortably comprehensive daily-changing menu starters and main dishes might include lamb koftas, beetroot and mascarpone risotto or crab-stuffed mushrooms, followed by honey-glazed

turkey with parsley and parsnip mash, or pork belly with caramel sauce. Light bites and interesting sandwiches are also available. In addition to the variety of real beers and ciders, there's an impressive range of malt whiskies and wines by the glass.

Open all day all wk 11-11 (Fri-Sat 11-mdnt) **Bar Meals** Av main course £10 food served all day **Restaurant** food served all day ⊕ GREENE KING ◀ Greene King IPA, Abbot Ale, Morland Best, Old Speckled Hen, St Austell Tribute Ŏ Westons Old Rosie, Inch's Stonehouse, Stowford Press. 🍷 20 **Facilities** Dogs allowed Garden Parking

WESTERHAM
Map 6 TQ45

The Fox & Hounds 🍷

Toys Hill TN16 1QG ☎ 01732 750328
e-mail: hickmott1@hotmail.com
dir: *Telephone for directions*

High up on Kent's Greensand Ridge, in an Area of Outstanding Natural Beauty, this late 18th-century ale house adjoins a large National Trust estate incorporating an old water tower now protected as a home for hibernating bats. The pub has a traditionally styled restaurant, where starters include smoked salmon and crab roulade, and deep-fried brie with cranberry sauce, while among the mains are fillet of pork stuffed with dates and apricots on horseradish mash, leg of lamb on bubble and squeak with rosemary jus, and daily specials. A children's menu is available.

Open 10-3 6-11 (Sat-Sun 10am-11pm) Closed: 25 Dec, Mon eve **Bar Meals** L served Mon-Sat 12-2, Sun 12-3 D served Tue-Sat 6-9 Av main course £11 **Restaurant** L served Mon-Sat 12-2, Sun 12-3 D served Tue-Sat 6-9 Av 3 course à la carte fr £20 ⊕ GREENE KING ◀ Greene King IPA, Abbot Ale, Ruddles County. 🍷 9 **Facilities** Children's menu Dogs allowed Garden Parking

WEST MALLING
Map 6 TQ65

PICK OF THE PUBS

The Farmhouse 🍷

97 The High St ME19 6NA
☎ 01732 843257 📠 01622 851881
e-mail: enquiries@thefarmhouse.biz
dir: *M20 junct 4, S on A228. Right to West Malling. Pub in village centre*

A modern gastro-pub, The Farmhouse occupies a handsome Elizabethan property at the heart of the village of West Malling. It has a relaxing atmosphere with a stylish bar and two dining rooms, while outside is a spacious walled garden with an area of decking. There are stone-baked pizzas and toasted paninis alongside the blackboard menu which changes regularly. Starters range from home-made soup with crusty bread to melon and Bayonne ham with blackcurrant dressing. Main courses might include pan-fried sea bass salad with sun-dried tomatoes; steak, Guinness and mushroom pie; or confit duck leg

continued on page 271

PICK OF THE PUBS

The Beacon ★★★★ INN 🍷

TUNBRIDGE WELLS (ROYAL) Map 6 TQ53

Tea Garden Ln, Rusthall TN3 9JH
☎ 01892 524252 📠 01892 534288
e-mail: beaconhotel@btopenworld.com
web: www.the-beacon.co.uk
dir: *From Tunbridge Wells take A264 towards East Grinstead. Pub 1m on left*

Set amid seventeen acres of grounds, the Beacon began life in 1895 as the country home of Sir Walter Harris. A former lieutenant of the City of London, he commissioned the finest craftsmen to create a host of impressive architectural features. The building still oozes with country house charm; the bar, with its moulded plaster ceiling, bookshelves and stained glass windows is a wonderful place to relax with a pint of Harveys or Larkins Traditional ales. After Harris's death the house passed through various hands until it became a hostel for Jewish refugees during the Second World War. Today, The Beacon's grounds encompass lakes, woodland walks and a chalybeate spring that was first used some 40 years before its more famous counterpart in Tunbridge Wells. Enjoy a drink on the terrace with amazing views in summer or by the fire in the bar on cooler days; here, you'll find draught and bottled cider, a range of beers and a good wine list offering plenty of choice by the glass. Food is served in both the bar and the elegant restaurant, or in one of three private dining rooms. The menus take full advantage of seasonal local produce to which, as a member of Kentish Fare, the kitchen is strongly committed. You could start with pork and apricot terrine with grape and apple chutney; or stilton and pine nut salad with Domino quails' eggs and herb croutons. Main course dishes include butter-roasted local cod with pea and smoked halibut ragout with poached egg, and seared rib-eye steak with caramelised onion mash and sautéed green vegetables. There are two double bedrooms and one single: the Georgian Room, the Colonial Room and the Contemporary Room.

Open Mon-Sat 11-11 (Sun 12-10.30) **Bar Meals** L served Mon-Thu 12-2.30, Fri-Sun 12-9.30 D served Mon-Thu 6.30-9.30, Fri-Sun 12-9.30 Av main course £9.50 **Restaurant** L served Mon-Thu 12-2.30, Fri-Sun 12-9.30 D served Mon-Thu 6.30-9.30, Fri-Sun 12-9.30 Av 3 course fr £22 FREE HOUSE Harveys Best, Timothy Taylor Landlord, Larkins Traditional Stowford Press Draught Cider, Weston's organic bottled pear cider. 🍷 12
Facilities Children's menu Play area Garden Parking **Rooms** 3

WEST MALLING *continued*

with sweet potato mash. Bar food is available all day. The 15th-century barn at the rear of the pub has been transformed into a deli/farmers' market.

Open all day all wk noon-11 **Bar Meals** Av main course £11 food served all day **Restaurant** Fixed menu price fr £11 Av 3 course à la carte fr £22 food served all day ⊕ FREE HOUSE ◀ Harvey's, Guinness, Youngs. ♀ 13 **Facilities** Children's menu Garden Parking

WHITSTABLE Map 7 TR16

PICK OF THE PUBS

The Sportsman ◎◎ ♀

Faversham Rd CT5 4BP ☎ 01227 273370
e-mail: contact@thesportsmanseasalter.co.uk
dir: *3.5m W of Whitstable, on the coast road between Whitstable and Faversham*

Reached via a winding lane across open marshland from Whitstable, and tucked beneath the sea wall, the Sportsman may seem an unlikely place to find such good food. The rustic yet comfortable interior, with its wooden floors, stripped pine furniture and interesting collection of prints has a warm and welcoming feel. A range of Shepherd Neame ales is served, including seasonal brews, and there is an excellent wine list. Remember that food is not served on Sunday evenings or Mondays, or you could be disappointed. The daily menu is based on local produce from farms, boats and game dealers. Fish dishes might include seared Thornback ray with cockles, sherry vinegar and brown butter. Starters also feature lots of seafood, typically rock oysters and hot chorizo. Amongst the mains is Monkshill Farm pork belly and apple sauce. There is also a tasting menu available for a maximum of 6 people.

Open all wk noon-3 6-11 Closed: 25 Dec **Bar Meals** Av main course £16 **Restaurant** L served Tue-Sun 12-2 booking required D served Tue-Sat 7-9 booking required Av 3 course à la carte fr £30 ⊕ SHEPHERD NEAME ◀ Shepherd Neame Late Red, Master Brew, Porter, Early Bird, Goldings, Whitstable Bay. ♀ 8 **Facilities** Children's menu Family room Dogs allowed Garden Parking

WYE Map 7 TR04

The New Flying Horse ♀

Upper Bridge St TN25 5AN
☎ 01233 812297 📠 01233 813487
e-mail: newflyhorse@shepherd-neame.co.uk
dir: *Telephone for directions*

This 17th-century posting house retains much of its original character after being refurbished. Winter log fires warm the bar and dining area, where you'll find a good selection of meals. In warmer weather, customers can

wine and dine in the prize-winning garden, which was featured at the 2005 Chelsea Flower Show. Expect a wide range of seasonal specials, classic dishes and vegetarian options, produced from the finest local ingredients.

Closed: Mon-Fri eve (Oct-May) ⊕ SHEPHERD NEAME ◀ Masterbrew Spitfire, Plus guests. ♀ 8 **Facilities** Play area Dogs allowed Garden

LANCASHIRE

BASHALL EAVES Map 18 SD64

PICK OF THE PUBS

The Red Pump Inn ♀

See Pick of the Pubs on page 272

BILSBORROW Map 18 SD53

Owd Nell's Tavern ♀

Guy's Thatched Hamlet, Canal Side PR3 0RS
☎ 01995 640010 📄 01995 640141
e-mail: info@guysthatchedhamlet.com
dir: *M6 junct 32 N on A6. In approx 5m follow brown tourist signs to Guy's Thatched Hamlet*

The Wilkinson family has owned and run Guy's Thatched Hamlet beside the Lancaster Canal for nearly 30 years, of which this country-style tavern forms a part. Flagstone floors, fireplaces and low ceilings create an authentic ambience. Excellent real ales are supplemented by a lovingly assembled collection of wheat beers, fruit beers and pilsners. All-day fare is typified by home-made steamed chicken, leek and mushroom pudding; famous steak and kidney pudding; spinach and cheese cannelloni; and bacon, brie and cranberry panini. Children's menus are available. There is a cider festival at the end of July.

Open all wk 7am-2am Closed: 25 Dec **Bar Meals** Av main course £7.50 food served all day **Restaurant** L served Mon-Sat 12-2.30, Sun 12-10.30 D served Mon-Sat 5.30-10.30, Sun 12-10.30 Fixed menu price fr £7.95 Av 3 course à la carte fr £17 ⊕ FREE HOUSE ◀ Boddingtons Bitter, Jennings Bitter, Copper Dragon, Black Sheep, Owd Nells Canalside Bitter, Moorhouses Bitter, Pendle Witch Ö Thatchers Heritage, Cheddar Valley. ♀ 40 **Facilities** Children's menu Play area Family room Dogs allowed Garden Parking

BLACKBURN Map 18 SD62

PICK OF THE PUBS

Clog and Billycock ♀

Billinge End Rd, Pleasington BB2 6QB
☎ 01254 201163
e-mail: enquiries@theclogandbillycock.com
dir: *M6 junct 29 onto M65 junct 3, follow signs for Pleasington*

The Clog and Billycock is named after the favoured attire of a landlord from the 1900s (a billycock is black felt hat, a predecessor of the bowler). The extensively renovated building stands in the quaint village of Pleasington on the quiet edges of Blackburn's western suburbs, where the River Darwen flows out of town. A warm and relaxing environment is provided for the appreciation of Thwaites ales, draught ciders, fine wines and good food prepared from quality Lancashire produce. Elm wood platters are a feature – ploughman's, house cured meats and local seafood – all with home-made bread and pickles. Hot and cold sandwiches, traditional pancakes and home-made organic ice cream and milkshakes are also fixtures. Other options might be Muncaster crab cakes or treacle-baked free range Middlewhite Garstang ribs with devilled black peas to start, followed by Lancashire hot pot, or Sandhams cheese and onion pie with sour cream jackets. A comprehensive young people's menu delivers real food and there is a great range of non-alcoholic drinks.

Open all wk noon-11 (Sun noon-10.30) Closed: 25 Dec **Bar Meals** L served Mon-Sat 12-2, Sun 12-8.30 D served Mon-Fri 6-9, Sat 5.30-9, Sun 12-8.30 Av main course £10.50 **Restaurant** L served Mon-Sat 12-2, Sun 12-8.30 D served Mon-Fri 6-9, Sat 5.30-9, Sun 12-8.30 ⊕ FREE HOUSE ◀ Thwaites Bomber, Wainwright, Original. ♀ 8 **Facilities** Children's menu Dogs allowed Garden Parking

PICK OF THE PUBS

The Red Pump Inn ♟

BASHALL EAVES   Map 18 SD64

Clitheroe Rd BB7 3DA
☎ **01254 826227**
e-mail: info@theredpumpinn.co.uk
web: www.theredpumpinn.co.uk
dir: *3m from Clitheroe, NW, follow
'Whitewell, Trough of Bowland & Bashall
Eaves' signs*

Enjoying panoramic views of Pendle Hill
and Longridge Fell, this is one of the
oldest inns in the Ribble Valley, its
name coming from the old red pump
that used to provide horses with water.
It was probably built in 1756, if you
accept the date on a door lintel. Public
areas divide into a snug with real fire,
dining rooms both large and small, a
comfy lounge and a bar, where you'll
find real ales from Timothy Taylor, Black

Sheep, Tirril Brewery and Moorhouses,
and ten wines by the glass. If you hear
music in the bar it'll probably be an
eclectic mix of 60s blues, jazz and
whatever else matches the relaxed,
slightly quirky atmosphere. The menu
changes to reflect the seasons and the
whims of the owners and chefs, while
the supporting daily specials boards
– which is where you'll find the fish -
may change during the day. Local
produce includes meat, game, cheeses,
vegetables, and the very popular extra-
matured local Pendle beef. Typical
dishes include Lancashire game pie in a
rich casserole; slow-braised Lancashire
lamb shank, served with mashed potato
and vegetables in a rich gravy; and
open lasagne with garlic-roasted
vegetables and tomato and herb sauce.
Children are catered for with a fresh
and healthy menu that's been known to
lead to cases of parental theft of food
from their child's plate! The bright and
sunny Coach House has a sumptuous
lounge that sells home-made breads,
cakes (try the chocolate and beetroot),
preserves and pâtés.

Open 12-3 6-11 Closed: Mon ex BH
Bar Meals L served Tue-Sat 12-2,
Sun 12-7.30 D served Tue-Sat 6-9,
Sun 12-7.30 **Restaurant** L served Tue-
Sat 12-2, Sun 12-7.30 D served
Tue-Sat 6-9, Sun 12-7.30 ⊕ FREE
HOUSE ◀ Timothy Taylor Landlord,
Black Sheep, Moorhouses, Tirril
Brewery. ♟ 10 **Facilities** Children's
menu Garden Parking

PICK OF THE PUBS

The Millstone at Mellor ★★ HL ⊛⊛ ☻

See Pick of the Pubs on page 274

BLACKO
Map 18 SD84

Moorcock Inn

Gisburn Rd BB9 6NG
☎ 01282 614186   ▤ 01282 614186
e-mail: boo@patterson1047.freeserve.co.uk
dir: *M65 junct 13, take A682 to Blacko*

Family-run country inn with traditional log fires and good views towards the Pendle Way, ideally placed for non-motorway travel to the Lakes and the Yorkshire Dales. Home-cooked meals are a speciality, with a wide choice including salads and sandwiches, and vegetarian and children's meals. Tasty starters like cheesy mushrooms, and garlic prawns are followed by lasagne, various steak choices, pork in orange and cider, and trout grilled with lemon and herb butter.

Closed: Mon eve ⊕ DANIEL THWAITES PLC ◀ Thwaites Best Bitter, Smooth. **Facilities** Garden Parking

---

BURROW
Map 18 SD67

PICK OF THE PUBS

The Highwayman ☻

LA6 2RJ ☎ 01524 273338
e-mail: enquiries@highwaymaninn.co.uk
dir: *M6 junct 36, A65 to Kirkby Lonsdale. Then A683 S. Burrow approx 2m*

This is a Ribble Valley inn and sister to the Three Fishes at Mitton. The building dates from the 18th century and, as a coaching inn, might well have been frequented by highwaymen as its name suggests. Handsome wooden furniture is set on stone floors by open fires, for this is a proper pub serving real beer by local brewer Daniel Thwaites. Food is very much at the heart of the operation, and the philosophy of head chef Michael Ward focuses on an attractive contemporary interpretation of traditional specialities using regional produce – the menu celebrates local food heroes on every line. The ingredients they supply appear in dishes such as Winnie Swarbrick's corn-fed Goosnargh chicken liver pâté; Muncaster crab cake; Sillfield Farm dry-cured gammon steak; and Andy Roe's tomato and red onion salad. Finish with burnt English custard and

stewed rhubarb; or bread and butter pudding with steeped apricots.

Open all wk noon-11 (Sun noon-10.30) Closed: 25 Dec **Bar Meals** L served Mon-Sat 12-2, Sun 12-8.30 D served Mon-Fri 6-9, Sat 5.30-9, Sun 12-8.30 Av main course £10.50 ◀ Lancaster Bomber, Double Century. ☻ 8 **Facilities** Children's menu Dogs allowed Garden Parking

---

CARNFORTH
Map 18 SD47

The Longlands Inn and Restaurant NEW ◬ ★★★★ INN

Tewitfield LA6 1JH ☎ 01524 781256   ▤ 01524 781004
e-mail: info@longlandshotel.co.uk
web: www.longlandshotel.co.uk
dir: *Please telephone for directions*

With its nooks and crannies, old beams and uneven floors, this family-run inn stands next to Tewitfield locks on the Lancaster canal. The bar comes to life for band night on Mondays, with a more relaxed feel during the rest of the week. The appetising menu includes slate platters with deli-style bread; and main course choices ranging from braised Silverdale lamb shank, and tamarind confit duck leg on Chinese noodles to the Longlands fish pie with melted cheese topping.

Open all day all wk 11am-1am **Bar Meals** L served Mon-Fri 12-2.30, Sat 12-4, Sun 12-9 D served Mon-Fri 5.30-9.30, Sat 5-9.30, Sun 12-9 Av main course £10 **Restaurant** L served Mon-Fri 12-2.30, Sat 12-4, Sun 12-9 D served Mon-Fri 5.30-9.30, Sat 5-9, Sun 12-9 booking required Av 3 course à la carte fr £18 **Facilities** Children's menu Dogs allowed Garden Parking **Rooms** 11

CHIPPING
Map 18 SD64

Dog & Partridge ☻

Hesketh Ln PR3 2TH ☎ 01995 61201   ▤ 01995 61446
dir: *M6 junct 31A, follow Longridge signs. At Longridge left at 1st rdbt, straight on at next 3 rdbts. At Alston Arms turn right. 3m, pub on right*

Dating back to 1515, this pleasantly modernised rural pub in the Ribble Valley enjoys delightful views of the surrounding fells. The barn has been transformed into a welcoming dining area, where home-made food on the comprehensive bar snack menu is backed by a specials board featuring fresh fish and game dishes. A typical menu shows duck and orange pâté; roast Lancashire beef and Yorkshire pudding; home-made steak and kidney pie; and broccoli and Stilton pancakes.

Open 11.45-3 6.45-11 (Sat 11.45-3 6-11 Sun 11.45-10.30) Closed: Mon **Bar Meals** L served Tue-Sat 12-1.45 **Restaurant** L served Tue-Sat 12-1.30, Sun 12-3 booking required D served Tue-Sat 7-9 Sun 3.30-8.30 booking required Fixed menu price fr £17.25 ⊕ FREE HOUSE ◀ Carlsberg-Tetley, Black Sheep. ☻ 8 **Facilities** Children's menu Parking

---

CLITHEROE
Map 18 SD74

PICK OF THE PUBS

The Assheton Arms ☻

See Pick of the Pubs on page 275

The Shireburn Arms ★★★ HL ☻

Whalley Rd, Hurst Green BB7 9QJ
☎ 01254 826518   ▤ 01254 826208
e-mail: sales@shireburnarmshotel.com
dir: *Telephone for directions*

A privately run, 17th-century inn with super views, in the heart of the Ribble Valley. *Lord of the Rings* author J R R Tolkien used to drink here when visiting his son at Stonyhurst College nearby, and the pub has become and home of the 'Tolkien Trail'. Using the finest local produce from around Lancashire, the menu ranges from sandwiches and salads to roasted Goosnargh duck with black cherry jus; wild sea trout on crushed peas; and mushroom, cranberry and brie Wellington. A conservatory links the restaurant with the patio and gardens.

Open all day all wk **Bar Meals** Av main course £8.50 food served all day **Restaurant** L served Mon-Fri 12-2, Sun 12-6 D served all wk 6-9 Fixed menu price fr £10.95 Av 3 course à la carte fr £20 ⊕ FREE HOUSE ◀ Theakstons Best Bitter, guest ales. ☻ 10 **Facilities** Children's menu Play area Family room Dogs allowed Garden Parking **Rooms** 22

PICK OF THE PUBS

The Millstone at Mellor ★★ HL ❀ ❀ ♟

BLACKBURN Map 18 SD62

Church Ln, Mellor BB2 7JR
☎ **01254 813333** 📠 **01254 812628**
e-mail: info@millstonehotel.com
web: www.millstonehotel.co.uk
dir: *M6 junct 31, A59 towards Clitheroe,*
past British Aerospace. Right at rdbt signed
Blackburn/Mellor. Next rdbt 2nd left. Hotel at
top of hill on right

In the 17th century the Millstone, set in the heart of Lancashire's glorious Ribble Valley, was a tithe barn, destined to become the original flagship of the Thwaites Blackburn brewery, whose real ales it sells to this day. Its landlord from 1948 to 1971 was former England cricket legend Big Jim Smith. The oak-panelled, fire-warmed restaurant has held two AA rosettes for a good few years, so you can expect to taste some excellent cooking, served by friendly and courteous staff. You'll also find chef/patron Anson Bolton on hand to answer your questions, not just about the food, but the wines too, from vin de pays to top-of-the-range Burgundies and Champagnes. In Millers Bar, lunch might start with chicken liver parfait with plum chutney and toast; and continue with deep-fried haddock tail in Thwaites beer batter with mushy peas, chips and tartare sauce. Very much setting the style in the restaurant are king prawn and anchovy fritters with spiced parsnip purée and cream sauce; woodland mushroom risotto with spinach, soft poached egg and shaved Parmesan; honey-roast Goosnargh duck breast with roasted parsnips, fondant potato and plum sauce; fresh market fish of the day; and baked ginger parkin with treacle sauce and clotted cream. Popular too are the traditional Sunday lunches, when the roast rump of Pendle lamb with bubble and squeak, fine green beans, port and mint jus, is just one of the many choices available. If you stay overnight you will be faced with a tough call: a Lancashire breakfast featuring black pudding and pork sausages, or the light and healthy alternative of fresh fruit, cereals and juices.

Open all week **Bar Meals** served Mon-Sat 12-9.30, Sun 12-9 Av main course £10.95 **Restaurant** L served all week 12-2.30 D served all week 6.30-9.30 Fixed menu price fr £31.50 Av 3 course à la carte fr £31.50 ⊞ SHIRE HOTELS LTD 🍺 Thwaites, Warsteiner, Lancaster Bomber, Thwaites Original Cash Bitter, Thwaites Premium Smooth. ♟ 12 **Facilities** Parking **Rooms** 23

PICK OF THE PUBS

The Assheton Arms ♗

CLITHEROE

Map 18 SD74

Downham BB7 4BJ
☎ 01200 441227 📠 01200 440581
e-mail: asshetonarms@aol.com
dir: *A59 to Chatburn, then follow Downham signs*

This stone-built country pub is well placed for a moorland walk up Pendle Hill, which looms over the village, and might be more familiar to viewers of the BBC serial *Born and Bred* set in the 1950s as The Signalman's Arms. The pub is named after Lord Clitheroe's family (they own the whole village), and the Assheton coat of arms on the sign above the inn's door includes a man holding a scythe incorrectly. The story behind this is that during the English Civil War the Asshetons supported Cromwell and one day a party of the kings' men was passing by. A prominent member of the family, not wishing to be discovered, leapt over a wall into a field where he picked up a scythe, meaning to pass himself off as a farm worker. His ruse worked, despite the fact that having never used a scythe before he was holding it the wrong way. Since that narrow escape the image of the scythe has been incorporated into the family emblem. Present-day visitors will find the single bar and sectioned rooms furnished with solid oak tables, wingback settees, the original stone fireplace, and a large blackboard listing the range of daily specials. Seafood is offered from the blackboard according to availability, and you can expect beer battered haddock and chips, and lemon sole with parsley butter. An interesting selection of small dishes includes Mrs Whelan's Burnley black pudding with piccalilli and mustard; and Leagrams organic Lancashire cheese platter with crusty bread and apple cider chutney. Main courses take in a choice of vegetarian dishes (broccoli bake; vegetarian chilli; cauliflower and mushroom provençale), as well as traditional Lancashire hot pot; venison casserole, and a range of steaks.

Bar Meals L served Mon-Sat 12-2, Sun 12-9 D served all wk 6-9 Av main course £11.50 **Restaurant** Av 3 course à la carte fr £20 ⊕ FREE HOUSE ◗ Lancaster Bomber, Wainwright Thwaites. ♗ 22 **Facilities** Children's menu Dogs allowed Parking

FENCE
Map 18 SD83

Fence Gate Inn ☆

Wheatley Lane Rd BB12 9EE
☎ 01282 618101 📄 01282 615432
e-mail: info@fencegate.co.uk
dir: *From M65 junct 13 towards Clayton-le-Moors, 1.5m, pub set back on right opposite T-junct for Burnley*

An extensive property, the Fence Gate Inn was originally a collection point for cotton delivered by barge and distributed to surrounding cottages to be spun into cloth. Food is served both in the bar and the Topiary Brasserie. Highlights are a selection of sausages starring Lancashire's champion leek and black pudding with a hint of sage. There is a good choice of pasta, and dishes like medallions of organic Salmesbury pork fillet.

Open all wk **Bar Meals** L served all wk D served all wk **Restaurant** L served all wk D served all wk ⊕ FREE HOUSE ◀ Theakston, Directors, Deuchars, Moorhouse, Bowland. ♟16 **Facilities** Garden Parking

Ye Old Sparrowhawk Inn ☆

Wheatley Lane Rd BB12 9QG
☎ 01282 603034 📄 01282 603035
e-mail: mail@yeoldsparrowhawk.co.uk
web: www.yeoldsparrowhawk.co.uk
dir: *M65 junct 13, A6068, at rdbt take 1st exit 0.25m. Turn right onto Carr Hall Rd, at top turn left 0.25m, pub on right*

Sipping a pint outside the half-timbered Sparrowhawk on a summer's evening is one of life's great pleasures. The pub stands at the gateway to Pendle Forest, famous for its witches, but here you'll find friendly service and stylish surroundings. The classically trained chefs work with locally sourced fresh ingredients to create menus that include stilton-glazed Pendle pork chop with Lyonnaise sauté potatoes and Mr Mellin's traditional sausages with mash and onion gravy.

Open all wk **Bar Meals** L served Mon-Sat 12-2.30, Sun 12-8 booking required D served Mon-Sat 5.30-9.30, Sun 12-8 booking required Av main course £10.50 **Restaurant** L served Mon-Sat 12-2.30, Sun 12-8 booking required D served Mon-Sat 5.30-9.30, Sun 12-8 booking required Fixed menu price fr £9 ◀ Thwaites Cask, Draught Bass, Moorhouse Blonde Witch, Black Sheep Best Ö Addlestones. ♟13 **Facilities** Children's menu Dogs allowed Garden Parking

FORTON
Map 18 SD45

PICK OF THE PUBS

The Bay Horse Inn ☆

LA2 0HR ☎ 01524 791204 📄 01524 791204
e-mail: yvonne@bayhorseinn.com
dir: *M6 junct 33 take A6 towards Garstang, turn left for pub, approx 1m from M6*

This charming, 18th-century pub is situated in the Trough of Bowland. Full of character, with mismatched furniture and a roaring log fire in winter in the handsome stone fireplace, you will find a warm welcome, real cask beers and a good selection of malt whiskies. It also specialises in simple, fresh and imaginative dishes from an award-winning chef, Craig Wilkinson. He exercises his culinary skills on the very best of local ingredients, elevating standard pub fare to unashamedly gastro levels. How else could a pub menu offer chicken liver and Garstang Blue cheese pâté with pear chutney or seafood platter (smoked, fresh and marinated), followed perhaps by slow-cooked corn-fed duck with potato purée, roast figs and Madeira sauce, or shank of lamb with parsnip purée, pearl barley and ale gravy. There are regular live music evenings, including jazz.

Open noon-3 6.30-mdnt Closed: Mon (ex BH L) **Bar Meals** L served Tue-Sat 12-1.45, Sun 12-3 D served Tue-Sat 7-9.15 booking required **Restaurant** L served Tue-Sat 12-1.45, Sun 12-3 D served Tue-Sat 7-9.15 booking required ◀ Thwaites Lancaster Bomber, Moorhouses Pendle Witch, Masham Brewery, Black Sheep. ♟11 **Facilities** Garden Parking

HASLINGDEN
Map 15 SD72

Farmers Glory

Roundhill Rd BB4 5TU
☎ 01706 215748 📄 01706 215748
dir: *On A667, 8m from Blackburn, Burnley & Bury, 1.5m from M66*

Stone-built 300-year-old pub situated high above Haslingden on the edge of the Pennines. Formerly a coaching inn on the ancient route to Whalley Abbey, it now offers locals and modern A667 travellers a wide-ranging traditional pub menu of steaks, roasts, seafood, pizzas, pasta, curries and sandwiches. Entertainment every Wednesday and Friday, and a large beer garden with ornamental fishpond.

Open all wk ⊕ PUNCH TAVERNS ◀ Tetley Bitter, Lees Speckled Hen, Jennings. **Facilities** Garden Parking

HESKIN GREEN
Map 15 SD51

Farmers Arms ☆

85 Wood Ln PR7 5NP
☎ 01257 451276 📄 01257 453958
e-mail: andy@farmersarms.co.uk
dir: *On B5250 between M6 & Eccleston*

Long, creeper-covered country inn with two cosy bars decorated with old pictures and farming memorabilia. Once known as the Pleasant Retreat, this is a family-run pub proud to offer a warm welcome and a traditional theme. Typical dishes include steak pie, fresh salmon with prawns and mushroom, rack of lamb, and chicken curry.

Open all wk ⊕ ENTERPRISE INNS ◀ Timothy Taylor Landlord, Pedigree, Black Sheep, Tetley, Tetley Bitter. ♟7 **Facilities** Play area Dogs allowed Garden Parking

HEST BANK
Map 18 SD46

Hest Bank Hotel ☆

2 Hest Bank Ln LA2 6DN
☎ 01524 824339 📄 01524 824948
dir: *From Lancaster take A6 N, after 2m left to Hest Bank*

Comedian Eric Morecambe used to drink at this canalside former coaching inn, first licensed in 1554. Awash with history and 'many happy ghosts', it now offers cask ales and a wide selection of meals all day, with local suppliers playing an important role in maintaining food quality. The good-value menu may range from a large pot of Bantry Bay mussels to the pub's own lamb hotpot made to a traditional recipe.

Open all day all wk 11.30-11.30 (Sun 11.30-10.30) **Bar Meals** L served Mon-Sat 12-9, Sun 12-8 D served Mon-Sat 12-9, Sun 12-8 food served all day ⊕ PUNCH TAVERNS ◀ Timothy Taylor Landlord, Blacksheep Bitter, Guest ales. ♟7 **Facilities** Garden Parking

LANCASTER
Map 18 SD46

The Stork Inn

Conder Green LA2 0AN
☎ 01524 751234 📄 01524 752660
e-mail: the.stork@virgin.net
dir: *M6 junct 33 take A6 north. Left at Galgate & next left to Conder Green*

White-painted coaching inn spread along the banks of the Conder Estuary, with a colourful 300-year-history that includes several name changes. The quaint sea port of Glasson Dock is a short walk along the Lancashire Coastal Way, and the Lake District is easily accessible. Seasonal specialities join home-cooked food like steak pie, locally-smoked haddock, salmon fillet with bonne femme sauce, and Cumberland sausage with onion gravy and mashed potatoes.

Open all day all wk 10am-11pm (Sat-Sun 8.30am-11pm) **Bar Meals** L served Mon-Fri 12-3, Sat-Sun 12-9 (Breakfast 8.30-10.30) D served Mon-Fri 5.30-9, Sat-Sun 12-9 ⊕ FREE HOUSE ◀ Marstons Pedigree, Black Sheep, Timothy Taylor Landlord, Cumberland Ales, Guest Ales. **Facilities** Play area Dogs allowed Garden Parking

PICK OF THE PUBS

The Sun Hotel and Bar ♀

LA1 1ET ☎ 01524 66006 📠 01524 66397
e-mail: info@thesunhotelandbar.co.uk
dir: 6m from M6 junct 33

By opening at 7.30am (a little later at weekends) and closing only when the last conversation dies, this city centre pub sees a steady and diverse flow of people throughout the day. The original inn was built in the 1600s, on the site of the medieval Stoop Hall, and is now Lancaster's oldest licensed premises. Its popular, award-winning bar serves a wide selection of cask ales, fifty bottled beers, two dozen wines by the glass and an excellent spirits selection. Attractive menus start with luxury breakfasts, and encompass reasonably priced lunches, with their acclaimed cheese and pâté boards, and evening meals. Typical main courses include beef chilli; Lancashire hotpot; steak, mushroom and oyster stout pie; moules marinière; and roasted butternut squash and sage risotto.

Open all day all wk from 7.30am until late **Bar Meals** Av main course £6 food served all day ⊕ FREE HOUSE ◀ Thwaites Lancaster Bomber, Lancaster Amber, Timmermans Strawberry, Lancaster Blonde, Warsteiner. ♀ 24 **Facilities** Children's menu Garden

PICK OF THE PUBS

The Waterwitch ♀

The Tow Path, Aldcliffe Rd LA1 1SU
☎ 01524 63828 📠 01524 34535
e-mail: thewaterwitch@mitchellsinns.co.uk
dir: 6m from M6 junct 33

The Waterwitch takes its name from three longboats that worked the adjacent Lancaster canal in the late 18th century. It occupies an old stables, tastefully converted to retain original features such as stone walls and interior slab floors. In just a few years the pub has acquired celebrity status and a clutch of awards, yet it still remains a genuine pub with the broad appeal of a wine bar and restaurant. It is noted for its ever-changing selection of fine cask-conditioned real ales, impressive wine list and guest cheeses. The talented team of chefs work with locally-sourced produce including fish that arrives daily from Fleetwood harbour. Traditional, classical and international influences combine on menus that might include king prawns with a Thai stir fry; Cumberland sausages on herb mash with red wine jus; or lamb steak with rosemary, mint and mustard on couscous.

Open all wk ◀ Thwaites Lancaster Bomber, Warsteiner, Moorhouse Ales, Lancaster Brewery Bitters, Beacon Ales. ♀ 27 **Facilities** Garden

ORMSKIRK **Map 15 SD40**

Eureka ♀

78 Halsall Ln L39 3AX ☎ 01695 570819
e-mail: siloutaylor@eurekaormskirk.co.uk
dir: 0.5m from town centre, at junct of County Rd & Southport Rd, turn left onto Halsall Ln

Although in a quiet housing estate (finding it is a clue to the name) this community pub attracts customers from a much wider area. In addition to a constantly changing specials board, the standard menu offers hot filled crispy baguettes; 'original' meals in a basket; baked jacket potatoes; 'mighty and meaty' mixed grill; and fresh haddock and chips. In August there's a beer festival with up to sixteen real ales on offer.

Open all wk ⊕ FREE HOUSE ◀ London Pride, Timothy Taylor Landlord, Black Sheep, Tetley Cask, Tetley Mild. ♀ 8 **Facilities** Play area Dogs allowed Garden Parking

PARBOLD **Map 15 SD41**

PICK OF THE PUBS

The Eagle & Child ♀

Maltkiln Ln, Bispham Green L40 3SG
☎ 01257 462297 📠 01257 464718
dir: 3m from M6 junct 27. Over Parbold Hill, follow signs for Bispham Green on right

Many years ago, legend has it, the local landowner Lord Derby and his wife were childless, but he fathered a child following an illicit liaison with a girl from the village. The child was placed in an eagle's nest so that when the lord and his wife were out walking they happened to hear the child cry. The lady insisted that the little boy was a gift from God, so they took him home and reared him as their son; hence the pub's name (known locally as the Bird and Bastard). The pub maintains its traditional atmosphere and offers five regularly changing guest ales, real ciders and a beer festival every May. All food is made on the premises with ingredients from local suppliers. The bar menu is extensive with the likes of crayfish and lemon risotto; chargrilled sweet cured gammon; and steak and real ale pie. The carte menu might include pan-fried Gressingham duck strips with orange and brandy sauce. There's a new deli shop in the barn next door.

Open all wk **Bar Meals** L served all wk 12-2 booking required D served Sun-Thu 5.30-8.30, Fri-Sat 5.30-9 booking required Av main course £12 **Restaurant** L served all wk 12-2 booking required D served Sun-Thu 5.30-8.30, Fri-Sat 5.30-9 booking required ⊕ FREE HOUSE ◀ Moorhouse Black Cat Mild, Thwaites Bitter, Southport Golden Sands, guest ales. ♀ 6 **Facilities** Children's menu Family room Dogs allowed Garden Parking

PRESTON **Map 18 SD52**

PICK OF THE PUBS

Cartford Country Inn & Hotel

Little Eccleston PR3 0YP ☎ 01995 670166
e-mail: info@thecartfordinn.co.uk
dir: Off A586

A former farmhouse, possibly 400 years old and a hostelry for probably 200 of them. Today the pleasantly rambling, three-storey inn stands sentinel by the toll bridge over the tidal River Wyre, a few miles from its meeting with the Irish Sea. Now run by Julie and Patrick Beaumé, the inn was completely refurbished in 2007 and offers a pleasant mix of traditional and gastro elements; a timeless log fire still burns in the winter grate, while polished wood floors and chunky dining furniture are decidedly up-to-date. Some of the ales are produced by the pub's own Hart Brewery at the back. Imaginative food starts with a choice of nibbles, continues with wood platters of antipasti or seafood, and culminates in the full menu experience: Lytham large prawns, followed by the chef's signature dish of oxtail and beef in real ale suet pudding, and finishing with chocolate fondant with mascarpone cream. There's a beer garden with river views, and live music some Friday nights.

Open all wk Closed: 25 Dec ⊕ FREE HOUSE ◀ Hart ales, Fuller's London Pride, Moorhouse, guest ales. **Facilities** Parking

RIBCHESTER **Map 18 SD63**

The White Bull ♀

Church St PR3 3XP ☎ 01254 878303
e-mail: enquiries@whitebullrib.co.uk
dir: M6 junct 31, A59 towards Clitheroe. B6245 towards Longridge. Pub 100mtrs from Roman Museum in town centre

Ancient Roman columns welcome patrons to this Grade II listed pub in the centre of Ribchester, with its beer garden overlooking the former Roman bathhouse. Despite its 18th-century origins as a courthouse, you'll find a warm and friendly atmosphere in which to sample the local hand-pumped beers. Lunchtime sandwiches and a variety of specials support a main menu that might include game rillette, cranberry chutney with toast;

continued

RIBCHESTER *continued*

bangers, mash and onion gravy; and grilled organic sea bass with spinach and lemon and parsley butter. Large walled garden available.

Open all wk Mon open 6pm **Bar Meals** L served Tue-Sun 12-2.30 D served Tue-Sun 6-9 Av main course £11 **Restaurant** L served Tue-Sun 12-2.30 D served Tue-Sun 6-9 Fixed menu price fr £14 Av 3 course à la carte fr £24 ⊕ ENTERPRISE INNS ◀ John Smiths, Copper Dragon Bitter, Bowland Brewery Bitter, Moorhouses. ♀ 8 **Facilities** Children's menu Garden Parking

---

SAWLEY   Map 18 SD74

The Spread Eagle ♀

BB7 4NH ☎ **01200 441202** 📄 **01200 441973**
e-mail: spreadeagle@zen.co.uk
dir: *Just off A159 between Clitheroe & Skipton, 4m N of Clitheroe*

This whitewashed pub stands on the banks of the River Ribble, affording lovely views from every table. There is a 17th-century bar with oak beams and a log fire, where a great choice of real ale, malt whiskies and wines by the glass is offered. Dishes served in the modern dining room might include smoked chicken salad; and seared fillet of sea bass with pumpkin velouté. Themed evenings (Turkish, Portuguese, Burns', Valentine's) are held regularly.

Open all day all wk 11-11 (Sun noon-10.30) **Bar Meals** L served Mon-Sat 12-2, Sun 12-7.30 D served Mon-Sat 6-9.30, Sun 12-7.30 ⊕ INDIVIDUAL INNS ◀ Timothy Taylor, Wainwrights. ♀ 16 **Facilities** Garden Parking

---

SLAIDBURN   Map 18 SD75

Hark to Bounty Inn ♀

Townend BB7 3EP ☎ **01200 446246** 📄 **01200 446361**
e-mail: manager@harktobounty.co.uk
web: www.harktobounty.co.uk
dir: *From M6 junct 31 take A59 to Clitheroe then B6478, through Waddington & Newton, onto Slaidburn*

A family-run 13th-century inn known as The Dog until 1875 when Bounty, the local squire's favourite hound, disturbed a post-hunt drinking session with its loud baying. The squire's vocal response obviously made a lasting impact. View the ancient courtroom, last used in 1937. The current family of landlords have been here some 25 years, and the kitchen offers the likes of black pudding with brandy and stilton; local organic pork with mustard and brown sugar; Bowland lamb shoulder with root vegetable and redcurrant gravy; or smoked mackerel kedgeree.

Open all day all wk 11-mdnt **Bar Meals** L served Mon-Sat 12-2, Sun 12-8 D served Mon-Sat 6-9, Sun 12-8 food served all day ⊕ SCOTTISH COURAGE ◀ Theakston Old Peculier, Theakstons Bitter, Moorhouses, Guest ale. ♀ 8 **Facilities** Dogs allowed Garden Parking

---

TUNSTALL   Map 18 SD67

PICK OF THE PUBS

The Lunesdale Arms ♀

LA6 2QN ☎ **015242 74203** 📄 **015242 74229**
e-mail: info@thelunesdale.co.uk
dir: *M6 junct 36. A65 Kirkby Lonsdale. A638 Lancaster. Pub 2m on right*

Set in a small village in the beautiful Lune Valley, The Lunesdale Arms has established quite a reputation for its food, wines and fine regional beers. Presided over by an ever-popular landlady, the pub is bright, cheery and welcoming. The food is freshly prepared, with bread baked on the premises. Most of the meat is supplied by local farms, and there is always roast lamb, beef or pork for Sunday lunch. Where possible the salad leaves and vegetables are grown organically. Both lunch and evening menus are likely to change on a daily basis according to the seasonality of ingredients and new ideas. Dishes range from Lancashire cheese rarebit with smoked Cumbrian ham; or free-range boiled egg with asparagus fingers and home-made brown bread, to roasted fillet of salmon on a bed of Puy lentils with roasted tomatoes, peppers and balsamic vinegar, or steak, Guinness and mushroom pie with chips.

Closed: 25-26 Dec, Mon (ex BH) **Bar Meals** L served Tue-Fri 12-2, Sat-Sun 12-2.30 booking required D served Tue-Sun 6-9 booking required Av main course £10.75 **Restaurant** L served Tue-Fri 12-2, Sat-Sun 12-2.30 booking required D served Tue-Sun 6-9 booking required Av 3 course à la carte fr £20 ⊕ FREE HOUSE ◀ Black Sheep, Dent Aviator, Guinness. ♀ 8 **Facilities** Children's menu Family room Dogs allowed Garden Parking

---

WHALLEY   Map 18 SD73

PICK OF THE PUBS

The Three Fishes ◉ ♀

Mitton Rd, Mitton BB7 9PQ
☎ **01254 826888** 📄 **01254 826026**
e-mail: enquiries@thethreefishes.com
dir: *M6 junct 31, A59 to Clitheroe. Follow signs for Whalley, take B6246 for 2m*

Mitton lies in a wedge of land between the Rivers Hodder and Ribble, the village name reflecting this position in a corruption of Midtown. The Three Fishes has been a public house for some 400 years, supposedly named after the 'three fishes pendant' in the coat of arms of the last abbot of Whalley Abbey, a carved stone from which is now incorporated over the pub entrance. The 21st-century interior very much respects the past and retains its most attractive features, including the big open fires. The strength of the menu of regional and British classics comes from using best quality produce from 'local food heroes'. A generous selection includes deep-fried Lancaster whitebait; braised shin of Ribble Valley beef; toad in the hole with Forager's Cumberland sausage; and breast of devilled Goosnargh chicken. Salads, lunchtime sandwiches and light meals are also available, while children have their own, quite grown-up, menu. Enjoy the sprawling sun terraces in summer.

Open all day all wk Closed: 25 Dec **Bar Meals** L served Mon-Sat 12-2, Sun 12-10.30 D served Mon-Fri 6-9, Sat 5.30-9, Sun 12-10.30 Av main course £10.95 food served all day ⊕ FREE HOUSE ◀ Thwaites Traditional, Thwaites Bomber, Bowland Brewery Hen Harrier. ♀ 13 **Facilities** Children's menu Dogs allowed Garden Parking

WHITEWELL Map 18 SD64

PICK OF THE PUBS

The Inn at Whitewell ★★★★★ INN ◉ ▼

Forest of Bowland BB7 3AT
☎ 01200 448222 📄 01200 448298
e-mail: reception@innatwhitewell.com
dir: From B6243 follow Whitewell signs

Whitewell lies in the heart of the Forest of Bowland surrounded by magnificent fell country. This ancient inn, parts of which date from the 13th century, stands on the east bank of the River Hodder. Approximately seven miles of water can be fished by guests, and the two acres of riverside grounds incorporate an extensive herb garden that supplies the kitchen. The somewhat eccentric interior is packed with a random collection of bric-a-brac and furnishings. Bar lunch dishes could include Whitewell fishcakes or chicken liver pâté à la Ballymaloe; more hearty plates may encompass Cumberland bangers and champ, or grilled Norfolk kipper. Bar suppers follow similar lines, or you can choose à la carte starters such as seared king scallops, and follow with chargrilled fillet of beef with home-made chipped potatoes; or breast of lamb slow-cooked with tomatoes and garlic. Children and dogs welcome.

Open all wk 10am-1am **Bar Meals** L served all wk 12-2 D served all wk 7.30-9.30 Av main course £9 **Restaurant** D served all wk 7.30-9.30 booking required Av 3 course à la carte fr £24 ⊕ FREE HOUSE 🍺 Marston's Pedigree, Bowland Bitter, Copper Dragon, Timothy Taylor Landlord ♂ Dunkerton's Organic Premium. ▼ 20 **Facilities** Dogs allowed Garden Parking **Rooms** 23

LEICESTERSHIRE

BELTON Map 11 SK42

PICK OF THE PUBS

The Queen's Head ★★★★ RR ◉◉ ▼

2 Long St LE12 9TP
☎ 01530 222359 📄 01530 224860
e-mail: enquiries@thequeenshead.org
web: www.thequeenshead.org
dir: On B5324 between Coalville & Loughborough

The clean, uncluttered exterior of this white-fronted, village centre pub suggests that its new owners might also have a fair idea of what constitutes good interior design. And so they have. The place has all-round appeal, whether you want to settle into a leather sofa in the contemporary bar, enjoy the food in the restaurant, garden or terrace, or stay overnight in a smartly designed bedroom. A Lite Bites/Classics menu incorporates club sandwiches; burger and fries; risotto of the day; and sausage and mash. The modern British set menu offers starters of grilled red mullet with

houmous and cucumber spaghetti; and carpaccio of beef, tarragon cream and rocket, with mains including fillet or rump of beef with smoked mash and cauliflower cheese; sweet potato curry with jasmine rice and home-made naan bread; and assiette of rabbit with beetroot purée. The two AA Rosettes the Queen's Head has earned speak volumes.

The Queen's Head

Open all day all wk Closed: 25-26 Dec **Bar Meals** L served all wk 12-2.30, Sat all day D served Mon-Fri 7-9.30, Sat all day Av main course £11 **Restaurant** L served all wk 12-2.30, Sun 12-4 D served Mon-Sat 7-9 Fixed menu price fr £13 Av 3 course à la carte fr £25 ⊕ FREE HOUSE 🍺 Worthington, Pedigree, Queens Special ♂ Merrydown. ▼ 14 **Facilities** Children's menu Play area Dogs allowed Garden Parking **Rooms** 6

BIRSTALL Map 11 SK50

PICK OF THE PUBS

The Mulberry Tree ▼

White Horse Ln LE4 4EF ☎ 0116 267 1038
dir: M1 junct 21A, A46 towards Newark 5.5m. Exit A46 at Loughborough

Set by Watermead Country Park in the heart of old Birstall, the Mulberry Tree offers peaceful waterside dining and a heated courtyard in addition to its bar and restaurant. The building, originally called the White Horse, dates from the 18th century when it was used for coal storage by the barges that plied the Grand Union canal. Today it's a sought-after gastro-pub whose executive head chef, Walter Blakemore,

counts Claridges and Le Caprice among his previous kitchens. Expect well-sourced food of a high order, with starters such as black pudding and crispy bacon salad; and spiced crab cake on green onion risotto. The main courses, each with a helpful wine recommendation, follow classic lines varying from pan-fried beef fillet (hung for 21 days) to pot roasted free range chicken; fish may include grilled swordfish or roast scallops. Desserts are all home made and irresistible, like warm Bakewell tart with raspberry ripple ice cream.

Open all wk winter 12-3 5.30-11, summer all day, everyday **Bar Meals** L served Mon-Sat 12-2.30, Sun 12-4 D served Mon-Sat 6-9 **Restaurant** L served Mon-Sat 12-2.30, Sun 12-4 D served Mon-Sat 6-9 🍺 Timothy Taylor Landlord, Jennings Cumberland, Guest. ▼ 10 **Facilities** Dogs allowed Garden Parking

BREEDON ON THE HILL Map 11 SK42

The Three Horseshoes

Main St DE73 8AN ☎ 01332 695129
e-mail: ian@thehorseshoes.com
dir: 5m from M1 junct 23a. Pub in village centre

Originally a farrier's – the stables can still be seen in the courtyard – the Three Horseshoes is around 250 years old. Opposite the pub is the village's original round house lockup. Numerous original features and old beams are supplemented by antique furniture, and sea-grass matting completes the warm and welcoming atmosphere. Typical dishes from the daily blackboard are chicken and spinach pancake; rib-eye beef with Stilton sauce; and favourite desserts like chocolate whisky trifle.

Closed: 25-26, 31 Dec-1 Jan, Sun eve **Bar Meals** L served Mon-Sat 12-2 D served Mon-Sat 5.30-9.15 Av main course £8.95 **Restaurant** L served Mon-Sat 12-2, Sun 12-3 booking required D served Mon-Sat 6.30-9.15 booking required Av 3 course à la carte fr £30 ⊕ FREE HOUSE 🍺 Marstons Pedigree, Speckled Hen, Theakstons. **Facilities** Dogs allowed Garden Parking

BRUNTINGTHORPE Map 11 SP68

Joiners Arms ▼

Church Walk LE17 5QH ☎ 0116 247 8258
e-mail: stephen@thejoinersarms.co.uk
dir: 4m from Lutterworth

More restaurant than village pub, with restored natural oak beams, tiled floor, pleasant decor, and lots of brassware and candles. Menus change constantly, and quality ingredients are sourced – beef from Scotland, Cornish lamb, Portland crab. Dishes might include roast rump of Scottish beef with Yorkshire pudding; supreme of chicken, mushroom and tarragon sauce; and sea bass with pea, leek and mustard grain sauce; and artichoke risotto, with specials boards offering additional choices.

continued

BRUNTINGTHORPE *continued*

Closed: Mon **Bar Meals** L served Tue-Sun 12-2 booking required **Restaurant** L served Tue-Sun 12-2 booking required D served 6.30-9.30 booking required Fixed menu price fr £13.50 Av 3 course à la carte fr £25 ⊕ FREE HOUSE ◀ Greene King IPA, John Smith's, Guinness. ₹ 8 **Facilities** Parking

EAST LANGTON | Map 11 SP79

PICK OF THE PUBS

The Bell Inn ₹

Main St LE16 7TW ☎ 01858 545278
e-mail: nickatthebell@btconnect.com
dir: *From Market Harborough on A6 N towards Leicester, 3rd right at rdbt 2m, follow The Langtons signs on B6047, 1.5m. Turn 1st right signed East Langton*

A creeper-clad, 16th-century listed building tucked away in a quiet village with good country walks all around. The cosy inn has a pretty walled garden, low beams and an open log fire. Nick and Shirley Gayton are enthusiastic owners, proud to offer local meats, vegetables and cheeses as well as locally brewed ales. The Langton micro-brewery operates from outbuildings, and produces two regular brews as well as seasonal ales. The wine list is carefully chosen too, and there is usually a selection of bin ends to add fun and variety to the decision-making. A wide range of food is displayed on menus which include light bites such as ciabattas, ploughman's, omelettes, and sausages with mash and onion gravy. A more hearty meal could start with a warm salad of goats' cheese with black pudding and beetroot; continue with monkfish, bacon and salmon kebabs; and conclude with one of the hot or cold puddings of the day.

Open all wk noon-3.30 5-11 (Fri-Sat noon-3 5-mdnt) Closed: 25 Dec **Bar Meals** L served all wk 12-2 D served Mon-Sat 6-9.30 booking required **Restaurant** L served all wk 12-3 booking required D served Mon-Sat 7-9.30 booking required ⊕ FREE HOUSE ◀ Greene King IPA & Abbot Ale, Langton Bowler Ale, Caudle Bitter, London Pride. ₹ 10 **Facilities** Garden Parking

EVINGTON | Map 11 SK60

The Cedars NEW ₹

Main St LE5 6DN ☎ 0116 273 0482
e-mail: cedars@king-henrys-taverns.co.uk
dir: *From London Road out of Leicester turn left at lights, follow road to Evington. Pub located in centre of Evington village*

King Henry's Taverns, the owners, like to say that you get two for the price of one here – and you can. The Bar Restaurant serves the group's usual range of competitively priced, freshly prepared steaks, fish and seafood, rumpburgers, traditional favourites, and international and vegetarian dishes. Take the Titanic Challenge – a 48oz (uncooked) rump steak, too big to be cooked 'well done'. Panoramic windows in the main eating area overlook a fountain and pond, and the gardens are a great place for alfresco dining. Friday nights here are devoted to karaoke – you have been warned!

Open all day all wk noon-11 **Bar Meals** Av main course £3 food served all day **Restaurant** food served all day ⊕ KING HENRY'S TAVERNS ◀ Guinness, IPA, Marstons Pedigree. ₹ 15 **Facilities** Children's menu Play area Family room Garden Parking

FLECKNEY | Map 11 SP69

The Old Crown ₹

High St LE8 8AJ ☎ 0116 240 2223
e-mail: old-crown-inn@fleckney7.freeserve.co.uk
dir: *Telephone for directions*

Close to the Grand Union Canal and Saddington Tunnel, a traditional village pub that is especially welcoming to hiking groups and families. Noted for good real ales and generous opening times (evening meals from 5pm) offering a wide choice of popular food. The garden has lovely views of fields and the canal, as well as a pétanque court.

Open all wk ⊕ EVERARDS BREWERY ◀ Everards Tiger & Beacon, Courage Directors, Adnams Bitter, Greene King Abbot Ale, Marston's Pedigree. ₹ 6 **Facilities** Play area Family room Dogs allowed Garden Parking **Notes** ⊛

GRIMSTON | Map 11 SK62

The Black Horse

3 Main St LE14 3BZ ☎ 01664 812358
e-mail: wymeswold@supanet.com
dir: *Telephone for directions*

A traditional 16th-century coaching inn displaying much cricketing memorabilia in a quiet village with views over the Vale of Belvoir. Overlooking the village green, there are plenty of opportunities for country walks, or perhaps a game of pétanque on the pub's floodlit pitch. Good home-cooked meals with daily specials, including lots of game. Fish choices and specials include monkfish, lemon sole, whole grilled plaice, and Arctic char. There is an alfresco eating area for warmer weather.

Open all wk 12-3 6-11 (Sun 12-6) **Bar Meals** L served Mon-Sat 12-2, Sun 12-3 booking required D served Mon-Sat 6-9 booking required **Restaurant** L served Mon-Sat 6-9 booking required D served Mon-Sat 6-9 booking required ⊕ FREE HOUSE ◀ Adnams, Marston's Pedigree, St Austell Tribute, Belvoir Mild, guest ales Ò Thatchers Gold. **Facilities** Children's menu Dogs allowed Garden

HATHERN | Map 11 SK52

The Anchor Inn ₹

Loughborough Rd LE12 5JB ☎ 01509 842309
dir: *M1 junct 24, A6 towards Leicester. Pub 4.5m on left*

The Anchor was once a coaching inn, with stables accessed through an archway off what is now the A6. Alongside a good range of real ales are snacks galore, a lengthy restaurant menu and plenty of vegetarian options. Rosemary and garlic coated brie wedges could be followed with Cajun chicken; fillet steak sizzler, or beef madras. Unquestionably family-friendly, there's a fenced-off children's play area in the garden.

⊕ EVERARDS BREWERY ◀ Everards Tiger, Original, Pitch Black, Abbot Ale. ₹ 20 **Facilities** Play area Garden Parking

KNOSSINGTON | Map 11 SK80

The Fox & Hounds ₹

6 Somerby Rd LE15 8LY ☎ 01664 454676
dir: *4m from Oakham in Knossington*

High quality food and helpful, friendly service are the hallmarks of this 500-year-old pub. Set in the village of Knossington close to Rutland Water, the building retains lots of traditional features, and the large rear garden and sitting area are ideal for al fresco summer dining. A typical lunch menu might include grilled lamb rump with ratatouille and tapenade; vegetable tart with stilton; or salmon with roasted aubergine, red pepper and coriander salsa.

Open noon-3 6-11 (Fri noon-3 5-11 Sat-Sun noon-11) Closed: Mon **Bar Meals** L served Tue-Sat 12-2, Sun 12-2.30 D served Tue-Sat 6.30-9 ⊕ ENTERPRISE INNS ◀ Bombardier, London Pride, IPA. ₹ 8 **Facilities** Play area Dogs allowed Garden Parking

LONG CLAWSON | Map 11 SK72

The Crown & Plough ₹

East End LE14 4NG
☎ 01664 822322 📄 01664 822322
e-mail: crownandplough@btconnect.com
dir: *In village centre, 3m from A606 (Melton Mowbray to Nottingham road)*

Following an extensive programme of refurbishment, the pub retains the atmosphere of a village local but with a contemporary flavour. It has a good reputation for the quality of its food served from one menu throughout the bar, snug, restaurant and landscaped garden. There's a good choice of fish (pan-fried sea bass with home-made tagliatelle, mussels and clams), and the likes of whole roast partridge with gratin potatoes and Savoy cabbage.

Open all wk ◀ Shepherd Neame, Spitfire, Lancaster Bomber, Marstons Pedigree, Adnams Explorer. ♥ 6 **Facilities** Garden Parking **Rooms** 5

LOUGHBOROUGH Map 11 SK51

The Falcon Inn NEW ★★★ INN

64 Main St, Long Whatton LE12 5DG
☎ 01509 842416 🖺 01509 646802
e-mail: enquiries@thefalconinnlongwhatton.com

Just ten minutes' drive from East Midlands airport and the M1, this traditional country inn offers great food, stylish en-suite accommodation in a converted stable and school house at the rear of the pub, and stunning award-winning flower displays in the outdoor areas in summer. Food choices range from classic pub favourites like filled jacket potatoes; roast rack of lamb; and steak and ale pie to more exotic dishes including a full Lebanese mezzeh that reflects the traditions of Lebanese-born proprietor Jad Otaki. Look out for the special events throughout the year.

Open all day all wk **Bar Meals** L served all wk 12-2 D served all wk 6.30-9 Av main course £9.50 **Restaurant** L served all wk 12-2 D served all wk 6.30-9 booking required Av 3 course à la carte fr £18 ⊕ EVERARDS ◀ Tiger Best Bitter, Everards Original, guest ale. **Facilities** Children's menu Family room Garden Parking **Rooms** 11

The Swan in the Rushes ♥

21 The Rushes LE11 5BE
☎ 01509 217014 🖺 01509 217014
e-mail: swanintherushes@castlerockbrewery.co.uk
dir: On A6 (Derby road). Pub in front of Sainsbury's, 1m from railway station.

A 1930s tile-fronted real ale pub, it was acquired by the Castle Rock chain in 1986, making it the oldest in the group. There's a first-floor drinking terrace, a function room and bar that seats 80, and a family/dining area. This real ale pub with a friendly atmosphere always offers ten ales, including seven guests, a selection of real ciders and hosts two annual beer festivals. Expect traditional pub grub. Music nights, folk club and a skittle alley complete the picture.

Open all day all wk 11-11 (Fri-Sat 11-mdnt Sun noon-11) **Bar Meals** L served all wk 12-3 D served Mon-Sat 6-9 Av main course £5.95 ⊕ CASTLE ROCK ◀ Castle Rock Harvest Pale, Castle Rock Sheriff's Tipple, Adnams Bitter, 7 guests ♂ Westons Old Rosie Scrumpy, Broadoak Moonshine. ♥ 11 **Facilities** Children's menu Family room Dogs allowed Parking

---

LUTTERWORTH Map 11 SP58

Man at Arms NEW ♥

The Green, Bitteswell LE17 4SB ☎ 01455 552540
e-mail: man@king-henrys-taverns.co.uk
dir: Take Ullesthorpe road out of Lutterworth, turn left at small white cottage. Pub on left after college on village green

This was the first pub bought by the King Henry's Taverns group, named after a bequest left by Henry VIII to the nearby village of Bitteswell to provide a 'man at arms' at times of war. Henry was indeed a big eater and, yes, some pretty sizeable meals are available here, but there are healthy options too. A change of decor and style is promised, modelled on sister pub The Ragley Boat Stop in Barrow-upon-Trent.

Open all day all wk noon-11 **Bar Meals** Av main course £3 food served all day **Restaurant** food served all day ⊕ KING HENRY'S TAVERNS ◀ Greene King IPA, Marstons Pedigree, Guinness. ♥ 15 **Facilities** Children's menu Play area Family room Garden Parking

---

MOUNTSORREL Map 11 SK51

The Swan Inn ★★★★ INN

10 Loughborough Rd LE12 7AT
☎ 0116 230 2340 🖺 0116 237 6115
e-mail: swan@jvf.co.uk
dir: On A6 between Leicester & Loughborough

A listed free house, originally two cottages built in 1688 of brick and Mountsorrel granite on the banks of the River Soar. Exposed beams, flagstone floors and roaring log fires in winter characterise the interior, while outside is a secluded riverside garden. Cask-conditioned beers and fine wines accompany mini saffron fishcakes with sweet cucumber and cinnamon salad; beef with onions casseroled in Old Peculier; and locally farmed Charolais steaks. Light lunches and snacks include pasta with a choice of sauces. There is a luxury suite available.

Open all wk 12-2.30 5.30-11 (Sat 12-11 Sun 12-3 7-10.30) **Bar Meals** L served all wk 12-2 D served all wk 6.30-9.30 Av main course £10 **Restaurant** L served all wk 12-2 D served all wk 6.30-9.30 Fixed menu price fr £10.95 Av 3 course à la carte fr £18 ⊕ FREE HOUSE ◀ Black Sheep Bitter, Theakston's XB, Old Peculier, Ruddles County, Abbot Ale. **Facilities** Dogs allowed Garden Parking **Rooms** 1

MOWSLEY Map 11 SP68

PICK OF THE PUBS

The Staff of Life ♥

See Pick of the Pubs on page 282

NETHER BROUGHTON Map 11 SK62

The Red House ♥

23 Main St LE14 3HB
☎ 01664 822429 🖺 01664 823805
e-mail: bernie@mulberrypubco.com
dir: M1 junct 21A take A46. Right onto A606. Or take A606 from Nottingham.

The Red House is a fine mixture of a 300-year-old village pub with log fires in winter and light contemporary design. The lounge bar opens into an airy restaurant, and a conservatory area overlooks the outdoor bar, terrace and courtyard grill. Immaculate gardens include a small play area and a permanent marquee for weddings, parties and corporate functions. Dishes range from locally sourced pork pie, or sausages of the week in the bar, to diver-caught scallops, or braised lamb shank in the restaurant. An ideal spot for walking, fishing and bird-watching.

Open all day all wk **Bar Meals** Av main course £10 food served all day **Restaurant** Av 3 course à la carte fr £25.30 food served all day ⊕ MULBERRY PUB CO LTD ◀ Guinness, Red House Special, Greene King IPA. ♥ 13 **Facilities** Children's menu Play area Dogs allowed Garden Parking

---

NEWTOWN LINFORD Map 11 SK50

PICK OF THE PUBS

The Bradgate ♥

37 Main St LE6 0AE
☎ 01530 242239 🖺 01530 249391
e-mail: john@thebradgate.co.uk
dir: M1 junct 22, A50 towards Leicester 1.5m. At 1st rdbt left towards Newton Linford 1.5m, at end of road turn right 0.25m. Pub on right

Long a favourite with locals and walkers, both as a watering hole and for fine dining. A recent makeover has left the pub with a modern, natural look, partly owing to the extensive use of light wood bar, flooring and furniture, and off-white walls. The food is very much in keeping, meeting the demand for style and innovation on the plate. Start with spiced crab cake, green onion risotto and sweet chilli oil; follow with braised pork with fondant potato and summer cabbage and light apple and white wine sauce; or roast scallops with pak choi and sweet potato; and finish with warm pear galette and almond and Armagnac ice cream.

continued on page 283

PICK OF THE PUBS

The Staff of Life 🍷

MOWSLEY **Map 11 SP68**

Main St LE17 6NT ☎ 0116 240 2359
dir: *M1 junct 20, A4304 to Market Harborough. Left in Husbands Bosworth onto A5199. In 3m turn right to pub*

Set back from the road, this well-proportioned building looks like a private Edwardian home – and that is exactly what it was before the village pub relocated here. A small patio area to the front and additional outside seating in the garden at the rear are ideal for alfresco supping. The interior has traditional features which include high-backed settles and flagstone floors in the bar. Here, if you look up, you'll see not only a fine wood-panelled ceiling but also the wine cellar. Wines served by the glass number nearly 20 at the last count; and there are usually four real ales to choose from. Overlooking the patio garden is the dining area where carefully prepared and presented dishes mix British and international influences. Daily-changing lunchtime blackboard menus from Tuesday to Saturday present a selection of good old-fashioned pub classics: sandwiches made with fresh white or granary bread; ploughman's with cheddar, stilton or home-cooked ham; and steaming plates of braised pheasant in red wine with herb dumplings; home-made fillet steak burger with bacon, cheese and hand-cut chips; and grilled salmon on buttered linguine. The more extensive evening carte uses seasonal produce; meats from surrounding farms is supplied by local butcher Joseph Morris. Expect to start with the likes of coarse pâté with spiced apricot and bramley apple chutney; or seared scallops on chorizo with lemon and Cointreau butter sauce. Main courses may include belly pork roasted with sage, onion and garlic on raisin mash; slow-cooked shin of beef; and chicken roulade with sun-kissed tomatoes and mozzarella wrapped in Parma ham. Desserts hand-crafted by Linda O'Neill, once a member of Ireland's Panel of Chefs, cannot be resisted. Will it be white chocolate and raspberry cheesecake with Chantilly cream? Or individual lemon meringue pie and burnt orange sauce? The choice, as they say, is yours.

Closed: Mon L (ex BH) FREE HOUSE Marstons, Banks Original. 🍷 19
Facilities Garden Parking

NEWTOWN LINFORD *continued*

The pub is family friendly with a children's menu and a large play area. Dogs on a lead are welcome in the beer garden.

Open all wk winter: 11.30-3 5.30-11 (Sun 12-9) summer: all day, every day **Bar Meals** L served Mon-Thu 12-2.30, Fri-Sun all day D served Mon-Thu 6-9, Fri-Sun all day **Restaurant** L served Mon-Thu 12-2.30, Fri-Sun all day D served Mon-Thu 6-9, Fri-Sun all day ⊕ EVERARDS ◀ Tiger, Beacon, Original, Guest ales. ♀ 10 **Facilities** Play area Family room Garden Parking

---

OADBY Map 11 SK60

PICK OF THE PUBS

Cow and Plough ♀

Gartree Rd, Stoughton Farm LE2 2FB
☎ 0116 272 0852 ☐ 0116 272 0852
e-mail: enquiries@steaminbilly.co.uk
dir: *3m Leicester Station A6 to Oadby. Turn off to BUPA Hospital, pub 0.5m beyond*

Formerly a Victorian dairy farm, this much-loved free house dates back to 1989, when licensee Barry Lount approached the owners of Stoughton Grange Farm, who were then in the process of opening the farm to the public. The farm park attraction has since closed, but the Cow and Plough continues to prosper, hosting functions and events such as beer festivals in the former farm buildings. The pub also brews its own award-winning Steamin' Billy beers, named after the owners' Jack Russell terrier. The interior is decorated with historic inn signs and brewing memorabilia, providing a fascinating setting in which to enjoy food from the regularly-changing menus. Typical choices include warm chicken, chorizo and spinach salad with pan juices followed by prawn, mussel and fennel linguini with salad. Heartier options include 21 day hung sirloin steak with black pudding, potatoes and peppercorn sauce; and a dessert of bramley apple pie.

Open all wk ⊕ FREE HOUSE ◀ Steamin Billy Bitter, Steamin Billy Mild, Skydiver, London Pride, Abbeydale. ♀ 8 **Facilities** Family room Dogs allowed Garden Parking

---

OLD DALBY Map 11 SK62

PICK OF THE PUBS

The Crown Inn ♀

Debdale Hill LE14 3LF ☎ 01664 823134
e-mail: oldcrown@castlerockbrewery.co.uk
dir: *A46 turn for Willoughby/Broughton. Right into Nottingham Ln, left to Old Dalby*

A classic creeper-covered, country pub dating from 1509, set in extensive gardens and orchards, with small rooms, all with open fires. The new owners have returned the pub to its former glory - traditional with a

---

contemporary feel. They place a strong emphasis on fresh seasonal produce: if the food doesn't all come from Leicestershire, the county's suppliers are nonetheless wholeheartedly supported. Expect dishes like pan-fried sea bass with lemon and crayfish risotto, or oven roasted rack and braised shoulder of lamb with minted pea purée. There's a good choice of real ales to help wash down a meal, or to enjoy without food: Castle Rock Hemlock and Harvest Pale are among the selection.

Open all wk noon-close Closed: Mon L **Bar Meals** L served Tue-Fri 12-2, Sat-Sun 12-3 booking required D served Tue-Sat 6-9 booking required Av main course £8 **Restaurant** L served Tue-Sun 12-2 booking required D served Tue-Sun 6-9 booking required Av 3 course à la carte fr £25 ⊕ FREE HOUSE ◀ Castle Rock Hemlock, Beaver, Harvest Pale, 3 Guest Ales ♂ Stowford Press. ♀ 10 **Facilities** Children's menu Family room Dogs allowed Garden Parking

---

REDMILE Map 11 SK73

Peacock Inn ★★★★ HL ♀

Church Corner, Main St NG13 0GA
☎ 01949 842554 ☐ 01949 843746
e-mail: reservations@thepeacockinnredmile.co.uk
web: www.thepeacockinnredmile.co.uk
dir: *From A1 take A52 towards Nottingham. Turn left, follow signs for Redmile & Belvoir Castle. In Redmile at x-rds turn right. Pub at end of village*

Set beside the Grantham Canal in the Vale of Belvoir, this 16th-century stone-built pub is only two miles from the picturesque castle. The inn has a local reputation for good quality food and real ales, and offers a relaxed setting for wining and dining. The menus are based on local seasonal produce; try smoked duck salad with orange and basil dressing; pan-fried pork fillet with fennel and apple calvados cream jus; chocolate crème brûlée served with fresh fruit. There are guest rooms if you would like to stay over.

Open all day all wk **Bar Meals** L served all wk 12-2.30 D served all wk 6-9 Av main course £8.95 **Restaurant** D served all wk 6-9 Fixed menu price fr £8.95 Av 3 course à la carte fr £16.95 ⊕ CHARLES WELLS ◀ Young's Bitter, Bombardier. ♀ 8 **Facilities** Children's menu Dogs allowed Garden Parking **Rooms** 10

SADDINGTON Map 11 SP69

The Queens Head

Main St LE8 0QH ☎ 0116 240 2536
dir: *Between A50 & A6 S of Leicester, NW of Market Harborough*

A traditional prize-winning English pub with terrific views from the restaurant and garden over the Saddington Reservoir. The inn specialises in real ale and good food, with four specials boards to supplement the evening menu. Foil-cooked cod fillet, roast Barbary duck, lamb shank with garlic mash, steak and ale pie, monkfish medallions with Parma ham, and pan-fried tuna steak with sweet pepper and oyster sauce guarantee something for everyone.

Open all wk noon-11 (Sun noon-10) **Bar Meals** L served all wk 12-2.30 D served all wk 6-9 ⊕ EVERARDS BREWERY ◀ Everards Tiger Best & Beacon Bitter, guests. **Facilities** Children's menu Garden Parking

---

SILEBY Map 11 SK61

The White Swan

Swan St LE12 7NW ☎ 01509 814832 ☐ 01509 815995
dir: *From Leicester A6 towards Loughborough, turn right for Sileby; or take A46 towards Newark-on-Trent, turn left for Sileby*

Behind the unassuming exterior of this 1930s building, you'll find a free house of some character, with a book-lined restaurant and a homely bar with an open fire. A wide selection of home-made rolls, baguettes and snacks is on offer; menus change twice weekly, and there are blackboard specials, too. Typical main course choices include baked pheasant with chestnut and cranberry stuffing; plaice with prawns in garlic butter; and roast lamb with garlic and rosemary.

Closed: 1-7 Jan, (Sun eve & Mon, May-Sep Sun L) **Bar Meals** L served Tue-Sun 12-1 D served Tue-Sat 7-8.30 Av main course £9 **Restaurant** L served Sun 12-1 D served Tue-Sat 7-8.30 Av 3 course à la carte fr £18 ⊕ FREE HOUSE ◀ Marston's Pedigree, Tetley's Smooth, Ansells, Banks, Fuller's London Pride. **Facilities** Garden Parking

SOMERBY — Map 11 SK71

Stilton Cheese Inn ♀

High St LE14 2QB ☎ 01664 454394

dir: *From A606 between Melton Mowbray & Oakham follow signs to Pickwell & Somerby. Enter village, 1st right to centre, pub on left*

This attractive 17th-century inn enjoys a good reputation for its food, beer, wine and malt whiskies. Built from mellow local sandstone, it stands in the centre of the village surrounded by beautiful countryside. An interesting range of food from the regularly-changing specials board includes smoked salmon and mascarpone roulade; Rutland Water trout with prawn and tarragon butter; liver, bacon, onion gravy with bubble and squeak; and ginger and walnut treacle tart.

Open all wk 12-3 6-11 (Sun 7-11) **Bar Meals** L served all wk 12-2 D served Mon-Sat 6-9, Sun 7-9 Av main course £9 **Restaurant** L served all wk 12-2 D served Mon-Sat 6-9, Sun 7-9 ⊕ FREE HOUSE ◀ Grainstore Ten Fifty, Brewster's Hophead, Belvoir Star, Tetley's Cask, Marston's Pedigree. ♀ 15 **Facilities** Children's menu Family room Garden Parking

STATHERN — Map 11 SK73

PICK OF THE PUBS

Red Lion Inn ◉ ♀

Red Lion St LE14 4HS
☎ 01949 860868 ▤ 01949 861579
e-mail: info@theredlioninn.co.uk
dir: *From A1 (Grantham), A607 towards Melton, turn right in Waltham, right at next x-rds then left to Stathern*

Whatever the season, there are treats to be enjoyed at the Red Lion Inn: Pimms on the terrace or Saturday barbecues in the summer, or mulled wine in winter, with chestnuts roasted on the open fires. The pub is located in the beautiful the Vale of Belvoir and comprises a stone-floored bar, a comfortable lounge with plenty of reading material, an elegant dining room and an informal dining area. Menus change daily in accordance with locally supplied produce and the menus offer a mixture of classic pub food and innovative country cooking. Typical dishes are Red Lion fish and chips with tartare sauce and mushy peas; and roast partridge with chestnut cabbage, caramelised pear, bread sauce and game chips. In collaboration with its sister pub, The Olive Branch at Clipsham, Red Olive Foods provides preserves, wholesale wines,

hampers and speciality dishes, available to purchase from the pubs. Outside catering can also be arranged.

Open 12-3 5.30-11 (Fri-Sat 12-11, Sun 12-6.30) **Closed:** 1 Jan, Mon **Bar Meals** L served Tue-Sat 12-2, Sun 12-3 booking required D served Tue-Thu 5.30-9, Fri 5.30-9.30, Sat 7-9.30 booking required Av main course £13.50 **Restaurant** L served Tue-Sat 12-2, Sun 12-3 booking required D served Tue-Thu 5.30-9, Fri 5.30-9.30, Sat 7-9.30 booking required Fixed menu price fr £10 Av 3 course à la carte fr £21.50 ⊕ RUTLAND INN COMPANY LTD ◀ Grainstore Olive Oil, Brewster's VPA, Exmoor Gold, London Pride. ♀ 8 **Facilities** Children's menu Dogs allowed Garden Parking

THORPE LANGTON — Map 11 SP79

The Bakers Arms ♀

Main St LE16 7TS ☎ 01858 545201 ▤ 01858 545924
dir: *Take A6 S from Leicester then left signed 'The Langtons', at rail bridge continue to x-rds. Straight on to Thorpe Langton. Pub on left*

A thatched pub set in a pretty village, with plenty of period charm and an enthusiastic following. The modern pub food is one of the key attractions, with the menu changing from week to week. Expect dishes like duet of salmon and monkfish with prawn jus or lamb fillet with white onion sauce and pea mash. An intimate atmosphere is created with low beams, rug-strewn quarry-tiled floors, large pine tables, and open fires. The area is popular with walkers, riders and mountain bikers.

Closed: Sun eve-Mon **Bar Meals** Av main course £14.95 **Restaurant** L served Sat-Sun 12-2.30 booking required D served Tue-Sat 6.30-21.15 booking required ⊕ FREE HOUSE ◀ Langton Brewery, Bakers Dozen Bitter. ♀ 9 **Facilities** Garden Parking

WELHAM — Map 11 SP79

The Old Red Lion NEW ♀

Main St LE16 7UJ ☎ 01858 565253
e-mail: redlion@king-henrys-taverns.co.uk

This old country pub is part of the King Henry's Taverns group. It was once a coaching inn, and the small area opposite the main bar was originally the archway where the coaches would swing in to offload their weary passengers. In winter the leather chesterfields around the log fires create a cosy feel, while in summer take an evening stroll along one of the many footpaths and bridleways. The menu goes in for traditional pub grub, burgers, curries, and vegetarian dishes. For those with a larger appetite it offers the Mary Rose Special, a 16oz T-bone steak.

Open all day all wk noon-11 **Bar Meals** Av main course £3 food served all day **Restaurant** food served all day ⊕ KING HENRY'S TAVERNS ◀ Greene King IPA, Marstons Pedigree, Guinness. ♀ 15 **Facilities** Children's menu Play area Family room Parking

WOODHOUSE EAVES — Map 11 SK51

The Wheatsheaf Inn ★★★ INN ♀

Brand Hill LE12 8SS
☎ 01509 890320 ▤ 01509 890571
e-mail: richard@wheatsheafinn.net
dir: *M1 junct 22, follow Quorn signs*

Around the turn of the 19th century, when local quarrymen wanted somewhere to drink, they built themselves the Wheatsheaf. It's what locals call a Dim's Inn, a succession of pubs run by three generations of the Dimblebee family. Bistro-style menus include chargrilled prime steaks and popular Wheatsheaf burgers. Fresh fish is a feature of the daily chalkboard - maybe linguine with prawns and salmon in creamy saffron sauce. An additional dining room is now available called The Mess. Three modern en suite bedrooms are available.

Closed: Sun eve in winter **Bar Meals** L served Mon-Fri 12-2, Sat 12-2.30, Sun 12-3.30 D served All wk 6.30-9.15 **Restaurant** L served Mon-Fri 12-2, Sat 12-2.30, Sun 12-3.30 D served All wk 6.30-9.15 ⊕ FREE HOUSE ◀ Greene King Abbot Ale, Draught Burton Ale, Timothy Taylor Landlord, Adnams Broadside, Tetley Smooth, guest ale. ♀ 14 **Facilities** Children's menu Dogs allowed Garden Parking **Rooms** 3

LINCOLNSHIRE

ALLINGTON — Map 11 SK84

The Welby Arms ★★★★ INN ♀

The Green NG32 2EA
☎ 01400 281361 ▤ 01400 281361
dir: *From Grantham take either A1 N, or A52 W. Allington 1.5m*

A creeper-covered inn overlooking the village green, the Welby Arms has a traditional country pub aspect. It is popular with travellers on the A1 as it also provides overnight accommodation. An excellent choice of real ales is offered alongside home-cooked food. Bar snacks take in home-made beef burgers, baguettes and chilli, and there is a full restaurant menu. Specials include steak and kidney pudding or monkfish wrapped in Parma ham with king prawns.

Open all wk 12-3 6-11 (Sun 12-10.30) **Bar Meals** L served Mon-Sat 12-2 D served Mon-Sun 6-9 Av main course £4.95 **Restaurant** L served Mon-Sun 12-2 booking required D served Mon-Sat 6-9, Sun 6-8.30 booking required Av 3 course à la carte fr £19.95 ⊕ FREE HOUSE ◀ John Smith's, Interbrew Bass, Timothy Taylor Landlord, Jennings Cumberland Ale, Badger Tanglefoot, Adnams Broadside. ▼ 22 **Facilities** Children's menu Garden Parking **Rooms** 3

ASWARBY   Map 12 TF03

The Tally Ho Inn ▼

NG34 8SA ☎ 01529 455170
e-mail: info@thetallyhoinn.com
dir: *3m S of Sleaford on A15 towards Bourne/ Peterborough*

Built from sturdy old pillars and beams and exposed stonework, this handsome inn is located on the Aswarby Estate and has strong connections with major hunts and other field sports. The old English garden, complete with fruit trees, overlooks estate parkland and grazing sheep. Favourite dishes at lunch and dinner include suet pudding with braised beef and mushrooms, and lamb and stilton casserole. Baguettes and toasted sandwiches are also served at lunchtime.

Open noon-2.30 5.30-11 (Tue 6-11 Sun noon-4) Closed: Tue L **Bar Meals** L served Mon-Sat 12-2.30, Sun 12-3.30 D served Mon-Sat 6-9.30 ⊕ FREE HOUSE ◀ Timothy Taylor Landlord, Abbott Ale, Guest Ales ♂ Westons Organic. ▼ 7 **Facilities** Garden Parking

BARNOLDBY LE BECK   Map 17 TA20

The Ship Inn ▼

Main Rd DN37 0BG ☎ 01472 822308   📄 01472 823706
e-mail: johnlinecaughtgy@aol.com
dir: *M180 junct 5, A18 past Humberside Airport. At Laceby Junction rdbt (A18 & A46) straight over follow Skegness/Boston signs. Approx 2m turn left signed Waltham & Barnoldby le Beck*

Fresh seafood is the star at this 300-year-old inn, whose own fishing boats bring in a daily haul of long-line caught fish (cod, turbot, plaice, skate and brill). The bar is filled with maritime bric-a-brac, while outside is a beautiful garden. Besides the line-caught fish options, typical dishes include oven-roasted lamb noisettes on rosemary rösti with a vegetable medley and a garlic and redcurrant jus; and gammon steak with egg, onion rings, grilled tomato and chips.

Open all wk 12-3 6-12 **Bar Meals** L served all wk 12-2 D served all wk 6.30-9.30 booking required **Restaurant** L served all wk 12-2 booking required D served all wk 6.30 booking required ⊕ PUNCH TAVERNS ◀ Black Sheep Best, Tetley's Smooth, Boddingtons, Timothy Taylor Landlord. ▼ 7 **Facilities** Children's menu Garden Parking

BELCHFORD   Map 17 TF27

The Blue Bell Inn

1 Main Rd LN9 6LQ ☎ 01507 533602
dir: *Off A153 between Horncastle & Louth*

This welcoming pub in the heart of the Wolds is run by husband and wife team Darren and Sue, with Darren as chef. Expect cask ales and comfortable armchairs, plus freshly cooked food written up on daily blackboards and a 'lunchbox' menu. Dishes range from pea, mint and watercress soup to saddle of wild fallow venison with sweet potato and smoked Austrian cheese purée; plus imaginative vegetarian choices too.

The Blue Bell Inn

Closed: 2nd & 3rd wk Jan, Sun eve-Mon **Bar Meals** L served Tue-Sun 12-2 D served Tue-Sat 6.30-9 **Restaurant** L served Tue-Sun 12-2 D served Tue-Sat 6.30-9 ⊕ FREE HOUSE ◀ Black Sheep, Timothy Taylor Landlord, guest. **Facilities** Garden Parking

BOURNE   Map 12 TF02

The Wishing Well Inn ▼

Main St, Dyke PE10 0AF
☎ 01778 422970   📄 01778 394508
e-mail: wishingwell@hotmail.com
dir: *Take A15 towards Sleaford. Inn in next village*

This Lincolnshire village free house started life in 1879 as a one-room pub called the Crown. Several extensions have since been sympathetically executed with recycled stone and timbers; the well that gives the pub its name,

continued

BOURNE *continued*

previously in the garden, is now a feature of the smaller dining room. Loyal customers return again and again to enjoy a comprehensive menu of traditional favourites in the warm and welcoming atmosphere. Outside, an attractive beer garden backs onto the children's play area.

Open all wk 11-3 5-11 (Fri-Sat 11-mdnt Sun 11-11 summer all wk 11-11) **Bar Meals** L served Mon-Thu 12-2.30, Fri-Sun 12-9 D served Mon-Thu 5.30-9, Fri-Sun 12-9 ⊕ FREE HOUSE ◀ Greene King Abbot Ale, Spitfire, 3 guest ales. ⬥ 7 **Facilities** Play area Dogs allowed Garden Parking

See advert on page 285

BRIGG   Map 17 TA00

The Jolly Miller ⬥

Brigg Rd, Wrawby DN20 8RH ☎ **01652 655658**
dir: *1.5m E of Brigg on A18, on left*

Popular country inn a few miles south of the Humber Estuary. The pleasant bar and dining area are traditional in style, and there's a large beer garden. The menu offers a good range of food: tuck into a chip butty; vegetable burger bap; home-made curry; or steak with onion rings. Puddings include hot chocolate fudge cake and banana split. Play area and children's menu. Coach parties accepted with advanced booking.

Open all wk ⊕ ENTERPRISE INNS ◀ Guinness, John Smith Extra Smooth, 2 guest ales. ⬥ 6 **Facilities** Play area Garden Parking

CONINGSBY   Map 17 TF25

The Lea Gate Inn ⬥

Leagate Rd LN4 4RS
☎ **01526 342370** ▤ **01526 345468**
e-mail: theleagateinn@hotmail.com
web: www.the-leagate-inn.co.uk
dir: *Off B1192 just outside Coningsby*

The oldest licensed premises in the county, dating from 1542, this was the last of the Fen Guide Houses that provided shelter before the treacherous marshes were drained. The oak-beamed pub has a priest's hole and a very old inglenook fireplace among its features. The same family have been running the pub for over 25 years. Both the bar and restaurant serve food and offer seasonal menus with lots of local produce (including game in season) and great fish choices, such as freshwater trout and lobster.

Open all wk **Bar Meals** L served all wk 12-2.15 D served all wk 6-9 Av main course £9 **Restaurant** D served all wk 6-9 Av 3 course à la carte fr £20 ⊕ FREE HOUSE ◀ Theakston's XB, Bombardier. ⬥ 7 **Facilities** Play area Garden Parking

DONINGTON ON BAIN   Map 17 TF28

The Black Horse Inn ★★★ INN ⬥

Main Rd LN11 9TJ ☎ **01507 343640** ▤ **01507 343640**
e-mail: mike@blackhorse-donington.co.uk
dir: *Telephone for directions*

Ideal for walkers, this old-fashioned country pub is set in a small village in the heart of the Lincolnshire Wolds on the Viking Way. A large grassed area surrounded by trees is ideal for enjoying a drink or dining alfresco on sunny days. Dining options include the non-smoking dining room, the Blue Room, and the Viking Snug. There are eight spacious bedrooms if you would like to stay over.

Open all wk ⊕ FREE HOUSE ◀ John Smiths, Greene King, Theakstons. ⬥ 6 **Facilities** Dogs allowed Garden Parking Rooms 8

EWERBY   Map 12 TF14

The Finch Hatton Arms

43 Main St NG34 9PH
☎ **01529 460363** ▤ **01529 461703**
e-mail: tel-c@supanet.com
dir: *From A17 to Kirkby-la-Thorne, then 2m NE. 2m E of A153 between Sleaford & Anwick*

Originally known as the Angel Inn, this 19th-century pub was given the family name of Lord Winchelsea, who bought it in 1875. After a chequered history and a short period of closure, it reopened in the 1980s and these days offers pub, restaurant and hotel facilities. It offers an extensive and varied menu to suit all tastes and budgets, but with its traditional ale and regular customers it retains a 'local' atmosphere.

Open all wk noon-3 6-11pm **Bar Meals** L served all wk 12-2.30 D served all wk 6-10 ⊕ FREE HOUSE ◀ Everards Tiger Best, Dixon's. **Facilities** Garden Parking

FREISTON   Map 12 TF34

Kings Head

Church Rd PE22 0NT ☎ **01205 760368**
dir: *From Boston towards Skegness on A52 follow signs for RSPB Reserve Freiston Shore*

Originally two tied cottages, this pub dates from the 15th century and retains its old world charm. According to the season, you'll be delighted by the award-winning flower displays outside or the large coal fire inside. The landlady, Ann, has been here 27 years and makes all the food, using only local produce, while partner Bill provides a warm welcome in the bar. Hearty dishes, such as steak or rabbit pie, are served with fresh vegetables. R.S.P.B. Freiston Shore is close by.

Open all wk 11.30-11 (Sun 11.45-4 Mon 11.30-3.30 7-11) **Bar Meals** L served Tue-Sun 12-2 Av main course £7.70 **Restaurant** L served Tue-Sun 12-2 booking required ⊕ BATEMANS ◀ Batemans XB & Dark Mild, Worthington Cream Flow, John Smiths, Guinness. **Facilities** Children's menu Parking **Notes** ⊛

FROGNALL   Map 12 TF11

The Goat ⬥

155 Spalding Rd PE6 8SA ☎ **01778 347629**
e-mail: graysdebstokes@btconnect.com
dir: *A1 to Peterborough, A15 to Market Deeping, old A16 to Spalding, pub approx 1.5m from A15 & A16 junct*

Families are welcome at this cosy, friendly country free house, which has an open fire, large beer garden and plenty to amuse the children. Main courses include beef stroganoff; pork in sweet and sour sauce; leek and mushroom pie; warm bacon and stilton salad; and home-made prawn curry. Beer is taken seriously, with five different guest ales each week and regular beer festivals throughout the year.

Open all wk 11.30-3 6-11.30 (Sun noon-11) Closed: 25 Dec, 1 Jan **Bar Meals** L served Mon-Sat 12-2 booking required D served Mon-Sat 6.30-9.30, Sun 12-9 booking required Av main course £9 **Restaurant** L served Mon-Sat 12-2, Sun 12-9 booking required D served Mon-Sat 6.30-9.30, Sun 12-9 booking required Fixed menu price fr £15.95 Av 3 course à la carte fr £18 ⊕ FREE HOUSE ◀ Guest ales: Elgoods, Batemans, Abbeydale, Nethergate, Hopshackle ◔ Westons Old Rosie, Broadoak Moonshine, Thatchers Cheddar Valley. ⬥ 16 **Facilities** Children's menu Play area Family room Garden Parking

GRANTHAM   Map 11 SK93

The Beehive Inn

10/11 Castlegate NG31 6SE ☎ **01476 404554**
dir: *A52 to town centre, left at Finkin St, pub at end*

Grantham's oldest inn (1550) is notable for having England's only living pub sign - a working beehive high up in a lime tree. Otherwise, this simple town hostelry offers a good pint of Newby Wyke and good-value, yet basic bar food. Kids will enjoy the bouncy castle that appears during the summer.

Open all wk ⊕ FREE HOUSE ◀ Newby Wyke Real Ales, Everards. **Facilities** Garden

HOUGH-ON-THE-HILL — Map 11 SK94

The Brownlow Arms ★★★★★ INN ◉

High Rd NG32 2AZ ☎ **01400 250234** 🖹 **01400 251993**
e-mail: armsinn@yahoo.co.uk
web: www.thebrownlowarms.com
dir: *Take A607 (Grantham to Sleaford road). Hough-on-the-Hill signed from Barkston*

Named after its former owner, Lord Brownlow, this 17th-century stone inn looks like a well-tended country house. A menu of modern classic dishes includes roast rack of lamb with dauphinoise potatoes or breast of chicken with melting Tallegio, oven-baked tomatoes and pesto. Alfresco dining can be enjoyed on the landscaped terrace that looks out over tree-lined fields. Take advantage of one of the four en suite double bedrooms.

Closed: 25-27 Dec, 1-20 Jan, 1wk Sep, Mon **Restaurant** L served Sun 12-2.15 booking required D served Tue-Sat 6.30-9.30 booking required ⊕ FREE HOUSE ◼ Timothy Taylor Landlord, Marston's Pedigree. **Facilities** Garden Parking **Rooms** 4

KIRTON IN LINDSEY — Map 17 SK99

The George NEW

20 High St DN21 4LX ☎ **01652 640600**
e-mail: enquiry@thegeorgekirton.co.uk
dir: *From A15 take B1205, turn right onto B1400*

Extensively restored in a modern traditional style by Glen and Neil McCartney, the George is an 18th-century former coaching inn offering locally brewed Bateman's ales and seasonally changing menus. From traditional Lincolnshire sausages with mash and gravy in the bar, the choice extends to beef stroganoff, braised lamb shank with mint pea sauce and rib-eye steak with peppercorn sauce. For pudding, indulge in sticky toffee pudding. Lincoln and The Wolds are within easy reach.

Open all wk 12-2 5-11 (Sun 11-3) **Bar Meals** Av main course £6.95 food served all day **Restaurant** Av 3 course à la carte fr £22 food served all day ⊕ FREE HOUSE ◼ Batemans XB. **Facilities** Children's menu Play area Garden

LINCOLN — Map 17 SK97

Pyewipe Inn

Fossebank, Saxilby Rd LN1 2BG
☎ **01522 528708** 🖹 **01522 525009**
e-mail: enquiries@pyewipe.co.uk
dir: *From Lincoln on A57 past Lincoln/A46 Bypass, pub signed in 0.5m*

First licensed in 1778, the Pyewipe (local dialect for lapwing) stands in four acres alongside the Roman-built Fossedyke Navigation. From the grounds there's a great view of nearby Lincoln Cathedral. All food is bought locally and prepared by qualified chefs. With up to eight menu boards to choose from, expect shank of lamb in braised in orange and rosemary; slow roasted aubergine gratin with ratatouille and gruyère; and smoked haddock with poached egg and grain mustard sauce.

Open all day all wk 11-11 **Bar Meals** Av main course £10.50 food served all day **Restaurant** Av 3 course à la carte fr £18.50 food served all day ⊕ FREE HOUSE ◼ Timothy Taylor Landlord, Greene King Abbot Ale, Interbrew Bass, Bombardier, Wadworth 6X. **Facilities** Children's menu Dogs allowed Garden Parking

The Victoria ☻

6 Union Rd LN1 3BJ ☎ **01522 541000**
e-mail: jonathanjpc@aol.com
dir: *From city outskirts follow signs for Cathedral Quarter. Pub 2 mins' walk from all major up-hill car parks*

Situated right next to the Westgate entrance of the Castle and within a stone's throw of Lincoln Cathedral, a long-standing drinkers' pub with a range of real ales, including six changing guest beers, ciders and perries, as well as two beer festivals a year. As well as the fantastic views of the castle, the pub also offers splendid meals made from exclusively home-prepared food including hot baguettes and filled bacon rolls, Saturday breakfast and Sunday lunches. House specials include sausage and mash, various pies, chilli con carne and home-made lasagne.

Open all day all wk 11-mdnt (Fri-Sat 11-1am) **Bar Meals** L served all wk 12-2.30 Av main course £4.50 ⊕ JPC ◼ Timothy Taylor Landlord, Batemans XB, Castle Rock Harvest Pale, guest ales ♂ Westons. ☻ 10 **Facilities** Children's menu Play area Dogs allowed Garden Parking

PICK OF THE PUBS

Wig & Mitre ☻

32 Steep Hill LN2 1LU
☎ **01522 535190** 🖹 **01522 532402**
e-mail: email@wigandmitre.com
dir: *At top of Steep Hill, adjacent to cathedral & Lincoln Castle car parks*

In the historic heart of Lincoln, the Wig & Mitre has been owned and managed by the same proprietors since 1977. The building is a mix of the 14th and 16th centuries, with some more recent parts too. But it all works, it's music-free, and real ales like Black Sheep and Batemans XB are on tap. Food is served in perpetual motion from 8.30am to around midnight every day, all year round. The comprehensive breakfast menu runs until noon. Light meals include hot chicken, parsley and red onion burger with horseradish mayonnaise in a hot ciabatta; and a plate of Scottish smoked salmon. Seasonal main menus offer starters such as creamed white onion soup with parmesan dumplings; main courses like Derbyshire beef with horseradish mash; and puds along the lines of russet apple and pear strudel with home-made custard. Wine recommendations are given on the menus. A specials board which may change as the day progresses completes the food options.

Open all day all wk 8.30am-mdnt **Bar Meals** Av main course £13.48 food served all day **Restaurant** Fixed menu price fr £12.50 Av 3 course à la carte fr £20.85 food served all day ⊕ FREE HOUSE ◼ Black Sheep Special, Batemans XB. ☻ 34 **Facilities** Children's menu Dogs allowed

LITTLE BYTHAM — Map 11 TF01

The Willoughby Arms NEW

Station Rd NG33 4RA ☎ **01780 410276**
e-mail: cdhulme@tiscali.co.uk
dir: *B6121 (Stamford to Bourne road), at junct follow signs to Careby/Little Bytham, inn 5m on right*

This 150 year-old traditional stone, beamed free house was originally built as the booking office and waiting room for Lord Willoughby's private railway line. Now, you'll find a selection of real ales - including several from local micro-breweries - with great, home-cooked food available every lunchtime and evening. Menu options include Lincolnshire sausage and mash; rabbit stew; and steak and kidney pie. There is a large beer garden with stunning views to enjoy on warmer days.

Open all day all wk 12-11 **Bar Meals** L served Mon-Sat 12-2, Sun 12-6 D served all wk 6-9 Av main course £7.50 **Facilities** Children's menu Dogs allowed Garden Parking

LOUTH — Map 17 TF38

Masons Arms

Cornmarket LN11 9PY
☎ 01507 609525 📠 0870 7066450
e-mail: info@themasons.co.uk
dir: *In town centre*

This Grade II listed building, located in the heart of Georgian Louth, dates back to 1725. In the days when it was known as the Bricklayers Arms, the local Masonic lodge met here. The CAMRA award-winning Market Bar is for beer lovers, while the 'upstairs' restaurant offers an à la carte menu where you might find honey roast ham, fried egg and home-made chips; steak and kidney pie; and cauliflower cheese.

Open all wk ⊕ FREE HOUSE ◀ Abbeydale Moonshine, Marston's Pedigree, Batemans XB Bitter, XXXB, 2 guest ales.

MARKET RASEN — Map 17 TF18

The Black Horse Inn NEW

Magna Mile LN8 6AJ
☎ 01507 313645 📠 01507 313645
e-mail: reedannam@aol.com
dir: *In village on A631, between Louth & Market Rasen*

New owners are breathing new life into this Wolds village inn, which dates back to 1730, having refurbished the bar and dining areas. Expect chunky tables, leather sofas fronting open fires and a relaxing atmosphere. There is also a display of RAF memorabilia connected with Squadron 101 who were stationed at Ludford airfield. Locals flock in for rustic, home-made food, perhaps game terrine with spiced tomato chutney, lamb hotpot with pickled red cabbage, halibut with caper and parsley butter, and white chocolate rice pudding with rhubarb jam, washed down with local Bateman's XB.

Open 12-2.30 5-11 Closed: 1 wk Jan, Sun eve-Mon **Bar Meals** L served Tue-Sat 12-2.30, Sun 12-6 D served Tue-Sat 5-10 Av main course £10 **Restaurant** L served Tue-Sat 12-2.30, Sun 12-6 D served Tue-Sat 5-10 Av 3 course à la carte fr £15.40 ⊕ FREE HOUSE ◀ Bateman's XB, Marston's Pedigree, Abott Ale, Fulstow Common, Tom Wood's Lincoln Red ♂ Westons Scrumpy, Skidbrooke Cyder. **Facilities** Children's menu Garden Parking

NEWTON — Map 12 TF03

The Red Lion

NG34 0EE ☎ 01529 497256
dir: *10m E of Grantham on A52*

Dating from the 17th century, the Red Lion is particularly popular with walkers and cyclists, perhaps because the flat Lincolnshire countryside makes for easy exercise. Low beams, exposed stone walls and an open fire in the bar help to create a very atmospheric interior. Popular dishes include haddock in beer batter, lemon sole with parsley butter sauce, breadcrumbed scampi, and home-made steak and ale pie. The carvery serves cold buffets on weekdays, hot ones on Friday and Saturday evenings, and Sunday lunchtime.

Open 12-3 6-11 Closed: Sun eve & Mon eve **Bar Meals** Av main course £12 **Restaurant** Av 3 course à la carte fr £20 ⊕ FREE HOUSE **Facilities** Children's menu Dogs allowed Garden Parking

PARTNEY — Map 17 TF46

Red Lion Inn

PE23 4PG ☎ 01790 752271 📠 01790 753360
e-mail: enquiries@redlioninnpartney.co.uk
dir: *On A16 from Boston, or A158 from Horncastle*

This peaceful village inn at the foot of the Lincolnshire Wolds offers a warm welcome. It also has a reputation for good home-cooked food using local produce, so walkers and cyclists take refreshment here between visits to the nearby nature reserves and sandy beaches. The comprehensive menu includes many favourites: starters such as prawn cocktail and deep-fried brie; main courses of lamb or pork chops, chicken curry, and beef casserole; and specials too, like half a honey-roast chicken.

Closed: Mon **Bar Meals** L served Tue-Sat 12-2, Sun 12-9 D served Tue-Sat 6-9.30 Av main course £7.50 **Restaurant** L served Tue-Sat 12-2, Sun 12-9 D served Tue-Sat 6-9.30 ⊕ FREE HOUSE ◀ Black Sheep, Guinness, Tetley's, guest ales ♂ Westons' 1st Quality Draught. **Facilities** Garden Parking

RAITHBY — Map 17 TF36

Red Lion Inn

PE23 4DS ☎ 01790 753727
dir: *A158 from Horncastle, right at Sausthorpe, left to Raithby*

Traditional beamed black-and-white village pub, parts of which date back 300 years. Log fires provide a warm welcome in winter. A varied menu of home-made dishes includes sea bass with lime stir fry vegetables, roast guinea fowl with tomato, garlic and bacon, and medallions of beef with peppercorn sauce. Meals can be taken in the garden in the warmer months.

Open all wk 12-2 6-11 (Mon 6-11) **Bar Meals** L served Tue-Sun 12-2 D served Tue-Sun 7-9 **Restaurant** L served Tue-Sun 12-2 D served Tue-Sun 7-9 ⊕ FREE HOUSE ◀ Raithby, Greene King IPA, Tetley Smooth. **Facilities** Children's menu Garden Parking

SKEGNESS — Map 17 TF56

Best Western Vine Hotel ★★★ HL ⊤

Vine Rd, Seacroft PE25 3DB
☎ 01754 763018 & 610611 📠 01754 769845
e-mail: info@thevinehotel.com
dir: *In Seacroft area of Skegness. S of town centre*

Substantially unchanged since 1770, the Vine is the second oldest building in Skegness. Set amid two acres of gardens, the ivy-covered hotel was bought by the brewer Harry Bateman in 1927. This charming hostelry offers comfortable accommodation and a fine selection of Bateman's own ales. The bar menu ranges from soup or a simple sandwich to bistro-style salads and substantial mixed grills; there's a traditional Sunday carvery, too.

Open all wk **Bar Meals** L served Mon-Sun 12-2 D served Mon-Sun 6-9 Av main course £10 **Restaurant** L served Sun 12-2 booking required D served Mon-Sun 6-9 booking required Fixed menu price fr £21.50 ⊕ FREE HOUSE ◀ Bateman's XB & XXXB, Valiant, Blacksheep, Dixon's ale. ⊤ 8 **Facilities** Dogs allowed Garden Parking **Rooms** 25

SOUTH RAUCEBY — Map 11 TF04

PICK OF THE PUBS

The Bustard Inn & Restaurant NEW ◉ ⊤

See Pick of the Pubs on opposite page

SOUTH WITHAM — Map 11 SK91

Blue Cow Inn & Brewery

High St NG33 5QB ☎ 01572 768432 📠 01572 768432
e-mail: enquiries@bluecowinn.co.uk
dir: *Between Stamford & Grantham on A1*

Just in Lincolnshire, with the Rutland border a few hundred yards away, this once-derelict, 13th-century inn stands close to the source of the River Witham. Part-timbered outside, the interior has a wealth of beamed ceilings and walls, stone floors and open log fires when the easterly winds whip across The Fens from Siberia. Simon Crathorn brews his own beers. The inn has a patio beer garden for warm evenings.

Open all day all wk 11-11 **Bar Meals** Av main course £8.50 food served all day **Restaurant** food served all day ⊕ FREE HOUSE **Facilities** Children's menu Family room Dogs allowed Garden Parking

PICK OF THE PUBS

The Bustard Inn & Restaurant NEW ◉ ♟

SOUTH RAUCEBY

44 Main St NG34 8QG ☎ 01529 488250
e-mail: info@thebustardinn.co.uk

Legend has it that the last great bustard to be shot in England met its fate in 1845 on Bustard Hill behind this fine Grade II listed pub. It was built by the owners of the Rauceby Hall Estate in 1860 to replace the Robin Hood Inn, which was removed to make way for the hall's new south gate. The Estate sold the inn in 1976, since when there have been several landlords, local residents Alan and Liz Hewitt acquiring it in 2006. They have renovated the inn in a big way to bring out the best features, namely the courtyard, old brewhouse, stable and ornate oriel window overlooking the beer garden. It was their vision to establish a much-needed

facility in the area providing, primarily, an elegant but informal restaurant serving delicious, freshly prepared food and, second, a public house serving perfect pints of real ales, as well as wines to suit all tastes. Mission accomplished. In the bar a pint of the whimsically named Cheeky Bustard might be accompanied by smoked haddock omelette with Lincolnshire cheese, or simply a round of sandwiches, while in the elegant but informal restaurant (incorporating the brewhouse and stable) award-winning chef Phil Lowe's freshly prepared dishes include pan-fried Gressingham duck with cider fondant and red cabbage; roasted sea bass with Mediterranean vegetable gateau and buttered spinach; and tomato and chickpea fondue with grilled aubergines, pan-fried halloumi and tzatziki. Children's portions and all dietary requirements are catered for. Prince Albert, later George VI, was a frequent visitor when he was stationed at nearby Cranwell, and Prince Charles also slipped in for a swift half when he was there. Gourmet evenings and live jazz evenings are arranged regularly.

Open 12-3 5.30-11 (Sun 12-3.30) Closed: Sun eve, Mon **Bar Meals** L served Tue-Sat 12-2.30, Sun 12-3 D served Tue-Sat 6-9.30 Av main course £9 **Restaurant** L served Tue-Sat 12-2.30, Sun 12-3 D served Tue-Sat 6-9.30 Fixed menu price fr £21.50 Av 3 course à la carte fr £32 ◀ Bateman's GHA, Guinness, Cheeky Bustard, Guest Ale. ♟ 13 **Facilities** Garden Parking

STAMFORD — Map 11 TF00

The Bull & Swan Inn ♟

24a High St, St Martin's PE9 2LJ ☎ 01780 763558
dir: A1 for B1081 towards Stamford. Pub on right in outskirts of town

A 17th-century coaching inn retaining many original features, close to historic Burghley House. There are two log fires in winter and a large patio garden for summer use. Live music is provided indoors every Sunday in winter and in the garden every Friday in summer. The menu ranges from sandwiches to steaks or moules marinière, while daily specials offer roasted smoked duck breast or medallions of pork.

Open all day all wk noon-11.30 (Sun noon-10.30) **Bar Meals** L served Mon-Fri 12-2.30, Sat 12-9, Sun 12-6 booking required D served Mon-Fri 5.30-9, Sat 12-9, Sun 12-6 booking required Av main course £8 **Restaurant** L served Mon-Fri 12-2.30, Sat 12-9, Sun 12-6 booking required D served Mon-Fri 5.30-9, Sat 12-9, Sun 12-6 booking required ⊕ PUNCH TAVERNS ◀ Greene King Abbot Ale, Adnams Bitter, guest ales ♂ Aspall. ♟ 7 **Facilities** Children's menu Dogs allowed Garden Parking

PICK OF THE PUBS

The George of Stamford ★★★ HL ☻ ♟

71 St Martins PE9 2LB
☎ 01780 750750   📄 01780 750701
e-mail: reservations@georgehotelofstamford.com
dir: From Peterborough take A1 N. Onto B1081 for Stamford, down hill to lights. Hotel on left

Forty coaches a day - 20 heading for London, 20 for York - once stopped at this 16th-century inn to change horses, which explains the doors marked with the names of the two cities. It is a magnificent building, full of fascinating rooms, and widely known for its famous gallows inn sign across the road that welcomed travellers, while warning highwaymen to keep going. Today's visitors will appreciate the welcoming log fires, oak-panelled restaurants, medieval crypt, walled Monastery Garden and cobbled courtyard. Various menus are available: in the bistro-style restaurant the food ranges from pastas to fish and chips; in the York Bar find sandwiches to goulash. Specific dishes include gruyère cheese fritters with Thai jelly; Grand Brittany seafood platter; Woodbridge duck with sage and onion stuffing and apple sauce; and English sirloin of beef carved off the bone at the table. The hotel has 47 individually designed, well-equipped bedrooms.

Open all day all wk 11-11 (Sun 12-11) **Bar Meals** L served all wk 11.30-2.30 Av main course £7.75 **Restaurant** L served all wk 12-2.30 (Garden Lounge all wk 11-11) booking required D served all wk 7-10.30 booking required Fixed menu price fr £19.55 Av 3 course à la carte fr £37.50 food served all day ⊕ FREE HOUSE ◀ Adnams Broadside, Fuller's London Pride, Greene King, Ruddles Bitter ♂ Aspall's Suffolk Cider. ♟ 15 **Facilities** Dogs allowed Garden Parking **Rooms** 47

SURFLEET SEAS END — Map 12 TF22

The Ship Inn

154 Reservoir Rd PE11 4DH
☎ 01775 680547   📄 01775 680541
e-mail: shipsurfleet@hotmail.com
dir: Off A16 (Spalding to Boston). Follow tourist signs towards Surfleet Reservoir then The Ship Inn signs

A fenland pub by the lock gates controlling the Rivers Glen and Welland, and Vernatti's Drain. Dating from only 2003, it occupies the footprint of an earlier hostelry, which the drainage-fixated Vernatti built in 1642. The bar is panelled in hand-crafted oak, while upstairs is the restaurant overlooking the marshes. Locally sourced food includes Whitby scampi; home-made pies; roast rib of Lincolnshire beef; and pan-fried salmon in the restaurant.

Open all wk 11-3 5-mdnt (Sat-Sun 11am-mdnt) **Bar Meals** L served Mon-Sat 12-3, Sun 12-6 D served Mon-Sat 5-9 ⊕ FREE HOUSE ◀ Hydes Smooth, local micro breweries. **Facilities** Dogs allowed Parking

SUSWORTH — Map 17 SE80

The Jenny Wren Inn NEW

East Ferry Rd DN17 3AS ☎ 01724 784000
e-mail: info@jennywreninn.co.uk
dir: Please telephone for directions

Like many other old inns, the Jenny Wren was once a farmhouse. Beamed ceilings, exposed brickwork, wood panelling and fireplaces make it easy to imagine an 18th-century farmer warming himself in front of some blazing logs drinking a pint of real ale. The menu offers typical starters of freshly prepared soup; and prawn cocktail with apple, celery and Marie Rose sauce; main courses include pan-fried salmon with prawn lemon cream; steak and ale pie; and oven-roasted chicken breast with dauphinoise potato. The River Trent flows past the front.

Open all wk noon-2.30 5.45-10.30 (Fri-Sun & BH noon-10.30) Closed: 1 Jan **Bar Meals** L served Mon-Thu 12-2, Fri-Sun 12-9 booking required D served Mon-Thu 5.45-9, Fri-Sun 12-9 booking required Av main course £10 **Restaurant** L served Mon-Thu 12-2, Fri-Sun 12-9 booking required D served Mon-Thu 5.45-9, Fri-Sun 12-9 booking required Fixed menu price fr £9.95 Av 3 course à la carte fr £20 ⊕ FREE HOUSE ◀ Old Speckled Hen, IPA Bitter, Theakstons. **Facilities** Children's menu Dogs allowed Garden Parking

WOODHALL SPA — Map 17 TF16

Village Limits Country Pub, Restaurant & Motel ♟

Stixwould Rd LN10 6UJ
☎ 01526 353312   📄 01526 352203
e-mail: info@villagelimits.co.uk
dir: At rdbt on main street follow Petwood Hotel signs. Motel 500yds past Petwood Hotel

The pub and restaurant are situated in the original part of the building, so expect bare beams and old world charm. Typical meals, championing the ingredients of many local Lincolnshire suppliers, include fillet steak with wild mushrooms; chargrilled rainbow trout; and gammon steak. There's a good choice of real ales to wash it all down.

Closed: Mon & Sun eve **Bar Meals** L served Tue-Sat 11.30-2 booking required D served Tue-Sat 6.30-9 booking required Av main course £10 **Restaurant** L served Tue-Sun 11.30-2 booking required D served Tue-Sat 6.30-9 booking required Av 3 course à la carte fr £19 ⊕ FREE HOUSE ◀ Batemans XB, Tetley's Smooth Flow, Highwood Tom Wood's Best, Fulstow IPA, Dixon's Major Bitter. ♟ 8 **Facilities** Children's menu Garden Parking

WOOLSTHORPE — Map 11 SK83

PICK OF THE PUBS

The Chequers Inn ★★★★ INN ☻ ♟

Main St NG32 1LU ☎ 01476 870701
e-mail: justinnabar@yahoo.co.uk
dir: Approx 7m from Grantham. 3m from A607. Follow heritage signs to Belvoir Castle

Modern style and traditional features rub along happily together in this atmospheric inn just a stone's throw from Belvoir Castle. The interior is warmed by five real fires, and there are further delights outside, including a cricket pitch, pétanque, and castle views from the mature garden. For refreshment, the fully-stocked bar meets every whim and taste, from ales to single malts. You can eat here too if you like, or try the Bakehouse Restaurant, which contains the oven from the pub's previous incarnation as the village bakery, built in 1646. Expect sophisticated pub food along the lines of macaroni of clams, mussels and squid with basil butter followed by pan-roasted Belvoir partridge, celeriac purée, game chips and sauté of sprout leaves. A separate list of traditional favourites includes beer-battered haddock with hand cut chips; and sausages and mash with onion gravy. Comfortable bedrooms can be found in the former stable block.

Open all wk Closed: 25 eve & 26 Dec, 1 Jan eve **Bar Meals** L served Mon-Sat 12-2.30, Sun 12-4 D served Mon-Sat 6-9.30, Sun 6-8.30 Av main course £10 **Restaurant** L served Mon-Sat 12-2.30, Sun 12-4 D served Mon-Sat 6-9.30, Sun 6-8.30 Fixed menu price fr £16.50 Av 3 course à la carte fr £25.50 ⊕ FREE HOUSE ◼ Woodforde's Wherry, Batemans ales Ò Aspall's Old Rosie Scrumpy. ♟ 25 **Facilities** Family room Dogs allowed Garden Parking **Rooms** 4

LONDON

E1

Town of Ramsgate ♟   PLAN 2 F4

62 Wapping High St E1W 2NP ☎ 020 7481 8000
dir: *0.3m from Wapping tube station & Tower of London*

A 500-year-old pub close to The City, decorated with bric-a-brac and old prints. Judge Jeffries was caught here while trying to flee the country and escape the kind of justice he dealt out. Press gangs used to work the area, imprisoning men overnight in the cellar. The owners continue to offer real ale and value for money bar food, which can be enjoyed on the decked terrace overlooking the River Thames.

Open all day all wk noon-mdnt (Sun noon-11) **Bar Meals** L served all wk 12-9 D served all wk 12-9 Av main course £8.50 food served all day ⊕ FREE HOUSE ◼ Adnams, Youngs, Fuller's London Pride Ò Brothers Pear Cider. ♟ 7 **Facilities** Dogs allowed Garden

E8

The Cat & Mutton NEW ♟   PLAN 2 F4

76 Broadway Market, Hackney E8 4QJ
☎ 020 7254 5599
e-mail: catandmutton@yahoo.co.uk
web: www.catandmutton.co.uk
dir: *Please telephone for directions*

A fixture in London's East End since the mid-1700s, when it was an ale house for cattle and sheep drovers, this once run-down street corner boozer was revamped and reinvented as a gastro-pub in 2003. At scrubbed tables in trendy, gentrified surroundings, order mussels with smoked haddock and bacon, or a ploughman's slate at lunch, with inventive evening extras taking in peppered venison steak with potato pancake and port jus, and pan-fried lemon sole with caper butter.

Open all day noon-11 (Fri-Sat noon-1am, Mon 6-11) Closed: 25-26 Dec & 1 Jan, Mon L **Bar Meals** L served Tue-Fri 12-3 D served Mon-Sat 6.30-10 booking required Av main course £14 **Restaurant** L served Tue-Sat 12-3, Sun 12-5 D served Mon-Sat 6-10 booking required ⊕ SEAMLESS LTD ◼ Adnams Bitter, Shepherd Neame Spitfire, San Miguel, Staropramen Ò Westons. ♟ 8 **Facilities** Children's menu Dogs allowed

E9

PICK OF THE PUBS

The Empress of India ♟   PLAN 2 F4

130 Lauriston Rd, Victoria Park E9 7LH
☎ 020 8533 5123 📄 020 8533 4483
e-mail: info@theempressofindia.com
dir: *From Mile End Station turn right onto Grove Rd, leads onto Lauriston Rd*

This archetypal East End pub was built a few years after Queen Victoria became Empress of India, and has in its time been a nightclub, a print works and, more recently, a floristry training school. The beautifully styled interior includes a carpet with the pub's name woven into it. The bar serves classic cocktails, draught beers and fine wines from around the globe. Modern British food, served from the open kitchen, offers options throughout the day, including breakfast, lunch, dinner, bar snacks, kids' menu, afternoon tea and a feast menu. Sunday lunchtime brings the likes of roast sirloin of Angus beef and all the trimmings: Yorkshire pudding, horseradish cream and seasonal vegetables, or whole roasted free-range Devonshire bronze chicken from the rotisserie with pigs in blankets, thyme stuffing and bread sauce. Rare breed meats, poultry and game are spit roasted daily; and shellfish figures prominently – pint o' prawns and Colchester oysters.

Open all wk Closed: 25-26 Dec ⊕ ROCHE COMMUNICATIONS ◼ Greenwich Meantime Helles Lager, Greenwich Meantime Indian Pale Ale, Paulaner Weiss ale. ♟ 30

E14

PICK OF THE PUBS

The Grapes ♟   PLAN 2 G4

76 Narrow St, Limehouse E14 8BP
☎ 020 7987 4396 📄 020 7987 3137
dir: *Telephone for details*

Charles Dickens once propped the bar up here, and so taken was he by its charms that the pub appears, thinly disguised, as The Six Jolly Fellowship Porters in his novel *Our Mutual Friend*. While the novelist might still recognise the interior, the surroundings have changed dramatically with the development of Canary Wharf and the Docklands Light Railway. However, the tradition of old-fashioned values is maintained by the provision of best cask conditioned ales in the atmospheric bar downstairs, while in the tiny upstairs restaurant only the freshest fish is served. This is a fish

lover's paradise with a menu that includes sea bass, monkfish, Dover sole and bream, all available with a range of different sauces. Meat eaters and vegetarians should not, however, be deterred from experiencing this evocative slice of old Limehouse; traditional roasts are served on Sundays, and sandwiches and salads are always available.

Open all day all wk noon-11 (Mon-Wed noon-3 5.30-11) Closed: 25-26 Dec, 1 Jan **Bar Meals** L served Mon-Sat 12-2.30, Sun 12-3.30 D served Mon-Sat 7-9.30 Av main course £7.95 **Restaurant** L served Mon-Fri 12-2.30 booking required D served Mon-Sat 7-9.30 booking required Av 3 course à la carte fr £35 ⊕ PUNCH TAVERNS ◼ Adnams, Marstons Pedigree, Timothy Taylor Landlord. ♟ 6 **Facilities** Dogs allowed

PICK OF THE PUBS

The Gun ◉ ♟   PLAN 2 G4

27 Coldharbour, Docklands E14 9NS
☎ 020 7515 5222 📄 020 7515 4407
e-mail: info@thegundocklands.com
dir: *From South Quay DLR, east along Marsh Wall to mini rdbt. Turn left, over bridge then 1st right*

Destroyed by fire several years ago, this Grade II listed 18th-century pub re-opened in 2004 following painstaking restoration work. It stands on the banks of the Thames in an area once home to the dockside iron foundries which produced guns for the Royal Navy fleets. The Gun itself used to shelter smugglers – a spy hole on the secret circular staircase was used when looking out for the 'revenue men'. Excellent real ales are backed by popular international beers at the bar, which can also seat 40 for food; a back bar has two snugs and two private dining rooms, while a fabulous riverside terrace accommodates up to 50. Bar snacks include Welsh rarebit; salt and pepper squid; and hot pig (crispy pork belly) with apple sauce. A concise selection of larger plates may include ox cheeks with mashed potato and onion jus, or pie of the week.

Open all wk Closed: 26 Dec ◼ Guinness. ♟ 22 **Facilities** Garden

EC1

PICK OF THE PUBS

The Bleeding Heart Tavern ✪ ♀ PLAN 1 E4

19 Greville St EC1N 8SQ
☎ 020 7242 8238 ▤ 020 7831 1402
e-mail: bookings@bleedingheart.co.uk
dir: *Close to Farringdon tube station, at corner of Greville St & Bleeding Heart Yard*

Standing just off London's famous Leather Lane, and dating from 1746, when Holborn had a boozer for every five houses and inns boasted that their customers could be 'drunk for a penny and dead drunk for twopence'. It traded until 1946, was a grill for 52 years, and reopened as The Tavern Bar in 1998. Today this Tavern offers traditional real ales and a light lunchtime menu if you're pressed for time. Downstairs, the warm and comforting dining room features an open rotisserie and grill serving free-range organic British meat, game and poultry alongside an extensive wine list. Typical menu choices might start with mackerel and whisky pâté as a prelude to braised beef in Adnams Ale with dumplings, or spit-roast suckling pig with sage apple and onion stuffing and crushed garlic potatoes. Desserts include steamed chocolate pudding, treacle tart and a jam roly-poly.

Open all day 7am-11pm Closed: BH, 10 days at Xmas, Sat-Sun **Bar Meals** Av main course £8.95 food served all day **Restaurant** L served Mon-Fri 12-2.30 booking required D served Mon-Fri 5.30-11 booking required Av 3 course à la carte fr £19.50 ⊕ FREE HOUSE ◀ Adnams Southwold Bitter, Broadside, Fisherman. ♀ 17

PICK OF THE PUBS

Coach & Horses NEW ♀ PLAN 1 E5

26-28 Ray St, Clerkenwell EC1 3DJ ☎ 020 7278 8990
e-mail: info@thecoachandhorses.com
dir: *From Farringdon tube station right onto Cowcross St. At Farringdon Rd turn right, after 500yds left onto Ray St. Pub at bottom of hill*

On this spot once stood Hockley-in-the-Hole bear garden, a popular entertainment venue in Queen Anne's day. Nearly two centuries later, in about 1855, this now classic Victorian London pub was built to serve the myriad artisans, many of them Italian, who populated this characterful area. What is now the public bar used to be a sweet shop, people lived in the beer cellars, and there was a secret passage to the long-buried River Fleet. Unsurprisingly there are a few ghosts, including an old man and a black cat. Among the reasonably priced dishes, look for herring roes on toast; black pudding hash with fried egg, plus these examples from a dinner menu: braised cuttlefish on toast; venison pie with mash; sea bream with roasted salsify, fennel, chervil and cucumber; cassoulet; and Jerusalem artichoke risotto. Over the road is the original Clerk's Well, from which this district takes its name.

Open all wk noon-11 (Sat 5-11 Sun noon-5) Closed: 23 Dec-1st Mon in Jan, BH **Bar Meals** L served Mon-Fri & Sun 12-3 D served Mon-Sat 6-10 Av main course £12.50 **Restaurant** L served Mon-Fri & Sun 12-3 D served Mon-Sat 6-10 Av 3 course à la carte fr £20 ◀ Timothy Taylor Landlord, Adnams Bitter, Guinness, Fuller's London Pride, Staropramen. ♀ 19 **Facilities** Children's menu Dogs allowed Garden

PICK OF THE PUBS

The Eagle ♀ PLAN 1 E4

159 Farringdon Rd EC1R 3AL ☎ 020 7837 1353
dir: *Angel/Farringdon tube station. Pub at north end of Farringdon Rd*

The Eagle, which opened in 1990, was a front-runner of a new breed of stylish eating and drinking establishments that we now know as gastro pubs. Farringdon Road was more downbeat in those days but Clerkenwell is quite a trendy district now. The Eagle is still going strong, despite considerable competition, and remains one of the neighbourhood's top establishments. The airy interior includes a wooden-floored bar and dining area, a random assortment of furniture, and an open-to-view kitchen that produces a creative, modern, daily-changing menu drawing on the worlds' cuisine. Typical of the range are escalivada, a Spanish-style roast vegetable salad with sherry vinegar and parsley; osso buco alla Milanese with saffron risotto; and Romney Marsh lamb chops with grilled artichokes and olives. A tapas selection is also available. Draught and bottled beers, and an international wine list are all well chosen.

Open all day noon-11 Closed: BH (not Good Fri eve), Sun eve **Bar Meals** L served Mon-Fri 12.30-3, Sat-Sun 12.30-3.30 D served Mon-Sat 6.30-10.30 ⊕ FREE HOUSE ◀ Wells Eagle IPA, Bombardier Ò Westons. ♀ 14 **Facilities** Dogs allowed

PICK OF THE PUBS

The Jerusalem Tavern PLAN 1 F4

55 Britton St, Clerkenwell EC1M 5NA
☎ 020 7490 4281
e-mail: beers@stpetersbrewery.co.uk
dir: *100mtrs NE of Farringdon tube station; 300mtrs N of Smithfield*

Named after the Priory of St John of Jerusalem, this historic tavern has been in four different locations since it was established in the 14th century. The current building dates from 1720, when a merchant lived here, although the frontage dates from about 1810, by which time it was the premises of one of Clerkenwell's many watch and clockmaker's workshops. A fascinating and wonderfully vibrant corner of London that has only recently been 'rediscovered', centuries after Samuel Johnson, David Garrick and the young Handel used to drink in this tavern. Its dark, dimly-lit Dickensian bar, with bare boards, rustic wooden tables, old tiles, candles, open fires and cosy corners, is the perfect film set - and that is what it has been on many occasions. The Jerusalem Tavern, a classic pub in every sense of the description, is open every weekday and offers the full range of bottled beers from St Peter's Brewery (which owns it), as well as a familiar range of pub fare, including game pie, risotto, sausage and mash and various roasts.

Open all day 11-11 Closed: 25 Dec-1 Jan, Sat-Sun **Bar Meals** L served Mon-Fri 12-3 D served Tue-Thu 6-9 ⊕ ST PETER'S BREWERY ◀ St Peters (complete range) Ò Aspalls.

PICK OF THE PUBS

The Peasant ♀ PLAN 1 D3

240 Saint John St EC1V 4PH
☎ 020 7336 7726 ▤ 020 7490 1089
e-mail: eat@thepeasant.co.uk
dir: *Exit Angel & Farringdon Rd tube station. Pub on corner of Saint John St & Percival St*

In the heart of Clerkenwell and dating from 1860, this gastro-pub retains many original Victorian features and is now Grade II listed. Customers delight in the lovingly restored mahogany horseshoe bar with its original inlaid mosaic floor, and a fabulous conservatory. The upstairs restaurant has had similar treatment and is beautifully lit by period chandeliers. An extensive range of pumped and bottled beers is supplemented by real ciders, rums, malt whiskeys and a good wine list. Light bites are served in the bar: mussels steamed in bacon, chilli and Leffe draught; fillet of haddock, Welsh rarebit crust, bubble and squeak; and sardine Caesar salad. The restaurant menu offers accomplished cooking in starters like sautéed lambs' kidneys with cassava gnocchi and walnut pesto; and main courses such as grass-fed Argentinian grilled rib-eye steak with roast shallots, red peppers and steamed curly kale. There is a garden terrace for alfresco dining.

Open all day all wk noon-11 (Sun noon-10.30) Closed: 24 Dec-2 Jan **Bar Meals** Av main course £11 food served all day **Restaurant** L served Tue-Fri 12-3 D served Tue-Sat 6-11 Fixed menu price fr £25 Av 3 course à la carte fr £30 ⊕ FREE HOUSE ◀ Bombardier, Dekonick Belgian Ale, Crouch Ale, Brewers Gold ♂ Thatchers Pear & Katy, Aspall. ♥ 12 **Facilities** Dogs allowed Garden

The Well ♥　　　　　　　　PLAN 1 F5

180 Saint John St, Clerkenwell EC1V 4JY
☎ 020 7251 9363 📠 020 7404 2250
e-mail: drink@downthewell.co.uk
dir: Farringdon tube station left to junct, left onto St John, pub on corner on right

A gastro-pub in trendy Clerkenwell offering a regularly changing, modern European lunch and dinner menu, an extensive wine selection, and lots of draught and bottled beers. The lower ground features a leather-panelled aquarium bar with exotic tropical fish in huge tanks. From the appealing menu, start with celeriac and black truffle oil soup or crayfish tails with avocado and shellfish cream; followed by roasted sea bream fillet with wild mushroom risotto or rabbit and whole grain mustard pie with creamed cauliflower.

Open all wk **Bar Meals** L served all wk 12-3 booking required D served all wk 6-10.30 booking required Av main course £12 **Restaurant** L served all wk 12-3 booking required D served all wk 6-10.30 booking required Av 3 course à la carte fr £25 ⊕ FREE HOUSE ◀ San Miguel, Paulaner, Red Stripe, Kronenbourg, Guinness. ♥ 6

Ye Olde Mitre ♥　　　　　　PLAN 1 E4

1 Ely Court, Ely Place, By 8 Hatton Garden EC1N 6SJ
☎ 020 7405 4751
dir: From Chancery Lane tube station exit 3 walk downhill to Holborn Circus, left into Hatton Garden. Pub in alley between 8 & 9 Hatton Garden

A famous old establishment, hidden up an alleyway off Hatton Garden, Ye Olde Mitre dates from 1546. Queen Elizabeth once danced around the cherry tree in the corner of the bar. These days there's also a lounge and an outside beer barrel area. Three permanent real ales are served and a minimum of two changing guest ales weekly. An 'English tapas' of toasted sandwiches, pork pies, scotch eggs, sausages, pickled eggs and gherkins is available from 11.30am to 9.30pm.

Open all day 11-11 Closed: 25 Dec, 1 Jan, BH, Sat-Sun (ex 2nd wknd Aug) **Bar Meals** Av main course £1.50 food served all day ⊕ PUNCH TAVERNS ◀ Adnams Bitter, Adnams Broadside, Deuchars IPA, Roosters, Orkney, guest ales ♂ Thatchers Scrumpy Jug. ♥ 9
Facilities Garden

EC2

Old Dr Butler's Head　　　　PLAN 1 F4

Mason's Av, Coleman St, Moorgate EC2V 5BT
☎ 020 7606 3504 📠 020 7600 0417
e-mail: olddrbutlershead@shepherdneame.co.uk
dir: Telephone for directions

This City pub is the only surviving tavern displaying the sign of Dr Butler, purveyor of 'medicinal ale'. It was rebuilt after the Great Fire, although the frontage is probably Victorian. Pub lunches and Shepherd Neame real ales are served in the Dickensian gas-lit bar, while upstairs, the Chop House restaurant offers a traditional English menu featuring steak and kidney pudding, and chargrilled lamb cutlets. The City is largely empty at weekends, so the pub closes.

Closed: Sat-Sun ⊕ SHEPHERD NEAME ◀ Shepherd Neame Spitfire, Bishops Finger Master Brew, Shepherd Neame Best.

EC4

The Black Friar ♥　　　　　　PLAN 1 F3

174 Queen Victoria St EC4V 4EG ☎ 020 7236 5474
dir: Opposite Blackfriars tube station

Located on the site of Blackfriar's monastery, where Henry VIII dissolved his marriage to Catherine of Aragon and separated from the Catholic church. The pub has made several TV appearances because of its wonderful Art Nouveau interior. It is close to Blackfriars Bridge and station and gets very busy with after-work drinkers. A traditional-style menu includes steak and ale pie, sausage and mash, and sandwiches, all washed down with a pint of Sharp's Doom Bar or St Austell Tribute.

Open all day all wk 10am-11pm (Thu-Fri 10am-11.30pm Sun noon-10.30) Closed: 25 Dec **Bar Meals** Av main course £6.95 food served all day ⊕ MITCHELLS & BUTLERS ◀ Fuller's London Pride, Adnams, Timothy Taylor, St Austell Tribute, Sharp's Doom Bar ♂ Westons Organic. ♥ 14 **Facilities** Garden

The Old Bank of England ♥　　PLAN 1 E4

194 Fleet St EC4A 2LT ☎ 020 7430 2255
e-mail: oldbankofengland@fullers.co.uk
dir: Pub by Courts of Justice

This magnificent building previously housed the Law Courts' branch of the Bank of England. Set between the site of Sweeney Todd's barbershop and his mistress' pie shop, it stands above the original bank vaults and the tunnels in which Todd butchered his unfortunate victims. Aptly, bar meals include an extensive range of pies, but other treats include soup, sandwiches, burgers, sharing platters, and hearty meals such as bangers and mash.

Open 11-11 Closed: BH, Sat-Sun **Bar Meals** L served Mon-Fri 12-8 D served Mon-Fri 12-8 ⊕ FULLER SMITH TURNER PLC ◀ London Pride, ESB, Chiswick, Discovery, Seasonal. ♥ 8 **Facilities** Garden

PICK OF THE PUBS

The White Swan ◉ ♥　　　　PLAN 1 E4

108 Fetter Ln, Holborn EC4A 1ES
☎ 020 7242 9696 📠 020 7404 2250
e-mail: info@thewhiteswanlondon.com
dir: Nearest tube: Chancery Lane. From station towards St Paul's Cathedral. At HSBC bank left into Fetter Lane. Pub on right

Transformed from the old Mucky Duck pub, this is now a handsome, traditional city watering hole. Upstairs is a mezzanine area and a beautifully restored dining room with mirrored ceiling and linen-clad tables. Of course, this being the ever busy City, eating can be a rushed business. No problem, the weekday Express Menu delivers two courses in one hour - in at twelve, out at one. Fish comes fresh from Billingsgate market each morning, including the pub menu's sardines on toast with a tomato and herb sauce, alongside pork and herb sausages, colcannon and onion gravy; and Jerusalem artichoke risotto. The Dining Room menu lists additional temptations such as braised pig's cheek, parsnip purée with thyme jus; twice cooked guinea fowl breast, Spanish ham, caramelized endive, game chips and sherry vinegar jus; pan-fried brill, truffled leeks, sautéed wild mushrooms, garlic chips and fish cream; and roasted Cox's apple Charlotte with cinnamon sauce.

Closed: Sat-Sun & BH **Bar Meals** L served Mon-Fri 12-3 D served Mon-Fri 6-10 Av main course £10 **Restaurant** L served Mon-Fri 12-3 booking required D served Mon-Fri 6-10 booking required Fixed menu price fr £23 Av 3 course à la carte fr £23 ⊕ ETM Group ◀ London Pride, Greene King IPA, Guinness, San Miguel. ♥ 10

N1

PICK OF THE PUBS

The Barnsbury ☻ PLAN 2 F4

209-211 Liverpool Rd, Islington N1 1LX
☎ 020 7607 5519 📄 020 7607 3256
e-mail: info@thebarnsbury.co.uk
dir: Please telephone for directions

The Barnsbury, a 'free house and dining room' in the heart of Islington, is a welcome addition to the London scene. It's a gastro-pub where both the food and the prices are well conceived – and its walled garden makes it a secluded and sought-after summer oasis for alfresco relaxation. At least two guest ales are backed by Thatchers Gold cider and an in-depth wine list. The food is cooked from daily supplies of fresh ingredients which have been bought direct from the market, itemised in refreshingly concise terms on the menu. Weekday lunches range from oysters to mushroom tagliatelle or lamb shank shepherd's pie. The à la carte dinner choice is also a no-nonsense selection of the day's produce: grilled sardines, caponata and basil oil could be your starter. Pork fillet with sweet potato purée and caramelised apples gives a flavour of the half dozen main course options. Pear and cranberry crumble with clotted cream rounds things off nicely.

Open all day all wk noon-11 (Sun noon-10.30) Closed: 25-26 Dec, 1 Jan Bar Meals L served Mon-Fri 12-3 Av main course £8 Restaurant L served Sat-Sun 12-4 D served all wk 6.30-10 Av 3 course à la carte fr £26 ⊕ FREE HOUSE ◀ Gravesend Shrimpers, 2 guest ales ⌀ Thatchers Gold. ☻ 12 Facilities Children's menu Dogs allowed Garden

The Compton Arms ☻ PLAN 2 F4

4 Compton Av, Off Canonbury Rd N1 2XD
☎ 020 7359 6883
e-mail: thecomptonarms@ukonline.co.uk
dir: Telephone for directions

George Orwell was once a customer at this peaceful pub on Islington's back streets. The late 17th-century building has a rural feel, and is frequented by a mix of locals, actors and musicians. One local described it as 'an island in a sea of gastro-pubs'. Expect real ales from the hand pump, and good value steaks, mixed grills, big breakfasts and Sunday roasts. The bar is busy when Arsenal are at home.

Open all wk Closed: 25 Dec afternoon Bar Meals L served Mon-Fri 12-2.30 D served Mon-Fri 6-8.30 Av main course £5 ⊕ GREENE KING ◀ Greene King IPA, Abbot Ale, Morlands, guest ale. ☻ 8 Facilities Family room Dogs allowed Garden

The Crown ☻ PLAN 2 F4

116 Cloudsley Rd, Islington N1 0EB ☎ 020 7837 7107
e-mail: crown.islington@fullers.co.uk
dir: From tube station take Liverpool Rd, 6th left into Cloudesley Sq. Pub on opposite side of Square

This Grade II listed Georgian building in the Barnsbury village conservation area of Islington boasts one of only two remaining barrel bars in London. It specialises in high quality gastro food, and has an unusual range of branded rums. The daily changing menu typically features starters to share like spare ribs or assorted platters with Turkish flatbreads, and mains such as lamb burgers, a variety of sausages, fishcakes, and steak and ale pie. Vegetarians are well catered for.

Open all day all wk noon-11 (Sun noon-10.30) Closed: 25 Dec Bar Meals L served Mon-Fri 12-3, Sat 12-5, Sun 12-9 D served Mon-Sat 6-10 ⊕ FULLERS BREWERY ◀ Fuller's London Pride, Organic Honeydew, ESB, Chiswick Bitter ⌀ Thatchers Gold. ☻ 12 Facilities Dogs allowed Garden

PICK OF THE PUBS

The Drapers Arms ☻ PLAN 2 F4

44 Barnsbury St N1 1ER ☎ 020 7619 0348
e-mail: nick@thedrapersarms.com
dir: Turn right from Highbury & Islington station, 10mins along Upper Street. Barnsbury St on right opposite Shell service station

The Drapers Company, one of the oldest City livery companies, owns this smart pub in one of North London's most prosperous districts. Speaking shortly before it reopened in May 2009, owner Nick Gibson was emphatic that the Drapers would be a 'pub pub, not a quasi-restaurant within a pub' and that the aim would be to delight customers with a robust, real food offering from one of London's top chefs, carefully chosen wines, and beers to include Spitfire, Harvey's Best, Black Sheep and Staropramen. The downstairs open plan bar is illuminated by large picture windows, its unfussy interior furnished with a mix of squashy sofas and solid wooden tables. If a more contemplative pint is sought, retire to the secluded and peaceful garden. Closely associated with the new enterprise is Ben Maschler, son of Fay, the doyenne of food writers.

Open all day all wk Closed: 24-27 Dec, 1-2 Jan Bar Meals L served all wk 12-3 D served all wk 6-11 Restaurant L served all wk 12-3 D served all wk 6-11 ⊕ FREE HOUSE ⌀ Aspall. ☻ 6 Facilities Dogs allowed Garden

PICK OF THE PUBS

The Duke of Cambridge ☻ PLAN 2 F4

30 Saint Peter's St N1 8JT
☎ 020 7359 3066 📄 020 7359 1877
e-mail: duke@dukeorganic.co.uk
dir: Telephone for directions

A pioneer in sustainable eating out, the Duke of Cambridge was the first UK pub certified by the Soil Association. Founder Geetie Singh has combined her passion for food and ethical business to create a leader in green dining. The company recycles and reuses wherever possible, and even the electricity is wind and solar sourced. The Marine Conservation Society has given its stamp of approval to the Duke's fish purchasing policy - and, with 100% organic wines and a daily-changing menu, you can feel really virtuous about tucking into a few courses with a glass of your favourite tipple. Try a delicious starter like langoustine with aioli and grilled bread, followed perhaps by mushroom and cavalo nero lasagne with beetroot and watercress salad; or slow roast mutton with rosemary and garlic roasted potatoes. Draft cider is on offer too.

Open all day all wk noon-11 Closed: 24-26 & 31 Dec, 1 Jan Bar Meals L served Mon-Fri 12.30-3, Sat-Sun 12.30-3.30 D served Mon-Sat 6.30-10.30, Sun 6.30-10 Av main course £13.50 Restaurant L served Mon-Fri 12.30-3, Sat-Sun 12.30-3.30 booking required D served Mon-Sat 6.30-10.30, Sun 6.30-10 booking required Av 3 course à la carte fr £27 ⊕ FREE HOUSE ◀ Pitfield SB Bitter & Eco Warrior, St Peter's Best Bitter, East Kent Golding, Red Squirrel London Porter ⌀ Westons, Dunkertons, Wiscombe. ☻ 12 Facilities Children's menu Dogs allowed

The House ☻ PLAN 2 F4

63-69 Canonbury Rd N1 2DG
☎ 020 7704 7410 📄 020 7704 9388
e-mail: info@inthehouse.biz
dir: Telephone for directions

This successful gastro-pub has featured in a celebrity cookbook and garnered plenty of praise since it opened its doors a few years ago. Situated in Islington's prestigious Canonbury district, expect a thoroughly modern menu at lunch and dinner. Enjoy roast salmon, red onion and basil risotto at lunchtime; or a starter of half dozen Colchester rock oysters and Cabernet Sauvignon dressing from the à la carte menu. Main courses include confit duck leg with warm Asian salad and hoi sin dressing; and traditional favourites like the House shepherd's pie.

Open all day Closed: Mon L (ex BH) Bar Meals Av main course £15 Restaurant L served Tue-Sun 12-2.30 D served all wk 6-9.30 Fixed menu price fr £10 Av 3 course à la carte fr £25 ◀ Adnams, Guinness. ☻ 8 Facilities Dogs allowed Garden

The Northgate ♀   PLAN 2 F4

113 Southgate Rd, Islington N1 3JS
☎ 020 7359 7392   📄 020 7359 7393
dir: *Nearest tube stations: Old Street & Angel. (7 mins from bus 21/76/141 from Old Street & 5 mins on bus 38/73 from Angel)*

This popular pub was transformed from a run-down community local into a friendly modern establishment serving excellent food. There's a regular guest beer, two real ales, and a good mix of draught lagers and imported bottled beers. The menu changes daily, and might include smoked haddock fishcake, slow-roast tomatoes with lemon butter; roast confit duck leg, mustard mash and Savoy cabbage; and roast aubergine, goats' cheese and onion tart with mixed leaves.

Open all wk 5-11 (Fri-Sat noon-mdnt Sun noon-10.30) Closed: 24-26 Dec, 1 Jan **Bar Meals** Av main course £13.50 food served all day **Restaurant** food served all day ⊕ PUNCH ◀ IPA, Fuller's London Pride, guest ales. ♀ 18 **Facilities** Dogs allowed Garden

N6

PICK OF THE PUBS

The Flask ♀   PLAN 2 E5

Highgate West Hill N6 6BU ☎ 020 8348 7346
e-mail: theflaskhighgate@london-gastros.co.uk
dir: *Nearest tube: Archway/Highgate*

A 17th-century former school in Highgate, one of London's loveliest villages. Dick Turpin hid from his pursuers in the cellars, and TS Elliot and Sir John Betjeman enjoyed a glass or two here. The pub is made up of a number of small rooms. There are two bars, one is listed and includes the original bar with sash windows which lift at opening time. Enjoy a glass of good real ale, a speciality bottled beer (choice of 15), or a hot toddy while you peruse the menu, which changes twice a day. Choices range through sandwiches and platters to char-grills and home-made puddings, with roasts on Sundays. There is a large seating area outside at the front of the pub which is extremely popular.

Open all day all wk 12-11 (Sun 12-10.30) **Bar Meals** L served Mon-Fri 12-3, Sat-Sun 12-5 D served Mon-Fri 6-10, Sat-Sun 6-9.30 ⊕ SIX CONTINENTS RETAIL ◀ Fuller's London Pride, ESB, Chiswick Bitter, Discovery Ŏ Thatchers Gold. ♀ 12 **Facilities** Dogs allowed Garden

N19

The Landseer ♀   PLAN 2 E5

37 Landseer Rd N19 4JU ☎ 020 7263 4658
e-mail: info@thelandseer.wanadoo.co.uk
dir: *Nearest tube stations: Archway & Tufnell Park*

Sunday roasts are a speciality at this unpretentious gastro-pub. Well-kept beers and a range of ciders are supported by 14 wines served by the glass. This is an ideal spot to relax with the weekend papers, or while away an evening with one of the pub's extensive library of board games. Weekend lunches and daily evening meals are served from separate bar and restaurant menus. Recent change of ownership.

Open all day all wk noon-mdnt (Mon-Tue & Sun noon-11) Closed: 25 Dec **Bar Meals** Av main course £11 food served all day **Restaurant** food served all day ⊕ FREE HOUSE ◀ Timothy Taylor Landlord, Abbot Ale, Adnams Ŏ Brothers Pear Cider, Aspall. ♀ 14 **Facilities** Children's menu Play area Dogs allowed

NW1

The Chapel   PLAN 1 B4

48 Chapel St NW1 5DP
☎ 020 7402 9220   📄 020 7723 2337
e-mail: thechapel@btconnect.com
dir: *By A40 Marylebone Rd & Old Marylebone Rd junct. Off Edgware Rd by tube station*

There's an informal atmosphere at this bright and airy Marylebone gastro-pub with stripped floors and pine furniture. The open-plan building derives its name from nothing more than its Chapel Street location, but it enjoys one of the largest gardens in central London with seating for over 60 customers. Fresh produce is delivered daily, and served in starters like broccoli and watercress soup, and mains such as pan-roasted chicken breast with sautéed ratte potatoes.

Open all day all wk noon-11 Closed: 25-26 Dec, 1 Jan, Etr **Bar Meals** Av main course £12 **Restaurant** L served all wk 12-2.30 D served all wk 7-10 Fixed menu price fr £14 Av 3 course à la carte fr £18 ⊕ PUNCH TAVERNS ◀ Greene King IPA, Adnams. **Facilities** Children's menu Dogs allowed Garden

PICK OF THE PUBS

The Engineer ♀   PLAN 2 E4

65 Gloucester Av, Primrose Hill NW1 8JH
☎ 020 7722 0950   📄 020 7483 0592
e-mail: info@the-engineer.com
dir: *Telephone for directions*

Situated in a very residential part of Primrose Hill close to Camden Market, this unassuming corner street pub is worth seeking out. Built by Isambard Kingdom Brunel in 1841, it attracts a discerning dining crowd for imaginative and well-prepared food and a friendly, laid-back atmosphere. Inside it is fashionably rustic, with a spacious bar area, sturdy wooden tables with candles, simple decor and changing art exhibitions in the restaurant area. A walled, paved and heated garden to the rear is extremely popular in fine weather. The regularly-changing menu features an eclectic mix of inspired home-made dishes and uses organic or free-range meats. Typical examples could be miso-marinated pollock with mash, bok choi and soy sherry sauce; baked Dolcelatte, walnut and beetroot cheesecake; and T bone pork chop with celeriac and red lentil mash. Side dishes include Baker fries or rocket and parmesan salad, while desserts include chocolate sticky toffee pudding.

Open all day all wk 9am-11pm (Sun & BH 9am-10.30pm) **Bar Meals** Av main course £15.50 food served all day **Restaurant** L served Mon-Fri 12-3, Sat-Sun 12.30-4 booking required D served Mon-Sat 7-11, Sun & BH 7-10.30 booking required Fixed menu price fr £30 Av 3 course à la carte fr £30 ◀ Erdinger, Bombardier, Amstel. ♀ 10 **Facilities** Children's menu Family room Dogs allowed Garden

The Globe ♀   PLAN 1 B4

43-47 Marylebone Rd NW1 5JY
☎ 020 7935 6368   📄 020 7224 0154
e-mail: globe.1018@thespiritgroup.com
dir: *At corner of Marylebone Rd & Baker St, opposite Baker St tube station*

The Globe Tavern is contemporaneous with the adjoining Nash terraces and the Marylebone Road itself. The first omnibus service from Holborn stopped here, and the Metropolitan Railway runs beneath the road outside. Built in 1735, the pub retains much of its period character, and the owners proudly serve traditional English fare. A good choice of real ales is offered alongside dishes such as posh bacon and eggs; city deli salad; and 8oz Aberdeen Angus burger.

Open all day all wk 10am-11pm (Fri-Sat 10am-11.30pm, Sun noon-10.30) Closed: 25 Dec, 1 Jan **Bar Meals** Av main course £6 food served all day **Restaurant** food served all day ⊕ PUNCH TAVERNS ◀ Scottish Courage Best, Bombardier, Young's, IPA, Old Speckled Hen, occasional guest ales. ♀ 17

PICK OF THE PUBS

The Lansdowne ▼   PLAN 2 E4

90 Gloucester Av, Primrose Hill NW1 8HX
☎ **020 7483 0409**
e-mail: thelansdownepub@thelansdownepub.co.uk
dir: *From Chalk Farm underground station cross Adelaide Rd, turn left up bridge approach. Follow Gloucester Ave for 500yds. Pub on corner*

In 1992, Amanda Pritchett started The Lansdowne as one of the earliest dining pubs in Primrose Hill. Stripping the pub of its fruit machines, TVs and jukebox, she brought in solid wood furniture and back-to-basics decor; today, it blends a light, spacious bar and outdoor seating area with a slightly more formal upper dining room. All that apart, however, its success depends on the quality of its cooking. All food is freshly prepared on the premises, using organic or free-range ingredients wherever possible, and portions are invariably generous. The seasonal menu offers spiced red lentil soup with Greek yoghurt; home-cured bresaola with rocket, capers and parmesan; pan-fried sardines on toast with watercress; confit pork belly with prunes, potatoes and lardons; poached sea trout with crushed herb potatoes; polenta with roast pumpkin, buffalo mozzarella and walnut; hot chocolate fondant with double cream; and peaches poached in saffron with yoghurt and nuts.

Open all day all wk noon–11 (Sun noon–10.30) **Bar Meals** L served Mon-Sat 12-10, Sun 12.30-9 D served Mon-Sat 12-10, Sun 12.30-9 food served all day **Restaurant** L served Mon-Sat 12-10, Sun 12.30-9 D served Mon-Sat 12-10, Sun 12.30-9 food served all day ⊕ FREE HOUSE ▼ 6 **Facilities** Dogs allowed

The Prince Albert NEW ▼   PLAN 2 E5

163 Royal College St NW1 0SG
☎ **020 7485 0270**   🖂 **020 7713 5994**
e-mail: info@princealbertcamden.com
web: www.princealbertcamden.com
dir: *From Camden tube station follow Camden Rd. Right onto Royal College St, 200mtrs on right.*

Standing solidly behind the picnic tables in its small, paved courtyard, the Prince Albert's welcoming interior features polished wooden floors and bentwood furniture. Addlestone's cider teams with Adnam's Broadside and Black Sheep bitters at the bar, whilst menu choices include roast butternut squash penne with goats' cheese and sprout tops; Charolais beef burger with aged

Cheddar on ciabatta; and sausages and mash with caramelised onion jus.

Open all day all wk noon–11 (Sun 12.30-10.30) Closed: 25-30 Dec **Bar Meals** L served Mon-Sat 12-3, Sun 12.30-6 D served Mon-Sat 6-10 Av main course £12.50 **Restaurant** L served Mon-Sat 12-3, Sun 12.30-6 D served Mon-Sat 6-10 Av 3 course à la carte fr £22.50 ⊕ FREE HOUSE ◀ Black Sheep, Adnams Broadside, Hoegaarden, Staropramen, Kirin Ichiban Ö Brothers, Addlestones. ▼ 20 **Facilities** Children's menu Dogs allowed Garden

The Queens ▼   PLAN 2 E4

49 Regents Park Rd, Primrose Hill NW1 8XD
☎ **020 7586 0408**   🖂 **020 7586 5677**
e-mail: thequeens@geronimo-inns.co.uk
dir: *Nearest tube - Chalk Farm*

In one of London's most affluent and personality-studded areas, this Victorian pub looks up at 206ft-high Primrose Hill from a beautiful balcony. Main courses may include seared calves' liver with bacon and sage mash, roast vegetable Yorkshire pudding, smoked chicken with mango and mange-tout peas, and whole roasted plaice with prawns and pancetta. On Sundays there's a selection of roasts, as well as fish, pasta and salad. Beers include Youngs and guests.

Open all day all wk 11-11 (Sun noon-10.30) **Bar Meals** L served Mon-Fri 10-3, Sat 10-5, Sun 10-8 D served Mon-Sat 7-10 Av main course £9 **Restaurant** L served Mon-Fri 10-3, Sat 10-5, Sun 10-8 D served Mon-Sat 7-10 Fixed menu price fr £10 ⊕ GERONIMO INNS LTD ◀ Young's Bitter & Special, Peroni. ▼ 12 **Facilities** Dogs allowed

NW3

The Holly Bush ▼   PLAN 2 E5

Holly Mount, Hampstead NW3 6SG
☎ **020 7435 2892**   🖂 **020 7431 2292**
e-mail: info@hollybushpub.com
dir: *Nearest tube: Hampstead. Exit tube station onto Holly Hill, 1st right*

The Holly Bush was once the home of English portraitist George Romney and became a pub after his death in 1802. The building has been investigated by 'ghost busters', but more tangible 21st-century media celebrities are easier to spot. Depending on your appetite, the menu offers snacks and starters - Colchester rock oysters, Dorset clam chowder, and Lincolnshire Farmhouse meat loaf. Main dishes might include Orkney Angus rump steak with creamy rosemary potatoes or

monkfish cheek, herb and cuttlefish risotto, including vegetarian options.

Open all day all wk noon–11 (Sun noon-10.30) Closed: 1 Jan **Bar Meals** booking required Av main course £10 food served all day **Restaurant** L served Sat-Sun 12-6 booking required D served Tue-Sun 6-10 booking required Av 3 course à la carte fr £22 ⊕ PUNCH RETAIL ◀ Harveys Sussex Best, Adnams Broadside, Fuller's London Pride, Brakspear Bitter, Hook Norton Old Hooky. ▼ 10 **Facilities** Dogs allowed

Spaniards Inn ▼   PLAN 2 E5

Spaniards Rd, Hampstead NW3 7JJ ☎ **020 8731 8406**
dir: *Nearest tube: Golders Green*

Believed to be the birthplace of highwayman Dick Turpin, this former tollhouse is a famous landmark beside Hampstead Heath. Named after two brothers who fought a fatal duel in 1721, it was mentioned by Bram Stoker in *Dracula*, and is still much frequented by celebrities. Traditional British fare is on offer, such as fish and chips, sausage and mash, and steamed steak and kidney pudding. In summer the stone flagged courtyard provides a shady retreat.

Open all day all wk 12-11 (Sun 10-11) **Bar Meals** food served all day ◀ Fuller's London Pride, Adnams Best, Oakhams JHB, guest ales Ö Westons Vintage, Aspalls. ▼ 16 **Facilities** Dogs allowed Garden Parking

Ye Olde White Bear ▼   PLAN 2 E5

Well Rd, Hampstead NW3 1LJ ☎ **020 7435 3758**
dir: *Telephone for directions*

A Victorian family-run pub with a Hampstead village feel and a clientele that spans workmen to Hollywood stars; there has been a pub here since 1704. Look out for the theatrical memorabilia, and there's a patio at the rear. However, the real reason to come is the beer: a rolling selection of regional ales, with the list of 20 beers changing every ten weeks, adds up to about 100 different brews in a year! Sandwiches, tempting salads, home-made pies, like salmon and haddock or beef and Guinness, and home-made burgers are on offer.

Open all day all wk 11.30-11 (Thu-Fri 11.30-11.30, Sat 11am-mdnt, Sun noon-11) **Bar Meals** food served all day **Restaurant** food served all day ⊕ PUNCH RETAIL ◀ A rolling selection of 6 ales from all over the UK. ▼ 12 **Facilities** Dogs allowed Garden

NW5

Dartmouth Arms ▼   PLAN 2 E5

35 York Rise NW5 1SP ☎ **020 7485 3267**
e-mail: info@darmoutharms.co.uk
dir: *5 min walk from Hampstead Heath*

Comedy nights, regular quizzes and themed food nights (perhaps steak or mussels) are popular fixtures at this welcoming pub close to Hampstead Heath. Food choices include a home-cooked breakfast, brunch menu, 'posh' sandwiches, a selection from the grill and platters themed by country (Spanish, Greek, English). Alongside the specials board, there are always hearty meals like bangers and mash or home-cooked pies. English ciders are a speciality – there are twenty to choose from.

Open all day all wk 11-11 (Sun 11-10.30) **Bar Meals** Av main course £6.50 food served all day **Restaurant** Av 3 course à la carte fr £15 food served all day ⊕ PUNCH TAVERNS ⬛ Adnams, Fuller's London Pride, Titanic Stout. ⏱ ♀ 7 **Facilities** Children's menu Dogs allowed

PICK OF THE PUBS

The Junction Tavern ♀   PLAN 2 E5

101 Fortess Rd NW5 1AG
☎ 020 7485 9400   📄 020 7485 9401
dir: *Between Kentish Town & Tufnell Park tube stations*

This friendly local, halfway between Kentish Town and Tufnell Park underground stations, is handy for Camden and the green spaces of Parliament Hill and Hampstead Heath. The pub specialises in real ales, with over a dozen usually on offer at any one time, from country-wide breweries based anywhere between Kent (Shepherd Neame) and Edinburgh (Deuchars). Regular beer festivals celebrate the amber liquid, when enthusiasts in the conservatory or large heated garden choose from a range of up to 50 beers hooked to a cooling system and served straight from the cask. The seasonal menus change daily to offer an interesting choice at lunch and dinner: duck liver and truffle parfait or grilled sardines could be followed by half a roast chicken with new potatoes, baby gem, broad beans, pancetta and aïoli. Finish with poached pear, chocolate pot, and peanut butter biscuits; or a straightforward steamed lemon sponge with custard.

Open all day all wk noon-11 (Sun noon-10.30) Closed: 24-26 Dec, 1 Jan **Bar Meals** L served Mon-Fri 12-3, Sat-Sun 12-4 D served Mon-Sat 6.30-10.30, Sun 6.30-9.30 Av main course £14 **Restaurant** L served Mon-Fri 12-3, Sat-Sun 12-4 booking required D served Mon-Sat 6.30-10.30, Sun 6.30-9.30 booking required Av 3 course à la carte fr £20 ⊕ ENTERPRISE INNS ⬛ Caledonian Deuchar's IPA, guest ales, 4 real ale pumps ⏱ Westons Organic. ♀ 12 **Facilities** Dogs allowed Garden

The Lord Palmerston ♀   PLAN 2 E5

33 Dartmouthhill Park NW5 1HU ☎ 020 7485 1578
e-mail: lordpalmerston@geronimo-inns.co.uk
dir: *From Tuffnel Park Station turn right. Up Dartmouth Park Hill. Pub on right, on corner of Chetwynd Rd*

Stylishly revamped London pub in the Dartmouth Park conservation area. It has two open fires in winter and fully opening windows in summer, plus a large front terrace and rear garden for dining. Food is taken seriously, with dishes ranging from beetroot and avocado tower with wasabi and balsamic reduction, to a lamb and mint burger with hand-cut chips. Saturday brunch is served from noon until 4pm, when the fish finger baguette and pea purée may prove too tempting.

Open all day all wk 12-11 (Sun 12-10.30) **Bar Meals** L served Mon-Fri 12-3, Sat 12-4 D served Mon-Sat 7-10, Sun 12-9 ⊕ GERONIMO INNS LTD ⬛ Adnams Best, Sharp's Eden Ale, Timothy Taylor Landlord, Sharp's Doom Bar ⏱ Aspalls, Breton. ♀ 25 **Facilities** Dogs allowed Garden

PICK OF THE PUBS

The Vine   PLAN 2 E5

86 Highgate Rd NW5 1PB
☎ 020 7209 0038   📄 020 7209 9001
e-mail: info@thevinelondon.co.uk
dir: *Telephone for directions*

The look of an Edwardian London pub on the outside belies the contemporary decor on the inside, with its copper bar, wooden floors, huge mirrors and funky art. Comfy leather sofas and an open fire make for a relaxed atmosphere. The Vine is billed as a bar, restaurant and garden, and the latter is a great asset – fully covered for year round use and popular for wedding receptions. Two dramatically decorated rooms are also available upstairs for private meetings or dinner parties. Lunchtime dishes range from antipasti or tuna carpaccio to start; to main courses such as caciucco de pesce – prawns, mussels, langoustines, baby octopus and squid in a chick pea stew with grilled garlic bread. The Italian flavours are particularly pronounced in a range of stone-baked pizzas, which can be ordered to take away and include a children's margherita. Addlestone cider competes with Bombardier and Brakspear ales at the bar.

Open all day all wk 11am-mdnt Closed: 26 Dec **Bar Meals** L served all wk 12-3 D served all wk 6-10 ⊕ PUNCH TAVERNS ⬛ Bombardier, Brakspear. **Facilities** Dogs allowed Garden Parking

NW6

The Salusbury Pub and   PLAN 2 D4
Dining Room ♀

50-52 Salusbury Rd NW6 6NN ☎ 020 7328 3286
e-mail: thesalusbury@london.com
dir: *100mtrs left from Queens Park tube & train station*

Gastro-pub with a lively and vibrant atmosphere, offering a London restaurant-style menu without the associated prices. The award-winning wine list boasts more than a hundred wines including mature offerings from the cellar. The owners are appreciated by a strong local following for continuity of quality and service. Example dishes are roast sea bream with Roman artichokes, leg of duck confit with lentils and cotechino, and Angus rib-eye steak.

Open all day 12-11 (Thu-Sat 12-12, Sun 12-10.30) Closed: 25-26 Dec & 1 Jan, Mon lunch **Bar Meals** L served all wk 12-3.30 D served all wk 7-10.15 ⬛ Broadside, Bitburger, Guinness, Staropramen ⏱ Aspalls. ♀ 13 **Facilities** Family room Dogs allowed

NW8

PICK OF THE PUBS

The Salt House ♀   PLAN 2 D4

63 Abbey Rd, St John's Wood NW8 0AE
☎ 020 7328 6626
e-mail: salthousemail@majol.co.uk
dir: *Turn right outside St Johns Wood tube. Left onto Marlborough Place, right onto Abbey Rd, pub on left*

Describing itself as a mere scuttle from the Beatles' famous Abbey Road zebra crossing, this 18th-century inn promises a two-fold commitment to good food: to source excellent ingredients and to home cook them. With the exception of the odd bottle of ketchup, everything – including bread, buns and pasta – is made on site. Meats are accredited by the Rare Breed Survival Trust, and most fish served has been caught by Andy in Looe. Representative starters are Thai-style fishcake with lemon aïoli; and pork pâté, apple jelly and toast. Main courses include comfort dishes such as beer-battered fish and chips with pea purée; and pork and leek sausages with mustard mash. Warm pear and almond tart with Chantilly cream is a nice finish, or look to the cheeseboard for three varieties served with grapes, crackers and home-made chutney. A function room can be hired for larger parties, while outside heaters allow for alfresco dining even when the weather is inclement.

Open all day all wk 12-12 (Sun 12-11) **Bar Meals** food served all day ⊕ MAJOL ⬛ Abbot Ale, Guinness. ♀ 14 **Facilities** Family room Dogs allowed

NW10

William IV Bar &   PLAN 2 D4
Restaurant ♀

786 Harrow Rd NW10 5JX
☎ 020 8969 5944   📄 020 8964 9218
e-mail: williamivw10@yahoo.co.uk
dir: *Nearest tube: Kensal Green*

The William IV is a large rambling gastro bar encompassing five distinct spaces, including a relaxed sofa area where people can chill out away from the music-orientated bar. Modern European food, hugely influenced by Spain, has starters of sautéed potatoes in rich spicy tomato sauce; rice dishes with chicken, chorizo sausages and roasted peppers; meat dishes such as chicken livers pan-fried with spring onions, ginger and Oloroso sherry; and desserts such as crema Catalana; and tarta de Santiago (almond tart) with ice cream.

Open all day all wk 12-11 (Sat-Sun noon-1am) Closed: 25 Dec, 1 Jan **Bar Meals** L served all wk 12.30-3.30 D served all wk 6-10.30 ⊕ FREE HOUSE ⬛ Fuller's London Pride, guest ales. ♀ 7 **Facilities** Dogs allowed Garden

SE1

The Anchor ☼ PLAN 1 F3

Bankside, 34 Park St SE1 9EF
☎ 020 7407 1577 & 7407 3003 📄 020 7407 7023
dir: *Telephone for directions*

In the shadow of the Globe Theatre, this historic pub lies on one of London's most famous tourist trails. Samuel Pepys supposedly watched the Great Fire of London from here in 1666, and Dr Johnson was a regular, with Oliver Goldsmith, David Garrick and Sir Joshua Reynolds. The river views are excellent, and inside are black beams, old faded plasterwork, and a maze of tiny rooms. A varied menu includes fish and chips, pan-fried halibut with olives, and cod in crispy bacon served on wilted spinach.

Open all wk Closed: 25 Dec ⊕ SPIRIT GROUP 🍺 Courage Directors, Greene King IPA, Adnams Broadside, Bombardier, guest ales. ☼ 14 **Facilities** Garden

PICK OF THE PUBS

The Anchor & Hope ◉◉☼ PLAN 1 E2

36 The Cut SE1 8LP
☎ 020 7928 9898 📄 020 7928 4595
e-mail: anchorandhope@btconnect.com
dir: *Nearest tube: Southwark & Waterloo*

It has picked up a long list of accolades for its cooking, but the Anchor and Hope remains a down-to-earth and lively place with a big bar; children, parents, and dogs with owners are all welcome. In fine weather, pavement seating allows you to watch the world go by as you enjoy a pint, or one of many wines sold by the glass. The wine list is notable for its straightforward approach to prices as many half bottles can be bought for half the cost of full ones - appreciated by the pub's faithful diners. A heavy curtain separates the bar from the dining area which has an open kitchen. The short menu, too, is refreshingly unembroidered. Expect robust, gutsy dishes along the lines of cock-a-leekie soup, braised rabbit with cider and bacon, or skate, lentils and green sauce. You could finish with a generous slice of lemon tart.

Open all day 11-11 Closed: BH, Xmas, New Year, Mon L **Bar Meals** L served Tue-Sat 12-2.30, Sun 2pm fixed time D served Mon-Sat 6-10.30 🍺 Bombardier, Youngs Ordinary, IPA, Erdinger, Kirin, Red Stripe. ☼ 18 **Facilities** Dogs allowed Garden

The Bridge House Bar & PLAN 1 G2
Dining Rooms ☼

218 Tower Bridge Rd SE1 2UP
☎ 020 7407 5818 📄 020 7407 5828
e-mail: the-bridgehouse@tiscali.co.uk
dir: *5 min walk from London Bridge/Tower Hill tube stations*

The nearest bar to Tower Bridge, The Bridge House has great views of the river and city and is handy for London Dungeons, Borough Market, Tate Modern, London Eye, Globe Theatre and Southwark Cathedral. It comprises a bar, dining room and new café, plus facilities for private functions. Typical dishes are chargrilled steak, beer battered haddock, and calves' liver with black pudding, smoked bacon, parsley mash and red wine gravy.

Open all wk Closed: 25-26 Dec ⊕ ADNAMS 🍺 Adnams Best Bitter, Adnams Broadside, Adnams Explorer, guest ale. ☼ 32 **Facilities** Family room

PICK OF THE PUBS

The Fire Station ☼ PLAN 1 D2

150 Waterloo Rd SE1 8SB ☎ 020 7620 2226
e-mail: firestation.waterloo@pathfinderpubs.co.uk
dir: *Turn right at exit 2 of Waterloo Station*

Close to Waterloo, and handy for the Old Vic Theatre and Imperial War Museum, this remarkable conversion of an early-Edwardian fire station has kept many of its former trappings intact. The rear dining room faces the open kitchen, and the menu offers gastro-pub favourites like collar of ham, mint and pea risotto, or vegetable curry with rice. The handy location means it can get very busy, but the friendly staff cover the ground with impressive speed.

Open all day all wk 9am-mdnt (Sun 10am-mdnt) Closed: 1 Jan **Bar Meals** L served Mon-Sat 9am-12am, Sun 10am-12am D served Mon-Sat 9am-12am, Sun 10am-12am food served all day **Restaurant** L served all wk 12-3 D served all wk 5-10.45 ⊕ PATHFINDER PUBS 🍺 Fuller's London Pride, Marstons Pedigree, Brakspear. ☼ 8

PICK OF THE PUBS

The Garrison ☼ PLAN 1 G2

99-101 Bermondsey St SE1 3XB
☎ 020 7407 3347 📄 020 7407 1084
e-mail: info@thegarrison.co.uk
dir: *From London Bridge tube station, E towards Tower Bridge 200mtrs, right onto Bermondsey St. Pub in 100mtrs*

Transformed from an old boozer to a great gastro-pub with a lively community vibe by Adam White and Clive Watson five years ago, the Garrison continues to thrive. It may look rather ordinary from the outside but expect an artfully restyled interior, a shabby-chic feel with a delightful hotch-potch of decorative themes more akin to a French brasserie. Antique odds and ends,

including mismatched chairs and tables, add to the quirky charm. The place bounces with life from breakfast through to dinner and beyond, when the downstairs room doubles as a mini cinema – a great space for a private party. Kick off the day with scrambled eggs and cured salmon or coffee and pastries, with lunchtime offerings taking in smoked haddock chowder, and salt and pepper squid with chilli jam. In the evening, tuck into ham hock terrine, roast garlic and rosemary lamb cutlet with Madeira jus, and baked pumpkin and maple cheesecake. To drink, there's Adnams ale, Breton cider and a raft of wines by the glass.

Open all day all wk 8am-11pm (Fri 8am-mdnt, Sat 9am-mdnt, Sun 9am-10.30pm) **Bar Meals** L served Mon-Fri 12-3.30, Sat-Sun 12.30-4 booking required D served Mon-Sat 6.30-10, Sun 6-9.30 booking required Av main course £14 **Restaurant** L served Mon-Fri 12-3.30, Sat-Sun 12.30-4 booking required D served Mon-Sat 6.30-10, Sun 6-9.30 booking required Av 3 course à la carte fr £23.90 ⊕ FREE HOUSE 🍺 Adnams, Franziskaner, Staropramen Ò Thatchers Pear Cider, Cidre Breton. ☼ 14

The George Inn PLAN 1 G3

77 Borough High St SE1 1NH
☎ 020 7407 2056 📄 020 7403 6956
e-mail: 7781@greeneking.co.uk
dir: *From London Bridge tube station, take Borough High St exit, left. Pub 200yds on left*

The only remaining galleried inn in London and now administered by the National Trust. This striking black and white building may have numbered one William Shakespeare among its clientele, and Dickens mentioned it in *Little Dorrit* - his original life assurance policy is displayed along with 18th-century rat traps. The honestly-priced pub grub includes hot and cold sandwiches, salads and Wiltshire ham, duck egg and chips; and salmon and broccoli fishcakes.

Open all day all wk 11-11 (Sun noon-10.30) Closed: 25-26 Dec **Bar Meals** L served all wk 12-5 D served Mon-Sat 6-9 Av main course £8 **Restaurant** D served Mon-Sat 5-10 booking required Av 3 course à la carte fr £22 ⊕ GREENE KING 🍺 Greene King Abbot Ale, George Inn Ale, IPA, Old Speckled Hen. **Facilities** Garden

The Market Porter ☼ PLAN 1 F3

9 Stoney St, Borough Market, London Bridge SE1 9AA
☎ 020 7407 2495 📄 020 7403 7697
dir: *Close to London Bridge Station*

Traditional tavern serving a market community that has been flourishing for about 1,000 years. Excellent choice of real ales. Worth noting is an internal leaded bay window unique in London. The atmosphere is friendly, if rather rough and ready, and the pub has been used as a location in *Lock, Stock and Two Smoking Barrels, Only Fools and Horses,* and *Entrapment.* Menu includes bangers and mash, roasted lamb shank, beetroot and lemon marinated salmon, and a hearty plate of fish and chips. Early morning opening.

Open all wk **Bar Meals** L served Sun-Fri 12-3
Restaurant L served Mon-Fri 12-3, Sat-Sun 12-5 booking required ⊕ FREE HOUSE ◀ Harveys Best, wide selection of international ales. ♟ 10

The Old Thameside ♟   PLAN 1 F3

Pickford's Wharf, Clink St SE1 9DG
☎ 020 7403 4243   📄 020 7407 2063
dir: Telephone for directions

Just two minutes' walk from Tate Modern, the Millennium Bridge and Shakespeare's Globe, this former spice warehouse is also close to the site of England's first prison, the Clink. The pub features a large outdoor seating area that overhangs the River Thames, and the friendly staff are always happy to point bewildered tourists in the right direction! Traditional pub fare includes fish and chips, sausage and mash, curries and vegetarian pies.

Open all wk Closed: 25 Dec ◀ Fuller's London Pride, Adnams Bitter, Landlords Ale. ♟ 10 **Facilities** Garden

SE5

The Sun and Doves ♟   PLAN 2 F3

61-63 Coldharbour Ln, Camberwell SE5 9NS
☎ 020 7733 1525
e-mail: mail@sunanddoves.co.uk
dir: On corner of Caldecot Rd & Coldharbour Ln

This attractive Camberwell venue is recognized for good food, drink and art – the pub mixes private views with wine tastings, jazz, film and music evenings. For a London pub it has a decent sized garden, planted in Mediterranean style, and a paved patio. The menu is stylishly simple, with great brunches all weekend and wonderful Sunday roasts representing excellent value. Comfort food lovers will love the six varieties of hand-made sausage served with three varieties of mash.

Open all wk Closed: 25-26 Dec ◀ Old Speckled Hen & Ruddles. ♟ 9 **Facilities** Dogs allowed Garden

SE10

The Cutty Sark Tavern ♟   PLAN 2 G3

4-6 Ballast Quay, Greenwich SE10 9PD
☎ 020 8858 3146
dir: Nearest tube: Greenwich. From Cutty Sark ship follow river towards Millennium Dome (10 min walk)

Originally the Union Tavern, this 1695 waterside pub was renamed when the world famous tea-clipper was dry-docked upriver in 1954. Inside, low beams, creaking floorboards, dark panelling and from the large bow window in the upstairs bar, commanding views of the Thames, Canary Wharf and the Millennium Dome. Well-kept beers, wines by the glass and a wide selection of malts are all available, along with bangers and mash, seafood, vegetarian specials and Sunday roasts. Busy at weekends, especially on fine days.

Open all wk ⊕ FREE HOUSE ◀ Fuller's London Pride, St Austells Tribute, Adnams Broadside. ♟ 8
Facilities Garden

PICK OF THE PUBS

Greenwich Union Pub   PLAN 2 G3

56 Royal Hill SE10 8RT
☎ 020 8692 6258   📄 020 8305 8625
e-mail: andy@meantimebrewing.com
dir: From Greenwich DLR & main station exit by main ticket hall, turn left, 2nd right into Royal Hill. Pub 100yds on right

Comfortable leather sofas and flagstone floors help to keep the original character of this refurbished pub intact. Interesting beers (including chocolate and raspberry!), lagers and even freshly-squeezed orange juice, along with a beer garden make this a popular spot. The food is an eclectic range of traditional and modern dishes drawn from around the world. Everything is freshly made and sourced locally where possible; for example the fish comes straight from Billingsgate Market. The lunch menu might include risotto of beetroot and parmesan, mackerel escabeche, or steak and Meantime London Stout pie. Try tempting bar snacks in the evening like crispy squid and home-made cocktail sauce, Spanish tortilla, or home-made Scotch egg and curry mayo. For heartier dishes expect slow roast shoulder of lamb, braised celeriac and mustard parsley crust. The Meantime Brewing Co., which brews the beers on offer, was the only UK brewery to win awards at the 2004 Beer World Cup.

Open all day all wk noon-11 (Sun noon-10.30) **Bar Meals** L served all wk 12-4 D served Mon-Fri & Sun 5.30-10, Sat 5.30-9 Av main course £9 **Restaurant** L served all wk 12-4 D served Mon-Fri & Sun 5.30-10, Sat 5.30-9 ⊕ FREE HOUSE ◀ Kolsch, Pilsener, Wheat ale, Raspberry ale, Chocolate ale. **Facilities** Dogs allowed Garden

PICK OF THE PUBS

North Pole Bar &   PLAN 2 G3
Restaurant ♟

See Pick of the Pubs on page 300

SE16

The Mayflower ♟   PLAN 2 F3

117 Rotherhithe St, Rotherhithe SE16 4NF
☎ 020 7237 4088   📄 020 7064 4710
dir: Exit A2 at Surrey Keys rdbt onto Brunel Rd, 3rd left onto Swan Rd, left at T-junct, pub 200mtrs on right

From the patio here you can see the renovated jetty from which the eponymous 'Mayflower' embarked on her historic voyage to the New World. Billed as 'London's riverside link with the birth of America' the pub has a collection of nautical memorabilia, as well as an unusual licence to sell both British and American postage stamps. Traditional pub fare includes old English sausages; and pan-fried lambs' liver and bacon. For something more adventurous, try chargrilled springbok

striploin, South Africa's most plentiful indigenous antelope.

Open all wk 11-3 5.15-11 (Sun 12-10.30, May-Oct 11-11) **Bar Meals** L served all wk 12-2.30 D served all wk 6-9.30 ⊕ GREENE KING ◀ Greene King Abbot Ale, IPA, Old Speckled Hen. ♟ 30 **Facilities** Dogs allowed Garden

SE21

The Crown & Greyhound ♟   PLAN 2 F2

73 Dulwich Village SE21 7BJ
☎ 020 8299 4976   📄 020 8693 8959
dir: Nearest tube: North Dulwich

With a tradition of service and hospitality reaching back to the 18th century, the Crown and Greyhound counts Charles Dickens and John Ruskin amongst its celebrated patrons. Modern day customers will find three bars and a restaurant in the heart of peaceful Dulwich Village. The weekly-changing menu might feature bean cassoulet with couscous; or an 8oz Angus burger with cheddar cheese and potato wedges. There are daily salads, pasta and fish dishes, too.

Open all day all wk 11-11 **Bar Meals** food served all day ⊕ MITCHELLS & BUTLERS ◀ Fuller's London Pride, Harveys Sussex Best, Adnams Broadside, Young's Ő Aspalls, Westons Organic. ♟ 15 **Facilities** Family room Dogs allowed Garden

SE22

PICK OF THE PUBS

Franklins ◉ ♟   PLAN 2 F2

157 Lordship Ln, Dulwich SE22 8HX ☎ 020 8299 9598
e-mail: info@franklinsrestaurant.com
dir: 0.5m S from East Dulwich station along Dog Kennel Hill & Lordship Lane

As much a pub as it is a bar/restaurant, Franklins offers real ales and lagers on tap, along with real ciders. The restaurant interior is stripped back, modern and stylish with bare floors, exposed brick walls and smartly clothed tables, while the bar has a more traditional feel. A great selection or real ales and ciders are served. The daily menu is available for both lunch and dinner, and there is a good-value set lunch Monday to Friday (except bank holidays and December), priced for two or three courses. Captivating combinations include pickled pigeon with watercress, pear and walnuts to start, and main courses such as leg of venison with sprouting broccoli and anchovy; or hake with chicory and brown shimp. Finish with chocolate nemesis, lemon meringue tart or a cheeseboard of Ashmore, Stinking Bishop and Norbury Blue. Traditional savouries are a feature: Scotch woodcock, Welsh rarebit, and black pudding on toast.

Open all wk Closed: 25-26 & 31 Dec, 1 Jan **Bar Meals** food served all day **Restaurant** food served all day ⊕ FREE HOUSE ◀ Whitstable Bay Organic Ale, Guinness, Meantime Pale Ale, Shepherd Neame's Orginal Porter Ő Westons, Aspalls, Biddendens. ♟ 11 **Facilities** Children's menu Dogs allowed

PICK OF THE PUBS

North Pole Bar & Restaurant ♥

SE10   **PLAN 2 G3**

**131 Greenwich High Rd, Greenwich
SE10 8JA**
☎ **020 8853 3020** 📄 **020 8853 3501**
e-mail:
natalie@northpolegreenwich.com
dir: *From Greenwich rail station turn right,
pass Novotel. Pub on right (2 min walk)*

You can do everything from dining to
dancing at this grand old corner pub,
which prides itself on offering a
complete night out under one roof.
Guests like to begin the evening with a
signature cocktail in the bar, then climb
the spiral staircase to the stylish Piano
Restaurant, where the resident pianist
tinkles away on the ivories Thursday to
Sunday evenings. If at this point you
happen to look up and see goldfish
swimming around in the chandeliers,
don't worry: they're for real and nothing
to do with any cocktail consumed

earlier. In the basement is the South
Pole club, where you can dance until
2am. To complete the picture there's
also a terrace, which makes an ideal
spot for a glass of Pimms on a summer
evening. An extensive bar menu is
available all day, every day from 12
until 10pm, with choices including filled
baguettes and mezze-style platters.
Using the best of local suppliers
produce, the cooking style in the Piano
Restaurant is modern European, with
starters typified by braised baby octopus
with chorizo, fennel and salad; oxtail
risotto; and smoked duck galette with
crispy salad and hoi sin dressing. Any
one of these could be followed by lamb
chump with potato gratin, roasted
parsnips and thyme jus; or perhaps
honey-roasted duck breast with spiced
red cabbage, raisins, sweet potato
fondant and chips, and duck jus. For
dessert, maybe choose sticky date
pudding with butterscotch sauce and
vanilla ice cream; or crème brûlée with
almond shortbread. Sundays bring roast
dinners in the bar and the restaurant
and live jazz, funk and Latin music
downstairs. Lager lovers might like to
know that the beers here include
Staropramen.

Open noon-2am **Bar Meals** L served all
wk 12-10 D served all wk 12-10 Av main
course £15 **Restaurant** L served Sat-
Sun 12-5 D served all wk 6-10.30 Fixed
menu price fr £17.95 Av 3 course à la
carte fr £25 ⊕ FREE HOUSE
🍺 Guinness, IPA, Staropramen. ♥ 20
Facilities Children's menu Garden

SE23

The Dartmouth Arms ☿   PLAN 2 F2

7 Dartmouth Rd, Forest Hill SE23 3HN
☎ 020 8488 3117 📠 020 7771 7230
e-mail: info@thedartmoutharms.com
dir: *800mtrs from Horniman Museum on South Circular Rd*

The long-vanished Croydon Canal once ran behind this transformed old pub, and you can still see the towpath railings at the bottom of the car park. Smart bars serve snacks, traditional real ales, continental lagers, cocktails, coffees and teas, while the restaurant might offer devilled ox kidneys with black pudding or smoked haddock tart for starters, and mains might be pork belly with cannellini beans or scallops with cauliflower purée and crispy pancetta.

Open all wk Closed: 25-26 Dec, 1 Jan **Bar Meals** food served all day **Restaurant** L served Mon-Sat 12-3.30, Sun 12-10 D served Mon-Sat 12-10.30, Sun 12-10 Fixed menu price fr £13.50 Av 3 course à la carte fr £23 ⊕ ENTERPRISE INNS ◀ Fuller's London Pride, Brakspears, Timothy Taylor Landlord. ♈ 10 **Facilities** Garden Parking

SW1

The Albert ☿   PLAN 1 D2

52 Victoria St SW1H 0NP
☎ 020 7222 5577 & 7222 7606
e-mail: thealbert.westminster@thespiritgroup.com
dir: *Nearest tube - St James Park*

Built in 1854, this Grade II Victorian pub is named after Queen Victoria's husband, Prince Albert. The main staircase is decorated with portraits of British Prime Ministers, from Salisbury to Blair, and the pub is often frequented by MPs. To make sure they don't miss a vote, there's even a division bell in the restaurant. The pub was the only building in the area to survive the Blitz of WWII, with even its old cut-glass windows remaining intact. The traditional menu includes a carvery, buffet, a selection of light dishes and other classic fare.

Open all day all wk 8-11pm (Sun 11am-10.30pm) Closed: 25 Dec, 1 Jan **Bar Meals** L served all wk 11-10 D served all day **Restaurant** food served all day ⊕ SPIRIT GROUP ◀ Bombardier, Courage Directors, London Pride, John Smiths, Greene King IPA, plus 2 guest ales. ♈ 14

The Buckingham Arms ☿   PLAN 1 D2

62 Petty France SW1H 9EU ☎ 020 7222 3386
e-mail: buckinghamarms@youngs.co.uk
dir: *Nearest tube: St James's Park*

Known as the Black Horse until 1903, this elegant, recently renovated Young's pub is situated close to Buckingham Palace. Retaining its old charm, this friendly pub is popular with tourists, business people and real ale fans alike. It offers a good range of simple pub food, including the 'mighty' Buckingham burger, nachos with chilli, chicken ciabatta and old favourites like ham,

egg and chips, in its long bar with etched mirrors. Recent change of landlord.

Open all day all wk 11-11 (Sat noon-9, Sun noon-6) **Bar Meals** L served all wk 12-3 D served Mon-Fri 3-8, Sat-Sun 3-6 Av main course £7.95 ⊕ YOUNG & CO BREWERY PLC ◀ Youngs Bitter, Special & Winter Warmer, Bombardier. ♈ 11 **Facilities** Dogs allowed

The Clarence ☿   PLAN 1 D3

55 Whitehall SW1A 2HP
☎ 020 7930 4808 📠 020 7321 0859
dir: *Between Big Ben & Trafalgar Sq*

This apparently haunted pub, situated five minutes' walk from Big Ben, the Houses of Parliament, Trafalgar Square and Buckingham Palace, has leaded windows and ancient ceiling beams from a Thames pier. Typical of the menu choice are sausage and mash; pesto penne pasta with brie or chicken; and pie of the day. Daily specials are available. The pub has a friendly atmosphere and is handy for the bus and tube.

Open all wk Closed: 25 Dec ⊕ SCOTTISH & NEWCASTLE ◀ Bombardier, Fuller's London Pride, Youngs, Adnams Broadside & guest ale. ♈ 17

The Grenadier ☿   PLAN 1 B2

18 Wilton Row, Belgravia SW1X 7NR ☎ 020 7235 3074
dir: *From Hyde Park Corner along Knightsbridge, left into Old Barracks Yd, pub on corner*

Regularly used for films and television series, the ivy-clad Grenadier stands in a cobbled mews behind Hyde Park Corner, largely undiscovered by tourists. Famous patrons have included King George IV and Madonna! Outside is the remaining stone of the Duke's mounting block. Expect traditional favourites on the blackboard, and keep an eye out for the ghost of an officer accidentally flogged to death for cheating at cards.

Open all wk ⊕ SPIRIT GROUP ◀ Fuller's London Pride, Wells Bombardier, Timothy Taylor Landord, Shepherd Neame Spitfire. ♈ 10 **Facilities** Dogs allowed

PICK OF THE PUBS

Nags Head   PLAN 1 B2

53 Kinnerton St SW1X 8ED ☎ 020 7235 1135
dir: *Telephone for directions*

Is this London's smallest pub? The award-winning Nags Head is certainly compact and bijou, with a frontage like a Dickens shop and an unspoilt interior. Located in a quiet mews near Harrods, its front and back bars, connected by a narrow stairway, boast wooden floors, panelled walls, and low ceilings. It was built in the early 19th-century to cater for the footmen and stable hands who looked after the horses in these Belgravia mews. The walls are covered with photos, drawings, mirrors and more: there are military hats and model aeroplanes too. There is a cosy, easy atmosphere here along with a bar that is only waist high. The full Adnams range is served, along with a

good value menu: daily specials, a help-yourself salad bar, and traditional favourites such as real ale sausages, mash and beans; steak and mushroom pie; and chilli con carne are all on offer. There are also ploughman's lunches and sandwiches.

Open all wk **Bar Meals** Av main course £7 food served all day **Restaurant** food served all day ⊕ FREE HOUSE ◀ Adnams Best, Broadside, Fisherman, Regatta.

The Wilton Arms ☿   PLAN 1 B2

71 Kinnerton St SW1X 8ED
☎ 020 7235 4854 📠 020 7235 4895
e-mail: wilton@shepherd-neame.co.uk
dir: *Between Hyde Park Corner & Knightsbridge tube stations*

This early 19th-century hostelry is named after the 1st Earl of Wilton, but known locally as The Village Pub. In summer it is distinguished by its fabulous flower-filled baskets and window boxes. High settles and bookcases create individual seating areas in the air-conditioned interior, and a conservatory covers the old garden. Shepherd Neame ales accompany traditional pub fare: house speciality - salt beef doorstep with horseradish and mustard dressing; chilli con carne; and steak and kidney pie.

Open all day all wk Closed: BH **Bar Meals** L served Mon-Fri 12-4, Sat 12-3 D served Mon-Fri 6-9.30 Av main course £6.95 ⊕ SHEPHERD NEAME ◀ Spitfire, Holsten, Orangeboom, Bishops Finger. ♈ 7

SW3

The Admiral Codrington ☿   PLAN 1 B2

17 Mossop St SW3 2LY
☎ 020 7581 0005 📠 020 7589 2452
e-mail: admiral.codrington@333holdingsltd.com
dir: *See website for directions*

The local nickname for this smart and friendly gastro-pub is, inevitably, The Cod. Although this old Chelsea boozer was given a complete makeover that resulted in a stylish new look when it re-opened, it still retains a relaxed and homely feel. The modern British menu runs to caramelised red onion soup; pumpkin and ricotta ravioli; confit Norfolk port belly; and organic Loch Duart salmon and crab cake. Also look out for the 21-day and 35-day aged steaks. A good proportion of the well-chosen wines are available by the glass.

Open all day all wk 11.30am-mdnt (Fri-Sat 11.30am-1am, Sun noon-10.30) **Bar Meals** L served Mon-Fri 12-2.30, Sat 12-3.30, Sun 12-4 D served all wk 6-10.30 Av main course £10 **Restaurant** L served Mon-Fri 12-2.30, Sat 12-3.30, Sun 12-4 booking required D served Mon-Sat 6.30-11, Sun 7-10.30 booking required Av 3 course à la carte fr £27 ⊕ 333 ESTATES LTD ◀ Guinness, Black Sheep, Spitfire. ♈ 20 **Facilities** Children's menu Garden

SW3 *continued*

PICK OF THE PUBS

The Builders Arms ☂   PLAN 1 B1

13 Britten St SW3 3TY ☎ 020 7349 9040
e-mail: buildersarms@geronimo-inns.co.uk
dir: *From Sloane Square tube station down Kings Rd. At Habitat turn right onto Chelsea Manor St, at end turn right onto Britten St, pub on right*

Just off Chelsea's famous Kings Road, a three-storey Georgian back-street pub built by the same crew that constructed St Luke's church over the way. Inside, leather sofas dot the spacious informal bar area, where your can enjoy a pint of Cornish Coaster or London Pride. A brief, daily changing menu offers a good choice of modern English food with a twist, but if further ideas are needed, consult the specials board and dine in the restaurant. Starters on the main menu might include mackerel and dill fishcake with spicy tomato ketchup; mussels and clams with cider, red onion and cream sauce; and sautéed chicken livers with smoked Black Forest bacon and broad beans. Typical main courses are baked codling fillet with Parmentier potatoes and mustard lentils; pan-fried sea bass with caramelised shallot and gremolata; and courgette, sun-blushed tomato and feta risotto. There are more than 30 bins, with French producers just about taking the lead, plus 16 wines by the glass. When the sun shines the outdoor terrace is highly popular.

Open all wk Closed: 25 Dec **Bar Meals** Av main course £12 food served all day **Restaurant** L served Mon-Fri 12-3, Sat-Sun 12-4 D served Mon-Thu 7-10, Fri-Sat 7-11, Sun 7-9 ◀ Adnams, London Pride, Sharp's Cornish Coaster ⚙ Aspall. ☂ 16 **Facilities** Dogs allowed

PICK OF THE PUBS

The Coopers of   PLAN 1 B1 Flood Street ☂

87 Flood St, Chelsea SW3 5TB
☎ 020 7376 3120 ▤ 020 7352 9187
e-mail: Coopersarms@youngs.co.uk
dir: *From Sloane Square tube station, straight onto Kings Road. Approx 1m W, opposite Waitrose, left. Pub half way down Flood St*

A quiet backstreet Chelsea pub close to the Kings Road and the river. Celebrities and the notorious rub shoulders with the aristocracy and the local road sweeper in the bright, vibrant atmosphere, while the stuffed brown bear, Canadian moose and boar bring a character of their own to the bar. Food is served here and in the quiet upstairs dining room, with a focus on meat from the pub's own organic farm. The fresh, adventurous menu also offers traditional favourites that change daily: seared king scallops and chorizo; grilled chicken, bacon, avocado and sunblushed tomato salad might precede chargrilled harissa lamb steak with Moroccan vegetable couscous; bangers and mash with onion gravy; and ricotta and spinach

tortellini. Good staff-customer repartee makes for an entertaining atmosphere.

Open all day all wk 11-11 (Sun 12-10.30) **Bar Meals** food served all day ⓦ YOUNG & CO BREWERY PLC ◀ Youngs Special, Youngs Bitter, Wells Bombardier, Guinness. ☂ 15 **Facilities** Dogs allowed Garden

The Cross Keys   PLAN 2 E3

1 Lawrence St, Chelsea SW3 5NB
☎ 020 7349 9111 ▤ 020 7349 9333
e-mail: xkeys.nicole@hotmail.co.uk
dir: *From Sloane Square walk down Kings Rd, left onto Old Church St, then left onto Justice Walk, then right*

A fine Chelsea pub close to the Thames and dating from 1765 that's been a famous bolthole for the rich and famous since the 1960s. The stylish interior includes the bar and conservatory restaurant, plus the Gallery and the Room at the Top - ideal for private parties. A set menu might offer porcini mushroom risotto, and smoked haddock and leek fishcake, while the carte goes for steamed mussels and clams marinière, and grilled swordfish steak with fennel and orange salad.

Open all day all wk 12-12 Closed: 23-29 Dec, 1-4 Jan & BH **Bar Meals** L served Mon-Fri 12-3, Sat-Sun 12-4 D served Mon-Sat 6-10, Sun 6-9 ⓦ FREE HOUSE ◀ Directors, Guinness. **Facilities** Dogs allowed

The Pig's Ear ☂   PLAN 2 E3

35 Old Church St SW3 5BS
☎ 020 7352 2908 ▤ 020 7352 9321
e-mail: thepigsear@hotmail.co.uk

An award-winning gastro-pub off the King's Road, specialising in traditional beers and continental cuisine, with food sourced from top quality suppliers. The lunch menu offers spinach and potato gnocchi with wild mushrooms, parmesan and truffle oil; and Angus rib-eye steak with French fries, leaf salad and café de Paris butter. In the Blue Room, main courses might include roast Berkshire grouse with parsnip purée, Agen prunes, game crisps and blackberries, or braised lamb shank with spiced pardina lentils.

Open all wk **Bar Meals** L served all wk 12-3.30 D served all wk 7-10 Av main course £15 **Restaurant** L served all wk 12-3.30 booking required D served Tue-Sat 7-10.30 booking required Av 3 course à la carte fr £30 ◀ Pigs Ear, Caledonian Deuchars IPA, Guinness. ☂ 10

SW4

PICK OF THE PUBS

The Belle Vue ☂   PLAN 2 E3

1 Clapham Common Southside SW4 7AA
☎ 020 7498 9473 ▤ 020 7627 0716
e-mail: sean@sabretoothgroup.com
dir: *Telephone for directions*

An independently owned freehouse overlooking the 220 acres of Clapham Common, one of South London's largest green spaces. Free internet access makes it a

great place to catch up on work or leisure pursuits, with a coffee, hot snack or some tapas-style nibbles close at hand. A daily changing bistro-style lunch and dinner menu specialises in fish and shellfish, such as pan-fried giant tiger prawns in Thai spices; grilled marlin steak with pepper sauce; dressed Cornish crab salad; and chef's special fish pie. Other possibilities are braised leg of rabbit; steak and kidney pie; Thai green chicken curry; and Mediterranean vegetarian lasagne. Sunday lunch is very popular, and in addition to all the regular roasts are fish and vegetarian dishes. The wine list features over 25 wines and champagnes by the glass, and Harvey's Sussex Bitter is the house real ale.

Open all wk Closed: 25-26 Dec ⓦ FREE HOUSE ◀ Harveys Sussex Bitter, Courage Directors Bitter. ☂ 35

The Coach & Horses ☂   PLAN 2 E3

173 Clapham Park Rd SW4 7EX
☎ 020 7622 3815 ▤ 020 7622 3832
e-mail: coach@coachandhorsesclapham.com
dir: *5 mins walk from Clapham High Street & Clapham Common tube station*

This traditional London pub has recently been renovated under new ownership. It offers an extensive choice of well-kept real ales, real ciders and fresh, simply cooked food using free-range produce. Aberdeen Angus burgers; wild mushroom risotto, and beer battered pollack with hand-cut chips are typical dishes. The pub is family friendly, and dogs are made welcome with water bowls and rawhide chews. Thursday night is quiz night and there is live acoustic music on a Friday.

Open all day all wk noon-11 (Fri-Sat noon-1am, Sun noon-10.30) Closed: 1 Jan **Bar Meals** L served Mon-Fri 12-2.30, Sat-Sun 12-9.30 D served Mon-Fri 6-9.30 Av main course £8.50 ⓦ S & B PUB COMPANY ◀ Timothy Taylor Landlord, Adnams Broadside, Hop Back Summer Lightning, Sharp's Doom Bar, Caledonian Deuchars IPA ⚙ Westons Stowford Press, Thatchers. ☂ 8 **Facilities** Dogs allowed Garden

The Windmill on the   PLAN 2 E2 Common ☂

Clapham Common South Side SW4 9DE
☎ 020 8673 4578 ▤ 020 8675 1486
e-mail: windmillhotel@youngs.co.uk
dir: *5m from London, just off South Circular 205 at junct with A24 at Clapham*

Crackling open fires in winter and soft leather sofas make this pub a popular place for friends to meet. The original part of the building was known as Holly Lodge and at one time was the property of the founder of Young's Brewery. The Windmill today offers a varied menu with something for all tastes and appetites: fresh fish, grilled or in Young's beer batter; grilled asparagus with roasted red peppers, butternut squash, rocket and pea shoots; and warm chocolate fondant are typical.

Open all wk ⊕ YOUNG & CO BREWERY PLC ◀ Youngs SPA & PA, Wells Bombardier. ♀ 17 **Facilities** Family room Garden Parking

PICK OF THE PUBS

The Atlas ♀   PLAN 2 D3

16 Seagrave Rd, Fulham SW6 1RX
☎ 020 7385 9129   📄 020 7386 9113
e-mail: theatlas@btconnect.com
dir: 2 mins walk from West Brompton tube station

This is one of only a handful of London pubs to have a walled garden. Located in a fashionable part of town where a great many pubs have been reinvented to become trendy diners or restaurants, here is a traditional local that remains true to its cause. The spacious bar area – split into eating and drinking sections – attracts what in rural enclaves would be quaintly referred to as outsiders, but to be a local here you can come from Chelsea, Hampstead or Hammersmith. Lunch might feature starters such as caldo verde (a Portuguese potato and kale soup with chorizo); and bruschetta al pomodoro (grilled 'Pugliese' bread with vine tomatoes and basil). Tempting mains continue the European influences in dishes such as braised oxtail with porcini, salsify, beef marrowbone and cannellini beans. Donald's chocolate and almond cake with cream, or apple crumble with vanilla ice cream conclude a flavoursome menu.

Open all day all wk 12-11 (Sun 12-10.30) Closed: 24 Dec-1 Jan **Bar Meals** L served Mon-Fri 12-2.30, Sat 12-4, Sun 12-10 D served Mon-Sat 6-10, Sun 12-10 ⊕ FREE HOUSE ◀ Fuller's London Pride, Caledonian Deuchars IPA, Timothy Taylor Landlord, guest ale. ♀ 13 **Facilities** Garden

The Imperial ♀   PLAN 1 B1

577 Kings Rd SW6 2EH
☎ 020 7736 8549   📄 020 7731 3874
dir: Telephone for directions

Mid 19th-century food pub in one of London's most famous and fashionable streets, with a paved terrace at the back. Vibrant and spacious inside, with wooden floors, striking features, and a lively and varied clientele. A selection of pizzas, sandwiches, salads, and burgers feature on the popular menu. Look out for the wild boar sausage with bubble and squeak.

Open all wk Closed: BH ◀ T.E.A, London Pride. ♀ 7 **Facilities** Garden

The Salisbury Tavern ♀   PLAN 2 D3

21 Sherbrooke Rd SW6 7HX ☎ 020 7381 4005
e-mail: events@thesalisbury.com
dir: Nearest tube: Fulham Broadway/Parsons Green

Since this sister pub to Chelsea's famous Admiral Codrington opened in 2003, it has established itself as one of Fulham's most popular bar-restaurants. Its elegantly simple triangular bar and dining area, fitted out with high-backed banquettes as well as individual chairs, is given a lofty sense of space by a huge skylight. Cosmopolitan flavours abound in snacks such as rabbit fritters or sticky chicken wings, and in main dishes such as rump of beef with gnocchi, greens and foie gras, venison pie, or curried sweet potato and spinach.

Open all day all wk 10am-mdnt Closed: 24-26 Dec **Bar Meals** L served Mon-Sat 12-3, Sun 12-6 D served Mon-Sat 6.30-10 ⊕ HONOR LTD ◀ Fuller's London Pride, Black Sheep. ♀ 16 **Facilities** Family room Dogs allowed

PICK OF THE PUBS

The White Horse ♀   PLAN 1 A1

1-3 Parson's Green, Fulham SW6 4UL
☎ 020 7736 2115
e-mail: info@whitehorsesw6.com
dir: 140mtrs from Parson's Green tube

This coaching inn has stood on this site since at least 1688, and has advanced impressively since then, with its polished mahogany bar and wall panels, open fires and contemporary art on the walls. A large modern kitchen is behind the imaginative, good value meals served in the bar and Coach House restaurant. For lunch, you might try basil-infused seared tuna with Greek salad, or pork sausages with mash, summer cabbage and beer onion gravy. In the evening there might be seared turbot with summer vegetable and black-eye bean broth, or chowder of gurnard, conger eel and smoked bacon. Every dish from the starters through to the desserts comes with a recommended beer or wine, and the choice of both is considerable. In fact the 2-day beer festival held annually in November with over 300 beers waiting to be sampled is a magnet for lovers of real ale and European beers.

Open all day all wk **Bar Meals** L served all wk 9.30am-10.30pm D served all wk 9.30am-10.30pm food served all day ◀ Adnams Broadside, Harveys Sussex Best Bitter ⓞ Aspalls. ♀ 20 **Facilities** Dogs allowed Garden

The Anglesea Arms ♀   PLAN 1 A1

15 Selwood Ter, South Kensington SW7 3QG
☎ 020 7373 7960
e-mail: enquiries@angleseaarms.com
dir: Telephone for directions

Feeling like a country pub in the middle of South Kensington, the interior has barely changed since 1827, though the dining area has been tastefully updated with panelled walls and leather-clad chairs, plus there's a heated and covered terrace. The Great Train Robbery was said to have been plotted here. Lunch and dinner menus place an emphasis on quality ingredients, fresh preparation and cosmopolitan flavours. From the daily changing menu expect perhaps a charcuterie plate with celeriac remoulade and capers; chicken and vegetable pie; lightly battered whiting and home-made chips; and apple and blackberry crumble with custard. Sunday lunches are popular, booking is advisable.

Open all wk Closed: 25-26 Dec **Bar Meals** L served Mon-Fri 12-3, Sat-Sun 12-5 D served Mon-Fri 6.30-10, Sat 6-10, Sun 6-9.30 Av main course £12 **Restaurant** L served Sat-Sun 12-5 booking required D served Mon-Fri 6.30-10, Sat 6-10, Sun 6-9.30 Av 3 course à la carte fr £19 ⊕ FREE HOUSE ◀ Fuller's London Pride, Adnams Bitter, Broadside, Brakspear, Hogs Back Tea. ♀ 21 **Facilities** Children's menu Dogs allowed Garden

The Masons Arms ♀   PLAN 2 E3

169 Battersea Park Rd SW8 4BT
☎ 020 7622 2007   📄 020 7622 4662
e-mail: masons.arms@london-gastros.co.uk
dir: Opposite Battersea Park BR Station

More a neighbourhood local with tempting food than a gastro-pub, the worn wooden floors and tables support refreshingly delightful staff and honest, modern cuisine. Here you'll find a warm and welcoming atmosphere, equally suited for a quiet romantic dinner, partying with friends, or a family outing. Open fires in winter and a summer dining terrace. Daily changing menus feature escobar fillet with paw paw and cucumber salad, pan-fried blackened tuna, and spinach and duck spring roll.

Open all day all wk 11-11 (Sun 12-10.30) **Bar Meals** L served all wk 12-3 D served all wk 6-10 ⊕ FULLERS ◀ Fuller's London Pride. ♀ 12 **Facilities** Dogs allowed Garden

SW10

PICK OF THE PUBS

The Chelsea Ram ♥   PLAN 2 E3

32 Burnaby St SW10 0PL ☎ 020 7351 4008
e-mail: bookings@chelsearam.co.uk
dir: Telephone for directions

A popular neighbourhood gastro-pub, The Chelsea Ram is located close to Chelsea Harbour and Lots Road, a little off the beaten track. There is a distinct emphasis on fresh produce in the monthly-changing menu, which includes fish and meat from Smithfield Market. Start with a selection of bread, marinated olives and balsamic vinegar, or enjoy a mezze selection or crispy fried calamari to share. Among the main courses, a modern approach to some old favourites includes battered haddock with minted pea purée and hand cut chips, or pork and leek sausages with creamy mash and caramelised red onion gravy. Alternatives are the Ram burger with Applewood cheddar, or hand-made sun-dried tomato and mascarpone ravioli with rocket and toasted pine nuts. Finish with a nostalgic knickerbocker glory topped with hot fudge sauce or a selection of English cheeses, oat biscuits and home-made chutney.

Open all wk ⊕ YOUNG & CO BREWERY PLC ◀ Young's Bitter, Bombardier, Guinness, Peroni. ♥ 16 Facilities Dogs allowed

PICK OF THE PUBS

The Hollywood Arms ♥   PLAN 1 A1

45 Hollywood Rd SW10 9HX ☎ 020 7349 7840
e-mail: hollywoodarms@youngs.co.uk
dir: 1 min from Chelsea & Westminster Hospital, 200mtrs down Hollywood Rd on right towards Fulham Rd

This listed building is one of Chelsea's hidden treasures. The interior has been elegantly refurbished, augmenting its original charm with rich natural woods, pastel shades and modern fabrics. The large upstairs lounge has elegant mouldings around the ceiling and large open fires at each end, with the bar centred on its length; four huge picture windows make the ambience light and airy. The ground floor pub and restaurant retains much of its traditional atmosphere. Here the chefs lovingly create menus from scratch using high quality ingredients; some, such as cheeses and cured meats, have won national or international recognition. Small plates will produce Rannoch Smokery smoked goose breast, or salt and pepper squid, while main courses offer the home-made half-pound beefburger and chips, Welsh lamb cutlets, or Muffs of Bromborough Old English herb sausages. Award-winning Burtree House Farm puddings are among the desserts.

Open all day all wk noon-11.30 (Thu-Sat noon-mdnt Sun noon-10.30) Bar Meals L served Mon-Sat 12-10.30, Sun 12-9.30 D served Mon-Sat 12-10.30, Sun 12-9.30 food served all day ⊕ YOUNG & CO BREWERY PLC ◀ Guinness. ♥ 12 Facilities Dogs allowed

PICK OF THE PUBS

Lots Road Pub and   PLAN 2 E3
Dining Room ♥

114 Lots Rd, Chelsea SW10 0RJ ☎ 020 7352 6645
e-mail: lotsroad@foodandfuel.co.uk
dir: 5-10 mins walk from Fulham Broadway Station

Located just off the bustling King's Road, opposite the entrance to Chelsea Harbour, the Lots Road is a real star of the gastro-pub scene, appealing to well-heeled locals for the relaxing vibe and a daily menu that lists imaginative, modern pub food. Expect a smart, comfortable, well-designed space, which segues smoothly between jaunty bar area and the more secluded dining area. Slate grey and cream walls and wooden tables create a light, pared-down feel, and attentive staff are set on making you feel comfortable. There's an excellent wine list, and cocktails both quirky and classic. Food takes in a mix of seasonal pub classics and more innovative dishes, perhaps carrot and broccoli soup or pork and apple terrine with home-made chutney, followed by chicken and leek pie with wilted spinach or braised lamb shank with celeriac mash, with baked rhubarb cheesecake for pudding. Don't miss Saturday brunch and the Sunday family roasts.

Open all day all wk 11-11 (Sun noon-10.30) Bar Meals L served Mon 12-3, Tue-Sat 12-4, Sun 12-5 D served Mon-Sat 6-10, Sun 6-9.30 Restaurant L served Mon 12-3, Tue-Sat 12-4, Sun 12-5 D served Mon-Sat 6-10, Sun 6-9.30 ⊕ FOOD AND FUEL ◀ Sharp's Doom Bar, Bombardier, IPA, Guinness. ♥ 33 Facilities Children's menu Dogs allowed

The Sporting Page ♥   PLAN 1 A1

6 Camera Place SW10 0BH
☎ 020 7349 0455 ▤ 020 7352 8162
e-mail: sportingpage@foodandfuel.co.uk
dir: Nearest tube - Sloane Square or South Kensington

A small whitewashed pub happily tucked away between the King's and Fulham Roads. Its smart interior of varnished pine and rosewood and sporting murals makes it easy to unwind there after a day's work. The popular modern British menu includes traditional comfort food such as Cumberland sausage and mash, cheese and bacon burger, and beer battered haddock and chips. Despite its side street location, there's seating for 60 outside.

Open all wk Closed: 25-26 Dec Bar Meals L served all wk 12-3 D served all wk 6-10 Av main course £7 Restaurant Fixed menu price fr £5 ⊕ FREE HOUSE ◀ Wells Bombardier, Fuller's London Pride. ♥ 12 Facilities Children's menu Dogs allowed Garden

SW11

The Castle ♥   PLAN 2 E3

115 Battersea High St SW11 3HS ☎ 020 7228 8181
e-mail: thecastlebattersea@youngs.co.uk
dir: Approx 10min walk from Clapham Junction

Built in the mid-1960s to replace an older coaching inn, this ivy-covered pub tucked away in 'Battersea Village', has rugs and rustic furnishings on bare boards inside, and an outside enclosed patio garden. A typical menu offers fresh salmon and dill fishcakes; Cajun chicken sandwich; organic lamb steak; and fresh swordfish steak with avocado salsa.

Open all day all wk noon-11 (Fri-Sat noon-mdnt Sun noon-10.30) Bar Meals L served Mon-Fri 12-3, Sat 12-10, Sun 12-8 D served Mon-Fri 6-10, Sat 12-10, Sun 12-8 ⊕ YOUNG & CO BREWERY PLC ◀ Youngs Original, Youngs Special, Guest Ales. ♥ 14 Facilities Dogs allowed Garden Parking

PICK OF THE PUBS

The Fox & Hounds ♥   PLAN 2 E3

66 Latchmere Rd, Battersea SW11 2JU
☎ 020 7924 5483 ▤ 020 7738 2678
e-mail: foxandhoundsbattersea@btopenworld.com
dir: From Clapham Junction exit onto High St turn left, through lights into Lavender Hill. After post office, left at lights. Pub 200yds on left

London still has hundreds of Victorian corner pubs, like the Queen Vic in EastEnders, and the Fox & Hounds is one of these. The style is simple, retaining the relaxed feel of a true neighbourhood local, with bare wooden floors, an assortment of furniture, a walled garden, extensive patio planting and a covered and heated seating area. With a good selection of real ales, the food, however, has changed immeasurably since the late 19th century. Fresh ingredients are delivered daily from the London markets, and the Mediterranean-style menu changes accordingly. You might start with an antipasti platter to share, or chicken and vegetable soup with Parmesan croutons. Pasta, available in starter or main course portions, includes penne with Italian sausage ragu, or pappardelle with roast pumpkin, pine nuts, goats' cheese and mascarpone, while going up the scale are dishes such as roast duck breast with apples and thyme, butternut squash gratin and orange hazelnut sauce.

Open noon-3 5-11 (Mon 5-11 Fri-Sat noon-11 Sun noon-10.30) Closed: 24 Dec-1 Jan, Etr wknd & 2nd Mon Aug, Mon L Bar Meals L served Fri-Sat 12.30-3, Sun 12.30-4 D served all wk 6-10 ⊕ FREE HOUSE ◀ Caledonian Deuchars IPA, Harveys Sussex Best Bitter, Fuller's London Pride. ♥ 14 Facilities Dogs allowed Garden

SW13

The Bull's Head ♥ PLAN 2 D3

373 Lonsdale Rd, Barnes SW13 9PY
☎ 020 8876 5241 📠 020 8876 1546
e-mail: jazz@thebullshead.com
dir: *Telephone for directions*

Facing the Thames and established in 1684, the Bull's Head has become a major venue for mainstream modern jazz and blues. Nightly concerts draw music lovers from far and wide, helped in no small measure by some fine cask-conditioned ales, over 200 wines, and more than 80 malt whiskies. Traditional home-cooked meals are served in the bar, with dishes ranging from haddock and crab to a variety of roasts and pies. Popular home-made puddings. An important and intrinsic feature of the pub is the Thai menu, available throughout the pub in the evening.

Open all day all wk noon-mdnt Closed: 25 Dec **Bar Meals** L served all wk 12-4 Av main course £8 food served all day **Restaurant** D served all wk 6-11 Av 3 course à la carte fr £12 ⊕ YOUNG & CO BREWERY PLC ◀ Young's Special, Bitter, Winter Warmer, St Georges, Ramrod, Guinness. ♥ 32 **Facilities** Children's menu Family room Dogs allowed Garden

PICK OF THE PUBS

The Idle Hour ♥ PLAN 2 D3

62 Railway Side, Barnes SW13 0PQ ☎ 020 8878 5555
e-mail: theidlehour@aol.com
dir: *Railway Side off White Hart Ln from rail crossing. No 62 just past school*

As the name suggests, this small organic gastro-pub is just the spot for whiling away an afternoon. The location - hidden away from the main drag - makes it a favourite with shy celebrities. The enclosed garden is stylishly designed, as is the interior with its roaring fire. The emphasis on organic produce extends from food to all the wines as well as many of the soft drinks. Sundays see all-day opening for an organic roast where the joint is brought to the table to be carved by the guests, or spit-roast pig in summer. The weekday menu changes regularly and features some traditional choices alongside more adventurous dishes. Typical starters include Cornish sardines, toast and butterbean and lemon purée or Moroccan style tomato soup with cumin and figs. Main courses might feature an organic burger, red onion marmalade and goose fat fries; home-made steak and ale pie; mixed mushroom and herb risotto. The dessert menu takes in sticky toffee pudding with toffee and rum sauce; and a selection of organic ice creams. Look out for the newly sourced Alaskan king crab legs.

Open all wk 5-mdnt (Sat-Sun noon-mdnt) **Bar Meals** L served Sat-Sun 1-9 D served all wk 7-10 Av main course £9 **Restaurant** L served Sat-Sun 1-9 D served all wk 7-10 Fixed menu price fr £12.50 ⊕ FREE HOUSE ◀ Adnams, Amstel. ♥ 12 **Facilities** Dogs allowed Garden

SW15

PICK OF THE PUBS

The Spencer Arms ♥ PLAN 2 D3

See Pick of the Pubs on page 306

SW18

PICK OF THE PUBS

The Alma Tavern ♥ PLAN 2 E3

499 Old York Rd, Wandsworth SW18 1TF
☎ 020 8870 2537
e-mail: alma@youngs.co.uk
dir: *Opposite Wandsworth town rail station*

Just a stone's throw from Wandsworth Town Station, The Alma is a classic example of Victorian pub architecture. The carefully restored building boasts shiny green tiles on its outside walls, and a second floor dome that makes it one of the Old York Road's most distinctive landmarks. Once inside, the buzzing central bar gives way to a large and airy dining room, with rustic tables and open French doors that lead into a secluded dining courtyard. The bar menu features some interesting sandwiches, as well as pub favourites such as burgers, or battered cod and chips. Meanwhile, the main menu offers pan-fried halibut on spring onion rosti with curly kale, and spiced pork tenderloin with roast garlic and apple mash. The pub is an established watering hole for rugby internationals at Twickenham, and has long associations with local rugby teams, too.

Open all wk **Bar Meals** food served all day **Restaurant** L served Mon-Fri 12-4, Sat 12-10.30, Sun 12-9.30 D served Mon-Fri 6-10.30, Sat 12-10.30, Sun 12-9.30 ⊕ YOUNG & CO BREWERY PLC ◀ Youngs Bitter, Youngs Special, Youngs Winter Warmer, Youngs guest/seasonal ales. ♥ 15 **Facilities** Children's menu Dogs allowed Garden Parking

PICK OF THE PUBS

The Cat's Back ♥ PLAN 2 D3

86-88 Point Pleasant, Putney SW18 1NN
☎ 020 8877 0818 & & 8874 2937
e-mail: info@thecatsback.com
dir: *2 min walk from Wandsworth Park, by river*

Some years ago, just before the landlord went on holiday, the pub cat disappeared, causing much concern among the regulars. A month later, after mine host's return, in strolled the wayward feline, prompting him to write a notice reading, somewhat prosaically, "The cat's back". Much relief all round. Built in 1865 for lightermen on the Thames and Wandle, this vestige of a once-busy riverside stands defiant among blocks of new apartments. Its eccentricity is exemplified by an old globe-topped petrol pump on the pavement, dodgy Victorian photographs, a Calypso fruit machine (one old penny a go), Barbie dolls in glass cases and more.

The bar offers a wide range of tempting food including lamb stew; Cumberland sausages and mash; cheese ravioli; spaghetti Bolognese; beef Stroganoff; and vegetarian spring rolls. Food is also served in the ornate first-floor dining room. Live music, from jazz to West African, can break out spontaneously.

Open all day all wk 11am-mdnt (Fri-Sat 11am-2am) **Bar Meals** L served all wk 11-10 D served all wk 11-10 food served all day **Restaurant** L served Sun 12-5 booking required D served all wk 6.30-10 booking required ⊕ FREE HOUSE ◀ Guinness, Moretti, guest ales. ♥ 6 **Facilities** Dogs allowed Garden

PICK OF THE PUBS

The Earl Spencer ♥ PLAN 2 D2

260-262 Merton Rd, Southfields SW18 5JL
☎ 020 8870 9244 📠 020 8877 2828
e-mail: theearlspencer@hotmail.com
dir: *Exit Southfields tube station, down Replingham Rd, left at junct with Merton Rd, to junct with Kimber Rd*

Located just five minutes from Southfields tube, this airy Edwardian pub has been renovated in true gastro-pub style. Traditional log fires and polished wood furnishings have been retained, and a good selection of wines and beers complements the high standard of cooking. It's child-friendly too, which is something of a rarity in establishments where food is taken seriously. The emphasis is on fresh cooking prepared from seasonal ingredients; the menu changes – and bread is baked – twice daily. A typical dinner choice could kick off with half a dozen Normandy oysters; or mackerel escabèche with roast pepper salsa. Continue with a warm salad of poached skate with frisée, green beans, croûtons, gherkins and soft egg; or chargrilled Barnsley lamb chop with creamed white beans. Round off with plum and almond tart or sticky ginger pudding. A large totally refurbished function room on the first floor has its own entrance, kitchen, bar and loos.

Open all day all wk 11am-1am (Sun 12-10) Closed: 25 Dec **Bar Meals** L served Mon-Sat 12.30-3, Sun 12.30-4 D served Mon-Sat 7-10.30, Sun 7-9.30 ⊕ FREE HOUSE ◀ Guinness, Hook Norton, Fuller's London Pride, Sharp's Doom Bar ♂ Aspalls. ♥ 12 **Facilities** Dogs allowed Garden

PICK OF THE PUBS

The Spencer Arms ♟

SW15   **PLAN 2 D3**

**237 Lower Richmond Rd, Putney
SW15 1HJ**
☎ **020 8788 0640**   📄 **020 8788 2216**
e-mail: info@thespencerarms.co.uk
dir: *Corner of Putney Common & Lower
Richmond Rd, opposite Old Putney Hospital*

The Spencer Arms was transformed a
few years ago from an attractive and
cosy Victorian tavern overlooking Putney
Common's leafy woods and dog-walking
trails into an equally attractive and cosy
gastro-pub. In the process owner Jamie
Sherriff has created a large sunlit bar
area and dining room, and a relaxed
fireside area with leather banquettes,
all done out in pastels and dark wood.
Parents with children to park quietly
while they enjoy a drink should do so
near the bookshelves and games chest.
On offer are daily-changing lunch and
dinner menus which incorporate the

best ingredients sourced from - and how
unusual is this? - not necessarily local
suppliers. For example, meats come
from a highly regarded butcher in
Coventry, fish is landed by day-boats
and trawlers into Falmouth, Plymouth
and Lowestoft, RSPCA-accredited
salmon is reared in Sutherland, Kentish
farms produce the cheeses, and fruit
and vegetables are delivered daily from
London's New Covent Garden market.
Lunch include small plates for sharing
– black pudding with apple and
horseradish coleslaw, Welsh rarebit,
sardines and tomato compote – and
dishes like lemon risotto with goats'
cheese, watercress soup, or buffalo
mozzarella with crayfish and rocket.
For dinner expect perhaps British-style
tapas such as seared scallops, blue
cheese and tomato tart and steak and
kidney pie, as well as starters like pea
soup, and black pudding on toast with
HP sauce. The mains might feature
braised turbot ragout; roast poussin;
confit of duck with curly kale. 'Staples'
such as macaroni cheese and
mushroom risotto also feature. Children
have their own menu. Parking might be
a bit tricky.

Open all week Closed: 25 Dec, 1 Jan
Bar Meals L served Mon-Thu 12-2.30,
Fri-Sun 12-6.30 D served Mon-Sat
6.30-10, Sun 6.30-9.30 Av main course
£12.95 **Restaurant** L served Mon-Thu
12-2.30, Fri-Sun 12-6.30 D served Mon-
Sat 6.30-10, Sun 6.30-9.30 Av 3 course
à la carte fr £25 ⊕ FREE HOUSE
◼ Guinness, London Pride, Adnams
Bitter ♻ Aspalls Draught. ♟ 18
Facilities Children's menu Dogs allowed
Garden

SW18 *continued*

The Old Sergeant ♥   PLAN 2 D2

104 Garrett Ln, Wandsworth SW18 4DJ
☎ 020 8874 4099 ▤ 020 8874 4099
dir: *Telephone for directions*

One of the first pubs bought by Young's in the 1830s.
Traditional, friendly and oozing with character, the Old
Sergeant enjoys a good reputation for its beers and pub
grub. Tuck into a full English breakfast while watching
the rugby on the big screen, or scan the frequently
changing specials list for something more considered.
Burgers, bangers and mash, fish and chips – all have a
place here alongside the great selection of world beers on
tap.

Open all wk ⊕ YOUNG & CO BREWERY PLC ◀ Youngs
Ordinary, Youngs Special. ♈ 12 **Facilities** Dogs allowed
Garden

The Roundhouse ♥   PLAN 2 E3

2 Northside, Wandsworth Common SW18 2SS
☎ 020 7326 8580

With new owners and a change of name from The
Freemasons, the aim of this laid back, popular pub is to
get back to basics; to provide excellent, affordable food
while maintaining all the ambience of the friendly local.
The space has been considered well, with details like a
round, black walnut bar, an open kitchen and eclectic art
on the walls. Both food and drink are taken seriously,
with daily-changing menus.

Open all day all wk Closed: 25-26 Dec, 1 Jan **Bar Meals** L
served all wk 12-3 D served all wk 6-10 Av main course
£10 ⊕ FREE HOUSE ◀ Timothy Taylor, Moretti Ò Westons
Organic. ♈ 20 **Facilities** Dogs allowed Garden

The Ship Inn ♥   PLAN 2 E3

Jew's Row SW18 1TB
☎ 020 8870 9667 ▤ 020 8874 9055
e-mail: drinks@theship.co.uk
dir: *Wandsworth Town BR station nearby. On S side of
Wandsworth Bridge*

Situated next to Wandsworth Bridge on the Thames, the
Ship exudes a lively, bustling atmosphere. The saloon bar
and extended conservatory area lead out to a large beer
garden, and in the summer months an outside bar is
open for business. There is a popular restaurant, and all-
day food is chosen from a single menu, with the
emphasis on free-range produce from the landlord's
organic farm. Expect the likes of lamb cutlets, chargrilled
marlin fillet, shepherds pie, and peppers stuffed with
hazelnuts and goat's cheese.

Open all wk ⊕ YOUNG & CO BREWERY PLC ◀ Youngs:
PA, SPA, Waggle Dance, Winter Warmer, Youngs Limited
Edition seasonal ales. ♈ 15 **Facilities** Dogs allowed
Garden

SW19

The Brewery Tap ♥   PLAN 2 D2

68-69 High St, Wimbledon SW19 5EE ☎ 020 8947 9331
e-mail: thebrewerytap@hotmail.com
dir: *Nearest tube station: Wimbledon*

A small, cosy one room pub, big on sports like football,
rugby and cricket. It is also the closest pub to the
Wimbledon tennis championships. Breakfast is served
until 12.30pm, and snacks take in wooden platters,
sandwiches and salad bowls. More substantial lunches
are hot salt beef, and bangers and mash (with veggie
sausage alternative). The only evening food is tapas on
Wednesday. Special events are held for Burns' Night,
Bastille Day etc.

Open all day all wk noon-11 (Fri-Sat noon-mdnt, Sun
noon-10.30) **Bar Meals** L served all wk 12-2.30 D served
Fri-Sun 7-10 Av main course £9 ⊕ ENTERPRISE INNS
◀ Fuller's London Pride, Adnams, guest ales Ò Aspalls.
♈ 13 **Facilities** Children's menu Dogs allowed

W1

The Argyll Arms ♥   PLAN 1 C4

18 Argyll St, Oxford Circus W1F 7TP ☎ 020 7734 6117
dir: *Nearest tube - Oxford Circus*

A tavern has stood on this site since 1740, but the
present building is mid-Victorian and is notable for its
stunning floral displays. The interior is divided into
'snugs' by wood and etched glass partitions dating from
the late 1800s. There's a popular range of sandwiches
and the hot food menu might offer vegetarian moussaka,
beef and Guinness pie, chicken and leek pie, haddock
and lasagne.

Open all day all wk 10am-11pm (Fri-Sat 10am-11.30pm)
Closed: 25 Dec **Bar Meals** Av main course £6.95 food
served all day **Restaurant** food served all day ⊕ FREE
HOUSE ◀ Fuller's London Pride, Timothy Taylor Landlord,
guest ales Ò Aspalls, Westons Organic. ♈ 15
Facilities Children's menu

French House ♥   PLAN 1 D4

49 Dean St, Soho W1D 5BG
☎ 020 7437 2477 ▤ 020 7287 9109
e-mail: fhrestaurant@aol.com
dir: *Telephone for directions*

Historic pub used by the Free French during World War II,
and Soho bohemians since the 1950s when the likes of
Dylan Thomas, Francis Bacon and Brendan Behan were
regulars. The bar is small - they do not serve pints - and
the music is the conversation. There is a small restaurant
on the first floor where the menu changes regularly,
including dishes like Chateaubriand with Lyonnaise
potatoes, spring greens and port gravy; and pan-fried
fillet of sea bream with saffron and pea risotto.

Open all day all wk noon-mdnt (Sun noon-10.30) **Bar
Meals** L served Mon-Sat 12-3 Av main course £17.50
Restaurant L served Mon-Sat 12-3 D served Mon-Sat
5.30-11 booking required Av 3 course à la carte fr
£30 ⊕ FREE HOUSE ◀ Budvar, Kronenbourg, Leffe,
Guinness, Becks, St Omer Ò Cidre Breton. ♈ 22

W2

The Cow ♥   PLAN 2 D4

89 Westbourne Park Rd W2 5QH
☎ 020 7221 5400 ▤ 020 7727 8687
e-mail: thecow@btconnect.com
dir: *Telephone for directions*

A gastro-pub popular with the Notting Hill glitterati, The
Cow has a bustling downstairs bar and a tranquil first-
floor dining room. 'Eat heartily and give the house a good
name' is the sound philosophy of The Cow, which
specialises in oysters and Guinness. Try Cow fish stew,
Londoner sausages and mash, or seafood platter in the
bar, or go upstairs for starters like baked razor clams,
soya, chilli and garlic, followed by hare leg with bashed
neeps and Swiss chard or Welsh mutton with mustard
and parsley crust and creamed leeks.

Open all wk Closed: 25 Dec **Bar Meals** L served all wk
12-3.30 D served all wk 6-10.30 Av main course £10
Restaurant L served Sat-Sun 12-3.30 booking required D
served all wk 7-10.30 booking required Fixed menu price
fr £22 Av 3 course à la carte fr £35 ⊕ FREE HOUSE
◀ Fuller's London Pride, Guinness, Courage Directors
Bitter, De Konick. ♈ 10

The Prince Bonaparte ♥   PLAN 2 D4

80 Chepstow Rd W2 5BE ☎ 020 7313 9491
e-mail: princebonaparte@realpubs.co.uk
dir: *Nearest tube: Notting Hill Gate*

A first-generation gastro pub where Johnny Vaughan
filmed the Strongbow ads. Renowned for its bloody Marys,
good music and quick, friendly service, the pub proves
popular with young professionals and has DJ nights on
Fridays and Saturdays. The building is Victorian, with an
airy and open plan interior. Typical meals include
sausages and mash, tomato and mozzarella bruschetta,
sea bass with spinach, and spicy chicken gnocchi.

Open all day all wk 12-11 **Bar Meals** L served Mon-Fri
12-3.30, Sat 12-4.30, Sun 12-9 D served Mon-Sat
6-10.30 ⊕ REAL PUBS ◀ Sharp's Doom Bar, 2 guest
ales Ò Aspalls. ♈ 13 **Facilities** Dogs allowed

W2 *continued*

The Westbourne ☻ PLAN 2 D4

101 Westbourne Park Villas W2 5ED
☎ 020 7221 1332 📄 **020 7243 8081**
dir: *On corner of Westbourne Park Rd & Westbourne Park Villas*

Bare floorboards and a long green and zinc bar characterise this classic Notting Hill pub/restaurant, much favoured by its bohemian and celebrity clientele. The popular terrace is sunny in summer and heated in winter. Robust and imaginative peasant-style dishes are listed on a large blackboard above the bar. Choose from the likes of braised cuttlefish; Gloucester Old Spot pork loin chop with chorizo and black cabbage; and honeycomb parfait with poached pears.

Open all wk Closed: 24 Dec-2 Jan ⊕ FREE HOUSE ◀ Leffe, Warsteiner, Hoegaarden, Old Speckled Hen, Flowers, Boddingtons. ♀ 9 **Facilities** Dogs allowed Garden

---

W4

PICK OF THE PUBS

The Devonshire House ◉ ☻ PLAN 2 C3

126 Devonshire Rd, Chiswick W4 2JJ
☎ 020 7592 7962 📄 **020 7592 1603**
e-mail: reservations@gordonramsay.com
dir: *150yds off Chiswick High Rd. 100yds from Hogarth rdbt & A4*

A laid back and unpretentious gastro-pub located in a leafy district of Chiswick, the Devonshire was formerly known as the Manor Tavern, and is now part of Gordon Ramsay's Holdings. Its transformation into an attractive, light and airy bar and restaurant happened a few years back returning it to its former glory. Expect high ceilings, large windows, original fireplaces and the restoration of its unique wood panelling and façade as well as an attractive landscaped garden to the rear of the pub. It serves an interesting mix of modern British and Mediterranean dishes, and changes daily depending on the fresh produce currently available. You can whet your appetite with some rabbit terrine with pear chutney, or warm mushroom and cheddar tart from the bar menu before launching in to the menu proper. A typical three courses might comprise swede and honey soup with pressed ham hock, or warm salad of quail and cured pork belly; followed by Gloucester pork sausages with champ and red onion gravy, or pan-fried sea bass with clams in a white bean winter broth; and cranberry and Clementine shortcake to finish. Children are made to feel welcome with a secure garden to play in, plus books, crayons and games to keep them entertained.

Open all day 12-11 (Wed-Thu 6-12, Sun 12-10.30) Closed: Mon-Tue **Bar Meals** L served Fri-Sun booking required D served Wed-Sun booking required Av main course £12 food served all day **Restaurant** L served Fri 12-3, Sat 12-4, Sun 12-10.30 booking required D served Fri 6-10.30, Sat 5-10.30, Sun 12-10.30 booking required ⊕ GORDON RAMSAY HOLDINGS LTD ◀ London Pride, Guinness, Caledonian Deuchars IPA, San Miguel, Kronenberg. ♀ 12 **Facilities** Children's menu Dogs allowed Garden

---

The Pilot ☻ PLAN 2 C3

56 Wellesley Rd W4 4BZ ☎ 020 8994 0828
e-mail: thepilot@london-gastros.co.uk
dir: *Nearest tube station: Gunnersbury*

A friendly pub and eating house, The Pilot has a simple, understated style with local artwork displayed on the walls, and a relaxed atmosphere. The large rear garden comes into its own during the barbecue season, serving unusual cuts of meat such as alligator and bison as well as traditional beef. Throughout the year, dishes from the daily-changing menu take full advantage of seasonal produce. A function room is available in the garden, away from the main building.

Open all wk Closed: 25-26 Dec **Bar Meals** L served Mon-Fri 12-3, Sat 12-4, Sun 12-9.30 booking required D served Mon-Fri 6-10, Sat-Sun 6-9.30 booking required Av main course £13.50 **Restaurant** L served Mon Fri 12 3, Sat 12-4, Sun 12-9.30 booking required D served Mon-Fri 6-10, Sat-Sun 6-9.30 booking required Fixed menu price fr £25 Av 3 course à la carte fr £30 ⊕ FULLERS SMITH AND TURNER ◀ Staropramen, Fuller's London Pride, Guinness, Peroni. ♀ 14 **Facilities** Children's menu Dogs allowed Garden

---

PICK OF THE PUBS

The Swan ☻ PLAN 2 C3

1 Evershed Walk, 119 Acton Ln W4 5HH
☎ 020 8994 8262 📄 **020 8994 9160**
e-mail: theswanpub@btconnect.com
dir: *Pub on right at end of Evershed Walk*

A friendly gastro-pub, The Swan is much appreciated by locals for its international range of beers and cosmopolitan atmosphere. A pub for all seasons, it has a welcoming wood-panelled interior and a large lawned garden and patio area for outdoor refreshments. Good food is at the heart of the operation, and you can sit and eat wherever you like. The menu of modern, mostly Mediterranean cooking has a particular Italian influence, and vegetarians are not forgotten. Start with perhaps roast pumpkin soup with crème fraîche and parsley; or stuffed quail, black pudding rice with fig and ginger jam; mains might be grilled salmon steak with Puy lentils and pancetta; roast guinea fowl with wild mushrooms and Madeira; or butternut squash and chestnut risotto. Still have an appetite, then finish off with peach and amaretti crumble with mascarpone or tarte Tatin with vanilla ice cream?

Open all wk 5-11.30 (Sat noon-11.30, Sun noon-10.30) Closed: 23 Dec-2 Jan, Etr **Bar Meals** L served Sat 12.30-3, Sun 12.30-4 D served Sun-Thu 6-10, Fri-Sat 6-10.30 Av main course £13.50 ⊕ FREE HOUSE ◀ Fuller's London Pride, Guinness, Harvey's Sussex Best Ô Westons Organic. ♀ 14 **Facilities** Children's menu Dogs allowed Garden

---

W5

The Red Lion ☻ PLAN 2 C3

13 St Mary's Rd, Ealing W5 5RA ☎ 020 8567 2541
dir: *Nearest tube: South Ealing*

The pub opposite the old Ealing Studios, the Red Lion is affectionately known as the 'Stage Six' (the studios have five), and has a unique collection of film stills celebrating the Ealing comedies of the 50s. Sympathetic refurbishment has broadened the pub's appeal, and the location by Ealing Green has a leafy, almost rural feel, plus there's an award-winning walled garden. Pub food ranges through oysters, burgers, bangers and mash, and fillet steak.

Open all day all wk 11-11 (Thu-Sat 11am-mdnt, Sun 12-11) **Bar Meals** L served all wk 12-3 D served all wk 7-9.30 ⊕ FULLERS BREWERY ◀ Fuller's London Pride, Chiswick & ESB, 2 guest ales. ♀ 10 **Facilities** Dogs allowed Garden

---

The Wheatsheaf ☻ PLAN 2 C4

41 Haven Ln, Ealing W5 2HZ ☎ 020 8997 5240
e-mail: wheatsheaf@fullers.co.uk
dir: *1m from A40 junct with North Circular*

Just a few minutes from Ealing Broadway, this large Victorian pub has a rustic appearance inside. Ideal place to enjoy a big screen sporting event or a drink among wooden floors, panelled walls, beams from an old barn, and real fires in winter. Traditional pub grub includes cottage pie; beer battered cod and chips; steak, ale and mushroom pie; pork and leek sausage and mash; and vegetable lasagne.

Open all day all wk noon-11 (Sun noon-10.30) **Bar Meals** L served Mon-Thu 12-3, Fri-Sat 12-10, Sun 12-8 D served Mon-Thu 6-10, Fri-Sat 12-10, Sun 12-8 ⊕ FULLER SMITH TURNER PLC ◀ Fuller's London Pride, ESB & Chiswick, seasonal ales Ô Pear Bulmers. ♀ 10 **Facilities** Dogs allowed Garden

W6

PICK OF THE PUBS

Anglesea Arms ⊛ ♀   PLAN 2 D3

35 Wingate Rd W6 0UR ☎ 020 8749 1291
dir: *Telephone for details*

Close to Ravenscourt Park tube station, and walkable from Goldhawk Road and Hammersmith. Real fires and a relaxed atmosphere are the attraction at this traditional corner pub, together with a terrace where drinks and food can be served. Behind the Georgian façade ales are dispensed from breweries as far apart as Suffolk and Cornwall, and the place positively hums with people eagerly seeking out the highly reputable food. Simple yet robust dishes may feature prawns, oysters, terrines and cheeses from the all-day menu. Light meal options could propose smoked eel with potato broth and poached egg; steamed razor clams in parsley and white wine; and whole Cornish crab with mayonnaise. Main courses step up a gear with sauté of rabbit with young artichokes and potatoes; roast woodcock, galette potato and braised endive; and Herdwick lamb chops with Pithiviers savoyarde and spring greens. Puddings such as mulberry and mascarpone tart are exemplary too.

Open all day all wk 11-11 (Sun noon-10.30) Closed: 25-27 Dec **Bar Meals** Av main course £12 food served all day **Restaurant** L served Mon-Fri 12-2.45, Sat 12-3, Sun 12-3.30 D served Tue-Sat 7-10.30, Sun-Mon 7-10 Av 3 course à la carte fr £22 ⊕ FREE HOUSE ◀ Fuller's London Pride, Timothy Taylor Landlord, Ringwood 49er, St Austell Tribute, Adnams East Green ♂ Westons Organic. ♀ 20 **Facilities** Dogs allowed Garden

PICK OF THE PUBS

The Dartmouth Castle ♀   PLAN 2 D3

26 Glenthorne Rd, Hammersmith W6 0LS
☎ 020 8748 3614 📄 020 8748 3619
e-mail: dartmouth.castle@btconnect.com
dir: *Nearest tube station: Hammersmith. 100yds from Hammersmith Broadway*

George and Richard Manners took over the Dartmouth Castle in Hammersmith a couple of years ago. While their aim is to keep the place very much a pub - somewhere to relax over a pint or two - the food is proving an even greater attraction. The monthly changing menu ranges from imaginative sandwiches (mozzarella and slow-roasted tomatoes with pesto) to dishes such as Marmitako (a Basque tuna and potato stew with tomatoes, saffron and peppers); roast pork loin with crackling, creamy borlotti beans and sautéed kale; Tuscan sausages, garlic mash and red onion marmalade. Vegetarian aren't forgotten either, with maybe rigatoni with sautéed greens, ricotta, chilli and pine nuts as a starter or main course. Typical desserts are pannacotta with wild red berries; and apple and pear crumble and ice cream. The range of beers includes two real ales on tap at any one time, and there's a good wine list with 14 available by the glass. Facilities extend to a beer garden and function room.

Open all day all wk noon-11 (Sun noon-10.30) Closed: Etr, 23 Dec-2 Jan & 2nd Mon Aug **Bar Meals** L served Mon-Sat 12-3, Sun 12-9.30 D served Mon-Sat 6-10, Sun 12-9.30 Av main course £12.50 **Restaurant** Av 3 course à la carte fr £22.50 ⊕ FREE HOUSE ◀ Fuller's London Pride, San Miguel, guest ales. ♀ 14 **Facilities** Dogs allowed Garden

The Stonemasons Arms ♀   PLAN 2 D3

54 Cambridge Grove W6 0LA
☎ 020 8748 1397 📄 020 8846 9636
e-mail: stonemasonsarms@london-gastros.co.uk
dir: *Hammersmith tube. Walk down King St, 2nd right up Cambridge Grove, pub at end*

A short walk from Hammersmith tube station and popular with local residents and business people. During warmer months a decking area can be used for alfresco dining. The pub boasts some of what must be the most unusual meat in the capital, which include kangaroo, ostrich and crocodile. They're among many innovations on a punchy menu inspired by traditional British and European dishes prepared with fresh seasonal produce.

Open all day all wk 11-11 (Sun noon-10.30) **Bar Meals** L served Mon-Fri 12-3, Sat 12-10, Sun 12-9.30 D served Mon-Fri 6-10, Sat 12-10, Sun 12-9.30 **Restaurant** L served Mon-Fri 12-3, Sat 12-10, Sun 12-9.30 D served Mon-Fri 6-10, Sat 12-10, Sun 12-9.30 ⊕ FULLERS BREWERY ◀ Fuller's London Pride & Organic Honeydew, Peroni. ♀ 12 **Facilities** Garden

W8

The Churchill Arms ♀   PLAN 2 D3

119 Kensington Church St W8 7LN ☎ 020 7727 4242
e-mail: churchill@fullers.co.uk
dir: *Off A40 (Westway). Nearest tube-Notting Hill Gate*

Thai food is the speciality at this traditional 200-year-old pub with strong emphasis on exotic chicken, beef, prawn and pork dishes. Try Kaeng Panang curry with coconut milk and lime leaves, or Pad Priew Wan stir-fry with sweet and sour tomato sauce. Oriental feasts notwithstanding, the Churchill Arms has many traditional British aspects including oak beams, log fires and an annual celebration of Winston Churchill's birthday.

Open all day all wk 11-11 (Tue-Sat 11am-mdnt, Sun 12-10.30) Closed: 25 Dec eve **Bar Meals** food served all day ⊕ FULLER SMITH TURNER PLC ◀ Fuller's London Pride, ESB, Chiswick Bitter. ♀ 25 **Facilities** Dogs allowed Garden

Mall Tavern ♀   PLAN 2 D4

71-73 Palace Gardens Ter, Notting Hill, Kensington W8 4RU ☎ 020 7727 3805 📄 020 7792 9620
e-mail: info@malltavern.co.uk
dir: *From Notting Hill Gate tube station E along Bayswater Rd, 2nd on right*

This 100-year-old pub in the heart of Notting Hill is run by two young chefs, so the focus on food is not unexpected. An extensive daily specials board backs up the menus of 'smaller bites', 'more substantial' and 'puds' dishes. Typical dishes are Cajun chicken skewers with lime mayo; ribeye steak, garlic mash and greens; and apple and pineapple crumble. The lunch menu includes a new 'super cheap' lunch along the lines of home-baked sourdough baguettes. There is also a Saturday and Sunday brunch menu served from 12-8pm. Drinks include continental beers and 20 wines served by the glass.

Open all day all wk noon-mdnt (Sat 11am-mdnt Sun noon-9) Closed: 25-26 Dec **Bar Meals** Av main course £12.50 food served all day **Restaurant** Fixed menu price fr £13.50 Av 3 course à la carte fr £23.50 food served all day ⊕ ENTERPRISE INNS ◀ Becks Vier, Staropramen, Leffe Blond, Tiger, Peroni. ♀ 20 **Facilities** Dogs allowed Garden

The Scarsdale ♀   PLAN 2 D3

23A Edwardes Square, Kensington W8 6HE
☎ 020 7937 1811 📄 020 7938 2984
dir: *Exit Kensington High Street Station, turn left, 10 mins along High St. Edwardes Sq next left after Odeon Cinema*

A 19th-century, free-standing local with a stone forecourt enclosed by railings, just off Kensington High Street. The Frenchman who developed the site was supposedly one of Bonaparte's secret agents. There's so much about this place, not least its intriguing mix of customers, that ensures you don't forget which part of London you are in. The food is modern European and highly praised, but the stupendous Bloody Marys are the real talking point.

Open all day all wk noon-11 (Sun noon-10.30) Closed: 25-26 Dec **Bar Meals** Av main course £8.95 food served all day **Restaurant** L served Mon-Sat 12-2.30, Sun 12-4 D served all wk 6-10 Av 3 course à la carte fr £26.95 ⊕ PUNCH TAVERNS ◀ London Pride, Old Speckled Hen, Young's, Greene King IPA, Bombardier, Shepherd Neame Spitfire. ♀ 20 **Facilities** Children's menu Dogs allowed Garden

W8 *continued*

The Windsor Castle 🍷   PLAN 2 D4

114 Campden Hill Rd W8 7AR ☎ 020 7243 8797
dir: From Notting Hill Gate, take south exit towards Holland Park, left onto Campden Hill Rd

Established in 1845, this pub takes its name from the royal castle, which could once be seen from the upper-floor windows. Unchanged for years, it boasts oak panelling and open fires, and is reputedly haunted by the ghost of Thomas Paine, author of *The Rights of Man*. A good variety of food is offered on a regularly changing menu – perhaps oven-baked camembert with rosemary and garlic; a wide selection of sausages accompanied by mash and red onion gravy; honey-roast pork belly with colcannon.

Open all day all wk noon-11 (Sun noon-10.30) **Bar Meals** L served Mon-Fri 12-3, Sat 12-10, Sun 12-9 D served Mon-Fri 5-10 (Sat 12-10, Sun 12-9) ⊕ MITCHELL'S AND BUTLERS ◀ Staropramen, Timothy Taylor Landlord, Fuller's London Pride, Greene King Abbot Ale, Paulaner ♂ Westons Old Rosie Scrumpy. 🍷 10 **Facilities** Dogs allowed Garden

W9

The Waterway 🍷   PLAN 2 D4

54 Formosa St W9 2JU
☎ 020 7266 3557   020 7266 3547
e-mail: info@thewaterway.co.uk

Trendy Maida Vale restaurant and bar in a canalside setting with a large decking area where popular barbecues are held. The bar is also a great place to relax with its comfy sofas and open fires, and there is a great choice of drinks, including cocktails and champagne by the glass, plus Burt's hand-fried potato chips. The restaurant menu offers a choice of modern European food – goats' cheese beignets with artichokes and chorizo; chargrilled squid with chilli sauce; wild mushroom and herb risotto.

Open all day all wk 12-11 (Sun 12-10.30) **Restaurant** L served Mon-Fri 12-3.30, Sat-Sun 12-4 D served Mon-Sat 6.30-10.30, Sun 6.30-10 ◀ Guinness, Hoegaarden, Fuller's London Pride ♂ Aspalls. 🍷 10 **Facilities** Dogs allowed Garden

W10

PICK OF THE PUBS

The Fat Badger   PLAN 2 D4

310 Portobello Rd W10 5TA ☎ 020 8969 4500
e-mail: fat_badger@me.com
dir: Nearest tube: Ladbroke Grove

Notting Hill's Portobello Road is famous for its antique shops and Saturday street market. Right at its heart is this former drinking pub, which once had a reputation for loud music but is now reborn as the place to relax with good beers and hearty food. Steve Ham and Bob Taylor took it over a couple of years ago and are building the pub's reputation for a friendly reception and comfortable surroundings. The wood-floored bar has plenty of tables and chairs to choose from and offers snacks such as Falmouth Bay rock oysters. The emphasis of the main menu is firmly on 'best of British' produce – including cuts of meat that have fallen from favour, fresh fish from day-boats, and regional ingredients from carefully chosen suppliers. Among the starters may be found crubbeens with sauce gribiche, and grilled mackerel with ginger dressing. Pork and prune pie or poached smoked haddock are typical main course options.

Open all day all wk 12-11 (Fri 12-12, Sat 10am-mdnt, Sun 10am-10.30pm) **Bar Meals** L served Mon-Fri 12-3.30, Sun 12-5 D served Mon-Thu 6-10, Fri-Sat 6-10.30, Sun 6-9 ⊕ ENTERPRISE INNS ◀ Guinness, Timothy Taylor Landlord. **Facilities** Dogs allowed

Golborne Grove 🍷   PLAN 2 D4

36 Golborne Rd W10 5PR
☎ 020 8960 6260   020 8960 6961
e-mail: golborne.house@hotmail.com
dir: From Ladbroke Grove tube, up Ladbroke Grove, right into Golborne Rd

A popular dining destination, this award-winning gastro-pub is located at the north end of Notting Hill, with a ground floor bar area and function room upstairs. Local architectural photos, 1920's Venetian mirrors and squashy 1960's sofas contribute to the appealing interior. The drinks range encompasses beers, cocktails and a reasonable wine list. Fish features strongly in dishes like pan-fried red snapper fillet with roast vegetables and pine kernels, cous cous and Greek salad.

Open all day all wk 12-12 **Bar Meals** L served all wk 12-3 D served all wk 6-9 ⊕ ENTERPRISE INNS ◀ Fuller's London Pride, Guinness. 🍷 10 **Facilities** Dogs allowed Garden

The North Pole 🍷   PLAN 2 D4

13-15 North Pole Rd W10 6QH
☎ 020 8964 9384   020 8960 3774
e-mail: northpole@massivepub.com
dir: Right from White City tube station, past BBC Worldwide, turn right at 2nd lights, 200yds on right. 10 mins walk

Recently refurbished, this trendy modern gastro-pub with large windows and bright decor was formerly owned by Jade Jagger. Its name could be considered appropriate given that it's just five minutes' walk from BBC Worldwide. Expect leather sofas, armchairs, daily papers, real ales, a good range of wines by the glass, cocktails and a lively atmosphere in the bar. Menus show real awareness of today's dietary requirements, with vegetarian and gluten-free options among the eclectic mix of snacks, favourites, great burgers and platters to share.

Open all day all wk 11am-11.30pm (Sun 12-10.30) **Bar Meals** L served Mon-Fri 12-3, Sat-Sun 12-9 D served Mon-Fri 5-9.30 ⊕ FREE HOUSE ◀ Fosters, Kronenbourg, Guinness, Kronenbourg Blanc. 🍷 14 **Facilities** Dogs allowed

W11

Portobello Gold 🍷   PLAN 2 D4

95-97 Portobello Rd W11 2QB ☎ 020 7460 4900
e-mail: reservations@portobellogold.com
dir: From Notting Hill Gate Tube Station, follow signs to Portobello Market

Born in the mid-1980s and still under the same ownership, this quirkily stylish Notting Hill pub cum brasserie retains its powerful appeal with a programme of live music, an internet café and monthly art exhibitions in the Gold Gallery. Add to this an eclectic range of beers and funky international menus for a winning package. Food is served in the bar or tropical-style conservatory, and oysters are a speciality. Booking is essential.

Open all wk Closed: 25 Dec-1 Jan **Bar Meals** Av main course £10 food served all day **Restaurant** Fixed menu price fr £6 Av 3 course à la carte fr £24 food served all day ⊕ PUB CO ◀ Staropramen, Guinness, Fuller's London Pride, Harveys Sussex Ales, Leffe, Meantime, Freedom ♂ Thatchers Gold, Katy & Spartan. 🍷 14 **Facilities** Children's menu Dogs allowed

W14

PICK OF THE PUBS

The Cumberland Arms ☻ PLAN 2 D3

29 North End Rd, Hammersmith W14 8SZ
☎ 020 7371 6806 📠 020 7371 6848
e-mail: thecumberlandarmspub@btconnect.com
dir: From Kensington Olympia, exit station, turn left, at
Hammersmith Rd right, at T-junct (North End Rd) left,
100yds, pub on left

A popular gastro-pub close to Olympia, the
Cumberland has an attractive blue-painted facade
with gold lettering and impressive floral displays in
season. Pavement benches and tables help to alleviate
the pressure inside, while mellow furniture and
stripped floorboards characterise the interior. Friendly
staff, an affordable wine list and well-kept ales are the
draw for those seeking after-work refreshment, but it is
also a great place for flavoursome plates of
unpretentious Mediterranean food offered from a
seasonal menu supported by daily specials. Hearty
dishes range through baked cod, with artichokes and
potatoes Napoletana; roast lamb steak with rosemary
and black olive tapenade; and roast pumpkin and
cinnamon risotto. Finish off with lemon tart and
mascarpone or a selection of French and English
cheeses. A set menu is available by pre-booking for a
minimum of eight people.

Open all day all wk noon-11 (Sun noon-10.30) Closed:
23 Dec-2 Jan **Bar Meals** Av main course £13.50
Restaurant L served Mon-Sat 12-3, Sun 12-10.30 D
served all wk 6-10 ⊕ THE PURPLE TIGER ◖ Fuller's
London Pride, Harvey's Sussex Best, Peroni. ☻ 12
Facilities Garden

The Havelock Tavern ☻ PLAN 2 D4

57 Masbro Rd, Brook Green W14 0LS ☎ 020 7603 5374
dir: Nearest tubes: Shepherd's Bush & Olympia

Despite being a gastro-pub for nearly fifteen years, the
Havelock is still run very much as a boozer – no table
bookings are taken and prices represent excellent value.
It is popular with both lunchtime and evening customers
who want a tasty plate of food before returning to work or
home. They can choose between the likes of deep-fried
monkfish cheeks and tiger prawns, with sweet chilli
dipping sauce; and slow roast belly of pork with
dauphinoise potatoes.

Open all day all wk 11-11 (Sun 12-10.30) Closed: 5 days
at Xmas & Etr Sun **Bar Meals** L served Mon-Sat 12-2.30,
Sun 12-3 D served Mon-Sat 7-10, Sun 7-9.30 ⊕ FREE
HOUSE ◖ Fullers London Pride, Sharp's Doom Bar,
Sambrook's Wandle. ☻ 11 **Facilities** Dogs allowed Garden

WC1

PICK OF THE PUBS

The Bountiful Cow ☻ PLAN 1 E4

51 Eagle St, Holborn WC1R 4AP ☎ 020 7404 0200
e-mail: manager@roxybeaujolais.com
dir: 230mtrs NE from Holborn tube station, via Procter
St. Walk through 2 arches into Eagle St. Pub between
High Holborn & Red Lion Square

Roxy Beaujolais, proprietor of the ancient Seven Stars
behind the Law Courts, acquired this 1960's pub a few
streets away and decided, here, to specialise in the
finest steaks and exceptionally large burgers. Her
architect husband's design achieves the right balance
between funky bistro and stylish saloon, aided by
dozens of pictures and posters celebrating beef. Five
cuts of beef feature on the menu: onglet (for
sandwiches), rib-eye, sirloin, fillet and T-bone, all aged
many weeks for tenderness and flavour, and all
available with melted goat's cheese, Béarnaise or
green peppercorn sauce. Non-beef options include
starters of Sephardic pâté (chopped chicken liver) with
toast, or tomato, mozzarella and basil salad, and
mains such as rump of lamb steak with sautéed
potatoes; charcuterie pork meats with ciabatta, and
bruschetta with tomatoes. Adnams and Harveys supply
the real ales, and there is free jazz on Saturday nights,
featuring the Shura Greenberg Trio.

Open all day 11-11 (Sun noon-8) Closed: BH
◖ Adnams Best, Adnams Broadside, Harveys Best,
Dark Star. ☻ 6

WC2

PICK OF THE PUBS

The Lamb ☻ PLAN 1 E4

94 Lamb's Conduit St WC1N 3LZ ☎ 020 7405 0713
e-mail: lambwc1@youngs.co.uk
dir: Russell Square, turn right, 1st right, 1st left,
1st right

This building was first recorded in 1729, was 'heavily
improved' between 1836-1876, and frequented by
Charles Dickens when he lived nearby in Doughty Street
(now housing the Dickens Museum). This really is a
gem of a place, with its distinctive green-tiled façade,
very rare glass snob screens, dark polished wood, and
original sepia photographs of music hall stars who
performed at the nearby Holborn Empire. The absence
of television, piped music and fruit machines allows
conversation to flow, although there is a working
polyphon. Home-cooked bar food includes a vegetarian
corner (vegetable curry, or burger), a fish choice
including traditional fish and chips; and steaks from the
griddle, plus pies and baked dishes from the stove.
Favourites are steak and ale pie (called the Celebration
1729 pie); sausage and mash; liver and bacon; and fried
egg and chips. For something lighter, try a ploughman's
or a vegetable samosa with mango chutney.

Open all day all wk noon-11 (Thu-Sat noon-mdnt, Sun
noon-10.30) **Bar Meals** L served all wk 12-9 D served
all wk 12-9 food served all day ⊕ YOUNG & CO
BREWERY PLC ◖ Youngs (full range). ☻ 11
Facilities Garden

WC2

The Lamb and Flag ☻ PLAN 1 D3

33 Rose St, Covent Garden WC2E 9EB
☎ 020 7497 9504
dir: Leicester Square, Cranbourne St exit, turn left into
Garrick St, 2nd left

Licensed during the reign of Elizabeth I, the Lamb and
Flag exudes a strong atmosphere, with low ceilings, wood
panelling and high-backed settles both striking features
of the bar. In 1679 the poet Dryden was almost killed in a
nearby alley. These days office workers and Covent
Garden tourists throng the surrounding streets. Typical
examples of the hot food served upstairs include beef
and Yorkshire pudding and lamb hot pot, with doorstep
sandwiches, jackets potatoes and sausages served in the
bar. There is a courtyard to enjoy in fine weather.

Open all day all wk 11-11 (Fri-Sat 11am-11.30pm, Sun
12-10.30) Closed: 25-26 Dec, 1 Jan **Bar Meals** L served
Mon-Fri 12-3, Sat-Sun 12-5 Av main course £6.50
⊕ FREE HOUSE ◖ Courage Best & Directors, Young's PA
& Special, Wells Bombardier, Greene King IPA. ☻ 10

WC2 *continued*

The Seven Stars   PLAN 1 E4

53 Carey St WC2A 2JB ☎ 020 7242 8521
e-mail: roxy@roxybeaujolais.com
dir: *From Temple N via The Strand & Bell Yard to Carey
St. From Holborn SE via Lincoln's Inn Fields & Searle
St to Carey St*

One of very few pubs in the square mile that opens
seven days per week, and a precious example of a
London pub that has escaped being tarted up. It
survived the Great Fire of 1666, eventually to become a
favourite with judges, barristers and litigants taking a
breather from duty in the Royal Courts of Justice over
the road. Pit musicians from West End shows also beat
a path here. It is a good bet for food thanks to the
efforts of chef, cookbook writer and broadcaster Roxy
Beaujolais, who owns the pub with Nathan Silver. Look
out for her inspiringly-named 'elegant fish pie', her
'Afghan beef and ginger pie', and 'marvellous meat
loaf' with salad. Even if you don't need the loo, pretend
you do for the fun of navigating the ridiculously narrow
Elizabethan stairs. Ms Beaujolais and Mr Silver also
own the Bountiful Cow off High Holborn.

Open all day all wk 11-11 (Sat noon-11, Sun noon-
10.30) Closed: 25-26 Dec, 1 Jan, Good Fri, Etr Sun **Bar
Meals** L served Mon-Fri 12-3, Sat-Sun 12-9 D served
Mon-Fri 5.30-9, Sat-Sun 12-9 ⊕ FREE HOUSE
◀ Adnams Best & Broadside, Dark Star Best, Hophead,
Harveys.

Greyhound Hotel ♀

2 High St SM5 3PE
☎ 020 8647 1511   ▤ 020 8647 4687
e-mail: greyhound@youngs.co.uk
dir: *5 min from Carshalton station on foot, 20 min train
journey from Victoria Station*

Standing directly opposite the ponds in Carshalton Park,
this distinctive former coaching inn has a welcoming fire
in the bar in winter months. Records dating back to 1706
show that the white-painted building was formerly a
centre for cock-fighters and race-goers. Today's visitors

---

will find an interesting range of filled ciabattas and
snacks, together with more substantial options like
home-made steak and kidney pudding; and hake fillet in
Young's beer batter, hand cut chips and mushy peas.

Open all wk ⊕ YOUNG & CO BREWERY PLC ◀ Youngs
Special, Winter Warmer, PA & Waggle Dance. ♀ 17
Facilities Parking

Fox and Hounds ♀

Barnston Rd CH61 1BW
☎ 0151 648 7685   ▤ 0151 648 0872
e-mail: ralphleech@hotmail.com
dir: *M53 junct 4 take A5137 to Heswell. Right to Barnston
on B5138. Pub on A551*

The pub, located in a conservation area, was built in
1911 on the site of an alehouse and barn. Its Edwardian
character has been preserved in the pitch pine woodwork
and leaded windows. Incredible collections of
1920s/1930s memorabilia include ashtrays, horse
brasses, police helmets and empty whisky cases. Real
ales and 12 wines by the glass are served alongside a
range of bar snacks such as toasted ciabattas, jacket
potatoes, sandwiches and meat or seafood platters. Daily
specials and desserts are posted on the chalkboard.

Open all wk 11-11 (Sun noon-10.30) **Bar Meals** L served
Mon-Sat 12-2, Sun 12-2.30 booking required Av main
course £6.50 ⊕ FREE HOUSE ◀ Websters Yorkshire Bitter,
Theakston's Best & Old Peculier, 3 guest ales. ♀ 12
Facilities Children's menu Family room Dogs allowed
Garden Parking

The Pheasant Inn NEW ♀

20 Moss Ln L38 3RA ☎ 0151 929 2106
dir: *Off the A565, on the B5193*

An original brick in the restaurant wall is dated 1719,
when the pub was known as the 'Ten Billets Inn'; the
present name was adopted in 1952. By the 19th century a
small on-site brewery was producing just 2½ barrels a
week, but today you'll find Timothy Taylor Landlord
alongside Aspall's cider. The menu starts with jacket
potatoes and sandwiches with interesting fillings, and
typical hot dishes include baked salmon fishcakes with

---

capers, smoked salmon and lemon chive crème fraîche;
corned beef hash with free-range eggs; and daily fish
special.

The Pheasant Inn

Open all day all wk noon-11pm (Sun noon-10.30pm) **Bar
Meals** Av main course £9.50 food served all day
Restaurant Fixed menu price fr £9.95 Av 3 course à la
carte fr £20 food served all day ⊕ MITCHELLS &
BUTLERS ◀ Timothy Taylor Landlord ♂ Aspall Draught &
Organic. ♀ 6 **Facilities** Children's menu Dogs allowed
Garden Parking

Everyman Bistro ♀

9-11 Hope St L1 9BH
☎ 0151 708 9545   ▤ 0151 703 0290
e-mail: bistro@everyman.co.uk
dir: *In front of Metropolitan Cathedral. Bistro in basement
of Everyman Theatre*

Celebrating 39 years in business, this is a favourite
haunt of Liverpool's media, academic and theatrical
fraternity - Bill Nighy and Julie Walters started out in the
theatre above. But you don't need to write erudite leader
columns, wear a mortar board, or worry about saying
'Macbeth' out loud to enjoy dishes from the twice-daily
changing menus, such as roast bacon with black
pudding, leek and potato hash and cider cream sauce;
Tom's lamb scouse with beetroot and red cabbage; or
Thai spinach and mushroom curry.

Open noon-mdnt (Fri-Sat noon-2am) Closed: Sun & BH
Bar Meals Av main course £8.50 food served all day
Restaurant food served all day ⊕ FREE HOUSE ◀ Cains
Bitter, Black Sheep, Derwent Pale Ale, Copper Dragon,
Timothy Taylor Landlord. ♀ 8

Kings Head ♀

See Pick of the Pubs on opposite page

PICK OF THE PUBS

Kings Head ♀

BAWBURGH   Map 13 TG10

Harts Ln NR9 3LS
☎ **01603 744977** 🖷 **01603 744990**
e-mail: anton@kingshead-bawburgh.
co.uk
dir: *From A47 W of Norwich take B1108 W*

A genuine village pub with heavy timbers and bulging walls, The Kings Head has stood beside the restful river Yare since the 17th century. Set opposite the village green, it is big on traditional charm in the form of wooden floors, log fires, comfy leather seating and pine dining furniture. Whatever the weather, this is an ideal place to relax after an exhausting shopping spree in nearby Norwich. The place to be on long summer evenings is the south-facing patio or the secluded, landscaped garden. Seasonal menus offer a wide choice of modern British, European and Oriental dishes, all using the best quality local produce, including herbs and vegetables from the pub garden and flour from nearby Letheringsett Mill. Lunch can be anything from the quick and easy, such as a filled roll or ciabatta, to heartier options such as roast breast of pheasant with sweet potato purée, wild mushroom polenta cake, truffled peas and crispy bacon; mille-feuille of Mediterranean vegetables with pesto, slow-cooked tomatoes, goats' cheese, rocket and parmesan; or baked gypsy eggs with chorizo, tomatoes, peas, spinach and smoked paprika. An evening meal could begin with smoked mackerel pâté, pickled cucumber, lemon and hot toast; seared breast of wood pigeon with bacon lardons, black pudding and pine nut salad; or Japanese-style slow-cooked sea bass with soy, chilli, ginger and pak choi. Follow with roast belly of pork with sage mash, black pudding apple relish, green beans and red wine jus; fish stew; or pan-roasted cod with squid ink risotto, tiger prawns, pak choi and oyster sauce. Eton mess or sticky toffee pudding are typical desserts. The famed Sunday roast lunch menu offers a choice of four local meats, all sourced from within 15 miles of the pub.

Open all week Closed: 25-27 Dec eve, 1 Jan eve **Bar Meals** L served all wk 12-2 D served Mon-Sat 5.30-9, Sun 5.30-8.30 **Restaurant** L served all wk 12-2 D served Mon-Sat 5.30-9, Sun 5.30-8.30 ⊕ FREE HOUSE ◾ Adnams, Woodforde's Wherry, Greene King IPA, Courage Directors. ♀ 18 **Facilities** Garden Parking

BINHAM
Map 13 TF93

Chequers Inn

Front St NR21 0AL ☎ 01328 830297
e-mail: steve@binhamchequers.co.uk
dir: *On B1388 between Wells-next-the-Sea & Walsingham*

The Chequers is home to the Front Street Brewery, but
even though they brew their own beer they still have
regular Norfolk/East Anglian guest ales, and a large
selection of bottled beers. The pub has been owned by a
village charity since the early 1640s, and was originally a
trade hall. Many stones from the nearby priory were used
in its construction. The daily changing menu offers dishes
such as Norfolk duck pâté, fresh lobster thermidor and
plum crumble.

Open all wk 11.30-2.30 6-11 (Fri-Sat 11.30-2.30 6-11.30
Sun noon-2.30 7-11) **Bar Meals** L served all wk 12-2 D
served all wk 6-9 ⊕ FREE HOUSE ◖ Binham Cheer 3.9%,
Callums Ale 4.3%, Unity Strong 5%, Seasonal specials,
micro brewery on site. **Facilities** Children's menu Garden
Parking

BLAKENEY
Map 13 TG04

The Kings Arms ♚

Westgate St NR25 7NQ
☎ 01263 740341 📄 01263 740391
e-mail: kingsarmsnorfolk@btconnect.com
dir: *From Hull or Fakenham take A148, then B1156 for
6m to Blakeney*

This Grade II listed free house is located on the beautiful
north Norfolk coast, close to the famous salt marshes.
Owners Marjorie and Howard Davies settled here after
long and successful showbiz careers and their son Nic,
now handles the day-to-day running of the pub. The Kings
Arms is an ideal centre for walking, or perhaps a ferry trip
to the nearby seal colony and world-famous bird
sanctuaries. Locally-caught fish and seasonal seafood
feature on the menu – crab in summer and mussels in
winter - together with local game, home-made lasagne
and steaks.

Open all day all wk 11-11 Closed: 25 Dec eve **Bar
Meals** Av main course £6 ⊕ FREE HOUSE ◖ Greene King
Old Speckled Hen, Woodforde's Wherry Best Bitter,
Marston's Pedigree, Adnams Best Bitter. ♚ 12
Facilities Children's menu Play area Family room Dogs
allowed Garden Parking

PICK OF THE PUBS

White Horse Hotel ♚

See Pick of the Pubs on opposite page

BLICKLING
Map 13 TG12

PICK OF THE PUBS

The Buckinghamshire Arms ♚

Blickling Rd NR11 6NF ☎ 01263 732133
e-mail: bucksarms@tiscali.com
dir: *A410 from Cromer exit at Aylsham onto B1354,
follow Blickling Hall signs*

Claimed to be Norfolk's most beautiful inn 'The Bucks'
stands by the gates of the National Trust's Blickling
Hall. A late 17th-century coaching inn, it is said to be
haunted by Anne Boleyn's ghost, who wanders in the
adjacent courtyard and charming garden. The lounge
bar and restaurant, with their solid furniture and wood-
burning stoves, have plenty of appeal. Meals can be
taken in either, with menus offering fresh local food
served in both traditional and modern styles. Dishes
from the dinner menu include Norfolk rump steak;
Gunton Park venison casserole; and Halvergate lamb
loin stuffed with apricot, pine nuts and rosemary with
braised lentils and smoked bacon. Alternatives might
be gnocchi with spinach, roast peppers and goats'
cheese, or poached smoked haddock with turmeric
crushed new potatoes. The Victorian cellar houses real
ales from Norfolk, Suffolk and Kent.

Open all day all wk 11-11 Closed: 25 Dec **Bar Meals** L
served Mon-Fri 12-2, Sat-Sun 12-2.30 booking required
D served all wk 7-9 booking required Av main course
£9.95 **Restaurant** L served Mon-Fri 12-2, Sat-Sun
12-2.30 booking required D served all wk 7-9 booking
required Fixed menu price fr £11.95 ⊕ FREE HOUSE
◖ Adnams Bitter & Regatta, Woodforde's Wherry,
Nelson's Revenge, Wolf Coyote Bitter ♻ Aspalls,
Norfolk. ♚ 7 **Facilities** Children's menu Garden Parking

BRANCASTER STAITHE
Map 13 TF74

PICK OF THE PUBS

The White Horse ★★★ HL ◉◉ ♚

PE31 8BY ☎ 01485 210262 📄 01485 210930
e-mail: reception@whitehorsebrancaster.co.uk
dir: *A149 (coast road), midway between Hunstanton &
Wells-next-the-Sea*

A popular gastro-pub gloriously situated in an Area of
Outstanding Natural Beauty, with panoramic views
from its conservatory restaurant and sun-deck over
tidal creeks and marshes to Scolt Head Island. If you
think these views are wonderful in daylight, then catch
them at sunrise and sunset. Scrubbed pine tables and
high-backed settles help to create a welcoming
atmosphere for diners ready for two AA Rosette-quality
food based on fresh local produce. The extensive, daily-
changing restaurant menus and specials offer cockles,
mussels and oysters, when in season, from the beds at
the bottom of the garden; slow-roasted belly of Norfolk
pork with caramelised root vegetables and apple
compote; confit duck leg with mixed beans and chorizo;
pan-fried fillet of sea bass with pancetta, broad beans,
peas and baby leeks; and wild mushroom and baby
spinach risotto. Tastefully furnished en suite bedrooms
look out over the ever ebbing and flowing tide.

Open all day all wk 9am-11pm (Sun 9am-10.30pm)
Bar Meals Av main course £7 food served all day
Restaurant L served all wk 12-2 booking required D
served all wk 6.30-9 booking required Av 3 course à la
carte fr £25 ⊕ FREE HOUSE ◖ Adnams Best Bitter,
Fuller's London Pride, Woodforde's Wherry, guest
♻ Aspall. ♚ 17 **Facilities** Children's menu Dogs
allowed Garden Parking **Rooms** 15

BRISLEY
Map 13 TF92

The Brisley Bell Inn &
Restaurant NEW ★★★ INN

The Green NR20 5DW ☎ 01362 668686
e-mail: info@brisleybell-inn.co.uk
dir: *On the B1145, between Fakenham and East Dereham*

Enjoying an isolated position close to the village centre,
this attractive, 16th-century warm brick-built pub
overlooks the largest piece of common land in Norfolk,
some 200 acres. Inside, you'll find a small, refurbished
bar area with old beams, large brick fireplace and
exposed brick walls, a separate, neatly laid-up dining
room, and a wide-ranging menu that takes in bar snacks,
stir-fries, steaks, daily fish specials, and popular Sunday
roast lunches. The bed and breakfast accommodation
makes a perfect country retreat.

Open noon-3 6-11 (Sat 11-11 Sun noon-10.30) Closed:
Mon **Bar Meals** L served Tue-Sun 12-2.30 D served Tue-
Thu & Sun 6-8, Fri-Sat 6-9 Av main course £5.95
Restaurant L served Tue-Sun 12-2.30 D served Tue-Thu
& Sun 6-8, Fri-Sat 6-9 booking required Fixed menu price
fr £8.25 **Facilities** Children's menu Dogs allowed Garden
Parking **Rooms** 3

PICK OF THE PUBS

White Horse Hotel ♉

4 High St NR25 7AL
☎ **01263 740574** 🖷 **01263 741303**
e-mail: info@blakeneywhitehorse.co.uk
dir: *From A148 (Cromer to King's Lynn road)
onto A149 signed to Blakeney*

Blakeney is a gem of a coastal village, a cluster of narrow streets lined with flint-built fishermen's cottages winding down to a small tidal harbour, with glorious views over creeks, estuary and salt marsh. A short stroll from the quayside stands the 17th-century White Horse, formerly a coaching inn, built of traditional brick-and-flint and set around the old courtyard and stables. Inside, the bar, dining room and airy conservatory are tastefully decorated in creams and darkwood with soft lamplight, and the informal bar is adorned with local artwork. The inn has a deserved reputation for its food. As befits its seaside location, fish dominates the constantly evolving menu, with lobster, crab and mussels sourced from local fishermen. It also delves into the rich larder of local produce available along the coast, including meat and game from nearby Holkham Estate, and soft fruit, salads and vegetables from small farms and suppliers, and both bread and puddings are made on the premises. At lunch, tuck into Cley Smokehouse prawns with chilli mayonnaise, deep-fried soft herring roes, fish pie, smoked haddock and crayfish kedgeree, or a smoked ham and mustard sandwich. From the evening carte, choose seared scallops with butternut squash purée, crab apple aioli and Parma ham, or pork belly with oriental broth and braised bok choi for a starter, then follow with roast red mullet, Morston mussel, bacon and tomato stew, confit duck leg with Lyonnaise potatoes, Savoy cabbage, chestnuts and bacon, or beer-battered haddock with hand-cut chips and tartare sauce. To finish, try the pumpkin tart with clotted cream, or the cinnamon pannacotta with roast plum coulis and cardamom ice cream. A 50-bin wine list, a dozen of which are available by the glass, and real ales from Adnams and Yetmans complete the picture.

Open all day all wk 10.30am-11pm
Closed: 25 Dec **Bar Meals** L served all wk 12-2.15 D served Thu-Sun 6-9, Fri-Sat 6-9.30 ⊕ FREE HOUSE ◀ Adnams Bitter, Woodforde's Wherry, Adnams Broadside, Yetmans Ŏ Aspalls. ♉ 12
Facilities Children's menu Family room Garden Parking

BURNHAM MARKET — Map 13 TF84

PICK OF THE PUBS

The Hoste Arms ★★★ HL ◉◉ ♟

See Pick of the Pubs on opposite page

BURNHAM THORPE — Map 13 TF84

PICK OF THE PUBS

The Lord Nelson ♟

Walsingham Rd PE31 8HN
☎ 01328 738241 📠 01328 738241
e-mail: simon@nelsonslocal.co.uk
web: www.nelsonslocal.co.uk
dir: *B1355 (Burnham Market to Fakenham road), pub 9m from Fakenham & 1.75m from Burnham Market. Pub near church opposite playing fields*

Horatio Nelson was born in Burnham Thorpe in 1758. The pub, then called the Plough, was already over 100 years old; in 1798 its name was changed to honour his victory over the French at the Nile. Visitors today can soak up an atmosphere that has changed little since; you can even sit on Nelson's high-backed settle. Upon the declaration of war against France in 1793, he celebrated being given a command by treating the whole village to a meal upstairs. There's no bar – drinks are served from the taproom, with real ales straight from the cask. The kitchen team aims to cook dishes with balance between flavours, so that the quality of the ingredients can be tasted. Traditional chunky fish broth; noisettes of minced lamb and aubergine with pasta; and pannacotta with limoncello cream are typical choices. Families are welcomed, and children will enjoy the huge garden. Dirty wellies and soggy doggies straight from the beach are no problem at all in 'Nelson's local'.

Open all day noon–11 Closed: Mon eve ex school hols **Bar Meals** L served all wk 12-2.30 D served Tue-Sun 6-9 Av main course £12 **Restaurant** L served all wk 12-2.30 D served Tue-Sun 6-9 booking required Fixed menu price fr £19.95 Av 3 course à la carte fr £25 ⊕ GREENE KING ◖ Greene King Abbot Ale & IPA, Woodforde's Wherry, Nelson's Blood Bitter. ♟ 15 **Facilities** Play area Dogs allowed Garden Parking

CLEY NEXT THE SEA — Map 13 TG04

PICK OF THE PUBS

The George Hotel ♟

High St NR25 7RN
☎ 01263 740652 📠 01263 741275
e-mail: info@thegeorgehotelatcley.co.uk
dir: *On A149 through Cley next the Sea, approx 4m from Holt*

Located near the sea and marshes, The George is stands on historic Cley's winding High Street. The beer garden backs onto the marshes, from where you can see Cley's famous mill, while the lovely oak-floored bar provides a year-round welcome. You can snack in the lounge bar or dine in the light, painting-filled restaurant. At lunchtime the menu runs from sandwiches (hot chicken, avocado, crispy bacon and red pesto mayonnaise; or brie, smoked ham and fresh mango) to starters and light meals such as warm pan-fried chicken liver, duck liver and rocket salad with balsamic dressing; or hearty main courses - perhaps home-made steak, kidney and suet pudding. Dinner brings starters of roast parsnip and honey soup laced with cream, followed by braised pork belly with spiced red cabbage, wilted spinach and honey glaze. Seafood is a real strength.

Open all day all wk 11-11 **Bar Meals** L served all wk 12-2.30 D served all wk 6.30-9 ⊕ FREE HOUSE ◖ Greene King IPA, Abbot Ale, Yetmans ales, Adnams Broadside, Woodforde's Wherry ♪ Aspalls. ♟ 8 **Facilities** Family room Dogs allowed Garden Parking

COLTISHALL — Map 13 TG21

Kings Head ♟

26 Wroxham Rd NR12 7EA
☎ 01603 737426 📠 01603 736542
dir: *A47 (Norwich ring road) onto B1150 to North Walsham at Coltishall. Right at petrol station, follow to right past church. Pub on right by car park*

This 17th-century free house stands on the banks of the River Bure, right in the heart of the Norfolk Broads. Hire cruisers are available at nearby Wroxham, and fishing boats can be hired at the pub. If you prefer to stay on dry land you'll find a warm welcome at the bar, with a range of real ales that includes Adnams Bitter, Directors and Marston's Pedigree. There's an inviting menu, too, served in both the bar and the restaurant.

Open all wk Closed: 26 Dec ⊕ FREE HOUSE ◖ Adnams Bitter, Directors, Marston's Pedigree. ♟ 10 **Facilities** Parking

DEREHAM — Map 13 TF91

Yaxham Mill ★★★★ INN ♟

Norwich Rd, Yaxham NR19 1RP
☎ 01362 851182 📠 01362 691482
e-mail: yaxhammill@hotmail.co.uk
dir: *From Norwich take A47 towards Swaffham. At East Dereham take B1135. Yaxham 2m*

A converted windmill in the middle of open Norfolk countryside and dating back to 1810. The miller's house and chapel were transformed into a restaurant and bar. Menus cater for all tastes, with grilled lemon sole, minted lamb steak, sweet and sour chicken, and chilli con carne among other dishes. Home-made pies, including steak and kidney and cottage, are something of a speciality.

Open all wk ⊕ FREE HOUSE ◖ Bombardier, Youngs, 2 guest ales. ♟ 8 **Facilities** Garden Parking **Rooms** 12

EAST RUSTON — Map 13 TG32

The Butchers Arms ♟

Oak Ln NR12 9JG ☎ 01692 650237
dir: *Off School Rd opp East Ruston allotment*

A quintessential village pub, originally three cottages built in the early 1800s. You won't find a jukebox, TV or pool table, but outside is 'Mavis', a 1954 Comma fire engine. Landlady Julie Gollop takes pride in creating a welcoming atmosphere, serving a good choice of real ales, and preparing a menu of traditional home-cooked favourites: mushrooms with garlic dip; and deep-fried whitebait; and grilled steaks.

Open all wk ⊕ FREE HOUSE ◖ Adnams, Woodforde's, Old Speckled Hen, Greene King IPA. ♟ 7 **Facilities** Dogs allowed Garden Parking **Notes** ◉

EATON — Map 13 TG20

The Red Lion ♟

50 Eaton St NR4 7LD
☎ 01603 454787 📠 01603 456939
e-mail: redlioneaton@hotmail.co.uk
dir: *Off A11, 2m S of Norwich city centre*

This heavily-beamed 17th-century coaching inn has bags of character, thanks to its Dutch gables, panelled walls and inglenook fireplaces. The covered terrace enables customers to enjoy one of the real ales or sample the extensive wine list outside during the summer months. The extensive lunch menu offers everything from steak and kidney suet pudding to grilled red snapper fillets with mango and sweet chilli salsa; or Swannington baked gammon with a Cumberland sauce.

Open all day all wk **Bar Meals** L served all wk 12-2.15 booking required D served all wk 6.30-9 booking required **Restaurant** L served all wk 12-2.15 booking required D served all wk 6.30-9 booking required ⊕ ENTERPRISE INNS ◖ Old Speckled Hen, Courage Directors, Greene King IPA, Adnams Bitter, Woodforde's Wherry, Fuller's London Pride. ♟ 10 **Facilities** Children's menu Garden Parking

PICK OF THE PUBS

The Hoste Arms ★★★ HL 🌹🌹 🍷

BURNHAM MARKET   Map 13 TF84

The Green PE31 8HD
☎ 01328 738777   📠 01328 730103
e-mail: reception@hostearms.co.uk
dir: *Signed off B1155, 5m W of Wells-next-the-Sea*

Over the centuries this building has been a courthouse, a livestock market, and even a Victorian brothel. Built as a manor house in 1550 in this lovely village close to the Norfolk coast, it has been an inn since 1720 but fell into decline during the last century. Indeed,

Horatio Nelson was once a regular. Paul Whittome rescued it 20 years ago and turned it into a beautifully presented hotel with striking interior design courtesy of his wife Jeanne. The inn now has 35 stylish bedrooms and several restaurant areas. The bar retains a traditional feel with its abundance of wood and log fire. The brasserie-style menu includes plenty of local specialities; perhaps roasted breast of local pigeon, rhubarb compote, toasted brioche and black pepper ice cream, followed by Arthur Howell's 21 day aged New York rib steak with hand-cut chips. Brancaster oysters are served many ways, from natural or with Bloody Mary shot to hot with tempura or rarebit glaze. Additional light lunch options include tempting sandwiches and salads. As well as a great choice of real ales, including the best from Woodforde's, Greene King and Adnams Breweries, the cellar houses over 100 fine wines in a temperature-controlled environment.

Open all day all week **Bar Meals** L served all wk 12-2 D served all wk 6-9 **Restaurant** L served all wk 12-2 D served all wk 6-9 ⊕ FREE HOUSE ◀ Woodforde's Wherry Best, Greene King Abbot Ale, Adnams Best Bitter, Adnams Broadside, Nelson's Revenge. 🍷 11 **Facilities** Dogs allowed Garden Parking **Rooms** 35

ERPINGHAM Map 13 TG13

PICK OF THE PUBS

The Saracen's Head

NR11 7LZ ☎ **01263 768909** 📠 **01263 768993**
e-mail: saracenshead@wolterton.freeserve.co.uk
dir: *A140, 2.5m N of Aylsham, left through Erpingham, pass Spread Eagle on left. Through Calthorpe bear left (do not follow rd to Aldborough), straight on to pub*

Lost among fields down Norfolk lanes, the privately owned Saracen's Head is an ideal escape from the rat race. A former coach house, built in Tuscan farmhouse style in 1806 for neighbouring Wolterton Hall, it is well known for its mellow atmosphere, created over 20 years by owner Robert Dawson-Smith and daughter Rachel, who has drawn on her years spent in Italy. There are wicker chairs, 19th century engravings, roaring log fires in winter and shelves of old books. The menus reflect owner Robert's enduring passion for Norfolk and its produce, although this doesn't preclude him from incorporating European influences in his cooking. The blackboards change daily in response to the many 'wild and tame' treats he and his team prepare. Seasonal availability permitting, these may include Morston mussels with cider and cream; crispy fried aubergine with garlic mayonnaise; baked Cromer crab with apple and sherry; roast Norfolk pheasant with Calvados and cream; vine leaves stuffed with feta; brown bread and butter pudding; and poached pears in spicy red wine. The delightful courtyard garden features the Shed, a small workshop run by Rachel, and sells furniture, 'retro and rustic' gifts and Rachel's own drawings and paintings.

Open all wk 11.30-3 6-11 (Sun noon-3 7-10.30) Closed: 25 Dec **Bar Meals** booking required Av main course £12.95 **Restaurant** booking required Av 3 course à la carte fr £25 ⊕ FREE HOUSE ◀ Adnams Best Bitter, Woodforde's Wherry. **Facilities** Children's menu Garden Parking

FAKENHAM Map 13 TF92

The Wensum Lodge Hotel

Bridge St NR21 9AY
☎ **01328 862100** 📠 **01328 863365**
e-mail: enquiries@wensumlodge.fsnet.co.uk
dir: *In town centre*

Wensum Lodge is a converted mill dating from around 1700, idyllically located by the River Wensum, for which the hotel has fishing rights. Home-cooked food is prepared from locally supplied ingredients, with baguettes, jacket potatoes and an all-day breakfast on the light bite menu. The carte might have baby peeled prawns on dressed leaves with chilli dip; and Wensum burger topped with bacon, cheese, salad and relish in a toasted bun served with fries.

Open all wk ⊕ FREE HOUSE ◀ Greene King Abbot Ale & IPA, Old Mill Bitter. **Facilities** Garden Parking

The White Horse Inn ★★★★ INN

Fakenham Rd, East Barsham NR21 0LH
☎ **01328 820645** 📠 **01328 820645**
e-mail: whitehorse@norfolkinns.co.uk
dir: *1.5m N of Fakenham on minor road to Little Walsingham*

Ideally located for birdwatching, walking, cycling, fishing, golf and sandy beaches, this refurbished 17th-century inn offers en suite rooms and a characterful bar with log-burning inglenook. Good range of beers and malt whiskies. Fresh ingredients are assured in daily specials, with fish especially well represented. Typical choices include chicken breast stuffed with stilton, peppered mackerel fillets, sweet and sour pork, and venison steak. There is also a grill menu. Birdwatching tours can be arranged.

Open all wk ◀ Adnams Best, Adnams Broadside, Tetley, Wells Eagle IPA. **Facilities** Garden Parking **Rooms** 3

GREAT RYBURGH Map 13 TF92

The Blue Boar Inn

NR21 0DX ☎ **01328 829212**
dir: *Off A1067 4m S of Fakenham*

Dating back to 1683, this whitewashed free house stands opposite the round towered Saxon church of St Andrew. A large magnolia tree ushers you into the rambling old building with its beams and inglenook fireplace. Adnams ales are offered at the bar, whilst local produce features strongly on the extensive chalkboard menu. Typical dishes include breast of Norfolk chicken with prawn thermidor; Ryburgh lamb cutlets with mustard mash; and steamed Brancaster mussels when in season. Recent change of Landlord.

Open 11.30-2.30 6.30-11.30 Closed: Tue **Bar Meals** L served Wed-Mon 11.30-2.30 D served Wed-Mon 6.30-10.30 Av main course £10 **Restaurant** L served Wed-Mon 11.30-2.30 D served Wed-Mon 6.30-10.30 ⊕ FREE HOUSE ◀ Adnams Bitter, Bass, Murphy's. **Facilities** Children's menu Play area Family room Garden Parking

HAPPISBURGH Map 13 TG33

The Hill House 🍷

NR12 0PW ☎ **01692 650004** 📠 **01692 650004**
dir: *5m from Stalham, 8m from North Walsham*

Expect to be corrected if you pronounce Happisburgh the way it's spelt - it's Haze-borough. Once the favourite haunt of the creator of Sherlock Holmes, Sir Arthur Conan Doyle, this Grade II listed, 16th-century coaching inn offers good value bar food including sandwiches, jacket potatoes, a range of ploughman's and local crab and fish dishes in season. The restaurant menu includes a wide selection of fish and seafood, steaks and other meat dishes, as well as a vegetarian selection. Look out for the Solstice Beer Festival in June for the chance to sample a wide range of real ales, ciders and perries.

Open all wk noon-11.30 (Mon-Wed noon-3 7-11.30 low season) **Bar Meals** L served all wk 12-2.30 D served Mon-Sat 7-9.30, Sun 7-9 booking required **Restaurant** L served all wk 12-2.30 D served Mon-Sat 7-9.30, Sun 7-9 booking required ⊕ FREE HOUSE ◀ Shepherd Neame Spitfire, Buffy's, Woodforde's Wherry, Adnams Bitter, House Bitter Ö Aspall, Westons Stowford Press. 🍷 10 **Facilities** Children's menu Play area Dogs allowed Garden Parking

HEVINGHAM Map 13 TG12

Marsham Arms
Freehouse ⚠ ★★★★ INN 🍷

Holt Rd NR10 5NP ☎ **01603 754268**
e-mail: nigelbradley@marshamarms.co.uk
web: www.marshamarms.co.uk
dir: *On B1149 N of Norwich airport, 2m through Horsford towards Holt*

Built as a roadside hostel for poor farm labourers by Victorian philanthropist and landowner Robert Marsham. Some original features remain, including the large open fireplace, and there's a spacious garden with paved patio and a dedicated family room. A good range of fresh fish dishes includes cod, haddock, sea bass, herrings and crab. Specialities such as beef stew with dumplings and beer battered haddock are backed by a daily blackboard. There are vegetarian and gluten-free dishes too. Look out for the monthly jazz nights and wine tasting evenings.

Open all wk **Bar Meals** L served all wk 12-2.30 D served all wk 6-9.30 **Restaurant** L served all wk 12-2.30 D served all wk 6-9.30 ⊕ FREE HOUSE ◀ Adnams Best, Woodforde's Wherry Best Bitter, Mauldens, Worthington, Broadside Ö Aspall. 🍷 6 **Facilities** Children's menu Play area Family room Dogs allowed Garden Parking **Rooms** 11

HEYDON Map 13 TG12

Earle Arms 🍷

The Street NR11 6AD ☎ **01263 587376**
e-mail: haitchy@aol.com
dir: *Signed between Cawston & Corpusty on B1149 (Holt to Norwich road)*

Heydon is one of only 13 privately owned villages in the country and is often used as a film location. It dates from the 16th century, and inside are log fires, attractive wallpapers, prints and a collection of bric-a-brac. One of the two rooms offers service through a hatch, and there are tables outside in the pretty back garden. Locally reared meat goes into dishes like braised lamb shank or fillet of beef marchand de vin. Fish choices include plaice goujons, crayfish omelette, and sea bass fillet with lemon butter.

Closed: Mon **Bar Meals** L served Tue-Sun 12-2 booking required D served Tue-Sun 7-9 booking required **Restaurant** L served Tue-Sun 12-2 booking required D served Tue-Sun 7-9 booking required ⊕ FREE HOUSE ◀ Adnams, Woodforde's Wherry. ♀ 8 **Facilities** Children's menu Dogs allowed Garden Parking

HOLKHAM   Map 13 TF84

PICK OF THE PUBS

Victoria at Holkham ★★ SHL ◉◉ ♀

Park Rd NR23 1RG
☎ 01328 711008 ▤ 01328 711009
e-mail: victoria@holkham.co.uk
dir: *On A149, 3m W of Wells-next-the-Sea*

The Victoria stands at the gates of landlord Tom Coke's Palladian ancestral home, Holkham Hall, just minutes from the golden sands of Holkham Beach. Its opulent, colonial-style interior is full of furniture and accessories from Rajahstan and other exotic places. Outside is a courtyard where summer barbecues are popular. Tom Coke would argue that the Victoria's main attraction is what he calls 'some of the most consistently good food in North Norfolk'. Key words here are fresh, local and seasonal, whether it be shellfish, fish or samphire from the north Norfolk coast, beef from farms on the Holkham estate, organic chickens from a tenant farmer, venison from the herd of fallow deer or, in the winter, wild game from family shoots. An eclectic, yet sensibly priced, wine list proves popular, and there are always several real ales on tap.

Open all day all wk 11-11 **Bar Meals** L served all wk 12-2.30 **Restaurant** L served all wk 12-2.30 D served Sun-Thu 7-9, Fri-Sat 7-9.30 ◀ Adnams Best, Woodforde's Wherry, guest ale ♡ Aspalls. ♀ 12 **Facilities** Play area Dogs allowed Garden Parking **Rooms** 10

HORSEY   Map 13 TG42

Nelson Head ♥

The Street NR29 4AD ☎ 01493 393378
dir: *On B1159 (coast road) between West Somerton & Sea Palling*

Located on a National Trust estate, which embraces nearby Horsey Mere, this 17th-century inn will, to many, epitomise the perfect country pub. It enjoys the tranquillity of a particularly unspoilt part of the Norfolk coast - indeed, the Broads are ½ mile away and glorious beaches only a mile - and the sheltered gardens look out towards the dunes and water meadows. Haddock and chips, cottage pie, and a selection of vegetarian choices are among the dishes available. Local beers are Woodforde's Wherry and Nelson's Revenge.

Open all day all wk 11-11 **Bar Meals** L served all wk 12-2.30 D served all wk 6-8.30 **Restaurant** L served all wk 12-2.30 D served all wk 6-8.30 ⊕ FREE HOUSE ◀ Woodforde's Wherry, Nelson's Revenge.
Facilities Children's menu Play area Family room Dogs allowed Garden Parking

HORSTEAD   Map 13 TG21

Recruiting Sergeant ♀

Norwich Rd NR12 7EE
☎ 01603 737077 ▤ 01603 736905
dir: *On B1150 between Norwich & North Walsham*

The name of this inviting country pub comes from the tradition of recruiting servicemen by giving them the King or Queen's shilling in a pint of beer. It offers good food, ales and wines in homely surroundings with a patio and lawned garden for alfresco dining. The menu is ever changing, with dishes such as pigeon breast, smoked lardoons and rocket salad; saddle of venison with honey-roast parsnips, mash and pepper sauce; and tagliatelle of roasted butternut with sage and Roquefort cream. There is also a vast daily specials menu, including fish and vegetarian dishes.

Open all day all wk 11-11 (Sun noon-10.30) **Bar Meals** L served Mon-Sat 12-2, Sun 12-9 booking required D served Mon-Sat 6-9, Sun 12-9 booking required Av main course £12.50 **Restaurant** L served Mon-Sat 12-2, Sun 12-9 booking required D served Mon-Sat 6-9, Sun 12-9 booking required ⊕ FREE HOUSE ◀ Adnams, Woodforde's, Greene King Abbot Ale, Scottish Courage. ♀ 13 **Facilities** Dogs allowed Garden Parking

HUNSTANTON   Map 12 TF64

The King William IV ◭ ★★★★ INN ♀

Heacham Rd, Sedgeford PE36 5LU
☎ 01485 571765 ▤ 01485 571743
e-mail: info@thekingwilliamsedgeford.co.uk
dir: *From A149 turn right at traffic lights in Heacham onto B1454. Pub 2m in village*

Despite being extensively refurbished and extended, The King William retains its traditional appeal. It is tucked away in the village of Sedgeford, conveniently close to the north Norfolk coastline. An ale house since 1836, it has winter log fires and a covered alfresco dining area for warmer months. A choice of light meals includes salads and pasta, while a longer visit might take in smoked salmon with lemon and dill dressing followed by duck breast in red wine and berry sauce.

Open all day 11-11 (Sun 12-10.30) Closed: Mon L (ex BH) **Bar Meals** L served Tue-Sat 12-2, Sun 12-2.30 booking required D served all wk 6.30-9 booking required Av main course £9.95 **Restaurant** L served Tue-Sat 12-2, Sun 12-2.30 booking required D served all wk 6.30-9 booking required Fixed menu price fr £18.95 Av 3 course à la carte fr £20 ⊕ FREE HOUSE ◀ Woodforde's Wherry, Adnams Bitter, Guinness, Greene King Abbot Ale, guest ale. ♀ 9 **Facilities** Children's menu Dogs allowed Garden Parking **Rooms** 9

ITTERINGHAM   Map 13 TG13

PICK OF THE PUBS

Walpole Arms ◉ ♀

See Pick of the Pubs on page 320

KING'S LYNN   Map 12 TF62

The Stuart House Hotel, Bar & Restaurant ★★★ HL

35 Goodwins Rd PE30 5QX
☎ 01553 772169 ▤ 01553 774788
e-mail: reception@stuarthousehotel.co.uk
web: www.stuarthousehotel.co.uk
dir: *Follow signs to town centre, pass under Southgate Arch, immediate right, in 100yds turn right*

A short walk from the historic town centre, the Stuart House is set in its own delightful grounds, with a patio and beer garden. Cask conditioned ales and home-cooked dishes are served in the bar, and there is a separate restaurant offering a carte menu and daily specials. A programme of events includes regular live music, murder mystery dinners and an annual beer festival.

Open all wk 5-11 **Bar Meals** D served all wk 6-9.30 **Restaurant** D served all wk 7-9.30 ⊕ FREE HOUSE ◀ Adnams, Woodforde's, Greene King, Oakham JHB, Timothy Taylor Landlord. **Facilities** Play area Garden Parking **Rooms** 18

LARLING   Map 13 TL98

PICK OF THE PUBS

Angel Inn ♀

NR16 2QU ☎ 01953 717963 ▤ 01953 718561
dir: *5m from Attleborough, 8m from Thetford. 1m from station*

Three generations of the Stammers family have been running this 17th-century free house for more than 80 years. The present generation is passionate about real ale, and Adnams Bitter is always supported by at least four guest ales from both Norfolk and elsewhere. There's a homely, local feel to the heavily-beamed public bar, whilst the lounge bar has wheel-back chairs, an oak settle, cosy log fire and a collection of over 100 water jugs. The cooking is underpinned by

continued on page 321

PICK OF THE PUBS

Walpole Arms ◉ ♀

ITTERINGHAM Map 13 TG13

NR11 7AR
☎ 01263 587258 📠 01263 587074
e-mail: goodfood@thewalpolearms.co.uk
web: www.thewalpolearms.co.uk
dir: *From Aylsham towards Blickling. After Blickling Hall take 1st right to Itteringham*

Long-term Norfolk residents Richard Bryan and Keith Reeves, together with their respective families, combined their talents in 2001 when they took over this traditional village pub in the beautiful north Norfolk countryside. Richard's lifetime passion for food has been partly channelled into broadcasting, notably as producer of BBC TV's *Masterchef*, while Keith is a highly respected wine merchant, supplying customers throughout East Anglia. With the addition of chef Andy Parle, a veteran of Michelin-starred restaurants in Norwich and London, the team seem to have every base covered, and the success of

this award-winning venture proves that they have indeed got the recipe right. The Walpole arms has been a pub since 1836, although the oak-beamed bar suggests something older. In fact, Robert Horace Walpole, a direct descendant of Britain's first prime minister, once owned it. Today it is both a real pub and a dining destination. Andy and his team use the best seasonal and local produce to create thoroughly modern and inspired pub food. Both restaurant and bar offer a daily changing three-course carte; on Saturdays a special brunch menu is served, and on Sundays there's a delicious roast. Typical starters include Moroccan style broad bean, feta and pomegranate salad; and ballotine of turkey, bacon and chestnut with cranberry relish. Follow with slow roast belly pork with saffron and chick pea stew and black kale; or Morston mussels with salsa rosso and crusty bread. Wash it down with wine from Keith's comprehensive wine list, and finish with desserts such as drop scones with quince compote, pistachio ice cream and crème fraîche. Outside are large grassy areas with tables and a vine-covered patio.

Open 12-3 6-11 (Sun noon-5) Closed: 25 Dec **Bar Meals** L served all week 12-2 D served all week 6-9.30 Av main course £9.25 **Restaurant** L served Thu-Sun 12-2 D served Thu-Sun 6-9.30 Av 3 course à la carte fr £25.50 ⊕ NOBLE ROT ASSOCIATES LTD ◀ Adnams Broadside & Bitter, Woodforde's Wherry Best Bitter & Walpole. ♀ 12
Facilities Children's menu Play area Dogs allowed Garden Parking

ARLING *continued*

local ingredients wherever possible, and the light bites menu supplements sandwiches and jacket potatoes with ham, eggs and chips; and sausages in French bread. Main menu options start with home-made pâté; and deep-fried Camembert; moving on to choices like lamb chops with mint sauce; grilled local trout; and pork in peppered cream sauce. The pub also offers camping in Angel meadow just across the road, and an annual beer festival in August.

Open all day all wk 10am-mdnt **Bar Meals** L served Sun-Thu 12-9.30, Fri-Sat 12-10 D served Sun-Thu 12-9.30, Fri-Sat 12-10 Av main course £9.95 food served all day **Restaurant** L served Sun-Thu 12-9.30, Fri-Sat 12-10 D served Sun-Thu 12-9.30, Fri-Sat 12-10 food served all day ⊕ FREE HOUSE ◀ Adnams Bitter, Wolf Bitter, Caledonian Deuchars IPA, Timothy Taylor Landlord, Mauldons Ŏ Aspall. ♀ 10 **Facilities** Children's menu Play area Garden Parking

---

LITTLE FRANSHAM   Map 13 TF91

The Canary and Linnet

Main Rd NR19 2JW ☎ 01362 687027
dir: *On A47 between Dereham & Swaffham*

A pretty, former blacksmith's cottage fulfilling the key requirements of a traditional English country pub - low ceilings, exposed beams and an inglenook fireplace. Its sign once showed footballers in Norwich City (Canaries) and Kings Lynn (Linnets) strips, but now features two birds in a cage. Food offered throughout the bar, conservatory restaurant and garden includes steak and ale pie, medallions of pork in stilton sauce, and seared cajun spiced swordfish steak with lime and coriander dressing.

Open all wk noon-3 6-11 (Sun noon-3 6.30-10.30) **Bar Meals** L served all wk 12-2 booking required D served all wk 6-9 booking required Av main course £10 **Restaurant** L served all wk 12-2 D served all wk 6-9 Av 3 course à la carte fr £20 ⊕ FREE HOUSE ◀ Greene King IPA, Adnams Bitter, Wolf Ŏ Aspall. **Facilities** Dogs allowed Garden Parking

---

LITTLE WALSINGHAM   Map 13 TF93

The Black Lion Hotel ♀

Friday Market Place NR22 6DB
☎ 01328 820235 ▤ 01328 821407
e-mail: lionwalsingham@btconnect.com
dir: *From King's Lynn take A148 & B1105. Or from Norwich take A1067 & B1105*

Parts of this former coaching inn date from 1310, when they were built to accommodate Edward III on his numerous pilgrimages to the shrine at Walsingham (the hotel's name comes from his wife's coat of arms). The friendly bar is warmed by a fire in winter. The menu offers something for every taste: light options include

---

soup and filled baps, while a full meal could feature goats' cheese melt, followed by mixed grill, and hot crumble or pie of the day.

Open all wk noon-3 6-mdnt (Sat noon-mdnt) **Bar Meals** L served all wk 12-2 D served all wk 7-9 Av main course £6 **Restaurant** L served all wk 12-2 D served all wk 7-9 booking required Av 3 course à la carte fr £15 ⊕ ENTERPRISE INNS ◀ Woodforde's Wherry, Blacksheep Special, Woodforde's Nelson's Revenge, Tetley's. ♀ 8 **Facilities** Children's menu Dogs allowed Garden

---

MARSHAM   Map 13 TG12

The Plough Inn ♀

Norwich Rd NR10 5PS
☎ 01263 735000 ▤ 01263 735407
e-mail: enq@ploughinnmarsham.co.uk
web: www.ploughinnmarsham.co.uk
dir: *on A140, 10m N of Norwich*

A warm welcome is assured at this 18th-century countryside inn, ideally located for the North Norfolk coast and the Broads. The pumps serve both real ales and lagers, while menus based on local and seasonal produce include traditional favourites such as pork sausages and mash; steak and ale pie; and home-made beefburgers. A specials board proffers fresh fish; gluten- and wheat-free meals are also a speciality.

Open all wk 12-2.30 6-11 **Bar Meals** L served all wk 12-2.30 D served all wk 6-9 ⊕ FREE HOUSE ◀ IPA, Adnams, John Smiths Ŏ Aspalls. ♀ 9 **Facilities** Garden Parking

---

MUNDFORD   Map 13 TL89

Crown Hotel ♀

Crown Rd IP26 5HQ
☎ 01842 878233 ▤ 01842 878982
dir: *A11 to Barton Mills junct, then A1065 to Brandon & onto Mundford*

Built in 1652, the Crown has been many things - a famous hunting lodge; the local magistrates' court; even a doctors' waiting room. Its most unusual feature, in these pancake-flat parts, is that it is set into a hill! Traditional food is served in the bar, and a more elaborate menu is available in the restaurant; perhaps tian of Brixham crab followed by lamb rump with flageolet purée, fondant potato, garlic confit and mint jus.

Crown Hotel

Open all wk **Bar Meals** L served all wk 12-3 D served all wk 6.30-10 Av main course £10.95 **Restaurant** L served all wk 12-3 D served all wk 6.30-10 booking required ⊕ FREE HOUSE ◀ Courage Directors, Marston Pedigree, Archers, Greene King IPA, guest ales. ♀ 6 **Facilities** Dogs allowed Garden Parking

---

NORWICH   Map 13 TG20

Adam & Eve ♀

Bishopsgate NR3 1RZ
☎ 01603 667423 ▤ 01603 667438
e-mail: theadamandeve@hotmail.com
dir: *Telephone for directions*

Norwich's oldest pub, the Adam & Eve welcomed its first customers in 1249. It stands in the shadow of the Anglican cathedral, and once welcomed the men who built it. These days it remains a traditional pub with no TV or games machines, and counts a few ghosts among its regulars. Decked with flowers in summer, it offers real ales, 50 whiskeys and plenty of traditional, home-made food: perhaps farmhouse pâté followed by lasagne.

Open all day all wk 11-11 (Sun noon-10.30) Closed: 25-26 Dec, 1 Jan **Bar Meals** L served Mon-Sat 12-7, Sun 12-5 Av main course £7 ⊕ ENTERPRISE INNS ◀ Adnams Bitter, Theakston Old Peculier, Greene King IPA, Wells Bombardier. ♀ 10 **Facilities** Parking

---

PICK OF THE PUBS

The Mad Moose Arms ◉◉ ♀

See Pick of the Pubs on page 322

PICK OF THE PUBS

The Mad Moose Arms ❀❀ ♛

NORWICH   Map 13 TG20

2 Warwick St NR2 3LB
☎ **01603 627687** 📠 **01508 494946**
e-mail: madmoose@animalinns.co.uk
web: www.themadmoose.co.uk

A warm neighbourhood pub, the result of a stunning refit that created a decidedly stylish ground floor bar, all vibrant red walls, exposed brickwork and gleaming wood. Locals and regular visitors know they can expect Norfolk real ales - Woodforde's Wherry and Wolf's Straw Dog - and a bar menu offering roast aubergine, coriander crust, spiced fruits and couscous; Caesar salad with chicken; seared salmon, niçoise salad and fresh herb oil; aromatic duck with noodles, ginger star anise, coconut and spring onions; green Thai curry with a choice of chicken, prawn or vegetable; and beefburger and chips. On the first floor is the elegant, two AA-Rosette, 1Up restaurant with chandeliers, sea-green drapes, and a feature wall depicting a

fairytale forest – the fine dining part of the operation. Confident and ambitious cooking is typified by starters of gravadlax of salmon, sweet pickled cucumber, baby capers and mustard dressing; balsamic cured beetroot, creamed goat's cheese, black olive and thyme biscotti; and truffled girolles with roast confit garlic, brioche toast, chicory and tarragon emulsion. To follow: pan-fried cod, braised Puy lentils, truffled savoy cabbage, seared scallops, red onion confit and crisp Parma ham; roast breast of Norfolk pheasant, herby gnocchi, braised red cabbage, confit salsify, baby onions and red wine sauce; pan-fried black bream, crushed new potatoes, warm confit fennel, crisp leeks, chorizo sausage and saffron butter sauce; and rump of English lamb, creamed white beans, Jerusalem artichokes, confit garlic wilted baby spinach and truffled herb jus. Among the desserts consider warm lemon polenta cake, fresh orange sorbet, orange syrup and candied zest; or caramelised banana tart Tatin, star anise ice-cream and caraway biscuit. Or you could always have just an interesting sandwich, served with skinny fries and salad. There is a stylish outdoor patio for alfresco dining in warmer weather.

Open all week noon-mdnt Closed: 25 Dec **Bar Meals** L served Mon-Fri 12-2, Sat-Sun 12-9 D served Mon-Fri 6-10, Sat-Sun 12-9 Av main course £7.50 **Restaurant** L served Sun 12-3 D served Mon-Sat 7-9.30 Av 3 course à la carte fr £25 ⊕ FREE HOUSE ◀ Woodforde's Wherry, Straw Dog. ♛ 9
Facilities Children's menu Garden

ORWICH continued

Ribs of Beef ♀

4 Wensum St NR3 1HY
☎ 01603 619517 📄 01603 625446
-mail: roger@cawdron.co.uk
ir: From Tombland (in front of cathedral) turn left at
Maids Head Hotel. Pub 200yds on right on bridge

nce used by the Norfolk wherry skippers, this welcoming
iverside pub is still popular among boat owners cruising
he Broads. Its structure incorporates remnants of the
riginal 14th-century building, which was destroyed in
he Great Fire in 1507. The pub is famous for its range of
ask ales, excellent wines and traditional English food
sing locally sourced produce. The menu offers a wide
ange of sandwiches, burgers and jacket potatoes, while
arger appetites should be satisfied with dishes such as
dnams' braised brisket of beef or vegetarian lasagne.

Open all day all wk 11-11 (Fri-Sat 11am-1am) Bar
Meals L served Mon-Fri 12-2.30, Sat-Sun 12-5 Av main
ourse £5.95 ⊕ FREE HOUSE ◀ Woodforde's Wherry,
dnams Bitter, Adnams Broadside, Marston's Pedigree,
lgoods Mild. ♀8 Facilities Children's menu Family room

REEPHAM   Map 13 TG12

The Old Brewery House Hotel ★★ HL

Market Place NR10 4JJ
☎ 01603 870881 📄 01603 870969
ir: Off A1067 (Norwich to Fakenham road), B1145
igned Aylsham

grand staircase, highly polished floors and wooden
anelling characterise this fine hotel, originally built as a
rivate residence in 1729. It became a hotel in the
970s, retaining many of its Georgian features. Alongside
he real ales and fine wines, there's a bar menu of freshly
roduced dishes.

pen all wk ⊕ FREE HOUSE ◀ IPA, Greene King Abbot Ale
x Old Speckled Hen. Facilities Dogs allowed Garden
arking Rooms 23

RINGSTEAD   Map 12 TF74

PICK OF THE PUBS

The Gin Trap Inn ★★★★ INN ◉ ♀

See Pick of the Pubs on page 324

SALTHOUSE   Map 13 TG04

The Dun Cow ♀

Coast Rd NR25 7XG ☎ 01263 740467
dir: On A149 (coast road). 3m E of Blakeney, 6m W of
Sheringham

Overlooking some of the country's finest freshwater
marshes, the front garden of this attractive pub is
inevitably popular with birdwatchers and walkers. The
bar area was formerly a blacksmith's forge, and many
original 17th-century beams have been retained.
Children are welcome, but there's also a walled rear
garden reserved for adults. The menu includes snacks,
pub staples like burgers and jacket potatoes, and main
courses like gammon steak, pasta and meatballs, plaice
and chips, and lasagne.

Open all wk ⊕ PUBMASTER ◀ Greene King IPA & Abbot
Ale, Adnams Broadside. ♀6 Facilities Family room Dogs
allowed Garden Parking

SNETTISHAM   Map 12 TF63

PICK OF THE PUBS

The Rose & Crown ♀

Old Church Rd PE31 7LX
☎ 01485 541382 📄 01485 543172
e-mail: info@roseandcrownsnettisham.co.uk
dir: 10m N from King's Lynn on A149 signed
Hunstanton. Inn in village centre between market
square & church

With its rose-covered façade, the 14th-century
whitewashed Rose & Crown is everything you'd expect
from a North Norfolk village inn - twisting passages
and hidden corners, low ceilings and old beams,
uneven pamment floors, log fires, excellent beers and
an informal atmosphere. The pretty walled garden was
once the village bowling-green. Each of the three
convivial bars has its own character (and characters!).
The single menu allies traditional pub favourites with
more exotic dishes, all prepared to a high standard and
using, wherever possible, locally supplied produce.
Beef, for example, comes from cattle that grazed the
nearby salt marshes; fishermen still in their waders
deliver Brancaster mussels and Thornham oysters; and
strawberries and asparagus are grown all around.
Typical dishes include chicken bhuna; braised pork
belly; Thai-style red snapper; and aubergine and lentil
moussaka.

Open all day all wk Bar Meals L served Mon-Fri 12-2,
Sat-Sun 12-2.30 booking required D served Sun-Thu
6-9, Fri-Sat 6-9.30 booking required Av main course
£12 Restaurant L served Mon-Fri 12-2, Sat-Sun
12-2.30 booking required D served Sun-Thu 6-9, Fri-
Sat 6-9.30 booking required Av 3 course à la carte fr
£18 ⊕ FREE HOUSE ◀ Adnams Bitter & Broadside,
Interbrew Bass, Fuller's London Pride, Greene King
IPA. ♀20 Facilities Play area Family room Dogs
allowed Garden Parking

STOKE HOLY CROSS   Map 13 TG20

PICK OF THE PUBS

The Wildebeest Arms ◉◉ ♀

See Pick of the Pubs on page 325

STOW BARDOLPH   Map 12 TF60

PICK OF THE PUBS

The Hare Arms ♀

PE34 3HT ☎ 01366 382229 📄 01366 385522
e-mail: trishmc@harearms222.wanadoo.co.uk
dir: From King's Lynn take A10 to Downham Market.
After 9m village signed on left

Trish and David McManus have been licensees at this
attractive ivy-clad pub for over 30 years. The pub was
built during the Napoleonic wars and takes its name
from the surrounding estate, ancestral home of the
Hare family since 1553. The Hare has preserved its
appeal and become deservedly popular. The L-shaped
bar and adjoining conservatory are packed with
decades-worth of fascinating bygones; the cat warms
itself by the fire and peacocks wander around outside.
An extensive menu of regular pub food is supplemented
by daily specials, including the award-winning steak
and peppercorn pie, and fish dishes like whole sea
bream with lemon and lime butter. The silver service
restaurant offers an à la carte menu Monday to
Saturday evening with a range of steaks, vegetarian
options and dishes such as slow-cooked lamb shank;
Gressingham duck in caramelised orange sauce, and
monkfish medallions with red pepper risotto.

Open all wk 11-2.30 6-11 (Sun noon-10.30) Closed:
25-26 Dec Bar Meals L served Mon-Sat 12-2, Sun
12-10 D served Mon-Sat 6.30-10, Sun 12-10 Av main
course £10 Restaurant D served Mon-Sat 7-9 booking
required Av 3 course à la carte fr £27 ⊕ GREENE
KING ◀ Greene King Abbot Ale, IPA & Old Speckled
Hen, guest ale. ♀7 Facilities Children's menu Play
area Family room Garden Parking

PICK OF THE PUBS

The Gin Trap Inn ★★★★ INN ✿ ♀

RINGSTEAD   Map 12 TF74

6 High St PE36 5JU ☎ **01485 525264**
e-mail: thegintrap@hotmail.co.uk
web: www.gintrapinn.co.uk
dir: *A149 from King's Lynn towards
Hunstanton. In 15m turn right at Heacham
for Ringstead*

The 17th-century, white-painted pub
stands in sleepy Ringstead on the
famous Peddars Way, just a few miles
inland from Hunstanton and the bird-
rich marshes of the North Norfolk coast.
From the early 70s until a re-fit just a
few years ago, the pub was festooned
with old gin traps and farm implements
(hence the name). A few gin traps
remain over the front door and
incorporated into light fittings in the oak
beamed-bar area. The pub has a relaxed
and friendly atmosphere with a blazing
log burner warming the bar throughout

the winter, a cosy dining room and
modern conservatory, and a pretty
garden for summer alfresco drinking
and dining. Walkers pop in for drinks
and a meal to fortify them on their way,
and dogs are very welcome - landlords
Steve Knowles and Cindy Cook have two
Great Danes. Food is taken very
seriously, and the snacks board
includes local mussels in season and a
selection of hand-cut sandwiches
including some based on speciality
breads, such as ciabatta and focaccia.
The menu is available throughout the
pub and makes good use of local
seasonal produce, from organic meats
reared at Courtyard Farm in the village,
and mussels and oyster delivered daily
in season from nearby Thornham.
Typically, start with six Thornham
oysters, served on ice with shallot and
red wine vinegar dressing, or chicken,
apricot and sage terrine with home-
made piccalilli and home-baked bread,
then move on to mustard-glazed ham
with free-range eggs and bubble-and-
squeak; dolcelatte and potato ravioli
with fresh sage and white truffle oil; or
confit Courtyard Farm organic
saddleback pork belly with creamed
leeks and wholegrain mustard velouté.

Desserts range from crème caramel with
poached fruits and mixed berries to
warm chocolate pudding with home-
made vanilla ice cream. There are three
individually appointed bedrooms
available.

Open 11.30am-mdnt (11.30-2.30 6-11
in winter) **Bar Meals** L served Mon-Fri
12-2, Sat-Sun 12-2.30 D served Sun-
Thu 6-9, Fri-Sat 6-9.30 Av main course
£10.50 **Restaurant** L served Mon-Fri
12-2, Sat-Sun 12-2.30 D served Sun-
Thu 6-9, Fri-Sat 6-9.30 Av 3 course à la
carte fr £20 ⊕ FREE HOUSE ◄ Adnams
Best, Woodforde's Wherry, guest
ales ♂ Aspall. ♀ 8 **Facilities** Children's
menu Dogs allowed Garden Parking
Rooms 3

PICK OF THE PUBS

The Wildebeest Arms ❀❀ ☿

STOKE HOLY CROSS Map 13 TG20

82-86 Norwich Rd NR14 8QJ
☎ 01508 492497 📄 01508 494946
e-mail: wildebeest@animalinns.co.uk
web: www.thewildebeest.co.uk
dir: *From A47 take A140, left to Dunston. At T-junct left, Wildebeest Arms on right*

Worth the short drive south of Norwich, this charming village local has been tastefully modernised, taking on a modern rustic chic look. Thick, chunky wooden tables, wooden floors and oak beams, vases of fresh lilies, potted plants, crackling log fires and yellow rag-washed walls create a good first impression. What is striking is the quirky collection of African tribal art, which adds a touch of exoticism, with colourful masks, primitive instruments, large carved hippos and a giraffe, and various spears and bold rugs. Although the emphasis has been placed firmly on delivering great food, drawing discerning Norwich diners, all are welcome to pop in for a pint of Adnams and a decent glass of wine (14 are available by the glass). The kitchen takes a modern approach – underpinned by a classical French theme – on the appealing carte and lunch and dinner menu du jour offers. From the latter, kick off with leek and potato soup with truffle oil and chives, or chicken liver and foie gras parfait with celeriac remoulade, and follow with honey-glazed confit duck leg with braised Puy lentils, or roast butternut squash and sage risotto with rocket salad. Pudding choice may include baked figs with mascarpone and port syrup, and vanilla pannacotta with apple purée and apple sorbet. Alternatively, look to the carte for starters of sautéed Dedham Vale lamb fillet or pan-fried scallops, and main dishes like braised shin of beef with oxtail ravioli, or pan-fried sea bass. Puddings may include rhubarb and vanilla mousse or vanilla and cardamom crème brûlée. The perfect retreat from the hustle and bustle of Norwich.

Open all week Closed: 25-26 Dec
🍺 FREE HOUSE ◀ Adnams. ☿ 14
Facilities Garden Parking

SWANTON MORLEY   Map 13 TG01

Darbys Freehouse

1&2 Elsing Rd NR20 4NY
☎ 01362 637647   📄 01362 637928
e-mail: louisedarby@hotmail.co.uk
dir: *From A47 (Norwich to King's Lynn) take B1147 to Dereham*

Built in the 1700s as a large country house, then divided into cottages in the late 19th century. In 1987, after the village's last traditional pub closed, it was converted into the pub you see today, while retaining its old beams and inglenooks. Traditional pub food includes steak and mushroom pudding, braised lamb shank, chargrilled pork loin, scampi, beer-battered haddock, steaks, curries and a vegetarian selection. Children have their own menu and a play area.

Open all wk 11.30-3 6-11 (Sat 11.30-11, Sun 12-10.30). Food served all day Sat-Sun ⊕ FREE HOUSE ◀ Woodforde's Wherry, Adnams Broadside & Best, 2 guest ales. **Facilities** Children's menu Play area Family room Dogs allowed Garden Parking

THOMPSON   Map 13 TL99

PICK OF THE PUBS

Chequers Inn ▲ ★★★★ INN ☗

See Pick of the Pubs on opposite page

THORNHAM   Map 12 TF74

PICK OF THE PUBS

Lifeboat Inn ★★ HL ☺ ☗

Ship Ln PE36 6LT ☎ 01485 512236   📄 01485 512323
e-mail: reception@lifeboatinn.co.uk
dir: *A149 from Hunstanton for approx 6m. 1st left after Thornham sign*

The Lifeboat is a 16th-century inn overlooking Thornham Harbour and the salt marshes. Despite being extended, its original character has been retained. Inside, the warm glow of paraffin lamps enhances the welcoming atmosphere, while the adjoining conservatory is renowned for its ancient vine and adjacent walled patio garden. The best available fish and game feature on the frequently changing menus, in the form of salmon and dill fishcakes with a sun dried tomato and pesto sauce, or Brancaster mussels

steamed in Chardonnay with lemon grass, ginger and cream. For a satisfying main course, try lightly bread-crumbed lamb cutlets with ratatouille and a minted garlic gravy, or local partridge casserole with Guinness and mushrooms. Nearby is Thornham Beach, Blakeney, Cley, Sandringham and Nelson's birthplace at Burnham Thorpe.

Open all wk **Bar Meals** food served all day ⊕ FREE HOUSE ◀ Adnams, Woodforde's Wherry, Greene King IPA & Abbot Ale, guest ales. ☗ 10 **Facilities** Children's menu Play area Family room Dogs allowed Garden Parking **Rooms** 13

PICK OF THE PUBS

The Orange Tree ☗

High St PE36 6LY ☎ 01485 512213   📄 01485 512424
e-mail: email@theorangetreethornham.co.uk

This refurbished country pub stands by the ancient Peddar's Way, opposite the church in one of North Norfolk's lovely coastal villages. Two large beer gardens and a children's play area add to the Orange Tree's family appeal; roast Sunday lunch is also popular, served from midday through to 6pm. The bar and restaurant are very stylish, but the building still has that special feel of a traditional rural pub. Lunchtime snacks start with a range of ciabattas, ploughman's, jacket potatoes and salads, and light lunches include baked oyster rarebit grilled with cheese, Guinness, Parma ham and Worcester sauce. Naturally the menu incorporates the best local seafood, which appears on the specials board as pan-fried hake with parsley mash, mussel and crayfish beurre blanc; and seared fillet of sea bass with gremolata potatoes and celeriac purée. Meats supplied by the butcher in Dersingham go into plates of Cumberland sausages served with champ mash and red onion; and traditional lasagne.

Open all wk ⊕ PUNCH TAVERNS ◀ Greene King IPA, Adnams Bitter, Guinness. ☗ 10 **Facilities** Play area Dogs allowed Garden Parking

TITCHWELL   Map 13 TF74

PICK OF THE PUBS

Titchwell Manor Hotel ★★★ HL ☺☺

PE31 8BB ☎ 01485 210221   📄 01485 210104
e-mail: margaret@titchwellmanor.com
dir: *A149 between Brancaster & Thornham*

In a stunning location on Norfolk's north coast and run by the Snaith family for 20 years, this Victorian manor has been tastefully updated with a light, modern decor. Expect to find a contemporary-styled lounge, an informal bar with stripped wooden floors, and a light and airy conservatory restaurant. From its pretty walled garden the sea views are glorious, and its proximity lends a major influence to the menus. The cooking is skilled and interesting, using local and seasonal ingredients to produce imaginative and well-presented

dishes. Lunch options include sandwiches, starters such as Brancaster oysters, and light cooked meals of pan-fried lemon sole with new potatoes, or deep-fried haddock with minted mushy peas. Evening additions may take in pollack or halibut, and Holkham venison with wild garlic and thyme jus. Families are welcome and stylish rooms are uncluttered, warmly decorated and split between the inn and a converted barn set around a courtyard.

Open all wk **Bar Meals** food served all day **Restaurant** food served all day ⊕ FREE HOUSE ◀ Greene King IPA. **Facilities** Dogs allowed Garden Parking **Rooms** 26

WARHAM ALL SAINTS   Map 13 TF94

PICK OF THE PUBS

Three Horseshoes

NR23 1NL ☎ 01328 710547
dir: *From Wells A149 to Cromer, then right onto B1105 to Warham*

This gem of a pub first opened its doors in 1725. Inside you'll find a gas-lit main bar, stone floors, scrubbed wooden tables and a grandfather clock ticking in the corner. Real ales are served directly from the cask through a hole in the bar wall, and the largely original interior includes a curious green and red dial in the ceiling - a rare example of Norfolk twister, an ancient pub game. Vintage posters, clay pipes, photographs and memorabilia adorn the walls, while down a step are old one-arm bandits. The pub is well known for its home cooking, with local game and shellfish; steak, kidney and Wherry bitter pie; Norfolk chicken and leek suet pudding; and woodman's pie (mushrooms and nuts in red wine sauce). Home-made puddings, such as spotted dick and syrup sponge, are listed over the fire in the main bar.

Open all wk **Bar Meals** L served all wk 12-1.45 D served all wk 6-8.30 Av main course £7.80 ⊕ FREE HOUSE ◀ Greene King IPA, Woodforde's Wherry. **Facilities** Children's menu Family room Dogs allowed Garden Parking **Notes** ☺

WELLS-NEXT-THE-SEA   Map 13 TF94

Carpenter's Arms ☗

High St, Wighton NR23 1PF ☎ 01328 820752

Gareth and Rebecca Williams took over the pub in April 2007 after six months' closure, and Gareth's cooking is proving very popular. The menu offers fresh, locally sourced classic British food (Adnams beer battered haddock with hand cut chips and mushy peas; home-made steak and kidney pudding; pan-fried calves' liver and bacon with mustard mash). The pub is family and pet friendly with quirky decor and a wood fire inside and large beer garden outside.

Closed: Mon lunch ⊕ FREE HOUSE ◀ Adnams, Woodforde's Wherry, Norfolk Honey Ale. ☗ 7 **Facilities** Dogs allowed Garden Parking

PICK OF THE PUBS

Chequers Inn A ★★★★ INN ♀

THOMPSON   Map 13 TL99

Griston Rd IP24 1PX
☎ 01953 483360   📄 01953 488092
e-mail:
richard@chequers_inn.wanadoo.co.uk
web: www.thompsonchequers.co.uk
dir: *Between Watton & Thetford off A1075*

This 17th-century free house, with its low-slung thatched roof, hides among the trees on the edge of Thompson village in the heart of Breckland. Like its namesakes elsewhere, it takes its name from a chequered cloth, which was probably used to explain wages and rents to not very numerate medieval agricultural workers. Our Chancellor of the Exchequer owes his title to this simple teaching aid. Manor courts, dealing with rents, lettings of land, and small crimes, were held at the inn in the 18th century, and at one stage it became a doctor's surgery. Original features inside include exposed beams and timbers, while old farming memorabilia hangs from the walls. Food may be chosen from the bar menu, carte or daily specials board, and there's a huge choice: snacks of jacket potatoes, baguettes and ploughman's; starters of devilled whitebait; locally smoked salmon and prawns; and deep-fried brie; lunchtime main courses of grilled breast of chicken with Cajun spices; beef or vegetable lasagne; and omelettes. In the evening there are local roast half duckling; beef Stroganoff; pan-roasted pork fillet; and grilled steaks, while baked field mushrooms with roasted vegetables, and Camembert cheese pancake are among the vegetarian possibilities. Finally, desserts may include home-made apple tart, treacle tart, or chocolate profiteroles. Nearby is the eight-mile Great Eastern Pingo Trail that navigates a succession of glacially formed swampy depressions in the ground. Dogs are welcome in the large rear garden, where there are also picnic tables and children's play equipment, and the views extend over open land and woods.

Open 11.30-3 6.30-11 **Meals** L served 12-2 D served 6.30-9 🍺 FREE HOUSE
🍺 Fuller's London Pride, Adnams Best, Wolf Best, Greene King IPA, Woodforde's Wherry Best Bitter. ♀ 7 **Facilities** Play area Dogs allowed Garden Parking

PICK OF THE PUBS

Wiveton Bell 🍷

WIVETON   Map 13 TG04

Blakeney Rd NR25 7TL
☎ **01263 740101**
e-mail: enquiries@wivetonbell.co.uk
web: www.wivetonbell.com
dir: *1m from Blakeney. Wiveton Rd off A149*

The Bell overlooks Wiveton's green and church, just a mile from glorious, bird-rich salt marshes and bustling Blakeney. The bucolic setting draws discerning pub-goers away from the thronging coast road - take the quiet back road beside Blakeney church to locate this thriving dining pub. A stunning, rustic-chic makeover has transformed the interior of the charming whitewashed inn. Think, stripped beams, chunky tables, oak planked floors, earthy, heritage colours, and bold, contemporary oil paintings (for sale) by local artists lining the walls of the cosy bar and the airy conservatory restaurant. Despite the emphasis on dining, the bar forms the focal point and attracts a good local drinking crowd, with the tables close to the inglenook fireplace remaining free of glasses and cutlery. To avoid a crush at the bar on busy summer days, a serving hatch delivers pints of Woodforde's Wherry and Yetmans Ale (brewed along the road) to drinkers enjoying the secluded rear garden. Chef Nick Anderson's extensive seasonal menu is bolstered by adventurous specials that make sound use of local fish and game, such as pan-fried scallops with cauliflower purée and pea cream, and roast partridge with red cabbage and red wine jus. More familiar offerings take in light lunches of wild mushroom risotto and a classic fisherman's pie, alongside local game and foie gras terrine, good salads, bangers and sage mash, huge bowls of local Morston mussels cooked in white wine, shallots and cream, and rib-eye steak with all the trimmings and béarnaise sauce. Leave room for apricot and chocolate St Emilion or rhubarb fool. There are baskets of cushions by the door for alfresco drinkers and diners to savour the food and church views from front benches in comfort, and wind-up torches and umbrellas in the bus shelter on the green to aid your stroll to the pub.

Open all week **Bar Meals** L served all week 12-2.15 D served all week 6-9 **Restaurant** L served all week 12-2.15 D served all week 6-9 ⊕ FREE HOUSE ◀ Woodforde's Wherry, Adnams Broadside, Yetmans ♂ Stowford Press. 🍷 18 **Facilities** Dogs allowed Garden Parking

WELLS-NEXT-THE-SEA *continued*

PICK OF THE PUBS

The Crown ⬗

The Buttlands NR23 1EX
☎ 01328 710209 📠 01328 711432
e-mail: reception@thecrownhotelwells.co.uk
dir: *10m from Fakenham on B1105*

Striking contemporary decor and furnishings blend effortlessly with the old-world charm of this 17th-century former coaching inn. The hotel overlooks a tree-lined green near the heart of the town, and has been refurbished to create a traditional atmosphere of uncluttered comfort. Beneath the bar's ancient beams, East Anglian ales and Aspall's Suffolk cyder accompany an informal menu. Lunchtime sandwiches might include smoked salmon, cream cheese and cucumber, or why not try the Crown black slate – a sampler of European and Asian appetizers served on a slate tile, whilst main course dishes such as seared liver and bacon with roast root vegetables, or butternut squash, Parmesan and sage risotto are also available in the evening. Meanwhile, dinner in the restaurant might begin with seared pigeon breast, mushroom and crouton salad, before a main course of baked salmon with tiger prawn, tomato and lemongrass brochette. Meals are also served in the new, warm and cheerful Orangery or outside with its great views.

Open all wk **Bar Meals** L served all wk 12-2.30 D served all wk 6.30-9.30 **Restaurant** D served all wk 7-9 booking required Av 3 course à la carte fr £34.95 ⬢ FREE HOUSE ◀ Adnams Bitter, Woodforde's Wherry, guest ale ♂ Aspall. ♒ 14 **Facilities** Children's menu Dogs allowed Garden Parking

---

WEST BECKHAM   Map 13 TG13

The Wheatsheaf ⬗

Manor Farm, Church Rd NR25 6NX ☎ 01263 822110
e-mail: danielclarejoe@tiscali.co.uk
dir: *2m inland from Sheringham on A148, turn opp Sheringham Park*

Former manor house converted to a pub over 20 years ago that retains many original features. Sample one of the real ales from Woodforde's Brewery and relax in the large garden. The extensive menu caters for all appetites, large or small, and may feature saddle of lamb stuffed with spinach and stilton with a brandy gravy, pork and oregano meatballs in a tomato sauce on tagliatelle with garlic bread, or chick pea, pepper and pineapple curry served with home-made chapattis.

Open all wk ⬢ FREE HOUSE ◀ Woodforde's Wherry Best Bitter, Nelson's Revenge, Norfolk Nog, Greene King IPA, guest ales. ♒ 7 **Facilities** Play area Family room Dogs allowed Garden Parking

---

WINTERTON-ON-SEA   Map 13 TG41

Fishermans Return ⬗

The Lane NR29 4BN ☎ 01493 393305
e-mail: fishermansreturn@yahoo.co.uk
web: www.fishermans-return.com
dir: *8m N of Great Yarmouth on B1159*

Long beaches and National Trust land are within 300 metres of this 350-year-old brick and flint pub – and it's dog-friendly too, making it an ideal spot to finish a walk. Behind the bar are Woodforde's Wherry and Adnams, with seasonal guests from Mauldons and Blackfriars. Menus include popular favourites, from toasted sandwiches to cottage pie. But look to the daily changing blackboard for fish and seafood specials, when freshly caught sea bass and mackerel may be on offer.

Open all wk **Bar Meals** L served all wk 12-2.30 D served all wk 6-9 Av main course £8 **Restaurant** L served all wk 12-2.30 D served all wk 6-9 ⬢ FREE HOUSE ◀ Woodforde's Wherry, Adnams Bitter & Broadside, John Smith's ♂ Westons Stowford Press, Old Rosie Scrumpy. ♒ 10 **Facilities** Children's menu Play area Family room Dogs allowed Garden Parking

---

WIVETON   Map 13 TG04

PICK OF THE PUBS

Wiveton Bell ⬗

See Pick of the Pubs on opposite page

WOODBASTWICK   Map 13 TG31

The Fur & Feather Inn ⬗

Slad Ln NR13 6HQ ☎ 01603 720003 📠 01603 722266
dir: *From A1151 (Norwich to Wroxham road), follow brown signs for Woodforde's Brewery. Pub next to Brewery*

This idyllic country pub is ideal for real ale lovers: Woodforde's Brewery is next door, and of course the ales are offered here, straight from the cask. The pub was originally two farm cottages, and now boasts three cosy bar areas and a smart restaurant where you can enjoy steak and ale pie, home baked ham, and goats' cheese, pepper and tomato lasagne, for example, followed by pannacotta and Norfolk honey or a baked vanilla cheesecake maybe.

Open all wk ⬢ WOODFORDE'S ◀ Woodforde's Wherry, Sundew, Norfolk Nog, Nelsons Revenge, Adnam's Reserve. ♒ 10 **Facilities** Garden Parking

---

NORTHAMPTONSHIRE

ASHBY ST LEDGERS   Map 11 SP56

The Olde Coach House Inn

CV23 8UN ☎ 01788 890349 📠 01788 891922
dir: *M1 junct 18 follow A361/Daventry signs. Village on left*

A late 19th-century farmhouse and outbuildings, skilfully converted into a pub with dining areas and meeting rooms, set in a village that dates way back to the Domesday Book of 1086. The village was home to Robert Catesby, one of the Gunpowder plotters. Beer is taken seriously here, with up to eight regularly changing real ales and legendary beer festivals. The pub also serves fresh, high quality food in comfortable surroundings, and holds summer barbecues.

Open all wk ⬢ FREE HOUSE ◀ Everards Original, Everards Tiger, Marstons Pedigree, guest ale. **Facilities** Play area Family room Garden Parking

---

ASHTON   Map 11 SP74

The Old Crown ⬗

1 Stoke Rd NN7 2JN ☎ 01604 862268
dir: *M1 junct 15. 1m from A508 from Roade*

Attractive 17th-century inn with traditional beamed interior and walls decorated with many prints and mirrors. Outside there are two attractively planted gardens for alfresco dining. Snacks such as soups, sandwiches and salads are available, along with main courses like seared fennel-crusted tuna on Mediterranean couscous; charred aubergine and coconut curry; five-herb roasted chicken breast with potato and celeriac mash; and steamed steak, mushroom, bacon, stilton and herb suet pudding.

Open all wk ◀ Wells, Bombardier, Red Stripe, guest ale. ♒ 7 **Facilities** Garden Parking

---

BADBY   Map 11 SP55

The Windmill Inn

Main St NN11 3AN ☎ 01327 702363 📠 01327 311521
e-mail: info@windmillinn-badby.com
dir: *M1 junct 16 take A45 to Daventry then A361 S. Village in 2m*

A traditional thatched pub dating back to the 17th century, with beamed and flagstone bars and a friendly, relaxed atmosphere. Theme nights are very popular, including a Winter Sportsmen's dinner, though the cask-conditioned ales and home-cooked food are a draw at any time. Close by are Blenheim Palace and Warwick Castle and nearby is the only thatched youth hostel in England and Wales.

Open all wk ⬢ FREE HOUSE ◀ Bass, Flowers OB, Boddingtons, Timothy Taylor Landlord. **Facilities** Dogs allowed Garden Parking

BULWICK
Map 11 SP99

PICK OF THE PUBS

The Queen's Head ♛

See Pick of the Pubs on opposite page

CHACOMBE
Map 11 SP44

PICK OF THE PUBS

George and Dragon

Silver St OX17 2JR
☎ 01295 711500 📄 01295 710516
e-mail: georgeanddragonchacombe@googlemail.com
dir: *From M40 junct 11 take A361 (Daventry road).*
Chacombe 1st right

An attractive, honey-stoned, 16th-century pub tucked away beside the church in a pretty village protected by Conservation Area status. There's a welcoming feel to the three comfortable bars, where the traditional atmosphere is upheld by an abundance of low beams, simple wooden chairs and settles, log fires (which really are lit), and warm terracotta decor. The blackboards list an interesting selection of food, from sandwiches and baked butternut squash or jacket potatoes (filled with flaked tuna and lemon mayonnaise, prawns with a lime dressing), to favourites and specials: you'll find fish pie at lunchtime, along with fish and chips; pork and apple burgers; root vegetable bake; smoked duck salad; and warm bacon and green leaf salad. In the evening the menu lists starters like goats' cheese and caramelised pears; with such main dishes as smoked salmon and avocado salad; steak and Everard Tiger beer pie; and wild mushroom risotto.

Open all day all wk noon–11 **Bar Meals** served Mon-Thu 12-8.30, Fri-Sat 12-9.30, Sun 12-7 food served all day **Restaurant** served Mon-Thu 12-8.30, Fri-Sat 12-9.30, Sun 12-7 food served all day ⊕ EVERARDS ◀ Everards Tiger, Everards Beacon, Guest ales. **Facilities** Garden Parking

CLIPSTON
Map 11 SP78

The Bulls Head ♛

Harborough Rd LE16 9RT
☎ 01858 525268 📄 01858 525268
e-mail: clipstonhead1@aol.co.uk
web: http://thebullshead.awardspace.com/index.htm
dir: *On B4036 S of Market Harborough*

American airmen once pushed coins between the beams as a good luck charm before bombing raids, and the trend continues with foreign paper money pinned all over the inn. In addition to its good choice of real ales, the pub

has an amazing collection of over 500 whiskies. The menu includes shark steaks, whole sea bass, hot toddy duck, and steak pie.

The Bulls Head

Open all wk 11.30am-2.30 6-mdnt (Fri-Sat 11.30-2 Sun noon-mdnt) **Bar Meals** L served Mon-Fri 11.30-2.30, Sat 11.30-9.30, Sun 12-4 D served Mon-Fri 6-9, Sat 11.30-9.30, Sun 6-9 ⊕ FREE HOUSE ◀ Tiger, Beacon, guest & seasonal ales. ♛ 14 **Facilities** Dogs allowed Garden Parking

COLLYWESTON
Map 11 SK90

PICK OF THE PUBS

The Collyweston
Slater ★★★★ INN ◉◉ ♛

See Pick of the Pubs on page 332

CRICK
Map 11 SP57

The Red Lion Inn

52 Main Rd NN6 7TX
☎ 01788 822342 📄 01788 822342
e-mail: ptm180@tiscali.co.uk
dir: *From M1 junct 18, 0.75m E on A428, follows signs for Crick from new rdbt*

A thatched, stone-built coaching inn dating from the 17th century, with beams and open fires. The Marks family, landlords here for over 25 years, give their regulars and visitors exactly what they want - a friendly atmosphere, real ales and traditional food. The daily home-made steak pie is a lunchtime favourite, while fillet and sirloin steaks are a speciality in the evening. Fish eaters will find trout, stuffed lemon sole, salmon and seafood platter.

Open all wk 11-2.30 6.15-11 (Sun 12-3 7-11) **Bar Meals** L served all wk 12-2 D served Mon-Sat 6.30-9 Av main course £8.75 ⊕ WELLINGTON PUB COMPANY ◀ Wells Bombardier, Greene King Old Speckled Hen, Theakston Best Bitter, guest ale. **Facilities** Dogs allowed Garden Parking

FARTHINGSTONE
Map 11 SP65

PICK OF THE PUBS

The Kings Arms

Main St NN12 8EZ
☎ 01327 361604 📄 01327 361604
e-mail: paul@kingsarms.fsbusiness.co.uk
dir: *M1 junct 16, A45 towards Daventry. At Weedon take A5 towards Towcester. Right signed Farthingstone*

Tucked away in perfect walking country near Canons Ashby (a National Trust property), this 18th-century Grade II listed inn is every inch the traditional country pub - albeit it a highly distinctive one. On fine days many come for the beautiful garden; in colder weather they warm themselves by the real fires, but there is always a warm welcome. The pub has a retail business specialising in Cornish fish, which is reflected in the short menu, available at weekend lunchtimes. British cheese and Loch Fyne fish platters are also available.

Open 7-11.30 (Sat-Sun 12-3.30 7-11.30) Closed: Mon **Bar Meals** L served Sat-Sun 12-2 Av main course £8.75 ⊕ FREE HOUSE ◀ Thwaites Original, Adnams, Brakspear Bitter, Young's Bitter, Hoggleys Northamptonshire Bitter Ở Westons Old Rosie Scrumpy. **Facilities** Children's menu Family room Dogs allowed Garden Parking **Notes** ☺

FOTHERINGHAY
Map 12 TL09

PICK OF THE PUBS

The Falcon Inn ◉ ♛

PE8 5HZ ☎ 01832 226254 📄 01832 226046
e-mail: info@thefalcon-inn.co.uk
dir: *N of A605 between Peterborough & Oundle*

King Richard III was born in Fotheringhay in 1452; 115 hundred years later the population balance was restored when Mary Queen of Scots was beheaded here. The attractive 18th-century, stone-built Falcon, in gardens redesigned by award-winning landscape architect, Bunny Guinness, overlooks the outstanding church, which looks truly magical at night when floodlit. It's a real local, with a tap bar regularly used by the real ale-fuelled village darts team. The menus, in both the bar and charming conservatory restaurant, rely extensively on locally sourced ingredients, offering pan-fried venison with parsnip mash; roast fillet of salmon with cannellini beans; and fricassée of mushrooms, leeks, and tagliatelle. Affogato (vanilla ice cream with espresso) is definitely worth trying for dessert, or stick with Bakewell tart, or some local cheeses.

Open all day all wk noon-11 **Bar Meals** L served Mon-Sat 12-2.15, Sun 12-3 D served Mon-Sat 6.15-9.15, Sun 6.15-8.30 **Restaurant** L served Mon-Sat 12-2.15, Sun 12-3 D served Mon-Sat 6.15-9.15, Sun 6.15-8.30 ⊕ FREE HOUSE ◀ Greene King IPA, Barnwell Bitter, Fools Nook, Guest ales Ở Westons Organic Vintage. ♛ 15 **Facilities** Dogs allowed Garden Parking

PICK OF THE PUBS

The Queen's Head ▾

BULWICK
Map 11 SP99

Main St NN17 3DY ☎ 01780 450272
e-mail: queenshead-bulwick@tiscali.co.uk
dir: *Just off A43, between Corby & Stamford*

Parts of this quintessential English free house date back to 1400, and the building is thought to have been a pub since the 17th century. The name comes from the Portuguese wife of Charles II, Katherine of Braganza, who was well known for her very elaborate hair-styles. Overlooking the village church, the pub is a warren of small rooms with exposed wooden beams, four open fireplaces and flagstone floors. Relax by the fire or on the patio with a pint of Spitfire or local Rockingham Ale, and some hearty pub food. Local shoots supply seasonal game such as teal, woodcock and partridge, and the other ingredients often include village-grown fruit and vegetables brought in by customers and friends. Lunchtime brings great sandwich choices and interesting snacks such as smoked Scottish salmon with shaved fennel, rocket, lemon and capers; and baked goat's cheese with garlic and roasted peppers. The evening menu opens with the likes of winter bean and vegetable soup with bread and olive oil; and home-cured salt beef with vine tomato and beetroot relish. Main course options might include slow-cooked Cornish lamb with root vegetables, pearl barley and herb suet dumpling; celeriac and porcini mushroom risotto with sage and gorgonzola; or pan-fried Scottish salmon with Portland crab and potato chowder. Typical desserts include dark chocolate terrine with toasted hazelnuts, caramel sauce and crème fraiche; or warm apple and caramel tart with clotted Devonshire cream. The menu is backed by a comprehensive wine list, whilst ale lovers will find guest ales sourced from microbreweries alongside the regular selection at the bar.

Closed: Mon **Bar Meals** L served Tue-Sun 12-2.30 D served Tue-Sat 6-9.30 **Restaurant** L served Tue-Sun 12-2.30 D served Tue-Sat 6-9.30 Fixed menu price fr £12.50 ⊕ FREE HOUSE ◀ Shepherd Neame, Spitfire, Elland, Rockingham Ales, Newby Wyke, Guest Ales. ▾ 9 **Facilities** Children's menu Dogs allowed Garden Parking

PICK OF THE PUBS

The Collyweston Slater ★★★★ INN ◉◉ 🍷

COLLYWESTON
Map 11 SK90

87-89 Main Rd PE9 3PQ
☎ **01780 444288**
e-mail: info@collywestonslater.co.uk
dir: *4m SW of Stamford, A43. 2m off A1 junct*

A traditional, 17th-century village coaching inn, enlarged several decades ago to incorporate the adjoining terraced houses. Although Collyweston slate is a limestone, the Romans discovered that, like the real McCoy, it also splits along natural cleavage lines and used it for roofing. As well as being used on the pub's roof, it also appears inside, where it offsets the original oak timbering, and helps to give the light, modern interior a convincing rustic look. Head chef Dameon Clarke, who has been running the business since early 2009, has introduced a bar menu that is strong on pies - chicken and tarragon,

corned beef hash, goats' cheese, roasted butternut squash and rosemary, steak and ale - all served with minted pease pudding and roasted sweet potato chips. But if pies aren't for you, there are light meals and sandwiches too. In the AA-Rosetted restaurant, the short, frequently-changing menus make the most of seasonal produce, and are backed by an extensive and well-chosen wine list, with plenty by the glass. Typical starters are goats' cheese parfait with figs, sour pear sorbet and fig jelly; and chicken liver parfait with sour plum chutney and toasted brioche. Seven mains are usually offered, among them, perhaps roast monkfish with ratatouille ravioli, creamed basil, aubergine caviar and red pepper coulis; Grasmere Farm sausages with caramelised onion, champ potatoes and rosemary and thyme juices; and confit of duck with fondant potato, roasted plums, spring cabbage, honey-roasted parsnips and thyme and garlic tortellini. Desserts include lemon tart with raspberry sorbet and fresh raspberries; and baked egg custard with green tea ice cream and raisin compote. Overnight guests have a choice of four rooms and one luxury suite.

Open all week Closed: 25 Dec, 2 Jan
🍺 Tiger, Bitter, Original Bitter, Sunchaser, Beacon. 🍷 8
Facilities Garden Parking **Rooms** 5

GRAFTON REGIS — Map 11 SP74

The White Hart ♀

Northampton Rd NN12 7SR ☎ **01908 542123**
e-mail: alan@pubgraftonregis.co.uk
dir: *M1 junct 15 onto A508 between Northampton & Milton Keynes*

A friendly village with approximately 96 residents is home to the White Hart, a thatched, stone-built property dating from the 16th century. In 1464 Edward IV married Elizabeth Woodville in this historic place. The pub has been owned by the same family for 12 years and Alan, one of the owners, is chef. Menus change frequently according to available produce. There are always at least three home-made soups, specials, fresh fish of the day, and dishes such as mature Welsh fillet steak, or roast chicken with creamy garlic mushroom sauce.

Open 12-2.30 6-11 Closed: Mon **Bar Meals** L served Tue-Sun 12-2 D served Tue-Sun 6-9.30 Av main course £7.10 **Restaurant** L served Tue-Sun 12-2 D served Tue-Sun 6.30-9 Av 3 course à la carte fr £25 ⊕ FREE HOUSE ◄ Greene King, Abbot Ale, IPA. ♀ 14 **Facilities** Garden Parking

GREAT OXENDON — Map 11 SP78

PICK OF THE PUBS

The George Inn ♀

LE16 8NA ☎ **01858 465205** 🖺 **01858 465205**
e-mail: info@thegeorgegreatoxendon.co.uk
dir: *A508 towards Market Harborough*

Parts of this country dining pub are up to 600 years old, and the building reputedly accommodated soldiers after the battle of Naseby. Original beams, a lovely log fire and old photographs lend stacks of charm. Today the George has a county-wide reputation for excellent food and service, but customers are still welcome to call in for a pint of Batemans or Stowford Press cider. Three dining areas comprise the cosy restaurant, a conservatory overlooking award-winning gardens, and a patio. Owner David Dudley and his son Philip offer lunchtime baguettes and 'little dishes' such as flat field mushroom, crispy spinach, roast garlic and Stilton; 'grazing boards' of Italian meats, cheeses and marinated olives; 'old comforts' such as battered cod, chunky chips and mushy peas; and 'big dishes' which comprise steaks with green peppercorn and brandy sauce. The good value Sunday lunch presents the usual roasts, with further options such as pheasant or duck.

Open Mon-Sat 12-3 5.30-11 (Sun 12-3) Closed: 25 Dec, Sun eve **Bar Meals** L served all wk 12-2 D served Mon-Sat 6-9.30 Av main course £12.95 **Restaurant** L served all wk 12-2 D served Mon-Sat 6-9.30 ⊕ FREE HOUSE ◄ Batemans guest ale, Adnams Bitter, Youngs Special, Timothy Taylor Landlord ♨ Stowford Press. ♀ 12 **Facilities** Children's menu Garden Parking

HARRINGTON — Map 11 SP78

PICK OF THE PUBS

The Tollemache Arms ♀

49 High St NN6 9NU ☎ **01536 710469**
e-mail: markandjo@tollemacheharrington.com
dir: *6m from Kettering, off A14 junct 3. Follow signs for Harrington*

A popular retreat from the nearby towns of Northampton, Kettering and Market Harborough, this thatched and whitewashed 16th-century pub stands in the lovely Northamptonshire village of Harrington. Refurbished but retaining its tradional charm, there are open fires in the winter months and panoramic views from the large garden. Food and drink are served all day, every day, from midday. Light bites include sandwiches, ploughman's and omelettes, while main menu dishes combine modern, classic and traditional influences. Start with rich coarse local pâté served with winter fruit chutney and toasted brioche, or black pearl scallops wrapped in oak smoked salmon, gently roasted, with vine tomatoes and a mango, sage and lime dressing. Mains range from a half pound sausage knot set on mustard crushed new potatoes with onion gravy; and pan-seared butter-flied sea bass on a cucumber and mint salsa. Skittles knockout evenings and quizzes are regular events.

Open all day all wk noon-11 (Sun noon-10.30) **Bar Meals** L served all wk 12-9.30 D served all wk 12-9.30 food served all day **Restaurant** L served all wk 12-9.30 D served all wk 12-9.30 food served all day ⊕ CHARLES WELLS ◄ Bombardier, Eagle IPA, Guest ales. ♀ 17 **Facilities** Garden Parking

KETTERING — Map 11 SP87

The Overstone Arms ♀

Stringers Hill, Pytchley NN14 1EU
☎ **01536 790215** 🖺 **01536 791098**
dir: *1m from Kettering, 5m from Wellingborough*

The 18th-century coaching inn is at the heart of the village and has been home to the Pytchley Hunt, which over the years has attracted many royal visitors. Years ago guests would travel up from London, staying here or at Althorp Hall, mainly for the hunting. Despite its rural location, the pub is just a mile from the busy A14. Home-made pies, grilled trout, steaks, lasagne and curry are typical dishes.

Open all wk ⊕ UNIQUE PUB CO LTD ◄ Greene King, Marston's Pedigree, Interbrew Bass, Adnams Bitter, Abbot Ale, Spitfire, IPA, Pedigree. ♀ 8 **Facilities** Garden Parking

NORTHAMPTON — Map 11 SP76

The Fox & Hounds ♀

Main St, Great Brington NN7 4JA
☎ **01604 770651** 🖺 **01604 770164**
e-mail: althorpcoachinn@aol.com
web: www.althorp-coaching-inn.co.uk
dir: *From A428 pass main gates of Althorp House, left before rail bridge. Great Brington 1m*

Flagstone floors, beams and open fires, not to mention a beautiful walled garden, are some of the charms of this 16th-century coaching inn, which stands on the Althorp Estate, ancestral home of the Spencer family. Equally praiseworthy are the numerous guest ales and reputation for quality food. Jacket potatoes and ciabatta sandwiches feature on the snack menu; other meals include chicken stuffed with haloumi cheese, and tom yam tiger prawns.

Open all day all wk 11-11 **Bar Meals** L served Mon-Fri 12-2.30, Sat-Sun 12-3 D served Sun-Thu 6.30-9.30. Fri-Sat 6.30-10 **Restaurant** L served Mon-Fri 12-2.30, Sat-Sun 12-3 D served Sun-Thu 6.30-9.30. Fri-Sat 6.30-10 ⊕ FREE HOUSE ◄ Greene King IPA, Speckled Hen, Fuller's London Pride, Abbot Ale, 5 guest ales. ♀ 8 **Facilities** Dogs allowed Garden Parking

OUNDLE — Map 11 TL08

The Chequered Skipper NEW

Ashton PE8 5LD ☎ **01832 273494**
e-mail: enquiries@chequeredskipper.co.uk
dir: *A605 towards Dundle, at rdbt follow signs to Ashton. 1m turn left into Ashton, pub in village*

At the heart of the Rothschild's glorious model village, all stone and thatch cottages nestling around the village green, the thatched, open-plan pub has a contemporary feel, with stone and oak flooring and an unusual flagstone bar top. Using the best of local produce with suppliers listed on the menu, beer-battered haddock and home-made stone-baked pizzas are available in the bar, while the restaurant menu might include slow braised belly of pork in Aspall's cider with demerara-glazed beetroot. On tap are local Rockingham and Oakham ales - don't miss the annual beer festivals.

Open all wk 11.30-3 6-11 (Sat 11.30-11 Sun 11.45-11) **Bar Meals** L served Mon-Fri 12-2, Sat 12-2.30, Sun 12-3 Av main course £8 **Restaurant** L served Mon-Fri 12-2, Sat 12-2.30, Sun 12-3 Av 3 course à la carte fr £25 ◄ Rockingham ale, Oakham ale **Facilities** Children's menu Dogs allowed Garden Parking

OUNDLE *continued*

The Montagu Arms ☻

Barnwell PE8 5PH ☎ **01832 273726** 📄 **01832 275555**
e-mail: ianmsimmons@aol.com
dir: *Off A605 opposite Oundle slip road*

One of Northamptonshire's oldest inns, the Montagu Arms was originally three cottages dating from 1601, housing the workmen building the nearby manor house. The inn has a large garden, well equipped for children's play, and overlooks the brook and village green of the royal village of Barnwell. An extensive menu serving the bar and restaurant ranges through snacks and sharing platters, and dishes such as Rutland sausages and mash, stuffed chicken, and crispy fish pie.

Open all wk ⊕ FREE HOUSE ◀ Digfield Ales, Adnams Broadside, Hop Back Summer Lightning, Fuller's London Pride, Oakham Ale, JHB. ☻ 14 **Facilities** Play area Garden Parking

SIBBERTOFT Map 11 SP68

PICK OF THE PUBS

The Red Lion ☻

43 Welland Rise LE16 9UD ☎ **01858 880011**
e-mail: andrew@redlionwinepub.co.uk
dir: *From Market Harborough take A4304, through Lubenham, left through Marston Trussell to Sibbertoft*

Wine is the special passion of owner Andrew Banks at this friendly 300-year-old free house. Over 200 bins are included on the ever-growing wine list, with many varieties available by the glass. Near the Naseby battle sites, the pub offers an appealing blend of contemporary and classic decor, with oak beams, leather upholstery and a smartly turned-out dining room. In fine weather, meals are served in the quiet garden, which is a favourite with local walkers and cyclists; there's also an outdoor play area for children. The same monthly-changing menu is served throughout, and features local and seasonal produce wherever possible. Choices might begin with crab and prawn fishcake with lime and sweet chilli dip, whilst typical main course options include pork T-bone with mash and stilton sauce; and roasted vegetables with melting mozzarella. Round off, perhaps, with meringue and mixed berry fool. Regular themed evenings include a weekly curry night.

Open 12-2 6.30-11 Closed: Mon & Tue lunch, Sun eve **Bar Meals** L served Wed-Sun 12-2 booking required D served Mon-Sat 6.30-9.30 booking required Av main course £10 **Restaurant** L served Wed-Sun 12-2 booking required D served Mon-Sat 6.30-9.30 booking required Fixed menu price fr £14.95 Av 3 course à la carte fr £19 ⊕ FREE HOUSE ◀ Adnams, Timothy Taylor Landlord, Black Sheep. ☻ 20 **Facilities** Children's menu Play area Garden Parking

STOKE BRUERNE Map 11 SP74

The Boat Inn

NN12 7SB ☎ **01604 862428** 📄 **01604 864314**
e-mail: info@boatinn.co.uk
web: www.boatinn.co.uk
dir: *In village centre, just off A508 or A5*

Just across the lock from a popular canal museum, this waterside free house has been run by the same family since 1877. Beneath its thatched roof you'll find cosy bars, open fires and flagstone floors, as well as a traditional skittle alley. Boat trips on the pub's narrowboat can be arranged. Home-made soups, sandwiches, jackets, salads and baguettes support more substantial meals such as pan-fried sea bream, supreme of chicken or Gressingham duck breast with apricot and bacon stuffing.

Open all day all wk 9.30am-11pm (Sun 9.30am-10.30pm) **Bar Meals** L served all wk 9.30-2.30 (all day Mar-Oct) D served all wk 6-9 (all day Mar-Oct) Av main course £8 **Restaurant** L served Tue-Sun 12-2 booking required D served all wk 7-9 booking required Fixed menu price fr £10 Av 3 course à la carte fr £15 ⊕ FREE HOUSE ◀ Banks Bitter, Marstons Pedigree, Frog Island Best, Marstons Old Empire, Wychwood Hobgoblin ☻ Thatcher's Traditional. **Facilities** Children's menu Dogs allowed Garden Parking

WADENHOE Map 11 TL08

PICK OF THE PUBS

The King's Head ☻

Church St PE8 5ST ☎ **01832 720024**
e-mail: info@kingsheadwadenhoe.co.uk
dir: *From A605, 3m from Wadenhoe rdbt. 2m from Oundle*

A haven for travellers since the 17th century, The King's Head is a stone-built, partially thatched inn situated at the end of a quiet country lane. Extensive gardens overlook the tranquil River Nene, and customers can sit and watch the boats pass by as they enjoy a pint of King's Head Bitter. The warm, welcoming interior has quarry-tiled and bare-boarded floors, heavy oak-beamed ceilings, pine furniture and open log fires. Indeed, the pub has lost none of its old world charm but with all the modern facilities. Here, you can challenge the locals to a game of Northamptonshire skittles - if you dare. The menu offers lunchtime sandwiches and panini, and hearty hot dishes such as beer-battered haddock with garden

peas, home-made tartare sauce and hand-cut chips, or roast partridge wrapped in bacon and stuffed with apricots and sage. Vegetables and herbs come from the inn's own garden, and other local sources supply most of the remaining produce.

Open all day 11-11 (Sun 12-10, winter 11-2.30 5.30-11 Sun 12-6) Closed: Sun eve in winter **Bar Meals** Av main course £6.50 food served all day **Restaurant** Fixed menu price fr £10 Av 3 course à la carte fr £25 food served all day ⊕ FREE HOUSE ◀ Kings Head Bitter, Barnwell Bitter, JHB, Black Sheep, Fuller's London Pride ☻ Westons Stowford Press. ☻ 18 **Facilities** Children's menu Dogs allowed Garden Parking

WESTON Map 11 SP54

PICK OF THE PUBS

The Crown ☻

See Pick of the Pubs on opposite page

WOLLASTON Map 11 SP96

PICK OF THE PUBS

The Wollaston Inn ☻

See Pick of the Pubs on page 336

WOODNEWTON Map 11 TL09

The White Swan ☻

22 Main St PE8 5EB ☎ **01780 470944**
dir: *5m off A605/A47*

The pub, which dates from the 1600s, is a stone-built, Grade II listed building set in the middle of an idyllic English village. It has recently been re-opened following major refurbishment and has wasted no time in establishing a reputation for its good modern British food, beers and wines. Entertainment is provided in the form of traditional pub games, such as dominoes and shove ha'penny, and speciality evenings are held throughout the year, including game suppers and wine dinners.

Open 11-2.30 6-11 (Sat 11-3 6-11, Sun 12-5) Closed: Sun eve, Mon **Bar Meals** L served Tue-Sat 12-2, Sun 12-2.30 D served Tue-Thu 6-9, Fri-Sat 6-9.30 Av main course £8.50 **Restaurant** Fixed menu price fr £12 Av 3 course à la carte fr £23 ⊕ FREE HOUSE ◀ Adnams, Timothy Taylor Landlord, Bass, Guinness, Greene King IPA, Woodforde's Wherry ☻ Aspall. ☻ 10 **Facilities** Children's menu Garden Parking

PICK OF THE PUBS

The Crown 🍷

WESTON   Map 11 SP54

Helmdon Rd NN12 8PX
☎ **01295 760310** 📠 **01295 760310**
e-mail: thecrown-weston@tiscali.co.uk
web: www.thecrownweston.co.uk
dir: *Accessed from A43 or B4525*

Following the brutal murder of his children's nanny at his London house in 1974, Lord Lucan was never seen again. Or was he? Some say he had a pint the following day in this attractive 16th-century inn, but we'll probably never know for sure. What is certain is that the inn has been serving ales since the reign of Elizabeth I, the first recorded owner being All Souls College, Oxford. Latest in a long line is Robert Grover, who took over in 2003 and who has ensured ever since that his pub features prominently in the life of the community by providing excellent beers, welcoming staff and a friendly atmosphere. Seasonal menus, a selection of freshly made snacks at lunchtime, and traditional roasts on Sundays have proved particular hits all round. A typical evening menu might start with game terrine, winter berry coulis and toasted ciabatta; duck spring rolls with sweet chilli dressing; or tiger prawn cocktail with Thousand Island dressing and crusty bread. Follow these with a main course such as pork sausages with buttered mash and onion gravy; beef, mushroom and ale pie with mixed leaves and chips; spicy lamb tagine with couscous and roasted root vegetables; salmon and smoked haddock fishcakes, paprika mayonnaise and chips; or roasted pear and goats' cheese tart. Smaller portions for children are available. Robert organises regular curry nights and other occasions. Wines are reasonably priced, from the unashamedly gluggable to sophisticated gems from top producers, with seven by the glass. Nearby attractions include Sulgrave Manor, the ancestral home of George Washington, and Silverstone racing circuit.

Open 6-11.30 (Fri-Sat noon-3.30 6-11.30, Sun noon-3.30 7-11) Closed: 25 Dec, Mon-Thu lunch **Meals** L served Fri-Sun 12-2.30 D served Tue-Sat 6-9.30 🛢 FREE HOUSE 🍺 Greene King IPA , Hook Norton Best, Black Sheep, Landlord, Church End Brewery & Goats Milk. 🍷 7 **Facilities** Family room Dogs allowed Garden Parking

PICK OF THE PUBS

The Wollaston Inn ♥

WOLLASTON   Map 11 SP96

87 London Rd NN29 7QS
☎ **01933 663161**
e-mail: info@wollaston-inn.co.uk
web: www.wollaston-inn.co.uk
dir: *From Wellingborough, onto A509*
towards Wollaston. After 2m, over rdbt, then
immediately left. Inn at top of hill.

Back in the late Sixties and early Seventies, when this was the Nags Head, the late John Peel was the resident Sunday night DJ here. Renowned for his love of live music, he attracted artists of the calibre of Rod Stewart and Led Zeppelin to this simple village pub. Then, then in 2003, Chris Spencer took over, reinvented it as a restaurant within a pub and gave it a name that immediately conferred on it a status perhaps formerly missing. If the name change was, dare it be suggested, cosmetic, he backed it up with a loving restoration of the 350-year-old building's interior to provide a

commendable backdrop to soft Italian leather sofas, casual tables and chairs, ambient lighting and gentle background music. The menus are prepared every day from only fresh ingredients and everything, from the bread and infused oils to the ice creams and rich, dark Belgian chocolate truffles, is made on the premises. The daytime menu is served until 7pm; this is the one for antipasti, charcuterie, burgers and club sandwiches, while the evening carte moves with the seasons to offer fresh linguini with mozzarella, sun-dried tomatoes, aubergine, courgette and pesto; spiced duck breast with port-glazed plum Tatin, puréed sweet potato, ginger and butternut squash, and port, citrus and red wine reduction; and liver and bacon with caramelised onion gravy, leeks and creamed potato. The fresh seafood menu is available all day and changes following daily deliveries from the markets. Ask for the all-day bar menu if you want fresh sandwiches and other snacks. A traditional Sunday lunch menu is served alongside the seafood and bar versions until 5pm. An extensive wine list recommends what to drink with your food, while the bar stocks draught Burton Bitter, Black Sheep and a good selection of bottled beers.

Open all week **Bar Meals** Av main course £9 **Restaurant** Av 3 course à la carte fr £25 ⊞ MARSTONS ◁ Burton Bitter, Black Sheep & Guinness. ♥ 12 **Facilities** Children's menu Garden Parking

NORTHUMBERLAND

ALLENHEADS — Map 18 NY84

The Allenheads Inn

NE47 9HJ ☎ 01434 685200 🖹 01434 685200
e-mail: philann@phomer.fsbusiness.co.uk
dir: From Hexham take B6305, then B6295 to Allenheads

An 18th-century free house with a lively atmosphere, the Allenheads Inn is situated in the fabulous countryside of the North Pennines, perfect for walking and exploring the nearby market towns and enjoying the many local attractions. Relax in the popular Antiques Bar, or the unusually-named Forces Room, and enjoy pies, chilli, curry, burgers, or one of the pub's seasonal specials.

Open all wk ⊕ FREE HOUSE ◀ Greene King Abbot Ale, Timothy Taylor Landlord, Black Sheep Bitter and guest ales. **Facilities** Dogs allowed Garden Parking

ALNWICK — Map 21 NU11

Masons Arms

Stamford, Nr Rennington NE66 3RX
☎ 01665 577275 🖹 01665 577894
e-mail: bookings@masonsarms.net
web: www.masonsarms.net
dir: NE of Alnwick on B1340, 0.5m past Rennington

A tastefully modernised 200-year-old coaching inn, known by the local community as Stamford Cott. It is a useful staging post for visitors to Hadrian's Wall, Lindisfarne and the large number of nearby golf courses. The substantial home-cooked food is available in the bar and the restaurant, and is made using the best of local produce. Typical examples include lemon sole with prawns and parsley sauce; Northumbrian game casserole; and curry.

Open all wk noon-2 6.30-11pm (Sun noon-2 6.30-10.30pm) **Bar Meals** L served all wk 12-2 D served all wk 6.30-9 ⊕ FREE HOUSE ◀ John Smiths's, Theakston Best, Secret Kingdom, Gladiator. **Facilities** Family room Dogs allowed Garden Parking

BELFORD — Map 21 NU13

Blue Bell Hotel ★★★ HL

Market Place NE70 7NE
☎ 01668 213543 🖹 01668 213787
e-mail: enquiries@bluebellhotel.com
dir: Off A1, 15m N of Alnwick , 15m S of Berwick-upon-Tweed

A touch of old-world charm with modern day comforts permeate this 17th-century coaching inn on the A1 London to Edinburgh route, and there are spectacular views across the hotel gardens to Belford church. The innovative menu takes its cue from the best of country kitchens, and choices from the restaurant menu might include mussels in Lindisfarne mead broth; Eyemouth fish pie; slow roasted lamb Henry with creamed potatoes and vegetables; or tempura vegetables with rice and sweet chilli dip.

Open all day all wk 11am-mdnt **Bar Meals** L served all wk 12-3 D served all wk 5-9 Av main course £8.95 **Restaurant** L served Sun 12-3 booking required D served all wk 6-9 booking required Fixed menu price fr £21 Av 3 course à la carte fr £40 ⊕ FREE HOUSE ◀ Calders, Tetleys Smooth, Black Sheep, Timothy Taylor Landlord. **Facilities** Children's menu Play area Family room Garden Parking **Rooms** 28

BLANCHLAND — Map 18 NY95

The Lord Crewe Arms

DH8 9SP ☎ 01434 675251 🖹 01434 675337
e-mail: lord@crewearms.freeserve.co.uk
dir: 10m S of Hexham via B6306

Built in the 12th century, once the private chapel of the abbot of Blanchland Abbey, and a significant location in the first Jacobite Rebellion in 1715, this is one of England's oldest inns. Antique furniture, blazing log fires and flagstone floors make for an atmospheric setting. Wide-ranging, good-value bar and restaurant menus with specials offer salads, savoury bean hot pot, and game pie. Watch out, there are lots of ghosts, and often filming crews too!

Open all day all wk 11-11 (Sun 12-10.30) **Bar Meals** L served all wk 12-2 D served all wk 7-9 Av main course £7 **Restaurant** D served all wk 7-9.15 booking required Av 3 course à la carte fr £21 ⊕ FREE HOUSE ◀ Black Sheep, John Smiths, Guinness, Boddingtons ♻ Thatchers. **Facilities** Children's menu Play area Family room Dogs allowed Garden Parking

CARTERWAY HEADS — Map 19 NZ05

PICK OF THE PUBS

The Manor House Inn ♀

DH8 9LX ☎ 01207 255268
dir: A69 W from Newcastle, left onto A68 then S for 8m. Inn on right

A very traditional free house enjoying spectacular views across open moorland and the Derwent Reservoir from its elevated position high on the A68. Built circa 1760, the completely refurbished inn is an ideal centre for exploring Northumberland's rolling hills and beautiful beaches; for a city visit, Newcastle and Durham are a short drive away. The cosy stone-walled bar, with its log fires, low-beamed ceiling and massive timber support, serves five well-kept real ales all year, among which may be found Ruddles County, Theakston's Best and Mordue Workie Ticket. The bar and lounge are ideal for a snack, while the restaurant is divided into two dining areas, the larger of which welcomes families with children. The focus on fresh local produce is typified by dishes such as smoked kippers with crisp side salad; slow-braised oxtail on a bed of black pudding mash; and supreme of chicken breast with sautéed leeks and Northumbrian nettle cheese sauce.

Open all day all wk 11-11 (Sun 12-10.30) **Bar Meals** food served all day **Restaurant** food served all day ⊕ FREE HOUSE ◀ Theakstons Best, Mordue Workie Ticket, Greene King Ruddles County, Courage Directors, Wells Bombardier ♻ Westons Old Rosie Scrumpy. ♀ 12 **Facilities** Children's menu Dogs allowed Garden Parking

CHATTON — Map 21 NU02

The Percy Arms Hotel ♀

Main Rd NE66 5PS ☎ 01668 215244 🖹 01668 215277
dir: From Alnwick take A1 N, then B6348 to Chatton

Traditional 19th-century forming coaching inn, situated in the heart of rural Northumberland. Expect a warm, traditional pub welcome, as well as a selection of fine beers, wines and tempting food. Bar menu includes Aberdeen Angus steaks, deep-fried haddock, steak and kidney pie and a wide selection of fish and seafood dishes. Bar games include snooker, pool and darts, but those who wish to can still enjoy a quiet pint in comfort.

Open all wk ⊕ JENNINGS BROTHERS PLC ◀ Jennings Cumberland Cream, guest ales. ♀ 7 **Facilities** Garden Parking

CORBRIDGE Map 21 NY96

The Angel of Corbridge ♛

Main St NE45 5LA ☎ **01434 632119** 📠 **01434 633496**
e-mail: info@theangelofcorbridge.co.uk
dir: 0.5m off A69, signed Corbridge

Stylish 17th-century coaching inn overlooking the River Tyne. Relax with the daily papers in the wood-panelled lounge or attractive bars, or enjoy a home-made dish or two from the extensive menu choice. Options include pan-fried chicken breast with spicy cous cous, salmon and lemon fish cakes and risotto of asparagus and leek.

Open all wk ⊕ FREE HOUSE ◀ Timothy Taylor Landlord, local ales. ♛ 10 **Facilities** Garden Parking

CRASTER Map 21 NU21

Cottage Inn ♛

Dunstan Village NE66 2UD
☎ **01665 576658** 📠 **01665 576788**
e-mail: enquiries@cottageinnhotel.co.uk
dir: NW of Howick to Embleton road

Set in six acres of woodland, in an Area of Outstanding Natural Beauty, this 18th-century inn lies in a hamlet close to the coast. Nearby is Dunstanburgh Castle, one of Northumberland's great historic landmarks. Inside is a beamed bar, together with a restaurant, conservatory and patio. One menu serves all and includes the ever-popular Craster kippers, steak and game pie, venison sausages, and vegetable risotto. Local ingredients are used wherever possible.

Open all wk ⊕ FREE HOUSE ◀ Mordue, Tetley's, Farne Island, Black Sheep, Timothy Taylor Landlord. ♛ 7 **Facilities** Play area Garden Parking

Jolly Fisherman Inn

Haven Hill NE66 3TR ☎ **01665 576461**
e-mail: muriel@silk8234.fsnet.co.uk
dir: Exit A1 at Denwick, follow Dunstanburgh Castle signs

The first landlord, in 1847, was a fisherman - presumably a jovial fellow. The pub stands right by the water in this tiny fishing village world-renowned for its kippers. The menu is not extensive, but it makes full use of the sea's bounty with home-made kipper pâté; crabmeat soup with whisky and cream; and oak-smoked or fresh salmon sandwiches. For something different, try Geordie stottie cake pizza. Nearby Dunstanburgh Castle is worth a visit.

Open all day all wk 11-11 **Bar Meals** L served all wk 11-2.30 ⊕ PUNCH TAVERNS ◀ Black Sheep, John Smith's, Mordue Workie Ticket. **Facilities** Dogs allowed Garden Parking **Notes** ⊛

ETAL Map 21 NT93

Black Bull ♛

TD12 4TL ☎ **01890 820200** 📠 **07092 367733**
dir: Off A697, left at junct for 1m then left into Etal

The Black Bull stands by the ruins of Etal Castle, not far from the River Till, with the grand walking country of the Cheviots on the doorstep. The only thatched pub in Northumberland, it serves traditional pub food such as mince and dumpling with potatoes and vegetables; or home-made steak and ale pie. Lighter options include soup, sandwiches, and toasted teacakes.

Closed: Mon (winter) ⊕ PUBMASTER ◀ Jennings, Deuchars, John Smith Smooth. ♛ 6 **Facilities** Garden Parking

FALSTONE Map 21 NY78

The Blackcock Inn ★★★ INN

NE48 1AA ☎ **01434 240200**
e-mail: thebcinn@yahoo.co.uk
dir: From Hexham take A6079, then B6320 to Bellingham, follow brown signs to Kielder & Falstone

Stone walls, log fires and original beams reflect the 17th-century origins of this traditional family-run free house. An ideal base for walking, boating and fishing, it sits close to Kielder Water and is handy for the Rievers cycle route. The food draws on excellent local produce, with options ranging from light lunchtime snacks through to full evening meals in the intimate Chatto's restaurant: perhaps Japanese-style king prawns followed by lamb shank in red wine and rosemary.

Closed: Tue in low season **Bar Meals** L served Wed-Sun 12-2 booking required Av main course £8.80 **Restaurant** L served Wed-Sun 12-2 booking required D served Wed-Mon 7-8.30 booking required Av 3 course à la carte fr £15.85 ⊕ FREE HOUSE ◀ John Smiths, Worthington, guest ale ♖ Westons. **Facilities** Children's menu Play area Family room Dogs allowed Garden Parking **Rooms** 6

PICK OF THE PUBS

The Pheasant Inn ★★★★ INN

See Pick of the Pubs on opposite page

GREAT WHITTINGTON Map 21 NZ07

PICK OF THE PUBS

Queens Head Inn ♛

NE19 2HP ☎ **01434 672267** 📠 **01434 672267**
dir: Turn off A69 towards Jedburgh, then N on A68. At rdbt take 3rd exit onto B6318, 1st left signed Great Whittington

At the heart of Hadrian's Wall country this old pub/restaurant, once a coaching inn, radiates a welcoming atmosphere in comfortable surroundings of beamed rooms, oak settles and open fires. In addition to real ales there are eleven wines by the glass. Menus combine the best of local and European ingredients, without losing touch with the classics. Expect starters like tempura of black pudding with a beetroot and red onion relish and crisp salad. Follow that with a main course such as pork tenderloin on an orange and onion marmalade with black pudding fritters and cider and sage jus. Traditional desserts include old favourites like sticky toffee pudding, bread and butter pudding, and baked vanilla cheesecake.

Open all wk ⊕ FREE HOUSE ◀ Farne Island, Auld Hemp, Nels Best. ♛ 11 **Facilities** Garden Parking

HALTWHISTLE Map 21 NY76

Milecastle Inn

Military Rd, Cawfields NE49 9NN ☎ **01434 321372**
e-mail: clarehind@aol.com
web: www.milecastle-inn.co.uk
dir: From A69 into Haltwhistle. Pub approx 2m at junct with B6318

There are good views of Hadrian's Wall from the garden of this rural inn, which sits close to some of the most interesting parts of this fascinating landmark. Inside you'll find open fires and, possibly, the resident ghost. Daily specials supplement separate bar and restaurant menus, which offer numerous home-made pies – wild boar and duckling, beef and venison - and grills, as well as please-all dishes such as roasted vegetable and Wensleydale bake; hot and spicy chicken wings; and lasagne with garlic bread.

Open all day noon-11 (noon-3 6-10 Nov-Mar) Closed: Sun eve in Jan-Mar **Bar Meals** L served all wk 12-2.30 D served all wk 6-8.30 **Restaurant** L served all wk 12-2.30 D served all wk 6-8.30 ⊕ FREE HOUSE ◀ Big Lamp, Prince Bishop, Carlsberg-Tetley, Castle Eden. **Facilities** Children's menu Garden Parking

PICK OF THE PUBS

The Pheasant Inn ★★★★ INN

FALSTONE Map 21 NY78

Stannersburn NE48 1DD
☎ **01434 240382** 📄 **01434 240382**
e-mail: enquiries@thepheasantinn.com
dir: *A69, B6079, B6320, follow signs for Kielder Water*

This sprawling stone-walled building in the north Tyne Valley dates back to 1624. It was originally a large farmstead, but for over 250 years one room was always used as a locals' bar. Its permanent change of use came about in 1974, and 1975 saw the conversion of some of the farm buildings into bedrooms. In 1985 it was taken over by the Kershaws, who have continually improved and upgraded it. However they have succeeded in keeping the rustic atmosphere intact - around the walls old photos record local people engaged in long-abandoned trades and professions. Robin and Irene's cooking is fresh, generous and tasty, producing wholesome traditionally English fare. Meals may be taken alfresco in the pretty grassed courtyard with a stream running through, or in the oak-beamed restaurant with its cottage style furnishings and warm terracotta walls. The bar menu changes daily according to season, but classic dishes like steak and kidney pie, home-made soups, lasagne, ploughman's and sandwiches are always available. Restaurant menu starters could embrace grilled fresh asparagus with a balsamic dressing; sweet marinated herrings; and creamy garlic mushrooms in puff pastry. Main courses from the blackboard might be slow-roasted Northumbrian lamb with rosemary and redcurrant jus; cider baked gammon; home-made game and mushroom pie; and fish from North Shields quay. Sandra's sticky toffee pudding is always an irresistible way to finish. Nearby is Kielder Water, the largest artificial lake in Europe and a magnet for walkers, cyclists and sailors. There's also Hadrian's Wall, some of England's least spoilt countryside and coastline, and sights such as Alnwick Castle and Gardens. Guests tempted to stay can book one of eight en suite bedrooms, with views over the stunning landscape.

Open 12-3 6.30-11 Closed: 25-26 Dec, Mon-Tue (Nov-Mar) **Bar Meals** L served Mon-Sat 12-2.30 **Restaurant** L served Mon-Sat 12-2.30 D served all week 6.30-8.30 ⊕ FREE HOUSE 🛢 Timothy Taylor Landlord, Wylam Gold, Wylam Rocket. **Facilities** Children's menu Play area Family room Dogs allowed by arrangement Garden Parking **Rooms** 8

HAYDON BRIDGE | Map 21 NY86

The General Havelock Inn ⬤

Ratcliffe Rd NE47 6ER
☎ 01434 684376 📠 01434 684283
e-mail: info@generalhavelock.co.uk
dir: On A69, 7m W of Hexham

In a riverside setting not far from Hadrian's Wall, the General Havelock is named after a 19th-century British Army officer. The pub, with its restaurant in a converted barn overlooking the River Tyne which teems with wildlife, is a favourite with show business personalities. The best of local ingredients inspires the adventurous menu, and typical dishes include steamed cod on mash with caper and parsley sauce; double-baked cheese soufflé with dressed salad; and roast rack of lamb with herb crust.

Open 12-2.30 7-10.30 Closed: Mon **Restaurant** L served 12-1 (Tue-Sun) D served 7-9 (Tue-Sat) ⬤ FREE HOUSE ◀ Hesket Newmarket Helvellyn Gold, Wylam Magic, High House Nel's Best, Durham Brewery Magus, Allendale Best Bitter. ▼ 9 **Facilities** Dogs allowed Garden

---

HEDLEY ON THE HILL | Map 19 NZ05

PICK OF THE PUBS

The Feathers Inn ⬤

See Pick of the Pubs on opposite page

HEXHAM | Map 21 NY96

PICK OF THE PUBS

Battlesteads Hotel & Restaurant

See Pick of the Pubs on page 342

PICK OF THE PUBS

Dipton Mill Inn ⬤

Dipton Mill Rd NE46 1YA ☎ 01434 606577
e-mail: ghb@hexhamshire.co.uk
dir: 2m S of Hexham on HGV route to Blanchland, B6306, Dipton Mill Rd

A former farmhouse, with the millstream running right through the gardens, the pub has recently celebrated its rebuilding 400 years ago. It is surrounded by farms and woodland with footpaths for pleasant country walks, and there is Hadrian's Wall and an assortment of other Roman sites in the area to explore. The Dipton Mill is home to Hexhamshire Brewery ales, including Devil's Water and Old Humbug. Food is served evenings and lunchtimes and all dishes are freshly prepared from local produce where possible. Start with home-made soup, such as carrot and celery served with a warm roll, followed by hearty dishes like mince and dumplings, lamb leg steak in wine and mustard sauce, or tomato, bean and vegetable casserole. Traditional desserts include bread and butter pudding or syrup sponge and custard. Salads, sandwiches and ploughman's are also always available.

Open noon-2.30 6-11 (Sun noon-3) Closed: 25 Dec, Sun eve **Bar Meals** L served all wk 12-2 D served Mon-Sat 6.30-8.30 Av main course £7.50 ⬤ FREE HOUSE ◀ Hexhamshire Shire Bitter, Old Humbug, Devil's Water, Devil's Elbow, Whapweasel ⬥ Westons Old Rosie. ▼ 17 **Facilities** Children's menu Garden **Notes** ✉

Miners Arms Inn

Main St, Acomb NE46 4PW ☎ 01434 603909
e-mail: info@theminersacomb.com
dir: 17m W of Newcastle on A69. 2m W of Hexham

Close to Hadrian's Wall in peaceful surroundings, this welcoming village pub with open hearth fire dates from 1746. Pride is taken in the range and quality of the ales and in the good home-cooked food. Sunday lunches are especially popular, when North Acomb beef or lamb roasts are accompanied by home-made Yorkshire puddings, roast potatoes and a selection of vegetables. There is a pleasant beer garden and families are welcome.

Open all wk **Bar Meals** L served Sat 12-2.30 booking required D served Thu-Sat 5-8.30 booking required **Restaurant** L served Sun 12-2.30 booking required D served Thu-Sat 5-8.30 booking required ⬤ FREE HOUSE ◀ Black Sheep, Wylam Bitter, Pilsner Urquell, Mordue, Yates Bitter ⬥ Wylam Perry's Farmhouse Cider. **Facilities** Children's menu Dogs allowed Garden

---

Rat Inn ⬤

NE46 4LN ☎ 01434 602814
e-mail: info@theratinn.com
dir: 2m from Hexham, Bridge End (A69) rdbt, take 4th exit signed Oakwood. Inn 500yds on right

Set in the picturesque hamlet of Anick, The Rat has spectacular views across Hexham and the Tyne Valley. A classic country pub with a stunning summer garden and log fires in winter, it offers a classy selection of traditional food cooked to order using local ingredients. Examples include pigeon and black pudding salad followed by herb-crusted rack of lamb with courgettes provençale and dauphinoise potatoes. Excellent real ales.

Open all wk noon-3 6-close (Sat-Sun noon-close) **Bar Meals** L served Tue-Sat 12-2, Sun 12-3 booking required D served Tue-Sat 6-9 booking required **Restaurant** L served Tue-Sat 12-2, Sun 12-3 booking required D served Tue-Sat 6-9 booking required ⬤ FREE HOUSE ◀ John Smiths, Guinness, Bass, Deuchars. ▼ 8 **Facilities** Children's menu Garden Parking

---

LONGFRAMLINGTON | Map 21 NU10

PICK OF THE PUBS

The Anglers Arms

See Pick of the Pubs on page 343

LONGHORSLEY | Map 21 NZ19

Linden Tree ★★★★ HL ⬤⬤

Linden Hall NE65 8XF
☎ 01670 500033 📠 01670 500001
e-mail: lindenhall@macdonald-hotels.co.uk
dir: Off A1 on A697, 1m N of Longhorsley

This popular pub was originally two large cattle byres. It takes its name from the linden trees near Linden Hall, the impressive Georgian mansion (now hotel) in whose grounds it stands. The brasserie-style menu might include a ham and pease pudding sandwich; a traditional Caesar salad; home-made Craster kipper pâté with brown bread, butter and lemon; spaghetti carbonara; and (from its Taste of Northumberland selection) home-made steak and suet pudding.

Open all wk Mon-Sat 11am-11pm (Sun 11am-10.30pm) **Bar Meals** L served Mon-Sat 12-9.30, Sun 12-9 D served Mon-Sat 12-9.30, Sun 12-9 **Restaurant** L served Mon-Sat 12-9.30, Sun 12-9 D served Mon-Sat 12-9.30, Sun 12-9 ⬤ FREE HOUSE ◀ Worthington, Greene King IPA, Caffreys, Guinness. **Facilities** Play area Garden Parking **Rooms** 50

PICK OF THE PUBS

The Feathers Inn 🍷

HEDLEY ON THE HILL   Map 19 NZ05

NE43 7SW
☎ 01661 843607 📄 01661 843607
e-mail: info@thefeathers.net
web: www.thefeathers.net
dir: *Telephone for directions*

Rhian and Helen Cradock, and Rhian's parents Richard and Jyll, took over this small, stone-built free house overlooking the splendid Cheviot Hills in 2007. Their three-roomed pub is well patronised by the local community, but visitors too are always charmed by its friendly and relaxed atmosphere. Old oak beams, coal fires, rustic settles, and stone walls decorated with local photographs of rural life make an ideal setting in which to appreciate the bar's mainly locally brewed cask ales, including the graphically named Mordue Workie Ticket and Big Lamp Bitter.

There's also a good selection of traditional pub games like shove ha'penny and bar skittles, but most people will be here for a meal. From the very outset, it was the Cradocks' intention to serve the very best food in an informal yet professionally run environment. Award-winning chef Rhian puts on daily-changing menus of great British classics and North East regional dishes, for whose ingredients he always knows the full provenance. On lunch menus you'll find beer-battered North Sea fish with chunky chips; jugged hare with tarragon; slow-roast Ravensworth Grange middle white pork; and lentil and chestnut shepherd's pie. In the evening, menus list grilled wild halibut; loin of Bill Fail's Currock Hill lamb stuffed with sweetbreads; and Doddington's cheese, spinach and beetroot pie. Rhian also believes in simply plated but flawlessly prepared desserts, such as gooseberry meringue pie and burnt Northumbrian cream. Groups might like to put together a feasting menu along the lines of, for example, home-made black pudding to begin, whole roast suckling pig as the main course, and a selection of Northumbrian cheeses to follow.

Open noon-11pm (Sun 12-10.30, Mon 6-11) **Bar Meals** L served Tue-Sun 12-2 D served Tue-Sat 6-8.30 Av main course £11 ⊕ FREE HOUSE ◀ Mordue Workie Ticket, Big Lamp Bitter, Fuller's London Pride, Northumberland Pit Pony, Orkney Red McGreggor, Hadrian Gladiator Ŏ Westons 1st Quality, Westons Old Rosie. 🍷 36 **Facilities** Children's menu Family room Parking

PICK OF THE PUBS

Battlesteads Hotel & Restaurant

HEXHAM Map 21 NY96

Wark NE48 3LS
☎ **01434 230209** 📄 **01434 230039**
e-mail: info@battlesteads.com
web: www.battlesteads.com
dir: *10m N of Hexham on B6320 (Kielder road)*

Flower tubs and hanging baskets greet travellers at this family-run hotel just a few miles north of Hadrian's Wall. Built as a farmhouse in 1747, Battlesteads became a temperance hotel in the early 20th century and still offers a tasty range of organic soft drinks and ginger beer from Fentimans of Newcastle. Nowadays, following a major renovation, cask ales like Durham Magus, Wylam Gold Tankard and Black Sheep are also available, together with a decent wine list. In winter, a cosy wood-burning stove warms the well-stocked bar, with its wood panelled walls and comfy leather settees. There's a new 80-seater restaurant, and a sunny conservatory

that leads out to the secret walled beer garden. Tasteful décor reflects the flavoursome menu, which is primarily modern British in character, but with a smattering of international choices for those with a more cosmopolitan palate. Head chef Eddie Shilton uses prime local ingredients for freshness and flavour, with free-range eggs, seasonal game, Cumbrian beef and Northumbrian lamb, plus fish from North Shields Fish Quay, and smoked fish and game from Bywell smokery. Fresh vegetables and herbs are grown in the hotel garden, and vegetarian choices are always available. The seasonal menu changes throughout the week, featuring starters such as king prawn and Cumbrian chorizo salad; pear, walnut and blue cheese salad; and local pheasant terrine with redcurrant jelly. Main course options might include tuna 'fuscha shichimi' with Japanese vegetable and noodle miso; wild mushroom risotto with fresh Parmesan shavings and truffle tartufata; or venison pie with local roe deer loin, pickled red cabbage and a rich jus. Hedgerow Trifle with liqueur-soaked Amaretti biscuits, and whisky and marmalade bread and butter pudding are typical home-made desserts.

Open all week ⊕ FREE HOUSE 🛢 Wylam Gold Tankard, Black Sheep Special, Durham White Velvet, Durham Magus, Black Sheep Bitter. **Facilities** Dogs allowed Garden Parking

PICK OF THE PUBS

The Anglers Arms

LONGFRAMLINGTON Map 21 NU10

Weldon Bridge NE65 8AX
☎ **01665 570271 & 570655**
🖷 **01665 570041**
e-mail:
johnyoung@anglersarms.fsnet.co.uk
dir: *From N, 9m S of Alnwick right Weldon Bridge sign. From S, A1 to by-pass Morpeth, left onto A697 for Wooler & Coldstream. 7m, left to Weldon Bridge*

This former coaching inn has commanded the picturesque Weldon Bridge over the River Coquet since the 1760s. The interior is full of nice little touches, antiques and quaint bric-a-brac; the walls are full of pictures and fishing memorabilia, and open log fires are a welcoming treat on winter days. Timothy Taylor Landlord and Theakstons Best Bitter are amongst the ales on offer to accompany a range of popular bar meals, where the main course choices include home-made steak and

ale pie; grilled salmon fillet with sweet chilli sauce; and vegetable stew with home-made dumplings. Outside, there's plenty of space for alfresco summer dining in the carefully-tended half-acre of garden, which also includes a children's play park. But for more style and a different set of options, the pub's own Pullman railway carriage provides an unusual restaurant experience. Silver service comes as standard here, and you can choose from starters like shredded duck salad with noodles and hoi sin sauce; twice-cooked belly pork with honey spiced apples; and garlic king prawns with a panache of fresh garden leaves. Moving on to the main course, the alternatives include pan-fried chicken breast on bubble and squeak with mushroom and red wine sauce; rack of Border lamb with roasted chateau potatoes; and vegetable stroganoff with basmati rice. Turn to the blackboard for a daily-changing dessert selection to complete your meal. The Anglers Arms is ideally situated for visiting Alnwick Castle, Cragside and Hadrian's Wall; or you can fish with a day permit on the inn's own mile stretch of the River Coquet.

Open 11-11 (Sun 12-11) **Bar Meals** Av main course £8 **Restaurant** Fixed menu price fr £20 Av 3 course à la carte fr £30 ⊕ FREE HOUSE ◀ Timothy Taylor Landlord, Abbot Ale Theakstons Best Bitter **Facilities** Children's menu Play area Family room Garden Parking

LOW NEWTON BY THE SEA — Map 21 NU22

The Ship Inn

The Square NE66 3EL ☎ 01665 576262
e-mail: forsythchristine@hotmail.com
dir: *NE from A1 at Alnwick towards Seahouses*

The beach is only a stroll away from this pretty inn, which overlooks the green. Low Newton was purpose-built as a fishing village in the 18th century and remains wonderfully unspoilt. Bustling in summer and a peaceful retreat in winter, The Ship offers plenty of fresh, locally caught fish and free-range meats, along with interesting vegetarian food and old fashioned puddings. The pub now has its own microbrewery, so expect some cracking real ales.

Open all wk **Bar Meals** L served all wk 12-2.30 D served all wk 7-8 (some seasonal variations, please telephone for details) booking required ⊕ FREE HOUSE ◀ Microbrewery - Sea Coal, Dolly Day Dream, Sea Wheat, Ship Hop Ale, Sandcastles at Dawn. **Facilities** Dogs allowed Garden **Notes** ☺

NETHERTON — Map 21 NT90

The Star Inn

NE65 7HD ☎ 01669 630238
dir: *7m from Rothbury*

Owned by the same family since 1917, this pub is situated in superb remote countryside and retains many original features. No food is served, but cask ales in the peak of condition are the speciality, served from a hatch in the entrance.

Closed: Mon, Thu ⊕ FREE HOUSE ◀ Castle Eden Ale. **Facilities** Parking **Notes** ☺

NEWTON-ON-THE-MOOR — Map 21 NU10

PICK OF THE PUBS

The Cook and Barker Inn ★★★★ INN ☂

See Pick of the Pubs on opposite page

ROWFOOT — Map 21 NY66

The Wallace Arms

NE49 0JF ☎ 01434 321872 ▤ 01434 321872
e-mail: www.thewallacearms@btconnect.com
dir: *Telephone for directions*

The pub was rebuilt in 1850 as the Railway Hotel at Featherstone Park station, when the now long-closed Haltwhistle-Alston line (today's South Tyne Trail) was engineered. It changed to the Wallace Arms in 1885. Sample menu includes modestly-priced haddock fillet in beer batter, salmon fillet in lemon and tarragon sauce, steak and ale pie, grilled sirloin steak, and smoked haddock and prawn pasta. There are light snacks, burgers and sandwiches, if you prefer.

Open all wk ⊕ FREE HOUSE ◀ Hook Norton Old Hooky, Young's Special, Greene King IPA, Greene King Abbot Ale, Jennings Cumberland Ale. **Facilities** Garden Parking

SEAHOUSES — Map 21 NU23

PICK OF THE PUBS

The Olde Ship Hotel ★★ SHL ☂

See Pick of the Pubs on page 346

WARDEN — Map 21 NY96

The Boatside Inn ☂

NE46 4SQ ☎ 01434 602233
e-mail: sales@theboatsideinn.com
web: www.theboatsideinn.com
dir: *Off A69 W of Hexham, follow signs to Warden Newborough & Fourstones*

A stone-built country inn, now under new ownership, the Boatside is situated where the North and South Tyne rivers meet, beneath Warden Hill Iron Age fort. The name refers to the rowing boat that ferried people across the river before the bridge was built. Children, walkers and cyclists are welcome, and the inn has fishing rights on the river opposite. Dishes include Boatside salads; lime, thyme and asparagus risotto; fresh seafood; and steak and ale pie.

Open all day all wk 11-11 (Sun 11-10.30) **Bar Meals** L served Mon-Sat 12-2.30, Sun 12-9 D served Mon-Sat 6-9, Sun 12-9 Av main course £9.95 **Restaurant** L served Mon-Sat 12-2.30, Sun 12-9 D served Mon-Sat 6-9, Sun 12-9 ⊕ FREE HOUSE ◀ Black Sheep, John Smiths, Mordue, Wylam. ☂ 15 **Facilities** Children's menu Dogs allowed Garden Parking

WARENFORD — Map 21 NU12

PICK OF THE PUBS

The White Swan ☂

NE70 7HY ☎ 01668 213453
e-mail: dianecuthbert@yahoo.com
dir: *100yds E of A1, 10m N of Alnwick*

This 200-year-old coaching inn stands near the original toll bridge over the Waren Burn. Formerly on the Great North Road, the building is now just a stone's throw from the A1. Inside, you'll find thick stone walls and an open fire for colder days; in summer, there's a small sheltered seating area, with further seats in the adjacent field. The Dukes of Northumberland once owned the pub, and its windows and plasterwork still bear the family crests. Visitors and locals alike enjoy the atmosphere and award-winning Northumbrian dishes: try Seahouses kippers with creamy horseradish sauce; venison pudding with lemon suet crust and fresh vegetables; or roast pork hock with wine and herbs. Vegetarians are well catered for, with interesting dishes like beetroot and potato gratin; artichoke and leek pancakes; and celeriac pan Haggarty with fresh tomato sauce.

Open all day all wk noon-mdnt **Bar Meals** L served all wk 12-3 D served all wk 6-9 ⊕ FREE HOUSE ◀ Black Sheep. ☂ 8 **Facilities** Garden Parking

WHALTON — Map 21 NZ18

PICK OF THE PUBS

Beresford Arms

NE61 3UZ ☎ 01670 775225 ▤ 01670 775351
e-mail: beresford.arms@btconnect.com
dir: *5m from Morpeth town centre on B6524*

Under the new management of landlady Wendy Makepeace, this ivy-covered coaching inn continues to maintain its country pub atmosphere, while at the same time conveying a modern feel. It lies in the picturesque village of Whalton, popular with cyclists and walkers enjoying the delights of nearby Kielder Forest and Northumberland National Park. Set opposite the village hall, it also provides a welcome focus for village life. Start with a pint of Black Sheep or Timothy Taylor Landlord while perusing the menu. Your meal could start with home-made soup, or prawn and avocado salad with Marie Rose sauce; follow with grilled Wallington Hall rib-eye steak with tomato, mushrooms, onion rings and chips; and finish with a crumble or something that involves whipped cream or chocolate sauce.

Open all wk **Bar Meals** L served Tue-Sat 12-2, Sun 12-3 D served Tue-Sat 12-2 6-9 Av main course £10 **Restaurant** L served Fri-Sat 12-2, Sun 12-3 D served Fri-Sat 6-9 Fixed menu price fr £9 Av 3 course à la carte fr £17.50 ⊕ FREE HOUSE ◀ Black Sheep, Timothy Taylor Landlord, John Smith's. **Facilities** Children's menu Dogs allowed Garden Parking

PICK OF THE PUBS

The Cook and Barker Inn ★★★★ INN ♟

NEWTON-ON-THE-MOOR   Map 21 NU10

NE65 9JY

☎ 01665 575234   📄 01665 575887

dir: *0.5m from A1 S of Alnwick*

From its elevated position in the picturesque village of Newton-on-the-Moor, this traditional country inn commands outstanding views of the Cheviot Hills and the Northumbrian coast. The Cook and Barker is a long-established family business run by Phil Farmer, who has set his sights well above the conventional 'pub grub with rooms'. To this end, highly skilled kitchen staff strive to prepare quality dishes that give value for money, while the front-of-house service team looks after guests with expertise and finesse.

A good choice of real ales – at least four ranging from Black Sheep to Timothy Taylor Landlord – is backed by a dozen wines served by the glass. Food can be served in the restaurant, bar, snug or lounge. The tempting bar lunch menu and mouthwatering à la carte evening menu are backed by daily specials on the blackboard, all served wherever the customer chooses to sit; a gourmet seven-course fixed-price menu is also available. Appetisers are along the lines of warm toasted muffin with black pudding, king scallop and fresh green pea purée; and pressed ham terrine with apricot and home-made chutney. For a main course, choose from the 'Seafood Selection' for the likes of seared tuna loin with a niçoise salad; or pan-roasted cod supreme with mushy peas. The 'Forest and Fields' listing may include noisettes of pork pan-fried with wild forest mushrooms deglazed with Madeira wine and set on a pillow of roasted vegetables; or roast rack of lamb with seasonal greens and rosemary. With 'Grills and Roasts' the

cooking technique comes as no surprise: perhaps a prime sirloin steak with balsamic tomatoes and sautéed button mushrooms; or surf-and-turf T-bone steak with garlic prawns. Finally look to the 'Oriental Dishes' for something a little spicy: beef fillet with ginger and spring onions, for example, or pork and prawn stir fry in a black bean sauce. There are 18 smartly furnished en suite bedrooms if you would like to stay over.

Open all week **Bar Meals** Av main course 8.95 **Restaurant** L served all wk 12-2 D served all wk 7-9 Fixed menu price fr £25 Av 3 course à la carte fr £35 🍺 FREE HOUSE 🍺 Timothy Taylor Landlord, Theakstons Best Bitter, Fuller's London Pride, Batemans XXXB, Black Sheep. ♟ 12 **Facilities** Children's menu Family room Garden Parking **Rooms** 18

PICK OF THE PUBS

The Olde Ship Hotel ★★ SHL ♟

SEAHOUSES Map 21 NU23

9 Main St NE68 7RD
☎ **01665 720200** 📄 **01665 721383**
e-mail: theoldeship@seahouses.co.uk
dir: *Lower end of main street above harbour*

A former farmhouse in an unusual position above the tiny bustling harbour, The Olde Ship owes its location to the grain export business of earlier times. On the right sort of day, you can enjoy a pint of Black Sheep in the garden while watching the local fishing boats bob up and down below. Built in 1745, it has been a pub since 1812 and is now a fully residential hotel with a long established reputation for good food and drink in comfortable, relaxing and old fashioned surroundings. Run by the present owner's family for nearly 100 years, its interior is nautically themed and the characterful main saloon bar is packed with memorabilia and lit by stained glass windows and the welcoming glow of the open fire. Next to this is the low, beamed Cabin Bar, with a wooden floor made of pine ships' decking. The hotel's corridors and boat gallery are also an Aladdin's cave of antique nautical artefacts and seafaring mementoes, including diving helmets, oars, fish baskets, branding irons, lamps and the nameplate from the 'Forfarshire' of Grace Darling fame. Popular bar foods include locally-caught seafood and pub classics such as sirloin steak and fried onions or scampi and chips, alongside appealing options such as mushroom and cashew nut pâté; fresh crab soup; chicken and mushroom casserole; smoked fish chowder; and lamb shank with a root vegetable mash. To follow, perhaps rhubarb upside-down pudding; clootie dumpling; lemon meringue ice cream; or banana and butterscotch pudding.

Bedrooms are neat and well appointed, and some have views over to the bird and seal sanctuary on the Farne Islands. Boats will take you there from the nearby pier.

Open 11-11 (Sun noon-11) **Bar Meals** L served all wk 12-2.30 D served all wk 7-8.30 (no D late Nov-late Jan) Av main course £10 **Restaurant** L served Sun 12-2 D served all wk 7-8.30 (no D late Nov-late Jan) Av 3 course à la carte fr £20 ⊕ FREE HOUSE ◼ Black Sheep, Theakstons, Best Scotch, Ruddles. ♟ 10 **Facilities** Children's menu Family room Garden Parking **Rooms** 18

NOTTINGHAMSHIRE

BEESTON — Map 11 SK53

Victoria Hotel ♟

Dovecote Ln NG9 1JG
☎ 0115 925 4049 📄 0115 922 3537
e-mail: hopco.victoriabeeston@btconnect.com
dir: *M1 junct 25, A52 E. Turn right at Nurseryman PH, right opp Rockaway Hotel into Barton St 1st left, next to railway station*

The Victoria dates from 1899 when it was built next to Beeston Railway Station, and the large, heated patio garden is still handy for a touch of train-spotting. It offers an excellent range of traditional ales, (up to 12 at a time) continental beers and lagers, traditional ciders, a good choice of wines by the glass and single malt whiskies. Home-cooked dishes on the menu might include Lincolnshire sausages, and smoked chicken and bacon pasta. There are always plenty of vegetarian options available.

Open all day all wk 11-11 (Sun 12-11) Closed: 26 Dec **Bar Meals** food served all day **Restaurant** food served all day ⊕ FREE HOUSE ◀ Batemans XB, Castle Rock Harvest Pale, Castle Rock Hemlock, Everards Tiger, 6 guest ales Ò Thatchers Traditional, Broadoak Medium, Biddendens. ♟ 30 **Facilities** Dogs allowed Garden Parking

BINGHAM — Map 11 SK73

The Chesterfield ♟

Church St NG13 8AL ☎ 01949 837342
e-mail: eat@thechesterfield.co.uk
dir: *6m E of Nottingham, Bingham off A52 & A46 junct. Pub just off market square*

One of the earliest buildings in the centre of this small market town, the Chesterfield has been refurbished in contemporary style. The pub now features a stylish bar and gastro-style restaurant, as well as a private dining room and garden. Lunchtime brings snacks and sandwiches, plus a traditional Sunday roast. Typical restaurant choices include rack of lamb with apricots and cheese; seared fresh salmon salad; and grilled haloumi with cous cous and curry sauce.

Open all wk ◀ Timothy Taylor Landlord, Marston Pedigree, Wells Bombardier, Shepherd Neame Spitfire, Fuller's London Pride. ♟ 12 **Facilities** Garden Parking

BLIDWORTH — Map 16 SK55

Fox & Hounds ♟

Blidworth Bottoms NG21 0NW ☎ 01623 792383
e-mail: info@foxandhounds-pub.com
dir: *Right off B6020 between Ravenshead & Blidworth*

A traditional country pub, extensively refurbished a few years ago to create attractive surroundings in which to eat and drink. It was probably built as a farmhouse in the 19th century, when Blidworth Bottoms was a thriving community, with shops and a post office. A reputation for good pub food comes from dishes such as steak and ale pie; Mediterranean chicken; blackened salmon in Cajun spices; home-made vegetarian cottage pie; and hot chilli con carne.

Open all day all wk 11.30am-11.30pm (Fri-Sat 11.30am-mdnt) **Bar Meals** L served Mon-Wed 11.30-8.30, Thu-Sun 11.30-9 D served Mon-Wed 11.30-8.30, Thu-Sun 11.30-9 food served all day ⊕ GREENE KING ◀ H&H Cask Bitter, Old Speckled Hen, Olde Trip H&H, seasonal guest ales. ♟ 9 **Facilities** Children's menu Play area Dogs allowed Garden Parking

CAUNTON — Map 17 SK76

PICK OF THE PUBS

Caunton Beck ♟

NG23 6AB ☎ 01636 636793 📄 01636 636828
e-mail: email@cauntonbeck.com
dir: *6m NW of Newark on A616 to Sheffield*

This civilised village pub cum restaurant opens daily for breakfast and carries on serving food until around midnight, just like its sister establishment, the Wig & Mitre in Lincoln. It is built around a beautifully restored 16th-century cottage with herb gardens and a colourful rose arbour. Real ales complement a worthy international wine list, including a wide choice by the glass. The main menu changes with the seasons and is served throughout. To start you might choose soup of the day or twice-baked Caunton Beck soufflé with portobello mushroom and Roquefort cheese. Mains include locally sourced rib-eye of beef with a choice of sauces, or whole roast sea bass stuffed with piri piri, coriander and lime. Dishes are accompanied with a wine suggestion. Vegetarian and gluten-free options

are clearly marked. A sandwich and light meal menu is also available, with tea, coffees and home-made fudge on offer.

Open all day all wk 8am-mdnt **Bar Meals** Av main course £16.10 food served all day **Restaurant** Fixed menu price fr £11 Av 3 course à la carte fr £22.20 food served all day ⊕ FREE HOUSE ◀ Batemans Valiant, Marston's Pedigree, Tom Woods Best Bitter. ♟ 34 **Facilities** Children's menu Dogs allowed Garden Parking

CAYTHORPE — Map 11 SK64

Black Horse Inn

NG14 7ED ☎ 0115 966 3520
dir: *12m from Nottingham off A612 towards Southwell*

Old-fashioned hospitality is guaranteed in this small, beamed country pub which has been run by three generations of the same family. It has its own brewery, producing Caythorpe Dover Beck bitter (named after the stream that runs past the pub), a coal fire in the bar, and delicious home-cooked food prepared from seasonal ingredients. Fresh fish dishes such as mussels or fish and chips are a speciality; other choices might include fresh asparagus or a generous mixed grill. Good local walks.

Open noon-2.30 6-11 (Sun noon-5 8-10.30) Closed: Mon L (ex BH) **Bar Meals** L served Tue-Sat 12-1.45 booking required D served Tue-Sat 6.30-8.30 booking required Av main course £10 **Restaurant** L served Tue-Sat 12-1.45 booking required D served Tue-Fri 6.30-8.30 booking required Fixed menu price fr £30 Av 3 course à la carte fr £30 ⊕ FREE HOUSE ◀ Greene King Abbot Ale, Dover Beck Bitter, Batemans XB, Adnams Ò Westons Stowford Press. **Facilities** Dogs allowed Garden Parking **Notes** ⊜

COLSTON BASSETT — Map 11 SK73

PICK OF THE PUBS

The Martin's Arms ♟

See Pick of the Pubs on page 348

PICK OF THE PUBS

The Martin's Arms ♀

COLSTON BASSETT   Map 11 SK73

School Ln NG12 3FD
☎ **01949 81361**   📄 **01949 81039**
e-mail: martins_arms@hotmail.co.uk
dir: *Off A46 between Leicester & Newark*

Harry Whinney

This award-winning 18th-century inn stands right at the heart of the village, next to a market cross that dates back to 1257. A listed building, it has a real country house feel, with period furnishings, traditional hunting prints, and winter fires in the Jacobean fireplace. Indeed, so charming is the place that it has often featured on TV. The acre of landscaped grounds, which back on to National Trust land, includes a herb garden and well-established lawns. As a free house, the inn can offer

an impressive range of real ales, including Black Sheep Best, Batemans and Timothy Taylor Landlord. Regional ingredients are a feature of appetising and inventive dishes in both the bar and the restaurant. For example, the ploughman's incorporates Melton Mowbray pork pie, that town being not too far away. Starters include Thai fish cakes with Asian coleslaw and sweet chilli sauce; and warm wood-pigeon salad, roasted beetroot and Puy lentils. From the main dishes come turkey saltimbocca with Marsala cream, herb roast potato, roasted Brussels sprouts and chestnuts; pan-fried scallops, chorizo and courgette risotto and tapenade dressing; and braised lamb shank with parsley mash, red cabbage, garlic and rosemary jus. Typical of the specials would be roast rump of lamb, mixed pepper and tomato stew, roasted new potatoes and mint jus. Among the desserts is dark chocolate and raspberry mousse with white chocolate sauce. For a quick snack try a ciabatta filled with roasted vegetables, pesto and goats' cheese; or warm bacon, brie and cranberry compote. More than 30 wines are grouped by dryness, richness, softness, heartiness and other essential qualities.

Open all week 12-3.30 6-11 Closed: 25 Dec eve **Bar Meals** L served Mon-Sat 12-2 (Sun 12-2.30) D served Mon-Sat 7-9.30 Av main course £14
Restaurant L served all week 12-2 D served Mon-Sat 7-9.30 Fixed menu price fr £15.95 Av 3 course à la carte fr £25 🍺 FREE HOUSE 🛢 Marston's Pedigree, Interbrew Bass, Greene King Abbot Ale, Timothy Taylor Landlord, Black Sheep Best, Batemans, IPA & London Pride. ♀ 7 **Facilities** Family room Dogs allowed Garden Parking

Matt Shepherd

EDWINSTOWE · Map 16 SK66

Forest Lodge NEW ★★★★ INN ☻

2-4 Church St NG21 9QA
☎ 01623 824443 📠 01623 824686
e-mail: audrey@forestlodgehotel.co.uk
web: www.forestlodgehotel.co.uk
dir: *A614 towards Edwinstowe, turn onto B6034. Opp church*

Refurbished by the Thompson family over the past five years, the 18th-century coaching inn stands opposite Edwinstowe church, reputedly where Robin Hood married Maid Marion. Quaff local ales, perhaps Kelham Island Pale Rider, with a plate of ham, egg and chips in the beamed bars, or linger over garlic king prawns and braised ham hock with smoked bacon and parsley sauce in the restaurant. Upgrading extends to the thirteen freshly decorated bedrooms.

Open all wk 11.30-3 5.30-11 (Fri 11.30-3 5-11, Sun 12-3 6-10.30) Closed: 1 Jan **Bar Meals** L served all wk 12-2 (booking recommended Thu-Sun) D served all wk 6-9 (booking recommended Thu-Sun) Av main course £8 **Restaurant** L served all wk 12-2 booking required D served all wk 6-9 (booking recommended Thu-Sun) Fixed menu price fr £15.75 Av 3 course à la carte fr £20 ⊕ FREE HOUSE ◀ Bombardier, Kelham Island Pale Rider, Abbeydale Moonshine. ☻ 9 **Facilities** Children's menu Dogs allowed Garden Parking **Rooms** 13

ELKESLEY · Map 17 SK67

Robin Hood Inn ☻

High St DN22 8AJ ☎ 01777 838259
e-mail: a1robinhood@aol.com
dir: *5m SE of Worksop off A1 towards Newark-on-Trent*

Parts of this unassuming village inn date back to the 14th century. Ceilings and floors are deep red, while the green walls are adorned with pictures of food. The comprehensive choice is served in both the bar and restaurant, and includes a fixed price menu, carte and daily specials board. Beef bourguignon; grilled rump or fillet steak; pan-fried Normandy style chicken breast, or sausages, onions and mustard mash will satisfy the heartiest of appetites.

Open 11.30-2.30 6-11 Closed: Sun eve & Mon lunch **Bar Meals** L served Tue-Sun 12-2 D served Mon-Sat 6-8 Av main course £9 **Restaurant** L served Tue-Sun 12-2 D served Mon-Sat 6-9 Fixed menu price fr £12.50 Av 3 course à la carte fr £15 ⊕ ENTERPRISE INNS ◀ John Smiths Extra Smooth, Black Sheep Best Bitter, guest ale. ☻ 6 **Facilities** Children's menu Play area Garden Parking

FARNDON · Map 17 SK75

PICK OF THE PUBS

The Farndon Boathouse NEW ☻

Riverside NG24 3SX
☎ 01636 676578 📠 01636 673911
e-mail: info@farndonboathouse.co.uk
dir: *From Newark follow A46 to Farndon x-rds, turn right and follow rd to river. Boathouse on riverside*

A major refurbishment of what used to be The New Ferry has produced a bar and restaurant very much in the style of, well, an old boathouse, albeit a very fashionable one. Clad in wood, with chunky exposed roof trusses, stone floors and an abundance of glass, this part-restored, part-new building sits really rather well on the banks of the River Trent, which the bar and restaurant overlook through an extensively glazed frontage. Fresh modern cooking uses local produce to provide reasonably priced dishes that include smoked haddock fishcakes with peas, rice and warm curry sauce; beef with Cropwell Bishop Stilton and baby onion pie with mash, garden peas and gravy; spiced bouillabaisse; bell pepper stuffed with mixed bean and vegetable chilli con carne; steaks and a variety of burgers. Add real ales, continental beers, fine wines and live music to complete a very appealing picture.

Open all day all wk 10am-11pm **Bar Meals** L served Mon- Fri 12-2.30, Sat-Sun 12-3 D served all wk 6-9.30 Av main course £10 **Restaurant** L served Mon-Fri 12-2.30, Sat-Sun 12-3 D served all wk 6-9.30 Fixed menu price fr £12 Av 3 course à la carte fr £20 ⊕ FREE HOUSE ◀ Black Sheep, Caythorpe Dover Beck. ☻ 16 **Facilities** Children's menu Garden Parking

HALAM · Map 17 SK65

PICK OF THE PUBS

The Waggon and Horses ☻

The Turnpike, Mansfield Rd NG22 8AE
☎ 01636 813109 📠 01636 816228
e-mail: info@thewaggonathalam.co.uk
dir: *From A614 at White Post Farm rdbt follow signs to Farnsfield. In Halam, pub on right*

Halam's dapper village local shines like a beacon in the Nottinghamshire countryside, drawing diners from far and wide for chef-patron Roy Wood's inventive pub food. In the smartened-up, open-plan bar and dining room, which oozes charm and character with heavy oak beams, chunky tables on wooden or tiled floors, and a wealth of cricketing memorabilia, you can sup a pint of Thwaites Bomber while perusing the day's chalkboard menu. Expect a modern approach to cooking classic pub dishes, which make good use of local seasonal ingredients, as seen in ham hock terrine with date and apple chutney, and main courses like slow-cooked lamb with garlic and thyme; pork fillet with fennel and mustard; and halibut with lemon and herb butter. Roy's Nottinghamshire pie, made with steak, leeks, mustard and stilton, flies out the door, it's that popular. For pudding, try the baked vanilla, lemon and ginger cheesecake. The set lunch menu is a steal.

Open 11.30-3 5.30-10 Closed: Mon **Bar Meals** L served Tue-Sat 11.30-2 booking required D served Tue-Sat 5.30-8.30 booking required Av main course £12 **Restaurant** L served Tue Sun 11.30-2 booking required D served Tue-Sat 5.30-8.30 booking required Fixed menu price fr £12 Av 3 course à la carte fr £25 ⊕ THWAITES ◀ Thwaites Bomber, Smooth & Wainwright, Warsteiner. ☻ 8 **Facilities** Children's menu Parking

HARBY · Map 17 SK87

Bottle & Glass ☻

High St NG23 7EB ☎ 01522 703438 📠 01522 703436
e-mail: email@bottleandglassharby.com
dir: *S of A57 (Lincoln to Markham Moor road)*

Situated in a charming village a few miles west of Lincoln, the pub's original beams and flagstone floors date back many years. Queen Eleanor reputedly died here in 1290. Proprietor Michael Hope aims to create the reassuringly civilised ambience of a music-free meeting house, reading room, watering hole and restaurant. Young's Bitter rubs shoulders with Farmer's Blonde and Black Sheep, while seasonal dishes of twice-baked cheese soufflé with roasted red onions may be followed by roast fillet of pollack with Puy lentils. There are wine suggestions with each dish.

Open all day all wk 12-12 **Bar Meals** Av main course £14.25 food served all day **Restaurant** Fixed menu price fr £12.50 Av 3 course à la carte fr £20.40 food served all day ⊕ FREE HOUSE ◀ Young's Bitter, Farmers Blonde, Black Sheep. ☻ 34 **Facilities** Children's menu Dogs allowed Garden Parking

The Nelson & Railway Inn

12 Station Rd NG16 2NR
☎ 0115 938 2177   📄 0115 938 2179
dir: 1m N of M1 junct 26

The landlord of more than 30 years gives this 17th-century pub its distinctive personality. Next door is the Hardy & Hanson brewery that supplies many of the beers, but the two nearby railway stations that once made it a railway inn are now sadly derelict. A hearty menu of pub favourites includes soup, ploughman's, and hot rolls, as well as grills and hot dishes like home-made steak and kidney pie; gammon steak; and mushroom stroganoff.

Open all day all wk 11am-mdnt **Bar Meals** L served all wk 12-2.30 D served all wk 5.30-9 Av main course £5.50 **Restaurant** L served all wk 12-2.30 D served all wk 5.30-9 ⊕ HARDY & HANSONS PLC ◀ Hardys, Hansons Best Bitter, Cool & Dark, Olde Trip, Morlands, Ruddles. **Facilities** Children's menu Family room Dogs allowed Garden Parking

The Dovecote Inn ☗

Moorhouse Rd NG22 0SX ☎ 01777 871586
e-mail: dovecote-inn@btconnect.com
dir: Exit A1 at Tuxford through Egmanton to Laxton

Like most of the village of Laxton, this family-run, 18th-century pub is Crown Estate property belonging to the Royal Family. Outside is a delightful beer garden with views of the church. The interior includes a bar and three cosy wining and dining rooms. Here the seasonal, home-cooked dishes could include wild Alaskan salmon, slow-roast belly pork with apple and onion compote, chicken breast and bacon, or 28-day matured steak. The village still practises the Medieval strip field farming method – there is a visitor centre in the pub car park.

Open all wk 11.30-3 6.30-11 (Sun 12-10.30) **Bar Meals** Av main course £9 **Restaurant** L served Mon-Sat 12-2, Sun 12.30-6 D served Mon-Sat 6.30-9.30 booking required Av 3 course à la carte fr £18 ⊕ FREE HOUSE ◀ Mansfield Smooth, John Smith's Smooth, Black Sheep, Greene King Old Speckled Hen, Adnams. ☗ 10 **Facilities** Children's menu Dogs allowed Garden Parking

PICK OF THE PUBS

The Full Moon Inn ☗

See Pick of the Pubs on opposite page

Cock & Hoop ☗

25 High Pavement NG1 1HE
☎ 0115 852 3231   📄 0115 852 3236
e-mail: drink@cockandhoop.co.uk
dir: Follow tourist signs for 'Galleries of Justice'. Pub opposite

Tasteful antiques, a real fire, a cellar bar and some striking bespoke artwork characterize this traditional Victorian alehouse. It stands opposite the Galleries of Justice, where Lord Byron is said to have watched hangings from his lodgings above the pub.

Open all wk Closed: 25-26 Dec ⊕ FREE HOUSE ◀ Deuchars IPA, Cock & Hoop, London Pride, Timothy Taylor Landlord, Old Speckled Hen. ☗ 7 **Facilities** Family room Dogs allowed

Fellows Morton & Clayton

54 Canal St NG1 7EH
☎ 0115 950 6795   📄 0115 953 9838
e-mail: info@fellowsmortonandclayton.co.uk
dir: Telephone for directions

Surrounded by the impressive Castle Wharf complex, with a cobbled courtyard overlooking the Nottingham canal, 'Fellows' was converted from a former warehouse in 1979. The pub, which has been under the same tenancy since 1990, is a regular Nottingham in Bloom award winner. The varied menu includes chargrilled chicken and bacon salad; spicy bean burger on toasted ciabatta; and Spanish haddock with smoked salmon and seafood. Sandwiches and lighter lunches too.

Open all wk ⊕ ENTERPRISE INNS ◀ Timothy Taylor Landlord, Fuller's London Pride, Nottingham EPA, Deuchars IPA, Mallard Bitter. **Facilities** Garden Parking

Ye Olde Trip to Jerusalem ☗

1 Brewhouse Yard, Castle Rd NG1 6AD
☎ 0115 947 3171
e-mail: 4925@greeneking.co.uk
dir: In town centre

Said to be Britain's oldest inn, the Trip is surely one of the most unusual. Parts of the building penetrate deep into the sandstone of Castle Rock, and customers are warned to look out for uneven steps, floors and low doorways. It also would be wise to avoid cleaning the Cursed Galleon. The menu caters for most tastes, ranging from burgers, wraps and jacket potatoes to main course dishes like stilton and vegetable crumble; smoked haddock fish pot; and hickory barbecue chicken.

Open all day all wk 10am-11pm (Fri-Sat 10am-mdnt) **Bar Meals** L served all wk 10-12, 12-8 D served all wk 12-8 ⊕ GREENE KING ◀ Ye Olde Trip Ale, guest ales, Greene King IPA, Abbot Ale, Old Speckled Hen. ☗ 11 **Facilities** Garden

Three Crowns ☗

23 Easthorpe St NG11 6LB ☎ 0115 921 3226
e-mail: simon@nottinghamthai.co.uk
dir: A60 towards Loughborough. Right at 1st lights then Ruddington, right & right again, pub 500yds on left

A modern pub with an authentic Thai restaurant next door, where traditionally attired waitresses from the Land of Smiles glide between the tables. Lunchtime pub snacks include baguettes, omelettes, burgers, traditional pies and Thai stir-fries. The restaurant serves pork, chicken, beef, duck, fish and seafood curries of various strengths, and other Thai dishes, as well as steaks. Traditional roasts and other non-Thai meals are served on Sundays.

Open all wk ⊕ FREE HOUSE ◀ Adnams, Nottingham Brewery, Timothy Taylor Landlord, Cottage Brewery, guest ales. ☗ 18 **Facilities** Dogs allowed

The Red Lion ☗

Southwell Rd NG14 7GP ☎ 01636 830351
dir: On A612 between Nottingham & Southwell

This 16th-century inn was once a monks' alehouse. Pub food can be enjoyed in the bar, restaurant or garden. Main courses include beef and Guinness casserole, chicken breast in garlic and mushroom sauce, or a variety of steaks. For a lighter option, try a salad with roast ham or poached salmon and prawn; or the cheese platter with local blue stilton. Look out for the 1936 newspaper cutting reporting the murder of a previous landlady by her niece!

Open all wk 11.30-2.30 6.30-11 (Sat-Sun & BH 11.30-11) **Bar Meals** L served all wk 12-2 D served all wk 6.30-9.30 Av main course £8.75 **Restaurant** L served all wk 12-2 D served all wk 6.30-9.30 ⊕ FREE HOUSE ◀ Greene King Abbot Ale, Jennings Cumberland, Carlsberg-Tetley, Black Sheep, Mansfield Cask. ☗ 7 **Facilities** Garden Parking

PICK OF THE PUBS

The Full Moon Inn ♟

MORTON   Map 17 SK75

Main St NG25 0UT
☎ **01636 830251** 📄 **01636 830554**
e-mail: info@thefullmoonmorton.co.uk
dir: *Newark A617 to Mansfield. Past Kelham, turn left to Rolleston & follow signs to Morton*

In January 2009 the The Full Moon emerged from a transformation by William and Rebecca White that they venture to suggest turned a dark and dated pub, once three cottages from the late 1700s, into one that is light, comfortable and contemporary. They exposed the old beams and brickwork, used reclaimed panels and furniture, and laid new carpets to help create what has fast become a destination pub in this Trent-side hamlet. Year-round appeal includes a charming garden for the summer and two roaring log fires for the winter. Five hand pulls prove that

William takes his real ales and freehouse status very seriously; the wines are good too and fairly priced, with eight served by the glass. Rebecca is in charge of the kitchen, where the emphasis is on farm-fresh food sourced mostly locally, with a set menu running alongside the pub menu at lunchtime and in the evenings. There's plenty on offer, from sandwiches, baguettes, pastas, burgers and omelettes to Gonalston Farm Shop bangers with mash, red cabbage and gravy; Moon pie with Nottingham beef and roast vegetables, red cabbage and chips; and fresh haddock in beer batter with minted pea purée and chips. On Friday and Saturday nights the set menu is replaced with a specials board, featuring fish chosen by a local fishmonger and only chalked up once he's actually delivered it. Some of Rebecca's popular casserole style dishes are available in takeaway foil containers – as she says: "We do the hard work and you take all the credit!". There's plenty here to keep children occupied too, with a designated indoor play area, an outdoor castle and a sand pit, while dogs are also welcome.

Open all week **Bar Meals** L served all week 12-2.30 D served all week 6-9.30 Av main course £10 **Restaurant** L served all week 12-2.30 D served all week 6-9.30 Fixed menu price fr £16 Av 3 course à la carte fr £22 🛢 FREE HOUSE 🍺 Bombardier, Dover Beck, Moonshine, guest ales. ♟ 8
Facilities Children's menu Play area Family room Dogs allowed Garden Parking

TUXFORD
Map 17 SK77

The Mussel & Crab ♟

NG22 0PJ ☎ 01777 870491 ▤ 01777 872302
e-mail: musselandcrab1@hotmail.com
dir: From Ollerton/Tuxford junct of A1& A57. N on B1164 to Sibthorpe Hill. Pub 800yds on right

Beautifully fresh fish and seafood dominate the menu at this quirky pub with a multitude of rooms, all decked out in inimitable style. The piazza room is styled as an Italian courtyard, with murals by artist Tony Cooke; the beamed restaurant is big on rustic charm; and the gents' toilets is brightened with a tank of fish! Countless blackboards offer ever-changing dishes such as crab chowder; and monkfish in a red wine and mushroom sauce, plus some fish you have never tasted.

Open all wk **Bar Meals** L served all wk 11-2.30 booking required D served Mon-Sat 6-10, Sun 6-9 booking required Av main course £10 **Restaurant** L served all wk 11-2.30 booking required D served Mon-Sat 6-10, Sun 6-9 booking required Av 3 course à la carte fr £28 ⊕ FREE HOUSE ◀ Tetley Smooth, Tetley Cask, Guinness. ♟ 16 **Facilities** Children's menu Family room Dogs allowed Garden Parking

---

OXFORDSHIRE

ABINGDON
Map 5 SU49

The Merry Miller ♟

Cothill OX13 6JW ☎ 01865 390390 ▤ 01865 390040
e-mail: rob@merrymiller.co.uk
dir: 1m from Marcham interchange on A34

Any inventory of the Merry Miller must include its wealth of risqué prints. Despite the beams, flagstones and stripped pine tables, the interior of this 17th-century former granary is more redolent of Tuscany - which at least ensures that the pasta dishes feel at home! But lunch could just as easily be a club sandwich or seafood salad bowl, whilst evening diners might choose roasted Gressingham duck; or tomato, goats' cheese and Puy lentil tartlettes.

Open all wk ⊕ GREENE KING ◀ Greene King IPA, Old Speckled Hen. ♟ 15 **Facilities** Dogs allowed Garden Parking

---

ADDERBURY
Map 11 SP43

Red Lion Ⓐ ★★ HL ♟

The Green OX17 3LU
☎ 01295 810269 ▤ 01295 811906
e-mail: 6496@greeneking.co.uk
dir: Off M40, 3m from Banbury

A fine stone-built coaching inn on the Banbury to Oxford road, overlooking the village green. Established in 1669, the Red Lion was once known as the King's Arms, and had a tunnel in the cellar used by Royalists in hiding during the Civil War. Enter the rambling, beamed interior to find daily newspapers, real ales, good wines and a varied menu, with plenty of fish choices like home-made Thai salmon fish cakes, chargrilled tuna steaks, and salmon steak parcels.

Open all day all wk 7am-11pm (Sat 8am-11.30pm, Sun 8am-11pm) **Bar Meals** food served all day **Restaurant** food served all day ⊕ GREENE KING ◀ Greene King IPA, Abbot Ale, Old Speckled Hen, Guest. ♟ 11 **Facilities** Garden Parking **Rooms** 12

ARDINGTON
Map 5 SU48

PICK OF THE PUBS

The Boar's Head ★★★★ INN ◉◉ ♟

See Pick of the Pubs on opposite page

BAMPTON
Map 5 SP30

The Romany

Bridge St OX18 2HA
☎ 01993 850237 ▤ 01993 852133
e-mail: romany@barbox.net
dir: Telephone for details

A shop until 20 years ago, The Romany is housed in an 18th-century building of Cotswold stone with a beamed bar, log fires and intimate dining room. The choice of food ranges from bar snacks and bar meals to a full carte restaurant menu, with home-made specials like hotpot, Somerset pork, or steak and ale pie. There is a good range of vegetarian choices. Regional singers provide live entertainment a couple of times a month.

Open all wk **Bar Meals** L served all wk 12-2.30 D served all wk 6-9.30 Av main course £10 **Restaurant** L served all wk 12-2.30 D served all wk 6-9.30 ⊕ PUNCH ◀ Archers Village, Fuller's London Pride, Brakspears, guest ales ♂ Westons Stowford Press. **Facilities** Children's menu Play area Dogs allowed Garden Parking

---

BANBURY
Map 11 SP44

The Wykham Arms ♟

Temple Mill Rd, Sibford Gower OX15 5RX
☎ 01295 788808
e-mail: info@wykhamarms.co.uk
dir: Between Banbury & Shipston-on-Stour off B4035. 20m S of Stratford-upon-Avon

A charming 18th-century thatched inn built of mellow stone with lovely countryside views, where drinkers and diners congregate in intimate beamed rooms. Along with well kept real ales and a good wine list, the bar menu, also available in the terrace and garden, offers great sandwiches like sirloin steak or Wykham club. Restaurant main courses may include Caesar salad with roasted maize-fed chicken or Salcombe crab and mango salad.

Open 12-2.30 6-11 Closed: Mon **Bar Meals** L served Tue-Sat 12-2.30 D served Tue-Sat 7-9.30 Av main course £15 **Restaurant** L served Tue-Sun 12-2.30 D served Tue-Sat 7-9.30 Av 3 course à la carte fr £26.50 ⊕ FREE HOUSE ◀ Hook Norton Best, Guinness, St Austell Tribute, Adnams Broadside, London Pride. ♟ 17 **Facilities** Children's menu Family room Dogs allowed Garden Parking

---

Ye Olde Reindeer Inn

47 Parsons St OX16 5NA
☎ 01295 264031 ▤ 01295 264018
e-mail: tonypuddifoot@aol.com
dir: 1m from M40 junct 11, in town centre just off market square

The oldest pub in Banbury, the Reindeer dates back to 1570. During the Civil War, Oliver Cromwell met his men here in the magnificent Globe Room, which still has its original panelling. A great range of cask ales is kept and a large selection of malt whiskies. Mulled wines are another house speciality. Pick of the menu is the very popular bubble and squeak and Yorkshire pudding filled with sausage, onion and gravy.

Open all wk **Bar Meals** L served Mon-Sat 11-2.30 Av main course £5.60 ⊕ HOOK NORTON BREWERY ◀ Hook Norton, Best, Hook Norton Haymaker, Old, 12 days, Dark & Gold. **Facilities** Family room Garden Parking

PICK OF THE PUBS

The Boar's Head ★★★★ INN ❀❀ ♟

ARDINGTON
Map 5 SU48

Church St OX12 8QA
☎ 01235 833254 📄 01235 833254
e-mail: info@boarsheadardington.co.uk
web: www.boarsheadardington.co.uk
dir: *Off A417 E of Wantage, next to village church*

Here is a combination of pub, first-class restaurant and excellent accommodation that works a treat in this lovely downland village. Ardington and its twin community, Lockinge, lie within the estate laid out in the 19th century by Lord Wantage, who would no doubt be tickled pinked that it remains very much as he left it. The half-timbered Boar's Head has been serving the local community for the past 150 years, its scrubbed pine tables, candles, fresh flowers and blazing log fires creating just the right atmosphere for today's pub-goer. Everything, from bread to ice cream, and from pasta to pastries, is made on the premises. The menu, which changes regularly, is varied and well known for the chef's fish specialities, featuring whatever comes up daily from Cornish ports. A typical meal might begin with Serrano ham with crazy salad and shaved Manchego; or a plate of Cornwall scallops; to be followed by Newlyn sea bass in pastry with girolle mushrooms in Chardonnay and tomato butter sauce; breast of duck with chorizo, rösti and port sauce; or roast rack of spring lamb with herb crust and minted pea risotto. Finish with a hot pistachio soufflé with iced chocolate cream; or tartlet of blackberry and apple crumble with vanilla. Should you feel inclined to take advantage of one of three well-appointed guest suites, you could explore the region further, since Ardington is an ideal base for walking or cycling, and footpaths wind through nearby villages and run up to the ancient Ridgeway. Golfers will appreciate the several excellent courses nearby, while fly-fishers can obtain a day-pass for the area's well-stocked trout lakes.

Open all week **Bar Meals** L served all week 12-2 D served all week 7-9.30 Av main course £11 **Restaurant** L served all week 12-2 D served all week 7-9.30 Fixed menu price fr £15 Av 3 course à la carte fr £30 ⊕ FREE HOUSE ◀ Hook Norton Old Hooky, West Berkshire Brewery Dr. Hexter's, Warsteiner, Butts Brewery, Barbus Barbus, Cotswold Lager. ♟ 8 **Facilities** Garden Parking **Rooms** 3

BARNARD GATE | Map 5 SP41

PICK OF THE PUBS

The Boot Inn ⚑

OX29 6XE ☎ 01865 881231
e-mail: info@theboot-inn.com
dir: *Off A40 between Witney & Eynsham*

The Boot is renowned for its celebrity boot collection – the Bee Gees, George Best and Jeremy Irons to name a few. Exposed beams, stone-flagged floors and two fabulous open fires set the scene at the inn, which is surrounded by beautiful countryside on the edge of the Cotswolds, near the ancient village of Eynsham, a few miles west of Oxford. There is a pleasant garden for summer use, a welcoming bar and secluded dining areas. Beers from well-known and reliable brewers are on tap, and the wine list would satisfy the most cosmopolitan of oenophiles. The lunch menu offers salads, doorstop sandwiches and a selection from the chargrill: burgers, sausages and steaks. Dinner options are along the lines of confit pork belly with Lyonnaise potatoes and balsamic roasted beetroot; ale battered fish with hand-cut chips; and butternut squash and feta cheese risotto.

Open all day all wk **Bar Meals** L served Mon-Sat 12-2.30, Sun 12-10 D served Mon-Sat 7-10, Sun 12-10 Av main course £12.95 **Restaurant** L served Mon-Sat 12 2.30, Sun 12 10 D served Mon-Sat 7-10, Sun 12-10 Av 3 course à la carte fr £23 ⊕ FREE HOUSE ◀ Hook Norton Best, Adnams Best, Fuller's London Pride, Youngs Best. ⚑ 7 **Facilities** Garden Parking

BECKLEY | Map 5 SP51

PICK OF THE PUBS

The Abingdon Arms ⚑

High St OX3 9UU ☎ 01865 351311
e-mail: chequers89@hotmail.com
dir: *M40 junct 8, follow signs at Headington rdbt for Beckley*

Expect a warm welcome at this cosy, traditional pub set in a pretty village to the north of Oxford. It has been smartly updated, and good food is also helping to put it on the map, backed by excellent beers from Brakspear. A range of sandwiches and bar snacks is available at lunchtime, while a full meal could include marinated crab with chilli, coriander and rocket, followed by chargrilled medallions of lamb with spinach mash and mustard cream sauce. The atmosphere in the pub is always friendly, and there are roaring log fires in winter. In the summer you can sit on the patio and enjoy the spectacular views of Otmoor. Some years ago this area was popular with the writer Evelyn Waugh, and today it is just round the corner from an RSPB bird reserve. There are opportunities for many pleasant walks in the area.

Open all wk ⊕ BRAKSPEAR ◀ Brakspears Bitter, Brakspear Special, Brakspear guest. ⚑ 8
Facilities Garden Parking

BLACK BOURTON | Map 5 SP20

PICK OF THE PUBS

The Vines ⚑

Burford Rd OX18 2PF
☎ 01993 843559 📠 01993 840080
e-mail: info@vineshotel.com
web: www.vinesblackbourton.co.uk
dir: *From A40 Witney, take A4095 to Faringdon, then 1st right after Bampton to Black Bourton*

A beautiful Cotswold village within easy reach of Burford, Witney and the Thames Path is the setting for the Vines, a traditional stone-built inn with an elegant, contemporary feel and surrounded by delightful gardens. The BBC's *Real Rooms* team famously designed and transformed the restaurant and bar, so expect a surprisingly stylish interior for a Cotswold pub, with murals, wooden floors, big plants in pots, and leather sofas fronting open log fires. Relax with a pint of Hooky or linger over lunch or dinner, the menus listing an imaginative choice of modern British dishes with an international twist, all freshly prepared using locally sourced produce. Typical examples from the carte include rump of lamb with tomato, garlic and rosemary; confit duck with Calvados sauce; baked halibut with seafood and cream sauce; and wild mushroom risotto. In addition, there's a good-value light bites menu, decent Sunday roasts, and a raft of Old and New World wines by the glass. On sunny days, dine alfresco on the sun-trap patio or play a nostalgic game of Aunt Sally.

Closed: Mon L **Bar Meals** L served Tue-Sun 12-2 D served Tue-Sun 6-9 Av main course £12.50 **Restaurant** L served Tue-Sun 12-2 D served Tue-Sun 6-9 Av 3 course à la carte fr £25 ⊕ FREE HOUSE ◀ Old Hooky, Tetley Smooth. ⚑ 7 **Facilities** Garden Parking

BLOXHAM | Map 11 SP43

The Elephant & Castle

OX15 4LZ ☎ 0845 873 7358
e-mail: elephant.bloxham@btinternet.com
dir: *M40 junct 11, pub just off A361, in village centre. 11m from Banbury*

The arch of this family-run 15th-century Cotswold-stone coaching inn used to straddle the former Banbury to Chipping Norton turnpike. At night the gates of the pub were closed, and no traffic could get over the toll bridge. Locals play Aunt Sally or shove-ha'penny in the big wood-floored bar, whilst the two-roomed lounge boasts a bar-billiards table and a large inglenook fireplace. The menu offers a range of sandwiches and crusty filled baguettes, plus pub favourites like roast chicken breast with stuffing, crispy battered cod and lasagne verdi.

Open all wk 10-3 5-12 (Fri 10-3 5-2am, Sat 10am-2am, Sun 10am-mdnt) **Bar Meals** L served Mon-Sat 12-2 Av main course £5 **Restaurant** L served Mon-Sat 12-2 ⊕ HOOK NORTON BREWERY ◀ Hook Norton Best Bitter, Hook Norton seasonal ales, guest ales ♂ Westons Old Rosie Scrumpy. **Facilities** Children's menu Play area Family room Dogs allowed Garden Parking

BRIGHTWELL BALDWIN | Map 5 SU69

PICK OF THE PUBS

The Lord Nelson Inn ⚑

See Pick of the Pubs on opposite page

BROUGHTON | Map 11 SP43

Saye and Sele Arms ⚑

Main Rd OX15 5ED ☎ 01295 263348
e-mail: mail@sayeandselearms.co.uk
dir: *3m from Banbury Cross*

Licensed for some 300 years, this pretty 16th-century free house stands just five minutes' walk from Broughton Castle, home to Lord and Lady Saye and Sele. Adnams is the resident beer, with three ever-changing guest ales and Stowford Press cider too. Chef/proprietor Danny McGeehan's 'proper' pies are always on the menu, whilst other dishes might include spinach, courgette and field mushroom lasagne; or venison steak on curly kale with juniper and port wine sauce.

Open 11.30-2.30 7-11 (Sat 11.30-3 7-11 Sun 12-5) Closed: 25 Dec, Sun eve **Bar Meals** L served Mon-Sat 12-2 booking required D served Mon-Sat 7-9.30 booking required **Restaurant** L served Mon-Sat 12-2, Sun 12-3 booking required D served Mon-Sat 7-9.30 booking required ⊕ FREE HOUSE ◀ Adnams Southwold, Hook Norton, Black Sheep, 2 guest ales ♂ Westons Stowford Press. ⚑ 8 **Facilities** Dogs allowed Garden Parking

PICK OF THE PUBS

The Lord Nelson Inn ♈

BRIGHTWELL BALDWIN   Map 5 SU69

OX49 5NP ☎ **01491 612497**
e-mail: ladyhamilton1@hotmail.co.uk
dir: *Off B4009 between Watlington & Benson*

In Nelson's day, this 17th-century pub was known as the Admiral Nelson, but when, in 1797, our naval hero was elevated to the peerage, its name was elevated too. For more than a century after that, passing travellers and villagers slaked their thirst here. In 1905, following complaints from the church and the local squire about over-indulgent estate workers, the inn was closed and it became a shop, a post office and then a private house. In 1971 a couple driving past liked the look of it,

bought it, renewed its licence and restored it to its former glory, decorating the interior in traditional style, in keeping with its age. These days, it's always full of fresh flowers and lit candles. During the summer the pretty, weeping willow-draped garden, and the rear terrace, are popular places to eat and drink. All the food is freshly cooked, using local produce where possible. The house menu begins with a complimentary basket of bread and olives. Starters might include seared scallops wrapped in Parma ham with baby spinach and watercress with lime and coriander dressing, or local pigeon breast with Puy lentils and wild mushrooms. For light main course options, try seafood pancake, tiger prawn tempura, mushroom omelette or crispy duck salad with oriental sauce. Calves' liver and bacon on black pudding mash; rack of English lamb stuffed with garlic and rosemary with red wine sauce; and fillets of sea bass on a crab mash with tomato and black olive tapenade are fine examples of

main courses. Weekly specials are shown on the boards. Real ales served in the beamed bar are supplied by Black Sheep, Brakspear, John Smiths and West Berkshire Brewery, and the comprehensive wine list includes 20 by the glass. In the early 1990s the RSPB chose the nearby Chiltern escarpment to reintroduce the red kite - you'll be unlucky not to see at least one.

Open 12-3 6-11 (Sun 12-10.30) **Bar Meals** L served all wk 12-2.30 D served all wk 6-10 Av main course 12 **Restaurant** L served all wk 12-2.30 D served all wk 6-10 Av 3 course à la carte fr £20 ⊕ FREE HOUSE ◖ West Berkshire Brewery, Brakspear, John Smiths, Black Sheep. ♈ 20 **Facilities** Garden Parking

BURCOT
Map 5 SU59

The Chequers ♟

OX14 3DP ☎ 01865 407771 📄 01865 407771
e-mail: enquiries@thechequers-burcot.co.uk
dir: *On A415 (Dorchester to Abingdon road) between Clifton Hampden & Dorchester on Thames*

Once a staging post for barges on the Thames, this 400-year-old thatched and timber framed pub now combines the best of old and new. On winter days the blazing fire surrounded by sofas is the favoured spot, especially for toasting marshmallows; in summer, the enclosed beer garden takes precedence. The food is serious, pubby home cooking: think pan-fried field mushrooms in garlic and herb butter on toast to start; then beer battered haddock with hand cut chips; or slow roasted lamb shank with mint and redcurrant gravy.

Open all day all wk 12-11 (Sun 12-4) **Bar Meals** L served all wk 12-3 D served Mon-Sat 6.30-9.30 Av main course £13 **Restaurant** L served all wk 12-3 booking required D served Mon-Sat 6.30-9.30 booking required Av 3 course à la carte fr £23 ⊕ FREE HOUSE ◀ Hook Norton Bitter, Ridgway, Young's, guest ales ♂ Westons Stowford Press. ♟ 21 **Facilities** Children's menu Garden Parking

BURFORD
Map 5 SP21

PICK OF THE PUBS

The Inn for All Seasons ★★ HL ♟
See Pick of the Pubs on opposite page

PICK OF THE PUBS

The Lamb Inn ★★★ SHL ◉◉ ♟
See Pick of the Pubs on page 358

CHADLINGTON
Map 10 SP32

The Tite Inn ♟

Mill End OX7 3NY ☎ 01608 676475 📄 01608 676475
dir: *2m S of Chipping Norton & 7m N of Burford*

Seventeenth-century Cotswold-stone free house where, in 1642, Royalist troops sank a few stiffeners before the Battle of Edgehill nearby. Situated in the beautiful countryside of the Cotswolds, the inn has a traditional, warm welcoming feel, with an open fire, flagstone floor and oak topped bar. The restaurant area is separate and the menu offers the finest range of home reared South Devon cross beef from fillet steak to burgers. Expect warm duck salad with redcurrant sauce, or pan fried scallops in lemon butter; followed by grilled ginger and coriander marinated tuna, or pan fried sirloin steak with peppercorn sauce.

Open 11-3 6-11 (Sun 12-3 7-10.30) Closed: Mon (ex BH) **Bar Meals** L served Tue-Sun 12-2.30 D served Tue-Sat 7-9 **Restaurant** L served Tue-Sun 12-2.30 booking required D served Tue-Sat 7-9 booking required ⊕ FREE HOUSE ◀ Sharp's, Timothy Taylor Landlord ♂ Westons Stowford Press. ♟ 6 **Facilities** Children's menu Dogs allowed Garden Parking

CHALGROVE
Map 5 SU69

PICK OF THE PUBS

The Red Lion Inn ♟

The High St OX44 7SS ☎ 01865 890625
e-mail: raymondsexton@btinternet.com
web: www.redlionchalgrove.co.uk
dir: *B480 from Oxford ring road, through Stadhampton, left then right at mini-rdbt. At Chalgrove Airfield right into village*

Rather unusually, the cruck-framed 15th-century Red Lion is one of only two pubs in the country owned by its local parish church. How appropriate, then, that the owners are Suzanne and Raymond Sexton; Raymond, incidentally, was Jamie Oliver's father's chef for 10 years. From the front garden there is a view of the memorial to Colonel John Hampden, a key political figure fatally wounded in a Civil War skirmish nearby. From a 'menu that tries to please everyone' come starters such as salad of spicy merguez sausage, potatoes and shallots topped with a crispy poached egg; and pan-fried pigeon breasts with wild rice and a port wine jus. Main dishes may include pan-fried kidneys served on a bed of bubble and squeak with bacon lardons and balsamic vinegar; and pork loin

chops grilled and served on a rich goats' cheese and sage cream. Sandwiches and side orders are also available at lunchtime.

Open all wk 11.30-3 6-mdnt (Sat 11.30-3 6-1am Sat 11.30am-1am Sun 11.30am-mdnt in summer) **Bar Meals** L served Mon-Sat 12-2, Sun 12-3 D served Mon-Sat 6-9 Av main course £11.50 **Restaurant** L served Mon-Sat 12-2, Sun 12-3 D served Mon-Sat 6-9 Fixed menu price fr £6.50 Av 3 course à la carte fr £21 ⊕ FREE HOUSE ◀ Fuller's London Pride, Adnams Best, Timothy Taylor Landlord, Boddingtons, guest ale ♂ Aspalls, Westons Stowford Press. ♟ 8 **Facilities** Children's menu Play area Dogs allowed Garden

CHARLBURY
Map 11 SP31

PICK OF THE PUBS

The Bull Inn ♟

Sheep St OX7 3RR ☎ 01608 810689
e-mail: info@bullinn-charlbury.com
dir: *M40 junct 8, A40, A44 follow Woodstock/Blenheim Palace signs. Through Woodstock take B4437 to Charlbury, pub at x-rds in town*

The mellow stone frontage of this fine 16th-century free house presides over Charlbury's main street. The beamed interior is full of period character, and log fires burn in the inglenook fireplaces in winter. There's a traditional bar with wooden floors, as well as a tastefully furnished lounge and dining room. Outside, the vine-covered terrace is a delightful spot to sit and enjoy a drink or a meal in summer. Food is served in both the bar and restaurant, with options ranging from lunchtime sandwiches and light meals in the bar, to a full restaurant menu. Diners might like to start with grilled goats' cheese on roasted red peppers with a pesto sauce, before tackling main course choices such as chargrilled swordfish with roasted asparagus and vine tomatoes, or rack of lamb with honey and mint sauce. Raspberry crush in a brandy snap basket is a typical option for dessert.

Open 11.30-2.30 6-11 Closed: Sun eve & Mon **Bar Meals** L served Tue-Sun 12-2 D served Tue-Sat 7-9 **Restaurant** L served Tue-Sun 12-2 D served Tue-Sat 7-9 Av 3 course à la carte fr £20 ⊕ FREE HOUSE ◀ Hook Norton, Wickwar, Wychwood, Goffs. ♟ 10 **Facilities** Garden Parking

PICK OF THE PUBS

The Inn for All Seasons ★★HL 🍷

The Barringtons OX18 4TN
☎ **01451 844324** 📄 **01451 844375**
e-mail: sharp@innforallseasons.com
dir: *3m W of Burford on A40*

Stagecoach travellers between London and West Wales in the 18th century would have been gasping for refreshment by the time they reached Burford. The New Inn, as it then was, was one of three coaching inns at which they could have stopped, all owned by the Barrington Park Estate. It remained estate-owned until the 1950s, when along with the nearby garage, it was bought by Shell, who sold it again in

1964 to a couple who had worked on the film *A Man for All Seasons* (hence the inn's name). In the mid-1980s the Sharp family took over and have been here ever since. Within its solid Cotswold stone walls is a treasure trove of ancient oak beams, inglenooks and coaching age mementoes, giving it that true country pub feel. Guest ales always include a Wychwood from nearby Witney. Matthew Sharp is a classically trained chef with a string of prestigious postings behind him; he selects only the best of everything for his British Continental cuisine, including game from the Barrington Estate. And he knows all the right people in Brixham to guarantee a daily supply of excellent fish for dedicated menus that feature roast John Dory on egg noodles with red wine and shallot sauce; and whole grilled lobster with lemon rice and sweet mustard and brandy sauce. Dinner might be rack of Cotswold lamb with a Provençal crust and caramelised garlic

and thyme sauce; tagliatelle with wild mushrooms, Parmesan and coriander and cherry tomato sauce; or confit of Gloucester pork with crisp stir-fry vegetables and plum and ginger dressing. At lunchtime there are grilled paninis, sandwiches and light meals. Blackberry pancake with crème fraîche; and hot chocolate fondant with vanilla ice cream are typical desserts. The 120 wines are chosen with the advice of local merchants to ensure a consistently high quality. There are 10 traditional country style inn bedrooms available if you would like to stay over.

Open all week 🍺 FREE HOUSE
🛢 Wadworth 6X, Interbrew Bass, Wychwood, Badger, Sharp's Doom Bar. 🍷 15 **Facilities** Play area Dogs allowed Garden Parking **Rooms** 10

PICK OF THE PUBS

The Lamb ★★★ SHL 🌸🌸 🍷

Sheep St OX18 4LR
☎ **01993 823155** 📠 **01993 822228**
e-mail: info@lambinn-burford.co.uk
web: www.cotswold-inns-hotels.co.uk/lamb
dir: *M40 junct 8, follow A40 & Burford signs, 1st turn, down hill into Sheep St*

The description 'charming old inn' may not always be fully deserved, but there's no question about the Lamb's right to use it. Lying just off the centre of Burford, this honey-coloured stone building was built in 1420 as weavers' cottages, but it's a long, long time since anyone threaded a weft through a warp here. The bar, with its stone-flagged floor and log fire, draws in hotel guests, visitors and locals alike, and is clearly a favourite spot to exchange news and views. The spacious, cream-walled, two-AA Rosette restaurant overlooks a walled cottage garden and courtyard, and its cheerful interior combines original features, such as mullioned windows, with modern fabrics, enhanced by flowers, candles and light jazz. The regularly-changing menus present contemporary English cooking with strong traditional influences, and owe their success almost entirely to locally sourced ingredients. Extensive lunch and dinner options include starters of carpaccio of beetroot with apple and walnut beignet; pressed confit pork belly and fig terrine with toasted blue cheese bread; and scallops, black pudding and mash. For a main course, try crispy duck leg with home-made spicy apricot chutney and sautéed potatoes; roast chicken breast with fettuccine and black olive salsa; or pan-fried sea bass with warm plum tomato and potato fricassée, sauce vierge. Among the desserts might be pear and apple crumble with ice cream; and pistachio soufflé with chocolate sorbet. A light bite might suffice: eggs Benedict with smoked salmon; or Cotswold Brie with cranberry sauce; or traditional sandwiches served with kettle chips and green salad, perhaps. On Sundays, there's Cotswold roast beef with Yorkshire pudding; roast pork with apple sauce; pan-fried salmon with olive-crushed potatoes and spinach froth; and twice-baked cheese soufflé with poached pear and walnut salad.

Open all week 11-11 **Bar Meals** L served all week 12-2.30 D served all week 6.30-9.30 **Restaurant** L served all week 12-2.30 D served all week 7-9.30 🍺 FREE HOUSE 🛢 Hook Norton Best, Brakspear. 🍷 9 **Facilities** Dogs allowed Garden **Rooms** 17

CHECKENDON — Map 5 SU68

The Highwayman ◉ ⛫

Exlade St RG8 0UA ☎ 01491 682020
dir: *On A4074 (Reading to Wallingford road)*

This early 17th-century listed inn has been beautifully restored and refurbished. The emphasis in the character bar is on wooden floors and open fireplaces, while the exterior has plenty of seating for fine days to enjoy a pint of Loddon Ferryman's Gold. The famous Maharajah's Well nearby is surrounded by numerous walks in the glorious Chiltern beechwoods. Eggs Benedict, trio of Cumberland sausages on bubble and squeak, and a superb list of local cheeses are typical examples from the inviting menu. A change of ownership has taken place.

Open all wk 11.30-3 5.30-11 **Bar Meals** L served all wk 11.30-2.30 D served all wk 5.30-9.30 Av main course £7 food served all day **Restaurant** L served all wk 11.30-2.30 D served Mon-Sat 5.30-9.30 Av 3 course à la carte fr £25 food served all day ⊕ FREE HOUSE ◀ Fuller's London Pride, Loddon Ferryman's Gold, Butlers Brewers, guest ale. ⛫ 6 **Facilities** Dogs allowed Garden Parking

CHINNOR — Map 5 SP70

PICK OF THE PUBS

The Sir Charles Napier ◉◉ ⛫

Spriggs Alley OX39 4BX
☎ 01494 483011 ▤ 01494 485311
dir: *M40 junct 6 to Chinnor. Turn right at rdbt, up hill to Spriggs Alley*

This is a true destination pub, but then it's probably always been one. After all, when the itinerant wood-turners, the bodgers, who once worked up in the hills wanted a beer, this was indeed their destination. Inside and out are stone, marble and wood sculptures by Michael Cooper – a statue of a naked woman particularly appealed to the Guardian's Matthew Norman. Huge log fires, comfortable sofas and an eclectic jumble of old furnishings characterise the interior, while the kitchen is proud of its two AA Rosettes. In summer, lunch is served on the vine- and wisteria-shaded terrace that overlooks extensive lawns and herb gardens. Try Bresse pigeon, wild mushroom ravioli, sausage roll and celeriac purée; or noisettes of venison, red onion tarte Tatin, girolles, nutmeg and orange jus. Skate wing with lemon and caper butter; and Lancashire hotpot are among the blackboard specials. A truly extensive wine list even includes bottles from Oregon and Lebanon.

Open noon-4 6-mdnt (Sun noon-6) Closed: 25-26 Dec, Mon, Sun eve **Bar Meals** L served Tue-Fri 12-2.30 D served Tue-Fri 6.30-9 Av main course £11.50 **Restaurant** L served Tue-Sat 12-2.30, Sun 12-3.30 booking required D served Tue-Sat 6.30-10 booking required Fixed menu price fr £14.50 Av 3 course à la carte fr £34 ⊕ FREE HOUSE ◀ Wadworth 6X, Wadworth IPA. ⛫ 15 **Facilities** Children's menu Dogs allowed Garden Parking

CHIPPING NORTON — Map 10 SP32

The Chequers ⛫

Goddards Ln OX7 5NP
☎ 01608 644717 ▤ 01608 646237
e-mail: info@chequers-pub.com/webmail
dir: *In town centre, next to theatre*

Log fires, low ceilings and soft lighting make for a cosy atmosphere in the bar of this popular 16th-century inn. By contrast, the courtyard restaurant is wonderfully bright and airy. Well-kept real ale, good wines and decent coffee are served along with freshly prepared contemporary dishes. Look for starters like wild mushroom risotto; and mains including baked cod in Parma ham with sun-dried tomato and pine nut cous cous; and chicken stir-fry with cashew nuts.

Open all day all wk 11am-11pm (Sun 11am-10.30pm) Closed: 25 Dec **Bar Meals** L served Mon-Sat 12-2.30. Sun 12-4 D served Mon-Sat 6-9.30 **Restaurant** L served Mon-Sat 12-2.30. Sun 12-4 D served Mon-Sat 6-9.30 ⊕ FULLERS BREWERY ◀ Fuller's Chiswick Bitter, London Pride & ESB, Organic Honeydew, Fullers Special Ale. ⛫ 18

CHISELHAMPTON — Map 5 SU59

PICK OF THE PUBS

Coach & Horses Inn — INN ⛫

Watlington Rd OX44 7UX
☎ 01865 890255 ▤ 01865 891995
e-mail: enquiries@coachhorsesinn.co.uk
dir: *From Oxford on B480 towards Watlington, 5m*

A young girl killed during the Civil War is believed to haunt this delightful 16th-century inn. Set in peaceful countryside on the old Roman road Icknield Street, the inn, as the name attests, once provided hospitality for the stage coaches travelling from Birmingham to London. Among the features inside are roaring log fires, quaint beams and an old bread oven. Start with deep fried brie with cranberry and orange chutney, before breast of chicken pancetta with creamy grain mustard sauce, or a steak from the grill. Vegetarians might like courgette and cherry tomato lasagne; or field and button mushrooms flamed in brandy with paprika. The daily specials fish board could include mixed seafood grill; fresh fillet of sea bass; and red snapper. Grills, poultry and game are also perennial favourites. There are nine chalet-style en suite bedrooms available, all with lovely rural views.

Open all wk 11-11 (Sun 11-10.30) **Bar Meals** L served Mon-Sat 12-2 booking required Av main course £10 **Restaurant** L served all wk 12-2 booking required D served Mon-Sat 7-9.30 booking required Av 3 course à la carte fr £12 ⊕ FREE HOUSE ◀ Hook Norton Best, London Pride, Old Hooky. ⛫ 8 **Facilities** Garden Parking **Rooms** 9

CHRISTMAS COMMON — Map 5 SU79

PICK OF THE PUBS

The Fox and Hounds ⛫

OX49 5HL ☎ 01491 612599
e-mail: kiran.daniels@btconnect.com
dir: *M40 junct 5, 2.5m to Christmas Common, on road towards Henley*

Renovations in recent years have transformed this charming 500-year-old inn into a stylish dining pub with an immaculate interior, a large restaurant complete with open-plan kitchen, and four cosy bar areas. Changing special and an imaginative menu that places a clear emphasis on quality ingredients, local where possible, produces lunchtime sandwiches (perhaps Welsh rarebit; or Scottish smoked salmon with cucumber and cream cheese) and excellent value hot dishes. Typical choices include roast red onion, oven-dried tomato, butternut, rocket and three cheese tart; and "lunch for a fiver" deals such as Angus beef and celeriac hash with a fried free-range egg and walnut mustard. From the evening menu come starters of chicken liver parfait with red onion marmalade and toast; and mains like roast local partridge with colcannon and rosemary gravy; or Aberdeen Angus rib-eye steak with sautéed potatoes, roast vine tomatoes, Spanish onion and parsley butter.

Open all wk Closed: 25 Dec, 31 Dec eve ⊕ BRAKSPEAR ◀ Brakspear Bitter, special, seasonal ales. ⛫ 14 **Facilities** Dogs allowed Garden Parking

CHURCH ENSTONE — Map 11 SP32

PICK OF THE PUBS

The Crown Inn ⛫

Mill Ln OX7 4NN ☎ 01608 677262
dir: *Off A44, 15m N of Oxford*

Award-winning chef Tony Warburton runs this stone-built 17th-century free house on the eastern edge of the Cotswolds with his wife Caroline. During the summer season you can while away the long evenings eating or drinking in the quiet and secluded rear garden, which is sheltered from the wind but enjoys the best of the late sunshine. Inside you'll find a traditional rustic bar with an open fire, a spacious slate floored conservatory, and a richly decorated beamed dining room. All meals are prepared on the premises using fresh produce, including pork, beef and game from the local farms and estates. Starters may include cream of

continued

CHURCH ENSTONE *continued*

spring vegetable soup; or warm salad of woodpigeon, bacon and quails' eggs. Main course choices range from steak and Hooky pie to fettuccini with wild mushrooms, cream and pesto. A home-made pudding such as cheesecake with blackcurrants will round things off nicely.

Open all wk 12-3 6-11 (Sun 12-4) Closed: 26 Dec, 1 Jan **Bar Meals** Av main course £9 food served all day **Restaurant** Fixed menu price fr £14.95 Av 3 course à la carte fr £17.95 food served all day ⊕ FREE HOUSE ◗ Hook Norton Best Bitter, Timothy Taylor Landlord, Wychwood Hobgoblin. ♚ 8 **Facilities** Children's menu Dogs allowed Garden Parking

CLIFTON — Map 11 SP43

Duke of Cumberland's Head

OX15 0PE ☎ **01869 338534** 📠 **01869 338643** **e-mail:** info@dukeatclifton.com **dir:** A4260 from Banbury, then B4031 from Deddington. 7m from Banbury

Built in 1645, this thatched and beamed stone pub was named to honour the Duke whose forces fought for his uncle, Charles I, at the nearby Battle of Edge Hill; important strategic decisions were supposedly made around the pub's inglenook fireplace. Today it offers a choice of real ales, two dining rooms, and a wonderful garden in summer. The menu may start with avocado and prawns, continue with beef braised in beer, and finish with tiramisu.

Closed: 25 Dec, Mon am, winter Sun pm ⊕ CLIFTON PUBLIC HOUSE MANAGEMENT LTD ◗ Hook Norton, Adnams, Deuchars, Black Sheep. **Facilities** Dogs allowed Garden Parking

CRAY'S POND — Map 5 SU68

PICK OF THE PUBS

The White Lion ♚

See Pick of the Pubs on opposite page

CUMNOR — Map 5 SP40

PICK OF THE PUBS

Bear & Ragged Staff ♚

See Pick of the Pubs on page 362

The Vine Inn ♚

11 Abingdon Rd OX2 9QN ☎ **01865 862567** 📠 **01865 862567** **dir:** A420 from Oxford, right onto B4017

An old village pub whose name, when you see the frontage, needs no explanation. In 1560, the suspicious death of an Earl's wife in Cumnor Place first had people asking 'Did she fall, or was she pushed?'. A typical menu here could include lamb shank with a red wine and mint sauce, pan-fried fillet steak with brandy and mushroom sauce, and the day's fresh fish. There's also a good range of snacks. Children love the huge garden.

Open all wk ⊕ PUNCH TAVERNS ◗ Adnams Bitter, Tetley Bitter, Hook Norton, guest ales. ♚ 7 **Facilities** Play area Dogs allowed Garden Parking

CUXHAM — Map 5 SU69

The Half Moon ♚

OX49 5NF ☎ **01491 614151** **e-mail:** info@thehalf-moon.com **dir:** M40 junct 6 follow Watlington signs. Right at T-junct, 2nd right to Cuxham. Across rdbt, Pub in 1m on right, just past Cuxham sign

Eilidh Ferguson grows the vegetables and salad leaves that end up on the dining plates at this 16th-century thatched pub. Her partner and chef Andrew Hill smokes the salmon and prepares the game from surrounding farms. Typically, you could expect dishes such as duck hearts on toast; fried Harlesford Farm organic mutton with bubble and squeak; roast chicken with Caesar salad; grilled dab with caper butter; mutton pie; and vegetable meze. Enjoy a pint of Brakspear Ordinary or Westons cider in the large beer garden in summer.

Open noon-3 6-11 (Sat noon-11 Sun noon-5) Closed: Mon ex BH Sun eve (winter) **Bar Meals** L served Tue-Sat 12-2, Sun 12-3 booking required D served Tue-Sat 6-9 booking required Av main course £14 **Restaurant** L served Tue-Sat 12-2, Sun 12-3 booking required D served Tue Sat 6-9 booking required Av 3 course à la carte fr £25 ⊕ BRAKSPEAR ◗ Brakspear Ordinary ♂ Westons Organic. ♚ 8 **Facilities** Children's menu Dogs allowed Garden Parking

DEDDINGTON — Map 11 SP43

PICK OF THE PUBS

Deddington Arms ★★★ HL 🍴 ♚

Horsefair OX15 0SH ☎ **01869 338364** 📠 **01869 337010** **e-mail:** deddarms@oxfordshire-hotels.co.uk **dir:** M40 junct 11 to Banbury. Follow signs for hospital, then towards Adderbury & Deddington, on A4260

This historic old coaching inn has been welcoming travellers since the 16th century. It overlooks the picturesque market square in Deddington, one of the gateways to the Cotswolds, and offers innovative, freshly prepared food served in friendly surroundings. Good quality ales and an international wine list add to the experience. Settle in the oak beamed bar with its flagstone floors and cosy fireplace for a bar snack, or move to the elegant restaurant where a meal might begin with pan-fried pigeon breast with apple fritters and Irish cider jus, followed by roasted rump of lamb with basil mash, Puy lentils and paysanne vegetables. A tempting dessert menu might offer espresso ice cream parfait with bitter chocolate sorbet, and there's also an enticing selection of traditional cheeses. Accommodation includes 27 en suite bedrooms with cottage suites and four-poster luxury.

Open all day all wk 11am-mdnt **Bar Meals** L served all wk 12-2 D served all wk 6.30-9 **Restaurant** L served all wk 12-2 D served Mon-Sat 6.30-10, Sun 7-9 ⊕ FREE HOUSE ◗ Black Sheep, Adnams, 2 Guest Ales. ♚ 8 **Facilities** Parking **Rooms** 27

The Unicorn Inn ♚

Market Place OX15 0SE ☎ **01869 338838** **e-mail:** robbie@theunicorninn.net **web:** www.theunicorninn.net **dir:** 6m S of Banbury on A4260

Populated by friendly locals and smiling staff, visitors feel welcome too in this Grade II listed 17th-century coaching inn overlooking the market square. Exposed beams and an open fire characterise the bar which serves award-winning cask ales and a large selection of wines by the glass. For warmer days the tranquillity of the secret walled garden is much enjoyed by couples and families alike. The restaurant offers excellent home-cooked food, using locally sourced fresh produce. The menu includes traditional pub favourites which compliment the more contemporary dishes. Fresh fish

continued on page 363

PICK OF THE PUBS

The White Lion 🍷

CRAY'S POND   Map 5 SU68

Goring Rd, Goring Heath RG8 7SH
☎ **01491 680471** 📄 **01491 684254**
e-mail: reservations@
thewhitelioncrayspond.com
dir: *From M4 junct 11 follow signs to
Pangbourne, through toll bridge to
Whitchurch. N for 3m into Cray's Pond*

Up in the Chilterns, in the hamlet of
Cray's Pond, the popular 250-year-old
White Lion enjoys views which extend
across the Thames Valley. A nearby field
is the home of the annual Woodcote
Rally, the third largest steam, vintage
and veteran transport fair in England.
As you might expect, while it's on, the
pub acts as the organisers' unofficial
headquarters. Photographs taken at
rallies during the last 40 or so years line
the deep terracotta walls. Also worth a
browse is the collection of fascinating
old menus from famous restaurants
around the world. The beamed ceilings
are low, so be prepared to stoop. The
dining area charms with open fires,
candles and oak floors, while the
conservatory looks out on to the garden
through its large bay windows. For
several reasons, the food is high in
quality: partly through the pub's close
working relationship with local
producers, partly because each dish is
prepared to order with fresh ingredients,
and partly because the kitchen team
bring in-depth experience and attention
to detail in their approach to modern
British cooking. A menu du jour offers
three choices at each stage for a meal
of excellent value. Among the carte's
eight starters and main courses,
supplemented by some specials, you
might find home-cured gravadlax with
pickled cucumbers; or celeriac
remoulade and prosciutto to start.
Follow with an Orkney rump burger,
which can have bacon or cheese added,
alongside a mound of hand-cut chips;
or Macey's Old English bangers and
mash served with onion red wine sauce.
The dessert choices follow classic lines:
mixed fruit trifle; sticky toffee pudding
with butterscotch sauce and Jersey
clotted cream; and warm chocolate
brownie with dark chocolate coulis and
bourbon vanilla Chantilly. Well-kept real
ales and an admirably concise wine list
complete the picture for this well
managed pub dining experience.

Closed: 25-26 Dec, 1 Jan, Sun eve, Mon
🍺 GREENE KING 🍺 IPA, Abbot Ale,
Guinness. 🍷 11 **Facilities** Play area
Dogs allowed Garden Parking

PICK OF THE PUBS

Bear & Ragged Staff 🍷

CUMNOR   Map 5 SP40

28 Appleton Rd OX2 9QH
☎ **01865 862329**   📠 **01865 862048**
e-mail: enquiries@bearandraggedstaff.com
dir: *A420 from Oxford, right onto B4017
signposted Cumnor*

After a seemingly lengthy hibernation, the Bear & Ragged Staff reopened early in 2009, its tenancy in the hands of a group led by Mark Greenwood, back in England after 30 years in Asia. As Mark explained at the time, it wasn't difficult to see its enormous possibilities – a recently renovated restaurant backed up by a first class kitchen, while the front part of the building, dating back to the 16th century, is a three-section pub. In a wooden lintel above a door in the main bar are the chiselled-out remains of what is believed to have been the Royal Crest, removed by none other than Richard Cromwell, Oliver's son, during

his stay here. The pub's name is inextricably linked with Warwickshire, particularly with the Earl of Warwick (the Kingmaker), whose mistress's ghost allegedly haunts the building. New menus reflect the cornucopia of wildlife with which the surrounding woods and farmland teem – pheasant, partridge, deer, muntjac, rabbit, duck and pigeon, for instance. The food is best described as hearty, country-style cooking, and casseroles, stews and pub classics, such as bangers and mash, will always be found on the menus, which change every five to six weeks. Lunch menus might offer a platter of charcuterie, or Greek mezze to share; home-made burger with bacon and Cheddar; ale, mushroom and beef pie; and salmon and dill fishcakes. There's just that little bit more sophistication in the evening, with roast venison loin, cavolo nero and juniper berry jus; confit duck leg with wild mushroom and braised chicory; and sea bass fillet with wilted mache lettuce, Japanese udon noodles and lime leaf and celery white bean broth. As for dessert, Chef says 'Don't forget to try the chocolate fondant'.

Open 11-11 **Bar Meals** L served all week 12-3 D served all week 6.30-10 Av main course £8.50 **Restaurant** L served all week 12-3 D served all week 6.30-10 Fixed menu price fr £10.50 Av 3 course à la carte fr £24 ⊕ GREENE KING ● IPA, Old Speckled Hen, Abbot Ale, guest ales. **Facilities** Children's menu Play area Dogs allowed Garden Parking

DEDDINGTON *continued*

deliveries six days per week make seafood a particular strength. Children have their own menu and dietary requirements are catered for.

Open all day all wk 11-11 (Fri-Sat 11am-12.30am, Sun noon-10.30) **Bar Meals** L served Mon-Sat 12-2.30 D served Mon-Thu 6-9, Fri-Sat 6-9.30 Av main course £9 **Restaurant** L served Mon-Sat 12-2.30, Sun 12-8 D served Mon-Thu 6-9, Fri-Sat 6-9.30, Sun 12-8 booking required Av 3 course à la carte fr £18 ⊕ Charles Wells Pub Co ◄ Hook Norton, Bombardier, Youngs Special, Guest Ale. ♈ 10 **Facilities** Children's menu Dogs allowed Garden Parking

DORCHESTER (ON THAMES) Map 5 SU59

Fleur De Lys ♈

9 High St OX10 7HH
☎ 01865 340502 📠 01865 340502
e-mail: info@fleurdorchester.co.uk

Dating from around 1525, this lovely old pub is located on the High Street of the picturesque village. It has retained much of its original character with a pretty garden and cosy bar and dining room. Traditional British fare is served, including steak, stilton and port wine pie; and crab and ginger fishcakes, all made in-house. Vegetarians are well catered for, too, with dishes such as baked aubergines stuffed with ratatouille, or steamed vegetarian pudding.

Open all wk noon-3 6-12.30am (Sat-Sun all day) Closed: Winter 3-6 **Bar Meals** L served all wk 12-2.30 booking required D served Mon-Sat 6.30-9.30 booking required ⊕ FREE HOUSE ◄ Brakspear, Hooky, Guinness, guest beer ⱺ Stowford Press. ♈ 8 **Facilities** Children's menu Dogs allowed Garden Parking

PICK OF THE PUBS

The George ★★ HL ♈

25 High St OX10 7HH
☎ 01865 340404 📠 01865 341620
e-mail: thegeorgehotel@fsmail.net
dir: *From M40 junct 7, A329 S to A4074 at Shillingford. Follow Dorchester signs. From M4 junct 13, A34 to Abingdon then A415 E to Dorchester*

DH Lawrence was a frequent visitor to this 15th-century coaching inn, believed to be one of the oldest public houses in Britain. The George stands at the centre of the picturesque village of Dorchester. Inside, oak beams and inglenook fireplaces help to create a welcoming atmosphere, while outside there is an attractive garden. The Potboys bar is a traditional taproom - just the spot to enjoy a pint of Brakspear while tucking into steak and Guinness pie; vegetable curry or goats' cheese and pesto roasted peppers. The Carriages restaurant, with its secret garden, serves a full menu with, for example, chicken and wild mushroom terrine or spiced sausage, black pudding and poached egg salad as starters. Main courses might be sea bass and mushroom risotto; pan-seared tuna steak or tian of roast vegetables with rocket pesto.

Open all day all wk 11am-mdnt **Bar Meals** L served all wk 12-3 D served all wk 6-9 **Restaurant** L served all wk 12-3 booking required D served all wk 6-9 booking required ⊕ CHAPMANS GROUP ◄ Butcombe Gold, Wadworth 6X. ♈ 6 **Facilities** Children's menu Garden Parking **Rooms** 17

PICK OF THE PUBS

The White Hart ★★★ HL ☕ ♈

High St OX10 7HN
☎ 01865 340074 📠 01865 341082
e-mail: whitehart@oxfordshire-hotels.co.uk
dir: *A4074 (Oxford to Reading), 5m from M40 junct 7/A329 to Wallingford*

If this picture-perfect hotel looks familiar, that could be because it has played a starring role in the TV series *Midsomer Murders*. Set seven miles from Oxford in heart of historic Dorchester-on-Thames, it has welcomed travellers for around 400 years, and the bars attract locals, residents and diners alike. There is a great choice of real beers available. Log fires and candlelight create an intimate atmosphere for the enjoyment of innovative dishes prepared from fresh ingredients. A good-value fixed-price lunch is available Monday to Saturday, with a choice of three starters, mains and desserts. The carte menu doubles your choice and includes imaginative dishes such as pumpkin risotto or Thai-style fish cakes, followed by roasted loin of pork with braised red cabbage, caramelised apple and sweet potato crisps; fish and chips in beer batter with crushed minted peas and hand cut chips; or grilled peppered rump steak with fat cut chips grilled tomato and salad.

Open all wk **Bar Meals** L served all wk 12-2.30 D served all wk 6.30-9.30 Av main course £7.95 **Restaurant** L served all wk 12-2.30 D served all wk 6.30-9.30 ⊕ FREE HOUSE ◄ Greene King, Marston's Pedigree, St Austell Tribute, Deuchars Caledonian IPA. ♈ 12 **Facilities** Children's menu Parking **Rooms** 26

EAST HENDRED Map 5 SU48

The Wheatsheaf ♈

Chapel Square OX12 8JN
☎ 01235 833229 📠 01235 821521
e-mail: info@thewheatsheaf.org.uk
dir: *2m from A34 Milton interchange*

Formerly used as a courthouse, this 16th-century pub stands in a pretty village close to the Ridgeway path. Spit-roasts and barbecues are popular summer features of the attractive front garden, which overlooks the village. Bar meals include baguettes; a venison burger with hand cut chips; and classic Greek salad with French bread. The restaurant menu might offer twice-baked cheddar, stilton and spinach soufflé, followed by noisette of lamb with mint and blackcurrant jus and dauphinoise potatoes.

Open all wk ⊕ GREENE KING ◄ IPA, 2 guest ales. ♈ 8 **Facilities** Family room Dogs allowed Garden Parking

FARINGDON Map 5 SU29

PICK OF THE PUBS

The Lamb at Buckland ♈

Lamb Ln, Buckland SN7 8QN ☎ 01367 870484
e-mail: enquiries@thelambatbuckland.co.uk
dir: *Just off A420, 3m E of Faringdon*

The 18th-century Lamb displays a fair few appropriately ovine artefacts. It has a village location on the fringe of the Cotswolds in the Vale of the White Horse and is renowned for its excellent food. A reliable menu, supplemented by daily specials, offers the likes of veal kidneys sautéed with shallots, smoked bacon, fresh herbs and mushrooms; and breast of Gressingham duck, roasted pink and served with apple and Calvados sauce. Items from the specials board might include brace of roast teal with sage and onion stuffing, or medallions of Scotch beef fillet with wild mushroom sauce. Friday night is fish night - a piscatorial extravaganza - with dishes like cullen skink, home-smoked sprats, monkfish and prawn ragout, and seared fillet of wild sea bass served with shrimp and saffron risotto.

Closed: Sun eve, Mon **Bar Meals** L served Tue-Sat 12-2, Sun 12-3 D served Tue-Sat 6-9.30 **Restaurant** L served Tue-Sat 12-2, Sun 12-3 D served Tue-Sat 6-9.30 ⊕ FREE HOUSE ◄ Hook Norton, Arkells 3Bs, Timothy Taylor Landlord. ♈ 12 **Facilities** Garden Parking

FARINGDON *continued*

PICK OF THE PUBS

AA PUB OF THE YEAR FOR ENGLAND 2009-2010

The Trout at Tadpole Bridge ★★★★ INN ☙

Buckland Marsh SN7 8RF ☎ **01367 870382**
e-mail: info@troutinn.co.uk
dir: *Halfway between Oxford & Swindon on A420 take road signed Bampton, pub approx 2m*

Sitting peacefully on the River Thames twenty minutes from Oxford is this historic, multi-award-winning free house with luxurious rooms. A destination in its own right, it offers log fires, cask ales, riverside walks, berthing for six boats and a kitchen that makes expert use of the best local ingredients. Having run several fine-dining restaurants, owners Gareth and Helen wanted somewhere to raise their family, so the need for games, toys, space and a decent children's menu is understood. The two of them take food seriously, but not so much as to marginalise the drinker, as the locals coming in every night for the fine range of regional beers would undoubtedly affirm. From a sample menu come smoked eel salad with Noilly Prat jelly and shallot purée; pithivier of ceps, leeks and red onion marmalade with red pepper sauce; steamed beef and ale pudding; and blue brie and sun-blushed tomato strudel.

Open 11.30-3 6-11 Closed: 25-26 Dec, Sun eve (1 Nov-30 Apr) **Bar Meals** L served all wk 12-2 booking required D served all wk 7-9 booking required Av main course £14 **Restaurant** L served all wk 12-2 booking required D served all wk 7-9 booking required Av 3 course à la carte fr £30 ⊕ FREE HOUSE ◀ Ramsbury Bitter, Youngs PA Bitter ♂ Stowford Press. ♟ 10 **Facilities** Children's menu Dogs allowed Garden Parking **Rooms** 6

FIFIELD   Map 10 SP21

Merrymouth Inn ☙

Stow Rd OX7 6HR ☎ **01993 831652**   📠 **01993 830840**
e-mail: tim@merrymouthinn.fsnet.co.uk
dir: *On A424 between Burford & Stow-on-the-Wold*

A beautifully restored Cotswold inn dating back to the 13th century. At that time it was owned by the monks of nearby Bruern Abbey, to which hitherto undiscovered underground passages are said to lead. A blackboard of fresh fish, vegetarian and other daily specials includes such dishes as a warm salad of scallops and bacon and gilt head sea bream with fennel and tomato. Home-made puddings include raspberry marshmallow meringue.

Closed: Sun eve in Winter ⊕ FREE HOUSE ◀ Hook Norton Best Bitter, Adnams Broadside. ♟ 7 **Facilities** Dogs allowed Garden Parking

---

FRINGFORD   Map 11 SP62

The Butchers Arms

OX27 8EB ☎ **01869 277363**
e-mail: butcherarms@aol.com
dir: *4m from Bicester on A4421 towards Buckingham*

Flora Thompson mentioned this traditional village pub in her 1939 novel *Lark Rise to Candleford* about life on the Northamptonshire/Oxfordshire border. A good selection of fresh fish and other seafood, including mussels, crab and king prawns, is offered, as well as liver, bacon and onions, peppered fillet steak, half a roast duck, and steak and kidney pie. Pumps display Adnams Broadside labels. From the patio watch the cricket during the summer.

Open all wk ⊕ PUNCH TAVERNS ◀ Adnams Broadside, Hooky Bitter, Old Speckled Hen. **Facilities** Dogs allowed Parking

---

FYFIELD   Map 5 SU49

PICK OF THE PUBS

The White Hart ☙

See Pick of the Pubs on opposite page

GORING   Map 5 SU68

PICK OF THE PUBS

Miller of Mansfield   RR ⊛ ☙

High St RG8 9AW ☎ **01491 872829**   📠 **01491 873100**
e-mail: reservations@millerofmansfield.com
dir: *From Pangbourne take A329 to Streatley. Right on B4009, 0.5m to Goring*

This beautiful old building has been stylishly renovated. There is a full bar menu and a restaurant open for breakfast, lunch and dinner 365 days a year. Modern European menus might offer ham hock terrine; slow roast belly pork; confit duck leg in the restaurant to steamed mussels or steak sandwich in the bar. There is a marble paved area in the garden with plants and statues under a canopy with gas heating. There are thirteen rooms available if you would like to stay over.

Open all day all wk 8am-11pm **Bar Meals** L served all wk 12-10 D served all wk 12-10 Av main course £8.95 food served all day **Restaurant** L served all wk 12-4.30 D served all wk 6.30-10 booking required Fixed menu price fr £14.95 Av 3 course à la carte fr £33.95 ⊕ FREE HOUSE ◀ Good Old Boy, Rebellion IPA, Organic Jester. ♟ 15 **Facilities** Children's menu Dogs allowed Garden Parking **Rooms** 13

GREAT TEW   Map 11 SP42

PICK OF THE PUBS

The Falkland Arms ☙

OX7 4DB ☎ **01608 683653**   📠 **01608 683656**
e-mail: falklandarms@wadworth.co.uk
dir: *Off A361, 1.25m, signed Great Tew*

This 500-year-old inn takes its name from Lucius Carey, 2nd Viscount Falkland, who inherited the manor of Great Tew in 1629. Nestling at the end of a charming row of Cotswold stone cottages, the Falkland Arms is a classic: flagstone floors, high-backed settles and an inglenook fireplace characterise the intimate bar, where a huge collection of beer and cider mugs hangs from the ceiling. Home-made specials such as baked cod with herb crust or sausages and mash supplement the basic lunchtime menu, served in the bar or the pub garden. In the evening, booking is essential for dinner in the small dining room. Expect Thai spiced crab cake or grilled goats' cheese salad, followed by creamy spinach and mushroom risotto, chicken breast with pan-fried bacon and mushroom with an Oxford blue cheese sauce, or haddock fillet with crushed new potatoes.

Open all wk 11.30-2.30 6-11 (Fri 11.30-2.30 6-mdnt Sat-Sun 11.30am-mdnt) **Bar Meals** L served Mon-Fri 12-2.30, Sat-Sun 12-10 D served Mon-Fri 6-10 **Restaurant** D served Mon-Sat 7-8 booking required ⊕ WADWORTH ◀ Wadworth 6X, Henry's IPA, guest ales. ♟ 12 **Facilities** Dogs allowed Garden

---

HAILEY   Map 11 SP31

Bird in Hand ★★★★ INN ☙

Whiteoak Green OX29 9XP
☎ **01993 868321**   📠 **01993 868702**
e-mail: welcome@birdinhandinn.co.uk
dir: *From Witney N onto B4022 through Hailey to Whiteoak Green for 5m. At Charlbury S onto B4022 for 5m*

Set in the Oxfordshire countryside just outside the village of Hailey, this classic Cotswold stone inn is Grade II listed and dates from the 16th century. The beamed interior has huge inglenook fireplaces, with log fires in winter. Food ranges from traditional rarebit on toast topped with a poached egg, to marinated Cotswold game casserole; or home-made faggots with onion gravy and mashed potato.

Open all wk noon-11.30 **Bar Meals** L served Mon-Sat 12-2.30, Sun 12-3 D served Mon-Sat 6.30-9.30, Sun 6-9 ⊕ Free House ◀ Ramsbury ♂ Stowford Press. ♟ 14 **Facilities** Children's menu Dogs allowed Garden Parking **Rooms** 16

PICK OF THE PUBS

The White Hart ♀

FYFIELD Map 5 SU49

Main Rd OX13 5LW ☎ **01865 390585**
e-mail: info@whitehart-fyfield.com
web: www.whitehart-fyfield.com
dir: *6m S of Oxford just off A420 (Oxford to Swindon road)*

Like so many pubs, the White Hart has quite a history. It was built in Henry VI's reign by the executors of the lord of the manor as accommodation for a chantry priest and five almsmen. By 1548, chantries had been abolished and it was sold to St John's College, Oxford, whose tenants converted it into a drinking establishment. The interior is breathtaking, with an arch-braced roof and a tunnel - probably an escape route for priests during the Dissolution of the Monasteries - running from the low-ceilinged bar to the manor house. The main restaurant is a grand hall of a place with soaring eaves and beams, huge stone-flanked windows and flagstone floors, overlooked by a minstrels' gallery. Mark and Kay are passionate about serving food that is fresh, using seasonal produce of the highest quality from mostly local suppliers (including their own kitchen garden) with meats sourced from trusted farms and estates; only fish, delivered fresh from Brixham needs to travel. Mark and his team prepare everything fresh daily, even the bread and pasta, which is made with flour from the local mill. Menus change frequently to offer fish, antipasti and mezze boards to share; salmon fillet with beetroot risotto and horseradish foam; slow-roasted belly of Kelmscott pork with celeriac purée, crackling and cider jus; and lentil, spinach and paneer cheese tart with spiced cauliflower and coriander yoghurt. Home-made ice creams and sorbets always slip down well to round things off. The wine list is varied and constantly evolving, with several 'wines of the month' allowing customers to try something a bit different. Two beer festivals are held during the May Day and August bank holiday weekends, with hog roasts, live music and at least 14 real ales.

Open Tue-Sun 12-3 5.30-11 (Sat noon-11pm, Sun noon-10.30pm) Closed: (Mon ex BHs) **Bar Meals** L served Tue-Sat 12-2.30 (Sun 12-4) D served Tue-Sat 7-9.30 Av main course £15
Restaurant L served Tue-Sat 12-2.30 (Sun 12-4) D served Tue-Sat 7-9.30 Fixed menu price fr £15 Av 3 course à la carte fr £28 ⊕ FREE HOUSE ◀ Hooky Bitter, Doom Bar, Hullabaloo, guest Ales ♂ Thatchers Cheddar Valley. ♀ 14
Facilities Children's menu Play area Garden Parking

HENLEY-ON-THAMES   Map 5 SU78

PICK OF THE PUBS

The Cherry Tree Inn   INN ⊛ ♟

Stoke Row RG9 5QA
☎ 01491 680430   📄 01491 682168
e-mail: info@thecherrytreeinn.com
dir: *B481 towards Reading & Sonning Common 2m,
follow Stoke Row sign*

There's a confident blend of ancient and modern inside
this 400-year-old listed building. Originally three flint
cottages, the Cherry Tree has been comprehensively re-
fitted, mixing the original flagstone floors, beamed
ceilings and fireplaces with contemporary decor, strong
colours and comfortable modern furnishings. The
contemporary theme continues throughout the pub,
which offers Brakspear real ales, fine malt whiskies
and over 40 different wines, including 12 served by the
glass. Service is informal, with a variety of classic
European dishes prepared from fresh local ingredients.
Lunchtime choices include grilled focaccia with goats'
cheese, peppers and pesto; as well as more substantial
dishes like belly of pork with black pudding and creamy
mash. À la carte options range from chargrilled rib-eye
steak, to grilled squid and chorizo salad. Outside, the
large south-facing garden is perfect for alfresco
summer dining, plus there are four bedrooms available.

Open all wk Closed: 25-26 Dec ⊕ BRAKSPEAR
◀ Brakspear Bitter, Brakspear Organic, Douvel, Orval,
Erdinger. ♟ 12 **Facilities** Garden Parking **Rooms** 4

PICK OF THE PUBS

The Five Horseshoes ♟

Maidensgrove RG9 6EX
☎ 01491 641282   📄 01491 641086
e-mail: admin@thefivehorseshoes.co.uk
dir: *From Henley-on-Thames take A4130, in 1m take
B480 to right, signed Stonor. In Stonor left, through
woods, over common, pub on left.*

This traditional 16th-century pub enjoys far-reaching
views across the surrounding countryside from its two
large beer gardens. Once inside, old pub games, log
fires, heavy beams and brasses set the scene; there are
two snug bar areas serving real ales, wines and
champagnes by the glass, as well as a large
conservatory restaurant. Food focuses on the freshest
produce, locally sourced where possible, and the menu
begins with pub classics like shepherd's pie with
market vegetables; and Berkshire sausages with
bubble and squeak. Other choices include smoked
haddock kedgeree with poached duck egg; and
butternut risotto with pumpkin seeds and Parmesan.
Walkers, cyclists and dogs are all welcome in this Area
of Outstanding Natural Beauty, and a special walkers'
snack menu includes soup; cheddar ploughman's; and
doorstep sandwiches with chunky chips. Summer
weekend barbecues and bank holiday hog roasts are
held in one of the gardens.

Open noon-3.30 6-11 (Sat noon-11 Sun noon-6)
Closed: Sun eve **Bar Meals** L served Mon-Fri 12-2.30,
Sat 12-3, Sun 12-4 booking required D served Mon-Sat
6.30-9.30 Av main course £10 **Restaurant** L served
Mon-Fri 12-2.30, Sat 12-3, Sun 12-4 booking required
D served Mon-Sat 6.30-9.30 booking required Av 3
course à la carte fr £25 ⊕ BRAKSPEAR ◀ Brakspear
Ordinary, Oxford Gold. ♟ 11 **Facilities** Children's menu
Dogs allowed Garden Parking

PICK OF THE PUBS

White Hart Nettlebed ★★★★ GA ⊛ ♟

High St, Nettlebed RG9 5DD
☎ 01491 641245   📄 01491 649018
e-mail: info@whitehartnettlebed.com
dir: *On A4130 between Henley-on-Thames &
Wallingford*

Royalist and parliamentary soldiers made a habit of
lodging in local taverns during the English Civil War;
this 15th-century inn reputedly billeted troops loyal to
the king. During the 17th and 18th centuries the area
was plagued by highwaymen, including the notorious
Isaac Darkin, who was eventually caught, tried and
hung at Oxford Gaol. These days the beautifully
restored property is favoured by a stylish crowd who
appreciate the chic bar and restaurant. Heading the
beer list is locally-brewed Brakspear backed by popular
internationals and a small selection of cosmopolitan
bottles. A typical three-course meal selection could
comprise sweet potato and gruyère tartlet with rocket;
spinach, feta and cumin spanakopita with
babaganouche; and lemon and thyme pannacotta with
red wine poached pear. Continental flavours are equally
abundant on the Sunday lunch menu: grilled sardines
with romesco sauce; confit of duck leg with butter
beans in tomato sauce; and chocolate pot and red wine
with Chantilly cream.

Open all day all wk 11am-11pm (Sun 11am-6pm) **Bar
Meals** L served Mon-Sat 12-2.30, Sun 12-3 booking
required D served Mon-Sat 6-9.30 booking required
Restaurant L served Mon-Sat 12-2.30, Sun 12-3
booking required D served Mon-Sat 6-9.30 booking
required ⊕ BRAKSPEAR ◀ Brakspear, Guinness. ♟ 12
Facilities Children's menu Play area Family room
Garden Parking **Rooms** 12

HOOK NORTON | Map 11 SP33

PICK OF THE PUBS

The Gate Hangs High ★★★★ INN

Whichford Rd OX15 5DF ☎ 01608 737387
e-mail: gatehangshigh@aol.com
dir: *Off A361 SW of Banbury*

This rural pub is set amid beautiful countryside near the mystical Rollright Stones and Hook Norton, where the cask-conditioned, dry-hopped ales served here are brewed. It is on the old drovers' road from Wales to Banbury and a tollgate that once stood outside was said to hang high enough for small creatures to pass under, although owners of larger beasts had to pay. In the low-beamed bar, polished horse brasses reflect the glow from the candles, pretty wall lights and roaring log fire. A good value set menu is offered October, November, January, February and March, from Monday to Friday - a typical example being bacon and mushroom salad, battered cod and chips, and bread pudding and custard. Otherwise popular options include lunchtime sandwiches served with chips and salad and dishes such as steak and Hooky ale pie; and swordfish steak with horseradish cream. The pub also has a cocktail menu.

Open all wk Closed: 25 Dec eve **Bar Meals** L served Mon-Fri 12-2.30, Sat-Sun 12-9.30 D served Mon-Fri 6-9.30, Sat-Sun 12-9.30 **Restaurant** L served Mon-Fri 12-2.30, Sat-Sun 12-9.30 D served Mon-Fri 6-9.30, Sat-Sun 12-9.30 ⊕ HOOK NORTON BREWERY ◀ Hook Norton - Best, Old Hooky, Gold Ö Stowford Press. **Facilities** Dogs allowed Garden Parking **Rooms** 4

Sun Inn ♀

High St OX15 5NH ☎ 01608 737570 ▤ 01608 737570
e-mail: thesuninnhooky@hotmail.co.uk
dir: *5m from Chipping Norton, 8m from Banbury, just off A361*

Set in picturesque Hook Norton, this welcoming Cotswold stone inn is just a 10 minute walk from the Hook Norton Brewery – ideal if you're planning a tour! Inside you'll find oak beams, flagstones, an inglenook fireplace and plenty of Hook Norton ales on tap. Food runs from sandwiches and British classics to more poised offerings such as cured haunch of smoked wild boar with parmesan, rocket and truffle oil followed by honey-glazed ham hock with roasted garlic and parsley mash and Meaux mustard sauce.

Open all wk 11-3 6-12 (Sun 12-12) **Bar Meals** L served all wk 11-3 D served all wk 6.30-9 **Restaurant** L served all wk 11-3 booking required D served all wk 6.30-9 booking required ⊕ HOOK NORTON BREWERY ◀ Hook Norton Best Bitter, Old Hooky, Hooky Gold, seasonal ales Ö Westons Organic. ♀ 8 **Facilities** Children's menu Dogs allowed Garden Parking

KELMSCOTT | Map 5 SU29

The Plough Inn

GL7 3HG ☎ 01367 253543 ▤ 01367 252514
e-mail: plough@kelmscottgl7.fsnet.co.uk
dir: *From M4 junct 15 onto A419 towards Cirencester then right onto A361 to Lechlade. A417 towards Faringdon, follow signs to Kelmscott*

The Plough dates from 1631 and is set in the beautiful village of Kelmscott a short walk from Kelmscott Manor, once home to William Morris. The inn is on the Thames Path midway between Radcot and Lechlade, so is a haven for walkers and boaters. Cotswold stone walls and flagstone floors set the scene for real ales and an extensive menu. Dishes include tempura of seafood with sweet chilli sauce, and pot roasted whole partridge.

Open all wk ⊕ FREE HOUSE ◀ Hook Norton, Timothy Taylor Landlord, Wychwood. **Facilities** Dogs allowed Garden Parking

LEWKNOR | Map 5 SU79

The Leathern Bottel ♀

1 High St OX49 5TW ☎ 01844 351482
dir: *0.5m from M40 junct 6 north or south*

Run by the same family for more than 25 years, this 16th-century coaching inn is set in the foothills of the Chilterns. Walkers with dogs, families with children, parties for meals or punters for a quick pint are all made equally welcome. In winter there's a wood-burning stove, a good drop of Brakspears ale, nourishing specials and a quiz on Sunday. Summer is the time for outdoor eating, the children's play area, Pimm's and Morris dancers.

Open all wk Closed: 25-26 Dec ⊕ BRAKSPEAR ◀ Brakspear Ordinary, Special. ♀ 12 **Facilities** Play area Family room Dogs allowed Garden Parking

LOWER SHIPLAKE | Map 5 SU77

The Baskerville Arms ★★★★ INN ♀

Station Rd RG9 3NY
☎ 0118 940 3332 ▤ 0118 940 7235
e-mail: enquiries@thebaskerville.com
dir: *Just off A4155, 1.5m from Henley*

This welcoming pub stands on the popular Thames Path, close to Shiplake station and just a few minutes from historic Henley-on-Thames. Brick-built on the outside, modern-rustic inside, it boasts an attractive garden where summer barbecues are a common fixture. Light meals are served in the bar, while the restaurant offers the likes of chargrilled tenderloin of marinated pork on a ragout of beans, lentils, tomato and paprika; and 'posh' fish and chips. Booking is essential during Henley Regatta (early July). There are four rooms available.

Open all wk 11.30-2.30 6-11 (Sun noon-4 7-10.30) **Bar Meals** L served Mon-Sat 11.30-2.30, Sun 12-3.30 Av main course £9 **Restaurant** L served Mon-Sat 11.30-2.30, Sun 12-3.30 D served Mon-Thu 7-9.30, Fri-Sun 7-10 booking required Fixed menu price fr £12.50 Av 3 course à la carte fr £28 ◀ London Pride, Loddon Hoppit, Timothy Taylor Landlord. ♀ 8 **Facilities** Children's menu Play area Dogs allowed Garden Parking **Rooms** 4

See advert on opposite page

LOWER WOLVERCOTE | Map 5 SP40

PICK OF THE PUBS

The Trout Inn ♀

195 Godstow Rd OX2 8PN ☎ 01865 510930
dir: *From A40 at Wolvercote rdbt (N of Oxford) follow signs for Wolvercote, through village to pub*

An old riverside inn on the banks of the Isis, as the Thames is known here. It was built around 1133 as a hospice to serve Godstow Nunnery, the ruins of which are on the opposite bank. With stone walls, slate roof, leaded windows, great oak beams, flagged floors and ancient fireplaces (always lit in winter), it is arguably Oxford's most atmospheric inn. Many visitors over the years have been happy just to sit on the terrace and watch the fast flowing waters while enjoying a drink and bite to eat. The menu kicks things off with dishes to share - boxed baked camembert and onion marmalade; plate of antipasti; or greek mezze. The starters might be baked crab and avocado al forno; or chicken liver pâté, onion jam and toast. Then the diverse menu divides into Salads and Pasta, Rotisserie (spit chicken or duck), Fired Pizzas and Stove – pork saltimbocca or red wine braised shoulder of lamb - so there's something for all tastes here.

Open all wk 11-11 **Bar Meals** food served all day **Restaurant** food served all day ⊕ FREE HOUSE ◀ Timothy Taylor Landlord, Adnams Best Bitter Ö Aspall Suffolk Draught. ♀ 14 **Facilities** Garden Parking

MARSTON
Map 5 SP50

Victoria Arms ☝

Mill Ln OX3 0PZ ☎ 01865 241382
e-mail: kyffinda@yahoo.co.uk
dir: *From A40 follow signs to Old Marston, sharp right into Mill Lane, pub in lane 500yds on left*

Friendly country pub situated on the banks of the River Cherwell, occupying the site of the old Marston Ferry that connected the north and south of the city. The old ferryman's bell is still behind the bar. Popular destinations for punters, and fans of TV sleuth *Inspector Morse*, as the last episode used this as a location. Typical menu includes lamb cobbler, steak and Guinness pie, spicy pasta bake, battered haddock, and ham off the bone.

Closed: Oct-Apr afternoons ⊕ WADWORTH ◀ Henrys IPA, Wadworth 6X, JCB, guest ales. ☝ 15 **Facilities** Family room Dogs allowed Garden Parking

MIDDLETON STONEY
Map 11 SP52

Best Western Jersey Arms Hotel ★★ HL ☝

OX25 4AD ☎ 01869 343234 📄 01869 343565
e-mail: jerseyarms@bestwestern.co.uk
dir: *3m from junct 9/10 of M4. 3m from A34 on B430*

This charming family-run free house was built as an ale house in the 13th century, on what used to be the estate of Lord Jersey. The cosy bar offers a good range of popular bar food with the extensive menu supplemented by daily blackboard specials. In the beamed and panelled Livingston's restaurant with its Mediterranean terracotta décor, the cosmopolitan brasserie-style menu features dishes like salad Niçoise; spinach and cream cheese pancakes; and duck confit with cherry and cinnamon sauce.

Open all wk ⊕ FREE HOUSE ◀ Interbrew Flower. ☝ 6 **Facilities** Garden Parking **Rooms** 20

MILTON
Map 11 SP43

PICK OF THE PUBS

The Black Boy Inn ☝

See Pick of the Pubs on opposite page

MURCOTT
Map 11 SP51

The Nut Tree Inn ⊛⊛ ☝

Main St OX5 2RE ☎ 01865 331253
dir: *M40 junct 9, A34 towards Oxford. Left onto B4027 signed Islip. At Red Lion turn left. Right signed Murcott, Fencott & Charlton-on-Otmoor. Pub on right in village*

A thatched 15th-century property, with oak beams, wood-burning stoves and unusual carvings, the Nut Tree stands in four acres overlooking the village pond. At the bar and in the garden, there are sandwiches made with home-made bread, soup of the day and triple cooked chips. There is a great selection of real ales to choose from, such as Vale Winter Solstice. The main menu uses free range, wild, organic or home produced ingredients wherever possible, including pork from the pigs in the garden and beef from the inn's own Dexter cattle. Try confit pork belly with potato purée and apple gravy, grilled rump steak with tarragon butter, or home-smoked salmon fish cake with creamed spinach and tomato butter sauce.

Open all day all wk noon-11 **Bar Meals** L served Mon-Sat 12-2.30, Sun 12-3 D served Mon-Sat 7-9 (Sun 6.30-8.30 (summer)) Av main course £8 **Restaurant** L served Mon-Sat 12-2.30, Sun 12-3 booking required D served Mon-Sat 7-9 booking required Fixed menu price fr £15 ⊕ FREE HOUSE ◀ Hook Norton, Vale Hadda's Winter Solstice, Fuller's London Pride, Brains Rev James, Wickwar Bob. ☝ 8 **Facilities** Dogs allowed Garden Parking

OXFORD
Map 5 SP50

The Anchor ☝

2 Hayfield Rd, Walton Manor OX2 6TT ☎ 01865 510282
dir: *A34 (Oxford ring road N), exit Peartree rdbt, 1.5m then right at Polstead Rd, follow road to bottom, pub on right*

This 1937 Art Deco-styled pub is particularly popular with North Oxford's well-heeled locals, firmly on the map for its well-kept ales, carefully chosen wines and good quality seasonal British food. Lunchtime specials include roast monkfish with courgettes, peas, bacon and spinach, while the main menu offers belly pork with black pudding and greens; and smoked haddock fishcakes with ginger lime mayo. Bar snacks and sandwiches are also available.

Open all day all wk noon-11 Closed: Xmas **Bar Meals** L served all wk 12-2.30 D served all wk 6-9.30 Av main course £11 **Restaurant** L served all wk 12-2.30 booking required D served all wk 6-9.30 booking required Av 3 course à la carte fr £23 ⊕ WADWORTH ◀ Wadworth 6X, Henrys IPA, Bishops Tipple ♂ Westons Stowford Press. ☝ 11 **Facilities** Children's menu Dogs allowed Garden Parking

Turf Tavern ☝

4 Bath Place, off Holywell St OX1 3SU
☎ 01865 243235 📄 01865 243838
e-mail: turftavern.oxford@laurelpubco.com
dir: *Telephone for directions*

Situated in the heart of Oxford, approached through hidden alleyways and winding passages, this famous pub lies in the shadow of the city wall and the colleges. It is especially popular in the summer when customers can relax in the sheltered courtyards. Eleven real ales are served daily, from a choice of around 500 over a year, along with some typical pub fare. The pub has been featured in TV's *Inspector Morse*, and was frequented by JRR Tolkien.

Open all wk ⊕ GREENE KING ◀ Traditional ales, changing daily. ☝ 6 **Facilities** Dogs allowed Garden

PISHILL
Map 5 SU78

PICK OF THE PUBS

The Crown Inn ☝

See Pick of the Pubs on page 370

RAMSDEN
Map 11 SP31

PICK OF THE PUBS

The Royal Oak ☝

See Pick of the Pubs on page 371

ROKE
Map 5 SU69

Home Sweet Home ☝

OX10 6JD ☎ 01491 838249 📄 01491 835760
dir: *Just off the B4009 from Benson to Watlington, signed on B4009*

Long ago converted from adjoining cottages by a local brewer, this pretty 15th-century inn stands in a tiny hamlet surrounded by lovely countryside. Oak beams and the large inglenook fireplace dominate a friendly bar with an old-fashioned feel. Starters might include spicy nachos topped with cheese for two to share; while main courses run to Cornish crab fishcakes with home-made tartare sauce; or calves' liver and bacon with an onion gravy. Extensive Sunday menu.

Open all wk Closed: 25-26 Dec ⊕ FREE HOUSE ◀ Black Sheep, Loddon Brewery ales- Hoppit & Branoc. ☝ 10 **Facilities** Dogs allowed Garden Parking

PICK OF THE PUBS

The Black Boy Inn ♥

MILTON   Map 11 SP43

OX15 4HH
☎ **01295 722111**   📠 **01295 722978**
e-mail: info@blackboyinn.com
web: www.blackboyinn.com
dir: *From Banbury take A4260 to Adderbury.*
After Adderbury turn right signed Bloxham.
Onto Milton Road to Milton. Pub on right

Nestling on the edge of picturesque
Milton, this gorgeous 16th-century long
building is set well back from the Milton
Road. The pub's name is thought to be
associated with the dark-skinned
Charles II; other popular theories
naturally include a reference to the
slave trade. A recently completed
refurbishment has created a charming
interior with solid pine furniture that's
entirely in keeping with the 400 year-old
building. The long room has a real wood
stove at one end and a comfortable
dining room at the other; in between is
the bar, from which extends a
conservatory-style dining room
overlooking a gravelled courtyard.
Outside, the patio and a lovely half-acre
garden offer plenty of seating and space
for children to run around. A rotating list
of guest ales and a selection of wines by
the glass ensure that drinkers can enjoy
the relaxed and informal atmosphere of
this quintessentially English free house.
Meanwhile, head chef Kevin Hodgkiss
produces modern British food based on
fresh, seasonal ingredients. There are
plenty of pub classics, including the
likes of cottage pie with wholegrain
mustard mash, and pan-fried liver and
bacon with a rich shallot sauce. On the
main menu, starters like pea and ham
hock soup, and spiced Thai fishcakes
with sweet mustard and herb
mayonnaise, herald choices that include
goats' cheese and fig tarte Tatin with
new potatoes; sea bream fillet on basil
tagliatelle with crayfish cream sauce;
and Cornish cannon of lamb with gratin
potato and roasted butternut squash.
Leave space for one of the excellent
desserts: Yorkshire rhubarb with vanilla
pannacotta is typical. A wide range of
fresh salads and interesting
sandwiches complete the choice.

Open 12-3 5.30-11.30 (Sat-Sun
12-11.30) **Bar Meals** L served all week
12-2.30 D served Mon-Thu 6.30-9, Fri-
Sat 6.30-9.30 **Restaurant** L served all
week 12-2.30 D served Mon-Thu 6.30-9,
Fri-Sat 6.30-9.30 ⊕ MERCHANT INNS
PLC ◀ Adnams, Abbot Ale, rotating
guest ales. ♥ 8 **Facilities** Children's
menu Play area Dogs allowed Garden
Parking

PICK OF THE PUBS

The Crown Inn ♀

PISHILL Map 5 SU78

RG9 6HH
☎ **01491 638364**
e-mail: enquiries@thecrowninnpishill.co.uk
web: www.thecrowninnpishill.co.uk
dir: *On B480 off A4130, 8m NW of Henley-on-Thames*

As it is bound to come up in conversation, perhaps we should first deal with the name of the village. Old maps show a second 's' in Pishill, which is why some people insist on separating the two syllables. Furthermore, in pre-combustion engine days waggon drivers would stop at the inn for a swift half after the stiff, six-mile climb from Henley-on-Thames, and their horses would relieve themselves while their masters were inside. (Quite why the horses waited so long isn't recorded.) On the other hand, maybe the word evolved from Peashill, because peas used to be grown round here. Take your pick, depending on whether Great Aunt

Gertrude is with you. This pretty, 15th-century brick and flint coaching inn contains a priest's hole (reputably the largest in the country), which was used extensively when Henry VIII was busy persecuting Catholics. Indeed, one of the many clerics who were smuggled in from the big house at nearby Stonor met a sticky end while hiding out at The Crown and his ghost still haunts the pub on the anniversary of his death. The bar is supplied by mostly local breweries, including Marlow. Under the ownership of Lucas Wood, menus and specials are revised daily, typically to provide medallions of beef tenderloin on rösti potato with wild mushrooms and port sauce; whole grilled lemon sole with herb butter and seasonal vegetables; breast of chicken stuffed with Brie and wrapped in smoked bacon; and wild mushroom and spinach risotto. On a fine day, enjoy the picturesque gardens overlooking the valley and watch the red kites circling overhead. In wintertime, enjoy the warmth and cosy atmosphere of the three log fires inside.

Open all week 11.30-3 6-11 (Sun noon-3 7-10) Closed: 25-26 Dec
Bar Meals L served all week 12-2.30 D served all week 7-9.30 **Restaurant** L served all week 12-2.30 D served all week 7-9.30 ⊕ FREE HOUSE
◧ Brakspears, West Berkshire Brewery, Loddon Brewery, Marlow Brewery, Hidden Brewery. ♀ 8 **Facilities** Dogs allowed Garden Parking

PICK OF THE PUBS

The Royal Oak ♀

RAMSDEN Map 11 SP31

High St OX7 3AU
☎ 01993 868213 📠 01993 868864
dir: *From Witney take B4022 towards Charlbury, then right before Hailey, through Poffley End*

Standing opposite the church in the pretty Cotswold village of Ramsden, this 17th-century former coaching inn was once a stopping off point for the London to Hereford stagecoach. These days the inn is more popular with walkers eager to explore the lovely surrounding countryside. Whether you are walking or not, the inn makes a fine place to stop for refreshment, and its old beams, warm fires and stone walls provide a very cosy welcome. The Royal Oak is a free house with beers sourced from local breweries, such as Hook Norton Old Hooky and Bitter, Adnam's Broadside and Young's Special. The wine list has over 200 wines, specialising in those from Bordeaux and Languedoc, many of them available by the glass. The bar menu regularly features a pie of the week, and there are other pub favourites such as chilli, beef curry, home-made beef burgers, and traditional British steak and kidney pudding. Every Thursday evening there is a special offer of steak with a glass of wine and dessert thrown in. The main menu features the very best of fresh, local, seasonal food, with regular fresh fish deliveries. A choice of fish dishes is always available, with the likes of seared yellow fin tuna; roast fillet of Atlantic cod with tapenade crust; and salmon with whisky and horseradish. A typical spring day might see some superb lemon sole offered alongside roast half shoulder of new season Westwell lamb with rosemary and garlic jus, or wild rabbit cooked with Armagnac and served with asparagus.

Open 11.30-3 6.30-11 (Sun 12-3 7-10.30) Closed: 25 Dec **Bar Meals** L served all wk 11.30-2 D served all wk 7-10 **Restaurant** L served all wk 11.30-2 D served all wk 7-10 ⊕ FREE HOUSE ◀ Hook Norton Old Hooky, Best, Adnams Broadside, Youngs Special, Hook Norton Bitter, Purity UBU. ♀ 30 **Facilities** Dogs allowed Garden Parking

SHIPTON-UNDER-WYCHWOOD — Map 10 SP21

PICK OF THE PUBS

The Shaven Crown Hotel ☉

High St OX7 6BA ☎ 01993 830330
e-mail: relax@theshavencrown.co.uk
dir: On A361, halfway between Burford & Chipping Norton opposite village green & church

As its name suggests, The Shaven Crown has a monastic past: it was built by the monks of Bruern Abbey as a hospice for the poor and needy. Following the Dissolution of the monasteries, Queen Elizabeth I used it as a hunting lodge before giving it to the village in 1580, when it became the Crown Inn. It was not until 1930 that a brewery with a touch of humour changed the name to reflect the hairstyles adopted by the monks. A 700-year-old honey-coloured Cotswold stone building set around a medieval courtyard, its interior is a feast of original features. Oxfordshire ales and light meals are served in the Monk's Bar, while the restaurant offers a more serious style of dining. Begin with drinks in the impressive Great Hall, then settle down to starters of deep-fried brie with raspberry coulis, followed perhaps by venison steak with wild mushroom and chive sauce. Fresh fish is delivered daily. Outside, apart from the enclosed courtyard, there is a tree-dotted lawned area.

Open all wk 11-3 6-11 (Sat-Sun 11-11) **Bar Meals** L served Mon-Fri 12-2, Sat-Sun 12-9.30 D served Mon-Fri 6-9.30, Sat-Sun 12-9.30 **Restaurant** L served Mon-Fri 12-2, Sat-Sun 12-9.30 D served Mon-Fri 6-9.30, Sat-Sun 12-9.30 ⊕ FREE HOUSE ◄ Hook Norton Best, guest ales including Old Hooky, Archers, Arkells Ö Westons Stowford Press. ☉ 10 **Facilities** Dogs allowed Garden Parking

SHUTFORD — Map 11 SP34

PICK OF THE PUBS

The George & Dragon NEW ☉

See Pick of the Pubs on opposite page

SOUTH MORETON — Map 5 SU58

The Crown Inn ☉

High St OX11 9AG ☎ 01235 812262
e-mail: dallas.family@ntlworld.com
dir: From Didcot take A4130 towards Wallingford. Village on right

Friendly village pub located midway between Wallingford and Didcot. It prides itself on its home-prepared food, and has real ale on tap. Families are welcome and customers come from far and wide. During the summer the garden is very popular. Dishes include steaks, shoulder of lamb, fresh battered haddock, and salmon fillet hollandaise.

Open noon-3 6-11pm (Fri noon-3 6-mdnt Sat noon-mdnt Sun noon-5) Closed: 1 Jan, Sun eve **Bar Meals** L served Mon-Sat 12-2.30, Sun 12-4.30 D served Mon-Sat 6.30-9.30 ⊕ WADWORTH ◄ Wadworth 6X, Henrys IPA. ☉ 12 **Facilities** Family room Dogs allowed Garden Parking

SOUTH STOKE — Map 3 SU58

The Perch and Pike ★★★ INN ☉

RG8 0JS ☎ 01491 872415 🖥 **01491 871001**
e-mail: info@perchandpike.co.uk
dir: On Ridgeway Hiking Trail. 1.5m N of Goring & 4m S of Wallingford on B4009

The Perch and Pike, just two minutes' walk from the River Thames, was the village's foremost beer house back in the 17th century. There is plenty of atmosphere in the original pub and in the adjoining barn conversion, which houses the 42-seater restaurant. Food ranges from a selection of salads, baguettes and ploughman's to the likes of Barbary duck breast with coriander and lemongrass couscous; braised pork belly with apple mash and onion gravy; and the South African dish, bobotie - a spicy minced beef.

Open all wk 11.30-3 5.30-11 (Sat-Sun 11.30-11) **Bar Meals** L served Mon-Sat 12-2.30 booking required D served Mon-Sat 7-9.30 booking required Av main course £9 **Restaurant** L served Sun 12-2.30 booking required D served Mon-Sat 7-9.30 booking required Av 3 course à la carte fr £24 ⊕ BRAKSPEAR ◄ Brakspear ales. ☉ 7 **Facilities** Children's menu Dogs allowed Garden Parking Rooms 4

STADHAMPTON — Map 5 SU69

PICK OF THE PUBS

The Crazy Bear ★★★★★ GA ⊛⊛ ☉

Bear Ln OX44 7UR
☎ 01865 890714 🖥 01865 400481
e-mail: enquiries@crazybear-stadhampton.co.uk
dir: M40 junct 7, A329. In 4m left after petrol station, left into Bear Lane

It's a fitting name for a fairly quirky place, but the 16th-century Crazy Bear likes to pride itself on being quirky, weaving its ancient features into a modern look within the utterly distinctive interior, which combines contemporary and art deco influences. The bar is quite traditional, except that it serves champagne and oysters as well as more conventional bar snacks. There are two restaurants, one serving Thai food, and the other modern British, as well as some stylish bedrooms and a wonderful garden with a waterfall and statues. The extensive menus should please everyone: 'all day' breakfasts and brunch dishes are served from 7am to 10am and classic English dishes from noon until 10pm. For breakfast/brunch choose duck eggs Benedict or farm-smoked haddock kedgeree; at lunch order a roast Angus beef and horseradish sandwich; or look to the main menu for seared scallops with a shallot and herb butter, or Old Spot ham hock terrine, followed by seared sea bass with shellfish bisque, or chicken and mushroom pie. Leave room for spiced plum crumble tart with clotted cream.

Open all day all wk 7am-mdnt **Bar Meals** Av main course £14 food served all day **Restaurant** Fixed menu price fr £10 food served all day ⊕ FREE HOUSE ◄ Old Speckled Hen, IPA, Timothy Taylor Landlord Ö Aspall, Stowford Press. ☉ 20 **Facilities** Children's menu Garden Parking **Rooms** 17

STANTON ST JOHN — Map 5 SP50

Star Inn ☉

Middle Rd OX33 1EX
☎ 01865 351277 🖥 01865 351006
e-mail: murwin@aol.com
dir: B4027 take Stanton exit, then 3rd left into Middle Rd, pub 200yds on left

Although the Star is only a short drive from the centre of Oxford, this popular pub still retains a definite 'village' feel. The oldest part dates from the early 17th century, and in the past, the building has been used as a butcher's shop and an abattoir. The garden is peaceful and secluded. A varied menu features shoulder of lamb in redcurrant and rosemary, spinach and mushroom strudel, or roast vegetable and goats' cheese tart.

Open all wk ⊕ WADWORTH ◄ Wadworth 6X, Henrys IPA, JCB. ☉ 7 **Facilities** Play area Family room Dogs allowed Garden Parking

PICK OF THE PUBS

The George & Dragon NEW ♟

SHUTFORD Map 11 SP34

Church Ln OX15 6PG ☎ 01295 780320
e-mail: info@thegeorgeanddragon.com
web: www.thegeorgeanddragon.com
dir: *Take A422 from Banbury. After 4m turn left at sign for Shutford, follow directly to pub*

This pretty, Cotswold stone country pub, dating back to the 13th century, is conveniently located at the start of the popular Shutford Walk. It is a favourite rest stop for ramblers who congregate in the beer garden overlooking the picturesque village. Legend has it that several ghosts haunt the pub, which is linked to the manor house by a secret tunnel. The bar (where dogs are welcome, and where in winter the locals play dominoes by the roaring fire) is

probably unique in that you are actually twelve feet underground as the pub is built into the side of a hill, with the village church directly above. That's surely something to think about when you order a pint of one of the five real ales, or maybe Dragon's Blood, a home-made mix of rum, herb and spice. Everything on the seasonal menus, except for the locally baked bread, is made from scratch; villagers bring in most game and vegetables. Predominantly English food is aimed at everyone: winter root vegetable soup; salmon en croûte, tarragon and lemon sauce; shank of Cotswold lamb braised in red wine; shallot and thyme tarte Tatin; Stilton, onion and potato hotpot; mulled wine-poached pear; and sticky ginger and golden syrup cake. If you just want a bar snack before heading off round the ancient tracks of the Shutford Walk, try a crayfish tails and herb mayonnaise bloomer.

Open 12-2.30 5.30-11 (Sat 12-11 Sun 12-10.30) Closed: Mon (ex BH) **Bar Meals** L served Tue-Sat 12-2, Sun 12-2.30 D served Tue-Sat 6.30-9 Av main course £8 **Restaurant** L served Tue-Sat 12-2, Sun 12-2.30 D served Tue-Sat 6.30-9 Fixed menu price fr £13 Av 3 course à la carte fr £22 🍺 Hooky Bitter, London Pride, Greene King IPA, Timothy Taylor Landlord. ♟ 9
Facilities Dogs allowed Garden

STANTON ST JOHN *continued*

The Talkhouse ♥

Wheatley Rd OX33 1EX ☎ 01865 351648
🖹 01865 351085
e-mail: talkhouse@fullers.co.uk
web: www.talkhouse.co.uk
dir: *Village signed from Oxford ring road*

First recorded as a pub in 1783, the Talkhouse comprises three bar and dining areas, all with a Gothic look and a welcoming atmosphere. A recently refurbished thatched property, it offers a good range of cask ales. Various bar meals (shepherd's pie, sausage and mash) are supplemented by a carte menu.

Open all day all wk noon-11pm (Sun noon-10.30pm)
Meals L served Mon-Sat 12-9, Sun 12-8 D served Mon-Sat 12-9, Sun 12-8 food served all day ⊕ FULLER SMITH TURNER PLC ◀ London Pride, ESB, Discovery, Guinness. ♥ 6 **Facilities** Dogs allowed Garden Parking

See advert on this page

STOKE ROW | Map 5 SU68

PICK OF THE PUBS

Crooked Billet ♥

See Pick of the Pubs on opposite page

SWALCLIFFE | Map 11 SP33

Stag's Head ♥

OX15 5EJ ☎ 01295 780232 🖹 01295 788977
dir: *6m W of Banbury on B4035*

This friendly, 600 year-old thatched village inn enjoys picture postcard looks and a pretty village setting. It seems that Shakespeare used to drink here, until he was barred! Blending a traditional pub feel with a family-friendly environment, the Stag also offers a beautiful terraced garden and play area. Freshly prepared dishes include goats' cheese tart with chips or salad; moules marinière with chorizo and crusty bread; and Oxfordshire liver and bacon with red wine and onion gravy. Look out for the landlord's own paintings of local scenes.

Closed: Mon ⊕ FREE HOUSE ◀ Adnams Bitter, Deuchars IPA, Wye Valley IPA, Badgers Gold, St Austell Tribute. ♥ 8 **Facilities** Play area Dogs allowed Garden

---

SWERFORD | Map 11 SP33

PICK OF THE PUBS

The Mason's Arms ◉ ♥

Banbury Rd OX7 4AP
☎ 01608 683212 🖹 01608 683105
e-mail: admin@masons-arms.com
dir: *Between Banbury & Chipping Norton on A361*

Originally a Masonic lodge, this award-winning 300-year-old pub is owned by Bill and Charmaine Leadbeater, and business partner, Tom Aldous. Seven years ago they refurbished the interior, added a new dining room and remodelled the gardens, all without upsetting its traditional, informal feel. 'Bill's Food' and 'Bill's Specials' menus confirm his supremacy in the kitchen, where the modern, personal twist he puts on his creations has earned him an AA Rosette. These range from chicken korma with pilau rice, naan bread

---

and onion bhaji, to 12-hour braised shin of shorthorn beef with cranberry and cinnamon red cabbage, herb roasties and red wine jus. His specials include chargrilled lamb cutlets with fondant potato, asparagus spears, honey and rosemary jus. Treacle tart and custard, and lemon and blueberry Pavlova are typical desserts. There is also a tempting children's menu. The bar dispenses well-kept Hook Norton and Brakspear's real ales, offers an extensive wine list and serves coffees and teas. A vegetable garden is planned for 2009.

Closed: 25-26 Dec, Sun eve **Bar Meals** L served Mon-Sat 12-2 booking required D served Mon-Sat 7-9 booking required Av main course £10.95 **Restaurant** L served Mon-Sat 12-2, Sun 12-3.30 booking required D served Mon-Sat 7-9 booking required Fixed menu price fr £14.95 Av 3 course à la carte fr £26 ⊕ FREE HOUSE ◀ Hook Norton Best, Brakspear Special. ♥ 14 **Facilities** Children's menu Garden Parking

---

SYDENHAM | Map 5 SP70

PICK OF THE PUBS

The Crown Inn ♥

Sydenham Rd OX39 4NB ☎ 01844 351634
e-mail: maxpettini@gmail.com
dir: *M49 junct 6 take B4009 towards Chinnor. Left at Kingston Blount. Or off B4445 (Thame to Chinnor road), 4m from Thame*

This pretty 17th-century inn lies in a picturesque village opposite its 900-year-old church. Refurbished to incorporate both traditional and modern styles, old photographs hang harmoniously on the walls alongside contemporary paintings. Croque monsieur and filled baguettes and jacket potatoes appear on the lunchtime snacks menu, while the regular carte offers a selection of British, French and Mediterranean-style food, with

continued on page 376

The Talkhouse

The Talkhouse is located in the picturesque village of Stanton-St-John, within easy reach of Oxford, Blenheim Palace and Bicester Village.

Owned & operated by Fullers, this beautiful building has been restored to offer a warm relaxed atmosphere from the moment you enter the bar.

Enjoy a range of Fullers ales at the bar complimented by the food and atmosphere of our Michelin recommended restaurant.

The Talkhouse also offers four extremely well appointed bedrooms for the perfect stay away.

Wheatley Road, Stanton-St-John, Oxford OX33 1EX
Tel: 01865 351648 · **Email:** talkhouse@fullers.co.uk · **Website:** www.thetalkhouse.co.uk

PICK OF THE PUBS

Crooked Billet 🍷

STOKE ROW   Map 5 SU68

RG9 5PU
☎ 01491 681048   📠 01491 682231
web: www.thecrookedbillet.co.uk
dir: *From Henley towards Oxford on A4130. Left at Nettlebed for Stoke Row*

It seems a shame to spoil the secret, but this charmingly rustic pub, tucked away down a single track lane in deepest Oxfordshire, is a popular hideaway for the well-heeled and the well known. It dates back to 1642 and was once the haunt of highwayman Dick Turpin; forced to hide here from local law enforcers, he whiled away the hours by courting the landlord's pretty daughter, Bess. Many of its finest features are unchanged, including the low beams, tiled floors and open fires that are so integral to its character. Famous customers, several of whom were introduced to the pub by the late George Harrison, have included Kate Winslet, who famously held her first wedding reception here; EastEnders cast members; and Jeremy Paxman. Menus are the work of award-winning chef/proprietor Paul Clerehugh. Local produce and organic fare are the mainstays of his kitchen, to the extent that he will even exchange a lunch or dinner for the locals' excess vegetables. Begin perhaps with roast scallops salad, artichoke and bacon; or partridge ham hock terrine, chutney served with a nip of sloe gin. To follow, there's a good range of fish mains, including lemon sole grilled on the bone with brown shrimp, watercress butter; whole baked Cornish mackerel with nutty green herb couscous; and monkfish baked in Serano ham, with roast sweet potato, confit tomato and roasted red onion.

Alternatives might include casserole of local rabbit, slow braised with white wine, vegetables, herbs, and mustard dumplings or pink carved venison steak, McSweens haggis, baby spinach, roast figs and juniper sauce. Notwithstanding the occasional famous face, the pub hosts music nights, free wine tastings and other events, and contributes some of its profit to the daily meals it provides for a local primary school.

Open noon-3 7-mdnt (Sat-Sun noon-mdnt) **Bar Meals** L served Mon-Fri 12-3, Sat-Sun all day D served Mon-Fri 7-10, Sat-Sun all day **Restaurant** L served Mon-Fri 12-3, Sat-Sun all day D served Mon-Fri 7-10, Sat-Sun all day Fixed menu price fr £3.95 ⊕ BRAKSPEAR 🛢 Brakspear Bitter. 🍷 12
Facilities Garden Parking

SYDENHAM *continued*

fish featuring regularly: perhaps monkfish with Parma ham, escalope of salmon, or fillets of sea bass. A Thai menu broadens the geographical purview even further.

Closed: Mon, Sun eve **Bar Meals** L served Tue-Sun 12-2.30 D served Tue-Sat 7-10 **Restaurant** L served Tue-Sun 12-2.30 D served Tue-Sat 7-10 ⊕ FREE HOUSE ◄ Greene King IPA, Ruddles County, Guinness, Brakspear, guest ales ♨ Westons. ☻ 6 **Facilities** Dogs allowed Garden Parking

---

TADMARTON   Map 11 SP33

The Lampet Arms ★★★ GA

Main St OX15 5TB ☎ 01295 780070 📄 **01295 788066**
dir: *Take B4035 from Banbury to Tadmarton, 5m*

Victorian-style free house offering well-kept ales and hearty home cooking. The pub is named after Captain Lampet, the local landowner who built it and mistakenly believed he could persuade the council to have the local railway line directed through the village, thereby increasing trade. Typical menu choices include steaks; chicken Kiev; steak and ale pie; chilli con carne; and a selection of sandwiches and baguettes.

Open all wk ⊕ FREE HOUSE ◄ Hook Norton, Theakstons, Guinness, John Smiths. **Facilities** Dogs allowed Garden Parking **Rooms** 4

TETSWORTH   Map 5 SP60

The Old Red Lion

40 High St OX9 7AS ☎ 01844 281274 📄 **01844 281863**
e-mail: fitz@the-red-lion-tetsworth.co.uk
dir: *Oxford Service area, turn right onto A40. At T-junct turn left then right onto A40 signed Stokenchurch, via Milton Common to Tetsworth*

This pink-washed pub is right on the village green, which conveniently has a large enclosed children's play area. Nemards restaurant comprises one eating areas behind the bar, the other in the quieter Library. In addition to dishes such as pan-fried potato gnocchi with tomato sauce, peas and mozzarella, the menu shows Afro-Caribbean influences with, for example, pan-fried barracuda on a bed of callaloo with coconut and ginger sauce. Check for live jazz and blues nights.

Open all wk ⊕ FREE HOUSE **Facilities** Dogs allowed Garden Parking

---

TOOT BALDON   Map 5 SP50

PICK OF THE PUBS

The Mole Inn ◉◉ ☻

OX44 9NG ☎ 01865 340001 📄 **01865 343011**
e-mail: info@themoleinn.com
dir: *5m SE from Oxford city centre off B480*

This stone-built, Grade II listed pub was the subject of an extensive renovation programme not long ago. The top-notch makeover has earned it a glowing and well-deserved reputation, due in no small measure to the efforts of award-winning chef/host Gary Witchalls. Inside, a great deal of care and attention has been lavished on this classic old local, and now customers can relax in black leather sofas amid stripped beams and solid white walls. The dining areas are equally striking with their intimate lighting and terracotta floors. Gary's inspired menu draws plenty of foodies from nearby Oxford and further afield, tempted by dishes such as 28-day, dry-aged Aberdeenshire rib steak; braised and roasted shoulder of Cornish lamb with clapshot and curly kale; or twice-cooked belly of Blythburgh pork in an apple jus, with gratin dauphinoise and purple sprouting broccoli.

Open all day all wk 12-12 (Sun 12-11) Closed: 25 Dec, 1 Jan **Restaurant** L served Mon-Sat 12-2.30, Sun 12-4 booking required D served Mon-Sat 7-9.30, Sun 6-9 booking required ⊕ FREE HOUSE ◄ Hook Norton, London Pride, Spitfire, Guinness. ☻ 11 **Facilities** Children's menu Garden Parking

---

WANTAGE   Map 5 SU38

The Hare ☻

Reading Rd, West Hendred OX12 8RH ☎ 01235 833249 📄 **01235 833268**
dir: *At West Hendred on A417 between Wantage & Didcot*

A late 19th-century inn mid-way between Wantage and Didcot, modernised in the 1930s by local brewers, Morland, and featuring a colonial-style verandah and colonnade. Inside it retains the more original wooden floors, beams and open fire.

Open all wk ⊕ GREENE KING ◄ Greene King Abbot Ale, IPA, Morland Original. ☻ 8 **Facilities** Dogs allowed Garden Parking

---

WHEATLEY   Map 5 SP50

Bat & Ball Inn ☻

**28 High St OX44 9HJ
☎ 01865 874379** 📄 **01865 873363**
e-mail: bb@traditionalvillageinns.co.uk
dir: *Through Wheatley towards Garsington, turn left signed Cuddesdon*

Do not be surprised to discover that the bar of this former coaching inn is packed to the gunnels with cricketing memorabilia. The owners claim that their collection puts to shame even that of Lords cricket ground! The comprehensive menu, supplemented by daily specials, is likely to feature steaks, fresh-baked pie of the day, herb-battered fresh cod, and maybe chargrilled Toulouse sausages. Lighter meals include lasagne, lamb Peshwari, and warm spinach and pancetta salad.

Open all wk ⊕ FREE HOUSE ◄ Marston's Pedigree, House LBW Bitter, Guinness. ☻ 10 **Facilities** Dogs allowed Garden Parking

---

WITNEY   Map 5 SP31

The Bell Inn

**Standlake Rd, Ducklington OX29 7UP
☎ 01993 702514** 📄 **01993 706822**
e-mail: danny@dpatching4.wanadoo.co.uk
dir: *1m S of Witney in Ducklington, off A415 (Abingdon road)*

Nearly 700 years have passed since the men building the adjacent church also erected their own living accommodation. Their hostel eventually became the Bell, and much extended over the years, it even embraces William Shepheard's former brewery, which closed in 1886. Today it is a popular, traditional village local, with many original features - and a collection of some 500 bells. Home-made pies, stews and burgers are a speciality, and there's a pig roast on Boxing Day.

Open all wk Closed: 25-26 Dec & 1 Jan ⊕ GREENE KING ◄ Greene King, IPA & Old Speckled Hen, Morland Original, Guinness. **Facilities** Play area Garden Parking

PICK OF THE PUBS

White Hart 🍷

WYTHAM   Map 5 SP40

OX2 8QA
☎ **01865 244372** 📠 **01865 248595**
e-mail:
whitehartwytham@btconnect.com
web: www.thewhitehartoxford.co.uk
dir: *Just off A34 NW of Oxford*

Just off the A34 in a sleepy hamlet west of Oxford, this Cotswold stone pub is worth remembering it you're stuck in traffic and in need of refreshment. If it looks familiar, it may be because it has featured in some of the *Inspector Morse* television programmes. The pub is more smart gastro-pub than traditional village local, the boldly refurbished interior blending flagged floors and big stone fireplaces with a contemporary, Mediterranean feel. Expect colourful walls and fabrics, painted floors and furniture, and modern artwork throughout the rambling rooms and plant-filled conservatory. You can pop in for a pint of Hooky but this is predominantly a place to eat, and boasts an extensive wine list. Landlord David Peever sources eggs, chicken, pork and bacon from a local farm less than a mile away, and all the meat is either free range or organic. The modern, Italian-inspired menu is supplemented by daily specials listing fresh fish and game dishes in season. To start, try the antipasti sharing plate (fish terrine, crab cake, chicken salad, soup, bread, dips and olives), or tuck into a warm asparagus and goats' cheese quiche with chervil dressing, or organic beef tomato, buffalo mozzarella and basil. Follow with lamb rump served with ratatouille and dauphinoise potatoes; pan-fried sea bass with wild rice, sugar snap peas and saffron velouté; or rib-eye steak with herb butter and chips; or roast halibut with saffron and herb risotto from the chalkboard. Leave room raspberry pannacotta with lemon and vanilla syrup; or pears poached in red wine with mascarpone cheese. There are also good lunchtime sandwiches and don't miss the Sunday roast lunches. In summer, dine alfresco on the rustic, Mediterranean-style terrace.

Open all week ⊕ SIX CONTINENTS RETAIL 🍺 Hook Norton & Timothy Taylor Landlord. 🍷 15 **Facilities** Garden Parking

WITNEY *continued*

The Three Horseshoes 🍷

78 Corner St OX28 6BS ☎ 01993 703086
e-mail: thehorseshoeswitney@hotmail.co.uk
web: www.threehorseshoes-witney.com
dir: *From Oxford on A40 towards Cheltenham take 2nd turn to Witney. At rdbt take 5th exit to Witney. Over flyover, through lights. At next rdbt take 5th exit into Corn St. Pub on left*

This traditional family-run pub sits on Witney's original main street. Built of Cotswold stone, the historic Grade II listed building has a charming interior with stone walls, low ceilings, wood and flagstone floors, and blazing log fires in winter. Traditional pub lunches include home-made cottage pie or chilli con carne, while evening menus may proffer cured calves' tongue or slow-roasted belly pork. Visit on the last Friday of the month (excluding December) for a complete fish menu.

Open all day all wk 11am-12.30am **Bar Meals** L served all wk 12-3 D served all wk 6-9.30 Av main course £13.50 **Restaurant** L served all wk 12-3 D served all wk 6-9.30 Av 3 course à la carte fr £16 ⊕ ADMIRAL TAVERNS ◧ Harveys Sussex Ale, Wychwood Hobgoblin, Brakspears Bitter, Hook Norton, St Austell Tribute ♻ Wychwood Green Goblin, Westons Stowford Press. 🍷 14 **Facilities** Dogs allowed Garden

WOOLSTONE   Map 5 SU28

The White Horse ★★★ INN

SN7 7QL ☎ 01367 820726 📠 01367 820566
e-mail: whitehorse@btconnect.com
dir: *Off A420 at Watchfield onto B4508 towards Longcot signed Woolstone*

Unusual windows add to the appeal of this black-and-white-timbered, thatched, Elizabethan village pub. Upholstered stools line the traditional bar, where a fireplace conceals two priest holes, visible to those who don't mind getting their knees dirty. Lunchtime bar snacks include fajitas, burgers and fish and chips. An extensive menu of freshly prepared English and international dishes in the oak-beamed restaurant

includes steak and ale pie, curries, steaks, fish pie and mushroom Stroganoff. There are five comfortable bedrooms in an annexe.

Closed: Sun eve ⊕ ARKELLS ◧ Arkells, Guinness ♻ Stowford Press. **Facilities** Dogs allowed Garden Parking **Rooms** 5

WYTHAM   Map 5 SP40

PICK OF THE PUBS

White Hart 🍷

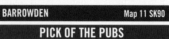

See Pick of the Pubs on page 377

RUTLAND

BARROWDEN   Map 11 SK90

PICK OF THE PUBS

Exeter Arms 🍷

LE15 8EQ ☎ 01572 747247 📠 01572 747247
e-mail: info@exeterarms.com
dir: *From A47 turn at landmark windmill, village 0.75m S. 6m E of Uppingham & 17m W of Peterborough*

This 17th-century pub-restaurant overlooks village green and duck pond in this pretty stone village not far from Rutland Water. With a half-acre garden for lazy summer days, it's a perfect country pub but it has been many other things in its long life, including a smithy, a dairy and a postal collection point. These days, ales are brewed in the barn next door and customers can rejoice in names such as Beech, Bevin, Hopgear, Owngear and Attitude Two. A typical menu opens with soup of the day or prosciutto, brie and tomato wrap with redcurrant and port dressing. Popular main courses are grilled sea bass fillets; fish pie; and steak and ale pie made with the pub's Barrowden beer. Desserts such as treacle tart and custard or chocolate brownies with chocolate sauce and ice cream ensure a happy ending.

Open 12-2.30 6-11 Closed: Sun eve, Mon L **Bar Meals** L served Tue-Sat 12-2 Av main course £9.95 **Restaurant** L served Sun 12-2 D served Tue-Sat 6.30-9 Av 3 course à la carte fr £19.50 ⊕ BARROWDEN BREWING COMPANY ◧ Beech, Bevin, Owngear, Hopgear, Attitude Two. 🍷 10 **Facilities** Dogs allowed Garden Parking

CLIPSHAM   Map 11 SK91

PICK OF THE PUBS

The Olive Branch ★★★★ INN ⊛⊛ 🍷

Main St LE15 7SH
☎ 01780 410355 📠 01780 410000
e-mail: info@theolivebranchpub.com
dir: *2m off A1 at B664 junct, N of Stamford*

Saved from closing well before the continuing decimation of Britain's pubs began in earnest, The Olive Branch shows what can be done with careful thought and determined effort. Outside, an attractive front garden and terrace; inside, a beautifully refurbished interior with bookshelves and an eclectic mix of antique and pine furniture. The bar serves local ales including Grainstore 1050, Olive Oil and Fenland, and Sheppy's and Stamford real ciders. From the two-AA Rosette kitchen come classics like fish and chips, and chargrilled rib-eye steak, holding their own alongside carpaccio of salmon with Thai-style salad; warm tartlet of wood pigeon with wild mushroom fricassée; braised shoulder of lamb with ratatouille and herb crust; and tandoori-baked halibut with lime and coriander rice. To follow: croissant and butter pudding; jam roly-poly, Clipsham custard and raspberry ripple ice cream; and chocolate marquise and mandarin sorbet. Check out the good selection of wines. Accommodation is available across the road at Beech House.

Open all wk noon-3.30 6-11 (Fri-Sun noon-11) Closed: 1 Jan, 25 & 26 Dec eve, 31 Dec L **Bar Meals** L served Mon-Fri 12-2, Sat 12-2 2.30-5.30, Sun 12-3 D served all wk 7-9 Av main course £9.50 **Restaurant** L served Mon-Sat 12-2, Sun 12-3 booking required D served Mon-Sat 7-9.30, Sun 7-9 booking required Fixed menu price fr £16.50 Av 3 course à la carte fr £26.50 ⊕ RUTLAND INN COMPANY LTD ◧ Grainstore 1050 & Olive Oil, Fenland, Brewster's, VPA, ♻ Sheppy's Dabinett Apple, Oakwood Special. 🍷 10 **Facilities** Dogs allowed Garden Parking **Rooms** 6

COTTESMORE — Map 11 SK91

The Sun Inn ♀

25 Main St LE15 7DH ☎ **01572 812321**
e-mail: cheviotinns@hotmail.co.uk
dir: *3m from Oakham on B668*

Dating back to 1610, this whitewashed, thatched pub boasts oak beams and a cosy fire in the bar. A well-priced menu supplemented by specials is on offer: chicken, leek and ham pie, steaks and grills, and plenty of fish choices like whole sea bass, swordfish steak and red snapper fillet are served. Lunchtime snacks include baguettes; ham, eggs and chips; and ploughman's. Apparently the ghost of a young girl is sometimes seen behind the bar.

Open all wk **Bar Meals** L served Mon-Sat 11.30-2.15, Sun 12-8 D served Mon-Sat 6-9, Sun 12-8 Av main course £9.50 **Restaurant** L served Mon-Sat 11.30-2.15, Sun 12-8 D served Mon-Sat 6-9, Sun 12-8 ⊕ EVERARDS BREWERY ◀ Adnams Bitter, Everards Tiger, Guinness, 2 guest ales. ♀ 9 **Facilities** Family room Dogs allowed Garden Parking

EMPINGHAM — Map 11 SK90

The White Horse Inn ★★★ INN ♀

Main St LE15 8PS ☎ **01780 460221** 🖹 **01780 460521**
e-mail: info@whitehorserutland.co.uk
dir: *From A1 take A606 signed Oakham & Rutland Water. From Oakham take A606 to Stamford*

An ideal place to recharge your batteries following a walk or cycle around Rutland Water, this former 17th-century courthouse has lost none of its period charm. The open fire, beamed bar and friendly staff are a recipe for total relaxation. The home-made food starts with sandwiches, home-made soup and baguettes and runs to hearty meals such as cheese and ale soup followed by Elizabethan pork casserole, or local trout fillets with a herb butter. Bedrooms are available.

Open all day all wk Closed: 25 Dec **Bar Meals** L served Mon-Thu 12-2.15, Fri-Sun 12-9 D served Mon-Thu 6.30-9, Fri-Sun 12-9 Av main course £9.50 **Restaurant** L served Mon-Thu 12-2.15, Fri Sun 12-9 D served Mon-Thu 6.30-9, Sun 12-9 Av 3 course à la carte fr £19 ⊕ ENTERPRISE INNS ◀ John Smith's, Adnams Best Bitter, Oakham Ales JHB & Bishops Farewell, Timothy Taylor Landlord. ♀ 9 **Facilities** Children's menu Dogs allowed Garden Parking **Rooms** 13

EXTON — Map 11 SK91

PICK OF THE PUBS

Fox & Hounds ♀

19, The Green LE15 8AP ☎ **01572 812403**
e-mail: sandra@foxandhoundsrutland.co.uk
dir: *Take A606 from Oakham towards Stamford, at Barnsdale turn left, after 1.5m turn right towards Exton. Pub in village centre*

A big and beautiful walled garden makes this former coaching inn a perfect spot for a sunny day. The imposing 17th-century building stands opposite the green in the centre of Exton, a charming village with countless stone and thatched cottages. The pub has a reputation for good food and hospitality, and is an ideal stopping-off point for those exploring the many good walks in the surrounding area. Its menu is the work of Italian chef/proprietor Valter Floris and his team, and combines the best of traditional English and Italian cuisine. In the evenings, there is an impressive list of over 25 authentic, thin-crust pizzas. The main menu features traditional options (chicken liver pâté followed by Grasmere sausages with creamy mashed potato and onion gravy) and further Italian flavours — perhaps mozzarella salad followed by porcini mushroom risotto.

Open all wk 11-3 6-11 **Bar Meals** L served all wk 12-2 D served Mon-Sat 6-9 ⊕ FREE HOUSE ◀ Greene King IPA & St Edmunds, Grainstore 1050, Ö St Helier Pear. ♀ 8 **Facilities** Play area Family room Dogs allowed Garden Parking

GLASTON — Map 11 SK80

The Old Pheasant ♀

Main Rd LE15 9BP ☎ **01572 822326** 🖹 **01572 823316**
e-mail: info@theoldpheasant.co.uk
dir: *On A47 between Leicester & Peterborough. Just outside Uppingham*

The stuffed head of a wild boar presides over the bar of this picture-perfect inn, which also features a smart stone-walled restaurant complete with evocative relics of farming history. Menus are constructed around quality produce, locally sourced where possible. Seasonal game from shoots is regularly featured, alongside trout from nearby rivers. Try home-cured gravadlax, honey glazed duck breast, and chocolate marquise, or an excellent range of cheeses.

Open all wk Closed: 2-7 Jan ⊕ FREE HOUSE ◀ Pheasant Ale, Timothy Taylor Landlord, Fuller's London Pride, Everards Original, Greene King Abbot Ale. ♀ 8 **Facilities** Garden Parking

LYDDINGTON — Map 11 SP89

Old White Hart ♀

51 Main St LE15 9LR
☎ **01572 821703** 🖹 **01572 821978**
e-mail: mail@oldwhitehart.co.uk
dir: *From A6003 between Uppingham & Corby take B672. Pub on main street opp village green*

Set amongst the sandstone cottages of rural Lyddington, this 17th-century free house close to Rutland Water has retained its original beamed ceilings, stone walls and open fires, and is surrounded by well-stocked gardens. Greene King and Timothy Taylor are amongst the beers on offer, along with interesting, freshly prepared food. The menu might include home cured gravadlax with horseradish dressing; and roast local pheasant breast with buttered mash. Fish and vegetarian choices plus daily specials and early bird menu also available.

Open all wk 12-3 6.30-11 (Sun 12-3 7-10.30) Closed: 25 Dec, 26 Dec eve **Bar Meals** L served Mon-Fri 12-2, Sat-Sun 12-2.30 booking required D served all wk 6.30-9, (Sun in summer 7-9) booking required Av main course £12.95 **Restaurant** L served Mon-Fri 12-2, Sat-Sun 12-2.30 booking required D served all wk 6.30-9 (Sun in summer 7-9) booking required Fixed menu price fr £10.95 Av 3 course à la carte fr £25 ⊕ FREE HOUSE ◀ Greene King IPA & Abbot Ale, Timothy Taylor Landlord, Fuller's London Pride, Timothy Taylor Golden Best. ♀ 8 **Facilities** Children's menu Play area Garden Parking

OAKHAM — Map 11 SK80

Barnsdale Lodge Hotel ★★★ HL ◉ ♀

The Avenue, Rutland Water, North Shore LE15 8AH
☎ **01572 724678** 🖹 **01572 724961**
e-mail: enquiries@barnsdalelodge.co.uk
dir: *A1 onto A606. Hotel 5m on right, 2m E of Oakham*

A former farmhouse, Barnsdale Lodge has been in the proprietor's family since 1760 as part of the adjoining Exton Estate. It stands overlooking Rutland Water in the heart of this picturesque little county. There's a cosy bar with comfortable chairs and a courtyard with outdoor seating. The bistro-style menu draws on local produce and offers dishes such as lobster bisque and individual Wellington of lamb fillet. There is also an attractive summer lunch menu.

Open all wk ⊕ FREE HOUSE ◀ Rutland Grainstore, Courage Directors, John Smith's, Guinness. ♀ 10 **Facilities** Play area Dogs allowed Garden Parking **Rooms** 44

PICK OF THE PUBS

The Jackson Stops Inn 🍷

Rookery Rd LE15 7RA
☎ **01780 410237**
dir: *1m off A1 pass Little Chef. Follow Stretton sign at B668 for Oakham*

For those keen on tracking down uniquely named pubs, this is a winner. You can guarantee nowhere else will have acquired its name by virtue of an estate agent sign that once hung outside for so long that locals dispensed with the original moniker of The White Horse Inn! The long, low, stone-built partly thatched building actually dates from 1721, and has plenty of appealing features: stone fireplaces with log fires, exposed stone and quarry tiled floors,

scrubbed wood tables and no fewer than four intimate dining rooms. In the timeless, black-beamed snug bar, you can order a pint of Adnams Bitter and play a rare pub game using old pennies – the traditional 'nurdling bench' is one of just two left in the country. Next door, in the cosy main bar, bag one of the comfy sofas and peruse the daily papers or the changing menu. For a snack, order a baguette or panini and create your own filling from interesting and mind-boggling list of 30 ingredients. For something more substantial, look to the main menu and specials board for starters of Thai fishcake with sweet chilli sauce, crayfish and avocado with capers and aioli, and chicken liver pâté with red onion marmalade. Follow with lamb shank with red wine gravy, steak and mushroom pie, pan-fried duck breast with confit rhubarb and ginger, or haddock wrapped in Parma ham with crayfish sauce. The two-course weekday lunch menu is great value.

Closed: Sun eve, Mon 🛢 FREE HOUSE
🍺 Oakham Ales JHB, Aldershaws Old Boy, Adnams Broadside, Timothy Taylor Landlord, Hop Back Summer Lightning.
🍷 7 **Facilities** Dogs allowed Garden Parking

PICK OF THE PUBS

Kings Arms ★★★★ INN ❀ ♟

Top St LE15 8SE
☎ **01572 737634** 📄 **01572 737255**
e-mail: info@thekingsarms-wing.co.uk
dir: *1m off B6003 between Uppingham &*
Oakham

Just one and a half miles from Rutland Water, the Kings Arms stands in the quaint village of Wing. Dating from 1649, this attractive free house is run by David and Gisa Goss, whilst their son James looks after the kitchen. After training in Switzerland and heading the team in a renowned Danish hotel restaurant, James took over as head chef when the family arrived in 2004. His excellent food has now earned an AA Rosette, and all bread, ice creams, terrines and sauces are made in-house. The pub has its own smoke house, and James cures bresaola, pancetta, corned beef and bacon on the premises. Because the family know what goes into their food, they can advise on ingredients and food allergies with confidence. The menus change twice a week and offer an extensive choice of dishes. Lunchtime brings soup and a range of filled organic rolls, whilst a selection from the main menu might begin with smoked pike Benedict; goat's cheese mousse with Parmesan crisp mille feuille; or smoked haddock, salmon and sea bass ravioli. Main dishes include Rutland trout supreme with saffron new potatoes; venison saddle with braised red cabbage; and butternut squash risotto with toasted pumpkin seeds and Cropwell Bishop goat's cheese. Beer drinkers can sample Shepherd Neame Spitfire and Grainstore Cooking. The eight en-suite letting rooms were freshly decorated in 2009, and are set away from the pub with their own private entrance. Guests with light boats and motorised campers are welcome to use the large off-road car park.

Open all week Closed: Sun eve, Mon (Oct-Mar), Mon L (Apr-Sep) **Bar Meals** L served Tue-Sun 12-2.30 D served Tue-Sat 6.30-8.30 Av main course £10 **Restaurant** L served Tue-Sun 12-2.30 D served Mon-Sat 6.30-8.30 Fixed menu price fr £12 Av 3 course à la carte fr £25 ⊕ FREE HOUSE ◣ Shepherd Neame Spitfire, Grainstore Cooking. ♟ 20 **Facilities** Garden Parking **Rooms** 8

OAKHAM *continued*

The Grainstore Brewery

Station Approach LE15 6RE
☎ 01572 770065 📠 01572 770068
e-mail: grainstorebry@aol.com
dir: *Next to Oakham rail station*

Founded in 1995, Davis's Brewing Company is housed in the three-storey Victorian grain store next to Oakham railway station. Finest quality ingredients and hops are used to make the beers that can be sampled in the pub's Tap Room. Filled baguettes and stilton and pork pie ploughman's are of secondary importance, but very tasty all the same. Go for the brewery tours and blind tastings; or attend the annual beer festival during the August Bank Holiday.

Open all day all wk 11am-1am **Bar Meals** L served all wk 11-3 ⊕ FREE HOUSE ◀ Rutlands Panther, Triple B, Ten Fifty, Silly Billy, Rutland Beast, Nip, seasonal beers Ö Sheppy's. **Facilities** Dogs allowed Garden Parking

SOUTH LUFFENHAM   Map 11 SK90

The Coach House Inn

3 Stamford Rd LE15 8NT
☎ 01780 720166 📠 01780 720866
e-mail: thecoachhouse123@aol.com
dir: *On A6121, off A47 between Morcroft & Stamford*

Horses were once stabled here while weary travellers enjoyed a drink in what is now a private house next door. Now elegantly refurbished, it offers a comfortable 40-cover dining room and a cosy bar. A short, appealing menu in the Ostler's Restaurant might feature goats' cheese, poached pear and walnut tart, followed by fillet of beef with chicken liver pâté and rösti potatoes.

Open noon-2 5-11 (Sat noon-11) Closed: 25 Dec, 1 Jan, Sun eve, Mon morning **Bar Meals** L served Tue-Sat 12-2 booking required D served Mon-Sat 6.30-9 booking required **Restaurant** L served Tue-Sun 12-2 booking required D served Mon-Sat 6.30-9 booking required ⊕ FREE HOUSE ◀ IPA, Adnams, Timothy Taylor Landlord, Guinness. **Facilities** Dogs allowed Parking

STRETTON   Map 11 SK91

PICK OF THE PUBS

The Jackson Stops Inn ♥

See Pick of the Pubs on page 380

Ram Jam Inn

The Great North Rd LE15 7QX
☎ 01780 410776 📠 01780 410361
dir: *On A1 N'bound carriageway past B668, through service station into car park*

The inn was originally a humble ale house called the Winchelsea Arms, and belonged to the Earl of that title who lived nearby. It is thought that its current name stems from a home-brew invented by a resident publican during the 18th century, when the pub sign advertised 'Fine Ram Jam'. Sadly no recipe survives, so its ingredients remain a mystery. Today's informal café-bar and bistro, with a patio overlooking orchard and paddock, welcomes visitors with its comprehensive daily-changing menu.

Open all day all wk 7.30am-10pm (Sun 8.30am-6pm) Closed: 25 Dec **Bar Meals** Av main course £9 food served all day **Restaurant** Av 3 course à la carte fr £15 food served all day ⊕ FREE HOUSE ◀ John Smith's Smooth, Fuller's London Pride. **Facilities** Children's menu Play area Garden Parking

WING   Map 11 SK80

PICK OF THE PUBS

Kings Arms ★★★★ INN ◉ ♥

See Pick of the Pubs on page 381

SHROPSHIRE

ADMASTON   Map 10 SJ61

The Pheasant Inn at Admaston NEW

TF5 0AD ☎ 01952 251989
e-mail: info@thepheasantadmaston.co.uk
web: www.thepheasantadmaston.co.uk
dir: *M54 junct 6 follow A5223 towards Whitchurch then follow B5063 towards Shawbirch & Admaston. Pub is on left of main rd*

Once owned by the Great Western Railway, this lovely old country pub dates from the 19th century. Stylish interior décor and a real fire add character to the dining areas, whilst the large enclosed garden is ideal for families. Using the best of local produce, expect pan-seared lamb's liver with crispy bacon and home-grown sage and red wine gravy; roast sea bass with prawn and cucumber butter; and broccoli, leek and field mushroom pie. There is also a very good 'Little People's' menu.

Open all day all wk **Bar Meals** L served Mon-Sat 12-2, Sun 12-3 D served Mon-Sat 6-9 Av main course £9 ◀ Shropshire Gold, Greene King IPA, Shropshire Lad, Guinness. **Facilities** Children's menu Play area Dogs allowed Garden Parking

BASCHURCH   Map 15 SJ42

The New Inn NEW ♥

Church Rd SY4 2EF ☎ 01939 260335
e-mail: bean.newinn@btconnect.com
dir: *8m from Shrewsbury, 8m from Oswestry*

Refurbished and revitalised by Marcus and Jenny Bean, this whitewashed village pub overlooks the parish church and draws the crowds for local ales and Marcus's home-cooked food. Sit at oak tables in the spick-and-span bar and dining room, or at teak tables on the landscaped patio, and tuck into lamb noisettes stuffed with rosemary and thyme, or slow roast Moor Farm pork belly with caramelised apples and cider jus, and milk chocolate and honeycomb mousse.

Open all wk 11-3 6-11 (Sun 12-4 7-11) Closed: 26 Dec, 1 Jan **Bar Meals** L served all wk 12-2 D served all wk 6.30-9.30 **Restaurant** L served all wk 12-2 booking required D served all wk 6.30-9.30 booking required ⊕ FREE HOUSE ◀ Greene King Abbot Ale, Banks Bitter, Stonehouse Station, Hobsons Best Bitter Ö Thatchers. ♥ 10 **Facilities** Children's menu Dogs allowed Garden Parking

PICK OF THE PUBS

The Sun at Norbury NEW INN

SY9 5DX ☎ **01588 650680**
dir: *10m from Church Stretton, 3m from Bishop's Castle off A489*

Discover the "blue remembered hills" that the poet A E Housman wrote about in *A Shropshire Lad*, today an Area of Outstanding Natural Beauty. The Sun is full of antiques and atmosphere, particularly in the bar, with its wealth of unusual artefacts, the 18th-century sitting room with log fires and elegant dining room. Food here includes a selection of baguettes with salad, local sausages with onion gravy, rump steaks, smoked trout and ploughman's. The chef/proprietors have established a restaurant with a reputation for good, unpretentious food using quality local produce, with choices such as starters of prawn and organic smoked salmon cocktail; and warm salsa of tomato, anchovy and olives; main courses including fillet and sirloin steaks; grilled lamb cutlets; roast Shropshire duck; chicken provençale; and fresh vegetable roulade; plus a range of home-made desserts. Stay overnight in one of the highly rated guest rooms.

Open 7pm-11pm (Sun 12-3) Closed: Sun eve, Mon **Bar Meals** L served Sat-Sun (summer) 12-2 D served Tue-Sat 7-9 booking required **Restaurant** L served Sun 12-2 booking required D served Tue-Sat 7-9 booking required ◀ Wye Valley Bitter, Woods Shropshire Lad Ö Westons Stowford Press. **Facilities** Garden Parking **Rooms** 6

The Three Tuns Inn ♀

Salop St SY9 5BW ☎ **01588 638797**
e-mail: timce@talk21.com
dir: *From Ludlow take A49 through Craven Arms, then left onto A489 to Lydham, then A488 to Bishop's Castle*

A traditional timber-framed town centre inn established in 1625, and a brewery since 1642; tours can be arranged. Refurbished and enlarged, the full range of Three Tuns ales can be enjoyed more or less in peace - without piped music or fruit machines, just occasional live jazz or summer Morris dancing. It still retains the public bar, snug bar and lounge bar with the addition of a classy oak framed, glass sided dining room. Well-priced menus may offer smoked venison and whisky pâté; award-winning Wenlock Edge sausages; or 28-day-hung rib eye steak with peppercorn sauce.

Open all wk ⊕ FREE HOUSE ◀ Tuns XXX, Steamer, Scrooge, Clerics Cure (all by Three Tuns), Three-eight. ♀ 10 **Facilities** Dogs allowed Garden

Halfway House Inn ★★★ INN ♀

Cleobury Rd, Eardington WV16 5LS
☎ **01746 762670** 📄 **01746 768063**
e-mail: info@halfwayhouseinn.co.uk
dir: *M5 junct 6, A449 towards Kidderminster. Follow ring road to right. At next rdbt take A442 N towards Bridgnorth. 12m, take A458 towards Shrewsbury. Follow brown tourist signs to pub*

An original Elizabethan wall mural is a fascinating feature of this former coaching inn, but the Halfway House owes its current name to a visit in 1823 by Princess Victoria and her entourage. (She was halfway between Shrewsbury and Worcester.) The pub is renowned for its locally sourced, home-cooked food, at least three local real ales, 40 malts, and around 100 wines. Dishes range from bar snacks to braised beef in Guinness, grilled local steaks and Astbury Falls rainbow trout. There is plenty of accommodation available if you want to stay over.

Open 5-11.30 (Fri & Sat 11am-11.30pm Sun 11-6) Closed: Sun eve ex BH **Bar Meals** L served Fri-Sun 12-2 D served Mon-Sat 6-9 Av main course £11.50 **Restaurant** D served Mon-Sat 6-9 booking required Fixed menu price fr £22.50 Av 3 course à la carte fr £25 ⊕ FREE HOUSE ◀ Holden's Golden Glow, Wood's Shropshire Lad, Hobson's Town Crier, Draught Guinness Ö Weston's Stowford Export. ♀ 10 **Facilities** Children's menu Play area Garden Parking **Rooms** 10

Pheasant Inn

Linley Brook WV16 4TA ☎ **01746 762260**
e-mail: pheasant-inn@tiscali.co.uk
dir: *From Bridgnorth take B4373 towards Broseley. At junct of B4373 & Briton's Ln follow brown & white tourist sign for pub. Pub in 400yds*

Run by a husband and wife team for over 25 years, this is a perfect, traditional country pub in a pretty location. There are no games machines or piped music there. Open fires and wood burners heat its two rooms, where locals play bar billiards, dominoes and card games. The beer range varies but the pub does support small breweries, usually local. Food includes battered haddock or plaice, home-made lasagne or curry or chilli con carne. Sorry, no small children. Local walks include one leading down to the River Severn.

Open all wk **Bar Meals** L served all wk 12-2 D served all wk 7-9 Av main course £7.50 ⊕ FREE HOUSE ◀ Hobson Bitter, Hobson Town Crier, Wye Valley HPA, Salopian Shropshire Gold, Cannon Royall Arrowhead. **Facilities** Garden Parking **Notes** ⊜

PICK OF THE PUBS

The Burlton Inn ♀

SY4 5TB ☎ **01939 270284**
e-mail: enquiries@burltoninn.com
dir: *10m N of Shrewsbury on A528 towards Ellesmere*

This pretty old building has been transformed into a classy, contemporary interpretation of an 18th-century inn, with a fresh looking dining area, a soft furnished space for relaxation, and a traditional bar - the perfect place for a pint of Robinson Unicorn among other real ales. A good choice of food is offered, including a list of starters doubling as light meals - maybe venison terrine or Thai style mussels. Among the main courses is a choice of steaks; pan-fried glazed belly pork with flavours of soy, coriander, celery, leek and onion, served with parsnip mash and fresh vegetables; and grilled sea bass fillets on pea, goats' cheese and pancetta risotto. Don't miss the home-made desserts. Outside there is a lovely patio area, carefully planted to provide a blaze of colour in summer.

Open all wk Closed: 25 Dec **Restaurant** L served all wk 12-2 D served all wk 6.30-9 ⊕ ROBINSONS ◀ Robinsons Unicorn, XB, seasonal beer Ö Stowford Press. ♀ 12 **Facilities** Family room Garden Parking

PICK OF THE PUBS

The Boyne Arms ♀

Bridgnorth Rd WV16 6QH ☎ **01746 787214**
e-mail: theboynearms@btconnect.com
dir: *On B4364 between Ludlow & Bridgnorth*

Set in the village of Burwarton amid idyllic Shropshire countryside, this Grade II listed Georgian former coaching inn is part of the Boyne estate, and has belonged to Lord Boyne's family for generations. It draws travellers and locals alike; a beautiful mature walled garden at the rear includes a children's playground, making it perfect for families. Four real ales plus a real cider are always available. The stable bar with its wood burning stove and solid beams hosts games and functions, while the tap room is the locals' favourite. Food offerings include filled freshly baked baguettes, traditional pies and a selection from the

continued

BURWARTON *continued*

grill, while the à la carte menu gives chef patron Jamie Yardley the chance to really strut his stuff, offering impressive dishes such as crisp smoked fish cake with sweet chilli mayonnaise and micro leaves followed by steamed supreme of salmon with lobster sauce and truffled pea mash.

Open all wk all day (wknds only) **Bar Meals** L served Mon-Sat 12-2 D served Tue-Sat 6.30-9 Av main course £7 **Restaurant** L served Fri-Sun 12-2 D served Tue-Sat 6.30-9 Fixed menu price fr £11.95 Av 3 course à la carte fr £25 ⊕ FREE HOUSE ◄ Timothy Taylor Landlord, Shropshire Lad, Bridgnorth Bitter, Town Crier, Queen Bee ○ Weston's Organic Scrumpy. ♇ 8 **Facilities** Play area Garden Parking

CHURCH STRETTON — Map 15 SO49

The Bucks Head NEW ★★★★ INN ♇

42 High St SY6 6BX ☎ 01694 722898
e-mail: lnutting@btinternet.com
dir: *12m from Shrewsbury & Ludlow*

Bring your boots, stay the night in one of the refurbished rooms, or walk off a hearty lunch with a ramble along the Long Mynd, just minutes from the front door of this recently revamped pub and restaurant. Fuel-up on or return from hills for home-made food using local produce. Expect home-made soups, steaks, lasagne, authentic curries or one of the daily fish specials. Expect Marston's and guest ales on tap, smart dining rooms, and an attractive summer garden for alfresco drinking.

Open all day all wk **Bar Meals** L served all wk 12-2.30 D served all wk 6-9 **Restaurant** L served all wk 12-2.30 D served all wk 6-9 ⊕ Marston's Pub Company ◄ Banks Original, Banks Bitter, Marston's Pedigree, Guinness, Guest Ale. ♇ 6 **Facilities** Children's menu Garden Parking **Rooms** 4

The Royal Oak

Cardington SY6 7JZ ☎ 01694 771266   📄 01694 771685
e-mail: inntoxicated@gmail.com
dir: *Turn right off A49 N of Church Stretton; 2m off B4371 (Church Stretton-Much Wenlock road)*

Reputed to be the oldest continuously licensed pub in the county, this 15th-century free house is set in a conservation village surrounded by lovely countryside close to the South Shropshire hills. It has a low-beamed bar with a vast inglenook, and a comfortable beamed dining room. Four cask ales are served alongside home-cooked food. Fidget pie (gammon, apples and cider) is a house speciality made from a recipe handed down from landlord to landlord.

Open 12-2.30 (Sun 12-3.30) 7-mdnt (Fri-Sat 1am) **Closed:** Mon (ex BH Mon L) **Bar Meals** L served Tue-Sat & BH Mon 12-2, Sun 12-2.30 D served Tue-Sun 7-9 **Restaurant** L served Tue-Sat 12-2, Sun 12-2.30 D served Tue-Sun 7-9 ⊕ FREE HOUSE ◄ Hobsons Best Bitter, Three Tuns XXX, Wye Valley Butty Bach, Bass, Six Bells 1859. **Facilities** Children's menu Garden Parking

CLEOBURY MORTIMER — Map 10 SO67

PICK OF THE PUBS

The Crown Inn ♇

Hopton Wafers DY14 0NB
☎ 01299 270372   📄 01299 271127
dir: *On A4117 8m E of Ludlow, 2m W of Cleobury Mortimer*

A quick glance at this 16th-century coaching inn suggests that it is constructed from Virginia creeper, so densely does foliage cover the exterior. The Crown is a great choice for a short break, especially if walking by tumbling streams through lush farmland and wooded valleys is your preferred relaxation. Alternatively special packages can be put together to cater for Ludlow racegoers. The Crown was once estate owned and its Rent Room bar is where local tenants used to pay whatever they owed. Off the bar is an informal eatery with relaxing views, where the daily menu, light bites and specials can be enjoyed. In the full service Poacher's Restaurant you can dine beneath exposed beams warmed, if necessary, by fires blazing in the large inglenooks. Fresh produce lies behind the seasonal menus, which specialise in local meat and game. The daily blackboards offer a dizzying choice, including an excellent array of fresh fish dishes.

Open all wk ⊕ FREE HOUSE ◄ Timothy Taylor Landlord, Hobsons Best, guest ales. ♇ 10 **Facilities** Play area Garden Parking

COCKSHUTT — Map 15 SJ42

The Leaking Tap ♇

Shrewsbury Rd SY12 0JQ
☎ 01939 270636   📄 01939 270746

This friendly pub in the centre of Cockshutt village features beamed bars and log fires, and serves a selection of guest ales and food cooked from local produce. Lunchtime or evening menus are available, including a vegetarian selection, might include oven-baked salmon with roasted fennel; almond crusted fish cakes; and baked cod with herbs and stilton.

Open all wk ⊕ PUNCH TAVERNS ◄ Banks Bitter, Banks Original, guest ales. ♇ 12 **Facilities** Parking

CRAVEN ARMS — Map 9 SO48

The Sun Inn ♇

Corfton SY7 9DF ☎ 01584 861239
e-mail: normanspride@aol.com
dir: *On B4368, 7m N of Ludlow*

First licensed in 1613, this historic pub has a public bar with pool table, jukebox and dartboard, along with a lounge and restaurant. Landlord Norman Pearce brews the Corvedale ales in what was the pub's old chicken and lumber shed, using local borehole water; Mahoral cider, from just down the road, is another drinks option. Teresa Pearce uses local produce in a delicious array of

traditional dishes, served with up to six fresh vegetables and a choice of chips or new potatoes. The pub has historic connection with the transportation of criminals to Australia.

Open all wk 12-2.30 6-11 (Sun 12-3 7-11) **Bar Meals** L served all wk 12-2 D served all wk 6-9 Av main course £9 **Restaurant** L served 12-2 D served 6-9 ⊕ FREE HOUSE ◄ Corvedale Normans Pride, Dark & Delicious, Julie's Ale, Katie's Pride, Farmer Rays ○ Mahoral. ♇ 14 **Facilities** Children's menu Play area Dogs allowed Garden Parking

CRESSAGE — Map 10 SJ50

The Riverside Inn ♇

Cound SY5 6AF ☎ 01952 510900   📄 01952 510926
dir: *On A458 7m from Shrewsbury, 1m from Cressage*

Originally a vicarage for St Peter's church in the village, the building also housed a girls' school and a railway halt before becoming a pub in 1878. Extensively refurbished, it sits in three acres of garden alongside the River Severn, offering customers delightful river views both outdoors and from a modern conservatory. Service with a smile delivers to the table wholesome plates of Moroccan chicken skewers; pork and leek pie; and treacle tart with cream or ice cream.

Open all wk all day (Sat-Sun May-Sep) **Bar Meals** L served all wk 12-2.30 D served all wk 6.30-9.30 Av main course £9 **Restaurant** L served all wk 12-2.30 D served all wk 6.30-9.30 Av 3 course à la carte fr £17 ⊕ FREE HOUSE ◄ Shropshire Gold, guest ales. ♇ 8 **Facilities** Dogs allowed Garden Parking

HODNET — Map 15 SJ62

The Bear at Hodnet

TF9 3NH ☎ 01630 685214   📄 01630 685787
e-mail: reception@bearathodnet.co.uk
dir: *At junct of A53 & A442 turn right at rdbt. Inn in village centre*

Standing opposite Hodnet Hall Gardens, Allison and Ben Christie's 16th-century coaching inn is steeped in history, with original beams and fireplaces in the character bar, and secret passages leading to the parish church. Famous for medieval banquets in the newly refurbished hall, food in the bar takes in rare breed meats (roast belly of Maynard's pork with sage and cider jus) and pub classics like ham, egg and chips, and liver and bacon with mash and onion gravy.

Open noon-3 6-mdnt (Fri-Sat noon-mdnt) Closed: Sun eve **Bar Meals** L served Mon-Sat 12-2.30 D served Mon-Sat 6-9.30 Av main course £7.95 **Restaurant** L served all wk 12-2.30 D served Mon-Sat 6-9.30 ⊕ FREE HOUSE ◀ Theakston, Worthers, Guest ales. **Facilities** Dogs allowed Garden Parking

IRONBRIDGE   Map 10 SJ60

The Malthouse ♀

The Wharfage TF8 7NH
☎ 01952 433712   📄 01952 433298
e-mail: enquiries@themalthouseironbridge.com
dir: Telephone for directions

An inn since the 1800s, the Malthouse is located in the village of Ironbridge next to the river, now a designated UNESCO World Heritage Site famous for its natural beauty and award-winning museums. Party menus are available for both the popular jazz bar and the restaurant, while the main menu ranges from lasagne or faggots to monkfish and pancetta baked and served with sweet chorizo, mussel and tomato cassoulet.

Open all wk **Bar Meals** food served all day **Restaurant** food served all day ⊕ PUNCH TAVERNS ◀ Directors, Greene King IPA, Badger. ♀ 10 **Facilities** Children's menu Dogs allowed Garden Parking

LLANFAIR WATERDINE   Map 9 SO27

PICK OF THE PUBS

The Waterdine ★★★★★ RR ◉◉ ♀

LD7 1TU ☎ 01547 528214
e-mail: info@waterdine.com
dir: 4.5m W of Knighton off B4355, turn right opposite Lloyney Inn, 0.5m into village, last on left opp church

There's an air of total peace and quiet, and there are fine views down the Teme Valley from this low, stone whitewashed pub-with-rooms, tucked away in a tiny hamlet smack on the border between England and Wales. The old parish church stands opposite, the Teme runs through the bottom of the garden, and chef-landlord Ken Adams proudly continues to provide sustenance and shelter for weary travellers at his 400-year-old former drover's inn. There are two dining rooms, the Garden Room looking out over the river, and the Taproom, tucked away in the oldest part of the building with heavy beams and a stone floor. Menus are based on home-grown and locally supplied organic produce, so dishes like Old Spot pork terrine with fig and raspberry chutney, pan-fried beef fillet with Dijon mustard sauce, and roast turbot on leek confit with girolle mushrooms are appropriately seasonal. Comfortable bedrooms are filled with thoughtful extras and have modern bathrooms.

Closed: 1wk winter, 1wk spring, Sun eve & Mon (ex BH) **Bar Meals** L served Thu-Sun 12.15-1.30 booking required **Restaurant** L served Thu-Sun 12.15-1.30 booking required D served Tue-Sat 7-8.30 booking required ⊕ FREE HOUSE ◀ Wood Shropshire Legends, Parish Bitter, Shropshire Lad. ♀ 8 **Facilities** Children's menu Garden Parking **Rooms** 3

LUDLOW   Map 10 SO57

The Church Inn ★★★★ INN ♀

Buttercross SY8 1AW
☎ 01584 872174   📄 01584 877146
dir: In town centre

The inn stands on one of the oldest sites in Ludlow, dating back some seven centuries, and through the ages has been occupied by a blacksmith, saddler, druggist and barber-surgeon. These days it enjoys a good reputation for decent beer and traditional pub food - cod in beer batter, locally made faggots, and three cheese pasta and broccoli bake. There are eight en suite bedrooms with televisions and tea-making facilities.

Open all wk **Bar Meals** L served Mon-Fri 12-2.30, Sat-Sun 12-3 D served Mon-Sat 6.30-9, Sun 6.30-8.30 ⊕ FREE HOUSE ◀ Hobsons Town Crier, Weetwood, Wye Valley Bitter, Ludlow Gold, Boilingwell Mild ♂ Stowford, Aspall. ♀ 14 **Facilities** Dogs allowed **Rooms** 8

The Clive Bar & Restaurant with Rooms ★★★★★ RR ◉◉ ♀

Bromfield SY8 2JR
☎ 01584 856565 & 856665   📄 01584 856661
e-mail: info@theclive.co.uk
web: www.theclive.co.uk
dir: 2m N of Ludlow on A49, between Hereford & Shrewsbury

This classy bar and eatery was once home to Robert Clive, who laid the foundations of British rule in India. Built as a farm house in the 18th-century, the building became a pub in the 1900s for the many workers of the Estate. These days it houses a bar with traditional ales, real ciders, a wide range of wines and light snacks. It separates into two sections - an 18th-century lounge area in traditional style with log fire and featuring the original coat of arms of Clive of India. A more contemporary upper area leads to an outside courtyard

with tables and parasols for warmer weather. There is also a stylish Rosetted restaurant and 15 en suite bedrooms.

Open all day all wk Mon-Sat 11-11 (Sun 12-10.30) Closed: 25-26 Dec **Bar Meals** L served Mon-Fri 12-3, Sat-Sun 12-6.30 booking required D served Mon-Sat 6.30-10, Sun 6.30-9.30 booking required Av main course £9.95 **Restaurant** L served all wk 12-3 booking required D served Mon-Sat 6.30-10, Sun 6.30-9.30 booking required Av 3 course à la carte fr £25 ⊕ FREE HOUSE ◀ Hobsons Best Bitter, Ludlow Gold Bitter, Guinness ♂ Dunkertons Original, Mahoral Farm. ♀ 10 **Facilities** Children's menu Garden Parking **Rooms** 15

PICK OF THE PUBS

The Roebuck Inn ★★★★ INN ◉◉

Brimfield SY8 4NE ☎ 01584 711230
e-mail: info@theroebuckludlow.co.uk
dir: Just off A49 between Ludlow & Leominster

Despite a façade that looks decidedly Victorian, this country inn dates from the 15th century. Its lounge bar retains the inglenook and wood panelling of the period, while the elegantly minimalist dining room is more contemporary. Customers have the choice of eating in either of these rooms from the imaginative menus of head chef-patron, the much-accolated Olivier Bossut, including two AA Rosettes for his modern-laced-with-classical French food. Expect his carte to offer starters of butternut squash risotto with aged Parmesan, roast pinenuts, cep oil; gateau of crab in a saffron beurre blanc; and main courses of saddle of lamb Wellington with Jerusalem artichoke and liquorice sauce; and fillet of beef en croûte with truffle sauce. Twice monthly, on Wednesday evenings, the Roebuck presents a French night in association with Ludlow's French Pantry, which specialises in providing the very best in regional food and wines from France.

Open all wk 11.30-3 6-mdnt (Sun eve times vary) **Bar Meals** L served Mon-Sat 11.30-2.30 D served Mon-Sat 6.30-9 Av main course £13.50 **Restaurant** L served all wk 11.30-2.30 D served Mon-Sat 6.30-9 ⊕ MARSTONS ◀ Bank's Bitter, Marstons Pedigree plus guests. **Facilities** Children's menu Dogs allowed Garden Parking **Rooms** 3

LUDLOW *continued*

PICK OF THE PUBS

The Unicorn ?

Corve St SY8 1DU
☎ 01584 873555 📄 01584 876268
e-mail: graham-unicorn@btconnect.com
dir: *A49 to Ludlow. From town centre down Corve St towards river*

This low, attractive, timber-framed building backs on to the once flood-prone River Corve. During the great flood of 1885 a photograph was taken of men sitting drinking around a table in the bar while water lapped the doorway. Apparently it wasn't unusual for empty beer barrels to float out of the cellar and down the river. These days, all is warm and dry: log fires in winter and the sunny riverside terrace in summer prove very appealing. The impressive food offerings run from sandwiches (brie and cranberry; home-cooked ham) to full meals such as home-made Shropshire pâté with sweet onion marmalade followed by the likes of fish pie – a house speciality – or braised local lamb shanks with proper gravy and fresh vegetables. For those seeking pub classics, there are home-made faggots, home-made rare breed steak burger and ale-battered fish with home-made chips. Home-made desserts include sticky toffee pudding and dark chocolate torte.

Open all day all wk 11am-mdnt **Bar Meals** L served all wk 12-2.15 D served all wk 6-9.15 Av main course £9 **Restaurant** L served all wk 12-2.15 D served all wk 6-9.15 Av 3 course à la carte fr £17.50 ⊕ Enterprise Inns PLC ◀ Ludlow Best Ale, Butty Bach, Guinness. ? 15 **Facilities** Dogs allowed Garden

---

MADELEY   Map 10 SJ60

All Nations Inn

20 Coalport Rd TF7 5DP
☎ 01952 585747 📄 01952 585747
dir: *On Coalport Rd, overlooking Blists Hill Museum*

Only three families have owned this friendly, largely unspoilt pub since it opened as a brewhouse in 1831. And a brewhouse it has remained. There's no jukebox, pool or fruit machine, although Six Nations rugby matches are shown on a TV perched on barrels. No restaurant either, but quality rolls and pork pies are available all day. From the outside seating area you can see Blists Hill Victorian Town open air museum.

Open all day all wk noon-mdnt **Bar Meals** Av main course £2.80 food served all day ⊕ FREE HOUSE ◀ Dabley Ale, Dabley Gold, Coalport Dodger Mild, Guest ales. **Facilities** Dogs allowed Garden Parking **Notes** ⊛

The New Inn

Blists Hill Victorian Town, Legges Way TF7 5DU
☎ 01952 601018 📄 01785 252247
e-mail: sales@jenkinsoncaterers.co.uk
dir: *Between Telford & Broseley*

Here's something different - a Victorian pub that was moved brick by brick from the Black Country and re-erected at the Ironbridge Gorge Open Air Museum. The building remains basically as it was in 1890, and customers can buy traditionally brewed beer at five-pence farthing per pint - roughly £2.10 in today's terms - using pre-decimal currency bought from the bank. The mainly traditional menu includes home-made soup, steak and kidney pudding, and ham and leek pie.

Open all wk Closed: 24-25 Dec, 1 Jan ⊕ IRONBRIDGE GORGE MUSEUMS ◀ Banks Bitter, Banks Original, Pedigree. **Facilities** Play area Family room Garden Parking

---

MARTON   Map 15 SJ20

The Sun Inn ?

SY21 8JP ☎ 01938 561211
e-mail: suninnmarton@googlemail.com
dir: *On B4386 (Shrewsbury to Montgomery road), in centre of Marton opp village shop*

This classic stone free house dates back to 1760 and is surrounded by glorious Shropshire countryside. Both bar and restaurant are attractively appointed, with the contemporary restaurant offering a modern English and Mediterranean menu and an impressive selection of fresh fish dishes. Typical main courses might include roasted fillet of hake with courgette and ouzo sauce or rabbit with two mustard sauce and prunes. The bar menu offers home-made pizzas, local cheese with pear and honey, and Wenlock Edge Farm sausages. Wash down your meal with a pint from the great selection of real ales or chose from one of the 12 wines by the glass.

Open 12-3 7-mdnt Closed: Mon, Tue L, Sun eve **Bar Meals** L served Wed-Sat 12-2.30 booking required D served Tue-Fri from 7pm booking required **Restaurant** L served Wed-Sun 12-2.30 booking required D served Tue-Sat from 7pm booking required ⊕ FREE HOUSE ◀ Hobsons Best Bitter, Worthington Creamflow, Guest ales. ? 12 **Facilities** Garden Parking

---

MUCH WENLOCK   Map 10 SO69

The Feathers Inn ?

Brockton TF13 6JR ☎ 01746 785202 📄 01746 712717
e-mail: feathersatbrockton@googlemail.com
dir: *From Much Wenlock follow signs to Ludlow on B4378 for 3m*

A vast inglenook, big mirrors, stone busts, reclaimed timbers from old ships and local art are all features of this Grade II listed, 16th-century pub. The Feathers also incorporates a mini shop, a children's cookery school, a ladies' luncheon club with cookery demonstrations on Friday lunchtimes, and a takeaway food service. Menus are based on fresh, largely local ingredients, with a regularly updated specials board, traditional Sunday roasts, and good value early suppers. Wines are sourced from all over the world.

Open 12-2 6.30-11 Closed: 26 Dec, 1-4 Jan, Mon **Bar Meals** L served Tue-Sun 12-2 D served Tue-Sun 6.30-11 Av main course £12 **Restaurant** L served Tue-Sun 12-2 D served Tue-Sun 6.30-11 Fixed menu price fr £10 Av 3 course à la carte fr £16 ⊕ FREE HOUSE ◀ Hobsons Ale, Guinness, Boddingtons, Worfield Brewery Ales. ? 6 **Facilities** Children's menu Garden Parking

---

The George & Dragon

2 High St TF13 6AA ☎ 01952 727312
e-mail: bevmason@btinternet.com
dir: *On A458 halfway between Shrewsbury & Bridgnorth*

The George & Dragon is an oak-beamed 17th-century inn at the heart of Much Wenlock. Sited next to the market square, Guildhall and ruined priory, the inn welcomes everyone, from locals to walkers. It oozes history, charm and character, and now and again the spirit of a mistreated 18th-century dog is felt as a cold chill around the legs or heard walking across the quarry tiles. Locals Bev and James have recently taken over the pub and pride themselves on serving good quality, home-cooked, traditional British food and real cask ales.

Open all day all wk 11-11 (Thu 11-mdnt Fri-Sat 11am-1am Sun 11am-11.30pm) **Bar Meals** L served all wk 12-2 D served Mon-Tue, Thu 6-9 Av main course £5.95 **Restaurant** L served all wk 12-2 D served Mon-Tue, Thu-Sat 6-9 Fixed menu price fr £6.95 Av 3 course à la carte fr £10.95 ⊕ PUNCH RETAIL ◀ Greene King Abbot Ale, Wadworth 6X, guest ales. **Facilities** Children's menu Dogs allowed

Longville Arms

Longville in the Dale TF13 6DT
☎ 01694 771206 📠 01694 771742
e-mail: jill.livingstone@btconnect.com
dir: *From Shrewsbury take A49 to Church Stretton, then B4371 to Longville*

Prettily situated in an Area of Outstanding Natural Beauty in Shropshire, ideally placed for walking and touring, this welcoming country inn has been carefully restored. Solid elm or cast-iron-framed tables, oak panelling and wood-burning stoves are among the features that help to generate a warm, friendly ambience. Favourite main courses on the bar menu and specials board include steak and ale pie, mixed fish platter, and a range of steaks. There are tethering facilities for horses and dogs are welcome.

Open all wk 12-3 6.30-11.30 (Sun 12-3 6.30-10.30) **Bar Meals** L served all wk 12-2.30 D served all wk 6.30-9.30 Av main course £10 **Restaurant** L served Sun & BH 12-2.30 D served Fri-Sat & BH 6.30-9.30 Fixed menu price fr £9.95 Av 3 course à la carte fr £22 ⊕ FREE HOUSE ◀ Local guest ales. **Facilities** Children's menu Play area Dogs allowed Garden Parking

The Talbot Inn ⓐ ★★★ INN ☙

High St TF13 6AA ☎ 01952 727077 🍷 01952 728436
e-mail: the_talbot_inn@hotmail.com
dir: *M54 junct 4, follow Ironbridge Gorge Museum signs, then Much Wenlock signs. Much Wenlock on A458, 11m from Shrewsbury, 9m from Bridgnorth*

Dating from 1360, the Talbot was once a hostel for travellers and a centre for alms giving. The delightful courtyard was used in the 1949 Powell and Pressburger film *Gone to Earth*. Daily specials highlighted on the varied menu may include steak and kidney pie, baked seabass, Shropshire pie and cod mornay.

Open all wk 11-11 **Bar Meals** L served all wk 12-2.30 D served Mon-Sat 6-9, Sun 6-8.30 ⊕ FREE HOUSE ◀ Bass, Guest Ales. 🍷 7 **Facilities** Garden Parking **Rooms** 6

PICK OF THE PUBS

Wenlock Edge Inn 🍷

Hilltop, Wenlock Edge TF13 6DJ
☎ 01746 785678 📠 01746 785285
e-mail: info@wenlockedgeinn.co.uk
dir: *4.5m from Much Wenlock on B4371*

Originally a row of 17th-century quarrymen's cottages, this inn perches at one of the highest points of Wenlock Edge's dramatic wooded ledge. The cosy interior contains a small country-style dining room and several bars, one with a wood-burning stove. Outside, a furnished patio takes full advantage of the views stretching across Apedale to Caer Caradoc and the Long Mynd. It even has its own fish pond from the Wenlock Edge fresh water spring. Traditional British pub food is served alongside Hobsons real ales, continental lagers and a good choice of wine by the glass. Local and regional produce is used and favourite dishes include local steaks with chunky hand-cut chips and home-made pies. There is also a daily fish board and special fish nights with specialities such as lobster and beer-battered scallops.

Closed: Mon **Bar Meals** Av main course £6.50 food served all day **Restaurant** Fixed menu price fr £22.50 Av 3 course à la carte fr £20 food served all day ⊕ FREE HOUSE ◀ Hobsons Best & Town Crier, Salopian Shropshire Gold, Three Tuns Brewery Edge Ale (exclusive to Wenlock Edge Inn). 🍷 8 **Facilities** Dogs allowed Garden Parking

MUNSLOW Map 10 SO58

PICK OF THE PUBS

The Crown Country Inn ★★★★ INN ☙☙ 🍷

See Pick of the Pubs on page 388

NORTON Map 10 SJ70

PICK OF THE PUBS

The Hundred House Hotel ★★ HL ☙☙ 🍷

See Pick of the Pubs on page 389

OSWESTRY Map 15 SJ22

The Bradford Arms NEW ★★★★ INN

Llanymynech SY22 6EJ
☎ 01691 830582 📠 01691 839009
e-mail: robinbarsteward@tesco.net
web: www.bradfordarmshotel.com
dir: *Situated on the A483 5m S of Oswestry*

On the Welsh border, close to Powis and Chirk Castles, this coaching inn offers newly refurbished rooms, and above-average eating in its spotless, quietly elegant bar and dining rooms. Arrive early to ensure a seat and then tuck into, say, a bowl of moules, lamb shank with mint gravy, steak and ale pie, and lemon meringue pie. Good lunchtime sandwiches, traditional Sunday roasts, and Black Sheep Bitter on tap. Once the coaching inn on the Earl of Bradford's estate, it is ideally situated for golfing, fishing and walking.

Open 11.30-3 6-mdnt Closed: 25 Dec L, Mon **Bar Meals** L served Tue-Sun 11.30-2 **Restaurant** L served Tue-Sun 11.30-2 D served Tue-Sun 6.30-9 ⊕ FREE HOUSE ◀ Black Sheep Best, Tetley Smooth, Guinness, 2 Guest ales. **Facilities** Children's menu Dogs allowed Garden Parking **Rooms** 5

The Red Lion Inn NEW ★★★ INN

Bailey Head SY11 1PZ
☎ 01691 656077 📠 01691 655932

A newly refurbished public house on the market square in the town centre with a listed, early 1800s frontage, and a modern, open-plan bar, where cask ales are changed every few days. A menu of inexpensive light meals includes home-made cottage pie; chilli con carne; chicken curry; jumbo cod in crispy batter; a wide range of burgers; jacket potatoes; sandwiches, toasted and au naturel; and salads. A Mediterranean-style courtyard acts as the perfect suntrap. There are five well-equipped en suite bedrooms available.

Open all day all wk 11am-11pm (Sun noon-10) Closed: 25-26 Dec **Bar Meals** L served Mon-Sat 11-3, Sun 12-3 D served Mon-Thu 5.30-8.30 booking required Av main course £5.50 ⊕ Punch Taverns ◀ John Smiths, Guinness. **Facilities** Children's menu Garden Parking **Rooms** 5

PICK OF THE PUBS

The Crown Country Inn ★★★★ INN 🌹🌹 🍷

MUNSLOW   Map 10 SO58

SY7 9ET
☎ **01584 841205**
e-mail: info@crowncountryinn.co.uk
dir: *On B4368 between Craven Arms & Much Wenlock*

The impressive, three-storey Crown stands in a lovely setting below the rolling hills of Wenlock Edge, in the Vale of the River Corve. A Grade II listed building, it retains in the main bar the sturdy oak beams, flagstone floors and prominent inglenook fireplace that must have been here since it was built in Tudor times. Initially, it was a Hundred House, where courts dished out punishment to local miscreants, including perhaps the black-clothed

Charlotte sometimes seen in the pub. Free house status means a good range of local beers, including Holden's Black Country Bitter, and Mahoral Farm ciders. Owners Richard and Jane Arnold have a strong commitment to good food. In fact, Richard is not only head chef but has also been a Master Chef of Great Britain for more than a decade. Meals are served in the main bar, the Bay dining area, and the Corvedale Restaurant. He acquires his top quality local produce from trusted sources and is proud to feature it in his dishes, many of which can be both starter or main course, such as risotto of prawns, basil and crayfish tails topped with home-grown dried cherry tomatoes; hot pavé of organic Clunbury smoked salmon with sweet pickled cucumber and horseradish potato salad; baked flat mushrooms topped with Shropshire Blue cheese and apricot and walnut crust; and roast breast of free-range Breckland duck with dauphinoise potatoes. The cheeseboard lists a dozen English and Welsh cheeses, while for something sweet there's warm spiced banana cake with caramelised banana, butterscotch sauce and The Crown's own home-made ice cream. Three large en suite bedrooms are located in a converted Georgian stable block.

Open Tue-Sun (ex Sun eve) Closed: 25 Dec **Bar Meals** L served Tue-Sun 12-2 D served Tue-Sat 6.45-8.45 Av main course £15 **Restaurant** L served Tue-Sun 12-2 D served Tue-Sat 6.45-8.45 Fixed menu price fr £18 Av 3 course à la carte fr £26 ⊕ FREE HOUSE ◀ Holden's Black Country Bitter, Holden's Golden Glow, Holden's Special Bitter & Three Tuns Brewery XXX ♂ Mahoral. ♟ 7 **Facilities** Children's menu Play area Garden Parking **Rooms** 3

PICK OF THE PUBS

The Hundred House Hotel ★★ HL 🌹🌹 🍷

NORTON   Map 10 SJ70

Bridgnorth Rd TF11 9EE
☎ 01952 580240   📠 01952 580260
e-mail:
reservations@hundredhouse.co.uk
web: www.hundredhouse.co.uk
dir: *On A442, 6m N of Bridgnorth, 5m S of Telford centre*

In medieval England the shires were subdivided into administrative areas called hundreds, and hundred houses were the courthouses. That's what the 14th-century, half-timbered, thatched barn outside the hotel used to be, and opposite are the remains of the old stocks and whipping post where offenders were punished. The hotel, which is mainly Georgian, has been lovingly run by the Phillips family for over two decades. Should the stained-glass panels on the swing doors stating 'Temperance Hall' induce a moment of panic as you enter, don't worry, it isn't! In fact, you enter an amazing interconnecting warren of lavishly decorated bars and dining rooms, with old quarry tiled floors, exposed brickwork, beamed ceilings and oak panelling. Oh, and one more thing to see is a display of twelve plates, each representing the annual award of AA Rosettes. Baskets of pumpkins and marrows are arranged in corners at harvest time, while in December huge decorated onions might occupy the same space. Dried herbs hang from beams, and chilli peppers, pot pourri and lavender bunches can all be found. Hearty food in the bar/brasserie includes traditional steak and kidney pie; spatchcock poussin marinated in rosemary and paprika, grilled and served with couscous, salad and harissa sauce; and tapas for two. And, from the main menu, roast Apley partridge stuffed with mushroom and cotechino (an Italian sausage); prime Bridgnorth sirloin steak; hake fillet baked with caponata (a Sicilian speciality); game pie; breast of Hereford duck with orange sauce, confit duck and black pudding; and sweet red and yellow peppers stuffed with bean casserole and salsa verde. The dessert menu offers raspberry and crème brûlée; pear and almond tart with cinnamon cream; and vanilla pannacotta with mulled red berries.

Open all wk 11-11 Closed: 25-26 Dec eve **Bar Meals** L served all wk 12-2.30 D served all wk 6-9.30 Av main course £9.95 **Restaurant** L served all wk 12-2.30 D served all wk 6-9.30 Fixed menu price fr £10 Av 3 course à la carte fr £22.50 ⊕ FREE HOUSE ◁ Heritage Bitter, Wells, Bombardier, Apley Ale. 🍷 16 **Facilities** Children's menu Garden Parking **Rooms** 10

PAVE LANE   Map 10 SJ71

The Fox ♟

TF10 9LQ ☎ 01952 815940 ▤ **01952 815941**
e-mail: fox@brunningandprice.co.uk
dir: *1m S of Newport, just off A41*

A big Edwardian-style pub, with a mix of private corners and sunny spacious rooms, all wrapped around a busy central bar. There's a large south-facing terrace with views over wooded hills. In addition to light bites and sandwiches, the comprehensive menu could include mushroom and Shropshire Blue soup; Wenlock Edge air-dried Shropshire ham and fig salad; Shropshire rabbit pie; artichoke heart tortelloni with watercress, caper and parmesan pesto. Desserts to try are chocolate and Shropshire stout cake; and passion fruit cheesecake with raspberry sauce.

Open all day all wk noon-11 (Sun noon-10.30) **Bar Meals** food served all day **Restaurant** food served all day ⊕ BRUNNING & PRICE ◀ Timothy Taylor Landlord, Woods Shropshire Lad, Thwaites Original, Titanic Mild, Hobsons Golden Glow. ♟ 6 **Facilities** Children's menu Dogs allowed Garden Parking

PICKLESCOTT   Map 15 SO49

Bottle & Glass Inn

SY6 6NR ☎ 01694 751345
dir: *Turn off A49 at Dorrington between Shrewsbury & Church Stretton*

The hamlet of Pickelscott lies in the northern foothills of the Long Mynd, or Mountain. The landlord of this 16th-century pub, who has been here for 30-odd years, occasionally hears the ghost of a wooden-legged predecessor tap-tapping around, somehow upsetting the pub's electrics. A typical starter is Roquefort-stuffed pear with green mayonnaise: homity pie; game and red wine casserole; and haddock with cheese sauce on spinach are among the main courses.

Closed: Sun eve, Mon ⊕ FREE HOUSE ◀ Hobsons, Three Tuns XXX, Wye Valley Butty Bach. **Facilities** Dogs allowed Parking

SHIFNAL   Map 10 SJ70

Odfellows Wine Bar ♟

Market Place TF11 9AU
☎ 01952 461517 ▤ **01952 463855**
e-mail: reservations@odley.co.uk
dir: *M54 junct 4, 3rd exit at rdbt, at next rdbt take 3rd exit, past petrol station, round bend under rail bridge. Bar on left*

Quirky, popular wine bar owned by Odley Inns, which explains the 'od' spelling. Drinks include regional real ales and ciders. The carefully prepared food, served in an elevated dining area and attractive conservatory, is ethically sourced from local suppliers. The bar and outdoor areas have now been extended and serve regional real ales and ciders as well as the great wine selection. Seasonal menus might offer devilled kidneys; potato, onion and chorizo soup; creamy, dreamy fish pie; chargilled Ludlow venison; and bacon wrapped pheasant breasts on bubble and squeak. Live music every Sunday.

Open all day all wk noon-mdnt Closed: 25-26 Dec, 1 Jan **Bar Meals** L served all wk 12-2.30 Av main course £6 **Restaurant** L served all wk 12-2.30 D served all wk 6-10 Av 3 course à la carte fr £15 ⊕ FREE HOUSE ◀ Salopian, Wye Valley, Holdens, Ludlow Gold, Three Tuns Ö Thatchers. ♟ 12 **Facilities** Children's menu Garden Parking

SHREWSBURY   Map 15 SJ41

The Armoury ♟

Victoria Quay, Victoria Av SY1 1HH
☎ 01743 340525 ▤ **01743 340526**
e-mail: armoury@brunningandprice.co.uk
dir: *Telephone for directions*

The converted Armoury building makes an impressive, large scale pub, just over the bridge on the opposite bank of the river from the new Theatre Severn. Large warehouse windows and huge bookcases dominate the interior of the bar and restaurant area. The comprehensive menu ranges through starters, light bites, main courses, sandwiches, puddings and cheese. Typical dishes are chilli and coriander crab cakes; wild boar and apricot sausages; and pan-fried salmon with crab risotto.

Open all day all wk 11am-mdnt Closed: 25-26 Dec **Bar Meals** Av main course £12 **Restaurant** L served 12-10 D served 12-10 food served all day ⊕ BRUNNING & PRICE ◀ Roosters APA, Salopian Shropshire Gold, Deuchars IPA, Woods Shropshire Lad, Three Tuns Steamer. ♟ 16 **Facilities** Children's menu

The Mytton & Mermaid Hotel ★★★ HL ◉◉♟

Atcham SY5 6QG ☎ 01743 761220 ▤ **01743 761292**
e-mail: admin@myttonandmermaid.co.uk
dir: *From M54 junct 7 signed Shrewsbury, at 2nd rdbt take 1st left signed Ironbridge/Atcham. In 1.5m hotel on right after bridge*

Food is a major attraction at this country house hotel on the banks of the Severn; its chef holds two AA rosettes for the quality of his cooking. The Grade II listed building's tastefully decorated interior recalls the atmosphere of its coaching inn days. Mad Jack's Bar, named after a colourful local squire, offers dishes such as naturally smoked haddock with crushed potatoes and hollandaise, or local venison and Shropshire Lad casserole with blue cheese dauphinoise and parsnip crisps.

Open all day all wk 7am-11pm Closed: 25 Dec **Bar Meals** L served all wk 12-2.30 D served all wk 6.30-10 Av main course £13.95 **Restaurant** L served all wk 12-2.30 booking required D served all wk 7-10 booking required Fixed menu price fr £29.50 Av 3 course à la carte fr £27.50 ⊕ FREE HOUSE ◀ Shropshire Lad, Shropshire Gold, Hobsons Best. ♟ 12 **Facilities** Children's menu Garden Parking **Rooms** 18

The Plume of Feathers

Harley SY5 6LP ☎ 01952 727360 ▤ **01952 728542**
e-mail: feathersatharley@aol.com
dir: *Telephone for directions*

Nestling under Wenlock Edge, this 17th-century inn has stunning views across the valley. Look for the Charles I oak bedhead, full size cider press and inglenook fireplace. Food reflects the seasons, with a changing fish menu; bar meals such as Shropshire baked ham with egg and chips; and restaurant dishes such as lamb en croûte stuffed with wild mushroom and leek gratin, with oxtail gravy; or pan-fried duck breast with black cherry sauce. We understand refurbishment was taking place as we went to press.

Open all wk ⊕ FREE HOUSE ◀ Worthingtons, Guinness, Directors, guest ales. **Facilities** Play area Garden Parking

STOTTESDON
Map 10 SO68

Fighting Cocks

1 High St DY14 8TZ ☎ **01746 718270** 📄 **01746 718270**
e-mail: sandrafc-5@hotmail.com
dir: *11m from Bridgnorth off B4376*

The pub, first licensed in 1850, was called the Cock Inn until the 1980s. The village name of Stottesdon means 'stud on the hill' and it used to be the administrative centre for the surrounding area. The unassuming 18th-century coaching inn once reputedly brewed an ale containing chicken for monks at the village church; called cock ale, it was also served to travellers along with chicken jelly. Today's food, home-made with locally-sourced produce, is rather more appealing. There is a good selection of real ales and ciders available.

Open all wk 6-mdnt (Fri 5pm-1am Sat-Sun noon-mdnt) **Bar Meals** L served Sat-Sun 12-2.30 booking required Av main course £10 **Restaurant** L served Sat-Sun 12-2.30 booking required D served Mon-Sat 7-9 booking required ⊕ FREE HOUSE 🍺 Hobsons Best, Hobsons Town Crier, Hobsons Mild, Wye Valley HPA, Wye Valley Bitter Ö Stowford Press. **Facilities** Children's menu Garden Parking

UPPER AFFCOT
Map 9 SO48

The Travellers Rest Inn 🍷

SY6 6RL ☎ **01694 781275** 📄 **01694 781555**
e-mail: reception@travellersrestinn.co.uk
web: www.travellersrestinn.co.uk
dir: *on A49, 5m S of Church Stretton*

Locals and passing trade enjoy the friendly atmosphere, great range of real ales and good pub grub at this traditional south Shropshire inn on the A49 between Church Stretton and Craven Arms. Food to suit the appetite and the pocket is served until 9pm. Expect to see starters of smoked mackerel or prawn cocktail, traditional mains like steak or chilli con carne, and spotted Dick or treacle sponge.

Open all day all wk 11.30-mdnt **Bar Meals** L served all wk 12-2 D served all wk 6-9 ⊕ FREE HOUSE 🍺 Wood Shropshire Lad, Wood Shropshire Lass, Wood Parish, Guinness. 🍷 14 **Facilities** Garden Parking

WENTNOR
Map 15 SO39

The Crown Inn

SY9 5EE ☎ **01588 650613** 📄 **01588 650436**
e-mail: crowninn@wentnor.com
dir: *From Shrewsbury A49 to Church Stretton, follow signs over Long Mynd to Asterton, right to Wentnor*

Outdoor enthusiasts of all persuasions will appreciate the location of this 17th-century coaching inn below the Long Mynd. Its homely atmosphere, which owes much to log fires, beams and horse brasses, makes eating and drinking here a pleasure. Meals are served in the bar or separate restaurant. Typical daily changing, traditional home-made dishes include pork tenderloin filled with marinated fruits; pan-fried breast of duck with a burnt orange sauce; and grilled sea bass with couscous.

Open all wk noon-3 6-11 (Sat noon-mdnt Sun noon-10) Closed: 25 Dec **Bar Meals** L served Mon-Fri 12-2 D served Mon-Fri 6-9 Av main course £7.50 **Restaurant** L served Sat-Sun 12-9 D served Sat-Sun 12-9 ⊕ FREE HOUSE 🍺 Hobsons, Old Speckled Hen, Three Tuns, Wye Valley Ö Westons Scrumpy. **Facilities** Children's menu Play area Garden Parking

WHITCHURCH
Map 15 SJ54

Willeymoor Lock Tavern 🍷

Tarporley Rd SY13 4HF ☎ **01948 663274**
dir: *2m N of Whitchurch on A49 (Warrington to Tarporley road)*

A former lock keeper's cottage idyllically situated beside the Llangollen Canal. Low-beamed rooms are hung with a novel teapot collection; there are open log fires and a range of real ales. Deep-fried fish and a choice of grills rub shoulders with traditional steak pie, chicken curry and vegetable chilli. Other options include salad platters, children's choices and gold rush pie for dessert.

Open all wk 12-2.30 6-11 (Sun 12-2.30 6-10.30) Closed: 25 Dec & 1 Jan **Bar Meals** L served all wk 12-2 D served all wk 6-9 **Restaurant** L served all wk 12-2 D served all wk 6-9 ⊕ FREE HOUSE 🍺 Abbeydale, Moonshine, Weetwood, Oakham JHB, Best & Eastgate, Timothy Taylor Landlord. 🍷 8 **Facilities** Children's menu Play area Garden Parking **Notes** ⊜

WISTANSTOW
Map 9 SO48

PICK OF THE PUBS

The Plough NEW 🍷

SY7 8DG ☎ **01588 673251**
e-mail: richardsys@btconnect.com
web: www.ploughwistanstow.co.uk
dir: *1m N of Craven Arms. Turn off A49 to Wistanstow*

Beers don't have to travel far to end up being drawn through century-old hand-pumps in the simply furnished bar of this traditional country pub. Located next to the award-winning Wood Brewery, it is effectively the brewery tap, serving Parish Bitter,

Shropshire Lad and Wood's other real ales. An ethically sourced menu includes the ever-popular fish and chips (made with Wood's beer batter, of course); Shropshire sirloin and gammon steaks; and scampi, as well as children's choices. The specials board changes regularly and might feature home-made curries (try the fish cooked in coconut milk and turmeric; or spicy lamb and spinach); and farmhouse pork, bacon and cheese pie. Local faggots, omelettes and baguettes appear on the lunchtime menu. On Sundays, as well as the regular menus, there are traditional beef, pork or free-range chicken roasts. Take your drinks and meals out to the patio and beer garden on fine days.

The Plough

Open all wk noon-2.30 5-mdnt (Sun noon-11) **Bar Meals** L served all wk 12-2 D served all wk 6.30-9 Av main course £7.50 ⊕ WOOD BREWERY 🍺 Wood's Shropshire Lad, Parish, Pot O' Gold Ö Thatchers, Stowford Press. 🍷 9 **Facilities** Children's menu Dogs allowed Garden Parking

WOORE
Map 15 SJ74

Swan at Woore 🍷

Nantwich Rd CW3 9SA ☎ **01630 647220**
dir: *A51 (Stone to Nantwich road). 10m from Nantwich*

Refurbished 19th-century dining inn by the A51 near Stapeley Water Gardens. Four separate eating areas lead off from a central servery. Daily specials boards supplement the menu, which might include crispy confit of duck, slow roast knuckle of lamb, roasted salmon on vegetable linguine, or red onion and garlic tarte Tatin. There's a separate fish menu, offering grilled red mullet fillets, perhaps, or seared tuna on roasted sweet peppers.

Open all day all wk noon-11 **Bar Meals** L served all wk 12-9 D served all wk 12-9 food served all day **Restaurant** L served all wk 12-9 D served all wk 12-9 food served all day ⊕ Punch Taverns 🍺 Wells Bomdardier, Boddingtons. 🍷 6 **Facilities** Dogs allowed Garden Parking

SOMERSET

APPLEY   Map 3 ST02

The Globe Inn ♥

TA21 0HJ ☎ **01823 672327**
e-mail: globeinnappley@btconnect.com
dir: *From M5 junct 26 take A38 towards Exeter. Village signed in 5m*

The Globe is known for its large collection of Corgi and Dinky cars, Titanic memorabilia, old advertising posters and enamel signs. The Grade II listed inn dates back 500 years and is hidden in maze of lanes on the Somerset-Devon border. Produce is sourced locally and using organic and Fair Trade goods where possible. Food from baguettes to main courses (including plenty for vegetarian options), like twice baked broccoli soufflé; lamb hot pot pie; Moroccan chicken and chickpea tagine; and 3 different varieties of 'multi chilli'.

Closed: Mon (ex BH) **Bar Meals** L served Tue-Sun 12-2 booking required D served Tue-Sun 7-9.30 booking required Av main course £11.95 **Restaurant** L served Tue-Sun 12-2 booking required D served Tue-Sun 7-9.30 booking required Fixed menu price fr £19.95 Av 3 course à la carte fr £22 ⊕ FREE HOUSE ◀ Palmers 200, Exmoor Ales, Appleys Ale, Doom Bar, Tribute ♂ Thatchers Gold. ♥ 8 **Facilities** Children's menu Play area Garden Parking

ASHCOTT   Map 4 ST43

The Ashcott Inn ♥

50 Bath Rd TA7 9QQ
☎ **01458 210282** 🖷 **01458 210282**
dir: *M5 junct 23 follow signs for A39 to Glastonbury*

Dating back to the 16th century, this former coaching inn has an attractive bar with beams and stripped stone walls, as well as quaint old seats and an assortment of oak and elm tables. Outside is a popular terrace and a delightful walled garden. A straightforward menu offers 'Home Favourites' such as Cumberland sausages, pasta carbonara, Spanish omelette and steak baguette, while poultry and seafood choices include chicken provençal, tuna steak with salad, or chicken tikka masala. Vegetarians may enjoy mushroom stroganoff with gherkins and capers, or stilton and walnut salad.

Open all wk ⊕ HEAVITREE ◀ Otter. ♥ 12 **Facilities** Play area Dogs allowed Garden Parking

Ring O'Bells ♥

High St TA7 9PZ ☎ **01458 210232**
e-mail: info@ringobells.com
dir: *M5 junct 23 follow A39 & Glastonbury signs. In Ashcott turn left, at post office follow church & village hall signs*

A free house run by the same family for 21 years. Parts of the building date from 1750, so the traditional village pub interior has beams, split-level bars, an old fireplace and a collection of bells and horse brasses. Local ales and ciders are a speciality, particularly guest ales from local breweries, while all food is made on the premises. Look to the good value specials board for ham and lentil soup; roast guinea fowl with apple and local cider sauce, then orange and rhubarb cheesecake to finish. An attractive patio and gardens are welcoming in warmer weather.

Open all wk noon-3 7-11 (Sun 7-10.30pm) Closed: 25 Dec **Bar Meals** L served all wk 12-2 D served all wk 7-10 Av main course £8 **Restaurant** L served all wk 12-2 D served all wk 7-10 ⊕ FREE HOUSE ◀ guest ales. ♥ 8 **Facilities** Children's menu Play area Garden Parking

ASHILL   Map 4 ST31

Square & Compass ♥

Windmill Hill TA19 9NX ☎ **01823 480467**
e-mail: squareandcompass@tiscali.co.uk
dir: *Turn off A358 at Stewley Cross service station (Windmill Hill) 1m along Wood Rd, behind service station*

There's a warm, friendly atmosphere at this traditional country pub, beautifully located overlooking the Blackdown Hills in the heart of rural Somerset. Lovely gardens make the most of the views, and the bar area features hand-made settles and tables. There is a good choice of home-cooked food (prepared in the state-of-the-art large kitchen). Dishes might include sweet and sour pork, lambs' kidneys braised with sherry and Dijon mustard, hot garlic king prawns, and mixed grill. The barn next door was built by the owners from reclaimed materials for use as a wedding and village events venue.

Closed: 25 Dec, Tue-Thu L **Bar Meals** L served Fri-Mon 12-3 D served all wk 6.30-late Av main course £8.50 **Restaurant** L served Fri-Mon 12-3 D served all wk 6.30-late Av 3 course à la carte fr £15 ⊕ FREE HOUSE ◀ Exmoor Ale & Gold Moor Withy Cutter, Wadworth 6X, Branscombe Bitter, WHB, HSD. ♥ 6 **Facilities** Children's menu Dogs allowed Garden Parking

AXBRIDGE   Map 4 ST45

Lamb Inn

The Square BS26 2AP
☎ **01934 732253** 🖷 **01934 733821**
dir: *10m from Wells & Weston-Super-Mare on A370*

Parts of this rambling 15th-century inn were once the guildhall, but it was licensed in 1830 when the new town hall was built. Standing across the medieval square from King John's hunting lodge, the pub's comfortable bars have log fires; there's also a skittle alley and large terraced garden. Snacks and pub favourites support contemporary home-made dishes like pan-fried salmon in cheese and chive coating; and Mediterranean roasted vegetable pancakes in stilton sauce.

Open all wk 11.30-11 (Mon-Wed 11.30-3 6-11) **Bar Meals** L served all wk 12-2.30 booking required D served Mon-Thu 6.30-9, Fri-Sat 6.30-9.30 booking required Av main course £9 ⊕ BUTCOMBE BREWERY ◀ Butcombe, Butcombe Gold, guest ales ♂ Thatchers. **Facilities** Children's menu Dogs allowed Garden

BABCARY   Map 4 ST52

Red Lion ♥

TA11 7ED ☎ **01458 223230** 🖷 **01458 224510**
e-mail: redlionbabcary@btinternet.com
dir: *Please telephone for directions*

The Red Lion is a beautifully refurbished, stone-built free house, with rich, colour-washed walls, heavy beams and simple wooden furniture setting the tone in the friendly bar, whilst French doors lead out into the garden from the restaurant. Granary sandwiches, ciabattas and hot pub favourites like fish pie and honey-glazed Somerset ham, egg and chips are served in the bar. In the restaurant, expect slow roasted pork belly with celeriac purée; butternut squash and sage risotto; and free range duck breast with wild mushroom cream sauce.

Open all wk **Bar Meals** L served all wk 12-2.30 D served Mon-Sat 7-9.30 **Restaurant** L served all wk 12-2.30 D served Mon-Sat 7-9.30 ⊕ FREE HOUSE ◀ Teignworthy Reel Ale, O'Hanlons, Otter, Bath Ales. ♥ 12 **Facilities** Children's menu Play area Dogs allowed Garden Parking

PICK OF THE PUBS

The Hop Pole

7 Albion Buildings, Upper Bristol Rd BA1 3AR
☎ 01225 446327
e-mail: hoppole@bathales.co.uk
dir: 20 min walk from City of Bath on A4 towards
Bristol. Pub opp Victoria Park

Opposite the Royal Victoria Park and just off the canal
path, this is a great spot for quaffing summer ales.
One of just nine pubs belonging to Bath Ales, a fresh
young microbrewery, the beers rejoice in names such
as Gem, Spa, Wild Hare and Barnstormer. Described as
a country pub in the heart of a city, The Hop Pole has a
stripped-down, stylish interior, and the lovingly
restored, spacious beer garden to the rear is complete
with patio heaters and pétanque pitch. The
atmospheric old skittle alley has been transformed into
a large restaurant, which can accommodate coach
parties if pre-booked. Home-cooked food ranges from
imaginative bar snacks and sandwiches through to full
meals. Children are served smaller portions from the
main menu. You could start with chicken liver parfait
before moving on to medallions of monkfish with
chargrilled Mediterranean vegetables, sun-dried
tomatoes and pesto. Monday night is quiz night.

Open all day all wk noon-11 (Fri-Sat noon-mdnt) Bar
Meals L served Mon-Sat 12-2, Sun 12-3 D served Mon-
Sat 6-9 Av main course £8.75 Restaurant L served
Mon-Sat 12-2, Sun 12-3 D served Mon-Sat 6-9 ⊕ BATH
ALES LTD ◀ Bath Ales: Gem, Spa, Barnstormer,
Festivity, Wild Hare. Facilities Children's menu Garden

PICK OF THE PUBS

King William ₹

36 Thomas St BA1 5NN ☎ 01225 428096
e-mail: info@kingwilliampub.com
dir: At junct of Thomas St & A4 (London Rd), on left
from Bath towards London. 15 mins walk from Bath
Spa main line station

In five years at this 19th-century city tavern, owners
Charlie and Amanda Digney have transformed it from a
run-down old boozer into a stylish and sophisticated
gastro-pub. It now offers the best of everything: four
real ales from local brewers, organic cider, and over 20
wines served by the glass. Occupying a corner site just
off the London Road, it has a cosy snug in the cellar
and a chic upstairs restaurant to showcase the
couple's passion for good food. Meat and poultry are
free range or organic, and seafood arrives daily from
the Cornish coastline. The bar menu might offer
upmarket burgers or beer-battered hake with chips and
tartare sauce. The dining room menu features dishes
such as pigeon breast with fig, bacon, walnuts and
apple syrup followed by grey mullet with bean
casserole, wild boar chorizo and rustic pesto. Finish
with a hot chocolate pot with malt ice cream.

Open noon-3 5-close (Sat-Sun noon-close) Closed: Mon
L Bar Meals Av main course £12.50 Restaurant L
served Sat-Sun 12-3 booking required D served Wed-
Sat 6-10 booking required Fixed menu price fr
£25 ⊕ FREE HOUSE ◀ Danish Dynamite, Otter Ale,
Dorset Gold ♻ Westons Stowford Press, Westons
Organic. ₹ 21 Facilities Children's menu Dogs allowed

PICK OF THE PUBS

The Marlborough Tavern NEW ₹

35 Marlborough Buildings BA1 2LY ☎ 01225 423731
e-mail: joe@marlborough-tavern.com
dir: 10m from M4 junct 18, 200mtrs from the western
end of Royal Crescent on the corner of Marlborough
Buildings and a short walk from Bath City Centre

Revamped from a dreary boozer to a contemporary
dining pub in 2006, this 18th-century corner pub
stands just a stone's throw from Bath's famous Royal
Crescent. Foot-weary from the city's tourist trail, then
seek rest and refreshment in the rustic-chic bars or
head for the attractive courtyard garden. Expect
Butcombe Bitter on tap, a raft of decent wines by the
glass, and a classy menu that delivers gutsy, full-
flavoured dishes prepared from local seasonal produce,
including organic meat from local farms and the
Neston Park estate, and fruit and vegetables grown by
Eades Greengrocers in fields at nearby Swainswick.
This translates to imaginative lunchtime sandwiches
(houmous, coriander and rocket), tapas-style dishes
like grilled chorizo and chicken skewers, classics like
braised beef and onions, and Lackfarm Farm rib-eye
steak with chips and mushroom sauce. Evening
additions may take in spiced pork and black pudding
terrine, whole plaice with caper brown butter and
spring onion mash, and lemon and saffron posset with
plum Eton mess.

Open all day all wk noon-11 (Fri-Sat noon-12.30am)
Closed: 25 Dec Restaurant L served Mon-Sat
12.30-2.30, Sun 12.30-4 booking required D served
Mon-Sat 6-9.30 booking required Av 3 course à la carte
fr £20 ⊕ PUNCH TAVERNS ◀ Butcombe Bitter, Sharp's
Doom Bar ♻ Westons Organic. ₹ 19
Facilities Children's menu Dogs allowed Garden

The Old Green Tree ₹

12 Green St BA1 2JZ ☎ 01225 448259
dir: In town centre

Loved for its faded splendour, this 18th-century, three-
roomed, oak-panelled pub has a dim and atmospheric
interior and a front room decorated with World War II
Spitfires. Food ranges from pub basics like soup and
bangers and mash ('probably the best sausages in Bath')
through to smoked duck and poached apple salad; or
mussels in white wine and cream sauce. Great for real
ales, German lager, malt whiskies and real coffee.

Open all wk Closed: 25 Dec ⊕ FREE HOUSE ◀ Spire Ale,
Brand Oak Bitter, Pitchfork, Mr Perrretts Stout & Summer
Lightning. ₹ 12 Notes ⊛

Pack Horse Inn ₹

Hods Hill, South Stoke BA2 7DU
☎ 01225 832060   ⊟ 01225 830075
e-mail: info@packhorseinn.com
dir: 2.5m from Bath city centre, take A367 (A37). Take
B3110 towards Frome. Take South Stoke turn on right

This country inn maintains a tradition of hospitality that
dates back to the 15th century. It was built by monks to
provide shelter for pilgrims and travellers, and still has
the original bar and inglenook fireplace. Outside an
extensive garden overlooks the surrounding countryside.
All the meals are home made, from sandwiches and
snacks to main courses of spinach, pea and forest
mushroom risotto; Normandy chicken, or pepper smoked
mackerel fillet with horseradish sauce.

Open all wk ⊕ INNSPIRED ◀ Butcombe Bitter, 6X,
London Pride. ₹ 6 Facilities Dogs allowed Garden

The Raven ₹

7 Queen St BA1 1HE ☎ 01225 425045
e-mail: enquiries@theravenofbath.co.uk
dir: Between Queen Sq & Milsom St

Real ale lovers flock to this traditional, family-owned free
house, set in two Georgian townhouses on a quiet
cobbled street in the centre of Bath. Two hundred ales
have been served in the last year alone, including the
exclusively brewed Raven and Raven's Gold. And what
better accompaniment for your pint than a home-made
pie with mash or chips, and gravy? Puddings are along
the lines of spotted Dick, lemon sponge and sticky toffee
pudding.

Open all wk 11.30-11.30 Closed: 25-26 Dec Bar Meals L
served Mon-Fri 12-2.30, Sat 12-8.30, Sun 12.30-4 D
served Sun-Fri 6-8.30, Sat 12-8.30 Av main course £8.20
⊕ FREE HOUSE ◀ Raven, Raven's Gold ♻ Stowford
Press. ₹ 7

The Star Inn

23 Vineyards BA1 5NA ☎ 01225 425072
e-mail: landlord@star-inn-bath.co.uk
dir: On A4, 300mtrs from centre of Bath

One of Bath's oldest pubs and of outstanding historic
interest, the Star was first licensed in 1760. Set amid
glorious Georgian architecture, it is an impressive
building in its own right, with original features including
19th-century Gaskell and Chambers bar fittings and a
barrel lift from the cellar. Long famous for its pints of
Bass served from the jug, these days Abbey Ales from
Bath's only brewery are also popular. Fresh filled rolls are
available and free snacks on Sundays.

Open all wk noon-2.30 5.30-mdnt (Fri noon-2.30
5.30-1am Sat noon-1am Sun noon-mdnt) ⊕ PUNCH
TAVERNS ◀ Bellringer, Bass, Bath Star, Doom Bar.
Facilities Dogs allowed

| **BAWDRIP** | Map 4 ST33 |

The Knowle Inn NEW

TA7 8PN ☎ **01278 683330**
e-mail: peter@matthews3.wanadoo.co.uk
dir: *M5 junct 23 or A39 from Bridgwater towards Glastonbury*

A mile off the M5 (Junct 23), this 16th-century pub nestles beneath the Polden Hills on the edge of the Somerset levels – a great place for walking and cycling. A true community pub, with live music, skittles and darts, it also specialises in fresh seafood, with possibly sea bass and gurnard among the catch delivered from Plymouth. Meat-eaters are not forgotten - try the steak and ale pie or a rib-eye steak with all the trimmings. Head for the Mediterranean-style garden, complete with fish pond, for summer alfresco meals.

Open all day all wk 11-11 **Bar Meals** L served all wk 11-3 booking required D served all wk 6-9 Av main course £8 **Restaurant** L served all wk 11-3 D served all wk 6-9 Fixed menu price fr £10 Av 3 course à la carte fr £20 ⊕ ENTERPRISE ◀ Otter, Champflower Ale, Revival, Somerland Gold ♂ Thatchers. **Facilities** Children's menu Dogs allowed Garden Parking

---

| **BECKINGTON** | Map 4 ST85 |

Woolpack Inn ⬡ ★★ SHL ♈

BA11 6SP ☎ **01373 831244** ▤ **01373 831223**
e-mail: 6534@greeneking.co.uk
dir: *Just off A36 near junction with A361*

Standing on a corner in the middle of the village, this charming, stone-built coaching inn dates back to the 1500s. Inside there's an attractive, flagstoned bar and outside at the back, a delightful terraced garden. The lunch menu offers soup and sandwich platters, and larger dishes such as home-made sausages and mash; fresh herb and tomato omelette; steak and ale pie; and beer-battered cod and chips. Some of these are also listed on the evening bar menu.

Open all day all wk 11am-11pm (Sun 11am-10pm) **Bar Meals** L served Mon-Sat 12-2.30, Sun 12-3 booking required D served Mon-Sat 6.30-9.30, Sun 6.30-9 booking required **Restaurant** L served Mon-Sat 12-2.30, Sun 12-3 booking required D served Mon-Sat 6.30-9.30, Sun 6.30-9 booking required ⊕ OLD ENGLISH INNS & HOTELS ◀ Greene King IPA, Abbot Ale, guest ale ♂ Moles Black Rat. ♈ 8 **Facilities** Children's menu Dogs allowed Garden Parking **Rooms** 12

| **BICKNOLLER** | Map 3 ST13 |

The Bicknoller Inn

32 Church Ln TA4 4EL ☎ **01984 656234**
e-mail: james_herd@sky.com
dir: *Telephone for directions*

A 16th-century thatched country inn set around a courtyard with a large garden under the Quantock Hills. Inside you'll find traditional inglenook fireplaces, flagstone floors and oak beams, as well as a theatre-style kitchen and restaurant. Meals range from sandwiches and pub favourites like hake in beer batter (priced for an 'adequate' or 'generous' portion), to the full three courses with maybe smoked salmon; chicken supreme cooked in red wine, and warm treacle tart.

Open all wk noon-3 6-11 (Fri-Sun all day) Closed: Mon L ex BH **Bar Meals** L served Tue-Thu 12-3, Fri-Sun all day booking required D served Tue-Thu 6.30-10, Fri-Sun all day booking required **Restaurant** L served Tue-Thu 12-3, Fri-Sun all day booking required D served Tue-Thu 6.30-10, Fri-Sun all day booking required ⊕ PALMERS BREWERY ◀ Palmers Copper, Palmers IPA, Palmers Gold, guest ales ♂ Thatchers Traditional. **Facilities** Children's menu Play area Dogs allowed Garden Parking

---

| **BLAGDON** | Map 4 ST55 |

The New Inn ♈

Church St BS40 7SB
☎ **01761 462475** ▤ **01761 463523**
e-mail: newinn.blagdon@tiscali.co.uk
dir: *From Bristol take A38 S then A368 towards Bath, through Blagdon left onto Church Ln, past church on right*

A lovely old country pub in the village of Blagdon at the foot of the Mendips, the New Inn offers open fires, traditional home-cooked food, and magnificent views across fields to Blagdon Lake. The menu is locally sourced, and ranges through snacks, salads and main meals such as brewer's beef (the meat marinated in Wadworth bitter); deep-fried breaded plaice, with chips, jacket or baby potatoes; and vegetable risotto served with a side salad.

Open all wk ⊕ WADWORTH ◀ Wadworth 6X, Henry's IPA, JCB, Guinness. ♈ 16 **Facilities** Dogs allowed Garden Parking

---

| **BLUE ANCHOR** | Map 3 ST04 |

The Smugglers ♈

TA24 6JS ☎ **01984 640385**
e-mail: info@take2chefs.co.uk
dir: *Off A3191, midway between Minehead & Watchet*

'Fresh food, cooked well' is the simple philosophy at this friendly 300-year-old inn, standing just yards from Blue Anchor's sandy bay with a backdrop of the Exmoor Hills. Food, using fresh produce locally sourced, can be enjoyed in the Cellar Bar or the Dining Room. Baguettes, filled baked potatoes, pizzas, pastas, grills, curries, salads, speciality sausages and fish and seafood are available. Honey-roast ham and minted lamb cutlets are listed among the 'comfort food' selection. In fine weather diners eat in the large walled garden, where children can enjoy the animals at the nearby farm and the bouncy castle.

Open noon-3 6-11 Closed: Nov-Etr, Sun eve, Mon-Tue L **Bar Meals** L served all wk 12-2.15 D served all wk 6-9 Av main course £8.95 **Restaurant** L served all wk 12-2.15 D served all wk 6-9 ⊕ FREE HOUSE ◀ Smuggled Otter, Otter Ale. ♈ 6 **Facilities** Children's menu Play area Dogs allowed Garden Parking

---

| **BRADFORD-ON-TONE** | Map 4 ST12 |

White Horse Inn ♈

Regent St TA4 1HF ☎ **01823 461239**
e-mail: donnamccann31@btinternet.com
dir: *N of A38 between Taunton & Wellington*

Dating back over 300 years, this stone-built inn stands opposite the church in the heart of a delightful thatched village. It has a bar area, restaurant, garden and patio, and serves real ales brewed in the southwest and home-cooked food prepared from locally sourced ingredients - try half shoulder of lamb with orange, cranberry and port jus; or vegetarian stuffed peppers. Pig roasts and barbecues are catered for, and there's a boules pitch in the garden.

Closed: Sun-Mon eve (Jan-Feb, Oct-Nov) ⊕ ENTERPRISE INNS ◀ Cotleigh Tawney, John Smith's, Whitbread Best, Sharp's Doom Bar, Exmoor ale, guest ales. ♈ 7 **Facilities** Dogs allowed Garden Parking

BUTLEIGH
Map 4 ST53

The Rose & Portcullis ▾

Sub Rd BA6 8TQ ☎ 01458 850287 📄 01458 850120
dir: *Telephone for directions*

This stone built 16th-century free house takes its name from the coat of arms granted to the local lord of the manor. Thatched bars and an inglenook fireplace are prominent features of the cosy interior; there's also a skittle alley, garden, and children's play area. Grills and pub favourites like ham, egg and chips rub shoulders on the menu with more adventurous fare: oriental duck with ginger and honey; and lentil moussaka are typical choices.

Open all wk ⊕ FREE HOUSE ◀ Interbrew Flowers IPA, Butcombe Bitter, Archers Best. ♈ 7 **Facilities** Play area Dogs allowed Garden Parking

CHEW MAGNA
Map 4 ST56

PICK OF THE PUBS

The Bear and Swan ▾

South Pde BS40 8SL ☎ 01275 331100
e-mail: bearandswan@fullers.co.uk
dir: *A37 from Bristol. Turn right signed Chew Magna onto B3130. Or from A38 turn left on B3130*

The Bear and Swan is a light and airy, oak-beamed gastro-pub with a large open fire, comfy chairs and tables, real ales, and a good selection of fine wines and beers in the bar. A big screen shows requested sports games. The restaurant offers a daily changing menu made from the finest locally sourced produce, along with an à la carte menu with a large range of fish, game, seafood, local meats and vegetarian dishes. A lunchtime menu at the bar highlights filled baguettes, soups and old favourites like locally made sausages, mash and mustard gravy; and gammon, free range eggs and chips. This list changes daily, too, to ensure that only the freshest produce is used. Fish aficionados will find different surprises everyday - from smoked haddock on wilted spinach with poached egg; and baked salmon en croute on chive butter sauce; to fresh scallops on risotto with pea purée; and pan-fried skate wing on caper salad.

Closed: Sun eve **Bar Meals** L served Mon-Sat 12-2, Sun 12-2.30 D served Mon-Thu 7-9.45 **Restaurant** L served Mon-Sat 12-2, Sun 12-2.30 D served Mon-Thu 7-9.45 ⊕ FULLERS ◀ London Pride, Seafarers Ale. ♈ 10 **Facilities** Dogs allowed Garden Parking

CHISELBOROUGH
Map 4 ST41

The Cat Head Inn ▾

Cat St TA14 6TT ☎ 01935 881231
e-mail: info@thecatheadinn.co.uk
dir: *1m off A303, take slip road to Crewkerne (A356)*

This creeper-clad hamstone pub was converted from a farmhouse in 1896. Today, the flagstone floors, open fires and contemporary artefacts create a unique atmosphere inside, while outside you will find an award-winning beer garden and play area. Sup real ales or local ciders while browsing the menu, with lunchtime options like scampi and chips, steak or salads like smoked chicken and pine nut, to evening dishes of crispy duck with scrumpy sauce, or saddle of rabbit with mustard and thyme.

Open all wk noon-3 6.30-11 **Closed:** 25 Dec eve, Sun eve **Bar Meals** L served all wk 12-2 D served Mon-Sat 7-10 Av main course £8.50 **Restaurant** Av 3 course à la carte fr £15 ⊕ ENTERPRISE INNS ◀ Butcombe, Otter, Old Speckled Hen, Tribute, London Pride ♂ Thatchers Cheddar Valley, Katy. ♈ 8 **Facilities** Play area Dogs allowed Garden

CHURCHILL
Map 4 ST45

The Crown Inn ▾

The Batch BS25 5PP ☎ 01934 852995
dir: *From Bristol take A38 S. Right at Churchill lights, left in 200mtrs, up hill to pub*

A gem of a pub, stone-built at the base of the Mendip Hills, the Crown was originally a coaching stop on the old Bristol to Exeter route. Constantly changing local brews are tapped straight from the barrel in the two rustic bars, where you'll find open fires, flagstone floors and stone walls. Freshly prepared food is served at lunchtime only, with options such as sandwiches, filled jacket potatoes, cauliflower cheese, beef casserole and chilli. There are beautiful gardens for outdoor eating in the summer.

Open all day all wk 11-11 (Fri 11-mdnt) **Bar Meals** L served all wk 12-2.30 Av main course £5.25 ⊕ FREE HOUSE ◀ Palmers IPA, Draught Bass, P G Steam, Butcombe, Batch Bitter. ♈ 7 **Facilities** Dogs allowed Garden Parking **Notes** ⊜

CLAPTON-IN-GORDANO
Map 4 ST47

PICK OF THE PUBS

The Black Horse ▾

Clevedon Ln BS20 7RH ☎ 01275 842105
e-mail: theblack.horse@tiscali.co.uk
dir: *M5 junct 19, 3m to village. 2m from Portishead, 10m from Bristol*

Down a little lane behind a stone wall is the pretty, whitewashed Black Horse, built in the 14th century and at one time what is now the small Snug Bar was the village lock up, as the surviving bars on one of the windows testify. The traditional bar features low beams with jugs and pint pots hanging from them, flagstone floors, wooden settles and old guns above the big open fireplace. The kitchen in this listed building is tiny, which limits its output to traditional pub food served lunchtimes only (and not at all on Sundays), but very tasty it is too. The repertoire includes hot filled baguettes and baps, moussaka, cottage pie, beef stew, chilli and lasagne. The large rear garden includes a children's play area, and there's a separate family room. There is a great atmosphere here and on Monday nights someone usually turns up with a guitar. Outside there's a large beer garden and children's play area.

Open all day all wk **Bar Meals** L served Mon-Sat 12-2 ⊕ ENTERPRISE INNS ◀ Courage Best, Wadworth 6X, Shepherd Neame Spitfire, Butcombe Best, St Austell Tribute ♂ Thatchers Dry, Moles Black Rat. ♈ 7 **Facilities** Play area Family room Dogs allowed Garden Parking **Notes** ⊜

CLUTTON — Map 4 ST65

PICK OF THE PUBS

The Hunters Rest INN ☕

See Pick of the Pubs on opposite page

COMBE HAY — Map 4 ST75

PICK OF THE PUBS

The Wheatsheaf Inn ☕

See Pick of the Pubs on page 398

CONGRESBURY — Map 4 ST46

The White Hart Inn NEW ☕

Wrington Rd BS49 5AR ☎ 01934 833303
e-mail: murat@simplywhitehart.co.uk
dir: *From M5 junct 21 take A370 through Congresbury, right towards Wrington. Inn in 2.3m on Wrington Road*

A handy M5 pit-stop a short drive from junction 21, this Badger dining pub has a secluded garden with views of the Mendip Hills, and the beamed bars are country-cosy with log fires in stone inglenooks. Refuel with simple, honest food such as steak and Badger ale pie, venison with blackberry and stilton sauce, or a lunchtime brie and bacon baguette, washed down with a pint of Tanglefoot. The gin list is impressive and don't miss the Turkish night – music and belly dancers.

Open all wk 11.30-3 6-11.30 (Fri-Sun 11.30-11.30) Closed: 25 Dec **Bar Meals** Av main course £8.95 food served all day **Restaurant** Av 3 course à la carte fr £17.50 food served all day ⊕ HALL & WOODHOUSE ◀ Badger, Tanglefoot ⬧ Westons Stowford Press. ☕ 8 **Facilities** Children's menu Play area Dogs allowed Garden Parking

CORTON DENHAM — Map 4 ST62

PICK OF THE PUBS

The Queens Arms ☕

DT9 4LR ☎ 01963 220317
e-mail: relax@thequeensarms.com
dir: *From A30 (Sherborne) take B3145 signed Wincanton. Approx 1.5m left at red sign to Corton Denham. 1.5m, left down hill, right at bottom into village. Pub on left*

Enjoy a pint of Abbeydale Riot, Moor Revival or a draft Somerset cider by the open fire of this late 18th-century village free house (AA Pub of the Year 2008-09), situated in beautiful countryside. Food is served throughout, as well as in the rear garden. Menus offer great variety: at lunch, Islay whisky-marinated smokey salmon, with pickled silverskins and gherkins; Old English sausages and mash with red onion marmalade; and pan-fried pollock on winter bean cassoulet, as well as sandwiches. In the evening, try seared scallops with

crispy Denhay ham, red pepper and shallot purée; the pub's own pig's liver with caramelised shallots and rich gravy; and slow-roasted shoulder of lamb with fondant parsnip, potato and cauliflower purée. Afterwards, 'proper' Somerset apple pie with cream; or the cheese plate and a Trappist beer, one of many world bottled beers available. The extensive wine and malt whisky lists make for good reading.

Open all wk 11-3 6-11 (Sat-Sun, BH, Xmas wk 11-11) **Bar Meals** L served Mon-Sat 12-3, Sun 12-4 D served Mon-Sat 6-10, Sun 6-9.30 Av main course £7.50 **Restaurant** L served Mon-Sat 12-3, Sun 12-4 D served Mon-Sat 6-10, Sun 6-9.30 Av 3 course à la carte fr £23 ⊕ FREE HOUSE ◀ Moor Revival, Abbeydale Riot, changing guests ⬧ Thatchers Cheddar Valley. ☕ 20 **Facilities** Children's menu Dogs allowed Garden Parking

CRANMORE — Map 4 ST64

Strode Arms ☕

BA4 4QJ ☎ 01749 880450
dir: *S of A361, 3.5m E of Shepton Mallet, 7.5m W of Frome*

Just up the road from the East Somerset Railway, this rambling old coaching inn boasts a splendid front terrace overlooking the village duck pond. Spacious bar areas are neatly laid-out with comfortable country furnishings and warmed by winter log fires. The bar menu features filled baguettes and pub favourites like Wiltshire ham, eggs and chips. Meanwhile, restaurant diners might choose roast guinea fowl; or bubble and squeak with asparagus.

Closed: Sun eve ⊕ WADWORTH ◀ Henry's IPA, Wadworth 6X, JCB. ☕ 9 **Facilities** Family room Dogs allowed Garden Parking

CREWKERNE — Map 4 ST40

The George Inn NEW ★★★ INN ☕

Market Square TA18 7LP
☎ 01460 73650 📠 01460 72974
e-mail: georgecrewkerne@btconnect.com
dir: *Please telephone for directions*

The George has been welcoming travellers in the heart of Crewkerne since the 16th century, though the present hamstone coaching inn dates from 1832. Using local produce where possible, the extensive menu includes something for everyone, starting with bar food like all-day breakfast, filled jacket potatoes, and steak and kidney pudding to Courtyard Restaurant dishes such as crispy duck with apple sauce, and poached salmon in white wine, plus grills and skillets. Thirteen comfortable en suite bedrooms are available.

Open all day all wk **Bar Meals** L served all wk 12-2 D served all wk 7-9 Av main course £8 **Restaurant** L served all wk 12-2 D served all wk 7-9 Av 3 course à la carte fr £16 ⊕ FREE HOUSE ◀ Old Speckled Hen, Doom Bar, Tribute, Boddington's ⬧ Thatchers Dry, Thatchers Gold. ☕ 8 **Facilities** Children's menu Dogs allowed Garden **Rooms** 13

The Manor Arms ★★★ INN ☕

North Perrott TA18 7SG
☎ 01460 72901 📠 01460 74055
e-mail: bookings@manorarmshotel.co.uk
dir: *From A30 (Yeovil/Honiton) take A3066 towards Bridport. North Perrott 1.5m*

On the Dorset-Somerset border, this 16th-century Grade II listed pub and its neighbouring hamstone cottages overlook the village green. The popular River Parrett trail runs by the door. The inn has been lovingly restored and an inglenook fireplace, flagstone floors and oak beams are among the charming features inside. Bar food includes fillet steak medallions, pan-fried whole plaice, and chicken supreme. There are eight comfortable rooms available.

Open all wk ⊕ FREE HOUSE ◀ Butcombe, Otter, Fuller's London Pride, 5 guest ales. ☕ 8 **Facilities** Garden Parking **Rooms** 8

CROSCOMBE — Map 4 ST54

The Bull Terrier ★★★ INN

Long St BA5 3QJ ☎ 01749 343658
e-mail: barry.vidler@bullterrierpub.co.uk
dir: *Half way between Wells & Shepton Mallet on A371*

Formerly known as the 'Rose and Crown', the name of this unspoiled village free house was changed in 1976. First licensed in 1612, this is one of Somerset's oldest pubs. The building itself dates from the late 15th century, though the fireplace and ceiling in the inglenook bar are later additions. One menu is offered throughout, including ginger chicken; bacon, mushroom and tomato pasta special; hot smoked mackerel with horseradish; and vegan tomato crumble. Accommodation consists of two brightly decorated bedrooms.

Open all wk ⊕ FREE HOUSE ◀ Butcombe, Courage Directors, Marston's Pedigree, Greene King Old Speckled Hen, Ruddles County. **Facilities** Family room Dogs allowed Garden Parking **Rooms** 2

DINNINGTON — Map 4 ST41

Dinnington Docks

TA17 8SX ☎ 01460 52397 📠 01460 52397
e-mail: hilary@dinningtondocks.co.uk
dir: *S of A303 between South Petherton & Ilminster*

Formerly known as the Rose & Crown, this traditional village pub on the old Fosse Way has been licensed for over 250 years. Rail or maritime enthusiasts will enjoy the large collection of memorabilia, and it is an ideal location for cycling and walking. Good quality cask ales and farmhouse cider are served, and freshly prepared food including the likes of crab cakes, Greek salad, faggots, snapper, steak, and lamb shank for two.

Open all wk 11.30-3.30 6-mdnt **Bar Meals** Av main course £6.95 food served all day **Restaurant** food served all day ⊕ FREE HOUSE ◀ Butcombe Bitter, Wadworth 6X guest ales ⬧ Burrow Hill, Stowford Press, Thatchers Gold. **Facilities** Children's menu Play area Family room Dogs allowed Garden Parking

PICK OF THE PUBS

The Hunters Rest ★★★★ INN 🍷

CLUTTON Map 4 ST65

King Ln, Clutton Hill BS39 5QL
☎ 01761 452303 📄 01761 453308
e-mail: info@huntersrest.co.uk
web: www.huntersrest.co.uk
dir: *On A37 follow signs for Wells through Pensford, at large rdbt left towards Bath, 100mtrs right into country lane, pub 1m up hill*

Paul Thomas has been running this popular free house for over 20 years, and has established a great reputation for its warm welcome and good home-made food. The views over the Cam Valley to the Mendip Hills and across the Chew Valley to Bristol are breathtaking - well worth a visit on their own account. The Hunters Rest was originally built around 1750 for the Earl of Warwick as a hunting lodge; when the estate was sold in 1872, the building became a tavern serving the growing number of coal miners working in the area. Mining has finished now and the inn has been transformed into an attractive place to eat and stay, with its five well-appointed bedrooms, including some four-poster suites. A range of real beers and a reasonably priced wine list are offered, with a good choice by the glass. The menu includes bakehouse filled rolls; oggies (giant filled pastries); grills using meat from local farms; and a variety of vegetarian dishes such as stilton and broccoli oggie, and breaded vegetable parcels. Dishes among the blackboard specials might include salmon and smoked haddock fishcakes with dill hollandaise; smoked local trout and king prawn salad with lime vinaigrette; rack of lamb with rosemary and garlic gravy; slow-roast belly pork, crackling, cider gravy and blackpud mash; and crispy duck breast with bramble sauce. There are some real old favourites among the desserts, such as blackcurrant cheesecake and sticky toffee pudding, alongside banoffee meringue roulade and lemon sorbet. In the summer you can sit out in the landscaped grounds and watch the miniature railway take customers on rides around the garden, while in winter you can cosy up to the crackling log fires.

Open noon-3 6-11 (Fri-Sun noon-11)
Bar Meals L served Mon-Thu 12-3, Fri-Sun 12-10 D served Mon-Thu 6-10, Fri-Sun 12-10 Av main course £10
Restaurant Av 3 course à la carte fr £20 ⊕ FREE HOUSE 🍺 Interbrew Bass, Otter Ale, Sharp's Own, Hidden Quest, Butcombe. 🍷 14 **Facilities** Play area Family room Dogs allowed Garden Parking **Rooms** 5

PICK OF THE PUBS

The Wheatsheaf Inn 🍷

COMBE HAY   Map 4 ST75

BA2 7EG
☎ **01225 833504**   📠 **01225 833504**
e-mail: info@wheatsheafcombehay.com
dir: *From Bath take A369 (Exeter road) to Odd Down, left at park towards Combe Hay. 2m to thatched cottage, turn left*

Standing close to the route of the former Somerset Coal Canal, this pretty black and white timbered free house nestles on its peaceful hillside just off the A367 south of Bath. The canal and the railway have come and gone, but the valley and its people survive; in fact, a newspaper recently named Combe Hay as one of England's most desirable villages. The Wheatsheaf was originally built as a farmhouse in 1576, and parts of the present building date back to the 16th century. It began opening its doors as a public house in the 18th century, and has been welcoming locals and travellers alike ever since. Today, real ales, local cider and an amazing European wine list (thanks to the passion of the owner) are available in the rambling but stylishly decorated bar with its massive wooden tables, sporting prints and open winter fires. The building is decorated with flowers in summer, when the gorgeous south-facing garden makes an ideal spot for alfresco dining. The daily menus feature ploughman's lunches, and an impressive selection of freshly-cooked hot dishes. Lunch or dinner might begin with slow-poached Combe Hay eggs with crisp pancetta and watercress, or Cornish crab lasagne with mango, lemon grass and ginger foam. For the main course, choices include pan-fried wild sea trout with samphire, scallops and sauce vièrge; spring lamb rump with wild garlic and goats' cheese; and Wiltshire duck breast with hispi cabbage and rhubarb tart. Don't miss dessert options like lemon meringue tart with lemon jelly and passion fruit ice, and dark chocolate mousse with pistachio ice cream. Polite dogs are welcome to join the pub's own spaniels, Milo and Brie.

Open Tue-Sun Closed: 25-26 Dec & 1st 2wks Jan, Sun eve & Mon (ex Mon BH) 🌐 FREE HOUSE 🍺 Butcombe Bitter, Butcombe Brunel 🍏 Cheddar Valley Cider. 🍷 13 **Facilities** Dogs allowed Garden Parking

DITCHEAT — Map 4 ST63

PICK OF THE PUBS

The Manor House Inn ♀

BA4 6RB ☎ 01749 860276 📠 0870 286 3379
e-mail: landlord@manorhouseinn.co.uk
dir: From Shepton Mallet take A371 towards Castle
Cary, in 3m turn right to Ditcheat

About 150 years ago this delightful 17th-century free house, constructed from Ditcheat red brick, belonged to the lord of the manor and was known as the White Hart. It's tucked away in a charming Mendip village offering easy access to the Royal Bath and West showground and the East Somerset steam railway. Inside you'll find roaring log fires in winter and flagstone floors, with the bar serving Butcombe Bitter and three regular guest ales, local apple brandies and up to eight wines by the glass. Menus are seasonal; in spring, for example, you may find starters such as pan-fried chicken livers with Madeira and wild mushrooms, or traditional prawn and seafood cocktail. Main courses may proffer rack of best British spring lamb with a minted herb crust on bubble and squeak; or roasted Somerset belly pork on leeks, spring greens and lardons with a cider sauce. Choose a home-made dessert from the board in the restaurant.

Open all day all wk 11.30-3 5.30-11 (Fri-Sun noon-mdnt) Bar Meals L served all wk 12-2 D served all wk 7-9.30 Av main course £7.50 Restaurant L served all wk 12-2 booking required D served all wk 7-9.30 booking required Av 3 course à la carte fr £25 ⊕ FREE HOUSE ◀ Butcombe, John Smiths's, guest ales. ♀ 8 Facilities Children's menu Dogs allowed Garden Parking

DUNSTER — Map 3 SS94

PICK OF THE PUBS

The Luttrell Arms ★★★ HL

High St TA24 6SG
☎ 01643 821555 📠 01643 821567
e-mail: info@luttrellarms.fsnet.co.uk
dir: From A39 (Bridgewater to Minehead), left onto A396 to Dunster (2m from Minehead)

Built in the 15th-century as a guest house for the Abbots of Cleeve, this beguiling hotel has retained all its atmospheric charms. Open fires and oak beams make the bar a welcoming place in winter, while the bedrooms are period pieces complete with leather armchairs and four-poster beds. A rib-sticking wild venison casserole with ale and horseradish sauce is just the thing for a chilly day, while in the more formal restaurant you could tuck into smoked haddock fishcakes, followed by wild pigeon and mushroom parcels with cider jus. Desserts include sticky ginger parkin with vanilla-steeped pineapple and ginger ice cream in the restaurant, and clotted cream rice pudding in the bar. Locally brewed beers and a good value wine list makes staying the night an appealing

---

option, especially since the murmuring of ghostly monks is rumoured to cure even the most stubborn insomnia.

Open all wk 8am-11pm Bar Meals L served all wk 11.30-3, all day summer D served all wk 7-10 Restaurant L served Sun 12-3 booking required D served all wk 7-10 booking required ⊕ FREE HOUSE ◀ Exmoor Gold Fox, Guest ale, ♻ Cheddar Valley Cider. Facilities Children's menu Family room Dogs allowed Garden Rooms 28

EAST COKER — Map 4 ST51

PICK OF THE PUBS

The Helyar Arms ★★★★ INN ◉

Moor Ln BA22 9JR
☎ 01935 862332 📠 01935 864129
e-mail: info@helyar-arms.co.uk
dir: 3m from Yeovil. Take A57 or A30, follow East Coker signs

Reputedly named after Archdeacon Helyar, a chaplain to Queen Elizabeth I, this Grade II listed building dates back in part to 1468. Log fires warm the old world bar in this charming inn, where Butcombe, Black Sheep and Hobgoblin ales are backed by Stowford Press and Taunton Traditional ciders. There's a skittle alley, accommodation and a separate restaurant occupying an original apple loft. The kitchen makes full use of local produce, including wood pigeon, rabbit, venison, pheasant and fish from the south Devon coast. Lunchtime bar snacks include salads such as chicken and bacon with toasted pine nuts; and hot beef and blue cheese with cherry tomatoes and red onion. A full meal could start with game keeper's terrine or home-smoked duck breast with beetroot and lentil salad. Main courses include pub classics in addition to the likes of whole roasted local partridge or confit chicken with sautéed thyme potatoes.

Open all wk Bar Meals L served all wk 12-2.30 D served all wk 6.30-9.30 Av main course £7 Restaurant L served all wk 12-2.30 D served all wk 6.30-9.30 Av 3 course à la carte fr £25 ⊕ PUNCH TAVERNS ◀ Butcombe Bitter, Black Sheep, Hobgoblin ♻ Stowford Press, Taunton Traditional. Facilities Children's menu Family room Dogs allowed Garden Parking Rooms 6

EXFORD — Map 3 SS83

PICK OF THE PUBS

The Crown Hotel ★★★ HL ◉◉♀

See Pick of the Pubs on page 400

FAULKLAND — Map 4 ST75

Tuckers Grave

BA3 5XF ☎ 01373 834230
dir: Telephone for directions

Tapped ales and farm cider are served at Somerset's smallest pub, a tiny atmospheric bar with old settles. Lunchtime sandwiches and ploughman's lunches are available, and a large lawn with flower borders makes an attractive outdoor seating area. The grave in the pub's name is the unmarked one of Edward Tucker, who hung himself here in 1747.

Open all wk 11.30-3 6-11 (Sun noon-3 7-10.30) Closed: 25 Dec ⊕ FREE HOUSE ◀ Interbrew Bass, Butcombe Bitter ♻ Cheddar Valley, Farmhouse Gold. Facilities Family room Dogs allowed Garden Parking Notes ◉

FRESHFORD — Map 4 ST76

The Inn at Freshford ♀

BA2 7WG ☎ 01225 722250 📠 01225 723887
dir: 1m from A36 between Beckington & Limpley Stoke

With its 15th-century origins, and log fires adding to its warm and friendly atmosphere, this popular inn in the Limpley Valley is an ideal base for walking, especially along the Kennet & Avon Canal. Extensive gardens. The à la carte menu changes weekly to show the range of food available, and a daily specials board and large children's menu complete the variety. Typical home-made dishes are pâtés, steak and ale pie, lasagne and desserts; a nice selection of fish dishes includes fresh local trout.

Open all wk ⊕ LATONA LEISURE LTD ◀ Butcombe Bitter, Courage Best, guest ale. ♀ 12 Facilities Dogs allowed Garden Parking

PICK OF THE PUBS

The Crown Hotel ★★★ HL 🌹🌹 🍷

Map 3 SS83

TA24 7PP
☎ **01643 831554** 📠 **01643 831665**
e-mail: info@crownhotelexmoor.co.uk
web: www.crownhotelexmoor.co.uk
dir: *From M5 junct 25 follow Taunton signs. Take A358 then B3224 via Wheddon Cross to Exford*

The family-run, 17th-century Crown Hotel was the first purpose-built coaching inn on Exmoor, strategically sited between Taunton and Barnstaple as a good place to change the horses. This venerable establishment, surrounded by beautiful countryside and moorland, is located in a pretty village in three acres of gardens and woodland, through which runs a fast-flowing trout stream. The cosy country bar remains very much the social heart of the village, many of whose patrons enjoy the Exmoor Ales from Wiveliscombe down

the road. Welcoming log fires are lit in the lounge and bar in winter, and there are lovely water and terrace gardens for summer use. Lunchtime snacks include a range of sandwiches and baguettes, and baked potatoes brimming with cheese and pickle, tuna and red onion, or chicken and bacon. Quality ingredients are sourced locally where possible and cooked to order. In the bar you'll find such dishes as Exmoor free-range duck leg and lentil salad; trio of organic sausages with mustard mash; seared Cornish scallops with lemon couscous; and pan-fried sea bass with creamed leek potatoes, black trumpet mushrooms, roasted shallots and orange sauce. Vegetarian options are delicious: try warm cep risotto with fresh Parmesan and mascarpone cheese. A fitting finish might be plum tart with frangipane, yoghurt sorbet and praline biscuit. There's also a two-Rosette restaurant for fine dining. If you fancy staying over and exploring the delights of this lovely area, accommodation is available in the en suite bedrooms. Not surprisingly, outdoor pursuits round here include walking, hunting, horse-riding and shooting. Bring your horse or dog – both can be accommodated.

Open all week noon-11pm **Bar Meals** L served all week 12-2.30 winter, 12-5.30 summer D served all week 6-9.30 Av main course £11 **Restaurant** D served all week 7-9 Av 3 course à la carte fr £37.50 🍺 FREE HOUSE ◀ Exmoor Ale, Exmoor Gold ♨ Thatchers Gold, Cornish Rattler. 🍷 12 **Facilities** Children's menu Dogs allowed Garden Parking **Rooms** 17

FROME
Map 4 ST74

PICK OF THE PUBS

The Horse & Groom ▼

East Woodlands BA11 5LY ☎ **01373 462802**
e-mail: kathybarrett@btconnect.com
dir: *A361 towards Trowbridge, over B3092 rdbt, take immediate right towards East Woodlands, pub 1m on right*

Located at the end of a single track lane, this attractive 17th-century building is adorned with colourful hanging baskets in summer and surrounded by lawns fronted by severely pollarded lime trees. The bar, furnished with pine pews and settles on a flagstone floor and a large inglenook fireplace, offers shove ha'penny, cribbage, dominoes and a selection of daily newspapers for your diversion. There's also a carpeted lounge, including three dining tables in addition to the conservatory-style garden room with 32 covers. A great choice of drinks includes smoothies and milkshakes, and designated drivers are provided with free soft drinks. The lunch and bar menu is offered at lunchtime along with baguettes, salads and daily specials. In the evening, the bar and baguette menus are complemented by a full carte served in all areas. Typical dishes are smoked salmon roulade followed by peppered venison with Cumberland sauce.

Open all wk **Bar Meals** L served all wk 12-2 D served Mon-Sat 6.30-9, Sun 7-9 **Restaurant** L served all wk 12-2 D served Mon-Sat 6.30-9, Sun 7-9 ⊕ FREE HOUSE ◀ Wadworth 6X, Butcombe Bitter, Timothy Taylor Landlord, Blindmans Brewery, Blindmans Buff, Yeovil Star Gazer ♂ Stowford Press. ▼ 9 **Facilities** Dogs allowed Garden Parking

---

HASELBURY PLUCKNETT
Map 4 ST41

PICK OF THE PUBS

The White Horse at Haselbury ▼

North St TA18 7RJ ☎ **01460 78873**
e-mail: haselbury@btconnect.com
dir: *Just off A30 between Crewkerne & Yeovil on B3066*

Set in the peaceful village of Haselbury Plucknett, the building started life as a rope works and flax store, later becoming a cider house. Its interior feels fresh and warm, but retains the original character of exposed stone and open fires. Patrick and Jan Howard have run the hostelry for over ten years, with the explicit promise to provide the best food, service and value for money possible. This is confirmed by the lunchtime set menu served from Tuesday to Saturday, when a vegetable soup could be followed by poached smoked hake with creamy spinach sauce, and rounded off with spiced fruit sponge and brandy sauce. However, an excellent selection of fish specials may tempt: lemon baked salmon fillet with lobster sauce; or fillet of cod baked with a pesto crust perhaps; or grilled fillet of turbot served on a mound of chargrilled Mediterranean vegetables. The eclectic carte also includes pork and three mustard Stroganoff, roasted breast of Aylesbury duck with plum sauce, and chunky Thai vegetable curry.

Open noon-2.30 6.30-11 Closed: Sun eve, Mon **Bar Meals** food served all day ⊕ FREE HOUSE ◀ Palmers IPA, Otter Ale. ▼ 10 **Facilities** Garden Parking

---

HINTON BLEWETT
Map 4 ST55

Ring O'Bells ▼

BS39 5AN ☎ **01761 452239** 📄 **01761 451245**
e-mail: jonjenssen@btinternet.com
dir: *11m S of Bristol on A37 toward Wells, small road signed in Clutton & Temple Cloud*

On the edge of the Mendips, this 200-year-old pub offers good views of the Chew Valley. An all-year-round cosy atmosphere is boosted by a log fire in winter, and a wide choice of real ales. The bar-loving shove ha'penny players attract a good following. Good value dishes include beef in Guinness served in a giant Yorkshire pudding, and chicken breast with stilton and bacon. Baguettes, sandwiches and ploughman's also available.

Open all wk ⊕ FREE HOUSE ◀ Butcombe, Fuller's London Pride, Badger Tanglefoot, Gem. ▼ 6 **Facilities** Play area Dogs allowed Garden Parking

---

HINTON ST GEORGE
Map 4 ST41

PICK OF THE PUBS

The Lord Poulett Arms ▼

High St TA17 8SE ☎ **01460 73149**
e-mail: steveandmichelle@lordpoulettarms.com
dir: *2m N of Crewkerne, 1.5m S of A303*

Beautifully restored by owners Michelle Paynton and Steve Hill, this 17th-century thatched pub fronts the street in one of Somerset's loveliest villages. The bar features bare flagstones and boarded floors and is furnished with a harmonious mixture of old oak and elm tables, and ladderback, spindleback and Windsor chairs. Similarly furnished, the dining room has real fires in open fireplaces, including one with a huge bressemer beam across the top. Most of the food is locally sourced: fish is organic or wild, free-range meat comes from the Somerset/Dorset border, and herbs are home-grown. The lunch menu offers soups, salads, gourmet sandwiches, bouillabaise and hot dishes like pan-roasted duck magret. In the evening you might expect chicken fillet stuffed with haggis; chowder of monkfish, langoustine and smoked bacon; and braised Somerset pork shoulder with carrot and ginger mash. In summer, enjoy a drink by the boule piste, under the wisteria shaded pergola or dine in the wild flower meadow.

Open all wk noon-3 6.30-11 Closed: 26 Dec, 1 Jan **Bar Meals** L served all wk 12-2 booking required D served all wk 7-9 booking required Av main course £14 **Restaurant** L served all wk 12-2 booking required D served all wk 7-9 booking required Av 3 course à la carte fr £22 ⊕ FREE HOUSE ◀ Hopback, Branscombe, Cotleigh, Archers, Otter ♂ Thatchers Gold. ▼ 7 **Facilities** Children's menu Dogs allowed Garden Parking

---

HOLCOMBE
Map 4 ST64

The Holcombe Inn ★★★★ INN ▼

Stratton Rd BA3 5EB ☎ **01761 232478** 📄 **01761 233737**
e-mail: bookings@holcombeinn.co.uk
dir: *On A367 to Stratton-on-the-Fosse, take concealed left turn opposite Downside Abbey signed Holcombe, take next right, pub 1.5m on left*

This country inn boasts comfortable accommodation and a large garden with views of nearby Downside Abbey and the Somerset countryside. The lunch menu runs to various sandwiches and wraps, while the evening choice is supplemented by a specials board: start with crispy squid with sweet chilli dip; or asparagus tips with tomato and basil hollandaise sauce, and move on to grilled Scottish salmon with cucumber and prawn cream; pork stroganoff; or spinach and ricotta ravioli.

Open all wk 11.30-11.30 (Sat 11.30-2.30 6.30-11 Sun noon-3 6.45-10.30) Closed: Sun eve & Mon in winter **Bar Meals** L served all wk 12-2 D served Mon-Sat 7-9, Sun 7-8.30 **Restaurant** L served all wk 12-2 D served Mon-Sat 7-9, Sun 7-8.30 ⊕ FREE HOUSE ◀ Otter Ale, Guinness, guest bitter ♂ Thatchers Old Rascal. ▼ 7 **Facilities** Children's menu Dogs allowed Garden Parking **Rooms** 8

ILCHESTER   Map 4 ST52

Ilchester Arms ♥

The Square BA22 8LN
☎ 01935 840220   📠 01935 841353
e-mail: mail@ilchesterarms.com
dir: *From A303 take A37 signed Ilchester/Yeovil, left at 2nd Ilchester sign. Hotel 100yds on right*

An elegant Georgian fronted house with lots of character, this establishment was first licensed in 1686 and was owned between 1962 and 1985 by the man who developed Ilchester cheese. Attractive features include open fires and a secluded garden. An extensive bistro menu offers the likes of smoked haddock fishcakes to start, medallions of venison with juniper onion compote, game sauce and pommes Anna, and passion fruit tart, in addition to snacks and salads, battered cod and steaks in the bar.

Open all day all wk 7am-11pm Closed: 26 Dec **Bar Meals** L served Mon-Sat 12-2.30 D served Mon-Sat 7-9 Av main course £6.50 **Restaurant** L served all wk 12-2.30 D served Mon-Sat 7-9 Av 3 course à la carte fr £35 ⊕ FREE HOUSE ◀ Butcombe, Flowers IPA, Bass, local ales Ŏ Thatchers Gold. ♥ 12 **Facilities** Children's menu Play area Family room Garden Parking

ILMINSTER   Map 4 ST31

New Inn ★★★★ INN ♥

Dowlish Wake TA19 0NZ ☎ 01460 52413
dir: *From Ilminster follow Kingstone & Perry's Cider Museum signs, in Dowlish Wake follow pub signs*

Deep in rural Somerset, you'll find this 350-year-old stone-built pub tucked away in the village of Dowlish Wake, close to Perry's thatched cider mill. Inside there are two bars with wood-burning stoves and a restaurant, and outside there is a large secluded beer garden. The menu of home-cooked food features local produce in dishes such as Perry's pork steak, with a rich cider, apple and cream sauce; and Aunt Sally's home-made apple pie. Four en suite bedrooms are available in an annexe.

Open all wk ⊕ ENTERPRISE INNS ◀ Butcombe Bitter, Poachers Bitter, Otter Ale Ŏ Thatcher's Gold. ♥ 10 **Facilities** Dogs allowed Garden Parking **Rooms** 4

KILVE   Map 3 ST14

The Hood Arms ★★★★ INN ♥

TA5 1EA ☎ 01278 741210   📠 01278 741477
e-mail: info@thehoodarms.com
dir: *From M5 junct 23/24 follow A39 to Kilve. Village between Bridgwater & Minehead*

This traditional, friendly 17th-century coaching inn is set among the Quantock Hills and provides thirsty walkers with traditional ales in the beamed bar and there are bedrooms available. A good range of fresh fish includes whole sea bass with apple and almond butter, and always on the menu are the inn's famous beef and ale pie, and stilton-topped steaks. Vegetarians get their own choice of dishes.

Open all day all wk 12-11 **Bar Meals** Av main course £9 food served all day **Restaurant** food served all day ⊕ FREE HOUSE ◀ Guinness, Otter Head, Palmers Copperdale, Fullers London Pride, Guest ales Ŏ Thatchers Gold. ♥ 13 **Facilities** Children's menu Play area Family room Dogs allowed Garden Parking **Rooms** 12

KINGSDON   Map 4 ST52

Kingsdon Inn ♥

TA11 7LG ☎ 01935 840543
e-mail: enquiries@kingsdoninn.co.uk
dir: *A303 onto A372, right onto B3151, right into village, right at post office*

Once a cider house, the three charmingly decorated, saggy-beamed rooms in this pretty thatched pub create a relaxed and friendly feel. Stripped pine tables and cushioned farmhouse chairs are judiciously placed throughout, and there are enough open fires to keep everywhere well warmed. Traditional country cooking includes pheasant, venison and other game in season; pork fillets with apricot and almonds, or roast half duck with local scrumpy cider sauce. There is always a wide selection of guest beers provided by local micro-breweries as well as more traditional ales.

Open all wk ⊕ FREE HOUSE ◀ Butcombe Cask, Otter Cask, guest ale. ♥ 10 **Facilities** Garden Parking

LANGLEY MARSH   Map 3 ST02

The Three Horseshoes

TA4 2UL ☎ 01984 623763
e-mail: mark_jules96@hotmail.com
dir: *M5 junct 25 take B3227 to Wiveliscombe. Turn right up hill at lights. From square, turn right, follow Langley Marsh signs, pub in 1m*

This handsome 17th-century red sandstone pub has had only four landlords during the last century. It remains a free house, with traditional opening hours, child-free bars and a good choice of ales straight from the barrel. The landlord's wife prepares home-cooked meals, incorporating local ingredients and vegetables from the pub garden. Typical specials include halibut steak baked with tomatoes and wine; and pheasant breast with smoked bacon and cranberries. There's an enclosed garden with outdoor seating.

Open noon-2.30 7-11 Closed: Mon, Sun eve **Bar Meals** L served Tue-Sun 12-1.45 D served Tue-Sat 7-9 ⊕ FREE HOUSE ◀ Palmer IPA, Otter Ale, Exmoor Ale, Cotleigh 25. **Facilities** Children's menu Garden Parking

LANGPORT   Map 4 ST42

The Old Pound Inn ★★★ INN ♥

Aller TA10 0RA ☎ 01458 250469   📠 01458 250469
e-mail: oldpoundinn@btconnect.com
dir: *2.5m N of Langport on A372. 8m SE of Bridgwater on A372*

Built as a cider house, the Old Pound Inn dates from 1571 and retains plenty of historic character with oak beams, open fires and a garden that used to be the village pound. It's a friendly pub with a good reputation for its real ale and home-cooked food, but also provides function facilities for 200 with its own bar. There is also a skittle alley, plus accommodation including a four-poster bedroom.

Open all wk **Bar Meals** L served all wk 12-2 D served all wk 6-9 **Restaurant** D served Fri-Sun 6-9 ◀ Tribute, Sharp's, Cotleigh, Branscombe, Glastonbury, Hopback Ŏ Burrow Hill Medium, Burrow Hill Pear. ♥ 8 **Facilities** Children's menu Dogs allowed Garden Parking **Rooms** 8

Rose & Crown

Huish Episcopi TA10 9QT ☎ 01458 250494
dir: *M5 junct 25, A358 towards Ilminster. Left onto A378. Village in 14m (1m from Langport). Pub near church in village*

This traditional, family-run inn (also known as Eli's) has no bar, just a flagstone taproom lined with casks of ales and farmhouse ciders, an upright piano and some fairly basic seating. No wonder folk music and storytelling evenings are a regular feature. Home-made food includes sandwiches, soups, jacket potatoes, pork cobbler and cottage pie. Vegetarian meals, such as cauliflower cheese, are always available, along with puddings like apple crumble. Burrow Hill Farmhouse cider available.

Open all wk 11.30-2.30 5.30-11 (Fri-Sat 11.30-11.30 Sun noon-10.30) **Bar Meals** L served all wk 12-2 D served Tue-Sat 5.30-7.30 Av main course £7.25 ⊕ FREE HOUSE ◀ Teignworthy Reel Ale, Mystery Tor, Hop Back Summer Lightning, Butcombe Bitter, Summathat Ŏ Burrow Hill Farmhouse. **Facilities** Play area Family room Dogs allowed Garden Parking **Notes** ⊛

LEIGH UPON MENDIP — Map 4 ST64

The Bell Inn �

BA3 5QQ ☎ 01373 812316 📄 01373 812434
e-mail: rodcambourne@aol.com
dir: From Frome take A37 towards Shepton Mallet. Turn right, through Mells, on to Leigh upon Mendip

The Bell was built in the early 16th century to house workers constructing the village church, and Pilgrims used to stop here en route to Glastonbury. There is a bar with two inglenook fireplaces, a 30-seat restaurant, a skittle alley/function room and a large garden with children's play equipment. Snacks and meals are served (mussels with Thai curry, lamb stew and dumplings). A three-mile walk around the lanes starts and finishes at the pub.

Open all wk ⊕ WADWORTH ◀ Wadworth 6X, Butcombe Bitter, Wadworths JCB, Henrys IPA, Bishops Tipple. �'12 Facilities Play area Family room Dogs allowed Garden Parking

LONG SUTTON — Map 4 ST42

PICK OF THE PUBS

The Devonshire Arms — INN ◎ �│

TA10 9LP ☎ 01458 241271 📄 01458 241037
e-mail: mail@thedevonshirearms.com
dir: Exit A303 at Podimore rdbt onto A372. Continue for 4m, left onto B3165.

A fine-looking, stone-built former hunting lodge on a pretty village green. Step through its imposing portico, decorated with the Devonshire family crest, to discover unexpectedly contemporary styling complementing the large open fire and other original features. Refreshments come in the form of increasingly popular regional brews from Bath Ales, Cheddar Ales and Yeovil Ales. The pub is also renowned for its daily changing menu based whenever possible on locally sourced produce. For lunch try a grilled mozzarella open sandwich with fennel, tomato and rocket salad, or a venison burger with local cheddar, home-cut chips and garlic mayonnaise. Desserts may include dark chocolate and pear clafoutis, and apple and frangipane tart. Dinner dishes are equally mouthwatering, with half a dozen choices at each course. Your can drink and dine alfresco in the courtyard, large walled garden or overlooking the green at the front. To complete the picture, nine en suite bedrooms, each with wide-screen TV, are designed in a fresh modern style, and benefit from the personal touch of hosts Philip and Sheila Mepham.

Open all wk noon-3 6-11 Closed: 25-26 Dec Bar Meals L served all wk 12-2.30 booking required D served all wk 7-9.30 booking required Av main course £9.75 Restaurant D served all wk 7-9.30 booking required Av 3 course à la carte fr £25 ⊕ FREE HOUSE ◀ Teignworthy Real Ale, Bath Spa, Cheddar Potholer, Yeovil Stargazer. ☐10 Facilities Children's menu Play area Dogs allowed Garden Parking Rooms 9

LOVINGTON — Map 4 ST53

PICK OF THE PUBS

The Pilgrims ★★★★ INN ☐

BA7 7PT ☎ 01963 240597
e-mail: jools@thepilgrimsatlovington.co.uk
dir: A303 onto A37 to Lyford, right at lights, 1.5m to The Pilgrims on B3153

With disarming honesty, owners Sally and Jools Mitchison admit that The Pilgrims will never be pretty from the outside. Step inside, however, and it's another story. Wicker and leather seating characterise the bar, and locals' pewter mugs hang ready for the next pint of Cottage ale, brewed just around the corner, or a real cider. 'Local' is a much-used word here; many herbs and vegetables are grown in the pub's own garden, and every effort is made to source nearby produce, particularly cheeses. Starters and light lunches include hot potted haddock in cheese sauce on tomato salsa; pan-fried pigeon breast on bubble and squeak; and baked Capricorn goats' cheese in filo pastry with tomato salsa. The dinner menu continues with stuffed free-range West Country chicken breast with bacon lardons and cider cream sauce; and pan-fried John Dory with pesto mash. There are now 5 highly individual king size guest rooms available if you would like to stay over.

Open noon-3 7-11 Closed: Oct, Sun eve, Mon Bar Meals L served Wed-Sun 12-2.30 D served Tue-Sat 7-9 Av main course £10 Restaurant L served Wed-Sun 12.30-2.30 D served Tue-Sat 7-9 booking required Av 3 course à la carte fr £30 ⊕ FREE HOUSE ◀ Cottage Brewing Champflower, Erdinger ♂ Burrow Hill Orchard Pig, Stowford Press. ☐12 Facilities Children's menu Dogs allowed Garden Parking Rooms 5

LOWER VOBSTER — Map 4 ST74

PICK OF THE PUBS

Vobster Inn — INN ◎ ☐

See Pick of the Pubs on page 404

MARTOCK — Map 4 ST41

The Nag's Head Inn

East St TA12 6NF ☎ 01935 823432
dir: Telephone for directions

This 200-year-old former cider house is set in a lovely hamstone street in a picturesque south Somerset village. The large rear garden is partly walled and has pretty borders and trees. Local real ales, wines and food are served in both the public and lounge bars, where crib, dominoes, darts and pool are available. The pub also has a skittle alley and a decked smoking area.

Open all wk noon-3 6-11 (Fri-Sun noon-mdnt) Bar Meals L served all wk 12-2 D served Mon-Thu 6-8, Sat-Sun 6-9 Av main course £5.50 Restaurant Av 3 course à la carte fr £14 ⊕ FREE HOUSE ◀ Guinness, Worthington, Toby. Facilities Children's menu Family room Dogs allowed Garden Parking

MILVERTON — Map 3 ST12

PICK OF THE PUBS

The Globe — INN ☐

See Pick of the Pubs on page 405

MONKSILVER — Map 3 ST03

PICK OF THE PUBS

The Notley Arms ☐

See Pick of the Pubs on page 406

MONTACUTE — Map 4 ST41

The Kings Arms Inn ☐

49 Bishopston TA15 6UU ☎ 01935 822513
e-mail: info@thekingsarmsinn.co.uk
dir: From A303 onto A3088 at rdbt signed Montacute. Hotel in village centre

Mons Acutus (thus Montacute) is the steep hill at whose foot the hamstone-built Kings Arms has stood since 1632. Have a snack in the fire-warmed bar or outside in warmer weather, or something more substantial chosen from the daily-changing restaurant menu; the restaurant was recently refurbished. At this welcoming inn, all food is cooked on the premises using the freshest of ingredients and served throughout the day.

Open all wk noon-3 6-11.30 (Sun noon-3 Oct-Feb) Bar Meals L served all wk 12-3 D served all wk 6-9 Av main course £4.75 Restaurant D served all wk 6-9 booking required Fixed menu price fr £15 ⊕ GREENE KING ◀ Ruddles County, Abbot Ale, Old Speckled Hen. ☐10 Facilities Children's menu Dogs allowed Garden Parking

PICK OF THE PUBS

Vobster Inn ★★★★ INN ✿ ▼

LOWER VOBSTER   Map 4 ST74

BA3 5RJ
☎ 01373 812920   📄 01373 812247
e-mail: info@vobsterinn.co.uk
dir: *4m W of Frome*

The original part of this long stone building, standing in four acres of grounds, dates back to the 17th century, though there was probably an inn here even before that. With warm support from their regulars and neighbours, Raf and Peta Davila have been making their mark here ever since, a process that includes being awarded one AA Rosette for the quality of their food and ingredients. The simple bar menu makes choosing easy with inexpensive suggestions such as roast chorizo sausages with fried eggs and crusty bread; cheese omelette and fries; and grilled goat's cheese bruschetta with Mediterranean vegetables and home-made crab apple jelly. On the main menu you'll find echoes of Raf's origins on Galicia's wild coast, including a selection of Spanish cured and smoked meats with salad, olives, houmous and crusty bread; and Somerset pork belly stuffed with Asturian black pudding, bubble and squeak and vanilla plum, as well as grilled open cap mushrooms with Welsh rarebit; and prawn, crab and mayonnaise cocktail. Typical among the mains options are mixed bean cottage pie; rack of lamb with black pudding, Savoy cabbage and pine nut sauté and scrumpy syrup; and grilled rib-eye with herb butter, mushrooms, cherry vine tomatoes and fries. Fish lovers will want to see what has come up fresh from St Mawes in Cornwall: brill, perhaps, saffron- and garlic-marinated and served with pak choi risotto. All desserts are home made, with choices like white chocolate and coconut cheesecake; pannacotta with fresh berries; and lemon posset. Children are particularly welcome and have their own menu, although they are also encouraged to try smaller portions from the main menus. Three individually furnished bedrooms are now available.

Open all week Closed: Sun eve **Bar Meals** L served all week 12-2 D served Mon-Sat 6.30-9 Av main course £12.50 **Restaurant** L served all week 12-2 D served Mon-Sat 6.30-9 Av 3 course à la carte fr £22.50 ⊕ FREE HOUSE ◀ Butcombe Blonde, Butcombe Bitter ☼ Ashton Press. ▼ 8 **Facilities** Children's menu Family room Garden Parking **Rooms** 3

PICK OF THE PUBS

The Globe ★★★ INN ♟

MILVERTON Map 3 ST12

Fore St TA4 1JX ☎ 01823 400534
e-mail: info@theglobemilverton.co.uk
dir: *On B3187*

Seven miles from Taunton in the heart of historic Milverton, The Globe is a village pub with a difference. Originally an old coaching inn, this Grade II listed free house has been refurbished in a contemporary style that creates a distinctive character and a warm, friendly atmosphere. Local artworks decorate the walls of the restaurant and bar area, whilst a wood-burning stove and an open air courtyard provide for all seasons. Local ales from Exmoor and Cotliegh alongside guest ales from brewers such as Otter and Quantock, plus local cider and English wine is also available. With the help of head chef Kaan Atasoy, husband and wife team Mark and Adele Tarry offer an extensive menu that covers all the bases. Everything is home made including the bread and all the desserts. Quick and easy lunch options feature baguettes and ciabattas with fillings like Parma ham, Brie and rocket; and roasted vegetables with feta cheese. Hot dishes such as West Country sausage and wholegrain mash with red wine gravy; mixed fish pie with leeks and gruyère cheese; and traditional steak and kidney pie and Sunday roasts are also available. À la carte choices might begin with a wide selection of fish specials such as sea trout and scallops or River Fowey mussels. For the main course, choose between honey roasted duck breast with Savoy cabbage and plum sauce; whole baked plaice with pine nut butter; and slow-roasted local Gloucester Old Spot pork. Mouth-watering home-made desserts include raspberry meringue. Milverton is an ideal base to explore the Somerset hills and nearby Exmoor; and you can stay over in one of the comfortable bedrooms.

Open 12-3 6-11 (Fri-Sat 6-11.30)
Closed: Sun eve, Mon L **Bar Meals**
L served Tue-Sun 12-2 D served Mon-Sat 6.30-9 Av main course £12
Restaurant L served Tue-Sun 12-2
D served Mon-Sat 6.30-9 Av 3 course à la carte fr £19.50 ◼ Exmoor Ale, Cotleigh 25, Guest Ales ○ Thatchers.
♟ 8 **Facilities** Children's menu Parking
Rooms 3

PICK OF THE PUBS

The Notley Arms ♀

MONKSILVER
Map 3 ST03

TA4 4JB ☎ 01984 656217
dir: *Village on B3227 N of Wiveliscombe towards Watchet & Minehead*

A country drinking and dining pub in a hamlet on the edge of Exmoor, built in the 1860s and named after the Revd George Notley, whose family purchased the local Combe Sydenham estate in 1796. The stream that runs by the pub garden is called the Silver, derived from silva, which is Latin for a wooded area. From that came Silva Monachorum, after monks from Monmouthshire arrived at nearby Cleeve Abbey, a name that then mutated over time to

Monksilver. Owners Jane and Russell Deary prepare and cook everything themselves, using fresh produce from the south west of England for their traditional English food, plus a bit of African cooking (that reflects the Dearys' Zimbabwean origins) and some other dishes from around the world. A quick glance at the menu reveals Exmoor sirloin steak; Somerset lamb shank braised in red wine jus; deerstalker pie; bobotie (an Afrikaans dish made with lightly curried lamb mince); West Country ostrich steaks; chicken teriyaki; and whole Cornish red mullet. For vegetarians, there's fresh pasta puttanesca; and shallot, date and apple tarte Tatin. Puddings include Somerset apple and hazelnut cake with toffee sauce and clotted cream; and raspberry ice cream meringue with raspberry coulis and toasted almonds. Well-tended flower borders make the garden look very pretty, and there's a

selection of outdoor toys to keep children happy. Should you need it, there's plenty of room to tie up your horse while you quench your thirst, or bring your dog – it'll be most welcome, and desperate to walk the nearby 36-mile Coleridge Way, which runs from Nether Stowey, the poet's one-time home, to Porlock.

Closed: Mon lunch in Summer
⊕ ENTERPRISE INNS ◫ Exmoor Ale, Wadworth 6X & Bath Ales. ♀ 10
Facilities Play area Family room Dogs allowed Garden Parking

MONTACUTE *continued*

The Phelips Arms ☻

The Borough TA15 6XB
☎ 01935 822557 📄 01935 822557
e-mail: phelipsarmsmontacute@talktalk.net
dir: *From Cartgate rdbt on A303 follow signs for Montacute*

A 17th-century listed ham stone building overlooking the village square and close to historic Montacute House (NT). The emphasis is on the quality of the food, and everything is prepared on the premises using the best local and West Country produce. The menu features dishes such as home-made steak and ale pie, stuffed oven-cooked pork belly with pear and apple jus; followed by rhubarb crumble or strawberry Pavlova.

Open noon-2.30 6-11 Closed: 25 Dec, Mon (ex BH) **Bar Meals** L served Tue-Sun 12-2 D served Tue-Sun 6.30-9 Av main course £7.95 **Restaurant** L served Tue-Sun 12-2 booking required D served Tue-Sun 6.30-9 booking required ⊕ PALMERS ◀ Palmers IPA & 200 Premium Ale, Copper Ale Ö Thatchers Gold. ☻ 9 **Facilities** Children's menu Dogs allowed Garden Parking

NORTH CURRY   Map 4 ST32

The Bird in Hand ☻

Queen Square TA3 6LT ☎ 01823 490248
dir: *5m from M5 junct 25*

A friendly 300-year-old village inn, with large stone inglenook fireplaces, flagstone floors, exposed beams and studwork. Cheerful staff provide a friendly welcome, and the place is atmospheric at night by candlelight. Blackboard menus feature local produce including vegetarian options and steak dishes, and the constantly changing seafood is supplied by a Plymouth fishmonger.

Open all wk ⊕ FREE HOUSE ◀ Badger Tanglefoot, Exmoor Gold, Otter Ale, Cotleigh Barn Owl, Hop Back Thunderstorm, Butcombe Gold, Teignworthy Old Moggie. ☻ 8 **Facilities** Dogs allowed Parking

NORTON ST PHILIP   Map 4 ST75

PICK OF THE PUBS

George Inn ☻

See Pick of the Pubs on page 408

NUNNEY   Map 4 ST74

The George at Nunney ☻

Church St BA11 4LW
☎ 01373 836458 📄 01373 836565
e-mail: enquiries@georgeatnunneyhotel.wanadoo.co.uk
dir: *0.5m N off A361, Frome/Shepton Mallet*

The garden was used in the Middle Ages as a place of execution, but this rambling old coaching inn is deservedly popular these days. Set in a historic conservation village, it serves a wide choice of food. Big steaks, mixed grill, steak and ale pie, and double chicken breasts with choice of sauces, plus a separate fish menu including brill, sea bass, hake, red mullet and fresh dressed crabs.

Open all wk ⊕ FREE HOUSE ◀ Highgate Brewery Saddlers Best Bitter, Wadworth 6X, Interbrew Bass, guest ales. ☻ 8 **Facilities** Family room Garden Parking

OVER STRATTON   Map 4 ST41

The Royal Oak ☻

TA13 5LQ ☎ 01460 240906
e-mail: info@the-royal-oak.net
dir: *Exit A303 at Hayes End rdbt (South Petherton). 1st left after Esso garage signed Over Stratton*

Blackened beams, flagstones, log fires, pews and settles set the scene in this welcoming old thatched inn built from warm Hamstone, which has the added attraction of a garden, children's play area and barbecue. Expect real ales, including Tanglefoot from the Badger brewery in Blandford Forum, and dishes ranging from beer battered haddock and chips with home-made tartare sauce to supreme of chicken in an apricot, ginger and white wine sauce.

Closed: Mon (ex BH) **Bar Meals** L served Tue-Sun 12-2 booking required D served Tue-Sun 6-9 booking required **Restaurant** L served Tue-Sun 12-2 booking required D served Tue-Sun 6-9 booking required ⊕ HALL & WOODHOUSE ◀ Badger Best, Tanglefoot, Sussex Best Bitter. ☻ 6 **Facilities** Children's menu Play area Family room Dogs allowed Garden Parking

PITNEY   Map 4 ST42

The Halfway House ☻

TA10 9AB ☎ 01458 252513
dir: *On B3153, 2m from Langport & Somerton*

This pub is largely dedicated to the promotion of real ale, and there are always six to ten available in tip-top condition, shown on a blackboard. This delightfully old-fashioned rural pub has three homely rooms boasting open fires, books and games, but no music or electronic games. Home-cooked meals (except Sundays when it is too busy with drinkers) include soups, local sausages, sandwiches and a good selection of curries and casseroles in the evening.

Open all wk 11.30-3 5.30-11 (Fri-Sat 5.30-mdnt Sun noon-3 7-11) Closed: 25 Dec **Bar Meals** L served Mon-Sat 12-2.30 D served Mon-Sat 7-9.30 ⊕ FREE HOUSE ◀ Butcombe Bitter, Teignworthy, Otter Ale, Cotleigh Tawny Ale, Hop Back Summer Lightning Ö Kingston Black, Burrow Hill, Wilkins Medium. ☻ 8 **Facilities** Play area Dogs allowed Garden Parking

PORLOCK   Map 3 SS84

The Anchor Hotel & Ship Inn

Porlock Weir TA24 8PB
☎ 01643 862753 📄 01643 862843
e-mail: info@theanchorhotelandshipinn.co.uk

A hotel, restaurant and 16th-century inn all in one, right on the harbour front at the point where the road ends. Just offshore is an ancient submarine forest, visible during only the lowest tides. Traditional pub food in Mariners Bar includes smoked mackerel; hot and fruity chicken curry; home-made steak and kidney pie; and four-cheese and roast onion quiche. Among dinner choices in the Harbourside Restaurant are rack of lamb; lobster thermidor; and cannelloni verde.

Open all wk ⊕ FREE HOUSE ◀ Exmoor Ale, Exmoor Fox, Cotleigh Barn Owl, Cotleigh 25, Taunton, Otter Ale. **Facilities** Dogs allowed Garden Parking

The Ship Inn

High St TA24 8QD ☎ 01643 862507
e-mail: enquiries@shipinnporlock.co.uk
dir: *A358 to Williton, then A39 to Porlock. 6m from Minehead*

Many travellers have been welcomed to this 13th-century inn, including Wordsworth, Coleridge and even Nelson's press gang. Nestling at the foot of Porlock's notorious hill, where Exmoor tumbles into the sea, its thatched roof and traditional interior provide an evocative setting for a meal, drink or overnight stay. Regularly changing menus include ploughman's, light bites and dishes such as supreme of salmon on horseradish mash with parsley and lemon crème. There's a beer garden with children's play area.

Open all day all wk 10am-mdnt **Bar Meals** L served 12-2.30 D served 6.30-8.45 ⊕ FREE HOUSE ◀ Tribute, Exmoor Ale, Otter, Proper Job Ö Thatchers. **Facilities** Play area Dogs allowed Garden Parking

PICK OF THE PUBS

George Inn 🍷

NORTON ST PHILIP — Map 4 ST75

High St BA2 7LH
☎ 01373 834224 📠 01373 834861
e-mail: georgeinnnsp@aol.com
dir: *From Bath take A36 to Warminster, after 6m take A366 on right to Radstock, village 1m*

Certainly one of the oldest licensed premises in the land, the Grade I listed George has been around since before liquor licences were introduced! A Carthusian guest house since its first building in the 13th century, it is of great historical and architectural interest, retaining its present architectural features for over 700 years now. Surviving to this day are the stone-slated roof, the massive Gothic doorway, sloping cobbled courtyard and the unique timbered galleries. On 12th June 1668 Samuel Pepys dined here, while in June 1685 the Duke of Monmouth occupied the village for a week prior to his defeat at Sedgemoor; twelve of his band were hanged at the crossroads on the orders of Judge Jeffreys, for they had tried to kill him as he stood shaving at the window. These days the outlook is more gently bucolic, with views over the local cricket pitch and the 13th-century church. Inside, at the heart of the pub, a huge open fire, wood floor and distinctive beams imbue the Monmouth bar with a timeless ambience in which to enjoy a pint of Wadworth 6X and some traditional pub food. Typical dishes include game terrine and chilli Thai fishcakes to start, with chicken and ham pie, beef Wellington, game casserole, sea bass with roasted vegetables, and venison steak with port sauce among the choice of main courses. For pudding, try the mixed berry cheesecake or the bread-and-butter pudding. Look out for special food evenings. You can also eat in the Norton (or Dungeon) bar, with its flagstone floor and arched stone ceiling, in the oak-beamed restaurant, or in the ancient and atmospheric courtyard. Beautifully restored by Wadworth a decade ago, it is a magnificent place to stay close to Bath.

Open all week ⊕ WADWORTH
🛢 Wadworth 6X, Henrys IPA, Wadworth Bishops Tipple, J.C.B. 🍷 30
Facilities Dogs allowed Garden Parking

PRIDDY   Map 4 ST55

New Inn

Priddy Green BA5 3BB ☎ **01749 676465**
dir: *M4 junct 18, A39 right to Priddy 3m before Wells. M4 junct 19 through Bristol onto A39. From M5 junct 21, A371 to Cheddar, then B3371*

Overlooking the village green high up in the Mendip Hills, this old, former farmhouse is popular with walkers, riders and cavers, and once served beer to the local lead miners. A typical dinner menu features liver and bacon, chargrilled steaks, Brixham plaice, and fillet of pork with braised red cabbage. There's also a skittle alley, and Priddy's 'friendliest folk festival in England' every July.

Open all wk ⊕ FREE HOUSE ◀ Interbrew Bass, Fuller's London Pride, Wadworth 6X, New Inn Priddy, 5 Real Ales. **Facilities** Play area Family room Dogs allowed Garden Parking

RODE   Map 4 ST85

The Mill at Rode ☻

BA11 6AG ☎ **01373 831100** ▤ **01373 831144**
e-mail: info@themillatrode.co.uk
dir: *6m S of Bath*

Less than 20 minutes' from the centre of Bath, this converted grist mill stands in a spectacular riverside setting with an original waterwheel that still turns. You'll find outside seating, patio heating and lovely nearby walks, while inside there is a 42-inch plasma screen and an upstairs children's den with PlayStation, X Box and Game Cube. Seasonal local fare includes pheasant pot-roasted with bacon and chestnuts; and rib-eye steak with red wine and horseradish butter.

Open all day all wk noon-11 Closed: 25 Dec **Bar Meals** Av main course £7.50 food served all day **Restaurant** Fixed menu price fr £7.97 Av 3 course à la carte fr £19.95 food served all day ⊕ FREE HOUSE ◀ Butcombe Bitter, Pedigree, Guinness, guest ales ♂ Black Rat, Inch's Stonehouse. ☻ 8 **Facilities** Play area Family room Garden Parking

RUDGE   Map 4 ST85

The Full Moon at Rudge ★★★ INN ☻

BA11 2QF ☎ **01373 830936** ▤ **01373 831366**
e-mail: info@thefullmoon.co.uk
dir: *From A36 (Bath to Warminster road) follow Rudge signs*

Strategically placed at the crossing of two old drove roads, this inn enjoys great views of Westbury White Horse. The venerable 16th-century building had been sympathetically updated and retains its small, stone-floored rooms furnished with scrubbed tables. Modern British cooking is the watchword with menus changing to reflect the seasons. Lamb chump chop with bubble and squeak and a rosemary jus or simple steak and kidney pie are examples of the fare. There are 17 comfortable bedrooms if you would like to stay over.

Open all day all wk 11.30-11 (Sun noon-10.30) **Bar Meals** L served Mon-Sat 12-2 D served Mon-Sat 6-9, Sun 7-9 **Restaurant** L served all wk 12-2 D served Mon-Sat 6-9 booking required ⊕ FREE HOUSE ◀ Butcombe Bitter, John Smith's, Potholer ♂ Stowford Press, Thatchers Cheddar Valley. ☻ 6 **Facilities** Children's menu Dogs allowed Garden Parking **Rooms** 17

SHEPTON BEAUCHAMP   Map 4 ST41

Duke of York ☻

TA19 0LW ☎ **01460 240314**
e-mail: sheptonduke@tiscali.co.uk
dir: *M5 junct 25 Taunton or A303*

In the lovely village of Shepton Beauchamp is this 17th-century free house, run by husband and wife team Paul and Hayley Rowlands, and Purdy, the 'famous' pub dog. The bar stocks some good West Country real ales while the restaurant's varied menu and blackboard specials offer something for everyone. Local chargrilled steaks and fresh fish from Bridport, as well as a selection of pub classics such as lamb moussaka and trio of lamb chops on minted creamed potato and redcurrant and port sauce, shows the style.

Open all day noon-3 6.30-mdnt (Mon 6-mdnt Fri noon-3 6-mdnt Sat noon-mdnt Sun noon-10.30) Closed: Mon L **Bar Meals** L served Tue-Sun 12-2 D served Tue-Sat 6.45-9 booking required **Restaurant** L served Tue-Sun 12-2 D served Tue-Sat 6.45-9 booking required ⊕ FREE HOUSE ◀ Teignworthy Reel Ale, Otter Bright. ☻ 7 **Facilities** Children's menu Family room Dogs allowed Garden Parking

SHEPTON MALLET   Map 4 ST64

PICK OF THE PUBS

The Three Horseshoes
Inn ★★★★ INN ◉ ☻

See Pick of the Pubs on page 410

PICK OF THE PUBS

The Waggon and Horses ☻

Frome Rd, Doulting Beacon BA4 4LA
☎ **01749 880302**
e-mail: dawncorp@yahoo.co.uk
dir: *1.5m N of Shepton Mallet at x-roads with Old Wells-Frome road, 1m off A37*

A pretty, whitewashed building with leaded windows, this rural coaching inn is now under new ownership. The pub, which has views over Glastonbury, is set in a large garden and a flower-filled paddock, and drinks and meals can be enjoyed outside in fine weather. Other attractions include the skittle alley, which together with a small bar, is available for hire, and free jazz nights (first Friday of the month) in the relaxed surroundings of the upstairs bar. A varying range of real beers, a good choice of wines by the glass and Addlestones cider are served alongside traditional home-made dishes. Expect the likes of fresh battered cod with chips; steak and ale pie; tarragon chicken with a creamy sauce, and home-made faggots. A great range of desserts includes raspberry cheesecake, spotted Dick, pineapple upside down pudding and apple crumble.

Open all wk Sat-Sun all day **Bar Meals** L served all wk 12-2.30 D served all wk 6-9 **Restaurant** L served all wk 12-2.30 D served all wk 6-9 ⊕ PUNCH TAVERNS ◀ Wadworth 6X, Butcombe ♂ Addlestones. ☻ 12 **Facilities** Children's menu Dogs allowed Garden Parking

PICK OF THE PUBS

Three Horseshoes Inn ★★★★ INN ⊛ ♆

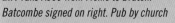

SHEPTON MALLET   **Map 4 ST64**

Batcombe BA4 6HE
☎ **01749 850359**   📄 **01749 850615**
dir: *Take A359 from Frome to Bruton. Batcombe signed on right. Pub by church*

Tucked away down a web of country lanes in the very rural Batcombe Vale, this honey-coloured stone inn enjoys a peaceful position and the lovely rear garden overlooks the old parish church. The long and low-ceilinged main bar has exposed stripped beams, deep window seats, a huge stone inglenook with log fire, and is warmly and tastefully decorated, with terracotta walls hung with old paintings, creating a relaxed and homely atmosphere. From gleaming handpumps on the bar come foaming pints of Butcombe, Adnams, Palmers, and locally brewed Bats in the Belfry. Menus draw on the wealth of

fresh seasonal produce available locally, with brasserie-style lunches taking in local pigeon breast with crispy ham and green pea vinaigrette; local sausages with mash and onion gravy; calves' liver on creamed potatoes with home-cured bacon and sage; and cassolette of shellfish and white fish. Choice at dinner extends to Coln Valley oak-smoked salmon with lemon and capers and Bagborough Farm goat's cheese with sun-blushed tomato pesto for starters, with the likes of whole Cornish plaice, slow-braised shoulder of organic Somerset lamb, fillet of West Country beef, and local free-range chicken with crispy bacon and bread sauce to follow. Desserts include sticky toffee pudding with butterscotch sauce and vanilla ice cream; classic treacle sponge with lemon zest, ginger and 'real English' custard; and local and continental cheeses with celery biscuits and home-made chutney. The wines are reasonably priced, with a more or less equal split between European and New World. There are three stylishly decorated letting bedrooms, two with en suite facilities and one with a private bathroom.

Open Tue-Sun Closed: Mon **Bar Meals** L served Tue-Sun 12-2 D served Tue-Sat 7-9 Av main course £10.50 **Restaurant** L served Tue-Sun 12-2 D served Tue-Sat 7-9 Av 3 course à la carte fr £25 ⊕ FREE HOUSE ◼ Butcombe Bitter, Bats in the Belfry, Adnams, Palmers 200. ♆ 8 **Facilities** Dogs allowed Garden Parking **Rooms** 3

SHEPTON MONTAGUE — Map 4 ST63

The Montague Inn ♥

BA9 8JW ☎ 01749 813213 📄 01749 813213
e-mail: themontagueinn@aol.com
dir: From Wincanton & Castle Cary turn right off A371

This comfortably refurbished, stone-built village inn nestles in rolling unspoilt Somerset countryside on the edge of sleepy Shepton Montague. Tastefully decorated throughout, with the homely bar featuring old dark pine and an open log fire, and a cosy, yellow-painted dining room. Menu choices include bacon and brie ciabatta, Scottish venison steak, home-made pies, mushroom lasagne, and organic lamb. Local beers and ciders are served directly from the cask. The attractive terrace with rural views is perfect for summer sipping.

Closed: Mon, Sun eve ⊕ FREE HOUSE ◀ Bath Ale, Butcombe Gold, Abbot Ale, guest ale Ď Local cider. ♥ 7 **Facilities** Dogs allowed Garden Parking

SPARKFORD — Map 4 ST62

The Sparkford Inn

High St BA22 7JH ☎ 01963 440218 📄 01963 440358
e-mail: sparkfordinn@sparkford.fsbusiness.co.uk
dir: Just off A303, 400yds from rdbt at Sparkford

A 15th-century former coaching inn with beamed bars and a fascinating display of old prints and photographs. It is set in an attractive garden just off the A303 between Wincanton and Yeovil. The restaurant offers a popular lunchtime carvery, light meals and a full evening menu, featuring steaks from the grill. Dishes include marinated Cajun chicken breast; smoked haddock and bacon au gratin; and bean, celery and coriander chilli.

Open all wk ⊕ FREE HOUSE ◀ Marstons Pedigree, Banks Bitter, guest ales. **Facilities** Play area Dogs allowed Garden Parking

STANTON WICK — Map 4 ST66

PICK OF THE PUBS

The Carpenters Arms ♥

See Pick of the Pubs on page 412

STOGUMBER — Map 3 ST03

The White Horse

High St TA4 3TA ☎ 01984 656277
e-mail: info@whitehorsestogumber.co.uk
dir: From Taunton take A358 to Minehead. In 8m left to Stogumber, 2m into village centre. Right at T-junct & right again. Pub opp church

Nestling between the Quantock Hills and Exmoor in an Area of Outstanding Natural Beauty, with the West Somerset Steam Railway only a mile away. The dining room of this traditional free house was once the historic village's Market Hall and Reading Room. Home-cooked menus change daily; typical dishes are smoked salmon tartare with cucumber salad, followed by pan-fried pheasant breast with caramelised apple and cider. The courtyard garden is a perfect place to sample one of the local ales.

Open all day all wk 11-11 (Sun 12-11) **Bar Meals** L served all wk 12-2 D served all wk 7-9 **Restaurant** L served all wk 12-2 D served all wk 7-9 ⊕ FREE HOUSE ◀ Cotleigh Tawny Bitter, Abbot Ale, Local West Country Guest Ales Ď Thatchers Cheddar Valley. **Facilities** Family room Dogs allowed Garden Parking

STOKE ST GREGORY — Map 4 ST32

Rose & Crown ♥

Woodhill TA3 6EW ☎ 01823 490296
e-mail: info@browningpubs.com
dir: M5 junct 25, A358 towards Langport, left at Thornfalcon, left again, follow signs to Stoke St Gregory

This 18th-century building, which became a pub in 1867, suffered a serious fire in March 2008. Everything internally has been re-designed and replaced. The pub has been run by the same family since 1979, and enjoys a well deserved reputation for good food, local produce and a warm reception. Fresh fish features on the specials board, alongside grills and roasts with a choice of sauces, vegetarian options and poultry dishes such as sizzling tandoori chicken.

Open all wk **Bar Meals** L served all wk 12-2 booking required D served all wk 7-9 booking required Av main course £10 **Restaurant** L served all wk 12-2 booking required D served all wk 7-9 booking required ⊕ FREE HOUSE ◀ Exmoor Fox, Stag, Butcombe, Otter Ale, Exmoor Ale, guest ales Ď Thatchers Gold. ♥ 8 **Facilities** Children's menu Garden Parking

TAUNTON — Map 4 ST22

The Hatch Inn ★★★ INN ♥

Village Rd, Hatch Beauchamp TA3 6SG
☎ 01823 480245
e-mail: jamie@thehatchinn.co.uk
dir: M5 junct 25, S on A358 for 3m. Left to Hatch Beauchamp, pub in 1m

This father and daughter-run pub prides itself on its friendly atmosphere and the quality of its beers and wines. Wholesome home-made food is served, prepared from West Country produce, with a good choice of snacks and meals served in the both the bar and restaurant. A children's menu is also offered. B&B accommodation is available to those who plan to stay over and explore this delightful corner of Somerset.

Closed: Mon L, D Oct-Feb **Bar Meals** L served all wk 12-2 D served all wk 6.30-9 **Restaurant** L served all wk 12-2 D served all wk 6.30-9 ⊕ FREE HOUSE ◀ Exmoor Ale, Sharp's Doom Bar, Cotleigh Ď Thatchers Stowford Press. ♥ 8 **Facilities** Children's menu Dogs allowed Parking **Rooms** 5

PICK OF THE PUBS

Queens Arms ♥

Pitminster TA3 7AZ
☎ 01823 421529 📄 01823 451068
e-mail: enquiries@queensarms-taunton.co.uk
dir: 4m from town centre. On entering Corfe, turn right signed Pitminster. 0.75m, pub on left

Situated in the heart of Pitminster, the Queens Arms even gets a mention in the Domesday Book of 1086, recording that this ancient building was then a mill. Today, the pub combines the traditional welcome of a classic country inn with a touch of continental influence. Oak and slate floors and roaring log fires in winter add to the appeal, while in summer the patio garden is the perfect spot for a cold drink or after-dinner coffee. The chef uses only the finest locally produced ingredients, with fish delivered daily from Brixham. Meat and game are produced in Somerset, and the vegetables are grown locally. Starters include smoked salmon, moules marinière, and mushroom and blue cheese bouchee. Among the main courses are beef and otter ale pie, fish and chips, traditional Irish stew, liver and bacon, Somerset lamb shank, and home-made fishcakes. Extensive and impresive wine list.

Closed: Mon L & Sun eve ⊕ ENTERPRISE INNS ◀ Otter Ale, Otter Bitter & Exmoor Ale. ♥ 8 **Facilities** Dogs allowed Garden Parking

PICK OF THE PUBS

The Carpenters Arms 🍷

STANTON WICK
Map 4 ST66

BS39 4BX
☎ **01761 490202** 📠 **01761 490763**
e-mail: carpenters@buccaneer.co.uk
web: www.the-carpenters-arms.co.uk
dir: *A37 to Chelwood rdbt, then A368. Pub 8m S of Bath*

Overlooking the Chew Valley, the hamlet of Stanton Wick provides a tranquil and picturesque setting for the Carpenters Arms. Formerly a row of miners' cottages, this delightful, stone-built free house is straight out of Central Casting's book of quintessential English pubs, plus combining the old with the new. Outside is a landscaped patio for alfresco drinks or meals, while behind the flower-bedecked façade lies a comfortable bar with low beams, a chatty, music-free atmosphere, and real ales, including Butcombe Bitter from

Wrington, not far away. Seasonal and local produce is a priority, so menus and daily specials change regularly to make the best of what's available, as well as (say the owners) to keep the chefs on their toes! There are certainly dishes to suit most tastes: among them you may see West Country barn-reared chicken on roasted root vegetables, butternut squash, red onion and sage; roasted fillet of cod on a sauté of cherry tomato, garlic and basil; confit of duck on bubble and squeak with port and redcurrant sauce; and steak and Butcombe ale pie. Among the specials might be fish stew in saffron cream sauce; and roast leg of pork with cider and apple gravy. Vegetarians could well be tempted by linguini with spinach, garlic, cherry tomatoes and toasted pine nuts, while children should be happy with golden fried scampi, pasta with tomato and herb sauce, or any of the other sensible options. Lighter snacks include baguettes and sandwiches. To complement the food, the extensive wine list combines New and Old World favourites.

Open 11-11 (Sun 12-10.30) Closed: 25-26 Dec **Bar Meals** L served Mon-Sat 12-2, Sun 12-9 D served Mon-Sat 7-10, Sun 12-9 Av main course £13.95 **Restaurant** L served Mon-Sat 12-2, Sun 12-9 D served Mon-Sat 7-10, Sun 12-9 Fixed menu price fr £23 Av 3 course à la carte fr £23.85 ⊕ BUCCANEER HOLDINGS ◀ Butcombe Bitter, Bath Gem, Sharps Doom Bar. 🍷 12 **Facilities** Children's menu Garden Parking

TRISCOMBE Map 4 ST13

PICK OF THE PUBS

The Blue Ball

TA4 3HE ☎ 01984 618242 01984 618371
e-mail: info@blueballinn.co.uk
dir: *From Taunton take A358 past Bishops Lydeard towards Minehead*

A converted 18th-century thatched barn, the Blue Ball Inn is hidden away down a narrow lane in the Quantock Hills. Inside you will find A-frame wooden ceilings, solid beech furniture, log fires and, from the windows, superb views south to the Brendon Hills. On fine days you can take a seat outside in the large beer garden or on the patio. The chefs produce dishes from fresh ingredients sourced with considerable care from local suppliers. Typical dishes are marinated Moroccan lamb with Mediterranean vegetables, lemon couscous and harissa sauce; five spice belly of pork with noodles and star anise broth; and corn-fed chicken with herb velouté and baby spring vegetables. Puddings are all home-made and might include dark chocolate tart, lemon and thyme pannacotta, and rhubarb syllabub with crushed meringue and shortbread. A range of real ales from the West Country is kept, and there's an extensive wine list.

Open all day noon-3.30 6.30-11 (Fri-Sat 12-11 Sun 12-9) Closed: 25-26 Dec eve, 1 Jan eve **Bar Meals** L served Mon-Sat 12-2.30, Sun 12-6 D served all wk 7-9.30 Av main course £8.50 **Restaurant** L served Tue-Sat 12-2.30, Sun 12-6 booking required D served Tue-Sun 7-9.30 booking required PUNCH TAVERNS Cotleigh Tawny, Exmoor Gold & Stag, St Austell, Tribute, Otter Head Ale. 8 **Facilities** Children's menu Dogs allowed Garden Parking

WASHFORD Map 3 ST04

The Washford Inn

TA23 0PP ☎ 01984 640256
e-mail: washfordinn@mail.com
dir: *Telephone for directions*

A pleasant family inn located beside Washford Station, a stop on the West Somerset Railway between Minehead and Bishop's Lydeard - the longest privately-owned line in Britain. A service runs all year, using both diesel and nostalgic old steam locos. A good range of beers and a simple menu of proven pub favourites such as omelette and chips, grilled steaks, and all-day breakfast. Chicken, sausages or pizzas for young trainspotters.

Open all wk all day from end of May **Bar Meals** L served all wk 12-9 D served all wk 12-9 SCOTTISH & NEWCASTLE Adnams Broadside, Spitfire, Old Speckled Hen. **Facilities** Play area Family room Dogs allowed Garden Parking

WATERROW Map 3 ST02

PICK OF THE PUBS

The Rock Inn ★★★★ INN

See Pick of the Pubs on page 414

WELLS Map 4 ST54

The City Arms

69 High St BA5 2AG ☎ 01749 673916
e-mail: query@thecityarmsatwells.com
dir: *Situated on the corner of Queen St & Lower High St, 2mins walk from St Cuthberts Church*

Dating from the 13th century, the pub was once the city jail (Judge Jeffreys passed sentence on William Penn here) and original features include barred windows, a solitary cell, chains and locks. Substantial alterations have brought the pub into the 21st century but traditional standards of quality and service apply, with seven real ales including local and award winning ones, draught ciders and freshly cooked food prepared from local produce. Specials include fish pie, butcher's faggots, and baked vegetable pasta.

Open all wk 9am-11pm (Sun 10am-11pm) **Bar Meals** Av main course £7.50 food served all day **Restaurant** food served all day FREE HOUSE Butcombe, Greene King, Sharps', Morland Old Speckled Hen, Potholer, Barbus Ashton Press. 16 **Facilities** Family room Dogs allowed Garden

PICK OF THE PUBS

The Fountain Inn & Boxer's Restaurant

1 Saint Thomas St BA5 2UU
☎ 01749 672317 01749 670825
e-mail: eat@fountaininn.co.uk
dir: *City centre, at A371 & B3139 junct. Follow signs for The Horringtons. Inn on junct of Tor St & Saint Thomas St*

Built during the 16th century to house the builders working on nearby Wells Cathedral, the award-winning Fountain Inn & Boxer's Restaurant has earned a well-deserved reputation for good food and exciting wine. A family-run business since Adrian and Sarah Lawrence took over in 1981, the front of house is now managed by their eldest daughter Kateley (who was born at the pub!) and her husband Andrew Kinnersley. Head chef Julie Pearce uses the finest local produce to create an impressive selection of quality home-cooked food for both the bar and the restaurant. Lunchtime favourites might include doorstep sandwiches with dressed salad and hand-cut chips; or oven-baked goats' cheese in Parma ham with tomato salad. Among the restaurant mains, try roasted cod with pesto and creamy leek mash; roast guinea fowl with chestnut and sage stuffing; or filo parcel with chargrilled Mediterranean vegetables, basil pesto and Greek salad.

The Fountain Inn & Boxer's Restaurant

Open all wk noon-2 6-11 Closed: 25-26 Dec **Bar Meals** L served all wk 12-2 D served all wk 6-9 Av main course £9.95 **Restaurant** L served all wk 12-2 D served all wk 6-9 Av 3 course à la carte fr £21 INNSPIRED Butcombe Bitter, Interbrew Bass, Courage Best. 23 **Facilities** Children's menu Parking

WEST BAGBOROUGH Map 4 ST13

The Rising Sun Inn

TA4 3EF ☎ 01823 432575
e-mail: jon@risingsuninn.info
dir: *Please telephone for directions*

Following a devastating fire, The Rising Sun was rebuilt in 2002 around the original 16th-century cob walls and magnificent door, and the craftsmen-led reincarnation is both bold and smart. Local ales are served and a good choice of food at lunch and dinner, with dishes ranging from goats' cheese, tomato and spinach tart or chicken and bacon salad to pan-fried monkfish with cream and mushroom sauce, or roast rump of Exmoor lamb with mint juices.

Open all wk **Bar Meals** L served all wk 12-2 D served all wk 6.30-9.30 Av main course £15 **Restaurant** L served all wk 12-2 D served all wk 6.30-9.30 Av 3 course à la carte fr £25 FREE HOUSE Exmoor Ale, Butcombe, Taunton Castle. **Facilities** Children's menu Dogs allowed

PICK OF THE PUBS

The Rock Inn ★★★★ INN 🍷

WATERROW Map 3 ST02

TA4 2AX
☎ **01984 623293** 📠 **01984 623293**
e-mail: lnp@rockinn.co.uk
web: www.rockinn.co.uk
dir: *From Taunton take B3227. Waterrow approx 14m W. Or from M5 junct 27, A361 towards Tiverton, then A396 N, right to Bampton, then B3227 to Waterrow*

In a lovely green valley beside the River Tone, this 400-year-old black and white inn was once a smithy, partly carved from the rock face, some of which is still visible behind the bar. And a proper bar it is too, with a dartboard which doesn't interfere with the tables and, at the back of the building, a pool room with its own jukebox - ideal for fractious kids. Everything served here is freshly sourced, prepared and cooked to order. Ever-changing blackboard menus feature the best and most succulent cuts of West Country meat (Aberdeen Angus beef comes from the Rock's own farm two miles away), locally caught fish daily from Brixham, and scrumptious puddings. In the bistro-style restaurant, with a spiral staircase that goes nowhere in particular, lunch could extend to whitebait or sun-blushed tomato, goats' cheese and spinach tartlet, followed by pie of the day, grilled fillets of Brixham lemon sole, or chargrilled Devon Red rib-eye steak. Dinner options are more extensive, with typical starters of moules marinière (from Exmouth); double-baked Jubilee gold soufflé; and pan-fried pigeon breasts with black pudding and quail's egg. For a main course, choose from chump of Somerset lamb, pea purée and Savoy cabbage; Barbary duck breast with caramelised Grand Marnier and orange sauce; fresh Ladram Bay crab and lobster (if available); and pea and mint risotto. There are pub classics too — lasagne and salad; beef and red wine pie with shortcrust pastry; and locally made sausages with mash and onion gravy. And finally, the puddings - try warm ginger Parkin and rhubarb compote, or vanilla crème brûlée. Miles of wonderful walking and fishing country make this region much cherished by outdoor types. Stop off for a night or two in one of the cosy bedrooms.

Open all week **Bar Meals** L served all week 12-2.30 D served all week 6.30-9.30 Av main course £11 **Restaurant** L served all week 12-2.30 D served all week 6.30-9.30 Av 3 course à la carte fr £20 ⊕ FREE HOUSE 🛢 Cotleigh Tawny, Exmoor Gold, Otter Ale, London Pride, Cotleigh Barn Owl. 🍷 11 **Facilities** Dogs allowed Parking **Rooms** 8

WEST CAMEL   Map 4 ST52

The Walnut Tree ★★ HL ◉

Fore St BA22 7QW ☎ 01935 851292 ▤ 01935 851292
e-mail: info@thewalnuttreehotel.com
dir: *Off A303 between Sparkford & Yeovilton Air Base*

Close to the border between Dorset and Somerset, this well-kept inn is in a quiet village. The Leyland Trail passes close by and brings plenty of walkers. The lounge bar and two restaurants entice the hungry with an imaginative menu that changes with the seasons and availability. Whole sea bass baked with lemon, capers and garlic on a bed of sautéed wild mushrooms or rump of spring lamb with black pudding and dauphinoise potatoes in a redcurrant sauce shows the style.

Open all wk Closed: 25-26 Dec, 1 Jan ⊕ FREE HOUSE
◼ Otter Ale, Bitter. **Facilities** Garden Parking **Rooms** 13

WEST HUNTSPILL   Map 4 ST34

PICK OF THE PUBS

Crossways Inn ♀

Withy Rd TA9 3RA
☎ 01278 783756 ▤ 01278 781899
e-mail: crossways.inn@virgin.net
dir: *On A38 3.5m from M5*

The Crossways Inn is a 17th-century coaching inn that forms an integral part of village life. A new skittle alley and pool table are available and live music, themed meals, and unusual competitions are regular events. Produce comes from local sources wherever possible, and dishes are from the menu or specials blackboards, from snacks like deep-fried whitebait and traditional pies, to lasagne, grilled duck breast with grilled peaches, lemon butter chicken or mushroom and brie Wellington. There's a family room, skittle alley and secluded garden. Recent change of management.

Open all wk 10-3.30 6-mdnt Closed: 25 Dec **Bar Meals** Av main course £7 food served all day **Restaurant** food served all day ⊕ FREE HOUSE ◼ Interbrew Bass, Flowers IPA, Fuller's London Pride, Exmoor Stag, Cotleigh Snowy, Butcombe Gold, Branscombe Bitter ♂ Ashton Press. ♀ 8 **Facilities** Children's menu Play area Family room Dogs allowed Garden Parking

---

WEST MONKTON   Map 4 ST22

PICK OF THE PUBS

The Monkton Inn NEW ♀

Blundells Ln TA2 8NP ☎ 01823 412414
web: www.themonkton.co.uk
dir: *M5 junct 25 to Taunton, right at Creech Castle for 1m, left into West Monkton Village*

Here is a village pub that, since 2006, has been completely rejuvenated by its owners, Eddie Street and Guy Arnold. The duo have invested a significant sum of money refurbishing the interior and kitchen, and adding a stylish patio area. Their mission statement requires staff to greet a customer within 30 seconds of entering, to "go the extra mile", and to have fun at work. Hear, hear! By serving freshly prepared, reasonably priced food they have built a loyal following, while taking good care of the drinks-only community too. Lunch and dinner menus change daily, which makes for a great many possibilities. Randomly selected are medallions of local pork with bacon, leek and sausage mash, apple and honey cider sauce; poached chicken with sweet potato and butternut squash mash, rich tomato sauce and fresh asparagus; and fresh fillet of plaice deep-fried in tempura batter, with home-made chips and tartare sauce.

Open noon-3 6-11 (Sat-Sun noon-11) Closed: Sun eve, Mon L **Bar Meals** L served Tue-Sun 12-2 Av main course £6 **Restaurant** L served Tue-Sun 12-2 D served Mon-Sat 6.30-9.30 booking required Fixed menu price fr £14.50 ⊕ ENTERPRISE INNS ◼ Butcombe Bitter, Cotleigh Tawny Exmoor Ale, Exmoor Gold. ♀ 7 **Facilities** Children's menu Play area Garden Parking

---

WHEDDON CROSS   Map 3 SS93

The Rest and Be Thankful Inn ★★★★ INN

TA24 7DR ☎ 01643 841222 ▤ 01643 841813
e-mail: stay@restandbethankful.co.uk
dir: *5m S of Dunster*

Years ago, travellers were grateful for a break at this coaching inn, nearly 1,000 feet up in Exmoor's highest village. Old world charm blends with friendly hospitality in the bar and spacious restaurant, where log fires burn in winter and home-cooked food is served. In addition to the restaurant menu there is a weekly specials board, a light lunch menu and a traditional Sunday carvery. The pub also has a skittle alley and pool table. There are comfortable, well-equipped bedrooms available.

Open all wk 10-3 6-close **Bar Meals** L served all wk 12-2 D served all wk 7-9 **Restaurant** L served all wk 12-2 booking required D served all wk 7-9 booking required ⊕ FREE HOUSE ◼ Exmoor Ale, Proper Job, Tribute, Guinness. **Facilities** Children's menu Garden Parking **Rooms** 8

WIVELISCOMBE   Map 3 ST02

PICK OF THE PUBS

White Hart NEW ★★★★ INN ♀

See Pick of the Pubs on page 416

PICK OF THE PUBS

White Hart NEW ★★★★ INN ♟

WIVELISCOMBE — Map 3 ST02

West St TA4 2JP
☎ **01984 623344** 📠 **01984 624748**
e-mail: reservations@
whitehartwiveliscombe.co.uk
web: www.whitehartwiveliscombe.co.uk
dir: *M5 junct 26. Pub in town centre*

Facing the square in Wiveliscombe
(Wivey to locals) is this 350-year-old
former coaching inn, transformed
throughout by recent major renovations.
Beers from both the village's breweries,
Cotleigh and Exmoor, are normally
served alongside each other in the
vibrant, friendly bar, as well as others
from around the country. Its reputation
for high quality, freshly cooked food
using locally sourced produce has led to
a number of prestigious accolades for
its pub classics, such as steak and
Tawny ale pie; and Beech Hayes Farm

Olde English sausages with apple mash
and rich onion gravy, as well as an ever-
changing menu that includes the
'famous' White Hart burger with home-
made chips. Other favourites are
starters such as chargrilled local
organic vegetable terrine with goats'
cheese and pesto salad; River Exe
mussels cooked in white wine and
cream; main dishes like pan-fried free-
range West Country duck breast on a
confit of garlic mash with orange and
rosemary sauce; fresh potato gnocchi
with local organic Mediterranean
vegetable and tomato sauce topped
with glazed Exmoor Blue cheese; and for
dessert, sticky toffee pudding; rhubarb
strudel with fresh home-made custard;
or the board of local cheeses. On offer at
lunchtime is a selection of sandwiches,
baguettes and omelettes, while Sundays
bring traditional roasts using finest,
21-day topside with thyme-herbed
Yorkshire pudding and goose fat-
roasted potatoes. The bar is open every
morning for a range of coffees. The inn's
refurbishment included the en suite
bedrooms, which display a blend of
original and contemporary features.

Open 10.30am-11pm (Fri-Sat 10am-
mdnt) **Bar Meals** L served Tue-Sun 12-2
D served all wk 6.30-9 Av main course
£8 **Restaurant** L served Tue-Sun 12-2
D served all wk 6.30-9 Av 3 course à la
carte fr £22.50 ⊕ FREE HOUSE
◀ Cotleigh Tawny Owl, Exmoor Gold,
Sharps Doom Bar, Fuller's London Pride,
Cotleigh Harrier ♂ Rattler. ♟ 10
Facilities Children's menu Dogs allowed
Garden Parking **Rooms** 16

WOOKEY
Map 4 ST54

The Burcott Inn

Wells Rd BA5 1NJ ☎ 01749 673874
e-mail: ian@burcottinn.co.uk
dir: *2m from Wells on B3139*

The 300-year-old stone building is set on the edge of a charming village with views of the Mendip Hills from the large garden. The inn features low beamed ceilings, a flagstone floor, log fires and a copper topped bar. Meals are served in the restaurant, and snacks and daily specials in the bar alongside quality local ales. Typical dishes include steaks with a choice of sauces, oven-baked Moroccan spiced sea bass; and wild mushroom and blue cheese alfredo.

Open all wk 11.30-2.30 6-11 (Sun 12-3 7-10.30) Closed: 25-26 Dec, 1 Jan **Bar Meals** L served all wk 12-2 D served Tue-Sat 6.30-9 Av main course £8.45 **Restaurant** L served all wk 12-2 D served Tue-Sat 6.30-9 Av 3 course à la carte fr £18 ⊕ FREE HOUSE ◀ Teignworthy Old Moggie, RCH Pitchfork, Branscombe BVB, Cotleigh 25, Cheddar Potholer. **Facilities** Family room Garden Parking

YARLINGTON
Map 4 ST62

The Stags Head Inn

Pound Ln BA9 8DG ☎ 01963 440393 📄 **01963 440393**
e-mail: mrandall1960@tiscali.co.uk
dir: *Leave A303 at Wincanton onto A37 signed Castle Carey. In 3m turn left signed Yarlington, take 2nd right into village. Pub opposite church*

Halfway between Wincanton and Castle Cary lies this completely unspoilt country inn with flagstones, real fires and no electronic intrusions. A sample menu includes slow-roasted lamb shank on creamed mash with redcurrant and rosemary; haddock fillet in beer batter; or chargrilled rump steak with chips, onion rings and mushrooms. Burgers and light bites also available.

Closed: 25 Dec, Sun (eve), Mon ⊕ FREE HOUSE ◀ Greene King, IPA, Bass, Guinness, guest ales Ď Inch's. **Facilities** Dogs allowed Garden Parking

YEOVIL
Map 4 ST51

PICK OF THE PUBS

The Masons Arms NEW
INN

41 Lower Odcombe BA22 8TX
☎ 01935 862591 📄 **01935 862591**
e-mail: paula@masonsarmsodcombe.co.uk
dir: *A3088 to Yeovil, right to Montacute, through village, 3rd right after petrol station to Odcombe*

Built of local hamstone, with four thatched 'eyebrows' above the upper windows, and dating back to the 15th century, this is the oldest building in the village. In the bar, sample a pint of Drew's (he's the co-owner and brewer) Odcombe No 1, the stronger Odcombe Spring or one of two seasonal ales from the pub's micro-brewery. Drew also runs the kitchen, producing freshly prepared traditional pub grub such as fish pie topped with chive mash; spicy meatball pasta; corned beef hash; and ham, egg and chips, while his daily-changing carte menu might feature lamb's liver and bacon, bubble 'n' squeak and onion gravy; sirloin steak with brandy, black pepper sauce and slow-cooked cabbage; cod fillet wrapped in prosciutto, provençale vegetables and pea purée; and red pepper and Parmesan risotto with oyster mushroom fritters. The comfortable en suite letting rooms are set back from the road in an extension overlooking the garden.

Open all wk noon-3 6-mdnt **Bar Meals** L served all wk 12-2 booking required D served all wk 6.30-9.30 booking required Av main course £10 **Restaurant** L served all wk 12-2 booking required D served all wk 6.30-9.30 booking required ⊕ FREE HOUSE ◀ Drew's Odcombe Ď Westons Bounds Brand. **Facilities** Children's menu Dogs allowed Garden Parking **Rooms** 6

STAFFORDSHIRE

ALSAGERS BANK
Map 15 SJ74

The Gresley Arms

High St ST7 8BQ ☎ 01782 720297 📄 **01782 720297**
dir: *3m from Newcastle-under-Lyme town centre on B5367*

A 200-year-old pub in a semi-rural location set between two country parks, making it a popular stopping off point for walkers and cyclists. It is a friendly local, with a traditional bar, separate lounge and large family room, serving real ale and real food at a reasonable price. The menu encompasses basket meals (chicken, scampi, beefburger), steaks with sauces, light bites, main meals and daily specials, such as braised lamb shank, and tagliatelle Nicoise.

Open all wk ◀ 6 guest ales. **Facilities** Family room Dogs allowed Garden Parking **Notes** ⊛

ALSTONEFIELD
Map 16 SK15

PICK OF THE PUBS

The George ▾

See Pick of the Pubs on page 418

ALTON
Map 10 SK04

Bulls Head Inn ▾

High St ST10 4AQ ☎ 01538 702307 📄 **01538 702065**
e-mail: janet@thebullshead.freeserve.co.uk
dir: *M6 junct 14, A518 to Uttoxeter. Follow Alton Towers signs. Onto B5030 to Rocester, then B5032 to Alton. Pub in village centre*

Traditional beers and home cooking are provided in the heart of Alton, less than a mile from Alton Towers theme park. Oak beams and an inglenook fireplace set the scene for the old world bar, the cosy snug and the country-style restaurant. Menus offer the likes of sirloin steak, deep fried breaded plaice, lasagne verde, steak, ale and mushroom pie, and hunter's chicken.

Open all wk ⊕ FREE HOUSE ◀ Guest ales. ▾ 6 **Facilities** Parking

ANSLOW
Map 10 SK22

The Burnt Gate Inn ▾

Hopley Rd DE13 9PY ☎ 01283 563664
e-mail: info@burntgate.co.uk
dir: *From Burton take B5017 towards Abbots Bromley. At top of Henhurst Hill turn right Inn on Hopley Rd, 2m from town centre*

Originally two cottages and a farmhouse, parts of this uniquely named pub are up to 300 years old. A refurbishment has given the interior some contemporary touches (Wi-Fi access, for example), while retaining the traditional elements of oak-floored bar, open fires and newspapers. As well as steaks and home-made pies, there is game (in season), Thai-style chicken and rice, fresh fish, tapas and deli boards and a gluten-free selection.

Open all wk ⊕ FREE HOUSE ◀ Pedigree, guest ales. ▾ 17 **Facilities** Parking

BURTON UPON TRENT
Map 10 SK22

Burton Bridge Inn ▾

24 Bridge St DE14 1SY ☎ 01283 536596
dir: *Telephone for directions*

A former coaching inn, the Burton Bridge is the oldest pub in Burton, and has its own brewery at the back in an old stable block. The old-fashioned interior has oak panelling, feature fireplaces, and a distinct lack of electronic entertainment. There is also thought to be a resident ghost. A full range of Burton Bridge ales is available on tap and the menu offers straightforward dishes. A skittle alley is also available for hire.

continued on page 419

PICK OF THE PUBS

The George ♀

Map 16 SK15

DE6 2FX ☎ 01335 310205
e-mail: emily@thegeorgeatalstonefield.com
web: www.thegeorgeatalstonefield.com
dir: *7m N of Ashbourne, signed Alstonefield to left off A515*

The nearby Manifold Valley is a famous haunt for ramblers and many seek well-earned refreshment at this friendly 18th-century coaching inn by the green in the heart of this picturesque stone village. Run by three generations of the same family since the 1960s, the current landlady Emily Hammond warmly welcome all-comers, as long as muddy boots are left at the door. She has undertaken a sympathetic restoration of the dining room, which revealed many features including a Georgian fireplace hidden for over a century. The place oozes warmth and charm, with fires crackling in the grate, tiled floors gleaming, and contented chatter from locals, walkers and diners. The appeal of this fine pub, other than the wonderful location and welcome, includes the cracking range real ales and wines by the glass, and the fantastic home-cooked food - the chef makes all his own jams, pickles and chutneys on the premises. The emphasis is on seasonal, regional and traditional dishes, with plenty of hearty options for walkers and fishermen: a range of sandwiches (roast beef and onion marmalade), steak and Guinness pie, home-made beef burger, and Tissington sausages with mash and gravy. By night, tuck into potted smoked mackerel or Devon crab with dill and radicchio risotto, and follow with roast duck breast with haricot bean casserole and kale, or whole baked bass with tomato salsa. Leave room for Bakewell pudding, dark chocolate tart with blueberry fool, and spotted Dick with honeyed figs and lashings of custard. Alternatively, round off with a plate of Hartington stilton with walnut and raisin loaf and a glass of port. A new vegetable patch supplies much of the produce. Allow time to visit Emily's farm shop, housed in the converted 18th-century coach house.

Open all week Closed: 25 Dec **Bar Meals** L served all week 12-2.30 D served Mon-Sat 7-9, Sun 6.30-8 Av main course £12 **Restaurant** L served all week 12-2.30 D served Mon-Sat 7-9, Sun 6.30-8 Av 3 course à la carte fr £25 ⊞ MARSTONS ◀ Marston's Bitter & Pedigree, Jennings Cumberland Ale, Brakspear Oxford Gold, Guest ale ♂ Thatchers. ♀ 8 **Facilities** Children's menu Dogs allowed Garden Parking

BURTON UPON TRENT *continued*

Open all wk 11.30-2.15 5-11 (Sun noon-2 7-10.30) **Bar Meals** L served Mon-Sat 12-2 Av main course £4 ⊕ BURTON BRIDGE BREWERY ◄ Burton Bridge - Gold Medal Ale, Festival Ale, Golden Delicious, Bridge Bitter. ♀ 15 **Facilities** Dogs allowed Garden **Notes** ☺

CAULDON
Map 16 SK04

Yew Tree Inn

ST10 3EJ ☎ 01538 308348 🖹 01782 212064
dir: *Between A52 & A523. 4.5m from Alton Towers*

The Yew Tree is so well known that people come from all over the world to see it. The pub dates back 300 years and has plenty of character and lots of fascinating artefacts, including Victorian music boxes, pianolas, grandfather clocks, a crank handle telephone, and a pub lantern. A varied snack menu offers locally made, hand-raised pork pies, sandwiches, baps, quiche and desserts.

Open all wk ⊕ FREE HOUSE ◄ Burton Bridge, Grays Mild, Bass. **Facilities** Family room Dogs allowed Parking **Notes** ☺

CHEADLE
Map 10 SK04

The Queens At Freehay

Counslow Rd, Freehay ST10 1RF
☎ 01538 722383 🖹 01538 723748
dir: *4m from Alton Towers*

Very much a family-run establishment, the pub dates from the 18th century and has a pretty setting surrounded by mature trees and garden. The interior is refreshingly modern in style, with elegant tables and chairs. The pub has established a good reputation for food, and dishes from the menu are supplemented by chef's specials from the fish or meat boards. Expect home-made beef and merlot pie; Moroccan lamb tagine; and fish and chips. Children have their own menu.

Open all wk noon-3 6-11 (Sun noon-4 6.30-11) Closed: 25-26, 31 Dec-1 Jan **Bar Meals** L served all wk 12-2 booking required D served all wk 6-9.30 booking required **Restaurant** L served all wk 12-2 booking required D served all wk 6-9.30 booking required ⊕ FREE HOUSE ◄ Draught Burton, Peakstones Alton Abbey. **Facilities** Children's menu Garden Parking

---

COLTON
Map 10 SK02

PICK OF THE PUBS

The Yorkshireman NEW ♀

Colton Rd WS15 3HB ☎ 01889 583977
e-mail: theyorkshireman@btconnect.com
dir: *10m from Stafford*

To know why the former Railway Tavern changed its name, look no further than the fact that a Yorkshireman once owned it, and rechristened it in his own honour. John and Jo Ashmore saw no reason to change it when they bought the pub in 2007, but gave it a complete makeover. Beers are brewed by Blythe's just up the road, the most popular being Palmer's Poison, named after Rugeley's famous serial-murdering doctor. Curled up on his bed in the corner of the bar you'll probably find Dahl, the pub's lazy greyhound. Locally sourced food can change daily to include gammon with free-range egg, fresh pineapple and chips; poached smoked haddock with sautéed new potatoes and creamy mustard and white wine sauce; and roasted pepper stuffed with pilau rice, and vegetable and chickpea tandoori. The Deli sells the Yorkshireman's own sauces and dishes, including fishcakes and beefburgers, to take away, plus local cheeses and vegetables.

Open all wk noon-2.30 5.30-11 (Sun noon-6) **Bar Meals** L served Mon-Sat 12-2.30, Sun 12-6 D served Mon-Sat 6-9.30 Av main course £10 **Restaurant** L served Mon-Sat 12-2.30, Sun 12-6 booking required D served Mon-Sat 6-9.30 booking required ⊕ FREE HOUSE ◄ Blythes, Black Sheep. ♀ 9 **Facilities** Children's menu Dogs allowed Garden Parking

---

ECCLESHALL
Map 15 SJ82

The George ♀

Castle St ST21 6DF ☎ 01785 850300 🖹 01785 851452
e-mail: vicki@slatersales.co.uk
dir: *6m from M6 junct 14*

A family-run, 16th-century former coaching inn with its own micro-brewery, where the owners' son produces award-winning Slater's ales. Occasional beer festivals are held, and the menu features a wide variety of dishes, including spicy chilli tortillas; fish stew; roast salmon with hoi sin sauce, chive mash and stir-fry veg; and cod in Slater's ale batter. A selection of salads, baked potatoes and sandwiches is also available.

Open all day all wk 11-11 (Sun 12-11) Closed: 25 Dec **Bar Meals** L served Sun-Thu 6.30-9.30. Fri-Sat 6.30-10 D served Mon-Fr 6-9 Sat 12-9, Sun 12-8 **Restaurant** L served Sun-Thu 6.30-9.30. Fri-Sat 6.30-10 D served Mon-Fr 6-9 Sat 12-9, Sun 12-8 ⊕ FREE HOUSE ◄ Slaters Ales. ♀ 6 **Facilities** Dogs allowed Parking

---

HOPEDALE
Map 16 SK15

PICK OF THE PUBS

The Watts Russell Arms NEW ♀

See Pick of the Pubs on page 420

KING'S BROMLEY
Map 10 SK11

Royal Oak ♀

Manor Rd DE13 7HZ ☎ 01543 472 289
e-mail: shropshall@btinternet.com
dir: *Off A515*

The Royal Oak looks and feels like a quaint village local but award-winning chef and licensee Mathew Shropshall offers cooking of serious intent alongside more familiar pub grub. There are lunchtime wraps, melts and sandwiches, and comfort food such as steak and ale pie or beer battered cod and chips. The serious stuff might

continued on page 421

PICK OF THE PUBS

The Watts Russell Arms NEW 🍷

HOPEDALE Map 16 SK15

Hopedale DE6 2GD ☎ 01335 310126
e-mail: contact@wattsrussell.co.uk
web: www.wattsrussell.co.uk
dir: *Take A515 N towards Buxton. In 6.5m left to Alstonefield & Mildale. Cross River Dove, take left fork to Mildale. 1.5m to pub*

Husband and wife team Bruce and Chris Elliott run this picture-postcard pub, originally a homestead dating from the 17th century. Later it became a beer-house called The New Inn, then in 1851 was renamed in honour of the wife of Jesse Watts-Russell, whose family owned Ilam Hall down the road, the surviving part of which is now a Youth Hostel. Maybe the dear lady wasn't that grateful, as her ghost reputedly still roams the area. Over the bar, where Chris holds sway, you may order a perfectly kept pint of Timothy Taylor Landlord, Black Sheep or the guest ale, a single malt from the selection of fifteen, or one of eight wines by the glass. In the kitchen, Bruce prepares everything from scratch, using mostly locally supplied produce and ingredients – nothing comes from a packet or a tin. Occasionally, neighbours supply herbs and vegetables and even something unusual like a giant puffball mushroom. At lunchtime there are tempting sandwiches, wraps, soups, hand-made pizzas and hot meals, while a typical evening meal might be seafood terrine with onion relish; breast of Gressingham duck cooked in cider and Calvados; and a home-made carrot and ginger, or cucumber and mint, ice cream. Vegetarian dishes might occasionally include a dish called vegetable whim, reflecting the latest neighbourly donation. Once a month, Bruce organises an evening devoted to Thai, Indian, Greek or another country's cuisine. A short walk from the pub is the River Dove and the beginning of Dovedale, one of the country's most beautiful walks.

Open 12-2.30 6.30-10.30 (Sat 12-11, Sun 12-9) Closed: Mon (ex BH) **Bar Meals** L served Tue-Fri 12-2, Sat-Sun 12-4 D served Tue-Sat 7-9, Sun 6-8 Av main course £9.50 🍺 Timothy Taylor Landlord, Black Sheep Best, guest ales. 🍷 8 **Facilities** Garden Parking

KING'S BROMLEY *continued*

include Barbary duck with a Seville orange and mustard sauce; or braised oxtail with sauce bourguignon and parsnip mash.

Closed: Mon ⊕ MARSTONS ◀ Pedigree Bitter, Banks Bitter, Sneck Lifter, Cocker Hoop, Cumberland Ale. ♀ 10 **Facilities** Dogs allowed Garden Parking

LEEK   Map 16 SJ95

Three Horseshoes Inn ★★★ HL ☺ ♀

Buxton Rd, Blackshaw Moor ST13 8TW
☎ 01538 300296   📄 01538 300320
e-mail: enquiries@threeshoesinn.co.uk
dir: on A53, 3m N of Leek

There are great views from the attractive gardens of this sprawling, creeper-covered inn. Inside, the main bar features wood fires in the winter, with a good selection of real ales. Visitors can choose from traditional decor and roast meats in the bar carvery, the relaxed atmosphere of the brasserie (one rosette), and the more formal restaurant. Choices include eggs Benedict with smoked haddock and spinach; and roasted vegetable, rosemary and goats' cheese tarte Tatin.

Open all wk ⊕ FREE HOUSE ◀ Theakstons XB Courage Directors, Morland Old Speckled Hen, John Smiths. ♀ 12 **Facilities** Play area Garden Parking **Rooms** 26

NORBURY JUNCTION   Map 15 SJ72

The Junction Inn

ST20 0PN ☎ 01785 284288
dir: From M6 junct 14 take A5013 for Eccleshall, left at Great Bridgeford onto B5405 towards Woodseaves, left onto A519 towards Newport, left for Norbury Junction

Not a railway junction, but a beautiful stretch of waterway where the Shropshire Union Canal meets the disused Newport arm. The inn's large beer garden gives a ringside view of everything happening on the canal, as well as hosting summer BBQs. Food ranges from baguettes to specials such as home-made rabbit stew with fresh crusty bread; traditional belly pork with black pudding; and bangers and mash with onion gravy. Disabled access at both front and rear.

Open all day all wk 11am-11pm (Fri-Sat 11am-mdnt Sun noon-11pm) Closed: afternoon in winter **Bar Meals** L served Mon-Fri 12-3, Sat-Sun 12-9 D served Mon-Fri 6-9, Sat-Sun 12-9 ⊕ FREE HOUSE ◀ Banks Mild, Banks Bitter, Junction Ale, guest ales. **Facilities** Play area Family room Dogs allowed Garden Parking

STAFFORD   Map 10 SJ92

PICK OF THE PUBS

The Holly Bush Inn ♀

See Pick of the Pubs on page 422

PICK OF THE PUBS

The Moat House ★★★★ HL ☺☺ ♀

Lower Penkridge Rd, Acton Trussell ST17 0RJ
☎ 01785 712217   📄 01785 715344
e-mail: info@moathouse.co.uk
dir: M6 junct 13 towards Stafford, 1st right to Acton Trussell

A Grade II listed mansion dating back to the 14th century, standing on a mound, scheduled as an Ancient Monument, beside the Staffordshire and Worcestershire Canal. Inside are oak beams and an inglenook fireplace, the stylish Brasserie Bar, and the Conservatory Restaurant. The food, for which the AA has awarded two Rosettes, is listed on a variety of menus offering, for example, beef tomato and buffalo mozzarella salad with crushed basil and extra virgin olive oil; 28-day, dry-aged Staffordshire sirloin steak with thick-cut chips, onion rings, field mushroom, tomato and a pepper sauce; free-range Tamworth pork cutlet with mashed potatoes, mustard carrots and cider velouté; and seared fillet of salmon served on a bed of wilted spinach with a sauce vierge and new potatoes. Quality bedrooms, conference facilities and corporate events are big attractions, and with four honeymoon suites, two with four-posters, the Moat House is a popular venue for weddings.

Open all day all wk 10am-11pm Closed: 25 Dec **Bar Meals** L served all wk 12-2.15 D served Sun-Fri 6-9 Av main course £10 **Restaurant** L served all wk 12-2 booking required D served all wk 6.30-9 booking required Av 3 course à la carte fr £40 ⊕ FREE HOUSE ◀ Old Speckled Hen, Greene King IPA, Guinness. ♀ 16 **Facilities** Children's menu Family room Garden Parking **Rooms** 41

STOURTON   Map 10 SO88

The Fox Inn ♀

Bridgnorth Rd DY7 5BL
☎ 01384 872614 & 872123   📄 01384 877771
e-mail: fox-inn-stourton@dial.pipex.com
dir: 5m from Stourbridge town centre. On A458 (Stourbridge to Bridgnorth road)

The Fox is a late 18th-century pub set amid beautiful countryside near Kinver village. Walkers from many nearby rambling areas are attracted by its warm atmosphere and historic surroundings, with many original features still in place. There's also a large garden, complete with weeping willow, gazebo and an attractive patio area. Landlord Stefan Caron has been here since 1971, and these days the pub holds

a civil wedding licence and offers a full wedding package.

Open all wk 10.30-3 5-11 (Sat-Sun 10.30am-11pm) **Bar Meals** L served Mon-Sat 12-2.30 D served Tue-Sat 7-9.30 Av main course £6.95 **Restaurant** L served Tue-Sat 12-2.30 D served Tue-Sat 7-9.30 booking required Fixed menu price fr £10.95 Av 3 course à la carte fr £20 ⊕ FREE HOUSE ◀ Bathams Ale, Enville Ale, Murphy's, Boddingtons. ♀ 8 **Facilities** Garden Parking

TAMWORTH   Map 10 SK20

The Globe Inn NEW ★★★ INN

Lower Gungate B79 7AT
☎ 01827 60455   📄 01827 63575
e-mail: info@theglobetamworth.com
dir: Please telephone for directions

A popular meeting place in the 19th century, the Globe was rebuilt in 1901. More recently, the building has been extended and refurbished to offer 18 en suite bedrooms, though retaining the elegant carved bar and fireplaces that reflect its period character. A range of light meals, salads and hot paninis liven up the snack menu, whilst main dishes include poached smoked haddock with Charlotte potatoes; lamb shank with mint gravy; and stilton and vegetable crumble.

Open all day all wk 11-11 (Thu-Sat 11am-mdnt Sun 11-4 7-11) **Bar Meals** L served all wk 11-2 D served Mon-Sat Av main course £6 **Restaurant** L served all wk D served Mon-Sat ⊕ FREE HOUSE **Facilities** Children's menu Parking **Rooms** 18

TATENHILL   Map 10 SK22

Horseshoe Inn ♀

Main St DE13 9SD ☎ 01283 564913
dir: From A38 at Branston follow signs for Tatenhill

Probably five to six hundred years old, this historic pub retains much original character, including evidence of a priest's hiding hole. In winter, log fires warm the bar and family area. In addition to home-made snacks like chilli con carne, and Horseshoe brunch, there are sizzling rumps and sirloins, chicken curry, moussaka, battered cod with chips and mushy peas, and a pasta dish of the week. And specials too - beef bourguignon, or steak and kidney pudding, for instance.

Open all day all wk 11am-11pm (Thu-Sat 11am-11.30pm) **Bar Meals** L served Mon-Sat 12-9.30, Sun 12-9 D served Mon-Sat 12-9.30, Sun 12-9 food served all day **Restaurant** food served all day ⊕ MARSTONS ◀ Marstons Pedigree. ♀ 14 **Facilities** Play area Family room Dogs allowed Garden Parking

PICK OF THE PUBS

The Holly Bush Inn 🍷

STAFFORD   Map 10 SJ92

Salt ST18 0BX
☎ **01889 508234**   📠 **01889 508058**
e-mail: geoff@hollybushinn.co.uk
web: www.hollybushinn.co.uk
dir: *Telephone for directions*

The Holly Bush is well known for the quality of its food and welcome, but it boasts two other notable distinctions. It is generally recognised as the second pub in the country to have been licensed. This event took place during Charles II's reign (1660-1685), though the building itself is far older, possibly dating back to 1190. Secondly, when landlord Geoff Holland's son became a joint licensee at the age of 18 years and 6 days, he was the youngest person ever to be granted a licence. The pub's comfortably old-fashioned interior contains all the vital ingredients: heavy carved beams, open fires, attractive prints and cosy alcoves. The team are more enthusiastic than ever in their attempts to reduce food miles and support local producers (named on the menu), with regular visits made to local farms to source new products - most recently Jersey milk ice cream and true free-range eggs. At lunchtime there are a good selection of sandwiches, hot sandwiches, toasties and filled jacket potatoes. On the main menu are traditional Staffordshire oatcakes filled with spiced black pudding and a herby tomato sauce; and a centuries' old recipe of slow cooked venison casserole. Other typical dishes include Forest Blue stuffed pears with raspberry and poppy seed vinaigrette; home-made steak and kidney pudding with onion gravy; braised lamb and apples. Seafood dishes attest to the excellent relationships developed with Brixham's fishermen; while local award-winning

cheeses and a great selection of locally farmed steaks complete the picture. The chalkboard displays the vegetarian options.

Open all week 12-11 (Sun 12-10.30) **Bar Meals** Av main course £10.50 ⊕ FREE HOUSE ◀ Adnams, Pedigree, guest ales. 🍷 12 **Facilities** Children's menu Garden Parking

PICK OF THE PUBS

The Crown Inn 🍷

WRINEHILL   Map 15 SJ74

Den Ln CW3 9BT
☎ 01270 820472   📠 01270 820547
e-mail: mark_condliffe@hotmail.com
dir: *Village on A531, 1m S of Betley. 6m S of Crewe; 6m N of Newcastle-under-Lyme*

Reputedly the longest-serving licensee in Staffordshire, Charles Davenhill and his wife Sue have owned this 19th-century former coaching inn for more than thirty years. Joined by their daughter and son-in-law Anna and Mark Condliffe in 2001, the family now run the Crown as a traditional country inn serving good beer and well-renowned pub food. The open plan interior boasts exposed oak beams, and the roaring open fire in the large inglenook fireplace is a welcome feature on cold winter nights. There's always a choice of six cask ales, including regularly changing guest beers. Food is a major part of the pub's success, famed locally not just for the generosity of its portions, but also for consistency in quality and use of seasonal produce. The appealingly organised menu offers a wide range of dishes for varying appetites. The not-so-hungry might prefer one of The Crown's signature soft floury baps, served open with salad and home-made coleslaw; fillings range from oven-baked free range chicken with lemon and pepper seasoning, to freshwater prawns in Marie Rose sauce with lemon and fresh chives. The more ravenous will find meat dishes that may encompass a 10-ounce rib-eye steak with mushrooms and battered onion rings; oven-baked chicken fillet with basil, oak-smoked bacon, cheddar and mozzarella; or Cumberland sausage. Fish comes in the form of sizzling tuna Thai style or baked whole silver bream with Parmesan, hazelnuts and mushrooms, whilst the comprehensive vegetarian selection is driven by Sue and Anna's own dietary lifestyle — vegetable burritos or Moroccan tagine. From the sweet menu, try iced lemon brulée; or hot chocolate pudding with chocolate orange sauce and fresh cream.

Open noon-3 6-11 (Sun noon-4 6-10.30)
Closed: 26 Dec **Bar Meals**
L served Mon-Sat 12-2, Sun 12-3
D served Mon-Fri 6.30-9.30, Sat 6-10, Sun 6-9 Av main course £10 ⊕ FREE HOUSE ◀▆ Marstons Pedigree & Bitter, Cumberland Ale, Sneck Lifter, Brakspear Gold, Guest ales. 🍷 9
Facilities Children's menu Garden Parking

TUTBURY | Map 10 SK22

Ye Olde Dog & Partridge Inn

High St DE13 9LS
☎ 01283 813030 📄 01283 813178
e-mail: info@dogandpartridge.net
dir: *On A50 NW of Burton-on-Trent, signed from A50 & A511*

A beautiful period building resplendent in its timbers and whitewashed walls, with abundant flower displays beneath the windows. The inn has stood in this charming village since the 15th century when Henry IV was on the throne. Five hundred years of offering hospitality has resulted in a well-deserved reputation for good food, served in two smart eating outlets.

Open all wk ⊕ FREE HOUSE ◀ Marston's Pedigree, Courage Director's. **Facilities** Family room Garden Parking

WATERHOUSES | Map 16 SK05

Ye Olde Crown

Leek Rd ST10 3HL ☎ 01538 308204 📄 01538 308204
e-mail: kerryhinton@hotmail.co.uk
dir: *From Ashbourne take A52 then A523 towards Leek. Village in 8m*

A traditional village local, Ye Olde Crown dates from around 1647 when it was built as a coaching inn. Sitting on the bank of the River Hamps, and on the edge of the Peak District National Park and the Staffordshire moorlands, it's ideal for walkers. Inside are original stonework and interior beams, and open fires are lit in cooler weather. Food choices, all home-cooked, are found on the specials board and à la carte menu.

Open all day (Sat noon-11.20 & Sun noon-10.30) Closed: Mon L **Bar Meals** L served Tue-Sun 12-2.30 D served all wk 6-8.30 booking required Av main course £5 **Restaurant** L served Tue-Sun 12-2.30 D served all wk 6-8.30 booking required ⊕ SCOTTISH & NEWCASTLE ◀ Guinness, Theakstons, Spitfire, Abbot Ale, Guest ales. **Facilities** Children's menu Parking

WETTON | Map 16 SK15

Ye Olde Royal Oak

DE6 2AF ☎ 01335 310287
e-mail: brian@rosehose.wanadoo.co.uk
dir: *A515 towards Buxton, left in 4m to Manifold Valley-Alstonfield, follow signs to Wetton*

The stone-built inn dates back over 400 years and features wooden beams recovered from oak ships at Liverpool Docks. It was formerly part of the Chatsworth Estate, and the Tissington walking and cycling trail is close by. Belvoir beers and other guest ales are served along with dishes such as home-made soup; large battered cod; and treacle sponge. Separate vegetarian and children's menus are available. The pub's moorland garden includes a campsite with showers and toilets.

Closed: Mon-Tue in winter **Bar Meals** L served Wed-Sun 12-2 D served Wed-Sun 7-9 Av main course £7.50 ⊕ FREE HOUSE **Facilities** Children's menu Family room Dogs allowed Garden Parking

WOODSEAVES | Map 15 SJ72

The Plough Inn

Newport Rd ST20 0NP ☎ 01785 284210
dir: *From Stafford take A5013 towards Eccleshall. Turn left onto B4505. Woodseaves at junct with A519. 5m from Eccleshall on A519 towards Newport*

Built in the mid-18th century for workers constructing the nearby canal, the Plough is a traditional country pub with winter fires and hanging baskets for the summer. There's a good selection of real ales, and the bar menu features favourites like sausages, mash and red wine gravy. The restaurant menu offers more adventurous options like deep-fried goat's cheese with ratatouille and chargrilled potatoes; or pan-fried duck with cranberry and orange sauce.

Closed: Mon-Tue ⊕ FREE HOUSE ◀ Spitfire, 6X, Grumpy Chef, Titanic Full Kiln Ale, Titanic Woodseaves Witch. **Facilities** Garden Parking

WRINEHILL | Map 15 SJ74

PICK OF THE PUBS

The Crown Inn ♀

See Pick of the Pubs on page 423

The Hand & Trumpet ♀

Main Rd CW3 9BJ ☎ 01270 820048 📄 01270 821911
e-mail: hand.and.trumpet@brunningandprice.co.uk
dir: *M6 junct 16 follow signs for Keele, continue onto A531, 7m on right*

A relaxed country pub, The Hand & Trumpet has a comfortable interior with original floors, old furniture, open fires and rugs. A deck to the rear overlooks the sizeable grounds, which include a large pond. Six cask ales and over 70 malt whiskies are served, along with a locally sourced menu of dishes such as braised lamb shoulder with honey roasted vegetables, rosemary and redcurrant gravy; or wild mushroom, celeriac, leek and thyme pie.

Open all day all wk 11.30-11 (Sun 11.30-10.30) Closed: 25 Dec **Bar Meals** L served all wk 12-10 booking required D served all wk 12-10 booking required Av main course £12.95 food served all day ⊕ FREE HOUSE ◀ Deuchars IPA, Hawkshead Lakeland Gold, Guest ales ♂ Stonehouse. ♀ 22 **Facilities** Children's menu Family room Dogs allowed Garden Parking

SUFFOLK

ALDEBURGH | Map 13 TM45

The Mill Inn ★★★ INN

Market Cross Place IP15 5BJ ☎ 01728 452563
e-mail: peeldennisp@aol.com
dir: *Follow Aldeburgh signs from A12 on A1094. Pub last building on left before sea*

A genuine fisherman's inn located less than 100 metres from the seafront, and a short walk from the town and bird sanctuaries. Seafood bought fresh from the fishermen on the beach is a speciality here, backed by pub favourites such as sirloin steak, ham and eggs, and lamb shank. Well-kept Adnams Bitter, Broadside, Regatta and Fisherman can all be enjoyed at this favourite haunt of the local lifeboat crew. There are four bedrooms available, some with sea views.

Open all wk 11-11 **Bar Meals** L served all wk 12-2.30 D served Tue-Sat 7-9.30 **Restaurant** L served all wk 12-2.30 D served Tue-Sat 7-9.30 ⊕ ADNAMS ◀ Adnams Bitter, Broadside, Regatta & Fisherman, OLD ♂ Aspall. **Facilities** Dogs allowed Garden **Rooms** 4

ALDRINGHAM | Map 13 TM46

The Parrot and Punchbowl Inn & Restaurant ♀

Aldringham Ln IP16 4PY ☎ 01728 830221
e-mail: paul@parrotandpunchbowl.fsnet.co.uk
dir: *On B1122, 1m from Leiston, 3m from Aldeburgh, on x-rds to Thorpeness*

Originally called The Case is Altered, it became the Parrot in 1604 and as such enjoyed considerable notoriety, particularly during the 17th century, as the haunt of Aldringham's smuggling gangs. Don't ask if there's any contraband rum on offer; just study the menu and try and decide between medallions of pork fillet, whole baked sea bass, deep-fried cod in Adnam's beer batter, or an Aberdeen Angus fillet steak. 'Parrot sandwiches' are generously overfilled.

Open all wk ⊕ ENTERPRISE INNS ◀ Adnams, guest ale. ♀ 10 **Facilities** Play area Family room Garden Parking

BARNBY
Map 13 TM49

PICK OF THE PUBS

The Swan Inn

See Pick of the Pubs on page 426

See Pick of the Pubs on page 426

BRANDESTON
Map 13 TM26

The Queens Head ₹

The Street IP13 7AD ☎ **01728 685307**
e-mail: thequeensheadinn@btconnect.com
dir: *From A14 take A1120 to Earl Soham, then S to Brandeston*

Originally four cottages, the pub has been serving ale to the villagers of Brandeston since 1811. A large open bar allows drinkers and diners to mix, and good use is made of the huge garden in summer. Local food, Adnams ales and award-winning Adnams wines are served, with dishes like herb-crusted and pressed shoulder of pork with wholegrain mustard; and confit duck leg with spring onion crushed potato and a rich berry jus.

Open noon-3 5-mdnt (Sun noon-5) Closed: Sun eve **Bar Meals** L served all wk 12-2 booking required D served Mon-Sat 6.30-9 booking required **Restaurant** L served all wk 12-2 booking required D served Mon-Sat 6.30-9 booking required ⊕ ADNAMS ◀ Adnams Broadside & Bitter, Explorer, seasonal ales Ö Aspall. ₹ 8
Facilities Children's menu Dogs allowed Garden Parking

BURY ST EDMUNDS
Map 13 TL86

The Linden Tree

7 Out Northgate IP33 1JQ ☎ **01284 754600**
e-mail: lindentree@live.com
dir: *Opposite railway station*

Built to serve the railway station, this is a big, friendly Victorian pub, with stripped pine bar, dining area, non-smoking conservatory and charming garden. The family-orientated menu ranges from beef curry, home-made pies, and liver and bacon, to crab thermidor, fresh sea bass, and mushroom and lentil moussaka. Youngsters will go for the burgers, scampi, or pork chipolatas. Freshly filled ciabattas at lunchtime.

Open all wk noon-11 (Fri-Sat 11-11 Sun noon-10) Closed: 25 Dec **Bar Meals** L served all wk 12-2.30 D served all wk 6-9.30 **Restaurant** L served all wk 12-2.30 booking required D served all wk 6-9.30 booking required ⊕ GREENE KING ◀ Greene King, IPA & Old Speckled Hen, guest. **Facilities** Children's menu Play area Dogs allowed Garden

The Nutshell

17 The Traverse IP33 1BJ ☎ **01284 764867**
dir: *Telephone for directions*

Unique pub measuring 15ft by 7ft, and said to be Britain's smallest. Somehow more than 100 people and a dog managed to fit inside in the 1980s. The bar's ceiling is covered with paper money, and there have been regular sightings of ghosts around the building, including a nun and a monk who apparently weren't praying! No food is available, though the pub jokes about its dining area for parties of two or fewer.

Open all wk ⊕ GREENE KING ◀ Greene King IPA, Abbot Ale, guest ales. **Facilities** Dogs allowed **Notes** ⊛

The Old Cannon Brewery ★★★ INN ₹

86 Cannon St IP33 1JR ☎ **01284 768769**
e-mail: info@oldcannonbrewery.co.uk
web: www.oldcannonbrewery.co.uk
dir: *From A14 (junct 43) follow signs to Bury St Edmunds town centre, at 1st rdbt take 1st left onto Northgate St, then 1st right onto Cadney Ln, left at end onto Cannon St, pub 100yds on left*

The Old Can is the only independent brewpub in the brewing town of Bury St Edmunds, and dominating the bar are the two giant stainless steel brewing vessels that remain the main feature after a recent refurbishment. There are beer tasting notes to help you decide. The Cannon Fodder menu is big on bangers, usually involving beer, and authentic Thai dishes regularly feature on the specials board. You can also expect fresh fish, game and traditional Sunday roasts. Overnight guests are treated to fresh Suffolk apple juice and a hearty farmhouse breakfast.

Open all wk noon-3 5-11 (Sun noon-4 7-10.30) Closed: 25-26 Dec, 1 Jan **Bar Meals** Av main course £3.75 **Restaurant** L served Tue-Sun 12-3 booking required D served Tue-Sat 5-11 booking required Fixed menu price fr £6 Av 3 course à la carte fr £20 ⊕ FREE HOUSE ◀ Old Cannon Best Bitter, Old Cannon Gunner's Daughter, Old Cannon Blonde Bombshell, Adnams Bitter, seasonal Old Cannon ales, guest ales Ö Aspall. ₹ 12 **Facilities** Garden Parking **Rooms** 5

The Three Kings ★★★★ INN ₹

Hengrave Rd, Fornham All Saints IP28 6LA
☎ **01284 766979**
e-mail: thethreekings@keme.co.uk
dir: *Bury St Edmunds (2m), A14 junct 42 (1m)*

A 17th-century coaching inn with a pretty village setting, the Three Kings features wood panelled bars, a conservatory, restaurant and courtyard. The Saturday night menu offers an elegant à la carte dining experience in additional to traditional bar food of burgers, beer battered fish and chips, and spicy vegetable chilli. There is also a popular Sunday roast carvery, for which booking is advised. Nine comfortable en suite bedrooms are available in converted outbuildings.

Open all wk ⊕ GREENE KING ◀ Greene King IPA, Abbot, Ridleys Rumps. ₹ 14 **Facilities** Garden Parking **Rooms** 9

CAVENDISH
Map 13 TL84

Bull Inn ₹

High St CO10 8AX ☎ **01787 280245**
dir: *A134 (Bury St Edmunds to Long Melford), then right at green, pub 3m on right*

A Victorian pub set in one of Suffolk's most beautiful villages, with an unassuming façade hiding a splendid 15th-century beamed interior. Expect a good atmosphere and decent food, with the daily-changing blackboard menu listing perhaps curries, shank of lamb, fresh fish and shellfish, and a roast on Sundays. Outside there's a pleasant garden.

Open all wk ⊕ ADNAMS ◀ Adnams Bitter, Broadside, Nethergate Suffolk County. ₹ 6 **Facilities** Dogs allowed Parking

CHILLESFORD
Map 13 TM35

The Froize Inn ⊛ ₹

The Street IP12 3PU ☎ **01394 450282**
e-mail: dine@froize.co.uk
dir: *On B1084 between Woodbridge (8m) & Orford (3m)*

A former gamekeeper's cottage, this free house and restaurant is housed in a distinctive red-brick building standing on the site of Chillesford Friary, and dates from around 1490. It is a thoroughly traditional pub with a modern dining room championing East Anglian growers and suppliers. The menu offers rustic English and French dishes, with plenty of fresh seafood in summer and game in winter. The pub stands on the popular Suffolk Coastal Path.

Closed: Mon **Restaurant** L served Tue-Sun 12-2 booking required D served Thu-Sat from 7pm booking required ⊕ FREE HOUSE ◀ Adnams Ö Aspall. ₹ 14 **Facilities** Children's menu Garden Parking

PICK OF THE PUBS

The Swan Inn

BARNBY   Map 13 TM49

Swan Ln NR34 7QF
☎ **01502 476646**   📄 **01502 562513**
dir: *Just off A146 between Lowestoft & Beccles*

Behind the distinctive pink-painted façade of this warm and friendly pub, located just off the A146 deep in the Suffolk countryside, is one of Suffolk's foremost fish restaurants, which is owned by Donald and Michael Cole, whose family have been fish wholesalers in Lowestoft since grandfather set up the business in 1936. With deep-sea trawling in steep decline by the mid-

1980s, Donald thought it prudent to diversify and bought the run-down Swan. It was during the refurbishment that he had a dinghy installed up in the rafters (although he might try and kid you there's just been a particularly high tide!). The property dates from 1690, and in the rustic Fisherman's Cove restaurant you'll find the original low beams and a collection of nautical memorabilia, including trawlers' bells, wheels and a binnacle, all placed on show as 'a tribute to the brave people who bring ashore the fruits of the sea'. The menu choice is mind-boggling, up to 80 different seafood dishes, so it's very much aimed at fish-lovers, with starters including smoked sprats, smoked trout pâté, dressed Cromer crab, locally-caught lobster, and main dishes such as whole grilled wild sea bass; grilled turbot with prawn and brandy sauce; the house speciality – a simply grilled 20oz Dover sole; monkfish

tails in hot garlic butter; and crab gratin. All are accompanied by salad, new potatoes or chips and peas. The Swan has its own smokehouse, one of just three remaining out of 200 in what was once one of Britain's busiest fishing ports. Anyone preferring meat to fish has a choice of fillet, rump and gammon steaks. The place gets packed, so book a table to avoid disappointment.

Open All week ⊕ FREE HOUSE ◾ Interbrew Bass, Adnams Best, Broadside, Greene King Abbot Ale, IPA, guest ales. **Facilities** Play area Garden Parking

COTTON
Map 13 TM06

PICK OF THE PUBS

The Trowel & Hammer Inn

Mill Rd IP14 4QL ☎ 01449 781234 📄 01449 781765
dir: From A14 follow signs to Haughley, then Bacton. Turn left for Cotton

A herd of nine carved teak elephants trekking through the main hall way to the outdoor swimming pool gives you a clue that this is no ordinary pub. At first sight the well maintained, wisteria-clad building belies its 16th-century origins; but, once inside, the old oak timbers and traditional fireplace give a better idea of its age. Nevertheless contemporary needs haven't been forgotten, and licensee Sally Burrows has created secluded areas within the main bars to cater for all age groups. In the summer months the garden, with its tropical theme and thatched poolside umbrellas, is a relaxing place for a drink and a bite to eat. The menus are a blend of traditional farmhouse cooking and international cuisine, so expect to find the regular Sunday roast rubbing shoulders with more exotic dishes that include crocodile and kangaroo.

Open all wk ⊕ FREE HOUSE ◀ Adnams Bitter & Broadside, Greene King IPA, Old Speckled Hen. **Facilities** Garden Parking

DENNINGTON
Map 13 TM26

The Queens Head

The Square IP13 8AB ☎ 01728 638241
e-mail: queenshead123@yahoo.co.uk
dir: From Ipswich A14 to exit for Lowestoft (A12). then B1116 to Framlingham then follow signs to Dennington

It may be recently refurbished, but this 500-year-old inn retains bags of old world charm including open fires, a resident ghost, a coffin hatch and a bricked-up tunnel to the neighbouring church. Locally brewed Aspall cider is available alongside real ales from Elgoods, Adnams and Mauldons. The menu centres around fresh food made with local produce and ingredients - perhaps cottage pie or fillet of plaice parcels.

Open all wk noon-3 6.30-11 Closed: 25-26 Dec **Restaurant** L served all wk 12-2 booking required D served all wk 6.30-9 booking required Fixed menu price fr £9 ⊕ FREE HOUSE ◀ Adnams, Elgoods, Mauldons Ò Aspall. **Facilities** Children's menu Garden Parking

DUNWICH
Map 13 TM47

The Ship Inn ★★ SHL

Saint James St IP17 3DT
☎ 01728 648219 📄 01728 648675
e-mail: info@shipatdunwich.co.uk
web: www.shipatdunwich.co.uk
dir: N on A12 from Ipswich through Yoxford, right signed Dunwich

The once-thriving medieval port of Dunwich has long since been claimed by the sea, but thankfully this old smugglers' haunt looks invulnerable. As one would expect, fresh fish usually features on the daily-changing menu, including plaice, mackerel, prawns, scampi and fishcakes, as do steak and ale pie; lamb, pea and mint casserole; and jam roly poly. In fine weather you can eat in the garden then slip down to the beach, two minutes away.

Open all day all wk 11am-11pm (Sun noon-10.30pm) **Bar Meals** L served all wk 12-3 D served all wk 6-9 ⊕ FREE HOUSE ◀ Adnams Ò Aspall. **Facilities** Family room Dogs allowed Garden Parking **Rooms** 20

EARL SOHAM
Map 13 TM26

Victoria

The Street IP13 7RL ☎ 01728 685758
dir: From A14 at Stowmarket take A1120 towards Yoxford

This friendly, down to earth free house is a showcase for Earl Soham beers, which for many years were produced from a micro-brewery behind the pub. Some nine years ago the brewery moved to the Old Forge building opposite the village green, where production still continues. The Victoria offers traditional pub fare, including ploughman's, jacket potatoes, macaroni cheese, and smoked salmon salad. Heartier meals include a variety of casseroles and curries, followed by home-made desserts.

Open all wk **Bar Meals** L served all wk 12-2 D served all wk 7-10 Av main course £9 ⊕ FREE HOUSE ◀ Earl Soham-Victoria Bitter, Albert Ale, Gannet Mild (all brewed on site), Earl Soham Porter Ò Aspall. **Facilities** Dogs allowed Garden Parking

ERWARTON
Map 13 TM23

The Queens Head

The Street IP9 1LN ☎ 01473 787550
dir: From Ipswich take B1456 to Shotley

This handsome 16th-century Suffolk free house provides an atmospheric stop for a pint of locally-brewed Adnams or Greene King ales. There's a relaxed atmosphere in the bar with its bowed black oak beams, low ceilings and cosy coal fires, and magnificent views over the fields to the Stour estuary. The wide-ranging menu offers traditional hot dishes and snacks, while daily specials include pheasant casserole, spinach and red lentil curry, Guinness-battered cod and chips, and home-made fishcakes. Booking is advised at weekends.

Open all wk Closed: Sun eve **Bar Meals** L served all wk 12-2.30 booking required D served all wk 6.30-9 booking required **Restaurant** L served all wk 12-2.30 booking required D served Mon-Sat 6.30-9 booking required ⊕ FREE HOUSE ◀ Adnams Bitter & Broadside, Greene King IPA, Guinness Ò Aspall. **Facilities** Children's menu Garden Parking

EYE
Map 13 TM17

The White Horse Inn ★★★★ INN

Stoke Ash IP23 7ET
☎ 01379 678222 📄 01379 678800
e-mail: mail@whitehorse-suffolk.co.uk
dir: On A140 between Ipswich & Norwich

A 17th-century coaching inn set amid lovely Suffolk countryside. The heavily-timbered interior accommodates an inglenook fireplace, two bars and a restaurant. There are eleven spacious motel bedrooms in the grounds, as well as a patio and secluded grassy area. An extensive menu is supplemented by lunchtime snacks, grills and daily specials from the blackboard. Try pan-fried chicken with bacon, leek and mushroom sauce; red mullet with chilli butter; or a venison steak when in season

Open all wk 7am-11pm (Sat 8am-11pm Sun 8am-10.30pm) **Bar Meals** Av main course £9.50 food served all day **Restaurant** Av 3 course à la carte fr £15 food served all day ⊕ FREE HOUSE ◀ Adnams, Greene King Abbot, IPA Smooth. **Facilities** Garden Parking **Rooms** 11

FRAMLINGHAM
Map 13 TM26

The Station Hotel ♟

Station Rd IP13 9EE ☎ 01728 723455
e-mail: framstation@btinternet.com
dir: Bypass Ipswich towards Lowestoft on A12. Approx 6m left onto B1116 towards Framlingham

Built as part of the local railway in the 19th century, The Station Hotel has been a pub since the 1950s, outliving the railway which closed in 1962. You will find scrubbed tables and an eclectic mix of furniture. During the last decade it has established a fine reputation for its gutsy and earthy food, such as home-cured meats, pies and suet puddings and beers from the Earl Soham brewery.

continued

FRAMLINGHAM continued

Open all wk noon-2.30 5-11 (Sun noon-3 7-10.30) **Bar Meals** L served all wk 12-2 D served Sun-Thu 6.30-9, Fri-Sat 6.30-9.30 booking required Av main course £8 **Restaurant** Fixed menu price fr £4 Av 3 course à la carte fr £23 ⊕ FREE HOUSE ◀ Earl Soham Victoria, Albert & Mild, Veltins, Crouch Vale, Guinness Ö Aspall. ♀ 6 **Facilities** Family room Dogs allowed Garden Parking

FRAMSDEN
Map 13 TM15

The Dobermann Inn

The Street IP14 6HG ☎ 01473 890461
dir: S off A1120 (Stowmarket to Yoxford road) 10m from Ipswich on B1077 towards Debenham

Previously The Greyhound, the pub was renamed by its current proprietor, a prominent breeder and judge of Dobermanns. The thatched roofing, gnarled beams, open fire and assorted furniture reflect its 16th-century origins. Food ranges from sandwiches, ploughman's and salads to main courses featuring game from a local estate when in season, and plenty of fish choices. Reliable favourites include North Sea plaice with prawn sauce stuffing, sirloin steak with sautéed mushrooms, and chicken and mushroom pie. Vegetarians can feast on mushroom stroganoff or spicy nut loaf.

Open noon-3 7-11 Closed: 25-26 Dec, Sun eve, Mon **Bar Meals** L served Tue-Sun 12-2 D served Tue-Sat 7-9 Av main course £9 ⊕ FREE HOUSE ◀ Adnams Bitter & Broadside, Mauldons Moletrap Bitter, Adnams Old WA Ö Aspall. **Facilities** Garden Parking **Notes** ⊜

GREAT BRICETT
Map 13 TM05

PICK OF THE PUBS

Red Lion

Green Street Green IP7 7DD
☎ 01473 657799 📄 01473 658492
e-mail: janwise@fsmail.net
dir: 4.5m from Needham Market on B1078

This charming 17th-century building may look like a traditional village pub and it was, arguably, just another hostelry until Jan Wise came along and turned it into East Anglia's only vegetarian pub. She has a fixed rule: nothing is served that means killing an animal, so there's no Sunday carvery, no mixed grill, no scampi in a basket. Wanting to 'celebrate the fantastic flavours that only vegetables can provide', Jan uses her 30 years' experience as a vegetarian caterer to create internationally-inspired starters such as dim sum, nachos or houmous, perhaps followed by oyster mushroom, leek and pine nut parcel; roasted vegetable and brie tart; or African sweet potato stew. She's back on more familiar territory with her desserts, which typically include chocolate brownies, rhubarb crumble and summer pudding. Not only is it advisable to book, you'll also need a healthy appetite.

Closed: Mon **Bar Meals** L served Tue-Sun 12-2 D served Tue-Sat 6-9 Av main course £7.90 ⊕ GREENE KING ◀ Greene King IPA, Old Speckled Hen. **Facilities** Children's menu Play area Dogs allowed Garden Parking

GREAT GLEMHAM
Map 13 TM36

The Crown Inn ⊛ ♀

IP17 2DA ☎ 01728 663693
e-mail: crown-i.cottle@btconnect.com
dir: A12 (Ipswich to Lowestoft), in Stratford-St-Andrew left at Shell garage. Pub 1.5m

A warm welcome, open fires and excellent food and ales make this cosy 17th-century village pub an appealing prospect. Set in Great Glemham, it overlooks the Great Glemham Estate and is within easy reach of the Suffolk Heritage Coast. You can eat in the extensively renovated bars and large flower-filled garden, where tiger prawns in tempura batter might be followed by slow-roasted pork belly with dauphinoise potatoes, roast parsnips and sage jus.

Open 11.30-3 6.30-11.30 Closed: Mon (ex BH) **Bar Meals** L served Tue-Sun 11.30-2.30 booking required D served Tue-Sun 6.30-9 booking required ⊕ FREE HOUSE ◀ Adnams Bitter, Tribute, Hobgoblin, Old Ale Ö Aspall. ♀ 7 **Facilities** Play area Dogs allowed Garden Parking

HALESWORTH
Map 13 TM37

PICK OF THE PUBS

The Queen's Head ♀

The Street, Bramfield IP19 9HT ☎ 01986 784214
e-mail: qhbfield@aol.com
dir: 2m from A12 on A144 towards Halesworth

A lovely old building in the centre of Bramfield on the edge of the Suffolk Heritage Coast near historic Southwold. The enclosed garden, ideal for children, is overlooked by the thatched village church which has an unusual separate round bell tower. The pub's interior welcomes with scrubbed pine tables, exposed beams, a vaulted ceiling in the bar and enormous fireplaces. In the same capable hands for over ten years, the landlord enthusiastically supports the 'local and organic' movement – reflected by the menu which proudly names the farms and suppliers from which the carefully chosen ingredients are sourced. Local produce notwithstanding, there's a definite cosmopolitan twist to many dishes, and vegetarian options are a particular strength: mushrooms baked in cream and garlic au gratin could be followed by fresh tagliatelle with pesto, roast red peppers and grilled goats' cheese. Local turkey, wild mushroom, bacon and chestnut pie or fillets of sea bass with rocket pesto mayonnaise are fine main course examples. Amanda's home-made desserts number half a dozen tempting options such as warm chocolate fudge cake or hot sticky toffee pudding. Look out for special dining evenings and live music.

Open all wk 11.45-2.30 6.30-11 (Sun noon-3 7-10.30) Closed: 26 Dec **Bar Meals** L served all wk 12-2 D served Mon-Fri 6.30-9.15, Sat 6.30-10, Sun 7-9 Av main course £10.95 **Restaurant** Av 3 course à la carte fr £20.95 ⊕ ADNAMS ◀ Adnams Bitter, Broadside. ♀ 8 **Facilities** Children's menu Family room Dogs allowed Garden Parking

HITCHAM
Map 13 TL95

The White Horse Inn ♀

The Street IP7 7NQ ☎ 01449 740981 📄 01449 740981
e-mail: lewis@thewhitehorse.wanadoo.co.uk
dir: 13m from Ipswich & Bury St Edmunds, 7m Stowmarket, 7m Hadleigh

There's a warm, friendly atmosphere at this family-run free house. Parts of the Grade II listed building are estimated to be around 400 years old, and make a perfect setting for traditional pub games and regular live entertainment. Freshly-prepared meals are served in the bar and restaurant and, in summer, the beer garden is open for barbecues. Three comfortable en suite bedrooms are also available.

Open all wk **Bar Meals** L served all wk 12-2.30 D served all wk 6-9 Av main course £9.50 **Restaurant** L served all wk 12-2.30 D served all wk 6-9 booking required Av 3 course à la carte fr £20 ⊕ FREE HOUSE ◀ IPA, Adnams Best Bitter, Rattlesden Best, Stowmarket Porter, Adnams Fisherman. ♀ 8 **Facilities** Children's menu Dogs allowed Garden Parking

HOLBROOK
Map 13 TM13

The Compasses

Ipswich Rd IP9 2QR
☎ 01473 328332 📄 01473 327403
e-mail: compasses.holbrook@virgin.net
dir: From A137 S of Ipswich, take B1080 to Holbrook, pub on left. From Ipswich take B1456 to Shotley. At Freston Water Tower right onto B1080 to Holbrook. Pub 2m right

Holbrook is bordered by the rivers Orwell and Stour, and this traditional country pub, which dates from the 17th century, is on the Shotley peninsula. A good value menu includes ploughman's, salads and jacket potatoes; pub favourites such as chilli con carne or chicken with cashew nuts; and a fish selection including seafood lasagne. Party bookings are a speciality, and look out for Wine of the Week deals. Pensioners' weekday lunches complete this pub's honest offerings.

Open all wk 11.30-2.30 6-11 (Sun noon-3 6-10.30) Closed: 25-26 Dec, 1 Jan, Tue eve **Bar Meals** L served all wk 12-2.15 booking required D served Wed-Mon 6-9.15 booking required **Restaurant** L served all wk 12-2.15 booking required D served Wed-Mon 6-9.15 booking required ⊕ PUNCH TAVERNS ◀ Greene King IPA, Adnams Bitter, Guinness Ö Aspall. **Facilities** Children's menu Play area Garden Parking

HONEY TYE	Map 13 TL93

The Lion ♥

CO6 4NX ☎ 01206 263434 📄 01206 263434
e-mail: enquiries@lionhoneytye.co.uk
dir: *On A134 midway between Colchester & Sudbury*

Located in an Area of Outstanding Natural Beauty this traditional country dining pub has low-beamed ceilings and an open log fire inside and a patio with tables and umbrellas for outside eating and drinking. The menu offers a good choice of daily fresh fish (oven baked red snapper supreme with tomato and prawn confit), pub favourites (home-made steak and ale pie), and main dishes such as braised lamb shank with rosemary, garlic and red wine jus.

Open all wk 11.30-3 6-11 (Sun noon-10) **Bar Meals** L served Mon-Sat 12-2, Sun 12-8 D served Mon-Sat 6-9, Sun 12-8 ⊕ FREE HOUSE ◀ Greene King IPA, Adnams Bitter, guest ale. ♥ 7 **Facilities** Garden Parking

HOXNE	Map 13 TM17

The Swan ♥

Low St IP21 5AS ☎ 01379 668275
e-mail: info@hoxneswan.co.uk
dir: *Telephone for directions*

This 15th-century Grade II listed lodge, reputedly built for the Bishop of Norwich, has large gardens running down to the River Dove, with a vast willow tree. Inside, the restaurant and front bar boast a 10ft inglenook fireplace, ornate beamed ceilings and old planked floors. Food ranges from lunchtime snacks like golden whitebait or soup of the day, to a weekly changing lunch and dinner menu. Traditional dishes include venison and wild mushroom pie, with innovative options like sweet potato and saffron fricassée.

Open all wk ⊕ ENTERPRISE INNS ◀ Adnams Best Bitter, 4 other real ales. ♥ 10 **Facilities** Dogs allowed Garden Parking

ICKLINGHAM	Map 13 TL77

The Plough Inn ♥

The Street IP28 6PL
☎ 01638 711770 📄 01638 583885
e-mail: info@ploughpubinn.co.uk

This old, flint-built village pub is part of the Iveagh Estate. Among the numerous fish dishes are grilled red snapper with rougail sauce; and pan-fried skate wing in rosemary and caper butter. Other main courses include beef fillet pie; cottage pie; pork and herb sausages; lemon basil chicken; and poacher's pot, which contains wild boar, rabbit, pheasant and venison in real ale and red wine.

Open all wk ⊕ FREE HOUSE ◀ IPA, Woodforde's Wherry, London Pride, Adnams. ♥ 26 **Facilities** Garden Parking

PICK OF THE PUBS

The Red Lion ♥

The Street IP28 6PS ☎ 01638 711698
dir: *A1101 from Bury St Edmunds, 8m. In Icklingham, pub on main street on left*

A sympathetically restored, 16th-century thatched country inn set back from the road behind a grassed area with flower beds and outdoor furniture. The interior, glowing by candlelight in the evening, features exposed beams, a large inglenook fireplace, wooden floors, and antique furniture. The pub backs onto the River Lark, and was formerly the site of a coal yard and a maltings. An interesting menu offers a variety of choices, and all dishes are freshly prepared.

Open all wk Closed: 25 Dec ⊕ GREENE KING ◀ Greene King Abbot Ale & IPA, Morlands Old Speckled Hen. ♥ 15 **Facilities** Garden Parking

IXWORTH	Map 13 TL97

Pykkerell Inn ♥

38 High St IP31 2HH
☎ 01359 230398 📄 01359 230398
dir: *On A143 from Bury St Edmunds towards Diss*

This former coaching inn dates from 1530 and still retains most of its original beams, inglenook fireplace and other features. The wood-panelled library is just off the lounge, and the 14th-century barn encloses a patio and barbecue. The extensive menu includes vegetarian options and children's meals, as well as traditional Sunday roast lunch. Menu boards highlight a variety of fresh fish, and may include red snapper, monkfish and Dover sole.

Open noon-3 5.30-11.30 Closed: Mon L **Bar Meals** L served Tue-Sun 12-2 D served all wk 7-9 ⊕ GREENE KING ◀ Greene King IPA, Abbot Ale, Old Speckled Hen. ♥ 6 **Facilities** Children's menu Dogs allowed Garden Parking

KETTLEBURGH	Map 13 TM26

The Chequers Inn

IP13 7JT
☎ 01728 723760 & 724369 📄 01728 723760
e-mail: info@thechequers.net
dir: *From Ipswich A12 onto B1116, left onto B1078 then right through Easton*

The Chequers is set in beautiful countryside on the banks of the River Deben. The landlord serves a wide range of cask ales, including two guests. In addition to snack and restaurant meals, the menu in the bar includes local sausages and ham with home-produced free-range eggs. The riverside garden can seat up to a hundred people.

Open all wk **Bar Meals** L served all wk 12-2 D served all wk 7-9.30 Av main course £6.50 **Restaurant** L served all wk 12-2 D served all wk 7-9.30 Av 3 course à la carte fr £18 ⊕ FREE HOUSE ◀ Greene King IPA, Black Dog Mild, 3 guest ales Ŏ Aspall. **Facilities** Children's menu Play area Dogs allowed Garden Parking

LAVENHAM	Map 13 TL94

PICK OF THE PUBS

Angel Hotel ★★★★ RR ◉ ♥

See Pick of the Pubs on page 430

LAXFIELD	Map 13 TM27

The Kings Head ♥

Gorams Mill Ln IP13 8DW ☎ 01986 798395
e-mail: bob-wilson5505@hotmail.co.uk
dir: *On B1117*

Beautifully situated overlooking the river, the garden of this thatched 16th-century alehouse was formerly the village bowling green. Beer is still served straight from the cask in the original tap room, whilst high-backed settles and wooden seats add to the charming atmosphere. Traditional home-cooked dishes complement the à la carte menu and chef's specials and, on warmer evenings, the rose gardens and arbour are perfect for al fresco dining.

Open all wk **Bar Meals** L served all wk 12-2.30 D served Mon-Sat 7-9.30 Av main course £7.50 **Restaurant** L served all wk 12-2.30 booking required D served Mon-Sat 7-9.30 booking required Fixed menu price fr £7.50 Av 3 course à la carte fr £15 ⊕ ADNAMS ◀ Adnams Best & Broadside, Adnams seasonal, guest ales Ŏ Aspall. ♥ 8 **Facilities** Children's menu Play area Family room Dogs allowed Garden Parking

PICK OF THE PUBS

Angel Hotel ★★★★ RR ❀ ♉

LAVENHAM **MAP 13 TL94**

Market Place CO10 9QZ
☎ 01787 247388 📄 01787 248344
e-mail: angel@maypolehotels.com
web: www.maypolehotels.com
dir: *7m from Sudbury on A1141 between Sudbury & Bury St Edmunds*

Licensed in 1420, the Angel overlooks the market place and famous timbered Guildhall in one of England's finest medieval towns. It was originally a 'high hall' house: smoke from a central fire would drift out through roof vents, then in around 1500 ventilation improved when two wings with brick chimneys were added to the building, along with a first-floor solar room, now the residents' lounge. Renovations over the years have revealed a rare Tudor shop window, which has been preserved for all to see, while the historic character of this famous inn can be seen in the beamed dining room and adjoining bar, with its huge inglenook fireplace and attractive plasterwork. Fresh produce from quality local suppliers highlight the daily-changing menus, and everything prepared on the premises. There are always home-made soups, pies and casseroles, fresh fish, game in season and vegetarian dishes. Typical starters from include twice-baked goats' cheese soufflé; shellfish linguine with a chive, lemongrass and ginger cream sauce; and pan-fried pigeon breast with blackberry cream sauce. Main courses might take in peppered rib-eye steak; slow-roasted pork belly with honey-roasted butternut squash and sherry sauce; grilled sea bass served with cabbage, bacon and white wine sauce; and pan-fried salmon with fennel and crab risotto. You could finish with a selection of English cheeses, or perhaps chocolate pannacotta with orange compôte. Expect sandwiches, ploughman's and lighter dishes at lunchtime, and tip-top ales from Suffolk brewers, including Adnams Broadside and Nethergate Suffolk. En suite rooms are full of character with old beams and sloping floors – perfect for lingering longer in this fabulous medieval wool town and exploring the unspoilt Suffolk villages and surrounding countryside.

Open 11-11 Sun 12-10.30 🍺 Adnams Bitter, Nethergate, Greene King IPA, Broadside & Old Growler. ♉ 10 **Facilities** Garden Parking

LEVINGTON
Map 13 TM23

PICK OF THE PUBS

The Ship Inn ♟

See Pick of the Pubs on page 432

LIDGATE
Map 12 TL75

PICK OF THE PUBS

The Star Inn

The Street CB8 9PP
☎ 01638 500275 📠 01638 500275
e-mail: tonyaxon@aol.com
dir: From Newmarket clocktower in High St follow signs towards Clare on B1063. Lidgate 7m

This pretty, pink-painted Elizabethan building is made up of two cottages with gardens front and rear; inside, two traditionally furnished bars with heavy oak beams, log fires and pine furniture lead into the dining room. Yet the Star's quintessentially English appearance holds a surprise, for here you'll find a renowned Spanish restaurant offering authentic Mediterranean cuisine. No mere gastro-pub, The Star provides an important meeting place for local residents. It's also popular with Newmarket trainers on race days, and with dealers and agents from all over the world during bloodstock sales. The menu offers appealingly hearty food: starters like Catalan spinach; and Mediterranean fish soup might precede Spanish meatballs; or hake a la vasca. English tastes are also catered for, with dishes such as smoked salmon and avocado; roast lamb with garlic; and fillet steak in pepper sauce. There's an extensive wine list, too.

Open all wk noon-3 6-mdnt Closed: 25-26 Dec, 1 Jan **Bar Meals** L served Mon-Sat 12-3 booking required D served Mon-Sat 7-10 booking required Av main course £11.50 **Restaurant** L served all wk 12-3 booking required D served Mon-Sat 7-10 booking required Fixed menu price fr £14 Av 3 course à la carte fr £28 ⊕ GREENE KING ◀ Greene King IPA, Ruddles County, Abbot Ale. **Facilities** Children's menu Garden Parking

MELTON
Map 13 TM25

Wilford Bridge ♟

Wilford Bridge Rd IP12 2PA
☎ 01394 386141 📠 01394 386141
e-mail: wilfordbridge@debeninns.com
dir: From A12 towards coast, follow signs to Bawdsey & Orford, cross rail lines, next pub on left

Just down the road from the famous Sutton Hoo treasure ship, Mike and Anne Lomas have been running the free house at Wilford Bridge for the last 17 years. As a former West End chef, Mike specialises in traditional cooking, especially seafood dishes; look out for local game, mussels and sprats in season, as well as crab, lobster, cod, salmon, trout, sea bass and others as available. At the bar, guest ales supplement the regular choice of beers.

Open all day all wk Closed: 25-26 Dec **Bar Meals** Av main course £10 food served all day **Restaurant** food served all day ⊕ FREE HOUSE ◀ Adnams Best, Broadside, John Smiths's, guest ales. ♟ 7 **Facilities** Garden Parking

MILDENHALL
Map 12 TL77

PICK OF THE PUBS

The Olde Bull Inn NEW ★★★ HL ◉ ♟

The Street, Barton Mills IP28 6AA
☎ 01638 711001 📠 01638 712003
e-mail: bookings@bullinn-bartonmills.com
dir: Off the A11 between Newmarket and Mildenhall, signed Barton Mills

Beautifully refurbished in contemporary style in 2007, the new-look Bull Inn stands just off the A11 on the Cambridge/Suffolk border. Rich in history and looking much the same as it did when it was built as a coaching inn in the 16th century, the pub is a popular pit-stop for travellers heading for Norwich or the Norfolk coast. Gleaming handpumps dispense tip-top East Anglian ales, so order a pint Brandon Rusty

Bucket and settle by the fire to peruse the menus. Everything is freshly prepared on the premises, so stay in the bar for classic award-winning Newmarket bangers and mash, a ciabatta filled with home-baked ham and mustard, or Denham Estate wild boar casserole served with dumplings. Linger over three courses in the Oak Room restaurant, perhaps following prawn and crayfish cocktail with braised lamb shank, and finishing with lemon tart. Well-appointed, individually designed bedrooms have flat-screen TVs, smart designer fabrics, and fresh bathrooms.

Open all day all wk 8am-11pm **Bar Meals** L served all wk 12-9 D served all wk 12-9 Av main course £8.75 food served all day **Restaurant** L served Sun 12-3 D served all wk 6-9 Av 3 course à la carte fr £22 ⊕ FREE HOUSE ◀ Adnams Broadside, Greene King IPA, Brandon Brewery Rusty Bucket, Humpty Dumpty, Wolf. ♟ 8 **Facilities** Children's menu Family room Garden Parking **Rooms** 14

MONKS ELEIGH
Map 13 TL94

PICK OF THE PUBS

The Swan Inn ◉◉ ♟

The Street IP7 7AU ☎ 01449 741391
e-mail: carol@monkseleigh.com
dir: On B1115 between Sudbury & Hadleigh

With its magnificent open fireplace, the main restaurant in this thatched free house may once have been used as the local manorial court. The pub welcomed its first customers in the 16th century when the interior would have been open to the roof; and, even today, you can still see evidence of the former smokehole. Other historical features include the original wattle and daub that was exposed during renovation work; it can now be seen behind a glass panel. The regularly changing menus reflect local ingredients wherever possible. Expect to find game in season, locally picked vegetables and fresh fish from the Suffolk coast. Starters like creamy pea and asparagus soup and dressed Cromer crab might precede main course options such as roast monkfish wrapped in Parma ham and sage leaves on buttered samphire, or chargrilled sirloin steak with aubergine, cherry tomato and basil compote.

Open noon-2.30 7-11 Closed: 25-26 Dec, 1-2 Jan, Mon-Tue (ex BH) **Bar Meals** L served Wed-Sun 12-2 D served Wed-Sat 7-9 Av main course £10 **Restaurant** L served Wed-Sun 12-2 D served Wed-Sat 7-9 Fixed menu price fr £13.50 Av 3 course à la carte fr £25 ⊕ FREE HOUSE ◀ Greene King IPA, Adnams Bitter, Broadside ⊙ Aspall, Thatchers Katy. ♟ 20 **Facilities** Children's menu Garden Parking

PICK OF THE PUBS

The Ship Inn ♀

LEVINGTON
Map 13 TM23

Church Ln IP10 0LQ ☎ **01473 659573**
dir: *Off A14 towards Felixstowe. Nr Levington Marina*

The Ship Inn stands within sight of the Orwell estuary and the Suffolk marshes, where old sailing vessels were beached and their hulks broken up for their precious beams. Indeed, the timbers of the part 14th-century thatched inn are impregnated with the salt of the sea. Attractive front and rear patios are adorned with hanging and potted plants. Walls and flat surfaces inside are full of seafaring pictures, curiosities and keepsakes, and the inn is so ordered and cosy that it is hard to imagine it as the smugglers' haunt it once was. But wait, read the old newspaper cuttings on the wall and you'll be left in no doubt that both contraband and excise men often

showed up here at The Ship. In summer, when shellfish comes into season, the kitchen buys huge quantities of lobster, crab, mussels, clams and oysters in addition to haddock, hake, salmon, mackerel and snapper from around the coast. This means a good choice of fish and seafood starters and main courses from the daily changing blackboard menu - perhaps something griddled in herb, lemon and garlic oil, or accompanied by a light sauce. Local game includes pigeon, pheasant, partridge, rabbit, hare and estate-reared venison, although the kitchen is also noted for its meats, including chargrilled chicken brochettes; fillet of pork or beef; and liver and bacon, served with black pudding and Madeira sauce. The home-made desserts are worth leaving room for, as is the good selection of British cheeses. Finish your meal with coffee (again, a good selection available) and home-made almond biscuits. Adnams Best and Broadside are served alongside a guest ale, plus a range of Scottish and Irish malts and wines by the glass, including champagne. Everything is served by smiling, attentive staff.

Open Apr-Sep 11.30-11 (Sun noon-10.30) Oct-Mar 11.30-3 6.30-11 (Sat 11.30-11 Sun noon-10.30) Closed: 25-26 Dec D only, 31 Dec-1 Jan seasonal hrs **Meals** L served Mon-Sat 12-2, Sun 12-3 D served Mon-Sat 6.30-9.30 ⊕ PUNCH TAVERNS ◀ Adnams Best, Broadside, guest ale ♂ Aspall. ♀ 11 **Facilities** Garden Parking

NAYLAND   Map 13 TL93

PICK OF THE PUBS

Anchor Inn

26 Court St CO6 4JL
☎ **01206 262313** 📄 **01206 264166**
e-mail: enquiries@anchornayland.co.uk
dir: *Follow A134 Colchester to Sudbury for 3.5m through Gt Horkesley, bottom of hill turn right to Nayland Horkesley road. Pub on right after bridge*

Nestling on the banks of the River Stour, this 15th-century free house is reputedly the last remaining place from which press gangs recruited their 'volunteers'. Visitors are welcome to wander around the adjoining Anchor Inn Heritage Farm, which provides the kitchen with most of its daily requirements. The farm is run on traditional lines, with working Suffolk Punch horses helping to produce good old-fashioned food in the time-honoured way. This farm-kitchen relationship is crucial to the quality of food. Everything from a variety of flavoured sausages to sauces is prepared here, and the regularly changing menus are shaped by the seasons. Try the breast of wild mallard duck with noodle stir-fry and sweet and sour sauce; Anchor Inn smoked platter from the smoke house; or IPA battered East Coast cod with fat chips and dressed leaf salad. Puddings might include apple and quince crumble with vanilla custard. There is a riverside deck for alfresco dining.

Open all wk 11-3 5-11 (all day spring and summer) **Bar Meals** L served Mon-Fri 12-2, Sat 12-2.30, Sun 12-3 D served Mon-Fri 6.30-9, Sat 6.30-9.30, Sun 5-8.30 Av main course £14 **Restaurant** L served Mon-Fri 12-2, Sat 12-2.30, Sun 12-3 D served Mon-Fri 6.30-9, Sat 6.30-9.30, Sun 5-8.30 Av 3 course à la carte fr £12.95 ⊕ FREE HOUSE ◀ Adnams, IPA, Mild, Local ales. **Facilities** Garden Parking

ORFORD   Map 13 TM45

Jolly Sailor Inn ★★★ INN

Quay St IP12 2NU ☎ **01394 450243** 📄 **0870 128 7874**
e-mail: hello@thejollysailor.net
web: www.thejollysailor.net
dir: *On B1084 E of Woodbridge, Orford signed from A12 approx 10m*

Until the 16th century, Orford was a bustling coastal port. This ancient, timber-framed smugglers' inn stood on the quayside - but, as Orford Ness grew longer, the harbour silted up and fell out of use. Nevertheless, the pub still serves visiting yachtsmen, and local fishermen supply fresh fish to the kitchen. There's also a daily roast, and other dishes might include seasonal local pheasant in red wine; or fresh pasta with a choice of sauces.

Open all wk 11-3 6-mdnt (Sat 11am-1am Sun noon-11 summer all wk 11am-mdnt) **Bar Meals** L served Mon-Fri 12-3, Sat-Sun 11-11 D served Mon-Fri 6-9.30, Sat-Sun 11-11 **Restaurant** L served Mon-Fri 12-3, Sat-Sun 11-11 D served Mon-Fri 6-9.30, Sat-Sun 11-11 ⊕ ADNAMS ◀ Adnams Bitter, Broadside, Explorer ♂ Aspalls. **Facilities** Dogs allowed Garden **Notes** ⊜

King's Head

Front St IP12 2LW ☎ **01394 450271**
e-mail: ian_thornton@talk21.com
dir: *From Woodbridge follow signs for Orford Castle on B1084. Through Butley & Chillesford on to Orford*

An inn with a smuggling history, The King's Head stands on the old market square, a short walk from the quay. The atmospheric interior includes a beamed bar serving Adnams ales, and a wood-floored restaurant offering plenty of local produce. Typical starters include garlic mushrooms, whitebait, and smoked mackerel, followed perhaps by 'boozy beef' (made with Adnams ale); cod in beer batter; or vegetable stir fry. Bar snacks include sandwiches, burgers and things with chips.

Open all wk ⊕ ADNAMS ◀ Adnams Bitter, Adnams Broadside, Adnams Regatta, Adnams Tally Ho, Adnams Explorer. **Facilities** Dogs allowed Garden Parking

REDE   Map 13 TL85

The Plough

IP29 4BE ☎ **01284 789208**
dir: *On A143 between Bury St Edmunds & Haverhill*

This picture-postcard, half-thatched, 16th-century pub has an old plough outside. The building has a cream exterior and restored beams, with a fresh, open feel to the interior. Light snacks in the form of carpaccio of wild boar or dressed Cromer crab are backed by an adventurous array of blackboard-listed dishes: grilled sea bass with a cream and bacon sauce; wild woodpigeon with lentils; and traditional country recipes with a Mediterranean twist like lamb, olive and artichoke stew. Menus change with the seasons and availability of fresh local produce.

Open all wk **Bar Meals** L served all wk 12-2 D served all wk 6-9 **Restaurant** L served all wk 12-2 D served Mon-Sat 6-9 ⊕ ADMIRAL TAVERNS ◀ Greene King IPA, Abbot Ale, London Pride, Adnams. **Facilities** Garden Parking

ST PETER SOUTH ELMHAM   Map 13 TM38

PICK OF THE PUBS

Wicked at St Peter's Hall 🍷

NR35 1NQ ☎ **01986 782288**
e-mail: mail@wickedlygoodfoodltd.co.uk
dir: *From A143/A144 follow brown signs to St Peter's Brewery*

This magnificent 13th-century moated hall is now home to one of Suffolk's most unusual and romantic pub/restaurants. The building was enlarged in 1539 using materials salvaged from nearby Flixton Priory, and the stunning conversion features period furnishings that make the most of original stone floors, Gothic windows and lofty ceilings. St Peter's Brewery was established in 1996 in an adjacent range of former agricultural buildings, and now produces traditional ales as well as some more unusual varieties like honey porter and fruit beer. The full range of cask and bottled beers is available alongside Aspalls cider in the bar. Locally sourced free range and organic produce is the mainstay of the menus, which range through dishes like pan-fried Barbary duck with brandy and cassis jus; baked salmon with Dijon mustard and herb crust; and breast of local pheasant in pancetta with redcurrant and spiced apple jus.

Open noon-3 6-11 (Sun noon-4) Closed: 1-12 Jan, Mon **Bar Meals** L served Tue-Sat 12-3 booking required Av main course £8 **Restaurant** L served Sun 12-4 booking required D served Tue-Sat 6-10 booking required Av 3 course à la carte fr £25 ⊕ ST PETERS BREWERY ◀ Golden Ale, Organic Ale, Grapefruit ale, Cream Stout, Organic Best Bitter ♂ Aspalls. 🍷 20 **Facilities** Children's menu Garden Parking

SNAPE
Map 13 TM35

PICK OF THE PUBS

The Crown Inn ♀

Bridge Rd IP17 1SL ☎ 01728 688324
e-mail: snapecrown@tiscali.co.uk
dir: *A12 N to Lowestoft, right to Aldeburgh, then right again in Snape at x-rds by church, pub at bottom of hill*

Visitors to Snape Maltings, home of the Aldeburgh Music Festival, will find this 15th-century former smugglers' inn perfect for a pre- or post-concert dinner. Set close to the River Alde, the pub is highly atmospheric, with abundant old beams, brick floors and, around the large inglenook, a very fine double Suffolk settle. Once installed, you'll realise (at least on a cold day) just how wonderful burning logs sound when there is no gaming machine or piped music to drown the crackles. Using local suppliers and produce from his own allotment, the landlord also rears livestock on site. His modern British menus, with daily specials, include starters of potted smoked haddock with green peppercorns and quail's egg salad; and pressed game terrine with pickled mushrooms. Main courses might be pheasant with pearl barley and root vegetable broth; home-reared pork sausages with mash and shallot gravy; and crisp battered cod and chips. For pudding, baked Seville orange marmalade cheesecake may be on the menu. Enjoy top quality Adnams ales, along with 18 wines available by the glass.

Open all wk **Bar Meals** L served all wk 12-2.30, Tue-Sun 12-2.30 (Nov-Apr) booking required D served all wk 6-9.30, Tue-Sat 6-9.30 (Nov-Apr) booking required Av main course £10.95 **Restaurant** L served all wk 12-2.30, Tue-Sun 12-2.30 (Nov-Apr) booking required D served all wk 6-9.30, Tue-Sat 6-9.30 (Nov-Apr) booking required Av 3 course à la carte fr £20 ⊕ ADNAMS ◑ Adnams Best, Broadside, Old Ale, Regatta, Explorer. ♀ 18 **Facilities** Children's menu Dogs allowed Garden Parking

The Golden Key ♀

Priory Ln IP17 1SQ ☎ 01728 688510
e-mail: info@snape-golden-key.co.uk
dir: *Telephone for directions*

The 17th-century building has seen many changes over the last couple of years with complete redecoration inside and out to provide an attractive and comfortable dining pub. Locally sourced food is key to the seasonal menus, which include fresh fish daily from Aldeburgh; Hogwarts Large Black rare-breed pork; and Simply Snape Jacob lamb. Typical dishes are dressed Aldeburgh crab; wild rabbit casserole; and Emmerdale Farm Suffolk Red Poll steak, mushroom and ale pie. A small shop has been established selling a range of local products.

Open all wk **Bar Meals** L served Mon-Sat 12-2, Sun 12-2.30 booking required D served Mon-Sat 6.30-9, Sun 7-9 booking required Av main course £10 **Restaurant** L served Mon-Sat 12-2, Sun 12-2.30 booking required D served Mon-Sat 6.30-9, Sun 7-9 booking required ⊕ ADNAMS ◑ Adnams Bitter, Broadside, Explorer, Old, Oyster Stout Ö Aspall. ♀ 14 **Facilities** Children's menu Family room Dogs allowed Garden Parking

Plough & Sail ♀

Snape Maltings IP17 1SR
☎ 01728 688413 ▤ 01728 688930
e-mail: enquiries@snapemaltings.co.uk
dir: *Snape Maltings on B1069 S of Snape. Signed from A12*

An enjoyable and popular part of any visit to Snape Maltings, the Plough and Sail rubs shoulders with the famous concert hall, art gallery and shops. The rambling interior includes a restaurant, and the large terrace provides summer seating. Sweet potato moussaka or wild boar sausages with green pea mash are typical light lunches, whilst evening diners might expect a slow braised lamb shank, or baked cod with Welsh rarebit and creamed leeks.

Open all wk ⊕ FREE HOUSE ◑ Adnams Broadside, Adnams Bitter, Explorer, Fishermans, Old Ale. ♀ 10 **Facilities** Dogs allowed Garden Parking

SOUTHWOLD
Map 13 TM57

PICK OF THE PUBS

The Crown Hotel ★★ HL ⊚ ♀

The High St IP18 6DP
☎ 01502 722275 ▤ 01502 727263
e-mail: crown.hotel@adnams.co.uk
dir: *A12 onto A1095 to Southwold. Into town centre, pub on left*

The multi-talented Crown fulfils the roles of pub, wine bar, eatery and small hotel. Originally a posting inn dating from 1750, it is now the flagship operation for Adnams brewery, so expect plenty of excellent ales on tap. Alternatively you can visit the cellar and kitchen store in the hotel yard for a full selection of bottled beers and over 200 wines. The whole place buzzes with lively informality as blue-shirted waiting staff attend to customers installed on green leather cushioned settles or at the green-washed oak-panelled bar. It's a popular place, especially in summer when customers are queueing at the door and can enjoy a pint or a meal outside. The high standard of cooking is recognised with an AA rosette. The seaside location brings impressive seafood options such as roasted fillet of hake or seared sea bass. Other options might include braised lamb sweetbreads or confit of rabbit ravioli. Excellent puddings include warm treacle tart with clotted cream.

Open all day all wk 8am-11pm (Sun 8am-10.30pm) Apr-Sep **Bar Meals** L served Sun-Fri 12-2, Sat 12-2.30 (12-3 summer) D served Sun-Fri 6-9, Sat 6-9.30 (5.30-9.30 summer) Av main course £15 ⊕ ADNAMS ◑ Adnams Ales. ♀ 20 **Facilities** Garden Parking **Rooms** 14

The Randolph ⊚ ♀

41 Wangford Rd, Reydon IP18 6PZ
☎ 01502 723603 ▤ 01502 722194
e-mail: reception@therandolph.co.uk
dir: *A1095 from A12 at Blythburgh 4m, Southwold 9m from Darsham train station*

This grand late-Victorian establishment with large gardens was built by Adnams the local brewer and named after Lord Randolph Churchill, Sir Winston's father. There is a traditional bar but the interior has more of a gastro-pub ambience. Modern British menus offer simple dishes full of flavour, such as deep-fried cod in Adnams batter with hand-cut chips; and confit of duck legs served on an egg noodle and vegetable stir-fry with hoi sin sauce.

Open all wk **Bar Meals** L served all wk 12-2 D served all wk 6.30-9 Av main course £10.95 **Restaurant** L served all wk 12-2 booking required D served all wk 6.30-9 booking required Av 3 course à la carte fr £21.50 ⊕ ADNAMS PLC ◑ Adnams Bitter, Adnams Broadside, Explorer, Old Ale Ö Aspall. ♀ 6 **Facilities** Children's menu Garden Parking

STANTON
Map 13 TL97

The Rose & Crown

Bury Rd IP31 2BZ ☎ 01359 250236
dir: *On A413 from Bury St Edmunds towards Diss*

Three acres of landscaped grounds surround this 16th-century coaching inn. Curl up on one of the comfy sofas in the split-level bar for a pint of locally brewed Adnams Broadside, before perusing a menu that offers the likes of seared scallop, chorizo and black pudding salad; glazed pork loin chops; and sea bass with crayfish and saffron risotto. The adjoining Cobbled Barn is a popular spot for weddings and parties.

Open all wk ⊕ PUNCH TAVERNS ◑ Greene King IPA, Adnams Broadside, Guinness. **Facilities** Play area Garden Parking

| STOKE-BY-NAYLAND | Map 13 TL93 |

PICK OF THE PUBS

The Angel Inn ☻

CO6 4SA ☎ 01206 263245 🖹 **01206 264145**
e-mail: info@theangelinn.net
dir: From Colchester take A134 towards Sudbury, 5m
to Nayland. Or from A12 between juncts 30 & 31 take
B1068, then B1087 to Nayland

Set in a landscape immortalised in the paintings of
local artist, John Constable, the Angel is a 16th-
century inn with beamed bars, log fires and a long
tradition of hospitality. The relaxed, modern feel
extends to the air-conditioned conservatory, the patio
and sun terrace. Tables for lunch and dinner may be
reserved in The Well Room, which has a high ceiling
open to the rafters, a gallery leading to the pub's
accommodation, rough brick and timber studded walls,
and the well itself, fully 52 feet deep. Eating in the bar,
by comparison, is on a strictly first-come, first-served
basis but the same menu is served throughout.
Starters might feature baked goats' cheese with
roasted field mushroom, beefsteak tomato and red
onion confit for example. Main courses offer a range of
meat, seafood and vegetarian options, typically
including griddled whole plaice served with salad and
French fries. There is an extensive wine list.

Open all day all wk 11-11 **Bar Meals** L served Mon-Sat
12-2.30, Sun 12-8.30 D served Mon-Sat 6-9.30, Sun
12-8.30 **Restaurant** L served Mon-Sat 12-2.30, Sun
12-8.30 D served Mon-Sat 6-9.30, Sun 12-8.30 ⊕ FREE
HOUSE ◖ Adnams Best. ☻ 9 **Facilities** Children's
menu Family room Garden Parking

PICK OF THE PUBS

The Crown ★★★ SHL ⊚⊚ ☻

CO6 4SE ☎ 01206 262001 🖹 **01206 264026**
e-mail: thecrown@eoinns.co.uk
dir: Exit A12 signed Stratford St Mary/Dedham.
Through Stratford St Mary 0.5m, left, follow signs to
Higham. At village green turn left, left again 2m, pub
on right

There are views across the beautiful Box Valley from
this modernised and extended mid-16th century village
inn. Wherever possible, local produce underpins dishes
on the monthly-changing modern British menu, all of
them freshly prepared by a team of eleven chefs. Being
so close to the coast means there is an excellent
selection of daily fish dishes on the blackboard –
perhaps grilled lemon sole with cherry vine tomatoes,
herb oil, new potatoes and fresh mixed salad or fish
cakes with chips. Lunch brings full meals or light
options such as goats' cheese and basil tart. An
evening meal might take in venison carpaccio with
rocket, crispy garlic and Parmesan; steak and kidney
pudding with horseradish mash and spring greens;
and fig tarte Tatin with clotted cream. Every dish is
given a wine match. A decent selection of ales sits
alongside a superb wine list; the inn even has its own
wine shop, offering wines to drink in or take away.

Open all day all wk 7.30am-11pm (Sun 8am-10.30pm)
Closed: 25-26 Dec **Bar Meals** L served Mon-Sat
12-2.30, Sun 12-9 D served Mon-Thu 6-9.30, Fri-Sat
6-10, Sun 12-9 Av main course £13.50 **Restaurant** L
served Mon-Sat 12-2.30, Sun 12-9 D served Mon-Thu
6-9.30, Fri-Sat 6-10, Sun 12-9 Av 3 course à la carte fr
£25 ⊕ FREE HOUSE ◖ Adnams Best Bitter, Brewers
Gold, Woodforde's Wherry, guest ales ⭕ Aspalls. ☻ 34
Facilities Children's menu Dogs allowed Garden
Parking **Rooms** 11

| STOWMARKET | Map 13 TM05 |

PICK OF THE PUBS

The Buxhall Crown ☻

Mill Rd, Buxhall IP14 3DW ☎ 01449 736521
e-mail: thebuxhallcrown@hotmail.co.uk
dir: 3m from Stowmarket and A14

A 17th-century building, The Buxhall Crown has a
classic old bar with intimate corners and an open fire,
and a second bar with a lighter, more modern feel. The
owners and staff pride themselves on the friendly
family feel of the pub, and the high quality of the food
they serve. Dishes are prepared from locally sourced
produce, and breads, biscuits, ice creams and sorbets
are all freshly made on the premises. Anything from a
little nibble to a full four-course meal is catered for,
with the likes of spring roll of duck confit, vegetables
and oriental dressing; grilled fillet of mackerel with
warm potato salad and salsa verde; and slow braised
English lamb with rosemary, root vegetables and lemon
sauce. A meat-free alternative might be tempura
battered vegetables with sweet chilli dipping sauce.
The menu changes regularly to suit the weather and
the availability of ingredients.

Open noon-3 7-11 (Sat noon-3 6.30-11) Closed: Sun
eve & Mon **Bar Meals** L served Tue-Sun 12-2 D served
Tue-Fri 7-10, Sat 6.30-10 Av main course £11.95
Restaurant L served Tue-Sun 12-2 D served Tue-Fri
7-10, Sat 6.30-10 Av 3 course à la carte fr £20.85
⊕ GREENE KING ◖ Greene King IPA, Old Trip, Old
Speckled Hen. ☻ 12 **Facilities** Children's menu Dogs
allowed Garden Parking

| STRADBROKE | Map 13 TM27 |

The Ivy House ☻

Wilby Rd IP21 5JN ☎ 01379 384634
e-mail: stensethhome@aol.com
dir: Please telephone for directions

A Grade II listed thatched pub just off the main street in
Stradbroke. The separate restaurant has beech tables
and chairs and white china. There's an extensive wine
list plus an impressive, daily-changing menu that makes
good use of local produce. Typical dishes include crayfish
salad with lemon dressing followed by roast Gressingham
duck breast with stir-fried vegetables, noodles and plum
sauce. Outside is a lawn and pond.

Open all wk **Restaurant** L served all wk 12-2 booking
required D served all wk 6.30-9 booking required ⊕ FREE
HOUSE ◖ Adnams, Woodforde's, Buffy's. ☻ 7
Facilities Dogs allowed Garden Parking

PICK OF THE PUBS

The Westleton Crown ★★★ HL 🌹🌹 ♟

WESTLETON Map 13 TM46

The Street IP17 3AD
☎ 01728 648777 📄 01728 648239
e-mail: info@westletoncrown.co.uk
web: www.westletoncrown.co.uk
dir: *A12 N, turn right for Westleton just after Yoxford. Hotel opposite on entering Westleton*

Guests have been accommodated on the site of the Crown since the 12th century when a priest in charge of Sibton Abbey lived here and took in travellers, and in the 17th century it was a thriving coaching inn. Over the years this attractive brick-built pub, located opposite the parish church in a peaceful village close to the RSPB's Minsmere Reserve, has evolved through careful renovation and refurbishment into a

well-appointed inn, combining historic character with contemporary charm, and providing a comfortable base for exploring Suffolk's glorious Heritage Coast. Inside you will find two crackling log fires, local real ales, a good list of wines (9 available by the glass), and an extensive menu that includes innovative daily specials and classic dishes with a twist, all freshly prepared from the best local produce available. You can eat in the cosy parlour, in the elegant dining room, or in the light and airy conservatory restaurant. Starters and lighter dishes may include free-range Blythburgh ham terrine with piccalilli, and baked butternut squash and onion tart. Main courses embrace braised shank of lamb with ratatouille, and local venison with sage creamed potatoes and blueberry sauce. Seafood lovers should look to the specials list for grilled bream with olive oil crushed potatoes and a clam and herb velouté; fresh battered haddock with tartare sauce, mushy peas and hand-cut chips; and the Crown's own smoked fish

platter. Save some space for accomplished desserts like warm chestnut and chocolate brownie with marshmallow ice cream; and caramelised blackberry crème brûlée. Retire to one of the 25 comfortable, individually styled and recently refurbished bedrooms complete with flat screen TV. Outside are large terraced gardens, floodlit in the evening.

Open 7am-11pm (Sun 7.30am-10.30pm) **Bar Meals** L served all week 12-2.30 D served all week 7-9.30 Av main course £16 **Restaurant** L served all week 12-2.30 D served all week 7-9.30 Av 3 course à la carte £28 🍺 FREE HOUSE 🛢 Adnams Bitter, range of real ales. ♟ 9 **Facilities** Children's menu Dogs allowed Garden Parking **Rooms** 25

SWILLAND
Map 13 TM15

Moon & Mushroom Inn ♥

High Rd IP6 9LR ☎ 01473 785320
e-mail: nikki@ecocleen.fsnet.co.uk
dir: 6m N of Ipswich on Westerfield road

This 300-year-old free house has a reputation as 'the pub that time passed by', and the owners intend to keep it that way. Winter fires, good company and a choice of East Anglian ales straight from the barrel all play their part. Steaks and fish and chips with mushy peas are staples, while ever popular are beef in ale with dumplings; pan-fried partridge breast; shoulder of lamb; and a good vegetarian selection.

Closed: Sun eve **Bar Meals** L served all wk 12-2 D served Tue-Sat 6-9 **Restaurant** L served all wk 12-2 D served Tue-Sat 6-9 ⊕ FREE HOUSE ◀ Nethergate Suffolk County, Woodforde's Wherry, Buffy's Hopleaf, Wolf Ale, Golden Jackal, Lavender Honey Ö Aspall. ♥ 10 **Facilities** Family room Dogs allowed Garden Parking

THORPENESS
Map 13 TM45

The Dolphin Inn ♥

Peace Place IP16 4NA ☎ 01728 454994
e-mail: info@thorpenessdolphin.com
dir: A12 onto A1094 & follow Thorpeness signs

A traditional inn and village shop in the heart of Thorpeness, The Dolphin offers Adnams ales, Aspall cider and lots of local food, including fish. In summer, you can enjoy a barbeque in the sprawling garden. The pub's interior is equally inviting, with a large fireplace and pine furniture. A meal might include potted Orford shrimps with toast; Musks pork and leek sausages with butternut mash and onion gravy; and lemon cheesecake with fig compote.

Closed: Sun eve & Mon in winter **Bar Meals** L served all wk 12-2.30 booking required D served all wk 6.30-9.30 booking required **Restaurant** L served all wk 12-2.30 booking required D served all wk 6.30-9.30 booking required ⊕ FREE HOUSE ◀ Adnams Best, Adnams Broadside, Rusty Bucket, Nautilus, Mid Summer Gold Ö Aspall. ♥ 8 **Facilities** Children's menu Dogs allowed Garden Parking

TOSTOCK
Map 13 TL96

Gardeners Arms

IP30 9PA ☎ 01359 270460
e-mail: brandon@brandonmchaledesigns.com
dir: A14 follow signs to Tostock, turn at slip road through Beyton. Left at T-junct over A14 turn left into Tostock. 1st right to end of road, pub on right

Parts of this charming pub, at the end of the village green, near the horse chestnut tree, date back 600 years. The basic bar menu - salads, grills, ploughman's, sandwiches, toasties, etc - is supplemented by specials boards offering six starters and 12 main courses in the evening. Look out for lamb balti, Thai king prawn green curry, steak and kidney pie, and chicken and stilton roulade. There's a large grassy garden.

Open 11.30-3 7-11 (Fri-Sat 11.30-3 7-12) Closed: Mon L **Bar Meals** L served Thu-Sun 11.30-3 D served Thu-Sat 7-9 ⊕ GREENE KING ◀ Greene King IPA, Greene King Abbot, Greene King seasonal ales. **Facilities** Dogs allowed Garden Parking

WALBERSWICK
Map 13 TM47

PICK OF THE PUBS

The Anchor NEW ◉◉ ♥

Main St IP18 6UA
☎ 01502 722112 ▤ 01502 724464
e-mail: info@anchoratwalberswick.com
dir: Please telephone for directions

A 1920s Arts and Crafts building located within earshot of the sea and run with passion and personality by Sophie and Mark Dorber. Her zealous dedication to local ingredients, including vegetables from her allotment, and skill in the kitchen is more than matched by his vast knowledge of beer and wines, the short perfectly seasonal menu pairing each flavour-packed dish with a different suggestion for beer and wine by the glass. Cooking is unpretentious, striking an interesting modern note, yielding the likes of double-baked Green's cheddar soufflé with caramelised onions, braised Blythburgh pork belly with Savoy cabbage and cider jus, and Hoegaarden braised rabbit's legs and peppered loin with buttered leeks and turnip gratin. Expect a relaxed atmosphere and a contemporary feel to the spruced-up bar, with its blue, sand and stone décor reflecting its seaside location, and rear dining room. The splendid rear terrace and garden overlook a beach-hut-dotted horizon.

Open all wk **Bar Meals** L served all wk 12-3 D served all wk 6-9 Av main course £13.25 **Restaurant** L served all wk 12-3 booking required D served all wk 6-9 booking required Av 3 course à la carte fr £24.50 ◀ Adnams Bitter, Broadside, Seasonal Ö Aspalls. ♥ 16 **Facilities** Children's menu Family room Dogs allowed Garden Parking

PICK OF THE PUBS

Bell Inn ♥

Ferry Rd IP18 6TN
☎ 01502 723109 ▤ 01502 722728
e-mail: thebell@adnams.co.uk
dir: From A12 take B1387, follow to beyond village green, bear right down track

The inn dates back 600 years and is located near the village green, beach and the ancient fishing harbour on the River Blyth. The large garden has beach and sea views, while the building's great age is evident from the interior's low beams, stone-flagged floors, high wooden settles and open fires. Adnams furnishes the bar with Broadside and Spindrift among others, while Suffolk cyder maker Aspall is also well represented. (Aspall has spelt its cyder with a 'y' since the 1920s, reputedly to reflect the refined quality of the family firm's multi-award-winning product.) Food is all home cooked with local produce featuring strongly, particularly fresh fish. Specialities include starters of locally smoked sprats or Suffolk smokies — flaked smoked haddock in a creamy cheese sauce — both served with granary toast and a salad garnish. There are non-fish dishes too, like baked Suffolk ham or lamb burger in toasted ciabatta.

Open all wk **Bar Meals** L served all wk 12-2 D served all wk 7-9 ⊕ ADNAMS ◀ Adnams Bitter, Broadside, Regatta, Old Ale, Explorer, Spindrift Ö Aspall. ♥ 15 **Facilities** Children's menu Family room Dogs allowed Garden Parking

WESTLETON
Map 13 TM46

PICK OF THE PUBS

The Westleton Crown ★★★ HL ◉◉ ♥

See Pick of the Pubs on opposite page

SURREY

ABINGER
Map 6 TQ14

PICK OF THE PUBS

The Stephan Langton ♥

Friday St RH5 6JR ☎ 01306 730775
e-mail: info@stephan-langton.co.uk
dir: *Exit A25 between Dorking & Guildford at Hollow Lane, W of Wootton. 1.5m then left into Friday St. At end of hill right at pond*

A brick and timber-built country pub, set in a tranquil valley, The Stephan Langton is named after a 13th-century local boy who later, as Archbishop of Canterbury, helped draw up the Magna Carta. A copy of the document is pinned to a wall by the bar. The current building dates from the 1930s, though looks older, and replaces its predecessor which burnt down. The lunchtime food, like the decor, is unpretentious, but will go down well following a strenuous walk through some of Surrey's most challenging terrain, not least Leith Hill, the highest summit in south-east England. From the daily blackboard come toasted panini with home-made soup; pork pie with piccalilli; and pan-fried pollock with crushed potatoes and leaf salad. From the dinner menu expect the likes of Aberdeen Angus rib-eye steak with horseradish layered potatoes; or confit belly of pork with cumin, haricot beans and chorizo.

Open all wk 11-3 5-10.30 (Sat 11-11 Sun 11-9) **Bar Meals** L served Tue-Sun 12-30-2.30 D served Tue-Sat 7-9 Av main course £10 **Restaurant** L served Tue-Sun 12.30-2.30 D served Tue-Sat 7-9 booking required Fixed menu price fr £18.50 Av 3 course à la carte fr £28.50 ⊕ FREE HOUSE ◀ Fuller's London Pride, Hogsback TEA, Shere Drop ♂ Stowford Press, Old Rosie Scrumpy. ♥ 14 **Facilities** Children's menu Dogs allowed Garden Parking

---

The Volunteer ♥

Water Ln, Sutton RH5 6PR
☎ 01306 730798 📠 01306 731621
dir: *Between Guildford & Dorking, 1m S of A25*

Enjoying a delightful rural setting with views over the River Mole, this popular village pub was originally farm cottages and first licensed about 1870. An ideal watering hole for walkers who want to relax over a pint in the attractive pub garden. Typical fish dishes include lobster thermidor, Mediterranean squid pasta and fillet of sea bass, while Thai coconut chicken, partridge with red wine and junipers and fillet of braised beef on fennel feature among the meat dishes.

Open all day all wk 11.30-11 (Sat 11-11 Sun noon-11) Closed: 25 Dec **Bar Meals** L served Mon-Sat 12-9.30, Sun & BH 12-8 D served Mon-Sat 12-9.30, Sun & BH 12-8 food served all day **Restaurant** L served Mon-Sat 12-9.30, Sun & BH 12-8 D served Mon-Sat 12-9.30, Sun & BH 12-8 food served all day ⊕ HALL & WOODHOUSE ◀ Badger Tanglefoot, King & Barns Sussex, plus guest ales ♂ Stowford Press. ♥ 9 **Facilities** Dogs allowed Garden Parking

---

ALBURY
Map 6 TQ04

The Drummond Arms Inn ♥

The Street GU5 9AG
☎ 01483 202039 📠 01483 205361
e-mail: drummondarms@aol.com
dir: *6m from Guildford*

Triple gables at the second-floor level add an interesting architectural twist to this village pub, set in an attractive garden overlooking the River Tillingbourne. The menu offers sandwiches, old favourites (fish and chips; sausage and mash), and regular main courses such as braised lamb shank, or chicken New Yorker (with barbecue sauce and mozzarella cheese); fish dishes feature strongly. There is also a choice of daily specials.

Open all day all wk 11-11 (Fri-Sat 11-mdnt, Sun noon-10.30) **Bar Meals** L served Mon-Fri 12-3, Sat-Sun 12-3.30 D served Mon-Sat 6-9.30, Sun 6-9 ⊕ MERLIN INNS LTD ◀ Courage Best, London Pride, Shere Drop. ♥ 8 **Facilities** Family room Dogs allowed Garden Parking

The Bat and Ball Freehouse

Bat and Ball Lane, Boundstone, Farnham, Surrey GU10 4SA
www.thebatandball.co.uk

Tel: 01252 792108
E-mail: info@thebatandball.co.uk

The Bat and Ball Freehouse nestles in the bottom of the Bourne valley in Boundstone near Farnham. Over 150 years old, the Pub has a relaxed, rural feel, surrounded by woodland and wildlife, and is the focal point of 5 footpaths which connect to local villages. Customers can eat or drink throughout the Pub, patio area and the large south-facing garden (which backs onto the Bourne stream and has a popular children's play structure). All the food is cooked in-house and this is very much a pub that serves restaurant quality food and not a restaurant that sells beer! The bar area has both a traditional and modern style to it to provide for our differing customer tastes, both young and old, and we have a tempting selection of 6 well-kept Cask Ales.

William IV

Little London GU5 9DG ☎ **01483 202685**
web: www.williamivalbury.com
dir: *Just off A25 between Guildford & Dorking. Near Shere*

This quaint country pub is just a stone's throw from Guildford yet deep in the heart of the Surrey Hills conservation area. It is great walking and riding country, and the attractive garden is ideal for post-ramble relaxation. A choice of real ales and a daily changing blackboard menu of proper home-cooked pub food are all part of the appeal. Home-produced, free-range, rare-breed pork usually features, alongside steak and chips and battered cod.

Open all wk 11-3 5.30-11 (Sun noon-3 7-11) Closed: 25 Dec **Bar Meals** L served all wk 12-2 booking required D served Mon-Sat 7-9 booking required Av main course €9.50 **Restaurant** Av 3 course à la carte fr £18.50 ⊕ FREE HOUSE ◀ Flowers IPA, Hogs Back, Surrey Hills Brewery Ö Westons Stowford Press, Bounds Brand Scrumpy. **Facilities** Dogs allowed Garden Parking

The Red Lion ★★★ INN ♀

Old Rd, Buckland RH3 7DS
☎ **01737 843336** ▯ **01737 845242**
e-mail: info@redlionbetchworth.co.uk
dir: *Telephone for directions*

The family-run Red Lion dates back to 1795 and is set in 18 acres with a cricket ground, a 230-year-old wisteria and rolling countryside views, all just 15 minutes from Gatwick Airport. A vaulted cellar accommodates a function room, and six en suite bedrooms are available in a separate self-contained block. The menu offers a pie of the week, fresh beer-battered pollack with hand cut chips, home-made burger, bangers and mash, and wild mushroom linguine. The area is ideal for walkers.

Open all day all wk 11am-11.30pm (Fri-Sat 11am-mdnt) **Bar Meals** L served Sun-Fri 12-2.30, Sat 12-4 **Restaurant** L served Mon-Fri 12-2.30, Sat-Sun 12-4 D served all wk 6-9 ⊕ PUNCH TAVERNS ◀ Fuller's London Pride, Adnams Broadside, Adnams Bitter, guest ale. ♀ 10 **Facilities** Children's menu Dogs allowed Garden Parking Rooms 6

The Villagers Inn ♀

Blackheath Ln GU4 8RB ☎ **01483 893152**
e-mail: info@thevillagersinn.co.uk

More than a hundred years old, this free house stands on the edge of Blackheath, a natural woodland area of several square miles in the heart of Surrey. A menu of traditional pub food includes steak and kidney pie, chicken pie, and fillet steak. A covered patio extends the opportunity for alfresco dining. Real ales are represented by London Pride, Surrey Hill Shere Drop and Weltons Horsham Best.

Open all wk 12-3 6-11 (Sun 12-11) **Bar Meals** L served Mon-Sat 12-2.30, Sun 12-3 D served Mon-Sat 6.45-9.30 ⊕ FREE HOUSE ◀ Surrey Hill Shere Drop, Weltons Horsham Best, Sussex Best, London Pride, guest ale Ö Stowford Press. ♀ 6 **Facilities** Play area Dogs allowed Garden Parking

Jolly Farmer Inn ♀

High St GU5 0HB ☎ **01483 893355** ▯ **01483 890484**
e-mail: enquiries@jollyfarmer.co.uk
dir: *From Guildford take A281 (Horsham road). Bramley 3.5m S of Guildford*

The family that own this friendly 16th-century free house (for nearly 40 years) have a passion for cask ales, and you'll always find up to eight real ales and six lagers, as well as an impressive range of Belgian bottled beers. All meals are freshly cooked to order: expect the likes of chargrilled swordfish loin steak, coq au vin, and butternut squash risotto on the specials board, alongside old favourites such as local pork and herb sausages.

Open all day all wk 11-11 **Bar Meals** L served all wk 12-2.30 D served all wk 6-9.30 **Restaurant** L served all wk 12-2.30 D served all wk 6-9.30 ⊕ FREE HOUSE ◀ 8 continually changing cask ales Ö Westons Stowford Press. ♀ 16 **Facilities** Children's menu Dogs allowed Garden Parking

The Crown Inn ★★★★★ INN ♀

The Green GU8 4TX ☎ **01428 682255** ▯ **01428 685736**
dir: *On A283 between Milford & Petworth*

Historic inn, dating back over 700 years, with lots of charming features, including ancient panelling, open fires, distinctive carvings, huge beams and eight comfortable bedrooms. Reliable food ranges from sausage and mash with onion gravy, chicken tagliatelle, freshly battered fish and chips, and decent sandwiches, warm salads and ploughman's at lunchtime, to Torbay sole, monkfish and tiger prawns pan-fried with ginger and lime cream sauce and served on tagliatelle, and roast duck with sweet plum sauce on the evening menu.

Open all wk ⊕ HALL & WOODHOUSE ◀ London Pride, Moon Dance, Crown Bitter, Summer Lightning. ♀ 9 **Facilities** Dogs allowed Garden **Rooms** 8

The Swan Inn & Restaurant ♀

Petworth Rd GU8 4TY
☎ **01428 682073** ▯ **01428 683259**
e-mail: the-swan-inn@btconnect.com
dir: *10m from Guildford city centre. Between Petworth & Godalming on A283*

This appealing 14th-century village pub successfully manages to balance the traditional and contemporary, with bare floors, wooden furniture and big leather sofas giving a relaxed, stylish feel. The chef makes impressive use of quality produce: look out for lamb shank; Cumberland sausages; tournedos of poached or roast salmon; and rib-eye steak with spinach, fries and peppercorn sauce.

Open all wk ⊕ FREE HOUSE ◀ Hogs Back TEA, Ringwood Best, Fuller's London Pride. ♀ 15 **Facilities** Garden Parking

CHURT
Map 5 SU83

PICK OF THE PUBS

Pride of the Valley ⬤

Tilford Rd GU10 2LH
☎ 01428 605799 📠 01428 605875
e-mail: reservations@prideofthevalleyhotel.com
dir: *4m from Farnham on outskirts of Churt Village. 3m from Haslemere town*

Built in 1867, the Pride of the Valley is a former coaching inn with its own lovely garden set in the heart of the Surrey countryside. Nearby are the Devil's Jumps beauty spot and Frensham Common for super walks and scenery, and the sculpture park for art appreciation. The inn was frequented by former Prime Minister David Lloyd George when he lived in the area, and then by Britain's first Formula One champion Mike Hawthorn. This association is celebrated with a number of period photos of Hawthorn in the bar. Locally brewed beers are served, and food is locally sourced from Surrey and Hampshire. The monthly changing menu reflects the current season, with dishes such trout rillettes with mini toasts and beetroot dressing; slow roast organic mutton pudding with braised Savoy cabbage and red wine sauce; and hot chocolate fondant with cinnamon ice cream and chocolate sauce.

Open all wk **Bar Meals** L served Mon-Sat 12-2.30, Sun 12-3 D served all wk 6.30-9.30 Av main course £8.95 **Restaurant** L served Tue-Sun 12-2.30 booking required D served Tue-Sat 6.30-9.30 booking required Av 3 course à la carte fr £26 ⊕ FREE HOUSE ◖ Hogs Back TEA, Hogs Back Bitter, Ringwood 49er. ⬤ 8 **Facilities** Children's menu Dogs allowed Garden Parking

CLAYGATE
Map 6 TQ16

Swan Inn & Lodge ⬤

2 Hare Ln KT10 9BS ☎ 01372 462582
e-mail: info@swaninn.net
web: www.theswanlodge.net
dir: *At Esher/Oxshott junct of A3 take A244 towards Esher. Right at 1st lights, pub 300yds on right*

Rebuilt in 1905 overlooking the village green and cricket pitch, yet barely 15 miles from Charing Cross. There's an attractively furnished Continental-style bar and a Thai restaurant offering nearly 75 starters, soups, curries, stir-fries, and seafoods. The Thai menu is available at lunchtime and in the evenings, as are calamari, Cajun chicken burgers, scampi, roast beef and lamb, and paninis. Dishes of the day appear on the specials board.

Open all day all wk noon-11 **Bar Meals** L served Mon-Sat 12-10, Sun 12-5 D served Mon-Sat 12-10 food served all day ⊕ WELLINGTON PUB COMPANY ◖ London Pride, Old Speckled Hen, Woodforde's Wherry. ⬤ 8 **Facilities** Play area Family room Dogs allowed Garden Parking

COBHAM
Map 6 TQ16

The Cricketers ⬤

Downside KT11 3NX
☎ 01932 862105 📠 01932 868186
e-mail: info@thecricketersdownside.co.uk
dir: *M25 junct 10, A3 towards London. 1st exit signed Cobham. Straight over 1st rdbt, right at 2nd. In 1m right opposite Waitrose into Downside Bridge Rd*

Traditional, family-run pub, parts of which date back to 1540, with beamed ceilings and log fires. The inn's charming rural setting makes it popular with walkers, and the pretty River Mole is close by. There is a salad and light meals menu, with dishes like fishcakes and Barnsley chops. The main menu offers pan-fried cod fillet with saffron mash, steamed mussels and creamy sorrel sauce, or lamb shank cooked in aromatics and red wine sauce.

Open all wk ⊕ ENTERPRISE INNS ◖ Old Speckled Hen, London Pride, IPA. ⬤ 9 **Facilities** Play area Dogs allowed Garden Parking

COLDHARBOUR
Map 6 TQ14

PICK OF THE PUBS

The Plough Inn ⬤

Coldharbour Ln RH5 6HD
☎ 01306 711793 📠 01306 710055
e-mail: ploughinn@btinternet.com
dir: *M25 junct 9, A24 to Dorking. A25 towards Guildford. Coldharbour signed from one-way system*

For 16 years, the husband-and-wife owners of this 17th-century pub have been slowly rebuilding, refurbishing and upgrading it to create a warm, welcoming hostelry with superb food, and - since 1996 - its own traditional English ales (Crooked Farrow, Tallywhacker). This labour of love perhaps results from the air here - the pub is 25 minutes walk from the top of Leith Hill, southern England's highest point. A well-worn smugglers' route from the coast to London once passed its door, which probably explains why the resident ghost is a matelot. The surrounding North Downs draw customers in the shape of walkers, horseback riders, cyclists, and Londoners simply anxious to escape the city and relax in convivial surroundings. Food is freshly prepared and home cooked, while three real fires in winter and candlelight in the evenings create a suitable ambience. Dishes might include steak and real ale pie; beef Wellington with rosemary roast potatoes; traditionally smoked haddock with herb mash and three cheese sauce. Home-made desserts like banoffee pie are irresistible;

and the collection of fine wines completes a thoroughly agreeable experience.

Open all day all wk 11.30am-mdnt (Fri-Sat 11.30am-1am) Closed: 25 Dec **Bar Meals** L served Mon-Fri 12-2.30, Sat-Sun 12-3 D served Mon-Sat 6.30-9.30, Sun 6.30-9 Av main course £10.95 **Restaurant** L served Mon-Fri 12-2.30, Sat-Sun 12-3 booking required D served Mon-Sat 6.30-9.30, Sun 6.30-9 booking required Fixed menu price fr £9.95 Av 3 course à la carte fr £18.15 ⊕ FREE HOUSE ◖ Crooked Furrow, Leith Hill Tallywhacker, Ringwood Old Thumper, Timothy Taylor Landlord, Shepherd Neame Best Bitter. ⬤ 8 **Facilities** Dogs allowed Garden Parking

COMPTON
Map 6 SU94

The Withies Inn ⬤

Withies Ln GU3 1JA ☎ 01483 421158 📠 01483 425904
dir: *Telephone for directions*

Set amid unspoiled country on Compton Common, just below the Hog's Back, this low-beamed, 16th-century pub has been carefully modernised to incorporate a small restaurant. There is also a splendid garden where meals are served in the pergola. Snacks are available in the bar, while in the restaurant there is a selection from the chargrill, and dishes such as poached halibut with prawns and brandy sauce; home-cooked steak, kidney and mushroom pie; and steak Diane flambé.

Open 11-3 6-11 (Fri 11-11) Closed: Sun eve **Bar Meals** L served all wk 12-2.30 D served Mon-Sat 7-10 **Restaurant** L served all wk 12-2.30 D served Mon-Sat 7-10 ⊕ FREE HOUSE ◖ TEA, Sussex, Adnams. ⬤ 8 **Facilities** Children's menu Dogs allowed Garden Parking

DUNSFOLD
Map 6 TQ03

The Sun Inn ⬤

The Common GU8 4LE
☎ 01483 200242 📠 01483 201141
e-mail: suninn@dunsfold.net
dir: *A281 through Shalford & Bramley, take B2130 to Godalming. Dunsfold on left after 2m*

A traditional 500-year-old family-run inn in a chocolate box village, set opposite the cricket green and village pond. Inside the welcome is warm, with blazing fires and an array of real ales including Adnams and Harveys. Home-made food includes the house speciality of Aberdeen Angus burgers, plenty of vegetarian options, and Sunday lunches brimming with fresh vegetables.

hildren have a menu of their favourites; alternatively
any main courses, such as beef lasagne or wholetail
campi, can be served in smaller portions.

pen all wk 11-3 5-mdnt (Fri-Sun 11am-mdnt) **Bar
Meals** L served all wk 12-2.30 D served Tue-Sat 5-9.15,
un 6-8.30 Av main course £8.85 **Restaurant** L served all
k 12-2.30 D served Tue-Sat 7-9.15, Sun 7-8.30 Fixed
enu price fr £5.95 ⊕ PUNCH TAVERNS ◼ Harveys
ussex, Adnams, Speckled Hen, Tribute, Guinness
Westons Old Rosie. ♈ 9 **Facilities** Children's menu
ogs allowed Garden Parking

EFFINGHAM   Map 6 TQ15

he Plough ♈

restan Ln KT24 5SW
☎ 01372 458121   🖨 01372 458121
r: *Between Guildford & Leatherhead on A246*

he Plough provides a peaceful retreat in a rural setting
ose to Polesden Lacy National Trust property. It is
cated on a no-through road in a picturesque village and
as a good crowd of regulars. The pub has a reputation
r freshly prepared food at reasonable prices. The
onthly changing menu might offer garlic and rosemary
mb leg; spicy mixed bean casserole; and sea bream
let with new potatoes and creamed leeks.

pen all wk 11.30-3 5.30-11 (Sun noon-3 7-10.30)
osed: 25- 26 Dec & 1 Jan eve **Bar Meals** L served all wk
2-2.30 booking required D served Mon-Sat 7-10, Sun
9 booking required Av main course £10.95
estaurant L served all wk 12-2.30 booking required D
rved Mon-Sat 7-10, Sun 7-9 booking required ⊕ YOUNG
CO BREWERY PLC ◼ Youngs IPA, Special, Winter
armer, Bombardier, Courage Directors. ♈ 12
acilities Garden Parking

EGHAM   Map 6 TQ07

he Fox and Hounds ♈

shopgate Rd, Englefield Green TW20 0XU
☎ 01784 433098   🖨 01784 438775
-mail: thefoxandhounds@4cinns.co.uk
r: *From village green left into Castle Hill Rd, then right
to Bishopsgate Rd*

e Surrey border once ran through the centre of this pub,
the edge of Windsor Great Park, convenient for walkers
nd riders. Features include a large garden, handsome
nservatory and weekly jazz nights. Menus offer a range
daily-changing fish specials as well as dishes like
ange and sesame chicken fillets on coriander and lime
odles, or roast pork with grain mustard glaze and
armesan crisps.

pen all wk ◼ Hogs Back Brewery Traditional English
e, Brakspears Bitter. ♈ 8 **Facilities** Dogs allowed
arden Parking

ELSTEAD   Map 6 SU94

PICK OF THE PUBS

The Woolpack ♈

The Green GU8 6HD
☎ 01252 703106   🖨 01252 705914
e-mail: woolpack.elstead@yahoo.co.uk
dir: *A3 S, take Milford exit, follow signs for Elstead
on B3001*

Originally a wool exchange dating to the 17th century,
The Woolpack has been many things, including a
butcher's shop and a bicycle repairer's, before
becoming the popular pub it is today. The surrounding
hundreds of acres of common land attract ramblers
galore, especially at lunchtime, and their arrival in the
bar is often heralded by the rustle of protective plastic
shopping bags over their muddy boots. In the carpeted
bar, weaving shuttles and other remnants of the wool
industry make appealing features, as do the open log
fires, low beams, high-backed settles, window seats
and spindle-backed chairs. A good range of cask-
conditioned beers is offered, and large blackboards
display frequently changing main meals, sandwiches,
ploughman's and burgers. Menus are planned around
the best local produce, taking account of the seasons,
and choices range from a traditional sausages and
mash to pan-fried sea bass with couscous. Leave room
for home-made dessert.

Open all wk noon-3 5.30-11 (Sat-Sun noon-11) **Bar
Meals** L served all wk 12.2.30 booking required D
served all wk 7-9.30 booking required Av main course
£12 **Restaurant** L served all wk 12-2.30 booking
required D served all wk 7-9.30 booking required Av 3
course à la carte fr £24 ⊕ PUNCH TAVERNS ◼ Greene
King Abbot Ale, Hobgoblin, Youngs, Spitfire, London
Pride Ò Old English. ♈ 40 **Facilities** Children's menu
Family room Dogs allowed Garden Parking

EPSOM   Map 6 TQ26

White Horse ♈

63 Dorking Rd KT18 7JU ☎ 01372 726622
e-mail: enquiries@whitehorseepsom.com
dir: *On A24 next to Epsom General Hospital*

The town's oldest surviving pub focuses on four areas -
real ales, freshly cooked traditional British food, being
family friendly and, as host of the Epsom Jazz Club on
Tuesday evenings, live entertainment. Typical starters are
hot smoked salmon pâté or creamy garlic mushrooms:
mains include chef's own pie of the week, fresh fish of
the week and curry of the day; or braised lamb shank on
herb mash. A carvery is available on Saturday and
Sunday.

Closed: Mon until 6pm **Bar Meals** Av main course £8 food
served all day **Restaurant** food served all day ⊕ PUNCH
TAVERNS ◼ guest ales. ♈ 7 **Facilities** Children's menu
Play area Family room Dogs allowed Garden Parking

FARNHAM   Map 5 SU84

The Bat & Ball Freehouse ♈

15 Bat & Ball Ln, Boundstone GU10 4SA
☎ 01252 792108
e-mail: info@thebatandball.co.uk
dir: *From A31 Farnham bypass follow signs for Birdworld.
Left at Bengal Lounge into School Hill. At top over
staggered x-rds into Sandrock Hill Rd. After 0.25m left
into Upper Bourne Lane, signed*

Tucked down a lane in a wooded valley south of Farnham,
this 150-year-old inn is worth hunting out. The interior
features oak beams, a roaring fire on colder days, and
plenty of cricketing memorabilia. Outside is a children's
play area and a lovely garden with vine-topped pergola
that backs onto the Bourne stream. Expect excellent ales,
a choice of six at any one time, and a varied selection of
home-cooked food: perhaps Wensleydale, apple and
walnut pâté followed by coq au vin, home-made pie or
half duck slow roasted in orange, apricots and vermouth.

Open all wk 11-11 (Sun noon-10.30) **Bar Meals** L served
Mon-Sat 12-2.15, Sun 12-3 booking required D served
Mon-Sat 7-9.30, Sun 6-8.30 booking required Av main
course £10.50 ⊕ FREE HOUSE ◼ Youngs Bitter, Tongham
TEA, Triple FFF, Harvey's Sussex Bitter, Hop Back. ♈ 8
Facilities Children's menu Play area Family room Dogs
allowed Garden Parking

See advertisement on page 438

FOREST GREEN   Map 6 TQ14

PICK OF THE PUBS

The Parrot Inn ♈

RH5 5RZ ☎ 01306 621339   🖨 01306 621255
e-mail: drinks@theparrot.co.uk
dir: *B2126 from A29 at Ockley, signed Forest Green*

Set opposite the village green and cricket pitch in a
rural hamlet, this attractive 17th-century building is in
many ways the archetypal British inn. But besides the
expected oak beams and huge fire, it also has its own
butchery, charcuterie and farm shop. The owners have
a farm just a couple of miles away where they raise
shorthorn cattle, saddleback pigs, Suffolk sheep and
Black Rock hens. The pub makes its own sausages,
preserves and chutneys, and much of the menu uses
home-grown or home-made produce. The dishes blend
modern, traditional and European influences: perhaps

continued

FOREST GREEN *continued*

coarse pork, hare and juniper berry terrine with fruit chutney and home-made bread, followed by slow-braised shorthorn beef in Guinness with sautéed potatoes and purple sprouting broccoli. Not to be forgotten is a good range of real ales, which can be enjoyed in the bar or one of the four pub gardens.

Open all day all wk **Bar Meals** L served Mon-Sat 12-3, Sun 12-5 D served Mon-Sat 6-10 Av main course £10 **Restaurant** L served Mon-Sat 12-3, Sun 12-5 booking required D served Mon-Sat 6-10 booking required Av 3 course à la carte fr £24 ⊕ FREE HOUSE ◀ Ringwood Best, Youngs PA, Timothy Taylor Landlord, Sharp's Doom Bar, Ringwood Old Thumper. ♀ 14 **Facilities** Dogs allowed Garden Parking

---

GUILDFORD Map 6 SU94

The Keystone ♀

3 Portsmouth Rd GU2 4BL ☎ 01483 575089
e-mail: drink@thekeystone.co.uk
dir: *0.5m from Guildford train station. Turn right from station. Cross 2nd pedestrian crossing, follow road downhill. Past Savills Estate Agents. Pub 200yds on left*

From its outdoor seating areas to the wooden floors and leather sofas in the bar, this town pub has a stylish, well-kept feel. Themed nights, live music and a book swap facility are just some of the distinctive ideas to look out for. Expect fairly priced, modern pub food, with award-winning home-made pies a speciality. Other dishes include pan-fried sea bass with ratatouille and rice; cherry tomato, black olive and melted brie tart; and wild boar sausages with braised red cabbage.

Open all wk noon-11 (Fri-Sat noon-mdnt Sun noon-7) Closed: 25-26 Dec, 1 Jan **Bar Meals** L served Mon-Fri 12-3, Sat-Sun 12-5 D served Mon-Thu 6-9 Av main course £8.50 ◀ Black Sheep, 6X, Guinness, guest ale Ö Westons Organic. ♀ 10 **Facilities** Children's menu Garden

---

HASCOMBE Map 6 TQ03

The White Horse ♀

The Street GU8 4JA ☎ 01483 208258 ▤ 01483 208200
dir: *From Godalming take B2130. Pub on left 0.5m after Hascombe*

Freshly prepared, locally sourced food is always on the menu at this friendly pub owned by John Beckett (a local farmer) and Ossie Gray (River Café). Surrounded by picturesque walking country, the 16th-century building is unmissable in summer thanks to its flower-filled garden. A meal might include field mushroom and spinach tart with roasted tomatoes, followed by grilled sea bass with roasted tomatoes and new potatoes; or grilled rib-eye steak with gratin dauphinoise.

Open all wk ⊕ PUNCH TAVERNS ◀ Harveys, Adnams Broadside, Black Sheep Bitter, Youngs. ♀ 6 **Facilities** Dogs allowed Garden Parking

---

HASLEMERE Map 6 SU93

The Wheatsheaf Inn ★★★ INN ♀

Grayswood Rd, Grayswood GU27 2DE
☎ 01428 644440 ▤ 01428 641285
e-mail: thewheatsheaf@aol.com
web: www.thewheatsheafgrayswood.co.uk
dir: *Exit A3 at Milford, A286 to Haslemere. Grayswood approx 7.5m N*

A stunning display of hanging baskets adorns this Edwardian village inn at the start of one of Surrey's loveliest walks. The three chefs provide a high standard of cuisine, showcased in themed evenings. You might encounter fillet of beef stroganoff; spinach, cherry tomatoes, pine nuts ad pesto on fusilli; or pan-fried lamb's liver and bacon on bubble and squeak. The magnificent viewpoint at Black Down, beloved of Alfred, Lord Tennyson, is nearby.

Open all wk 11-3 6-11 (Sun noon-3 7-10.30) **Bar Meals** L served all wk 12-2 booking required D served all wk 7-9.45 booking required **Restaurant** L served all wk 12-2 booking required D served all wk 7-9.45 booking required ⊕ FREE HOUSE ◀ Greene King, London Pride, Sharp's Eden Ale, Old Speckled Hen Ö Thatchers. ♀ 8 **Facilities** Garden Parking **Rooms** 7

HINDHEAD Map 6 SU83

Devil's Punchbowl Inn ★★ HL ♀

London Rd GU26 6AG
☎ 01428 606565 ▤ 01428 605713
e-mail: hotel@punchbowlhotels.co.uk
dir: *A3 N of Hindhead, opp National Trust car park for Devils Punch Bowl*

The hotel, which dates from the early 1800s, stands 900 above sea level with wonderful views as far as London o a clear day. The 'punchbowl' is a large natural bowl in the ground across the road. The menu, while not large, has something for everybody, with chilli con carne, steal and Guinness pie, Surrey shepherds pie, sausage and mash, and hand-made burger with chunky chips.

Open all wk ⊕ ELDRIDGE POPE ◀ Bass, 6X, Tetleys, Bombardier. ♀ 15 **Facilities** Family room Garden Parking **Rooms** 32

LEIGH Map 6 TQ24

The Plough ♀

Church Rd RH2 8NJ ☎ 01306 611348 ▤ 01306 6112[9]
e-mail: sarah@theploughleigh.wanadoo.co.uk
dir: *Telephone for directions*

This welcoming country pub stands opposite St Bartholomew's Church overlooking the village green. There is always a great atmosphere here and the quaint low beams are conveniently padded! The comprehensive menu is supplemented by daily specials, and dishes range from nachos, jacket potatoes and salads like war bacon, black pudding and potato in the bar to braised lamb shank in redcurrant and mint gravy, or sea bass fillet with champagne and asparagus sauce from the main menu in the restaurant area. Home-made pies go down well, as do puddings like Mars bar cheesecake. Children and dogs welcome.

Open all wk 11-11 (Sun noon-11) **Bar Meals** Av main course £9.50 food served all day **Restaurant** Av 3 cours à la carte fr £22.50 food served all day ⊕ HALL & WOODHOUSE ◀ Badger Best, Tanglefoot, Sussex Bitter. ♀ 10 **Facilities** Children's menu Dogs allowed Garden Parking

PICK OF THE PUBS

Hare and Hounds ♥

Common Rd RH7 6BZ
☎ 01342 832351　📠 01342 832351
e-mail: info@hareandhoundspublichouse.co.uk
dir: From A22 follow signs for Lingfield Racecourse into
Common Rd

An 18th-century country pub close to Lingfield Park
racecourse, the Hare and Hounds has great charm and
character. Enjoy the relaxing atmosphere by the fire,
the candlelit snug or just propping up the bar. The pub
has a good name for its modern and classic food. The
new owners have worked in the UK and France and
developed some great seasonal recipes. Using local
suppliers of produce where possible, the dinner menu
may start with light curried parsnip soup with deep-
fried chervil root, or pressed duck terrine with tarragon,
smoked magret and cress salad. Caramelised swede
ravioli with thyme and goats' cheese on toast and
swede linguini is an innovative sample of the
vegetarian fare. For a main course, expect dishes like
roast breast of free range chicken with potato gnocchi,
sweetcorn and baby gem, or confit belly pork and roast
Braeburn apples with celery and macaroni gratin. The
blackboard menu offers braised blade of beef,
seasonal vegetables and tarragon, turmeric dumpling,
or 7 hour roasted lamb shoulder with apricots and figs
and provencal couscous. Head for the split-level
decked garden for a drink in the sun.

Closed: 1 Jan, Sun Eve **Bar Meals** L served Mon-Sat
12-3 D served Mon-Sat 7-10 Av main course £12
Restaurant L served Mon-Sat 12-3 D served Mon-Sat
7-10 Fixed menu price fr £12 Av 3 course à la carte fr
£30 ⊕ PUNCH TAVERNS ◀ Greene King IPA, Flowers
Original, Old Speckled Hen, Guinness. ♥ 8
Facilities Dogs allowed Garden Parking

The Ditton NEW ♥

4 Ditton Hill Rd KT6 5JD ☎ 020 8339 0785
e-mail: goodfood@theditton.co.uk
dir: Please telephone for directions

The old Plough & Harrow has been given a facelift to
return the pub to its former glory and a trendy new name,
the rambling village pub now sports a fresh,
contemporary feel throughout the bar and interconnecting
dining areas. The focus is on family dining and wide-
ranging menus take in classic bar snacks, a mezze
menu, home-made pies, roasts on Sundays, and more
adventurous dishes like pan-fried pork with mash and
sherry sauce. The barbecue menu draws the crowds to
the large garden on warm summer days.

Open all day all wk noon-11 **Bar Meals** L served all wk
12-9 D served all wk 12-9 Av main course £8.95 food
served all day **Restaurant** L served Sat-Sun 12-9 booking
required D served Mon-Sat 12-9 booking required Av 3
course à la carte fr £22.50 ⊕ ENTERPRISE INNS
◀ Bombardier, Youngs, Tanglefoot. ♥ 8
Facilities Children's menu Play area Dogs allowed
Garden Parking

King William IV ♥

Byttom Hill RH5 6EL ☎ 01372 372590
dir: From M25 junct 9, A24 signed to Dorking, pub just
before Mickleham

The former ale house, built in 1790 for workers on Lord
Beaverbrook's estate, has a panelled snug and larger
back bar with an open fire, cast iron tables and
grandfather clock. The terraced garden, ideal for summer
dining, offers panoramic views of the Mole Valley. The
chef proprietor serves good food alongside real ales, with
specials such as roast pheasant breast with red wine jus;
and seared king scallops on crayfish in tomato sauce. An
ideal location for outstanding local walks.

Open all wk Closed: 25 Dec **Bar Meals** L served Mon-Fri
11.45-2, Sat 12-2, Sun 12-5 booking required D served
Tue-Sat 7-9 booking required Av main course £10
Restaurant L served Mon-Fri 11.45-2, Sat 12-2, Sun 12-5
booking required D served Tue-Sat 7-9 booking required
Av 3 course à la carte fr £17 ⊕ FREE HOUSE ◀ Hogs
Back TEA, Adnams Best, guest ales ♻ Stowford
Press. ♥ 11 Facilities Children's menu Garden Parking

The Running Horses ♥

Old London Rd RH5 6DU
☎ 01372 372279　📠 01372 363004
e-mail: info@therunninghorses.co.uk
dir: 1.5m from M25 junct 9. Off A24 between Leatherhead
& Dorking

The Running Horses has been welcoming travellers for
more than 400 years and has a history of sheltering
highwaymen. It stands amid Natural Trust countryside
close to Box Hill. The interior resonates with history, right
down to the bare beams and real fires, but the menus
have a modern edge. Bar food takes in venison and beef
burgers, local sausages, and tempura fish in beer batter,
while the restaurant might offer seared monkfish
wrapped in Parma ham or roast rump of lamb with
beetroot chips.

Open all wk 11.30-11 (Sun noon-10.30) Closed: 25-26
Dec, 31 Dec-1 Jan eve **Bar Meals** L served Mon-Fri
12-2.30, Sat-Sun 12-3 D served Mon-Sat 7-9.30, Sun
6.30-9 Av main course £10 **Restaurant** L served Mon-Fri
12-2.30, Sat-Sun 12-3 booking required D served Mon-
Sat 7-9.30, Sun 6.30-9 booking required Av 3 course à la
carte fr £28 ⊕ PUNCH TAVERNS ◀ Fuller's London Pride,
Young's Bitter, Adnams Bitter, Spitfire. ♥ 9
Facilities Dogs allowed Garden

The Surrey Oaks ♥

Parkgate Rd RH5 5DZ
☎ 01306 631200　📠 01306 631200
e-mail: ken@surreyoaks.co.uk
dir: From A24 follow signs to Newdigate, at T-junct turn
left, pub 1m on left

Picturesque oak-beamed pub located one mile outside
the village of Newdigate. Parts of the building date back
to 1570, and it became an inn around the middle of the
19th century. There are two bars, one with an inglenook
fireplace, as well as a restaurant area, patio and beer
garden with boules pitch. The great selection of beers are
mainly from micro-breweries. A typical specials board
features Barnsley lamb chop with minted gravy, chicken
and ham pie, and grilled plaice with parsley butter.

Open all wk 11.30-2.30 5.30-11 (Sat 11.30-3 6-11 Sun
noon-10.30) **Bar Meals** L served Mon-Fri 12-2, Sat-Sun
12-2.15 D served Tue-Sat 6.30-9.30 Av main course £9
Restaurant L served Mon-Fri 12-2, Sat-Sun 12-2.15 D
served Tue-Sat 6.30-9.30 ⊕ ADMIRAL TAVERNS
◀ Harveys Sussex Best, Surrey Hills Ranmore Ale,
rotating guest ales ♻ Moles Black Rat, Weston's Country
Perry. ♥ 8 Facilities Children's menu Play area Dogs
allowed Garden Parking

PICK OF THE PUBS

Bryce's at The Old School House ◉ ♥

RH5 5TH ☎ 01306 627430　📠 01306 628274
e-mail: bryces.fish@virgin.net
dir: 8m S of Dorking on A29

Formerly a boarding school, this Grade II listed building
dates back to 1750 and was bought by Bill Bryce some
16 years ago. He's passionate about fresh fish and
offers a huge range, despite the location in rural
Surrey. It's more of a restaurant than a pub, although

continued

OCKLEY *continued*

there is a bar with its own interesting menu (chilli salt soft shell crab; half a dozen Loch Fyne oysters; pan-fried herring roes). The dishes on the restaurant menu are nearly all fish - with some non-fish daily specials. Options to start include langoustine bisque and grilled Cornish sardines, while mains take in herb-crusted fillet of pollock with minted pea purée and roast cherry tomatoes; and pan-seared scallops with butternut squash purée, honey roast carrots and ginger foam. Private parties are a speciality.

Open noon-3 6-11 Closed: 25-26 Dec, 1 Jan, (Sun pm Nov, Jan-Feb) **Bar Meals** L served all wk 12-2.30 D served all wk 6-9.30 Av main course £11 **Restaurant** L served all wk 12-2.30 D served all wk 7-9.30 Fixed menu price fr £10 Av 3 course à la carte fr £31 ⊕ FREE HOUSE ◀ London Pride, W J King Sussex, John Smith's Smooth. ♚ 15 **Facilities** Children's menu Dogs allowed Parking

The Kings Arms Inn ♚

Stane St RH5 5TS ☎ 01306 711224
e-mail: enquiries@thekingsarmsockley.co.uk
dir: *From M25 junct 9 take A24 through Dorking towards Horsham, A29 to Ockley*

The many charms of this heavily-beamed 16th-century inn include welcoming log fires, a priest hole, a friendly ghost, and an award-winning garden. Set in the picturesque village of Ockley and overlooked by the tower of Leith Hill, it's an ideal setting in which to enjoy a pint and home-cooked food. Using the best of local produce where possible, expect dishes fillet of beef Stroganoff, pan-fried duck breast with honey and mustard sauce, or roast salmon fillet with cucumber and chorizo salad. Every Saturday and Sunday there is a credit crunch brunch. Sunday roasts include whole hog roast, back by popular demand.

Open all wk noon-2.30 5-11 **Bar Meals** L served all wk 12-2.30 D served all wk 6.30-9.30 Av main course £11 **Restaurant** L served all wk 12-2.30 D served all wk 6.30-9.30 Av 3 course à la carte fr £25 ⊕ CROSSOAK INNS ◀ Horsham Best, Doom Bar, Old Speckled Hen. ♚ 10 **Facilities** Children's menu Garden Parking

PIRBRIGHT   Map 6 SU95

The Royal Oak ♚

Aldershot Rd GU24 0DQ ☎ 01483 232466
dir: *M3 junct 3, A322 towards Guildford, then A324 towards Aldershot*

A genuine old world pub specialising in real ales (up to nine at any time), and well known for its glorious prize-winning garden. The Tudor cottage pub has an oak church door, stained glass windows and pew seating, and in winter there are welcoming log fires in the rambling bars. The menu may include smoked salmon and pesto, braised lamb shoulder, steak and ale pie, and penne pasta Alfredo, along with various specials.

Open all wk ⊕ LAUREL PUB PARTNERSHIPS ◀ Flowers IPA, Hogs Back Traditional English Ale, Bass Ringwood Ale, Abbots Ales, Old Speckled Hen. ♚ 18 **Facilities** Dogs allowed Garden Parking

RIPLEY   Map 6 TQ05

The Talbot Inn NEW ★★★★ INN ⊛

High St GU23 6BB ☎ 01483 225188 📄 01483 211332
e-mail: info@thetalbotinn.com
dir: *Please telephone for directions*

The latest addition to Merchant Inns impressive pub portfolio is this stunningly renovated 15th-century coaching inn. The classic beamed bar contrasts spectacularly with the chic dining room, with its copper ceiling and modern glass conservatory extension. Good food blends pub classics like liver and bacon with more innovative dishes like grilled bream with crab and spring onion risotto and shellfish sauce. Bedrooms are smart and contemporary, ranging from beamed rooms in the inn to new-build rooms overlooking the garden.

Open all day all wk noon-11 (Sun noon-10) **Bar Meals** D served all wk 6-11 booking required Av main course £10 food served all day **Restaurant** L served all wk 12-3 booking required D served all wk 6-9.30 booking required Fixed menu price fr £16 Av 3 course à la carte fr £35 ⊕ MERCHANT INNS ◀ Shere Drop, IPA, Abbot Ale ♖ Stowford Press. **Facilities** Children's menu Dogs allowed Garden Parking **Rooms** 39

SOUTH GODSTONE   Map 6 TQ34

Fox & Hounds ♚

Tilburstow Hill Rd RH9 8LY ☎ 01342 893474
dir: *4m from M25 junct 6*

Parts of this cosy, traditional inn date back to 1368, though Thomas Hart first opened it as a pub in 1601. There's a large inglenook in the restaurant, and a real fire in the lower bar. Specialising in fish and seafood, regular visitors to the specials board might find supremes of marlin pan-fried in Cajun spices; home-made cheese-topped shepherd's pie; and brochettes of sole and tiger prawns. Outside is a large garden with pleasant rural views. The pub is said to have a resident ghost who might once have been a smuggler.

Open all day all wk noon-11 (25 Dec noon-2) **Bar Meals** food served all day **Restaurant** food served all day ⊕ GREENE KING ◀ All Greene King. ♚ 13 **Facilities** Children's menu Dogs allowed Garden Parking

---

STAINES   Map 6 TQ07

The Swan Hotel ♚

The Hythe TW18 3JB
☎ 01784 452494 📄 01784 461593
e-mail: swanhotel@fullers.co.uk
dir: *Just off A308, S of Staines Bridge. 5m from Heathrow*

This 18th-century inn stands just south of Staines Bridge and was once the haunt of river bargemen who were paid in tokens which could be exchanged at the pub for food and drink. It has a spacious, comfortable bar, and a menu based on traditional home-cooked food. Examples range from sausage and mash; pot-roast lamb shank; and steak and ale pie, to seafood risotto or vegetarian noodle bowl.

Open all wk 11-11 **Bar Meals** L served Mon-Sat 12-3, Sun 12-8 D served Mon-Sat 6-10, Sun 12-8 **Restaurant** L served Mon-Sat 12-3, Sun 12-8 D served Mon-Sat 6-10, Sun 12-8 ⊕ FULLER SMITH TURNER PLC ◀ Fuller's London Pride, ESB, Discovery. ♚ 10 **Facilities** Children's menu Dogs allowed Garden

VIRGINIA WATER   Map 6 TQ06

The Wheatsheaf Hotel ♚

London Rd GU25 4QF
☎ 01344 842057 📄 01344 842932
e-mail: wheatsheaf.hotel.4306@thespiritgroup.com
dir: *From M25 junct 13, take A30 towards Bracknell*

The Wheatsheaf dates back to the second half of the 18th century and is beautifully situated overlooking Virginia Water on the edge of Windsor Great Park. Chalkboard menus offer a good range of freshly prepared dishes with fresh fish as a speciality. Popular options are beer battered cod and chips, roast queen fish with pesto crust and braised lamb shank on mustard mash.

Open all wk ⊕ CHEF & BREWER ◀ guest ales. ♚ 6 **Facilities** Family room Garden Parking

WEST CLANDON   Map 6 TQ05

Onslow Arms ♚

The Street GU4 7TE ☎ 01483 222447 📄 01483 211127
e-mail: onslowarms@massivepub.com
dir: *A3 then A247, approx 7m from Guildford*

An old English pub with a French restaurant attached, the Onslow Arms dates from 1623. For the high flying clientele a helipad is provided, and there's a large patio and even larger car park. The Cromwell Bar has a good choice of real ales, and the beamed interior provides a contrast to the contemporary restaurant. L'Auberge serves traditional French cuisine while the separate rotisserie offers an appetising range of soups, salads, omelettes and baguettes.

Open all wk ⊕ MASSIVE LTD ◀ Courage Best & Directors Bombardier Premium, Hogs Back TEA, Pedigree, 2 rotating guest ales. ♚ 11 **Facilities** Dogs allowed Garden Parking

PICK OF THE PUBS

The Inn @ West End ♥

WEST END   Map 6 SU96

42 Guildford Rd GU24 9PW
☎ **01276 858652**
e-mail: greatfood@the-inn.co.uk
web: www.the-inn.co.uk
dir: *On A322 towards Guildford. 3m from M3 junct 3, just beyond Gordon Boys rdbt*

Gerry and Ann Price's unassuming, 200-year-old roadside pub stands three miles from the M3 (J3) and is a culinary beacon in a desert for decent pub food. Hard work for nearly a decade has created a thriving destination dining pub as well as a cracking local for those who love a tip-top pint of Fuller's London Pride and a decent glass of wine. You'll find a light, modern and airy interior, with wooden floors, yellow walls, tasteful check fabrics, crisp linen-clothed tables in the dining area, a warming wood-burner, daily papers and magazines in the bar, and a relaxed and informal atmosphere. An eclectic mix of discerning diners, from ladies who lunch, shooters from the nearby Bisley ranges, business folk and well-heeled locals, beat a path to the door for the excellent modern British dishes listed on imaginative seasonal menus, which are enhanced by daily specials. The kitchen makes good use of home-grown herbs, vegetables and pigs, and locally sourced ingredients, with organic meat from Hyden Organic Farm, game shot by Gerry (the pub has its own game room and plucking machine), and fresh fish collected from the south coast in the pub's own chiller van. This translates to such starters as salmon and dill fishcakes with tartare sauce; wild mushrooms on toast; and chicken liver pâté with Cumberland sauce, and main courses like roast pheasant with redcurrant and thyme jus; slow-roasted lamb with dauphinoise potato and mint jus; roast cod with peas, bacon, basil, lemon oil and herb mash; and Cumberland sausages with mash and caramelised onion gravy. Leave room for chocolate cheesecake with orange-scented anglaise, and crème brûlée with clove and plum shortbread. Explore the extensive, enthusiasts' list of wines (17 by the glass) and don't miss Gerry's wine tasting suppers.

Open all week ⊕ FREE HOUSE ◧ Youngs Bitter, Fuller's London Pride. ♥ 17
Facilities Dogs allowed Garden Parking

WEST END | Map 6 SU96

PICK OF THE PUBS

The Inn @ West End ⬤

See Pick of the Pubs on page 445

WEST HORSLEY | Map 6 TQ05

PICK OF THE PUBS

The King William IV ⬤

83 The Street KT24 6BG
☎ 01483 282318 📠 01483 282318
e-mail: kingbilly4th@aol.com
dir: *On The Street off A246 (Leatherhead to Guildford)*

When laws limiting the consumption of gin were passed in the 1830s, the King William IV began a swift trade in ale through its street-level windows. Fortunately, many of the original Georgian features have been preserved, giving this traditional countryside local a warm and welcoming atmosphere, augmented by open fires in winter and a light and airy conservatory restaurant. Today it's popular with walkers, not least for the large garden and terrace to the rear, with colourful tubs and floral baskets. Beers include several lagers, while the generously proportioned wine list proffers a good selection by the glass. The well-priced menu ranges over reliable starters such as deep-fried French brie or crispy garlic mushrooms, and leads on to equally popular mains like seared tuna, or marinated minty lamb rumps. Children can tuck into home-made lasagne and a shot of sugar-free 'safari juice'.

Open all day all wk 11.30am-mdnt (Sun noon-10.30) **Bar Meals** L served all wk 12-3 D served Mon-Sat 6.30-9.30 Av main course £9.50 **Restaurant** L served all wk 12-3 D served Mon-Sat 6.30-9.30 Fixed menu price fr £9.50 ⬤ ENTERPRISE INNS ◀ Shere Drop, Courage Best. ⬤ 12 **Facilities** Children's menu Family room Dogs allowed Garden Parking

WITLEY | Map 6 SU93

The White Hart ⬤

Petworth Rd GU8 5PH ☎ 01428 683695
e-mail: thewhitehartwitley@yahoo.co.uk
dir: *From A3 follow signs to Milford, then A283 towards Petworth. Pub 2m on left*

A delightfully warm and welcoming pub, built in 1380 as a hunting lodge for Richard II; the white hart became his personal emblem. Licensed since 1700, the three log fires, oak beams, Shepherd Neame ales and hearty portions of good value home-cooked food continue to attract. Soups, sandwiches, salads and pastas make a light lunch; steak and kidney pudding, venison casserole, and sausages and mash are some of the main course options. Families and dogs welcome.

Open 11-3 5.30-11 (Sat 11-11 Sun noon-6) Closed: Sun eve **Bar Meals** L served all wk 12-2.30 D served Tue-Sat 6.30-9.30 ⬤ SHEPHERD NEAME ◀ Shepherd Neame Master Brew, Spitfire, Guinness, seasonal ale. ⬤ 7 **Facilities** Play area Dogs allowed Garden Parking

SUSSEX, EAST

ALCISTON | Map 6 TQ50

PICK OF THE PUBS

Rose Cottage Inn ⬤

BN26 6UW ☎ 01323 870377 📠 01323 871440
e-mail: ian@alciston.freeserve.co.uk
dir: *Off A27 between Eastbourne & Lewes*

This traditional Sussex pub, with roses round the door, is situated in a cul-de-sac village below the South Downs. Ramblers will find it a good base for long walks in unspoilt countryside, especially along the old traffic-free coach road to the south. The inn has been in the same family for over 40 years, and is well known for its good, 'fresh daily' home-cooked food. This includes the best local meats, poultry and game, served in rambling dining rooms, in the bar or in the patio garden. The local butcher's sausages and steaks are particularly excellent, and the wide-ranging fish selection includes fresh Scottish mussels delivered every Friday (when in season) and cooked French or Italian-style. From the choices you might choose an authentic chicken curry using fresh spices; home-made steak and ale pie; red wine braised Sherrington Manor pheasant; or fillet of local cod topped with Welsh rarebit. Lunchtime eating is primarily casual, with booking necessary only in the restaurant.

Open all wk Closed: 25-26 Dec **Bar Meals** L served all wk 12-2 D served all wk 7-9.30 Av main course £10 **Restaurant** L served all wk 12-2 booking required D served all wk 12-2 booking required Av 3 course à la carte fr £20 ⬤ FREE HOUSE ◀ Harveys Best, Dark Star. ⬤ 9 **Facilities** Dogs allowed Garden Parking

ALFRISTON | Map 6 TQ50

George Inn ⬤

High St BN26 5SY ☎ 01323 870319 📠 01323 871384
e-mail: info@thegeorge-alfriston.com
dir: *Telephone for directions*

Splendid 14th-century, Grade II listed flint and half-timbered inn set in a magical South Downs village. The George boasts heavy oak beams, an ancient inglenook fireplace and a network of smugglers' tunnels leading from its cellars. The team of three chefs create delights such as rosemary pot roast chicken supreme with sweet potato; rack of South Downs lamb with tomato and olive sauce; and fillet of sea bass poached in white wine, ginger, lime and coriander.

Open all wk 11-11 Closed: 25-26 Dec **Bar Meals** L served all wk 12-2.30 D served all wk 6.30-9.30 Av main course £10 **Restaurant** L served all wk 12-2.30 booking required D served all wk 6.30-9.30 booking required Av 3 course la carte fr £25 ⬤ GREENE KING ◀ Greene King Old Speckled Hen, Abbot Ale, 2 guests. ⬤ 12 **Facilities** Dogs allowed Garden

The Sussex Ox ⬤

Milton St BN26 5RL ☎ 01323 870840
e-mail: mail@thesussexox.co.uk
dir: *Off A27 between Wilmington & Drusillas. Follow brown signs to pub*

Idyllically situated pub, tucked away down a meandering country lane and set in almost two acres of gardens. In recent years, improvements and adjustments have been made, but the friendly welcome and cosy atmosphere of country pub have been retained. You can eat in the bar, the Garden Room, or the more formal Dining Room. A typical menu includes char-grilled breast of Gressingham duck with a raspberry and fig reduction, and upside down beef, ale and mushroom pie. Bar snacks, sandwiches and Sussex cheddar ploughman's are also available.

Open all wk 11.30-3 6-11 Closed: 25-31 Dec **Bar Meals** L served all wk 12-2 booking required D served all wk 6-9 booking required Av main course £9.50 **Restaurant** L served all wk 12-2 booking required D served all wk 6-9 booking required ⬤ FREE HOUSE ◀ Harveys Best, Dark Star Hophead, Golden Gate, Hop Back Summer Lightning, Crouch Vale Brewers Gold Ȯ Westons Perry. ⬤ 15 **Facilities** Children's menu Family room Dogs allowed Garden Parking

ASHBURNHAM PLACE | Map 6 TQ61

Ash Tree Inn

Brownbread St TN33 9NX ☎ 01424 892104
dir: *From Eastbourne take A271 at Boreham Bridge towards Battle. Next left, follow pub signs*

The Ash Tree is a friendly old pub with three open fires, plenty of exposed beams and a traditional local atmosphere. Bar food includes ploughman's, salads and sandwiches, while the restaurant serves steaks, local lamb, steak and ale pie, or salmon in a variety of sauces.

Open noon-4 7-11 (Sat-Sun 11.30am-mdnt) Closed: Mon **Bar Meals** L served Tue-Sun 12-3 booking required D served Tue-Sun 7-9 booking required Av main course £9 **Restaurant** L served Tue-Sun 12-3 booking required D served Tue-Sun 7-9 booking required Av 3 course à la carte fr £16 ⬤ FREE HOUSE ◀ Harveys Best, Greene King Old Speckled Hen, Brakspear Bitter, guest ales. **Facilities** Dogs allowed Garden Parking

BERWICK
Map 6 TQ50

PICK OF THE PUBS

The Cricketers Arms ♀

BN26 6SP ☎ 01323 870469 ▤ 01323 871411
e-mail: pbthecricketers@aol.com
dir: Off A27 between Polegate & Lewes, follow signs for
Berwick Church

A traditional flint and stone cottage pub in beautiful
gardens close to many popular walks, including the
South Downs Way running along the crest of the chalk
scarp to the south. In the 16th century it was two
farmworkers' cottages, which then became an
alehouse for the next 200 years before Harvey's of
Lewes bought it around 50 years ago and turned it into
a 'proper' pub. Three beamed, music-free rooms with
stone floors and open fires are simply furnished with
old pine furniture. Home-made food, using local
produce, found on the bar menu includes starters such
as whole crevettes pan fried in garlic and herb butter,
and apple and smoked mackerel pâté, with main
courses like steak and Harvey's Ale pie; and Cricketer's
fish pie with salmon, white fish and prawns. Nearby is
Charleston Farmhouse, the country rendezvous of the
London writers, painters and intellectuals known as the
Bloomsbury Group, and scene of an annual literary
festival.

Open all wk Closed: 25 Dec Bar Meals Av main course
£8 food served all day ⊕ HARVEYS OF LEWES
◀ Harveys Best Bitter, Pale, Armada. ♀ 11
Facilities Children's menu Family room Dogs allowed
Garden Parking

BLACKBOYS
Map 6 TQ52

The Blackboys Inn ♀

Lewes Rd TN22 5LG
☎ 01825 890283 ▤ 01825 890283
e-mail: blackboys-inn@btconnect.com
dir: From A22 at Uckfield take B2102 towards Cross in
Hand. Or from A267 at Esso service station in Cross in
Hand take B2102 towards Uckfield. Village in 1.5m at
junct of B2102 & B2192

Set in 12 acres of beautiful countryside, the rambling,
black-weatherboarded inn comprises two restaurant
rooms and two cosy bar areas full of endearingly historic
features but up to date with interior design. Menus offer
freshly prepared food - fish, game, roasts and vegetarian
specialities – with home-grown vegetables where
possible; while the bar snack selection is known for its
famous range of burgers. Grounds include a large duck
pond, a secret garden for adults only and a separate
party venue.

Open all wk noon-mdnt Bar Meals L served Mon-Fri 12-3,
Sat 12-10, Sun 12-9 D served Sun-Mon 6-9, Tue-Sat
6-10 Av main course £8.50 Restaurant L served Mon-Fri
12-3, Sat 12-10, Sun 12-9 D served Sun-Mon 6-9, Tue-
Sat 6-10 Av 3 course à la carte fr £22 ⊕ HARVEYS OF
LEWES ◀ Harveys Sussex Best Bitter, Sussex Halow,
Sussex XXXX Old Ale, seasonal ♂ Stowford Press. ♀ 8
Facilities Children's menu Dogs allowed Garden Parking

BRIGHTON & HOVE
Map 6 TQ30

The Basketmakers Arms

12 Gloucester Rd BN1 4AD
☎ 01273 689006 ▤ 01273 682300
e-mail: bluedowd@hotmail.co.uk
dir: From Brighton station main entrance 1st left
(Gloucester Rd). Pub on right at bottom of hill

This Victorian corner pub in the North Laine conservation
area has had the same landlord for 22 years. At least
seven real ales are offered, 90-100 malt whiskies and a
large selection of vodkas and gins. All the food is made
on the premises from locally sourced produce, organic
where possible. The home-made burgers, including a
veggie version, are famously locally, plus there is at least
one seafood special per day with fish sourced straight
from the local fishermen.

Open all wk 11-11 (Fri-Sat 11am-mdnt Sun noon-11) Bar
Meals L served Mon-Thu 12-8.30, Fri-Sat 12-6, Sun 12-5
D served Mon-Thu 12-8.30, Fri-Sat 12-6, Sun 12-5 Av
main course £6.95 ⊕ FULLERS BREWERY ◀ Fuller's HSB,
Butser Bitter, London Pride, ESB & Discovery, seasonal
ales. Facilities Dogs allowed

The Chimney House ♀

28 Upper Hamilton Rd BN1 5DF ☎ 01273 556708
e-mail: info@chimneyhousebrighton.co.uk
dir: Please telephone for directions

Taken over by Andrew and Helen Coggings early in 2009,
the Chimney House was given a facelift prior to
reopening. It's primarily a family-friendly pub serving the
local community, but word of mouth is spreading its
popularity beyond the neighbourhood. In addition to
reliable Harveys ales, the food is fresh, seasonal, bought
locally if possible and reasonably priced. You'll find
different menus for lunch and dinner, children have their
own selections, and Sunday roasts feature prime Sussex
pork, lamb and beef.

Open all wk noon-3 5-11 (Sat noon-11 Sun noon-8) Bar
Meals L served Mon-Fri 12-2.30, Sat 12-4, Sun 12-6 D
served Mon-Sat 6-9.45 ⊕ FREE HOUSE ◀ Harvey's
Sussex Best Bitter, Guinness. ♀ 21 Facilities Children's
menu Dogs allowed

PICK OF THE PUBS

The Greys

105 Southover St BN2 9UA ☎ 01273 680734
e-mail: chris@greyspub.com
dir: 0.5m from St Peters Church in Hanover area of
Brighton

For the last 20 years The Greys has been a popular
community pub in the bohemian area of Hanover in
central Brighton, frequented by hearty locals,
celebrities and students. Stripped wood and flagstone
floors and timber panelled walls give the sense of a
country pub in the town, and with the wood-burning
stove glowing in the fireplace, there is no finer place to
relax with a pint of Harveys bitter. There is a great
selection of Belgian beers, too. Food is prepared by ex-
Claridge's chef Roz Batty, with dishes such as
cassoulet with goose fat roast potatoes and braised
red cabbage; mussel, leek and bacon chowder with
home-made garlic bread; and winter vegetable and
aduki bean stew with herb dumplings. The Greys is
also known for its live country/folk/bluegrass music on
Monday nights.

Open all wk 4-11 (Sat noon-mdnt Sun noon-11) Bar
Meals D served Tue-Thu & Sat 6-9 Av main course
£6.50 Restaurant L served Sun 12-4.30 D served Tue-
Thu & Sat 6-9 Av 3 course à la carte fr £20
⊕ ENTERPRISE INNS ◀ Timothy Taylor Landlord,
Harveys Best Bitter ♂ Stowford Press, Westons
Organic. Facilities Dogs allowed Parking

The Market Inn ★★ INN ♀

1 Market St BN1 1HH
☎ 01273 329483 ▤ 01273 777227
e-mail: marketinn@reallondonpubs.com
dir: In The Lanes area, 50mtrs from junct of North St &
East St

This Victorian corner pub in the North Laine conservation
area has had the same landlord for 22 years. At least
seven real ales are offered, 90-100 malt whiskies and a
large selection of vodkas and gins. All the food is made
on the premises from locally sourced produce, organic
where possible. The home-made burgers, including a
veggie version, are famously locally, plus there is at least
one seafood special per day with fish sourced straight
from the local fishermen. There are two attractively
decorated en suite rooms available.

Open all wk 11-11 (Fri-Sat 11am-mdnt Sun noon-10.30)
Bar Meals L served Mon-Sat 11-9, Sun 12-7 D served
Mon-Sat 11-9, Sun 12-7 Av main course £6.50 food
served all day ⊕ SCOTTISH COURAGE ◀ Harveys, Wells
Bombardier. ♀ 7 Facilities Children's menu Dogs allowed
Rooms 2

CHAILEY
Map 6 TQ31

The Five Bells Restaurant and Bar ♀

East Grinstead Rd BN8 4DA
☎ 01825 722259 📄 01825 723368
e-mail: info@fivebellschailey.co.uk
dir: *5m N of Lewes on A275*

Handy for Sheffield Park, the Bluebell Railway, Plumpton racecourse and walks around Chailey. With origins in the 15th century and serving ale since the 17th, this country pub cum wine bar cum smart restaurant has many original features, including a large inglenook fireplace. The highly qualified kitchen team create modern European dishes rooted in English tradition from fresh, organic and free-range ingredients. Friday evenings host live jazz, and in summer the large bar terrace and secluded restaurant garden come into their own.

Open all wk noon-3 6-11 (Sun-Mon noon-3) Closed: Sun & Mon eve **Bar Meals** L served all wk 12-2.30 D served Tue-Thu 6-9, Fri-Sat 6-9.30 Av main course £11.95 **Restaurant** L served all wk 12-2.30 D served Tue-Thu 6-9, Fri-Sat 6.9.30 ⊕ ENTERPRISE INNS ◀ Harvey's Best, Youngs Special ♂ Stowford Press. ♀ 7
Facilities Children's menu Dogs allowed Garden Parking

CHIDDINGLY
Map 6 TQ51

The Six Bells

BN8 6HE ☎ 01825 872227
dir: *E of A22 between Hailsham & Uckfield. Turn opp Golden Cross PH*

Inglenook fireplaces and plenty of bric-a-brac are to be found at this large characterful free house which is where various veteran car and motorbike enthusiasts meet on club nights. The jury in the famous Onion Pie Murder trial sat and deliberated in the bar before finding the defendant guilty. Live music at weekends. Exceptionally good value bar food includes stilton and walnut pie, lemon peppered haddock, Six Bells Yorkshire pudding with beef or sausage, vegetarian lasagne, cannelloni, lasagne, and shepherd's pie.

Open all wk ⊕ FREE HOUSE ◀ Courage Directors, John Smiths, Harveys Best. **Facilities** Family room Dogs allowed Garden Parking

COOKSBRIDGE
Map 6 TQ41

PICK OF THE PUBS

The Rainbow Inn NEW ♀

Resting Oak Hill BN8 4SS
☎ 01273 400334 📄 01273 401667
e-mail: lwilson@sterlinggroupltd.com
dir: *3m outside Lewes on A275 towards Haywards Heath*

Built of brick and flint and making the most of its pretty corner site, the 17th-century Rainbow boasts a sun-trap enclosed rear terrace with views to the South Downs – a super spot to unwind with a cracking pint of Harveys on lazy summer days. On cooler days, head inside and cosy-up by the blazing fire in the rustic bar, or peruse the chalkboard specials and settle in one of three warmly decorated dining areas, all sporting wooden floors, an eclectic mix of tables and chairs, tasteful artwork, and a relaxing atmosphere. Look out for Newhaven fish (sea bass with herb butter), confit of Sussex pork belly with mixed bean cassoulet, and local estate game, perhaps roast saddle of venison with sweet potato rösti and port jus. Simpler, lighter bar meals take in filled rolls and ploughman's platters. Leave room for baked lemon and lime tart or the impressive cheese selection. Upstairs are two charming little private dining rooms.

Open all wk noon-3 5-11 (Sat-Sun noon-11) **Bar Meals** Av main course £6.50 food served all day **Restaurant** Fixed menu price fr £12.95 Av 3 course à la carte fr £21 food served all day ⊕ STERLING PUB COMPANY ◀ Harveys Best Bitter, Guinness ♂ Stowford Press. ♀ 10 **Facilities** Children's menu Dogs allowed Garden Parking

COWBEECH
Map 6 TQ61

PICK OF THE PUBS

The Merrie Harriers ♀

BN27 4JQ ☎ 01323 833108 📄 01323 833108
e-mail: rmcotton@btopenworld.com
dir: *Off A271, between Hailsham & Herstmonceux*

A Grade II listed, 17th-century, white clapboard building at the centre of the village with great country views. The beamed bar has a large inglenook fireplace, and there is another open fire in the lounge bar/dining room, which leads into the restaurant. The latter opens on to a pretty terrace with garden tables among the flowering tubs. A good choice of real ales and nine wines by the glass are served, and all the food is prepared on the premises using local suppliers and produce - free range and organic wherever possible. Dishes, prepared from local free-range and organic produce where possible, might include slow roasted lamb shank with parsnip purée, Sussex steak and kidney pie with shortcrust pastry, and pan-fried fillet of sea bass with roast Mediterranean vegetables. Starters like wild mushroom risotto can double as mains.

Open all wk 11.30-3 6-11 **Bar Meals** L served Tue-Sun 12-2.30 D served Tue-Sun 6.30-9 **Restaurant** L served Tue-Sun 12-2.30 D served Tue-Sun 6.30-9 ⊕ FREE HOUSE ◀ Harveys, Timothy Taylor ♂ Stowford Press. ♀ 9 **Facilities** Children's menu Dogs allowed Garden Parking

DANEHILL
Map 6 TQ42

PICK OF THE PUBS

The Coach and Horses ♀

RH17 7JF ☎ 01825 740369 📄 01825 740369
dir: *From East Grinstead, S through Forest Row on A22 to junct with A275 (Lewes road), right on A275, 2m to Danehill, left onto School Lane, 0.5m, pub on left*

Set on the edge of Ashdown forest with access to miles of footpaths, The Coach and Horses has provided hospitality since 1847. It was built as an ale house with stabling and a courtyard between two large country estates; these days the stables form part of a comfortable country-style restaurant, and the original bars remain busy with locals: proof that some classic hostelries still exist in an age when the traditional village local is under threat. Open fires and neatly tended gardens add colour to a characterful setting: expect half-panelled walls, highly polished wooden floorboards and vaulted beamed ceilings. Food plays a key role in its success. Typical choices include confit rabbit terrine with shallot chutney; spicy Portland crab and saffron risotto with Parmesan; and hot chocolate fondant with pistachio crème Anglaise. In addition to the main menu and blackboard dishes, sandwiches are available at lunchtime. The landlady now sells her own preserves under the name of Ladypots.

Open all wk 11.30-3 6-11 (Sat-Sun 11.30-11) **Bar Meals** L served all wk 12-2 D served Mon-Sat 7-9 Av main course £12.50 **Restaurant** L served all wk 12-2 D served Mon-Sat 7-9 Av 3 course à la carte fr £23.75 ⊕ FREE HOUSE ◀ Harveys Best & Old Ale, Wadworth IPA, WJ King & Co, Hammerpot, Dark Star ♂ Stowford Press. ♀ 10 **Facilities** Children's menu Play area Dogs allowed Garden Parking

DITCHLING
Map 6 TQ31

PICK OF THE PUBS

The Bull ★★★★ INN ♀

See Pick of the Pubs on opposite pag

PICK OF THE PUBS

The Bull ★★★★ INN 🍷

DITCHLING   Map 6 TQ31

2 High St BN6 8TA
☎ **01273 843147** 📄 **01273 843147**
e-mail: info@thebullditchling.com
web: www.thebullditchling.com
dir: *S on M23/A23 5m. N of Brighton follow
signs to Pyecombe/Hassocks then signs to
Ditchling, 3m*

Dating back to 1563, the Bull is one of
the oldest buildings in this picture-
postcard Sussex village, which nestles
below Ditchling Beacon, a key landmark
on the South Downs. First used as an
overnight resting place for travelling
monks, the inn has also served as a
courthouse and staging post for the
London-Brighton coach. Restored with
passion and a contemporary touch by

Dominic Worrall, it still retains its
historic charm and character, including
four charming bedrooms. Real ale lovers
can quaff four top-notch beers,
including the local Harvey's Best, while
wine drinkers can enjoy 20 regularly-
changing wines by the glass. The
modern British menu also changes
frequently to make the most of the
freshest local supplies, be it game from
the Balcombe Estate, South Downs lamb
from village farms or fish from the
nearby coast. These appear in such
dishes as pan-roasted lamb rump with
green beans and red cabbage; and
bouillabaisse of cockles, squid, tiger
prawns, haddock and samphire, in
addition to starters of duck breast salad
with honey dressing; and seared smoked
salmon with gazpacho salad; and mains
like veal, ham and mushroom pie;
haddock in Harveys ale batter with
hand-cut chips, and local sausages
with bubble-and-squeak and onion
gravy. No one should miss the rare
opportunity to sample Sussex pond
pudding, a local speciality made with

an alarming amount of butter, and here
served with lemon and lime crème
anglaise. Caramelised orange and
toffee bread-and-butter pudding and
chocolate and hazelnut brownie are
equally alluring. For a snack, share a
camembert, baked in its box and served
with crusty bread. Families are made
very welcome and the garden
commands stunning views over the
South Downs.

Open 11-11 (Sun 12-10.30) **Meals**
L served Mon-Fri 12-2.30 6-9.30 (Sat
12-9.30 Sun 12-9) 🛢 FREE HOUSE
🍺 Harveys Best, Timothy Taylor
Landlord, Hop Back Summer Lightning,
Dark Star. 🍷 20 **Facilities** Play area
Dogs allowed Garden Parking **Rooms** 4

EAST CHILTINGTON   Map 6 TQ31

The Jolly Sportsman ☺

Chapel Ln BN7 3BA ☎ **01273 890400** 🖹 01273 890400
e-mail: thejollysportsman@mistral.co.uk
dir: *From Lewes take A275, left at Offham onto B2166 towards Plumpton, take Novington Ln, after approx 1m left into Chapel Ln*

Secluded and romantic, this sympathetically upgraded dining inn is tucked away down a quiet no-through road surrounded by downland. The bar retains some of the character of a Victorian ale house, while the dining room strikes a cool, modern pose, and there is a terrace with Moroccan-tiled tables overlooking the garden. Typical dishes are mussel, tomato and herb risotto; roast partridge with cabbage, bacon and Lyonnaise potatoes; and almond custard fritter with roast plums.

Closed: 25-26 Dec, Mon ex BH **Bar Meals** L served Tue-Sat 12.15-2.30, Sun 12.15-3 D served Tue-Thu & Sun 7-9.30, Fri-Sat 7-10 booking required Av main course £13.50 **Restaurant** L served Tue-Sat 12.15-2.30, Sun 12.15-3 booking required D served Tue-Thu & Sun 7-9.30, Fri-Sat 7-10 booking required Fixed menu price fr £15.75 Av 3 course à la carte fr £25 ⊕ FREE HOUSE ◀ Dark Star Hophead, guest ales. ☺ 9 **Facilities** Children's menu Play area Dogs allowed Garden Parking

FLETCHING   Map 6 TQ42

PICK OF THE PUBS

The Griffin Inn ☺

TN22 3SS ☎ **01825 722890** 🖹 01825 722810
e-mail: info@thegriffininn.co.uk
dir: *M23 junct 10 to East Grinstead, then A22, then A275. Village signed on left, 15m from M23*

The Griffin's superbly landscaped gardens boast one of the best views in Sussex, looking out over the Ouse Valley towards Sheffield Park. Indeed, in the summer months, the terrace forms an important part of the restaurant. The Grade II listed Griffin is reputedly the oldest licensed building in Sussex and, since it's been at the heart of this unspoilt village for over 400 years, the claim sounds reasonable. Old beams, wainscotting, open fires and pews make up the character of the main bar. Menus change daily, with the emphasis on fresh Rye Bay fish and organic, locally sourced ingredients wherever possible. Modern British dishes are given a Mediterranean twist, and a typical restaurant meal might start with spiced beef carpaccio with black olives and caper dressing; followed by roast rack of Sussex lamb, chargrilled courgette and cavalo nero. Puddings include roast apples and pears with mascarpone and pine nuts.

Open all wk noon-11 Closed: 25 Dec **Bar Meals** L served Mon-Fri 12-2.30, Sat-Sun 12-3 D served all wk 7-9.30 Av main course £11.50 **Restaurant** L served Mon-Fri 12-2.30, Sat-Sun 12-3 booking required D served Mon-Sat 7-9.30 booking required Fixed menu price fr £30 Av 3 course à la carte fr £30 ⊕ FREE HOUSE ◀ Harvey Best, Kings of Horsham, Hepworths. ☺ 15 **Facilities** Children's menu Play area Garden Parking

GUN HILL   Map 6 TQ51

PICK OF THE PUBS

The Gun Inn ☺

TN21 0JU ☎ **01825 872361** 🖹 01622 851881
e-mail: enquiries@thegunhouse.co.uk
dir: *5m S of Heathfield, 1m off A267 towards Gun Hill. 4m off A22 between Uckfield & Hailsham*

A lovely 17th-century building and former courthouse set in delightful East Sussex countryside, with extensive views from a pretty terrace and garden. Wood dominates the interior, with beams, a beautiful wooden floor, and lots of hideaway places for quiet eating and drinking. A separate panelled dining room with a stunning fireplace is ideal for private parties. Three deli board selections can be shared by a gathering of friends - the cold meat board, for example, includes garlic sausage, salami, chorizo, honey roast ham and farmhouse terrine. From the menu come starters of stuffed mushroom with stilton and bacon, and The Gun Sussex smokie – oven-baked smoked haddock with mozzarella and mustard sauce. Main dishes include home-made Dublin pie (beef, mushrooms and Guinness gravy), and chef's favourite Sussex beef cuts (rib-eye, sirloin) with sauce of your choice. Game dishes are available when in season. The Old Coach House behind The Gun has been transformed into a farmer's market offering a wide selection of fresh local fruits and vegetables, organic foods, fish and meats.

Open noon-3 6-11 (Sat-Sun noon-11) **Bar Meals** L served Mon-Fri 12-3, Sat-Sun 12-10 D served Mon-Fri 6-9.30, Sat-Sun 12-10 Av main course £9.95 **Restaurant** L served Mon-Fri 12-3, Sat-Sun 12-10 D served Mon-Fri 6-9.30, Sat-Sun 12-10 Fixed menu price fr £10 Av 3 course à la carte fr £19 ⊕ FREE HOUSE ◀ Harveys, Guinness, Youngs. ☺ 13 **Facilities** Children's menu Play area Garden Parking

HARTFIELD   Map 6 TQ43

Anchor Inn

Church St TN7 4AG ☎ **01892 770424**
dir: *On B2110*

A 14th-century inn at the heart of Winnie the Pooh country, deep within the scenic Ashdown Forest. Inside are stone floors enhanced by a large inglenook fireplace Sandwiches and salads are among the bar snacks, while for something more substantial you could try whole Dover sole; grilled pork loin on a bed of spaghetti; or medallion of beef fillet. Puddings include crème brûlée; ice cream gâteau; and orange marmalade bread and butter pudding.

Open all day all wk **Bar Meals** L served all wk 12-2 booking required D served all wk 6-10 booking required Av main course £8 **Restaurant** L served all wk 12-2 booking required D served all wk 6-10 booking required ⊕ FREE HOUSE ◀ Harveys Sussex Best Bitter, Larkins. **Facilities** Children's menu Family room Dogs allowed Garden Parking

PICK OF THE PUBS

The Hatch Inn ☺

See Pick of the Pubs on opposite page

ICKLESHAM   Map 7 TQ81

The Queen's Head ☺

Parsonage Ln TN36 4BL
☎ **01424 814552** 🖹 01424 814766
dir: *Between Hastings & Rye on A259. Pub in village on x-rds near church*

A 17th-century tile-hung building, full of exposed oak beams, the pub has a magnificent view across the Bred valley to Rye. The traditional atmosphere has been conserved, with vaulted ceilings, large inglenook fireplaces, church pews, old farm implements, and a bar from the old Midland Bank in Eastbourne. Typical of the home-made dishes are a choice of pies; Thai vegetable curry; steaks and grills; salads and snacks. Gardens include a playhouse, climbing frame and boule pitch.

Open all wk 11-11 (Sun 11-10.30) **Bar Meals** L served Mon-Fri 12-2.30, Sat-Sun 12-9.30 D served Mon-Fri 6-9.30, Sat-Sun 12-9.30 Av main course £8.95 ⊕ FREE HOUSE ◀ Rother Valley Level Best, Greene King Abbot Ale, Harveys Best, Dark Star, Ringwood 49r Ö Biddenden ☺ 10 **Facilities** Children's menu Play area Garden Parking

PICK OF THE PUBS

The Hatch Inn 🍷

Coleman's Hatch TN7 4EJ
☎ 01342 822363 📠 01342 822363
e-mail: nickad@bigfoot.com
dir: *A22, 14m, left at Forest Row rdbt, 3m to Colemans Hatch, right by church. Straight on at next junct, pub on right*

Nicholas Drillsma and his partner Sandra have built quite an enviable reputation over the past fourteen years for this classically picturesque, weatherboarded pub. Reputedly dating from 1430, it was converted in the 18th century from three cottages probably used by workers at the local water-driven hammer mill. It is named after one of the hatches, or gates, into what used to be the Royal Ashdown Forest, and was probably a smugglers' haunt. Only minutes' away is the restored Poohsticks Bridge, immortalised in A.A. Milne's *Winnie the Pooh* stories. There are two large beer gardens for alfresco summer dining, one of which enjoys views out over the forest. Ingredients of the highest quality are sourced locally and, under the hands-on guidance of head chef Greg Palmer, exciting menus are produced that include a good selection of light bites and traditional dishes. If you're stopping for lunch, try a starter of fresh Shetland Isles mussels in cider and tarragon, and roast sirloin of beef with mixed dressed leaves to follow. Lighter options include sandwiches and traditional ploughman's. In the evening (for which booking is essential) starters of goats' cheese and leek tartlet, or gravadlax of Scottish salmon might tempt, as could main courses of chargrilled Angus fillet steak with hand-cut fries, vine tomatoes and Béarnaise sauce; roast fillet of pork wrapped in filo pastry and served with sweet mustard seed sauce; naturally smoked fillet of haddock topped with Welsh rarebit; or fresh wild mushroom pasta with roasted vine tomato and olive and basil sauce. For dessert, try the Belgian chocolate pot, or Bakewell tart with custard.

Open 11.30-3 5.30-11 (Sat-Sun all day)
Meals L served all week 12-2.30
D served all week 7-9 (Fri & Sat 7-9.30)
Closed: 25 Dec ⊕ FREE HOUSE
◆ Harveys, Fuller's London Pride, Larkins & Harvey's Old. ♟ 10
Facilities Play area Dogs allowed Garden

KINGSTON (NEAR LEWES)   Map 6 TQ30

The Juggs ♀

The Street BN7 3NT ☎ 01273 472523   📄 **01273 483274**
e-mail: juggs@shepherd-neame.co.uk
dir: *E of Brighton on A27*

Named after the women who walked from Brighton with baskets of fish for sale, this rambling, tile-hung 15th-century cottage, tucked beneath the South Downs, offers an interesting selection of freshly-cooked food. The area is ideal for walkers, and families are very welcome.

Open all day all wk 11am-11pm (Sun 11am-10.30pm)
Bar Meals L served Mon-Fri 12-2.30, Sat-Sun 12-8 (Sun winter 12-4) D served Mon-Fri 12-6.9, Sat-Sun 12-8 (Sun winter 12-4) ⊕ SHEPHERD NEAME ◧ Shepherd Neame Spitfire, Best, Bishops Finger, Seasonal. ♀ 7
Facilities Family room Dogs allowed Garden Parking

MAYFIELD   Map 6 TQ52

PICK OF THE PUBS

The Middle House ♀

See Pick of the Pubs on opposite page

OFFHAM   Map 6 TQ41

The Blacksmiths Arms ★★★★ INN ♀

London Rd BN7 3QD ☎ 01273 472971
e-mail: blacksmithsarms@tiscali.co.uk
dir: *2m N of Lewes on A275*

An attractive, mid-18th-century free house popular with walkers and cyclists on the South Downs Way. Harvey's ales are served in the bar, where log fires burn in the inglenook. Bernard and Sylvia Booker's use of excellent local produce is shown in dishes like Auntie Kate's crispy roast duckling with spiced orange and Cointreau sauce; rack of South Downs lamb with poached pear and apricot sauce; and locally caught seafood. There is comfortable accommodation available.

Closed: Mon **Bar Meals** L served Tue-Sun 12-2 Av main course £6 **Restaurant** L served Tue-Sun 12-2 booking required D served Tue-Sun 6.30-9 booking required Fixed menu price fr £10 Av 3 course à la carte fr £22.50
⊕ FREE HOUSE ◧ Harveys Ales. ♀ 10
Facilities Children's menu Garden Parking **Rooms** 4

RINGMER   Map 6 TQ41

The Cock ♀

Uckfield Rd BN8 5RX
☎ **01273 812040**   📄 **01273 812040**
e-mail: matt@cockpub.co.uk
web: www.cockpub.co.uk
dir: *On A26 approx 2m N of Lewes just outside Ringmer*

Built in the 16th-century, this former coaching inn was a mustering point during the Civil War for the siege of Arundel. Original oak beams, flagstone floors and a blazing fire set a cosy scene. Harveys ales and guest beers accompany an extensive menu. Frequent specials include pot roasted pheasant, organic sausage and onion pie, whole fresh brill, and vegetarian quiche. The west-facing restaurant and garden have views to the South Downs and some wonderful sunsets.

Open all wk 11-3 6-11.30 (Sun 11-11) Closed: 26 Dec
Bar Meals L served Mon-Sat 12-2, Sun 12-9.30 D served Mon-Sat 6-9.30, Sun 12-9.30 Av main course £9.50
Restaurant L served Mon-Sat 12-2, Sun 12-9.30 booking required D served Mon-Sat 6-9.30, Sun 12-9.30 booking required Av 3 course à la carte fr £18.50 ⊕ FREE HOUSE ◧ Harveys Sussex Best Bitter, Sussex XXXX Old Ale, Fuller's London Pride, Dark Star Hophead ○ Westons 1st Quality. ♀ 9 **Facilities** Children's menu Play area Dogs allowed Garden Parking

---

RUSHLAKE GREEN   Map 6 TQ61

PICK OF THE PUBS

Horse & Groom ♀

TN21 9QE ☎ 01435 830320   📄 **01435 830310**
e-mail: chappellhatpeg@aol.com
dir: *Telephone for directions*

Just across the road from the village green, this whitewashed inn dates from around 1650. The building was first licensed in 1775, and two years later it was listed as the Horse and Groom. Today you'll find a welcoming atmosphere surrounded by old beams, with Shepherd Neame ales dispensed from a row of hand pumps in the bar. Antique shotguns decorate the walls of the Gun Room restaurant, where you can choose an entirely fishy flavour for your meal: monkfish and organic salmon baked in parchment vanilla and vermouth; scallops sautéed with smoked bacon, spring onions, white wine and a butter oyster sauce; wild seabass fillets pan-fried and served with crushed olive, potato and white wine sauce; and mussels steamed in leeks, onions, white wine and pink peppercorns. On warmer days, meals are served in the garden, with fantastic views of the Sussex countryside.

Open all wk ⊕ SHEPHERD NEAME ◧ Master Brew, Spitfire, Kent Best, Late Red, Bishop's Finger. ♀ 8
Facilities Dogs allowed Garden Parking

RYE   Map 7 TQ92

The Globe Inn ♀

10 Military Rd TN31 7NX ☎ 01797 227918
e-mail: info@theglobe-inn.com
dir: *M20 junct 11 onto A2080*

A small, informal free house just outside the ancient town walls. An absence of gaming machines, jukeboxes and TV screens encourages even husbands and wives to talk to each other over their drinks; or while they enjoy their contemporary British food in the modern, wood-floored bar and restaurant area. Fresh fish comes from a local fisherman, organic meat from a National Trust farm at Winchelsea, and fruit and vegetables from Kent, the Garden of England.

Closed: 2wks Jan, Mon, Sun eve & Tue Jan-Mar ⊕ FREE HOUSE ◧ ESB, Harveys & Guinness. ♀ 20 **Facilities** Dogs allowed Garden Parking

PICK OF THE PUBS

The Middle House 🍷

MAYFIELD   Map 6 TQ52

High St TN20 6AB
☎ 01435 872146   📠 01435 873423
e-mail: kirsty@middle-house.com
web: www.middlehousehotel.co.uk
dir: *E of A267, S of Tunbridge Wells*

This Grade I listed, 16th-century village inn dominates the High Street. Described as 'one of the finest examples of a timber-framed building in Sussex', it has survived since 1575, when it was built for Sir Thomas Gresham, Elizabeth I's Keeper of the Privy Purse, and founder of the London Stock Exchange. A private residence until the 1920s, when it still incorporated a private chapel, it retains a fireplace by master carver Grinling Gibbons, and a splendid oak-panelled restaurant. A truly family-run business from start to finish, the Middle House is owned by Monica and Bryan Blundell; their son Darren is general manager, and daughter Kirsty manages the restaurant, while son-in-law Mark is the head chef. Well known for its exceptionally good, hand-made food, the extensive menus change on a weekly basis, with specials changing daily. All meats, poultry and game come from local farms and producers. The bar menu consists of over 40 dishes including traditional classics, fresh salads and vegetarian options, with fresh fish and daily specials displayed around the huge working fire. During the lunch period ploughmans', baguettes, ciabattas and a 'ladies lunch menu' are available. The menu in the beautifully panelled restaurant offers a carte menu with over twenty main courses to choose from: expect starters of pan-seared lamb fillet with mixed leaves and croutons, rosemary and garlic oil; and smoked fish trio – tuna, marlin and swordfish served on horseradish and dill Bellini with chive crème fraîche. Others are roasted boneless quail with mixed forest mushrooms, pancetta and pinenut farci and Madeira cream sauce; whole grilled Cornish sardines with garlic butter, green salad and new potatoes; and, for vegetarians, corn fritter and harissa-roasted vegetable stack with toasted feta cheese and Provençal new potatoes.

Open all week ⊕ FREE HOUSE ◀ Harveys Best, Greene King Abbot Ale, Black Sheep Best, Theakston Best, Adnams Bitter. 🍷 9 **Facilities** Play area Garden Parking

RYE *continued*

PICK OF THE PUBS

Mermaid Inn ★★★ HL ◉ ☻

Mermaid St TN31 7EY
☎ 01797 223065 📄 01797 225069
e-mail: info@mermaidinn.com
dir: *A259, follow signs to town centre, then into Mermaid St*

Destroyed by the French in 1377 and rebuilt in 1420 (on foundations dating back to 1156), the Mermaid is steeped in history and stands among the cobbled streets of Rye. Once famous for its smuggling associations, the infamous Hawkhurst Gang used to meet here, it remains strong on romantic, old-world appeal, with beams hewn from ancient ships' timbers, antique furnishings, linenfold panelling, and huge fireplaces carved from French stone ballast rescued from the harbour. There is also a priest's hole in the lounge bar. Food is served in the bar and atmospheric restaurant, and in the summer you can relax under sunshades on the patio. Bar food ranges from sandwiches or baked fish pie, to smoked haddock and salmon fishcakes and sirloin steak with chips and blue cheese sauce. Bedrooms ooze character and include eight four-poster rooms – book the Elizabethan Chamber, an impressive panelled room with a magnificent carved four-poster bed.

Open all wk noon–11 **Bar Meals** L served all wk 12-2.30 D served all wk 6-9 Av main course £8.50 **Restaurant** L served all wk 12-2.30 booking required D served all wk 7.30-9.30 booking required Fixed menu price fr £24 Av 3 course à la carte fr £35 ⊕ FREE HOUSE ◀ Greene King Old Speckled Hen, Courage Best, Fuller's London Pride. ☻ 11 **Facilities** Children's menu Garden Parking **Rooms** 31

PICK OF THE PUBS

The Ypres Castle Inn ☻

Gun Garden TN31 7HH ☎ 01797 223248
e-mail: info@yprescastleinn.co.uk
dir: *Behind church & adjacent to Ypres Tower*

'The Wipers', as locals call it, was once the haunt of smugglers. Built in 1640 in weather-boarded style and added to in Victorian times, it's the only pub in the citadel area of Rye. Another plus is its garden - the roses, shrubs and views to the 13th-century Ypres Tower and River Rother make it an ideal spot for a pint

from the range of tapped ales. Colourful art and furnishings help give the interior a warm and friendly atmosphere. The seasonal, regularly-changing menu is largely sourced locally, including Winchelsea pork, Romney Marsh lamb and Rye Bay caught seafood, especially the famous Rye Bay scallop. The evening menu may propose starters of cracked Dungeness crab, a theme which could be continued with grilled Rye Bay plaice or pan-fried fillets of lemon sole. Meaty options are no less appealing: grilled rack of Romney salt marsh lamb, or local ham cooked in cider.

Open all wk **Bar Meals** L served all wk 12-3 D served Mon-Sat 6-9 **Restaurant** L served all wk 12-3 booking required D served Mon-Sat 6-9 booking required ⊕ FREE HOUSE ◀ Harveys Best, Adnams Broadside, Wells Bombardier, Timothy Taylor Landlord, Fuller's London Pride. ☻ 11 **Facilities** Garden

PICK OF THE PUBS

The Peacock Inn ☻

TN22 3XA ☎ 01825 762463 📄 01825 762463
e-mail: enquiries@peacock-inn.co.uk
dir: *Just off A272 (Haywards Heath to Uckfield road) & A26 (Uckfield to Lewes road)*

Mentioned in Samuel Pepys' diary, this traditional inn dates from 1567 and is full of old world charm, both inside and out. Today it is renowned for its food (created by no fewer than three chefs), and also the resident ghost of Mrs Fuller. The large rear patio garden is a delightful spot in summer. Food choices include toasted ciabatta and toasted foccacia with a variety of fillings. For the hungry there are starters such as chicken and duck liver pâté, or crayfish tails and smoked salmon, followed by seafood crêpe, pan-fried sea bass fillets; steak, Guinness and mushroom pie or fillet steak with garlic and stilton butter. For the non-meat eaters there's Mediterranean vegetable and mozzarella tartlet, or vegetarian tagine. Look out for chefs' specials.

Open all wk Mon-Fri 11-3 (Sat-Sun all day) Closed: 25-26 Dec **Bar Meals** L served Mon-Fri 12-3, Sat-Sun all day D served Mon-Fri 6-10, Sat-Sun all day ⊕ FREE HOUSE ◀ Abbot Ale, Harveys Best Bitter, Fuller's London Pride. ☻ 8 **Facilities** Children's menu Dogs allowed Garden Parking

The Bull ☻

Dunster Mill Ln TN5 7HH
☎ 01580 200586 📄 01580 201289
e-mail: enquiries@thebullinn.co.uk
dir: *From M25 exit at Sevenoaks toward Hastings, right at x-rds onto B2087, right onto B2099 through Ticehurst, right for Three Legged Cross*

The Bull is based on a 14th-century Wealden hall house, set in a hamlet close to Bewl Water. The interior features oak beams, inglenook fireplaces, quarry tiled floors, and a mass of small intimate areas in the bar. The extensive gardens are popular with families who enjoy the duck pond, petanque pitch, aviary and children's play area. Menus offer pub favourites ranging from freshly baked baguettes and bar snacks to hearty dishes full of comfort, such as bangers and mash and treacle tart.

Open all wk noon-11 Closed: 25-26 Dec eve **Bar Meals** L served Mon-Fri 12-2.30, Sat 12-3, Sun 12-8 D served Mon-Sat 6.30-9, Sun 6.30-8 **Restaurant** L served Mon-Fri 12-2.30, Sat 12-3, Sun 12-8 D served Mon-Sat 6.30-9, Sun 6.30-8 ⊕ FREE HOUSE ◀ Harveys, Sussex Best, Harveys Armada, Timothy Taylor, 1066, guest ales ⊙ Stowford Press. ☻ 7 **Facilities** Children's menu Play area Dogs allowed Garden Parking

The Plough ☻

Coldharbour Rd BN27 3QJ ☎ 01323 844859
dir: *Off A22, W of Hailsham*

17th-century former farmhouse which has been a pub for over 200 years, and now comprises two bars and two restaurants. Excellent wheelchair facilities, a large beer garden and a children's play area add to the appeal, and the Plough is also a handy stop for walkers. Expect such fish dishes as Sussex smokie or prawn, brie and broccoli bake, while other options include duck breast in spicy plum sauce, veal in lemon cream, or lamb cutlets in redcurrant and rosemary.

Open all day all wk 11am-11pm (Sun noon-10.30pm) **Bar Meals** L served Mon-Fri 12-2.30, Sat-Sun 12-9.30 D served Mon-Fri 6-9.30, Sat-Sun 12-9.30 ⊕ SHEPHERD NEAME ◀ Shepherd Neame Spitfire Premium Ale, Best, Kent Best. ☻ 6 **Facilities** Play area Family room Dogs allowed Garden Parking

PICK OF THE PUBS

The Lamb Inn 🍷

WARTLING Map 6 TQ60

BN27 1RY ☎ 01323 832116
web: www.lambinnwartling.co.uk
dir: *A259 from Polegate to Pevensey rdbt. Take 1st left to Wartling & Herstmonceux Castle. Pub 3m on right*

This family-run, classic country pub and restaurant was built in 1526, although it did not begin dispensing ale until 1640. Since then it has provided a welcome rest stop to everyone from 18th-century smugglers to today's birdwatchers, walkers and locals who enjoy the nearby Pevensey Levels and surrounding East Sussex countryside. Draw up one of the comfortable cream sofas to the fire and, as your well-behaved dog settles down at your feet, enjoy a real ale from Sussex breweries or a glass of wine. Aside from liquid refreshment, the pub is well known for its food. Everything is made on the premises, including the bread, and, as far as possible, makes use of top quality produce sourced locally from places like Chilley Farm, which specialises in raising Gloucester Old Spot pigs, Southdown and Kent Cross lamb, and Sussex beef without additives and in unhurried fashion. Fish makes the short journey from Hastings and Newhaven to become house specialities, offered daily on the specials board. An easy-to-assimilate menu offers plenty of variety, so that a meal might begin with pancake of creamy garlic mushrooms glazed with Stilton; smoked mackerel, prawn and crayfish terrine with horseradish cream and Melba toast; or grilled fresh figs. For a main course, there could be seafood platter; fillet of lemon sole stuffed with spinach and crab, dill and Champagne sauce; chargrilled Tottingworth Farm Barnsley chop with dauphinoise potatoes, garlic and parsley butter; rib-eye of Sussex Limousin beef with home-made wedges, mushrooms and fried onions; or, for vegetarians, risotto and dressed salad; or winter vegetable casserole with Parmesan and breadcrumb crust. Traditional home-made desserts are represented by iced chocolate and Tia Maria parfait, and lemon and sultana bread and butter pudding with clotted cream. Look out for year round events and special nights.

Open all week Closed Sun eve, Mon in winter **Bar Meals** L served all week 12-2.15 D served Tue-Sat 7-9 Av main course £8.95 **Restaurant** L served all week 12-2.15 D served Tue-Sat 7-9 Fixed menu price fr £11.95 Av 3 course à la carte fr £22.95 🍺 Harveys, Red River, Horsham Best, Toff's, Level Best. 🍷 8 **Facilities** Children's menu Dogs allowed Garden Parking

PICK OF THE PUBS

The Dorset Arms ♗

WITHYHAM Map 6 TQ43

TN7 4BD
☎ 01892 770278 📄 01892 770195
e-mail: pete@dorset-arms.co.uk
dir: *4m W of Tunbridge Wells on B2110 between Groombridge & Hartfield*

This white, weather-boarded building has been an inn since the 18th century, although 300 years earlier it was Somers, an open-halled farmhouse with earth floors. Today's name comes from the arms of the Sackville family, once the Earls of Dorset, of nearby Buckhurst Park. Set on the borders of Kent and Sussex, the inn is ideally situated for explorations of nearby Ashdown Forest, home to everybody's favourite bear, Winnie the Pooh. It has many interesting features, including a massive wall and ceiling beams in the restaurant, an oak-floored bar, a huge open fireplace, and

an old ice-house buried in the hillside at the back. The prize-winning beers come from Harveys of Lewes, and a good number of wines from the extensive wine list are available by the glass. Where possible, the owners source all their ingredients locally, especially meats, fish and vegetables. Bar snacks and daily specials are among the food choices, and the carte menu lists starters such as oak-smoked salmon with brown bread and butter; mushrooms in garlic, white wine and cream; and deep-fried tempura battered king prawns with chilli dip. Main courses can include pan-fried fillets of sea bass with parsley butter; sliced boneless breast of chicken with bacon and onions in tomato and herb sauce; half shoulder of English lamb with red wine gravy and mint sauce; and vegetable risotto with garlic bread. Blackboard specials might feature chilli con carne with rice; rich steak and ale pie; and cheese-topped ratatouille bake. The pub is a popular venue for local fishing and cricket teams, and holds regular quiz nights and music evenings.

Open 11.30-3, 6-11 Closed: Mon L **Bar Meals** L served Tue-Sun 12-2 D served Tue-Sun 7.30-9 Av main course £8 **Restaurant** L served Tue-Sun 12-2 D served Tue-Sat 7.30-9 Fixed menu price fr £16.50 Av 3 course à la carte fr £19 ⊕ HARVEYS OF LEWES ◀ Harveys Sussex Best, seasonal ales. ♗ 8 **Facilities** Dogs allowed Garden Parking

WADHURST   Map 6 TQ63

PICK OF THE PUBS

The Best Beech Inn ♀

Mayfield Ln TN5 6JH ☎ 01892 782046
dir: *7m from Tunbridge Wells. On A246 at lights turn left onto London Rd (A26), left at mini rdbt onto A267, left then right onto B2100. At Mark Cross signed Wadhurst, 3m on right*

The unusually-named Best Beech Inn is going from strength to strength. The inn dates back to 1680, and has been sympathetically refurbished in recent years to preserve the essentially Victorian character of its heyday. The result is a place bursting with personality, characterised by comfy chairs, exposed brickwork and open fireplaces. Ideally situated near the Kent and Sussex border, in an Area of Outstanding Natural Beauty, the inn includes a fine à la carte restaurant offering excellent European cuisine with a French influence. For those who prefer a more informal atmosphere, there is the bar bistro with a comprehensive menu available from the blackboard. Dinner could begin with pork rillette and apricot chutney, move on to bouillabaisse with saffron new potatoes, and finish with tarte au chocolate, marmalade syrup and vanilla ice cream.

Open all day all wk noon–11pm **Bar Meals** L served Mon-Sat 12-3, Sun 12-4 booking required D served Mon-Sat 6-9.30 booking required **Restaurant** L served Mon-Sat 12-3, Sun 12-4 booking required D served Mon-Sat 6-9.30 booking required ⊕ SHEPHERD NEAME ◀ Kent Best, Master Brew. ♀ 7
Facilities Children's menu Family room Dogs allowed Garden Parking

WARBLETON   Map 6 TQ61

The War-Bill-in-Tun Inn

Church Hill TN21 9BD
☎ 01435 830636 🖺 01435 830636
e-mail: whitton@thewarbillintun.wanadoo.co.uk
dir: *From Hailsham take A267 towards Heathfield. Turn right for village. 15m from Hailsham*

A 400-year-old smugglers' haunt, visited by The Beatles when they came to see their manager, Brian Epstein, who lived half a mile away. Locals still recall meeting Lennon and McCartney, as well as the resident ghost. Family run, the owners aim to offer good food and friendly service. Representative dishes include Gressingham duck, grilled trout with an almond and wine sauce, and light lunch dishes like jacket potatoes and scampi.

Open all wk ⊕ FREE HOUSE ◀ Harveys Best, Bishop's Finger, Tanglefoot, Spitfire Smooth. **Facilities** Dogs allowed Garden Parking

WARTLING   Map 6 TQ60

PICK OF THE PUBS

The Lamb Inn ♀

See Pick of the Pubs on page 455

WILMINGTON   Map 6 TQ50

The Giants Rest ♀

The Street BN26 5SQ
☎ 01323 870207 🖺 01323 870207
e-mail: abecjane@aol.com
dir: *2m outside Polegate on A27 towards Brighton*

With the famous chalk figure of the Long Man of Wilmington standing guard opposite, this family-owned, Victorian free house is admirably committed to home-prepared, seasonal food. Sit at a pine table, play a game or puzzle, and order roast chicken and leek pie; beef in Guinness with rosemary dumplings; hake with coriander, spring onion and chilli fishcakes; or haloumi warm salad. There are daily specials too. Harveys real ales from Lewes are among those offered.

Open all wk 11am-3 6-11pm (Sat-Sun all day) **Bar Meals** L served Mon-Fri 11.30-2, Sat-Sun all day booking required D served Mon-Fri 6.30-9, Sat-Sun all day booking required **Restaurant** L served Mon-Fri 11.30-2, Sat-Sun all day booking required D served Mon-Fri 6.30-9, Sat-Sun all day booking required ⊕ FREE HOUSE ◀ Harveys Best, Timothy Taylor Landlord, Summer Lightning, Harveys Best Ŏ Stowford Press. ♀ 7
Facilities Children's menu Dogs allowed Garden Parking

WINCHELSEA   Map 7 TQ91

The New Inn ♀

German St TN36 4EN ☎ 01797 226252
dir: *Telephone for directions*

Elegant Winchelsea has seen much change over the centuries, not least the sea's retreat that ended its days as a thriving seaport. The 18th-century New Inn has witnessed change of a far more beneficial nature and is known today for its comfort, hospitality and excellent cuisine. Chalkboard specials include lobster tails with chips and salad, Rye Bay lemon sole, and chicken Kiev. The lovely walled garden is a delight on a sunny day.

Open all wk ⊕ GREENE KING ◀ Morlands Original, Abbots Ale, Greene King IPA, Old Speckled Hen. ♀ 10
Facilities Family room Dogs allowed Garden Parking

WITHYHAM   Map 6 TQ43

PICK OF THE PUBS

The Dorset Arms ♀

See Pick of the Pubs on opposite page

SUSSEX, WEST

AMBERLEY   Map 6 TQ01

Black Horse ♀

High St BN18 9NL ☎ 01798 831700
dir: *Please telephone for directions*

A traditional 17th-century tavern with a lively atmosphere in a beautiful South Downs village. Look out for the display of sheep bells donated by the last shepherd to have a flock on the local hills. Food is served in the large restaurant and bar or in the beer garden complete with pond, and there's plenty of choice for everyone including a children's menu. Great beer, good local walks, and nice views of the South Downs. Dogs (on leads) are welcome in the bar.

Open all day all wk **Bar Meals** L served all wk 12-3 D served Sun-Thu 6-8.30, Fri-Sat 6-9.30 Av main course £10 **Restaurant** L served Sun only booking required D served Sun-Mon & Wed-Thu 6-8.30, Fri-Sat 6-9.30 booking required ⊕ ADMIRAL TAVERNS ◀ Greene King IPA, Harveys Sussex, guest ale. ♀ 9 **Facilities** Children's menu Dogs allowed Garden

The Bridge Inn ♀

Houghton Bridge BN18 9LR ☎ 01798 831619
e-mail: bridgeamberley@btinternet.com
web: www.bridgeinnamberley.com
dir: *5m N of Arundel on B2139. Next to Amberley main line station*

Standing alongside the River Arun at the mid-point of the South Downs Way National Trail, this traditional free house dates from 1650. The pretty pub garden and patio are summer favourites, whilst the candle-lit bar and log fires come into their own on cold winter evenings. Drinkers will find Westons ciders and a good range of real ales, whilst daily chalkboard specials and an extensive range of pub classics sustain the heartiest appetites.

continued

AMBERLEY *continued*

Open all day all wk noon-11 (Sun noon-10.30) **Bar Meals** L served Mon-Fri 12-2.30, Sat-Sun 12-4 D served Sun-Mon 6-8, Tue-Sat 6-9 Av main course £9 **Restaurant** Av 3 course à la carte fr £17 ⊕ FREE HOUSE ◀ Harveys Sussex, Fuller's London Pride, Hopback Summer Lightning, Sharps Cornish Coaster ♻ Westons Stowford Press, Westons Old Rosie. ♚ 8 **Facilities** Children's menu Dogs allowed Garden Parking

ASHURST Map 6 TQ11

PICK OF THE PUBS

The Fountain Inn ♚

BN44 3AP ☎ 01403 710219
e-mail: fountainashurst@aol.com
dir: *On B2135 N of Steyning*

This 16th-century free house is located just north of Steyning in a picturesque setting in the historic village of Ashurst. The interior features flagstone floors, low beams and a fantastic inglenook fireplace. There are two large garden areas in a delightfully tranquil setting by the large duck pond with seating for 200 people. The inn offers an extensive selection of home-made dishes to delight your taste buds, including its renowned burgers and steak and ale pies, and the regular range of well-kept real ales is supplemented by a weekly guest ale from local breweries. At lunchtime there are ploughman's, salads, freshly cut sandwiches, and Sussex smokie - smoked haddock and prawns in a cheese sauce. In the evening there is a good choice from the chargrill, notably steaks, and dishes like chicken breast with a sunblush tomato and pesto dressing. A fishy option might be sea bass, or a choice from the specials board.

Open all day all wk 11.30am-11pm (Sun noon-10.30pm) **Bar Meals** L served Mon-Sat 11.30-2.30, Sun 12-3 D served Mon-Sat 6-9.30, Sun 6-8.30 **Restaurant** L served Mon-Sat 11.30-2.30, Sun 12-3 D served Mon-Sat 6-9.30, Sun 6-8.30 ⊕ FREE HOUSE ◀ Harveys Sussex, Fuller's London, Seasonal ales, Guest ales ♻ Stowford Press. ♚ 10 **Facilities** Dogs allowed Garden Parking

BALCOMBE Map 6 TQ33

The Cowdray NEW

RH17 6QD ☎ 01444 811280
e-mail: alexandandy@hotmail.co.uk
dir: *Please telephone for directions*

Just a mile from the M23 (junct 10a), the once run-down village boozer has been transformed into cosy dining pub, with Alex and Andy Owen, who once worked for Gordon Ramsay, re-opening the doors in early 2008. Expect wood floors, a fresh, crisp decor, and a pub menu that's a cut above average and boasts 85% Sussex produce. Follow wild mushroom risotto with pan-fried squid with chorizo, prawns and clams, or Old Spot pork belly with root vegetables, and pear Tatin.

Open all wk noon-3 5.30-11 Closed: 25 Dec eve, 1 Jan eve **Bar Meals** L served Mon-Sat 12-3, Sun 12-4 D served Mon-Thu 6-9, Fri-Sat 6-10 Av main course £8.50 **Restaurant** L served Mon-Sat 12-3, Sun 12-4 booking required D served Mon-Thu 6-9, Fri-Sat 6-10 booking required Av 3 course à la carte fr £25 ⊕ GREENE KING **Facilities** Children's menu Play area Family room Dogs allowed Garden Parking

BARNHAM Map 6 SU90

The Murrell Arms ♚

Yapton Rd PO22 0AS ☎ 01243 553320
dir: *From Brighton follow A27 through Arundel for 2m, left at The Oaks, follow road to end. Turn right at The Olive Branch*

Lavish window boxes and hanging baskets mark out this attractive white-painted pub in the summer. Built in 1750 as a farmhouse, it became an inn shortly after the railway station opened over 100 years later. With the briefest of menus at the lowest of prices, there's no more affordable place to sit down for a ploughman's, bacon hock with new potatoes and green beans, or cockles and mussels, washed down with a reliable pint of Fuller's.

Open all wk 11-2.30 5.30-11 (Sat 11-11 Sun noon-10.30) **Bar Meals** L served all wk 12-2 D served all wk 6-9 Av main course £3.75 ⊕ FULLERS BREWERY ◀ Fuller's London Pride, ESB & Butser Best - Horndean Special Brew. ♚ 28 **Facilities** Play area Dogs allowed Garden Parking **Notes** ⊚

BURGESS HILL Map 6 TQ31

The Oak Barn NEW ♚

Cuckfield Rd RH15 8RE
☎ 01444 258222 📄 01444 258388
e-mail: enquiries@oakbarnrestaurant.co.uk
web: www.oakbarnrestaurant.co.uk
dir: *Please telephone for directions*

Beautifully restored six years ago, using old timbers salvaged from wooden ships, acres of oak flooring and fine stained glass, this 250-year-old barn has been transformed into a popular pub-restaurant. Lofty, raftered ceilings, a galleried restaurant, and leather chairs fronting a huge fireplace set the atmospheric scene for supping pints of Harveys and tucking into mussels in garlic, cream and white wine, pork belly with caramelised apples, and banoffee pie, or one of the all-day bar meals.

Open all day all wk 10am-11pm (Sun 11-11) **Bar Meals** L served all wk 12-2.30 D served all wk 6-9.30 Av main course £13 **Restaurant** L served all wk 12-2.30 booking required D served all wk 6-9.30 booking required Av 3 course à la carte fr £21 ⊕ FREE HOUSE ◀ Guinness, Harveys. ♚ 12 **Facilities** Children's menu Garden Parking

BURPHAM Map 6 TQ00

PICK OF THE PUBS

George & Dragon ⊚

See Pick of the Pubs on opposite page

BURY Map 6 TQ01

The Squire & Horse ♚

Bury Common RH20 1NS
☎ 01798 831343 📄 01798 831343
dir: *On A29, 4m S of Pulbrough, 4m N of Arundel*

The original 16th-century building was extended a few years ago, with old wooden beams and country fireplaces throughout. All the food is freshly cooked to order. The fish specials change daily and main courses are served with a selection of vegetables. These could include barbecued barracuda fillet on a bed of prawn risotto, or calves' liver with bacon and red wine glaze. Thai food is a speciality, and the pub is renowned for its desserts.

Open all wk ◀ Greene King IPA, Harveys Sussex, guest ales. ♚ 8 **Facilities** Garden Parking

PICK OF THE PUBS

George & Dragon ✹

BURPHAM
Map 6 TQ00

BN18 9RR ☎ **01903 883131**

e-mail: sara.cheney@btinternet.com

dir: *Off A27 1m E of Arundel, signed Burpham, 2.5m pub on left*

Tucked away down a long 'no through road', Burpham looks across the Arun valley to the mighty Arundel Castle. There are excellent riverside and downland walks on the doorstep of this 300 year-old free house, and walkers and their dogs are welcome in the bar: but please, leave any muddy footwear in the porch. Step inside, and you'll find beamed ceilings and modern prints on the walls, with worn stone flags on the floor. The original rooms have been opened out to form a large space that catches the late sunshine, but there are still a couple of alcoves with tables for an intimate drink. Look a little further, and you'll also discover a small bar hidden around a corner. This is very much a dining pub, attracting visitors from far and wide. The à la carte menu and specials board offer a good choice of dishes between them: for starters you could try caramelised red onion, fig and pear tartlet with Stilton dressing, or game terrine with Arundel ale chutney. Main courses might include honey roasted Scotch salmon on citrus cous cous with pan-roasted vegetables and soy sauce; wild mushroom, garlic, leek and thyme crumble with Sussex Cheddar topping and side salad; or pan roasted English lamb rump on red onion confit with black pepper, red wine and cranberry sauce, served with dauphinoise potatoes and fresh vegetables. There are tables outside, ideal for whiling away an afternoon or evening in summer, listening to the cricket being played on the green a few steps away.

Open 11.30-3, 6-mdnt **Bar Meals** L served Mon-Fri 12-2, Sat-Sun 12-3 D served all week 6-9 Av main course £13.95 **Restaurant** L served Mon-Sat 12-2 D served Mon-Sun 6-9 Av 3 course à la carte fr £24.95 ⊕ FREE HOUSE ◼ Brewery-on-Sea Spinnaker Bitter, Fuller's London Pride, Arundel Ales and guest ales. ♻ Stowford Press.
Facilities Children's menu Dogs allowed Garden Parking

CHARLTON — Map 6 SU81

PICK OF THE PUBS

The Fox Goes Free ☂

See Pick of the Pubs on opposite page

CHICHESTER — Map 5 SU80

Crown and Anchor ☂

Dell Quay Rd PO20 7EE ☎ 01243 781712
e-mail: crown&anchor@thespiritgroup.com
dir: *Take A286 from Chichester towards West Wittering, turn right for Dell Quay*

Nestling at the foot of the Sussex Downs with panoramic views of Chichester harbour, this unique hostelry dates in parts to the early 18th century when it also served as a custom house for the old port. It has a superb terrace overlooking the quay for al fresco dining. Menu choices include fish (battered to order) and chips, grilled steaks, and steak and ale pie.

⊕ PUNCH TAVERNS ◄ Bombardier, Theakstons, Guinness. ☂ 17 **Facilities** Dogs allowed Garden Parking

PICK OF THE PUBS

Royal Oak Inn ★★★★★ INN ☺ ☂

Pook Ln, East Lavant PO18 0AX
☎ 01243 527434 🖷 01243 775062
e-mail: enquiries@royaloakeastlavant.co.uk
web: www.royaloakeastlavant.co.uk
dir: *A286 from Chichester signed Midhurst, 2m then right at mini-rdbt, pub over bridge on left*

Set just outside Chichester in the picturesque village of East Lavant, this coaching inn offers a friendly welcome, real ales and award-winning food all within easy reach of the rolling hills of Sussex. The Royal Oak was a regular pub for many years, but has been exceptionally well converted to offer stylish, sleekly furnished guest accommodation complete with state of the art entertainment systems. The brick-lined restaurant and bar achieve a crisp, rustic brand of chic: details include fresh flowers, candles, and wine attractively displayed in alcoves set into the walls. Favourite dishes include tempura vegetables with teriyaki and sweet chilli dipping sauce; seared scallops on parsnip purée with crisp pancetta; risotto of wild mushrooms with marinated artichokes and shaved pecorino; and fillet steak with a creamy pepper sauce,

chestnut mushrooms and bordelaise potatoes A lengthy wine list will delight any connoisseur.

Open all day all wk 7am-11.30pm Closed: 25 Dec **Bar Meals** Av main course £15.50 **Restaurant** L served all wk 12-3 booking required D served all wk 6.30-11 booking required Av 3 course à la carte fr £30 ⊕ FREE HOUSE ◄ Ballards, HSB, Sussex, Arundel. ☂ 20 **Facilities** Children's menu Garden Parking **Rooms** 8

CHILGROVE — Map 5 SU81

PICK OF THE PUBS

The Fish House Ⓤ ☂

High St PO18 9HX ☎ 01243 519444
e-mail: info@thefishhouse.co.uk
dir: *On B2141 between Chichester & Petersfield*

Low ceilings, beams and decorative brickwork combine with leather sofas in the bar of this recently refurbished wisteria-covered building. Here, too, you'll find a crustacean counter, Irish Marble topped bar and a 300 year-old French fireplace. Besides its signature Guinness and oysters, the Fish House offers a daily set lunch menu and Sunday roasts in the bar. Meanwhile the sumptuous fine dining restaurant features paintings by John Holt, as well as hand-made furniture and contrasting linen drapes. From their tables, diners can watch head chef Alan Gleeson preparing dishes from an à la carte menu where fish and seafood naturally top the bill. Typical dishes include whole baby plaice, baked mash and fine beans; steamed fillet of hake, glass noodles and enoki mushrooms; and local game pie, red cabbage and crushed parsnips.

Open all day all wk **Bar Meals** L served all wk 12-2.30 D served all wk 6-10 Av main course £12.50 **Restaurant** L served all wk 12-2.30 booking required D served all wk 6-10 booking required Fixed menu price fr £17 Av 3 course à la carte fr £40 ⊕ FREE HOUSE ◄ Black Sheep, Harveys Best ♂ Westons Organic. ☂ 24 **Facilities** Children's menu Dogs allowed Garden Parking **Rooms** 15

COMPTON — Map 5 SU71

Coach & Horses

The Square PO18 9HA ☎ 02392 631228
dir: *On B2146 S of Petersfield, to Emsworth, in centre of Compton*

The 16th-century pub is set quite remotely in the prettiest of Downland villages, a popular spot for walkers and cyclists. The front bar features two open fires and a bar billiards table, while the restaurant is in the oldest part of the pub, with many exposed beams. Up to five guest beers from independent breweries are usually available, plus Stowford Press and Thatchers ciders. There is an extensive menu of home-cooked dishes, all made to order.

Open all wk 11.30-3 6-11 **Bar Meals** L served all wk 12-2 D served all wk 7-9 Av main course £10 **Restaurant** L served all wk 12-2 booking required D served all wk 7-9 booking required Fixed menu price fr £17.75 Av 3 course à la carte fr £25 ⊕ FREE HOUSE ◄ Fuller's ESB, Ballard's Best, Dark Star Golden Gate, Oakleaf Brewery Nuptu'ale, Dark Star Hophead ♂ Stowford Press, Thatchers. **Facilities** Children's menu Dogs allowed

DUNCTON — Map 6 SU91

The Cricketers ☂

GU28 0LB ☎ 01798 342473
dir: *On A285, 3m from Petworth, 8m from Chichester*

Dating back to the 16th century, this attractive white-painted pub is situated in fine cricket walking country at the western end of the South Downs. Rumoured to be haunted, the inn has changed little over the years. There is a delightful and very popular garden with extensive deck seating and weekend barbecues. The menus sometimes change four times a day, offering good hearty meals like beer-battered haddock or rib-eye steak, both with hand-cut chips; all washed down with quality real ales from micro-breweries. An ideal stop-off point for coach parties visiting Goodwood.

Open all day all wk **Bar Meals** L served Mon-Fri 12-2.30, Sat-Sun 12-6 D served Mon-Fri 6-9, Sat-Sun 12-9 **Restaurant** L served Mon-Fri 12-2.30, Sat-Sun 12-6 D served Mon-Fri 6-9, Sat-Sun 12-9 ⊕ FREE HOUSE ◄ Betty Stogs, Horsham Best, Arundel Gold, Guest ale ♂ Thatchers Heritage. ☂ 8 **Facilities** Children's menu Play area Dogs allowed Garden Parking

EAST ASHLING — Map 5 SU80

Horse and Groom ★★★★ INN ☂

East Ashling PO18 9AX
☎ 01243 575339 🖷 01243 575560
e-mail: info@thehorseandgroomchichester.co.uk
dir: *3m from Chichester on B1278 between Chichester & Rowland's Castle. 2m off A27 at Fishbourne*

A substantially renovated 17th-century inn located at the foot of the South Downs. This is good walking country, and top tourist attractions lie within easy reach. The flagstone floor and beamed bar is cosy, with a working range at one end and an open fire at the other. The underground cellar keeps ales at a constant temperature, and there are bar snack, blackboard and full carte menus. The enclosed garden is great place for alfresco

continued on page 462

PICK OF THE PUBS

The Fox Goes Free 🍷

CHARLTON Map 6 SU81

PO18 0HU
☎ 01243 811461 📠 **01243 811712**
e-mail: enquiries@thefoxgoesfree.com
web: www.thefoxgoesfree.com
dir: *A286, 6m from Chichester towards Midhurst. 1m from Goodwood racecourse*

Nestling in unspoilt countryside, this lovely old brick and flint free house was a favoured hunting lodge of William III. With its three huge fireplaces, old pews and brick floors, the 16th-century building simply exudes charm and character. The pub, which hosted the first Women's Institute meeting in 1915, lies close to the rambling Weald and Downland open-air museum, where fifty historic buildings from around southern England have been reconstructed to form a unique collection. Goodwood estate is also close by, and The Fox attracts many a punter during the racing season and the annual Festival of Speed. Away from the high life, you can watch the world go by from the solid timber benches and tables to the front, or relax under the apples trees in the lawned rear garden. And, lest all this sounds rather fancy, you'll find that The Fox is nonetheless a friendly and welcoming drinkers' pub. There is a good selection of real ales – including the eponymous Fox Goes Free bitter – and eating here is not prohibitive either. Everything is homemade and, whether you're looking for a quick bar snack or something more substantial, the daily changing menus offer plenty of choice. Baguettes filled with sausage and caramelised onions or smoked salmon with mascarpone will fill the odd corner, whilst fresh battered cod and chips; or steak and mushroom pie are tempting alternatives from the bar menu. À la carte choices include roast shoulder of lamb with braised red cabbage and olives; and pan-fried chicken with Parma ham, creamed leeks and red wine sauce.

Open 11-11 (Sun noon-11pm) Closed: 25 Dec eve **Bar Meals** L served Mon-Fri 12-2.30, Sat-Sun 12-10 D served Mon-Fri 6.30-10, Sat-Sun 12-10 Av main course £10 **Restaurant** L served all week 12-2.30 D served all week 6.30-10 Av 3 course à la carte fr £25 ⊞ FREE HOUSE ■ Ballards Best & The Fox Goes Free, Harvey's Sussex. 🍷 8
Facilities Children's menu Dogs allowed Garden Parking

EAST ASHLING *continued*

eating in warmer weather. There are eleven comfortable and spacious rooms available if you would like to stay over.

Open noon-3 6-11 (Sun noon-6) Closed: Sun eve **Bar Meals** L served all wk 12-2.15 D served Mon-Sat 6.30-9.15 Av main course £10.95 **Restaurant** L served all wk 12-2.15 D served Mon-Sat 6.30-9.15 booking required ⊕ FREE HOUSE ◀ Youngs, Harveys, Summer Lightning, Hop Head Ö Stowford Press. ♀ 6 **Facilities** Children's menu Dogs allowed Garden Parking **Rooms** 11

EAST DEAN Map 6 SU91

PICK OF THE PUBS

The Star & Garter ♀

PO18 0JG ☎ 01243 811318 ▤ 01243 811826 **e-mail:** thestarandgarter@hotmail.com **dir:** *On A286 between Chichester & Midhurst. Exit A286 at Singleton. Village in 2m*

Close to Goodwood Racecourse and motor racing venues, the pub is located in the pretty downland village of East Dean just above the village pond. It was built in 1740 from traditional Sussex napped flint and the interior has been opened out to give a light and airy atmosphere, with original brickwork, oak flooring, antique panelling, scrubbed tables and a wood-burning stove. The menu changes almost daily, with a wide choice of fish and shellfish listed on a large blackboard above the fire. Shellfish platters are available from Easter to October, featuring Selsey crab, lobster, hand-carved salmon, crevettes and other shellfish as available. A Star Platter serves two and a Garter Platter serves four. A wide selection of meat, game and vegetarian dishes is also offered. Game grill is a popular choice, comprising a whole roasted partridge, pheasant breast, pigeon breasts and venison sausage with red wine jus.

Open all wk **Bar Meals** Av main course £13 food served all day **Restaurant** Av 3 course à la carte fr £25 food served all day ⊕ FREE HOUSE ◀ Ballards Best, Guinness, Arundel Castle & Gold Ö Westons 1st Quality, Westons Scrumpy, Stowford Press. ♀ 10 **Facilities** Children's menu Dogs allowed Garden Parking

---

ELSTED Map 5 SU81

PICK OF THE PUBS

The Three Horseshoes

GU29 0JY ☎ 01730 825746 **dir:** *A272 from Midhurst towards Petersfield, after 2m left to Harting & Elsted, after 3m pub on left*

A 16th-century former drovers' ale house tucked below the steep scarp slope of the South Downs in the peaceful village of Elsted. It's one of those quintessential English country pubs that Sussex specialises in, full of rustic charm, with unspoilt cottagey bars, worn stone-flagged floors, low beams, latch doors, a vast inglenook, and a motley mix of antique furnishings. On fine days the extensive rear garden, with roaming chickens and stunning southerly views, is hugely popular. Tip-top real ales, including Bowman's from across the Hampshire border, are drawn from the cask, and a daily-changing blackboard menu offers classic country cooking. Starters such as devilled kidneys or potted shrimps are followed by main courses likely to include venison; stalked locally and hung by the landlord, it may be served roasted with a redcurrant sauce reduction. Game such as pheasant is abundant in season; alternatively fish of the day comes with dauphinoise potatoes.

Open all wk **Bar Meals** L served all wk 12-2 D served Mon-Sat 6.30-9, Sun 7-8.30 Av main course £12.50 **Restaurant** L served all wk 12-2 D served Mon-Sat 6.30-9, Sun 7-8.30 ⊕ FREE HOUSE ◀ Flowerpots Ale, Ballard's Best, Fuller's London Pride, Timothy Taylor Landlord, Hop Back Summer Lightning, Bowman Ales Swift One. **Facilities** Dogs allowed Garden Parking

---

FERNHURST Map 6 SU82

PICK OF THE PUBS

The King's Arms ♀

Midhurst Rd GU27 3HA ☎ 01428 652005 ▤ 01428 658970 **dir:** *On A286 between Haslemere & Midhurst, 1m S of Fernhurst*

A Grade II listed, 17th-century free house and restaurant set amidst rolling Sussex farmland, which can be seen at its best from the garden. The pub and its outbuildings are built from Sussex stone and decorated with hanging baskets, flowering tubs, vines and creepers. The L-shaped interior is very cosy, with beams, lowish ceilings, and a large inglenook fireplace, with the bar one side and restaurant and small dining room the other. Everything is home made and freshly prepared on the premises, from salad dressings to sorbets. Fish is an important commodity, and Michael regularly visits the south coast to buy direct from the boats, bringing back what later appears on the menu as, for instance, goujons of plaice with tartare sauce; monkfish loin in Parma ham with courgette ribbons,

---

prawn and saffron sauce; or perhaps seared scallops with bacon and pea risotto. Alternatives to fish usually include Barbary duck breast with Savoy cabbage, baby roast potatoes and orange and port sauce; rack of English lamb with redcurrant and rosemary mash with lightly minted gravy; and fillet steak with dauphinoise potatoes, wild mushrooms and rich red wine jus. In addition to the monthly changing menu, there are daily changing specials such as steak, kidney and mushroom pudding. The large garden has some lovely trees, including a mature willow and pretty white lilacs, and views over surrounding fields. A wisteria-clad barn is used for the pub's annual three-day beer festival at the end of August.

Open all day all wk 11am-11pm (Sun noon-10.30pm) **Bar Meals** L served Mon-Sat 12-2.30, Sun 12-4 booking required D served Mon-Sat 6-9.30 booking required **Restaurant** L served Mon-Sat 12-2.30, Sun 12-4 booking required D served Mon-Sat 6-9.30 booking required ⊕ FREE HOUSE ◀ Hepworth Sussex, Skinners Betty Stogs. ♀ 10 **Facilities** Children's menu Dogs allowed Garden Parking

---

The Red Lion ♀

The Green GU27 3HY ☎ 01428 643112 ▤ 01428 643939 **dir:** *Just off A286 midway between Haslemere & Midhurst*

An attractive 16th-century inn with oak beams and open fires, The Red Lion is set in its own lovely gardens on the village green. The pub is renowned for the quality of its beers, with the likes of Fuller's ESB, Chiswick and London Pride along with seasonal guest ales. Freshly cooked, traditional English food is offered from a regularly changing specials menu featuring seafood, with dishes such as deep-fried Selsey cod in beer batter.

Open all wk 11.30am-11pm (closed Mon-Wed 3-5) **Bar Meals** L served all wk 12-2.30 D served all wk 6-9.30 **Restaurant** L served all wk 12-2.30 D served all wk 6-9.30 ⊕ FULLER SMITH TURNER PLC ◀ Fuller's ESB, Chiswick, London Pride, Guest Ale. ♀ 8 **Facilities** Dogs allowed Garden Parking

---

GRAFFHAM Map 6 SU91

PICK OF THE PUBS

The Foresters Arms ♀

The Street GU28 0QA ☎ 01798 867202 **e-mail:** info@forestersgraffham.co.uk **dir:** *Telephone for directions*

Clare and Robert Pearce bought this 16th-century country freehouse in 2007. In the bar you'll find old beams and a large smoke-blackened fireplace while, in the restaurant, a move back to basics results in a short, daily-changing menu using produce sourced from within a 50-mile radius. Thus, panfried skate wing; salt beef; and mushroom and leek fritta are among Robert's repertoire. Sixteen wines by the glass on a personally chosen list from selected vintners.

Open all wk 11am-2.30 6-late **Bar Meals** L served all wk 12-2.15 booking required D served all wk 6.15-9.15 booking required **Restaurant** L served all wk 12-2.15 booking required D served all wk 6.15-9.15 booking required ⊕ FREE HOUSE ☕ 16 **Facilities** Children's menu Dogs allowed Garden Parking

---

HALNAKER   Map 6 SU90

PICK OF THE PUBS

The Anglesey Arms at Halnaker ☕

See Pick of the Pubs on page 464

HEYSHOTT   Map 6 SU81

PICK OF THE PUBS

Unicorn Inn

GU29 0DL ☎ 01730 813486   🖺 01730 814896
e-mail: unicorninnheyshott@hotmail.co.uk
dir: *Telephone for directions*

This cosy village pub dates from 1750, although it was not granted its first licence until 1839, has a good view of the Downs from the beautiful, south-facing rear gardens. It is set within the South Downs Area of Outstanding Natural Beauty, scheduled to re-designated as a National Park in 2010. The Unicorn is popular not just with locals, but with walkers and cyclists detouring from the South Downs Way. The bar, with beams and large log fire, is part of the original building, and very atmospheric it is too. The subtly lit, cream-painted restaurant, with matching table linen, is also in perfect historical tune. Locally sourced food is important, although some of the meats come from Smithfield, while fish arrives daily from Selsey a few miles away, and Portsmouth.

Open 11.30-3 7-11 (Sun 12-4) Closed: Sun eve & Mon **Bar Meals** L served Tue-Sat 12-2, Sun 12-2.30 booking required D served Tue-Sat 7-9 booking required Av main course £6.50 **Restaurant** L served Tue-Sat 12-2, Sun 12-2.30 booking required D served Tue-Sat 7-9 ⊕ FREE HOUSE ◀ Horsham Best Bitter, Fuller's London Pride ☕ Stowford Press. **Facilities** Dogs allowed Garden Parking

---

HORSHAM   Map 6 TQ13

The Black Jug ☕

31 North St RH12 1RJ
☎ 01403 253526   🖺 01403 217821
e-mail: black.jug@brunningandprice.co.uk
dir: *Telephone for directions*

This busy town centre pub is close to the railway station and popular with Horsham's well-heeled. Here you'll find a congenial atmosphere with friendly staff, an open fire, large conservatory and courtyard garden. Meals are freshly prepared using local ingredients wherever possible; light bites include bacon and black pudding hash, or grilled minute steak with Stilton mayonnaise, whilst larger appetites might go for smoked haddock and salmon fishcakes or steak and kidney pudding with new potatoes and curly kale.

Open all day all wk 11.30am-11pm (Sun 12-10.30) **Bar Meals** Av main course £10.95 food served all day **Restaurant** food served all day ⊕ BRUNNING & PRICE ◀ Harveys, Adnams Broadside, Greene King IPA, Guest ales. ☕ 30 **Facilities** Dogs allowed Garden

---

KINGSFOLD   Map 6 TQ13

The Dog and Duck

Dorking Rd RH12 3SA ☎ 01306 627295
e-mail: info@thedogandduck.fsnet.co.uk
dir: *On A24, 3m N of Horsham*

A 16th-century, family-run country pub with a very large garden, children's play equipment and a summer ice cream bar. The pub has been steadily building a reputation for wholesome home-made food, such as liver and bacon, breaded plaice with prawns, chicken curry, chilli con carne and lasagne. It hosts many events, including quizzes, darts evenings, a big beer festival and fundraising activities for St George's Hospital.

Open all wk ⊕ HALL & WOODHOUSE ◀ King & Barnes Sussex, Badger Best, seasonal variations, guest ales. **Facilities** Play area Dogs allowed Garden Parking

---

KIRDFORD   Map 6 TQ02

PICK OF THE PUBS

The Half Moon Inn

See Pick of the Pubs on page 465

LAMBS GREEN   Map 6 TQ23

The Lamb Inn ☕

RH12 4RG
☎ 01293 871336   & 871933   🖺 01293 871933
e-mail: lambinnrusper@yahoo.co.uk
dir: *6m from Horsham between Rusper & Faygate. 5m from Grawley*

Purchased by the former tenants, the Lamb remains unchanged, with an emphasis on sourcing real ales from independent breweries and using as much local produce as they can get their hands on. Everything on the menu from starters to puddings is home made. Baguettes, omelettes, a fresh fish board and 28-day matured steaks feature, along with specials such as wild rabbit casserole; and chicken breast in a creamy stilton and Madeira sauce.

Open all wk Mon-Thu 11.30am-3 5.30-11pm (Fri-Sat 11.30am-11pm Sun noon-10.30pm) Closed: 25-26 Dec **Bar Meals** L served Mon-Fri 12-2, Sat 12-9.30, Sun 12-9 booking required D served Mon-Fri 6.30-9.30, Sat 12-9.30, Sun 12-9 booking required **Restaurant** L served Mon-Fri 12-2, Sat 12-9.30, Sun 12-9 booking required D served Mon-Fri 6.30-9.30, Sat 12-9.30, Sun 12-9 booking required ⊕ FREE HOUSE ◀ Horsham Best Bitter, Kings Old Ale, Dark Star Original, Hepworth Prospect, Hogs Back TEA ☕ Stowford Press. ☕ 12 **Facilities** Children's menu Family room Dogs allowed Parking

---

LICKFOLD   Map 6 SU92

PICK OF THE PUBS

The Lickfold Inn ☕

GU28 9EY ☎ 01798 861285
e-mail: lickfold@evanspubs.co.uk
dir: *From A3 take A283, through Chiddingfold, 2m on right signed 'Lurgashall Winery', pub in 1m*

In the capable hands of Camilla Hansen and Mark Evans, this thriving free house dates back to 1460. Period features include an ancient timber frame with attractive herringbone-patterned bricks, and a huge central chimney. Inside are two restaurant areas with oak beamed ceilings, and a cosy bar dominated by a large inglenook fireplace, Georgian settles and moulded panelling. Look for the recurring garlic motif, reflecting the village's Anglo-Saxon name, 'leac fauld', which means an enclosure where garlic grows. The pub is heavily food oriented, offering tempting lunchtime sandwiches, Sunday roasts, and seasonal dishes complemented by a choice of well-kept real ales and a comprehensive wine list. Expect Lickfold Inn fish pie; grilled aubergine with spinach and ricotta; and roast guinea fowl in bacon with potato rosti and redcurrant sauce. The large courtyard and rambling terraced gardens are ideal for alfresco dining. Fifty per cent of the pub's profits go to a children's hospice.

Open all day all wk noon-11 (Sun noon-5) Closed: 25 Dec **Bar Meals** Av main course £10 food served all day **Restaurant** Av 3 course à la carte fr £26 food served all day ⊕ FREE HOUSE ◀ Hogs Back TEA, Guinness, Old Speckled Hen. ☕ 12 **Facilities** Children's menu Dogs allowed Garden Parking

PICK OF THE PUBS

The Anglesey Arms at Halnaker 🍷

HALNAKER   Map 6 SU90

PO18 0NQ
☎ 01243 773474   🖨 01243 530034
e-mail: angleseyarms@aol.com
web: www.angleseyarms.co.uk
dir: *From centre of Chichester 4m E on A285 (Petworth road)*

Whether you pop in for a quick drink or a full meal, you'll find a warm welcome in the wood-floored bar of this charmingly old-fashioned Georgian inn. The Anglesey stands in two acres of landscaped grounds on the Goodwood estate, just a mile from the famous Boxgrove archaeological site - home to the 500,000-year-old remains of the Boxgrove Man. Bowman Swift One and Youngs Bitter are amongst the hand-pulled ales at the bar; cider drinkers will find Stowford Press, and the extensive wine list includes unusual wines from small vineyards. Hand-cut sandwiches, ploughman's with unpasteurised cheese, local sausages, and other traditional pub favourites will fill the odd corner, or you could sample something from the à la carte menu. The kitchen team makes skilful use of meat from fully traceable and organically raised animals, as well as locally-caught fish from sustainable stocks. The Anglesey has built a special reputation for its steaks, cut from British beef and hung for at least 21 days. Additional meats are supplied by the Estate's Home Farm, while vegetables come from Wayside Organics. The area is noted for shooting, so game birds and venison are also available in season. Dinner might begin with Sussex rarebit; toasted goats' cheese and red onion marmalade with salad leaves; or freshwater crayfish and mango salad with chilli dressing. Main course options include slow roasted English pork belly, plum sauce and cucumber salad; king prawns with Thai-style curry sauce and rice; and free range chicken breast on crushed new potatoes with seasonal greens, smoked bacon and mushroom sauce. Home-made puddings are listed on the blackboard, or you might choose hand-made cheeses with water biscuits and home-made chutney.

Open 11-3 5.30-11 (Sat-Sun 11-11) **Bar Meals** L served Mon-Sun 12-2.30 D served Mon-Sat 6.30-9.30 Av main course £9.50 **Restaurant** L served Mon-Sun 12-2.30 D served Mon-Sat 6.30-9.30 Av 3 course à la carte fr £24 ⊕ PUNCH TAVERNS ⬛ Young's Bitter, Bowman Swift One, Black Sheep Bitter ♂ Stowford Press. 🍷 14 **Facilities** Children's menu Dogs allowed Garden Parking

PICK OF THE PUBS

The Half Moon Inn

KIRDFORD   Map 6 TQ02

RH14 0LT
☎ **01403 820223**
web: www.halfmoonkirdford.co.uk
dir: *Off A272 between Billingshurst & Petworth. At Wisborough Green follow Kirdford signs*

This picturesque, red-tiled 16th-century village inn is covered in climbing rose bushes, and sits directly opposite the church in this quiet unspoilt Sussex village near the River Arun. A bit off the beaten track, the pub is made up of cottages that were once craftsmen's workshops. Although drinkers are welcome, the Half Moon is mainly a dining pub. The interior consists of an attractive bar with adjoining wooden-floored restaurant area. The furniture and paintings charmingly reflect the oak beams, tiled floors, open fireplaces and log fires in winter. The chef serves honest wholesome food, locally sourced from healthy well-reared stock, with creative twists. The à la carte and daily set menu reflect the best of the season's ingredients. Lunch choices from the menu might include medallions of lobster, followed by pan-fried venison with black pudding mash, or pan-fried medallions of pork; plus traditional Sunday lunches with a minimum of two roasts. Lunchtime snacks reflect the seasons, for example salads in summer and hotpots in winter. At dinner, the menu is broadly similar, although the atmosphere changes, with candlelight, linen tablecloths and polished glassware. Private dining is available. Well-tended gardens at the front and rear are an added draw in the summer, and a pamphlet featuring local country walks is available. Look out for the monthly themed music-to-dine-to evenings. There are also a number of cycle routes in the area.

Open 11-3 6-11 Closed: Sun eve & Mon eve **Meals:** L served Mon-Sun 12-2.30 D served Tue-Sat 6-9.30 ◼ Local ale **Facilities** Garden Parking

LODSWORTH
Map 6 SU92

PICK OF THE PUBS

The Halfway Bridge Inn ☂

See Pick of the Pubs on opposite page

PICK OF THE PUBS

The Hollist Arms ☂

The Street GU28 9BZ ☎ 01798 861310
e-mail: george@thehollistarms.co.uk
dir: *0.5m between Midhurst & Petworth, 1m N of A272, adjacent to Country Park*

The Hollist Arms, a pub since 1823, is full of traditional charm and character. The 15th-century building overlooks a lawn where a grand old tree stands ringed by a bench. Step through the pretty entrance porch and you'll find roaring open fires, leather sofas and a blissful absence of fruit machines. You'll probably need to book to enjoy dishes such as tiger prawns and leek gratin with fresh bread; home-made steak, Guinness and mushroom pie; or hoi sin duck in soy sauce with ginger, mushrooms and spring onions. Bar snacks range from toasties to sausages and mash. Wash it down with real ales such as Timothy Taylor Landlord; Horsham Best or the locally-brewed Langham's Halfway to Heaven. The Hollist Arms is conveniently situated for Goodwood, Cowdray Park and Petworth House, and has its own business providing picnic hampers for any event.

Open all day all wk 11am-11pm **Bar Meals** L served all wk 12-9 booking required D served all wk 12-9 booking required food served all day **Restaurant** L served all wk 12-9 booking required D served all wk 12-9 booking required food served all day ⊕ FREE HOUSE ◀ Langham, Timothy Taylor Landlord, Horsham Best ♂ Stowford Press. ☂ 7 **Facilities** Children's menu Dogs allowed Garden Parking

LURGASHALL
Map 6 SU92

The Noah's Ark ☂

The Green GU28 9ET ☎ 01428 707346
e-mail: amy@noahsarkinn.co.uk
dir: *B2131 from Haslemere follow signs to Petworth/Lurgashall. A3 from London towards Portsmouth. At Milford take the A283 signed Petworth. Follow signs to Lurgashall*

Set in a picturesque village, beneath Blackdown Hill, this attractive 16th-century inn overlooks the cricket green. The revitalised interior is full of charm and character, thanks to the enthusiastic owners, with old beams and a large inglenook fireplace. Three ales are offered along with a regularly changing guest beer, and traditional British food with a contemporary twist and the occasional French influence. Ingredients are carefully sourced from the best local suppliers for dishes ranging from Sussex beef bourguignon to Noah's ale battered cod and chips.

Open all day Closed: Mon (ex Summer) **Bar Meals** L served Tue-Sat 12-2.30 booking required D served Tue-Sat 7-9.30 booking required Av main course £13 **Restaurant** L served Tue-Sun 12-2.30 booking required D served Tue-Sat 7-9.30 booking required ⊕ GREENE KING ◀ Greene King IPA , Abbot, Guest ale ♂ Stowford Press. ☂ 8 **Facilities** Children's menu Family room Dogs allowed Garden Parking

MAPLEHURST
Map 6 TQ12

The White Horse ☂

Park Ln RH13 6LL ☎ 01403 891208
dir: *5m SE of Horsham, between A281 & A272*

In the tiny Sussex hamlet of Maplehurst, this traditional pub offers a break from modern life: no music, no fruit machines, no cigarette machines, just hearty, home-cooked pub food and an enticing range of ales. Sip Harvey's Best, Welton's Pride & Joy, or Dark Star Espresso Stout in the bar or whilst admiring the rolling countryside from the quiet, south-facing garden. Village-brewed cider is a speciality.

Open all wk 12-2.30 6-11 (Sun 12-3 7-11) **Bar Meals** L served all wk 12-2 D served all wk 6-9 Av main course £5.50 ⊕ FREE HOUSE ◀ Harvey's Best, Welton's Pride & Joy, Dark Star Espresso Stout, King's Red River, Station Pullman ale ♂ Local cider. **Facilities** Play area Family room Dogs allowed Garden Parking **Notes** ☺

MIDHURST
Map 6 SU82

The Angel Hotel ☂

North St GU29 9DN ☎ 01730 812421 🖹 **01730 815928**
dir: *Telephone for directions*

An imposing and well-proportioned, late-Georgian façade hides the true Tudor origins of this former coaching inn. Its frontage overlooks the town's main street, while at the rear attractive gardens give way to meadowland and the ruins of Cowdray Castle. Bright yellow paintwork on local cottages means they are Cowdray Estate-owned. Gabriel's is the main restaurant, or try The Halo Bar where dishes range from snacks and pasta to sizzlers and steaks, with additional specials.

Open all wk ⊕ FREE HOUSE ◀ Fuller's HSB, Best. ☂ 6 **Facilities** Dogs allowed Garden Parking

NUTHURST
Map 6 TQ12

PICK OF THE PUBS

Black Horse Inn ☂

Nuthurst St RH13 6LH ☎ 01403 891272
e-mail: clive.henwood@btinternet.com
dir: *4m S of Horsham, off A281, A24 & A272*

Built of clay tiles and mellow brick, this one time smugglers' hideout is still appropriately secluded in a quiet backwater. It is a lovely old building, half masked by impressive window boxes in summer, forming part of what was originally a row of workers' cottages on the Sedgwick Park estate. The building was first recorded as an inn in 1817, and plenty of its history remains. Inside you'll find stone-flagged floors, an inglenook fireplace and an exposed wattle and daub wall. The place is spotlessly maintained with a warm and cosy atmosphere that's perfect for dining or just enjoying a drink. The pub has a reputation for good beers, including Harveys, London Pride and numerous guest beers. On sunny days, visitors can sit out on the terraces at the front and rear, or take their drinks across the stone bridge over a stream into the delightful back garden. The blackboard menu changes regularly.

Black Horse Inn

Open all wk **Bar Meals** L served all wk 12-2.30 booking required D served all wk 6-9.30 booking required **Restaurant** L served all wk 12-2.30 booking required D served all wk 6-9.30 booking required ⊕ FREE HOUSE ◀ Harveys Sussex, W J King, Fuller's London Pride, Hepworths, guest ales ♂ Westons Stowford Press. ☂ 7 **Facilities** Children's menu Dogs allowed Garden Parking

OVING
Map 6 SU90

The Gribble Inn ☂

PO20 2BP ☎ 01243 786893 🖹 **01243 786893**
e-mail: dave@thegribble.co.uk
dir: *From A27 take A259. After 1m left at rdbt, 1st right to Oving, 1st left in village*

Named after local schoolmistress Rose Gribble, the inn retains all of its 16th-century charm. Large open fireplaces, wood burners and low beams set the tone. There's no background music at this peaceful hideaway, which is the ideal spot to enjoy any of the half dozen real ales from the on-site micro-brewery. Liver and bacon; spinach lasagne with red peppers; and special fish dishes are all prepared and cooked on the premises.

Open all wk 11-3 5.30-11 (Fri-Sun 11-11) **Bar Meals** L served all wk 12-2.30 D served all wk 6.30-9.30 Av main course £9 **Restaurant** L served all wk 12-2.30 booking required D served all wk 6.30-9.30 booking required ⊕ HALL & WOODHOUSE ◀ Gribble Ale, Reg's Tipple, Fursty Ferret, Badger First Gold, Pigs Ear. ☂ 10 **Facilities** Children's menu Family room Dogs allowed Garden Parking

PICK OF THE PUBS

The Halfway Bridge Inn ♟

LODSWORTH   Map 6 SU92

Halfway Bridge GU28 9BP
☎ **01798 861281**
e-mail: enquiries@halfwaybridge.co.uk
web: www.halfwaybridge.co.uk
dir: *Between Petworth & Midhurst, next to Cowdray Estate & Golf Club on A272*

On the A272 midway between Petworth and Midhurst, hence its name, the mellow, red-brick inn stands in glorious Sussex countryside and was originally built as a coaching inn in 1740. It's an ideal pit-stop for antique hunters drawn to Petworth's fabled shops, as well as the polo crowd heading for nearby Cowdray Park. Locally it is popular, not

least because owners Paul and Sue Carter have made the inn an attractive destination for diners. Winter cosiness is guaranteed: rambling, tastefully furnished interconnecting rooms boast open fires, wooden floors, old beams and a casual and relaxed atmosphere, while in summer the sheltered patio and lawn is perfect for alfresco dining. Traditional pub dishes are given a modern twist and the emphasis is on local crab and Sussex pork, alongside fresh meats, fish and vegetables from the London markets. Daily specials are chalked up on the blackboards. The lunchtime bar menu consists of sandwiches - roast beef and horseradish, fresh crab - or a choice of appetizers from the main menu. These may include grilled mackerel with home-made foccacia bread and horseradish mousse; poached scallops with fennel, shallot and caper salad; and partridge and pheasant terrine with fruit chutney. Typical of the vegetarian main courses is chargrilled vegetable millefeuille layered with parmesan crisps and served with a Roquefort cream. Otherwise you may find game suet pudding with red wine jus; seafood risotto with rocket and

parmesan salad; whole baked sea bass with roasted butternut squash, garlic and shallot butter; and roast pork belly with red wine jus. Puddings may include vanilla Cambridge burnt cream with chocolate chip cookie; and dark chocolate and pistachio nut tart with vanilla mascarpone. To drink, you'll find Ringwood Best Bitter on tap and a raft of 14 wines by the glass.

Open 11-11 (Sun 12-10.30) Closed: 25 Dec **Bar Meals** L served all wk 12-2.30 D served all wk 6.30-9.15 **Restaurant** L served all wk 12-3 D served all wk 6.30-9.15 ⊕ FREE HOUSE ◼ Skinners Betty Stogs, Ballards Best Bitter, Ringwood Best Bitter. ♟ 14
Facilities Children's menu Dogs allowed Garden Parking

PETWORTH
Map 6 SU92

The Black Horse

Byworth GU28 0HL ☎ 01798 342424
dir: *A285 from Petworth, 2m, turn right signed Byworth, pub 50yds on right*

An unspoilt 16th-century village pub, once part of the old tanneries, The Black Horse retains a rustic feel with exposed beams, flagstone floors, scrubbed wooden tables and open fires. The former kitchen has been transformed into a snug dining area including the original Aga, whilst the large garden offers views to the South Downs. Expect a range of home-made fresh pizza, light bites and daily specials. A function room and separate bar accommodates larger parties.

Open all day all wk 11-11 (Sun 12-11) **Bar Meals** L served all wk 12-3 D served Mon-Thu 6-9, Fri-Sat 6-9.30, Sun 6-8.30 **Restaurant** L served all wk 12-3 booking required D served Mon-Thu 6-9, Fri-Sat 6-9.30, Sun 6-8.30 booking required ⊕ FREE HOUSE ◀ Fuller's London Pride, Sharp's Doom Bar, Flowerpots, Hophead. **Facilities** Children's menu Dogs allowed Garden Parking

PICK OF THE PUBS

The Grove Inn

Grove Ln GU28 0HY ☎ 01798 343659
e-mail: steveandvaleria@tiscali.co.uk
dir: *On outskirts of town, just off A283 between Pullborough & Petworth. 0.5m from Petworth Park*

A 17th-century free house a stone's throw south of historic Petworth. Idyllically sited, it nestles in beautiful gardens with views to the South Downs; a patio area with shady pergola is ideal for alfresco drinks. Inside is a bar with oak-beamed ceilings and large fireplace, while the conservatory restaurant is the place to sample a seasonal menu revised every six to eight weeks. The pub is hosted by a husband and wife partnership: Valeria looks after front of house, warmly welcoming locals and visitors alike, while husband Stephen runs the kitchen operation. His simple objective is to serve quality dishes at prices that do not detract from their enjoyment. Typical starters include moules marinière and baked asparagus wrapped in Parma ham. Among the main courses you may find roasted lamb cannon with rosemary, or crayfish tail and penne pasta. Expect desserts along the lines of hot chocolate mousse or apple crumble.

Closed: Sun eve & Mon **Bar Meals** L served Tue-Sun 12-2.30 booking required D served Tue-Sat 6-9.15 booking required Av main course £9.20 **Restaurant** L served Tue-Sun 12-2.30 booking required D served Tue-Sat 6-9.15 booking required Av 3 course à la carte fr £26 ⊕ FREE HOUSE ◀ Youngs, Betty Stogs, Arundel Gold, Hogs Back TEA. **Facilities** Children's menu Dogs allowed Garden Parking

POYNINGS
Map 6 TQ21

PICK OF THE PUBS

Royal Oak Inn ☝

The Street BN45 7AQ
☎ 01273 857389 📄 01273 857202
e-mail: ropoynings@aol.com
dir: *N on A23 just outside Brighton, take A281 signed Henfield & Poynings, then follow signs into Poynings*

Tucked away in a fold of the South Downs below the Devil's Dyke, the Royal Oak has eye-catching window blinds and cream-painted exterior and roaring winter fires within. Solid oak floors and old beams hung with hop bines blend effortlessly with contemporary decor and comfy sofas. In the bar, Sussex-bred Harveys real ales rub shoulders with offerings from Greene King and Morland, and a decent wine list includes a red and a white from a Sussex vineyard. The menu combines local and seasonal produce with sometimes ambitious international twists. Starters and light meals include sharing platters and sandwich platters, or more elaborate preparations such as potted Selsey crab with spring onion and garlic, lemon and lime toasts. For a main course you might choose hand-made Henfield sausages, creamed potato, rich gravy and red onion jam; or basil and pine nut risotto with a fried egg and balsamic syrup. Puddings are ordered at the bar – pear, apple and ginger crumble perhaps.

Open all day all wk 11-11 (Sun 11.30-10.30) **Bar Meals** food served all day **Restaurant** food served all day ⊕ FREE HOUSE ◀ Harveys Sussex, Abbot Ale, Greene King Morland Old Speckled Hen, Fuller's London Pride Ò Westons Herefordshire Country Perry, Old Rosie Scrumpy. ☝ 12 **Facilities** Children's menu Play area Dogs allowed Garden Parking

ROWHOOK
Map 6 TQ13

The Chequers Inn ◉ ☝

RH12 3PY ☎ 01403 790480 📄 01403 790480
e-mail: thechequersrowhook@googlemail.com
dir: *Off A29 NW of Horsham*

A hamlet on the Sussex, Surrey border provides the setting for this 15th-century inn of great character, with 'mind your head' original beams, flagstones and open fires. Master Chef Tim offers a good choice of food such as a restaurant starter of risotto of crayfish and feves with Parmesan and virgin olive oil; or terrine of smoked ham hock with fried quail's egg and home-made pineapple chutney. Mains might be sauté local venison with buttered Savoy cabbage, roasted beetroot and garlic fondant potato; or pan-fried fresh haddock on petit pois à la Francoise. The bar menu takes in home-made sausages of the day, and steak and kidney pie, plus to a variety of tempting baked ciabattas.

Open 11.30-3.30 6-11.30 Closed: 25 Dec, Sun eve **Bar Meals** L served all wk 12-2 booking required D served Mon-Fri 7-9 booking required **Restaurant** L served all wk 12-2 booking required D served Mon-Sat 7-9 booking required ⊕ FREE HOUSE ◀ Harvey's Sussex Ale, Fuller's London Pride, guest ale Ò Thatchers Gold. ☝ 7 **Facilities** Children's menu Dogs allowed Garden Parking

RUDGWICK
Map 6 TQ03

The Fox Inn ☝

Guildford Rd, Bucks Green RH12 3JP
☎ 01403 822386 📄 01403 823950
e-mail: seafood@foxinn.co.uk
dir: *on A281 midway between Horsham & Guildford*

'Famous for Fish!' is the claim of this attractive 16th-century inn, a message borne out by the extensive menu. Food offered includes all-day breakfast and afternoon tea, while the bar menu focuses on seafood, from fish and chips to the huge fruits de mer platter. Dishes include Foxy's famous fish pie; roasted cod loin with chorizo; and hand-made Cumberland sausage on stilton mash. A horse is apparently walked through the pub each Christmas day!

Open all wk ⊕ HALL & WOODHOUSE ◀ King & Barnes Sussex, Badger Tanglefoot, Fursty Ferret. ☝ 8 **Facilities** Play area Dogs allowed Garden Parking

SHIPLEY
Map 6 TQ12

PICK OF THE PUBS

The Countryman Inn ☝

See Pick of the Pubs on opposite page

PICK OF THE PUBS

The Countryman Inn 🍷

SHIPLEY   Map 6 TQ12

Countryman Ln RH13 8PZ
☎ 01403 741383   📠 01403 741115
e-mail: countrymaninn@btopenworld.com
web: www.countrymanshipley.co.uk
dir: *From A272 at Coolham into Smithers Hill Ln. 1m to junct with Countryman Ln*

This inn, close to the small village of Shipley, is surrounded by 3,500 acres of farmland owned by the Knepp Castle Estate. Nearly ten years ago the estate embarked on a series of regeneration and restoration projects aimed primarily at nature conservation and a less intensive way of meat production. This is why today fallow deer, Tamworth pigs, Exmoor ponies and longhorn cattle roam free. In fine weather, the inn's garden is a great place to watch birds, attracted by the estate's wild grasses, and enjoy the open air kitchen and barbecues.In the cosy bar you'll find warming log fires, and cask-conditioned locally brewed ales, together with a great choice of wines from around the world. Local produce is used wherever possible, and free-range meat and vegetables from local farms make their appearance on the menu alongside home-grown herbs, fresh fish from Shoreham and Newhaven, and local game in season. Day-to-day menus change frequently, although expect all-year pub classics such as sausage casserole; ham, egg and chips; and beef and ale pie. From a typical main lunch menu come chicken Caesar salad; Sussex lamb hotpot; and battered cod and chips, while the dinner menu might offer roast belly of saddleback pork; plaice and Serrano paupiette; aromatic roast duck; and pappardelle arrabbiata. Among the representative desserts are lemon posset; winter berry cheesecake; and coconut rice pudding. Do note, however, that the restaurant is not suitable for very young children. Shipley's historic eight-sided smock mill is the fictional home of the BBC's *Jonathan Creek*, and is just a mile's walk along a woodland bridle path from the pub.

Open 10-4, 6-11 Closed: Sun eve (Jan) **Bar Meals** L served all week 11.30-3.30 D served all week 6-10 Av main course £12 **Restaurant** L served all week 11.30-3.30 D served all week 6-10 ⊕ FREE HOUSE 🛢 Harveys, Kings, London Pride. 🍷 20 **Facilities** Garden Parking

SHIPLEY *continued*

George & Dragon ⬤

Dragons Green RH13 7JE ☎ 01403 741320
dir: *Signed from A272 between Coolham & A24*

Set amid beautiful Sussex countryside, this 17th-century cottage is a haven of peace and quiet, especially on balmy summer evenings when the garden is a welcome retreat. Its interior is all head-banging beams and inglenook fireplaces, with an excellent choice of real ales at the bar. Food-wise, expect pub classics such as local ham with egg and chips or a Yorkshire pudding filled with sausage, mash and gravy. Shipley is famous for its smock mill.

Open all wk **Bar Meals** L served all wk 12-2 booking required D served all wk 6-9 Av main course £7.50 **Restaurant** L served all wk 12-2 D served all wk 6-9 ⬤ HALL & WOODHOUSE ◀ Badger Best, Sussex Best, Hall and Woodhouse Fursty Ferret & Pickled Partridge, Guest ale ⭕ Westons Stowford Press. ⬤ 8 **Facilities** Children's menu Play area Family room Dogs allowed Garden Parking

SINGLETON   Map 5 SU81

The Partridge Inn

PO18 0EY ☎ 01243 811251   ▤ 0870 804 4566
dir: *Telephone for directions*

Once known as the Fox and Hounds, the building probably dates from the 16th century, when it would have been part of a huge hunting park owned by the Fitzalan family, Earls of Arundel. Today, it is popular with walkers enjoying the rolling Sussex countryside and visitors to Goodwood for motor and horse-racing. A menu of typical pub fare includes liver and bacon, steak and ale pie, Goodwood gammon, salmon fishcakes, fish and chips, and home-made puddings.

Open all wk ⬤ ENTERPRISE INNS ◀ London Pride, Ringwood Best Bitter, Hopworths Sussex. **Facilities** Dogs allowed Garden Parking

SLINDON   Map 6 SU90

The Spur ⬤

BN18 0NE ☎ 01243 814216   ▤ 01243 814707
dir: *Off A27 on A29 outside Slindon*

Nestling on top of the South Downs, just outside the village of Slindon, sits this 17th-century pub. Inside this free house is an open-plan bar and restaurant, warmed by log fires that create a friendly atmosphere. If you book in advance you can use the skittle alley, or enjoy a game of pool or other pub games.

Open all wk 11.30-3 6-11 (Sun noon-3 7-10.30) **Bar Meals** L served all wk 12-2 D served Sun-Tue 7-9, Wed-Sat 7-9.30 Av main course £11.50 **Restaurant** L served all wk 12-2 booking required D served Sun-Tue 7-9, Wed-Sat 7-9.30 booking required Av 3 course à la carte fr £24 ⬤ FREE HOUSE ◀ Greene King IPA, Courage Directors. ⬤ 9 **Facilities** Children's menu Dogs allowed Garden Parking

SOUTH HARTING   Map 5 SU71

The Ship Inn

GU31 5PZ ☎ 01730 825302
dir: *From Petersfield take B2146 towards Chichester. Inn in 5m*

A 17th-century inn made from a ship's timbers, hence the name. There is a great selection of real ales and Thatchers Gold cider available. Home-made pies are a feature, and other popular dishes include fish pie, mussel chowder, calves' liver, rack of lamb, ham and asparagus mornay, and Hungarian goulash, all washed down with a pint of Palmer IPA. A range of vegetarian dishes and bar snacks is also available.

Open all day all wk 11.30-11 (Sun noon-11) **Bar Meals** L served all wk 12-2.30 D served Mon & Wed-Thu 7-9, Fri-Sat 7-9.30 booking required Av main course £8.95 **Restaurant** L served all wk 12-2.30 booking required D served Mon & Wed-Sat 7-9 booking required Av 3 course à la carte fr £20 ⬤ FREE HOUSE ◀ Palmer IPA, Dark Star Brewery Hophead, Ballards Wassail, Palmers Copper Ale ⭕ Thatchers Gold. **Facilities** Dogs allowed Garden Parking

STEDHAM   Map 5 SU82

Hamilton Arms/Nava Thai Restaurant ⬤

Hamilton Arms School Ln GU29 0NZ
☎ 01730 812555   ▤ 01730 817459
e-mail: hamiltonarms@hotmail.com
web: www.thehamiltonarms.co.uk
dir: *Off A272 between Midhurst & Petersfield*

The Hamilton Arms is one of the first traditional English country pubs to serve authentic Thai food. The pub is set in a pretty village in beautiful South Downs countryside, and is also the base for a charitable trust to help prevent child prostitution in Thailand. The huge menu offers soups, curries, salads and speciality meat, seafood and vegetarian dishes, also available to takeaway. Oriental beers, too, are available alongside local real ales. There is a patio to enjoy in warmer weather.

Open 11-3 6-11 (Sun noon-4 7-11, Fri-Sat 11am-11.30pm) Closed: Mon (ex BH) **Bar Meals** L served Tue-Sun 12-2.30 D served Tue-Sun 6-10 **Restaurant** L served Tue-Sun 12-2.30 D served Tue-Sun 6-10 booking required ⬤ FREE HOUSE ◀ Ballard's Best, Fuller's London Pride, Everards Tiger Best, Fuller's HSB, Wadworth 6X, Sussex King, Barnes ⭕ Westons Vintage. ⬤ 8 **Facilities** Children's menu Play area Dogs allowed Garden Parking

TROTTON   Map 5 SU82

PICK OF THE PUBS

The Keepers Arms ⬤

GU31 5ER ☎ 01730 813724
e-mail: nick@keepersarms.co.uk
dir: *5m from Petersfield on A272, pub on right just after narrow bridge*

This charming 17th-century free house is tucked onto a hillside just above the river Rother, in an Area of Outstanding Natural Beauty. A log fire provides a warm welcome in the lovely, low-ceilinged bar, and the stylish dining room is also a treat with its warm colours, modern oak dining tables, comfortable upholstered chairs and tartan fabrics. By day, there are fabulous views over the South Downs. Food is taken seriously, with real efforts made to source local and seasonal produce. Blackboard menus offer pub favourites such as chargrilled sirloin steak and chips or Cumberland sausages and mash, while the frequently changing à la carte menu features starters such as warm salad of wild rabbit or carpaccio of yellowfin tuna with soy vinaigrette, followed by slow-roasted pork belly with seared scallops and cauliflower purée or poached turbot with crab and coriander ravioli and pak choi. As well as taking meals in the bar or dining room, you can sit outside on the sun terrace with those great views.

Open all wk **Bar Meals** L served all wk 12-2 D served all wk 7-9 Av main course £13 **Restaurant** L served all wk 12-2 D served all wk 7-9 Av 3 course à la carte fr £23 ⬤ FREE HOUSE ◀ Dark Star Hophead, Ringwood Best, Ballards Best, Ringwood 49'er, Horsham Best ⭕ Westons 1st Quality. ⬤ 8 **Facilities** Dogs allowed Garden Parking

WALDERTON   Map 5 SU71

The Barley Mow ⬤

PO18 9ED ☎ 023 9263 1321   ▤ 023 9263 1403
e-mail: mowbarley@aol.co.uk
dir: *B2146 from Chichester towards Petersfield. Turn right signed Walderton, pub 100yds on left*

Set in the rolling Sussex Downs, this ivy-clad, 18th-century pub is famous locally for its skittle alley and was used by the local Home Guard as its HQ in World War II. Its secluded, stream-bordered garden is a real sun trap, perfect for a pint of Old Thumper. The menu takes in a daily pie, grills, fish and a choice of vegetarian dishes. There is also a snack menu of sandwiches, jacket potatoes and panini.

Open all wk 11-3 6-11 (Sun 12-10.30) **Bar Meals** L served all wk 12-2 D served all wk 6-9 **Restaurant** L served all wk 12-2 D served all wk 6-9 ⬤ FREE HOUSE ◀ Ringwood Old Thumper & Fortyniner, Fuller's London Pride, Harveys Best. ⬤ 8 **Facilities** Dogs allowed Garden Parking

WARNHAM
Map 6 TQ13

The Greets Inn

47 Friday St RH12 3QY
☎ 01403 265047   📄 01403 265047
dir: *Off A24 N of Horsham*

A fine Sussex hall house dating from about 1350 and built for Elias Greet, a local merchant. A magnificent inglenook fireplace and low beams will be discovered in the flagstone-floored bar. There is a rambling series of dining areas where diners can sample the wares of the kitchen team. Look out for some good pasta and fish dishes.

Open all wk ⊕ LAUREL PUB PARTNERSHIPS ◀ Interbrew, Greene King IPA, Fuller's London Pride, Abbot Ale. ♀ 6 **Facilities** Dogs allowed Garden Parking

WARNINGLID
Map 6 TQ22

The Half Moon ♀

The Street RH17 5TR ☎ 01444 461227
e-mail: info@thehalfmoonwarninglid.co.uk
dir: *1m from Warninglid/Cuckfield junct of A23 & 6m from Haywards Heath*

The first phase of building work has been completed at this 19th-century pub, and customers love the new areas, but the place has not lost its traditional feel. Enjoy a pint of Harveys or a real cider while perusing the menu. The business is food-led with a menu of snacks, specials and pub classics, such as red Thai chicken curry; beer battered fish and chips, and beef and mushroom pie. Daily specials include south coast brill fillet with green beans and herb cream, and venison cottage pie.

Open all wk 11.30-2.30 5.30-11 (Sun 11.30-11) **Bar Meals** L served Mon-Sat 12-2, Sun 12-3 D served Mon-Sat 6-9.30 Av main course £10 **Restaurant** L served Mon-Sat 12-2, Sun 12-3 booking required D served Mon-Sat 6-9.30 booking required Av 3 course à la carte fr £24 ⊕ FREE HOUSE ◀ Harveys Sussex, Black Sheep, Ringwood Best, Dark Star, Harvey's Old Ale Ŏ Westons Stowford Press, Sheppy's Dabinet, Oakwood Special. ♀ 8 **Facilities** Children's menu Dogs allowed Garden Parking

WEST CHILTINGTON
Map 6 TQ01

The Queens Head NEW ♀

The Hollow RH20 2JN
☎ 01798 812244   📄 01798 815039
e-mail: enquiries@thequeenshead.info
dir: *Please telephone for directions*

A traditional, mainly 17th-century country pub with two bars, a restaurant and ample outside space. The interior is pure textbook –beams, low ceilings, an open fire and a bar serving three well-kept real ales. Mainly locally sourced, freshly cooked traditional dishes include Harvey's beer-battered haddock and chips with mushy peas; Caesar salad with chicken and bacon; slow-roasted lamb shank with fresh herb mash; and mushroom Stroganoff with rice. Up to five home-made pies appear as specials.

Open all day all wk noon-11 (Mon 5-11 ex BH noon-11 Sun noon-10.30) **Bar Meals** L served Tue-Sat 12-2.30, Sun & BH 12-4 D served Tue-Sat 6-9.30 Av main course £10.50 **Restaurant** L served Tue-Sat 12-2.30, Sun & BH 12-4 D served Tue-Sat 6-9.30 Av 3 course à la carte fr £18 ⊕ ENTERPRISE INNS PLC ◀ Harveys Sussex Best Bitter, Fuller's London Pride, Ballards Best Bitter, Itchen Valley Godfathers, Langhams Halfway to Heaven. ♀ 7 **Facilities** Children's menu Dogs allowed Garden Parking

WINEHAM
Map 6 TQ22

The Royal Oak ♀

BN5 9AY ☎ 01444 881252
e-mail: theroyaloakwineham@sky.com
dir: *Wineham between A272 (Cowfold to Bolney) & B2116 (Hurst to Henfield)*

After dispensing ale straight from the barrels for more than two centuries, this delightful 14th-century half-timbered cottage still retains its traditional, unspoilt character. It is a true rural alehouse - so expect rustic furnishings, and food like venison sausage toad-in-the-hole; cauliflower cheese; steak and ale pie; and home-made soups. Snacks of potted and smoked mackerel, and ploughman's on a wooden board are served weekdays, with roasts on Sundays. Outside, the extensive gardens are ideal for summer drinking.

Open all wk 11-2.30 5.30-close (Sat 11-3.30 6-close Sun noon-4 7-10.30) **Bar Meals** L served Mon-Sat 12-2.30, Sun 12-3 booking required D served Mon-Sat 7-9.30 booking required **Restaurant** L served Mon-Sat 12-2.30, Sun 12-3 booking required D served Mon-Sat 7-9.30 booking required ⊕ PUNCH TAVERNS ◀ Harveys Sussex Best Bitter, Guest ales Ŏ Stowford Press. ♀ 20 **Facilities** Children's menu Dogs allowed Garden Parking

WISBOROUGH GREEN
Map 6 TQ02

Cricketers Arms ♀

Loxwood Rd RH14 0DG ☎ 01403 700369
e-mail: craig@cricketersarms.com
dir: *On A272 between Billingshurst & Petworth. In centre of Wisborough Green turn at junct next to village green, pub 100yds on right*

A traditional village pub dating from the 16th century with oak beams, wooden floors and open fires. Fans of extreme sports should be aware that the Cricketers is the home of the British Lawn Mower Racing Association. A full bar menu ranges from snacks to three course meals and Sunday roasts, with a large selection of specials.

Typical dishes include steak pie, sea bass in a prawn and oyster sauce, game dishes in season, and 'mega' salads.

Open all wk ⊕ ENTERPRISE INNS ◀ Harveys Sussex, Fuller's London Pride, Swift One. ♀ 34 **Facilities** Dogs allowed Garden Parking

TYNE & WEAR

NEWCASTLE UPON TYNE
Map 21 NZ26

Shiremoor House Farm ♀

Middle Engine Ln, New York NE29 8DZ
☎ 0191 257 6302   📄 0191 257 8602
dir: *Telephone for directions*

A swift pint of Jarrow River Catcher in New York? Since that's the name of the village, it's eminently feasible at this popular North Tyneside pub, brilliantly converted from an old farm. Particularly appealing is the glazed former granary where a wide range of traditional pub food is served, including steak, ale and mushroom casserole; fillet of salmon with prawn and dill sauce; and sizzling strips of chicken with sweet chilli sauce.

Open all wk ⊕ FREE HOUSE ◀ Timothy Taylor Landlord, Mordue Workie Ticket, Theakston BB, John Smiths, Jarrow River Catcher. ♀ 12 **Facilities** Family room Garden Parking

TYNEMOUTH
Map 21 NZ36

Copperfields ★★★ HL

Grand Hotel, Hotspur St NE30 4ER
☎ 0191 293 6666   📄 0191 293 6665
e-mail: info@grandhotel-uk.com
dir: *On NE coast, 10m from Newcastle upon Tyne*

The bar is at the rear of the imposing Grand Hotel, where Stan Laurel and Oliver Hardy always stayed when they played Newcastle's Theatre Royal. Worth a visit for the great views up and down the coast, as well as an extensive bar menu that includes home-made ham, leek and cheddar clanger (a steamed pudding); smokie fish pie; sticky chilli belly pork; Mexican beefburger; and riccia pasta ribbons. A blackboard lists daily specials.

Open all wk ◀ Bass '9', Black Sheep, Durham Brewery ales. **Facilities** Parking **Rooms** 45

WHITLEY BAY — Map 21 NZ37

The Waterford Arms

Collywell Bay Rd, Seaton Sluice NE26 4QZ
☎ 0191 237 0450
e-mail: les47@bt.connect.com
dir: *From A1 N of Newcastle take A19 at Seaton Burn then follow signs for A190 to Seaton Sluice*

The building dates back to 1899 and is located close to the small local fishing harbour, overlooking the North Sea. Splendid beaches and sand dunes are within easy reach, and the pub is very popular with walkers. Seafood dishes are the speciality, including seared swordfish, lemon sole, halibut, crab-stuffed plaice, and very large portions of fish and chips.

Open all wk noon-11.30 (Thu-Sat noon-mdnt Sun noon-10.30) **Bar Meals** Av main course £8 **Restaurant** L served Mon-Sat 12-9, Sun 12-4 booking required D served Mon-Sat 12-9, Sun 12-4 booking required food served all day ⊕ PUNCH ◗ Tetleys, John Smiths, Scotch, Guinness. 🍷 6 **Facilities** Children's menu Parking

WARWICKSHIRE

ALCESTER — Map 10 SP05

PICK OF THE PUBS

The Holly Bush NEW

37 Henley St B49 5QX
☎ 01789 762482 & 0788 4342363
e-mail: thehollybushpub@btconnect.com
dir: *M40 junct 15 for Warwick/Stratford, take A46 to Stratford*

Situated between Alcester's parish church and historic town hall, the 17th-century Holly Bush has been transformed from a one-bar boozer to a thriving pub serving great ales and delicious food by Tracey-Jane Deffley over the past six years. Handpumps dispense eight real ales – try a pint of Purity Mad Goose or Uley Bitter – and farm cider at the central bar, beyond which lie four panelled rooms. Menus blend traditional pub classics with more contemporary dishes and the emphasis on using locally sourced ingredients, including herbs and vegetables from the pub's allotment garden. Extensive menus range from lunchtime sandwiches (bacon and stilton) ham, egg and chips, and beer-battered cod and chips, to chorizo and clam risotto, roast pork belly with apple mash and sweet cabbage, and monkfish wrapped in Parma ham with pea mash and red wine sauce. For pudding, choose perhaps chocolate mousse with fresh raspberries, or lemon tart with bitter chocolate sorbet. This is a cracking town centre pub run with passion and panache – and there's a great garden, too.

Open all day all wk noon-mdnt (Fri-Sat noon-1am) **Bar Meals** L served Mon-Sat 12-2.30, Sun 12-4 D served Tue-Sat 7-9.30 Av main course £7.50 **Restaurant** L served Mon-Sat 12-2.30, Sun 12-4 D served Tue-Sat 7-9.30 Av 3 course à la carte fr £23 ⊕ FREE HOUSE ◗ Sharpe's Doom Bar, Black Sheep, Purity Gold, Purity Mad Goose, Uley Bitter Ø Local farm cider. **Facilities** Children's menu Dogs allowed Garden

ALDERMINSTER — Map 10 SP24

PICK OF THE PUBS

The Bell

CV37 8NY ☎ 01789 450414 📠 01789 450998
e-mail: info@thebellald.co.uk
dir: *On A3400 3.5m S of Stratford-upon-Avon*

An 18th-century coaching inn whose interior blends modern touches with traditional charms. The spacious conservatory restaurant overlooks a delightful old courtyard with views of the Stour Valley beyond. A good selection of starters and 'little dishes' could include avocado and crayfish tails with tomato vinaigrette on mixed leaves; pan-fried duck livers with Grand Marnier, spiced apple and toasted brioche; and a platter of mixed hors d'oeuvres. Follow with pork fillet filled with apricots and lemongrass, wrapped in Parma ham and served with Madeira jus and vegetables; or fillet of beef mignon with green beans, cherry tomatoes and a Jack Daniels and gorgonzola sauce. If you prefer a snack, there is also a selection of baguettes and light bites including hot cheese and bacon bruschetta; smoked salmon and cream cheese baguette with mixed leaves; and bacon, lettuce and tomato baguette. Those fond of fresh fish should keep an eye on the blackboard menu.

Open 11.30-2.30 6-11 (Fri-Sat 11.30-11 Sun noon-4.30) Closed: Sun eve **Bar Meals** L served Mon-Fri 12-2, Sat 12-2.30, Sun 12-3 booking required D served Mon-Thu 7-9, Fri-Sat 6-9 booking required **Restaurant** L served Mon-Fri 12-2, Sat 12-2.30, Sun 12-3 booking required D served Mon-Thu 7-9, Fri-Sat 6-9 booking required ⊕ FREE HOUSE ◗ Hook Norton, Lady Godiva. 🍷 11 **Facilities** Children's menu Dogs allowed Garden Parking

ALVESTON — Map 10 SP25

PICK OF THE PUBS

The Baraset Barn

See Pick of the Pubs on opposite page

ARDENS GRAFTON — Map 10 SP15

PICK OF THE PUBS

The Golden Cross

See Pick of the Pubs on page 474

BARFORD — Map 10 SP26

PICK OF THE PUBS

The Granville @ Barford NEW

52 Wellesbourne Rd CV35 8DS
☎ 01926 624236 📠 01926 624806
e-mail: info@granvillebarford.co.uk
dir: *1m from M40 junct 15. Take A429 signed Stow. Located at furthest end of Barford village*

This friendly and stylish village dining pub in the heart of Shakespeare country is owned and run by Val Kersey. Relax on the leather sofas in the lounge with a drink - a pint of Hooky or Purity perhaps. Everything on your plate here is home made from local produce delivered daily, except for the rustic bread, which arrives freshly-baked each morning from a neighbouring village. At lunchtime, try one of the larger size starters, such as warm black pudding with bubble and squeak, crispy bacon and stilton sauce; or a smoked salmon, dill and cucumber crème fraîche doorstop sandwich. In the evening, home in on crispy beer-battered fish of the day with chips, mushy peas and tartare sauce; home-made chicken Kiev with sauté potatoes and vegetables of the day; or butternut squash and herb risotto with Parmesan crisps. The manageable wine list embraces Europe, South America and South Africa. Enjoy alfresco dining in the spacious patio garden.

Open all wk noon-3 5.30-11 (Fri-Sat noon-11.30 noon-11) **Bar Meals** Av main course £12 **Restaurant** Fixed menu price fr £14.50 Av 3 course à la carte fr £18 ⊕ ENTERPRISE INNS PLC ◗ Hooky Bitter, Purity Gold, Purity UBU. 🍷 18 **Facilities** Children's menu Dogs allowed Garden Parking

PICK OF THE PUBS

The Baraset Barn ♟

ALVESTON
Map 10 SP25

1 Pimlico Ln CV37 7RF
☎ 01789 295510 📠 01789 292961
e-mail: barasetbarn@lovelypubs.co.uk

Surrounded by glorious Warwickshire countryside close to Stratford-upon-Avon, the hugely impressive Baraset Barn is part of Lovely Pubs, a select group established in 1995 by visionary operators Paul Salisbury and Paul Hales, who now have six quality dining destinations in the area. Converted from an old barn, this is a unique gastro-pub, a light, modern venue with a distinct continental feel and a dramatic interior styled from granite, pewter and oak. The original flagstones remind customers of its 200-year history as a barn, but the glass-fronted kitchen introduces a stylish, up-to-the-minute visual appeal. From the bar, stone steps lead to the main dining area with high oak beams and brick walls, and the open mezzanine level makes for a perfect vantage point, while the luxurious lounge area sports sumptuous sofas for a relaxing morning coffee with the papers. The crowd-pleasing menu successfully blends classic British dishes with an eclectic Mediterranean choice, offering sharing plates, dishes from the stove and rotisserie, and a chalkboard listing daily fish dishes. Typically, begin with devilled kidneys on toast, or chilli, honey-seared tuna with fennel, rocket and lemon olive oil, or share a camembert, baked in its box and served with onion toast and pear chutney. For main course, try the spit-roast chicken with lemon and tarragon butter; lamb rump Provençal with fondant potato and basil jus; bouillabaisse; or a rib-eye steak with stilton cream sauce. Leave room for treacle tart with vanilla custard or share a hot chocolate and orange fondue, served with dipping strawberries, marshmallows and bananas. The continental-style patio garden is perfect for summer alfresco dining and sipping champagne.

Open 11am-mdnt Closed: 25 Dec & 1 Jan, Sun eve, Mon (Jan-Feb) **Bar Meals** L served all week 12-2.30 D served Mon-Sat 6.30-9.30 Av main course £17 **Restaurant** L served Mon-Sat 12-2.30 (Sun 12-3.30) D served Mon-Sat 6.30-9.30 Fixed menu price fr £10 Av 3 course à la carte fr £22 ◀ UBU. ♟ 12 **Facilities** Children's menu Dogs allowed Garden Parking

PICK OF THE PUBS

The Golden Cross ♥

ARDENS GRAFTON   Map 10 SP15

B50 4LG
☎ 01789 772420   📄 01789 773697
e-mail: info@thegoldencross.net
web: www.thegoldencross.net
dir: *Telephone for directions*

This beautiful 18th-century building has seen a few changes since Pat and Steve Wainwright took over the reins five years ago. The patio has been given a complete makeover, making it just the place to relax with friends over a drink or a meal in the warmer months. Come indoors when the weather turns, to thaw out in the mellow, rug-strewn bar with its flagstone floor, massive beams and open fires. Wells Bombardier and Purity Brewing ales are amongst the beers on offer here, together with regular guest ales. The light, airy dining room offers a complete contrast, with its soft pastel decor and elegant plaster ceiling. The same menu is served throughout the pub, whether in the bar, the dining room or the garden. Traditional pub favourites are always available, and the blackboards reflect an ever-changing selection of specials. The kitchen team works tirelessly to prepare a completely home-cooked menu, using the best local produce and fresh Brixham fish. There's strong emphasis on seasonal changes; a steak option is always available, together with an interesting choice of fish and vegetarian dishes. Starters from the main menu include baked mushrooms and stilton with rocket salad; creamy smoked haddock pots; and crispy duck with orange salad. Main course choices are just as appealing; choose steak and kidney suet pudding with roasted root vegetables and new potatoes; or butternut squash and wild rocket risotto with basil oil and Parmesan shavings from the main menu, or switch to the specials board for grilled fillet of sea bass, spring onion mash and green beans with citrus cream. Typical desserts include bread and butter pudding with ice cream and custard, or lemon cheesecake with raspberry purée and tuile biscuit. Tuesday night is curry night along with live music.

Open May-Sep noon-11 **Bar Meals** L served all week 12-3 D served all week 5-9.30 Av main course £9 **Restaurant** L served all week 12-3 D served all week 5-9.30 Fixed menu price fr £12 ⊕ CHARLES WELLS ◄ Wells Bombardier, Purity Brewing, guest ales. ☙ 8 **Facilities** Garden Parking

BROOM
Map 10 SP05

Broom Tavern ♥

High St B50 4HL ☎ 01789 773656 📠 01789 773656
e-mail: webmaster@broomtavern.co.uk
dir: *N of B439 W of Stratford-upon-Avon*

Once a haunt of William Shakespeare, this 16th-century brick and timber inn is smartly furnished, with a large beer garden where barbecues are held in summer. Very much at the heart of village life, it is home to the Broom Tavern Golf Society, and fun days, charity events and outings are a feature. The menu offers a large selection of vegetarian dishes and seafood specials.

Open all wk noon-3 5.30-11 **Bar Meals** L served all wk 12-2.30 D served all wk 6-9 Av main course £8.25 **Restaurant** L served all wk 12-2.30 D served all wk 6-9 booking required ⊕ PUNCH TAVERNS ◀ Greene King IPA, Black Sheep, Timothy Taylor Landlord, Wells Bombardier. ♥ 20 **Facilities** Children's menu Dogs allowed Garden Parking

---

EDGEHILL
Map 11 SP34

The Castle Inn ♥

OX15 6DJ ☎ 01295 670255 📠 01295 670521
e-mail: info@thecastle-edgehill.com
dir: *M40 junct 11 then A422 towards Stratford-upon-Avon. 6m to Upton House, next right, 1.5m to Edgehill*

A fascinating property, the inn was built as a copy of Warwick Castle in 1742 to commemorate the centenary of the Battle of Edgehill, and stands on the summit of Edgehill, 700 feet above sea level. It opened on the anniversary of Cromwell's death in 1750, was first licensed in 1822, and acquired by Hook Norton a hundred years later. Bar snacks, sandwiches, hot platters and steaks are served.

Open all wk ⊕ HOOK NORTON BREWERY ◀ Hook Norton Best, Old Hooky & Generation, Hooky Dark, guest ales. ♥ 6 **Facilities** Garden Parking

---

ETTINGTON
Map 10 SP24

The Houndshill ♥

Banbury Rd CV37 7NS
☎ 01789 740267 📠 01789 740075
dir: *On A422 SE of Stratford-upon-Avon*

Family-run inn situated at the heart of England, making it a perfect base for exploring popular tourist attractions such as Oxford, Blenheim, Stratford and the Cotswolds.

The pleasant tree-lined garden is especially popular with families. Typical dishes range from poached fillet of salmon, and faggots, mash and minted peas, to supreme of chicken and ham and mushroom tagliatelle. Alternatively, try cold ham off the bone or home-made steak and kidney pie.

Open all wk Closed: 25-28 Dec **Bar Meals** L served all wk 12-2 D served all wk 7-9.30 Av main course £7.50 **Restaurant** L served all wk 12-2 D served all wk 7-9.30 Av 3 course à la carte fr £15 ⊕ FREE HOUSE ◀ Hook Norton Best, Spitfire. ♥ 7 **Facilities** Children's menu Play area Dogs allowed Garden Parking

---

FARNBOROUGH
Map 11 SP44

PICK OF THE PUBS

The Inn at Farnborough ♥

OX17 1DZ ☎ 01295 690615
e-mail: enquiries@innatfarnborough.co.uk
dir: *M40 junct 11 towards Banbury. Right at 3rd rdbt onto A423 signed Southam. 4m & onto A423. Left onto single track road signed Farnborough. Approx 1m turn right into village, pub on right*

Serving as an ale house for at least 200 years, this Grade II listed, 16th-century property enjoys a picturesque setting in a National Trust village. Formerly known as the Butcher's Arms, it was once the butcher's house on the Farnborough Estate and original features include a fine inglenook fireplace. A good choice of real ales and wines by the glass are offered alongside dishes based on high quality Heart of England produce. Dishes range from great British classics – beef and Hook Norton ale stew, bangers of the day, and poached salmon fishcakes – to dishes from the land (chargrilled Aubrey Allen rump steak), sea (baked fillet of sea bass), air (roast breast of guinea fowl) and earth (basil tagliatelle). The selection is supplemented by daily specials and a good value fixed-price menu of one to three courses. A funky private function room is available, with claret walls and a zebra print ceiling.

Open all wk Closed: 25 Dec **Bar Meals** L served all wk 12-3 booking required D served Tue-Sun 6-10 booking required Av main course £10 **Restaurant** L served all wk 12-3 booking required D served Tue-Sun 6-10 booking required Fixed menu price fr £10.95 Av 3 course à la carte fr £22 ⊕ FREE HOUSE ◀ Old Speckled Hen, Greene King IPA, Guinness, Hook Norton. ♥ 16 **Facilities** Dogs allowed Garden Parking

---

GREAT WOLFORD
Map 10 SP23

PICK OF THE PUBS

The Fox & Hounds Inn

CV36 5NQ ☎ 01608 674220 📠 01608 674160
e-mail: enquiries@thefoxandhoundsinn.com
dir: *Off A44 NE of Moreton-in-Marsh*

This unspoilt village hostelry nestles in Warwickshire's glorious countryside on the edge of the Cotswolds.

Among the excellent ales on offer are some from the county's Purity Brewing Company, to be supped at leisure whilst enjoying the quintessential English inn ambience – old settles, Tudor inglenook fireplaces and solid ceiling beams adorned with jugs or festooned with hops. The busy kitchen uses fresh local produce such as Dexter beef and seasonal game from local shoots, herbs and vegetables from the garden, and locally gathered mushrooms; only fresh fish comes from further afield, with deliveries from Scotland and Cornwall. Sausages, bacon, chutneys and pickles are all prepared on site – even the bread is baked using fresh yeast and organic flour milled in the Cotswolds. A typical selection from the menu could include Windrush goats' cheese and beetroot salad; Kitebrook lamb loin with home-made black pudding, celeriac purée and braised Puy lentils; and honey and lavender crème brûlée. There are three thoughtfully furnished, en suite bedrooms available.

The Fox & Hounds Inn

Closed: 1st 2wks Jan, Mon **Bar Meals** L served Tue-Sun 12-2 D served Tue-Sat 6.30-9 ⊕ FREE HOUSE ◀ Hook Norton Best, guest ales. **Facilities** Dogs allowed Garden Parking

---

HATTON
Map 10 SP26

The Case is Altered

Case Ln, Five Ways CV35 7JD ☎ 01926 484206
dir: *Please telephone for directions*

This traditional free house proudly carries the standard for the old style of pub. It serves no food and does not accept children or dogs. That aside, it's a thoroughly welcoming spot for adults who appreciate the pleasures of a quiet pint. Greene King beers have a strong presence, and there is always a local and national guest ale to sup while enjoying lively conversation or just appreciating the atmosphere.

Open all wk noon-2.30 6-11 (Sun 12-2 7-10.30) ⊕ FREE HOUSE ◀ Greene King IPA, Sharp's Doom Bar, guest ales. **Facilities** Parking Notes ⊛

ILMINGTON
Map 10 SP24

PICK OF THE PUBS

The Howard Arms ♥

Lower Green CV36 4LT
☎ 01608 682226 📄 01608 682226
e-mail: info@howardarms.com
dir: Off A429 or A3400, 7m from Stratford-upon-Avon

The 17th-century Cotswold stone inn is a rambling building with five arched windows overlooking the pretty village green. Centuries of connections with one of England's most illustrious families who resided at nearby Foxcote House add a touch of history to this Cotswold gem. The flagstoned bar and open-plan dining room create a civilised look without sacrificing period charm, and it is all imbued with an informal atmosphere. A blackboard above the inglenook fireplace lists an imaginative weekly-changing menu that utilises garden herbs and a host of quality local suppliers. Rare-breed pork and chicken from Chesterton Farm, Cirencester, vegetables and soft fruit from around Ebrington, and local estate game all feature in a repertoire that may take in duck liver and sage pâté with red onion chutney; lamb, cider and rosemary cobbler; Arbroath smokie fishcake with pea and mint mash and caper tartare sauce, and pear and apple flapjack crumble. There's local ale on tap and a super terrace and flower-filled garden for summer sipping.

Open all wk ⊕ FREE HOUSE ◀ Everards Tiger Best, Hook Norton Gold, Purity Brewing UBU, Bard's Brewery Nobel Fool, Timothy Taylor Landlord, Black Sheep Bitter. ♥ 20 Facilities Garden Parking

LAPWORTH
Map 10 SP17

PICK OF THE PUBS

The Boot Inn ♥

Old Warwick Rd B94 6JU
☎ 01564 782464 📄 01564 784989
e-mail: bootinn@hotmail.com
dir: Telephone for directions

Beside the Grand Union Canal in the unspoilt village of Lapworth, this lively and convivial 16th-century former coaching inn is well worth seeking out. Apart from its smartly refurbished interior, the attractive garden is a great place to relax on warm days, while a canopy and patio heaters make it a comfortable place to sit even on cooler evenings. But the main draw is the modern brasserie-style food, with wide-ranging menus that deliver home-produced dishes. A selection from the menu might include prawn, smoked haddock and spring onion fishcake, served with lemon gremolata and herb aioli; haddock in tempura batter with pea purée, sauce gribiche and frites; and fillet steak with smoked roast garlic, spinach and mascarpone mash.

Open all day all wk 11-11 (Thu-Sat 11am-mdnt Sun 11-10) Closed: 25 Dec Bar Meals L served all wk 12-2.30 D served Mon-Fri 7-9.30, Sat 6.30-9.30, Sun 7-9 Restaurant L served all wk 12-2.30 D served Mon-Fri 7-9.30, Sat 6.30-9.30, Sun 7-9 ⊕ LAUREL PUB PARTNERSHIPS ◀ Morland Old Speckled Hen, Fuller's London Pride, Hobgoblin. ♥ 8 Facilities Children's menu Dogs allowed Garden Parking

LONG ITCHINGTON
Map 11 SP46

PICK OF THE PUBS

The Duck on the Pond ♥

The Green CV47 9QJ
☎ 01926 815876 📄 01926 815766
dir: On A423 in village centre, 1m N of Southam

Children will be delighted to discover that the name of this attractive village inn does indeed indicate the presence of a pond replete with drakes and mallards. Adults, meanwhile, will be comforted to learn that the inn's appearance, which is reminiscent of a French bistro, is entirely substantiated by the food. Winter fires light an entirely intriguing interior, crammed with French artwork, road signs and bottles, not to mention an unusual willow baton ceiling. The passion is evident in an appealing and well thought out menu that mixes traditional dishes with more innovative selections. Start with an impressive tower of prawns and filo pastry; or fresh Scottish mussels steamed with chorizo, garlic and tomato sauce. Follow on with breast of chicken stuffed with spinach and brie; roast pork with nettle stuffing on apple mash with cider cream; or grilled salmon with braised fennel and a caramelised lime, mango and pineapple salsa. Specials might include seared scallops with sautéed black pudding, or Thai-marinated red snapper stir fry.

Closed: Mon (ex BH) ⊕ CHARLES WELLS ◀ Wells Bombardier, Young's Winter Warmer, Guinness. ♥ 10 Facilities Garden Parking

MONKS KIRBY
Map 11 SP48

The Bell Inn

Bell Ln CV23 0QY ☎ 01788 832352 📄 01788 832352
e-mail: belindagb@aol.com
dir: Off The Fosseway junct with B4455

The Spanish owners of this quaint, timbered inn, once a Benedictine priory gatehouse and then a brewhouse cottage, describe it as "a corner of Spain in the heart of England". Mediterranean and traditional cuisine play an important role on the menu. Red snapper gallega, saddle of lamb, fillet Catalan, chicken piri piri, and Mexican hot pot are popular favourites. Extensive range of starters and speciality dishes.

Closed: 26 Dec, 1 Jan, Mon ⊕ FREE HOUSE ◀ Boddingtons, IPA, Ruddles. Facilities Garden Parking

NAPTON ON THE HILL
Map 11 SP46

The Bridge at Napton ♥

Southam Rd CV47 8NQ ☎ 01926 812466
e-mail: info@thebridgeatnapton.co.uk
dir: At Bridge 111 on Oxford Canal on A425, 2m from Southam & 1m from Napton on the Hill

This is an ideal place to moor the narrow boat, though travellers by car or bike are equally welcome. Built as a stabling inn at Bridge 111 on the Oxford canal, the pub has a restaurant, three bars and a large garden, plus its own turning point for barges. There are some excellent ales, and food choices range from Aberdeen Angus beefburger with chips to the likes of honey-roasted belly pork with caramelised onions.

Open noon-3 6-11 (Sun noon-8) Closed: Mon (ex BH & summer school hols) Bar Meals L served Mon-Sat 12-2, Sun 12-7 booking required D served Mon-Sat 6-9, Sun 12-7 booking required Av main course £9 Restaurant L served Mon-Sat 12-2, Sun 12-7 booking required D served Mon-Sat 6-9, Sun 12-7 booking required ⊕ PUNCH TAVERNS ◀ Guinness, John Smith, Black Sheep, Guest ales. ♥ 6 Facilities Children's menu Play area Family room Dogs allowed Garden Parking

PRESTON BAGOT
Map 10 SP16

The Crabmill ♥

B95 5EE ☎ 01926 843342 📄 01926 843989
e-mail: thecrabmill@lovelypubs.co.uk
dir: M42 junct 8, A3400 towards Stratford-upon-Avon. Take A4189 Henley-in-Arden lights. Left, pub 1.5m on left

The name is a reminder that crab apple cider was once made at this 15th-century hostelry, which is set in beautiful rural surroundings. Restored to create an upmarket venue, the pub has a light, open feel. Even the menu seems fresh and stylish, with dishes ranging from a lunchtime croque monsieur or panini, to evening dishes such as Moroccan chicken with spiced potatoes and cucumber yogurt relish, and crab, crayfish and saffron risotto.

Open all day 11-11 Closed: 25 Dec, Sun eve Bar Meals L served Mon-Fri 12-2.30, Sat 12-3, Sun 12-3.30 D served all wk 6.30-9.30 ⊕ ENTERPRISE INNS ◀ Wadworth 6X, Tetleys, Greene King Abbot Ale ⱷ Stowford Press. ♥ 8 Facilities Dogs allowed Garden Parking

PRIORS MARSTON — Map 11 SP45

PICK OF THE PUBS

The Hollybush Inn ☎

Hollybush Ln CV47 7RW ☎ 01327 260934
dir: *From Southam A425, off bypass, 1st right, 6m to Priors Marston. Left after war memorial, next left, 150yds left again*

Many pubs are central to their communities, but this one goes a step further - it provides lunches for the local school and is committed to supporting the village sports club. Set in the beautiful village of Priors Marston in the heart of Warwickshire, the Hollybush was a farmhouse that started selling beer in 1927 and became fully licensed twenty years later. Recent extensions have added the 40-seat restaurant and a games room. With its large fireplace burning brightly, it's a warm hub of village social activity with a very relaxed atmosphere; people can eat and/or drink wherever they choose. The bar menu ranges from baguettes to steak, Guinness and mushroom pie; and a dish of charcuterie is served with olives, spicy cornichons and bread. A three-course dinner could comprise pan-fried pigeon breast with beetroot salad; medallions of pork fillet; and blackberry and apple crumble - with custard of course!

Open all wk Sun-Fri noon-3 5-11 (Sat noon-3 5-12)
Bar Meals L served all wk 12-2.30 D served Mon-Sat 6.30-9.30 ⊕ Punch Taverns ◀ Hook Norton, Pedigree ♂ Stowford Press. ♀8 **Facilities** Dogs allowed Garden Parking

RATLEY — Map 11 SP34

The Rose and Crown

OX15 6DS ☎ 01295 678148
e-mail: k.marples@btinternet.com
dir: *Follow Edgehill signs, 7m N of Banbury (13m SE of Stratford-upon-Avon) on A422*

Following the Battle of Edgehill in 1642, a Roundhead was discovered in the chimney of this 12th-century pub and beheaded in the hearth. His ghost reputedly haunts the building. Enjoy the peaceful village location and the traditional pub food, perhaps including beef and ale pie, scampi and chips, chicken curry and the Sunday roast, plus vegetarian options.

Closed: Mon L **Bar Meals** L served Tue-Sun 12-2.30 booking required D served Mon-Sat 6.30-9 booking required Av main course £9.95 ⊕ FREE HOUSE ◀ Wells Bombardier, Eagle IPA, Greene King Old Speckled Hen, Guest ale. **Facilities** Children's menu Family room Dogs allowed Garden Parking

RED HILL — Map 10 SP15

The Stag at Redhill ☎

Alcester Rd B49 6NQ
☎ 01789 764634 📠 01789 764431
e-mail: info@thestagatredhill.co.uk
web: www.thestagatredhill.co.uk
dir: *On A46 between Stratford-upon-Avon & Alcester*

A family-run business, The Stag is a 16th-century coaching inn, which has also been a court house and prison (you can still see a cell door in the court room restaurant). Food is freshly prepared and service begins with breakfast from 7.30am. From Mondays through to Saturday you might be tempted by the value 'Credit Crunch Lunch' (1, 2 or 3 courses). There is a large patio eating area, popular in fine weather. A helipad facility allows customers to fly in for a meal at their convenience.

Open all day all wk 7am-11pm **Bar Meals** L served all wk 12-5 D served all wk 5-9 Av main course £8.50 food served all day **Restaurant** L served all wk 12-5 D served all wk 5-9 Fixed menu price fr £12 food served all day ⊕ GREENE KING ◀ Greene King IPA, Abbot Ale, Old Speckled Hen, Ruddles, Morland Original ♂ Stowford Press. ♀8 **Facilities** Children's menu Garden Parking

See advert on this page

The Stag at Redhill
Alcester Road, Redhill, Alcester, Warwickshire B49 6NQ

The Stag at Redhill is a family run business that really does care; we always offer that personal touch to ensure you have a fabulous time.

All our food is fresh and our menu is very extensive – whether it's dinner for two or more, a relaxed Sunday roast or a business lunch, there's something wholesome and delicious to suit. The excellent children's menu will have younger guests licking their lips as well – and there'll be a whole host of special daily menus and themed evenings happening right through the week.

The Stag couldn't be easier to find as it sits proudly on the A46 between Stratford and sleepy Alcester. There's plenty of parking – as well as ten comfortable rooms that guarantee a relaxed stay.

• Tel: (01789) 764634 • www.thestagatredhill.co.uk • info@thestagatredhill.co.uk •

RUGBY
Map 11 SP57

PICK OF THE PUBS

Golden Lion Hotel ★★★ HL ▾

Easenhall CV23 0JA
☎ 01788 832265 📄 01788 832878
e-mail: reception@goldenlionhotel.org
dir: *From Rugby take A426, take 1st exit Newbold road B4112. Through Newbold. At Harborough Parva follow brown sign, turn left, pub in 1m*

This charming 16th-century free house with low oak-beamed ceilings and narrow doorways was built on the trading route between London and the Welsh borders. The development of the canal network saw the village grow into a thriving rural community, with the Golden Lion at its heart. James and Claudia are the third generation of the Austin family at the helm. You'll find traditional ales, roaring winter fires and an extensive wine list, as well as excellent food and service. Almost a dozen varieties of sandwich and baguette are served at lunchtime, or from the main menu you can choose the likes of fresh melon and Parma ham; pan-seared fillet of sea bream with ratatouille and crushed new potatoes; and lemon meringue pie with double cream. The pub is set amidst idyllic countryside in one of Warwickshire's best-kept villages, and its 20 en suite bedrooms, some with four-poster beds, offer outstanding accommodation.

Open all day all wk 11-11 (Sun noon - 11) **Bar Meals** L served Mon-Sat 12-2, Sun 12-2.30 D served Mon-Sat 4.30-9.30, Sun 3-8.45 Av main course £10.95 **Restaurant** L served Mon-Sat 12-2, Sun 12-2.30 D served Mon-Sat 4.30-9.30, Sun 3-8.45 Av 3 course à la carte fr £20 ⊕ FREE HOUSE ◀ Guinness, Ruddles Best, 2 real ales. ▾ 7 **Facilities** Children's menu Garden Parking **Rooms** 20

Old Smithy NEW ▾

1 Green Ln, Church Lawford CV23 9EF ☎ 02476 542333
e-mail: smithy@king-henry-taverns.co.uk
dir: *Take the Coventry to Rugby Road, The Old Smithy is on the green in Church Lawford*

Anyone asked to draw their idyllic 'roses round the door' village pub might produce something looking like The Old Smithy. As with all King Henry's Taverns pubs, the menu features a huge choice of traditional favourites, such as gammon steak, fish and seafood, to haddock in batter; chicken dishes, and a selection for those with larger appetites, including Brontosaurus lamb shank. Vegetarians will welcome a six-way choice, including tomato and basil penne pasta.

Open all day all wk noon-11 **Bar Meals** Av main course £3 food served all day **Restaurant** food served all day ⊕ KING HENRY'S TAVERN ◀ Guinness, IPA, Marstons Pedigree. ▾ 15 **Facilities** Children's menu Play area Family room Garden Parking

SHIPSTON ON STOUR
Map 10 SP24

The Cherington Arms ▾

Cherington CV36 5HS ☎ 01608 686233
dir: *12m from Stratford-upon-Avon. 14m from Leamington & Warwick. 10m from Woodstock. 4m from Shipston on Stour*

An attractive 17th-century inn with exposed beams and Cotswold stone walls, stripped wood furniture and roaring log inglenook fire. The carte menu might announce crab fishcakes with mango and chilli salsa; or breast of chicken stuffed with sun-dried tomato and cream pesto, all washed down with a pint of Hook Norton. There's also a snack menu and specials board. Outside there are large riverside gardens with a mill race, ideal for alfresco dining. Horse riders and walkers are welcome.

Open all wk **Bar Meals** L served Mon-Fri 12-2, Sat-Sun 12-2.30 D served Sun, Tue-Thu 7-9, Fri-Sat 7-9.30 **Restaurant** L served Mon-Fri 12-2, Sat-Sun 12-2.30 D served Sun, Tue-Thu 7-9, Fri-Sat 7-9.30 ⊕ HOOK NORTON BREWERY ◀ Hook Norton Best Bitter, guest ales ⓒ Stowford Press. ▾ 11 **Facilities** Children's menu Dogs allowed Garden Parking

PICK OF THE PUBS

The Red Lion ★★★★ INN ▾

See Pick of the Pubs on opposite page

White Bear Hotel ▾

High St CV36 4AJ ☎ 01608 661558 📄 01608 662612
dir: *From M40 junct 15, follow signs to Stratford-upon-Avon, then take A3400 to Shipston on Stour*

Open fires and wooden settles give the bars of this Georgian hotel a comfortable, timeless appeal. You'll find a range of real ales and keg beers, with up to eight wines available by the glass. The refurbished restaurant with its crisp white tablecloths makes dining a delicious experience: starters like pan-fried kidneys with black pudding precede main course options that include rack of lamb; and haddock with spinach and Welsh rarebit.

Open all wk Mon-Thu & Sun 11am-mdnt (Fri-Sat 11am-2am) **Bar Meals** food served all day **Restaurant** food served all day ⊕ PUNCH TAVERNS ◀ Adnams Hobgoblin, Bass, guest ales. ▾ 8 **Facilities** Children's menu Dogs allowed Garden Parking

SHREWLEY
Map 10 SP26

PICK OF THE PUBS

The Durham Ox Restaurant and Country Pub ▾

Shrewley Common CV35 7AY ☎ 01926 842283
e-mail: enquiries@durham-ox.co.uk
dir: *M40 junct 15 onto A46 towards Coventry. 1st exit signed Warwick, turn left onto A4177. After Hatton Country World, pub signed 1.5m*

An award-winning pub/restaurant in a peaceful village just four miles from Warwick and Leamington. Warm and inviting, its old beams, roaring fire and traditional hospitality combine with a city chic that give it a competitive edge. Success is in no small measure due to the restaurant, where Master Chef Simon Diprose prepares impressive, seasonally changing classic and contemporary dishes. A meal might consist of deep-fried Boursin with ratatouille and basil sorbet; roast fillet of five-spice salmon with sweetcorn, pak choi and coriander dressing; and hot chocolate and Snickers fondant with vanilla ice cream. For more examples of his style, consider roast vegetables with North African spices, couscous and yoghurt dressing; and fresh plaice fillet in crispy Cajun coating with buttered peas and chunky chips. Children are offered penne pasta, and home-made fishcakes from their own menu. Extensive gardens incorporate a safe children's play area.

Open all wk 12-2.30 6-9.30 (Sat 12-9.30) **Bar Meals** food served all day ⊕ GREENE KING ◀ Ruddles, Abbot Ale, guest ales ⓒ Stowford Press. ▾ 21 **Facilities** Play area Garden Parking

STRATFORD-UPON-AVON
Map 10 SP25

The Dirty Duck

Waterside CV37 6BA ☎ 01789 297312
dir: *Telephone for directions*

Frequented by members of the Royal Shakespeare Company from the nearby theatre, this traditional, partly Elizabethan inn has a splendid raised terrace overlooking the River Avon. In addition to the interesting range of real ales, a comprehensive choice of food is offered. Light bites, pastas, salads and mains at lunchtime, plus pub classics and 'make it special' dishes at night, from rustic sharing bread with herbs, garlic and olives to roast rack of lamb.

Open all day all wk 11am-mdnt (Sun 11am-10.30pm) **Bar Meals** L served Mon-Sat 12-9, Sun 12-7 D served Mon-Sat 12-9, Sun 12-7 food served all day ⊕ GREENE KING ◀ Morland Old Speckled Hen, Greene King IPA ⓒ Stowford Press. **Facilities** Dogs allowed Garden

PICK OF THE PUBS

The Red Lion ★★★★ INN ♀

Main St, Long Compton CV36 5JS
☎ **01608 684221** 📄 **01608 684968**
e-mail:
info@redlion-longcompton.co.uk
web: www.redlion-longcompton.co.uk
dir: *On A3400 between Shipston on Stour & Chipping Norton*

The newly refurbished interior of this Grade II listed free house blends old-world charm with a smart contemporary feel. High backed settles, stone walls and oak beams set the scene, with warming log fires in winter. Originally built as a coaching inn in 1748, the Red Lion stands in an Area of Outstanding Natural Beauty. Though it is ideally situated for such major attractions as Stratford-upon-Avon, Warwick, Oxford and the Cotswold Wildlife Park, tales of witches in the village and a nearby prehistoric stone circle mean there is as

much to interest the historian as the tourist. The pub's walls are decorated with original paintings by Katharine Lightfoot, and there are several distinct areas in which to dine or simply relax with a good pint. The bar is full of atmosphere, and visitors can eat there or in the restaurant area. In summer, it's a real treat to sit out in the garden, or take a leisurely lunch on the pretty, flower-bordered patio. The menu and blackboard specials cater for all tastes, from interesting sandwiches like crayfish, rocket and lemon mayonnaise on ciabatta to an open goats' cheese omelette with caramelised onions, spinach and salad. The adventurous starters include wild boar terrine with spiced pear chutney, whilst main course dishes range from venison with roasted winter vegetables to pan-fried scallops with creamed parsnips, crisp pancetta and a vermouth and chive sauce. Round off with warm treacle tart and clotted cream, or hazelnut cream and raspberry Pavlova with raspberry sauce. Five elegant en suite bedrooms all feature such modern luxuries as Egyptian cotton bed linen, fluffy towels and flat-screen televisions.

Open all week 11-11 **Bar Meals** L served Mon-Thu 12-2.30, Fri-Sun 12-9.30 D served Mon-Thu 6-9, Fri-Sun 12-9.30 Av main course £15.95 **Restaurant** L served Mon-Thu 12-2.30, Fri-Sun 12-9.30 D served Mon-Thu 6-9, Fri-Sun 12-9.30 Fixed menu price fr £11.95 ⊕ FREE HOUSE ◀ Hook Norton Best, Adnams, Timothy Taylor. ♀ 7 **Facilities** Children's menu Play area Dogs allowed Garden Parking **Rooms** 5

STRATFORD-UPON-AVON *continued*

PICK OF THE PUBS

The Fox & Goose Inn ★★★ INN ⬤

CV37 8DD ☎ 01608 682293 📄 01608 682293
e-mail: mail@foxandgoose.co.uk
dir: *1m off A3400, between Shipston on Stour & Stratford-upon-Avon*

Formerly two cottages and a blacksmith's forge, the Fox & Goose is located in Armscote, a beautiful village south of Stratford-upon-Avon. The inn was given a total refurbishment a few years ago, and the result is stylish and utterly distinctive. It includes a smart dining room and a cosy bar. The bar has lots of squishy velvet cushions, an open fire, flagstone floors and piles of reading matter to enjoy while supping a pint of real ale. If you prefer wine or champagne, there is a good selection by the glass or bottle. For more solid sustenance, look to the country-style menu: sautéed garlic mushroom pepperpot with garlic nibbles; grilled chicken breast with fresh asparagus and chef's creamy risotto; and a home-made dessert from the daily changing board will undoubtedly suffice. Out in the garden there's a large grassy area, decking with 20 seats for dining under the vines, and lovely countryside views. Accommodation is available.

Open all wk 12-3 6-11 (Fri-Sun 12-11) **Bar Meals** L served Mon-Thu 12-2, Fri-Sun 12-9.30 D served Mon-Thu 6-9.30, Fri-Sun 12-9.30 ⊕ FREE HOUSE ◀ local guest ales ☼ Westons, Thatchers Gold. ⬤ 8 **Facilities** Garden Parking **Rooms** 3

The One Elm ⬤

1 Guild St CV37 6QZ ☎ 01789 404919
e-mail: theoneelm@peachpubs.com
dir: *In town centre*

Standing on its own in the heart of town, the One Elm has two dining rooms: downstairs is intimate, even with the buzzy bar close by, while upstairs feels grander. The menu features chargrilled côte de beouf for two, Aberdeen Angus rump steak, and tuna, as well as other main courses. The deli board offers all-day nuts and seeds, cheeses, charcuterie and antipasti. The secluded terrace induces in some a feeling of being abroad.

Open all wk 11-11 (Thu-Sat 11am-mdnt) Closed: 25 Dec **Bar Meals** Av main course £11 food served all day **Restaurant** Av 3 course à la carte fr £18 food served all day ⊕ PEACH PUB CO ◀ London Pride, UBU Purity, Purity Gold. ⬤ 9 **Facilities** Children's menu Dogs allowed Garden Parking

---

STRETTON ON FOSSE   Map 10 SP23

The Plough Inn ⬤

GL56 9QX ☎ 01608 661053
e-mail: saravol@aol.com
dir: *From Moreton-in-Marsh, 4m on A429 N. From Stratford-upon-Avon, 10m on A429 S*

A classic village pub built from mellow Cotswold stone, The Plough has the requisite bare beams and real fire, plus a friendly resident cat, Alfie, to add to the welcome. It's a family-run affair, with French chef and co-owner Jean Pierre in charge of the kitchen. Expect traditional French cooking from the specials board, while other choices might include beer-battered cod with chips and salad. There's a spit roast in the inglenook on Sundays (September-May).

Open all wk 11.30-2.30 6-11.30 (Sun 12-2.30 7-11) Closed: 25 Dec eve **Bar Meals** L served all wk 12-2 D served Mon-Sat 7-9 Av main course £9.95 ⊕ FREE HOUSE ◀ Hook Norton, Ansells Mild, Spitfire, Purity, local ales ☼ Old Katy, Black Rat, Thatchers Traditional. ⬤ 9 **Facilities** Children's menu Play area Garden Parking

---

TEMPLE GRAFTON   Map 10 SP15

The Blue Boar Inn ⬤

B49 6NR ☎ 01789 750010 📄 01789 750635
e-mail: info@theblueboar.co.uk
dir: *From A46 (Stratford to Alcester) turn left to Temple Grafton. Pub at 1st x-rds*

The oldest part of the inn is 17th century, and has been an alehouse since that time. The restaurant features a 35-foot glass-covered well, home to a family of koi carp, from which water was formerly drawn for brewing. There are four open fires in the bar and restaurant areas, and a patio garden with views of the Cotswold Hills. A menu of traditional dishes is served, with variety provided by daily specials prepared from local produce, game in particular.

Open all day all wk **Bar Meals** L served all wk 12-3 D served all wk 6-10 **Restaurant** L served all wk 12-3 D served all wk 6-10 ⊕ MARSTONS PUB COMPANY ◀ Marstons Banks Original, Pedigree, Guinness ☼ Thatchers Gold. ⬤ 6 **Facilities** Children's menu Garden Parking

---

WARWICK   Map 10 SP26

The Rose & Crown ⬤

30 Market Place CV34 4SH
☎ 01926 411117 📄 01926 492117
e-mail: roseandcrown@peachpubs.com
dir: *M40 junct 15 follow signs to Warwick. Pass castle car park entrance up hill to West Gate, left into Bowling Green St, 1st right*

Stylish gastro-pub located in the centre of Warwick with large leather sofas in the bar, a good choice of real ales and wines by the glass. Breakfast, lunch and dinner are served in the vibrant red restaurant. The deli board is a popular feature, with nuts and seeds, cheese, charcuterie, antipasti, fish and bread. Mains take in free range coq au vin, Porterhouse steak, roast hake, and sausage of the week.

Open all day all wk 8am-11pm (Fri-Sat 8am-mdnt) Closed: 25 Dec **Bar Meals** food served all day **Restaurant** food served all day ⊕ PEACH PUBS ◀ Black Sheep, London Pride, Old Hooky. ⬤ 8 **Facilities** Children's menu Dogs allowed

---

WELFORD-ON-AVON   Map 10 SP15

PICK OF THE PUBS

The Bell Inn ⬤

Binton Rd CV37 8EB
☎ 01789 750353 📄 01789 750893
e-mail: info@thebellwelford.co.uk
dir: *Please telephone for directions*

In the heart of the Warwickshire countryside, this 17th-century inn has all the classic touches, including open fires, flagstone floors, exposed beams and oak furniture. Legend has it that William Shakespeare contracted fatal pneumonia after stumbling home from here in the pouring rain. In addition to an extensive list of wines, at least five real ales are always on offer, including two local brews such as Pure Gold and Pure UBU (named after the brewery's dog, pronounced Oo-Boo) from the Purity Brewing Company in Great Alne just a few miles away. Food is taken seriously here and the local suppliers of quality ingredients are credited on the menu. In addition to the main menu, a specials carte tempts with prawn and ginger fritters in a sweet chilli and smoked garlic sauce; pan-roasted partridge on sautéed cabbage and potato with a sun blush tomato jus; and sticky fig and date pudding with butterscotch and walnut sauce.

Open all wk Sat 11.30-11 Sun noon-10.30 **Bar Meals** L served Mon-Sat 11.30-2.30, Sun all day booking required D served Mon-Thu 6-9.30, Fri-Sat 6-10, Sun all day booking required Av main course £12 **Restaurant** L served Mon-Sat 11.30-2.30, Sun all day booking required D served Mon-Thu 6-9.30, Fri-Sat 6-10, Sun all day booking required Av 3 course à la carte fr £22.95 ⊕ ENTERPRISE INNS ◀ Hook Norton (various), Flowers Original, Hobsons Best, Wadworth 6X, Flowers Best, Purity Gold, UBU. ⬤ 16 **Facilities** Children's menu Garden Parking

PICK OF THE PUBS

The Bulls Head ♀

WOOTTON WAWEN Map 10 SP16

Stratford Rd B95 6BD
☎ 01564 792511
dir: *On B3400, 4m N of Stratford-upon-Avon, 1m S of Henley-in-Arden*

Non-locals may like to know that the village name is pronounced Woot'n Worn. Ideally placed for touring and exploring the lovely landscapes of Warwickshire and the Cotswolds, the Bulls Head is one of several notable buildings. Originally two separate cottages, it displays a stone with the date 1317, and the bar and snug areas feature beams, leather sofas, open fires and old church pews. The same tone and style are maintained in the magnificent 'great hall' restaurant, with its vaulted ceiling and yet more exposed beams. Outside, you'll find a lawned garden and paved patio surrounded by mature trees. Since taking over in 2006, Andrew and Wendy Parry have developed the pub into a serious dining destination, the attraction being what they describe quite simply as 'food we love to eat and food we love to cook.' They visit local suppliers personally in order to ensure that the very best of the county's produce finds its way to their kitchen. Start with fresh Scottish mussels in white wine and garlic; chicken and apricot terrine with fruit chutney; or fresh home-made soup with crusty bread. Among the mains might be Lashford's award-winning sausages of the week with mash and gravy; Lighthorne shoulder of lamb stuffed with apricots, prunes and pistachios; grilled sea bass on leek and spinach mash with balsamic roasted tomatoes; or chef's risotto of the day. Look to the blackboard for the daily specials. The wine list tours the globe to offer bins from Europe to South America, and from New Zealand to California.

Closed: Mon (ex BH) **Restaurant**
⌖ WOLVERHAMPTON & DUDLEY BREWERIES PLC ◗ Marston's Pedigree, Banks Bitter, Banks Original plus guest ales. ♀ 10 **Facilities** Garden Parking

WITHYBROOK — Map 11 SP48

The Pheasant ▼

Main St CV7 9LT ☎ 01455 220480 🖨 01455 221296
e-mail: thepheasant01@hotmail.com
dir: *7m from Coventry*

This well-presented 17th-century free house stands beside the brook where withies were once cut for fencing. An inglenook fireplace, farm implements and horse-racing photographs characterise the interior. Under the same ownership since 1981, the pub has a varied menu with a wealth of popular choices. Alongside a blackboard of specials, a typical menu includes pan-fried pork cutlets, fisherman's pie, braised faggots, and chicken and mushroom pie. Outside tables overlook the Withy Brook.

Open all wk 11-3 6-11.30 (Sun & BH 11-11) Closed: 25-26 Dec **Bar Meals** L served Mon-Sat 12-2, Sun 12-9 booking required D served Mon-Sat 6-10, Sun 12-9 booking required **Restaurant** L served Mon-Sat 12-2, Sun 12-9 booking required D served Mon-Sat 6-10, Sun 12-9 booking required ⊕ FREE HOUSE ◀ Courage Directors, Theakstons Best, John Smiths Smooth. ▼ 9
Facilities Children's menu Dogs allowed Garden Parking

WOOTTON WAWEN — Map 10 SP16

PICK OF THE PUBS

The Bulls Head ▼

See Pick of the Pubs on page 481

WEST MIDLANDS

BARSTON — Map 10 SP27

PICK OF THE PUBS

The Malt Shovel at Barston ⊛ ▼

Barston Ln B92 0JP
☎ 01675 443223 🖨 01675 443223
web: www.themaltshovelatbarston.com
dir: *M42 junct 5, take turn towards Knowle. 1st left on Jacobean Ln, right at T-junct (Hampton Ln). Sharp left into Barston Ln. Restaurant 0.5m*

Handily close to Solihull, this bustling, award-winning country pub has been converted from an early 20th century mill where malt was ground. The bar is cosy and relaxed with log fires in winter, and the restaurant

---

is housed in a converted barn next door – both are stylishly decorated with modern soft furnishings and interesting art and artefacts. Fresh local produce is cooked to order, with some imaginative, modern British dishes making the best of seasonal ingredients. Seafood is a particular strength, and dishes include roast masala monkfish; grilled plaice with roast sweet potato, crab and black Tuscan olive dressing; and baked cod on black pudding with pea purée, smoked bacon and béarnaise. An alternative might be beef fillet with peppercorn cream and sauté potatoes, followed by apple tarte Tatin with pistachio ice cream, or dark chocolate fondant with cherries, Kirsch and vanilla bean ice cream. There's a super rear garden for summer alfresco dining.

The Malt Shovel at Barston

Open all day all wk **Bar Meals** L served Mon-Sat 12-2.30, Sun 12-4 booking required D served Mon-Sat 6-9.30 booking required Av main course £12.95 **Restaurant** L served Sun 12-4 booking required D served Mon-Sat 7-9.30 booking required Fixed menu price fr £21.95 Av 3 course à la carte fr £20 ⊕ FREE HOUSE ◀ Tribute, Brew XI, Timothy Taylor Landlord. ▼ 8 **Facilities** Garden Parking

BIRMINGHAM — Map 10 SP08

The Peacock ▼

Icknield St, Forhill, nr King's Norton B38 0EH
☎ 01564 823232 🖨 01564 829593
dir: *Telephone for directions*

Despite its out of the way location, at Forhill just outside Birmingham, the Peacock keeps very busy serving traditional ales and a varied menu, (booking essential). Chalkboards display the daily specials, among which you might find braised partridge on a bed of pheasant sausage and mash, whole sea bass with crab, grilled shark steak with light curry butter, pan-fried sirloin steak with mild mushroom and pepper sauce, or lamb fillet with apricot and walnut stuffing. Several friendly ghosts are in residence, and one of their tricks is to disconnect the taps from the barrels. Large gardens with two patios.

Open all wk ⊕ CHEF & BREWER ◀ Hobsons Best Bitter, Theakstons Old Peculier, Enville Ale. ▼ 20
Facilities Garden Parking

CHADWICK END — Map 10 SP27

PICK OF THE PUBS

The Orange Tree ▼

Warwick Rd B93 0BN
☎ 01564 785364 🖨 01564 782988
e-mail: theorangetree@lovelypubs.co.uk
dir: *3m from Knowle towards Warwick*

Relaxation is the name of the game at this pub/restaurant in peaceful countryside, only minutes away from the hustle and bustle of the National Exhibition Centre. The interior is light, airy and warm with open kitchens, stone-fired ovens and log burning fires. Real ales are backed by Thatchers Gold cider on tap, so settle with a pint while choosing from the menu. Comfort springs to mind here too, where sharing plates of antipasti or Greek mezze can be followed by fired pizzas – try the sloppy Guiseppe with hot spiced beef and green peppers. Alternatively half a dozen different pastas range from tagliatelle bolognese to macaroni with smoked haddock and cauliflower cheese. Other sections on the carte promise grills, spit-roast chicken from the rotisserie, salads and dishes such as braised beef in Barolo from the oven. The sunny lounge area, al sumptuous leather sofas and rustic decor, opens up through oversized French doors to the patio.

Open all day all wk 11-11 Closed: 25 Dec **Bar Meals** L served all wk 12-2.30 D served all wk 6-9.30 Av main course £13.50 **Restaurant** L served all wk 12-2.30 booking required D served all wk 6-9.30 booking required Av 3 course à la carte fr £25 ⊕ FREE HOUSE ◀ IPA, Old Hooky, Black Sheep ◔ Thatchers. ▼ 8 **Facilities** Children's menu Play area Dogs allowed Garden Parking

HAMPTON IN ARDEN — Map 10 SP28

PICK OF THE PUBS

The White Lion

10 High St B92 0AA ☎ 01675 442833
e-mail: info@thewhitelioninn.com
dir: *Opposite church*

A listed 400-year-old timber-framed village pub, originally a farmhouse although licensed since at least 1836. The lounge bar has the more comfortable furniture and open fires, and provides an appealing range of traditional bar food. In the attractively designed and furnished restaurant you'll find modern English cuisine based on local, seasonal produce, including fresh fish on daily specials boards. For dinner, try a starter of spicy lamb koftas with Greek salad, followed by pan-fried duck breast with braised red cabbage, orange and blackberry and port jus; chargilled chicken supreme and confit chicken leg with red wine, bacon and mushroom sauce; or salmon and prawn fishcakes with fine green beans and hollandaise sauce. Plenty of choice for children, and roasts on Sundays.

Open all wk noon-12.30am (Sun noon-10.30) **Bar Meals** L served all wk 12-2.30 D served all wk 5.30-9.30 ⊕ PUNCH TAVERNS ◀ Brew XI, Black Sheep, Adnams, guest ale ⓑ Thatchers Gold. **Facilities** Garden Parking

OLDBURY
Map 10 SO98

Waggon & Horses

7a Church St B69 3AD ☎ 0121 552 5467
e-mail: andrew.gale@unicombox.co.uk
dir: *Telephone for directions*

listed back-bar, high copper-panelled ceiling and riginal tile work are among the character features to be und at this real ale pub in the remnants of the old town entre. Traditional pub food includes faggots and mash, ork and leek sausages, lasagne, chilli, and fish and hips. Beers from Brains of Cardiff and regular guests es available.

pen all wk ⊕ S A BRAIN ◀ Enville White, Brains IPA, akham JHB, 3 guest ales. **Facilities** Family room arking

SEDGLEY
Map 10 SO99

Beacon Hotel & Sarah Hughes Brewery ⬤

29 Bilston St DY3 1JE
☎ 01902 883380 ▤ 01902 884020
dir: *Telephone for directions*

ttle has changed in 150 years at this traditional rewery tap, which still retains its Victorian atmosphere. he rare snob-screened island bar serves a taproom, nug, large smoke-room and veranda. Proprietor John ughes reopened the adjoining Sarah Hughes Brewery in 987, 66 years after his grandmother became the censee. Flagship beers are Sarah Hughes Dark Ruby, urprise and Pale Amber, with guest bitters also vailable.

pen all wk noon-2.30 5.30-11 (Sat-12-3 6-11 Sun 12-3 -10.30) **Bar Meals** food served all day ⊕ SARAH UGHES BREWERY ◀ Sarah Hughes Dark Ruby, Surprise Pale Amber, plus guest, seasonal ales. ⬤ 8 acilities Play area Family room Dogs allowed Garden arking **Notes** ⊜

SOLIHULL
Map 10 SP17

The Boat Inn ⬤

222 Hampton Ln, Catherine-de-Barnes B91 2TJ
☎ 0121 705 0474 ▤ 0121 704 0600
dir: *Telephone for directions*

Village pub with a small, enclosed garden located right next to the canal in Solihull. Real ales are taken seriously and there are two frequently changing guest ales in addition to the regulars. There is also a choice of 14 wines available by the glass. Fresh fish is a daily option, and other favourite fare includes chicken cropper, Wexford steak, and beef and ale pie.

Open all wk ◀ Bombardier, Greene King IPA, 2 guest ales. ⬤ 14 **Facilities** Family room Garden Parking

WEST BROMWICH
Map 10 SP09

The Vine

Roebuck St B70 6RD ☎ 0121 553 2866
e-mail: bharat@thevine.co.uk
dir: *0.5m from M5 junct 1. 2m from town centre*

Well-known, family-run business renowned for its good curries and cheap drinks. Since 1978 the typically Victorian alehouse has provided the setting for Suresh 'Suki' Patel's eclectic menu. Choose from a comprehensive range of Indian dishes (chicken balti, lamb saag), a barbecue menu and Thursday spit roast, offered alongside traditional pub fare. The Vine boasts the Midlands' only indoor barbeque, plus it is a stone's throw from The Hawthorns, West Bromwich Albion's football ground.

Open all wk **Bar Meals** L served Mon-Fri 12-2 D served Mon-Fri 5.30-10.30 Av main course £4.95 **Restaurant** L served Sat-Sun 1-10.30 D served Sat-Sun 1-10.30 ⊕ FREE HOUSE ◀ Mild Banks, Brew XI, John Smiths. **Facilities** Family room Garden

WIGHT, ISLE OF

ARRETON
Map 5 SZ58

The White Lion

PO30 3AA ☎ 01983 528479
e-mail: chrisandkatelou@hotmail.co.uk
dir: *B3056 (Newport to Sandown road)*

Sited in an outstandingly beautiful conservation area, this 300-year-old former coaching inn offers a genuinely hospitable welcome. Oak beams, polished brass and open fires set the cosy tone inside, while a safe outside seating area enjoys views of the Arreton scenery. Well-priced pub grub is served all day, ranging from traditional snacks to specials such as nasi goreng - Indonesian spicy rice with chicken and prawns. Favourite puddings of spotted dick and jam roly poly sell out quickly.

Open all day all wk **Bar Meals** Av main course £7.95 food served all day **Restaurant** Av 3 course à la carte fr £10 food served all day ⊕ ENTERPRISE INNS ◀ Badger Best, Fuller's London Pride, Timothy Taylor Landlord, John Smiths Smooth, Flowers Best. **Facilities** Children's menu Play area Family room Dogs allowed Garden Parking

BEMBRIDGE
Map 5 SZ68

The Crab & Lobster Inn ★★★★ INN ⬤

32 Foreland Field Rd PO35 5TR ☎ 01983 872244
▤ 01983 873495
e-mail: crab.lobster@bluebottle.com
dir: *From Bembridge Village, 1st left after Boots down Forelands Rd to the Windmill Hotel. Left into Lane End Rd, 2nd right into Egerton Rd, left into Forelands Rd & immediately right into Foreland Field Rd*

Originally a fisherman's cottage, this refurbished, award-winning beamed pub sits just yards from the popular 65-mile coastal path. A raised deck and patio area offer superb sea views. Locally caught seafood is one of the pub's great attractions; typical choices include a pint of prawns; lobster salad; home-made crab cakes; and seafood platters. For meat eaters there are pub classics such as steaks or ham, egg and chips. The AA rated bedrooms are light and airy, with some having stunning views.

Open all wk summer 11-11 (Sun 11-10.30) winter 11-3 6-11 (Sun 6-10.30) **Bar Meals** L served all wk 12-2.30 booking required D served Sun-Thu 6-9, Fri-Sat 6-9.30 booking required Av main course £8.50 **Restaurant** L served all wk 12-2.30 booking required D served Sun-Thu 6-9, Fri-Sat 6-9.30 booking required ⊕ ENTERPRISE INNS ◀ Interbrew Flowers Original, Goddards Fuggle-Dee-Dum, Greene King IPA, John Smiths. ⬤ 12 **Facilities** Children's menu Dogs allowed Garden Parking **Rooms** 5

BEMBRIDGE *continued*

The Pilot Boat Inn ☻

Station Rd PO35 5NN ☎ **01983 872077 & 874101**
dir: *On corner of harbour at bottom of Kings Rd*

Just a stone's throw from Bembridge harbour, this strikingly designed free house enjoys a strong local following, whilst being handy for yachtsmen and holidaymakers. Owners Nick and Michelle Jude offer an attractive menu of traditional favourites, including cod in beer batter with chips and peas; and bangers and mash with red wine and onion gravy. There's also a children's menu, together with specials like vegetable balti with rice; and chunky lamb stew and mash.

Open all day all wk 11-11 (Wed 11am-mdnt Fri 11am-late Sat 11am-11.30pm Sun noon-11) **Bar Meals** L served all wk 12-2.30 (summer food all day) booking required D served all wk 6.30-9 (summer food all day) booking required **Restaurant** L served all wk 12-2.30 (summer food all day) booking required D served all wk 6.30-9 (summer food all day) booking required ⊕ FREE HOUSE ◄ London Pride, Guinness, guest ale. ☻ 8 **Facilities** Children's menu Dogs allowed Parking

BONCHURCH Map 5 SZ57

The Bonchurch Inn

Bonchurch Shute PO38 1NU
☎ **01983 852611** ▤ **01983 856657**
e-mail: gillian@bonchurch-inn.co.uk
dir: *Off A3055 in Bonchurch*

In its quiet, off the road location, this small family-run free house inn lies tucked away in a secluded Dickensian-style courtyard. You won't be disturbed by juke boxes or gaming machines, for little has changed here since this former coaching inn and stables was granted its first licence in the 1840s. Food is available lunchtime and evenings in the bar; choices range from sandwiches and ploughman's to fresh fish, juicy steaks and Italian specialities.

Open all wk 11-3 6.30-11 Closed: 25 Dec **Bar Meals** L served all wk 12-2 D served all wk 6.30-9 booking required Av main course £10 **Restaurant** D served all wk 7-8.45 booking required ⊕ FREE HOUSE ◄ Courage Directors, Best. **Facilities** Children's menu Family room Dogs allowed Garden Parking

COWES Map 5 SZ49

The Folly ☻

Folly Ln PO32 6NB ☎ **01983 297171**
dir: *Telephone for directions*

Reached by land and water, and very popular with the boating fraternity, the Folly is one of the island's more unusual pubs. Timber from an old sea-going French barge was used in the construction, and wood from the hull can be found in the bar. The menus are wide ranging with something for everyone. House specialities include venison Wellington, prime British beef ribs and slow cooked lamb.

Open all wk **Bar Meals** Av main course £8 food served all day **Restaurant** food served all day ⊕ GREENE KING ◄ Greene King IPA, Old Speckled Hen, Goddards Best Bitter. ☻ 10 **Facilities** Children's menu Dogs allowed Garden Parking

FRESHWATER Map 5 SZ38

PICK OF THE PUBS

The Red Lion ☻

Church Place PO40 9BP
☎ **01983 754925** ▤ **01983 754483**
dir: *In Freshwater follow signs for parish church*

An unashamedly English pub where 'tradition and care' is the motto of owners Michael and Lorna Mence. Origins go back to the 11th century, although today's climber-clad building is clearly more recent. A garden at the rear is well furnished with hardwood chairs and tables, and a canvas dome comes into its own for candlelit alfresco dinners. The bar is comfortable with settles and chairs around scrubbed pine tables, the log fire burns throughout the winter, and peace and quiet is preferred to music. Lorna is the talented head chef who prepares a mix of favourite and more unusual dishes for lunch and dinner seven days a week. You may find that starters include herring roes on toast; smoked haddock pâté; or scrambled eggs with smoked salmon. Main courses range from rib-eye steak with brandy cream and chive sauce to whole lobster salad, while the daily-changing blackboard lists the day's home-made puds.

Open all wk 11.30-3 5.30-11 (Sun noon-3 7-10.30) **Bar Meals** L served all wk 12-2 booking required D served all wk 6.30-9 booking required **Restaurant** L served all wk 12-2 booking required D served all wk 6.30-9 booking required ⊕ ENTERPRISE INNS ◄ Interbrew Flowers Original, Spitfire, Goddards, Wadworth 6X. ☻ 16 **Facilities** Children's menu Dogs allowed Garden Parking

GODSHILL Map 5 SZ58

The Taverners NEW ☻

High St PO38 3HZ ☎ **01983 840707**
web: www.thetavernersgodshill.co.uk
dir: *Please telephone for directions*

Tucked away in picture-perfect Godshill, the Island's 'honeypot' village, the Taverners has been wowing locals and tourists with top-notch pub food since locals Roger Serjent and Lisa Choi took over in May 2008. Changing menus champion local seasonal produce, from local allotment fruit and vegetables and Bembridge crab to village-reared organic pork and lamb. Take baked crab pot, braised ox cheek with horseradish mash, finishing with treacle tart, with roast rib of beef for Sunday lunch. One to watch!

Open all day all wk 11-11 (Fri 11am-mdnt Sun 11-10.30) Closed: 1st 2wks Jan **Bar Meals** L served all wk summer 11.30-3.30, Mon-Sat 12-3, Sun 12-4 winter D served all wk summer 6-9.30, Mon-Sat winter 6-9 Av main course £10 **Restaurant** L served all wk summer 12-3.30, Mon-Sat 12-3, Sun 12-4 winter booking required D served Sun-Thu 6-9.30, Fri-Sat 6-10 summer, Sun-Thu 6-9, Fri-Sat 6-9.30 winter booking required Av 3 course à la carte fr £20 ⊕ PUNCH ◄ Undercliff, London Pride, John Smiths ○ Stowford Press, Old Rosie. ☻ 8 **Facilities** Children's menu Play area Family room Dogs allowed Garden Parking

NITON Map 5 SZ57

Buddle Inn ☻

St Catherines Rd PO38 2NE ☎ **01983 730243**
dir: *Take A3055 from Ventnor. In Niton take 1st left signed 'to the lighthouse'*

A spit away from the English Channel one way and the Coastal Path the other, this 16th-century, former cliff-top farmhouse can claim to be one of the island's oldest hostelries. Popular with hikers and ramblers (and their muddy boots and dogs), the interior has the full traditional complement - stone flags, oak beams and large open fires as well as great real ales on tap. Simple but well prepared food is served, including beef Wellington and venison casserole. Recent change of hands.

Open all day all wk 11-11 (Fri-Sat 11-mdnt Sun noon-10.30) **Bar Meals** L served all wk 12-2.45 D served all wk 6-9 **Restaurant** L served all wk 12-2.45 D served all wk 6-9 ⊕ ENTERPRISE INNS ◄ Bombardier, Fortyniner, Spitfire. ☻ 8 **Facilities** Children's menu Family room Dogs allowed Garden Parking

NORTHWOOD
Map 5 SZ49

ravellers Joy

Pallance Rd PO31 8LS ☎ 01983 298024
-mail: tjoy@globalnet.co.uk

uth and Derek Smith run this 300-year-old alehouse,
st a little way inland from Cowes. They keep eight real
es on hand pump all year round. Don't expect dishes
escribed on the menu as 'drizzled' or 'pan-roasted' here
ecause the food is home cooked and uncomplicated but
ith all the trimmings - grilled gammon steak, salmon
eak, breaded plaice, double sausage with egg, chips
nd beans, honey-roast ham, home-made steak and
dney pie, and children's meals. Outside is a pétanque
rrain, pets' corner and play area.

pen all wk **Bar Meals** L served all wk 12-2 D served all
k 6.30-9.30 Av main course £6.45 ⊕ FREE HOUSE
Goddards Special Bitter, Courage Directors, Ventnor
olden Bitter, Deuchars IPA, St Austell Tribute.
acilities Children's menu Play area Family room Dogs
lowed Garden Parking

ROOKLEY
Map 5 SZ58

he Chequers

ton Rd PO38 3NZ ☎ 01983 840314 📄 01983 840820
-mail: richard@chequersinn-iow.co.uk
r: Telephone for directions

orses in the neighbouring riding school keep a watchful
e on comings and goings at this 250-year-old family-
iendly free house. In the centre of the island,
urrounded by farms, the pub has a reputation for good
od at reasonable prices. Fish, naturally, features well,
ith sea bass, mussels, plaice, salmon and cod usually
vailable. Other favourites are mixed grill, pork
edallions, T-bone steak, and chicken supreme with BBQ
uce and cheese.

pen all wk ⊕ FREE HOUSE ◀ John Smiths, Courage
rectors, Best, Wadworth 6X, 3 guest ales.
acilities Play area Family room Dogs allowed Garden
arking

SEAVIEW
Map 5 SZ69

PICK OF THE PUBS

he Seaview Hotel &
Restaurant ★★★ HL ☺☺

See Pick of the Pubs on page 486

SHALFLEET
Map 5 SZ48

PICK OF THE PUBS

The New Inn ♥

Mill Ln PO30 4NS ☎ 01983 531314 📄 01983 531314
e-mail: info@thenew-inn.co.uk
dir: 6m from Newport to Yarmouth on A3054

This is one of Wight's best-known dining pubs, and its
location on the National Trust-owned Newtown River
estuary makes it an absolute mecca for yachties. Its
name reflects how it rose phoenix-like from the charred
remains of an older inn, which burnt down in 1743;
original inglenook fireplaces, flagstone floors and low-
beamed ceilings give it bags of character. The
waterside location helps explain its reputation for
excellent fish and seafood dishes, with lobster and
cracked local crab usually featuring on the specials
carte. For meat lovers there are prime steaks; steak
and local ale pie; chicken; slow-roasted pork belly with
cider and bacon sauce; and gammon with egg and
chips. Alternatively choose from a range of home-
cooked baguettes, freshly-cut sandwiches, traditional
ploughman's and seasonal salads. At the bar you'll
find Goddards Special, Marston's Pedigree and Ventnor
Golden among others, and with over 60 worldwide
wines, the New Inn offers one of the island's most
extensive selections.

Open all day all wk **Bar Meals** L served all wk 12-2.30
booking required D served all wk 6-9.30 booking
required Av main course £12 **Restaurant** L served all
wk 12-2.30 booking required D served all wk 6-9.30
booking required Av 3 course à la carte fr £20
⊕ ENTERPRISE INNS ◀ Interbrew Bass, Goddards
Special Bitter, Greene King IPA, Marston's Pedigree,
Ventnor Golden. ♥ 6 **Facilities** Children's menu Dogs
allowed Garden Parking

SHORWELL
Map 5 SZ48

PICK OF THE PUBS

The Crown Inn

Walkers Ln PO30 3JZ
☎ 01983 740293 📄 01983 740293
e-mail: info@crowninnshorwell.co.uk
dir: Turn left at top of Carisbrooke High Street, Shorwell
approx 6m

Set in a pretty village in picturesque West Wight, with
thatched cottages, a small shop, three manor houses,
and the church opposite. In summer, arum lilies
decorate the garden stream, and a Wendy house, slide
and swings keep youngsters amused. The building
dates in part from the 17th century, and different floor
levels attest to many alterations. Log fires, antique
furniture and a friendly female ghost, who disapproves
of card playing, complete the picture of this traditional
family-run pub. Beers on tap include an island brew,
and food consists of home-made favourites based on
locally sourced lamb, beef, plus game in winter and
fish in summer. Tempting pub grub, plus an award-
winning specials board offer cottage pie, steak and
kidney pie, and game dishes when in season. There are
also great fish, pasta and vegetarian dishes too. Enjoy
your meal with a great selection of beers, including
local Goddards, Ringwood and Adnams Broadside.

Open all wk **Bar Meals** food served all day
⊕ ENTERPRISE INNS ◀ Goddards (local), Ringwood
Fortyniner, Ringwood Best, Doom Bar, Adnams
Broadside. **Facilities** Children's menu Play area Family
room Dogs allowed Garden Parking

VENTNOR
Map 5 SZ57

The Spyglass Inn ♥

The Esplanade PO38 1JX
☎ 01983 855338 📄 01983 855220
e-mail: info@thespyglass.com
dir: Telephone for directions

For centuries this area was a haunt of smugglers, and
echoes of these activities can be seen in the huge
collection of nautical memorabilia on the walls of this
continued on page 487

PICK OF THE PUBS

The Seaview Hotel & Restaurant ★★★ HL ❀❀

SEAVIEW   Map 5 SZ69

High St PO34 5EX
☎ **01983 612711**   📄 **01983 613729**
e-mail: reception@seaviewhotel.co.uk
dir: *B3330 (Ryde to Seaview road), left via
Puckpool along seafront road, hotel on left*

The Pump Bar is a unique English pub
situated at the heart of a hotel that for
many years has been welcoming locals
and visitors alike in traditional style.
Even a log fire blazes to keep out the
winter chill. In a sailing-mad village
this smart, sea-facing hotel is crammed
with nautical associations. Amidst the
lobster pots, oars, masts and other
nautical memorabilia in the bar you'll
find traditional and local real ales,
complemented by wines and an
extensive menu of traditional and
innovative dishes from the bar menu. In
summer, the terrace or the Front Bar are

the places to relax and watch the world
go by. Modelled on a naval wardroom,
the Front Bar is home to a magnificent
collection of naval pictures,
photographs and artefacts – one of the
most extensive private collections to be
found on the Island. The hotel offers a
choice of dining venues; there's the
small Victorian dining room, and the
more contemporary Sunshine
restaurant, complete with its own
conservatory. Both dining rooms offer
the same menu, which reflects the
hotel's close relationship with the
Island's farmers and fishermen,
ensuring that the chefs are always
working with the very best seasonal
produce. Polish up your taste-buds with
Isle of Wight crab with green chilli, lime
and coriander tagliatelle, or wild
mushroom soup with truffle jelly; before
moving on to the main course. Options
might encompass New Close Farm
venison with braised red cabbage,
creamed potato and sultana and thyme
sauce, or pan-fried pollack with beetroot
mash, spinach and lemon balm. For
dessert, choose chocolate mousse, or
apple crumble with home-made
custard.

Open all week **Bar Meals** L served all
week 12-2.20 D served all week
6.30-9.30 **Restaurant** L served all week
(summer) 12-2, Sat-Sun (winter) 12-2
D served all week 6.30-9.30 ⊕ FREE
HOUSE ◼ Goddards, Ventnor Bitter,
guest ale. **Facilities** Children's menu
Dogs allowed **Rooms** 28

ENTNOR *continued*

amous 19th-century inn. It has a superb position, right t the end of Ventnor Esplanade. Much of the food here s, naturally, fish, with home-made fish chowder, Ventnor rab and lobster, but other dishes might include several arieties of pie; local sausages; or ham and leek bake.

pen all day all wk 10.30am-11pm **Bar Meals** L served ll wk 12-9.30 D served all wk 12-9.30 food served all ay **Restaurant** L served all wk 12-9.30 D served all wk 2-9.30 food served all day ⊕ FREE HOUSE ◀ Ventnor olden, Goddards Fuggle-Dee-Dom, Yates Undercliff xperience, Ringwood Best, Ringwood Fortyniner. ♀ 8 acilities Children's menu Family room Dogs allowed arden Parking

WILTSHIRE

ALDBOURNE   Map 5 SU27

he Crown at Aldbourne NEW ⓤ ♀
he Square SN8 2DU
☎ 01672 540214   ▤ 01672 541050

-mail: info@crownataldbourne.co.uk
ir: *M4 Junct 15 go N on A419 direction of Swindon. At rst junct Aldbourne is signed on B4192. The Crown is ituated in centre of village opposite the pond*

verlooking the village square and duck pond, the Crown s a spick-and-span 18th-century inn with a cosy, raditional beamed bar and a comfortable, wooden- oored dining room. Very much the village inn, smartly efurbished and with local Ramsbury Gold on tap, it ffers a good selection of home-cooked dishes, from soup nd sandwiches to Sunday roasts and a popular tapas enu, and four comfortable, well decorated bedrooms. he courtyard is a pleasant spot for summer sipping.

pen all wk noon-3 6-11 (Sat-Sun noon-11) **Bar Meals** L erved all wk 12-3 D served Mon-Sat 7-9.30 **Restaurant** L erved all wk 12-3 D served Mon-Sat 7-9.30 ⊕ ENTERPRISE INNS ◀ Spitfire Shepherds Neame, harp's Cornish Coaster, Ramsbury Gold Ŏ Westons towford Press. ♀ 8 **Facilities** Children's menu Play area ogs allowed Garden Parking **Rooms** 4

ALDERBURY   Map 5 SU12

he Green Dragon ♀
ld Rd SP5 3AR ☎ 01722 710263
ir: *1m off A36 (Southampton to Salisbury road)*

here are fine views of Salisbury Cathedral from this 5th-century pub, which is probably named after the eroic deeds of Sir Maurice Berkeley, the Mayor of lderbury, who slew a green dragon in the 15th century. ickens wrote *Martin Chuzzlewit* here, and called the pub he Blue Dragon. An interesting and daily changing menu eatures home-made meat and vegetarian dishes using ocally sourced produce.

Open all wk **Bar Meals** L served all wk 12-2 D served all wk 6.30-9.30 **Restaurant** L served all wk 12-2 D served all wk 6.30-9.30 ⊕ HALL & WOODHOUSE ◀ Badger First Gold, Tanglefoot, Fursty Ferret Ŏ Stowford Press. ♀ 14 **Facilities** Children's menu Dogs allowed Garden Parking

AXFORD   Map 5 SU27

Red Lion Inn ♀
SN8 2HA ☎ 01672 520271
e-mail: info@redlionaxford.com
web: www.redlionaxford.com
dir: *M4 junct 15, A246 Marlborough centre. Follow Ramsbury signs. Inn 3m*

A pretty, 16th-century brick and flint pub with fine views over the Kennet Valley, now under new ownership. In the bar there's a large inglenook, and a pleasing mix of sofas and more solid seating. The inn specialises in seasonal game and fish dishes, and in addition to bar snacks, the regularly-changing menus offer plenty of choice. Perhaps a starter of warm salad of wood pigeon with smoked bacon lardons and black pudding; or seared scallops with sauce vierge, sweet and sour greens to begin. Mains might be a classic lobster thermidor; oven-roasted cod pavé with shellfish bisque; fillet of venison with Cumberland sauce; or roast rump of lamb with redcurrant, red wine and port wine reduction. Vegetarians can look forward to dishes like the sweet potato, blue cheese and leek tart.

Open 12-3 6-11 Closed: Sun eve, Mon **Bar Meals** L served Tue-Sat 12-2.30 D served Tue-Fri 6-9 **Restaurant** L served Tue-Sun 12-2.30 D served Tue-Sun 12-9 ⊕ FREE HOUSE ◀ Axford Ale, Ramsbury Gold, Guest ales Ŏ Stowford Press. ♀ 16 **Facilities** Children's menu Garden Parking

BARFORD ST MARTIN   Map 5 SU03

Barford Inn ♀
SP3 4AB ☎ 01722 742242   ▤ 01722 743606
e-mail: thebarfordinn@btconnect.com
dir: *On A30 5m W of Salisbury 1.5m from Wilton*

There's been a recent change of management at this 16th-century former coaching inn five miles outside Salisbury, but the welcoming lounge, lower bar area and intimate snug have greeted visitors for generations. During World War II the Wiltshire Yeomanry dedicated a tank to the pub, known then as The Green Dragon. Meals are served in the bar or restaurant, and in warmer months in the garden or patio area. Alongside ploughman's, hot baguettes, jackets and sandwiches, you'll find gammon steak, sausage and mash, beef stroganoff or grilled sea bass fillet.

Open all day all wk **Bar Meals** L served all wk 12-2.30 D served Sun-Thu 6-9, Fri-Sat 6-9.30 **Restaurant** L served all wk 12-2.30 booking required D served Sun-Thu 6-9, Fri-Sat 6-9.30 booking required ⊕ HALL & WOODHOUSE ◀ Badger Dorset Best, Fursty Ferret, Festive. ♀ 6 **Facilities** Children's menu Dogs allowed Garden Parking

BOX   Map 4 ST86

The Northey ♀
Bath Rd SN13 8AE ☎ 01225 742333
e-mail: office@ohhcompany.co.uk
dir: *4m from Bath on A4 towards Chippenham. Between M4 juncts 17 & 18*

Following a magnificent transformation, this former station hotel is now a favourite in the area for eating, drinking and listening to the soothing tones of Sinatra and Fitzgerald. Designed throughout by owner Sally Warburton, the interior makes good use of wood and flagstone flooring, high-backed oak chairs, leather loungers and handcrafted tables around the bar, where interesting sandwiches, ciabattas and Italian platters hold sway. The main menu ranges from pork, duck and Toulouse sausage cassoulet to aromatic tagine of salmon and cod with curried potatoes and spinach.

Open all wk **Bar Meals** L served all wk 11-3 D served all wk 6-10 Av main course £11 **Restaurant** L served all wk 11-3 D served all wk 6-10 Fixed menu price fr £10 Av 3 course à la carte fr £15 ⊕ WADWORTH ◀ Wadworth 6X, IPA, Malt 'n' Hops, Old Father Timer. ♀ 10 **Facilities** Children's menu Dogs allowed Garden Parking

BOX *continued*

The Quarrymans Arms ☞

Box Hill SN13 8HN ☎ 01225 743569 📠 01225 742610
e-mail: john@quarrymans-arms.co.uk
dir: *Telephone for directions*

Built above Brunel's famous Box railway tunnel, this 300-year-old pub is packed with stone-mining memorabilia (take a tour of the old mine workings). Great views through the restaurant window of the valley, abundantly laced with marked paths and trails. In addition to the regular menu – sizzling stir-fry, pork Dijonnaise, tuna niçoise – look out for the vegetarian menu and specials board. Some good hand-pumped West Country beers, real ciders, good wines and over sixty malt whiskies are available.

Open all wk 11am-11.30pm **Bar Meals** L served all wk 11-3 booking required D served all wk 6- last booking booking required Av main course £10 **Restaurant** L served all wk 11-last booking booking required D served all wk 6-last booking booking required Av 3 course à la carte fr £19 ⊕ FREE HOUSE ◀ Butcombe Bitter, Wadworth 6X, Moles Best, Local guest ales ♂ Stowford Press. ☞ 12 **Facilities** Children's menu Family room Dogs allowed Garden Parking

---

BRADFORD-ON-AVON **Map 4 ST86**

The Dandy Lion ☞

35 Market St BA15 1LL
☎ 01225 863433 📠 01225 869169
e-mail: Dandylion35@aol.com
dir: *Telephone for directions*

The owners have refurbished this 17th-century town centre pub. But the spirit of the original Dandy Lion lives on through its well-kept ales and continental lagers, together with a mix of traditional English and rustic European food. The café-bar menu offers grazing boards ideal for sharing, hot-filled flatbreads, and thick-cut sandwiches alongside old comforts like home-baked Wiltshire ham with double free-range eggs and rustic chips. A meal in the air-conditioned restaurant could start with deep fried baby squid with chilli and garlic mayonnaise, and continue with braised lamb shank with root vegetables and creamy mash. Desserts are home made and are shown on the blackboard.

Open all wk 11-3 6-11 (Fri-Sat 11-11 Sun 11.30-10.30) **Bar Meals** L served all wk 12-2.30 D served all wk 6-9 Av main course £8.95 **Restaurant** D served Fri-Sat 7-9.30 booking required Av 3 course à la carte fr £21.50 ⊕ WADWORTH ◀ Wadworth 6X, Henrys IPA, Wadworth Seasonal ♂ Stowford Press, Westons Organic. ☞ 11 **Facilities** Children's menu

---

PICK OF THE PUBS

The Kings Arms ☞

Monkton Farleigh BA15 2QH ☎ 01225 858705
e-mail: enquiries@kingsarms-bath.co.uk
dir: *Off A363 (Bath to Bradford-on-Avon road), follow brown tourist signs to pub*

Dating back to the 11th century, this historic Bath stone building is situated in an attractive village just outside Bradford-on-Avon. Conversion into an alehouse took place in the 17th century, but original features remain, including the mullioned windows, flagged floors and a vast inglenook - said to be the largest in Wiltshire - in the medieval-style Chancel restaurant, which is hung with tapestries and pewter plates. The Bar and Garden menu offers light lunches such as Bath sausages, spring onion and smoked bacon mash; steak frites; three-egg omelette (with various fillings) and chips; and wild mushroom, spinach and asparagus lasagne. From the à la carte menu come main dishes such as duck breast with balsamic glaze, mascarpone and almond dauphinoise; game casserole with herb dumplings; brochette of sirloin steak and tiger prawns (known as the 'Trawler and Tractor'), while specials may include roast poussin with smoked bacon, parsley mash and cheddar cheese sauce; pork schnitzel with sesame-fried potatoes and dolcelatte cheese sauce; and chicken piri piri sizzle with white and wild rice.

Open all wk 12-3 6-11 (Sat-Sun 12-11) **Bar Meals** L served Mon-Fri 12-3, Sat 12-10. Sun 12-9 D served Mon-Fri 6-10, Sat 12-10, Sun 12-9 ⊕ Punch Taverns ◀ Butcombe Bitter, Tribute, guest ale ♂ Addlestone, West Scrumpy. ☞ 8 **Facilities** Dogs allowed Garden Parking

---

The Swan NEW ☞

1 Church St BA15 1LN
☎ 01225 868686 📠 01225 868681
e-mail: theswan-hotel@btconnect.com
web: www.theswan-hotel.com
dir: *From train station turn left, over bridge, on left adjacent to river*

Smack beside the medieval bridge that spans the River Avon, the Swan is a striking, 15th-century honey-stoned inn that has been refurbished with style and flair. Bar and dining areas exude an elegant, contemporary feel, with rugs on stripped boards and flagged floors and comfy sofas fronting blazing log fires. Modern touches

---

extend to the short menus, from a lunchtime deli board to ham hock terrine with piccalilli crostinis and seared tuna with crab risotto at dinner. A sunny terrace completes the picture.

The Swan

Open all day all wk 7am-11pm (Sun 7am-10.30pm) **Bar Meals** L served all wk 12-2.30 booking required D served all wk 6.30-9.30 booking required Av main course £12 **Restaurant** L served all wk 12-2.30 booking required D served all wk 6.30-9.30 booking required Fixed menu price fr £12 Av 3 course à la carte fr £20 ⊕ GREENE KING ◀ Old Speckled Hen, Old Trip ♂ Stowford Press. ☞ **Facilities** Children's menu Garden Parking

---

PICK OF THE PUBS

The Tollgate Inn ★★★★ INN ◉◉ ☞

See Pick of the Pubs on opposite page

BRINKWORTH **Map 4 SU08**

PICK OF THE PUBS

The Three Crowns ☞

SN15 5AF ☎ 01666 510366
dir: *From Swindon take A3102 to Wootton Bassett, then B4042, 5m to Brinkworth*

Facing the church across the village green, the Three Crowns has been run by the same licensees for over 20 years. The building extends into a large, bright conservatory and garden room, then out onto a heated patio and garden that offers extensive views of the Dauntsey Vale. In winter, a welcoming log fire burns in the lounge. The Drinkers' Bar is dominated by two giant forge bellows and a wheelwright's bellow, all now converted into tables; settle there for a pint of Wadworth 6X or Abbey Ales Bellringer, and perhaps a game of cribbage or chess. When it's time to eat, the

continued on page 49

PICK OF THE PUBS

The Tollgate Inn ★★★★ INN

BRADFORD-ON-AVON Map 4 ST86

Holt BA14 6PX
☎ 01225 782326 01225 782805
e-mail: alison@tollgateholt.co.uk
dir: *M4 junct 18, A46 towards Bath, then A363 to Bradford-on-Avon, then B3107 towards Melksham, pub on right*

Built in the 16th century, The Tollgate used to be a cider house known as the White Hart - and a den of iniquity it was, by all accounts. As with many old buildings, it has a chequered history, having been part weaving mill, part Baptist chapel, and even the village school. When the nearby Kennet and Avon Canal was cut, some of the building was knocked down to make way for an approach road. The bar serves a rotating selection of guest ales, mostly from small West Country micro-breweries. You can eat in a small adjoining room with wood-burning stove and country-style decoration. The restaurant proper is up wooden stairs in what was originally the chapel for the weavers working below. Regular customers are attracted by modern British cooking with Mediterranean influences, locally sourced and supplied whenever possible. For example, hand-reared beef comes from the lush pastures of nearby Broughton Gifford; the lamb from Limpley Stoke; pork from Woolley Farm and village shoots provide the game; vegetables are grown in the surrounding fertile soils; and fish is delivered daily from Brixham. Lunchtime light bites (Tuesday to Saturday only) include corned beef hash with fried egg; Church Farm sausages with Dijon mash; eggs Benedict. The carte menu is full of temptation – Cornish crab ravioli on a pea and mint velouté; goats' cheese bruschetta with figs and local honey to start; with mains such as oven roasted Brixham halibut; risotto of local squashes; and rack of lamb with dauphinoise potatoes and rosemary sauce. The well-established garden and terrace (out of bounds to children under 12) is a tranquil and delightful place to eat when the weather permits. There are four en suite bedrooms if you would like to stay over.

Open 11.30-3 5.30-11 (Sun 11.30-3) Closed: Mon **Bar Meals** L served Tue-Sun 12-2 D served Tue-Sat 7-9 Av main course £13.50 **Restaurant** L served Tue-Sun 12-2 D served Tue-Sat 7-9 Fixed menu price Tue-Fri fr £18.75 Av 3 course à la carte fr £22 FREE HOUSE Exmoor Gold, Glastonbury Ales Mystery Tor, York Ales, Sharp's Doom Bar, Eden, Yorkshire Terrier Thatchers Gold, Thatchers Scrumpy. 9 **Facilities** Children's menu Dogs allowed Garden Parking **Rooms** 4

BRINKWORTH *continued*

imaginative blackboard menus may offer locally smoked chicken with sherry and cream sauce; rack of English lamb with garlic breadcrumbs; poached halibut in white wine with a julienne of crispy leeks and seared scallops; or a baked vegetarian parcel with fresh tomato and basil sauce. The home-made dessert selection could feature strawberry shortbread; melon sorbet; or tangy lemon and Cointreau cheesecake.

Open all day all wk 10am-mdnt **Closed**: 25-26 Dec **Bar Meals** L served Mon-Sat 12-2, Sun 12-3 **Restaurant** L served Mon-Sat 12-2, Sun 12-3 D served all wk 6-9.30 ⊕ ENTERPRISE INNS ◖ Wadworth 6X, Greene King IPA, Wells Bombardier, Abbey Ales Bellringer ♨ Stowford Press. ♉ 20 **Facilities** Children's menu Play area Dogs allowed Garden Parking

BROAD CHALKE　　　　Map 5 SU02

The Queens Head Inn ♉

1 North St SP5 5EN ☎ **01722 780344 & 0870 770 6634**
dir: *A354 from Salisbury towards Blandford Forum, at Coombe Bissett right towards Bishopstone, pub in 4m*

Attractive 15th-century-inn with friendly atmosphere and low-beamed bars, once the village bakehouse. On sunny days, enjoy the flower-bordered courtyard, whilst in colder weather the low beams and wood burner in the bar provide a cosy refuge. Menus include light snacks such as sandwiches, ploughman's lunches and home-made soups, as well as more substantial main courses: perhaps grilled trout with almonds, sirloin steak with a choice of vegetables, or wild game casserole.

Open all wk noon-3 6-11.30 (Fri-Sat 6-mdnt Sun noon-10.30) **Bar Meals** L served Mon-Sat 12-2.30, Sun 12-6 D served Mon-Sat 6-9, Sun 12-6 **Restaurant** L served Mon-Sat 12-2.30, Sun 12-6 D served Mon-Sat 6-9, Sun 12-6 ⊕ Hall & Woodhouse ◖ Badgers Best, Badger Tanglefoot, Hopping Hare ♨ Stowford Press. ♉ 7 **Facilities** Children's menu Family room Dogs allowed Garden Parking

BURCOMBE　　　　Map 5 SU03

The Ship Inn ♉

Burcombe Ln SP2 0EJ
☎ **01722 743182** 📠 **01722 743182**
e-mail: theshipburcombe@mail.com
dir: *In Burcombe, off A30, 1m from Wilton & 5m W of Salisbury*

A 17th-century village pub with low ceilings, oak beams and a large open fire. In summer the riverside garden is a great place to enjoy a leisurely meal in the company of the resident ducks. Seasonal menu examples include home-made fishcakes; braised lamb shank with mustard mash and Savoy cabbage; grilled field mushroom with talegio; stuffed chicken supreme with brie and basil; or pumpkin curry with chickpeas and spinach. Daily changing specials, sandwiches and light bites are also available.

The Ship Inn

Open all wk **Bar Meals** L served all wk 12-2.30 D served all wk 6-9 Av main course £9 **Restaurant** L served all wk 12-2.30 D served all wk 6-9 Av 3 course à la carte fr £25 ◖ Wadworth 6X, Courage Best, Butcombe. ♉ 10 **Facilities** Children's menu Dogs allowed Garden Parking

BURTON　　　　Map 4 ST87

The Old House at Home ♉

SN14 7LT ☎ **01454 218227**
e-mail: office@ohhcompany.co.uk
dir: *On B4039 NW of Chippenham*

This stone, ivy-clad pub has beautiful landscaped gardens and a waterfall, and inside, low beams and an open fire. Overseen by the same landlord for some twenty years, the crew here are serious about food. The kitchen offers a good fish choice, vegetarian and pasta dishes, and traditional pub meals. Favourites include lighter dishes such as roast red pepper and feta salad or smoked salmon and crab salad, and a heartier venison casserole.

Open all wk **Closed**: 25 & 26 Dec **Bar Meals** L served all wk 12-2 D served all wk 7-10 Av main course £15.50 **Restaurant** L served all wk 12-2 D served all wk 7-10 ⊕ FREE HOUSE ◖ Maiden Voyage, Doom Bar, Wadworth Ale ♨ Stowford Press. ♉ 46 **Facilities** Dogs allowed Garden Parking

COLLINGBOURNE DUCIS　　　　Map 5 SU25

The Shears Inn & Country Hotel ♉

The Cadley Rd SN8 3ED
☎ **01264 850304** 📠 **01264 850301**
e-mail: info@the-shears-inn.co.uk
dir: *On A338 NW of Andover & Ludgershall*

As the name attests, this thatched 16th-century building was formerly a shearing place for market-bound sheep. Now a thriving country inn, the daily chalkboard menus round up all the usual suspects as well as more unusual dishes such as poached chicken, spinach and Parma ham roulade; roasted goose breast and sweet cherry gravy; or oxtail in red wine.

Open all wk ⊕ BRAKSPEAR ◖ Brakspear Bitter, Hobgoblin, guest ales. ♉ 12 **Facilities** Family room Dogs allowed Garden Parking

CORSHAM　　　　Map 4 ST87

PICK OF THE PUBS

The Flemish Weaver ♉

63 High St SN13 0EZ ☎ **01249 701929**
dir: *Next to town hall on Corsham High St*

Standing opposite the historic Corsham Court, this stone-built town centre inn takes its name from a nearby row of original Flemish weavers' cottages. Drinkers and diners are all welcome to enjoy the winter log fires and candlelit interior - though it's advisable to book a table. Thatchers Gold and Stowford Press ciders complement a good range of real ales, some of which are served straight from the barrel. There's also an extensive wine list, with many choices available by the glass. Menus are changed daily, and you might start with hand-crumbed Somerset brie and cranberry compote before making the choice between tagliatelle in dolcelatte cream sauce with spinach and toasted pine nuts; and cod with leek and potato gratin. Typical desserts include bread and butter pudding laced with Bailey's; and summer fruits and jelly terrine. Enjoy them in the large outdoor eating area on warmer days.

Open 11-3 5.30-11 (Sun noon-3) **Closed**: Sun eve **Bar Meals** L served Mon-Sat 11.30-2.30 booking required Av main course £5 **Restaurant** L served Mon-Sat 11.30-2.30, Sun 12-2.30 booking required D served Mon-Sat 6.30-9.30 booking required Fixed menu price fr £7.20 Av 3 course à la carte fr £14.95 ⊕ ENTERPRISE INNS ◖ Bath Spa, Doom Bar, Bath Gem, Bob, HPA Wye Valley, Hook Norton ♨ Thatchers Gold, Stowford Press. ♉ 10 **Facilities** Children's menu Dogs allowed Garden Parking

CORTON　　　　Map 4 ST94

PICK OF THE PUBS

The Dove Inn ★★★ INN ♉

BA12 0SZ ☎ **01985 850109** 📠 **01985 851041**
e-mail: info@thedove.co.uk
dir: *A36 (Salisbury towards Warminster), in 14m turn left signed Corton & Boyton. Cross rail line, right at T-junct. Corton approx 1.5m, turn right into village*

Tucked away in a lovely Wiltshire village near the River Wylye, this thriving traditional pub is a haven of tranquillity. A striking central fireplace is a feature of the refurbished bar, and the spacious garden is the perfect spot for barbecues or a drink on long summer

days. The award-winning menu is based firmly on West Country produce, with many ingredients coming from within just a few miles. Popular lunchtime bar snacks give way to a full evening carte featuring a classy but hearty take on pub food. Typical starters include pan-fried pigeon breast with a redcurrant jus; and garlic king prawns with a sweet chilli dip. Main courses range from oven-baked sea bass stuffed with fresh herbs to spicy chicken curry with basmatic rice. Five en suite bedrooms arranged around a courtyard make The Dove an ideal touring base. Bath, Salisbury and Stonehenge are all close by.

Open all wk noon-2.30 6-11 **Bar Meals** L served all wk 12-2 D served Sun-Thu 7-9, Fri-Sat 7-9.30 Av main course £6 **Restaurant** L served all wk 12-2 D served Sun-Thu 7-9, Fri-Sat 7-9.30 Av 3 course à la carte fr £18 ⊕ FREE HOUSE ◀ Spitfire, Youngs, Butcombe, Hop Back GFB Ö Stowford Press. ☘ 10 **Facilities** Children's menu Dogs allowed Garden Parking **Rooms** 5

DEVIZES Map 4 SU06

The Bear Hotel ★★★ HL ☘

The Market Place SN10 1HS
☎ 0845 456 5334 📄 01380 722450
e-mail: info@thebearhotel.net
dir: In town centre, follow Market Place signs

Right in the centre of Devizes, home of Wadworth's Brewery, this old coaching inn dates from at least 1559 and lists Judge Jeffreys, George III and Harold Macmillan amongst its notable former guests. You'll find old beams, log fires, fresh flowers, Market and Lansdowne bars, two restaurants and a courtyard in summer. The menu offers pot-roasted partridge perhaps, and broccoli and mushroom strudel. Music fans should check out the weekly jazz sessions in the cellar.

Open all day all wk 9.30am-11pm Closed: 25-26 Dec **Bar Meals** L served Mon-Sat 11.30-2.30 D served all wk 7-9.30 Av main course £6 **Restaurant** L served Sun 12-2.30 D served Mon-Sat 7-9.45 Fixed menu price fr £23.95 ⊕ WADWORTH ◀ Wadworth 6X, Wadworth IPA, Wadworth JCB, Old Timer, Malt & Hops, Summersault, seasonal ales. ☘ 18 **Facilities** Dogs allowed Garden Parking **Rooms** 25

The Raven Inn ☘

Poulshot Rd SN10 1RW
☎ 01380 828271 📄 01380 828271
dir: A361 from Devizes towards Trowbridge, left at Poulshot sign

A characterful half-timbered 18th-century pub in an attractive village - an easy walk to the Kennet and Avon Canal and the towpath by the famous Caen Hill flight of locks. The extensive menu of home-cooked food includes light bites such as avocado, prawn and apple salad; and deep-fried tiger prawns in filo pastry. There are usually a trio of vegetarian options, perhaps four fish dishes, main courses of steak and kidney pie or pork stroganoff, and traditional desserts like banana split.

Open 11.30-2.30 6.30-9 (Sun 12-3 7-10.30) Closed: Mon **Bar Meals** L served Tue-Sun 12-2 D served Tue-Sat 6.30-9, Sun 7-9 **Restaurant** L served Tue-Sun 12-2 D served Tue-Sat 6.30-9, Sun 7-9 ⊕ WADWORTH ◀ Wadworth 6X, Wadworth IPA, Summersault, Wadworth Old Timer Ö Stowford Press. ☘ 8 **Facilities** Garden Parking

---

DONHEAD ST ANDREW Map 4 ST92

PICK OF THE PUBS

The Forester ☘

Lower St SP7 9EE ☎ 01747 828038
e-mail: possums1@btinternet.com
dir: 4.5m from Shaftesbury off A30 towards Salisbury

The Forester is a lovely old country pub located in the Donheads close to Wardour Castle in beautiful walking country. Traditional in style, it has warm stone walls, a thatched roof, original beams and an inglenook fireplace. An extension provides a restaurant and a restaurant/meeting room, with double doors opening on to the lower patio area. The garden and large patio area are furnished with hardwood chairs and tables as well as bench seating. The restaurant has a good reputation for its freshly cooked food and specialises in Cornish seafood, with deliveries five times a week. A Taste of the Sea lunch might offer pan-fried herring roes with smoked bacon, capers and parsley, followed by fillet of plaice with herb butter and new potatoes. Alternatives might be Kashmiri-style duck leg curry, or rump of local lamb with goats' cheese gnocchi, tomato and black olive jus. The wine list has been carefully compiled by the landlord.

Open noon-2 6.30-11 Closed: Sun eve **Bar Meals** L served all wk 12-2 booking required D served Mon-Sat 7-9 booking required Av main course £12.50 **Restaurant** L served all wk 12-2 D served Mon-Sat 7-9 booking required Fixed menu price fr £15.50 Av 3 course à la carte fr £20 ⊕ FREE HOUSE ◀ Ringwood, Butcombe, Butts Ö Stowford Press, Ashton Press. ☘ 17 **Facilities** Children's menu Dogs allowed Garden Parking

---

EAST KNOYLE Map 4 ST83

PICK OF THE PUBS

The Fox and Hounds ☘

See Pick of the Pubs on page 492

EBBESBOURNE WAKE Map 4 ST92

PICK OF THE PUBS

The Horseshoe

Handley St SP5 5JF ☎ 01722 780474
dir: Telephone for directions

A genuine old English pub, The Horseshoe dates from the 17th century. The village is not that easy to find, but a good navigator and perseverance pay dividends. The original building has not changed much, except for a necessary conservatory extension to accommodate more diners, and there's a pretty, flower-filled garden. Beyond the climbing roses are two rooms filled with simple furniture, old farming implements and country bygones, linked to a central servery where cask-conditioned ales are dispensed straight from their barrels. Good value bar food is freshly prepared from local produce, including watercress from the beds down the road. Favourites are pies, such as wild boar and apricot; liver and bacon casserole; beef in red wine; fresh fish bake; and watercress and mushroom lasagne. Meals are accompanied by plenty of vegetables and there are some great home-made desserts: seasonal fruit crumble, treacle tart, and lemon meringue roulade among them.

Open all wk Closed: 26 Dec, Sun eve & Mon L **Bar Meals** L served Tue-Sat 12-2 booking required D served Tue-Sat 7-9 booking required Av main course £10.95 **Restaurant** L served Sun 12-2 D served Tue-Sat 7-9 booking required Fixed menu price fr £10.75 Av 3 course à la carte fr £25 ⊕ FREE HOUSE ◀ Otter Best bitter, Bowmans Swift One, Palmers Copper Ö Thatchers Farm, Thatchers Gold. **Facilities** Play area Garden Parking

PICK OF THE PUBS

The Fox and Hounds ♀

EAST KNOYLE
Map 4 ST83

The Green SP3 6BN
☎ 01747 830573 📠 01747 830865
e-mail:
pub@foxandhounds-eastknoyle.co.uk
web:
www.foxandhounds-eastknoyle.co.uk
dir: *1.5m off A303 at the A350 turn off,
follow brown signs*

East Knoyle and this picturesque, late-15th-century thatched and beamed, black and white free house are situated on a greensand ridge, from which there are magnificent views of Blackmore Vale. Add an imaginative menu and you have an ideal lunch or dinner venue. The village was home to the family of Jane Seymour, Henry VIII's third wife, as well being where Sir Christopher Wren grew up, his father the local vicar. The pub's interior is quaint and comfortable, with wooden flooring, natural stone walls, flagstones, and sofas within toasting

distance of a winter fire. In the bar you'll find real ales from the Palmer's, Cottage and Butcombe breweries, the latter also producing Ashton Press cider. A varied and appetising specials menu points out that all meat, chicken and game is sourced from local farms and suppliers. In it, depending on daily availability, you can expect dishes such as Lizzie's lamb chump on mash and bacon with a rosemary/mint jus; aubergine filled with spinach, tomato, pecorino and mozzarella cheeses; chicken salad with basil and mango dressing; Moroccan vegetable tagine; fresh haddock in beer batter; crab and prawn risotto; slow-cooked lamb shanks in red wine; pan-fried calf's liver and bacon on mash with onion gravy; venison haunch steak with port and cranberry sauce; and Thai green chicken curry. You'll also find a range of ploughman's, and pizzas from a clay oven. If you're ready for more, desserts include chocolate lumpy bumpy and cream; apple and caramel pancake stack with vanilla ice cream; and bread and butter pudding laced with Bailey's. The sweeping views across Dorset and Somerset are particularly good from The Green outside.

Open 11.30-3 5.30-11 **Bar Meals** L served all week 12-2.30 D served all week 6-9 **Restaurant** L served all week 12-2.30 D served all week 6-9 ⊕ **FREE HOUSE** ◖ Butcombe, Cottage, Palmer's Durdle Door, Cheer up, Copper Ale, Golden Arrow Ŏ Thatchers Cheddar Valley, Ashton Press. ♀ 10
Facilities Children's menu Dogs allowed Garden Parking

GREAT BEDWYN — Map 5 SU26

PICK OF THE PUBS

The Three Tuns ♀

High St SN8 3NU ☎ **01672 870280**

e-mail: jan.carr2@btinternet.com

dir: *Off A4 between Marlborough & Hungerford*

You'll find this popular country inn in the centre of the village, close to the Ridgeway Path and the Kennet and Avon Canal. A roaring winter fire in the inglenook and lovely beer garden in summer attract a healthy year-round trade. Food is served at candlelit tables in the open plan bar area and there is a choice of lunch dishes, traditional bar food and a full evening carte menu. Local meat and game, augmented by twice-weekly deliveries of fresh Devon fish, feature in such dishes as slow-roasted lamb shank with cinnamon and red wine sauce; chicken, chorizo, belly pork and mixed sausage cassoulet; Spanish-style rabbit with peppers, tomatoes, white wine, onions and garlic; and tagliatelle with clams, slightly spicy tomato sauce and basil sauce. Chargrills are available every day except Sunday. Out back is a pleasant raised garden.

Open 12-3 6-11 (Sun 12-6) Closed: Sun eve **Bar Meals** L served Mon-Sat 12-2, Sun 12-2.30 D served Mon-Sat 7-9 ⊕ PUNCH TAVERNS ◀ Wadworth 6X, Fuller's London Pride, Flowers IPA. ♀ 9 **Facilities** Dogs allowed Garden Parking

GREAT CHEVERELL — Map 4 ST95

PICK OF THE PUBS

The Bell Inn ♀

High St SN10 5TH ☎ **01380 813277**

e-mail: gillc@clara.co.uk

dir: *N side of Salisbury plain. A360 from Salisbury through West Lavington, 1st left after black & yellow striped bridge to Great Cheverell*

Famous for its television appearance on *Location, Location, Location*, this former coaching inn stands on the northern edge of Salisbury Plain. Sit by the log fire in the 18th-century bar and musé through the daily papers, or get involved with the varied programme of entertainment. Home-cooked West Country food is served in the elegantly styled restaurant, and the imaginative and varied menu makes use of the best local ingredients where possible. Lunchtime brings filled ciabattas and baguettes, as well as old favourites like ham, eggs and chips. Main course dishes include baked sea bass with dill and white wine sauce; slow-cooked lamb shank with spring onion mash; and roasted vegetable, sun-dried tomato and goats' cheese parcel. The sunny, secluded garden is set in tranquil surroundings with lots of wooden benches and a patio area, enjoyed by families and locals long into the evening.

Closed: 26 Dec, 1 Jan **Bar Meals** L served all wk 12-2.30 D served all wk 6-9 Av main course £10 **Restaurant** L served all wk 12-2.30 D served all wk 6-9 Fixed menu price fr £13 Av 3 course à la carte fr £17 ⊕ FREE HOUSE ◀ 6X, IPA, Doom Bar, guest ale. ♀ 9 **Facilities** Children's menu Dogs allowed Garden Parking

GREAT HINTON — Map 4 ST95

PICK OF THE PUBS

The Linnet ♀

BA14 6BU ☎ **01380 870354** ▤ **01380 870354**

dir: *Just off A361 (Devizes to Trowbridge road)*

A former woollen mill in a picturesque setting, The Linnet was converted into a village local circa 1914. Chef/landlord Jonathan Furby and his staff have been here for nine years (every year winning an award), and the locals are friendly and supportive. The pub prides itself on using the best of local produce and serving freshly prepared food at an honest price. Everything is made on the premises - bread, ice cream, pasta and sausages. The lunch menu offers a daily soup, warm salads and a good choice of steaks. A signature dish from the evening menu is baked tenderloin of pork filled with prunes and spinach wrapped in smoked bacon on a wild mushroom sauce and dauphinoise potatoes. A vegetarian alternative might be wild mushroom and tarragon risotto cake with tomato sauce, rocket salad and shaved parmesan. In summer there are seats on the large front patio area.

Open 11-2.30 6-11 Closed: 25-26 Dec, 1 Jan, Mon **Bar Meals** L served Tue-Sat 12-2, Sun 12-2.30 D served Sun, Tue-Thu 6.30-9, Fri-Sat 6.30-9.30 booking required Av main course £8.50 **Restaurant** L served Tue-Sat 12-2, Sun 12-2.30 booking required D served Tue-Sun 6.30-9 booking required Fixed menu price fr £14.95 Av 3 course à la carte fr £26.95 ⊕ WADWORTH ◀ Wadworth 6X, Henrys IPA ♂ Stowford Press. ♀ 11 **Facilities** Children's menu Dogs allowed Garden Parking

GRITTLETON — Map 4 ST88

The Neeld Arms

The Street SN14 6AP

☎ **01249 782470** ▤ **01249 782168**

e-mail: neeldarms@zeronet.co.uk

dir: *Telephone for directions*

This 17th-century Cotswold stone pub stands at the centre of a pretty village in lush Wiltshire countryside. Quality real ales and freshly prepared food are an equal draw to diners who will eagerly tuck in to lamb shanks, home-made steak and kidney pie or sausage and mash. Children are welcome and the small garden is especially popular for alfresco eating in fine weather.

Open all wk ⊕ FREE HOUSE ◀ Wadworth 6X, Buckleys Best, Brakspear Bitter, IPA. **Facilities** Dogs allowed Garden Parking

HANNINGTON — Map 5 SU19

The Jolly Tar ♀

Queens Rd SN6 7RP

☎ **01793 762245** ▤ **01793 765159**

e-mail: info@jollytar.co.uk

dir: *M4 junct 15, A419 towards Cirencester. At Bunsdon/Highworth sign follow B4109. Towards Highworth, left at Freke Arms, follow Hannington & Jolly Tar pub signs*

Although it's a fair old trek to the sea, there is a connection - the marriage of a lady from a local land-owning family to a 19th-century battleship captain. Inside are old timbers, a log fire and locally brewed Arkells ales. On the menu, chicken, olive and prosciutto ribbon pasta; home-made lamb burger; Gloucester Old Spot sausages; and Jolly Fantastic fish pie. Specials may include tuna, prawn and red pepper chowder; and shepherd's pie.

Open all wk ⊕ ARKELLS ◀ Arkells 3B, Noel Ale, Kingsdown. ♀ 11 **Facilities** Play area Family room Dogs allowed Garden Parking

HEYTESBURY — Map 4 ST94

PICK OF THE PUBS

The Angel Coaching Inn ♀

See Pick of the Pubs on page 494

PICK OF THE PUBS

The Angel Coaching Inn ♀

HEYTESBURY　　　Map 4 ST94

High St BA12 0ED
☎ **01985 840330**　📄 **01985 840931**
e-mail: admin@theangelheytesbury.co.uk
dir: *From A303 take A36 towards Bath, 8m,*
Heytesbury on left

A 16th-century inn surrounded by
stunning countryside. If you have the
time, discover one of the walks which
start and end here before settling down
with a real ale or glass of house
champagne. The Angel itself has been
transformed by a complete
refurbishment into a striking blend of
original features and contemporary
comfort. The beamed bar has scrubbed
pine tables, warmly decorated walls and
an attractive fireplace with a wood-
burning stove. Although very much a
dining pub, it has not forsaken the
traditional charm and character of its
coaching inn past. You can eat in the
restaurant, the bar, or, during the
summer months, alfresco in the
secluded courtyard garden which leads
off the restaurant. The focus is on
offering customers fresh seasonal and
local ingredients at wallet-friendly
prices. Steaks are a speciality – they are
sourced either from nearby Pensworth
Farm or from Castle Brae in Scotland;
then hung for 35 days in the pub's
ageing rooms for the best possible
quality and taste, before being served
with chunky chips, salad and sauce
béarnaise. A typical choice from the
dinner carte may start with steamed
River Fowey mussels with shallots,
garlic, wine and cream; or chorizo with a
broad bean salad. Follow with confit
duck hash with wilted greens and fried
egg; or pan-fried sea bass with
ratatouille. Passion fruit cheesecake
brings a happy ending. Popular Sunday
lunches are based on a fixed-price carte
of two or three courses, with five choices
at each stage. In addition to the
traditional main courses of roast beef
and lamb, a fish dish and a vegetarian
option can always be found.

Open Tues-Sun Closed: Mon (ex BH)
🌐 GREENE KING 🍺 Morlands, Greene
King IPA, 6X. ♀ 10 **Facilities** Dogs
allowed Garden Parking

HINDON · Map 4 ST93

PICK OF THE PUBS

Angel Inn ?

High St SP3 6DJ ☎ 01747 820696
e-mail: info@theangelathindon.com
dir: *1.5m from A303, on B3089 towards Salisbury*

An elegant gastro-pub where rustic charm meets urbane sophistication in a beautifully restored Georgian coaching inn. Outside is an attractive paved courtyard and garden furniture, where food can be served in fine weather. The interior is characterised by natural wood flooring, beams, large stone fireplace and comfortable leather seating. Behind the bar can be found Sharp's and Ringwood ales, and more than a dozen wines served by the glass; pine country-style tables and chairs, together with the day's newspapers, lend a friendly and relaxed atmosphere. An eclectic mix of traditional and modern dishes characterise the brasserie-style menu, based on quality seasonal ingredients. Typical starters are scallops, pea purée and crispy pancetta, and devilled lambs' kidneys on toast. Main courses such as venison sausages with creamy mash and rich gravy are augmented by rib-eye steaks from the grill, hand-cut to order by the chef. Desserts are on the blackboard, as are the day's set menu and specials.

Open all wk 11-3 5-11 (Sun noon-4) **Bar Meals** L served all wk 12-2.30 D served Mon-Sat 6-9.30 Av main course £11 **Restaurant** L served all wk 12-2.30 D served Mon-Sat 6-9.30 Av 3 course à la carte fr £22 ⊕ FREE HOUSE ◀ Sharp's, Ringwood, Bass. ? 14 **Facilities** Dogs allowed Garden Parking

PICK OF THE PUBS

The Lamb at Hindon ★★★★ INN ⓘ ?

High St SP3 6DP ☎ 01747 820573 ▤ 01747 820605
e-mail: info@lambathindon.co.uk
dir: *From A303 follow signs to Hindon. At Fonthill Bishop right onto B3089 to Hindon. Pub on left*

Wisteria clings to one corner of the mellow 17th-century coaching inn, tucked away in a charming village just minutes from the A303. At its height, 300 post horses were kept here to supply the coaches plying to and from London to the West Country. Inside, the long bar is divided into several cosy areas and oozes old-world charm, with sturdy period furnishings, flagstone floors, terracotta walls hung with old prints and paintings, and a splendid old stone fireplace with a crackling log fire creates a warm, homely atmosphere, especially on cold winter nights. Add tip-top ale from Youngs on tap, extensive wine and whisky lists, and a chalkboard menu offering hearty modern pub dishes, then it's worth lingering over a meal by the fire. Typically, tuck into lambs' kidneys with balsamic shallots and red wine jus, followed by roast salmon with Jerusalem artichokes and Puy lentils, or slow-cooked salt beef with horseradish dumplings, and butterscotch tart

for pudding. Upstairs, there are 14 individually furnished bedrooms.

Open all day all wk 7.30am-mdnt **Bar Meals** L served all wk 12-2.30 D served all wk 6.30-9.30 booking required Av main course £10 **Restaurant** L served all wk 12-2.30 D served all wk 6.30-9.30 booking required Av 3 course à la carte fr £25 ⊕ BOISDALE ◀ Youngs Bitter, Wells Bombardier, 2 guest ales. ? 6 **Facilities** Children's menu Family room Dogs allowed Garden Parking **Rooms** 14

HORNINGSHAM · Map 4 ST84

PICK OF THE PUBS

The Bath Arms NEW ★★★ HL ⓘ ?

BA12 7LY ☎ 01985 844308 ▤ 01985 845187
e-mail: enquiries@batharms.co.uk
dir: *Off B3092 S of Frome*

This impressive, creeper-clad stone inn is situated by one of the entrances to Lord Bath's Longleat Estate. It was built in the 17th century, becoming a public house with rooms in 1732, initially called the New Inn, later the Weymouth Arms, and then, in 1850, the Marquess of Bath Arms. It has been comfortably refurbished and features a fine beamed bar with settles and old wooden tables, and a terracotta-painted dining room with an open fire. The lunch and bar menu offers Wiltshire ham and piccalilli sandwich; tuna niçoise; and sirloin steak with tarragon sauce and thick chips, while in the evening a short menu might suggest chump of Dorset lamb with roast shallot purée and grilled courgettes; rolled saddle of rabbit with garden peas wrapped in pancetta; and grilled lemon sole with white truffle mash and saffron sauce. Finish with raspberry crème brûlée or South West Country cheeses.

Open all day all wk **Bar Meals** L served all wk 12-2.30 D served all wk 7-9 Av main course £9.50 **Restaurant** L served all wk 12-2.30 booking required D served all wk 7-9 booking required Fixed menu price fr £9.50 Av 3 course à la carte fr £29.50 ⊕ HILLBROOKE HOTELS ◀ Horningsham Pride, guest ales Ö Stowford Press. ? 9 **Facilities** Children's menu Dogs allowed Garden Parking **Rooms** 15

HORTON · Map 5 SU06

The Bridge Inn ?

Horton Rd SN10 2JS ☎ 01380 860273
e-mail: bridge.innhorton@talktalkbusiness.net
dir: *A361 from Devizes, right at 3rd rdbt. Follow brown signs*

This waterside pub, built around 1800, pre-dates the neighbouring Kennet and Avon Canal. Situated in an idyllic setting, the interior is cosy with open fires and the canal-side garden is the perfect place to enjoy a pint while watching the narrow boats cruise by. The pub keeps excellent cask ales, some served straight from the wood. Menus offer traditional home-made English food, from filled rolls to hearty hot meals.

Open 11.30-3 6-11 (summer Sat-Sun & BH 11.30-11) Closed: Mon Oct-Mar **Bar Meals** L served all wk 12-2 (ex Mon winter) D served Mon-Sat 6-9 Av main course £8 **Restaurant** L served all wk 12-2 (ex Mon winter) D served Mon-Sat 6-9 Av 3 course à la carte fr £17 ⊕ WADWORTH ◀ Wadworth Henry's original IPA, 6X, Old Father Timer Ö Stowford Press. ? 8 **Facilities** Children's menu Dogs allowed Garden Parking

KILMINGTON · Map 4 ST73

The Red Lion Inn

BA12 6RP ☎ 01985 844263
dir: *B3092 off A303 N towards Frome. Pub 2.5m from A303 on right on B3092 just after turn to Stourhead Gardens*

There's a good local pub atmosphere at this 14th-century former coaching inn, which once provided spare horses to assist coaches in the climb up nearby White Sheet Hill. Inside, you'll find flagstone floors, beams, antique settles and blazing log fires, and outside a large garden and a smoking shelter. Good value meals are served, such as home-made chicken casserole; and steak and kidney pie, plus snacks at lunchtime.

Open all wk 11.30-2.30 6.30-11 (Sun noon-3 7-11) **Bar Meals** L served all wk 12-1.50 Av main course £5.95 ⊕ FREE HOUSE ◀ Butcombe Bitter, Jester, Guest ale Ö Thatchers Cheddar Valley, Ashton Press. **Facilities** Garden Parking **Notes** ⊛

LACOCK · Map 4 ST96

The George Inn ?

4 West St SN15 2LH
☎ 01249 730263 ▤ 01249 730186
dir: *M4 junct 17 take A350, S*

Steeped in history and much used as a film and television location, this beautiful National Trust village includes an atmospheric inn. The George dates from 1361 and boasts a medieval fireplace, a low-beamed ceiling, mullioned windows, flagstone floors and an old tread wheel by which a dog would drive the spit. Wide selection of steaks and tasty pies, and fish options include specials in summer; finish with home-made bread and butter pud.

Open all day all wk 9am-11pm **Bar Meals** L served all wk 12-2 D served all wk 6-9 **Restaurant** L served all wk 12-2 D served all wk 6-9 ⊕ WADWORTH ◀ Wadworth 6X, Henrys IPA, J.C.B, Henrys Smooth. ? 13 **Facilities** Play area Dogs allowed Garden Parking

LACOCK *continued*

Red Lion Inn ?

1 High St SN15 2LQ ☎ 01249 730456 📠 01249 730766
e-mail: redlionlacock@wadworth.co.uk
dir: *Just off A350 between Chippenham & Melksham. Follow Lacock signs*

This historic 18th-century inn has kept its original features intact, from the large open fireplace to the flagstone floors and Georgian interior. Wadworth ales and a varied wine list accompany the home-cooked meals and daily specials. Lunchtime menu offers sandwiches or organic baguettes, small plates like breaded whitebait, home comforts, and ploughman's boards, whilst more substantial evening dishes include goats' cheese and cheddar terrine; braised shoulder of lamb, port and redcurrant sauce; beef and garlic casserole; and butternut squash and parmesan risotto.

Open all day all wk 11-11 (Sun 11-10.30) **Bar Meals** L served Mon-Sat 12-2.30, Sun 12-3 D served all wk 6-9.30 Av main course £10.50 **Restaurant** L served Mon-Sat 12-2.30, Sun 12-3 D served all wk 6-9.30 Av 3 course à la carte fr £20 ⊕ WADWORTH ◀ Wadworth 6X, Henrys IPA, seasonal ales ♂ Stowford Press, Thatchers Gold. ♀15 **Facilities** Children's menu Dogs allowed Garden Parking

The Rising Sun ?

32 Bowden Hill SN15 2PP ☎ 01249 730363
e-mail: the.risingsun@btinternet.co.uk

The pub is located close to the National Trust village of Lacock, on a steep hill, providing spectacular views over Wiltshire from the large garden. Beer festivals, live music, hog roasts and barbecues are a regular feature, and games and reading material are provided in the bar. Thai curries and stir-fries are popular options, alongside traditional liver, bacon and onions, steaks, and beef, ale and Stilton pie. Enjoy a pint of Moles ale or Black Rat cider.

Open all wk noon-3 6-11 **Bar Meals** L served all wk 12-2 booking required D served all wk 6-9 booking required **Restaurant** L served all wk 12-2 booking required D served all wk 6-9 booking required ⊕ MOLES BREWERY ◀ Moles Best, Molecatcher, Tap Bitter, Rucking Mole, guest ale ♂ Thatchers Gold, Black Rat. ♀10 **Facilities** Children's menu Play area Dogs allowed Garden Parking

---

LIMPLEY STOKE   **Map 4 ST76**

The Hop Pole Inn ?

Woods Hill, Lower Limpley Stoke BA2 7FS
☎ 01225 723134 📠 01225 723199
dir: *Telephone for directions*

Set in the beautiful Limpley Stoke valley, the Hop Pole dates from 1580 and takes its name from the hop plant that still grows outside the pub. Eagle-eyed film fans may recognise it as the hostelry in the 1992 film *Remains of the Day*. A hearty menu includes Thai vegetable curry; home-made pies; fresh local trout; and steaks. Giant filled baps and other light bites are available too.

Open all wk 11-2.30 6-11 (Sun noon-3 7-10.30) Closed: 25 Dec **Bar Meals** L served Mon-Sat 12-2, Sun 12-2.15 D served Mon-Thu 6-9, Fri-Sat 6-9.30, Sun 7-9 ⊕ FREE HOUSE ◀ Courage Best, Butcombe Bitter, Sharps Doom Bar, Guest ales ♂ Ashton Press. ♀8 **Facilities** Family room Dogs allowed Garden Parking

---

LITTLE CHEVERELL   **Map 4 ST95**

The Owl

Low Rd SN10 4JS ☎ 01380 812263
dir: *A344 from Stonehenge, then A360, after 10m left onto B3098, right after 0.5m. Pub signed*

Sit in the pretty garden after dark and you'll discover that this pub is aptly named. As well as the hoot of owls, woodpeckers can be heard in summer. A brook runs at the bottom of the garden and there are views of Salisbury Plain. The pub itself is a cosy hideaway with oak beams and a fire in winter. Typical dishes include lasagne; Thai chicken curry; sizzling beef Szechwan; and stilton and mushroom pork.

Open all day all wk noon-11 **Bar Meals** L served all wk 12-9 D served all wk 12-9 food served all day ⊕ ENTERPRISE INNS ◀ Hop Back Summer Lightning, Bath Gem. **Facilities** Children's menu Play area Dogs allowed Garden Parking

---

LOWER CHICKSGROVE   **Map 4 ST92**

PICK OF THE PUBS

Compasses Inn ★★★★ INN ◉ ?

SP3 6NB ☎ 01722 714318
e-mail: thecompasses@aol.com
dir: *On A30 (1.5m W of Fovant) take 3rd right to Lower Chicksgrove. In 1.5m turn left into Lagpond Lane, pub 1m on left*

This picture-perfect 14th-century thatched inn is full of character and stands in a tiny hamlet on the old drovers' track from Poole to Birmingham - a route that can still be traced today. The rolling countryside that unfolds around is part of a designated Area of Outstanding Natural Beauty. Inside there's a long, low-beamed bar with stone walls, worn flagstone floors and a large inglenook fireplace with a wood-burning stove for colder days. Be sure to try the food: the kitchen team have won an AA rosette for their efforts. Dishes

---

from the ever-changing blackboard menu are freshly made using seasonal produce. A meal might take in potted crab and avocado; venison steak with mixed berry sauce and dauphinoise potatoes; and brioche bread and butter pudding with banana and rum. The garden has a large grassed area with some lovely views and seats for 40 people. Five bedrooms are available, providing an ideal base for exploring the beautiful surrounding countryside.

Open all wk noon-3 6-11 (Sun noon-3 7-10.30) Closed: 25-26 Dec **Bar Meals** L served all wk 12-2 D served all wk 6.30-9 Av main course £15 ⊕ FREE HOUSE ◀ Keystone Large One & Solar Brew, Hidden Potential, Bass ♂ Stowford Press. ♀8 **Facilities** Children's menu Dogs allowed Garden Parking **Rooms** 5

LUDWELL   **Map 4 ST92**

The Grove Arms ?

SP7 9ND ☎ 01747 828328 📠 01747 828960
e-mail: info@grovearms.com
dir: *On A30 (Shaftesbury to Salisbury road), 3m from Shaftesbury*

The Grove Arms is a 16th century village inn once owned by the aristocratic Grove family. David Armstrong-Reed, chef and owner, is passionate about local produce, which is sourced from local farms and estates. Dishes are freshly made, including the popular home-made breads and chutneys, and fresh fish features strongly. Popular dishes, such as meat pies, chicken curry, and Badger beer battered haddock with tartare sauce are also available to take away during the week.

Open all day all wk **Bar Meals** L served all wk 12-3 D served all wk 6-9.30 Av main course £7 **Restaurant** L served Mon-Fri 12-3, Sat-Sun 12-9.30 booking required D served Mon-Fri 6-9.30, Sat-Sun 12-9.30 booking required ⊕ HALL & WOODHOUSE ◀ Badger Gold, Festive Feasant, Hopping Hare. ♀6 **Facilities** Children's menu Family room Dogs allowed Garden Parking

---

MALMESBURY   **Map 4 ST98**

PICK OF THE PUBS

Horse & Groom Inn ?

See Pick of the Pubs on opposite page

PICK OF THE PUBS

Horse & Groom Inn ▾

MALMESBURY Map 4 ST98

The Street, Charlton SN16 9DL
☎ **01666 823904**
e-mail: info@horseandgroominn.com
web: www.horseandgroominn.com
dir: *M4 junct 17 follow signs to Cirencester on A429. Through Corston & Malmesbury. Straight on at Priory rdbt, at next rdbt take 3rd exit to Cricklade, then to Charlton*

Owned by a small, private pub company, and with a new landlord holding the reins, this Cotswold stone, 16th-century coaching inn stands well back from the road from Malmesbury to Cricklade, fronted by a tree-sheltered lawn. A refurbishment a little while back ensured that it lost none of its charm and character, which is why you will still find the original stone flags and fireplaces in the popular Charlton Bar, and in the dining room furnishings that include solid oak tables and a rug-strewn wooden floor. Outside space is plentiful, including a lovely walled garden and a separate play area. In the dog-friendly indoor bar, the house beer is Archer's, holding its corner against a weekly changing guest ale chosen by customers. Snacks include tempting sandwiches, deli platters to share, ploughman's and salads, and the more substantial home-made crab cakes with dill mayonnaise; double-cooked Cotswold lamb with whole-grain mustard mash; fresh battered pollack with hand-cut chips and crushed peas; and pan-fried liver with smoked bacon, mash and shallot sauce. The focus on sensibly priced, modern British cooking continues on the carte menu which offers St George's mushroom risotto with Parmesan and chives; roasted Cotswold chicken breasts marinated in lemon and thyme with truffle mash and Evesham asparagus; and grilled fillet of wild brown trout, herb-crushed potatoes and cherry tomato and fennel salad. Resident chef Paul Nicholson is passionate about flying the flag for Wiltshire produce, such as the beef, which comes from a family butcher's that recently celebrated its 200th anniversary, and the pork belly, which comes from nearby Bromham. The wine list may not be that long, but it is comprehensive and offers a good number by the glass.

Open 11-11 (Sun 11-10.30) **Bar Meals** L served Mon-Sat 12-2.30 D served Sun-Thu 6.30-9, Fri-Sat 6.30-9.30 Av main course £11 **Restaurant** L served Mon-Sat 12-2.30, Sun 12-3 D served Sun-Thu 6.30-9, Fri-Sat 6.30-9.30 Av 3 course à la carte fr £25 ⊕ MERCHANT INNS LTD ◪ Archers, Morland Original, Old Speckled Hen, guest ales. ▾ 8 **Facilities** Children's menu Play area Dogs allowed Garden Parking

MALMESBURY *continued*

The Smoking Dog 🍸

62 The High St SN16 9AT ☎ 01666 825823
e-mail: smokindog@sabrain.com
dir: *5m N of M4 junct 17*

A winged wheel on the outside front wall greets visitors to this refined 17th-century stone-built pub, right in the heart of Malmesbury. Inside log fires and wooden floors make for a warm and cosy atmosphere. Freshly cooked food and live music have broad appeal, while the wide choice of refreshments includes continually changing guest ales and scrumpy ciders. A renowned beer and sausage festival over Whitsun weekend is the time to sample over 30 brews and 15 banger varieties.

Open all day all wk noon–11 (Fri-Sat noon-mdnt, Sun noon-10.30) **Bar Meals** L served Mon-Sat 12-2.30, Sun 12-3 D served Mon-Sat 6.30-9.30, Sun 6.30-8.30 **Restaurant** L served Mon-Sat 12-2.30, Sun 12-3 ⊕ S A BRAIN ◀ Archers Best, Buckleys Best, Reverend James, 3 guest bitters. 🍸 7 **Facilities** Dogs allowed Garden

PICK OF THE PUBS

The Vine Tree 🍸

Foxley Rd, Norton SN16 0JP ☎ 01666 837654
e-mail: tiggi@thevinetree.co.uk
dir: *M4 junct 17, A429 towards Malmesbury. Turn left for village*

The Vine Tree used to be a mill, and workers apparently passed beverages out through front windows to passing carriages - an early drive-through it would seem. These days, it is well worth seeking out for its interesting modern pub food and memorable outdoor summer dining. In today's central bar a large open fireplace burns wood all winter, and there's a wealth of old beams, flagstone and oak floors. Ramblers and cyclists exploring Wiltshire's charms are frequent visitors, and the inn is situated on the official county cycle route. Cooking is modern British in style, with menus changing daily in response to local produce availability. Everything on the menus is produced in-house, including bread. Dishes include light bites and vegetarian options, local game and well-sourced fish and meats. There's also a terrific stock of wines. In addition to the suntrap terrace, there's a two-acre garden with two boules pitches.

Open all wk noon-3 6-11 (Sun noon-4 6-11) **Bar Meals** L served Mon-Fri 12-2.30, Sun 12-3.30 D served Mon-Thu 7-9.30, Fri-Sat 7-10, Sun 7-9 ⊕ FREE HOUSE ◀ Tinners, Butcombe, guest ales Ö Stowford Press. 🍸 30 **Facilities** Play area Dogs allowed Garden Parking

---

MARDEN   Map 5 SU05

The Millstream 🍸

SN10 3RH ☎ 01380 848308   📄 01380 848337
e-mail: mail@the-millstream.net
dir: *Signed from A342*

The Millstream sits in lovely countryside in the Vale of Pewsey, within sight of both Salisbury Plain and the Marlborough Downs. It was tastefully refurbished a few years ago without losing its traditional feel: wooden floors, beamed ceilings, log fires and pretty muted colours create a cosy, welcoming interior. Books, games and comfy sofas add their own homely touch. A good choice of hand-pulled beers and an impressive wine list are an ideal accompaniment for the contemporary menu, where locally sourced seasonal produce, plus fish from Cornwall, hold sway. Look out for braised lamb shank, and spatchcock poussin, with all the trimmings.

Open noon-3 6-late (Fri-Sun noon-late) Closed: Mon (ex BH) **Bar Meals** L served Tue-Sat 12-3, Sun 12-4 booking required D served Tue-Sat 6.30-10 booking required **Restaurant** L served Tue-Sat 12-3, Sun 12-4 booking required D served Tue-Sat 6.30-10 booking required ⊕ WADWORTH ◀ 6X, Henry's IPA, Bishops Tipple, Malt & Hops Ö Stowford Press. 🍸 14 **Facilities** Children's menu Play area Family room Dogs allowed Garden Parking

---

MINETY   Map 5 SU09

PICK OF THE PUBS

Vale of the White Horse Inn 🍸

SN16 9QY ☎ 01666 860175   📄 01666 860175
dir: *On B4040 (3m W of Cricklade, 6m & E of Malmesbury)*

This eye-catching, beautifully restored inn overlooks its own lake. In summer, sitting out on the large raised terrace surrounded by rose beds, it's hard to think of a better spot. The lower ground floor originally provided stabling for horses, and nowadays the village bar still serves the local community well. Here you'll find a good selection of real ales and a range of sandwiches and simple bar meals. Upstairs, lunch and dinner are served in the stone-walled restaurant with its polished tables and bentwood chairs. The menus offer something for most tastes, with starters including leek, stilton and sun-dried tomato quiche, and crayfish tail and king prawn cocktail. Main courses range from beer-battered cod and chips to confit duck leg on braised red cabbage with mustard mash and Madeira sauce. Finish with crumble or treacle tart with ice cream.

Open all day all wk 11-11 **Bar Meals** L served all wk 12-2.30 D served all wk 6-9.15 Av main course £8 **Restaurant** L served all wk 12-2.30 D served all wk 6-9.15 Av 3 course à la carte fr £16.50 ⊕ FREE HOUSE ◀ Wadworth, Henrys IPA, Three Castle Vale Ale, Hancocks, Archers Chrystal Clear Ö Stowford Press. 🍸 12 **Facilities** Children's menu Family room Dogs allowed Garden Parking

---

NEWTON TONY   Map 5 SU24

PICK OF THE PUBS

The Malet Arms

SP4 0HF ☎ 01980 629279   📄 01980 629459
e-mail: maletarms@hotmail.com
dir: *8m N of Salisbury on A338, 2m from A303*

Off the beaten track, in a quiet village on the River Bourne, this 17th-century inn was originally built as a dwelling house. Much later it became The Three Horseshoes, named after a nearby smithy. An earlier Malet Arms, owned by lord of the manor Sir Henry Malet, closed in the 1890s and its name was transferred. It's not just the village that's quiet: the pub is too, as fruit machines and piped music are banned. There is a good range of real ales and all the food on the ever-changing blackboard menu is home cooked. Game is plentiful in season, often courtesy of the landlord who shoots pheasant and deer. The landlady makes all the puddings, often sourced from obscure old English recipes. In fine weather you can sit outside in the garden, where there is a children's play area. Dogs are also welcome.

Open all wk Closed: 25-26 Dec, 1 Jan **Bar Meals** D served all wk 6.30-10 booking required **Restaurant** D served all wk 6.30-10 booking required ⊕ FREE HOUSE ◀ Ramsbury, Stonehenge, Triple FFF, Palmers, Archers Ö Old Rosie. **Facilities** Play area Dogs allowed Garden Parking

---

NUNTON   Map 5 SU12

The Radnor Arms 🍸

SP5 4HS ☎ 01722 329722
dir: *From Salisbury ring road take A338 to Ringwood. Nunton signed on right*

A popular pub in the centre of the village dating from around 1750. In 1855 it was owned by the local multi-talented brewer/baker/grocer, and bought by Lord Radnor in 1919. Bar snacks are supplemented by an extensive fish choice and daily specials, which might include braised lamb shank, wild mushroom risotto, tuna with noodles, turbot with spinach or Scotch rib-eye fillet, all freshly prepared. Fine summer garden with rural views. Hosts an annual local pumpkin competition.

Open all wk **Bar Meals** L served all wk 12-2.15 D served all wk 7-9 Av main course £8.95 **Restaurant** L served all wk 12-2.15 D served all wk 7-9 Av 3 course à la carte fr £25 ⊕ HALL & WOODHOUSE ◀ Badger Tanglefoot, Best, Golden Champion. ♀ 6 **Facilities** Children's menu Play area Family room Dogs allowed Garden Parking

---

OAKSEY   Map 4 ST99

PICK OF THE PUBS

The Wheatsheaf Inn ◉◉ ♀

Wheatsheaf Ln SN16 9TB ☎ 01666 577348
e-mail: info@thecompletechef.co.uk
dir: *Off A419, 6m S of Cirencester*

A 14th-century village inn built of mellow Cotswold stone, the Wheatsheaf has a traditional feel, with a big inglenook fireplace, flagstone floors and dark beams. It also has something rather bizarre - an 18th-century 'royal' coffin lid displayed above the open fireplace. The restaurant is light and modern, with a sisal carpet, wooden tables and painted walls decorated with wine racks and jars of preserved vegetables. Modern British food - all made on the premises from fresh local produce, and behind the award of two AA Rosettes – is displayed on daily blackboards that may include delicately flavoured chestnut soup; followed by succulent belly pork with braised red cabbage, creamy mash and shallot jus; and baked rice pudding with cinnamon and cranberry jam to finish. On Fridays fish and chips are available to eat in or take away - at chip shop prices! Look out too for the Britain's Best Burger menu. There are quality real ales on tap and varied wine selection.

Open all wk **Bar Meals** L served Tue-Sun 12-2 D served Tues-Sat 6.30-9 **Restaurant** L served Tue-Sun 12-2 D served Tue-Sat 6.30-9 ⊕ FREE HOUSE ◀ Sharp's Doom Bar, Hook Norton, Bath Gem. ♀ 9 **Facilities** Children's menu Dogs allowed Garden Parking

---

PEWSEY   Map 5 SU16

The Seven Stars ♀

Bottlesford SN9 6LU
☎ 01672 851325   🖹 01672 851583
e-mail: info@thesevenstars.co.uk
dir: *Off A345*

This thatched 16th-century free house stands in a splendid seven acre garden. Its front door opens straight onto the low-beamed, oak-panelled bar, now tastefully refurbished. Expect well-kept ales and an extensive menu of home-cooked food. With pheasant and pigeon on the menu when available, typical dishes include roast pork belly; smoked haddock risotto; and mutton shepherd's pie with greens. Finish with rice pudding with Bramley compote and crumble topping, then walk it off with a stroll in the garden.

Open noon-3 6-11 Closed: Mon **Bar Meals** food served all day **Restaurant** food served all day ⊕ FREE HOUSE ◀ Wadworth 6X, Brakspear, London Pride, Guest ales ♂ Stowford Press. ♀ 6 **Facilities** Children's menu Dogs allowed Garden Parking

---

PITTON   Map 5 SU23

PICK OF THE PUBS

The Silver Plough ♀

White Hill SP5 1DU
☎ 01722 712266   🖹 01722 712262
e-mail: thesilverplough@hotmail.co.uk
dir: *From Salisbury take A30 towards Andover, Pitton signed. Approx 3m*

Surrounded by rolling countryside and with a peaceful garden, this popular pub at the heart of a thatched village is within easy reach of many lovely downland and woodland walks. Converted from a farmstead around 60 years ago, the interior is full of bucolic character. The bar has an unusual carved front, while the multitude of beams are strung with antique glass rolling pins – said to bring good luck – along with bootwarmers, Toby jugs and various other artefacts. A skittle alley can be found adjacent to the snug bar, and traditional darts and board games are available. When it comes to food, expect products from the local Fjordling smokery on the menu, including chicken and mackerel. Bar snacks and blackboard specials served at lunchtime include favourites such as filled jackets, baguettes and home-made steak and kidney pie. In the evening look for hot starters such as pan-fried scallops, and main events such as veal à la crème.

Open all wk 11-3 6-11 **Bar Meals** Av main course £8.95 food served all day **Restaurant** Fixed menu price fr £12.95 Av 3 course à la carte fr £22.95 food served all day ⊕ HALL & WOODHOUSE ◀ Badger Tanglefoot, Badger Gold, King Barnes Sussex, guest ale. ♀ 9 **Facilities** Family room Dogs allowed Garden Parking

---

RAMSBURY   Map 5 SU27

PICK OF THE PUBS

The Bell ♀

The Square SN8 2PE
☎ 01672 520230   🖹 01672 520832
e-mail: jeremy@thebellramsbury.com
dir: *Telephone for directions*

The Bell, originally a 16th-century coaching inn, stands on ancient crossroads in the centre of the village, probably the site of a hostelry since medieval times. Head chef Paul Kinsey's passion for cooking stems from a training background in France and Hampshire, and two years working for celebrity chef, Antony Worrall-Thompson. Paul sources food from within Wiltshire or neighbouring Berkshire wherever possible, and delivers an impressive array of dishes. A typical meal might start with Wiltshire pigeon breast with roasted garlic polenta, squash purée and pickled

---

shitake mushrooms; continue with River Kennet crayfish, venison and redcurrant sausages, or a 28-day Aberdeen Angus steak; and finish with Bramley apple, strawberry and raspberry crumble with roasted hazelnut and vanilla mascarpone. Private dining is available in the Chapter Room, and regular wine-tasting events are worth looking out for.

Closed: 25 Dec, Sun eve (ex BH) **Bar Meals** L served Mon-Sat 12-2 D served Mon-Sat 7-9 Av main course £10.50 **Restaurant** L served all wk 12-2 booking required D served Mon-Sat 7-9 booking required Fixed menu price fr £13.95 Av 3 course à la carte fr £30 ⊕ FREE HOUSE ◀ Ramsbury Gold, Bell Bitter ♂ Black Rat. ♀ 8 **Facilities** Dogs allowed Garden Parking

---

ROWDE   Map 4 ST96

PICK OF THE PUBS

The George & Dragon ★★★★ RR ◉◉ ♀

High St SN10 2PN ☎ 01380 723053
e-mail: thegandd@tiscali.co.uk
dir: *1m from Devizes, take A342 towards Chippenham*

Winter log fires warm the panelled bars and dining room of this 15th-century free house, not far from the Caen Hill lock flight on the Kennet and Avon Canal. Real ales dispensed at the bar are several in number, while wine lovers will have nearly a dozen by the glass to choose from. Rooms are cosy, welcoming and full of character. Bearing witness to the pub's age, a Tudor rose is carved on one of the beams in the restaurant, where tables are replete with crisp white linen and glowing candles. The pub specialises in seafood from Cornwall, so take your pick from the catch of the day chalked up on the blackboard. The list of starters is augmented by half a dozen dishes that can be served either as starters or as main courses, such as Cajun spiced fishcakes with hollandaise, or from the main course selection chargrilled tuna steak with an olive, green bean and soft-boiled egg salad. Home-made puddings may include glazed creamy rice pudding with apple compote.

Closed: Sun eve **Bar Meals** L served Mon-Sat 12-3, Sun 12-4 booking required D served Mon-Fri 7-10, Sat 6.30-10 booking required Av main course £12.50 **Restaurant** L served Mon-Sat 12-3, Sun 12-4 booking required D served Mon-Fri 7-10, Sat 6.30-10 booking required Fixed menu price fr £15.50 Av 3 course à la carte fr £26.50 ⊕ FREE HOUSE ◀ Butcombe Bitter, Milk Street Brewery Ales, Bath Ales Gem, ESB, London Pride, Ringwood 49er. ♀ 11 **Facilities** Children's menu Dogs allowed Garden Parking **Rooms** 3

SALISBURY
Map 5 SU12

PICK OF THE PUBS

The Haunch of Venison ☕

See Pick of the Pubs on opposite page

SEEND
Map 4 ST96

Bell Inn

Bell Hill SN12 6SA ☎ 01380 828338
e-mail: bellseend@aol.com

According to local tradition, Oliver Cromwell and his troops enjoyed breakfast at this inn, quite possibly on 18 September 1645 when he was advancing from Trowbridge to attack Devizes Castle. The extensive menu runs to poached salmon with a prawn and cream sauce; spicy bean burgers; and barbecue pork ribs, while the specials board highlights liver and bacon casserole; chicken balti; and Highland sausages in whisky. The two-floor restaurant has lovely valley views.

Open all wk ⊕ WADWORTH ◀ Wadworth 6X, Henry's IPA, Henrys Smooth. **Facilities** Play area Dogs allowed Garden Parking

SEMINGTON
Map 4 ST86

The Lamb on the Strand ☕

99 The Strand BA14 6LL
☎ 01380 870263 & 870815 🖷 01380 871203
e-mail: lamb@eyno.co.uk
dir: *1.5m E on A361 from junct with A350*

An 18th-century farmhouse that later became a beer and cider house. Today's popular dining pub typically offers starters of grilled goats' cheese with spiced beetroot; and grilled fig, chorizo and parmesan salad. Almost sure to be found on the generous list of main courses are sausages, mash and onion gravy; fillet of cod with herb crust, leeks and new potatoes; medallions of venison, parsnip purée, vegetables and Madeira jus; and cheesy pudding, salad and sauté potatoes.

Open noon-3 6.30-11 Closed: 25-26 Dec & 1 Jan, Sun eve **Bar Meals** L served all wk 12-2.30 D served Mon-Sat 6.30-9 Av main course £11 **Restaurant** L served all wk 12-2.30 D served Mon-Sat 6.30-9 ⊕ FREE HOUSE ◀ Butcombe Bitter, Ringwood Bitter, Shepherd Neame Spitfire, Guinness Ō Thatchers. ☕ 12 **Facilities** Children's menu Dogs allowed Garden Parking

SHERSTON
Map 4 ST88

The Rattlebone Inn NEW ☕

Church St SN16 0LR ☎ 01666 840871
e-mail: eat@therattlebone.co.uk
dir: *M4 junct 17 go N to Malmesbury. 2m N after passing petrol station at Stanton St. Quentin, take rd to left signed Sherston*

Named after the legendary Saxon hero John Rattlebone, this lovely 16th-century pub boasts roaring winter fires and bags of character. A lively drinkers' pub serving real ales and organic cider, the Rattlebone also has a reputation for its country bistro menu. Expect locally sourced ingredients, summer spit roasts, and seasonal game, featuring dishes like venison marinated with port and juniper berries. The pub has two garden areas, two boules pistes and a well-used skittles alley.

Open all wk noon-3 5-11 (Fri noon-3 5-mdnt Sat noon-mdnt Sun noon-11) **Bar Meals** L served Mon-Sat 12-3 D served Mon-Sat 6-7.30 Av main course £8 **Restaurant** L served all wk 12-3 D served Mon-Sat 6-9.30 Fixed menu price fr £10.95 Av 3 course à la carte fr £18 ⊕ YOUNG & CO ◀ Youngs Bitter, Bombardier, St Austell Tribute Ō Stowford Press, Westons Organic. ☕ 14
Facilities Children's menu Dogs allowed Garden

STOFORD
Map 5 SU03

The Swan Inn ★★★ INN ☕

Warminster Rd SP2 0PR
☎ 01722 790236 🖷 01722 444972
e-mail: info@theswanatstoford.co.uk
dir: *From Salisbury take A36 towards Warminster. Stoford on right 4m from Wilton*

The Swan is a landmark coaching inn, close to the cathedral city of Salisbury, with attractive gardens overlooking the River Wylye to meadow and farmland. There is a welcoming log fire, four cask ales and a popular wine and cocktails selection. Traditional home cooked food includes Wiltshire pork sausages with mash and onion gravy, Lancashire hot pot, and oven baked whole sea bass with dill butter sauce. As well as lovely riverside gardens, a marquee is now available for riverside wedding receptions. There are nine comfortable guest rooms.

Open all day all wk 8am-11pm (Sun 9am-10.30pm) **Bar Meals** Av main course £10 food served all day **Restaurant** Fixed menu price fr £10 Av 3 course à la carte fr £17 food served all day ⊕ FREE HOUSE ◀ Ringwood Best, Fuller's London Pride, Odyssey Best Bitter, Old Speckled Hen. ☕ 7 **Facilities** Children's menu Dogs allowed Garden Parking **Rooms** 9

STOURTON
Map 4 ST73

PICK OF THE PUBS

Spread Eagle Inn ★★★★ INN ☕

BA12 6QE ☎ 01747 840587 🖷 01747 840954
e-mail: enquiries@spreadeagleinn.com
dir: *N of A303 off B3092*

Built at the beginning of the 19th century, this charming inn stands in the heart of the 2,650-acre Stourhead Estate, one of the country's most-visited National Trust properties. Before or after a walk through the magnificent gardens and landscapes there is plenty on offer here, including locally produced beers and traditional food. Expect perhaps Wiltshire pasty with onion gravy and chips; lamb casserole and roasted root vegetables; and Old Spot sausages with bubble and squeak mash and sweet mustard sauce. The restaurant menu shifts things up a gear with breast of Gressingham duck with parsnip purée and apple sauce; escalope of cod with lentils and bacon; and chump of Cotswold lamb with spiced apricots and rosemary. Finish with treacle tart with clotted cream; hot sticky toffee pudding; or chocolate roulade. The interior is smartly traditional, and in the bedrooms, antiques sit side by side with modern comforts.

Open all wk ⊕ FREE HOUSE ◀ Kilmington, Butcombe, Wadworth 6X. ☕ 8 **Facilities** Garden Parking **Rooms** 5

TOLLARD ROYAL
Map 4 ST91

King John Inn ☕

SP5 5PS ☎ 01725 516207
e-mail: info@kingjohninn.co.uk
dir: *On B3081 (7m E of Shaftesbury)*

A Victorian building dating from 1859, named after one of King John's hunting lodges. The pub was rescued from an advanced state of dereliction in 2008 and comprehensively refurbished. The interior of quarry-tiled floors, open fire and solid oak bar complete with Belfast sink is stylishly uncluttered. The kitchen's output seeks the freshest of flavours from locally sourced produce. A typical meal selection could comprise smoked fillet of trout; pan-fried brill with saffron potatoes; and apple, date and sultana crumble.

Open all wk noon-3 6-11 **Bar Meals** L served Mon-Fri 12-2.30, Sat-Sun 12-3 booking required D served all wk 7-9.30 booking required **Restaurant** L served Mon-Fri 12-2.30, Sat-Sun 12-3 booking required D served all wk 7-9.30 booking required ⊕ FREE HOUSE ◀ Ringwood Best, Fuller's London Pride, Summer Lightning, guest ales Ō Stowford Press. ☕ 12 **Facilities** Dogs allowed Garden Parking

PICK OF THE PUBS

The Haunch of Venison 🍷

1-5 Minster St SP1 1TB
☎ **01722 411313**
e-mail: oneminsterst@aol.com
dir: *In city centre. Opposite Poultry Cross Monument, adjacent to market place*

Dating from 1320, this is (probably) Salisbury's oldest hostelry. Heavily beamed, it once housed craftsmen working on the cathedral spire, although it is closer to St Thomas's Church, whose clergy used to visit via a tunnel to avoid the unseemly goings on in some of the rooms. The arrangement of floor levels is supposed to reflect ecclesiastical hierarchy, the so-called House of Lords room being for the higher orders. The bar has a small, intimate 'Horsebox', originally for ladies, and reputedly used by Churchill and Eisenhower when planning the D-Day

landings. Charming details include what is believed to be the country's only surviving complete pewter bar top, as well as original gravity-fed spirit taps. With such history, ghosts are inevitable, a favourite being the one-handed Demented Whist Player, whose hand, severed for cheating at cards, was found mummified in the 19th century and remains to this day. He is usually seen in the private bar, which has the only licensed landing in England. There is also the Grey Lady, who is searching for her child. In the main dining room is a working fireplace dating back to 1588. Here, modern and classic lunch dishes include cottage pie; garlic sausage, smoked bacon and mushroom pasta with parmesan; smoked salmon and chive crème fraîche wrap with crab slaw and salad; and Mediterranean vegetable pasta with Provençal sauce. In the evening, try pan-fried sea bass with a warm French green bean salad and tomato, onion and coriander salsa; roasted quail stuffed with foie gras and wild mushroom forcemeat; and, of course, haunch of venison with colcannon potato and thick onion and Madeira sauce.

Open 11-11 Closed: 25 Dec eve **Bar Meals** L served all wk 12-2.30 D served Sun-Wed 6-9.30 (Thu-Sat 6-10) **Restaurant** L served all wk 12-2.30 D served Sun-Wed 6-9.30 (Thu-Sat 6-10) ⊕ ENTERPRISE INNS 🛢 Courage Best, Summer Lightning, Greene King IPA, Ringwood guest ale. 🍷 12 **Facilities** Children's menu Dogs allowed

UPPER WOODFORD
Map 5 SU13

The Bridge Inn NEW ☙

SP4 6NU ☎ 01722 782323
e-mail: enquiries@thebridgewoodford.co.uk
dir: *5m N of Salisbury, situated in the Woodford Valley, off the A360*

Hidden away on a quiet lane beside the Wiltshire Avon just north of Salisbury, this charming pub has been completely refurbished to include a modern, theatre-style kitchen. As well as a riverside garden and winter fires, you'll find flowers and candles on the tables at any time of year. Seasonal menu choices might include braised lamb shank with gruyère mash; or home-made fish cakes with herbed chips, mixed leaves and tartare sauce.

Open all wk 11-3 6-11 (Sun 11-11 summer) **Bar Meals** L served all wk 12-2.30 D served all wk 6-9 Av main course £13 **Restaurant** L served all wk 12-2.30 D served all wk 6-9 Av 3 course à la carte fr £24 ⊕ ENTERPRISE INNS ◀ Summer Lightning, Wadworth 6X, Ringwood Best. ☙ 10 **Facilities** Children's menu Dogs allowed Garden Parking

UPTON LOVELL
Map 4 ST94

Prince Leopold Inn ☙

BA12 0JP ☎ 01985 850460
e-mail: Princeleopoldinn@btconnect.com
dir: *From Warminster take A36 after 4.5m turn left into Upper Lovell*

Built in 1887 as the local shop, post office and store to service the then prosperous woollen industry, the inn's name was chosen to honour Prince Leopold who lived nearby. Possibly unique in England, the Mediterranean-style restaurant has an eye-level fireplace with a charcoal barbecue grill. Seafood features strongly on a wide ranging menu, offering brill fillet on champ mash with hollandaise sauce and thyme scented onions alongside Thai green chicken curry.

Open winter noon-3 7-11 (Sun noon-4 7-10.30) summer noon-11 Closed: winter Mon all day Tue L **Bar Meals** L served all wk 12-2, Sun 12-4 D served Mon-Sat 7-9 ⊕ FREE HOUSE ◀ Ringwood Best, John Smiths's, guest ales ♉ Stowford Press. ☙ 8 **Facilities** Dogs allowed Garden Parking

WARMINSTER
Map 4 ST84

PICK OF THE PUBS

The Angel Inn ☙

Upton Scudamore BA12 0AG
☎ 01985 213225 ▤ 01985 218182
e-mail: mail@theangelinn.co.uk
dir: *From Warminster take A350 towards Westbury or A36 towards Bath*

The Angel is a restored 16th-century coaching inn located in a small village close to Warminster; ideally placed for visits to Longleat, Stonehenge, Amesbury and the Cotswolds. Access to the pub is via a walled

garden and terrace, where meals and drinks can be served in fine weather. Inside, open fires and natural wood flooring create a relaxed atmosphere. Dishes from the lunch menu vary from modern to traditional -- you might, for example, find a starter of sesame crusted tuna loin, mango and chilli salsa, with mango purée and wasabi dressing; and a main course of braised lamb shank on a tomato and thyme cassoulet. For dinner the eclectic range of flavours continues in such dishes as confit guinea fowl terrine with an orange vinaigrette and toasted brioche; and roast fillet of pollack on wilted greens, with a mussel, lemongrass and coconut broth. Desserts, including ice creams and sorbets, are freshly made on the premises by the kitchen team.

Open all wk Closed: 25-26 Dec, 1 Jan **Bar Meals** Av main course £16 **Restaurant** Av 3 course à la carte fr £25 ⊕ FREE HOUSE ◀ Wadworth 6X, Butcombe, John Smith's Smooth, guest ales. ☙ 8 **Facilities** Children's menu Garden Parking

The Bath Arms NEW ☙

Clay St, Crockerton BA12 8AJ
☎ 01985 212262 ▤ 01985 218670
e-mail: batharms@aol.com
web: www.batharmscrockerton.co.uk
dir: *From Warminster on A36 take A350 towards Shaftesbury then left to Crockerton, follow signs for Shearwater*

Standing close to the Shearwater Lake on the Longleat Estate, this well-known free house attracts locals, walkers and tourists. The garden has been landscaped to provide a pleasant spot for outdoor dining, and the Garden Suite, with views across the lawn, provides additional seating on busy weekends. Expect steak and horseradish baguettes; shepherd's pie with crushed peas; or Bath Arms fish cake with Cornish crab and broad beans.

Open all wk **Bar Meals** L served all wk 12-2 D served all wk 6.30-9 **Restaurant** L served all wk 12-2 D served all wk 6.30-9 ⊕ FREE HOUSE ◀ Crockerton Classic, Naughty Ferret, Guest ales. ☙ 10 **Facilities** Play area Dogs allowed Garden Parking

The George Inn ★★★★ INN ☙

BA12 7DG ☎ 01985 840396 ▤ 01985 841333
e-mail: info@the-georgeinn.co.uk
dir: *Telephone for directions*

A 17th-century coaching inn at the heart of the pretty village of Longbridge Deverill. Customers can enjoy a pint of real ale by the fire in the oak-beamed Longbridge bar, or sit outside in the two-acre garden on the banks of the River Wylye. Food is served in a choice of two restaurants and there is a Sunday carvery in the Wylye Suite. Function facilities are available, plus accommodation in 11 en suite bedrooms.

Open all day all wk 11-11 (Sun noon-10.30) Closed: 25 Dec from 3, 26 Dec (open 11-3 Jan 1) **Bar Meals** L served Mon-Thu 11-3, Fri-Sat 11-6, Sun 12-6 D served Mon-Thu 6-9.30, Fri-Sat 11-6, Sun 6-9 Av main course £9.95 **Restaurant** L served Mon-Thu 11-3, Fri-Sat 11-6, Sun 12-6 D served Mon-Thu 6-9.30, Fri-Sat 11-6, Sun 6-9 ⊕ FREE HOUSE ◀ John Smiths's, Wadworth 6X, Hobdens Doverills Advocat. ☙ 11 **Facilities** Play area Garden Parking **Rooms** 11

WEST LAVINGTON
Map 4 SU05

PICK OF THE PUBS

The Bridge Inn ☙

26 Church St SN10 4LD
☎ 01380 813213 ▤ 01380 813213
e-mail: portier@btopenworld.com
dir: *Approx 7m S of Devizes on A360 towards Salisbury. On edge of village, beyond church*

The Bridge is an attractive food-led pub in a village setting on the edge of Salisbury Plain. Inside you'll find a beamed bar with a log fire and displays of local paintings for sale, while outside there is a large garden featuring a boule pitch. The pub is owned by Cyrille and Paula Portier; Cyrille, heading up the kitchen,

continued on page 504

PICK OF THE PUBS

The Pear Tree Inn ★★★★★ RR 🏵🏵 ♗

Top Ln SN12 8QX
☎ **01225 709131** 📠 **01225 702276**
e-mail: enquries@thepeartreeinn.com
dir: *A365 from Melksham towards Bath, at Shaw right onto B3353 into Whitley, 1st left in lane, pub at end*

No great stretch of the imagination is required to picture the Pear Tree, surrounded by acres of wooded farmland, as the farmhouse it once was. The agricultural antiques that adorn its interior help to maintain a connection with those very different times, while its laid-back, comfortable feel comes from the flagstone floors, two log fires, and a bar that's open all day. Like other establishments in the Maypole Group, it cares deeply about its real ales, (Sharp's Doom Bar, Wadworth 6X,

Fuller's London Pride) and a carefully selected worldwide wine list that features many by the glass. The home-made food on its popular menu of hearty, traditional British dishes has earned generous praise, not least from the AA, which has awarded two Rosettes for the obvious attention paid to the quality and selection of ingredients. Indeed, everything comes from locally based suppliers - nearby farms and growers for the top quality fruit and vegetables - but some things have to come from further afield, such as the lemons from the Amalfi coast that provide the basis for the delicious lemon tart. There is also a healthy children's menu. Food is served throughout the pub, giving customers the option to choose a dining style to suit their mood and dress. Outside, an extensive patio area and a cottage garden make alfresco relaxation particularly agreeable. You can work up a thirst or an appetite by visiting Lacock Abbey, Avebury or Silbury Hill, which are close by, or Stonehenge which is a lovely drive across Salisbury Plain. Afterwards you can stay in one of the luxury bedrooms.

Open all week breakfast-11 **Bar Meals** L served all week 12-2.30
D served all week 6.30-9.30 Av main course £13.95 **Restaurant** L served all week 12-2.20 D served all week 6.30-9.30 Fixed menu price fr £12
🍺 Wadworth 6X, Fuller's London Pride, Sharp's Doom Bar. ♟ 19
Facilities Children's menu Dogs allowed Garden Parking **Rooms** 8

WEST LAVINGTON *continued*

brings a French influence to the menu, with dishes such as l'assiette de charcuterie for one or two to share; cassoulet with roast duck leg and sausage, or soufflé with Emmental cheese and tomato pesto. Pub favourites offered from the specials board include soup of the day with crème fraiche and croutons; moules marinière; haddock in organic beer batter, or Wiltshire ham with organic free-range eggs and pommes frites. Annual event are now a regular feature at The Bridge, from Harvest Supper in September to the Charity Beer Festival over the August Bank Holiday weekend.

Open noon-3 6.30-11 Closed: 2wks Feb, Sun eve & Mon **Bar Meals** L served Tue-Sun 12-2 booking required D served Tue-Sat 7-9 booking required **Restaurant** L served Tue-Sun 12-2 booking required D served Tue-Sat 7-9 booking required ⊕ ENTERPRISE INNS ◀ Brakspear Organic Oxford Gold, Hobgoblin, Wadworth Henry's IPA, Greene King IPA, Maiden Voyage. ☻ 12 **Facilities** Children's menu Garden Parking

---

WHITLEY   Map 4 ST86

PICK OF THE PUBS

The Pear Tree Inn ★★★★★ RR ⊚⊚ ☻

See Pick of the Pubs on page 503

WINTERBOURNE BASSETT   Map 5 SU07

The White Horse Inn ☻

SN4 9QB ☎ 01793 731257 🖹 01793 739030
e-mail: ckstone@btinternet.com
dir: *5m S of Swindon on A4361 (Devizes road)*

Lying just two miles north of the mysterious Avebury stone circle, the White Horse is an ideal base for walks on the historic Ridgeway path. Food is served in the bar and conservatory restaurant, as well as in the safe, lawned garden. Budget lunches and snacks are supported by a full menu and daily specials: look out for baked cod topped with tomato, herbs and mozzarella; mushroom Stroganoff; and beef, ale and mushroom pie.

Open all wk 11.30-3 6-11 **Bar Meals** L served all wk 12-2 D served all wk 6-7.30 **Restaurant** L served all wk 12-2 D served all wk 6-9.30 ⊕ WADWORTH ◀ Wadworth 6X, IPA, Hophouse Brews ♂ Stowford Press. ☻ 20 **Facilities** Children's menu Garden Parking

---

WOODFALLS   Map 5 SU12

The Woodfalls Inn ☻

The Ridge SP5 2LN ☎ 01725 513222 🖹 01725 513220
e-mail: enquiries@woodfallsinn.co.uk
dir: *B3080 to Woodfalls*

Located on an old coaching route on the northern edge of the New Forest, the Woodfalls Inn has provided hospitality to travellers since the early Victorian era. A more recent extension accommodates a purpose built function suite, in addition to the bar areas, conservatory, lounge and restaurant. Home-made dishes include chicken curry, beef or vegetable lasagne, and steak and ale pie. There is also a comprehensive selection of grills.

Open all day all wk 11am-11pm (Sun noon-11pm) Closed: 1 Jan **Bar Meals** L served all wk 12-2.30 D served all wk 6-9 ⊕ FREE HOUSE ◀ Ringwood 49er, Best, 2 guest ales. ☻ 9 **Facilities** Dogs allowed Garden Parking

---

WOOTTON RIVERS   Map 5 SU16

PICK OF THE PUBS

Royal Oak ☻

SN8 4NQ ☎ 01672 810322 🖹 01672 811168
e-mail: royaloak35@hotmail.com
dir: *3m S from Marlborough*

Just 100 yards from the Kennet and Avon Canal, this 16th-century thatched and timbered inn presents a picture of rural idyll. It's also very handy for exploring the 2600 ancient oaks of Savernake Forest, as well as visiting Stonehenge, Avebury, Bath and Marlborough. The interior is as charming as the setting, comprising low-beamed ceilings, exposed brickwork and toasty open fires. Menus tend to be flexible, with an array of starters, main courses and fish dishes. Typical examples include starters of fresh pan-fried scallops with bacon and mushrooms; or home-made chicken liver and brandy pâté with berry compote, followed by green Thai chicken curry; Gloucester Old Spot pork with mustard mash; or rich beef and Burgundy casserole with a parsley dumpling. The Royal Oak has 20 years experience in hosting weddings, and holds a licence for civil ceremonies. Discos, parties, film screenings and meetings can also be accommodated.

Open all wk ⊕ FREE HOUSE ◀ Wadworth 6X, Guest ales inc local Ramsbury Bitter. ☻ 7 **Facilities** Family room Dogs allowed Garden Parking

---

WYLYE   Map 4 SU03

The Bell Inn ☻

High St BA12 0QP ☎ 01985 248338 🖹 01985 248491
dir: *From Salisbury take A36 N'bound to Warminster, then Wylye & A303 Honiton signed off A36. Follow signs for Wylye*

There's a wealth of old oak beams, log fires and an inglenook fireplace at this 14th-century coaching inn, situated in the pretty Wylye valley. Owned by the Hidden Brewery (located just two miles away in Dinton), and so Hidden beers are available, but thankfully, not too well hidden. Lunch and dinner menus feature mainly local ingredients.

Open all wk ⊕ FREE HOUSE ◀ Hidden Pint, Hidden Quest Hidden Oldsarum, Hidden Fantasy, Hidden Treasure, Hidden Pleasure. ☻ 10 **Facilities** Dogs allowed Garden Parking

---

WORCESTERSHIRE

ABBERLEY   Map 10 SO76

The Manor Arms at Abberley ☻

WR6 6BN ☎ 01299 896507 🖹 01299 896723
e-mail: themanorarms@btconnect.com
dir: *Signed from A443, Abberley B4202 towards Clows Top, right at village hall*

Set in the historic village of Abberley overlooking a picturesque valley, this 300-year-old inn has plenty of original features, including oak beams and a log-burning fire. Food options range from bar snacks to a full à la carte menu. Themed evenings include home-made curries on Monday nights and fresh fish and chips on Fridays. Fish and chips are also available to take away on Monday to Saturday evenings. Good choice of real ales.

Open noon-3 6-11.30 (Sat-Sun noon-11.30) Closed: Mon L **Bar Meals** L served Tue-Sun 12-2.30 booking required D served Mon-Sat 6-9 booking required Av main course £8.95 **Restaurant** L served Tue-Sun 12-2.30 D served Mon-Sat 6-9 Fixed menu price fr £10 ⊕ ENTERPRISE INNS ◀ Timothy Taylor, Hooky Bitter, Hereford HPA, Flowers IPA. ☻ 11 **Facilities** Children's menu Dogs allowed Garden Parking

BECKFORD Map 10 SO93

The Beckford ★★★ INN ♀

Cheltenham Rd GL20 7AN
☎ 01386 881532 📠 01386 882021
e-mail: norman@thebeckford.com
dir: On A46 (Evesham to Cheltenham road) 5m from M5 Junct 9

Parts of this traditional, family-run coaching inn date back to the 18th century, but extensive refurbishment has made sure things keep up to date without losing their charm. Field Marshall Montgomery was a welcome guest here in the 1960s when his niece was landlord. There's a pleasant bar area with a real fire, an attractive formal dining room and beautiful gardens. Menu choices include grilled seabass fillet in a seafood broth; venison steak on a confit of leeks; and wild mushroom risotto. There are ten rooms available.

Open all wk 11-11 (Sat-Sun 11am-11.30pm) Closed: 25 Dec eve & 26 Dec eve Bar Meals L served Mon-Fri 12-2.30, Sat-Sun 12-9.40 booking required D served Mon-Fri 6.30-9.40, Sat-Sun 12-9.40 booking required Av main course £13 Restaurant L served Mon-Fri 12-2.30, Sat-Sun 12-9.40 booking required D served Mon-Fri 6.30-9.40, Sat-Sun 12-9.40 booking required Fixed menu price fr £10 Av 3 course à la carte fr £13.95 ⊕ FREE HOUSE ◀ London Pride, Greene King Abbot, Marstons Pedigree Ō Stowford Press. ♀ 8 Facilities Children's menu Dogs allowed Garden Parking Rooms 10

BEWDLEY Map 10 SO77

Little Pack Horse ♀

31 High St DY12 2DH
☎ 01299 403762 📠 01299 403762
e-mail: enquires@littlepackhorse.co.uk
dir: From Kidderminster follow ring road & signs for Safari Park. Then follow signs for Bewdley over bridge, turn left, then right, right at top of Lax Lane. Pub in 20mtrs

The interior of this historic timber-framed inn is warmed by cosy log fires and lit by candles at night. There are low beams, an elm bar, and a small outside patio for alfresco summer dining. There are a great selection of real ales and ciders, and the finest, local produce is sourced with an emphasis on seasonality. Expect an impressive range of roasts like Packhorse mix roast using lamb, beef, pork, turkey and slow roasted duck leg.

Open all wk noon-2.30 6-11.30 (Sat-Sun noon-mdnt) Bar Meals food served all day Restaurant food served all day ⊕ PUNCH TAVERNS ◀ Theakstons Best Wye Valley HPA, Dorothy Goodbodies Golden Ale, Black Sheep Bitter, Shepherd Neame Spitfire Ō Stowford Press, Westons Organic, Thatchers Katy. ♀ 21 Facilities Children's menu Family room Dogs allowed Garden

The Mug House Inn & Angry Chef Restaurant ★★★★ INN ◉ ♀

12 Severnside North DY12 2EE
☎ 01299 402543 📠 01299 402543
e-mail: drew@mughousebewdley.co.uk
dir: A456 from Kidderminster to Bewdley. Pub in town on river

Nestled beside the River Severn in picturesque Bewdley, the inn's riverside seating area is popular on warmer days. The unusual name dates back to the 17th century, when 'mug house' was a popular term for an alehouse. Nowadays, visitors will find an extensive lunchtime bar menu, with carte options in the restaurant (a speciality is lobster cooked direct from a tank in the restaurant). Typical choices include chicken breast with chorizo, red pepper and tomato; and braised blade of beef with oxtail casserole. Why not stay over in one of the seven comfortable bedrooms?

Open all wk noon-11 Bar Meals L served Sun-Sat 12-2.30 Av main course £7.95 Restaurant L served Mon-Sat 12.2.30, Sun 12-5 D served Mon-Sat 6.30-9 booking required Av 3 course à la carte fr £20 ⊕ PUNCH TAVERNS ◀ Timothy Taylor Landlord, Wye Valley, Hereford Pale Ale, 2 guest ales Ō Westons Traditional Scrumpy. ♀ 10 Facilities Dogs allowed Garden Rooms 7

Woodcolliers Arms NEW ★★★ INN

76 Welch Gate DY12 2AU ☎ 01299 400589
e-mail: roger@woodcolliers.co.uk
dir: 2mins walk from No2 bus stop in Load Street, Bewdley. 3m from Kidderminster

Dating from before 1780, this family-run free house stands close to the centre of Bewdley and just across the river from the Severn Valley steam railway. Russian trained chef Boris Rumba serves a unique blend of freshly-prepared pub favourites and authentic Russian dishes. The regularly changing menu might offer mustard and herb crusted rack of lamb; steak and ale pie; Boyarsky salmon; or Sidrovka - loin of pork in cider and onion sauce. In winter there are warming bowls of Borsch or Imperial soup. Five generously-sized guest bedrooms are available.

Open all wk 5-12.30 (Sat 12.30pm-12.30am Sun 12.30-11) Bar Meals L served Sat-Sun 12.30-3 D served all wk 6-9 booking required Av main course £8.95 Restaurant L served Sat-Sun 12.30-3 booking required D served all wk 6-9 booking required Fixed menu price fr £8.95 Av 3 course à la carte fr £15 ⊕ OLIVERS INNS LTD ◀ Ludlow Gold, Hobsons Bitter, St George Friar Tuck Ō Thatchers Gold. Facilities Children's menu Dogs allowed Garden Parking Rooms 5

BRANSFORD Map 10 SO75

The Bear & Ragged Staff ♀

Station road WR6 5JH
☎ 01886 833399 📠 01886 833106
e-mail: mail@bear.uk.com
dir: 3m from Worcester or Malvern, clearly signed from A4103 or A449

Built in 1861 as an estate rent office, this lovely old pub's reputation is founded on good food. Wide choices are available: in the bar, beef pasanda curry and beer-battered, deep-fried haddock, for example and, in the restaurant, shallow-fried calf's liver in sage and black pepper butter; trio of English lamb; grilled Cornish Dover sole; and baked red onion savoury cheesecake. Sunday roast could be loin of Woodland pork, or prime Herefordshire beef.

Open all wk Closed: 25 Dec eve, 1 Jan eve ⊕ FREE HOUSE ◀ St Georges Best, Shepherd Neame Spitfire. ♀ 10 Facilities Garden Parking

BRETFORTON Map 10 SP04

PICK OF THE PUBS

The Fleece Inn ♀

The Cross WR11 7JE ☎ 01386 831173
e-mail: nigel@thefleeceinn.co.uk
dir: From Evesham follow signs for B4035 towards Chipping Campden. Through Badsey into Bretforton. Right at village hall, past church, pub in open parking area

Owned by the National Trust and its first licensed property, The Fleece, or The Ark as it is known locally, has been part of Cotswold history for six centuries. The beautiful timbered building was originally a longhouse, and its last private owner, Lola Taplin, who died in front of the fire in the snug in 1977, was a direct descendant of the man who built it. The pub is well known for its British Asparagus festival day, held in

continued

BRETFORTON *continued*

May every year, and fresh asparagus naturally features in the menu when in season. Typical dishes from a winter menu include oven-baked camembert with cranberry jelly followed by traditional local faggots with chive creamed potatoes: an evening-only treat is a choice of matured steaks served with hand cut chips and all the trimmings. There is always an impressive selection of guest ales. Look out for events throughout the year such as vintage and classic car meets, Fox's Morris (dancers) weekend and regular folk singers.

Open all wk 11-3 6-11 (11-11 in summer) **Bar Meals** L served Mon-Sat 12-2.30, Sun 12-4 D served Mon-Sat 6.30-9, Sun 6.30-8.30 ⊕ FREE HOUSE ◀ Buckle Street no 1 Bitter, Pig's Ear, Dog in the Fog, Pandora's Box ☼ Thatchers, Priors Tipple. ♈ 12 **Facilities** Play area Garden

---

CLENT	Map 10 SO97

The Bell & Cross ♈

Holy Cross DY9 9QL
☎ 01562 730319   📄 01562 731733
dir: *Telephone for directions*

Several rooms make up this award-winning pub at the foot of the Clent Hills, and there's a covered patio for pleasant alfresco dining. Recently refurbished, the building dates from the early 19th century, and today Roger Narbett serves modern British food in a traditional setting. Light bar lunches include toasted paninis, pasta and daily specials like cream of sweetcorn and coriander soup, or slow braised lamb with herb dumplings. The main menu might feature grilled sea bass with prawns; faggots, cheesy mash and mushy peas; or chargrilled sirloin steak.

Open all wk noon-3 6-11 Closed: 25 Dec **Bar Meals** L served all wk 12.2 D served Mon-Sat 6.30-9.15 booking required Av main course £11.03 **Restaurant** L served Mon-Sat 12-2, Sun 12-7 booking required D served Mon-Sat 6.30-9.15, Sun 12-7 booking required Fixed menu price fr £13.95 Av 3 course à la carte fr £18.50 ⊕ ENTERPRISE INNS ◀ Pedigree, Mild, Bitter, Timothy Taylor Landlord, guest ales. ♈ 14 **Facilities** Dogs allowed Garden Parking

---

CLOWS TOP	Map 10 SO77

PICK OF THE PUBS

The Colliers Arms ♈

Tenbury Rd DY14 9HA ☎ 01299 832242
e-mail: thecolliersarms@aol.com
dir: *On A456.11 Pub 4m from Bewdley & 7m from Kidderminster*

This is a popular, family-owned, traditional country free house with a bar, lounge area and separate restaurant. From the outside patio and beer garden you can enjoy the views of the largest Norman church in England at neighbouring Rock. The Colliers Arms has earned an

excellent reputation for the quality of its freshly prepared, home-made food, well-kept cask ales like Town Crier and first-class wines. At least half the ingredients used in cooking are sourced locally, a proportion that will increase with the pub's addition of a hugely productive vegetable, herb and fruit garden. On the lunch menu are beef Stroganoff with wild rice; and pork, apple and Shropshire Blue pie, while at dinner you might wish to order lamb cutlets with croquette potatoes and rosemary reduction; battered cod with coarse pea purée and home-made chips; papillote of gilthead bream with orange and fennel; and potato, spinach and cauliflower ragout.

Open noon-3 6-11 (Sat 11-11 Sun noon-4) Closed: Sun eve **Bar Meals** L served Mon-Fri 12-2, Sat 12-2.30, Sun 12-3 booking required D served Mon-Fri 6.30-9, Sat 6.30-9.30 booking required Av main course £10.95 **Restaurant** L served Mon-Fri 12-2, Sat 12-2.30, Sun 12-3 booking required D served Mon-Fri 6.30-9, Sat 6.30-9.30 booking required Fixed menu price fr £10.50 Av 3 course à la carte fr £20 ⊕ FREE HOUSE ◀ Hobsons Best, Town Crier, Guinness, guest ale. ♈ 14 **Facilities** Children's menu Dogs allowed Garden Parking

---

DROITWICH	Map 10 SO86

PICK OF THE PUBS

The Chequers ♈

Cutnall Green WR9 0PJ
☎ 01299 851292   📄 01299 851744
dir: *Telephone for directions*

A display of football memorabilia on the bar wall reveals that this is the home of Roger Narbett, chef to the England football team. He runs the Chequers with his wife Joanne, retaining its charming and traditional village pub atmosphere with open fire, panelled bar and richly coloured furnishings. A goodly range of real ales includes Banks and Enville ales. Next to the bar is the Garden Room with warmly painted walls, a plush sofa and hanging tankards. Lunchtime sandwiches and toasted paninis are backed by classics such as Scotch beef steak pie with neeps, mash and onion gravy; and slow braised lamb with herb dumplings and root vegetables. The carte includes starters of carrot, sweet potato and red lentil soup with garlic toasty. Typical main courses may proffer breast of pot roast Jimmy Butler's belly of pork, while desserts like treacle tart with granny's thick custard should not be missed.

Open all wk Closed: 25 Dec, 1 Jan **Bar Meals** L served Mon-Sat 12-2, Sun 12-2.30 D served Mon-Sun 6.30-9.15 Av main course £10.75 **Restaurant** L served Mon-Sat 12-2, Sun 12-2.30 booking required D served Mon-Sun 6.30-9.15 booking required Fixed menu price fr £11.50 Av 3 course à la carte fr £18.50 ⊕ ENTERPRISE INNS ◀ Timothy Taylor, Enville Ale, Banks Bitter, Banks Mild, Hook Norton, Ruddles. ♈ 11 **Facilities** Children's menu Family room Dogs allowed Garden Parking

The Honey Bee NEW ♈

Doverdale Ln, Doverdale WR9 0QB ☎ 01299 851620
e-mail: honey@king-henrys-taverns.co.uk
dir: *Please telephone for directions*

'It's buzzin' at The Honey Bee but you won't get stung!' So say King Henry's Taverns, which owns this beekeeping-themed pub, with working beehives and a children's area containing an enormous beehive plaything. All the group's establishments offer a standard menu that covers most pub grub eventualities - steak and ale pie; whole roast chicken; pan-fried fillets of plaice; rump, fillet and rib steaks; lamb rogan josh; vegetarian balti; and broccoli and cream cheese bake.

Open all day all wk noon-10 **Bar Meals** Av main course £3 food served all day **Restaurant** food served all day ⊕ KING HENRY TAVERNS ◀ Guinness, Greene King IPA, Marstons Pedigree. ♈ 15 **Facilities** Children's menu Play area Family room Garden Parking

---

The Old Cock Inn ♈

Friar St WR9 8EQ ☎ 01905 774233
dir: *M5 junct 5, A449 in Droitwich town centre opposite theatre*

Three stained-glass windows, rescued from a church destroyed during the Civil War, are a feature of this charming pub, first licensed during the reign of Queen Anne. The stone carving above the front entrance is believed to portray Judge Jeffreys, who presided over the local magistrates' court. A varied menu, including snacks and more substantial dishes - beer battered fish and chips, vegetarian risotto, and local sausages and mash - is supplemented by the daily specials.

Open all wk ⊕ MARSTONS ◀ 3 guest ales. ♈ 8 **Facilities** Dogs allowed Garden

---

FLADBURY	Map 10 SO94

Chequers Inn

Chequers Ln WR10 2PZ ☎ 01386 860276
e-mail: chequersinn@btinternet.com
dir: *Off A4538 between Evesham & Pershore*

The Chequers is a 14th-century inn with plenty of beams and an open fire, tucked away in a pretty village with views of the glorious Bredon Hills. Local produce from the Vale of Evesham provides the basis for home-cooked dishes offered from the monthly-changing menu, plus a choice of daily specials. There is also a traditional Sunday carvery. The pretty walled garden enjoys outstanding views, and the nearby River Avon is ideal for walking.

Open all wk 11.30-2.30 6-11 (Sun 11.30-3.30) **Bar Meals** L served all wk 12-2 D served Mon-Sat 6-9 ⊕ Enterprise Inns ◀ Purity, Bombadier Real Ales. **Facilities** Children's menu Garden Parking

FLYFORD FLAVELL Map 10 SO95

The Boot Inn ★★★★ INN 🍽

Radford Rd WR7 4BS
☎ 01386 462658 📠 01386 462547
e-mail: enquiries@thebootinn.com
web: www.thebootinn.com
dir: From Worcester take A422 towards Stratford. Turn right to village

Parts of this family-run coaching inn date back to the 13th century, as heavy beams and slanting doorways attest. The large bar area is comfortable, with pool table and TV in a separate room. Good food is served by friendly staff, and may include mains like minted lamb and spinach curry or grilled swordfish steak with pink peppercorn sauce. Outside are gardens front and back, with a heated patio and sheltered smoking area. Five charming bedrooms in the converted coach house complete the picture.

Open all wk noon-mdnt (25 Dec noon-2) Bar Meals L served all wk 12-2 D served all wk 6.30-10 Restaurant L served all wk 12-2 D served all wk 6.30-10 ⊕ PUNCH TAVERNS ◀ Old Speckled Hen, London Pride, John Smith's Tribute. 🍷 8 Facilities Children's menu Dogs allowed Garden Parking Rooms 5

KEMPSEY Map 10 SO84

PICK OF THE PUBS

Walter de Cantelupe Inn ★★★ INN

See Pick of the Pubs on page 508

KINGTON Map 10 SO95

PICK OF THE PUBS

The Red Hart 🍽

Stratford Rd WR7 4DD
☎ 01386 792559 📠 01386 793748
dir: M5 junct 6, A4538. Then A422 towards Stratford-upon-Avon. Right for Kington. From Redditch A441, right onto A422, left for Kington

This beautiful, easy-going country pub and restaurant was created from a derelict shell in 2001 by a team of local craftsmen. The interior has been stripped to reveal its original looks, while some stunning contemporary touches have been added. The main bar is furnished in wine bar style, while the secondary bar area boasts deep leather sofas surrounding a log burner. The restaurant is also smart and full of atmosphere. Like the interior, the food is classy yet unpretentious. You could start with moules marinière and crusty bread or sweet potato and rosemary risotto, then move on to local game casserole with suet dumplings; beer battered fish and chips; or grilled sea bass with saffron linguine and Provençale vegetables. Lunch brings home-made soup, simple pasta dishes and perhaps bangers and mash. Heated log burners are dotted strategically around the outside decking.

Open all wk ⊕ MARSTONS ◀ Banks, Marstons, Pedigree. 🍷 10 Facilities Dogs allowed Garden Parking

KNIGHTWICK Map 10 SO75

PICK OF THE PUBS

The Talbot 🍽

WR6 5PH ☎ 01886 821235 📠 01886 821060
e-mail: admin@the-talbot.co.uk
dir: A44 (Leominster road) through Worcester, 8m W right onto B4197 at River Teme bridge

The late 14th-century coaching inn has been owned by the Clift family for over 25 years and is run by Annie Clift and her team. Over the years they have developed their own style and are firmly rooted in the traditions and produce of the Teme Valley. Nearly everything is made in house, including bread, preserves, black pudding, raised pies and so on. The inn has a large kitchen garden run on organic principles, which produces a wide range of salads, herbs and, of course, vegetables. Sausages, hams, bacon and cheeses are sourced from local suppliers. The Talbot is also the home of The Teme Valley Brewery, started in 1997, using hops grown in the parish. The cask conditioned ales, all on hand pump in the bar, are called This, That, T'Other and Wot. Wot is a seasonal brew, so there is Spring Wot, Wassail Wot, and Wotever Next.

Open all day all wk 7.30am-11.30pm Closed: 25 Dec pm Bar Meals L served all wk 12-2 D served all wk 6.30-9 Av main course £16 Restaurant D served all wk 6.30-9 booking required Fixed menu price fr £27 Av 3 course à la carte fr £38 ⊕ FREE HOUSE ◀ Teme Valley This, That , T'Other & Wot, Hobsons Best Bitter Choice. 🍷 9 Facilities Children's menu Dogs allowed Garden Parking

MALVERN Map 10 SO74

The Anchor Inn 🍽

Drake St, Welland WR13 6LN ☎ 01684 592317
e-mail: theanchor13@hotmail.com
dir: M50 junct 1, A38 follow signs for Upton upon Severn. Left onto A4104, through Upton upon Severn, 2.5m. Pub on right

The attractive 17th-century Anchor Inn has spectacular views of the Malvern Hills. There's a garden for warmer weather and a welcoming winter fire in the dining room. Fresh, quality food is cooked to order. Light bites and main meals are marked up on the chalkboard, with dishes such as pork loin stuffed with apple in stilton sauce, steak and kidney pie, and shank of lamb simmered in mint and rosemary gravy. Themed menus and quiz nights feature regularly. The inn has won awards from Britain in Bloom.

Closed: Sun eve Bar Meals L served all wk 12-2 D served Mon-Sat 7-9 booking required Av main course £9.99 Restaurant L served all wk 12-2 D served Mon-Sat 7-9 booking required ⊕ FREE HOUSE ◀ Black Sheep, Woods, Hook Norton, Greene King, Malvern Hills. 🍷 20 Facilities Children's menu Family room Garden Parking

The Red Lion

4 St Ann's Rd WR14 4RG ☎ 01684 564787
e-mail: johnholmes25@btintenet.com
dir: In town centre

An authentic Thai restaurant complete with chefs and waitresses from the Land of Smiles has been added to this thriving pub. The existing pub menu continues to be available, offering a wide choice of snacks, starters and main courses, all freshly cooked to order. Seafood is a particular speciality: try pan-fried king prawns, or a hearty paella. One of the main walking routes in the Malvern Hills runs right by, so expect plenty of ramblers.

Open all wk ⊕ MARSTONS ◀ Marstons Bitter, 4 guest ales. Facilities Garden

PICK OF THE PUBS

Walter de Cantelupe Inn ★★★ INN

KEMPSEY   Map 10 SO84

Main Rd WR5 3NA ☎ **01905 820572**
dir: *4m S of Worcester city centre on A38.
Pub in village centre*

With its whitewashed walls bedecked with flowers, this privately owned and run free house dates in part from the 17th century. One of the bedrooms in the oldest part of the inn is said to be haunted. Outside, a walled and paved garden has been fragrantly planted with clematis, roses and honeysuckle, and its south-facing position can be a real sun-trap. The inn commemorates a 13th-century Bishop of Worcester, who was strongly against his parishioners' habit of brewing and selling ales as a way to raise church funds, so its naming three centuries later was probably a bit of 16th-century irony on the part of the locals. The menu is written up each day on a blackboard, with choices to appeal to both traditionalists and those seeking something more contemporary. You could begin with leek and potato soup served with crusty granary bread; or perhaps king prawns with Marie Rose sauce. Main courses might include baked sea bass with lemon butter sauce; beef and local ale pie with shortcrust pastry; seared duck breast with honey and thyme sauce; and wild mushroom, spinach and ricotta filo parcel. Then you could finish with hot banana bread and butter pudding with chocolate sauce; or a plate of British cheeses with Cantelupe chutney (in good years grapes from the pub's own vines appear alongside). Three or four cask ales are usually on offer, including Cannon Royal Brewery's King's Shilling from nearby Uphampton. The pub's en suite accommodation is modelled on 'a friend's home' rather than a 'stereotypical motel'.

Closed: 25-26 Dec, 1 Jan, Mon (ex BHs)
Restaurant ⊕ FREE HOUSE ◀ Timothy Taylor Landlord, Cannon Royal, Kings Shilling, Hobsons Best Bitter.
Facilities Dogs allowed Garden Parking
Rooms 3

MARTLEY
Map 10 SO76

Admiral Rodney Inn ★★★★ INN

Berrow Green WR6 6PL ☎ **01886 821375**
e-mail: rodney@admiral.fslife.co.uk
web: www.admiral-rodney.co.uk
dir: M5 junct 7, A44 signed Leominster. Approx 7m at
Knightwick right onto B4197. Inn 2m on left at Berrow
Green

This early 17th-century farmhouse-cum-alehouse stands
in the heart of the countryside on the Worcester Way
footpath. The stylishly traditional interior includes a
split-level restaurant housed in an old barn.
Herefordshire steaks feature strongly, along with dishes
like lamb shank with mustard mash, home-made pies,
fish and chips, and a choice of vegetarian fare; all
washed down with a pint of Wye Valley Bitter. En suite
bedrooms and a skittle alley are also available.

Open all wk noon-3 5-11 (Mon 5-11 Sat noon-11 Sun
noon-10.30) **Bar Meals** L served Tue-Sat 12.30-2.30, Sun
12-4 D served all wk 6.30-9 Av main course £10
Restaurant L served Tue-Sat 12.30-2.30, Sun 12-4 D
served all wk 6.30-9 Fixed menu price fr £7.95 ⊕ FREE
HOUSE ◀ Wye Valley Bitter, local guest ales eg Black
Pear, Malvern Hills Brewery, Muzzle Loader, Cannon
Royal. **Facilities** Children's menu Dogs allowed Garden
Parking **Rooms** 3

The Crown Inn

Berrow Green Rd WR6 6PA ☎ **01886 888840**
dir: 7m W of Worcester on B4204

Once the scene of an unlikely gig by Eric Clapton, the
Crown is a Victorian village pub with a large extension
formed from redundant outbuildings, which now houses
the dining area. In one bar is an open fire, Sky TV, pool
table and jukebox, while the other has dining tables and
French windows to the garden. This great community pub
is on the Worcester Way, so many visitors tend to be
walkers. Locally sourced, freshly cooked food includes
10oz Kobe beefburger; lamb and mint sausages; Thai fish
curry; and penne pasta with creamy goats' cheese sauce.

Open all wk noon-11 (Fri-Sat noon-mdnt Sun noon-
10.30) **Bar Meals** L served Mon-Sat 12-2, Sun 12-3 D
served Mon-Sat 6-9 Av main course £8.50 **Restaurant** L
served Mon-Sat 12-2, Sun 12-3 D served Mon-Sat 6-9 Av
3 course à la carte fr £17.65 ⊕ MARSTONS ◀ Banks
Bitter, Banks Mild. **Facilities** Children's menu Play area
Dogs allowed Garden Parking

OMBERSLEY
Map 10 SO86

PICK OF THE PUBS

Crown & Sandys Arms ♥

Main Rd WR9 0EW
☎ **01905 620252** 📠 **01905 620769**
e-mail: enquiries@crownandsandys.co.uk
dir: 3m from Droitwich, off A449, 6m off junct 6 &
junct 5 of M5

After being closed for nearly a year for complete
refurbishment, this classy establishment run by
Richard and Rachael Everton reopened its doors in May
2009. The decor is bang up-to-date, yet the original
beams and fireplaces seem to blend effortlessly with
the trendy furnishings. Expect the same focus on well-
kept real ales, ciders from Thatchers and Aspall, a
smoothly managed food operation and excellent
service. Regular 'wine dinners' and themed evenings
continue, complementing the modern menus which
burst with the latest flavours. The full carte is backed
by a weekly specials list, and customers can choose
between three dining areas: the Orangery, the Bistro
and the Bar. Starters may include potted salmon and
crab with hot toasted crumpets. Main dishes offer
favourites like fish and home-cut chips; steak and
kidney pudding; and steaks of best Scottish beef.
Desserts such as lemon, sultana and treacle steamed
sponge with custard will not be resisted.

Open all wk noon-3 5-11 (ex BH) **Bar Meals** L served
all wk 12-2.30 D served all wk 6-9.30 booking required
Av main course £10 **Restaurant** L served all wk
12-2.30 booking required D served all wk 6-9.30
booking required Av 3 course à la carte fr £20 ⊕ FREE
HOUSE ◀ Sadlers Ale, Marstons, Woods Shropshire
Lad, Burtons Bitter, Marstons Pedigree, Greene King
IPA Ò Thatchers, Aspall. ♥ 16 **Facilities** Children's
menu Garden Parking

POWICK
Map 10 SO85

The Halfway House Inn

Bastonford WR2 4SL
☎ **01905 831098** 📠 **01905 831704**
dir: From A15 junct 7 take A4440 then A449

Situated on the A449 between Worcester and Malvern,
this delightful pub is just a few minutes' drive from the
picturesque spa town of Malvern, a popular centre for
exploring the Malvern Hills. The menu choice ranges from
Herefordshire fillet steak or roasted Gressingham duck
breast to baked fillet of Scottish salmon and spinach,
ricotta and beef tomato lasagne.

Open noon-3 6-11 Closed: Mon L (ex BH) **Bar Meals** Av
main course £6 **Restaurant** Av 3 course à la carte fr
£20 ⊕ FREE HOUSE ◀ Abbot Ale, St Georges Bitter,
Fuller's London Pride, Timothy Taylor. **Facilities** Play area
Garden Parking

STONEHALL
Map 10 SO84

The Inn at Stonehall

Stonehall Common WR5 3QG ☎ **01905 820462**
dir: 2m from M5 junct 7. Stonehall Common 1.5m from St
Peters Garden Centre Norton

Formerly The Fruiterer's Arms, because local fruit pickers
used to drink here, the name change follows the new
owner's refurbishment that has created a comfortable
bar area with open log fire, private dining room in
addition to the restaurant and an open kitchen. Here,
Rick Stein and Shaun Hill disciple Dwight Clayton, works
his magic preparing modern British cooking with a
French influence, such as lamb and rosemary pie,
sautéed potatoes and mangetout; pan-fried bream,
sautéed spinach and fish nage; and sweet potato and
parsnip tarte Tatin.

Open all wk noon-2.30 6-11 (Sun & Mon noon-2.30)
Closed: Sun & Mon eve **Bar Meals** L served Tue-Sat
12-2.30, Sun 12-3 Av main course £7 **Restaurant** L
served Tue-Sat 12-2.30, Sun 12-3 D served Tue-Sat
6.30-9.30 Av 3 course à la carte fr £25 ⊕ FREE
HOUSE ◀ St Austell Tribute, guest ales. **Facilities** Play
area Garden Parking

TENBURY WELLS
Map 10 SO56

PICK OF THE PUBS

The Peacock Inn

WR15 8LL ☎ **01584 810506**
e-mail: info@the-peacock-at-boraston.co.uk
dir: On A456 (Kidderminster to Tenbury Wells)

A 14th-century coaching inn with a sympathetic
extension overlooking the River Teme. A pleasant patio
eating area means you can relax outside and enjoy the
views over the valley in summer. The inviting bars and
oak-panelled restaurant are enhanced by oak beams,
dried hops and open log fires, while upstairs the ghost
of Mrs Brown, a former landlady, does her best to make
her presence felt. Produce from local markets and
specialist suppliers is used for the menus, which cover
an eclectic mix of reasonably priced dishes. The bar
menu ranges from a three-egg omelette with choice of
fillings and served with chips; to chilli con carne; or
rendang pedis - a home-made Indonesian beef curry
made to a traditional family recipe. Other main courses
tend towards the more usual: spicy meatballs;
wholetail scampi; creamy pasta bake; and barbecued
chicken fillet are among the choices.

Open noon-3 6-11 Closed: Sun eve **Bar Meals** L served
all wk 12-2.30 D served Mon-Sat 6.30-8.30
Restaurant L served all wk 12-2.30 booking required D
served Mon-Sat 7-8.30 booking required ⊕ PUNCH
TAVERNS ◀ Hobsons Best Bitter, Spitfire, guest
ale Ò Stowford Press, Westons Organic.
Facilities Children's menu Dogs allowed Garden
Parking

UPTON SNODSBURY — Map 10 SO95

Bants ★★★★ INN ☕

Worcester Rd WR7 4NN
☎ 01905 381282 📠 01905 381173
e-mail: info@bants.co.uk
dir: *Exit M5 junct 6, follow Evesham signs. At 2nd rdbt left onto A422 towards Stratford. Bants 2m on left*

Named after the owners, Sue and Steve Bant, who have been running the pub for nearly 25 years, this is a 16th-century free house serving traditional ales, with real fires in winter warming an eclectic mix of ancient beams and modern furnishings. Traditional dishes are served with a modern twist and are served in three lounge bars and the dedicated conservatory restaurant which has a high comfort factor: you may find faggots with garlic mash, or corned beef hash on bubble and squeak with fried egg. There are eight en suite rooms available.

Open all wk **Bar Meals** Av main course £8 **Restaurant** Fixed menu price fr £12 Av 3 course à la carte fr £20 ⊕ FREE HOUSE ◀ Guinness, London Pride, Cats Whiskas, Pettermans. ☕ 6 **Facilities** Garden Parking **Rooms** 8

YORKSHIRE, EAST RIDING OF

BEVERLEY — Map 17 TA03

White Horse Inn

22 Hengate HU17 8BN ☎ 01482 861973
dir: *A1079 from York to Beverley*

Gas lighting, open fires, old cartoons and high-backed settles add to the charm of this classic 16th-century local. John Wesley preached in the back yard in the mid-18th century, and the pub's atmospheric little rooms arranged around the central bar are probably much as they were back then. Traditional bar food might include pasta dishes, fresh jumbo haddock, bangers and mash, and steak and ale pie. Toasted and plain sandwiches and daily specials also feature.

Open all day all wk 11am-11pm (Sun noon-10.30pm) **Bar Meals** L served all wk 12-2.30 ⊕ SAMUEL SMITH ◀ Samuel Smith Old Brewery Bitter, Sovereign Bitter. **Facilities** Play area Family room Garden Parking **Notes** ⊗

DRIFFIELD — Map 17 TA05

Best Western The Bell ★★★ HL

46 Market Place YO25 6AN
☎ 01377 256661 📠 01377 253228
e-mail: bell@bestwestern.co.uk
dir: *Enter town from A164, right at lights. Car park 50yds on left behind black railings*

A delightful 18th-century coaching inn furnished with antiques, with an oak-panelled bar serving a good range of cask beers and 300 whiskies. Food ranges through broiled salmon fillet cooked with red peppers, lemon, garlic and capers; roasted whole pork fillet coated with honey and Dijon mustard; and oven roasted breast of English duckling with spicy plum sauce. Fresh coffee is served in the mornings 9.30-11.30 with scones, jam and cream.

Open all wk Closed: 25 Dec, 1 Jan ⊕ FREE HOUSE ◀ Wold Top, Falling Stones, Mars Magic, Hambleton Stallion & Stud, Tom Wood Shepherds Delight. **Facilities** Parking **Rooms** 16

FLAMBOROUGH — Map 17 TA27

The Seabirds Inn ☕

Tower St YO15 1PD ☎ 01262 850242 📠 01262 851874
dir: *On B1255 E of Bridlington, 6m from train station*

Head westwards from famous Flamborough Head and you'll swiftly arrive at this 200-year-old village pub. Good eating is the emphasis here, with a daily changing specials board that includes seasonal fresh fish: typical examples are sea bass served whole with garlic butter prawns; halibut supreme in a prawn and champagne sauce; and home-made luxury fish pie with monkfish, scallops and salmon. Meat options include steaks, loin of pork, and chicken breast stuffed with apricot stilton.

Open noon-3 6-11 Closed: Mon (winter) **Bar Meals** L served all wk 12-2 D served Sun-Fri 6-8.30, Sat 6-9.30 Av main course £7 **Restaurant** L served all wk 12-2 D served Sun-Fri 6-8.30, Sat 6-9.30 booking required Fixed menu price fr £6.95 Av 3 course à la carte fr £18 ⊕ FREE HOUSE ◀ John Smith's, Interbrew Boddingtons Bitter, Tetleys Creamflow. ☕ 9 **Facilities** Children's menu Dogs allowed Garden Parking

HOLME UPON SPALDING MOOR — Map 17 SE83

Ye Olde Red Lion Hotel ☕

Old Rd YO43 4AD ☎ 01430 860220 📠 01430 861471
dir: *Off A1079 (York to Hull road). At Market Weighton take A614. Right at painted rdbt in village centre, 100yds, right then 1st left*

A historic 17th-century coaching inn that once provided hospitality for weary travellers who were helped across the marshes by monks. It's still a great refuge, with a friendly atmosphere, oak beams and a cosy fire. The inspiring menu could include oven-baked duck breast with star anise sauce, corn fed chicken coq-au-vin or pan-seared sea bass with wilted greens and vièrge sauce.

Open 11-3 5-11 (Mon 5-11) Closed: Mon until 5pm **Bar Meals** L served Tue-Sun 12-2 D served Tue-Sun 5.30-9 ⊕ Enterprise Inns ◀ John Smiths, Black Sheep, Guinness. ☕ 9 **Facilities** Children's menu Garden Parking

HUGGATE — Map 19 SE85

The Wolds Inn ★★★ INN ☕

YO42 1YH ☎ 01377 288217
e-mail: huggate@woldsinn.freeserve.co.uk
dir: *S off A166 between York & Driffield*

Probably the highest inn on the Yorkshire Wolds, this family-run hostelry is 16th century in origin, with tiled roofs and white-painted chimneys, and a wood-panelled interior with open fires and gleaming brassware. The robust menu includes dishes such as steak pie, fillet of plaice, chicken breast wrapped in bacon, grills, or a selection of jackets, baguettes and sandwiches. For a "mixed grill to remember", try the Wolds Topper.

Open noon-2 6.30-11 (Fri-Sat 5-11 Sun 5-10.30) Closed: Mon (ex BH) **Bar Meals** L served Tue-Sun 12-2 D served Tue-Thu 6.30-9, Fri-Sun 5-9 booking required Av main course £8 **Restaurant** L served Sun 12-2 D served Tue-Thu 6.30-9, Fri-Sun 5-9 booking required Av 3 course à la carte fr £18 ⊕ FREE HOUSE ◀ Tetley Bitter, Timothy Taylor Landlord. ☕ 10 **Facilities** Children's menu Garden Parking **Rooms** 3

KILHAM   Map 17 TA06

The Old Star Inn ♛

Church St YO25 4RG ☎ 01262 420619
e-mail: oldstarkilham@hotmail.com
dir: *Between Driffield & Bridlington on A164. 6m from Driffield. 9m from Bridlington*

Situated in the historic village of Kilham, with easy access to Bridlington, Scarborough and the Yorkshire Wolds, this quaint pub offers home-cooked food, a good selection of real ales and a warm welcome. Food is sourced from local suppliers, with particular attention to reducing the travelling time of ingredients. Special diets are catered for, and children have half price portions. John Smiths is the resident beer, the three other pumps operating a rotation of guest ales.

Open all wk 5-11 (Mon 6-11 Fri noon-2 4-11 Sat noon-2.30 5.30-11 Sun noon-10.30) Closed: Mon-Thu L **Bar Meals** L served Fri-Sat 12-2, Sun 12-5 D served Tue-Fri 5-8.30, Sat 5.30-8.30 Av main course £8 **Restaurant** L served Sun 12-5 booking required booking required Av 3 course à la carte fr £20 ⊕ FREE HOUSE ◀ John Smiths Cask, Deuchars, Theakstons, Black Sheep, Daleside, guest ales. ♛ 7 **Facilities** Children's menu Dogs allowed Garden Parking

LOW CATTON   Map 17 SE75

The Gold Cup Inn ♛

YO41 1EA ☎ 01759 371354
dir: *1m S of A166 or 1m N of A1079, E of York*

Solid tables and pews - reputedly made from a single oak tree - feature in the restaurant of this 300-year-old, family-run free house. There's a large beer garden, and the adjoining paddock drops down to the River Derwent. On the menu expect to find braised beef in red wine gravy on mashed potato; grilled gammon with port and mushroom sauce; baked cod loins with herb crust; and deep-fried brie with cranberry and orange dip.

Open noon-2.30 6-11 (Sat-Sun noon-11) Closed: Mon L **Bar Meals** L served Tue-Fri 12-2.30, Sat-Sun 12-6 D served all wk 6-9 Av main course £8.25 **Restaurant** L served Sun 12-5.30 booking required D served all wk 6-9 booking required Fixed menu price fr £12.5 Av 3 course à la carte fr £20 ⊕ FREE HOUSE ◀ John Smiths, Theakstons. ♛ 15 **Facilities** Children's menu Play area Dogs allowed Garden Parking

LUND   Map 17 SE94

The Wellington Inn ♛

19 The Green YO25 9TE
☎ 01377 217294   📠 01377 217192
dir: *On B1248 NE of Beverley*

Nicely situated opposite the picture-postcard village green, the Wellington Inn is popular with locals and visitors alike, whether for a pint of real ale, a glass of house wine, or a plate of decent food. You can choose to eat from the bar menu or à la carte, and there's an extensive wine list. Expect king scallops with bacon and garlic risotto; or perhaps beef, mushroom and red onion suet pudding.

Closed: Mon L **Bar Meals** L served Tue-Sun 12-2 D served Tue-Sat 6.30-9 Av main course £13.95 **Restaurant** D served Tue-Sat 7-9 booking required Av 3 course à la carte fr £26 ⊕ FREE HOUSE ◀ Timothy Taylor Landlord, Black Sheep Best, John Smiths, regular guest, Copper Dragon. ♛ 8 **Facilities** Children's menu Garden Parking

SOUTH CAVE   Map 17 SE93

The Fox and Coney Inn ♛

52 Market Place HU15 2AT
☎ 01430 424336   📄 01430 421552
e-mail: foxandconey@mail.com
dir: *4m E of M62 on A63. 4m N of Brough mainline railway*

Right in the heart of South Cave, this family run pub dates from 1739 and is probably the oldest building in the village. The inn, which is handy for walkers on the nearby Wolds Way, was known simply as The Fox until William Goodlad added the Coney (rabbit) in 1788. Sample starters such as smoked fishcakes or grilled field mushroom with goats' cheese, before moving on to steak and ale pie, pasta carbonara, Thai red curry or Toulouse sausage. Vegetarians and other dietary requirements are well catered for.

Open all wk 11.30-11 **Bar Meals** L served Mon-Sat 12-2.30, Sun 12-8 D served Mon-Sat 5-9, Sun 12-8 Av main course £7.50 **Restaurant** L served Mon-Sat 12-2.30, Sun 12-8 D served Mon-Sat 5-9, Sun 12-8 Av 3 course à la carte fr £20 ⊕ ENTERPRISE INNS ◀ Timothy Taylor Landlord, John Smiths & Theakston Cool Cask, Deuchars IPA, guest ales. ♛ 10 **Facilities** Family room Dogs allowed Garden Parking

SOUTH DALTON   Map 17 SE94

PICK OF THE PUBS

The Pipe & Glass Inn ◉ ♛

See Pick of the Pubs on page 512

SUTTON UPON DERWENT   Map 17 SE74

St Vincent Arms ♛

Main St YO41 4BN ☎ 01904 608349
e-mail: enquiries@stvincentarms.co.uk
dir: *From A64 follow signs for A1079. Turn right, follow signs for Elvington on B1228. Through Elvington to Sutton upon Derwent*

The name comes from John Jervis, created the first Earl of St Vincent in the 18th century, and mentor to Admiral Lord Nelson. This is a warm family-run pub with an old-fashioned welcoming atmosphere, minus music or gaming machines but plus great food and good selection of beer. Food options include sandwiches, ciabatta, salads, steaks and scampi at lunch, and in the evening dishes such as loin of cod with tomato and pepper stew, or rabbit pie.

Open all wk **Bar Meals** L served all wk 12-2 D served all wk 6.30-9.30 **Restaurant** L served all wk 12-2 D served all wk 6.30-9.30 ⊕ FREE HOUSE ◀ Timothy Taylor Landlord, Fuller's ESB, Yorkshire Terrier, Wells Bombardier, Fuller's London Pride, Old Mill Bitter, York Brewery Terrier. ♛ 19 **Facilities** Garden Parking

PICK OF THE PUBS

The Pipe & Glass Inn ⊛ ♉

SOUTH DALTON   Map 17 SE94

West End HU17 7PN ☎ 01430 810246
e-mail: email@pipeandglass.co.uk
web: www.pipeandglass.co.uk
dir: *Just off B1248 (Beverley to Malton road). 7m from Beverley*

The present building, part 15th century, part 17th, stands on the site of the original gatehouse to Dalton Hall, the family seat of Lord Hotham. It was where visitors to the 'great house' stayed. When James and Kate Mackenzie took over in 2006, they undertook a full refurbishment, making sure they kept a country pub feel in the bar, while giving the restaurant a more contemporary look. A large conservatory looking out over the garden houses a magnificent long table seating twenty-four, and there is also plenty more room for dining in the garden. James uses as much local and seasonal produce as possible for his regularly changing menus, from which come starters of oak-smoked salmon with smoked eel, potato and horseradish salad; and potted spiced Gloucester Old Spot pork with sticky apples and crackling salad. Mains include roast Burdass lamb (from the Yorkshire Wolds) with braised mutton and kidney faggot, champ potato, broad beans and nettle and mint sauce; grilled sirloin steak with sautéed sea salt and thyme potatoes, green peppercorn sauce, ox tongue and shallot salad; fillet of Filey Bay sea bass with braised gem lettuce, ceps and oyster sauce; and baked Yorkshire field mushroom and spinach tart with 'Lincolnshire poacher' rarebit, poached egg and hazelnut pesto. Desserts are equally tempting, with lemon verbena burnt cream and spiced summer berries; sticky toffee pudding with stout ice cream and walnut praline; and fresh strawberries, syllabub and sorbet with elderflower shortbread. The wines are sourced entirely from small producers, so there's an interesting story behind every one. Regularly changing hand-pulled ales include guests from the Copper Dragon, Wold Top and Black Sheep. Westons Old Rosie scrumpy cider has nothing to do with Laurie Lee, but is named after a traction engine owned by its makers.

Open 12-3 6.30-11 (Sun 12-10.30) Closed: 1 week Jan, Mon (ex BHs) **Bar Meals** L served Tue-Sun 12-2 D served Tue-Sat 6.30-9.30 Av main course £14.95 **Restaurant** L served Tue-Sat 12-2 (Sun 12-4) D served Tue-Sat 6.30-9.30 Av 3 course à la carte fr £29 ⊕ FREE HOUSE ◖ Wold Top, Copper Dragon, Black Sheep, Cropton, John Smiths ♻ Old Rosie. ♉ 10 **Facilities** Children's menu Garden Parking

YORKSHIRE, NORTH

AKEBAR
Map 19 SE19

The Friar's Head ☙

Akebar Park DL8 5LY
☎ 01677 450201 & 450591 ▯ 01677 450046
e-mail: info@akebarpark.com
dir: From A1 at Leeming Bar onto A684, 7m towards Leyburn. Entrance at Akebar Park

A typical stone-built Dales pub at the entrance to a stunning, peaceful holiday park, The Friar's Head overlooks beautiful countryside and grounds, where bowls or croquet can be played on the lawn. The large south-facing conservatory dining room called The Cloister is a stunning feature, particularly by candlelight, with its stone flags, lush planting and fruiting vines. Hand-pulled local ales are served, and typical dishes include beef and mushrooms in Dijon mustard cream sauce, and halibut steak with white wine cream sauce.

Open all wk 10-3 6-11.30 (Fri-Sun 10am-11.30pm Jul-Sep) Closed: 25 Dec, 26 Dec eve & 1 Jan **Bar Meals** L served all wk 12-2.30 D served all wk 6-9.30 **Restaurant** L served all wk 12-2.30 booking required D served all wk 6-9.30 booking required ⊕ FREE HOUSE ◀ John Smiths & Theakston Best Bitter, Black Sheep Best, Timothy Taylor Landlord. ☙ 14 **Facilities** Children's menu Garden Parking

APPLETON-LE-MOORS
Map 19 SE78

The Moors Inn

YO62 6TF ☎ 01751 417435
e-mail: enquiries@moorsinn.co.uk
dir: On A170 between Pickering & Kirbymoorside

Whether you're interested in walking or sightseeing by car, this family-run inn is a good choice for its location and good home-cooked food. Set in a small moors village with lovely scenery in every direction, in summer you can sit in the large garden and enjoy the splendid views. Dishes include pheasant casserole and fish pie, and in addition to hand-pumped Black Bull and Black Sheep, there is a selection of 50 malt whiskies.

Open 7-close (Sun noon-2 7-close) Closed: Mon **Bar Meals** L served Sun 12-2 booking required D served Tue-Sun 7-9 booking required **Restaurant** L served Sun 12-2 booking required D served Tue-Sun 7-9 booking required ⊕ FREE HOUSE ◀ Black Sheep, Black Bull Ŏ Stowford Press. **Facilities** Children's menu Dogs allowed Garden Parking **Notes** ⊛

APPLETREEWICK
Map 19 SE06

The Craven Arms ☙

BD23 6DA ☎ 01756 720270
e-mail: thecravenarms@ukonline.co.uk
dir: From Skipton take A59 towards Harrogate, B6160 N. Village signed on right. Pub just outside village

This 16th-century Dales pub, with spectacular views of the River Wharfe and Simon's Seat, was originally a farm and later used as a weaving shed and courthouse. The village stocks are still outside. The building retains its original beams, flagstone floors and magnificent fireplace. Ten cask beers are served all year round, and the menu changes frequently. A cruck barn to the rear serves as restaurant and function room, ideal for weddings and medieval banquets.

Open all day all wk **Bar Meals** L served all wk 12-2.30 D served all wk 6.30-8.30 Av main course £12 **Restaurant** L served all wk 12-2.30 D served all wk 6.30-8.30 ⊕ FREE HOUSE ◀ Timothy Taylor, Golden Best, Hetton Pale Ale, Wold Top Bitter. ☙ 8 **Facilities** Children's menu Dogs allowed Garden Parking

ASENBY
Map 19 SE37

PICK OF THE PUBS

Crab & Lobster ⊛⊛ ☙

Dishforth Rd YO7 3QL
☎ 01845 577286 ▯ 01845 577109
e-mail: reservations@crabandlobster.co.uk
web: www.crabandlobster.co.uk
dir: From A1(M) take A168 towards Thirsk, follow signs for Asenby

Amid seven acres of garden, lake and streams stands this unique 17th-century thatched pub and adjacent small hotel. It is an Aladdin's cave of antiques and artefacts from around the world. Equally famous for its innovative cuisine and special gourmet extravaganzas, the menus show influences from France and Italy, with occasional oriental spices too. Starters leave no doubt you are in seafood heaven: crispy fishcakes of local codling and oak-smoked salmon, with creamed greens and poached hen's egg; a classic prawn cocktail with lobster and langoustine; and steamed Shetland mussels. The theme continues into main courses with the likes of lobster, scallop and prawn thermidor; and crab-crusted Wester Ross salmon. For those who prefer meat, the range of locally-sourced ingredients will not disappoint: prime Yorkshire fillet steak; herb-crusted loin of lamb; and roasted loin of venison are typical offerings.

Open all wk 11-11 **Bar Meals** L served all wk 12-2.30 D served Sun- Mon 7-9, Sat 6.30-9.30 Av main course £15 **Restaurant** Fixed menu price fr £16 Av 3 course à la carte fr £35 ⊕ FREE HOUSE ◀ John Smiths, Scots 1816, Golden Pippin, Guinness. ☙ 16 **Facilities** Children's menu Garden Parking

ASKRIGG
Map 18 SD99

Kings Arms ☙

Market Place DL8 3HQ ☎ 01969 650817
▯ 01969 650597
dir: N off A684 between Hawes & Leyburn

At the heart of the Yorkshire Dales, Askrigg's pub was known as The Drovers in the TV series All Creatures Great and Small. Built in 1762 as racing stables and converted to a pub in 1860, today it boasts a good range of real ales and an extensive menu and wine list. Favourites are roasted rack of Dales lamb with a mustard and herb crust, beer-battered haddock fillet with chips, chicken breast with linguini, seared sea bass on fresh pasta with a shellfish nage, or grilled gammon steak with eggs or pineapple rings. Look our for the spectacular inglenook fireplace in the main bar.

Open all wk 10-3 6-mdnt (Sat-Sun 11am-mdnt) **Bar Meals** L served all wk 12-2 D served all wk 6-9 ⊕ FREE HOUSE ◀ John Smiths, Black Sheep, Theakstons Best Bitter. ☙ 6 **Facilities** Dogs allowed Garden

AUSTWICK
Map 18 SD76

The Game Cock Inn

The Green LA2 8BB ☎ 015242 51226
e-mail: richardlord495@hotmail.com
dir: Telephone for directions

Richard and Trish Lord offer a warm welcome to this award-winning pub, set in the limestone village of Austwick. There's a large garden and children's play area, with winter log fires in the cosy bar. Expect real ale, a range of malt whiskies, and an imaginative menu. Typical dishes include giant ham shank with mash and pickled red cabbage, whilst one of the regular French evenings might feature fresh Toulouse sausage on provençale couscous.

Open all wk ⊕ THWAITES ◀ Thwaites Best Bitter & Smooth, Warfsteiner. **Facilities** Play area Family room Garden Parking

AYSGARTH — Map 19 SE08

PICK OF THE PUBS

The George & Dragon Inn ★★★★ RR ⊛ ♥

DL8 3AD ☎ 01969 663358 📄 01969 663773
e-mail: info@georgeanddragonaysgarth.co.uk
web: www.georgeanddragonaysgarth.co.uk
dir: *On A684 midway between Leyburn & Hawes. Pub in village centre*

The George & Dragon Inn is a 17th-century Grade II listed building in a superb location in the Yorkshire Dales National Park, near the beautiful Aysgarth Falls. The area is perfect for walking, touring and visiting local attractions, including Forbidden Corner, the Wensleydale Railway, and the cheese factory. The owners are proud to continue a centuries-long tradition of Yorkshire hospitality at the inn, with customers keeping cosy in winter by the fireside, and in summer enjoying their drinks and meals out on the furnished flower-filled patio. Well-kept real ales are served, and the inn has a great reputation for its traditional food. Open sandwiches, home-made soups and plates of roast beef and Yorkshire pudding or Wensleydale sausages and mash are the order of the day at lunchtime. In the early evening a fixed-price menu meets the needs of ravenous walkers, while a broader à la carte choice comes into force after 7pm.

Open all wk Closed: 2wks Jan ⊕ FREE HOUSE ◀ Black Sheep Best, John Smith's Cask, Smooth, Theakstons Bitter, Black Sheep Emmerdale & Special. ♥ 16 **Facilities** Dogs allowed Garden Parking **Rooms** 7

BAGBY — Map 19 SE48

The Roebuck Inn NEW ♥

Main St YO7 2PF ☎ 01845 597315
e-mail: info@roebuckinn.bagby.co.uk
dir: *2m SE of Thirsk. Easily accessed from A19 & A170. Follow signs for Bagby, Balk & Kilburn*

Owners Nicholas Stanley and Paul Taylor have recently refurbished this 18th century whitewashed free house. Yorkshire flavours predominate here, with regular guest ales supporting John Smith's and Black Sheep at the bar. Chef Helen Green also relies on local suppliers to create dishes such as ocean medley pancakes with Yorkshire Blue sauce; and pork belly with apricot and cider sauce. As you'd expect, the Sunday roast beef comes with Yorkshire pudding as standard!

Open noon-2.30 6-11 (Fri-Sat noon-2.30 6-mdnt Sun noon-10.30) Closed: 25 Dec, Mon L **Bar Meals** L served Tue-Sat 12-2.30, Sun 12-4.30 D served Tue-Sat 6-9, Sun 5-8 **Restaurant** L served Tue-Sat 12-2.30, Sun 12-4.30 booking required D served Tue-Sat 6-9, Sun 5-8 booking required ⊕ FREE HOUSE ◀ John Smiths Cask, Black Sheep Best, guest ales. ♥ 7 **Facilities** Children's menu Garden Parking

BILBROUGH — Map 16 SE54

PICK OF THE PUBS

The Three Hares Country Inn & Restaurant ♥

Main St YO23 3PH
☎ 01937 832128 📄 01937 834626
e-mail: info@thethreehares.co.uk
dir: *Off A64 between A659 Tadcaster & A1237 York junct*

Renowned for the quality of its food, this 18th-century country pub draws race-goers, foodies and locals alike. A light and smartly decorated brick-walled dining room provides an elegant setting for the culinary delights in store. The menu offers British fare alongside a selection of Thai dishes, so a meal might include Thai fishcakes followed by Penang curry with sticky rice, or whitefish goujons with fresh leaves followed by rib eye steak with hand cut chips and red cabbage. Desserts such as apple and pear tarte Tatin with cinnamon ice cream maintain the momentum, and the selection of Yorkshire cheeses is excellent. Race-goers should look out for the racing brunch, which is just the thing to toast a win or console oneself after a loss. On Sunday there's a traditional roast, and any day of the week you'll find an excellent selection of real ales, such as Copper Dragon. A heated terrace completes the package.

Open all wk noon-3 6-11 (Tue 6-11) **Bar Meals** L served Wed-Sun booking required D served Wed-Sun booking required Av main course £11.95 **Restaurant** L served Wed-Sun booking required D served Wed-Sun booking required Av 3 course à la carte fr £25 ⊕ FREE HOUSE ◀ Copper Dragon, Rudgate Viking, Classic. ♥ 10 **Facilities** Garden Parking

BOROUGHBRIDGE — Map 19 SE36

PICK OF THE PUBS

The Black Bull Inn ♥

See Pick of the Pubs on opposite page

BREARTON — Map 19 SE36

PICK OF THE PUBS

Malt Shovel Inn ♥

See Pick of the Pubs on page 516

BROMPTON-BY-SAWDON — Map 17 SE98

The Cayley Arms NEW ♥

YO13 9DA ☎ 01723 859372
e-mail: joannabou@hotmail.co.uk
dir: *Situated on the A170 in Brompton-by-Sawdon between Pickering and Scarborough*

Standing in the heart of picturesque Brompton-by-Sawdon, the pub is named after pioneering aviator Sir George Cayley. Its cosy log fire and friendly atmosphere has been the centre of village life for over a century, and is well-known to travellers between Pickering and Scarborough. Chunky lunchtime sandwiches with home-made crisps and hot baguettes are supplemented by hot dishes like Yorkshire pudding and boozey beef. In the evening expect spinach and ricotta tortellini; fisherman's pie with potato topping; or oven-baked chicken with leek and blue cheese sauce.

Open noon-3 5-close (Mon 6-close) Closed: Mon L **Bar Meals** L served Tue-Sun 12-2 D served Mon-Sat 6-9 **Restaurant** L served Tue-Sat 12-2 D served Mon-Sat 6-9 ⊕ PUNCH TAVERNS ◀ Tetley Cask, Black Sheep Cask. ♥ 20 **Facilities** Children's menu Play area Dogs allowed Garden Parking

PICK OF THE PUBS

The Black Bull Inn ♀

BOROUGHBRIDGE   Map 19 SE36

6 St James Square YO51 9AR
☎ **01423 322413**   📄 **01423 323915**
dir: A1(M) junct 48, B6265 E for 1m

Standing in a quiet corner of the market square, the Black Bull was one of the main watering holes for travellers on the long road between London and the north of England. Today you have to turn off the A1(M), but it's worth it to discover an inn built in 1258 that retains its ancient beams, low ceilings and roaring open fires, not to mention one that also gives houseroom to the supposed ghosts of a monk, a blacksmith and a small boy. Tony Burgess is the landlord, the man responsible for setting and

maintaining the high standards you'll enjoy at this popular place. Traditional pub fare is the order of the day, with a menu listing 10oz fillet steak in creamy whisky sauce with wild mushroom and smoked bacon lardons; chicken breast wrapped in Parma ham with pan-fried wild mushrooms in port and garlic sauce; and salmon steak on a bed of fried noodles with spicy oriental sauce. On the Sizzlers menu are Mexican spiced vegetables in a hot sweet salsa sauce; and pan-fried duck breast topped with water chestnuts, peppers, mushrooms and bamboo shoots, with a sweet and sour sauce. Frequently changing blackboard specials widen the choice even more. What could possibly follow but chocolate fudge cake and cream; baked jam sponge with hot custard sauce; or mixed ice creams, brandy snaps and fruit purées. In the bar, real ale drinkers will find Timothy Taylor Landlord, Cottage Brewing and rotating guest beers, while the wine list shows all the signs of careful selection.

Open all week 11-11 (Fri-Sat 11am-mdnt, Sun noon-11pm) **Bar Meals** L served all week 12-2 D served all week 6-9 Av main course £7.50 **Restaurant** L served all week 12-2 D served all week 6-9 Av 3 course à la carte fr £18.65 ⊕ FREE HOUSE ◼ Black Sheep, John Smiths, Timothy Taylor Best Bitter, Cottage Brewing, Wells Bombardier Premium Bitter, guest. ♀ 10 **Facilities** Children's menu Dogs allowed Parking

PICK OF THE PUBS

Malt Shovel Inn ♗

BREARTON | Map 19 SE36

HG3 3BX ☎ 01423 862929
e-mail:
bleikers@themaltshovelbrearton.co.uk
dir: *From A61 (Ripon/Harrogate) onto B6165*
towards Knaresborough. Left & follow
Brearton signs. In 1m right into village

The Bleiker family took over this 16th-century beamed free house in 2006, having previously run the Old Deanery in Ripon and established the hugely successful Bleiker's Smokehouse. Swiss-born Jurg's fine cooking specialises in fresh fish, classic sauces and well-sourced local produce. He and his wife Jane draw on their wealth of experience in food, hospitality and entertainment to create an ambience that combines elegance and theatricality. Their son and daughter-in-law are international opera soloists, and the pub's 'Dinner with Opera' evenings are a unique and thrilling part of life at the Malt Shovel. However it's their commitment to great food and wine, impeccable service and the warmest of welcomes that brings customers back again and again. Lunch from the popular new bistro menu, which features dishes like oxtail and kidney pudding; calves' liver and bacon; and fresh fish cakes may suffice for some. Others may plump for the authentic Thai dishes served in the conservatory on Wednesday to Saturday evenings: the choices include salt and chilli squid with sweet chilli sauce; and fresh crab and mango on fine herb salad. There are also lunchtime and evening cartes, when Jurg's sophisticated cooking techniques are given full rein: Dover sole meunière, for instance, or rösti with Gruyère cheese and green salad. With its open winter fires, flagstoned floors and pianos, the Malt Shovel exudes both atmosphere and character. The rural setting has some good examples of ancient strip farming, and although the pub is surrounded by rolling farmland, it's just fifteen minutes from Harrogate and within easy reach of both Knaresborough and Ripon.

Open Wed-Sun Closed: Mon-Tue & Sun eve **Bar Meals** L served Wed-Sat 12-2, Sun 12-3 D served Wed-Sat 6-9 Av main course £12.95 **Restaurant** L served Wed-Sat 12-2, Sun 12-3 D served Wed-Sat 6-9 Av 3 course à la carte fr £30 ⊕ FREE HOUSE ◀ Black Sheep Best, Timothy Taylor Landlord, guest beer. ♗ 21 **Facilities** Children's menu Garden Parking

BROUGHTON
Map 18 SD95

The Bull ♈

BD23 3AE ☎ **01756 792065**
e-mail: janeneil@thebullatbroughton.co.uk
web: www.thebullatbroughton.co.uk
dir: *3m from Skipton on A59*

Like the village itself, the pub is part of the 3,000-acre Broughton Hall estate, owned by the Tempest family for 900 years. Now part of Ribble Valley Inns, whose philosophy is to obtain the finest local ingredients for traditional fare with modern twists, the finest local ales and a great atmosphere. The locally brewed Bull Bitter and guest ales are backed by a dozen wines served by the glass. Head chef Neil Butterworth has been working with acclaimed chef Nigel Haworth to create a unique Yorkshire menu.

Open all wk noon-2.30 5.30-11 (Mon noon-2.30 5.30-10 Fri-Sat noon-11 Sun noon-7.30) **Bar Meals** L served Mon-Fri 12-2, Sat 12-2.30, Sun 12-6 D served Mon-Thu 6-9, Fri-Sat 5.30-9 **Restaurant** L served Mon-Fri 12-2, Sat 12-2.30, Sun 12-6 booking required D served Mon-Thu 6-9, Fri-Sat 5.30-9 booking required ⊕ FREE HOUSE ◀ John Smith's Smooth, Bull Bitter (Local), guest ales, Copper Dragon. ♈ 12 **Facilities** Children's menu Family room Dogs allowed Garden Parking

BURNSALL
Map 19 SE06

PICK OF THE PUBS

The Red Lion ★★ HL ◉ ♈

By the Bridge BD23 6BU
☎ 01756 720204 📠 01756 720292
e-mail: redlion@daelnet.co.uk
dir: *From Skipton take A59 E, take B6160 towards Bolton Abbey, Burnsall 7m*

This 16th-century ferryman's inn overlooks the River Wharfe as it gently curves under a magnificent five-arch bridge. Large gardens and terraces make it an ideal spot for sunny days. The Grayshon family have sympathetically upgraded the interior, retaining its beamed ceilings and creaky sloping floors. The original 'one-up, one-down' structure, now the oak-panelled and floored main bar, is the focal point of the hotel. The Grayshons like to namecheck Jim, the head chef, not just because he's their son-in-law, but also because he is the reason for their AA Rosette. Bar food includes lunchtime sandwiches and light meals such as ham hock terrine with shallot compote; and shepherd's pie or pork belly with a spring vegetable

and smoked bacon jardinière in the evening. The main menu ups the ante with the likes of Thai style fish fritters, followed by oxtail and potato pie. If you are staying over in one of the bedrooms look out for the horse trough – it was easier to build the steps around it.

Open all wk **Bar Meals** L served Mon-Sat 12-2.30, Sun 12-9 D served all wk 7-9 ⊕ FREE HOUSE ◀ Timothy Taylor Golden Best, Theakston Best Bitter, Copper Dragon. ♈ 14 **Facilities** Play area Family room Dogs allowed Garden Parking **Rooms** 25

BYLAND ABBEY
Map 19 SE57

PICK OF THE PUBS

Abbey Inn ★★★★★ RR ◉ ♈

See Pick of the Pubs on page 518

CARTHORPE
Map 19 SE38

PICK OF THE PUBS

The Fox & Hounds

DL8 2LG ☎ **01845 567433**
dir: *Off A1, signed on both N'bound & S'bound carriageways*

The Fox and Hounds has been standing in the sleepy village of Carthorpe for over 200 years. The restaurant was once the village smithy, and the old anvil and other tools of the trade are still on display, giving a nice sense of history to the place. The pub has an excellent reputation for its food, which might include starters of honey roast ham hock terrine with home-made piccalilli; caramelised onion and goats' cheese tart; or Loch Fyne smoked salmon. Typical main courses include half roasted Gressingham duckling; or chicken breast with Yorkshire blue cheese and leeks. Vegetarians won't go hungry - there's a dedicated menu of five dishes, each available as a starter or main course. Leave room for desserts such as meringue with lemon curd ice cream served with seasonal fruit. All wines are available by the glass.

Open 12-3 7-11 Closed: 25-26 Dec eve & 1st wk Jan, Mon **Bar Meals** L served Tue-Sat 12-2 D served Tue-Sat 7-9.30 ⊕ FREE HOUSE ◀ Black Sheep Best, Worthington's Bitter ♂ Thatchers Gold.
Facilities Parking

CHAPEL LE DALE
Map 18 SD77

The Old Hill Inn

LA6 3A4 ☎ **015242 41256**
dir: *From Ingleton take B6255 4m, on right*

Parts of this ancient inn date from 1615. Built as a farm it later served as a stopping place for drovers. It is run by a family of chefs, three prepare the savoury dishes and one, a pastry chef, is renowned for his spectacular sugar sculptures. Lunch includes hot or cold home-cooked ham and local sausages. From the main menu, try beetroot and mascarpone risotto topped with Wensleydale cheese or beef and ale casserole, finishing with chocolate indulgence. Lovely Dales views are offered, with good walks from the pub.

Closed: 24-25 Dec, Mon (ex BH) **Bar Meals** L served Tue-Sun 12-2.30 booking required D served Tue-Sun 6.30-8.45, Sat 6-8.45 booking required **Restaurant** L served Tue-Sun 12-2.30 booking required D served Tue-Sun 6.30-8.45, Sat 6-8.45 booking required ⊕ FREE HOUSE ◀ Black Sheep Best & Ale, Timothy Taylor Landlord, Theakstons Best, Dent Aviator ♂ Thatchers Gold. **Facilities** Children's menu Dogs allowed Garden Parking

CLAPHAM
Map 18 SD76

New Inn ♈

LA2 8HH ☎ **01524 251203** 📠 **01524 251496**
e-mail: info@newinn-clapham.co.uk
dir: *On A65 in Yorkshire Dale National Park*

Set in the charming village of Clapham beneath the famous summit of Ingleborough, this 18th-century inn offers a delightful blend of old and new. Expect a warm welcome from outdoors enthusiasts Keith and Barbara Mannion, who have run the inn since 1987. The honest, wholesome food ranges from traditional crusty steak pie with vegetables and mash to the likes of Vietnamese chilli chicken with stir-fried vegetables and noodles. This is a popular base for walking holidays.

Open all day all wk 11am-mdnt (Fri-Sat 11am-1am) **Bar Meals** L served all wk 12-2 D served all wk 6.30-8.30 Av main course £9 **Restaurant** L served all wk 12-1.30 booking required D served all wk 6.30-8 booking required Fixed menu price fr £10 Av 3 course à la carte fr £22 ⊕ ENTERPRISE INNS ◀ Black Sheep Best, Timothy Taylor Landlord, Copper Dragon Pippin, Copper Dragon Best, Bowland Hen Harrier. ♈ 18 **Facilities** Children's menu Dogs allowed Garden Parking

See advert on page 519

PICK OF THE PUBS

Abbey Inn ★★★★★ RR 🌹 🍷

BYLAND ABBEY Map 19 SE57

YO61 4BD
☎ 01347 868204 📄 01347 868678
e-mail: abbeyinn@english-heritage.org.uk
web: www.bylandabbeyinn.com
dir: *From A19 Thirsk/York follow signs to Byland Abbey/Coxwold*

The ivy-clad Abbey Inn was built as a farmhouse in 1845 by Fr Alban Molyneux and a team of monks, using 'borrowed' stones from the ruined Cistercian monastery just across the road. In its day, Byland Abbey was probably Europe's largest ecclesiastical building; but, thanks to Henry VIII, it is now just a beautiful ruin in the shadow of the Hambleton Hills. Perhaps unconsciously, Fr Molyneux chose an appropriate location for his building – for the medieval abbey guesthouse where monks once entertained King Edward II

was recently discovered beneath the foundations of the inn. You might not meet Royalty on your own visit, but be sure to reserve a table well in advance, as the renowned Sunday lunch is often booked up to four weeks ahead. Two dining rooms at the front overlook the haunting profile of the abbey itself; a third, known as the Piggery, stands on the site of the original back yard. The award-winning gastro-pub uses only fresh seasonal Yorkshire produce, and the daily-changing menu might offer starters and light bites such as organic parsnip and honey soup; Gloucester Old Spot and chestnut sausages with creamed mash; or potted brown shrimps in blade mace butter with lemon and home-made granary bread. Main course dishes include braised wild rabbit in red wine with creamed mash and wilted curly kale; crispy feta and spinach pastries with tomato and chickpeas; and pan-fried black bream with Yorkshire potato tartiflette, clams and samphire. Leave room for dessert: Yorkshire Parkin with black treacle ice cream is a typical choice. Children are offered the same healthy food but in half-size portions, whilst early evening diners may choose a three-course set menu. Three en suite bedrooms are available.

Open noon-2.30 6-11 (Sun noon-3)
Closed: 25-26 Dec, 24 & 31 Dec eve, 1 Jan, Sun eve, Mon-Tue **Bar Meals** Av main course £14.50 **Restaurant** L served Wed-Sat 12-2.30, Sun 12-3 D served Wed-Sat 6-11 Fixed menu price fr £12.50 Av 3 course à la carte fr £20.95 ⊕ FREE HOUSE ◀ Black Sheep Best, Timothy Taylor. 🍷 8
Facilities Children's menu Garden Parking **Rooms** 3

New Inn Clapham

As relaxed as you like

Clapham LA2 8HH
Yorkshire Dales National Park

This family run Inn is set amidst a geological wonderland of limestone, cavern and fell country.

Being a true 18th-century village coaching inn, experience the warmth and friendliness that we give to the New Inn. Now a

19-bedroomed inn with four poster and kingsize beds, 2 bars with open fires, cask beers, quality wines and malt whiskies, restaurant and residents lounge.

A wonderful blend of old and new, to retain the ambience of a true Dales village Inn.

Nestling beneath Ingleborough mountain, the beautiful Dales village straggles either side of Clapham Beck, one half linked to the other by three bridges – the church is at the top, the New Inn at the bottom.

Walk from our doorstep or tour the Dales or Lakes, Windermere being only 40 minutes drive away.

Contact us now for details of our special offers

Tel: 015242 51203
Email: www.info@newinn-clapham.co.uk
Website: www.newinn-clapham.co.uk

Pets welcome.

COLTON
Map 16 SE54

Ye Old Sun Inn ♥

Main St LS24 8EP ☎ 01904 744261 ▤ 01904 744261
e-mail: kelly.mccarthy@btconnect.com
dir: 3-4m from York, off A64

Dating from the 18th-century, this whitewashed local stands at the heart of the village with tables and chairs on the lawn overlooking rolling countryside. The pub prides itself on serving fine local food and ales – restaurant-style dishes without the fuss. Ingredients are locally sourced and mentioned on the menu and everything is cooked from fresh. Typical dishes are lime and ginger chicken, smoked venison and beetroot, haddock with Yorkshire Blue cheese, and mixed bean fricassee topped with a herb scone; all dishes come with a wine recommendation.

Closed: 1-26 Jan, Mon **Bar Meals** L served Tue-Sat 12-2, Sun 12-4 booking required D served Tue-Sat 6-9.30 booking required Av main course £13.50 **Restaurant** Fixed menu price fr £17.95 ⊕ ENTERPRISE INNS ◀ Timothy Taylor Landlord, Timothy Taylor Golden Best, Black Sheep, guest ale. ♥ 18 **Facilities** Children's menu Garden Parking

CRAY
Map 18 SD97

PICK OF THE PUBS

The White Lion Inn ♥

Cray BD23 5JB ☎ 01756 760262
e-mail: admin@whitelioncray.com
dir: B6265 from Skipton to Grassington, then B6160 towards Aysgarth. Or from Leyburn take A684 towards Hawes. At Aysgarth take B6160 towards Grassington. Cray in 10m

Nestling beneath Buckden Pike, The White Lion is Wharfedale's highest inn. It also boasts some spectacular scenery, since it's set right at the heart of the Yorkshire Dales. Indeed, the celebrated fell-walker Wainwright once described this former drovers' hostelry as a 'tiny oasis', a claim that's just as accurate today. All the qualities of a traditional Yorkshire inn have been maintained here, from warm hospitality to oak beams, log fire and flagstone floors. A good choice of hand-pulled real ales is offered and 20-plus malt whiskies. You can eat and drink in the bar or dining room, though the sight of the cascading Cray Gill, which runs past the inn, is sure to entice children out to the garden. Before or after a meal, you can also make your way across the stepping-stones in the gill to

the open fells and many walks, long and short. In the bar, lunchtime options include filled baguettes, ploughman's, and plate-sized Yorkshire puddings with a choice of fillings. Also available, lunchtime and evenings, is a variety of substantial dishes such as pork fillet in a honey and mustard cream sauce; whole steamed Kilnsey trout, or steak and mushroom casserole. A children's menu is also on offer.

Open all wk Closed: 25 Dec ⊕ FREE HOUSE ◀ Timothy Taylor Golden Best, Copper Dragon Golden Pippin, Copper Dragon 1816, Wensleydale Brewery Semerwater. ♥ 9 **Facilities** Family room Dogs allowed Garden Parking

CRAYKE
Map 19 SE57

PICK OF THE PUBS

The Durham Ox ★★★★ ⒜ RR ♥

See Pick of the Pubs on opposite page

CROPTON
Map 19 SE78

The New Inn ♥

YO18 8HH ☎ 01751 417330 ▤ 01751 417582
e-mail: info@croptonbrewery.co.uk
dir: Telephone for directions

Home of the award-winning Cropton micro-brewery, this family-run free house on the edge of the North York Moors National Park is popular with locals and visitors alike. Meals are served in the restored village bar and in the elegant Victorian restaurant: choices could include Whitby cod with mushy peas and home-made chips; three cheese and roasted vegetable frittata; an extensive range from the grill; plus lunchtime sandwiches and ciabatta rolls.

Open all wk ⊕ FREE HOUSE ◀ Cropton Two Pints, Monkmans Slaughter, Yorkshire Moors Bitter, Honey Gold Bitter, Theakstons Best Bitter. ♥ 7 **Facilities** Play area Family room Dogs allowed Garden Parking

EAST WITTON
Map 19 SE18

PICK OF THE PUBS

The Blue Lion ♥

DL8 4SN ☎ 01969 624273 ▤ 01969 624189
e-mail: enquiries@thebluelion.co.uk
dir: From Ripon take A6108 towards Leyburn

This former coaching inn has welcomed travellers since the days when cattle drovers rested here on their journey through glorious Wensleydale. Built towards the end of the 18th century, the pub's stone facade can hardly have changed since it first opened, while inside an extensive but sympathetic refurbishment has created rural chic interiors with stacks of atmosphere and charm. The bar with its open fire and flagstone floor is a beer drinker's haven, where the best of North Yorkshire's breweries present a pleasant dilemma for the real ale lover. A blackboard displays imaginative

but unpretentious bar meals. Diners in the candlelit restaurant can expect award-winning culinary treats incorporating a variety of Yorkshire ingredients. A fulfilling repast may comprise a Provencale stew of fresh mussels and clams, followed by cassoulet of duck leg, Toulouse sausage and belly pork, and apple tarte Tatin with vanilla ice cream to finish.

The Blue Lion

Open all day all wk 11-11 Closed: 25 Dec Bar Meals L served all wk 12-2.15 D served all wk 7-9.30 Av main course £15 **Restaurant** L served Sun 12-2.15 D served all wk 7-9.30 Av 3 course à la carte fr £27 ⊕ FREE HOUSE ◀ Black Sheep Bitter, Theakston Best Bitter, Black Sheep Riggwetter, Worthingtons. ♥ 12 **Facilities** Dogs allowed Garden Parking

EGTON
Map 8 NZ80

PICK OF THE PUBS

The Wheatsheaf Inn

YO21 1TZ ☎ 01947 895271
e-mail: info@wheatsheafegton.com
dir: Off A169 NW of Grosmont

This unassuming old pub sits back from the wide main road, so be careful not to miss it. The main bar is cosy and traditional, with low beams, dark green walls and comfy settles. There's a locals' bar too, but it only holds about twelve, so get there early. The pub is very popular with fishermen, as the River Esk runs along at the foot of the hill, and is a big draw for fly-fishers in particular. The menu offers white nut and artichoke heart roast with mushroom stroganoff, and chicken and smoked bacon puff pastry pie among others.

Open 11.30-3 5.30-11.30 (Sat 11.30-11.30 Sun 11.30-11) Closed: Mon Bar Meals L served Tue-Sun 12-2 D served Tue-Sat 6-9 ⊕ FREE HOUSE ◀ Black Sheep Bitter, Black Sheep Golden, John Smith, Timothy Taylor Landlord, Guest Ales ○ Thatchers Gold. **Facilities** Dogs allowed Garden Parking

PICK OF THE PUBS

The Durham Ox ★★★★ A RR ♟

CRAYKE Map 19 SE57

Westway YO61 4TE
☎ 01347 821506 📄 01347 823326
e-mail: enquiries@thedurhamox.com
dir: *Off A19 from York to Thirsk, then to Easingwold. From market place to Crayke, turn left up hill, pub on right*

From this historic village in the heart of Herriot Country, there are breathtaking views over the Vale of York on three sides, yet York city centre is less than 20 minutes away. Three hundred years old, and family owned for the last ten, this was the AA's Pub of the Year (England) in 2007/8; other award-making bodies like it a lot too. Priding itself on friendly and efficient service, and with menus showcasing the best of local produce, as well as stocking an extensive range of wines and cask ales, it deserves all its accolades. With flagstone floors, exposed beams, oak panelling and roaring fires in the main bar in winter, it ticks all the boxes on the 'traditional country pub' checklist. The menus tell us the eponymous ox was born in 1796 and grew to enormous proportions - five feet six inches tall, 11 feet from nose to tail, the same around its girth, and weighing 171 stone - little wonder the beast created such a sensation. Another claim to fame is that the hill outside is reputedly the one the Grand Old Duke of York marched his men up and down. The menus and blackboard specials are known locally for their game, meats, fresh fish and seafood dishes; they change regularly to incorporate seasonal varieties. Typically, you would find spiced roasted root vegetable casserole with 'wartime' herb dumplings; grilled plaice with brown shrimp butter sauce; corn-fed chicken with piri-piri and aioli dipping sauce; and Portobello mushroom and wild garlic risotto. Sundays provide a much talked-about traditional rib of beef and Yorkshire puddings, as well as other options. There also are snacks on toast, burgers and open sandwiches. Outside is a beautiful water garden. Smart overnight accommodation is provided in converted farm cottages, with exposed brickwork and original quarry tiles.

Open 12-2.30 6-11 Closed: 25 Dec **Bar Meals** L served Mon-Sat 12-2.30, Sun 12-3 D served Mon-Sat 6-9, Sun 6-8.30 **Restaurant** L served Mon-Sat 12-2.30, Sun 12-3 D served Mon-Sat 6-9, Sun 6-8.30 Fixed menu price fr £12.95 ⊕ FREE HOUSE 🛢 John Smiths, Theakstons, Timothy Taylor Landlord, Black Sheep Best. ♟ 9 **Facilities** Dogs allowed Garden Parking

EGTON BRIDGE — Map 19 NZ80

Horseshoe Hotel ♀

YO21 1XE ☎ 01947 895245
e-mail: paul@thehorseshoehotel.co.uk
dir: *From Whitby take A171 towards Middlesborough. Village signed in 5m*

An 18th-century country inn by the River Esk, handy for visiting the North Yorkshire Moors Railway. Inside are oak settles and tables, local artists' paintings and, depending on the weather, an open fire. Lunchtime bar food consists of sandwiches in granary bread and hot baguettes. The main menu includes starters like crab cakes with a sweet chilli dip, and mains like lasagne, scampi, or pie of the day. There is also a specials board.

Open all wk 11.30-3 6.30-11 (Sat 11.30-11 Sun noon-10.30) **Bar Meals** L served all wk 12-2 D served all wk 7-9 ⊕ FREE HOUSE ◀ John Smiths Cask, Durham, Black Sheep, Archers, Theakstons. ♀ 7 **Facilities** Family room Dogs allowed Garden Parking

FADMOOR — Map 19 SE68

PICK OF THE PUBS

The Plough Inn ♀

See Pick of the Pubs on opposite page

FELIXKIRK — Map 19 SE48

PICK OF THE PUBS

The Carpenters Arms

YO7 2DP ☎ 01845 537369 📄 01845 537889
dir: *2m from Thirsk on A170*

This 18th-century inn stands in the pretty hamlet of Felixkirk, a mere skip away from the market town of Thirsk, where much-loved writer and vet James Herriott once practised. The inn has been in the capable hands of mother and daughter team Linda and Karen Bumby since 2000, and very welcoming they've made it too. The Bistro bar is a cosy spot, with soft seating and big cushions, oil lamps, coloured checked tablecloths, carpenters' tools, old-fashioned toy balloons and various other knick-knacks on display. Tuck into home-made fisherman's pie; Indonesian chicken curry; or venison and beef casserole with suet dumplings. In the slightly more formal restaurant, with its white linen cloths and napkins, crystal glasses and locally made furniture, the menu also moves up a notch. Try duck breast with port wine sauce and parsnip crisps; or bacon-wrapped pork fillet stuffed with black pudding and apple, with wholegrain mustard sauce.

Open 11.30-3 6.30-11 (Sun 12-3) Closed: 1wk Feb, 25 Dec, Mon, Sun eve **Bar Meals** L served Tue-Sun 12-2 D served Tue-Sat 6.30-9 ⊕ FREE HOUSE ◀ Black Sheep, Theakstons, Guest Ale. **Facilities** Parking

GIGGLESWICK — Map 18 SD86

Black Horse Hotel

32 Church St BD24 0BE ☎ 01729 822506
dir: *Telephone for directions*

Set in the 17th-century main street, this traditional free house stands next to the church and behind the market cross. Down in the warm and friendly bar you'll find a range of hand-pulled ales. The menu of freshly-prepared pub favourites ranges from hot sandwiches or giant filled Yorkshire puddings to main course dishes like steak and ale pie; broccoli and sweetcorn vol-au-vent; and crispy battered haddock.

Closed: Mon 12-2.30 ⊕ FREE HOUSE ◀ Carlsberg-Tetley Bitter, Timothy Taylor Landlord, John Smiths, Timothy Taylor Golden Best. **Facilities** Garden Parking

GOATHLAND — Map 19 NZ80

Birch Hall Inn

Beckhole YO22 5LE ☎ 01947 896245
e-mail: glenys@birchhallinn.fsnet.co.uk
dir: *9m from Whitby on A169*

This delightful little free house, tucked away in a remote valley close to the North York Moors steam railway, has been in the same ownership for 25 years. With just two tiny rooms separated by a sweet shop, it offers an open fire in the main bar, well-kept local ales and a large garden with tempting views of the local walks. The simple menu features locally-baked pies, butties, home-made scones and buttered beer cake.

Open 11-3 7.30-11 (11-11 summer) Closed: Mon eve & Tue in winter **Bar Meals** food served all day **Restaurant** food served all day ⊕ FREE HOUSE ◀ Black Sheep Best, Theakstons Black Bull, Cropton Yorkshire Moors Bitter, Daleside Brewery Legover, Durhams Black Velvet. **Facilities** Family room Dogs allowed Garden **Notes** ⊛

GREAT AYTON — Map 19 NZ51

The Royal Oak ★★★ INN ♀

123 High St TS9 6BW
☎ 01642 722361 📄 01642 724047
e-mail: info@royaloak-hotel.co.uk
dir: *Telephone for directions*

Real fires and a relaxed atmosphere are part of the attraction at this traditional 18th-century former coaching inn now corner pub, run by the Monaghan family since 1978. The public bar and restaurant retain many original features and offer a good selection of real ales, and an extensive range of food is available all day. There are five comfortable bedrooms if you would like to stay over.

Open all wk Closed: 25 Dec **Bar Meals** L served Mon-Sat 12-2, Sun 12-6 D served Mon-Sat 6.30-9.30 **Restaurant** L served Mon-Sat 12-2, Sun 12-6 booking required D served Mon-Sat 6.30-9.30 ⊕ SCOTTISH & NEWCASTLE ◀ Theakstons, John Smiths Smooth, Directors. ♀ 10 **Facilities** Children's menu Garden **Rooms** 5

GREEN HAMMERTON — Map 19 SE45

The Bay Horse Inn

York Rd YO26 8BN ☎ 01423 330338
dir: *Telephone for directions*

A 200-year-old coaching inn located in a small village near the A1 and close to both York and Harrogate. Food served in the bar and restaurant, and there is further seating outside, sheltered by the boundary hedge. Dishes might include local sausages and mash, fresh battered haddock and hand-cut chips, home-made lasagne, and home-made pie of the day. Tuesdays and Fridays are fish and chips nights to eat in or take away.

Open all wk ⊕ GREENE KING ◀ Timothy Taylor, Black Sheep, Guest ale. **Facilities** Dogs allowed Garden Parking

GRINTON — Map 19 SE09

PICK OF THE PUBS

The Bridge Inn ♀

See Pick of the Pubs on page 52

HAROME — Map 19 SE68

PICK OF THE PUBS

The Star Inn ⊛⊛

YO62 5JE ☎ 01439 770397 📄 01439 771833
dir: *From Helmsley take A170 towards Kirkbymoorside 0.5m. Turn right for Harome*

A fine 14th-century cruck-framed longhouse is home to this award-winning gastro-pub with a bar full of Mousey Thompson hand-carved oak furniture. Recent additions to the inn include a new dining area, a chef's table, a private dining room upstairs, a summer dining terrace and a kitchen garden. A further new property comprises an indoor swimming pool and a 40-seater dining room within 200 yards of the inn. Produce sourced directly from nearby farms and estates, and fish and shellfish from Whitby and Hartlepool, are used to good effect in the regional menu. Dishes might include risotto of red-legged partridge with yellow chanterelles, white truffle oil and wilted garden rainbow chard; and pan-roasted Duncombe Park roe deer with little venison cottage pie, York ham lardons, girolle mushrooms and tarragon juices.

Open 11.30-3 6-11 (Sun noon-11) Closed: 25 Dec, Mon L **Bar Meals** L served Tue-Sun 11.30-2 D served Mon-Sat 6-9.30 Av main course £20 **Restaurant** L served Tue-Sun 11.30-2 booking required D served Mon-Sat 6-9.30 booking required Av 3 course à la carte fr £40 ⊕ FREE HOUSE ◀ Black Sheep Special, Copper Dragon, Hambleton Ales, John Smith's, Theakstons Best. **Facilities** Children's menu Garden Parking

PICK OF THE PUBS

The Plough Inn ♟

FADMOOR   Map 19 SE68

Main St YO62 7HY
☎ **01751 431515**   📠 **01751 432492**
e-mail:
enquiries@theploughfadmoor.co.uk
web: www.ploughrestaurant.co.uk
dir: *1m N of Kirkbymoorside on A170 (Thirsk to Scarborough road)*

With dramatic views over Ryedale and the Wolds, the setting of this stylish country pub and restaurant overlooking the village green could hardly be more idyllic. Lovingly restored a few years ago, the inn's 18th-century feel is strongly conveyed by its low, beamed ceilings, comfortable wall benches and log fires in winter – just the place for a pint of Black Sheep Best or one of the guest ales. Neil Nicholson is head chef and creator of an extensive and varied menu reliant on local meats, vegetables, herbs and salad crops, and fish straight from East Coast quaysides.

His wife Rachael looks after front of house, with a team of staff providing a level of service that encourages people to come back again and again. The Plough has built up a reputation for good food served either in the bar, in one of the intimate dining rooms, or on the terrace. Lunch and dinner menu starter options include creamy button mushroom and blue Stilton pot with toasted onion bread; and timbale of fresh Scottish salmon and Greenland prawns with home-made Marie Rose sauce. These could be followed by slow-roasted boneless half Gressingham duckling with orange, mandarin and brandy sauce; paupiette of plaice, stuffed with fresh spinach and prawns with tarragon, white wine and cream sauce; or Thai green vegetable curry with steamed, flavoured basmati rice. Desserts made on the premises offer choices of Neapolitan parfait with fresh fruit; baked American cheesecake with fresh raspberries; and warm treacle tart with white chocolate ice cream. The Sunday lunch menu goes way beyond traditional roasts to include lamb and vegetable casserole, and mushroom and brie Wellington. The wine list makes for rewarding reading, with a good value house selection.

Open noon-2.30 6.30-11 (Sun noon-5) Closed: Mon-Tue (ex BH), Sun eve, 25-26 Dec, 1 Jan **Bar Meals** L served Wed-Sat 12-2 Sun 12-2.30 D served Wed-Sat 6.30-8.45 Av main course £10.50 **Restaurant** L served Wed-Sat 12-2 Sun 12-3.30 D served Wed-Sat 6.30-8.45 booking required Fixed menu price fr £13.75 Av 3 course à la carte fr £22 ⊞ FREE HOUSE ◄ Black Sheep Best, John Smith's, Tetley Cask, guest ales ♂ Stowford Press. ♟ 8
Facilities Children's menu Garden Parking

PICK OF THE PUBS

The Bridge Inn 🍷

DL11 6HH ☎ 01748 884224
e-mail: atkinbridge@btinternet.com
web: www.bridgeinngrinton.co.uk
dir: *Exit A1 at Scotch Corner towards
Richmond. In Richmond take A6108 towards
Reeth, 10m*

Situated on the banks of the River Swale
in the heart of the Yorkshire Dales
National Park, the Bridge Inn stands
opposite St Andrew's church in the
picturesque village of Grinton. Dating
from the 13th century, this former
coaching inn with its beamed ceilings
and open fires has now been tastefully
restored. Most visitors head for the
Dales in search of country pursuits, and
a range of activities can be found on the
pub's doorstep. Walking, horse riding
and mountain biking are all close at
hand, and fishermen can buy their day
tickets from the hotel. The Bridge Inn is
well known for its great food and ales,
and customers are invited to sample
Jennings award-winning cask ales, or
maybe try something a little different
from a micro-brewery. There is also a
fine extensive cellar of handpicked
wines. Menus are based on seasonal
local produce under the experienced eye
of resident chef John Scott, and
flavoured with herbs plucked from the
pub's own garden. Hot or cold baguettes
are served in the bar with a handful of
chips, and baked jacket potatoes are
also on offer. In the fine à la carte
restaurant, starters include courgette
and tomato bake; smoked mackerel
pâté; and black pudding with chorizo,
red chard and three pepper dressing.
Typical main course choices include
garlic and sage roasted belly pork
served on a stew of lentils, smoked
bacon, tomato, onions and white wine;
cod in cider and dill batter; or Grinton
lamb and barley casserole with minted
dumplings on a bed of mash. If you've
room to spare, the dessert menu
includes a daily choice of old-fashioned
traditional puddings.

Open all week **Bar Meals** Av main
course £10 food served all day
Restaurant Av 3 course à la carte fr
£25 food served all day ⊕ JENNINGS
BROTHERS PLC ◀ Cumberland Ale,
Cocker Hoop, Deuchars IPA, Adnams,
Yorkshire Terrier. 🍷 7 **Facilities** Dogs
allowed Garden Parking

HARROGATE
Map 19 SE35

PICK OF THE PUBS

The Boars Head Hotel ★★★ HL @@ ♥

Ripley Castle Estate HG3 3AY
☎ 01423 771888 📇 01423 771509
e-mail: reservations@boarsheadripley.co.uk
dir: On A61 (Harrogate/Ripon road). Hotel in village centre

Dating back to 1830 when the Lord of the Manor rebuilt the village next to his castle, this lovely old coaching inn, originally called The Star, in the cobbled village square was refurbished by the present Lord (Sir Thomas Ingilby) in 1990 and turned into an impressive hotel. Sir William Ingilby closed all three of Ripley's inns when he inherited the estate some time after the First World War, and Ripley remained dry until the Star was re-opened as the Boar's Head Hotel. Oil paintings and furniture from the castle help to create the country-house feel in tranquil drawing and morning rooms and the individually decorated bedrooms. Stable partitions in the pubby bar and bistro bring intimacy to the relaxed, candlelit atmosphere, where an array of handpumps dispense some cracking Yorkshire ales. Food options begin with classic sandwiches (poached salmon with lemon and dill crème fraiche), and starters like goats' cheese and pepper terrine, or chicken liver parfait. For main course, choose pork and leek sausages on crushed potatoes, breast of estate pheasant wrapped in bacon with herb potatoes, and haddock with butterbean and tomato salad. In the restaurant, main course prices are inclusive of a starter, dessert and coffee, so the price of your meal depends on your choice of main course. Mains range from roast duck breast with confit shallots to pan-seared sea bass with crab beignet and braised fennel.

Open all wk Bar Meals L served all wk 12-2 D served all wk 6-9.30 Restaurant L served all wk 12-2 D served all wk 7-9 booking required ⊕ FREE HOUSE ◀ Theakston Best & Old Peculier, Daleside Crackshot, Hambleton White Boar, Black Sheep Best. ♥ 10 Facilities Children's menu Dogs allowed Garden Parking Rooms 25

HAWES
Map 18 SD88

The Moorcock Inn ♥

Garsdale Head LA10 5PU
☎ 01969 667488 📇 01969 667488
e-mail: admin@moorcockinn.com
dir: On A684 5m from Hawes, 15m from Sedbergh at junct for Kirkby Stephen (10m). Garsdale Station 1m

A heart-warming 18th-century hostelry, where owners Liz and Simon welcome weary walkers with or without muddy boots and dogs. Candles glow in the windows, while inside fairy lights pick out a cosy blend of original stonework and bright colours, furnished with comfy sofas and traditional wooden chairs. Savour the pub's local ales around the wood-burning stove, or enjoy the spectacular views from the garden. Traditional fare

ranges from Whitby scampi; lamb and root vegetable hotpot; to steak, mushroom and ale pie. Vegetarians and children are not forgotten with their own choices.

Open all day all wk 11am-mdnt Bar Meals food served all day Restaurant food served all day ⊕ FREE HOUSE ◀ Black Sheep, Copper Dragon, Boddingtons Cask, guest ales. ♥ 7 Facilities Children's menu Family room Dogs allowed Garden Parking

HELMSLEY
Map 19 SE68

The Crown Inn NEW ⚠ ★★★★ INN

Market Square YO62 5BJ ☎ 01439 770297
e-mail: info@tchh.co.uk
dir: Please telephone for directions

The family-run 16th-century inn overlooking Helmsley's beautiful square has been refurbished with style and taste, without losing the inn's historic charm. You can order a pint of Black Sheep and tuck into some fresh home-made food using local produce in the cosy bar and lounge, each warmed by an open log fire. Choose to stay to explore the North York Moors and visit nearby Castle Howard; you have the choice of smart, well-appointed rooms in the inn, or in a converted barn with views of Helmsley Castle.

Open all day all wk 7.30am-11.30pm Bar Meals Av main course £9 food served all day Restaurant Fixed menu price fr £14.95 Av 3 course à la carte fr £20 ⊕ FREE HOUSE ◀ Black Sheep, John Smith Cask, Guest ale. Facilities Children's menu Family room Dogs allowed Garden Parking Rooms 19

HETTON
Map 18 SD95

PICK OF THE PUBS

The Angel ♥

BD23 6LT ☎ 01756 730263 📇 01756 730363
e-mail: info@angelhetton.co.uk
dir: A59 onto B6265 towards Grassington. Left at Rylstone Pond (signed) then left at T-junct

Much loved for its modern British food, this ivy-clad Dales inn has a long and interesting history. Built in the 15th century, it welcomed drovers in the early 1800s, and some local residents remember it as a traditional farmhouse pub in the 1950s. Denis and Juliet Watkins took the reins in 1985 and made it a landmark gastro-pub; since Denis' death in 2004, Juliet and her dedicated team, with chef Bruce Elsworth, have stayed true to his vision of 'good food and great value'. The interior is all oak beams, nooks and crannies, and winter log fires; in summer you can sit on the flagged forecourt and enjoy views of Cracoe Fell. Locally-sourced meats, seasonal game and fresh Fleetwood fish are the foundation of the varied menus. The brasserie blackboard menu might offer pea and prosciutto risotto followed by Lancashire hotpot, whilst à la carte diners might enjoy goats' cheese soufflé; and monkfish roasted in Parma ham.

Open all wk noon-3 6-11 Closed: 25 Dec & 1wk Jan Bar Meals L served all wk 12-2.15 D served all wk 6-9.30 (6-9 in winter) Restaurant L served Sun 12-1.45 booking required D served Mon-Fri 6-9, Sat 6-9.30 booking required Fixed menu price fr £25 Av 3 course à la carte fr £29 ⊕ FREE HOUSE ◀ Blacksheep Bitter, Timothy Taylor Landlord, Hetton Pale Ale. ♥ 24 Facilities Children's menu Garden Parking

HOVINGHAM
Map 19 SE67

The Malt Shovel

Main St YO62 4LF ☎ 01653 628264 📇 01653 628264
e-mail: info@themaltshovelhovingham.co.uk
dir: 18m NE of York, 5m from Castle Howard

Tucked away in the Duchess of Kent's home village, the stone-built 18th-century Malt Shovel offers a friendly atmosphere with good value food prepared from quality local ingredients. Popular options include Whitby wholetail scampi, vegetarian pancake, chicken stroganoff and steak pie. Fresh vegetables, hand-cut chips and daily specials board featuring game dishes complete the picture. Recent change in ownership.

Open all wk 11.30-2 6-11 (winter), 11.30-2.30 5.30-11 (summer) Bar Meals L served Mon-Sat 11.30-2 (winter) 11.30-2.30 (summer), Sun 12-2.30 D served Mon-Sat 6-9 (winter) 5.30-9 (summer), Sun 5.30-8 Av main course £8.50 Restaurant L served Mon-Sat 11.30-2 (winter) 11.30-2.30 (summer), Sun 12-2.30 booking required D served Mon-Sat 6-9 (winter) 5.30-9 (summer), Sun 5.30-8 booking required Fixed menu price fr £8.75 ⊕ PUNCH TAVERNS ◀ Tetley's, Black Sheep, Guest Ale. Facilities Children's menu Garden Parking

PICK OF THE PUBS

The Worsley Arms Hotel ★★★ HL ♥

Main St YO62 4LA
☎ 01653 628234 📇 01653 628130
e-mail: enquiries@worsleyarms.co.uk
dir: On B1257 between Malton & Helmsley

In 1841 Sir William Worsley thought he would turn the village of Worsley into a spa to rival Bath, and built a spa house and a hotel. However, he reckoned without the delicate nature of his guests who disliked the muddy track between the two. Inevitably the spa failed, but the hotel survived and, together with the separate pub, forms part of the Worsley family's historic Hovingham Hall estate, birthplace of the Duchess of Kent, and currently home to her nephew. You can eat in the restaurant or the Cricketer's Bar (the local team has played on the village green for over 150 years). Hambleton Stallion beer from nearby Thirsk is on tap, and food choices include seared Gressingham duck with celeriac and potato dauphinoise, Worsley Arms fishcakes with lemon fish cream, Waterford Farm sausages with mash and red onion confit, or rack of North Yorkshire lamb with fondant potato, roast garlic and fresh mint.

continued

HOVINGHAM *continued*

Open all day all wk **Bar Meals** L served all wk 12-2 booking required D served all wk 6.30-9 booking required Av main course £11 **Restaurant** L served Sun 12-2 booking required D served all wk 6.30-9 required Fixed menu price fr £29.50 Av 3 course à la carte fr £23.50 ⊕ FREE HOUSE ◼ Tetleys, Hambleton Ales. ♀ 20 **Facilities** Children's menu Dogs allowed Garden Parking **Rooms** 20

HUBBERHOLME   Map 18 SD97

The George Inn

BD23 5JE ☎ 01756 760223

dir: *From Skipton take B6265 to Threshfield. B6160 to Buckden. Follow signs for Hubberholme*

To check if the bar is open, look for a lighted candle in the window. Another old tradition is the annual land-letting auction on the first Monday night of the year, when local farmers bid for 16 acres of land owned by the church. Stunningly located beside the River Wharfe, this pub has flagstone floors, stone walls, mullioned windows, an open fire and an inviting summer terrace. Lunches include chicken and cheese melt and maybe a pint of Black Sheep; evening choices include pork escalope topped with spiced cheese and Wensleydale cheese.

Open noon-3 7-11 Closed: 1st 2wks Dec, Mon **Bar Meals** L served Tue-Sun 12-2 D served Tue-Sun 7-8.30 booking required Av main course £9 ⊕ FREE HOUSE ◼ Black Sheep Best, Black Sheep Special, Skipton Brewery ♂ Thatchers Gold. **Facilities** Children's menu Garden Parking

---

KILBURN   Map 19 SE57

The Forresters Arms Inn ♀

YO61 4AH ☎ 01347 868386

e-mail: admin@forrestersarms.com

dir: *From Thirsk take A170, after 3m turn right signed Kilburn. At Kilburn Rd junct, turn right, Inn on left in village square*

A sturdy stone-built former coaching inn still catering for travellers passing close by the famous White Horse of Kilburn on the North York Moors. Next door is the famous Robert Thompson workshop; fine examples of his early work, with the distinctive mouse symbol on every piece, can be seen in both bars. Visiting coachmen would undoubtedly have enjoyed the log fires, cask ales and good food as much as today's visitors.

Open all day all wk 9am-11pm **Bar Meals** L served all wk 12-3 booking required D served all wk 6-9 booking required Av main course £7.95 **Restaurant** L served all wk 12-3 booking required D served all wk 6-9 booking required ⊕ ENTERPRISE INNS ◼ John Smiths Cask, Guinness, Hambleton Bitter, Guest ales. ♀ 6 **Facilities** Children's menu Dogs allowed Garden Parking

---

KIRBY HILL   Map 19 NZ10

The Shoulder of Mutton Inn

DL11 7JH ☎ 01748 822772 ◻ 01325 718936

e-mail: info@shoulderofmutton.net

dir: *From A1 Scotch Corner junct take A66. Approx 6m follow signs for Kirby Hill on left*

A traditional ivy-clad 18th-century inn with panoramic views over Holmedale and beyond. Two open log fires burn in the bar, adding to the enjoyment of a pint of Daleside or Copper Dragon. The separate stone-walled restaurant, replete with original beams and white linen, makes just the right kind of setting for renowned daily-changing home-cooked dishes. A typical selection could comprise warm kidney and bacon salad, followed by roast breast of duck on an apple compote, with a home-made pastry to round everything off.

Open all wk 6-11 (Sat-Sun noon-3 6-11) **Bar Meals** L served Sat-Sun 12-2 booking required D served Wed-Sun 6.30-9 booking required Av main course £10 **Restaurant** L served Sun 12-2 booking required D served Wed-Sun 6.30-9 booking required Av 3 course à la carte fr £25 ⊕ FREE HOUSE ◼ Daleside, Black Sheep, Copper Dragon, Deuchars, Yorkshire Dales. **Facilities** Garden Parking

---

KIRKBYMOORSIDE   Map 19 SE68

PICK OF THE PUBS

George & Dragon Hotel ♀

17 Market Place YO62 6AA
☎ 01751 433334 ◻ 0870 7060004

e-mail: reception@georgeanddragon.net

dir: *Just off A170 between Scarborough & Thirsk. In town centre*

A former cornmill, rectory and 17th-century coaching inn have been seamlessly combined to make this welcoming hotel in the heart of Kirkbymoorside. Its beamed, olde worlde interior is full of character and comfy chairs. Visitors can sit by the log fire and sample hand-pulled real ales, wines by the glass and a choice of 30 malt whiskies. Food is served all day using fresh local produce, and includes a bar lunchtime menu, à la carte and specials board. Dishes range from pub food favourites (fried Whitby scampi, steak and stilton pie) to classy offerings such as duck liver pâté with home-made chutney or fillets of east coast bass and red mullet with mussel and prawn risotto and asparagus. Light options include filled baguettes; mussel cassoulet; and home-made soup with home-made bread. A haven for real ale lovers, the bar offers guest ales alongside regulars from Black Sheep and Copper Dragon.

Open all day all wk 10.30am-11pm **Bar Meals** Av main course £12 food served all day **Restaurant** Av 3 course à la carte fr £20 food served all day ⊕ FREE HOUSE ◼ Black Sheep Best, Tetley, Copper Dragon, Guest ale. ♀ 10 **Facilities** Children's menu Dogs allowed Garden Parking

---

KIRK DEIGHTON   Map 16 SE35

The Bay Horse Inn ♀

Main St LS22 4DZ ☎ 01937 580058 ◻ 01937 582443

e-mail: gailmoscicki@yahoo.co.uk

dir: *1m N of Wetherby on B6164 towards Knaresborough*

This building's two front doors are a legacy from the day when it comprised two pubs, one for men and one for ladies. These days about a third of the building is a bar while the rest is dedicated to dining. With an emphasis on local produce, lunchtime offerings might include smoked salmon Benedict, or queenie scallop gratin. With an Early Bird offer available, in the evening you could try Swaledale George Fells lamb saddle.

Open noon-3 5-11 Closed: Mon L **Bar Meals** L served Tu-Sat 12-3, Sun 12-5 D served Mon-Sat 6-9 Av main course £15 **Restaurant** L served Tue-Sat 12-3, Sun 12-5 D served Mon-Sat 6-9 booking required Fixed menu price fr £12.95 ⊕ FREE HOUSE ◼ Timothy Taylor Landlord, Black Sheep Bitter, John Smiths Cask. ♀ 12 **Facilities** Children's menu Parking

---

KIRKHAM   Map 19 SE76

PICK OF THE PUBS

Stone Trough Inn ♀

Kirkham Abbey YO60 7JS
☎ 01653 618713 ◻ 01653 618819

e-mail: info@stonetroughinn.co.uk

dir: *1.5m off A64, between York & Malton*

This free house has a great reputation for its friendliness, fine food and real ales. It stands high above Kirkham Priory and the River Derwent, and was sympathetically converted from licensed premises in the early 1980s from Stone Trough Cottage. The cottage took its name from the base of a cross erected by a 12th-century French knight to commemorate a son killed in a riding accident. The cross has long since disappeared, but its hollowed-out base now stands at the entrance to the car park. A real fire, bare beams and wooden settles make for a pleasingly traditional interior. Food-wise there's a menu of serious intent that includes roast breast of guinea fowl with confit leg and a chanterelle sauce; whole grilled lemon sole with a shrimp beurre noisette dressing; and fillet of turbot with a basil and ginger sauce.

Closed: 25 Dec & 2-5 Jan, Mon ⊕ FREE HOUSE ◼ Tetle Cask, Timothy Taylor Landlord, Black Sheep Best, Malton Brewery Golden Chance, guest ales. ♀ 14 **Facilities** Garden Parking

KNARESBOROUGH · Map 19 SE35

PICK OF THE PUBS

The General Tarleton
nn ★★★★★ RR ☺☺ ♀

See Pick of the Pubs on page 528

LANGTHWAITE · Map 19 NZ00

he Red Lion Inn ♀

.11 6RE ☎ 01748 884218 📄 01748 884133
mail: rlionlangthwaite@aol.com
: Through Reeth into Arkengarthdale, 18m from A1

e Red Lion is a traditional country pub owned by the
me family for 44 years. It hosts two darts teams in
nter, a quoits team in summer and bar snacks are
rved all year round. There are some wonderful walks in
s part of the Dales and relevant books and maps are
sale. In the tiny snug there are photographs relating to
e various films and TV programmes filmed at this
usually photogenic pub.

en all wk 11-3 7-11 **Bar Meals** L served all wk 11-3
FREE HOUSE ◄ Black Sheep Bitter, Riggwelter,
rthington Cream Flow, Tetleys, Guinness ○ Thatchers
ld. ♀ 8 **Facilities** Family room Garden Parking

LASTINGHAM · Map 19 SE79

lacksmiths Arms ♀

62 6TL ☎ 01751 417247 📄 01751 417247
mail: pete.hils@blacksmithslastingham.co.uk
*: 7m from Pickering & 4m from Kirbymoorside. A170
ickering to Kirbymoorside road), follow Lastingham &
pleton-le-Moors signs*

is 17th-century pub stands opposite St Mary's Church
nowned for its Saxon crypt) in the National Park area.
e stone-built free house retains its original low-
amed ceilings and open range fireplace, and outside
ere's a cottage garden and decked seating area. Home-
oked dishes prepared from locally supplied ingredients
clude lamb casserole served with Yorkshire pudding,
d beer-battered jumbo cod. Snacks range through
nini, luxury salad, filled roll platters and buckets of
ps. Look out for daily specials.

Open all day noon-11.30 Closed: Tue L (Nov-May) **Bar
Meals** L served all wk (not Tue Nov-May) 12-5 D served
all wk 6.30-8.45 Av main course £8.50 **Restaurant** L
served Mon-Sat 12-2 (not Tue Nov-May), Sun 12-5
booking required D served all wk 6.30-8.45 booking
required ⊕ FREE HOUSE ◄ Theakstons Best Bitter, 2
rotating guest ales. ♀ 10 **Facilities** Children's menu
Family room Garden

LEYBURN · Map 19 SE19

The Old Horn Inn

Spennithorne DL8 5PR ☎ 01969 622370
e-mail: desmond@furlong1706.fsbusiness.co.uk
*dir: From Leyburn on A684 approx 1.5m E. Turn right
signed Spennithorne. From Bedale & A1 on A684 approx
9m W. Turn left signed Spennithorne*

Low beams and open log fires characterise this
traditional 17th-century free house. The former
farmhouse, which has been a pub for at least 100 years,
is named after the horn that summoned the farmer's
workers to lunch. Today's customers enjoy good food in
the dining room. Expect local hog and hop sausages with
mash and red onion marmalade; baked salmon with
prawns and basil sauce; or roasted vegetable lasagne
with garlic ciabatta bread.

Closed: Mon (ex BH) ◄ Black Sheep Bitter & Special,
John Smiths Cask, Coors Worthington's Cream Flow.
Facilities Dogs allowed Garden **Notes** ☺

PICK OF THE PUBS

Sandpiper Inn ♀

Market Place DL8 5AT
☎ 01969 622206 📄 01969 625367
e-mail: hsandpiper99@aol.com
dir: From A1 take A684 to Leyburn

Although it has been a pub for only 30 years, the
building that houses the Sandpiper Inn is the oldest
in Leyburn, dating back to around 1640. It has a
beautiful summer garden, and inside, a bar where you
can enjoy a pint of Black Sheep or Copper Dragon, a
snug and dining room where an exciting and varied mix
of traditional and more unusual dishes is served.
Lunch brings sandwiches (brie, salami and rocket for
example); and Masham sausage and mash with onion
gravy. An evening meal could start with warm pigeon
on a butternut squash risotto or terrine of game with
apple chutney, and continue with fish pie topped with
Berwick Edge cheese or slow-cooked Dales lamb with

---

winter vegetables and dauphinoise potatoes. Sunday
lunch includes roasted rib of Dales beef with onion
gravy and Yorkshire pudding.

Open 11.30-3 6.30-11 (Sun noon-2.30 7-10.30)
Closed: Mon & occasionally Tue **Bar Meals** L served all
wk 12-2.30 Av main course £8.50 **Restaurant** L served
all wk 12-2.30 booking required D served all wk
6.30-9.30 booking required ⊕ FREE HOUSE ◄ Black
Sheep Best, Black Sheep Special, Daleside, Copper
Dragon, Archers. ♀ 8 **Facilities** Children's menu Family
room Dogs allowed Garden

LITTON · Map 18 SD97

Queens Arms ♀

BD23 5QJ ☎ 01756 770208
e-mail: info@queensarmslitton.co.uk
dir: N of Skipton

Surrounded by the beauty of the Yorkshire Dales, this is
an ideal refreshment stop for everyone from walkers to
potholers. This drover's inn dates from the 18th century
and is full of original features including flagstones and
beams. An open fire provides a warm winter welcome. The
pub serves its own cask-conditioned ales, which are
brewed on the premises, as well as fine wines and
excellent home-cooked food made with ingredients from
local farms.

Open noon-3 6.30-11.30 (Sun 7-11) Closed: Mon **Bar
Meals** L served Tue-Sun 12-2.30 D served Tue-Sun
6.30-9 Av main course £9.50 **Restaurant** L served Tue-
Sun 12-2.30 D served Tue-Sun 6.30-9 booking required
Av 3 course à la carte fr £18.50 ⊕ FREE HOUSE ◄ Litton
Ale, Tetley Cask, guest ales ○ Stowford Press. ♀ 12
Facilities Family room Dogs allowed Garden Parking

LONG PRESTON · Map 18 SD85

Maypole Inn ♀

Maypole Green BD23 4PH
☎ 01729 840219 📄 01729 840727
e-mail: landlord@maypole.co.uk
dir: On A65 between Settle & Skipton

This inn has been welcoming visitors since 1695, when
Ambrose Wigglesworth welcomed his first customers.
Hand-drawn ales and traditional home cooking underpin
the operation. Located at the edge of the Yorkshire Dales
National Park, it's a good base for walking and cycling.
Relax in the beamed dining room or cosy bar over a pint
and a simple snack, sandwich, steak or salad; or try a
'special' like beef in ale pie, braised shoulder of lamb, or
pork in Pernod.

Open all wk ⊕ ENTERPRISE INNS ◄ Timothy Taylor
Landlord, Moorhouses Premier, Jennings, Cumberland,
Bombardier, Guest ale. ♀ 10 **Facilities** Dogs allowed
Garden Parking

PICK OF THE PUBS

The General Tarleton ★★★★★ RR 🌹🌹 ♉

KNARESBOROUGH — Map 19 SE35

Boroughbridge Rd, Ferrensby HG5 0PZ
☎ 01423 340284 📠 01423 340288
e-mail: gti@generaltarleton.co.uk
web: www.generaltarleton.co.uk
dir: A1(M) junct 48 at Boroughbridge, take
A6055 to Knaresborough. Inn 4m on right

What started in the 18th-century as a coaching inn is now known for its contemporary comforts, unstuffy atmosphere, and top-class dining, endorsed by two AA Rosettes. The 'Butcher General' himself, Sir Banastre Tarleton, distinguished himself during the American War of Independence, and a member of his platoon probably asked to name the inn in his honour. Step inside to find a reception lounge with large sofas, daily papers, glossy magazines and a warm and welcoming, low-beamed bar with log fires and cosy corners, the perfect setting in which to enjoy some Yorkshire real ales. Menus

subtitled 'Food with Yorkshire Roots' change daily to reflect the seasons and the day's pick of the crop or catch. The chef gets a call most days from the fishing boats as they return to ports on both coasts and within hours the fish is in the kitchen. In the Bar Brasserie, from where you can spill out into the light and airy covered courtyard, try The General's home-made black pudding with crispy bacon, lightly poached egg and sherry vinegar reduction; hotch-potch of Yorkshire pork with mock goose pie; or the signature dish of seafood parcels in lobster sauce, known as Little Moneybags. In the chic Tarleton restaurant start with warm shredded duck with chorizo, pancetta, croutons and salad leaves; follow with grilled fillet of brill with pak choi, fondant potato, brown shrimp and sauce vièrge; and end with iced nougatine parfait, passionfruit sorbet and raspberry coulis. The wine list features some fine bottles at bargain prices, as well as an impressive selection of house wines. Children are very welcome, as the menu of home-made dishes road-tested by the owners' three offspring testifies. The bedrooms are individually decorated and well equipped.

Open 12-3 6-11 **Bar Meals** L served all week 12-2 D served all week 6-9.15 Av main course £13.95 **Restaurant** L served Sun 12-1.45 D served Mon-Sat 6-9.15 Av 3 course à la carte fr £30 🍺 FREE HOUSE 🍺 Black Sheep Best, Timothy Taylor Landlord. ♉ 8 **Facilities** Children's menu Garden Parking **Rooms** 14

e Punch Bowl Inn ★★★★ INN ♀

.11 6PF ☎ 01748 886233 📠 01748 886945
mail: info@pbinn.co.uk
eb: www.pbinn.co.uk
r: A1 from Scotch Corner take A6108 to Richmond.
rough Richmond then right onto B6270 to Low Row

ting from the 17th-century, The Punch Bowl is located
Swaledale with Wainwright's Coast to Coast Walk on
doorstep. During a refurbishment a couple of years
o, the bar and bar stools were hand-crafted by Robert
e Mouseman Thompson (see if you can spot the mice
ound the bar). The menu, written on a large mirror,
lects the availability of seasonal produce, with game
m the surrounding moors and fish from Whitby. Local
sk conditioned ales from Theakston's and Black Sheep
eweries also feature. There are 11 en suite bedrooms if
u would like to stay over.

en all day all wk 11am-mdnt Closed: 25 Dec **Bar
als** L served all wk 12-2 booking required D served all
. 6.30-9 booking required Av main course £11.95
staurant L served all wk 12-2 booking required D
ved all wk 6.30-9 booking required Av 3 course à la
rte fr £22 ⊕ FREE HOUSE ◀ Theakstons Black Bull,
ack Sheep Best Bitter, John Smiths Cask & Smooth,
ack Sheep Riggwelter ♂ Thatchers Gold. ♀ 14
cilities Children's menu Parking **Rooms** 11

e Black Sheep Brewery

4 4EN
01765 689227 & 680100 📠 01765 689746
mail: sue.dempsey@blacksheep.co.uk
r: Off A6108, 9m from Ripon & 7m from Bedale

ul Theakston, of Masham's famous brewing family,
unded the Black Sheep Brewery in the early nineties
cording to traditional brewing principles. The complex

boasts a visitor centre where you can enjoy a
'shepherded' tour of the brewhouse, before popping into
the cosy bistro and 'baa...r' to sample the ales. The beers
also find their way into a range of hearty dishes,
including steak and Riggwelter casserole served with
jacket potato.

Open all wk 10.30-4.30 (Thu-Sat 10.30-late) **Bar Meals**
food served all day **Restaurant** food served all day
⊕ BLACK SHEEP BREWERY ◀ Black Sheep Best Bitter,
Riggwelter, Black Sheep Ale. **Facilities** Children's menu
Family room Garden Parking

Kings Head Hotel ★★ HL ♀

Market Place HG4 4EF
☎ 01765 689295 📠 01765 689070
dir: B6267 towards Masham, 7m from A1

Overlooking Masham's large market square with its cross
and maypole, this tastefully renovated Georgian inn
boasts open fires in the public rooms and a pleasant
terrace for summer dining. Unwind over a pint of
Theakstons in the bar, or sample a range of traditional
and contemporary dishes in the wood panelled
restaurant. Options might include minted lamb shoulder
with creamy mash; chicken with thyme dumplings and
Savoy cabbage; and smoked salmon penne pasta.

Open all day all wk 10.30am-1am **Bar Meals** L served
Mon-Fri 12-2.30, Sat-Sun & BH 12-9.30 D served Mon-Fri
6-9.30 Sat-Sun & BH 12-9.30 **Restaurant** L served Mon-
Fri 12-2.30, Sat-Sun & BH 12-9.30 D served Mon-Fri
6-9.30 Sat-Sun & BH 12-9.30 ⊕ SPIRIT GROUP
◀ Theakstons Best Bitter, Black Bull & Old Peculier,
Theakstons XB, Black Sheep. ♀ 14 **Facilities** Garden
Rooms 27

Black Swan Hotel ♀

Market Place DL8 4NP
☎ 01969 622221 📠 01969 622221
e-mail: blackswanmiddleham@breathe.com
dir: Telephone for directions

Dating back to the 17th-century and backing onto
Middleham Castle, home of Richard III, this historic pub
is at the heart of Yorkshire's racing country. Horses can
be seen passing outside every morning on their way to
the gallops. The emphasis here is on good food, with an
appealing choice including Black Swan grill, chicken
curry, bangers and mash, lasagne, and Kilnsey trout
roasted with parsley and thyme dressing. There's also a
good vegetarian choice.

Open all wk ⊕ FREE HOUSE ◀ John Smiths, Theakstons
Best Bitter, Black Bull, Old Peculier, guest ales. ♀ 7
Facilities Family room Dogs allowed Garden

The White Swan NEW ♀

Market Place DL8 4PE
☎ 01969 622093 📠 01969 624551
e-mail: enquiries@whiteswanhotel.co.uk
dir: From A1, take A684 towards Leyburn then A6108 to
Ripon, 1.5m to Middleham

Overlooking the town's picturesque market square and
boasting lovely rural views, the White Swan has recently
been extended and refurbished. An old-fashioned
flagstone floor adds to the atmosphere of the cosy public
bar, with its welcoming winter fire. A range of hand-
pulled Yorkshire ales, Thatchers cider and quality wines
complement the very best modern cuisine, from pizzas
and pasta dishes to seasonal game, daily fresh fish and
tempting puddings. All meals are freshly prepared using
mostly Yorkshire ingredients.

Open all day all wk 10.30am-11pm (mdnt at wknds)
Restaurant L served all wk 12-2.15 booking required D
served all wk 6.30-9.30 booking required ⊕ FREE HOUSE
◀ Black Sheep Best, John Smith's, Theakstons
♂ Thatchers Gold. ♀ 10 **Facilities** Children's menu
Family room Dogs allowed Parking

Crown Hotel ♀

HG3 5ST ☎ 01423 755204
dir: Telephone for directions

The original building dates back to the 17th century; today
it offers the chance to enjoy a good pint of local beer by a
cosy, roaring log fire, or in a sunny pub garden. Standing
on a breezy 900ft hilltop with good views towards
Gouthwaite Reservoir, the pub is in an ideal spot for anyone
potholing or following the popular Nidderdale Way.

Open all wk noon-2 7-8.30 **Bar Meals** L served all wk
12-2 D served all wk 7-8.30 ⊕ FREE HOUSE ◀ Black
Sheep Best, Guinness, Wensleydale Bitter. ♀ 20
Facilities Dogs allowed Garden Parking

The Middleton Arms ♀

Church Ln YO18 8PB ☎ 01751 475444
e-mail: themiddletonarms@aol.com
dir: 1m W of Pickering on A170

Formerly known as The New Inn, the pub dates from the
17th century and retains much of its traditional charm.
Menus draw on the best local produce and food is
prepared to order by chef proprietor Andy Green. Seasonal
fish and meat dishes are featured on the daily specials
board, while regulars might include oriental chicken stir
fry, Italian meatballs, or beef and ale stew with cheesy
scones.

Open 6-11 (Sun noon-3 6-10.30) Closed: Mon **Bar
Meals** Av main course £12 **Restaurant** L served Sun 12-3
D served Tue-Sun 6-9 Av 3 course à la carte fr £17
⊕ FREE HOUSE ◀ Timothy Taylor Landlord, Tetleys
Smooth, Nick Stafford Hambleton Ales, Black Sheep. ♀ 7
Facilities Children's menu Parking

MOULTON — Map 19 NZ20

Black Bull Inn

DL10 6QJ ☎ 01325 377289 📠 01325 377422

e-mail: info@blackbullmoulton.com

dir: *1m S of Scotch Corner off A1, 5m from Richmond*

Old pews, settles and fresh flowers all lend character to this civilised free house. If you want more, try booking an evening table in 'Hazel', the pub's immaculate Pullman dining carriage that was built in 1932 for service on the Brighton Belle. The food is just as impressive, specialising in seafood. Lunchtime bar snacks include smoked salmon baguettes and Welsh rarebit with bacon, whilst evening choices range from wild bass on fennel purée; griddled diver-caught scallops with smoked bacon and lentils; to pan-fried liver with colcannon.

Open noon-3 6-mdnt Closed: Sun eve **Bar Meals** L served Mon-Fri 12-2.30, Sat 12-2 Av main course £7.50 **Restaurant** L served Mon-Fri 12-2.30, Sun 12-4 booking required D served Mon-Thu 6.30-9.30, Fri-Sat 6.30-10 booking required Fixed menu price fr £19.95 Av 3 course à la carte fr £36.50 ⊕ FREE HOUSE ◀ Theakstons Best, John Smiths Smooth. **Facilities** Garden Parking

MUKER — Map 18 SD99

The Farmers Arms 🍷

DL11 6QG ☎ 01748 886297 📠 01748 886375

dir: *From Richmond take A6108 towards Leyburn, turn right onto B6270*

The last remaining pub in the village of Muker, at the head of beautiful Swaledale, The Farmers Arms is understandably popular with walkers. A welcoming coal fire burns in the stone-flagged bar in cooler weather, while in summer the south facing patio is a relaxing place to sit. Award-winning ales are served along with good home-cooked food (the steak pie is a particular favourite). Dogs on leads are welcome in the bar.

Open all day all wk 11am-11.30pm **Bar Meals** L served all wk 12-2.30 Av main course £8 ⊕ FREE HOUSE ◀ Theakstons Best, Old Peculier, John Smith's, Black Sheep, guest ales Ò Thatchers Gold. 🍷 10 **Facilities** Dogs allowed Garden Parking

NUNNINGTON — Map 19 SE67

The Royal Oak Inn 🍷

Church St YO62 5US ☎ 01439 748271
📠 01439 748271

dir: *Village centre, close to Nunnington Hall*

A short walk through the village from Nunnington Hall brings you to this Grade II listed country inn. The sign on the front door says it all – 'Real ale, real food, real people'. Traditional decor, with open fires in winter and fresh flowers in summer, make for a welcoming atmosphere, and the patio garden is a welcome recent addition. Hearty home-cooked meals are prepared from seasonal vegetables, locally reared meats and game from local farms and estates. Expect main dishes like

Fisherman's pot or steak and kidney casserole. Home-made desserts such as sticky toffee pudding or triple chocolate mousse are a proper treat.

Open 11.45-2.30 6.30-11 (Sun noon-2.30 7-11) Closed: Mon **Bar Meals** L served Tue-Sun 12-2 Av main course £11 **Restaurant** D served Tue-Sun 6.30-9 ⊕ FREE HOUSE ◀ Black Sheep, Wold Top, John Smiths, Theakstons XB. 🍷 11 **Facilities** Children's menu Dogs allowed Garden Parking

OLDSTEAD — Map 19 SE57

PICK OF THE PUBS

The Black Swan ⓤ ☺☺ 🍷

Main St YO61 4BL ☎ 01347 868387

e-mail: enquiries@blackswanoldstead.co.uk

dir: *A1 junct 49, A168, A19S of A19N to Coxwold then Byland Abbey. In 2m left for Oldstead, pub 1m on left*

The Black Swan, which dates from the 16th century, is owned and run by the Banks family, who have lived and farmed in the village for generations. The bar is full of character with a log fire, flagstone floor, window seats, antique furniture and oak fittings by Robert 'Mousey' Thompson. Choice at the bar includes real ales, good wines by the glass, malt whiskies and old port. Both lunch and evening menus offer home-made fare including traditional and more sophisticated dishes. Options include pub classics (fish and chips; beef casserole; steak and chips) plus starters such as celeriac velouté with grilled pancetta, capers and shallots; followed by fillet of turbot with salmon and crab ravioli; or haunch of venison with button onion tart. Ingredients are fresh, and the beef, pork and lamb comes from local farms. Printed details of walks from the pub are available at the bar, and you are welcome to leave your vehicle in the car park while you enjoy your walk.

Open all wk noon-3 6-11 **Bar Meals** L served all wk 12-2 D served all wk 6-9 Av main course £11.50 **Restaurant** L served all wk 12-2 booking required D served all wk 6-9 booking required Av 3 course à la carte fr £21.95 ⊕ FREE HOUSE ◀ Black Sheep, Copper Dragon, Guinness Ò Thatchers Gold. 🍷 19 **Facilities** Children's menu Garden Parking Rooms 4

OSMOTHERLEY — Map 19 SE49

PICK OF THE PUBS

The Golden Lion

6 West End DL6 3AA ☎ 01609 883526

The Golden Lion is a cosy sandstone building of some 250 years standing. The atmosphere is warm and welcoming, with open fires and wooden flooring on one side of the downstairs area. Furnishings are simple with a wooden bar, bench seating and tables, whitewashed walls, mirrors and fresh flowers. The extensive menu ranges through basic pub grub to more refined dishes. The starters are divided between fish, soups, vegetarian, pastas and risottos, meat and salads, and might include smoked salmon; buffalo mozzarella with tomato and basil; spicy pork ribs; and avocado and king prawn salad. Mains are along the lines of grilled seabass with new potatoes and peas; coq au vin; calves' liver with fried onions and mash; home-made beef burger with Mexican salsa; and spicy chilladas with fresh tomato sauce. Also interesting specials like pork stroganoff and rice, or lamb and feta lasagne. Sherry trifle, and bread and butter pudding with cream, are popular desserts.

Open 12-3 6-11.30 Closed: 25 Dec, Mon L, Tue L **Bar Meals** L served Wed-Sun 12-2.30 D served all wk 6-9 ◀ Timothy Taylor Landlord, Jennings Bitter, York Guzzler. **Facilities** Dogs allowed Garden

Queen Catherine

7 West End DL6 3AG ☎ 01609 883209

dir: *Please telephone for directions*

Nestling in the heart of a picturesque village, this traditional inn is believed to be the only one in Britain called 'Queen Catherine'. The name is a reference to Henry VIII's wife Catherine of Aragon, who reputedly left her horse and carriage here while sheltering from her husband in a nearby priory. There's no sense of menace around nowadays and visitors can enjoy comforting food locally sourced where possible, such as crab-stuffed chicken breast, lamb shank with minted gravy and breaded Whitby scampi.

Open all wk **Bar Meals** L served all wk 12-2.30 D served all wk 6-9 **Restaurant** L served all wk 12-2.30 booking required D served all wk 6-9 booking required ⊕ FREE HOUSE ◀ Tetleys Smooth & Extra Cold, Tetleys Cask Bitter, guest ale. **Facilities** Children's menu Dogs allowed

PADSIDE   Map 19 SE15

The Stone House Inn ▾

Thruscross HG3 4AH
☎ 01943 880325   📠 01943 880347
e-mail: info@stonehouseinn.co.uk

Throughout its 300-year history, the Stone House Inn has been a place of refreshment for travellers as well as a community hub. Run by John McEwan since 2007, it features open fires, exposed beams and stone flagged floors. Locally sourced ingredients are the starting point for varied, home made dishes; expect specials such as Ramsgill oxtail casserole with root vegetables; black pudding salad; and wild mushroom and feta lasagne. Lunchtime sandwiches are also available.

Closed: Mon (Jan-Etr) ⊕ FREE HOUSE ◀ Black Sheep Bitter, Deuchars IPA, Old Bear Honeypot, Riggwelter, Daleside. ▾ 7 Facilities Dogs allowed Garden Parking

PATELEY BRIDGE   Map 19 SE16

PICK OF THE PUBS

The Sportsmans Arms Hotel ▾

See Pick of the Pubs on page 532

See Pick of the Pubs on page 532

PICKERING   Map 19 SE78

PICK OF THE PUBS

Fox & Hounds Country Inn ★★ HL ☻ ▾

Sinnington YO62 6SQ
☎ 01751 431577   📠 01751 432791
e-mail: foxhoundsinn@easynet.co.uk
dir: *3m W of town, off A170 between Pickering & Helmsley*

This handsome 18th-century coaching inn lies in Sinnington, on a quiet road between Pickering and Kirkbymoorside. A gentle walk from the pub passes the village green to the pretty riverside where ducks swim in the shallows and an ancient packhorse bridge leads to more footpaths through the woods. Proprietors Andrew and Catherine Stephens and friendly efficient staff ensure a warm welcome. As you settle down with a pint of Theakstons or Black Sheep, you can relax and enjoy the oak-beamed ceilings, old wood panelling and open fires. The inn has ten well equipped en suite bedrooms, and a residents' lounge where guests can relax by the fire before dinner. The menu is full of

locally farmed produce, and many of the starters are also available as main courses. Expect the likes of pan-crisp braised belly pork with ginger and honey noodles; Gressingham duck leg, roast beetroot and rocket; and Swaledale 'Old Peculiar' cheese soufflé.

Open all wk noon-2 6.30-9 Closed: 25-26 Dec Bar Meals L served all wk 12-2 booking required D served all wk 6.30-9 booking required Av main course £13.95 **Restaurant** L served all wk 12-2 booking required D served all wk 6.30-9 booking required Av 3 course à la carte fr £25 ⊕ FREE HOUSE ◀ Theakstons Best, Black Sheep Special, Worthingtons Creamflow. ▾ 7 **Facilities** Children's menu Dogs allowed Garden Parking **Rooms** 10

The Fox & Rabbit Inn NEW ▾

Whitby Road, Locton YO18 7NQ
☎ 01751 460213   📠 01751 460052
e-mail: info@foxandrabbit.co.uk
dir: *Four miles north of Pickering on A169, at Thornton-le-Dale junct*

In a lovely location at the edge of Dalby Forest, the Fox & Rabbit Inn enjoys great views across the valley of the North York Moors Railway. Owners Charles and Toby Wood have been at the helm here since 2004, and they pride themselves on their use of local produce. Try the popular Whitby haddock and chips, or Dalby sausage and mash with red onion gravy featuring pork from forest pigs. You can eat in the cosy bar with its open fire or the sunny restaurant which has panoramic views.

Open all day (Etr-Oct) please phone for winter opening times Bar Meals L served all wk 12-2 D served all wk 5-8.30 av main course £11 **Restaurant** L served all wk 12-2 D served all wk 5-8.30 à la carte fr £19 ⊕ FREE HOUSE ◀ Black Sheep, Best Bitter, Camerons, John Smiths Smooth, Cropton Brewery Ŏ Thatchers Gold ▾ 10 **Facilities** Dogs allowed Children's menu Garden Parking

Horseshoe Inn ▾

Main St, Levisham YO18 7NL
☎ 01751 460240   📠 01751 460052
e-mail: info@horseshoelevisham.co.uk
dir: *A169, 5m from Pickering. 4m, pass Fox & Rabbit Inn on right. In 0.5m left to Lockton. Follow steep winding road to village*

At the head of a tranquil village deep in *Heartbeat* country on the edge of the North York Moors National Park, this spruced-up 16th-century inn makes an ideal pit-stop or base for walking, cycling and touring the moors – don't miss a trip on the nearby steam railway. Charles and Toby Wood have created in inviting atmosphere in the beamed bar, with its polished plank floor and roaring log fire, offering tip-top Yorkshire ales and hearty country cooking – pork belly with cider gravy, steak and mushroom pie, roast beef and horseradish sandwiches.

Open all wk Bar Meals L served all wk 12-2 booking required D served all wk 6-8.30 booking required Av main course £11 **Restaurant** L served all wk 12-2 booking required D served all wk 6-8.30 booking required Av 3 course à la carte fr £19 ⊕ FREE HOUSE ◀ Black Sheep Best, Timothy Taylor Landlord Ŏ Thatchers. ▾ 9 **Facilities** Children's menu Dogs allowed Garden Parking

PICKHILL   Map 19 SE38

PICK OF THE PUBS

Nags Head Country Inn ★★ HL ☻ ▾

YO7 4JG ☎ 01845 567391   📠 01845 567212
e-mail: enquiries@nagsheadpickhill.co.uk
dir: *1m E of A1. 4m N of A1/A61 junct*

This region of Yorkshire is known as 'Herriot country', after the books by the famous country vet. A direct descendant of the coaching inn tradition, the Nag's Head is a 200-year-old free house set in the village of Pickhill. It's perfectly situated for exploring the local fells, playing a round of golf, fishing or having a flutter at nearby Thirsk, Ripon and Catterick races. Once you've worked up an appetite, head inside where beamed ceilings, stone-flagged floors and winter fires make for a most welcoming atmosphere. A lengthy but thoughtful menu is equally appealing. Starters like potted brown shrimps with five spice and lime herb croutons precede main course options that include luxury fish pie; saddle of Pickhill hare with confit leg; and pan-fried calves' liver with crispy bacon. Desserts too rise above the usual; individual apple tarte Tatin, for example, is served with blackberry ice cream.

Open all wk 11-11 (Sun 11-10.30) Closed: 25 Dec Bar Meals L served Mon-Sat 12-2, Sun 12-2.30 booking required D served Mon-Sat 6-9.30, Sun 6-9 booking required Av main course £12.95 **Restaurant** L served Mon-Sat 12-2, Sun 12-2.30 booking required D served Mon-Sat 6-9.30, Sun 6-9 booking required Av 3 course à la carte fr £22.50 ⊕ FREE HOUSE ◀ Black Sheep Best, Old Peculier, Theakstons Best Bitter, Black Bull, York Brewery Guzzler Ŏ Thatchers Gold. ▾ 8 **Facilities** Children's menu Dogs allowed Garden Parking **Rooms** 14

PICK OF THE PUBS

The Sportsmans Arms Hotel ♈

PATELEY BRIDGE   Map 19 SE16

Wath-in-Nidderdale HG3 5PP
☎ **01423 711306** 🖹 **01423 712524**
dir: *A59/B6451, hotel 2m N of Pateley Bridge*

Nidderdale is one of the most beautiful of the Yorkshire Dales; Wath is a conservation village, picturesque and unspoilt. Ray and June Carter have been running their 17th-century restaurant with bedrooms, reached by a packhorse bridge across the Nidd, for 30 years, although son Jamie and daughter Sarah have leading roles too these days. Enter the hallway and find open log fires,
comfortable chairs, a warm and welcoming bar and a calm, softly lit restaurant, dominated at one end by a Victorian sideboard and substantial wine rack. As much of the food as possible is locally sourced, but Ray has no qualms about buying foreign produce if he thinks it better. Always good, though, are the Nidderdale lamb, pork, beef, fresh trout and game (season permitting) from the moors. Fish arriving daily from Whitby and other East Coast harbours typically appear on the plate as turbot with spinach and mousseline; seared tuna with rocket salsa and Greek salad; or maybe as lightly-cooked halibut with beurre blanc glazed with fresh Parmesan. Best end of Nidderdale lamb is perfectly accompanied by creamy garlic mash, natural jus and tomato concassé; and chestnuts, cranberries and pancetta go well with saddle of venison. The wine list offers a wide selection of styles and
prices from traditional wine-making areas, plus some new and interesting examples. As well as fine vintage ports, brandies, and liqueurs, a special interest in whiskies is shown and some excellent Champagnes are also available. The Sportsmans Arms stands on the 53-mile, circular Nidderdale Way, hard by the dam over the River Nidd (some fishing rights belong to the hotel) that creates Gouthwaite Reservoir.

Open 12-2.30 6.30-11 Bar meals L served Mon-Sat 12-2 D served all week 7-9 Closed: 25 Dec **Restaurant** L served Sun 12-2 D served Mon-Sat 7-9 ⊕ FREE HOUSE ◼ Black Sheep, Worthingtons, Timothy Taylor Landlord, Folly Ale. ♈ 12 **Facilities** Garden Parking

PICTON
Map 19 NZ40

The Station Hotel ♥

TS15 0AE ☎ 01642 700067

dir: 1.5m from A19

'Hotel' by name only, this is family-run and family-friendly village pub has had the same owner for 20 years. Offering real food at reasonable prices, just about everything is home made from locally sourced produce, with one menu serving both bar and dining room. While the children enjoy the outdoor play area in the beer garden, parents can relax in front of the open fire and scan the extensive specials board over a pint of John Smiths.

Open all wk 6-11.30 (Sat noon-2.30 6-11.30 Sun noon-4 6-11.30) **Bar Meals** L served Sat 12-2.30, Sun 12-4 booking required D served all wk ⊕ FREE HOUSE ◀ John Smiths Cask, John Smiths Smooth, Guinness. ♥ 6 **Facilities** Children's menu Play area Garden Parking

REETH
Map 19 SE09

PICK OF THE PUBS

Charles Bathurst Inn ★★★★ INN ♥

Arkengarthdale DL11 6EN
☎ 01748 884567 📠 01748 884599
e-mail: info@cbinn.co.uk
web: www.cbinn.co.uk
dir: From A1 leave at Scotch Corner, take A6108 to Richmond then B6270 to Reeth. At Buck Hotel turn N to Langthwaite, pass church on right, Inn 0.5m on right

Cosy fires and antique pine furniture greet customers entering this 18th-century free house. Strategically located on the edge of the Pennine Way and close to the mid-point of the coast-to-coast walk, the inn is set in remote and beautiful Arkengarthdale. The building was formerly a bunkhouse for lead miners employed by Charles Bathurst, an 18th-century lord of the manor and son of Oliver Cromwell's physician. Today, the owners pride themselves on knowing the provenance of all their food, and the daily menu is written up on an imposing mirror hanging at the end of the bar. Starters might include butternut squash and Parmesan risotto; and pan-fried mackerel on Greek salad. For a hearty lunch try steamed steak and red wine suet pudding with parsnip mash; or the lighter goats' cheese, tomato and red onion tartlet; followed, perhaps, by plum crumble with crème Anglaise. There are 19 en suite bedrooms if you would like to stay over for a spot of walking, mountain biking, horse riding or angling.

Open all wk 11am-mdnt Closed: 25 Dec **Bar Meals** L served all wk 12-2 booking required D served all wk 6.30-9 booking required Av main course £11.95 **Restaurant** L served all wk 12-2 booking required D served all wk 6.30-9 booking required Av 3 course à la carte fr £22 ⊕ FREE HOUSE ◀ Theakstons, John Smiths Bitter, John Smiths Smooth, Black Sheep Best, Riggwelter. ♥ 12 **Facilities** Children's menu Play area Garden Parking **Rooms** 19

ROBIN HOOD'S BAY
Map 19 NZ90

Laurel Inn ♥

New Rd YO22 4SE ☎ 01947 880400

dir: Telephone for directions

Picturesque Robin Hood's Bay is the setting for this small, traditional pub which retains lots of character features, including beams and an open fire. The bar is decorated with old photographs, and an international collection of lager bottles. This coastal fishing village was once the haunt of smugglers who used a network of underground tunnels and secret passages to bring the booty ashore.

Open all wk ⊕ FREE HOUSE ◀ Old Peculier, Theakstons Best, Deuchars IPA. **Facilities** Family room Dogs allowed **Notes** ⊛

SAWDON
Map 17 SE98

The Anvil Inn ♥

Main St YO13 9DY ☎ 01723 859896
e-mail: theanvilinnsawdon@btinternet.com
web: www.theanvilinnsawdon.co.uk
dir: 1.5m N of Brompton-by-Sawdon, on A170 8m E of Pickering & 6m W of Scarborough

Set on the edge of Dalby Forest, this is a walkers' and birdwatchers' paradise. It was a working forge for over 200 years until 1985; many artefacts remain, including the original furnace. Local ales and ciders are always available. Local produce, nicely handled and well priced, appears in dishes such as fresh crab and leek terrine with avocado dressing; pan-roasted lamb loin with a ragout of chorizo, beans, tomatoes and olives; and steamed marmalade sponge pudding. Two self-catering cottages are available.

Closed: 26 Dec & 1 Jan, Mon **Bar Meals** L served Tue-Sat 12-2, Sun 12-3 booking required D served Tue-Sat 6.30-9 booking required Av main course £13.75 **Restaurant** L served Tue-Sat 12-2, Sun 12-3 booking required D served Tue-Sat 6.30-9 booking required Av 3 course à la carte fr £19 ⊕ FREE HOUSE ◀ Daleside Blonde, Hobgoblin Ale, Copper Dragon, Wold Top, Daleside Old Leg Over ♂ Stowford Press. ♥ 11 **Facilities** Children's menu Dogs allowed Garden Parking

SAWLEY
Map 19 SE26

The Sawley Arms ♥

HG4 3EQ ☎ 01765 620642
e-mail: junehawes1@aol.co.uk
dir: A1(M) junct 47, A59 to Knaresborough, B6165 to Ripley, A61 towards Ripon, left for Sawley. Or from Ripon B6265 towards Pateley Bridge, left to Sawley. Pub 1m from Fountains Abbey

This delightful 200-year-old pub stands just a mile from Fountains Abbey. Run by the same owners for 40 years, it was a frequent haunt of the late author and vet James Herriot. Surrounded by its own stunning gardens, the pub is big on old world charm. The menu is suitably traditional, with dishes ranging from pies and casseroles to fresh plaice mornay with sautéed leeks, creamed potatoes and a rich cheese glaze.

Open 11.30-3 6-10.30 Closed: 25 Dec, Sun eve & Mon eve in winter **Bar Meals** L served all wk 12-2.30 booking required D served all wk 6.30-9.30 booking required **Restaurant** L served all wk 12-2.30 booking required D served all wk 6.30-9.30 booking required ⊕ FREE HOUSE ◀ Theakston Best, John Smiths. ♥ 8 **Facilities** Children's menu Garden Parking

SCAWTON
Map 19 SE58

PICK OF THE PUBS

The Hare Inn ⊛ ♀

YO7 2HG ☎ 01845 597769
e-mail: info@thehareinn.co.uk
dir: *Telephone for directions*

Mentioned in the Domesday Book, and once frequented by the abbots and monks of Rievaulx Abbey. In the 17th century, ale was brewed here for local iron workers. Inside, as you might expect, are low-beamed ceilings and flagstone floors, a wood-burning stove providing a warm welcome in the bar, and an old-fashioned kitchen range in the dining area. Eating here promises food of AA Rosette standard, with the kitchen ringing the changes according to availability, but sourcing ingredients locally from seafood specialists in Hartlepool, beef and lamb from Masham, and chicken and duck from Pateley Bridge. The full à la carte menu is complemented by light lunch and early bird possibilities, offering quality dining at value prices. A representative choice could start with smoked haddock with Montgomery cheddar rarebit; continue with roast rack of Sutton Bank lamb with fresh tarragon; and finish with hazelnut and raspberry Pavlova.

Closed: Mon **Bar Meals** L served Tue-Sat 12-2, Sun 12-4 Av main course £13.95 **Restaurant** L served Tue-Sat 12-2, Sun 12-4 booking required D served Tue-Sat 6-9 booking required Fixed menu price fr £12.50 Av 3 course à la carte fr £30 ⊕ FREE HOUSE ◀ Black Sheep, Timothy Taylor Landlord, guest ales Ö Thatchers. ♀ 14 **Facilities** Garden Parking

SETTLE
Map 18 SD86

Golden Lion ♀

Duke St BD24 9DU ☎ 01729 822203 ▤ 01729 824103
e-mail: info@goldenlion.yorks.net
dir: *Telephone for directions*

This traditional Dales coaching inn has been the silent witness to incalculable comings and goings in Settle's market place since around 1640. Its cosy bars, open fire, commodious restaurant and comfy bedrooms often meet the needs of travellers on the spectacular Settle-Carlisle railway line. There is a good choice of beers and a strong emphasis on food prepared from fresh ingredients, with specials such as moules marinière, Moroccan lamb curry and vegetable stirfry.

Open all day all wk 11-11 (Sun noon-10.30) **Bar Meals** L served Mon-Fri 12-2.30 Sat 12-10, Sun 12-9.30 D served Mon-Thu 6-9.30, Fri 6-10, Sat 12-10, Sun 12-9.30 ⊕ DANIEL THWAITES PLC ◀ Thwaites Bitter, Bomber, Guest ales. ♀ 9 **Facilities** Parking

SKIPTON
Map 18 SD95

Devonshire Arms ♀

Grassington Rd, Cracoe BD23 6LA
☎ 01756 730237 ▤ 01756 730142
dir: *Telephone for directions*

A convivial 17th-century inn convenient for the Three Peaks, and original setting for the Rhylstone Ladies WI calendar. There are excellent views of Rhylstone Fell. A wide range of cask ales plus extensive wine list will wash down a menu that includes steak and mushroom pie cooked in Jennings Snecklifter ale, lamb Jennings, chicken Diane, and haddock and chips.

Open all wk ⊕ WOLVERHAMPTON & DUDLEY BREWERIES PLC ◀ Jennings, Jennings Cumberland, Snecklifter, Tetley. ♀ 7 **Facilities** Garden Parking

SNAINTON
Map 17 SE98

Coachman Inn ♀

Pickering Road West YO13 9PL
☎ 01723 859231 ▤ 01723 850008
e-mail: james@coachmaninn.co.uk
dir: *5m from Pickering, off A170 onto B1258*

The Coachman is an imposing Grade II listed Georgian coaching inn, run by James and Rita Osborne. It was once the last staging post before Scarborough for the York mail. As well as the varied main menu, there is a daily specials board including dishes like smoked local venison with asparagus and quail egg; and seared scallops with gruyère and chive mash, grilled pancetta and lemon oil. Outside is a large lawned area with flowers, trees and seating.

Closed: Mon **Bar Meals** L served Wed-Sun 12-2 D served Tue-Sun 6.30-9 **Restaurant** L served Wed-Sun 12-2 booking required D served Tue-Sat 7-9 booking required ⊕ FREE HOUSE ◀ John Smiths, Wold Top, Guinness Ö Stowford Press. ♀ 7 **Facilities** Children's menu Garden Parking

STARBOTTON
Map 18 SD97

Fox & Hounds Inn ♀

BD23 5HY ☎ 01756 760269 ▤ 760367
e-mail: starbottonfox@aol.com
dir: *Telephone for directions*

Situated in a picturesque limestone village in Upper Wharfedale in the heart of the Yorkshire Dales, this ancient pub was originally built as a private house, but has been a pub for more than 160 years. Make for the cosy bar, with its solid furnishings and flagstones, and enjoy a pint of Black Sheep or one of the guest ales. The menu offers steak and ale pie, minted lamb shank, pork medallions in brandy and mustard sauce, and a selection of steaks.

Open noon-3 6-11 (Sun noon-3.30 5.30-10.30) Closed: 1-22 Jan, Mon **Bar Meals** Av main course £10.45 ⊕ FREE HOUSE ◀ Black Sheep, Timothy Taylor Landlord, Moorhouse, guest ales. ♀ 8 **Facilities** Children's menu Garden Parking

SUTTON-ON-THE-FOREST
Map 19 SE56

PICK OF THE PUBS

The Blackwell Ox Inn
INN ⊛ ♀

Huby Rd YO61 1DT
☎ 01347 810328 ▤ 01347 812738
e-mail: enquiries@blackwelloxinn.co.uk
dir: *7m from centre of York off A1237. Take B1363, at T-junct left. Pub on right*

Set in the picturesque village of Sutton-on-the-Forest, the Blackwell Ox blends modern elegance with period charm. Visitors will find hand-pulled ales and an open fire in the bar, as well as a terrace for sitting out in the warmer months. Meanwhile, restaurant diners can relax in the lounge area before or after their meal. The chef believes in simple, honest cooking, and sources local North Yorkshire produce to create his dishes. Substantial 'knife and fork' sandwiches appear at lunchtime, alongside a fixed price menu that might include salmon fritters with aïoli; or confit of pork with cassoulet. A typical evening meal might start with pea and mint soup, followed by sea bass with braised endive, and finishing with lemon posset and butter shortbread. Overnight, the Blackwell Ox offers comfortable, individually designed bedrooms, just 7 miles from the centre of York.

Open all wk noon-3 5.30-11 (Sun close 10.30) **Bar Meals** Av main course £11.45 food served all day **Restaurant** Fixed menu price fr £10.95 Av 3 course à la carte fr £25 food served all day ⊕ FREE HOUSE ◀ Black Sheep, John Smiths Cask, Guinness, Timothy Taylor Landlord, Copper Dragon. ♀ 9 **Facilities** Children's menu Garden Parking **Rooms** 7

THORNTON LE DALE
Map 19 SE88

The New Inn

Maltongate YO18 7LF ☎ 01751 474226
e-mail: enquire@the-new-inn.com
dir: *A64 N from York towards Scarborough. At Malton take A169 to Pickering. At Pickering rdbt right onto A170, 2m, pub on right*

This Georgian coaching inn stands at the heart of a picturesque village complete with stocks and a market cross. The old world charm of the surroundings is echoed inside the bar and restaurant, whose large windows illuminate real log fires and exposed beams. Well-behaved dogs sit patiently while their owners ponder the array of guest ales, bitters, lagers and wines. Freshly cooked food ranges from ploughman's to prime fillet steaks and roast of the day.

Open all wk ⊕ SCOTTISH & NEWCASTLE ◀ Theakston Best, Bombardier, Black Sheep, guest ales. **Facilities** Dogs allowed Garden Parking

THORNTON WATLASS
Map 19 SE28

PICK OF THE PUBS

The Buck Inn ★★★ INN ♀

See Pick of the Pubs on page 536

TOPCLIFFE
Map 19 SE37

The Angel Inn ♀

YO7 3RW ☎ 01845 577237 📠 01845 578000
e-mail: info@topcliffeangelinn.co.uk
web: www.topcliffeangelinn.co.uk
dir: *On A168(M), 3m from A1*

A refurbishment has given this old country inn a more contemporary feel, but with more than a nod to tradition. The restaurant has a good local reputation for creative dishes such as fillet of red mullet with warm potato, celeriac and beetroot salad; pheasant pot au feu with stuffed cabbage and spätzle; and, for two, seafood casserole under puff pastry.

Open all day all wk 9am-11pm (Fri-Sat 9am-mdnt) **Bar Meals** L served all wk 12-3 booking required D served all wk 5-9 booking required ⊕ CAMERONS ◀ John Smith, Black Sheep, Timothy Taylor. ♀ 8 **Facilities** Children's menu Dogs allowed Garden Parking

WASS
Map 19 SE57

PICK OF THE PUBS

Wombwell Arms ♀

See Pick of the Pubs on page 537

WEAVERTHORPE
Map 17 SE97

PICK OF THE PUBS

The Star Country Inn

YO17 8EY ☎ 01944 738273 📠 01944 738273
e-mail: starinn.malton@btconnect.com
dir: *From Malton take A64 towards Scarborough. 12m, at Sherborn right at lights. Weaverthorpe 4m, inn opposite junct*

Situated in the village of Weaverthorpe in the heart of the Yorkshire Wolds, this 200-year-old inn has a rustic interior with large winter fires and a welcoming, convivial atmosphere. Theakstons is the major real ale on tap in the bar, alongside beers from Wold Top and John Smiths. Food is fresh and locally sourced where possible, and pride is taken in everything from fresh-baked breads to home-made ice cream. Even the tomato ketchup is made on site! A meal might include ham hock terrine followed by beer battered Whitby fish with hand cut chips, mushy peas and tartare sauce, while spicier options include vegetable balti with pilau rice or green Thai prawn curry. A classy selection of specials might include pan-fried pigeon breast with watercress salad and walnut dressing; or pan-seared Shetland king scallops with curried parsnip purée and parsnip chips. The Star is an ideal base for visiting local attractions such as Castle Howard, and the area is also popular with cyclists and bird-watchers.

Open all day noon-mdnt Closed: Mon **Bar Meals** L served Tue-Sat 12-6, Sun 12-3 booking required Av main course £8 food served all day **Restaurant** L served Sun 12-3 booking required D served Tue-Sun 6-9 booking required ⊕ FREE HOUSE ◀ Bitter, John Smiths, Wold Top, Theakstons. **Facilities** Children's menu Garden Parking

WEST BURTON
Map 19 SE08

Fox & Hounds

DL8 4JY ☎ 01969 663111 📠 01969 663279
web: www.fhinn.co.uk
dir: *A468 between Hawes & Leyburn, 0.5m E of Aysgarth*

The Fox and Hounds is a traditional pub in a beautiful Dales setting overlooking the village green, which has swings and football goals for children, and its own hidden waterfalls. The pub is a proper local, hosting men's and women's darts teams and a dominoes team. In summer customers play quoits out on the green. Real ales, some from The Black Sheep Brewery down the road,

and home-made food prepared from fresh ingredients are served. Dishes include chicken curry, steak and kidney pie, lasagne, steaks and other pub favourites.

Open all day all wk **Bar Meals** L served all wk 12-2 D served all wk 6-8.30 Av main course £7.95 **Restaurant** L served all wk 12-2 booking required D served all wk 6-8.30 booking required Av 3 course à la carte fr £16 ⊕ FREE HOUSE ◀ Black Sheep, John Smiths, Theakstons Best, Copper Dragon ♂ Stowford Press. **Facilities** Children's menu Family room Dogs allowed Parking

WEST TANFIELD
Map 19 SE27

PICK OF THE PUBS

The Bruce Arms ♀

See Pick of the Pubs on page 538

WESTOW
Map 19 SE76

The Blacksmiths Inn

Main St YO60 7NE ☎ 01653 618365
dir: *From A64, Westow signed from top of Whitwell Hill. Turn right, to T-junct. Pub right on Main St*

A 19th-century free house in the old village blacksmith's, where nothing much has changed and the old oven, anvil and bellows are still in place. Tuesday night is pie night, when the owners serve a selection of home-made pies, washed down with Jennings' Bitter or Cumberland.

Closed: Sun eve, Mon & Tue L ⊕ FREE HOUSE ◀ Jennings Bitter, Jennings Cumberland, Guinness. **Facilities** Garden Parking

WHASHTON
Map 19 NZ10

Hack & Spade

DL11 7JL ☎ 01748 823721
e-mail: info@hackandspade.com
dir: *From Scotch Corner A66 W towards Penrith for 5m. Left exit towards Ravensworth, follow for 2m. Left at x-rds for Whashton*

Set amid rolling hills in the heart of North Yorkshire, this pub has fantastic views over Holmedale and the surrounding area. Its name relates to the quarry that used to be opposite; nowadays it has been filled in to form part of the village green. The menu is built on local ingredients, and might include grilled black pudding and goats' cheese stack followed by pan-fried pork loin, spring onion and pea mash and mustard sauce.

Open all wk 6.30-11.30 **Restaurant** D served all wk 6.30-8.45 Av 3 course à la carte fr £20 ⊕ FREE HOUSE ◀ John Smith's Smooth, Theakstons. **Facilities** Children's menu Parking

PICK OF THE PUBS

The Buck Inn ★★★ INN ♟

THORNTON WATLASS   Map 19 SE28

HG4 4AH
☎ 01677 422461   📠 01677 422447
e-mail: innwatlass1@btconnect.com
web: www.buckwatlass.co.uk
dir: *From A1 at Leeming Bar take A684 to Bedale, then B6268 towards Masham. Village 2m on right, inn by cricket green*

The Buck Inn doesn't just overlook the village green and cricket pitch; players score four runs for hitting the pub wall, and six if the ball goes over the roof! Very much the quintessential village scene in beautiful Thornton Watlass, Bedale is where Wensleydale, gateway to the Yorkshire Dales National Park, begins, and this glorious area is where much of the television programme *Heartbeat* was filmed. The pub is a traditional, well run, friendly institution that has been in experienced hands of Michael and Margaret Fox for over 20 years, so they have no trouble in maintaining its welcoming and relaxed atmosphere. There are three separate dining areas - the bar for informality, the restaurant for dining by candlelight, and on busy days the large function room is opened. The menu ranges from traditional, freshly prepared pub fare to exciting modern cuisine backed by daily changing blackboard specials. Typical bar favourites are Masham rarebit (Wensleydale cheese with local ale topped with bacon and served with pear chutney); steak and ale pie; oven-baked lasagne; lamb cutlets with rosemary and redcurrant sauce, and beer-battered fish and chips. Hearty and wholesome daily specials may take in chicken liver parfait with red onion marmalade; beef Wellington with Madeira sauce; game casserole, and roast cod with mash and saffron cream. Beer drinkers have a choice of five real ales pulled from handpumps, including Masham-brewed Black Sheep, while whisky drinkers have a selection of some forty different malts to try, ideal when relaxing by the real coal fire, and there's live jazz most Sunday lunchtimes. Cottage-style bedrooms provide a comfortable night's sleep.

Open all week Closed: 25 Dec eve ⌖ FREE HOUSE ◗ Theakston Best, Black Sheep Best, Theakston Black Bull & guest ales. ♟ 7 **Facilities** Play area Dogs allowed Garden Parking **Rooms** 7

PICK OF THE PUBS

Wombwell Arms 🍷

WASS Map 19 SE57

YO61 4BE
☎ **01347 868280**
e-mail: wombwellarms@btconnect.com
web: www.wombwellarms.co.uk
dir: *From A1 take A168 to A19 junct. Take York exit, then left after 2.5m, left at Coxwold to Ampleforth. Wass 2m*

Ian and Eunice Walker recently took over this character country pub in breathtaking surroundings on the southern edge of the North York Moors National Park. The building was constructed around 1620 as a granary, probably using stone from nearby Byland Abbey, but 25 years or so later it had became an alehouse. There are two bars, one with a huge open fire, and the Poachers, with a wood-burning stove, where dogs are welcome to sprawl

across the floor, no doubt wondering why it takes their owners so long to put away a pint of Timothy Taylor Landlord, Black Bull or Old Peculier. High quality, freshly prepared meals are available in both bars, as well as in the two restaurants, and the Walkers have established North Yorkshire suppliers for most of the produce used. Light lunches include tempting filled ciabatta and granary bread sandwiches, salads, ploughman's and smoked salmon and scrambled eggs. On a very manageable menu, starters such as pigeon bruschetta with mushrooms; trio of smoked fish; and twice-baked cheese soufflé could be followed with king prawn risotto and pan-fried scallops; roasted chicken breast with creamy leek and stilton sauce; poacher's casserole; or vegetarian chickpea curry. Then there are the Wombwell Classics, including Wass steak pie; a 10-oz sirloin steak; or haddock, chips and garden or mushy peas. Children get their look-in too with home-made fish fingers and chips with peas and beans; pizza Margherita; and pasta Bolognaise with salad. This is a great location for those planning to walk the Cleveland Way.

Open all week 12-3 6-11 (Sat 12-11, Sun 12-4) **Bar Meals** L served Mon-Thu 12-2, Fri-Sat 12-2.30, Sun 12-3 D served Mon-Thu 6.30-9, Fri-Sat 6.30-9.30 Av main course £10.95 **Restaurant** L served Mon-Thu 12-2, Fri-Sat 12-2.30, Sun 12-3 D served Mon-Thu 6.30-9, Fri-Sat 6.30-9.30 Av 3 course à la carte fr £17.15 ⊕ FREE HOUSE ◀ Timothy Taylor Landlord, Theakstons Black Bull, Theakstons Old Peculier. ♥ 9 **Facilities** Children's menu Dogs allowed Garden Parking

PICK OF THE PUBS

The Bruce Arms 🍷

WEST TANFIELD   Map 19 SE27

Main St HG4 5JJ
☎ **01677 470325** 📠 **01677 470925**
e-mail: info@bruce-arms.co.uk
web: www.bruce-arms.co.uk
dir: *On A6108 between Ripon & Masham*

The Bruce Arms is a stone-built house dating from 1820. It's handy for racing at both Ripon and Thirsk, as well as visiting famous sights such as Fountains Abbey and Staley Royal Water Garden. Situated in the heart of the pretty village of West Tanfield, just five miles northwest of Ripon, the pub is rapidly earning a reputation for providing great food in relaxed surroundings. Its bistro-style interior exudes charm with traditional exposed beams, log fires and candles on the tables. The pub is run by husband and wife team Russell and Rosie Caines, who between them have a keen eye for quality food and first-class customer service. A good wine list and real ales such as Black Sheep guarantee that customers find what they would like to drink. The restaurant is split into two traditionally furnished areas: one with a real fire is slightly more informal, while the other is ideal for family celebrations or private functions. Russell's menu is best described as modern British, but his flair is also exercised by some international dishes; he uses only the finest ingredients, sourcing them locally whenever possible. A typical meal choice based on seafood may start with 'simply seared' scallops with apple-ginger and coriander salad. This could be followed by a fried fillet of smoked haddock with langoustine chowder. Alternatively try the terrine of ham hock with sweet and sour onions and potato purée, followed by a roast breast of Goosnargh duck with honeyed drumstick and spiced apple. Round off with an orange and passion fruit salad, or a platter of English and French cheeses with fruit and biscuits.

Closed: Mon 🛢 FREE HOUSE 🍺 Black Sheep Best, Black Sheep Ale & Worthington Smooth. 🍷 10
Facilities Dogs allowed Garden Parking

WHITBY
Map 19 NZ81

The Magpie Café ☻

14 Pier Rd YO21 3PU
☎ 01947 602058 ☐ 01947 601801
e-mail: ian@magpiecafe.co.uk
dir: *Telephone for directions*

More a licensed restaurant than a pub, the award-winning Magpie has been the home of North Yorkshire's best-ever fish and chips since the late 1930s when it moved to its present site in Pier Road. The dining rooms command excellent views of the harbour, the Abbey and St Mary's Church. Given its proximity to the Fish Market, fresh fish dishes abound - up to 10 daily. Ranges of salads and over 20 home-made puddings continue the choice.

Open all day all wk 11.30-11 Closed: 1-21 Jan **Bar Meals** L served all wk 11.30-9pm D served all wk 11.30-9pm food served all day ⊕ FREE HOUSE ◀ Crompton, Scoresby Bitter, Tetley Bitter. ☻ 11

WIGGLESWORTH
Map 18 SD85

The Plough Inn ☻

BD23 4RJ ☎ 01729 840243 ☐ 01729 840638
web: www.ploughinn.info
dir: *From A65 between Skipton & Long Preston take B6478 to Wigglesworth*

Dating back to 1720, the bar of this traditional country free house features oak beams and an open fire. There are fine views of the surrounding hills from the conservatory restaurant, where the pub's precarious position on the Yorkshire/Lancashire border is reflected in a culinary 'War of the Roses'. Yorkshire pudding with beef casserole challenges Lancashire hotpot and pickled red cabbage - the latest score is published beside the daily blackboard specials!

Open all wk **Bar Meals** L served Mon-Sat 12-2, Sun 12-8.30 D served Mon-Sat 6-9, Sun 12-8.30 ⊕ FREE HOUSE ☻ 6 **Facilities** Family room Garden Parking

YORK
Map 16 SE65

PICK OF THE PUBS

Blue Bell ☻

53 Fossgate YO1 9TF ☎ 01904 654904
e-mail: robsonhardie@aol.com
dir: *In city centre*

Its narrow frontage makes it easy to miss, but don't walk past this charming pub – the smallest in York – which has been serving customers in the ancient heart of the city for 200 years. In 1903 it was given a typical Edwardian makeover, and since then almost nothing has changed - this includes the varnished wall and ceiling panelling, the two cast-iron tiled fireplaces, and the old settles. The layout is original too, with the taproom at the front and the snug down a long corridor at the rear, both with servery hatches. Quite fittingly, the whole interior is now Grade II listed. The only slight drawback is that the pub's size leaves no room for a kitchen, so don't expect anything more complicated than sandwiches. However, there's a good selection of real ales: no fewer than six are usually on tap, including rotating guests. The pub has won awards for its efforts in fund-raising.

Open all day all wk 11-11 (Sun noon-10.30) **Bar Meals** L served Mon-Sat 12-2.30 ⊕ PUNCH TAVERNS ◀ Deuchars IPA, Timothy Taylor Landlord, Adnams Bitter, Abbot Greene King, Tetleys Dark Mild. ☻ 10 **Facilities** Dogs allowed **Notes** ◉

Lysander Arms ☻

Manor Ln, Shipton Rd YO30 5TZ
☎ 01904 640845 ☐ 01904 624422
dir: *Telephone for directions*

The Lysander Arms is a recently constructed pub built on the site of an old RAF airfield. The contemporary feel of the pub's interior includes a long, fully air-conditioned bar with modern furnishings, brick-built fireplace and large-screen TV. The lunch menu features a choice of ciabatta, melted bloomer and poppy bagel sandwiches; specialities such as blackened Cajun chicken with chargrilled peppers; and in the evening, beef from the char grill, accompanied by thick chips.

Open all wk ◀ John Smiths Cask, Deuchars IPA, John Smiths Smooth, Bombardier. ☻ 18 **Facilities** Play area Dogs allowed Garden Parking

YORKSHIRE, SOUTH

BRADFIELD
Map 16 SK29

The Strines Inn

Bradfield Dale S6 6JE ☎ 0114 2851247
dir: *N off A57 between Sheffield & Manchester*

Nestled amid the breathtaking moorland scenery of the Peak District National Park, overlooking Strines Reservoir, this popular free house feels a world away from nearby Sheffield but is in fact within its border. Although it was built as a manor house in the 13th century, most of the present building is 16th century. It has been an inn since 1771. Traditional home-made fare ranges from sandwiches, salads and jacket potatoes, to substantial Yorkshire puddings with a choice of fillings, plus grilled steaks, mammoth mixed grill, or pie of the day.

Open all wk 10.30-3 5.30-11 (Sat-Sun 10.30am-11pm) Closed: 25 Dec **Bar Meals** L served all wk 12-2.30 D served all wk 5.30-9 Av main course £8.25 ⊕ FREE HOUSE ◀ Marston's Pedigree, Kelham Island, Mansfield Cask, Bradfield Bitter, Old Speckled Hen. **Facilities** Children's menu Play area Dogs allowed Garden Parking

CADEBY
Map 16 SE50

PICK OF THE PUBS

Cadeby Inn ☻

Main St DN5 7SW ☎ 01709 864009
e-mail: info@cadeby-inn.co.uk

Before being converted into a picturesque whitewashed pub, with a stone-walled traditional bar and a more contemporary restaurant with stylish yet comfortable chairs, this was a farmhouse. Sandstone walls enclose the large front garden, while a patio and smaller garden lie at the rear; ideal for enjoying a meal or a pint of John Smiths in the warmer weather. The lunch menu offers interesting sandwiches like classic minute steak and onion, or open sandwich of smoked salmon, prawn and lemon mayonnaise; or crisp warm brie with Waldorf salad and cranberry sauce. In the evening you might start with creamy parsnip and apple soup, followed by main courses such as Whitby cod fillet, creamy mash, parsley sauce and crisp bacon; confit duck leg, stew of white beans, Savoy cabbage, shallots and thyme; and simple wild mushroom and parmesan risotto.

continued on page 541

PICK OF THE PUBS

Cubley Hall ♍

PENISTONE   Map 16 SE20

Mortimer Rd, Cubley S36 9DF
☎ **01226 766086** 📠 **01226 767335**
e-mail: info@cubleyhall.co.uk
dir: *M1 junct 37, A628 towards Manchester, or M1 junct 35a, A616. Hall just S of Penistone*

Please say hello to Flo if you see her wandering about; she'll be dressed in Edwardian clothes and may not reply. Flo, or Florence Lockley to be precise, married here in 1904 and has become the resident ghost in this fine-looking mansion. Since the 1700s it has been used for a variety of purposes, from moorland farm to today's freehouse pub, by way of gentleman's residence and, for 50 years, a children's home. Despite those decades of youthful assault, many original features such as mosaic floors, ornate plasterwork, oak panelling and stained glass have somehow survived.

The restaurant, massively oak-beamed and solidly slate-floored, was once the barn; old pine tables, chairs and pews add to the ambience. There are plenty of snacks and light meals, such as creamy garlic mushrooms; pork and leek sausage with creamy mash and rich onion gravy; a 'sizzlin' platter of spicy chicken wings; pizzas and pastas; and chargrilled beefburger, rump steak; gammon and chicken fajitas. Main courses include chilli con carne with rice, sour cream and nachos; 'classic British' pie of the day with shortcrust pastry, salted steak fries and a panache of vegetables; pan-fried lamb's liver with onions and lardons; chargrilled chicken breast marinated in cumin and coriander with steamed rice, sultanas and pinenuts, topped with natural yoghurt; Whitby wholetail breaded scampi with home-made tartare sauce; risotto with mixed beans, fresh herbs, Parmesan and pesto; and seasonal salads. Ten daily specials on blackboards, several 'credit munch' options and a children's menu complete the picture. The hotel, particularly its garden pavilion, is a popular wedding venue.

Open all week **Bar Meals** L served all week, all day D served all week, Mon-Fri until 9.30, Sat-Sun until 10 Av main course £8 **Restaurant** L served Sun 12.30-3.30 D served Sun, last orders at 5.45 Fixed menu price fr £9.75 Av 3 course à la carte fr £21 ⊕ FREE HOUSE ◖ Tetley Bitter, Burton Ale, Greene King Abbot Ale, Young's Special. ♍ 7 **Facilities** Children's menu Play area Family room Garden Parking

CADEBY continued

Open all wk noon-11 **Bar Meals** L served all wk 12-5.30 food served all day **Restaurant** L served all wk 12-9.30 D served Mon-Sat 12-9.30, Sun 12-8 food served all day ⊕ FREE HOUSE ◀ John Smiths Cask, Black Sheep Best Bitter, Guinness. ♥ 6 **Facilities** Children's menu Garden Parking

---

DONCASTER   Map 16 SE50

Waterfront Inn ♥

Canal Ln, West Stockwith DN10 4ET ☎ **01427 891223** **dir:** *From Gainsborough take either A159 N, then minor road to village. Or A631towards Bawtry/Rotherham, then right onto A161, then minor road*

Built in the 1830s overlooking the Trent Canal basin and the canal towpath, the pub is now popular with walkers and visitors to the nearby marina. Real ales and good value food are the order of the day, including pasta with home-made ratatouille, broccoli and cheese bake, deep fried scampi, half honey-roasted chicken, and lasagne.

Open noon-2.30 6-11 (Sat noon-11 Sun noon-9) Closed: Mon (ex BH) **Bar Meals** L served Tue-Sun, 12-2.30 D served Tue-Sun 6.30-9 Av main course £7.99 **Restaurant** L served Tue-Sun 12-2.30 D served Tue-Sun 6.30-9 ⊕ ENTERPRISE INNS ◀ John Smiths Cask, Greene King Old Speckled Hen. ♥ 9 **Facilities** Children's menu Play area Dogs allowed Garden Parking

---

PENISTONE   Map 16 SE20

PICK OF THE PUBS

Cubley Hall ♥

See Pick of the Pubs on opposite page

The Fountain Inn Hotel ♥

Wellthorne Ln, Ingbirchworth S36 7GJ ☎ **01226 763125** ◻ **01226 761336** **e-mail:** enquiries@fountain-Ingbirchworth.co.uk **dir:** *M1 junct 37, A628 to Manchester then A629 to Huddersfield*

Parts of this former coaching inn date from the 17th century; it is attractively located by Ingbirchworth Reservoir in the foothills of the southern Pennines. The interior is cosy and stylish, the locals' bar has real log fires and traditional games, and the food focus is on quality with value for money: expect the likes of prawn cocktail, roast sirloin of local beef, and apple and blackberry crumble with custard. Garden with large decking and seating area.

Open all wk ⊕ ENTERPRISE INNS ◀ Tetleys Cask, Theakstons Best, Black Sheep, John Smiths Smooth. ♥ 8 **Facilities** Play area Garden Parking

---

SHEFFIELD   Map 16 SK38

PICK OF THE PUBS

The Fat Cat

23 Alma St S3 8SA ☎ **0114 249 4801** ◻ **0114 249 4803** **e-mail:** info@thefatcat.co.uk **dir:** *Telephone for directions*

This reputedly haunted three-storey, back street pub was built in 1832, and is Grade II listed. Beer-wise, it's hard to imagine anywhere better: a constantly changing range of guest beers from across the country, especially from micro-breweries, makes for a real ale heaven. Two hand-pumped ciders, unusual bottled beers and 21 country wines (the likes of elderberry and cowslip) are also sold, while the Kelham Island Brewery, owned by the pub, accounts for at least four of the ten traditional draught real ales on offer. The number of different beers sold since the concept was introduced now exceeds 4,500. The smart interior is very much that of a traditional, welcoming city pub; outside there's an attractive walled garden complete with Victorian-style lanterns, bench seating and shrubbery. Real fires in winter complete the cosy feel. Home-cooked food from a simple weekly menu is available except on Sunday evenings – nutty mushroom pie or Mexican chicken casserole. Look out for special events such as beer and food evenings.

Open all wk noon-11 (Sat-Sun noon-mdnt) Closed: 25 Dec **Bar Meals** L served all wk 12-2.30 D served Mon-Sat 6-8 ⊕ FREE HOUSE ◀ Timothy Taylor Landlord, Kelham Island Bitter, Pale Rider, Pride of Sheffield, Kelham Island Gold ♂ Stowford Press, Guest ciders. **Facilities** Children's menu Family room Dogs allowed Garden Parking

---

TOTLEY   Map 16 SK37

PICK OF THE PUBS

The Cricket Inn ♥

Penny Ln, Totley Bents S17 3AZ ☎ **0114 236 5256** **e-mail:** info@brewkitchen.co.uk **dir:** *Follow A621 from Sheffield 8m. Turn right onto Hillfoot Rd, 1st left onto Penny Ln*

Being so close to the Peak District means that The Cricket is a natural choice for sustenance when you have completed your ten-mile tramp or fell run. Muddy running shoes, walking boots, children and dogs are all welcome. The pub is owned by the Thornbridge Brewery, so expect to find four of its ales on tap as well as a small selection of bottled Belgians. The building was originally a farmhouse which started selling beer to navvies building the Totley Tunnel on the nearby Sheffield to Manchester railway. It opened for business in its current guise in 2007 and today it's a forward-looking venture that links the innovative beers with great pub food. Fill the odd corner with tasty snacks like fresh (rather than frozen) whitebait; main course offerings include steak and kidney pie with home-made ham hock. Whatever you order, the chips, fried in beef dripping the way nature intended, are not to be missed.

Open all day all wk 11-11 **Bar Meals** L served Mon-Fri 12-2.30, Sat-Sun all day D served Mon-Fri 5-8.30, Sat-Sun all day Av main course £12 **Restaurant** L served Mon-Fri 12-2.30, Sat-Sun all day D served Mon-Fri 5-8.30, Sat-Sun all day Fixed menu price fr £12 Av 3 course à la carte fr £20 ⊕ BREWKITCHEN LTD ♥ 8 **Facilities** Children's menu Dogs allowed Garden Parking

---

YORKSHIRE, WEST

ADDINGHAM   Map 19 SE04

PICK OF THE PUBS

The Fleece ♥

154 Main St LS29 0LY ☎ **01943 830491** **dir:** *Between Ilkley & Skipton*

A 17th-century coaching inn popular with walkers, situated at the intersection of several well-tramped footpaths. Food and drink can be served on the front terrace in summer. At other times the stone-flagged interior welcomes with an enormous fireplace, wooden settles and a friendly bunch of locals. A pint of Copper Dragon might be all you're seeking, but if you feel peckish, be sure to consult the daily chalkboard. Much of the produce is local and organic, with beef and lamb coming from a nearby farm, surplus vegetables brought along by allotment holders, and seasonal game delivered straight from the shoot. Simple flavoursome dishes are the speciality here. The lunchtime offerings include sandwiches, omelettes and traditional plates such as sausages and mash; Wharfedale shepherd's pie; or Whitby haddock, chips

continued

ADDINGHAM *continued*

and mushy peas. For a full meal, choose from the likes of pigeon prune terrine to start, a Bolton Abbey steak au poivre, and dessert of the day from the blackboard.

Open all wk noon–11 (Sun noon–10.30) **Bar Meals** L served Mon-Sat 12-2.15, Sun 12-8 D served Mon-Sat 6-9.15, Sun 12-8 booking required **Restaurant** L served Mon-Sat 12-2.15, Sun 12-8 booking required D served Mon-Sat 6-9.15, Sun 12-8 booking required ⊕ PUNCH TAVERNS ◀ Black Sheep, Copper Dragon, Timothy Taylor Landlord, Tetleys ⓣ Stowford Press. ♟ 15 **Facilities** Children's menu Dogs allowed Parking

BRADFORD · Map 19 SE13

New Beehive Inn

171 Westgate BD1 3AA
☎ **01274 721784** ▤ 01274 735092
e-mail: newbeehiveinn@talk21.com
dir: *A606 into Bradford, A6161 200yds B6144, left after lights, pub on left*

Classic Edwardian inn, dating from 1901 and retaining its period atmosphere with separate bars and gas lighting. Outside, with a complete change of mood, you can relax in the Mediterranean-style courtyard. The pub offers a good range of unusual real ales and a selection of over 100 malt whiskies, served alongside some simple bar snacks.

Open all wk ⊕ FREE HOUSE ◀ Timothy Taylor Landlord, Kelham Island Bitter, Hop Back Summer Lightning, Abbeydale Moonshine, Salamander Mudpuppy. **Facilities** Family room Garden Parking

CLIFTON · Map 16 SE12

The Black Horse Inn ◉ ♟

HD6 4HJ ☎ **01484 713862** ▤ 01484 400582
e-mail: mail@blackhorseclifton.co.uk
dir: *1m from Brighouse town centre. 0.5m from M62 junct 25*

The white-painted, 15th-century building was originally a farmhouse, which helps to explain why a six-inch layer of chicken droppings was found here during conversion in the 1970s. At the pub's heart is a well-kept bar serving traditional Yorkshire ales and a wide-ranging wine selection. Three separate dining areas provide a seasonal menu of locally sourced food, such as slow-braised lamb shank; pan-fried breast of chicken; beer-battered Whitby haddock; and leek and pea tartlet.

Open all day all wk noon-mdnt **Bar Meals** L served Mon-Sat 12-2.30, Sun 12-8 D served Mon-Sat 5.30-9.30, Sun 12-8 ⊕ ENTERPRISE INNS ◀ Black Sheep, Timothy Taylor Landlord. ♟ 18 **Facilities** Garden Parking

HALIFAX · Map 19 SE02

PICK OF THE PUBS

The Old Bore NEW ◉ ♟

Oldham Rd, Rishworth HX6 4QU ☎ **01422 822291**
dir: *M62 junct 22, follow signs to Halifax 0.75m on left hand side*

Affectionately known as the Bore, this self-styled "Anything but boring" pub sports flagged floors, oak beams, antique furniture and a wealth of interesting details. The bar, with Black Sheep, Timothy Taylor Landlord and Bore Bitter, is a popular local haunt, while the extensive wine list shows off owner Scott Hessel's passion for gold medal winners, single estate producers and rare class acts. His impressive restaurant CV means you can expect equally notable modern British food using, wherever possible, seasonal produce from a network of committed suppliers. A typical three-courser might include Colchester oysters with lemon and cucumber; braised brisket with horseradish mash, watercress purée, caramelised vegetables, mini Yorkshire puddings and shallot sauce; and passionfruit crème brûlée with piña colada sorbet. A 'Credit Crunch' bistro menu offers two courses – crispy duck spring roll, and Mediterranean chunky fish stew, perhaps - plus a half bottle of wine for £15.

Open noon-2.15 6-11 (Sun noon-11) Closed: 1st 2wks Jan, Mon-Tue **Bar Meals** L served Wed-Sat 12-2.15, Sun 12-4 D served Wed-Sat 6-9.30, Sun 5.30-8 booking required Av main course £16.95 **Restaurant** L served Wed-Sat 12-2.15, Sun 12-4 D served Wed-Sat 6-9.30, Sun 5.30-8 booking required Fixed menu price fr £10 ⊕ FREE HOUSE ◀ Timothy Taylor, Black Sheep Best, Bore Bitter. ♟ 11 **Facilities** Dogs allowed Garden Parking

The Rock Inn Hotel

Holywell Green HX4 9BS
☎ **01422 379721** ▤ 01422 379110
e-mail: enquiries@therockhotel.biz
dir: *From M62 junct 24 follow Blackley signs, left at x-rds, approx 0.5m on left*

Substantial modern extensions have transformed this attractive 17th-century wayside inn into a thriving hotel and conference venue in the scenic valley of Holywell Green. All-day dining in the brasserie-style conservatory is truly cosmopolitan; kick off with freshly prepared parsnip and apple soup or crispy duck and seaweed, followed by liver and bacon, Thai-style steamed halibut, or vegetables jalfrezi.

Open all day all wk noon-11 **Bar Meals** L served Mon-Sat 12-2, Sun 12-6.30 D served Mon-Sat 6-9 ⊕ FREE HOUSE ◀ Timothy Taylor Landlord, John Smiths. **Facilities** Garden Parking

PICK OF THE PUBS

Shibden Mill Inn ★★★★ INN ♟

See Pick of the Pubs on opposite page

HAWORTH · Map 19 SE03

The Old White Lion Hotel ★★ HL ♟

Main St BD22 8DU ☎ **01535 642313** ▤ 01535 646222
e-mail: enquiries@oldwhitelionhotel.com
dir: *A629 onto B6142, hotel 0.5m past Haworth Station*

This traditional 300-year-old coaching inn is set in the famous Brontë village of Haworth, looking down onto the famous cobbled Main Street. In the charming bar the ceiling beams are held up by timber posts. Bar food includes all the usual favourites plus a great selection of filled giant Yorkshire puddings. From the carte in the candlelit restaurant choose between game casserole of rabbit, venison, wild boar and pigeon in red wine; and mango, stilton and sweet chilli topped chicken.

Open all wk 11-11 (Sun noon-10.30) **Bar Meals** L served Mon-Fri 12-2.30, Sat-Sun all day D served Mon-Fri 6-9.30, Sat-Sun all day Av main course £8.30 **Restaurant** L served Sun 12-2.30 booking required D served all wk 7-9.30 booking required Fixed menu price fr £17 Av 3 course à la carte fr £17.90 ⊕ FREE HOUSE ◀ Theakstons Best (Green Label), Tetley Bitter, John Smiths, Websters, guest beer. ♟ 6 **Facilities** Children's menu Parking **Rooms** 15

HORBURY · Map 16 SE21

The Quarry Inn

70 Quarry Hill WF4 5NF ☎ **01924 272523**
dir: *On A642 approx 2.5m from Wakefield*

In the hollow of a disused quarry, this creeper-clad pub is built with stone actually quarried here, as are the bar fronts. Just beyond the main road outside are the River Calder and the Calder and Hebble Navigation. A good range of simple but appetising dishes in the bar and restaurant includes cottage pie, steaks, gammon, fish and chips, liver and onions, and Yorkshire puddings with various fillings.

Open all wk ⊕ MARSTON, THOMPSON & EVERSHED PLC ◀ Marston's Pedigree, Mansfield Smooth. **Facilities** Parking

PICK OF THE PUBS

Shibden Mill Inn ★★★★ INN ♍

HALIFAX   Map 19 SE02

Shibden Mill Fold HX3 7UL
☎ 01422 365840 📠 01422 362971
e-mail: enquiries@shibdenmillinn.com
web: www.shibdenmillinn.com
dir: *From A58 turn into Kell Ln. After 0.5m left into Blake Hill*

A 17th-century free house tucked into a fold of the Shibden Valley, overlooking Red Beck. The first mention by name of an ancient manorial water corn mill on this site is found in Wakefield's court rolls dating it to the second year of Edward II's reign, 1308. (Curiously the rolls also tell us that Shibden used to be spelled Schepedene, and that Chippendale derives from Schepedendale.) It appears that the mill was used for corn right up to the 19th century. In 1845 a change of ownership brought a change of use - machinery for spinning worsted was installed.

However a disastrous fire in 1859 closed the business, and the mill was sold in 1890 to a Halifax brewer. The original mill pond was filled in, possibly to prevent water leaking into the local mine shafts; today this area is the inn's car park. The interior has been sympathetically renovated while retaining much of the character of these long-gone times, particularly in the log fire-warmed, oak-beamed bar and candlelit restaurant. Real ales include two guests, and the wine list cheers the hearts of all oenophiles. The menus offer plenty of options, including an excellent value early bird served Monday to Friday at lunchtime and between 6 and 7pm: warm terrine of smoked haddock, roast rump of English lamb, and dark chocolate and cherry cheesecake could be a typical selection. The bar menu has antipasti; starters such as steak tartare with warm toast; fish in the form of grilled tuna steak niçoise or seared supreme of salmon; and traditional mains such as steak and kidney pudding and home-made cottage pie. Vegetarian options are equally attractive, and can be served as starters or main courses; one possibility is poached egg with asparagus, hollandaise and sautéed spinach. Children tuck into haddock goujons or crispy chicken strips with potato wedges and peas. Stylish bedrooms are available.

Open 12-2.30 5.30-11 (Sat-Sun noon-11pm) Closed: 25-26 Dec eve & 1 Jan eve **Bar Meals** L served Mon-Sat 12-2, Sun all day D served Mon-Sat 6-9.30 Av main course £11 **Restaurant** L served Sun 12-7.30 D served Fri-Sat 6-9.30 Av 3 course à la carte fr £24 ⊕ FREE HOUSE ◀ John Smiths, Theakston XB, Shibden Mill, 2 guest ales. ♍ 14 **Facilities** Dogs allowed Garden Parking **Rooms** 11

KIRKBURTON — Map 16 SE11

The Woodman Inn ★★★★ INN ℙ

Thunderbridge HD8 0PX
☎ 01484 605778 📠 01484 604110
e-mail: thewoodman@connectfree.co.uk
dir: Approx 5m S of Huddersfield, just off A629

Lovely old stone-built inn set in the wooded hamlet of Thunderbridge. One menu is offered throughout, but customers can eat in the bar downstairs or the more sophisticated ambience of the restaurant upstairs. Dishes include daily fresh fish (grilled brill with chilli), and the likes of wild boar and apple sausages. Wine is selected by the owners, whose family has been in the licensed trade since 1817. Accommodation is provided in adjacent converted weavers' cottages.

Open all wk ⌖ FREE HOUSE ◁ Timothy Taylor Best Bitter, Tetleys Bitter. ℙ 13 **Facilities** Parking **Rooms** 12

LEDSHAM — Map 16 SE42

The Chequers Inn ℙ

Claypit Ln LS25 5LP
☎ 01977 683135 📠 01977 680791
e-mail: cjwrath@btconnect.com
dir: Between A1(M) & A656 N of Castleford. 1m from A1(M) junct 42

A quaint, creeper-clad inn located in an old estate village, with low beams, wooden settles, and a history traceable back to 1540. Ever since the lady of the manor was offended by her over-indulgent farm workers over 160 years ago, the pub has been closed on Sundays. But otherwise, you can tuck into peppered escalope of venison, monkfish tail in pancetta, steak and mushroom pie, steak sandwich, or smoked salmon crumble.

Closed: Sun **Bar Meals** L served Mon-Sat 12-9 D served Mon-Sat 12-9 Av main course £12 food served all day **Restaurant** D served Mon-Sat 12-9 ⌖ FREE HOUSE ◁ Theakston, John Smiths, Timothy Taylor Landlord, Brown Cow, Golden Best. ℙ 10 **Facilities** Dogs allowed Garden Parking

LEEDS — Map 19 SE23

PICK OF THE PUBS

The Cross Keys NEW ℙ

107 Water Ln LS11 5WD ☎ 0113 243 3711
e-mail: info@the-crosskeys.com
dir: 0.5m from Leeds Station: right onto Neville St, right onto Water Lane. Pass Globe Rd, pub on left

Just across the river from Leeds city station, the Cross Keys stands huddled between converted industrial buildings enjoying a second lease of life as fashionable offices. So if the open fires, exposed brick walls and beamed ceilings put you in mind of some old-world rural backwater, think again. For this cosy city pub with its fine outdoor courtyard is firmly geared towards the Wi-Fi generation. Yet with ales from local independent breweries, Weston's organic cider, and a menu that

captures long lost recipes and traditional British classics, it is well worth a visit. Lunchtime brings salt beef sandwiches with English mustard and pickles; devilled mushrooms on toast; and a range of hot dishes like home-made faggots with bubble and squeak. In the evenings, fresh seafood and herb broth might precede slow-cooked wild rabbit with herb dumplings and colcannon, followed by rice pudding with caramelised apples.

Open all wk noon-11 (Fri-Sat noon-mdnt, Sun noon-10.30) **Bar Meals** L served Mon-Sat 12-4, Sun 12-8 D served Mon-Sat 6-10 Av main course £7.50 **Restaurant** L served Mon-Sat 12-4, Sun 12-8 D served Mon-Sat 6-10 Fixed menu price fr £14 Av 3 course à la carte fr £17.95 ⌖ FREE HOUSE ◁ Roosters, Duvel, Liefmans Frambogen ⌕ Westons Organic, Westons Medium Dry. ℙ 13 **Facilities** Children's menu Dogs allowed Garden

Whitelocks ℙ

Turks Head Yard, Briggate LS1 6HB
☎ 0113 245 3950 📠 0113 242 3368
e-mail: whitelocks@live.co.uk
dir: Next to Marks & Spencer in Briggate

First licensed in 1715 as the Turks Head, this is the oldest pub in Leeds. Restoration has highlighted its classic long bar with polychrome tiles, stained-glass windows, advertising mirrors and a mid-Victorian-style Top Bar known as Ma'Gamps. Food is along the lines of home-made soup; roast of the day; ham, egg and chips; home-made tray pie (steak; steak and stilton or vegetable); treacle sponge and apple pie. There is a children's menu too. Guest ales are on a weekly rotation – sometimes daily.

Open all wk 11-11 (Sun noon-6 winter Sun noon-10.30 summer) Closed: 25-26 Dec, 1 Jan **Bar Meals** food served all day **Restaurant** booking required ⌖ CHENNELL & ARMSTRONG ◁ Theakston Best, Old Peculier, John Smiths, Deuchars, Leeds & York Brewery Ales, Guest ales. ℙ 16

LINTHWAITE — Map 16 SE11

The Sair Inn

Hoyle Ing HD7 5SG ☎ 01484 842370
dir: From Huddersfield take A62 (Oldham road) for 3.5m. Left just before lights at bus stop (in centre of road) into Hoyle Ing & follow sign

You won't be able to eat here, but this old hilltop ale house has enough character in its four small rooms to make up for that. Three are heated by hot (landlord Ron Crabtree's word) Yorkshire ranges in winter. Ron has brewed his own beers for 25 years and much sought after they are by real ale aficionados. In summer the outside drinking area catches the afternoon sun and commands views across the Colne Valley.

Open all wk 5-11 (Sat noon-11 Sun noon-10.30) ⌖ FREE HOUSE ◁ Linfit Special Bitter, Linfit Bitter, Linfit Gold Medal, Autumn Gold, Old Eli. **Facilities** Family room Dogs allowed **Notes** ⊖

LINTON — Map 16 SE34

The Windmill Inn ℙ

Main St LS22 4HT ☎ 01937 582209 📠 01937 587518
web: www.thewindmillinnwetherby.co.uk
dir: From A1 exit at Tadcaster/Otley junct, follow Otley signs. In Collingham follow Linton signs

A coaching inn since the 18th century, the building actually dates back to the 14th century, and originally housed the owner of the long-disappeared windmill. Stone walls, antique settles, log fires, oak beams and lots of brass set the scene in which to enjoy good bar food prepared by enthusiastic licensees. Expect the likes of chicken breast on mustard mash with onion jus, sea bass on pepper mash with tomato and basil sauce, baked salmon on Italian risotto, or king prawns in lime and chilli butter. While you're there, ask to take a look at the local history scrapbook.

Open all wk 11-3 5.30-11 (Sat-Sun 11-11) Closed: 1 Jan **Bar Meals** L served Mon-Fri 12-2, Sat 12-2.30, Sun 12-5.45 Av main course £8.95 **Restaurant** L served Mon-Fri 12-2, Sat 12-2.30, Sun 12-5.45 D served Mon-Tue 5.30-8.30, Wed-Sat 5.30-9, Sun 12-5.45 Fixed menu price fr £9.95 Av 3 course à la carte fr £13.95 ⌖ SCOTTISH COURAGE ◁ John Smiths, Theakston Best, Daleside, Greene King Ruddles County. ℙ 12 **Facilities** Children's menu Dogs allowed Garden Parking

MARSDEN — Map 16 SE01

The Olive Branch ★★★★ RR ⌖ ℙ

Manchester Rd HD7 6LU ☎ 01484 844487
e-mail: mail@olivebranch.uk.com
dir: On A62 between Marsden & Slaithwaite, 6m from Huddersfield

This old moorland inn by a former packhorse route offers daily-changing, seasonally dependent brasserie-style menus. Choice is wide, with starters such as king scallops and chorizo; foie gras and Armagnac terrine; and Roquefort soufflé; and mains that include roast wild sea bass fillet; crispy pork belly; aged Hartshead Moor beef served with a choice of sauces. Locally brewed real ales are always available. Four designer bedrooms include one with ducks - plastic, one assumes - in the bath.

Open all wk Closed: 1st 2wks Jan **Restaurant** D served Mon-Sat 6.30-9.30, Sun 1-8 booking required Fixed menu price fr £13.95 Av 3 course à la carte fr £28 ⌖ FREE HOUSE ◁ Dogcross Bitter, Greenfield Red Ale, Boddingtons. ℙ 16 **Facilities** Garden Parking **Rooms** 3

MYTHOLMROYD
Map 19 SE02

Shoulder of Mutton ♀

New Rd HX7 5DZ ☎ **01422 883165**
dir: *A646 Halifax to Todmorden, in Mytholmroyd on B6138, opposite rail station*

Award-winning Pennines' pub situated by a trout stream in the village where Ted Hughes was born. Popular with walkers, cyclists, families and visitors to the area, the pub's reputation for real ales and hearty fare using locally sourced ingredients remains intact after 33 years of ownership. The menu ranges from snacks and sandwiches to vegetarian quiche; filled giant Yorkshire pudding; Cumberland sausages; and beef in ale. Look out for the 17th-century counterfeit golden guineas on display in the bar.

Closed: Tue L **Bar Meals** L served Wed-Mon 11.30-2 D served Wed-Sun 7-8.15 Av main course £4.50 ⊕ ENTERPRISE INNS ◀ Black Sheep, Copper Dragon, Greene King IPA, Timothy Taylor Landlord, Castle Eden. ♀ 10 **Facilities** Children's menu Play area Family room Dogs allowed Garden Parking **Notes** ⊜

RIPPONDEN
Map 16 SE01

Old Bridge Inn ♀

Priest Ln HX6 4DF ☎ **01422 822595**
dir: *5m from Halifax in village centre by church, over a pack horse bridge*

An award-winning whitewashed traditional pub prettily situated in a lovely Pennine conservation village. It serves fine real ales in three separate bars, with antique furniture and open fires in winter, and boasts tranquil landscaped seating next to the River Ryburn for summer days. Only home-cooked food is served, seasonal and locally sourced when possible. Popular since 1963 is the weekday salad and cold meat carvery lunches available Monday to Friday. Other options may include garlic tiger prawns on lemon and coriander couscous; and braised chicken leg on fondant potatoes.

Open all wk **Bar Meals** L served all wk 12-2 booking required D served Mon-Fri 6.30-9.30 booking required Av main course £9.50 ⊕ FREE HOUSE ◀ Timothy Taylor Landlord, Golden Best & Best Bitter, Black Sheep Best, guest ales. ♀ 12 **Facilities** Garden Parking

SHELLEY
Map 16 SE21

PICK OF THE PUBS

The Three Acres Inn ♀

See Pick of the Pubs on page 546

SOWERBY
Map 16 SE02

PICK OF THE PUBS

The Travellers Rest ♀

Steep Ln HX6 1PE
☎ **01422 832124** 📠 **01422 831365**
dir: *M62 junct 22 or 24*

The stone-built Travellers Rest was built in 1730 and fully renovated in 2001 by current owner, Caroline Lumley. It sits high on a steep hillside with glorious views, a dining terrace, duck pond, huge car park and helipad. The cosy stone-flagged bar boasts fresh flowers and an open fire, while in the restaurant, beams, animal print sofas, more warmth from a wood-burning stove, and exposed stonework continue the emphasis on comfort and relaxation. Dishes cooked to order from local produce are rooted in Yorkshire tradition yet refined with French flair, yielding an immaculate and happy mix of classic and contemporary cooking, overseen by head chef, Mark Lilley. Start with ham hock terrine with home-made piccalilli, belly pork with truffled new potatoes, or salmon tapas; continue with lamb loin with cabbage and Parma ham, breast of pigeon with bacon and thyme risotto, or venison with sweet potato crisps. Resist the sticky toffee pudding if you can.

Closed: Mon-Tue **Bar Meals** L served Sat 12-2, Sun 12-7 D served Wed-Thu 5-9, Fri 5-9.30, Sat 5.30-9.30, Sun 12-7 **Restaurant** L served Sat 12-2, Sun 12-7 D served Wed-Thu 5-9, Fri 5-9.30, Sat 5.30-9.30, Sun 12-7 ⊕ FREE HOUSE ◀ Timothy Taylor Landlord, Timothy Taylor, Best Bitter. ♀ 8 **Facilities** Children's menu Dogs allowed Garden Parking

SOWERBY BRIDGE
Map 16 SE02

The Alma Inn NEW

Cotton Stones HX6 4NS ☎ **01422 823334**
e-mail: info@almainn.com
dir: *Turn off A58 at Triangle Twixt Sowerby Bridge & Ripponden. Follow signs for Cotton Stones*

The old stone inn stands in a dramatic rural location in the heart of Calderdale with views across the glorious Rydale Valley from its terrace and garden. Inside, stone-flagged floors, oak beams, glowing fires, and rustic pine tables set the informal, traditional scene for supping pints of Taylor Landlord and, surprisingly, for tucking into Italian-inspired dishes. Expect great value pizzas and pasta dishes, or fillet steak Rossini, and pubby bar meals, from the Alma burger to fish pie.

Open all day all wk noon-11 **Bar Meals** Av main course £8 food served all day **Restaurant** Fixed menu price fr £7.50 Av 3 course à la carte fr £14 food served all day ⊕ FREE HOUSE ◀ Tetley Bitter, Timothy Taylor Landlord, Timothy Taylor Golden Best.
Facilities Children's menu Dogs allowed Garden Parking

PICK OF THE PUBS

The Millbank ♀

HX6 3DY ☎ **01422 825588**
e-mail: eat@themillbank.com
dir: *A58 from Sowerby Bridge to Ripponden, right at Triangle*

This contemporary pub-cum-restaurant retains the function and traditional feel of the village free house it's always been. It stands in the Pennine conservation village of Mill Bank in the scenic Ryburn Valley, home since 1971 to writer and poet Glyn Hughes; you can read one of his sonnets, The Rock Rose, in the churchyard, engraved on a slate slab in the wall. Back in the pub, head for the cosy stone-flagged tap room with roaring fire in winter for a real ale, or the main wooden-floored drinking area for more of a wine bar feel and stunning views of the gardens and valley. The dining room chairs are recycled mill and chapel seats, complete with prayer-book racks. The food has won plenty of praise in the press; expect modern British cooking with bistro touches - perhaps pork rillettes with grape chutney followed by fish pie with green beans. As a lighter option, sandwiches are available until 7pm. Enjoy in the views in the spacious garden in warmer weather.

Open noon-3 5.30-11 (Sun noon-10.30) **Closed:** 1st 2 wks Oct & 1st wk Jan, Mon **Bar Meals** L served Tue-Sun 12-2.30 D served Tue-Sun 6-9.30 Av main course £11.95 **Restaurant** L served Tue-Sun 12-2.30 D served Tue-Sun 6-9.30 booking required Fixed menu price fr £13.95 Av 3 course à la carte fr £21 ⊕ FREE HOUSE ◀ Timothy Taylor Landlord, Tetley Bitter, Erdinger. ♀ 20 **Facilities** Children's menu Garden

THORNTON
Map 19 SE03

PICK OF THE PUBS

Ring O'Bells Country Pub & Restaurant ♀

See Pick of the Pubs on page 547

PICK OF THE PUBS

The Three Acres Inn

SHELLEY Map 16 SE21

HD8 8LR
☎ 01484 602606 📠 01484 608411
e-mail: info@3acres.com
web: www.3acres.com
dir: *From Huddersfield take A629 then B6116, turn left for village*

Well into their fourth decade here, Brian Orme and Neil Truelove have built a reputation for good quality food, tasteful accommodation, and a welcoming atmosphere. In a sense, perhaps, nothing changes for it was once a favourite with drovers bringing their sheep to market from their Pennine pastures. Today's visitors may be drawn to the National Mining Museum and Yorkshire Sculpture Park, both within easy reach, or a Three Acres activity break, such as golf, clay pigeon shooting or wine tasting. The inn's spacious interior is lavishly traditional - all rich reds, greens and yellows, exposed beams and large fireplaces. On summer evenings, sit out on the deck with a pint of Black Sheep, or a glass of wine. The food, including plenty of fresh fish, is served in both bar and restaurant and successfully fuses traditional English and international influences. Starter firm favourites include fresh rope-grown Hebridean mussels with shallots, dry white wine, cream and parsley; and chicken liver parfait and rillettes of duck on toasted onion bread, autumn fruit chutney and a shot of Sauternes. Among popular main courses are seared monkfish tail with curried mussels, spinach and saffron rice; roast half Lunesdale duck with Bramley apple purée, sage and onion stuffing, parsnip and potato mash and buttered cabbage; and braised field mushrooms, tarragon and buttered leek cottage pie with tomato and basil sauce. The three-course Sunday lunch menu offers seven or eight choices at each stage, enabling you to begin with Yorkshire pudding with onion gravy; follow with creamy fish pie, crispy potato and Gruyère crust; and finish with scrunchy brown bread ice cream with brandy snap and hot toffee sauce. A generous range of hot open and other sandwiches and light meals makes for a great lunchtime choice. There are also rooms available for private dining.

Open noon-2 6.30-9.30 Closed: evening 25-26 Dec, 1 Jan eve FREE HOUSE Timothy Taylor Landlord, Black Sheep, Tetley Smooth, Tetley Bitter. 16
Facilities Garden Parking

PICK OF THE PUBS

Ring O'Bells Country Pub & Restaurant 🍷

THORNTON Map 19 SE03

212 Hilltop Rd BD13 3QL
☎ 01274 832296 📄 01274 831707
e-mail: enquiries@theringobells.com
dir: *From M62 take A58 for 5m, right onto A644. 4.5m follow Denholme signs, onto Well Head Rd into Hilltop Rd*

On a clear day, views from the Ring O'Bells stretch up to 30 miles across rugged Pennine moorland. It stands just minutes away from the village of Thornton, where the Brontë sisters were born and their father was curate. The pub was converted from a Wesleyan chapel, and the restaurant was formerly two mill workers' cottages. It has been successfully run by Ann and Clive Preston for the past 17 years, and their cuisine, service and professionalism have been recognised with accolades from visitors far and wide. The wood-panelled and welcoming bar and dining area serves Black Sheep cask-conditioned ales and a fine selection of malt whiskies, speciality liqueurs and wines by the glass. The fully air-conditioned Brontë restaurant has a new contemporary look; a conservatory running its whole length rewards diners with stunning valley views. Meat, fish, game and vegetables sourced from local farmers and suppliers are carefully prepared and served by a team of award-winning chefs. The à la carte menu and daily specials board offer traditional British dishes with European influences. Expect starters such as lamb and spinach meatballs on a tsatziki sauce; turkey, lemon and rice soup; and leek and mushroom tart with creamy blue cheese sauce. Main courses may include poached haddock with prawn mornay sauce; chicken breast filled with garlic wild mushrooms; diced pork with apricots and celery casserole; or pork, coriander and plum sausages with mustard mash. Imaginative vegetarian options are on the blackboard, and all dietary requirements can be catered for. A range of desserts is made to order, from chef's creative crème brûlée to traditional warm lattice apple pie served with vanilla ice cream and toffee sauce.

Open 11.30-4 5.30-11.30 (Sat-Sun 6.15-11.30) Closed: 25 Dec **Bar Meals** Av main course £10.95 **Restaurant** Fixed menu price fr £7.95 Av 3 course à la carte fr £19.95 food served all day FREE HOUSE John Smiths, Courage Directors, Black Sheep ales. 🍷 12 **Facilities** Children's menu Parking

WAKEFIELD — Map 16 SE32

PICK OF THE PUBS

Kaye Arms Inn & Brasserie ▮

29 Wakefield Rd, Grange Moor WF4 4BG
☎ 01924 848385 ▤ 01924 848977
e-mail: kayearms@hotmail.co.uk
dir: On A642 between Huddersfield & Wakefield

This family-run dining pub stands alone on the Huddersfield to Wakefield road. Its bar menu offers the likes of cold rare roast beef with celeriac remoulade; braised veal and mushroom pasta; and honey-baked ham sandwiches. Over in the brasserie, try crab tart or chicken liver parfait; then confit of duck leg with French-style peas and dauphinoise potatoes; smoked haddock and poached egg with beetroot and spinach; or mature cheddar cheese soufflé with roquefort salad. Specials might take in braised shin beef or grilled fillet of John Dory with Greek salad. Raspberry soufflé is the house speciality, though bread and butter pudding with whisky and honey cream or almond tart with vanilla crème anglaise are equally appealing. An extensive wine list comprehensively roams the world. The popular National Coal Mining Museum is close by.

Open noon-2.30 5.30-11 (Sat-Sun noon-11) Closed: 25 Dec-2 Jan, Mon Bar Meals L served all wk 12-2.30 D served all wk 5.30-9.30 ⊕ FREE HOUSE ◀ John Smiths, Theakstons Best, Guinness, guest ales. ▮ 15 Facilities Parking

WIDDOP — Map 18 SD93

Pack Horse Inn ▮

HX7 7AT ☎ 01422 842803 ▤ 01422 842803
dir: Off A646 & A6033

The Pack Horse is a converted Laithe farmhouse dating from the 1600s, complete with welcoming open fires. A beautiful location just 300 yards from the Pennine Way makes it popular with walkers, but equally attractive are the home-cooked meals, good range of real ales and fabulous choice of 130 single malt whiskies. Please note that from October to Easter the pub is only open in the evening.

Closed: Mon & Tue-Fri lunch (Oct-Etr) ⊕ FREE HOUSE ◀ Thwaites, Theakston XB, Morland Old Speckled Hen, Black Sheep Bitter. ▮ 8 Facilities Dogs allowed Parking

CHANNEL ISLANDS

GUERNSEY

CASTEL — Map 24

PICK OF THE PUBS

Fleur du Jardin ▮

Kings Mills GY5 7JT
☎ 01481 257996 ▤ 01481 256834
e-mail: info@fleurdujardin.com
dir: 2.5m from town centre

This friendly hotel, bar and restaurant stands in a picturesque village, a short stroll from the island's finest sandy beaches. Dating from the 15th century, it has been restyled with an eye for contemporary shabby chic design, but historical features such as granite walls, solid wood beams and real fireplaces remain intact. Those taller than the average might have to stoop in the bar, but that needn't prevent enjoyment of a pint of Roquette cider. In fact imaginative use of local produce is what sets the restaurant apart; it is not unusual to see a local fisherman delivering his catch to the kitchen. You could start with prawn and crab timbale in cocktail sauce; or baked Portobello mushroom stuffed with Boursin cheese. Main courses may include pan-fried calves' liver on a bed of caramelised red onion, topped with crispy bacon; or Meadow Court pork and veal sausages served with apple and sage mash.

Open all wk Bar Meals food served all day Restaurant food served all day ⊕ FREE HOUSE ◀ Sunbeam, Guernsey Special, London Pride, Guest ales ♂ Roquette cider. ▮ 12 Facilities Dogs allowed Garden Parking

Hotel Hougue du Pommier ★★★ HL

Hougue du Pommier Rd GY5 7FQ
☎ 01481 256531 ▤ 01481 256260
e-mail: hotel@houguedupommier.guernsey.net
dir: Telephone for directions

An 18th-century Guernsey farmhouse with the only feu du bois (literally 'cooking on the fire') in the Channel Islands. Eat in the beamed Tudor Bar with its open fire or the more formal restaurant. Menu options may include dishes from the spit-roast menu, baked aubergine and Mediterranean vegetable ragout; chargrilled supreme of chicken; or Chef's seafood fishcake. The 8-acre gardens have a swimming pool, barbecue and medieval area, where banquets are held the first Saturday of the month.

Open all day all wk Bar Meals L served all wk 12-2 booking required D served all wk 6.30-9 booking required Av main course £9.50 Restaurant L served all wk 12-2 booking required D served all wk 6.30-9 booking required Fixed menu price fr £19.50 Av 3 course à la carte fr £25 ⊕ FREE HOUSE ◀ John Smiths, Extra Smooth, Guernsey Best Bitter, Guinness. Facilities Children's menu Dogs allowed Garden Parking Rooms 40

ST PETER PORT — Map 24

The Admiral de Saumarez NEW ★★ HL

Duke of Normandie Hotel, Lefebure St GY1 2JP
☎ 01481 721431 ▤ 01481 711763
e-mail: dukeofnormandie@cwgsy.net
dir: Hotel located in town centre 5 mins from harbour & 20 mins from airport

Part of the Duke of Normandie Hotel, this thoughtfully restored bar is full of architectural salvage, including old timbers (now painted with well-known amusing sayings), and maritime memorabilia. Details of the great naval victories of the Admiral himself are engraved on the tables. On the menu are corned beef hash with free-range egg and meaty veal sauce; pavé of cod with buttered vegetables and cream white wine reduction; and pea and asparagus risotto.

Open all wk Bar Meals L served all wk 12-2 D served all wk 6-9 Restaurant D served all wk 6.15-9 ⊕ FREE HOUSE ◀ Guinness, John Smith. Facilities Garden Parking Rooms 37

JERSEY

GOREY — Map 24

Castle Green Gastropub ▮

La Route de la Cote JE3 6DR
☎ 01534 840218 ▤ 01534 840229
e-mail: enquiries@jerseypottery.com
dir: Opposite main entrance of Gorey Castle

A superbly located pub overlooking Gorey harbour and, in turn, overlooked by dramatic Mont Orgueil Castle. The views from the wooden sun terrace are breathtaking. An imaginative menu offers pan-Pacific-style dishes like Moroccan spiced lamb shoulder; Thai chicken burger; sushi and sashimi plate with pickled ginger and wasabi; along with fresh fillets of the day's catch , and summer seafood platter.

Closed: Sun eve & Mon ◀ Directors, John Smiths Extra Smooth, Theakstons. ▮ 8

ST AUBIN Map 24

Old Court House Inn ▾

St Aubin's Harbour JE3 8AB
☎ 01534 746433 📄 01534 745103
e-mail: info@oldcourthousejersey.com
dir: *From Jersey Airport, right at exit, left at lights, 0.5m to St Aubin*

The original courthouse at the rear of the property dates from 1450 and was first restored in 1611. Beneath the front part are enormous cellars where privateers stored their plunder. Three bars offer food, and there are two restaurants, the Granite and the Mizzen, with terrific views over the harbour, plus an attractive courtyard. There's lots of locally caught fish on the menus of course, plus real ales including Jersey Brewery, and the wine list incorporating a worthy Director's Bin.

Closed: 25 Dec, Mon Jan-Feb **Bar Meals** L served all wk 12.30-2.30 D served Mon-Sat 7-10 Av main course £8 **Restaurant** L served all wk 12.30-2.30 D served all wk 7-10.30 Fixed menu price fr £10 Av 3 course à la carte fr £20 ⊕ FREE HOUSE ◀ Directors, Theakstons, John Smiths, Jersey Brewery. ▾ 8 **Facilities** Children's menu Dogs allowed Garden

ST MARTIN Map 24

Royal Hotel ▾

La Grande Route de Faldouet JE3 6UG
☎ 01534 856289 📄 01534 857298
e-mail: johnbarker@jerseymail.co.uk
dir: *2m from Five Oaks rdbt towards St Martyn. Pub on right next to St Martin's Church*

A friendly atmosphere, value for money, and great food and drink are the hallmarks of this friendly local in the heart of St Martin. John Barker, the landlord, has been extending a welcome for 23 years at this former coaching inn. Roaring log fires warm winter visitors, and there's a sunny beer garden to relax in during the summer months. Among the traditional home-made favourites are steak and ale pie, fresh grilled trout, monkfish and prawn Thai curry, and vegetarian lasagne. Ploughman's lunches, filled jacket potatoes, grills and children's choices are also on offer.

Open all day all wk **Bar Meals** L served Mon-Sat 12-2.15 D served Mon-Sat 6-8.30 Av main course £8.50 **Restaurant** L served Mon-Sat 12-2.15 D served Mon-Sat 6-8.30 ⊕ RANDALLS VAUTIER ◀ John Smiths Smooth, Theakstons Cool, Guinness, Ringwood Real Ale. ▾ 9 **Facilities** Children's menu Play area Garden Parking

ISLE OF MAN

PEEL Map 24 SC28

The Creek Inn ▾

Station Place IM5 1AT
☎ 01624 842216 📄 01624 843359
e-mail: jeanmcaleer@manx.net
dir: *On quayside opposite House of Mannanan Museum*

Ideal for walkers, wildlife lovers and yachting enthusiasts, this family-run free house overlooks the harbour at Peel. Expect live music on Friday and Saturday nights, and a good selection of beers including locally brewed Okells ales. Fish and seafood dominate the menu, with the following available on any given day: Manx kippers, crab, lobster, seafood lasagne, salmon and broccoli bake, and king prawn thermidor.

Open all wk ⊕ FREE HOUSE ◀ Okells Bitter, Okells Seasonal, Bushy's Bitter, 4 guest ales. ▾ 9 **Facilities** Garden Parking

PORT ERIN Map 24 SC26

Falcon's Nest Hotel ★★ HL

The Promenade, Station Rd IM9 6AF
☎ 01624 834077 📄 01624 835370
e-mail: falconsnest@enterprise.net

A popular hotel overlooking a beautiful, sheltered harbour and beach. In 1865 Gladstone, then prime minister, stayed here with his son, and was responsible for what he called 'an amusing incident' involving a teapot. The lounge and saloon bars serve local beers, over 150 whiskies, snacks and meals, although there is also a restaurant with carvery option. Fish include local crab, prawns, sea bass, lobster and local scallops known as 'queenies'.

Open all wk **Bar Meals** L served all wk 12-2 D served all wk 6-9 Av main course £8 **Restaurant** L served all wk 12-2 D served all wk 6-9 Fixed menu price fr £15 Av 3 course à la carte fr £21 ⊕ FREE HOUSE ◀ Manx guest ale, Guinness, John Smiths, guest ales. **Facilities** Children's menu Family room Dogs allowed Parking **Rooms** 35

Scotland

Ben Venue reflecting in Loch Achray,
Trossachs National Park

SCOTLAND

ABERDEEN, CITY OF

| ABERDEEN | Map 23 NJ90 |

Old Blackfriars

52 Castle St AB11 5BB
☎ **01224 581922** 📠 **01224 582153**
dir: *From train station down Deeside to Union St. Turn right. Pub at end on right*

Stunning stained glass and a warm, welcoming atmosphere are features of this traditional city centre pub, situated in Aberdeen's historic Castlegate. It is built on the site of property owned by Blackfriars Dominican monks, hence the name. The menu runs from sandwiches and filled potatoes through to hearty dishes such as bangers and mash; chicken tikka masala; and beef au poivre. Finish with sticky toffee pudding or pancakes in maple syrup.

Open all wk Closed: 25 Dec, 1 Jan ⊕ BELHAVEN ◀ Abbot Ale, Deuchars IPA, Caledonian 80/-, Inveralmond, Ossian, Guest ales. 🍷 12

ABERDEENSHIRE

| BALMEDIE | Map 23 NJ91 |

The Cock & Bull Bar & Restaurant ◉ 🍷

Ellon Rd, Blairton AB23 8XY
☎ **01358 743249** 📠 **01358 742466**
e-mail: info@thecockandbull.co.uk
dir: *11m N of city centre, on left of A90 between Balmedie junct & Foveran*

What was once a coaching inn has been developed into a cosy gastro-pub. The bar area, warmed by a cast-iron range, has big sofas and a hotchpotch of hanging junk, from a ship's lifebelt to a trombone. The menu ranges from bar dishes of fish and chips, and cheese and bacon burger to restaurant fare like loin of monkfish wrapped in Parma ham with tarragon and chilli couscous and roasted red pepper reduction.

Open all day all wk 11.30-11.30 Closed: 25-26 Dec, 1-2 Jan **Bar Meals** L served Mon-Sat 12-9, Sun 12-6.45 D served Mon-Sat 12-9, Sun 12-6.45 food served all day ⊕ FREE HOUSE ◀ Directors Ale, Caledonian 80, Guinness. 🍷 7 **Facilities** Play area Garden Parking

| MARYCULTER | Map 23 NO89 |

Old Mill Inn

South Deeside Rd AB12 5FX
☎ **01224 733212** 📠 **01224 732884**
e-mail: Info@oldmillinn.co.uk
dir: *5m W of Aberdeen on B9077*

This delightful family-run 200-year-old country inn stands on the edge of the River Dee, five miles from Aberdeen city centre. A former mill house, the 18th-century granite building has been tastefully modernised to include a restaurant where the finest Scottish ingredients feature on the menu: venison stovies, peppered carpaccio of beef, cullen skink, and chicken and venison terrine are typical.

Open all wk **Bar Meals** L served all wk 12-2 D served all wk 5.30-9 **Restaurant** L served all wk 12-2 D served all wk 5.30-9 ⊕ FREE HOUSE ◀ Interbrew Bass, Caledonian Deuchars IPA, Timothy Taylor Landlord.
Facilities Children's menu Garden Parking

| NETHERLEY | Map 23 NO89 |

PICK OF THE PUBS

The Lairhillock Inn 🍷

AB39 3QS ☎ **01569 730001** 📠 **01569 731175**
e-mail: info@lairhillock.co.uk
dir: *From Aberdeen take A90. Right towards Durris on B9077 then left onto B979 to Netherley*

Set in beautiful rural Deeside yet only 15 minutes drive from Aberdeen, this award-winning 200-year-old former coaching inn offers real ales in the bar and real fires in the lounge to keep out the winter chill. Dishes are robust and use a bounty of fresh, quality, local and regional produce such as langoustines from Gourdon, mussels from Shetland, scallops from Orkney, wild boar and venison from the Highlands and salmon from the Dee and Don, not forgetting certified Aberdeen Angus beef. For lunch, try the Lairhillock lasagne which layers pasta with minced venison, beef and pork topped with wild mushroom sauce. For a more formal dining option, the atmospheric Crynoch restaurant menu might feature shredded confit duck leg and beetroot timbale, followed by chicken supreme filled with sage and sausagemeat. Quality abounds on the children's menu too, where spicy spare ribs and Finnan haddock fishcakes can be found.

Open all wk 11am-mdnt Closed: 25-26 Dec, 1-2 Jan **Bar Meals** L served all wk 12-2 booking required D served all wk 6-9.30 booking required Av main course £9.95 **Restaurant** D served Tue-Sat 7-9.30 booking required Av 3 course à la carte fr £27.50 ⊕ FREE HOUSE ◀ Timothy Taylor Landlord, Courage Directors, Cairngorm, Tradewinds, Greene King IPA. 🍷 7 **Facilities** Children's menu Dogs allowed Garden Parking

| OLDMELDRUM | Map 23 NJ82 |

The Redgarth

Kirk Brae AB51 0DJ ☎ **01651 872353** 📠 **01651 873763**
e-mail: redgarth1@aol.com
dir: *On A947 (bypass) Oldmeldrum located east side. Follow signs to golf club/pleasure park*

A family-run inn, The Redgarth was built as a house in 1928 and has an attractive garden offering magnificent views of Bennachie and the surrounding countryside. Cask-conditioned ales, such as Orkney Scapa and Isle of Skye Red Cullin, and fine wines are served along with dishes prepared on the premises using fresh local produce. A typical selection might start with duo of hot and cold salmon with horseradish mayonnaise, or game terrine; continue with pork fillet stuffed with black pudding served with red cabbage in pear cider gravy, or pan-fried Barbary duck breast with Grand Marnier and orange glaze; and finish with apple pie or chocolate fudge cake.

Open all wk 11-3 5-11 (Fri-Sat 11-3 5-11.45) Closed: 25-26 Dec, 1-3 Jan **Bar Meals** L served all wk 12-2 D served Sun-Thu 5-9, Fri-Sat 5-9.30 **Restaurant** L served all wk 12-2 booking required D served Sun-Thu 5-9, Fri-Sat 5-9.30 booking required ⊕ FREE HOUSE ◀ Inveralmond Thrappledouser, Caledonian Deuchars IPA, Timothy Taylor Landlord, Isle of Skye Red Cullin, Orkney Scapa. **Facilities** Garden Parking

ARGYLL & BUTE

| ARDUAINE | Map 20 NM71 |

PICK OF THE PUBS

Loch Melfort Hotel ★★★ HL ◉◉ 🍷

See Pick of the Pubs on opposite page

PICK OF THE PUBS

Loch Melfort Hotel ★★★ HL ❀❀ ♉

ARDUAINE   Map 20 NM71

PA34 4XG ☎ **01852 200233**
e-mail: reception@lochmelfort.co.uk
web: chartroom2.com
dir: On A816, 20m south of Oban

Standing in 26 acres of grounds next to the National Trust for Scotland's Arduaine Gardens, this award-winning hotel and restaurant offers the perfect place for a relaxing holiday or short break at any time of year. The hotel is framed by woodlands and the magnificent mountains of Argyll and, from its waterside location on the Scottish west coast, guests can enjoy spectacular views across Asknish Bay and the Sound of Jura. There's a uniquely informal and relaxed atmosphere as you step into the warmth and tranquillity of this comfortable country house with its cosy bar, welcoming sitting rooms and squashy sofas beside the log fire. The main house is principally Victorian, built by J. Arthur Campbell in 1896; some of the beautiful original features remain, including oak panelling and 19th-century family portraits. Fresh scented flowers adorn the treasured occasional tables and bookcases, whilst the latest lifestyle magazines are available in the lounges. Choose to dine in the formal Arduaine Restaurant, where tian of Asknish Bay crab with apple and sweet pepper sauce; or marinated Islay scallops with pea pesto, lime and chilli dressing might introduce main courses like pan-fried loin of Argyll venison with dauphinoise potatoes, creamed leeks and a thyme and juniper jus; or sea trout fillet with braised fennel, and pea and chervil risotto. The more relaxed atmosphere of the modern Chartroom 2 bar and bistro is the place to enjoy all-day drinks, teas, coffees and home baking, as well as light lunches and suppers. It has the finest views on the West Coast and serves home-made Scottish fare including plenty of locally landed seafood. You can sit outside and enjoy a drink in warmer weather or crowd around the cosy fire in winter and watch the waves crashing against the rocks.

Open 11-11 **Bar Meals** L served all week 12-2.30 D served all week 6-8.30 Av main course £8.95 ⊕ FREE HOUSE ☎ 80/- Ale Belhaven, Fyne Ale. ♉ 8 **Facilities** Children's menu Play area Dogs allowed Garden Parking **Rooms** 25

CLACHAN-SEIL — Map 20 NM71

PICK OF THE PUBS

Tigh an Truish Inn

PA34 4QZ ☎ **01852 300242**
dir: *14m S of Oban take A816. 12m, onto B844 towards Atlantic Bridge*

Following the Battle of Culloden in 1746, kilts were outlawed on pain of death. In defiance of this edict the islanders wore their kilts at home; but, on excursions to the mainland, they would stop at the Tigh an Truish — the 'house of trousers' — to change into the hated trews. Now popular with tourists and members of the yachting fraternity, the inn is handy for good walks and lovely gardens. Ales from local brewers stock the bar, along with a range of single malts, while an appetising menu based on the best local produce is particularly well endowed with fresh seafood: moules marinière, locally caught prawns served with garlic mayonnaise and salad, and smoked salmon of course. Look out for venison, perhaps prepared in a pepper cream and Drambuie sauce. If this all sounds rather sophisticated, families need not worry; a separate lounge off the main bar is furnished with children's books — another indication of the pub's genuinely warm welcome.

Open all wk 11-11 (Mon-Fri 11-2.30 5-11 Oct-Mar) **Closed:** 25 Dec & 1 Jan **Bar Meals** L served all wk 12-2 D served all wk 6-8.30 (Apr-Oct) Av main course £7.50 ⊕ FREE HOUSE ◀ Local guest ales changing regularly. **Facilities** Family room Dogs allowed Garden Parking

CONNEL — Map 20 NM93

PICK OF THE PUBS

The Oyster Inn NEW

PA37 1PJ ☎ **01631 710666** 📄 **01631 710042**
e-mail: stay@oysterinn.co.uk
dir: *Please telephone for directions*

A comfortable, informal hotel overlooking the tidal whirlpools and white water of the Falls of Lora, and enjoying glorious views of the mountains of Mull. It was built in the 18th century to serve ferry passengers, but the ferry is no more, superseded by the modern road bridge. Years ago it was known as The Glue Pot, because canny locals knew they could be 'stuck' here between ferries, and thus get round complicated Sunday licensing laws. Food is served all day, using

locally-sourced, quality produce, particularly from the sea and lochs, such as West Coast mussels marinière; Ferryman's ocean pie; and seafood pancakes. Other dishes include steak and ale pie; bangers and mash; local lamb shank; and tempura battered vegetables. There's a log fire in the bar, where regular live music is performed, and where your companions are reasonably certain to be walkers, divers, canoeists, fishermen or yachting enthusiasts.

Open all wk noon-mdnt **Bar Meals** L served all wk 12.30-2.30 D served all wk 5.30-8.30 Av main course £9.95 **Restaurant** D served all wk 6-8.30 booking required ⊕ FREE HOUSE ◀ Guinness.
Facilities Children's menu Dogs allowed Garden Parking

CRINAN — Map 20 NR79

PICK OF THE PUBS

Crinan Hotel

See Pick of the Pubs on opposite page

DUNOON — Map 20 NS17

Coylet Inn

Loch Eck PA23 8SG ☎ **01369 840426**
e-mail: reservations@coylet-locheck.co.uk
dir: *9m N of Dunoon on A815*

Overlooking the shores of Loch Eck, this beautifully refurbished 17th-century coaching inn is a blissful hideaway with no television or games machines to disturb the peace. The inn is famous for its ghost, the Blue Boy; a film was even made of the story, starring Emma Thompson. Unwind by one of three log fires or plunder the impressive menus, where choices range from venison burger and chips to grilled sole with mussel cream.

Closed: 25 Dec, Mon & Tue (Oct-Mar) ⊕ FREE HOUSE ◀ Caledonian Deuchars IPA, Highlander.
Facilities Garden Parking

KILFINAN — Map 20 NR97

Kilfinan Hotel Bar

PA21 2EP ☎ **01700 821201** 📄 **01700 821205**
e-mail: kilfinanhotel@btconnect.com
dir: *8m N of Tighnabruaich on B8000*

The hotel, on the eastern shore of Loch Fyne set amid spectacular Highland scenery on a working estate, has been welcoming travellers since the 1760s. The bars are cosy with log fires in winter, and offer a fine selection of malts. There are two intimate dining rooms, with the Lamont room for larger parties. Menus change daily and offer the best of local produce: Loch Fyne oysters, of course, and langoustine grilled in garlic butter; cullen skink soup; and moules marinière, plus game, Aberdeen Angus beef and a variety of Scottish sweets and cheeses. Enjoy the views from the garden on warmer days.

Open all wk **Bar Meals** L served all wk 12.30-4 D served all wk 6.30-9.30 Av main course £7.95 **Restaurant** L served all wk 12.30-4 booking required D served all wk 6.30-9.30 booking required Av 3 course à la carte fr £22 ⊕ FREE HOUSE ◀ McEwens 70/-, McEwens 80/-.
Facilities Children's menu Family room Dogs allowed Garden Parking

LOCHGILPHEAD — Map 20 NR88

PICK OF THE PUBS

Cairnbaan Hotel ★★★ HL ⊛ ♥

See Pick of the Pubs on page 556

LUSS — Map 20 NS39

PICK OF THE PUBS

AA PUB OF THE YEAR FOR SCOTLAND 2009-2010

The Inn at Inverbeg NEW — INN ♥

G83 8PD ☎ **01436 860678** 📄 **01436 860203**
e-mail: inverbeg.reception@loch-lomond.co.uk
dir: *12m N of Balloch*

Situated just off the A82 and commanding stunning views across Loch Lomond and its surrounding hills, the Inn is Scotland's first boutique inn. Dating from 1814, it has been remodelled and refurbished in contemporary style, yet retains its old-world charm and character — typically find roaring log fires fronted by swish leather and cow hide seating. At the Whisky Bar you have over 200 malts and real ales like Deuchars IPA to choose from. In Mr C's, the relaxed and informal dining room, you can tuck into fresh, sustainable fish caught off Scottish shores. Start with steamed mussels, Loch Fyne oysters or chilli-coated squid with garlic mayonnaise, move on to fishcakes with spinach and lemon hollandaise or simply grilled cod or haddock served with chips, or Buccleuch sirloin steak with herb butter. Comfortable, individually styled rooms are split between the inn and a sumptuous beach house beside loch, the latter featuring wooden floors, hand-crafted furniture, crisp linen, and a hot tub.

Open all day all wk 11-11 **Bar Meals** Av main course £9.95 food served all day **Restaurant** food served all day ◀ Killellan, Highlander, Deuchars IPA. ♥ 30
Facilities Children's menu Parking **Rooms** 20

PICK OF THE PUBS

Crinan Hotel

CRINAN Map 20 NR79

PA31 8SR
☎ 01546 830261 📄 01546 830292
e-mail: reservations@crinanhotel.com
dir: *From M8, at end of bridge take A82, at Tarbert left onto A83. At Inverary follow Campbeltown signs to Lochgilphead, follow signs for A816 to Oban. 2m, left to Crinan on B841*

At the north end of the Crinan Canal which connects Loch Fyne to the Atlantic Ocean, the Crinan is a romantic retreat enjoying fabulous views across the sound of Jura. It's a long-standing place of welcome at the heart of community life in this tiny fishing village. The hotel dates back some 200 years and has been run by owners Nick and Frances Ryan for nearly 40 of them. The Panther Arms is the hotel's public bar, where you can sample Scottish beers or whiskies while chatting to the locals. You can eat here too, or in the Mainbrace Bar which has a menu served both at lunchtime and in the evening. The award-winning cuisine is firmly based on the freshest of seafood — it's landed daily just 50 metres from the hotel. Some bar meals can be served in either starter or main course quantities: warm tart of Loch Crinan scallops and smoked bacon is served with organic leaves and a goats' cheese cream; Loch Etive mussels are classically steamed in lemon, thyme and garlic; and oak-smoked salmon from Rothesay are three examples. If in the evening a full à la carte dinner is required, head for the Westward restaurant on the ground floor with its views over Loch Crinan to Jura, Scarba and the mountains of Mull. If you've eaten enough seafood, a typical choice could start with pithiviers of free range chicken and wood pigeon, with winter truffles and salsify; continue with roasted saddle of Argyll venison with slow-cooked haunch, Savoy cabbage and confit potatoes; and finish with hot chocolate fondant, poached mandarins and vanilla ice cream. Boat trips can be arranged to the islands, and there is a classic boats regatta in the summer.

Open all week Closed: 25 Dec ⊕ FREE HOUSE ◀ Belhaven, Interbrew, Worthington Bitter, Tennents Velvet, Guinness, Loch Fyne Ales.
Facilities Dogs allowed Garden Parking

PICK OF THE PUBS

Cairnbaan Hotel ★★★ HL 🌹🍷

LOCHGILPHEAD Map 20 NR88

Cairnbaan PA31 8SJ
☎ 01546 603668 📠 01546 606045
e-mail: info@cairnbaan.com
web: www.cairnbaan.com
dir: *2m N, take A816 from Lochgilphead, hotel off B841*

Originally a coaching inn, the Cairnbaan was built in the latter part of the 18th century during the construction of the Crinan Canal. At one point it was considered the wildest pub in Mid-Argyll, with goats and other animals sharing space at the bar, but time was finally called on the last of the livestock years ago and the hotel is now stylish,

relaxed and particularly popular with the waterway-cruising fraternity. It's owned by ex-QE2 catering officer Darren Dobson, ashore now for 20-plus years, and wife Christine, a former teacher, who plans the menus and does all the baking. Enjoy a meal in their serene restaurant, holder of an AA Rosette, where the carte specialises in the use of fresh local produce, notably seafood and game. For a lunchtime snack, opt for ciabatta rolls with fillings such as pastrami, with mustard mayonnaise and gherkin. On the main menu, look for starters of seared scallops with Stornoway black pudding and pea purée; tempura of haggis with root vegetable slaw in whisky and grain mustard dressing; and Cajun-spiced chicken Caesar salad. Mains might include monkfish tail stuffed with rosemary pesto and wrapped in Parma ham, with roast tomato, green vegetables and crushed potatoes; Argyll game pie with chestnuts, chive mash

and rich port gravy; Cairnbaan fish pie; and crêpes stuffed with mixed vegetables, glazed with Mull cheddar and spinach cream. See the specials board for an ever-changing range of home-made desserts. From nearby Oban there are sailings to the islands of Mull, Tiree, and Coll, while Inveraray Castle is well worth a visit, as is Dunadd Fort where the ancient kings of Scotland were crowned. With so much to see and do in the area, the en suite bedrooms could be worth investigating.

Open all week ⊕ FREE HOUSE 🍺 Local Ales. 🍷 8 **Facilities** Garden Parking **Rooms** 12

PICK OF THE PUBS

Pierhouse Hotel & Restaurant ★★★ SHL

PORT APPIN Map 20 NM94

PA38 4DE
☎ 01631 730302 📠 01631 730509
e-mail: reservations@pierhousehotel.co.uk
dir: *A828 from Ballachulish to Oban. In Appin right at Port Appin & Lismore ferry sign. After 2.5m left after post office, hotel at end of road by pier*

Situated in a quiet village on the shores of Loch Linnhe, this family-run, 12-bedroom hotel, bar and renowned seafood restaurant is surrounded by the raw beauty of Scotland's magnificent West Coast. With breathtaking views to the islands of Lismore and Mull, it would be hard to imagine a more spectacular setting. You arrive along a narrow road from Appin, or by boat, tying up to one of the hotel's ten moorings near the pier. It prides itself on the freshness and quality of its seafood, game and meats, and sources virtually all such produce locally. Once the piermaster's home, it now houses a popular bar, pool room, terrace and dining area, and offers a selection of menus featuring oysters hand-picked from the Lismore beds; mussels and langoustines harvested from Loch Linnhe and Loch Etive; and lobsters and crab kept mouth-wateringly fresh in creels at the end of the pier. As well as fish of the day, there are several seafood platters – the Pierhouse, for example, consists of those local langoustines and mussels, as well as plump grilled Mull scallops, oysters, fresh and smoked salmon and a roll mop. There are alternatives to seafood, such as Highland fillet steak served on creamy herb mash with a whisky and peppercorn sauce; and pappardelle with fresh mushrooms, herbs, white wine, garlic and cream topped with gruyère cheese. Twelve individually designed bedrooms include two with four-poster beds and superb loch views, and three triple family rooms. Country sports enthusiasts will love the deer-stalking and fly-fishing, both of which the hotel will arrange with a small number of private estate owners.

Open 11-11 Closed: 25 & 26 Dec **Bar Meals** L served all week 12.30-2.30 D served all week 6.30-9.30 Av main course £9 **Restaurant** L served all week 12.30-2.30 D served all week 6.30-9.30 Fixed menu price fr £35 Av 3 course à la carte fr £23 ⊕ FREE HOUSE ◀ Calders 80/-, Belhaven Best, Guinness. **Facilities** Children's menu Family room Dogs allowed Garden Parking **Rooms** 12

PORT APPIN Map 20 NM94

PICK OF THE PUBS

The Pierhouse Hotel & Seafood Restaurant ★★★ SHL

See Pick of the Pubs on page 557

STRACHUR Map 20 NN00

PICK OF THE PUBS

Creggans Inn ★★★ HL ☻ ♀

PA27 8BX ☎ **01369 860279** 📄 **01369 860637**
e-mail: info@creggans-inn.co.uk
dir: *A82 from Glasgow, at Tarbet take A83 towards Cairndow, left onto A815 to Strachur*

From the hills above this informal family-friendly house on the shores of Loch Fyne, you can gaze across the Mull of Kintyre to the Western Isles beyond. It has been a coaching inn since the days of Mary Queen of Scots. Current proprietors Archie and Gill MacLellan were preceded years ago by Sir Fitzroy Maclean, reputedly the man upon whom Ian Fleming based his most famous character. A good selection of real ales, wines by the glass and malt whiskies are all served at the bar. There's a formal terraced garden and patio for alfresco summer enjoyment, and regional produce plays a key role in the seasonal menus: the famed Loch Fyne oysters of course, but also salmon from the same waters, smoked or grilled. Robust main courses may feature fillet of Aberdeenshire beef; haddock in a crisp beer batter; or pot-roasted chicken. Apple and bramble tart with home-made cinnamon ice cream makes a fulfilling conclusion.

Open all wk 11am-mdnt **Bar Meals** L served all wk 12-2.30 D served all wk 6-8.30 Av main course £9.50 **Restaurant** D served all wk 7-8.30 booking required Fixed menu price fr £37.50 ⊕ FREE HOUSE ◀ Fyne Ales Highlander, Atlas Latitude, Deuchars IPA, Harviestoun Bitter & Twisted. ♀ 7 **Facilities** Children's menu Dogs allowed Garden Parking **Rooms** 14

TAYVALLICH Map 20 NR78

PICK OF THE PUBS

Tayvallich Inn

PA31 8PL ☎ **01546 870282**
dir: *From Lochgilphead take A816 then B841/B8025*

Following a change of hands in recent times, the Tayvallich Inn is now run by Glen and Lynne Hyde. The property was converted from an old bus garage in 1976. The name translates as 'house in the pass' and it has the most spectacular setting. The inn stands by a natural harbour at the head of Loch Sween with stunning views over the anchorage, particularly from the outside area of decking, where food and drinks can be enjoyed. Those seated inside can gaze out over the village and Tayvallich Bay from the large picture windows. A selection of fine wines and single malts are served as well as Loch Fyne Ales. Not surprisingly given the location, fresh seasonal seafood is the house speciality, available along with good quality pub food. Those interested in the works of 19th-century engineer Thomas Telford will find plenty of bridges and piers in the area.

Closed: 25-26 Dec, Mon (Nov-Mar) **Bar Meals** L served all wk 12-2.15 D served all wk 6-8.45 **Restaurant** L served all wk 12-2.15 booking required D served all wk 6-8.45 booking required ⊕ FREE HOUSE ◀ Tennents, Guinness, Loch Fyne Ales. **Facilities** Children's menu Dogs allowed Garden Parking

CLACKMANNANSHIRE

DOLLAR Map 21 NS99

Castle Campbell Hotel ★★★ SHL ♀

11 Bridge St FK14 7DE
☎ **01259 742519** 📄 **01259 743742**
e-mail: bookings@castle-campbell.co.uk
dir: *A91 (Stirling to St Andrews road). In Dollar centre by bridge overlooking clock tower*

Find a real taste of Scotland at this 19th-century coaching inn, handy for the romantic castle and Dollar Glen's spectacular gorges. Recognised as a Whisky Ambassador, the hotel has over 50 malts; local ale is always on tap and the wine list runs to several pages. Prime Scottish produce features on both bar and restaurant menus, with options ranging from lunchtime sandwiches to Arbroath haddock fillet in crisp beer batter, or lamb with minted mash.

Open all wk ⊕ FREE HOUSE ◀ Harviestoun Bitter & Twisted, Deuchars IPA (guest), McEwans 70'. ♀ 7 **Facilities** Dogs allowed Parking **Rooms** 9

DUMFRIES & GALLOWAY

ISLE OF WHITHORN Map 20 NX43

PICK OF THE PUBS

The Steam Packet Inn ♀

Harbour Row DG8 8LL
☎ **01988 500334** 📄 **01988 500627**
e-mail: steampacketinn@btconnect.com
dir: *From Newton Stewart take A714, then A746 to Whithorn, then Isle of Whithorn*

This lively quayside pub stands in a picturesque village at the tip of the Machars peninsula. Sit by the picture windows and watch the fishermen at work, then look to the menu for a chance to sample the fruits of their labours. Extensive seafood choices - perhaps local lobster thermidor or a kettle of fish with vermouth crème fraîche - are supported by the likes of steak and baby onion suet pudding or Thai pork ciabatta.

Open all wk 11-11 (Sun noon-11) Closed: 25 Dec, winter Tue-Thu 2.30-6 **Bar Meals** L served all wk 12-2 D served all wk 6.30-9 ⊕ FREE HOUSE ◀ Timothy Taylor Landlord, Caledonian Deuchars IPA, Black Sheep Best Bitter, Houston Killellan. ♀ 9 **Facilities** Dogs allowed Garden Parking

KIRKCUDBRIGHT Map 20 NX65

Selkirk Arms Hotel ★★★ HL ♀

Old High St DG6 4JG
☎ **01557 330402** 📄 **01557 331639**
e-mail: reception@selkirkarmshotel.co.uk
web: www.selkirkarmshotel.co.uk
dir: *M74 & M6 to A75, halfway between Dumfries & Stranraer on A75*

Robert Burns is reputed to have written the Selkirk Grace at this privately owned hotel, and the proprietors have created their own real ale, The Selkirk Grace, in conjunction with Sulwath Brewers. There are two bars, and a great choice of dishes is offered in The Bistro or more intimate Artistas Restaurant, including pan-seared Kirkcudbright king scallops; slow roast lamb shank; and Eccelfechan butter tart. Accommodation is provided in 17 en suite bedrooms.

Selkirk Arms Hotel

Open all wk **Bar Meals** L served all wk 12-2 D served all wk 6-9 Av main course £9.95 **Restaurant** L served Sun 12-2 booking required D served all wk 7-9 booking required Fixed menu price fr £19 Av 3 course à la carte fr £30 ⊕ FREE HOUSE ◀ Youngers Tartan, John Smiths Bitter, Criffel, Timothy Taylor Landlord, The Selkirk Grace. ♀ 8 **Facilities** Children's menu Dogs allowed Garden Parking **Rooms** 17

MOFFAT — Map 21 NT00

Black Bull Hotel ♀

Churchgate DG10 9EG
☎ 01683 220206 📄 01683 220483
e-mail: hotel@blackbullmoffat.co.uk
dir: *Telephone for directions*

This historic pub was the headquarters of Graham of Claverhouse during the 17th-century Scottish rebellion, and was frequented by Robert Burns around 1790. The Railway Bar, in former stables across the courtyard, houses a collection of railway memorabilia and traditional pub games. Food is served in the lounge, Burns Room or restaurant. Dishes include Black Bull sizzlers (steak, chicken fillets, gammon) served on a cast iron platter; the daily roast, and deep-fried breaded haddock fillet.

Open all wk ⊕ FREE HOUSE ◀ McEwans, Theakston. ♀ 10 **Facilities** Garden Parking

NEW ABBEY — Map 21 NX96

Criffel Inn

2 The Square DG2 8BX
☎ 01387 850305 & 850244 📄 01387 850305
e-mail: criffelinn@btconnect.com
dir: *A74/A74(M) exit at Gretna, A75 to Dumfries, A710 to New Abbey*

A former 18th-century coaching inn set on the Solway Coast in the historic conservation village of New Abbey close to the ruins of the 13th-century Sweetheart Abbey. Expect a warm welcome and excellent home-cooked food

using local produce. There's a lawned beer garden overlooking the corn-mill and square; ideal for touring Dumfries and Galloway.

Open all wk noon-2.30 5-11 (Mon-Tue 5-11 Fri-Sat noon-2.30 5-mdnt) **Bar Meals** L served Wed-Sun 12-2 D served Wed-Sun 5-8 Av main course £7.95 **Restaurant** L served Wed-Sun 12-2 D served Wed-Sun 5-8 ⊕ FREE HOUSE ◀ Belhaven Best, McEwans 60-, Guinness. **Facilities** Children's menu Family room Dogs allowed Garden Parking

NEW GALLOWAY — Map 20 NX67

Cross Keys Hotel ♀

High St DG7 3RN ☎ 01644 420494 📄 01644 701071
e-mail: enquiries@thecrosskeys-newgalloway.co.uk
dir: *At N end of Loch Ken, 10m from Castle Douglas on A712*

An 18th-century coaching inn with a beamed period bar, where food is served in restored, stone-walled cells (part of the hotel was once the police station). The à la carte restaurant offers hearty food with a Scottish accent, chicken stuffed with haggis and served with whisky sauce being a prime example. Real ales are a speciality, and there's a good choice of malts in the whisky bar.

Open all wk ◀ Houston, guest real ales. ♀ 9 **Facilities** Dogs allowed Garden

NEWTON STEWART — Map 20 NX46

PICK OF THE PUBS

Creebridge House Hotel ▲ ★★★ SHL

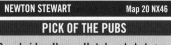

Minnigaff DG8 6NP
☎ 01671 402121 📄 01671 403258
e-mail: info@creebridge.co.uk
dir: *From A75 into Newton Stewart, turn right over river bridge, hotel 200yds on left*

A listed building dating from 1760, this family-run hotel is set in three acres of idyllic gardens and woodland at the foot of Kirroughtree forest. It was formerly the Earl of Galloway's shooting lodge and part of his estate. The refurbished Bridge's bar and brasserie offers malt whiskies, real ales and an interesting menu, perfect for an informal lunch. For a candlelit dinner the alternative dining venue is the Creebridge Garden Restaurant. The emphasis is on fresh Scottish produce, and both menus feature Kirkcudbrightshire beef, hung for 14 days, and an award-winning house speciality: best loin of lamb with creamed kale and roulade of braised shin. Fish dishes range from the brasserie's local sea bass set on chive mash with dill butter sauce, to the restaurant's seared Solway salmon with lemon risotto and chive velouté.

Open all wk noon-2 6-11.30 (Fri-Sat noon-2 6-1am) **Bar Meals** L served all wk 12-2 D served all wk 6-9 ⊕ FREE HOUSE ◀ Tennents, Deuchars, Guinness, guest ales. **Facilities** Dogs allowed Garden Parking **Rooms** 18

The Galloway Arms NEW ★★★ INN ♀

54-58 Victoria St DG8 6DB
☎ 01671 402653 📄 01671 401202
e-mail: info@gallowayarmshotel.com
dir: *In the centre of Newton Stewart opposite town clock*

Established in 1750, the Galloway Arms is older than the town of Newton Stewart, which was built around it. The newly refurbished Earls Room lounge offers an unrivalled range of over 100 malt whiskies, as well as real ale and traditional Scottish beers. Local produce from a 20-mile radius is the foundation of most dishes, which might feature fresh Kirkcudbright scallops, beef sourced from only five local farms or Galloway venison. There are 17 en suite bedrooms if you would like to stay over.

Open all day all wk 11am-mdnt (Fri-Sat 11am-1am) **Bar Meals** L served all wk 12-2 D served all wk 6-9 Av main course £8 **Restaurant** D served all wk 6-9 Av 3 course à la carte fr £17.95 ⊕ FREE HOUSE ◀ Belhavan Best, Guinness, Caledonian Deuchars IPA. ♀ 11 **Facilities** Children's menu Dogs allowed Garden Parking **Rooms** 17

PORTPATRICK — Map 20 NW95

Crown Hotel ♀

9 North Crescent DG9 8SX ☎ 01776 810261
e-mail: info@crownportpatrick.com
dir: *Take A77 from ferry port at Stranraer*

Just a few yards from the water's edge in one of the region's most picturesque villages, the Crown has striking views across the Irish Sea. The rambling old bar has seafaring displays and a warming winter fire. Naturally seafood is a speciality: starters range from crab and scallop fish soup, to fresh local crab claws in dill sauce; main courses continue the briny celebration with a hot seafood platter, or whole fresh pan-fried sea bass.

Open all wk ⊕ FREE HOUSE ◀ John Smiths, McEwans 80/-, McEwans 70/-, Guinness. ♀ 8 **Facilities** Family room Garden Parking

DUNDEE, CITY OF

BROUGHTY FERRY   Map 21 NO43

The Royal Arch Bar ▼

285 Brook St DD5 2DS
☎ **01382 779741** 📄 **01382 739174**
dir: *3m from Dundee. 0.5 min from Broughty Ferry rail station*

In Victorian times, the jute industry made Broughty Ferry the 'richest square mile in Europe'. Named after a Masonic lodge which was demolished to make way for the Tay road bridge, the pub dates from 1869. The deep, dry cellars are ideal for conditioning ale so look forward to a nice pint in the bar with its original hand-carved oak bar, sideboard and counter. An extensive selection of meals range from light snacks to three-course meals, served in the bar, lounge, restaurant or pavement café.

Open all wk Closed: 1 Jan **Bar Meals** L served Mon-Fri 12-2.15, Sat-Sun 12-5 booking required D served All wk 5-7.30 booking required Av main course £8 ⊕ FREE HOUSE ◀ McEwans 80/-, Belhaven Best, Guinness, Caledonian, Deuchars IPA. ▼ 12 **Facilities** Children's menu Family room Dogs allowed Garden

DUNDEE   Map 21 NO43

Speedwell Bar ▼

165-167 Perth Rd DD2 1AS ☎ **01382 667783**
e-mail: jonathan_stewart@fsmail.net
dir: *From city centre along Perth Rd, pass university, last bar on right*

Popularly known as Mennies, this surviving Edwardian pub is listed for an interior that has no need of imported nicknacks to give it period character. The same family owned it for 90 years, until the present landlord's father bought it in 1995. The bar offers 157 whiskies. A kitchen would be good, but since the pub is listed this is impossible, so signs encourage customers to bring in pies from next door.

Open all wk ⊕ FREE HOUSE ◀ McEwans, Belhaven Best. ▼ 10 **Facilities** Dogs allowed **Notes** ☺

EAST AYRSHIRE

DALRYMPLE   Map 20 NS31

The Kirkton Inn

1 Main St KA6 6DF ☎ **01292 560241** 📄 **01292 560835**
e-mail: kirkton@cqm.co.uk
dir: *6m SE from centre of Ayr just off A77*

This inn's motto is, 'There are no strangers here, only friends who have never met', and the welcoming atmosphere makes it easy to feel at home. It's a stoutly traditional setting, with open fires and polished brasses, set in the village of Dalrymple. As we went to press we understand there was a change of hands.

Open all wk ⊕ FREE HOUSE ◀ Belhaven Best, Tennents. **Facilities** Dogs allowed Garden Parking

GATEHEAD   Map 20 NS33

The Cochrane Inn

45 Main Rd KA2 0AP ☎ **01563 570122**
dir: *From Glasgow A77 to Kilmarnock, then A759 to Gatehead*

There's a friendly, bustling atmosphere inside this traditional village centre pub, which sits just a short drive from the Ayrshire coast. The menus combine British and international flavours. At lunch this might translate as cullen skink with crayfish tails followed by penne Arrabiata or spicy lamb curry. In the evening, maybe crispy bacon and houmous on toast ahead of a hearty steak pie with carrots and mash.

Open all wk noon-2.30 5.30 onwards (Sun noon-9) **Bar Meals** food served all day **Restaurant** food served all day ⊕ FREE HOUSE ◀ John Smiths. **Facilities** Children's menu Garden Parking

SORN   Map 20 NS52

PICK OF THE PUBS

The Sorn Inn ★★★★ RR ◉◉ ▼

35 Main St KA5 6HU
☎ **01290 551305** 📄 **01290 553470**
e-mail: craig@sorninn.com

Now a gastro-pub with rooms, the Sorn was built in the 18th century as a coaching inn on the old Kilmarnock to Edinburgh route. A completely new style of menu in both the Chop House and Restaurant offers a fusion of fine dining and brasserie-style food using the best seasonal and fresh local ingredients. From a dinner menu come starters of rillette of salmon with cucumber salsa and lemon dressing; Macsween haggis beignets with creamed leeks; and pan-fried foie gras with chargrilled brioche and rum and raisin syrup. Main courses include pan-fried lamb's liver with Tuscan sausage, shallots and pinto beans; fillet of pink bream with saffron, lemon pasta, leeks and asparagus sauce; and confit rib of beef with horseradish mash and honey-glazed root vegetables. To follow, try coconut rice pudding with caramelised pineapple; or mango and passion fruit crème brûlée. The Sorn has held its two AA Rosettes for seven years. Four comfortable bedrooms are available.

Open noon-2.30 6-10 (Fri 6-mdnt Sat noon-mdnt Sun 12.30-10) Closed: 2wks Jan, Mon **Bar Meals** L served Tue-Fri 12-2.30, Sat 12-9, Sun 12.30-7.30 D served Tue-Fri 6-9, Sat 12-9, Sun 12.30-7.30 Av main course £12 **Restaurant** L served Tue-Fri 12-2.30, Sat 12-9, Sun 12.30-7.30 booking required D served Tue-Fri 6-9, Sat 12-9, Sun 12.30-7.30 booking required Fixed menu price fr £23.95 Av 3 course à la carte fr £25 ⊕ FREE HOUSE ◀ John Smiths, McEwans 60/-. ▼ 13 **Facilities** Children's menu Dogs allowed Parking **Rooms** 4

EDINBURGH, CITY OF

EDINBURGH   Map 21 NT27

Bennets Bar ▼

8 Leven St EH3 9LG ☎ **0131 229 5143**
e-mail: knight@hotmail.com
dir: *Next to Kings Theatre. Please phone for more detailed directions*

Bennets is a friendly pub, popular with performers from the adjacent Kings Theatre, serving real ales, over 120 malt whiskies and a decent selection of wines. It's a listed property dating from 1839 with hand-painted tiles and murals on the walls, original stained glass windows and brass beer taps. Reasonably priced home-made food ranges from toasties, burgers and salads to stovies, steak pie, and macaroni cheese. There's also a daily roast and traditional puddings.

Open all wk 11-11 (Sun noon-1am) Closed: 25 Dec **Bar Meals** L served Mon-Sat 12-2 D served Mon-Sat 5-8.30 Av main course £6.25 ⊕ IONA PUB ◀ Caledonian Deuchars IPA, Guinness, Caledonian 80/-. ▼ 14 **Facilities** Children's menu Family room

The Bow Bar ▼

80 The West Bow EH1 2HH ☎ **0131 226 7667**
dir: *Telephone for directions*

Located in the heart of Edinburgh's old town, the Bow Bar reflects the history and traditions of the area. Tables from decommissioned railway carriages and a gantry from an old church used for the huge selection of whiskies create interest in the bar, where 150 malts are on tap, and eight cask ales are dispensed from antique equipment. Bar snacks only are served, and there are no gaming machines or music to distract from conversation.

Open all wk Closed: 25-26 Dec, 1-2 Jan ⊕ FREE HOUSE ◀ Deuchars IPA, Belhaven 80/-, Timothy Taylor Landlord, Harviestown Bitter & Twisted, Atlas Lattitude, Trade Winds, Stewarts Pentland IPA. ▼ 6 **Facilities** Dogs allowed

PICK OF THE PUBS

Doric Tavern

15-16 Market St EH1 1DE ☎ **0131 225 1084**
e-mail: info@the-doric.com
dir: *In city centre opp Waverly Station & Edinburgh Dungeons*

The property dates from 1710, when it was built as a private residence. It became a pub in the mid-1800s and takes its name from a language that used to be spoken in north-east Scotland, mainly in Aberdeenshire. It's conveniently located for Waverley Station, just a short walk from Princes Street and Edinburgh Castle. Public rooms include a ground-floor bar, and a wine bar and bistro upstairs. In these pleasantly informal surroundings a wide choice of fresh, locally sourced food is prepared by the chefs on site. While sipping a pint of Deuchars, you can nibble on home-made roasted red pepper houmous served with warm pitta bread. For those in need of something with chips, a home-made cheeseburger or chicken fillet burger will suffice. Starter options include steamed mussels; stuffed aubergines; and pan-seared king scallops. Main dishes range from herb-crusted sea bream to medallions of venison. Haggis, neeps and tatties covered with a whisky jus will certainly satisfy traditionalists. There is a pre-theatre menu available.

Open all wk 11.30am-mdnt (Thu-Sat 11.30am-1am) Closed: 25-26 Dec, 1 Jan **Bar Meals** Av main course £7.20 food served all day **Restaurant** Fixed menu price fr £9.95 Av 3 course à la carte fr £22 food served all day ⊕ FREE HOUSE ◀ Deuchars IPA, Tennents, Guinness. **Facilities** Family room

---

The Shore Bar & Restaurant ⚲

Shore, Leith EH6 6QW
☎ 0131 553 5080 ▤ 0131 553 5080
-mail: info@theshore.biz
ir: *Please telephone for directions*

'art of this historic pub was a 17th-century lighthouse nd, befitting its location beside the Port of Leith, it has fine reputation for fish and seafood. The carte changes t every sitting during the day to ensure the freshest roduce is on offer. A typical meal could be roast rabbit vith gnocchi and blue cheese sauce, followed by hargrilled tuna with roasted vegetables, Sardinian cous ous and black olive tapenade. Recent change of hands.

pen all wk noon-1am (Sun 12.30-1am) Closed: 25-26 ec, 1 Jan **Bar Meals** L served all wk 12-2.30 booking quired D served all wk 6-10.30 booking required Av ain course £12 **Restaurant** L served all wk 12-2.30 ooking required D served all wk 6-10.30 booking quired Fixed menu price fr £8.95 Av 3 course à la carte £22 ⊕ FREE HOUSE ◀ Belhaven 80/-, Deuchars IPA, uinness. ⚲ 14 **Facilities** Dogs allowed

---

RATHO Map 21 NT17

PICK OF THE PUBS

The Bridge Inn ⚲

27 Baird Rd EH28 8RA
☎ 0131 333 1320 ▤ 0131 333 3480
e-mail: info@bridgeinn.com
dir: *From Newbridge at B7030 junct, follow signs for Ratho and Edinburgh Canal Centre*

An 18th-century former farmhouse was converted to create this canal-side pub in 1820 with the opening of the Union Canal. It was once owned by the family of the last man to be hanged in public in Edinburgh, and his ghost is still reputed to haunt the building. In addition to the restaurant and two bars, The Bridge Inn also has a restaurant barge on the canal, providing the perfect venue for wedding parties, dinner dances, birthdays and other special events. Dishes range from bar snacks and light bites, such as mushrooms stuffed with haggis and black pudding, battered, deep-fried and served with red onion marmalade, to main courses

---

of smoked haddock fishcakes with lime and tarragon dressing, or pork and beef medallions with wholegrain mustard sauce and roasted potatoes. The canal's towpath is ideal for walkers and cyclists.

Open all day all wk 11-11 (Fri-Sat 11am-mdnt) Closed: 25-26 Dec, 1-2 Jan **Bar Meals** L served Mon-Sat 11-9, Sun 12-30-9 D served Mon-Sat 11-9, Sun 12-30-9 Av main course £9 food served all day **Restaurant** L served Mon-Sat 12-2.30, Sun 12.30-8.30 booking required D served Mon-Sat 6.30-9.30, Sun 12.30-8.30 booking required Fixed menu price fr £9.50 Av 3 course à la carte fr £16 ⊕ FREE HOUSE ◀ Belhaven, Deuchars IPA, Tennents, Stewarts Pentland. ⚲ 6
Facilities Children's menu Family room Garden Parking

FIFE

ANSTRUTHER Map 21 NO50

The Dreel Tavern ⚲

16 High Street West KY10 3DL
☎ 01333 310727 ▤ 01333 310577
e-mail: dreeltavern@aol.com
dir: *From Anstruther centre take A917 towards Pittenweem*

Complete with a local legend concerning an amorous encounter between James V and a local gypsy woman, the welcoming 17th-century Dreel Tavern has plenty of atmosphere. Its oak beams, open fire and stone walls retain much of the distant past, while home-cooked food and cask-conditioned ales are served to hungry visitors of the present. Peaceful gardens overlook Dreel Burn.

Open all wk 11am-mdnt **Bar Meals** L served all wk 12-3 D served all wk 5.30-9.30 **Restaurant** L served all wk 12-3 D served all wk 5.30-9.30 ⊕ FREE HOUSE ◀ Deuchars IPA, 2 guest ales. ⚲ 20 **Facilities** Children's menu Family room Dogs allowed Garden Parking

---

BURNTISLAND Map 21 NT28

Burntisland Sands Hotel

Lochies Rd KY3 9JX ☎ 01592 872230 ▤ 01592 872230
e-mail: clarkelinton@hotmail.com
dir: *Towards Kirkcaldy, Burntisland on A921. Hotel on right before Kinghorn*

This small, family-run hotel, just 50 yards from an award-winning sandy beach, was once a highly regarded girls' boarding school. Reasonably priced breakfasts, snacks, lunches and evening meals are always available, with a good selection of specials. Try breaded haddock and tartare sauce; gammon steak Hawaii; or crispy shredded beef. Desserts include hot naughty fudge cake, and banana boat. There is also an excellent choice of hot and cold filled rolls, and a children's menu.

Open all wk ⊕ FREE HOUSE ◀ Scottish Courage ales, Guinness, guest ales. **Facilities** Play area Garden Parking

---

CRAIL Map 21 NO60

The Golf Hotel ⚲

4 High St KY10 3TD ☎ 01333 450206 ▤ 01333 450795
e-mail: enquiries@thegolfhotelcrail.com
dir: *At the end of High Street opposite Royal Bank*

The present day Golf Hotel occupies a striking 18th-century Grade I listed building, but the first inn on the site opened its doors 400 years earlier. The characterful bars have an old world atmosphere. Well known for its traditional Scottish high tea with home-made pancakes and cakes, the inn is also popular for its home cooking. Choices range from fresh Crail crab salad and macaroni cheese through to steak and Deuchars ale pie or grilled fresh haddock in garlic butter from the carte menu.

Open all day all wk 11am-mdnt (Sun noon-mdnt) **Bar Meals** Av main course £6.50 food served all day **Restaurant** Av 3 course à la carte fr £15 food served all day ⊕ FREE HOUSE ◀ McEwans 60/-, 80/-, 70/-, Belhaven Best, real ale. ⚲ 6 **Facilities** Children's menu Dogs allowed Garden Parking

---

ELIE Map 21 NO40

The Ship Inn ⚲

The Toft KY9 1DT ☎ 01333 330246 ▤ 01333 330864
e-mail: info@ship-elie.com
dir: *Follow A915 & A917 to Elie. From High Street follow signs to Watersport Centre & The Toft*

Standing right on the waterfront at Elie Bay, this lively free house has been a pub since 1838 and run by the enthusiastic Philip family for 20 years. The cricket team plays regular fixtures on the beach, live music is performed, and there is a regular programme of summer barbecues and other eagerly anticipated events throughout the year. Local bakers, butchers and fishmongers and their produce feature in the pub's colourful and concise menu.

Open all wk Closed: 25 Dec ⊕ FREE HOUSE ◀ Caledonian Deuchars IPA, Belhaven Best, Tetleys Xtra Cold, Caledonian 801, Tartan Special. ⚲ 7 **Facilities** Play area Family room Dogs allowed Garden

---

KINCARDINE Map 21 NS98

The Unicorn ⚲

15 Excise St FK10 4LN ☎ 01259 739129
e-mail: info@theunicorn.co.uk
dir: *Exit M9 junct 7 towards Kincardine Bridge. Cross bridge, bear left. 1st left, then sharp left at rdbt*

This 17th-century pub-restaurant in the heart of the historic port of Kincardine used to be a coaching inn. And it was where, in 1842, Sir James Dewar, inventor of the vacuum flask, was born. Leather sofas and modern decor blend in well with the older parts of the building. There is a comfortable lounge bar, a grillroom, and a more formal dining room upstairs. In decent weather, have a drink by the old well in the walled garden.

continued

KINCARDINE *continued*

Open noon-2.30 5.30-mdnt (Sun 12.30-mdnt) Closed: 3rd wk Jul, Mon **Bar Meals** L served Tue-Sat 12-2.30, Sun 12.30-8 D served Tue-Sat 5.30-9.30, Sun 12.30-8 ⊕ FREE HOUSE ◄ Bitter & Twisted. ☻ 8 **Facilities** Children's menu Parking

---

LOWER LARGO   Map 21 NO40

The Crusoe Hotel

2 Main St KY8 6BT ☎ 01333 320759 ▤ 01333 320865
e-mail: relax@crusoehotel.co.uk
dir: *A92 to Kirkcaldy East, A915 to Lundin Links, then right to Lower Largo*

This historic inn is located on the sea wall in Lower Largo, the birthplace of Alexander Selkirk, the real-life castaway immortalised by Daniel Defoe in his novel, *Robinson Crusoe*. In the past the area was also the heart of the once-thriving herring fishing industry. Today it is a charming bay ideal for a golfing break. A typical menu may include 'freshly shot' haggis, Pittenweem haddock and a variety of steaks.

Open all day all wk 11am-mdnt (Fri-Sat 11am-1am) **Bar Meals** L served all wk 11-9 D served all wk 11-9 food served all day ⊕ FREE HOUSE ◄ Belhaven 80/-, Best, Deuchars, Abbot Ale, Old Speckled Hen. **Facilities** Play area Dogs allowed Parking

---

ST ANDREWS   Map 21 NO51

PICK OF THE PUBS

The Inn at Lathones ★★★★ INN ◉◉ ☻

Largoward KY9 1JE
☎ 01334 840494 ▤ 01334 840694
e-mail: lathones@theinn.co.uk
dir: *5m from St Andrews on A915*

St Andrews' oldest coaching inn – parts of the building date back over 400 years. Belhaven Best on tap is backed by eleven bottled Orkney beers served in pewter tankards in the bar lounge, which welcomes with leather sofas and log burning fires; the pewter theme continues with the restaurant's water goblets. A consistent winner of AA rosettes for over ten years, the kitchen team prepares the best fresh local produce in seasonal menus. A typical carte selection could start with hare fillet and scallops on a rocket salad; and follow with a tempura of salmon, halibut and haddock with home-made chips and tartare sauce. Puddings of the day are usually old favourites, but more exotic options also tempt. The inn is an award-winning live music venue, a considerable achievement when maximum capacity is limited to just 50 people; the walls of the inn display one of the best collections of music memorabilia in the country. There are smart contemporary bedrooms in two separate wings.

Open all wk Closed: 2wks Jan **Bar Meals** Av main course £10.50 food served all day **Restaurant** L served all wk 12-2.30 D served all wk 6-9.30 Av 3 course à la carte fr £25 ⊕ FREE HOUSE ◄ Dark Island, Three Sisters, Belhaven Best. ☻ 11 **Facilities** Children's menu Dogs allowed Garden Parking **Rooms** 13

PICK OF THE PUBS

The Jigger Inn NEW ☻

The Old Course Hotel KY16 9SP
☎ 01334 474371 ▤ 01334 477688
dir: *Please telephone for directions*

Once the stationmaster's lodge on a railway line that disappeared many years ago, the Jigger is in the grounds of the Old Course Hotel. St Andrew's is renowned, of course, throughout the world as the Home of Golf, so don't be surprised by the golfing memorabilia, or by sharing bar space with a caddy or two, fresh in from a long game. Even Tiger Woods has been seen here. Open-hearth fires are the backdrop for a selection of Scottish beers, including St Andrew's Ale from Belhaven Brewery in Dunbar. All-day availability is one advantage of a short, simple menu that lists soup, sandwiches and barbecued chicken salad wrap with honey mustard dressing as starters, and continues with beer-battered fish and chips; sausage and mash with onion gravy; warm sunblushed tomato with goats' cheese and rocket tart, and gremolata dressing; and grilled Speyside steak with seasoned fries and onion rings.

Open all day all wk 11-11 (Sun noon-11) Closed: 25 Dec **Bar Meals** L served all wk 12-9.30 Av main course £11 food served all day **Restaurant** D served all wk 12-9.30 booking required ⊕ FREE HOUSE ◄ Guinness, St Andrews Best. ☻ 8 **Facilities** Children's menu Garden Parking

---

GLASGOW, CITY OF

GLASGOW   Map 20 NS56

Rab Ha's

83 Hutchieson St G1 1SH
☎ 0141 572 0400 ▤ 0141 572 0402
e-mail: management@rabhas.com
dir: *Telephone for directions*

In the heart of Glasgow's revitalised Merchant City, Rab Ha's takes its name from Robert Hall, a local 19th-century character known as 'The Glasgow Glutton'. This hotel, restaurant and bar blend Victorian character with contemporary Scottish decor. Pre-theatre and set menus show extensive use of carefully sourced Scottish produce in starters like poached egg on grilled Stornoway black pudding, and pan-seared Oban scallops, followed by roast saddle of Rannoch Moor venison.

Open all day all wk noon-mdnt (Sun 12.30pm-mdnt) **Bar Meals** L served Sun-Thu 12-9, Fri-Sat 12-10 D served Sun-Thu 12-9, Fri-Sat 12-10 food served all day ⊕ FREE HOUSE ◄ Tennents.

Stravaigin NEW ◉◉ ☻

28 Gibson St G12 8NX
☎ 0141 334 2665 ▤ 0141 334 4099
e-mail: stravaigin@btinternet.com
dir: *Please telephone for directions*

Whether feasting in the ground-floor restaurant or grazing in the upstairs bar, it's the warm hospitality and service that makes Stravaigin the place to eat in Glasgow. The bar was intended to be where diners had pre-dinner drinks but for the last 15 years it has a life and clientele of its own. Deuchars IPA joins ciders from Westons at the bar. Diners can look forward to fresh Scottish ingredients cooked with imagination and flair. Expect everything from haggis; steamed West Coast mussels; to spice route curry of the moment, and a great variety of nibbles.

Open all day all wk 11-11 Closed: 25-26 Dec, 1 Jan **Bar Meals** L served all wk 11-5 D served all wk 5-11 Av main course £10.95 food served all day **Restaurant** L served Fri-Sun 12-11 D served all wk 5-11 Fixed menu price fr £10 Av 3 course à la carte fr £25 ⊕ FREE HOUSE ◄ Deuchars IPA ♂ Westons Premium Organic, Addlestones. ☻ 23 **Facilities** Children's menu Dogs allowed

PICK OF THE PUBS

Ubiquitous Chip ◉◉ ☻

12 Ashton Ln G12 8SJ
☎ 0141 334 5007 ▤ 0141 337 6417
e-mail: mail@ubiquitouschip.co.uk
dir: *In West End of Glasgow, off Byres Rd. Beside Hillhead subway station*

Situated in a unique, glass-covered mews, with cobbled floors, water fountains and a fabulous array of lush green plants, this culinary legend combines Scottish tradition with an imaginative touch. Glasgow residents have been treated to some top-notch Scottish cooking for 38 years and the place is as popular as ever. Traditional draught beers, over a hundred malt whiskies and excellent wines are served from three bars; the stunning roof terrace is a quiet space in which to enjoy them. The original upper level bar with its coal fire and the sound of no music is a regular haunt for the city's media types. The Wee bar, reputed to be the smallest in Scotland, is intimate and cosy. Finally the Corner bar boasts an imported tin ceiling and a granite bar top reclaimed from a mortuary. The food continues to showcase the best of Scotland's produce, take Orkney organic salmon with spinach sauce, Angus fillet steak au poivre, Seil Island crab salad, and Scrabster ling on clapshot with chillied seaweed.

Open all wk 11am-mdnt Closed: 25 Dec, 1 Jan **Bar Meals** L served all wk 12-11 D served all wk 12-11 Av main course £5.50 food served all day **Restaurant** L served Mon-Sat 12.30-2.30, Sun 12.30-3 booking required D served all wk 5.30-11 booking required Fixed menu price fr £23.85 Av 3 course à la carte fr £15 food served all day ⊕ FREE HOUSE ◁ Deuchars IPA, The Chip 71 Ale. ₹ 21 **Facilities** Children's menu

HIGHLAND

ACHILTIBUIE   Map 22 NC00

PICK OF THE PUBS

Summer Isles Hotel & Bar ◉◉

IV26 2YG ☎ 01854 622282 📠 01854 622251
e-mail: info@summerisleshotel.com
dir: Take A835 N from Ullapool for 10m, Achiltibuie signed on left, 15m to village. Hotel 1m on left

Located in a stunningly beautiful and unspoilt landscape, it would be hard to discover a more individual and relaxing place in which to unwind. The bar at the side of the hotel is the original crofters' meeting place, and dates back to the mid-19th century. Highland real ales and a huge selection of malt whiskies head the choice of refreshments, but wine lovers will need time to study the list too – there are over 400 to choose from. The seafood platter is the hotel's signature dish, served at lunchtime in both the bar and the hotel; lighter offerings include sandwiches; smoke-roasted salmon steaks; and desserts such as bannoffee pie, strawberry millefeuille, and home-made ice creams. For dinner a single five-course balanced menu is presented, for which suitable wines are selected and made available by the glass; typical dish examples would be warm scallop mousse; pan-fried breast of wood pigeon; grilled fillet of Lochinver halibut; dessert; and cheeses.

Open all wk ⊕ FREE HOUSE ◁ Red Cuillin, Misty Isle, Hebridean Gold, Young Pretender, IPA Deuchars. **Facilities** Dogs allowed Garden Parking

AVIEMORE   Map 23 NH81

he Old Bridge Inn ₹

alfaber Rd PH22 1PU ☎ 01479 811137
-mail: nigel@oldbridgeinn.co.uk
r: Exit A9 to Aviemore, 1st left to Ski Rd, then 1st left gain 200mtrs

et in the spectacular Scottish Highlands, in an area ell-known for its outdoor pursuits, this friendly Aviemore ub overlooks the River Spey. Dine in the relaxing bars ith roaring log fire, the comfortable restaurant, or in the tractive riverside garden. A tempting chargrill menu cludes lamb chops in redcurrant jelly, Aberdeen Angus rloin or rib-eye steaks, and butterflied breast of chicken arinated in yoghurt, lime and coriander. Other choices

include braised guinea fowl with brandy or potato gnocchi with butternut squash in a filo basket. Fine cask ales and large selection of malt whiskies available.

Open all wk 11-11 (Fri-Sat 11am-mdnt Sun 12.30-11) **Bar Meals** L served all wk 12-2 D served all wk 6-9 **Restaurant** L served all wk 12-2 D served all wk 6-9 booking required D ⊕ FREE HOUSE ◁ Caledonian 80/-, Cairngorm Highland IPA, Deuchars IPA, Timothy Taylor, Atlas Avalanche. ₹ 18 **Facilities** Children's menu Play area Family room Garden Parking

BADACHRO   Map 22 NG77

The Badachro Inn ₹

IV21 2AA ☎ 01445 741255 📠 01445 741319
e-mail: Lesley@badachroinn.com
dir: From Kinlochewe A832 towards Gairloch. Onto B8056, right to Badachro after 3.25m, towards quay

Great views from one of Scotland's finest anchorages are afforded at this convivial waterside pub, with two mooring available free for visitors. Decking, with nautical-style sails and rigging, runs right down to the water overlooking Loch Gairloch. Interesting photographs and collages adorn the bar walls, where there is a dining area by a log fire. Friendly staff serve a couple of beers from the An Teallach or Caledonian breweries and a farm cider. A further dining conservatory overlooks the bay. Excellent fresh fish is the speciality of the house, along with dishes such as local venison terrine and chicken breast on crushed haggis, neeps and tatties.

Open all wk Closed: 25 Dec **Bar Meals** L served all wk 12-3 D served all wk 6-9 **Restaurant** L served all wk 12-3 D served all wk 6-9 ⊕ FREE HOUSE ◁ Red Cullen, An Teallach, Blaven, 80/-, Guinness. ₹ 11 **Facilities** Dogs allowed Garden Parking

CARRBRIDGE   Map 23 NH92

The Cairn NEW 🄰 ★★★ INN ₹

PH23 3AS ☎ 01479 841212 📠 01479 841362
e-mail: info@cairnhotel.co.uk
dir: Village centre on old A9 close to historic 1717 Pack Horse bridge

The Highland village of Carrbridge and this family-run inn make the perfect base for exploring the Cairngorms, the Moray coast and the Malt Whisky Trail. In the homely, tartan-carpeted bar, you'll find cracking Isle of Skye and Cairngorm ales on handpump, blazing winter log fires, all-day sandwiches, and hearty bar meals, including sweet marinated herring with oatcakes, venison sausage casserole, and sticky toffee pudding.

Open all day all wk 11-11 (Fri-Sat 11am-1am) **Bar Meals** L served all wk 12-2 D served all wk 6-8.30 Av main course £7 ⊕ FREE HOUSE ◁ Cairngorm, Orkney. ₹ 8 **Facilities** Children's menu Dogs allowed Garden Parking **Rooms** 7

CAWDOR   Map 23 NH85

PICK OF THE PUBS

Cawdor Tavern ₹

The Lane IV12 5XP
☎ 01667 404777 📠 01667 404777
e-mail: enquiries@cawdortavern.info
dir: From A96 (Inverness-Aberdeen) take B9006 & follow Cawdor Castle signs. Tavern in village centre

Standing close to the famous castle in a beautiful conservation village, the tavern was formerly a joinery workshop for the Cawdor Estate. Oak panelling from the castle, gifted by the late laird, is used to great effect in the lounge bar. Roaring log fires keep the place cosy and warm on long winter evenings, while the garden patio comes into its own in summer. A single menu is offered for both restaurant and bar, where refreshments include a choice of real ales and 100 malt whiskies. The pub's reputation for seafood draws diners from some distance for dishes like fresh Wester Ross salmon with potatoes and parsley butter. Other favourites include smooth chicken liver pâté with home-made apple jelly and crostini; a trio of Scottish puddings – black pudding, white pudding and haggis served with home-made chutney; and prime beef steak pie and mash.

Open all wk 11-3 5-11 (Sat 11am-mdnt Sun 12.30-11) Closed: 25 Dec, 1 Jan **Bar Meals** L served Mon-Sat 12-2, Sun 12.30-3 D served all wk 5.30-9 booking required Av main course £8.95 **Restaurant** D served all wk 5.30-9 booking required Av 3 course à la carte fr £18.95 ⊕ FREE HOUSE ◁ Red McGregor, 3 Sisters, Orkney Dark Island, Raven Ale, Latitude Highland Pilsner. ₹ 8 **Facilities** Children's menu Family room Dogs allowed Garden Parking

CONTIN   Map 23 NH45

Achilty Hotel ★★★ SHL ◉ ♟

IV14 9EG ☎ 01997 421355 🖩 01997 421923
e-mail: info@achiltyhotel.co.uk
dir: On A835, at N outskirts of Contin

The original stone walls and log fire keep this former drovers' inn warm when the Highlands weather closes in. On the edge of the village near a fast-flowing mountain river, the cosy Achilty Hotel serves good Scottish food made from fresh local produce. The bar/restaurant menu offers an extensive choice with a seafood slant: bouillabaisse (Scottish style), scampi provençal, seafood thermidor, halibut and monkfish, plus chicken with haggis in a creamy whisky and onion sauce, duck breasts, mushroom stroganoff, and a large selection of steaks and home-made desserts.

Open all day all wk 11-11 Closed: 25 Dec & 2nd wk Jan
Bar Meals L served all wk 12-2 D served all wk 5-8.30
⊕ FREE HOUSE ◀ Calders Cream, Calders 70/-,
Guinness. ♟ 8 **Facilities** Garden Parking **Rooms** 11

FORT WILLIAM   Map 22 NN17

Moorings Hotel ★★★ HL ◉

Banavie PH33 7LY ☎ 01397 772797 🖩 01397 772441
e-mail: reservations@moorings-fortwilliam.co.uk
dir: From A82 in Fort William follow signs for Mallaig, then left onto A830 for 1m. Cross canal bridge then 1st right signed Banavie

This modern hotel lies alongside Neptune's Staircase, on the coast-to-coast Caledonian Canal. The canal is a historic monument, its eight locks able to raise even sea-going craft a total of 64 feet. Most hotel bedrooms and the Upper Deck lounge bar have good views of Ben Nevis (1344m) and Aonach Mor (1219m). A range of eating options includes Mariners cellar bar, and the Caledonian split-level lounge bar overlooking the canal, plus the fine-dining Jacobean Restaurant.

Open all wk ⊕ FREE HOUSE ◀ Calders 70/-, Tetley Bitter,
Guinness. **Facilities** Dogs allowed Garden Parking
Rooms 27

GAIRLOCH   Map 22 NG87

PICK OF THE PUBS

The Old Inn ♟

See Pick of the Pubs on opposite page

GARVE   Map 23 NH36

Inchbae Lodge Guesthouse ★★ INN

IV23 2PH ☎ 01997 455269 🖩 01997 455207
e-mail: contact@inchbae.co.uk
dir: 30m from Inverness, 26m from Ullapool, A835 from Tore rdbt

You can watch stags feeding in the garden of this 19th-century hunting lodge, and residents can fish for free in the river Blackwater, which flows just outside. Inside you'll find a bistro and a conservatory dining room with panoramic views, and a large residents' lounge warmed by a log fire on cooler days. The international menu includes hearty traditional choices such as venison casserole or liver and onions, and an extensive list of curries. Accommodation and a good selection of local ales are available.

Open all day all wk **Bar Meals** Av main course £7 food served all day **Restaurant** Fixed menu price fr £7 food served all day ⊕ FREE HOUSE ◀ Guinness, Isle of Skye Red Cullin, An Teallach Brewhouse Special.
Facilities Garden Parking **Rooms** 7

GLENELG   Map 22 NG81

Glenelg Inn

IV40 8JR ☎ 01599 522273 🖩 01599 522283
e-mail: glenelg-inn.info.com
dir: From Shiel Bridge (A87) take unclassified road to Glenelg

The inn is a conversion of 200-year-old stables set in a large garden stretching down to the sea, with stunning views across the Sound of Sleat. Musicians are frequent visitors to the bar, where at times a ceilidh atmosphere prevails. Menus offer traditional Scottish fare based on local produce, including plenty of fresh fish and seafood, hill-bred lamb, venison and seasonal vegetables. In the bar are seafood casserole and pies, while the dinner menu offers West Coast turbot with fennel and new potatoes.

Open all day all wk noon-mdnt **Bar Meals** L served all wk 12.30-2 D served all wk 6-9 ◀ Guest Ales.
Facilities Dogs allowed Garden Parking

INVERIE   Map 22 NG70

The Old Forge

PH41 4PL ☎ 01687 462267 🖩 01687 462267
e-mail: info@theoldforge.co.uk
dir: From Fort William take A830 (Road to the Isles) towards Mallaig. Take ferry from Mallaig to Inverie (boat details on website)

Britain's most remote mainland pub, The Old Forge is accessible only by boat, and stands literally between heaven and hell (Loch Nevis is Gaelic for heaven and Loch Hourn is Gaelic for hell). It's popular with everyone from locals to hillwalkers, and is renowned for its impromptu ceilidhs. It is also the ideal place to sample local fish and seafood, and other specialities such as haunch of estate venison. There are nine boat moorings and a daily ferry from Mallaig.

Open all wk **Bar Meals** L served all wk 12-3 D served all wk 6-9.30 Av main course £10 food served all day **Restaurant** L served all wk 12-3 D served all wk 6-9.30 ⊕ FREE HOUSE ◀ 80 Shilling, Guinness, Red Cuillin, real ales. **Facilities** Children's menu Play area Family room Dogs allowed Garden Parking

KYLESKU   Map 22 NC23

PICK OF THE PUBS

Kylesku Hotel

e-mail:
See Pick of the Pubs on page 566

LYBSTER   Map 23 ND23

Portland Arms ★★★★ INN ♟

KW3 6BS ☎ 01593 721721 🖩 01593 721722
e-mail: manager.portlandarms@ohiml.com
dir: Exit A9 signed Latheron, take A99 to Wick. Then 4m to Lybster

A former coaching inn, just half a mile from the North Sea coastline, the welcoming Portland Arms has evolved into a comfortable modern hotel. The bar and dining areas serve fresh local produce and extensive menus cater for all tastes, with everything from home-made soup with freshly baked baguette to flash-fried langoustine in garlic and brandy butter. Look out for delicious desserts and home baking with morning coffee and afternoon tea. Sunday lunch is a speciality. Take time for a nostalgic walk around this historic fishing town and stay over in one of the bedrooms.

Open all day all wk 7am-11pm **Bar Meals** food served all day **Restaurant** food served all day ⊕ FREE HOUSE ◀ McEwans 70/-, Guinness. ♟ 6 **Facilities** Children's menu Parking **Rooms** 22

PICK OF THE PUBS

The Old Inn 🍷

GAIRLOCH Map 22 NG87

IV21 2BD

☎ 01445 712006 📠 01445 712933

e-mail: info@theoldinn.net

dir: *Just off A832, near harbour at south end of village*

Gairloch's oldest hostelry enjoys a fabulous setting at the foot of the Flowerdale Valley by the harbour, looking out across Gairloch Harbour to the isles of Rona, Raasay and Skye, and was built by the estate in 1750 as a changing house for horses. On a good day, you might be able to spy the Outer Hebrides from this attractive inn, which makes a popular base for the many local activities - walking, fishing, golf, bird-watching and boat trips to see whales and bottlenose dolphins — or for simply resting and lolling about on the golden beaches. In the two bars you'll find the inn's own beer, the Blind Piper of Gairloch, which was created by the landlord and enthusiastic locals, alongside a good range of real ales, from Isle of Skye Red Cullin to Wildcat, a full-bodied and strong brew from Cairngorm Brewery. If you fancy a wee dram, then you have an extensive range of Highland malts to choose from. Seafood is the main draw in an area where Gairloch lobster, Loch Ewe scallops, Minch langoustines, mussels, brown crab and fresh fish are regularly landed. Tuck into the traditional Cullen skink, a soup of smoked haddock, potato and cream, or crispy-fried squid, before launching into smoked haddock risotto; pan-seared scallops with smoked bacon mash and tamarind sauce, or Cajun-spiced cod. Carnivores will not be disappointed with pork belly served with herb-roasted vegetables, or venison steak with braised red cabbage, garlic confit, basil mash, and Highland blue cheese and whisky cream. A large grassy area by the pretty stream with picnic tables is an attractive place to eat and enjoy the views. Dogs are more than welcome, with bowls, baskets and rugs to help them feel at home.

Open 11am-mdnt (Sun noon-mdnt) **Bar Meals** L served all week 12-2.30 (summer 12-4.30) D served all week 5-9.30 Av main course £9.50 **Restaurant** D served all week 6-9.30 Fixed menu price fr £25 Av 3 course à la carte fr £17.50 ⊕ FREE HOUSE 🍺 Adnams Bitter, Isle of Skye Red Cullin, Blind Piper, An Teallach, Deuchars IPA, Wildcat. 🍷 8 **Facilities** Children's menu Play area Family room Dogs allowed Garden Parking

PICK OF THE PUBS

Kylesku Hotel

KYLESKU Map 22 NC23

IV27 4HW
☎ **01971 502231** 📄 **01971 502313**
e-mail: info@kyleskuhotel.co.uk
web: www.kyleskuhotel.co.uk
dir: *A835, then A837 & A894 into Kylesku.*
Hotel at end of road at Old Ferry Pier

The Kylesku Hotel now finds itself at the centre of Scotland's first designated Global Geopark, a 2,000-square kilometre area of lochs, mountains and coastal scenery with an abundance of wildlife and a wide range of outdoor activities. On the shores of two sea lochs, Glendhu and Glencoul, it certainly is a delightful place with truly memorable views. A former coaching inn, the Kylesku dates from 1680; it stands by the former ferry slipway between the two expanses of water, which furnish the restaurant and bar with splendid vistas over to the mountains. The chef uses fresh local produce wherever possible, and with local fishing boats landing their catch regularly on the slipway beside the hotel, seafood is the mainstay – langoustines, spineys, lobster, crab, scallops, haddock and mussels don't travel far to appear on the carte. Salmon is hot- and cold-smoked on the premises, beef and lamb come from the Highlands, and wild venison is delivered in season. Bar meal alternatives to all that fish and seafood could be starters such as a ramekin of haggis topped with a whisky and onion sauce, or parfait of chicken liver with tomato and onion chutney. Non-fish main dishes are along the lines of grilled rib-eye steak with peppercorn sauce, or wild venison and root vegetable casserole with new potatoes. Puddings range from lime cheesecake to sticky toffee pudding. Dinner takes the form of a set menu at a fixed price for two or three courses. This enables the chef to use the day's fresh ingredients in dishes such as seared hand-dived scallops with garlic butter, and pan-fried fillets of Lochinver haddock with lemon butter. If a cheese platter takes your fancy, try the Isle of Mull cheddar, made by traditional methods from unpasteurised milk. To wash it all down, choose between Highland real ales, Skye Cuillin bottled beers, 40 wines and 50 malt whiskies.

Open all week Closed: Nov-Feb 🛢 FREE HOUSE 🍺 Tennents Ember 80/-, Selection of Black Isle Brewery and Skye Cuillin bottled ales. **Facilities** Garden

NORTH BALLACHULISH   Map 22 NN06

..och Leven Hotel

..ld Ferry Rd PH33 6SA
☎ 01855 821236   📠 01855 821550
-mail: reception@lochlevenhotel.co.uk
..ir: *Off A82, N of Ballachulish Bridge*

..Vith its relaxed atmosphere, beautiful loch-side setting,
..nd dramatic views, this privately owned hotel lies in the
..eart of Lochaber, 'The Outdoor Capital of the UK', and
..roves popular with walkers and climbers. It began life
..ver 300 years ago, accommodating travellers using the
..allachulish Ferry. Food is available in the restaurant
..nd the bar, both of which offer spectacular views over
..he fast-flowing narrows to the mountains. Home-cooked
..eals are built around local produce, especially fresh
..eafood, game and other traditional Scottish dishes.

..pen 11-11 (Thu-Sat 11am-mdnt Sun 12.30-11) Closed:
..fternoons in winter **Bar Meals** L served all wk 12-3 D
..erved all wk 6-9 Av main course £8.95 **Restaurant** L
..erved all wk 12-3 D served all wk 6-9 Fixed menu price
..·£12.95 Av 3 course à la carte fr £15 ⊕ FREE HOUSE
..◀ John Smith's Extra Smooth, MacEwans 80%.
..acilities Children's menu Play area Family room Dogs
..Jlowed Garden Parking

See advert on this page

PLOCKTON   Map 22 NG83

PICK OF THE PUBS

The Plockton Hotel ★★★ SHL ♟

Harbour St IV52 8TN
☎ 01599 544274   📠 01599 544475
e-mail: info@plocktonhotel.co.uk
web: www.plocktonhotel.co.uk
dir: *On A87 to Kyle of Lochalsh take turn at Balmacara.
Plockton 7m N*

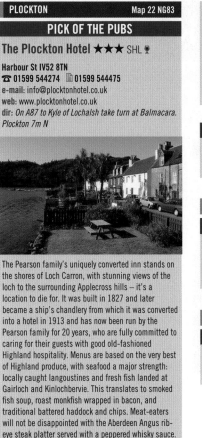

The Pearson family's uniquely converted inn stands on
the shores of Loch Carron, with stunning views of the
loch to the surrounding Applecross hills – it's a
location to die for. It was built in 1827 and later
became a ship's chandlery from which it was converted
into a hotel in 1913 and has now been run by the
Pearson family for 20 years, who are fully committed to
caring for their guests with good old-fashioned
Highland hospitality. Menus are based on the very best
of Highland produce, with seafood a major strength:
locally caught langoustines and fresh fish landed at
Gairloch and Kinlochbervie. This translates to smoked
fish soup, roast monkfish wrapped in bacon, and
traditional battered haddock and chips. Meat-eaters
will not be disappointed with the Aberdeen Angus rib-
eye steak platter served with a peppered whisky sauce.
A fine range of malts is available to round off that
perfect Highland day.

Open all day all wk 11am-mdnt (Sun 12.30pm-11pm)
Bar Meals L served all wk 12-2.15 D served all wk 6-10
Av main course £9.75 **Restaurant** L served all wk
12-2.15 D served all wk 6-10 booking required Av 3
course à la carte fr £20 ⊕ FREE HOUSE ◀ Caledonian
Deuchars IPA, Hebridean Gold - Isle of Skye Brewery,
Harvieston Blonde Ale, Crags Ale. ♟ 6
Facilities Children's menu Family room Garden
Rooms 15

PICK OF THE PUBS

Plockton Inn & Seafood Restaurant

See Pick of the Pubs on page 568

SHIELDAIG   Map 22 NG85

PICK OF THE PUBS

Shieldaig Bar & Coastal Kitchen ★ SHL ◉◉ ♟

See Pick of the Pubs on page 569

TORRIDON   Map 22 NG95

PICK OF THE PUBS

The Torridon Inn ♟

See Pick of the Pubs on page 570

PICK OF THE PUBS

Plockton Inn & Seafood Restaurant

PLOCKTON   Map 22 NG83

Innes St IV52 8TW
☎ **01599 544222**   📄 **01599 544487**
e-mail: info@plocktoninn.co.uk
dir: *On A87 to Kyle of Lochalsh take turn at Balmacara. Plockton 7m N*

Mary Gollan and her brother Kenny, the proprietors of this attractive stone-built free house, were born and bred in Plockton. Their great grandfather built this property as a manse, just 100 metres from the harbour in the fishing village where BBC Scotland's *Hamish Macbeth* series was filmed in the mid-1990s. Mary, Kenny and his partner, Susan Trowbridge, bought the inn over ten years ago, Mary and Susan doing the cooking, Kenny running the bar. The atmosphere is relaxed and friendly, with winter fires in both bars, and a selection of more than 50 malt whiskies. Taking pride of place on the regular and daily-changing specials menus in the dining room and the lounge bar are fresh West Coast fish and shellfish and West Highland beef, lamb and game. Starters include fish-based soup of the day; hot Plockton prawns (landed by the barman himself) with garlic butter; and roasted red pepper pâté. Haggis and clapshot is a particular speciality (including a vegetarian version), served with neeps, tatties and home-made pickled beetroot. Seafood main dishes take in creel-caught langoustines from the waters of Loch Carron, served cold with Marie Rose sauce; and hake fillet with pesto crust, as well as the famous seafood platter. The finest seafood is taken to the smokehouse on the premises and can later be enjoyed from the menu. Other dishes include braised lamb shank; venison in ale; chicken Caesar salad; and aubergine parmigiana. Among some truly mouth-watering desserts is lemon and ginger crunch pie, as well as a selection of Scottish cheeses served with Orkney oatcakes. The National Centre of Excellence in Traditional Music is based in Plockton, which is why the inn's public bar resonates with fantastic live sounds on Tuesdays and Thursdays.

Open all week **Bar Meals** L served all wk 12-2.30 D served all wk 6-9 **Restaurant** D served all wk 6-9 Av 3 course à la carte fr £18 ⊕ FREE HOUSE ◧ Greene King Abbot Ale, Fuller's London Pride, Isle of Skye Blaven, Caledonian 80/-, Plockton Crag Ale. **Facilities** Children's menu Play area Dogs allowed Garden Parking

PICK OF THE PUBS

Shieldaig Bar & Coastal Kitchen ★ SHL ◉◉ ♉

IV54 8XN
☎ 01520 755251 📄 01520 755321
web: www.tighaneilean.co.uk
dir: Off A896, in village centre

This rustic, no-nonsense waterfront bar belongs to a rather special league, one that might be called the League of Bars with Stunning Views Across a Loch. The loch is Torridon, which leads to the open sea and it is from the first floor eating area - the Coastal Kitchen, with its balcony and open decks — that you will be most impressed by these views. As part of the two-AA Rosette Tigh an Eilean Hotel next door in a charming, mostly 18th century fishing village, the bar positively jumps at weekends with live traditional Gaelic music. In fact, all over Wester Ross you are likely to find a ceilidh taking place somewhere. Throughout the day a full range of alcoholic and non-alcoholic beverages is served to suit the hour, and there's always a ready supply of newspapers and magazines to read. Bar snacks include sandwiches, home-made soups, and steak and onion baguette with gravy and chips, but it's for fine seafood that the bar has earned its reputation, with daily menus ensuring the freshest of catches, such as Loch Torridon spiny lobsters with lemongrass and coriander dressing; Shieldaig crab salad; fresh razor clam fritters with Romesco sauce; and the speciality Shieldaig bar seafood stew. It's all caught locally, some from local prawn-fishing grounds that have won a sustainable fishery award. Alternatives to fish include steaks and pizzas from the Coastal Kitchen's wood-fired oven; local venison sausages with mash and red wine and onion gravy; and shallot and goats' cheese tart with salad and new potatoes. A resident pastry cook prepares superb desserts using both traditional and unusual ingredients. Food is served all day in summer, when you can also dine in the lochside courtyard, on the balcony or on the decks. A good range of real ales is on tap from the Isle of Skye Brewery and Black Isle Ales, plus malt whiskies and a choice of wines by the glass.

Open all week ⊕ FREE HOUSE ◖ Isle of Skye Brewery Ales, Black Isle. ♉ 8
Facilities Dogs allowed Garden Parking **Rooms** 11

PICK OF THE PUBS

The Torridon Inn 🍷

TORRIDON	Map 22 NG95

IV22 2EY
☎ **01445 791242** 📄 **01445 712253**
e-mail: inn@thetorridon.com
dir: *From Inverness take A9 N, then follow signs to Ullapool. Take A835 then A832. In Kinlochewe take A896 to Annat. Pub 200yds on right after village*

Once a grand shooting lodge, built for the first Earl of Lovelace in 1887, The Torridon enjoys one of the most impressive coastal positions in the Scottish Highlands. The inn was created by converting the stable block, buttery and farm buildings of nearby Ben Damph House, now known as The Torridon Hotel. Whether you use it as a base to enjoy some of the many activities on offer, or simply want to unwind with a warm fire and relaxing pint from the good selection of local real ales after a hard day's walking, you can be sure of a memorable visit. Newly refurbished, the cosy bar offers a Highland welcome from both staff and locals: choose from a range of over 60 malt whiskies, or recount the day's adventures over a pint of local real ale. Entertainment ranges from indoor games to regular traditional live music sessions. The inn has its own restaurant, also refurbished, where you can sample high quality, locally sourced food at any time. Hearty soups, sandwiches and bar meals are available during the day, and in the evening there's a delicious choice of starters, main courses and desserts. Local produce drives menus that might feature venison, salmon, haggis and home-made specials. Dinner could begin with caramelised onion tart with fresh rocket and olive oil, or double-baked Beauly wild boar belly with Loch Ewe scallops and caramelised apple. Typical main course choices include game casserole served with creamy mashed potatoes and seasonal baby vegetables; butternut squash, ricotta and pine nut pasta parcels in a creamy pesto sauce; and whole baked trout with almond, breadcrumb and spring onion stuffing, served with new potatoes and garden salad. Tea and coffee is available throughout the day.

Open all week Closed: Nov-27 Mar **Bar Meals** L served all week all day D served all week 6-9 Av main course £13.50 **Restaurant** Av 3 course à la carte fr £22 🍺 Isle of Skye Red Cuillin, Torridon Ale & Blaven; Cairngorm Stag & Tradewinds. 🍷 8 **Facilities** Children's menu Play area Dogs allowed Garden Parking

ULLAPOOL — Map 22 NH19

PICK OF THE PUBS

The Ceilidh Place ♥

14 West Argyle St IV26 2TY
☎ 01854 612103   📠 01854 613773
e-mail: stay@theceilidhplace.com
dir: *On entering Ullapool, along Shore St, pass pier, take 1st right. Hotel straight ahead at top of hill*

Organic growth has seen this old boatshed café metamorphose over 37 years into an all-day bar, coffee shop, restaurant, bookshop and art gallery. The late founder Robert Urquhart had aspirations for a place for serious writing - life histories, not postcards; a place for eating, meeting, talking and singing. This all came to pass and it is now known mostly for live traditional Scottish music, although some jazz slips in. The heart of The Ceilidh Place is the café/bar, with its big open fire and solid wooden furniture. It's a place to stay all day, and some do. Simple delights conjured up by the menu include mince and tatties, kedgeree, homity pie, and bone-warming cullen skink. Among the main dishes are braised venison chop; pan-roasted whole Loch Broom prawns; and seafood platter. A specials board offering seasonally available fish, meat, vegetables and fruits complements the printed menu.

Open all wk Closed: 2wks mid-Jan ⊕ FREE HOUSE
🍺 Belhaven Best, Guinness, Scottish ales. ♥ 8
Facilities Dogs allowed Garden Parking

MIDLOTHIAN

PENICUIK — Map 21 NT25

The Howgate Restaurant ♥

Howgate EH26 8PY ☎ 01968 670000   📠 01968 670000
e-mail: peter@howgate.com
dir: *10m N of Peebles. 3m E of Penicuik on A6094 between Leadburn junct & Howgate*

A short drive from Edinburgh, the Howgate was once a racehorse stables and a dairy. These days this long, low building makes a warm and welcoming bar and restaurant, overseen by chefs Steven Worth and Sean Blake. There is an impressive wine list from all the corners of the world, great real ales, a regularly changing menu, and a 'dishes of the moment' selection. Options might include Borders venison and cranberry pie, pan-fried duck breast with asparagus, pan-fried trio of sea bass, salmon and king prawns, or mushroom and red pepper stroganoff.

Open all wk Closed: 25-26 Dec, 1 Jan **Bar Meals** L served all wk 12-2 D served all wk 6-9.30 Av main course £9.95 **Restaurant** L served all wk 12-2 booking required D served all wk 6-9.30 booking required Fixed menu price fr £15 Av 3 course à la carte fr £25 ⊕ FREE HOUSE
🍺 Belhaven Best, Hoegaarden Wheat Biere. ♥ 12
Facilities Children's menu Garden Parking

MORAY

FOCHABERS — Map 23 NJ35

Gordon Arms Hotel

80 High St IV32 7DH
☎ 01343 820508   📠 01343 829059
e-mail: gordonarmsfochabers@live.co.uk
dir: *A96 approx halfway between Aberdeen & Inverness, 9m from Elgin*

This 200-year-old former coaching inn, close to the River Spey and within easy reach of Speyside's whisky distilleries, is understandably popular with salmon fishers, golfers and walkers. Its public rooms have been carefully refurbished, and the hotel makes an ideal base from which to explore this scenic corner of Scotland. The cuisine makes full use of local produce: venison, lamb and game from the uplands, fish and seafood from the Moray coast, beef from Aberdeenshire and salmon from the Spey - barely a stone's throw from the kitchen!

Open all day all wk 11-11 (Thu 11-mdnt Fri-Sat 11am-12.30am) **Bar Meals** L served all wk 12-2 D served all wk 5-9 ⊕ FREE HOUSE 🍺 Caledonian Deuchars IPA, John Smiths Smooth, Guest Ales. **Facilities** Dogs allowed Parking

NORTH LANARKSHIRE

CUMBERNAULD — Map 21 NS77

Castlecary House Hotel ★★★ HL ♥

Castlecary Rd G68 0HD
☎ 01324 840233   📠 01324 841608
e-mail: enquiries@castlecaryhotel.com
dir: *A80 onto B816 between Glasgow & Stirling. 7m from Falkirk, 9m from Stirling*

Run by the same family for over 30 years, this friendly hotel is located close to the historic Antonine Wall and Forth and Clyde Canal. Meals in the lounge bars plough a traditional furrow with options such as home-made steak pie; oven-baked Scottish salmon fillet with a sun-dried tomato and herb brioche crust; and a range of flame-grilled steaks. There is an excellent selection of real ales on offer. More formal restaurant fare is available in Camerons Restaurant.

Open all wk **Bar Meals** Av main course £8.50 food served all day **Restaurant** Av 3 course à la carte fr £22 ⊕ FREE HOUSE 🍺 Arran Blonde, Harviestoun Brooker's Bitter & Twisted, Inveralmond Ossian's Ale, Housten Peter's Well, Caledonian Deuchars IPA. ♥ 8 **Facilities** Children's menu Dogs allowed Garden Parking **Rooms** 60

PERTH & KINROSS

GLENDEVON — Map 21 NN90

PICK OF THE PUBS

An Lochan Tormaukin Country Inn and Restaurant ★★★★ INN ⊛ ♥

FK14 7JY ☎ 01259 781252   📠 01259 781526
e-mail: info@anlochan.co.uk
dir: *M90 junct 6 onto A977 to Kincardine, follow signs to Stirling. Exit at Yelts of Muckhard onto A823/Crieff*

This attractive whitewashed building was built in 1720 as a drovers' inn, at a time when Glendevon was frequented by cattlemen making their way from the Tryst of Crieff to the market place at Falkirk. The name Tormaukin is Gaelic for 'hill of the mountain hare', which reflects its serene, romantic location in the midst of the Ochil Hills. Sympathetically refurbished throughout, it still bristles with real Scottish character and charm. Original features like stone walls, exposed beams and blazing winter fires in the cosy public rooms ensure a warm and welcoming atmosphere. Expect fresh, locally sourced food. Lunch might bring scallops, Stornoway black pudding and rocket followed by a home-made beef and venison burger with chips. In the evening, perhaps wild boar terrine, then Aberdeen Angus beef Wellington with spinach and wild mushrooms. Live music is a regular feature at the inn, and golfing breaks are available.

Open all day all wk **Bar Meals** L served all wk 12-3 D served all wk 5.30-9 food served all day **Restaurant** L served all wk 12-3 D served all wk 5.30-9 Fixed menu price fr £20.95 Av 3 course à la carte fr £19.90 ⊕ FREE HOUSE 🍺 Bitter & Twisted, Thrappledouser ♨ Aspall. ♥ 8 **Facilities** Children's menu Dogs allowed Garden Parking **Rooms** 13

GLENFARG — Map 21 NO11

The Famous Bein Inn ★★ SHL ⊛

PH2 9PY ☎ 01577 830216   📠 01577 830211
e-mail: enquiries@beininn.com
dir: *On the intersection between A912 & B996. 2m N of Glenfarg just off junct 8, M90*

Situated in a wooded glen overlooking the river, the inn is now owned by a local farming family, well known for the quality of their beef, and maintains a nearly 150-year-old tradition of catering for travellers between Perth and Edinburgh. Locally sourced and freshly prepared food is served in the restaurant or bistro. Expect dishes such as North Sea mackerel fillet with Arran wholegrain mustard potato salad, or pan roast rump of black face Perthshire lamb with bacon and cabbage and sesame potatoes. Visitors might also enjoy coffee and a scone by a log fire or a refreshing pint of Belhaven Best on the sundeck.

continued on page 573

PICK OF THE PUBS

Moulin Hotel ★★★ SHL 🍷

PITLOCHRY Map 23 NN95

**11-13 Kirkmichael Rd, Moulin
PH16 5EH**
☎ **01796 472196** 📄 **01796 474098**
e-mail: enquiries@moulinhotel.co.uk
web: www.moulinhotel.co.uk
dir: *From A924 at Pitlochry take A923.
Moulin 0.75m*

Built in 1695 at the foot of Ben Vrackie on the old drove road from Dunkeld to Kingussie, the inn faces Moulin's square, a rewarding three-quarters of a mile from the busy tourist centre of Pitlochry. A great all-round inn, popular as a walking and touring base, it offers comfortable accommodation, extensive menus, and conference and function room facilities. Locals are drawn to the bar for the excellent home-brewed beers, with Ale of Atholl, Braveheart, Moulin Light, and Old Remedial served on handpump. A major refurbishment of the building in the 1990s opened up old fireplaces and beautiful stone walls that had been hidden for many years, and lots of cosy niches were created using timbers from the old Coach House (now the brewery). The courtyard garden is lovely in summer, while blazing log fires warm the Moulin's rambling interior in winter. Menus partly reflect the inn's Highlands location, and although more familiar dishes are available such as seafood pancake, lamb shank and fish and chips, you also have the opportunity to try something more local, such as haggis, neeps and tatties; venison Braveheart; Scotsman's bunnet, which is a meat and vegetable stew-filled batter pudding; or game casserole. You might then round off your meal with ice cream with Highland toffee sauce, or bread-and-butter pudding. A specials board broadens the choice further. Around 20 wines by the glass and more than 30 malt whiskies are available. Moulin may look like a French word but it is actually derived from the Gaelic 'maohlinn', meaning either smooth rocks or calm water.

Open 11-11 (Fri-Sat 11am-11.45pm, Sun noon-11pm) **Bar Meals** L served all week 12-9.30 D served all week 12-9.30 Av main course £9.50 **Restaurant** D served all week 6-9 Fixed menu price fr £23.50 Av 3 course à la carte fr £27 ⊕ FREE HOUSE ◀ Moulin Braveheart, Old Remedial, Ale of Atholl & Moulin Light. 🍷 20
Facilities Children's menu Garden Parking **Rooms** 15

GLENFARG *continued*

Open all day all wk Closed: 25 Dec **Bar Meals** Av main course £9.95 food served all day **Restaurant** Fixed menu price fr £17.95 Av 3 course à la carte fr £21.95 food served all day ⊕ FREE HOUSE ◼ Belhaven Best, Inveralmond Ale, Guinness. **Facilities** Children's menu Parking **Rooms** 11

GUILDTOWN
Map 21 NO13

Anglers Inn ★★★ INN ⊛ ♥

Main Rd PH2 6BS ☎ **01821 640329**
e-mail: info@theanglersinn.co.uk
dir: *6m N of Perth on A93*

Refurbished by Shona and Jeremy Wares, formerly of 63 Tay Street (an AA-Rosetted restaurant in Perth), as a contemporary gastro-pub, the Anglers provides a relaxing venue in a country setting just six miles from Perth. Comfortable leather chairs and a log fire maintain a homely atmosphere. Jeremy is the accomplished chef, offering the likes of Angler's fishcakes with chilli jam and herb salad; and roast marinated rump of lamb with haggis haché, spinach and rosemary vinaigrette. This is the perfect stop before or after the races at Perth Race Course, and you can stay over in one of the comfortable bedrooms if you like.

Open all day all wk 11am-mdnt **Bar Meals** L served all wk 12-2 D served all wk 6-9 Av main course £13 **Restaurant** L served all wk 12-2 booking required D served all wk 6-9 booking required Fixed menu price fr £15 Av 3 course à la carte fr £25 ⊕ FREE HOUSE ◼ Ossian, Liafail, Boddingtons. ♥ 13
Facilities Children's menu Dogs allowed Garden Parking **Rooms** 5

KILLIECRANKIE
Map 23 NN96

PICK OF THE PUBS

Killiecrankie House Hotel ⊛⊛ ♥

PH16 5LG ☎ **01796 473220** 🖨 **01796 472451**
e-mail: enquiries@killiecrankiehotel.co.uk
dir: *Take B8079 N from Pitlochry. Hotel in 3m after NT Visitor Centre*

Built in 1840 as a dower house, this small, friendly hotel is set in four sprawling acres of wooded grounds at the northern end of the historic Killiecrankie Pass, scene of the famous battle. The cosy, wood-panelled bar is a popular haunt of both locals and visitors, while the snug sitting room opens on to a small patio and a fine herbaceous border. At lunchtime options include open sandwiches and bar meals of deep-fried haddock with chips, and game pie. The restaurant gains ever-wider recognition for the quality of its food and not only retains two AA Rosettes, but was also recognised for its Notable Wine List in the 2009 AA Restaurant Guide. Grilled fillet of sea trout with roasted asparagus; roasted supreme of guinea fowl stuffed with walnut mousse; and leek, pea and stilton risotto are typical of the restaurant menu. The Conservatory Bar also serves lunches and dinners.

Open all wk Closed: Jan & Feb ⊕ FREE HOUSE ◼ Tennents Velvet Ale, Red McGregor, Deuchars IPA, Brooker's Bitter & Twisted. ♥ 8 **Facilities** Dogs allowed Garden Parking

---

KINNESSWOOD
Map 21 NO10

PICK OF THE PUBS

Lomond Country Inn ♥

KY13 9HN ☎ **01592 840253** 🖨 **01592 840693**
e-mail: info@lomondcountryinn.co.uk
dir: *M90 junct 5, follow signs for Glenrothes then Scotlandwell, Kinnesswood next village*

A small, privately owned hotel on the slopes of the Lomond Hills that has been entertaining guests for more than 100 years. It is the only hostelry in the area with uninterrupted views over Loch Leven to the island on which Mary Queen of Scots was imprisoned. The cosy public areas offer log fires, a friendly atmosphere, real ales and a fine collection of single malts. If you want to make the most of the loch views, choose the charming restaurant, a relaxing room freshly decorated in country house style. Now under new management, the focus is on serving well kept real ales such as Orkney Dark Island, and a mix of traditional and favourite pub dishes which are all competitively priced. Starters may feature home-made pâté; sautéed mushrooms; and North Atlantic prawn cocktail. Main courses include steak and Guinness pie; mince and tatties; Cajun chicken breast; and home-made locally sourced game stew.

Open all day all wk 7am-1am **Bar Meals** L served all wk 7am-9pm D served all wk 5-9 Av main course £5.95 food served all day **Restaurant** L served all wk 7am-9pm D served all wk 5-9 Fixed menu price fr £9.95 Av 3 course à la carte fr £18.95 food served all day ⊕ FREE HOUSE ◼ Deuchars IPA, Calders Cream, Tetleys, Orkney Dark Island, Bitter & Twisted. ♥ 6
Facilities Children's menu Play area Family room Dogs allowed Garden Parking

---

PITLOCHRY
Map 23 NN95

PICK OF THE PUBS

Moulin Hotel ★★★ SHL ♥

See Pick of the Pubs on opposite page

RENFREWSHIRE

HOUSTON
Map 20 NS46

Fox & Hounds ♥

South St PA6 7EN
☎ **01505 612448** & **612991** 🖨 **01505 614133**
e-mail: jonathon.wengel@btconnect.com
dir: *A737, W from Glasgow. Take Johnstone Bridge off Weir exit, follow signs for Houston. Pub in village centre*

Run by the same family for over thirty years, this charming 18th-century village inn is home to the award-winning Houston Brewing Company. Sample a pint of Jock Frost or Warlock Stout in one of the three bars. There is a micro-brewery malt of the month, wine of the week to sample too. From the appealing bar or restaurant menus, choose from charred sausage du jour with creamy mash and onion gravy, tagliatelle with fresh peas and courgette, Houston ale-battered haddock, or slow braised game casserole. Look out for gourmet evenings and live music nights.

Open all day all wk 11am-mdnt (Fri-Sat 11am-1am Sun from 12.30) **Bar Meals** Av main course £8 food served all day **Restaurant** Av 3 course à la carte fr £25 food served all day ⊕ FREE HOUSE ◼ Killelan, Warlock Stout, Texas, Jock Frost, Peter's Well. ♥ 10 **Facilities** Children's menu Dogs allowed Garden Parking

SCOTTISH BORDERS

ALLANTON — Map 21 NT85

Allanton Inn

TD11 3JZ ☎ 01890 818260
e-mail: info@allantoninn.co.uk
dir: *From A1 at Berwick take A6105 for Chirnside (5m). At Chirnside Inn take Coldstream Rd for 1m to Allanton*

Highly acclaimed for its food, this award-winning establishment is housed in an 18th-century coaching inn. Outside is a large lawned area with fruit trees overlooking open countryside. Inside are two restaurants and a cosy bar serving real ales and a range of malt whiskies. Daily changing menus may offer braised beef and Guinness casserole with a puff pastry crust at lunch, and monkfish tail sautéed onto a risotto of asparagus, mussels and rocket for dinner.

Open 6pm-10.30pm (Sat-Sun noon-2) Closed: Mon **Bar Meals** L served Sat-Sun 12-2 D served Tue-Sat 6.30-8 booking required **Restaurant** L served Sat-Sun 12-2 D served Tue-Sat 6.30-8 booking required ⊕ FREE HOUSE ◀ Ossian, Trade Winds, Pentland IPA. **Facilities** Dogs allowed Garden Parking

ETTRICK — Map 21 NT21

Tushielaw Inn

TD7 5HT ☎ 01750 62205 📠 01750 62205
e-mail: robin@tushielaw-inn.co.uk
dir: *At junct of B709 & B711(W of Hawick)*

An 18th-century former toll house and drovers' halt on the banks of Ettrick Water, making a good base for touring the Borders, trout fishing (salmon fishing can be arranged) and those tackling the Southern Upland Way. An extensive menu is always available with daily-changing specials. Fresh produce is used according to season, with local lamb and Aberdeen Angus beef regular specialities. Home-made steak and stout pie and sticky toffee pudding are popular choices.

Open all wk **Bar Meals** Av main course £10 ⊕ FREE HOUSE **Facilities** Children's menu Dogs allowed Parking

GALASHIELS — Map 21 NT43

Kingsknowes Hotel ★★★ HL

1 Selkirk Rd TD1 3HY
☎ 01896 758375 📠 01896 750377
e-mail: enquiries@kingsknowes.co.uk
dir: *Off A7 at Galashiels/Selkirk rdbt*

In over three acres of grounds on the banks of the Tweed, a splendid baronial mansion built in 1869 for a textile magnate. There are lovely views of the Eildon Hills and Abbotsford House, Sir Walter Scott's ancestral home. Meals are served in two restaurants and the Courtyard Bar, where fresh local or regional produce is used as much as possible. The impressive glass conservatory is the ideal place to enjoy a drink.

Open all wk ⊕ FREE HOUSE ◀ McEwans 80/-, John Smiths. **Facilities** Play area Dogs allowed Garden Parking Rooms 12

LAUDER — Map 21 NT54

PICK OF THE PUBS

The Black Bull ★★★★ INN ☻

See Pick of the Pubs on opposite page

LEITHOLM — Map 21 NT74

The Plough Hotel ☻

Main St TD12 4JN ☎ 01890 840252 📠 01890 840252
e-mail: theplough@leitholm.wanadoo.co.uk
dir: *5m N of Coldstream on A697. Take B6461, Leitholm in 1m*

The only pub remaining in this small border village (there were originally two), the Plough dates from the 17th century and was once a coaching inn. Food is traditional with the likes of parsnip soup or pâté and Melba toast followed steak and Guinness pie; home-made lasagne; or local sausages with Yorkshire pudding. Tuesdays and Fridays are fish and chip nights.

Open all day all wk noon-mdnt **Bar Meals** Av main course £12 food served all day **Restaurant** food served all day ⊕ FREE HOUSE ◀ Guinness. ☻ 8 **Facilities** Children's menu Garden Parking

MELROSE — Map 21 NT53

PICK OF THE PUBS

Burts Hotel ★★★ HL ◉◉ ☻

Market Square TD6 9PL
☎ 01896 822285 📠 01896 822870
e-mail: enquiries@burtshotel.co.uk
dir: *A6091, 2m from A68 3m S of Earlston*

Facing Melrose's picturesque 18th-century market square, Burts was built in 1722 as a comfortable home for a local dignitary, and still displays much period charm. For a while it was a temperance hotel, but today's selection of real ales, 80 single malt whiskies and a good range of wines by the glass, suggests a rather more liberal attitude. The Henderson family have been running this award-winning business for 40 years, their personal attention ensuring the highest standards. The food in both the Bistro Bar and formal restaurant - holder of two AA Rosettes since 1995 - offers a true taste of the Borders that you might sample by beginning with lobster and scallop terrine, following with roast fillet of Scottish beef, or pan-roasted turbot fillet with tiger prawn ravioli, and finishing with pear tart Tatin and white chocolate parfait. The bar menu also includes grills, vegetarian dishes and toasted sandwiches.

Open all wk noon-2.30 5-11 **Bar Meals** L served all wk 12-2 D served all wk 6-9.30 Av main course £11 **Restaurant** L served all wk 12-2 booking required D served all wk 7-9 booking required Fixed menu price fr £22 ⊕ FREE HOUSE ◀ Caledonian 80/-, Deuchars IPA, Timothy Taylor Landlord, Fuller's London Pride. ☻ 8 **Facilities** Dogs allowed Garden Parking Rooms 20

ST BOSWELLS — Map 21 NT53

PICK OF THE PUBS

Buccleuch Arms Hotel ☻

The Green TD6 0EW
☎ 01835 822243 📠 01835 823965
e-mail: info@buccleucharms.com
dir: *On A68, 10m N of Jedburgh. Hotel on village green*

This smart and friendly country-house hotel, dating from the 16th century, sits next to the village cricket pitch. There is a large and comfortable, log fire-warmed lounge to enjoy in winter, and a spacious, enclosed garden for the warmer months. Food plays a pivotal role, from breakfast through award-winning bar meals to dinner. Menus change seasonally, but the specials may well change twice daily to reflect the availability of local ingredients from the Scottish Borders countryside, such as the beef, which is sourced from the Buccleuch estates and then hung for a minimum of 21 days. Burnside Farm Foods in Rutherford three miles away supply other meats including poultry and game, and when it comes to fish, it falls to a fishmonger in Eyemouth, who delivers six days a week, to decide on the roll-call. With the provenance outlined, here are examples of what to expect: steak, ale and mushroom pie, using slowly braised prime beef from Craig Douglas in the village; chargrilled gammon steak; breaded scampi tails; and home-made nut loaf.

Open all day all wk 7am-11pm Closed: 25 Dec **Bar Meals** L served all wk 12-2 D served all wk 6-9 Av main course £8 food served all day **Restaurant** D served all wk 6-9 booking required ⊕ FREE HOUSE ◀ John Smiths, Guinness, Broughton, guest ales. ☻ 8 **Facilities** Play area Dogs allowed Garden Parking

PICK OF THE PUBS

The Black Bull ★★★★ INN ♓

LAUDER   **Map 21 NT54**

Market Place TD2 6SR
☎ **01578 722208**   📄 **01578 722419**
e-mail:
enquiries@blackbull-lauder.com
dir: *In centre of Lauder on A68*

Just twenty minutes from Edinburgh, The Black Bull nestles in the heart of the Scottish Borders. This dazzling white, three-storey coaching inn dates from 1750: now, as an independent family-owned business, the hotel's dining rooms and Harness Room bar are open to residents and non-residents alike. Priding itself on a warm and welcoming atmosphere, great food and comfortable accommodation, The Black Bull makes an ideal country retreat. Whatever your passions – country sports, walking, golfing, shopping, or the arts – there are all sorts of wonderful places to visit nearby. While

you're working up an appetite, the kitchen brigade will be busy preparing flavoursome, seasonal dishes for you to enjoy. Choose between the informal surroundings of the Harness Room bar for a gastro-pub lunch, or get around a table in the cosy lounge bar after a day on the hills. Either way, you can choose from the same seasonal menu, prepared to order from the best quality local meat, fish and seasonal game. A light lunch menu of snacks and sandwiches is served from midday, whilst a typical supper menu might start with deep-fried mushrooms in sweet potato and coriander butter, or chicken liver and cognac pâté with gooseberry jelly and Scottish oatcakes. Follow with venison bourguignon with highland burgundy mash, or mushroom risotto cakes with sun-dried tomato, pine nuts, Parmesan shavings and side salad. Round off, perhaps, with sticky toffee pudding and cream, or baked lemon and raspberry cheesecake with winter berry salad. Alternatively, if you're staying in one of the inn's eight superb en suite rooms and have a successful day on the river, the kitchen will happily prepare your catch for dinner while you put your feet up in the cosy bar.

Open all week 🍺 PERTHSHIRE TAVERNS LTD 🛢 Broughton Ales, Guinness, Worthington, Caffreys, Timothy Taylor Landlord, Tetley. ♓ 16 **Facilities** Parking **Rooms** 8

SWINTON Map 21 NT84

PICK OF THE PUBS

The Wheatsheaf at Swinton ★★★★ RR ◉◉ ♥

Main St TD11 3JJ ☎ **01890 860257** 📄 **01890 860688**
e-mail: reception@wheatsheaf-swinton.co.uk
dir: From Edinburgh A697 onto B6461. From East Lothian A1 onto B6461

In the past few years, the award-winning Wheatsheaf has built up an impressive reputation as a dining destination. Run by husband and wife team Chris and Jan Winson, this popular venue is tucked away in the picturesque village of Swinton. A consistent winner of AA Rosettes for over ten years, the Wheatsheaf's secret is to use carefully sourced local ingredients in imaginative combinations. In addition to wild mushrooms and organic vegetables, wild salmon, venison, partridge, pheasant, woodcock and duck are all likely menu contenders subject to seasonal availability. Lunchtime offers the likes of sautéed Paris brown mushrooms and bacon in a tarragon crêpe with a Mull cheddar glaze; and open omelette of Dunsyre Blue cheese and confit cherry tomatoes. In the evening settle back, enjoy the friendly service, and tuck into plates of seared scallops with a lemon and chive butter sauce; and braised shank of Border lamb, gratin dauphinoise and creamed Savoy.

Open all wk Closed: 25-27 & 31 Dec-1 Jan **Bar Meals** Av main course £17 **Restaurant** L served all wk 12-2 booking required D served Mon-Sat 6-9, Sun 6-8.30 booking required Av 3 course à la carte fr £30 ⊕ FREE HOUSE ◀ Deuchars IPA, Broughton Greenmantle Ale, Belhaven Best. ♥ 12 **Facilities** Parking **Rooms** 10

TIBBIE SHIELS INN Map 21 NT22

PICK OF THE PUBS

Tibbie Shiels Inn

St Mary's Loch TD7 5LH
☎ **01750 42231** 📄 **01750 42302**
dir: From Moffat take A708. Inn 14m on right

On the isthmus between St Mary's Loch and the Loch of the Lowes, this waterside hostelry is named after the woman who first opened it in 1826. Isabella 'Tibbie' Shiels expanded the inn from a small cottage to a hostelry capable of sleeping around 35 people, many of them on the floor! Famous visitors during her time included Walter Scott, Thomas Carlyle and Robert Louis Stevenson. Tibbie Shiels herself is rumoured to keep watch over the bar, where the selection of over 50 malt whiskies helps sustain long periods of ghost watching. Now under new ownership, meals can be enjoyed in either the bar or the dining room. The inn will also prepare packed lunches for your chosen activity – be it walking (the inn now lies on the coast-to-coast Southern Upland Way walking trail), windsurfing or fishing (residents fish free of charge).

Open all day all wk 9am-mdnt **Bar Meals** Av main course £10 food served all day **Restaurant** Fixed menu price fr £16 Av 3 course à la carte fr £20 food served all day ⊕ FREE HOUSE ◀ Broughton Greenmantle Ale, Belhaven 80/- ♂ Stowford Press. **Facilities** Children's menu Play area Dogs allowed Garden Parking

WEST LINTON Map 21 NT15

The Gordon Arms ♥

Dolphinton Rd EH46 7DR
☎ **01968 660208** 📄 **01968 661852**
e-mail: info@thegordon.co.uk

Set in the pretty village of West Linton but within easy reach of the M74, this 17th-century inn has a real log fire in the cosy lounge bar, and a lovely sun-trap beer garden. Enjoy a local ale alongside your meal, which may start with feta cheese and cous cous fritters with a spicy red schoog, or cullen skink; continue with steak and ale pie, haggis, or collops of venison with a rustic butternut squash and sweet potato purée; and finish with sticky toffee pudding.

Open all day all wk 11-11 (Fri-Sat 11-1am Tue 11-mdnt) **Bar Meals** L served Mon-Fri 12-3, Sat-Sun all day D served Mon-Fri 6-9, Sat-Sun all day **Restaurant** L served Mon-Fri 12-3, Sat-Sun all day D served Mon-Fri 6-9, Sat-Sun all day ⊕ SCOTTISH & NEWCASTLE ◀ John Smiths, Guinness, real ales. ♥ 7 **Facilities** Children's menu Play area Dogs allowed Garden Parking

SOUTH AYRSHIRE

SYMINGTON Map 20 NS33

Wheatsheaf Inn

Main St KA1 5QB ☎ **01563 830307** 📄 **01563 830307**
dir: Telephone for directions

This 17th-century inn lies in a lovely village setting close to the Royal Troon Golf Course, and there has been a hostelry here since the 1500s. Log fires burn in every room and the work of local artists adorns the walls. Seafood dominates the menu - maybe pan-fried scallops in lemon and chives - and alternatives include honey roasted lamb shank; haggis, tatties and neeps in Drambuie and onion cream, and the renowned steak pie.

Open all day all wk 11-11 (Fri-Sat 11am-mdnt) Closed: 25 Dec, 1 Jan **Bar Meals** food served all day **Restaurant** food served all day ⊕ BELHAVEN ◀ Belhaven Best, Old Speckled Hen, Guinness. **Facilities** Garden Parking

STIRLING

ARDEONAIG Map 20 NN63

The Ardeonaig Hotel ♥

South Lock Tay Side FK21 8SU
☎ **01567 820400** 📄 **01567 820282**
e-mail: info@ardeonaighotel.co.uk
dir: In Kenmore take road to S of Loch Tay signed Acharn. 6m. Or from Killin, next Falls of Dochart, take South Rd through Achmore & on to Ardeonaig, 6m

A romantic retreat with a difference, on the south shore of Loch Tay with views of the Ben Lawers mountains. The difference is that chef/owner Pete Gottgens has totally refurbished the inn and introduced many elements dear to his heart from his native Southern Africa. Developments include a new kitchen; five thatched colonial-style garden lodges (called rondawels); a fine dining wine cellar which houses Europe's largest collection of South African wines; a new dining room called the Study, where light lunches or afternoon teas are served; and the landscaping of 13 acres of grounds. African influences notwithstanding, the Ardeonaig has a solid reputation for using the best of seasonal Scottish produce in the kitchen. A typical dinner selection could start with poached Loch Tarbet lobster salad; continue with a main course of Ardtalnaig Estate hare fillets with caramelised onions, Puy lentils and seasonal vegetables.

Open all day all wk 11-10 (Fri-Sat 11-11) **Bar Meals** Av main course £8 food served all day **Restaurant** L served all wk 12-6 D served all wk from 7pm booking required Fixed menu price fr £26.50 Av 3 course à la carte fr £32 ⊕ FREE HOUSE ◀ Arran Blonde, Tusker, Castle Lager, Windhoek Lager. ♥ 10 **Facilities** Family room Dogs allowed Garden Parking

CALLANDER Map 20 NN60

The Lade Inn ♥

Kilmahog FK17 8HD ☎ 01877 330152
e-mail: info@theladeinn.com
dir: *From Stirling take A84 to Callander. 1m N of Callander, left at Kilmahog Woollen Mills onto A821 towards Aberfoyle. Pub immediately on left*

First licensed in the 1960s, this family-run free house was built as a tea room in 1935. Today, it offers a friendly welcome and the highest standards of food and drink. Beside the usual range at the bar, the pub's own Scottish real ale shop stocks over 120 ales from Scotland's 26 micro-breweries. Soak them up with haggis, neeps and tatties; whole baked Trossachs trout; or penne pasta with wild mushroom sauce.

Open all day all wk noon-11 (Fri-Sat noon-1am Sun 12.30-10.30) **Bar Meals** L served May-Sep all wk, all day, Oct-Apr all wk 12-3 D served May-Sep all wk, all day, Oct-Apr Sun-Thu 5-9 Av main course £8 **Restaurant** L served May-Sep all wk, all day, Oct-Apr all wk 12-3 D served May-Sep all wk, all day, Oct-Apr all wk 5-9 booking required Fixed menu price fr £14.25 Av 3 course à la carte fr £15 ⊕ FREE HOUSE ◀ Waylade, LadeBack, LadeOut, Bellhaven Best. ♥ 9 **Facilities** Play area Family room Dogs allowed Garden Parking

DRYMEN Map 20 NS48

The Clachan Inn

2 Main St G63 0BG ☎ 01360 660824
dir: *Telephone for directions*

Quaint, white-painted cottage, believed to be the oldest licensed pub in Scotland, situated in a small village on the West Highland Way, and once owned by Rob Roy's sister. Locate the appealing lounge bar for freshly-made food, the varied menu listing filled baked potatoes, salads, fresh haddock in crispy breadcrumbs, spicy Malaysian lamb casserole, vegetable lasagne, a variety of steaks, and good daily specials.

Open all wk Closed: 25 Dec & 1 Jan ⊕ FREE HOUSE ◀ Caledonian Deuchars IPA, Belhaven Best, Guinness. **Facilities** Dogs allowed Parking

KIPPEN Map 20 NS69

Cross Keys Hotel

Main St FK8 3DN ☎ 01786 870293
e-mail: info@kippencrosskeys.co.uk
dir: *10m W of Stirling, 20m from Loch Lomond off A811*

Refurbished by owners Debby and Brian, this cosy inn now serves food and drink all day. Nearby Burnside Wood is managed by a local community woodland group, and is perfect for walking and nature trails. The pub's interior, warmed by three log fires, is equally perfect for resting your feet afterwards. Regular events include a weekly Tuesday folk night.

Open all day noon-11 (Fri-Sat noon-1am Sun noon-11) Closed: 25 Dec, 1-2 Jan, Mon **Bar Meals** L served Tue-Sun 12-9 D served Tue-Sun 12-9 food served all day **Restaurant** L served Tue-Sun 12-9 D served Tue-Sun 12-9 food served all day ⊕ FREE HOUSE ◀ Belhaven Best, Harviestoun Bitter & Twisted, Guinness. **Facilities** Children's menu Family room Dogs allowed Garden Parking

WEST LOTHIAN

LINLITHGOW Map 21 NS97

PICK OF THE PUBS

Champany Inn - The Chop and Ale House ◉◉

Champany EH49 7LU
☎ 01506 834532 🖷 01506 834302
e-mail: reception@champany.com
dir: *2m N.E of Linlithgow on corner of A904 & A803*

At Champany Corner a collection of buildings, some 16th century, has been turned into two splendid restaurants. The more informal is the easy chair and couch-strewn Chop and Ale House bar, where your eyes will alight on the rock pond, where you'll find fresh Loch Gruinart oysters and lobsters before preparation for the pot. In the elegant, octagonal restaurant starters include Highland black pudding with onion marmalade; triple-smoked rump of beef with single-vineyard olive oil and fresh oregano; and fillet of salmon hot smoked over woodchips. In winter try cullen skink, a soup made from smoked haddock. Walking from the bar to the restaurant takes you past a chilled counter filled with a selection of steaks for the charcoal grill. Although Aberdeen Angus holds centre-stage, the two-AA Rosette menu also offers baked chicken filled with smoked bacon and tarragon mousse; and grilled salmon, langoustines and deep-fried organic cod.

Open all wk noon-2 6.30-10 (Fri-Sun noon-10) Closed: 25-26 Dec, 1 Jan **Bar Meals** food served all day **Restaurant** food served all day ⊕ FREE HOUSE ◀ Belhaven. **Facilities** Children's menu Garden Parking

SCOTTISH ISLANDS
COLL, ISLE OF

ARINAGOUR   Map 22 NM25

PICK OF THE PUBS

Coll Hotel

PA78 6SZ ☎ 01879 230334   🖹 **01879 230317**
e-mail: info@collhotel.com
dir: *Ferry from Oban. Hotel at head of Arinagour Bay, 1m from Pier (collections by arrangement)*

The Coll Hotel is the only inn on the Isle of Coll, and commands stunning views over the sea to Jura and Mull. The island only has 170 inhabitants, so is perfect for a holiday away from it all. The hotel is a popular rendezvous for locals, and food is served in the Gannet Restaurant, bar or garden. Fresh produce is landed and delivered from around the island every day and features on the specials board. Try local seafood open sandwiches; or Coll crab and local prawn spaghetti with chilli and parmesan at lunch, and for dinner perhaps Argyll venison casserole with port, juniper and clove gravy; or roasted locally caught monkfish tail with crispy Parma ham, tomato and basil sauce, and rice. The hotel has a private helipad in the garden, and guests are welcome to land and enjoy a meal or an overnight stay.

Open all wk 11am-11.45pm **Bar Meals** L served all wk 12-2 D served all wk 6-9 ⊕ FREE HOUSE ◖ Loch Fyne Ale, Pipers Gold, Guinness. **Facilities** Play area Dogs allowed Garden Parking

SKYE, ISLE OF

ARDVASAR   Map 22 NG60

Ardvasar Hotel ★★ HL ♚

IV45 8RS ☎ 01471 844223   🖹 **01471 844495**
e-mail: richard@ardvasar-hotel.demon.co.uk
web: www.ardvasarhotel.com
dir: *From ferry terminal, 50yds & turn left*

An early 1800s white-painted cottage-style inn, the second oldest on Skye, renowned for its genuinely friendly hospitality and informal service. Sea views over the Sound of Sleat reach the Knoydart Mountains beyond. Malt whiskies are plentiful, but beer drinkers will not be disappointed. Food is served in the informal lounge bar throughout the day and evening, with a sumptuous four-course dinner in the dining room during high season. Local produce figures prominently, particularly freshly-landed seafood, venison, and Aberdeen Angus beef.

Open all day all wk 11am-mdnt (Sun noon-11pm) **Bar Meals** L served all wk 12-2.30 D served all wk 5.30-9 ⊕ FREE HOUSE ◖ IPA, Isle of Skye Red Cuillin. ♚ 6 **Facilities** Dogs allowed Garden Parking **Rooms** 10

CARBOST

CARBOST   Map 22 NG33

The Old Inn

IV47 8SR ☎ 01478 640205   🖹 **01478 640205**
e-mail: reservations@oldinn.f9.co.uk

Two-hundred-year-old free house on the edge of Loch Harport with wonderful views of the Cuillin Hills from the waterside patio. Not surprisingly, the inn is popular with walkers and climbers. Open fires welcome winter visitors, and live music is a regular feature. With a great selection of real ales, the menu includes daily home-cooked specials, with numerous fresh fish dishes, including local prawns and oysters and mackerel from the loch.

Open all day all wk 11am-mdnt **Bar Meals** L served Mon-Sat 11-9, Sun 12.30-11.30 D served Mon-Sat 11-9, Sun 12.30-11.30 food served all day **Restaurant** L served Mon-Sat 11-9, Sun 12.30-11.30 D served Mon-Sat 11-9, Sun 12.30-11.30 food served all day ⊕ FREE HOUSE ◖ Red Cuillin, Black Cuillin, Hebridean ale, Cuillin Skye Ale, Pinnacle Ale. **Facilities** Children's menu Family room Dogs allowed Garden Parking

ISLE ORNSAY   Map 22 NG71

PICK OF THE PUBS

Hotel Eilean Iarmain ★★★ SHL ◉◉

IV43 8QR ☎ 01471 833332 📄 01471 833275
e-mail: hotel@eileaniarmain.co.uk
dir: A851, A852 right to Isle Ornsay harbour front

An award-winning Hebridean hotel with its own pier, overlooking the Isle of Ornsay harbour and Sleat Sound. The old-fashioned character of the hotel remains intact, and decor is mainly cotton and linen chintzes with traditional furniture. More a small private hotel than a pub, the bar and restaurant ensure that the standards of food and drinks served here - personally chosen by the owner Sir Iain Noble - are exacting. The head chef declares: "We never accept second best, it shines through in the standard of food served in our restaurant." Here you can try dishes like Eilean Iarmain estate venison casserole, pan-seared sirloin steak, or grilled fillet of cod with hollandaise sauce. If you call in at lunchtime, a more humble range of baked potatoes, sandwiches and toasties is also available. Half portions are served for children, or the chef can usually oblige with fish fingers or sausages.

Open all wk ⊕ FREE HOUSE ◀ McEwans 80/-, Guinness, Isle of Skye real ale. **Facilities** Dogs allowed Garden Parking **Rooms** 16

STEIN   Map 22 NG25

Stein Inn ♀

Macleod's Ter IV55 8GA ☎ **01470 592362**
e-mail: angus.teresa@steininn.co.uk
dir: A87 from Portree. In 5m take A850 for 15m. Right onto B886, 3m to T-junct. Turn left

The oldest inn on the island, set in a lovely hamlet right next to the sea, the Stein Inn provides a warm welcome, fine food, and an impressive selection of drinks: fine wines, real ales and no fewer than a hundred malt whiskies. Highland meat, game and local seafood feature strongly on daily-changing menus, ranging from lunchtime haggis toastie and smoked salmon platter to West Coast moules marinière, Highland venison pie, and salmon in a vermouth and tarragon sauce.

Open all day all wk 11am-mdnt Closed: 25 Dec, 1 Jan **Bar Meals** L served all wk 12-4 D served all wk 6-9.30 Av main course £7.50 **Restaurant** D served all wk 6-9.30 Av 3 course à la carte fr £15 ⊕ FREE HOUSE ◀ Red Cuillin, Trade Winds, Reeling Deck, Deuchars IPA, Dark Island. ♀ 8 **Facilities** Family room Dogs allowed Garden Parking

SOUTH UIST

LOCHBOISDALE   Map 22 NF71

The Polochar Inn

Polochar HS8 5TT ☎ **01878 700215** 📄 **01878 700768**
e-mail: polocharinn@aol.com
dir: W from Lochboisdale, take B888. Hotel at end of road

Overlooking the sea towards the islands of Eriskay and Barra, this superbly situated 18th-century inn enjoys beautiful sunsets. The bar menu offers fresh seafood dishes and steaks with various sauces, while restaurant fare includes venison, fresh scallops or steak pie. There is always a great choice of guest ales.

Open all day all wk 11-11 (Fri-Sat 11am-1am Sun 12.30pm-1am) **Bar Meals** L served Mon-Sat 12.30-8.30, Sun 1-8.30 (winter all wk 12-2.30) D served Mon-Sat 12.30-8.30, Sun 1-8.30 (winter all wk 5-8.30) ⊕ FREE HOUSE ◀ Guest Ales. **Facilities** Family room Garden Parking

Wales

Tintern Abbey viewed from the Devil's Pulpit

WALES

ANGLESEY, ISLE OF

BEAUMARIS Map 14 SH67

PICK OF THE PUBS

Ye Olde Bulls Head Inn ★★★★★ INN ⊛⊛ ♈

Castle St LL58 8AP
☎ 01248 810329 📠 01248 811294
e-mail: info@bullsheadinn.co.uk
web: www.bullsheadinn.co.uk
dir: *From Britannia Road Bridge follow A545. Inn in town centre*

Situated a stone's throw from the gates of imposing Beaumaris castle, The Bull (as it is commonly known) is inextricably linked to Anglesey's history. Built in 1472 as a coaching house, it has welcomed such distinguished guests as Samuel Johnson and Charles Dickens. Inside there's a traditional bar leading on to the popular brasserie which offers modern European cuisine - perhaps shredded duck salad with plum sauce, followed by pork saltimbocca with celeriac purée and Marsala sauce. Or it's up the stairs to the smartly modern, first-floor Loft restaurant which offers a more formal menu. Try a terrine of wild rabbit, foie gras and Parma ham, followed by fillet of Anglesey black beef with spinach, red wine, shallots, ceps, fine beans, pancetta, fondant potatoes and Madeira jus. Delectable desserts like caramelised hazelnut and sweet apple semifreddo with Bramley apple fritters and hazelnut tuile will be hard to resist. If you'd like to stay and explore the area, there are richly decorated guest rooms available.

Open all wk Mon-Sat 11am-11pm (Sun noon-10.30pm) Closed: 25 Dec **Bar Meals** L served Mon-Sat 12-2, Sun 12-3 D served Mon-Sat 6-9, Sun 6.30-9.30 **Restaurant** D served Mon-Sat 7-9.30, Sun 6.30-9.30 booking required ⊕ FREE HOUSE ◾ Bass, Hancocks, Worthingtons, guest ales. ♈ 16 **Facilities** Children's menu Parking **Rooms** 13

RED WHARF BAY Map 14 SH58

PICK OF THE PUBS

The Ship Inn ♈

LL75 8RJ ☎ 01248 852568 📠 01248 851013
dir: *Telephone for directions*

Wading birds in their hundreds flock to feed on the extensive sands of Red Wharf Bay, making The Ship's waterside beer garden a birdwatcher's paradise on warm days. Before the age of steam, sailing ships landed cargoes here from all over the world; now the boats bring fresh Conwy Bay fish and seafood to the kitchens of this traditional free house. A single menu covers the bars and the restaurant, and specials always include a catch of the day. Lunchtime sandwiches are a cut above the usual: choose from the likes of open prawn on granary bloomer with lemon and dill mayonnaise; or a baguette of roast turkey with sage and apricot stuffing. Starters range from salmon fishcakes to hot-smoked duck and spring onion salad with teriyaki dressing. A main course of baked half shoulder of Welsh spring lamb with celeriac dauphinoise could be rounded off by lemon tart with fruit compote.

Open all wk **Bar Meals** L served all wk 12-2.30 D served all wk 6-9 booking required Av main course £10 **Restaurant** D served Sat-Sun booking required Fixed menu price fr £17.50 Av 3 course à la carte fr £20 ⊕ FREE HOUSE ◾ Brains SA, Adnams, guest ales. ♈ 16 **Facilities** Children's menu Play area Family room Garden Parking

BRIDGEND

KENFIG Map 9 SS88

Prince of Wales Inn ♈

CF33 4PR ☎ 01656 740356
dir: *M4 junct 37 into North Cornelly. Left at x-rds, follow signs for Kenfig & Porthcaw. Pub 600yds on right*

A 16th-century property, this stone-built inn has been many things in its time: a school, town hall and courtroom among others. The town hall, incorporated into the inn, has recently been restored and one of the landlord's family will happily show it to you. Local fare on the menu includes award-winning sausages, Welsh minted lamb chops and Welsh braised faggots. Also worth attention are the daily specials on the blackboard and traditional Sunday lunches.

Open all wk ⊕ FREE HOUSE ◾ Bass Triangle, Worthington Best, guest ales. ♈ 15 **Facilities** Dogs allowed Garden Parking

CARDIFF

CREIGIAU Map 9 ST08

PICK OF THE PUBS

Caesars Arms ♈

See Pick of the Pubs on opposite page

Gwaelod-y-Garth Inn ♈

Main Rd, Gwaelod-y-Garth CF15 9HH
☎ 029 2081 0408 & 07855 313247
dir: *From M4 junct 32, N on A470, left at next exit, at rdbt turn right 0.5m. Right into village*

Meaning 'foot of the garth (mountain)', this welcoming pub was originally part of the Marquess of Bute's estate. Every window of the pub offers exceptional views, and it's a much favoured watering hole for ramblers, cyclists and hang-gliders as well as some colourful locals. Real ales change every week, and the pub offers Gwynt y Ddraig award-winning ciders. Starters might include mussels in

continued on page 584

PICK OF THE PUBS

Caesars Arms ♀

Cardiff Rd CF15 9NN
☎ **029 2089 0486** 📄 **029 2089 2176**
e-mail: caesarsarms@btconnect.com
dir: *1m from M4 junct 34*

Just ten miles outside Cardiff, Caesars Arms sits tucked away down winding lanes. A whitewashed building that is probably older than it looks, it has an appealing interior. With fine views of the surrounding countryside from its heated patio and terrace, it attracts a well-heeled clientele. And it is little wonder, as its restaurant has a vast selection of fresh fish, seafood, meat and game taking pride of place. The emphasis

here is on locally sourced food, displayed on shaven ice. Starters might include imaginative choice such as Bajan fishcakes, scallops with leek julienne or cherry-smoked duck breast with organic beetroot. Main courses take in hake, halibut, Dover sole and lobster, as well as a show-stopping Pembrokeshire sea bass baked in rock salt, which is cracked open and filleted at your table. But is not all about fish - other choices include steak from slow-reared, dry-aged pedigree Welsh Blacks plus lamb and venison from the Brecon Beacons and free-range chickens from the Vale of Glamorgan. Home-grown organic herbs, salads and vegetables are all used as much as possible, and the inn has its own smokery. Another attraction is the farm shop, which provides a range of home-produced honey, free-range eggs, Welsh cheeses, home-baked bread and chef's ready-prepared meals to take away.

Open noon-2.30 6-10 (Sun noon-4) Closed: 25 Dec, 1 Jan **Bar Meals** L served Mon-Sat 12-2.30 Av main course £6.95 **Restaurant** L served Mon-Sat 12-2.30, Sun 12-4 D served Mon-Sat 6-10 Fixed menu price fr £6.95 Av 3 course à la carte fr £25 ⊕ FREE HOUSE ◂ Felinfoel Double Dragon, Guinness. ♀ 8 **Facilities** Children's menu Dogs allowed Garden Parking

CREIGIAU *continued*

a tomato and garlic sauce; and main courses like rack of lamb with a herb crust, or duck breast with a kumquat and blackcurrant sauce.

Open all wk 11am-mdnt (Sun noon-11) **Bar Meals** food served all day **Restaurant** L served Mon-Thu 12-2, Fri-Sat 11am-mdnt, Sun 12-3 booking required D served Mon-Sat 6.30-9 booking required ⊕ FREE HOUSE ◀ HPA (Wye Valley), Otley OI, RCH Pitchfork, Vale of Glamorgan, Crouch Vale Brewers Gold ♂ Local cider. ☂ 7
Facilities Children's menu Family room Dogs allowed Garden Parking

See advert on this page

CARMARTHENSHIRE

ABERGORLECH   Map 8 SN53

The Black Lion

SA32 7SN ☎ 01558 685271
e-mail: georgerashbrook@hotmail.com
dir: *A40 E from Carmarthen, then B4310 signed Brechfa & Abergorlech*

A family-run establishment in the Brechfa Forest, this 16th-century former coaching inn has an award-winning beer garden overlooking the Cothi River and an ancient stone-built Roman bridge. Flagstone floors, settles and a grandfather clock grace the antique-furnished bar, while the dining room is more modern in style. Lots of home-made food and puddings are served, prepared from locally sourced produce, with Welsh steaks as a speciality.

Open all day Closed: Mon (ex BH) **Bar Meals** L served Tue-Sun 12-2.30 D served Tue-Sun 7-9 booking required Av main course £7.50 **Restaurant** D served Tue-Sun 7-9 booking required ⊕ FREE HOUSE ◀ Rhymney ♂ Stowford Press. **Facilities** Children's menu Dogs allowed Garden Parking

LLANDDAROG   Map 8 SN51

White Hart Thatched Inn & Brewery

SA32 8NT ☎ 01267 275395
e-mail: bestpubinwales@aol.com
web: www.thebestpubinwales.co.uk
dir: *6m E of Carmarthen towards Swansea, just off A48 on B4310, signed Llanddarog*

The Coles family invites you to try a pint from the micro-brewery that adjoins their ancient thatched free house. Built in 1371, the pub's thick stone walls and heavy beams enclose a cosy log fire and converted barn restaurant. The menu ranges far and wide, using the best of local produce. Expect Welsh lamb chops and Black Beef steaks from the grill; duck sizzling in orange sauce; and swordfish in Spanish sauce. In summer, the flower-filled patio garden is perfect for alfresco dining.

Open all wk 11.30-3 6.30-11 (Sun noon-3 7-10.30) **Bar Meals** L served all wk 11.30-3 D served all wk 6.30-11 **Restaurant** L served all wk 11.30-3 D served all wk 6.30-11 ⊕ FREE HOUSE ◀ Roasted Barley Stout, Llanddarog Ale, Bramling Cross. **Facilities** Children's menu Play area Garden Parking

LLANDEILO   Map 8 SN62

The Angel Hotel ☂

Rhosmaen St SA19 6EN
☎ 01558 822765 ▤ 01558 824346
e-mail: capelbach@hotmail.com
dir: *In town centre next to post office*

This popular pub in the centre of Llandeilo has something for everyone. Real ales are available in the bar area, which hosts regular live music nights. Upstairs, the Yr Eglwys function room ceiling is decorated with soaring frescoes inspired by Michelangelo's Sistine Chapel, and at the rear is an intimate bistro with warm terracotta walls, where dishes might include warm chorizo and potato salad, followed by slowly roasted Welsh beef in a sweet baby onion gravy.

Open 11.30-3 6-11 Closed: Sun **Bar Meals** L served Mon-Sat 11.30-2.30 D served Mon-Sat 6-9 Av main course £5 **Restaurant** L served Mon-Sat 11.30-2.30 booking required D served Mon-Sat 6-9 booking required Fixed menu price fr £9.95 Av 3 course à la carte fr £16 ⊕ FREE HOUSE ◀ Evan Evans Ales, Tetleys, Butty Bach. ☂ 12
Facilities Children's menu Garden

The Castle Hotel

113 Rhosmaen St SA19 6EN
☎ 0871 917 0007 ▤ 01558 822290
dir: *Telephone for directions*

A 19th-century Edwardian-style hotel within easy reach of Dinefwr Castle and wonderful walks through classic parkland. A charming, tiled and partly green-painted back bar attracts plenty of locals, while the front bar and side area offer smart furnishings and the chance to relax in comfort over a drink. A good range of Tomas Watkins ales is available, and quality bar and restaurant food is prepared with the finest of fresh local ingredients.

Open all wk ⊕ CELTIC INNS ◀ Tomas Watkins, Hancoats Bitter, Archers Golden, London Pride, Bombardier.
Facilities Family room Garden Parking

LLANWRDA Map 9 SN73

The Brunant Arms NEW ⬤

Caio SA19 8RD ☎ 01558 650483 📄 01558 650832
e-mail: thebrunantarms@yahoo.co.uk
dir: 1.4m of the main A482

Tucked away at the foot of a small valley, the village of Caio lies safely off the road from Lampeter to Llandovery. Here, the Brunant Arms offers a relaxed welcome with some unusual real ales, Taffy Apples cider, guest beers and good food. The menu features soft floured baps and filled jacket potatoes, as well as daily choices that might include Welsh cawl with herb dumplings; locally sourced venison steaks; sweet potato and butternut korma; or home-cooked Carmarthen ham, egg and chips. There is an impressive 30 wines by the glass.

Open noon-3 6-11 (Fri-Sat noon-3 6-1am Sun noon-11) Closed: Mon Bar Meals L served Tue-Sun 12-2 D served Tue-Sun 6.30-9 Av main course £4.95 Restaurant L served Tue-Sun 12-2 D served Tue-Sun 6.30-9 Av 3 course à la carte fr £18.50 ⊕ FREE HOUSE ◀ Ramblers Ruin, Wolvers Ale, Cribyn, Jacobi Dark Ale ♂ Taffy Apples. ⬤ 30 Facilities Children's menu Dogs allowed Garden Parking

NANTGAREDIG Map 8 SN42

PICK OF THE PUBS

Y Polyn ⬤⬤ ⬤

SA32 7LH ☎ 01267 290000
e-mail: ypolyn@hotmail.com
dir: From A48 follow signs to National Botanic Garden of Wales. Then follow brown signs to Y Polyn

Handily placed by a fork in the roads between Aberglasney and the National Botanic Garden of Wales, this 250-year-old inn is set in a lovely spot in the verdant Towy Valley. Long ago it was a tollhouse - its name means 'pole', probably after the original barrier across the road. Though drinkers are undoubtedly welcome to call in for a quick pint by the fire, in reality Y Polyn is pretty much a restaurant in a pub setting. Everything is made on the premises, and there's an emphasis on buying locally. The fixed-price dinner menu could begin with crispy pig's ear salad with capers and red onion, before main course offerings like Y Polyn fish pie; baked peppers with cous cous, pine kernels and feta cheese; and Welsh mountain lamb hot pot. Treacle tart with vanilla ice cream and Y Polyn rhubarb fool are typical desserts.

Closed: Mon, Sun eve Restaurant L served Tue-Sun 12-2 D served Tue-Sat 7-9 ⊕ FREE HOUSE ◀ Deuchars IPA, Ffos-y-ffin ales. ⬤ 7 Facilities Garden Parking

CEREDIGION

ABERAERON Map 8 SN46

PICK OF THE PUBS

The Harbourmaster INN ⊚ ⬤

Pen Cei SA46 0BA ☎ 01545 570755
e-mail: info@harbour-master.com
dir: From A487. In Aberaeron follow Tourist Information Centre signs. Pub next door on harbour

A renovated Grade II listed harbourmaster's residence, the inn has been a landmark on the Aberaeron quayside since 1811. A recent extension into the adjoining grain warehouse has greatly increased the bar capacity, and the bar, restaurant and inn all enjoy fabulous views of the harbour – there is no better place to enjoy a pint of Cwrw Haf or Tomas Watkins. The light interior decor is complemented by original features like the Welsh slate masonry and listed spiral staircase. Typical bar dishes include warm beetroot salad with Welsh goats' cheese; and Harbourmaster fish stew with croutons and aïoli. A set lunch could comprise Harbourmaster fishcake; boiled ham, parsley sauce and Savoy cabbage; and Bramley apple crumble with ice cream. There are plenty of opportunities to sample fresh local produce in the restaurant, with the likes of Welsh Black fillet steaks; locally-landed lobster; and organic vegetables and salad leaves.

Open all day all wk 10am-11.30pm Closed: 25 Dec Bar Meals L served Tue-Sun 12-2.30 D served Mon-Sun 6-9 Av main course £10.50 Restaurant L served Tue-Sun 12-2.30 booking required D served Mon-Sun 6.30-9 booking required Av 3 course à la carte fr £23 ⊕ FREE HOUSE ◀ Tomas Watkins Cwrw Haf, Evan Evans Best Bitter. ⬤ 14 Facilities Children's menu Parking Rooms 13

LLWYNDAFYDD Map 8 SN35

The Crown Inn & Restaurant ⬤

SA44 6BU ☎ 01545 560396
e-mail: www.the-crown-inn.moonfruit.com
dir: Off A487 NE of Cardigan

A traditional Welsh longhouse dating from 1799, with original beams, open fireplaces and a pretty restaurant. Rob and Monique, the young owners, have been there for 18 months now, and are having a great time. A varied menu offers a good selection of dishes, including lamb and root vegetable casserole with rosemary cobbler; or whole trout stuffed with pine nuts and bacon with rosemary and lemon butter. Blackboard specials and bar meals are available lunchtimes and evenings. Outside is a delightful, award-winning garden. An easy walk down the lane leads to a cove with caves and National Trust cliffs.

Open all day all wk noon-11 Bar Meals L served all wk 12-3 D served all wk 6-9 Av main course £8.95 Restaurant L served all wk 12-3 D served all wk 6-9 ⊕ FREE HOUSE ◀ Flowers IPA , Greene King Old Speckled Hen, Honey Ales, Envill Ale, Fuller's London Pride, guest ale. ⬤ 11 Facilities Children's menu Play area Family room Dogs allowed Garden Parking

NEW CROSS Map 8 SN67

New Cross Inn NEW

SY23 4LY ☎ 01974 261526
dir: Left on A487 to Cardigan for 1.09m, left onto A4120 Devils Bridge, right onto B4340. Continue for 3.16m, New Cross Inn on right hand side

The history of this small, family-run, rural Welsh free house goes back to the 1930s, and is documented in a collection of photos displayed in the bar. Brains beers and Thatchers cider accompany James Ward's reliable, honest cooking using the best of local produce: the daily specials board might feature mussels; slow-roast belly pork; or chicken livers in Madeira, whilst typical choices from the main menu include local trout Almandine marinated in red wine and herbs; and pan-seared duck breast with sweet plum sauce.

Open all day all wk Closed: 1 Jan Bar Meals Av main course £6.95 food served all day Restaurant booking required booking required Fixed menu price fr £19.95 Av 3 course à la carte fr £25 food served all day ⊕ Free House ◀ Brains Dark, Brains S.A, Rev James, Worthington's, Pedigree ♂ Thatchers Gold. Facilities Children's menu Parking

CONWY

BETWS-Y-COED   Map 14 SH75

PICK OF THE PUBS

Ty Gwyn Inn   INN

LL24 0SG
☎ 01690 710383 & 710787   📠 01690 710383
e-mail: mratcl1050@aol.com
dir: *At junct of A5 & A470, 100yds S of Waterloo Bridge*

Set in the heart of the Snowdonia National Park, this atmospheric inn overlooks the Conwy River and enjoys some beautiful views of the mountains. It began life in 1636 as a coaching inn on the London to Holyhead road, and in 1815 Thomas Telford built the impressive cast iron Waterloo Bridge opposite. The interior, refurbished over the past three years, has retained the character of its exposed beams, so minding your head

is recommended. Real ales come from near and far, while food is home-cooked and full of imagination – a blend of international themes and quality Welsh produce. There's no shortage of flavour in a starter of Thai marinated julienne fillet steak with chilli, lemongrass, ginger, garlic, coriander and soy sauce. Alternatively you could leave the steak until the main course, and tuck into the dish entitled mature Welsh fillet tower block – which comprises fillet steak, black pudding, salami, garlic croûton, Welsh cheddar and sauce au poivre. If you would like to stay over, there are 13 refurbished en suite rooms available, some with four poster beds.

Open all wk 12-2 6.30-11 Closed: 1wk Jan **Bar Meals** L served all wk 12-2 D served all wk 6.30-9 booking required Av main course £7.95 **Restaurant** L served all wk 12-2 D served all wk 6.30-9 booking required Av 3 course à la carte fr £22 ⊕ FREE HOUSE 🍺 Adnams Broadside, Reverend James, Old Speckled Hen, Bombardier, IPA, Orms Best. **Facilities** Children's menu Parking **Rooms** 13

See advert on this page

White Horse Inn

Capel Garmon LL26 0RW
☎ 01690 710271   📠 01690 710721
e-mail: r.alton@btconnect.com
web: www.whitehorseinnsnowdonia.co.uk
dir: *Telephone for directions*

Picturesque Capel Garmon perches high above Betws-y-Coed, with spectacular views of the Snowdon Range, a good 20 kilometres away. To make a detour to find this cosy 400-year-old inn with its original exposed timbers, stone walls, and log fires, is to be rewarded by a menu featuring fresh local produce. Home-cooked food is available in the bars and cottage-style restaurant.

Open all wk 6-11pm Closed: 25 Dec **Bar Meals** L served Sun 12-2 D served all wk 6-9 **Restaurant** L served Sun 12-2 D served all wk 6-9 ⊕ FREE HOUSE 🍺 Tetley Smoothflow, Rev James 🍏 Old English.
Facilities Children's menu Family room Dogs allowed Parking

BETWS-YN-RHOS — Map 14 SH97

The Wheatsheaf Inn ☐

LL22 8AW ☎ 01492 680218 ☐ 01492 680666
e-mail: wheatsheafinn@hotmail.co.uk
web: www.thewheatsheafinn.org.uk
dir: A55 to Abergele, take A548 to Llanrwst from High
Street. 2m turn right B5381, 1m to Betws-yn-Rhos

The Wheatsheaf, licensed as a coaching inn during the
17th century, stands in the picturesque village of Betws-
yn-Rhos opposite the famous twin towered church of St
Michael. The inn has plenty of historic character with
splendid oak beams adorned with brasses, stone pillars
and plenty of cosy, old world charm. Bar snacks are
served in addition to the restaurant menu where choices
range from local Welsh Black beef steaks or pork
medallions with black pudding and Stilton sauce, to a
house speciality: Welsh lamb joint slow roasted with
rosemary and thyme.

Open all day all wk noon-11 (Fri-Sat noon-mdnt) Bar
Meals L served all wk 12-2 booking required D served all
wk 6-9 booking required Av main course £10
Restaurant L served all wk 12-2 booking required D
served all wk 6-9 booking required ⊕ ENTERPRISE
INNS ◀ John Smiths, Brains, Hobgoblin, Old Speckled
Hen, Guinness. ☐ 6 Facilities Children's menu Play area
Dogs allowed Garden Parking

CAPEL CURIG — Map 14 SH75

Cobdens Hotel ★★ SHL

LL24 0EE ☎ 01690 720243 ☐ 01690 720354
e-mail: info@cobdens.co.uk
dir: Telephone for directions

Situated in a beautiful mountain village in the heart of
Snowdonia, this 250-year-old inn offers wholesome,
locally sourced food and real ales. Start with local rabbit
and pancetta carbonara; or leek and potato terrine.
Mains include roasted Welsh lamb with garlic and thyme
mash; Welsh beef steaks; and pasta with roasted
courgette, blue cheese and chestnut. Snacks and
sandwiches also available.

Open all day all wk noon-11pm (Sun noon-10.30pm)
Closed: 6-26 Jan Bar Meals L served all wk 12-2 D served
all wk 6-9 ⊕ FREE HOUSE ◀ Conwy Castle ale, Cobdens
ale, guest ale. Facilities Dogs allowed Garden Parking
Rooms 17

COLWYN BAY — Map 14 SH87

PICK OF THE PUBS

Pen-y-Bryn ☐

Pen-y-Bryn Rd LL29 6DD ☎ 01492 533360
e-mail: pen.y.bryn@brunningandprice.co.uk
dir: 1m from A55. Follow signs to Welsh Mountain Zoo
and estab at top of hill

Don't be put off by the simple exterior of this 1970s
building – the interior has character in spades, with
oak floors, open fires, rugs and old furniture. The
atmosphere is friendly and chatty, with local ales,
Inch's Stonehouse cider, and good, straightforward
food cooked and served throughout the day. Outside,
the stunning rear garden and terrace have panoramic
views over the sea and the Great Orme headland. The
modern British menu offers a great choice of
sandwiches, rolls and wraps like sausage bap with
mustard fried onions; warm crispy lamb and feta
cheese wrap; and a simple smoked salmon sandwich
with lemon and chive cream cheese. Main course
options range from green pea and mint risotto with
char-grilled asparagus and Parmesan, to slow-roasted
belly pork with roasted sweet potatoes, chorizo and
spiced apple sauce. Leave space for strawberries with
vanilla cream and shortbread, or white chocolate and
raspberry trifle.

Open all day all wk noon-11pm (Sun noon-10.30pm)
Bar Meals D served Mon-Sat 12-9.30, Sun 12-9 Av
main course £9.95 food served all day Restaurant D
served Mon-Sat 12-9.30, Sun 12-9 food served all
day ⊕ BRUNNING & PRICE ◀ Timothy Taylor Landlord,
Thwaites Original, Ormes Best, Flowers Original,
Ö Stonehouse. ☐ 17 Facilities Children's menu Dogs
allowed Garden Parking

CONWY — Map 14 SH77

PICK OF THE PUBS

The Groes Inn   INN ⊛ ☐

See Pick of the Pubs on page 588

DOLWYDDELAN — Map 14 SH75

Elen's Castle NEW

LL25 0EJ ☎ 01690 750207
e-mail: stay@hotelinsnowdonia.co.uk
dir: 5m S of Betws-Y-Coed, follow A470

Once an 18th-century coaching inn and a part of the Earl
of Ancaster's Welsh Estate, this family-run free house
now boasts an old world bar with a wood-burning stove.
The intimate restaurant offers breathtaking views of the
mountains and Lledr River, which can also be enjoyed
from the garden. Sample dishes include wild rice,
spinach and honey roast with summer vegetable
ratatouille; and Conwy valley lamb shank on mashed
potato and leek with rosemary jus.

Open vary by season Closed: 2wks Jan, wk days in quiet
winter periods Bar Meals L served all wk 12-2 (summer
holidays) D served all wk 6.30-9 Av main course £7.95
Restaurant D served all wk 6.30-9 Fixed menu price fr
£17.50 Av 3 course à la carte fr £20 ⊕ Free House
◀ Brains, Worthington, Black Sheep, Spitfire Ö Stowford
Press. Facilities Children's menu Play area Family room
Dogs allowed Garden Parking

LLANDUDNO JUNCTION — Map 14 SH77

PICK OF THE PUBS

AA PUB OF THE YEAR FOR WALES 2009-2010

The Queens Head ☐

Glanwydden LL31 9JP
☎ 01492 546570 ☐ 01492 546487
e-mail: enquiries@queensheadglanwydden.co.uk
dir: From A55 take A470 towards Llandudno. At 3rd
rdbt right towards Penrhyn Bay, then 2nd right into
Glanwydden, pub on left

Just five minutes from the seaside at Llandudno, this
charming free house is perfectly situated for country
walks, cycling, or a day on the beach. Owners Rob and
Sally Cureton have created one of North Wales' best-
kept secrets: a smart country pub with creative,
appealing menus, a good selection of wines and beers,
and a team of attentive staff. The stylish terrace is
great for summer evenings, whilst on colder nights the
relaxed atmosphere in the bar makes it just the place
for a pre-dinner drink by the log fire. The talented chefs
clearly have a passion for their art and make excellent
use of local produce in traditional and modern dishes.
The varied menus range from light lunchtime bites
such as warm brie and crispy bacon on ciabatta bread,
with balsamic drizzle and vine tomatoes; to more
substantial fare that reflects the inn's surroundings –
try Welsh lamb shank with rosemary and redcurrant
jus; Conwy mussels with brown bread and butter; or
fresh asparagus risotto with poached egg. Extravagant
home-made desserts complete the picture.

Open all wk 11.30-3 6-10.30 (Sat-Sun 11.30-10.30) Bar
Meals L served Mon-Fri 12-2, Sat-Sun 12-9 D served
Mon-Fri 6-9, Sat-Sun 12-9 Av main course £11
Restaurant L served Mon-Fri 12-2, Sat-Sun 12-9 D
served Mon-Fri 6-9, Sat-Sun 12-9 ⊕ FREE HOUSE
◀ Carlsberg-Tetley, Weetwood Ales, Great Orme
Brewery. ☐ 7 Facilities Children's menu Garden Parking

PICK OF THE PUBS

The Groes Inn ★★★★★ INN ◉ ♟

CONWY   Map 14 SH77

LL32 8TN
☎ **01492 650545** 🖷 **01492 650855**
e-mail: reception@groesinn.com
dir: *Exit A55 to Conwy, left at mini rdbt by Conwy Castle onto B5106, 2.5m inn on right*

The backdrop to this 15th-century inn, the earliest licensed house in Wales, is the mountain ridge known as Tal-y-Fan, the last spur of Snowdonia's Carnedd Llewelyn range. Built as a small two-storey house, it has flourished as an inn since the 16th century; in 1889 its sale was witnessed by the grandson of the Iron Duke, an event now commemorated by the Wellington Room. The deeds he signed remain on display at the top of the stairs. Rambling rooms, beamed ceilings, historic settles, military hats, historic cooking utensils, a stag's head over an open fire - this inn has all the credentials that make for an interesting visit. Don't expect a jukebox, gaming machines or pool table – instead study the display of saucy Victorian postcards. Food at The Groes Inn has a character all of its own: a strong influence of traditional British and local Welsh dishes, enhanced by continental tastes and a flair for creativity and the unusual. Visitors have a wealth of choice – stylish dining in the award-winning restaurant, bar snacks from the chalkboard menu, or light snacks. The head chef insists that fresh ingredients are the heart of good cooking – lamb from the salt marshes of the Conwy Valley, fine Welsh beef, game from nearby estates, farm-cured hams and poultry, and mussels and oysters from the waters around Anglesey - all are menu regulars. Puddings and desserts are well renowned – indeed for many, the inn's ice creams, made with fresh free-range eggs and cream, are the main reason for a visit. Rounding everything off is an imaginative, well-priced wine list, great real ales, and some unusual Welsh cheeses. Beneath a jaunty clock tower lie the guest rooms, some with private terrace or balcony from which to enjoy the afternoon and evening sun across open fields.

Open all week **Bar Meals** Av main course £9 **Restaurant** Av 3 course à la carte fr £22 ⊕ FREE HOUSE ◀ Tetley, Burton Ale, Ormes Best, Welsh Black. ♟ 10 **Facilities** Children's menu Family room Dogs allowed Garden Parking **Rooms** 14

LLANNEFYDD — Map 14 SH97

The Hawk & Buckle Inn

L16 5ED ☎ 01745 540249 ▤ 01745 540316
e-mail: enquiries@hawkandbuckleinn.com
web: www.hawkandbuckleinn.co.uk
dir: Telephone for directions

A 17th-century coaching inn 200m up in the hills, with wonderful views to the sea beyond. Traditional dishes using local produce - shoulder of Welsh lamb, chicken breast stuffed with Welsh cheese or duck breast with port and redcurrant sauce - sit comfortably alongside international flavours - lamb pasanda, beef and Guinness casserole or chicken tikka masala, for example.

Open all wk winter 6-11, Sat-Sun noon-mdnt (summer 12-3 6-11 Sat-Sun noon-mdnt) **Bar Meals** L served winter Sat-Sun 12-9, summer Mon-Fri 12-3, Sat-Sun 12-9 D served Mon-Fri 6-9, Sat-Sun 12-9 ⊕ FREE HOUSE ◀ Brains, Guest Ales ♻ Taffy Apple Cider. **Facilities** Dogs allowed Parking

DENBIGHSHIRE

LLANGOLLEN — Map 15 SJ24

The Corn Mill ♥

Dee Ln LL20 8PN ☎ 01978 869555 ▤ 01978 869930
e-mail: corn.mill@brunningandprice.co.uk

The first two things to strike you as you walk through the door are the great jumble of old beams, and the waterwheel turning slowly behind the bar. The decks outside are built directly over the millrace and the rapids, and on the opposite bank of the river, steam trains huff and puff in the restored railway station: the perfect place to enjoy a pint. Mains include cold honey-roast ham; Cumberland sausage; lamb and vegetable suet pudding; and macaroni cheese.

Open all wk **Bar Meals** food served all day **Restaurant** food served all day ⊕ FREE HOUSE ◀ Boddingtons, Flassey ales ♻ Inch's Stonehouse. ♥ 12

PRESTATYN — Map 15 SJ08

Nant Hall Restaurant & Bar ♥

Nant Hall Rd LL19 9LD
☎ 01745 886766 ▤ 01745 886998
e-mail: mail@nanthall.com
dir: E towards Chester, 1m on left opposite large car garage

Nant Hall, a Grade II listed Victorian country house in seven acres of grounds, operates as a gastro-pub with a great variety of food, beers and wines. The menu offers local and regional dishes alongside recipes from around the world: Thai green chicken curry, pan-seared fillet of salmon with a creamy herb risotto, chargrilled steaks, Chinese chicken and vegetable satay, or creamy fish pie in a parsley sauce. The large outdoor eating area is great in summer.

Open all day noon-11pm Closed: Mon **Bar Meals** Av main course £9.95 food served all day **Restaurant** Fixed menu price fr £10.95 Av 3 course à la carte fr £15 food served all day ⊕ FREE HOUSE ◀ Bass Smooth, Boddingtons. ♥ 14 **Facilities** Children's menu Family room Garden Parking

RHEWL — Map 15 SJ16

The Drovers Arms, Rhewl ♥

Denbigh Rd LL15 2UD
☎ 01824 703163 ▤ 01824 703163
dir: 1.3m from Ruthin on A525

A small village pub whose name recalls a past written up and illustrated on storyboards displayed inside. Main courses are divided on the menu into poultry, traditional meat, fish, grills and vegetarian; examples from each section are chicken tarragon; Welsh lamb's liver and onions; Vale of Clwyd sirloin steak; home-made fish pie; and mushroom stroganoff. Desserts include treacle sponge pudding.

Open all wk noon-3 5.30-11 (Sat noon-3 5.30-mdnt Sun noon-11pm Open all day Jun-Sep) Closed: Tue L **Bar Meals** L served all wk 12-2 booking required D served all wk 6-9 booking required **Restaurant** L served all wk 12-2 booking required D served all wk 6-9 booking required ⊕ J W Lees ◀ J W Lees bitter. ♥ C **Facilities** Children's menu Play area Garden Parking

RUTHIN — Map 15 SJ15

The Wynnstay Arms NEW ★★★★ RR ◉◉ ♥

Well St LL15 1AN ☎ 01824 703147 ▤ 01824 705428
e-mail: reservations@wynnstayarms.com

This 460-year-old, timber-framed inn once hosted secret meetings of the Jacobites. It was here too that wandering 19th-century author George Borrow, after walking from Llangollen, treated his trusty guide, John Jones the Weaver, to "the best duck he had ever tasted". Much of the food, which has earned two AA Rosettes, is sourced from Wales, while bread and hams are baked, and pâtés and desserts are made in-house. Bar W provides space for a quiet drink and a read of the papers, as well as a daily gastro-pub-style menu offering lunchtime sandwiches, paninis and main meals. In Fusions Brasserie, typical are teriyaki chicken; pasta carbonara with crispy bacon and sautéed mushrooms; slow-braised shank of Welsh lamb with bubble and squeak and red wine gravy; roast gurnard with white wine, watercress and herb potatoes; and asparagus, roasted pepper and spinach risotto. En suite rooms have been recently refurbished to a high standard.

Open all day all wk **Bar Meals** L served all wk 12-2 booking required D served Mon-Sat 5.30-9.30, Sun 12-7 booking required Av main course £10.95 **Restaurant** L served Sun booking required D served Tue-Sat booking required Av 3 course à la carte fr £25.25 ⊕ FREE HOUSE ◀ Old Speckled Hen, Tetleys. ♥ 8 **Facilities** Children's menu Dogs allowed Parking Rooms 7

Ye Olde Anchor Inn

Rhos St LL15 1DY ☎ 01824 702813 ▤ 01824 703050
e-mail: info@anchorinn.co.uk
dir: At junct of A525 and A494

In the centre of town, this impressive-looking old inn has 16 windows at the front alone - all with award-winning window boxes. An extensive bar snack menu is available lunchtimes and evenings, while the main menu offers two types of lasagne, baked beef or Mediterranean vegetable; honey-spiced Welsh lamb shank; trinity of grilled fish; carpetbag fillet steak; and chestnut, mushroom and asparagus linguine, all eminently worth following with one of the freshly prepared desserts.

Open all wk ⊕ FREE HOUSE ◀ Timothy Taylor, Worthington, guest ales. **Facilities** Dogs allowed Parking

ST ASAPH
Map 15 SJ07

The Plough Inn ☆

The Roe LL17 0LU ☎ **01745 585080** 🖹 **01745 585363**
dir: *Exit A55 at Rhyl/St Asaph signs, left at rdbt, pub 200yds on left*

An 18th-century former coaching inn, the Plough has been transformed. The ground floor retains the traditional pub concept, cosy with open fires and rustic furniture, while upstairs there are two very different restaurants: an up-market bistro and an Italian-themed art deco restaurant, divided by a wine shop. All the kitchens are open so you can see the food being prepared. Desserts are a great strength throughout.

Open all wk ⊕ FREE HOUSE ◀ Greene King Old Speckled Hen, Shepherd Neame Spitfire, Plassey brewery. ☆ 9 **Facilities** Garden Parking

FLINTSHIRE

BABELL
Map 15 SJ17

Black Lion Inn ☆

CH8 8PZ ☎ **01352 720239**
e-mail: theblacklioninn@btinternet.com
dir: *A55 junct 31 to Caerwys turn left at crossroads signed Babell. Travel 3m turn right at fork*

Ancient inns spawn ghost stories, but the 13th-century Black Lion boasts more than its fair share. Ask about them when you visit, but don't be put off savouring a local real ale on the outside decking while the children enjoy the play area. Alternatively tuck into good home-cooked dishes like black pudding layered with crisp back bacon; and pork escalope with fresh asparagus sauce. Irish music keeps the spirits awake on the last Wednesday of the month.

Open all wk 6pm-close (Sat-Sun noon-close) **Bar Meals** L served Sat-Sun 12-9 D served Thu-Sun 6-9 Av main course £12.95 **Restaurant** L served Sat-Sun 12-9 D served Thu-Sun 6-9 Av 3 course à la carte fr £22 ⊕ FREE HOUSE ◀ Thwaites Lancaster Bomber, Thwaites Smooth Bitter, Purple Moose Brewery - Traeth Mawr, Thirstquencher Spitting Feathers. ☆ 7 **Facilities** Children's menu Play area Garden Parking

CILCAIN
Map 15 SJ16

White Horse Inn

CH7 5NN ☎ **01352 740142** 🖹 **01352 740142**
e-mail: christine.jeory@btopenworld.com
dir: *From Mold take A541 towards Denbigh. After approx 6m turn left*

A 400-year-old pub, which is the last survivor of five originally to be found in this lovely hillside village - no doubt because it was the centre of the local gold-mining industry in the 19th century. Today the White Horse is popular with walkers, cyclists, and horse-riders. The dishes are home made by the landlord's wife using the best quality local ingredients, including filled omelettes, grilled ham and eggs, breaded fillet of trout, cig oen Cymraeg (Welsh lamb pie), and various curries.

Open all wk noon-3 6.30-11 (Sat noon-11 Sun noon-10.30) **Bar Meals** L served all wk 12-2 D served all wk 7-9 Av main course £7.50 ⊕ FREE HOUSE ◀ Marston's Pedigree, Bank's Bitter, Timothy Taylor Landlord, Draught Bass, Archers Golden. **Facilities** Dogs allowed Garden Parking

MOLD
Map 15 SJ26

PICK OF THE PUBS

Glasfryn ☆

Raikes Ln, Sychdyn CH7 6LR
☎ **01352 750500** 🖹 **01352 751923**
e-mail: glasfryn@brunningandprice.co.uk
dir: *From Mold follow signs to Theatr Clwyd, 1m from town centre*

Built as a judge's residence in around 1900, later a farm and then divided into bedsits, this building was rescued by the present owners ten years ago and transformed into a wonderful pub. It attracts a variety of visitors from farmers and business people to holidaymakers along the north Wales coast. Outside, the newly landscaped garden is maturing well, while inside is a bright open space with lots of polished wooden tables and chairs. The comprehensive daily menu runs from sandwiches and snacks through to meals such as Pen Llyn bacon with roasted sweet potato and honey mustard dressing, followed by smoked haddock and salmon fishcakes with chive mayonnaise; or perhaps smoked duck with rhubarb and ginger chutney, followed by Edwards of Conwy lamb and leek sausages with mash and gravy. Puddings and cheeses are not to be missed.

Open all day noon-11 Closed: 25 Dec, Sun **Bar Meals** Av main course £9 food served all day **Restaurant** food served all day ⊕ BRUNNING & PRICE ◀ Timothy Taylor, Thwaites, Snowdonia Ale. ☆ 20 **Facilities** Children's menu Dogs allowed Garden Parking

NORTHOP
Map 15 SJ26

Stables Bar Restaurant ☆

CH7 6AB ☎ **01352 840577** 🖹 **01352 840382**
e-mail: info@soughtonhall.co.uk
dir: *From A55, take A119 through Northop*

Converted stables at the magnificent 17th-century Soughton Hall provide the setting for this destination pub. Many original features remain intact, including the cobbled floors, stalls and roof timbers, and the tables are named after famous racecourses and their winners. There is a great selection of real ales such as Stables Bitter and Dick Turpin. Menus embrace the racing theme with punters' mains and final furlong sweets. Start with chicken liver parfait with brioche and chutney, followed by trio of champion sausages with champ potato and caramelised red onion gravy, and chocolate brownie with lavender custard.

Open all day all wk **Bar Meals** L served all wk 12-9.30 D served all wk 12-9.30 Av main course £12 food served all day **Restaurant** D served all wk 7-9.30 booking required Av 3 course à la carte fr £25 ⊕ FREE HOUSE ◀ Shepherd Neame Spitfire, Shepherd Neame Bishops Finger, Coach House Honeypot, Dick Turpin, Plassey Bitter, Stables Bitter. ☆ 6 **Facilities** Family room Garden Parking

GWYNEDD

ABERDYFI
Map 14 SN69

PICK OF THE PUBS

Penhelig Arms Hotel & Restaurant ☆

Terrace Rd LL35 0LT
☎ **01654 767215** 🖹 **01654 767690**
e-mail: info@penheligarms.com
dir: *On A493 W of Machynlleth*

The Penhelig Arms has been in business since the late 18th century. It enjoys glorious views over the tidal Dyfi estuary, and is idyllically placed for breezy sea strolls or hill walks. Cader Idris and a variety of majestic mountains and historic castles are within easy reach. In the summer months many customers relax on the sea wall opposite the pub. Locals and visitors alike experience a warm welcome in the wood-panelled Fisherman's bar, where traditional ales and home-cooked bar meals are served. Alternatively take a seat in the popular waterfront restaurant, and relax as your decision-making skills are put to the test: will it be half a dressed Aberdyfi lobster with salad and mayonnaise, or melon and crayfish tails with chilli and lime dressing? Follow up with the likes of grilled monkfish wrapped in pancetta; or roast rump of lamb with root vegetable mash and rosemary gravy.

Open all day all wk 11-11 Closed: 25-26 Dec **Bar Meals** L served all wk 12-2 D served all wk 6-9 booking required Av main course £12.50 **Restaurant** L served all wk 12-2 booking required D served all wk 7-9 booking required Fixed menu price fr £29 Av 3 course à la carte fr £25 ⊕ S A BRAIN & CO LTD ◀ Adnams Broadside, Brains Reverend James & SA, Brains SA, Everards Toger. ♀ 22 **Facilities** Children's menu Dogs allowed Garden Parking

BLAENAU FFESTINIOG   Map 14 SH74

The Miners Arms

Llechwedd Slate Caverns LL41 3NB
☎ 01766 830306 📠 01766 831260
e-mail: quarrytours@aol.com
dir: *From Llandudno take A470 south. Through Betwys-y-Coed, 16m to Blaenau Ffestiniog*

Slate floors, open fires and staff in Victorian costume emphasise the heritage theme of this welcoming pub nestling in the centre of a Welsh village. On the site of Llechwedd Slate Caverns, one of the country's leading tourist attractions, it caters for all comers and tastes: expect steak and ale casserole, pork pie and salad, various ploughman's lunches, and hot apple pie, as well as afternoon tea with scones and cream.

Open all wk Closed: Oct-Etr **Bar Meals** food served all day **Restaurant** food served all day ⊕ FREE HOUSE **Facilities** Play area Family room Dogs allowed Garden Parking

LLANBEDR   Map 14 SH52

Victoria Inn ★★★ INN ♀

LL45 2LD ☎ 01341 241213 📠 01341 241644
e-mail: junevicinn@aol.com
web: www.victoriainnllanbedr.co.uk
dir: *On A496 between Barmouth and Harlech*

Fascinating features for pub connoisseurs are the circular wooden settle, ancient stove, grandfather clock and flagged floors in the atmospheric bar of the Victoria. Home-made food is served in the lounge bar and restaurant, complemented by a range of Robinson's traditional ales. A children's play area has been incorporated into the well-kept garden, with a playhouse, slides and swings. The Rhinog mountain range and the famous Roman Steps are right on the doorstep. Newly redecorated bedrooms are all en suite.

Open all day all wk 11-11 (Sun noon-10.30) **Bar Meals** Av main course £9 food served all day **Restaurant** Fixed menu price fr £10.50 food served all day ⊕ FREDERIC ROBINSON ◀ Robinson's Best Bitter, guest bitters ♂ Stowford Press. ♀ 10 **Facilities** Children's menu Play area Dogs allowed Garden Parking **Rooms** 5

NANTGWYNANT   Map 14 SH65

Pen-Y-Gwryd Hotel

LL55 4NT ☎ 01286 870211
dir: *A5 to Capel Curig, left on A4086 to T-junct*

This slate-roofed climbers' pub and rescue post in the heart of Snowdonia has long been the home of British mountaineering. The 1953 Everest team used it as their training base, and etched their signatures on the ceiling. The appetising and inexpensive menus make good use of Welsh lamb and local pork; other options include home-made pâté with pickles, salad and crusty bread; or ham and cannellini bean spaghetti with home-made olive and herb flatbread.

Closed: Nov-1 Jan & mid wk (Jan-Feb) ⊕ FREE HOUSE ◀ Interbrew Bass, Boddingtons Bitter. **Facilities** Play area Family room Dogs allowed Garden Parking

TUDWEILIOG   Map 14 SH23

Lion Hotel ♀

LL53 8ND ☎ 01758 770244
e-mail: martinlee1962@hotmail.com
dir: *A487 from Caernarfon onto A499 towards Pwllheli. Right onto B4417 to Nefyn, onto Edern then onto Tudweiliog*

The beach is only a mile away from this friendly inn, run by the Lee family for over 30 years. The large garden and children's play area makes the pub especially popular with the cyclists, walkers and families who flock to the Lleyn Peninsula. The bar features an extensive list of over 80 malt whiskies. A typical menu might consist of Tuscan bean soup, Welsh lamb bake, and rice pudding.

Open all wk **Bar Meals** L served all wk 12-2 D served all wk 6-9 Av main course £8.25 ⊕ FREE HOUSE ◀ Purple Moose Brewery Ale, Boddingtons. ♀ 6 **Facilities** Children's menu Play area Family room Garden Parking

WAUNFAWR   Map 14 SH55

Snowdonia Parc Brewpub & Campsite

LL55 4AQ ☎ 01286 650409 & 650218
e-mail: info@snowdonia-park.co.uk
dir: *Telephone for directions*

This pub stands 400 feet above sea level at Waunfawr Station on the Welsh Highland Railway. There are steam trains on site (the building was originally the stationmaster's house), plus a micro-brewery and campsite. The foot of Mount Snowdon is four miles away. Expect home-cooked food based on locally produced and traditionally reared beef, lamb, chicken and pork. In addition to its own brews, the bar serves guest ales and popular lagers, cider and Guinness. Children and dogs welcome.

Open all day all wk 11-11 (Fri-Sat 11-11.30) **Bar Meals** food served all day **Restaurant** food served all day ⊕ FREE HOUSE ◀ Marston's Pedigree, Welsh Highand Bitter (own brew). **Facilities** Play area Family room Dogs allowed Garden Parking

MONMOUTHSHIRE

ABERGAVENNY   Map 9 SO21

PICK OF THE PUBS

Clytha Arms ♀

Clytha NP7 9BW ☎ 01873 840209 📠 01873 840209
e-mail: theclythaarms@tiscali.co.uk
dir: *From A449/A40 junction (E of Abergavenny) follow signs for 'Old Road Abergavenny/Clytha'*

Andrew and Beverley Canning have now celebrated 30 years of marriage, 18 of which have been spent at the Clytha. They are as enthusiastic as ever about their hostelry, despite the trials and tribulations of the weather and the economy. This former dower house is heavily involved with the Welsh Cider Festival in May

continued

ABERGAVENNY *continued*

and the Beer and Cheese Festival in August. Hardly surprising then that the bar offers Weston ciders and the Clytha's own perry, as well as local beers from the Rhymney Brewery and Crow Valley — at least four are always on offer. Whisky, gin and vodka come from the Penderyn Distillery just 20 miles away. As for food, Andrew cooks up a storm on his new oak-fired grill, starting the day by baking his own bread and muffins. The menu offers treats for every taste, from rabbit and cider pie to bacon, laverbread and cockles. Treacle pudding and home-made custard to finish is a must.

Open noon-3 6-mdnt (Fri-Sun noon-mdnt) Closed: 25 Dec, Mon L **Bar Meals** L served Tue-Sun 12.30-2.30 D served Mon-Sat 7-9.30 Av main course £10 **Restaurant** L served Tue-Sun 12.30-2.30 D served Mon-Sat 7-9.30 Fixed menu price fr £16.95 Av 3 course à la carte fr £25 ⊕ FREE HOUSE ◀ Felinfoel Double Dragon, Rhymney Bitter, 4 guest ales (300+ per year) Ŏ Westons Old Rosie, Westons Perry, Clytha Perry. ♀ 10 **Facilities** Children's menu Play area Dogs allowed Garden Parking

---

CHEPSTOW
Map 4 ST59

Castle View Hotel ★★★ HL ♀

16 Bridge St NP16 5EZ
☎ 01291 620349 ▤ 01291 627397
e-mail: castleviewhotel@btconnect.com
dir: *Opposite Chepstow Castle*

Standing opposite Chepstow Castle and built as a private house in the 17th-century, the inn boasts walls that are five feet thick and a delightful secluded walled garden. Using quality ingredients from local suppliers the menus may list moules marinière, braised lamb shank with redcurrant and rosemary jus, wild mushrooms risotto, and traditional bar snacks like sandwiches, ploughman's lunches and omelettes.

Open all wk **Bar Meals** L served all wk 12-3 D served all wk 6.30-9.30 Av main course £12 **Restaurant** L served all wk 12-3 D served all wk 6.30-9.30 Av 3 course à la carte fr £20 ⊕ FREE HOUSE ◀ Wye Valley Real Ale, Double Dragon, Felinfoel Best Bitter Ŏ Stowford Press. ♀ 6 **Facilities** Children's menu Dogs allowed Garden Parking **Rooms** 13

LLANGYBI
Map 9 ST39

PICK OF THE PUBS

The White Hart Village Inn

See Pick of the Pubs on opposite page

LLANTRISANT
Map 9 ST39

PICK OF THE PUBS

The Greyhound Inn Ⓐ ★★★ INN ♀

NP15 1LE
☎ 01291 672505 & 673447 ▤ 01291 673255
e-mail: enquiry@greyhound-inn.com
dir: *M4 junct 24, A449 towards Monmouth, exit at 1st junct signed Usk. 2nd left for Llantrisant. Or from Monmouth A40, A449 exit for Usk. In Usk left into Twyn Sq follow Llantrisant signs. 2.5m under A449 bridge. Inn on right*

A traditional 17th-century Welsh longhouse, once part of a 400-acre farm. In 1845 the milk parlour was converted into an inn, and over the years the land was sold off. By 1980, the whole complex was in a sorry state, as pictures hanging in the Cocktail and Llangibby lounges bear witness. Today, after 27 years in the same family's hands, the Greyhound has two acres of award-winning gardens, a four-acre paddock, accommodation and an array of restored outbuildings. Owner Nick Davies heads the kitchen team, serving customers in the four eating areas, one of which is a candlelit dining room. The regular menu ranges over old favourites such as prawn cocktail, home-made curries, pies and lasagne. It is complemented by a daily specials blackboard offering unusual and seasonal dishes: chicken veronique; local pheasant; pork roberto; and Usk salmon. The vegetarian selection, with eight choices, is particularly notable. Home-made sweets include hazelnut meringue gateau, peach Melba and profiteroles.

Open all day 11-11 Closed: 25 & 31 Dec, 1 Jan, Sun eve **Bar Meals** L served all wk 12-2.15 D served Mon-Sat 6-10 Av main course £11 **Restaurant** L served all wk 12-2.15 D served Mon-Sat 6-10 ⊕ FREE HOUSE ◀ Interbrew Flowers Original & Bass, Greene King Abbot Ale, guest ale. ♀ 10 **Facilities** Children's menu Family room Dogs allowed Garden Parking **Rooms** 10

LLANVAIR DISCOED
Map 9 ST49

PICK OF THE PUBS

The Woodland Tavern Country Pub & Dining ♀

NP16 6LX ☎ 01633 400313 ▤ 01633 400313
e-mail: info@thewoodlandstavern.co.uk
dir: *5m from Caldicot & Magor*

This old inn has been extended to accommodate a growing number of diners, but remains at heart a friendly family-run village local. The pub is located close to the Roman fortress town of Caerwent and Wentworth's forest and reservoir; it was nicknamed 'the war office' when Irish navvies held bare-knuckle fights here while building the reservoir. A patio area with seating ensures that food and drink can be served outside in fine weather. A good range of guest ales is backed by a regular supply of Brains beers, ideal to go with a classic ploughman's or home-made pasty. A short fixed-price lunch menu offers a couple of choices at each stage: tomato, basil and mozzarella salad; deep-fried fillet of haddock; and creamed rice pudding with apple compote would be typical. The more extensive restaurant menu proffers the likes of baked flat mushrooms with red onion marmalade topped with goats' cheese; followed by roast rump of Welsh lamb served on mash.

Closed: Mon, Sun eve **Bar Meals** L served Tue-Sat 12-2, Sun 12-3 D served Tue-Fri 6-9, Sat 6-9.30 Av main course £11.50 **Restaurant** L served Tue-Sat 12-2, Sun 12-3 booking required D served Tue-Fri 6-9, Sat 6-9.30 booking required Fixed menu price fr £9.95 Av 3 course à la carte fr £20 ⊕ FREE HOUSE ◀ Brains, Felinfoel Double Dragon, Tomas Watkins OSB, Guest ales. ♀ 8 **Facilities** Children's menu Dogs allowed Parking

PICK OF THE PUBS

The White Hart Village Inn

LLANGYBI   Map 9 ST39

NP15 1NP ☎ **01633 450258**
e-mail: info@whitehartvillageinn.com
www: www.whitehartvillageinn.com
dir: *M4 junct 25 onto B4596 (Caerleon road) through town centre on High St, straight over rdbt onto Usk Rd, continue to Llangybi*

This historic inn was originally built in the 12th century for Cistercian monks. Early in the 1500s it became the property of Henry VIII as part of Jane Seymour's wedding dowry and, a century later, Oliver Cromwell is said to have used it as his headquarters in Gwent. The pub has literary connections, too. For years, students were mystified by a couple of lines from TS Eliot's poem *Usk*: 'Do not hope to find the white hart behind the white well...'. Recently it emerged that Eliot wasn't referring to

an animal, but to The White Hart Village Inn; the pub stands not far from the ruined village well, which was formerly painted white. Today, the White Hart has been sensitively restored by the Pell family, who have retained a wealth of historic features including exposed beams, original Tudor plasterwork and 16th-century fireplaces — just the place to while away a winter's evening with a pint from the Wye Valley Brewery beside a crackling open fire. On warmer days, the extensive rear flagstone seating area offers far reaching views to the Wentwood Hills. During the summer months this area also hosts barbecues and special events including a hog roast and live jazz band. Lunchtime brings a range of informal main course dishes like corned beef hash with crispy bacon and poached egg; or beer battered cod and chips with peas and tartare sauce. Evening diners might sample the home-made Cajun fishcakes and sweet chilli sauce, followed by honey-glazed five-spice crispy duck with stir-fried plum and ginger vegetables. Round off with a look at the daily dessert board, or a selection of cheeses.

Open Wed-Sun Closed: Mon-Tue
🍺 Timothy Taylor Landlord, Rhymney Brewery Bevan's Bitter, Hobby Horse, Wye Valley Butty Bach and Sharps Doom Bar. **Facilities** Garden Parking

MAMHILAD	Map 9 SO30

PICK OF THE PUBS

Horseshoe Inn ♟

NP4 8QZ ☎ **01873 880542**
e-mail: horseshoe@artizanleisure.com
dir: *A4042 (Pontypool to Abergavenny road),
at Mamhilad Estate rdbt take 1st exit onto Old
Abergavenny road. 2m over canal bridge on right*

Bordering the Brecon to Monmouth canal and sited on
the Pontypool to Abergavenny turnpike, the Horseshoe
started providing welcome sustenance for canal
navigators and horse-drawn coach passengers over
200 years ago. The ambience of its history is recalled in
its original oak beams, stone walls and huge
fireplaces. Today it continues the tradition of serving
fine real ales, good value wines and tasty locally
produced food in the relaxed surroundings of crackling
wood fires, cosy armchairs and informal dining rooms.
Rymney Bitter and Butty Bach are among the beer
choices, while wine lovers can choose between ten
served by the glass. Typical starters are home-cured
gravadlax with citrus crème fraîche; haddock and
spring onion fishcakes with tomato butter sauce; and
blue cheese panacotta with redcurrant syrup and
rocket salad. Main courses vary from chorizo sausage
cassoulet to trio of Gloucester Old Spot sausages with
bubble and squeak and onion gravy. Desserts are all
home made.

Open all wk **Bar Meals** L served all wk 12-2.30 D
served all wk 6.30-9.30 Av main course £9
Restaurant L served all wk 12-2.30 D served all wk
6.30-9.30 Av 3 course à la carte fr £25 ⊕ FREE
HOUSE ◢ Abbot Ale, London Pride, Rymney Bitter, Butty
Bach, Guest Ales. ♟10 **Facilities** Children's menu Dogs
allowed Garden Parking

PANTYGELLI	Map 9 SO31

The Crown NEW ♟

Old Hereford Rd NP7 7HR ☎ **01873 853314**
e-mail: crown@pantygelli.com
dir: *Please telephone for directions*

Reputedly an old coaching inn dating back to the 16th
century, this charming family-run free house is a genuine
community local. Located on the edge of the Brecon
Beacons National Park, it's popular with walkers, cyclists
and general visitors. Stowford Press cider supports the
range of local ales, and the food offering ranges from hot
roast pork and apple sauce ciabattas to herb-crusted
baked mussels; or Welsh black beef with bubble and
squeak.

Open noon-2.30, 6-11 (Sat-Sun noon-3, Sun 6-10.30)
Closed: Mon lunch **Bar Meals** L served Tue-Sun 12-2
booking required D served Tue-Sat 7-9 booking required
Restaurant L served Tue-Sun 12-2 booking required D
served Tue-Sat 7-9 booking required ⊕ FREE HOUSE
◢ Rhymney Bitter, Wye Valley HPA ♂ Westons Stowford
Press. ♟7 **Facilities** Children's menu Dogs allowed
Garden Parking

PENALLT	Map 4 SO51

The Boat Inn

Lone Ln NP25 4AJ ☎ **01600 712615** 📄 **01600 719120**
dir: *From Monmouth take A466. In Redbrook, pub car park
signed. Access by foot across rail bridge over River Wye*

Dating back over 360 years, this riverside pub has served
as a hostelry for quarry, mill, paper and tin mine workers,
and even had a landlord operating a ferry across the Wye
at shift times. The unspoilt slate floor is testament to the
age of the place. The excellent selection of real ales and
local ciders complements the menu well, with choices
ranging from various ploughman's to lamb steffados or
the charmingly-named pan haggerty. Ideal for walkers
taking the Offa's Dyke or Wye Valley walks.

Open all wk ⊕ FREE HOUSE ◢ Freeminer Bitter,
Wadworth 6X, Abbot Ale & Old Speckled Hen, Wye Valley
Butty Bach, Wye Valley guest ales. **Facilities** Dogs
allowed Garden Parking

RAGLAN	Map 9 SO40

PICK OF THE PUBS

The Beaufort Arms Coaching Inn &
Restaurant ★★★ HL ◉ ♟

High St NP15 2DY
☎ **01291 690412** 📄 **01291 690935**
e-mail: enquiries@beaufortraglan.co.uk
dir: *0.5m from junct of A40 & A449 Abergavenny/
Monmouth*

The Beaufort has been an inn since the time of the Civil
War, when its proximity to Raglan Castle meant that
Roundhead soldiers supped here during the siege of
1646. Later it became a coaching inn on the London to
Fishguard route. The inn has been beautifully
refurbished with many delightful design features, while
holding strong to its traditional roots. A handsome
display of fishing trophies dominates the country bar,
where locals and visitors alike gather. Food is served in
the lounge, with its carved bar, large stone fireplace
and deep leather settees, as well as in the brasserie
and private dining room. Bar meals range from light
bites of classic Welsh rarebit, hot chorizo salad and
paninis to local faggots served with chunky chips,
crushed peas and red onion jus. The brasserie offers
the likes of roasted pork belly with beetroot fondant
and peppercorn sauce. A south-facing patio and
terrace, and 15 individually decorated bedrooms,
complete the package.

Open all day all wk **Bar Meals** Av main course £8.95
food served all day **Restaurant** L served all wk 12-3
booking required D served all wk 6-9.30 booking
required Av 3 course à la carte fr £22 ⊕ FREE
HOUSE ◢ London Pride, Reverend James, Warsteiner,
Old Speckled Hen ♂ Stowford Press. ♟12
Facilities Children's menu Garden Parking **Rooms** 15

SHIRENEWTON
Map 9 ST49

The Carpenters Arms

Usk Rd NP16 6BU ☎ 01291 641231 ▤ 01291 641231
dir: *M48 junct 2, A48 to Chepstow then A4661, B4235.
Village 3m on left*

A 400-year-old hostelry, formerly a smithy and
carpenter's shop, with flagstone floors, open fires and
antiques. It's set in a pleasant wooded location in the
valley of the Mounton Brook which lies between the
bigger valleys of the Wye and Usk. Straightforward bar
food is typified by chicken in leek and stilton sauce, steak
and mushroom pie, smoked haddock and potato pie,
guinea fowl in orange sauce, and lamb rogan josh.

Open all wk ⊕ PUNCH TAVERNS ◀ Fuller's London Pride,
Wadworth 6X, Marston's Pedigree, Theakston Old
Peculier. **Facilities** Family room Dogs allowed Parking

SKENFRITH
Map 9 SO42

PICK OF THE PUBS

The Bell at
Skenfrith
RR ◉◉ ♟

NP7 8UH ☎ 01600 750235 ▤ 01600 750525
e-mail: enquiries@skenfrith.co.uk
dir: *M4 junct 24 onto A449. Exit onto A40, through
tunnel & lights. At rdbt take 1st exit, right at lights
onto A466 towards Hereford Road. Left onto B4521
towards Abergavenny, 3m on left*

From its setting by the historic arched bridge over the
River Monnow, this 17th-century coaching inn has
views of Skenfrith Castle. An oak bar, flagstone floors,
comfortable sofas and old settles ooze plenty of
character, and 11 individually decorated and well-
equipped bedrooms, some with four-poster beds,
provide high-quality accommodation. Real ales include
Wye Valley brews, backed by hand-pumped local cider.
The pub flies the flag for fine food and wines. Locally
sourced and mainly organic ingredients, many from the
inn's very own kitchen garden, are used in regularly
changing menus. One day's selection could include
warm duck salad; slow braised shoulder of Talgarth
lamb with pan-seared lambs' liver and mashed potato;
and lemon meringue pie. The fixed priced carte proffers
exquisite dishes which carefully combine finely judged
flavours: an entrée of locally picked wild garlic served
as a vichyssoise, with a warm fricassée of Hereford
snails and spring rabbit ballotine bound with tarragon
mustard is an excellent example.

Closed: last wk Jan & 1st wk Feb, Mon Nov-Mar **Bar
Meals** L served all wk 12-2.30 booking required D
served Mon-Sat 7-9.30, Sun 7-9 booking required Av
main course £15 **Restaurant** L served all wk 12-2.30
booking required D served Mon-Sat 7-9.30, Sun 7-9
booking required Fixed menu price fr £19 Av 3 course à
la carte fr £28 ⊕ FREE HOUSE ◀ Timothy Taylor
Landlord, St Austell Tribute, Wye Valley Bitter ♻ Local
cider. ♟ 13 **Facilities** Children's menu Dogs allowed
Garden Parking **Rooms** 11

TINTERN PARVA
Map 4 SO50

Fountain Inn ♟

Trellech Grange NP16 6QW ☎ 01291 689303
e-mail: fountaininntintern@btconnect.com
dir: *From M48 junct 2 follow Chepstow then Tintern
signs. In Tintern turn by George Hotel for Raglan. Bear
right, inn at top of hill*

A fire failed to destroy this fine old early 17th-century inn,
and its charming character remains unspoilt. It enjoys
views of the Wye Valley from the garden, and is close to
Tintern Abbey. Home-cooked food includes grilled
sardines with balsamic vinegar and cherry tomatoes; leek
and Caerphilly sausages with onion gravy; and beef and
Guinness pie. Also a good selection of steaks, omelettes,
and seafood choices are available. Recent change of
landlord.

Closed: Mon (ex BH) **Bar Meals** L served Wed-Sun
12-2.30 D served all wk 6-9 **Restaurant** L served Wed-
Sun 12-2.30 D served all wk 6-9 ⊕ FREE HOUSE ◀ Hook
Norton, Spinning Dog, Ring of Bells, Interbrew Bass,
Hobgoblin, Rev James, Kingstone Classic, Cats
Whiskers. ♟ 10 **Facilities** Children's menu Family room
Dogs allowed Garden Parking

TREDUNNOCK
Map 9 ST39

PICK OF THE PUBS

The Newbridge ★★★★ RR ◉ ♟

NP15 1LY ☎ 01633 451000 ▤ 01633 451001
e-mail: newbridge@evanspubs.co.uk
dir: *M4 junct 24 follow Newport signs. Right at Toby
Carvery, B4236 to Caerleon. Right over bridge, through
Caerleon to mini rdbt. Straight ahead onto Llnagibby/
Usk road*

The Newbridge occupies an idyllic riverside location: to
be there in the early morning and watch the mist over
the river is magical. The decor is warm and welcoming,
with comfortable sofas and subtle lighting. Head Chef
Iain Sampson has worked in some of the country's
finest kitchens and the quality and consistency of his
modern British with Mediterranean-influenced food is
well reflected in exciting seasonal menus, based
extensively on local produce. Expect a typical meal of
Welsh oak-smoked haddock risotto with parmesan
wafer and herb oil; mustard-crusted rack of local
Penperlleni lamb with fondant potatoes and carved
vegetables; and banana Tatin with caramel ice cream.
Dinner could be watercress, spinach and goats' cheese
tart with beetroot coulis; Gloucestershire Old Spot pork
loin with potato cake, baby vegetables and buttered
tarragon jus; and home-made ice cream. The day's
catch, purchased from the quayside in Cornwall, is
displayed on the specials board.

Open all wk 11am-mdnt **Bar Meals** L served all wk
12-2.30 booking required D served Mon-Sat 6.30-10,
Sun 6-8.30 booking required **Restaurant** L served all
wk 12-2.30 booking required D served Mon-Sat
6.30-10, Sun 6-8.30 booking required ⊕ FREE HOUSE
◀ Brains Rev James, Hobby Horse, guest ale
♻ Aspalls. ♟ 12 **Facilities** Children's menu Garden
Parking **Rooms** 6

TRELLECH
Map 4 SO50

PICK OF THE PUBS

The Lion Inn

NP25 4PA ☎ 01600 860322 ▤ 01600 860060
e-mail: debs@globalnet.co.uk
dir: *From A40 S of Monmouth take B4293, follow signs
for Trellech. From M8 junct 2, straight across rdbt, 2nd
left at 2nd rdbt, B4293 to Trellech*

Summer drinkers enjoy supping in the garden of this
well established free house, which features a stream,
large aviary and views over fields. The former
brewhouse and coaching inn has won many awards,
and its growing reputation is soundly based on all
that's best about a good British pub: a warm welcome,
beams, wood fires in winter, as well as wholesome
food, traditional ales, ciders and games. For hearty
appetites, the menu embraces bar snacks and basket
meals. Blackboard specials include fresh fish but,
proving that homage to tradition is not total, ostrich or
kangaroo may also be found here. Look out, too, for
authentic Hungarian dishes, and hedgerow 'poacher's
pocket' ingredients such as pigeon and wild boar
harvested from the surrounding countryside. Children
have plenty of favourites to choose from, while walkers'
dogs are fussed over with biscuits and a bowl of fresh
water. There are plenty of activities to enjoy most
nights, plus a summer and winter beer festival.

Open 12-3 6-11 (Fri-Sat noon-mdnt Sun 12-4.30 Mon
eve 7-11pm Thu eve 6-mdnt) Closed: Sun eve **Bar
Meals** L served Mon-Fri 12-2, Sat-Sun 12-2.30 D
served Mon 7-9.30, Tue-Sat 6-9.30 booking required Av
main course £12 **Restaurant** L served Mon-Fri 12-2,
Sat-Sun 12-2.30 D served Mon 7-9.30, Tue-Sat 6-9.30
booking required Av 3 course à la carte fr £23 ⊕ FREE
HOUSE ◀ Bath Ales, Wye Valley Butty Bach, Sharp's
Cornish Coaster, Rhymney Best, Butcombe Gold.
Facilities Children's menu Dogs allowed Garden
Parking

USK
Map 9 SO30

The Nags Head Inn ☕
Twyn Square NP15 1BH
☎ 01291 672820 📠 01291 672720
dir: *On A472*

Owned by the Key family for 40 years, this 15th-century coaching inn overlooks the square just a short stroll from the River Usk, and boasts magnificent hanging flower baskets. The traditional bar is furnished with polished tables and chairs, and decorated with collections of horse brasses, farming tools and lanterns hanging from exposed oak beams. Game in season figures strongly among the speciality dishes, including whole stuffed partridge, pheasant in port, home-made rabbit pie and brace of quails. There is a good choice for vegetarians, too, such as Glamorgan sausage filled with cheese and leek and served with a chilli relish.

Open all wk Closed: 25 Dec **Bar Meals** L served all wk 11.45-1.45 D served all wk 5.30-9.30 **Restaurant** L served all wk 11.45-1.45 D served all wk 5.30-9.30 ⊕ FREE HOUSE ◀ Brains Bitter, Dark, Buckleys Best, Reverend James, Bread of Heaven Ö Thatchers Gold. ☕ 8 **Facilities** Children's menu Dogs allowed Garden Parking

PICK OF THE PUBS

Raglan Arms ◉ ☕
Llandenny NP15 1DL
☎ 01291 690800 📠 01291 690155
e-mail: raglanarms@aol.com
dir: *From Monmouth take A449 to Raglan, left in village*

This cosy, part-stone, part-wooden-floored, flint-built pub is tucked away in a small, attractive village. While the choice of dishes is limited, menus are changed daily and a good selection of Welsh and English cheeses supports a well-chosen range of starters, mains and puddings. Dine at rustic tables around the bar, or in the conservatory extension, on modern British dishes with a Gallic influence. Expect longhorn rib-eye of beef from a local breeder-cum-butcher; langoustines from Scotland, and scallops and turbot from Cornwall; slow-roasted pork with apples; and, compromising somewhat the modern British/Gallic theme, there's imam bayaldi, a Middle Eastern spiced aubergine and tomato-based dish, a long-standing favourite in the repertoire here. Try the deliciously creamy crème brûlée with red berry compote for dessert. In the bar you'll find Wye Valley Bitter and the same brewery's Butty Bach.

Open noon-3 6.30-9.30 Closed: Sun eve & Mon **Bar Meals** L served Tue-Sun 12-3 D served Tue-Sat 6.30-9.30 Av main course £11 **Restaurant** L served Tue-Sun 12-3 booking required D served Tue-Sat 6.30-9.30 booking required Av 3 course à la carte fr £25 ⊕ FREE HOUSE ◀ Wye Valley Bitter, Butty Bach, Guinness Ö Thatchers Gold. ☕ 12 **Facilities** Children's menu Garden Parking

PEMBROKESHIRE

ABERCYCH
Map 8 SN24

Nags Head Inn
SA37 0HJ ☎ 01239 841200
dir: *On B4332 (Carmarthen to Newcastle Emlyn road)*

Crossing into Pembrokeshire from the Teifi Falls at Cenarth, the Nags Head is the first building you see over the county boundary. The famous old inn, with its beamed bars and riverside gardens, is located at the entrance to an enchanted valley immortalised in Welsh folklore. Old Emrys Ale is brewed on the premises and good food options include coracle caught Teifi sewin; hungry farmer's mixed grill; and home-made faggots with chips and mushy peas.

Closed: Mon **Bar Meals** L served Tue-Sun 12-2 D served Tue-Sun 6-9 Av main course £8.95 **Restaurant** L served Tue-Sun 12-2 D served Tue-Sun 6-9 ⊕ FREE HOUSE ◀ Old Emrys. **Facilities** Play area Dogs allowed Garden Parking

AMROTH
Map 8 SN10

The New Inn ☕
SA67 8NW ☎ 01834 812368
dir: *A48 to Carmarthen, A40 to St Clears, A477 to Llanteg then left*

A 400-year-old inn, originally a farmhouse, belonging to Amroth Castle Estate. It has old world charm with beamed ceilings, a Flemish chimney, a flagstone floor and an inglenook fireplace. It is close to the beach, and local lobster and crab are a feature, along with a popular choice of home-made dishes including steak and kidney pie, soup and curry. Enjoy food or drink outside on the large lawn complete with picnic benches.

Open all day all wk Mar-Oct 11am-11pm Closed: Oct-Mar **Bar Meals** food served all day **Restaurant** food served all day ⊕ FREE HOUSE ◀ Brains, Old Speckled Hen, Guinness, guest ales. ☕ 8 **Facilities** Children's menu Family room Dogs allowed Garden Parking **Notes** ◉

CAREW
Map 8 SN00

Carew Inn
SA70 8SL ☎ 01646 651267
e-mail: mandy@carewinn.co.uk
dir: *From A477 take A4075. Inn 400yds opp castle & Celtic cross*

A traditional stone-built country inn situated opposite the Carew Celtic cross and Norman castle. Enjoy the one-mile circular walk around the castle and millpond. A good range of bar meals includes Welsh Black steak and kidney pie; chilli con carne; Thai red chicken curry; and seafood pancakes. Fruit crumble and old favourite jam roly poly feature among the puddings. Live music every Thursday night under the marquee.

Open all wk Closed: 25 Dec ⊕ FREE HOUSE ◀ Worthington Best, SA Brains Reverend James, guest ales. **Facilities** Play area Dogs allowed Garden Parking

CILGERRAN
Map 8 SN14

Pendre Inn
Pendre SA43 2SL ☎ 01239 614223
dir: *Off A478, S of Cardigan*

Dating back to the 14th century, this is a pub full of memorabilia and featuring exposed interior walls, old beams, slate floors and an inglenook fireplace. An ancient ash tree grows through the pavement in front of the white stone, thick-walled building. Typical menu includes lamb steaks with red wine and cherries, rump and sirloin steaks, pork loin with honey and mustard glaze, and salmon with hollandaise.

Closed: Sun eve ⊕ FREE HOUSE ◀ Tomas Watkins, OSB, Murphys, Worthington. **Facilities** Garden Parking

LAMPHEY
Map 8 SN00

The Dial Inn ☕
Ridgeway Rd SA71 5NU
☎ 01646 672426 📠 01646 672426
dir: *Just off A4139 (Tenby to Pembroke road)*

The Dial started life around 1830 as the Dower House for nearby Lamphey Court, and was converted into a pub in 1966. It immediately established itself as a popular village local, and in recent years the owners have extended the dining areas. Food is a real strength, and Pembrokeshire farm products are used whenever possible. You can choose from traditional bar food, the imaginative restaurant menu, or the daily blackboard.

Open all wk ⊕ FREE HOUSE ◀ Coors ale, Runmey Bitter. ☕ 8 **Facilities** Family room Garden Parking

LETTERSTON Map 8 SM92

The Harp Inn ?

31 Haverfordwest Rd SA62 5UA
☎ 01348 840061 📄 01348 840812
dir: On A40

This 15th-century free house was once a working farm, as well as home to a weekly market. After remaining largely unchanged for 500 years, the inn is now firmly grounded in the 21st century with disabled facilities and a 130-seater restaurant. Two comprehensive menus and a chalkboard offer dishes ranging from grilled sea bass to tenderloin pork in red plum sauce; and Welsh steaks garni to stir-fried vegetables in black bean sauce.

Open all day all wk Jul-Sep (ex Sun) **Bar Meals** food served all day ⊕ FREE HOUSE ◀ Tetleys, Greene King, Abbot Ale. ? 8 **Facilities** Play area Garden Parking

LITTLE HAVEN Map 8 SM81

PICK OF THE PUBS

The Swan Inn ?

Point Rd SA62 3UL
☎ 01437 781880 📄 04137 781880
e-mail: enquiries@theswanlittlehaven.co.uk
dir: From Haverfordwest take B4341 (Broad Haven road). In Broad Haven follow signs for seafront & Little Haven, 0.75m

Follow the footpath to reach this unspoilt, 200-year-old seaside gem, perched above a rocky cove overlooking St Bride's Bay. The views across the water to Solva and Ramsay Island are spectacular, particularly from the terrace, the sea wall outside or even from the sought-after bay window in the beamed bar. A couple of years back the Swan was boarded up, now it buzzes with chatter and contented diners, thanks to Paul Morris who has revitalised the pub. Expect a rustic and relaxed bar, with old settles, polished oak tables, and leather armchairs fronting a blazing log fire, an intimate dining room and, upstairs, an elegant, contemporary-style restaurant. Cooking is modern British with a commitment to seasonal and local produce, so bag a table with a grand view and tuck into open soda bread sandwiches (Caerfai cheese and chutney) and St Bride's Bay dressed crab, at lunch, or venison casserole, brill with marsh samphire and sherry butter, or Welsh rib-eye steak with red onion confit and béarnaise in the evening.

Open 11-3 5.30-mdnt (Sat-Sun 11am-mdnt) Closed: Mon (Jan) **Bar Meals** L served all wk 12-2 D served Mon-Sat 6-9 Av main course £10 **Restaurant** L served all wk 12-2 booking required D served Mon-Sat 6-9 booking required Av 3 course à la carte fr £28 ⊕ FREE HOUSE ◀ Worthington Best Bitter, Old Speckled Hen, Guinness, S A Brains. ? 8 **Facilities** Children's menu Dogs allowed Garden

NEWPORT Map 8 SN03

Salutation Inn ▲ ★★★ INN

Felindre Farchog, Crymych SA41 3UY
☎ 01239 820564 📄 01239 820355
e-mail: JohnDenley@aol.com
web: www.salutationcountryhotel.co.uk
dir: On A487 between Cardigan & Fishguard

Set right on the banks of the River Nevern, this 16th-century coaching inn stands in a quiet village in the heart of the Pembrokeshire Coast National Park. The oak-beamed bars are full of old world charm and country atmosphere. There is an emphasis on fresh local produce on the varied menu, including meat, poultry, fish, cheese and fruit and vegetables. Asparagus and smoked Cerwyn cheese, or rustic game pâté to start, with perhaps prime fillet of Welsh Black beef on rösti and roasted shallots to follow are fine examples of the fare. There are eight en suite bedrooms available.

Open all day all wk **Bar Meals** L served all wk 12.30-2.30 D served all wk 6.30-9 **Restaurant** L served Sun 12.30-2.30 booking required D served Sat-Sun 7-9 booking required ⊕ FREE HOUSE ◀ Felinfoel, Brains, Local guest ales ♂ Thatchers Gold. **Facilities** Children's menu Dogs allowed Garden Parking **Rooms** 8

PEMBROKE DOCK Map 8 SM90

Ferry Inn

Pembroke Ferry SA72 6UD ☎ 01646 682947
dir: A477, off A48, right at garage, signs for Cleddau Bridge, left at rdbt

There are fine views across the Cleddau estuary from the terrace of this 16th-century free house. Once the haunt of smugglers, the riverside inn has a nautical-themed bar with a 'great disaster' corner highlighting pictures of local catastrophes! The pub is also said to be haunted. Fresh fish features strongly on the menu: favourites include locally caught trout; salmon fillet with dill butter; and brill with cherry tomatoes and crème fraîche.

Open all wk noon-2.30 6.30-10.30 **Bar Meals** L served all wk 12-2 D served all wk 6.30-9 ⊕ FREE HOUSE ◀ Worthington, Bass, Felinfoel Double Dragon, guest ale ♂ Stowford Press. **Facilities** Garden Parking

PORTHGAIN Map 8 SM83

The Sloop Inn

SA62 5BN ☎ 01348 831449 📄 01348 831388
e-mail: matthew@sloop-inn.freeserve.co.uk
dir: Take A487 NE from St David's for 6m. Left at Croesgooch for 2m to Porthgain

Possibly the most famous pub on the North Pembrokeshire Coast, the Sloop Inn is located in beautiful quarrying village of Porthgain. The walls and ceilings are packed with pictures and memorabilia from nearby shipwrecks. The harbour is less than 100 metres from the door and there is a village green to the front and a large south-facing patio. A varied menu includes breakfasts, snacks, pub favourites, steaks from the grill and as much home-caught fish as possible.

Open all day all wk 9.30am-11pm Closed: 25 Dec **Bar Meals** L served all wk 12-2.30 D served all wk 6-9.30 booking required **Restaurant** L served all wk 12-2.30 D served all wk 6-9.30 booking required ⊕ FREE HOUSE ◀ Reverend James, Brains Draught, Felinfoel, IPA. **Facilities** Children's menu Garden Parking

ROSEBUSH Map 8 SN02

Tafarn Sinc

Preseli SA66 7QT ☎ 01437 532214
dir: Please telephone for directions

The looming presence of this large red corrugated-iron free house stands testament to its rapid construction in 1876. Now deserted by the railway it was built to serve, this idiosyncratic establishment boasts wood-burning stoves, a sawdusted floor, and a charming garden. Set high in the Preseli Hills amid stunning scenery, it is popular with walkers, who can stoke up on traditional favourites like home-cooked Glamorgan sausage with chutney, Welsh sirloin steak and chips, faggots and Preseli lamb burgers.

Open all day noon-11 Closed: Mon ex BH & summer **Bar Meals** L served Tue-Sat 12-2 D served Tue-Sat 6-9 **Restaurant** L served Tue-Sat 12-2 D served Tue-Sat 6-9 ⊕ FREE HOUSE ◀ Worthington, Tafarn Sinc, guest ale. **Facilities** Children's menu Dogs allowed Garden Parking

PICK OF THE PUBS

The Stackpole Inn 🍷

STACKPOLE   Map 8 SR99

SA71 5DF
☎ **01646 672324** 📠 **01646 672716**
e-mail: info@stackpoleinn.co.uk
dir: *From Pembroke take B4319 & follow
signs for Stackpole, approx 4m*

Locations don't come much more
exciting than this 17th-century inn. It is
particularly well blessed, standing as it
does in beautiful gardens within the
Pembrokeshire Coast National Park a
mere walk or short drive away from
stunning beaches, cliff faces just made
for climbing, a huge natural arch, a bird
watchers' paradise, and entertaining
things for children to do. In the mellow
stone wall outside is a rare George V
post box, a leftover from when one of the
two original stone cottages was a post
office. It's a freehouse, so there's always
a guest beer from elsewhere in the UK to
accompany three Welsh ales. The bar
surface is made from slate, while the
wood for the ceiling beams came from
ash trees grown on the estate. Warmth
is provided by a wood-burning stove set
within the stone fireplace. Local produce
from the surrounding countryside and
fish from the coast play a major part in
the home-cooked menu. From its lunch
menu come wholetail scampi, chips and
peas; Thai green chicken curry;
spaghetti bolognaise; and a vegetarian
dish of the day. Starters at dinner
include soft-cured chorizo with crusty
bread; chicken liver with toasted
hazelnut and roast garlic parfait; and
pan-seared halloumi on bitter leaf salad
with pickled walnuts and grapes
poached in sauternes. Typical main
courses are locally smoked cheese-filled
breast of organic chicken on pesto
linguine with vine tomato fondue; rack
of Welsh lamb with parsnip beignets,
compote and rosemary jus; king prawn
and cherry tomato Thermidor tossed
with linguine; and caramelised red
onion, sweet potato and gruyère
pithivier with roasted red pepper coulis.
Specials are likely to include local
mackerel, fresh lobster and whole fresh
sea bass.

Closed: Sun eve (winter) 🛢 FREE
HOUSE 🍺 Brains Reverend James,
Felinfoel, Double Dragon, Best Bitter &
Variable guest ale. 🍷 12 **Facilities** Dogs
allowed Garden Parking

ST DOGMAELS — Map 8 SN14

Webley Waterfront Inn & Hotel ♀

Poppit Sands SA43 3LN ☎ **01239 612085**
e-mail: webleyhotel@btconnect.com
dir: A484 from Carmarthen to Cardigan, then to St Dogmaels, right in village centre to Poppit Sands on B4546

From its spectacular location at the start of the Pembrokeshire Coast National Park, the inn offers outstanding views across the River Teifi and Poppit Sands to Cardigan Bay. Being where it is naturally means fresh seafood, with specialities such as line-caught sea bass, dressed crab and lobster, and Teifi sewin (sea trout), while fresh lamb and beef comes from local farms, and organic ice cream from Mary's Farmhouse in nearby Crymych.

Open all wk ⊕ FREE HOUSE ◀ Brains Buckleys Bitter, Worthington, Rev James, DSB, guest ales. ♀ 8
Facilities Dogs allowed Garden Parking

SOLVA — Map 8 SM82

The Cambrian Inn ♀

Main St SA62 6UU ☎ **01437 721210** 🖨 **01437 720661**
e-mail: thecambrianinn@btconnect.com
dir: 13m from Haverfordwest on A487 towards St David's

Something of an institution in this pretty fishing village is a Grade II listed 17th-century inn that attracts local and returning visitors alike. A sample bar menu offers Welsh Black beef curry, vegetable pancakes topped with melted cheese or Welsh sirloin steak, while the carte dinner menu offers lots of fresh fish dishes. Sandwiches, jackets, salads and ploughmans also available.

Open all wk ⊕ FREE HOUSE ◀ Tomas Watkins OSB & Cwrw Braf/Haf, Butty Bach, guest ales. ♀ 15
Facilities Garden Parking

STACKPOLE — Map 8 SR99

PICK OF THE PUBS

The Stackpole Inn ♀

See Pick of the Pubs on opposite page

WOLF'S CASTLE — Map 8 SM92

The Wolfe Inn ♀

SA62 5LS ☎ **01437 741662** 🖨 **01437 741676**
dir: On A40 between Haverfordwest & Fishguard. 7m from both towns

The Wolfe is an oak-beamed, stone-built property in a lovely village setting. The bar-brasserie and restaurant comprise four interconnecting but distinctly different rooms: the Victorian Parlour, Hunters' Lodge, the Brasserie and a conservatory. The inn uses mainly local produce in its 'robust, real food'. Example dishes are fillet of beef Bordelaise, lamb all'aglio e menta, chicken piccante, salmon fillet with cream and Pernod sauce, and mussels in garlic, white wine and cream. Award-winning local cheeses and scrumptious home-made desserts follow.

Open all wk ⊕ FREE HOUSE ◀ Interbrew Worthington Bitter, guest ale. ♀ 11 **Facilities** Garden Parking

POWYS

BERRIEW — Map 15 SJ10

The Lion Hotel

SY21 8PQ ☎ **01686 640452** 🖨 **01686 640604**
e-mail: trudi.jones@btconnect.com
dir: 5m from Welshpool on A483, right to Berriew. In village centre next to church

Behind the black and white timbered grid of this 17th-century family-run coaching inn lie bars and dining areas where yet more old timbers testify to its age. Menus, based on local produce, include loin of venison with wild mushrooms and redcurrant jus, and slow-roasted Welsh lamb shoulder with red wine mint gravy; and a fish board with sea bream, halibut, red snapper and salmon dishes. There is a separate bar area where you can enjoy a pint of real ale from the selection on tap including Banks, Pedigree and Old Empire.

Open all wk noon-3 5-11 (Fri-Sat noon-11 Sun noon-3 6-10.30) **Bar Meals** L served all wk 12-2 D served all wk 6-9 Av main course £12.50 **Restaurant** L served all wk 12-2 D served all wk 6-9 booking required
⊕ MARSTONS ◀ Banks Bitter, Pedigree, Old Empire, guest ales. **Facilities** Children's menu Parking

BRECON — Map 9 SO02

PICK OF THE PUBS

The Felin Fach Griffin ★★★★★ INN ⊛⊛ ♀

Felin Fach LD3 0UB ☎ **01874 620111**
e-mail: enquiries@eatdrinksleep.ltd.uk
dir: 4.5m N of Brecon on A470 (Brecon to Hay-on-Wye road)

This much-feted country inn exemplifies owner Charles Inkin's passion for 'the simple things, done well'. The ethos is applied to food, wines, beers and en suite bedrooms. In the bar are deep leather sofas surrounding a newspaper-strewn table and open fire. Food is served in rambling bare-floored rooms where original features, including an Aga, are teamed with tasteful modern touches. Set on the edge of the Brecon Beacons, the Griffin draws much of its ingredients from the surrounding area, while the garden keeps up a steady flow of organic produce. The all important lunchtime menu includes Gorwydd Caephilly ploughman's with home-made soda bread and pickles, or Welsh pork and leek sausages. The freshest seafood could feature wild halibut fillet with young spring vegetables and fresh creamed morels. Other mains include rack of Herdwick lamb, shepherd's pie and carrot purée, and oak roast salmon on crushed Witchill potato and spinach. Quality draught beers, 20 wines by the glass and beer tasting with the breweries complete the experience.

Open all day all wk 11-11 Closed: 24-25 Dec **Bar Meals** L served Mon-Sat 12.30-2.30, Sun 12-2.30 Av main course £11 **Restaurant** L served Mon-Sat 12.30-2.30, Sun 12-2.30 D served Mon-Sat 6.30-9.30, Sun 6.30-9 Fixed menu price fr £15 Av 3 course à la carte fr £35 ⊕ FREE HOUSE ◀ Breconshire Breweries, Wye Valley Butty Bach ♂ Thatchers. ♀ 20
Facilities Children's menu Dogs allowed Garden Parking **Rooms** 7

BRECON *continued*

The Old Ford Inn

Llanhamlach LD3 7YB ☎ 01874 665391
📠 01874 665391
e-mail: lynxcymru@aol.com
dir: *2.5m from Brecon on A40 towards Abergavenny*

The Old Ford is a 900-year-old inn set in the foothills of the Brecon Beacons, affording outstanding views over the mountains, the River Usk and the canal. The business is family run and offers cosy beamed bars and a cottage-style restaurant serving home-cooked food using local produce. Chef's specials include Old Ford cow pie, with beef, vegetables and ale under a puffed pastry lid; and braised Welsh lamb shank with mint and rosemary sauce. There is a beer garden to relax in when the weather permits.

Closed: 3-6 months winter, Mon **Bar Meals** L served all wk 12-3 booking required D served all wk 6-9 booking required Av main course £8.95 **Restaurant** L served all wk 12-3 booking required D served all wk 6-9 booking required ⊕ FREE HOUSE ◀ Worthington, Guinness. **Facilities** Garden Parking

PICK OF THE PUBS

The Usk Inn ★★★★ INN ◉ ♀

Talybont-on-Usk LD3 7JE
☎ 01874 676251 📠 01874 676392
e-mail: stay@uskinn.co.uk
dir: *6m E of Brecon, just off A40 towards Abergavenny & Crickhowell*

The inn was established in the 1840s, just as the Brecon to Merthyr Railway arrived. In 1878 the locomotive Hercules failed to stop at the former station opposite and crashed into the street, seriously disrupting conversations and beer consumption in the bar. The owner Andrew Felix is making sure you can still partake of interesting food like fried haggis and chilli dressing. This haggis, by the way, is prefixed by the all-important word Celtic. Alternatively, opt for risotto of smoked garlic and porcini mushrooms, then half a honey-roast duck with apricot and tarragon, or a fish special, and home-made treacle tart to finish. The Brecon to Monmouth Canal runs through the village, in some places at rooftop level. Enjoy a stay in one of the en suite bedrooms; one room has a four-poster bed.

Open all day all wk 11am-11.30pm Closed: 25-26 Dec **Bar Meals** D served all wk 12-2.30 **Restaurant** D served all wk 6.30-9.30 ⊕ FREE HOUSE ◀ Hancocks HB, Brains, Guinness, Worthington, Rev James, Gold SA ⬭ Thatchers. ♀ 11 **Facilities** Children's menu Garden Parking **Rooms** 11

PICK OF THE PUBS

The White Swan Inn ♀

See Pick of the Pubs on opposite page

The Old Hand and Diamond Inn

SY5 9AR ☎ 01743 884379 📠 01743 884379
e-mail: moz123@aol.com
web: www.oldhandanddiamond.co.uk
dir: *9m from Shrewsbury*

Set in beautiful countryside close to the River Severn and the Welsh border, this 17th-century inn retains much of its original character. Open winter fires crackle in the beamed interior, whilst outside you'll find a children's play area and a beer garden with plenty of seating on the patio. You can enjoy a pint of Woods Shropshire Lad and Stones Station Bitter. Local produce underpins the extensive restaurant menu, offering dishes like braised haunch of venison with juniper berry and sloe gin, and whole sea bass filled with crab, soy and honey.

Open all day all wk 11am-1am **Bar Meals** L served Mon-Thu 12-2.30, Fri-Sun 12-9.30 D served Mon-Thu 6-9.30, Fri-Sun 12-9.30 Av main course £10.95 **Restaurant** L served Mon-Thu 12-2.30, Fri-Sun 12-9.30 D served Mon-Thu 6-9.30, Fri-Sun 12-9.30 Av 3 course à la carte fr £22 ⊕ FREE HOUSE ◀ Worthington, Shropshire Lad, guest ales. **Facilities** Children's menu Play area Dogs allowed Garden Parking

PICK OF THE PUBS

The Bear Hotel ★★★ HL ◉ ♀

See Pick of the Pubs on page 602

PICK OF THE PUBS

Nantyffin Cider Mill Inn ♀

Brecon Rd NP8 1SG
☎ 01873 810775 📠 01873 810986
e-mail: info@cidermill.co.uk
dir: *At junct of A40 & A479, 1.5m W of Crickhowell*

Originally a drovers' inn, located at the foot of the Black Mountains between Crickhowell and Brecon, the Nantyffin dates from the 16th century. It became well known for the cider it produced in the 19th century and the original cider press, fully working until the 1960s, has been incorporated into the Mill Room Restaurant. These days the Nantyffin is renowned for its successful pairing of traditional pub values with acclaimed French bistro-style food. The bars are full of character and offer a range of ales, draught and bottled Welsh ciders, and a comprehensive wine list. Menus are based on locally sourced produce such as beef, pork, lamb and poultry from a farm only six miles away.

Open noon-3 6-11 Closed: Mon (ex BH), Sun eve Oct-Mar **Bar Meals** L served Tue-Sun 12-2.30 D served Tue-Sun 6.30-9.30 **Restaurant** L served Sun 12-2.30 booking required D served Fri-Sat 6.30-9.30 booking required ⊕ FREE HOUSE ◀ Reverend James, Rhymney Best Bitter, Felinfoel Stout ⬭ Stowford Press, Taffy Apples. ♀ 12 **Facilities** Children's menu Dogs allowed Garden Parking

PICK OF THE PUBS

The White Swan Inn ♇

BRECON
Map 9 SO02

Llanfrynach LD3 7BZ
☎ 01874 665276 📄 01874 665362
dir: *3m E of Brecon off A40, take B4558, follow Llanfrynach signs*

The Brecon Beacons provide an awesome backdrop to this converted row of white-painted stone cottages, which stands opposite the ancient church of St Brynach. Originally a 17th-century coaching inn, it is now an unpretentious gastro-pub with character and atmosphere, featuring stone walls, exposed oak beams, stone-flagged floors, wooden furniture and bar counter, plus log fires, leather sofas, atmospheric lighting, and a warm and cosy feel. Eat in the spacious dining room, or more informally in the bar, which also offers a lighter snack menu and Brains Bitter on handpump. Eat crisp, honest dishes in the

unpretentious gastro-pub mould, all freshly prepared using locally sourced produce - Welsh beef, lamb, pork and venison — with daily fish specials listed on the chalkboard. Lunchtime bar meals begin with home-made open ravioli filled with ham hock and leeks and served with a grain mustard cream, or twice-baked goats' cheese soufflé, and go on to pan-fried pork loin with caramelised red onions and apples and a green peppercorn and cider jus. Evening additions may take in roast scallops with spiced black pudding and a saffron and orange reduction, and chicken liver and foie gras parfait with home-made piccalilli to start, followed by venison with beetroot mash and red wine jus; rump of Welsh lamb with steamed leek and mutton pudding, minted sweet potato purée and a rich lamb jus; or pan-fried supreme of pollack. Puddings take in baked pear, plum and almond Bakewell tart with amaretti anglaise, or try a slate of Welsh cheeses with chutney. There's trout fishing on the nearby Usk, the Monmouthshire and Brecon Canal runs close by, and Brecon, noted for its famous August Jazz Festival, is two miles away.

Closed: 25-26 Dec, 1 Jan, Mon (ex Summer, Dec & BH) ⊕ FREE HOUSE ◀ HB, Brains SA, Brains Smooth, Guinness, Rev James. ♇ 8
Facilities Garden Parking

PICK OF THE PUBS

The Bear Hotel ★★★ HL 🏵 🍷

CRICKHOWELL — Map 9 SO21

Brecon Rd NP8 1BW
☎ 01873 810408 📄 01873 811696
e-mail: bearhotel@aol.com
dir: *On A40 between Abergavenny & Brecon*

The Bear is an ageless classic that has stood hard by the A40 at the heart of this quaint market town since the days of the London to Aberystwyth mail coach. In the Hindmarsh family for over 30 years, who treat all-comers with genuine hospitality, it bristles with personality and honest endeavour, successfully ignoring the passage of time whilst forever staying abreast of the best trends and traditions of good innkeeping. Continual improvements have seen expansion deep into its 15th-century fabric and every available nook and cranny has been put into good use as bar, bistro and restaurant. Front bars, a hive of activity, are resplendent with oak panelling, thick beams, ornamental sideboards, stone walls and

welcoming log fires, while the more formal dining rooms are filled with antiques, candles, fresh flowers and linen-draped tables. Add to this the comfortable bedrooms, divided between the historic inn and the coach house facing the cobbled courtyard, and its fully deserved reputation becomes clear. Cooking is modern British but the trend is towards the wholesome dishes of the past, and top-notch locally sourced ingredients are used to full effect on appealing lunch and dinner menus, bolstered by daily specials, including Brecon lamb, Usk and Wye salmon, Welsh Black beef and local game. The bar menu goes from strength to strength, offering hearty traditional dishes, such as lamb hotpot, daube of beef with mash, cottage pie, faggots with onion gravy and smoked salmon sandwiches, alongside specials like venison pie and chicken casserole. Dinner in the restaurant may take in pan-fried scallops on black pudding with cauliflower purée and tomato salsa, rack of lamb with ratatouille and rosemary jus, or skate with lemon and caper butter, and a classic lemon tart to finish. Accompany with top-class cask ales and well-chosen wines by the glass.

Open 11-3 6-11 **Bar Meals** L served all week 12-2 D served Mon-Sat 6-10, Sun 7-9.30 **Restaurant** L served Sun 12-2 Av 3 course à la carte fr £30 ⊕ FREE HOUSE 🛢 Interbrew Bass, Ruddles Best, Brains Reverend James, John Smiths. 🍷 12 **Facilities** Family room Dogs allowed Garden Parking **Rooms** 34

DYLIFE
Map 14 SN89

Star Inn

SY19 7BW ☎ 01650 521345 📠 01650 521345

dir: *Between Llanidloes & Machynlleth on mountain road*

Situated at 1300 feet in some of Wales' most breathtaking countryside, the inn is in an area favoured by Dylan Thomas and Wynford Vaughn Thomas; red kites swoop overhead, and the magnificent Clywedog reservoir is close by. A varied choice of wholesome pub fare includes cottage pie, big banger and chips, chicken in mushroom cream sauce, and gammon with egg or pineapple. Between November and March the inn is not open for weekday lunch.

Closed: Mon-Fri lunch (winter) ⊕ FREE HOUSE ◀ Tetley Smooth, Abbots. **Facilities** Family room Dogs allowed Parking

GLADESTRY
Map 9 SO25

The Royal Oak Inn ▾

HR5 3NR ☎ 01544 370669 & 370342

e-mail: brianhall@btinternet.com

dir: *4m W of Kington, 10m from Hay-on-Wye on B4594*

The huge inglenook fireplace, heavily beamed ceilings and a flagstone floor set a scene befitting a 400-year-old inn that once welcomed drovers taking store cattle from Wales to England. Offa's Dyke footpath is nearby, and there's an exhilarating four-mile walk from Kington along Hergest Ridge with its breathtaking views. Home-made fare is served in the lounge bar/dining area, including bar snacks, soups, jacket potatoes, sandwiches and salads. A roast is served every Sunday.

Open all wk Oct-Mar reduced hrs **Bar Meals** L served all wk 12-2.30 D served all wk 7-9.30 booking required **Restaurant** L served all wk 12-2.30 D served all wk 7-9.30 booking required ⊕ FREE HOUSE ◀ Brains Reverend James, Butty Bach, S A, Worthingtons Ö Stowford Press. ▾ 8 **Facilities** Children's menu Dogs allowed Garden Parking **Notes** ⊛

HAY-ON-WYE
Map 9 SO24

Kilverts Inn ▾

The Bullring HR3 5AG
☎ 01497 821042 📠 01497 821580

e-mail: info@kilverts.co.uk

dir: *From A438 take B4351 to Hay. Turn right after bridge, left towards park and left again*

In the summer months, be sure to visit this pub's lovely garden, with its lawns, flower beds, pond and fountain. Indoors, there's a timber-framed, olde-worlde style bar offering a range of local beers. Expect robust, generous food, with worldwide influences – typical dishes include grilled goats' cheese with a pesto crust; Kilvert's famous home-made steak and pudding; home-made fisherman's pie and chilli con carne. At the bar there's an impressive selection of ales and ciders. There is an annual beer festival too.

Open all wk **Bar Meals** L served all wk 12.30-2.30 D served all wk 6.30-9 Av main course £8.95 **Restaurant** D served Fri-Sat 6.30-9 ⊕ FREE HOUSE ◀ Wye Valley Butty Bach, The Reverend James, Pedigree, Guest Ales Ö Westons Old Rosie. ▾ 8 **Facilities** Children's menu Family room Dogs allowed Garden Parking

---

PICK OF THE PUBS

The Old Black Lion ★★★★ INN ⊛ ▾

See Pick of the Pubs on page 604

LLANDRINDOD WELLS
Map 9 SO06

The Gold Bell Country Inn

Llanyre LD1 6DX ☎ 01597 823959 📠 01597 825618

e-mail: info@bellcountryinn.co.uk

dir: *1.5m NW of Llandrindod Wells on A4081*

Set in the hills above Llandrindod Wells, this former drovers' inn has been extensively refurbished, creating a smart, modern interior. Two bars and a restaurant serve a range of beers and seasonally changing menus. A meal might include terrine of guinea fowl, organic chicken and woodland mushrooms on brioche followed by pork tenderloin stuffed with cider-soaked apricots, wrapped in ham and served with apple purée and cider sauce. Finish with sticky toffee pudding.

Open all wk noon-2 6-11.30 **Bar Meals** L served all wk 12-2 D served Mon-Sat 6-9 **Restaurant** D served Mon-Sat 6-9 booking required ⊕ FREE HOUSE ◀ Guinness, guest ales. **Facilities** Children's menu Garden Parking

LLANFYLLIN
Map 15 SJ11

Cain Valley Hotel ★★ HL

High St SY22 5AQ ☎ 01691 648366 📠 01691 648307

e-mail: info@cainvalleyhotel.co.uk

dir: *From Shrewsbury & Oswestry follow signs for Lake Vyrnwy & onto A490 to Llanfyllin. Hotel on right*

Family-run coaching inn dating from the 17th century, with a stunning Jacobean staircase, oak-panelled lounge bar and a heavily beamed restaurant with exposed hand-made bricks. A full bar menu is available at lunchtime and in the evening. Local lamb steak with red wine and rosemary sauce, Mediterranean vegetable risotto, prime steak braised in real ale, or tenderloin of pork pan-fried with cider, apples and cream may be on the menu.

Open all day all wk 11.30am-mdnt (Sun noon-11pm) Closed: 25 Dec **Bar Meals** L served all wk 12-2 booking required D served all wk 7-9 booking required **Restaurant** D served all wk 7-9 booking required ⊕ FREE HOUSE ◀ Worthington's, Ansells Mild, Guinness Ö Stowford Press. **Facilities** Children's menu Dogs allowed Parking **Rooms** 13

LLANGATTOCK
Map 9 SO21

The Vine Tree Inn ▾

The Legar NP8 1HG ☎ 01873 810514

dir: *Take A40 W from Abergavenny then A4077 from Crickhowell*

A pretty pink pub on the River Usk, at the edge of the National Park and within walking distance of Crickhowell. The large garden overlooks the river, bridge and Table Mountain. It is predominantly a dining pub serving a comprehensive menu, with traditional roast lunches on Sundays. Tuesdays now feature the weekly Mexican evening, when authentic Latin dishes cooked to order include nachos, spicy bean soup, a choice of fajitas and enchiladas, and chilli con carne.

Open all wk noon-3 6-11 (Sun noon-8) **Bar Meals** L served Mon-Sat 12-3 D served Mon-Sat 6-10 Av main course £9 **Restaurant** Av 3 course à la carte fr £20 ⊕ FREE HOUSE ◀ Fuller's London Pride, Coors, Worthington's, Golden Valley. ▾ 8 **Facilities** Garden Parking

LLANGYNIDR
Map 9 SO11

The Coach & Horses ▾

Cwmcrawnon Rd NP8 1LS ☎ 01874 730245

dir: *A40 from Brecon to Abergavenny, 12m from Brecon. Through Bwlch, pub after bend turn right*

This free house stands just two minutes' walk from the nearby canal moorings. Now under new ownership, the talented chefs offer such dishes as smoked haddock, broccoli and mature cheese tart; roast peppered local venison haunch steak with juniper and redcurrant sauce; slow cooked Welsh lamb shoulder on minted mushy peas; and fillet of hake in crispy Welsh beer batter. There is a beer garden on the side of the canal.

Open all day all wk noon-mdnt (closed Mon in Winter) **Bar Meals** L served all wk 12-2 booking required D served all wk 6-9 booking required Av main course £6.50 **Restaurant** L served Mon-Sat 12-2, Sun 12-4 booking required D served Sun 6-9 booking required Av 3 course à la carte fr £16 ⊕ FREE HOUSE ▾ 6 **Facilities** Children's menu Dogs allowed Garden Parking

PICK OF THE PUBS

The Old Black Lion ★★★★ INN ⊛ ♟

HR3 5AD
☎ **01497 820841**   📄 **01497 822960**
e-mail: info@oldblacklion.co.uk
web: www.oldblacklion.co.uk
dir: *In town centre*

Close to the centre of Hay-on-Wye, this charming old inn dates back in part to the 1300s, although structurally most of it is 17th century. Nearby is the Lion Gate, one of the original entrances to this ancient walled town, with the Brecon Beacons to the west and the Black Mountains to the south. Hay is the world's largest second-hand book

centre, with bookshops at every turn, and it also hosts a renowned annual literary festival. Oliver Cromwell is reputed to have stayed at the inn during the siege of Hay Castle, although he would not have found a teddy bear in his room as guests do today. The oak-timbered bar is furnished with scrubbed pine tables and comfy armchairs - an ideal setting in which to enjoy beers from Rhymney and Wye Valley Breweries (including the latter's Old Black Lion) beside the log-burning stove. The inn has a long-standing reputation for its food, and the pretty dining room overlooking the garden terrace provides the perfect environment for enjoying a meal. Bar favourites include Moroccan lamb with couscous; steak and kidney pie with cabbage, smoked bacon and creamed potatoes; and sea bass fillets on vegetable egg-fried rice with sweet plum sauce. In the restaurant the menu typically offers Gressingham duck

breast on parsnip purée with pink peppercorn sauce; supreme of guinea fowl with spinach, sun-blushed tomatoes and Madeira sauce; and wild mushroom and leek crêpes topped with cheese sauce and Parmesan. An extensive wine list starts at £12.95 for house reds and whites. Accommodation includes rooms in the recently refurbished Coach House.

Open all week Closed: 24-26 Dec
🍺 FREE HOUSE ◀ Old Black Lion Ale, Rhymney Export, General Picton. ♟ 8
Facilities Garden Parking **Rooms** 10

MACHYNLLETH   Map 14 SH70

PICK OF THE PUBS

Wynnstay Hotel ♥

SY20 8AE ☎ **01654 702941** 🖃 **01654 703884**
e-mail: info@wynnstay-hotel.com
dir: At junct A487 & A489. 5m from A470

Famous visitors to this attractive old 18th-century coaching inn have included David Lloyd-George, who addressed the town from the hotel's balcony. Set in the heart of Machynlleth, the Wynnstay is now in the capable hands of brothers Gareth and Paul Johns. Head chef Gareth has created a menu based firmly on good Welsh produce, with French and Italian influences. Drop in to the lively bars for tea, coffee and cakes, or stay for a pint of beer and something more substantial to eat. The light lunch menu features Welsh beef salad with mustard pickle, and vegetable strudel with parsley and garlic dressing. Evening diners might start with Rhydlewis trout and haddock parcel with yoghurt and berry sauce; followed by Pembroke turkey escalope with rosemary and sage dressing and rosti potato. Whinberry curd parfait with raspberry coulis and chocolate risotto is just one of the mouthwatering desserts.

Open all wk noon-4 6-11 **Closed:** 1wk over New Year **Restaurant** L served all wk 12-2 booking required D served all wk 6.30-9 booking required Av 3 course à la carte fr £19.50 ⊕ FREE HOUSE ◀ Greene King IPA, Reverend James, Butty Bach, Guinness. ♥ 6 **Facilities** Children's menu Dogs allowed Parking

MONTGOMERY   Map 15 SO29

PICK OF THE PUBS

Dragon Hotel ★★ HL ◉

SY15 6PA ☎ **01686 668359** 🖃 **0870 011 8227**
e-mail: reception@dragonhotel.com
web: www.dragonhotel.com
dir: A483 towards Welshpool, right onto B4386 then B4385. Behind town hall

In a small quiet town amidst the stunning countryside of the Welsh Marches, this family-run black and white timber-framed coaching inn offers a friendly welcome. An enclosed patio has been created from the former coach entrance, while the bar, lounge and most bedrooms contain beams and masonry allegedly removed from the ruins of Montgomery Castle after Oliver Cromwell destroyed it in 1649. Ales from Wood's

brewery, wines from the Penarth Vineyard and whisky from the Penderyn Distillery are all served at the bar. The hotel prides itself on its use of fresh local produce in the kitchen too. In addition to daily blackboard specials and soups, the bar menu includes warm ciabattas; beef, chicken or vegetarian fajitas; and home-made fish pie. The carte may start perhaps with leek-laced Welsh cakes topped with a Perl Las cheese sauce, and continue with breast of local pheasant wrapped in prosciutto, with blackcurrant jus and honey-roasted vegetables.

Open all wk noon-2 6-11 **Bar Meals** L served all wk 12-2 D served all wk 7-9 Av main course £8 **Restaurant** L served all wk 12-2 booking required D served all wk 7-9 booking required Fixed menu price fr £25 Av 3 course à la carte fr £29 ⊕ FREE HOUSE ◀ Wood Special, Interbrew Bass, guest. **Facilities** Children's menu Dogs allowed Garden Parking **Rooms** 20

NEW RADNOR   Map 9 SO26

PICK OF THE PUBS

Red Lion Inn

Llanfihangel-nant-Melan LD8 2TN
☎ **01544 350220** 🖃 **01544 350220**
e-mail: theredlioninn@yahoo.co.uk
dir: A483 to Crossgates then right onto A44, 6m to pub. 3m W of New Radnor on A44

Old habits die hard here: this ancient drover's inn still provides water, though nowadays it's for hosing down the bike. Next door is one of four churches named after St Michael that encircle the burial place of the last Welsh dragon. According to legend, should anything happen to them the dragon will rise again. The inn has a lounge and a locals' bar, two small restaurants and a sun-trap garden. A broad menu draws extensively on local produce, including herbs from the garden. Mussels, usually served as a starter in white wine, garlic and cream, come from the River Conwy up north. Main courses might include game terrine with Cognac and grape preserve; Welsh Black beef fillet with béarnaise sauce; organic salmon fish cakes; and leek, wild mushroom and chestnut gâteau. Round off with Welsh cheeses and home-made walnut bread.

Open noon-11.30 (Sun noon-7.30) **Closed:** Tue **Bar Meals** L served Mon-Sat 12-3, Sun 12-7.30 D served Mon-Sat 6-11.30, Sun 12-7.30 ⊕ FREE HOUSE ◀ Guest Ales Ď Thatchers. **Facilities** Children's menu Family room Dogs allowed Garden Parking

OLD RADNOR   Map 9 SO25

PICK OF THE PUBS

The Harp

LD8 2RH ☎ **01544 350655** 🖃 **01544 350655**
e-mail: info@harpinnradnor.co.uk
dir: Old Radnor signed off A44 (Kington to New Radnor)

Just yards from Old Radnor's fine parish church of St Stephen you'll find this seemingly untouched village inn with spectacular views over the Radnor countryside. The building is a Welsh longhouse made from local stone and slate, dating back to the 15th century. Open the simple wooden door and you'll step into a cosy lounge and bars with oak beams, open log fires, semi-circular wooden settles, flagstone floors, and lots of guide books to browse through. Pictures of local history adorn the walls. A lively menu, available in the two dining rooms, of modern pub food includes starters such as venison and juniper berry terrine or broccoli and celeriac soup, followed perhaps by spinach and ricotta cannelloni or Welsh Black rump steak with hand cut chips and roasted seasonal vegetables. Deserts range from apple and pear crumble to pannacotta with caramelised clementines. At the bar there's an impressive selection of real ales and ciders.

Open 6-11 (Sat-Sun noon-3 6-11) **Closed:** Mon **Bar Meals** L served Sat-Sun 12-2.30 booking required D served Tue-Sun 6-9 booking required Av main course £11.95 **Restaurant** L served Sat-Sun 12-2.30 booking required D served Tue-Sun 6-9 booking required ⊕ FREE HOUSE ◀ Timothy Taylor, Three Tuns, Hopback, Wye Valley, Hobsons Ď Kingston Rosie, Dunkertons, Stowford Press. **Facilities** Children's menu Dogs allowed Garden Parking

PICK OF THE PUBS

The Castle Coaching Inn

TRECASTLE Map 9 SN82

LD3 8UH
☎ **01874 636354** 📠 **01874 636457**
e-mail:
enquiries@castle-coaching-inn.co.uk
web: www.castle-coaching-inn.co.uk
dir: *On A40 W of Brecon*

A Georgian coaching inn on the old London to Carmarthen coaching route, in the northern part of the Brecon Beacons National Park. Owned and run by John and Val Porter and their son Andrew, the hotel has been carefully restored in recent years, and has lovely old fireplaces and a remarkable bow-fronted bar window. The inn also offers a peaceful terrace and garden. An open log fire burns in the bar throughout the winter, where with a pint of one of the weekly changing real ales or a glass of wine in your hand, you may savour the pub's great atmosphere. Some guests prefer to stay in the bar to eat, where the menu is the same as in the restaurant, but which additionally offers fresh sandwiches, ploughman's, hot filled baguettes and filled jackets. Thus in both locations there will be minestrone or leek and potato soup; smoked haddock topped with ham and tomato in Cheddar cheese sauce; and Japanese-style prawns with sweet chilli dip as starters. There will be main courses of fillet steak with melted Stilton and roasted red onions; supreme of chicken with mushroom, Gruyère and white wine sauce; Welsh lamb chops with rosemary and redcurrant sauce; steak and Guinness pie; chilli con carne with rice and garlic bread; chicken curry served with rice; pan-fried salmon with orange and tarragon; and Mediterranean vegetable bake. And finally, there will be desserts of Dutch apple flan; cool mint fling; banana and Amaretto cheesecake; and treacle sponge pudding and custard.

Open all week noon-3 6-11 (Sun 7-10.30) **Bar Meals** L served Sat-Sun 12-2 D served Mon-Sat 6.30-9, Sun 7-9 Av main course £10 **Restaurant** L served Sat-Sun 12-2 D served Mon-Sat 6.30-9, Sun 7-9 Av 3 course à la carte fr £18 ⊕ FREE HOUSE ◖ Fuller's London Pride, Evan Evan Cwrw, Timothy Taylor Landlord, Spitfire.
Facilities Children's menu Garden Parking

TALGARTH	Map 9 SO13

Castle Inn

Pengenffordd LD3 0EP
☎ 01874 711353 📄 01874 711353
e-mail: castleinnwales@aol.com
dir: 4m S of Talgarth on A479

Named after the Iron Age hill fort that tops the hill behind
it – Castell Dinas, this welcoming inn enjoys a
spectacular location in the heart of the Black Mountains,
in the Brecon Beacons National Park. Numerous walks
and mountain bike routes begin and end at its door,
making it popular with outdoor enthusiasts. With a good
selection of real local ales, substantial pub food includes
sausage and mash and fisherman's pie. The pub also
offers bunkhouse accommodation and a campsite.

Open noon-11.30 Closed: Mon (Nov-Etr) **Bar Meals** L
served Sat-Sun 12-3 D served Wed-Sun 6.30-9 Av main
course £7.95 **Restaurant** L served Sat-Sun 12-3 D served
Wed-Sun 6.30-9 ⊕ FREE HOUSE ◀ Butty Bach, Rhymney
Bitter, Rev James, Hobby Horse, guest ales ♂ Stowford
Press. **Facilities** Children's menu Garden Parking

TALYBONT-ON-USK	Map 9 SO12

Star Inn

LD3 7YX ☎ 01874 676635
dir: Telephone for directions

With its pretty riverside garden, this traditional 250-year-
old inn stands in a picturesque village within the Brecon
Beacons National Park. The pub, unmodernised and with
welcoming fireplace, is known for its constantly changing
range of well-kept real ales, and hosts quiz nights on
Monday and live bands on Wednesday. Hearty bar food
with dishes such as chicken in leek and stilton sauce,
Hungarian pork goulash, traditional roasts, salmon fish
cakes, and vegetarian chilli.

Open all wk ⊕ FREE HOUSE ◀ Felinfoel Double Dragon,
Theakston Old Peculier, Hancock's HB, Bullmastiff Best,
Wadworth 6X, regular guest ales. **Facilities** Dogs allowed
Garden

TRECASTLE	Map 9 SN82

PICK OF THE PUBS

The Castle Coaching Inn

See Pick of the Pubs on opposite page

SWANSEA

REYNOLDSTON	Map 8 SS48

King Arthur Hotel 🍷

Higher Green SA3 1AD
☎ 01792 390775 📄 01792 391075
e-mail: info@kingarthurhotel.co.uk
dir: Just N of A4118 SW of Swansea

A traditional country inn, with real log fires, in a village
lying at the heart of the beautiful Gower Peninsula. Eat in
the restaurant, main bar or family room, choosing main
menu or specials board dishes including seasonal game,
Welsh Black beef, locally caught fish and vegetarian
options. Try whole trout with cockle and laverbread
sauce; crisp garlicky chicken Kiev; or tuna and bean
salad.

Open all day all wk Closed: 25 Dec **Bar Meals** food
served all day **Restaurant** L served all wk 12-2.30 D
served Sun-Thu 6-9, Fri-Sat 6-9.30 ⊕ FREE HOUSE
◀ Felinfoel Double Dragon, Worthington Bitter & Bass,
Tomas Watkins OSB, King Arthur Ale. 🍷 9
Facilities Children's menu Family room Garden Parking

LLANGENNITH	Map 8 SS49

Kings Head NEW ★★★★ INN

SA3 1HX ☎ 01792 386212 📄 01792 386477
e-mail: info@kingsheadgower.co.uk
dir: M4 junct 47, follow signs for Gower A483, 2nd exit at
rndbt, right at lights onto B495 towards Old Walls, left at
fork to Llangennith, pub is on right.

Standing opposite the largest parish church on the Gower
Peninsular and protected by a rough stone wall, the
King's Head has been in the same family since the
1980s. Originally a row of three 17th century buildings,
the interior retains its old beams, exposed stonework and
a large winter fire. Home-cooked pizzas and Thai dishes
are house specialities, with more traditional choices
including home-made burgers; minted salt marsh lamb
pie; and venison and blueberry pie. Look out for the large
collection of whiskies. Comfortable bedrooms are
available in a separate building.

Open all day all wk 9am-11pm (Sun 9am-10.30pm) **Bar
Meals** L served all wk 9-9.30 D served all wk 9-9.30 Av
main course £8 food served all day **Facilities** Children's
menu Dogs allowed Parking **Rooms** 27

COWBRIDGE	Map 9 SS97

PICK OF THE PUBS

Hare & Hounds NEW 🍷

Aberthin CF71 7LG ☎ 01446 774892
e-mail: nicholasmassey@hotmail.com
dir: 1m from Cowbridge

Transformed from a run-down boozer to a popular
dining pub by Nick and Suzanne Massey two years ago,
this 15th-century former mint stands in the pretty
village of Aberthin. The bar remains traditional, a cosy
haven for drinking pints of Ringwood or Pedigree by the
open fire, while the dining room sports a fresh,
contemporary look, with a warm decor and modern
furnishings. Local diners now beat a path to the door
for hearty food prepared from Welsh ingredients, local
and organic where possible. At lunch, tuck into chicken
liver parfait with plum chutney or quail's egg and
bacon salad for starters or a light bite, or a main dish
like cottage pie and gammon, egg and home-made
chips. More imaginative evening dishes may take in
pan-fried venison with fondant potato and roasted
pear jus; braised pork belly with cider apple jus; and
wild mushroom risotto with basil dressing. On fine days
dine alfresco by the stream in the garden.

Open all day all wk noon-mdnt (Mon 4-mdnt Fri-Sat
noon-1am) **Bar Meals** L served Tue-Sat 12-3
Restaurant L served Tue-Sun 12-3 booking required D
served Tue-Sat 6-9 booking required ⊕ MARSTONS
◀ Ringwood Best, Pedigree. 4 guests ♂ Thatchers
Gold. 🍷 11 **Facilities** Children's menu Family room
Dogs allowed Garden Parking **Notes** ⊛

Victoria Inn

Sigingstone CF71 7LP
☎ 01446 773943 📄 01446 776446
dir: Off B4270 in Sigingstone

A quiet, attractively furnished old village inn with a fine
reputation for good quality home-prepared food. The
beamed interior, decorated with old photographs, prints
and antiques, has a good feel about it. The daily menu is
extensive, with some 40 different dishes on offer, plus
specials and vegetarian boards, and the likes of red
snapper, sea bass, salmon and more. Tomos Watkins
Bitter is brewed in Swansea.

Open all wk ⊕ FREE HOUSE ◀ Tomos Watkins Best
Bitter, Hancocks HB, Worthington Creamflow.
Facilities Garden Parking

PICK OF THE PUBS

Blue Anchor Inn ♉

EAST ABERTHAW — Map 9 ST06

CF62 3DD
☎ 01446 750329 📠 01446 750077
web: www.blueanchoraberthaw.com
dir: *From Barry take A4226, then B4265 towards Llantwit Major. Follow signs, turn left for East Aberthaw. 3m W of Cardiff Airport*

This pretty inn has a history spanning some 700 years, having first opened its doors for business in 1380. It has been trading almost continuously since, the only break being in 2004 when a serious fire destroyed the top half of the building, forcing its closure for restoration. The grandfather of the present owners, Jeremy and Andrew Coleman, acquired the property in 1941, when he bought it from a large local estate. Legend has it that this stone-built and heavily thatched inn has an underground passage leading down to the shore, once used by the wreckers and smugglers who roamed this once-wild coastline. The interior comprises a warren of small rooms separated by thick walls, low, beamed ceilings, and a number of open fires, including a large inglenook. A good selection of regional real ales is always on tap and an enticing range of food is offered in both the bar and the upstairs restaurant. Staying downstairs in the bar, expect starters such as chorizo, wild mushroom salad and poached egg; River Exe steamed mussels; and truffled macaroni cheese; then follow with a main course of lamb and mint sausages with butter mash and onion gravy; or aubergine and sweet potato curry. In the restaurant, find pan-seared wood pigeon with pickled walnut, celeriac and beetroot salad; and tomato fondue, wild mushroom and aubergine bake to start, followed by maize-fed chicken supreme with sweetcorn purée and Madeira cream sauce; rump of Welsh lamb with honey-roasted chantenay carrots and red wine jus; and fresh fish, such as monkfish tail alla gremolata with tomato, garlic and orange sauce; and pan-fried red mullet with mussel and saffron linguine. Desserts are well exemplified by iced blackcurrant and clotted cream bavarois, and baked lemon and sultana cheesecake.

Open all week 11-11 (25 Dec noon-2)
Bar Meals L served Mon-Sat 12-2
D served Mon-Fri 6-9 Av main course £8
Restaurant L served Sun 12.30-2.30
D served Mon-Sat 7-9.30 Fixed menu price fr £10.50 Av 3 course à la carte fr £22 ⊕ FREE HOUSE ◀ Theakston Old Peculier, Wadworth 6X, Wye Valley Hereford Pale Ale, Brains Better. ♉ 7
Facilities Dogs allowed Garden Parking

EAST ABERTHAW Map 9 ST06

PICK OF THE PUBS

Blue Anchor Inn

See Pick of the Pubs on opposite page

MONKNASH Map 9 SS97

he Plough & Harrow

F71 7QQ ☎ 01656 890209
-mail: info@theploughmonknash.com
r: *M4 junct 35 take dual carriageway to Bridgend. At ıbt follow St Brides sign, then brown tourist signs. Pub m NW of Llantwit Major*

a peaceful country setting on the edge of a small llage with views across the fields to the Bristol hannel, this low, slate-roofed, 14th-century building as originally built as the chapter house of a monastery, though it has been a pub for 500 of its 600-year xistence. Expect an atmospheric interior, open fires, real ders, up to eight guest ales on tap, and home-cooked ood using fresh local ingredients. Great area for walkers.

pen all wk noon-11 **Bar Meals** L served all wk 12-2.30 D erved all wk 6-9 Av main course £7.50 **Restaurant** L erved all wk 12-2.30 D served all wk 6-9 Fixed menu rice fr £9 Av 3 course à la carte fr £18 FREE HOUSE Archers Goldon, Shepherd Neame Spitfire, Hereford ale ale, Sharp's IPA, Bass, guest ales Black Dragon, ery Fox, Barnstormer. **Facilities** Children's menu Garden arking

ST HILARY Map 9 ST07

PICK OF THE PUBS

The Bush Inn

CF71 7DP ☎ 01446 772745
e-mail: bush@artizanleisure.com
dir: *S of A48, E of Cowbridge*

Built in the 16th century, this thatched village pub in the Garden of Wales displays bare stone walls, flagstone floors, original oak beams and a huge fireplace beside which a stone spiral staircase leads to the first floor. An interesting former customer was Edward Williams, a charlatan who died in 1826, having established a faux 'Welsh' ceremony that has become the premier artistic event in Wales, the National Eisteddfod. Bar menus offer choices of light bites, sandwiches and salads, chargrilled steaks, a fresh fish special of the day and vegetarian options. A typical restaurant menu may include glazed Pant Ysgawn goats' cheese with tomato and basil salad and balsamic reduction; slow-roasted shank of salt marsh lamb with swede mash and rosemary potatoes; and sticky apricot pudding with clotted cream. French windows lead out from the pretty restaurant to the garden. In the bar, drink Hancock's HB and Weston's Old Rosie scrumpy cider.

Open all day all wk **Bar Meals** L served all wk 12-2.30 D served all wk 6.30-9.30 Av main course £12 **Restaurant** L served all wk 12.30-2.30 D served all wk 6.30-9.30 Av 3 course à la carte fr £27 PUNCH TAVERNS Hancock's HB, Greene King Abbot Ale, Interbrew Worthington Bitter & Bass, guest ale Westons Old Rosie. 10 **Facilities** Dogs allowed Garden Parking

WREXHAM

GRESFORD Map 15 SJ35

PICK OF THE PUBS

Pant-yr-Ochain

Old Wrexham Rd LL12 8TY
☎ 01978 853525 01978 853505
e-mail: pant.yr.ochain@brunningandprice.co.uk
dir: *From Chester take exit for Nantwich. Holt off A483. Take 2nd left, also signed Nantwich Holt. Turn left at 'The Flash' sign. Pub 500yds on right*

A sweeping drive lined by majestic trees leads to this 16th-century, decoratively gabled manor house overlooking a lake and award-winning gardens. The interior fulfils this initial promise, with an inglenook fireplace, wattle and daub walls, and a host of nooks and crannies. A daily changing menu offers starters of smoked chicken, mango and cashew salad; Moroccan couscous with chargrilled vegetable and chickpea salad; and sea bass tempura with avocado salsa. Among the wealth of main courses, try spinach with butternut squash and Shropshire Blue filo pie with gazpacho dressing; shoulder of lamb with herb mash, garlic and mint gravy; battered haddock with mushy peas and hand-cut chips; and game and steak suet pudding with red wine sauce. Follow with mango fool and shortbread; or Welsh and English cheeses. There are also plenty of light bites, sandwiches and ploughman's. The bar dispenses Weetwood Eastgate real ale and Taffy Apples strong cider.

Open all wk noon-11.30 (Sun noon-11) Closed: 25 Dec **Bar Meals** Av main course £10.20 food served all day **Restaurant** Av 3 course à la carte fr £22 food served all day BRUNNING & PRICE Timothy Taylor Landlord, Interbrew Flowers Original, Thwaites Original, Weetwood Eastgate, Ruddles County Stonehouse, Taffy Apples. 22 **Facilities** Garden Parking

HANMER Map 15 SJ43

The Hanmer Arms NEW ★★★★ INN

SY13 3DE ☎ 01948 830532 01948 830740
e-mail: hanmerarms@brconnect.com
web: www.hanmerarms.co.uk
dir: *Between Wrexham & Whitchurch on A539, off A525*

Standing beside the parish church in a peaceful, rural location on the borders of Shropshire, Wales and Cheshire, this traditional inn is the heart of the community. Locals fill the beamed and wooden floored bars, warmed by log fires, for pints of local Stonehouse Cambrian Gold, and plates of pork terrine with home-made chutney, lamb rump with mustard mash and thyme gravy, and sticky toffee pudding. Contemporary-styled rooms, including a loft suite, provide a good touring base.

Open all day all wk **Bar Meals** L served all wk 12-2.30 D served all wk 6-9.30 Av main course £11 **Restaurant** L served Mon-Sat 12-2.30, Sun 12-9 D served all wk 6-9.30 Fixed menu price fr £11.95 Av 3 course à la carte fr £20 FREE HOUSE Timothy Taylor, Adnams, Stonehouse Stowford Press. 12 **Facilities** Children's menu Dogs allowed Garden Parking **Rooms** 12

LLANARMON DYFFRYN CEIRIOG Map 15 SJ13

PICK OF THE PUBS

The Hand at Llanarmon INN ◉ ☻

LL20 7LD ☎ 01691 600666 📄 01691 600262
e-mail: reception@thehandhotel.co.uk
web: www.thehandhotel.co.uk
dir: *Exit A5 at Chirk follow B4500 for 11m. Through Ceiriog Valley to Llanarmon D C. Pub straight ahead*

Built beside the old drovers' road from London to Anglesey, this 16th-century farmhouse was a natural stopping place for drovers and their flocks. Yet The Hand only became a fully-fledged inn as recently as the late 1950s, and it still retains its original oak beams and large fireplaces. Make the journey up the remote Ceiriog Valley, and you'll find a classic country inn with a unique dining room and 13 comfortable en suite bedrooms. Chef Grant Mulholland has built a strong reputation for superb cuisine, and the pub menu includes traditional favourites such as traditional ploughman's with Welsh cheeses and home-made bread; as well as hot dishes like gammon, eggs and chips. Restaurant diners can expect starters like grilled red mullet with celeriac and ginger purée; followed, perhaps, by leg of Welsh lamb with cranberries and red wine. Desserts are just as inviting; try sticky date pudding, or honey and cranberry pannacotta.

Open all wk **Bar Meals** L served Mon-Sat 12-2.20, Sun 12.30-2.45 booking required D served all wk 6.30-8.45 booking required **Restaurant** L served Mon-Sat 12-2.20, Sun 12.30-2.45 booking required D served all wk 6.30-8.45 booking required ⊕ FREE HOUSE ◄ Worthington Cream Flow, Guinness, guest ale. ☻ 7 **Facilities** Children's menu Dogs allowed Garden Parking **Rooms** 13

PICK OF THE PUBS

West Arms INN ◉◉ ☻

LL20 7LD ☎ 01691 600665 📄 01691 600622
e-mail: gowestarms@aol.com
dir: *Leave A483 at Chirk, follow signs for Ceiriog Valley B4500, 11m from Chirk*

Take slate-flagged floors, ancient timberwork, inglenooks and open fires. Add some period furniture and warm hospitality, and the precious traditions of this 17th-century drovers' inn are kept well and truly alive. Long ago the drovers would come down from the Welsh hills by way of three tracks that converged here. After resting for the night they continued their slow, arduous journeys to markets in Chirk, Oswestry, Wrexham and as far away as London. Award-winning chef Grant Williams has travelled too, working in kitchens around the world, appearing on several TV cookery programmes, and even cooking for Prince Charles. Grant's seafood dishes are sheer indulgence: grilled fillets of Dover sole with thyme-roasted asparagus; truffled scallops with Anglesey lobster; grilled rosettes of sole and wild River Dee smoked salmon. Or you can simply relax outside with a pint, view the Berwyn mountains, and lose track of time as the Ceiriog River burbles away in the valley. Comfortable accommodation is available.

Open all day all wk noon-11pm **Bar Meals** L served all wk 12-2 D served all wk 7-9 ⊕ FREE HOUSE ◄ Flowers IPA, Guinness, guest ales. ☻ 11 **Facilities** Dogs allowed Garden Parking **Rooms** 15

MARFORD Map 15 SJ35

Trevor Arms Hotel ☻

LL12 8TA ☎ 01244 570436 📄 01244 570273
e-mail: info@trevorarmsmarford.fsnet.co.uk
dir: *Off A483 onto B5102 then right onto B5445 into Marford*

The early 19th-century coaching inn takes its name from Lord Trevor of Trevallin, who was killed in a duel; public executions, both by beheading and hanging, took place in the village. Grisly history notwithstanding, today's Trevor Arms is a charming hostelry, offering a selection of real ales and a varied menu. Bar specials may include deep-fried breaded plaice; minted lamb steak with home-made chips; or braised steak cooked in a rich mushroom and red wine gravy.

Open all wk ⊕ SCOTTISH COURAGE ◄ Greenalls, Bombardier, John Smiths, Morland Old Speckled Hen, 2 guest ales. ☻ 12 **Facilities** Play area Family room Garden Parking

How to Find a Pub in the Atlas Section

Pubs are located in the gazetteer under the name of the nearest town or village. If a pub is in a small village or rural area, it may appear under a town within fives miles of its actual location. The black dots and town names shown in the atlas refer to the gazetteer location in the guide. Please use the directions in the pub entry to find the pub on foot or by car. If directions are not given, or are not clear, please telephone the pub for details.

Key to County Map

The county map shown here will help you identify the counties within each country. You can look up each county in the guide using the county names at the top of each page. Towns featured in the guide use the atlas pages and index following this map.

England

1 Bedfordshire
2 Berkshire
3 Bristol
4 Buckinghamshire
5 Cambridgeshire
6 Greater Manchester
7 Herefordshire
8 Hertfordshire
9 Leicestershire
10 Northamptonshire
11 Nottinghamshire
12 Rutland
13 Staffordshire
14 Warwickshire
15 West Midlands
16 Worcestershire

Scotland

17 City of Glasgow
18 Clackmannanshire
19 East Ayrshire
20 East Dunbartonshire
21 East Renfrewshire
22 Perth & Kinross
23 Renfrewshire
24 South Lanarkshire
25 West Dunbartonshire

Wales

26 Blaenau Gwent
27 Bridgend
28 Caerphilly
29 Denbighshire
30 Flintshire
31 Merthyr Tydfil
32 Monmouthshire
33 Neath Port Talbot
34 Newport
35 Rhondda Cynon Taff
36 Torfaen
37 Vale of Glamorgan
38 Wrexham

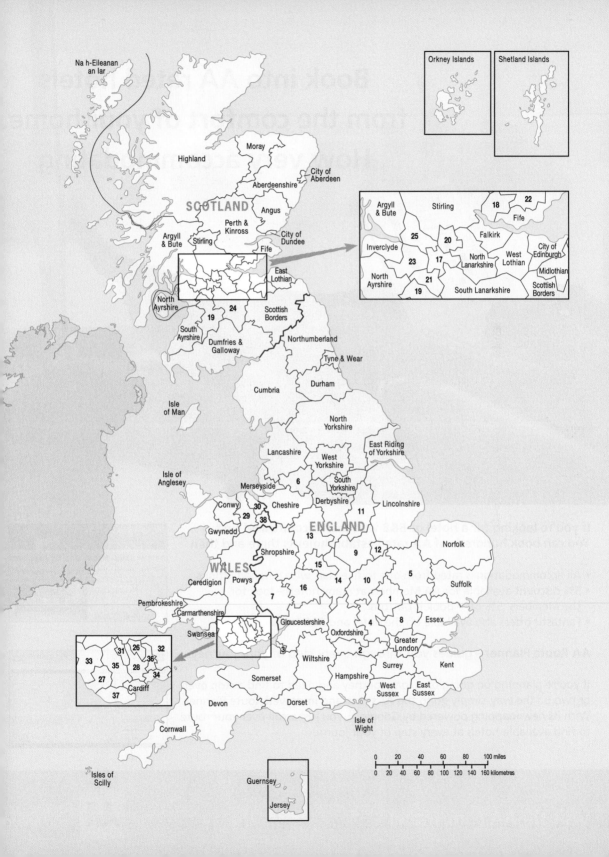

Book into AA rated hotels from the comfort of your home. How very accommodating

If you're looking for a hotel or B&B visit theAA.com/travel first. You can book hundreds of AA rated establishments there and then

- All accommodation is rated from one to five stars with detailed listings
- 5% discount available for AA Members at many hotels – look for the Members' 5% off – book it buttons
- Fantastic offers also available on the hotel and B&B homepage

AA Route Planner – guides you through every step of your journey

If you're planning on going on a long journey and need to find a stop over or two on the way, simply go to the AA's new and improved Route Planner. With its new mapping powered by Google™, you just scroll over your route to find available hotels at every step of your journey.

Visit **theAA.com/travel**

For the road ahead

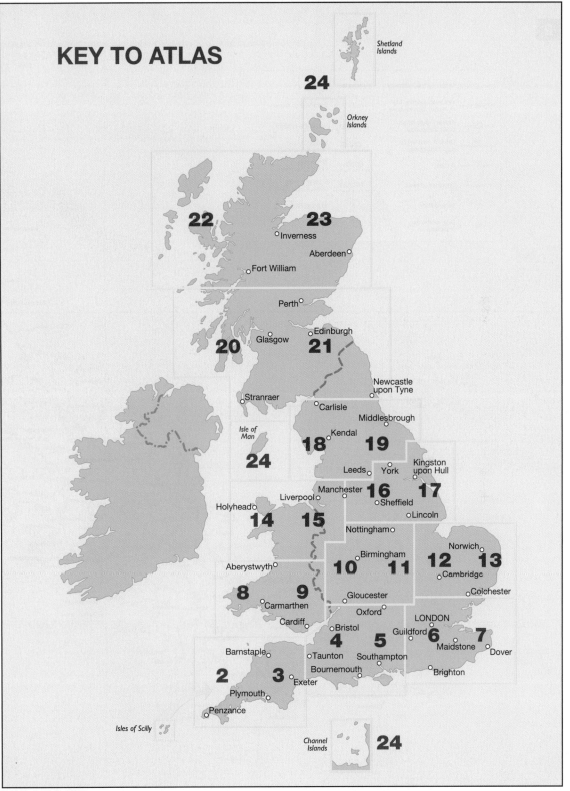

KEY TO ATLAS

Shetland
Islands

24

Orkney
Islands

22

23

Inverness

Aberdeen

Fort William

Perth

20

Glasgow

Edinburgh

21

Stranraer

Newcastle
upon Tyne

Carlisle

Middlesbrough

Isle of
Man

Kendal

18

19

24

Leeds

York

Kingston
upon Hull

Liverpool

Manchester

16

17

Holyhead

Sheffield

Lincoln

14

15

Nottingham

Norwich

Aberystwyth

Birmingham

12

13

10

11

Cambridge

8

9

Gloucester

Colchester

Carmarthen

Oxford

LONDON

Cardiff

Bristol

Guildford

6

7

Barnstaple

4

5

Maidstone

Taunton

Southampton

Dover

2

3

Bournemouth

Brighton

Exeter

Plymouth

Penzance

Isles of Scilly

Channel
Islands

24

2

═══ M6 ═══	Motorway/toll motorway
═══	Motorway junction full/restricted. Service area
A30	Primary route single/dual carriageway
A34	Other A road single/dual carriageway
B3400	B road
	Unclassified road
– V –	Vehicle ferry
– C –	Fast vehicle ferry or catamaran
● Oundle	Pub/Inn
○ King's Cliffe	Town/Village name
	National boundary
ESSEX	English county name & boundary
CONWY	Welsh county name & boundary
MORAY	Scottish county name & boundary
	National Park

ISLES OF SCILLY

Bryher · New Grimsby · Tresco · St Martin's · Higher Town · Hugh Town · St Mary's · Middle Town · Old Town · St Agnes

ISLES OF SCILLY (ST MARY'S)

SV

SW

Lundy

Hartland Point
Hartla

Morwenstow

Kilkhampt

Bude
Bay
Bude
Widemouth Bay

Crackington Haven
Week
St Mar

Boscastle
Tintagel
Trebarwith
Delabole
Camelford
Port Isaac · Port Gaverne
Polzeath
Pendoggett
St Breward · Bolvento
St Tudy · BODMIN MOOR
Harlyn · Rock
St Merryn · Padstow · Blisland
Porthcothan · Wadebridge
Dunmere · Bodmin · St Neot · St Clee
CORNWALL
Mawgan Porth · St Mawgan · St Columb Major · Lanivet · Dobwalls
Newquay · Roche · Lanlivery · St Keyne
West Pentire · Bugle · Lostwithiel · Duloe
Cubert · St Blazey · Tywardreath · Pelynt
Perranporth · Mitchell · Summercourt · St Austell · Bodinnick
Ladock · St Stephen · Polkerris · Fowey · Polperro
St Agnes · Marazanvose · Polruan
Porthtowan · Grampound · Pentewan
Portreath · St Day · Truro · St Ewe · Mevagissey
Gwithian · Malpas · Ruan Lanihorne · Tregony · Gorran Haven
St Ives · Redruth · Carnon Downs · Feock · Veryan · Portloe
Zennor · Camborne · St Just-in-Roseland · Portscatho
Lelant · Hayle · Mylor Bridge · Penryn · Portscatho
Ludgvan · Falmouth · St Mawes
Marazion · Goldsithney · Constantine · Mawnan Smith
St Just · Penzance · Perranuthnoe · Helston · Gweek
Newlyn · Praa Sands · Porthleven · Manaccan
Land's End · Sennen · St Buryan · Mousehole · St Keverne
Porthcurno · Treen · Lamorna · Gunwalloe
Mullion
Coverack
Lizard · Cadgwith
Lizard Point

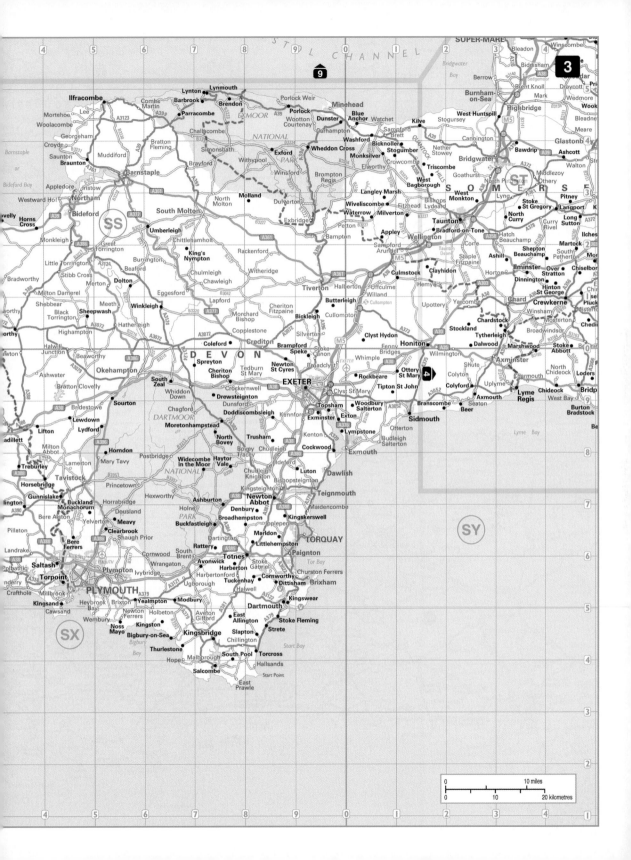

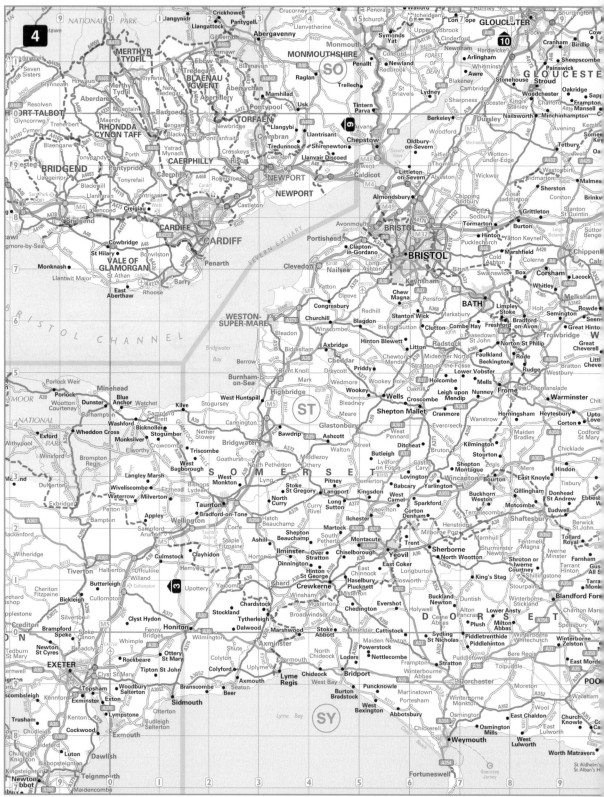

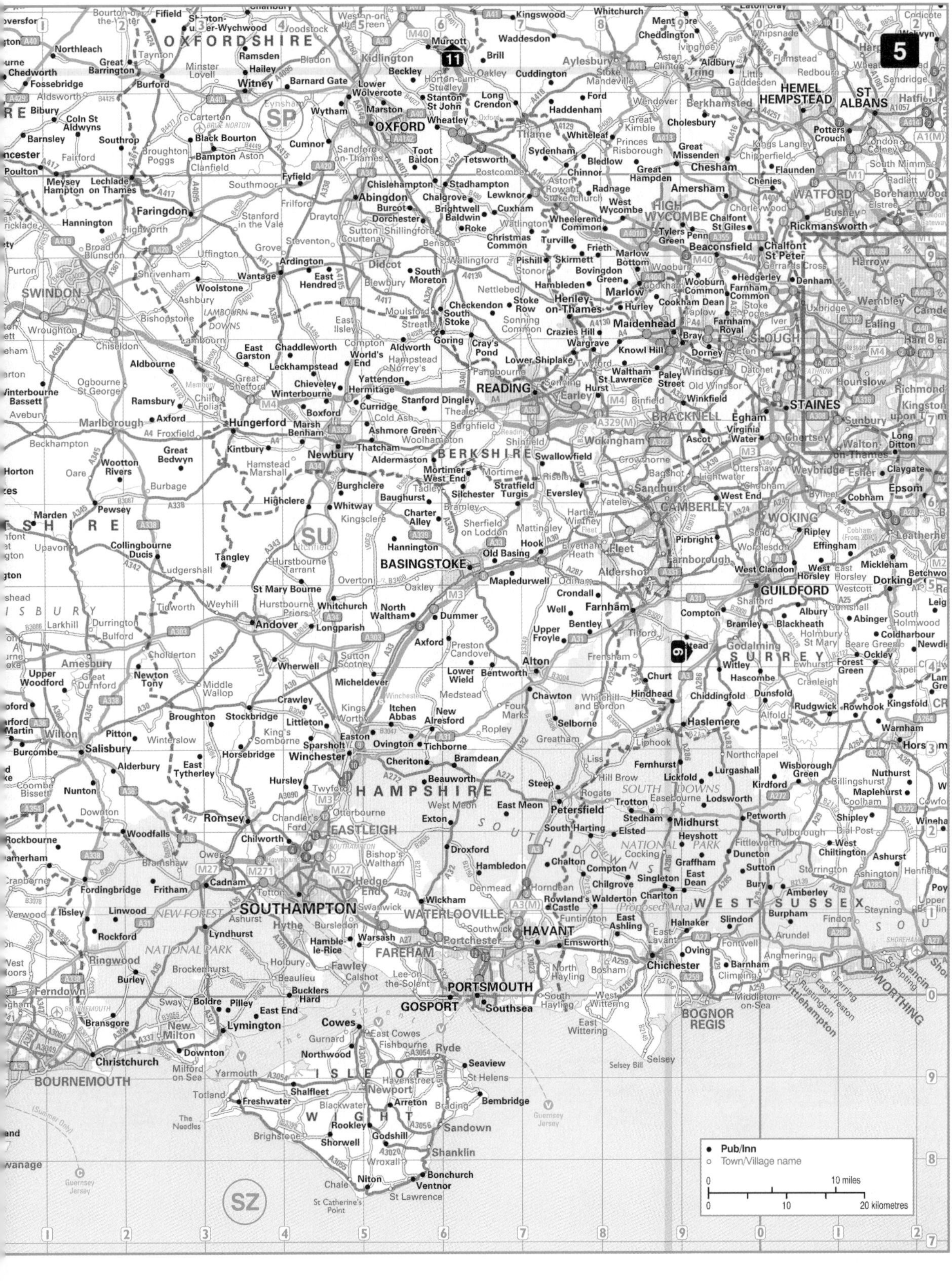

5

Pub/Inn
Town/Village name

0   10 miles
0   10   20 kilometres

OXFORDSHIRE
BERKSHIRE
HAMPSHIRE
SURREY
WEST SUSSEX
ISLE OF WIGHT

OXFORD
READING
BASINGSTOKE
SOUTHAMPTON
PORTSMOUTH
GUILDFORD
WINCHESTER
SALISBURY
ANDOVER
NEWBURY
BOURNEMOUTH
CHRISTCHURCH
ST ALBANS
HEMEL HEMPSTEAD
WATFORD
HIGH WYCOMBE
SLOUGH
STAINES
BRACKNELL
CAMBERLEY
WOKING
EASTLEIGH
WATERLOOVILLE
HAVANT
FAREHAM
GOSPORT
PORTSMOUTH
SOUTHSEA
COWES
NEWPORT
RYDE
SANDOWN
SHANKLIN
VENTNOR
CHICHESTER
BOGNOR REGIS
WORTHING

SP SU SZ

11
6

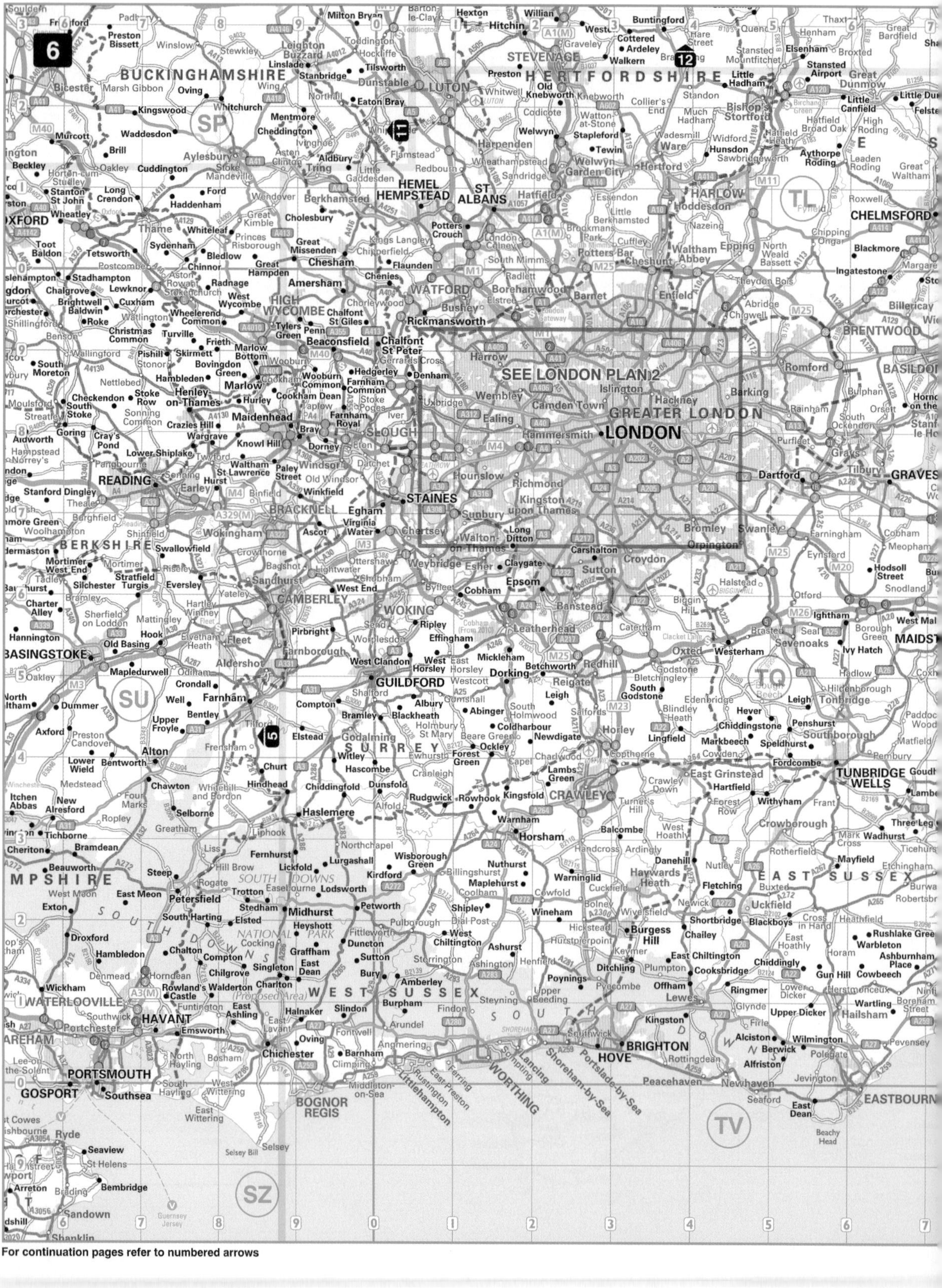

For continuation pages refer to numbered arrows

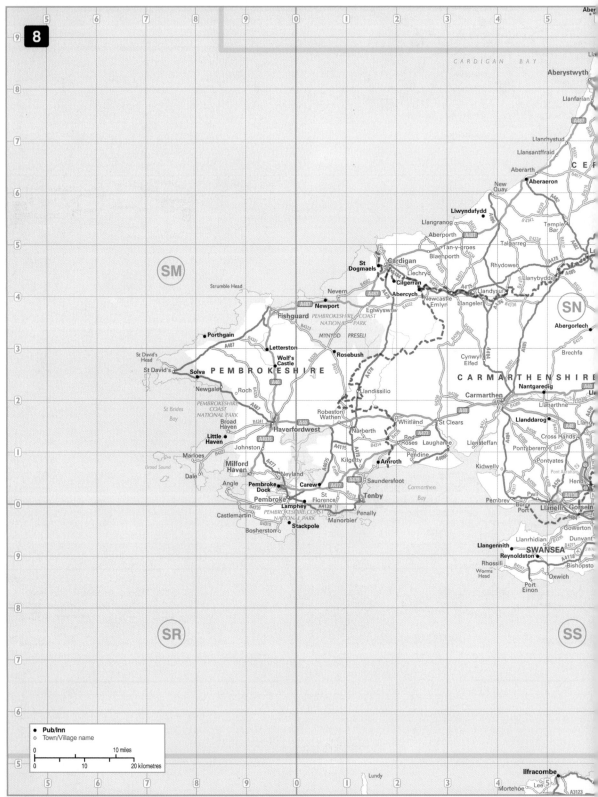

CARDIGAN BAY

Aberystwyth

Llanfarian

Llanrhystud

Llansantffraid

Aberarth

New Quay

Aberaeron

CEF

Llwyndafydd

Llangranog

Aberporth

Tan-y-groes

Blaenporth

Temple Bar

Talgarreg

Rhydower

Llanybydder

Cardigan

St Dogmaels

Llechryd

Cilgerran

Abercych

Newcastle Emlyn

Nevern

Eglwyswrw

Langeler

Llandysul

SN

Abergorlech

SM

Strumble Head

Fishguard

Newport

PEMBROKESHIRE COAST NATIONAL PARK

MYNYDD PRESELI

Cynwyl Elfed

Brechfa

Porthgain

Letterston

Wolf's Castle

Rosebush

CARMARTHENSHIRE

St David's Head

St David's

Solva

PEMBROKESHIRE

Llandissilio

Carmarthen

Nantgaredig

Llanarthne

Newgale

Roch

Llanddarog

St Brides Bay

PEMBROKESHIRE COAST NATIONAL PARK

Broad Haven

Robeston Wathen

Whitland

St Clears

Cross Hands

Pontyberem

Haverfordwest

Narberth

Red Roses

Laugharne

Llansteffan

Pontyates

Little Haven

Johnston

Kilgetty

Pendine

Kidwelly

Broad Sound

Marloes

Milford Haven

Neyland

Dale

Angle

Pembroke Dock

Carew

Saundersfoot

Pembroke

St Florence

Amroth

Tenby

Pembrey

Pwll

Llanelli

Gorsein

Lamphey

Penally

Carmarthen Bay

Burry Port

Castlemartin

Manorbier

PEMBROKESHIRE COAST NATIONAL PARK

Bosherston

Stackpole

Gowerton

Dunvant

Llanrhidian

SWANSEA

Llangennith

Reynoldston

Rhossili

Bishopsto

Worms Head

Oxwich

Port Einon

SR

SS

● Pub/Inn
○ Town/Village name

0   10 miles
0   10   20 kilometres

Lundy

Ilfracombe

Mortehoe   Lee

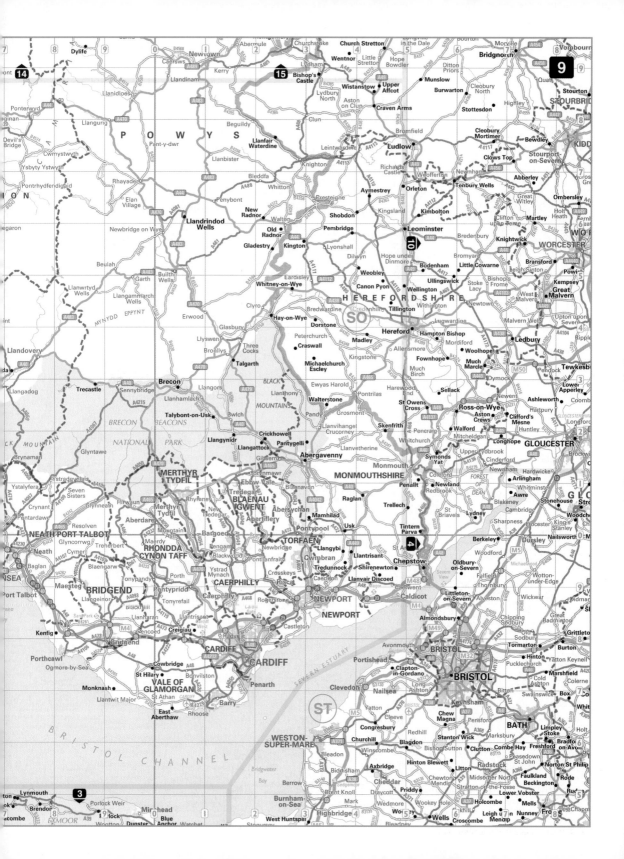

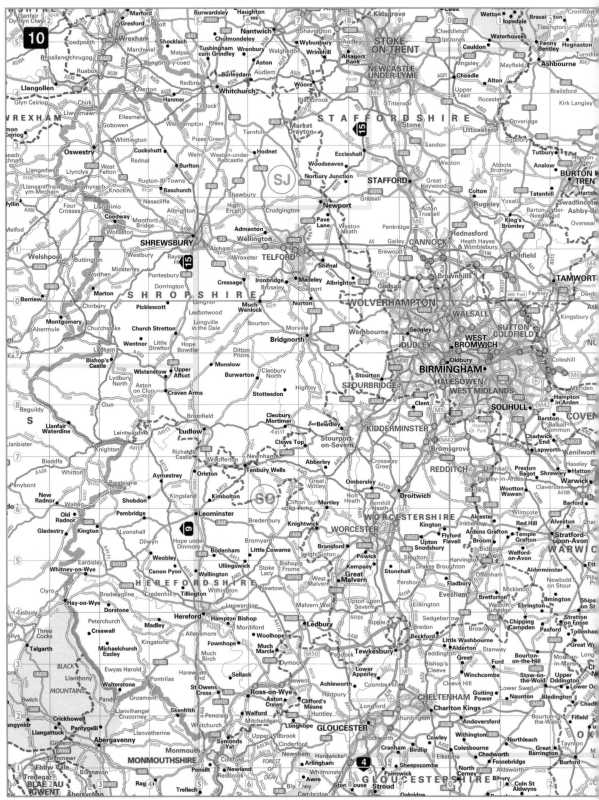

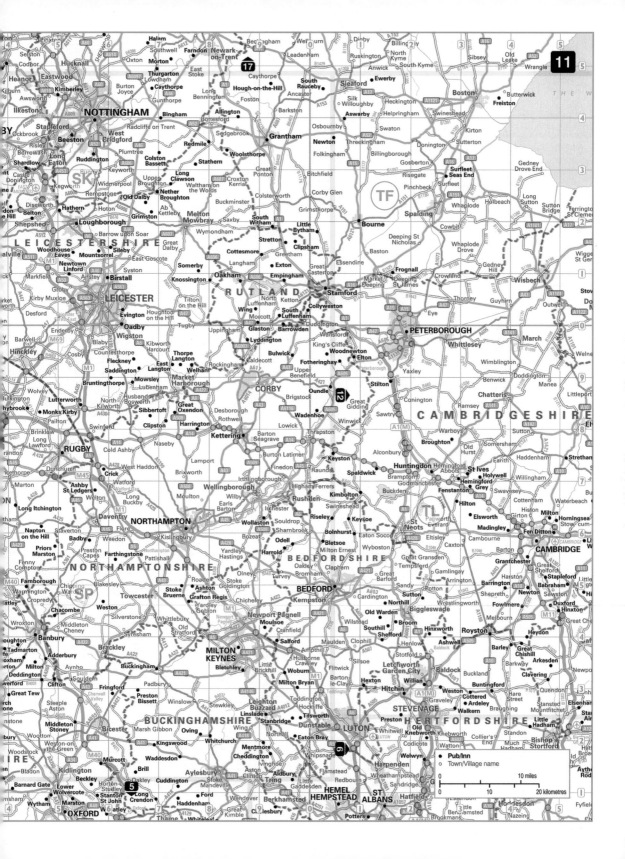

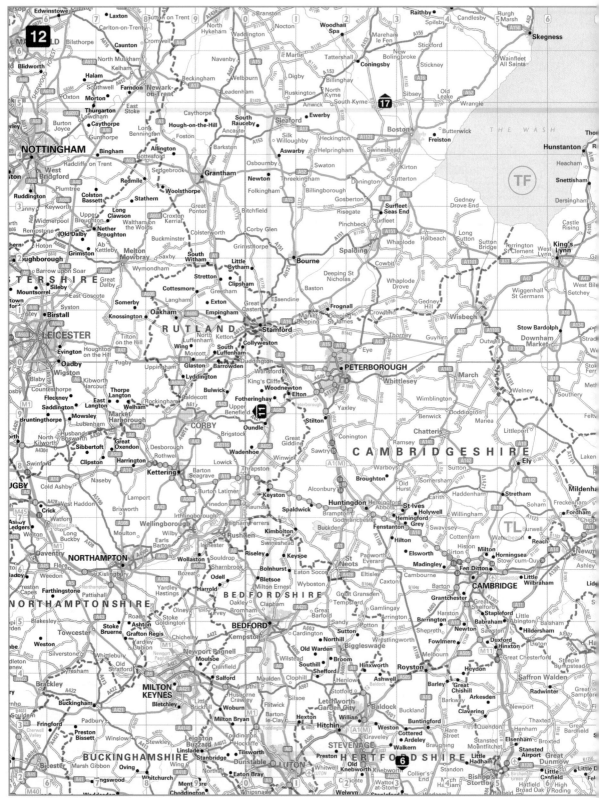

13

Legend:
- ● Pub/Inn
- ○ Town/Village name

0 ─── 10 miles
0 ─── 10 ─── 20 kilometres

Pub/Inn
Town/Village name

0   10 miles
0   10   20 kilometres

ISLE OF
ANGLESEY

Cemaes
Amlwch
Llanerchymedd
Holyhead
Llanfachraeth
Benllech
Red Wharf Bay
Llandudno
Rhôs-on-Sea
Colwyn Bay
Llanddulas
Trearddur Bay
Pentraeth
Langoed
Deganwy
Llandudno Junction
Holy Island
Penmaenmawr
Conwy
Llansantffraid Glan Conwy
Llangefni
Beaumaris
Rhosneigr
Menai Bridge
Bangor
Llanfairfechan
Betws-yn-Rhos
Llanfair P G
Llanfairpwll
Llanllechid
Tal-y-Cafn
Aberffraw
Y Felinheli
Bethesda
Tal-y-Bont
Llangernyw
Llanfair Talhaiarn
Newborough
Caernarfon
Llanrug
Trefriw
Llanrwst
Bylch
Bontnewydd
Llanberis
CONWY
Waunfawr
Capel Curig
Llandwrog
Llanwnda
Betws-y-Coed
Caernarfon Bay
Penygroes
Rhyd-Ddu
Dolwyddelan
Pentrefoelas
Clynnog-fawr
Nantgwynant
Penmachno
Cerrigydrudion
Llanaelhaearn
SNOWDONIA
Beddgelert
SH
Blaenau Ffestiniog
Morfa Nefyn
Prenteg
Ffestiniog
Nefyn
Tremadog
Maentwrog
LLEYN PENINSULA
Bodfuan
Llanystumdwy
Porthmadog
Renrhyndeudraeth
Tudweiliog
Criccieth
Borth-y-Gest
Talsarnau
NATIONAL
Bala
Sarn
Pwllheli
Trawsfynydd
GWYNEDD
Llanbedrog
Harlech
Llanuwchllyn
Y Rhiw
Abersoch
PARK
Aberdaron
Llanbedr
Ganllwyd
Bardsey Island
Dyffryn Ardudwy
Tal-y-bont
Barmouth
Dolgellau
Dinas-Mawddwy
Fairbourne
Mallwyd
Llwyngwril
Corris
Cemmaes Road
Llanbrynm
Bryncrug
Pennal
Tywyn
Machynlleth
Carno
SN
Aberdyfi
Dylife
Borth
Tal-y-bont
CARDIGAN BAY
Llandre
Llanidloes
Aberystwyth
Capel Bangor
Ponterwyd
9

For continuation pages refer to numbered arrows

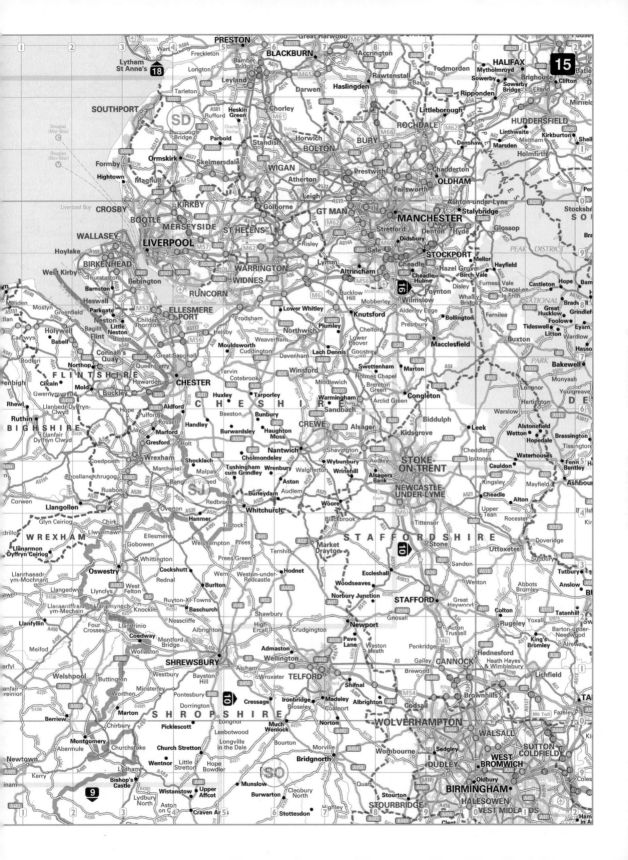

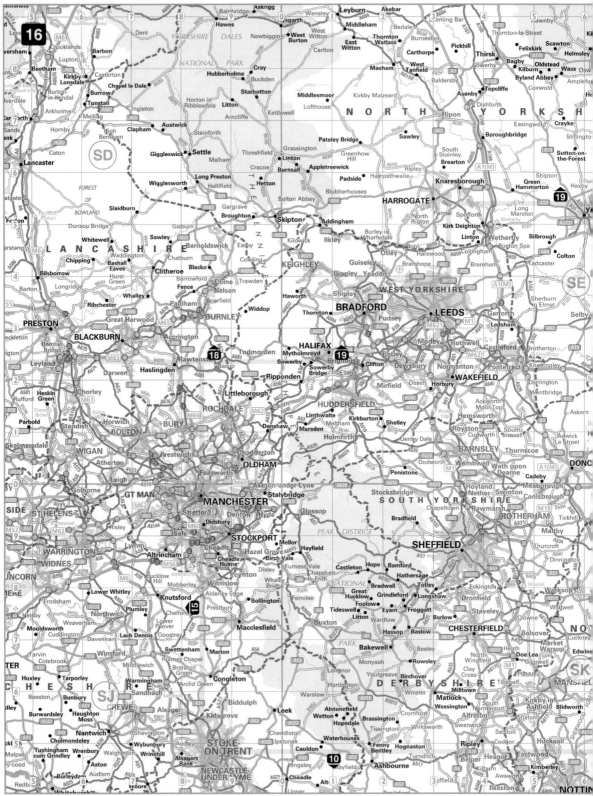

For continuation pages refer to numbered arrows

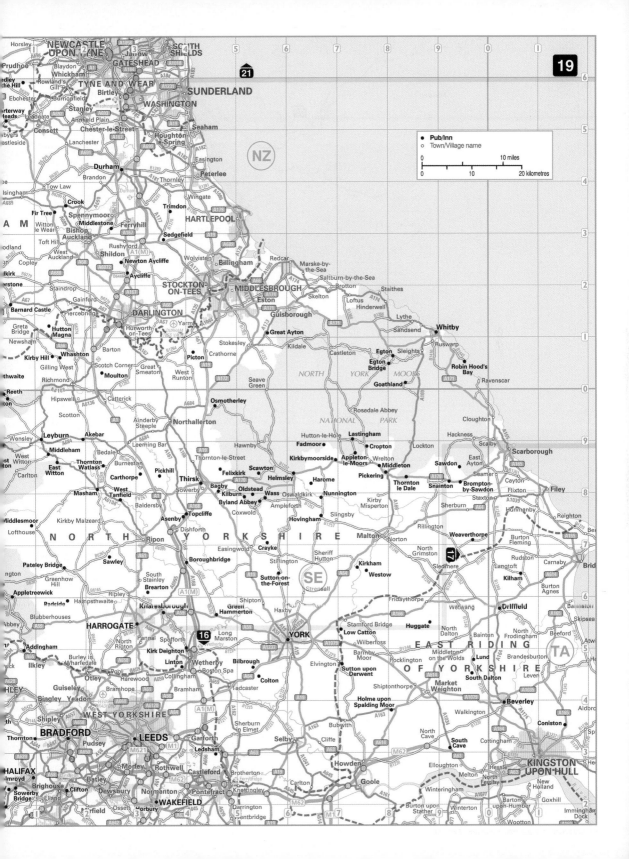

C EDIN	City of Edinburgh
C GLAS	City of Glasgow
CLACKS	Clackmannanshire
C DUND	City of Dundee
E DUNS	East Dunbartonshire
E RENS	East Renfrewshire
INVER	Inverclyde
MDLOTH	Midlothian
N LANS	North Lanarkshire
RENS	Renfrewshire
W DUNS	West Dunbartonshire
W LOTH	West Lothian

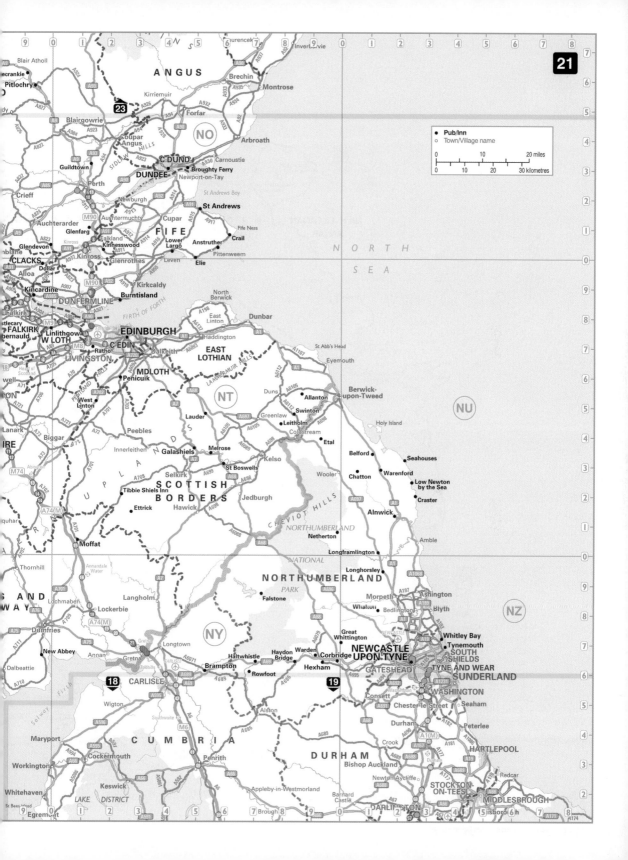

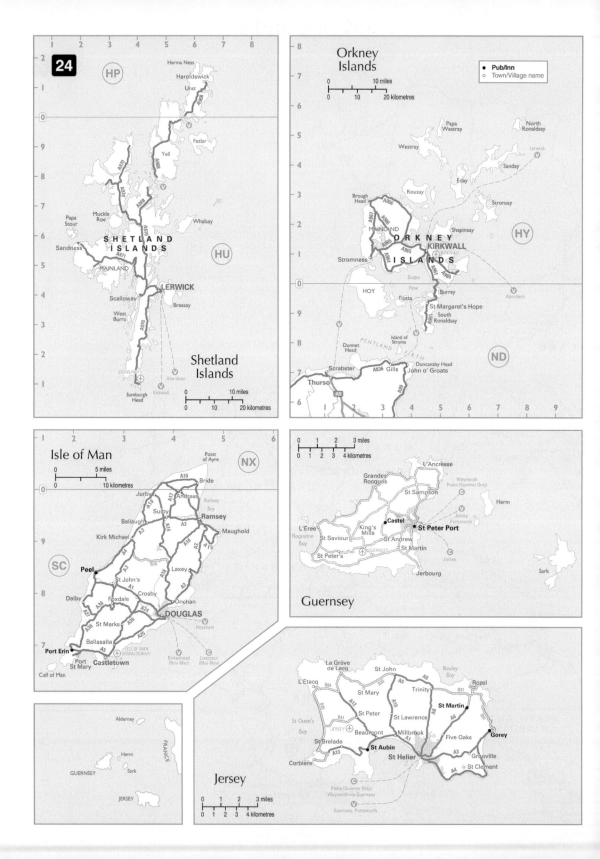

24

Shetland Islands

SHETLAND ISLANDS

MAINLAND

LERWICK

Herma Ness
Haroldswick
Unst
Fetlar
Yell
Whalsay
Papa
Stour
Muckle
Roe
Sandness
Scalloway
West
Burra
Bressay
SUMBURGH
Sumburgh
Head
Aberdeen
Kirkwall

HP
HU

Orkney Islands

● Pub/Inn
○ Town/Village name

Papa
Westray
North
Ronaldsay
Westray
Lerwick
Sanday
Eday
Rousay
Stronsay
Brough
Head
Shapinsay
MAINLAND
ORKNEY
KIRKWALL
Stromness
ISLANDS
Scapa
Flow
Burray
HOY
Flotta
Aberdeen
St Margaret's Hope
South
Ronaldsay
Island of
Stroma
Dunnet
Head
PENTLAND FIRTH
Duncansby Head
Scrabster
Gills
John o' Groats
Thurso

HY
ND

Isle of Man

Point
of Ayre
NX
Bride
Jurby
Andreas
Ramsey
Bay
Sulby
Ballaugh
Ramsey
Kirk Michael
Maughold
Dalby
St John's
Laxey
Crosby
Foxdale
Onchan
St Marks
DOUGLAS
Ballasalla
Heysham
Port Erin
Port
St Mary
Castletown
Calf of Man
ISLE OF MAN
(RONALDSWAY)
Birkenhead
(Nov-Mart)
Liverpool
(Mar-Nov)

Peel
SC

Guernsey

L'Ancresse
Grandes
Rocques
St Sampson
Weymouth
Poole (Summer Only)
Herm
L'Eree
Castel
St Peter Port
King's
Mills
Jersey
Portsmouth
Roquaine
Bay
St Saviour
St Andrew
St Peter's
St Martin
Jerbourg
Sark

Jersey

La Grève
de Lecq
St John
Bouley
Bay
L'Etacq
Rozel
St Mary
Trinity
St Martin
St Peter
St Lawrence
Five Oaks
Gorey
St Ouen's
Bay
Beaumont
Millbrook
St Brelade
Grouville
St Aubin
St Helier
St Clement
Corbière
Guernsey, Portsmouth
Poole (Summer Only)
Weymouth via Guernsey

Alderney
Herm
FRANCE
Sark
GUERNSEY
JERSEY

Central London

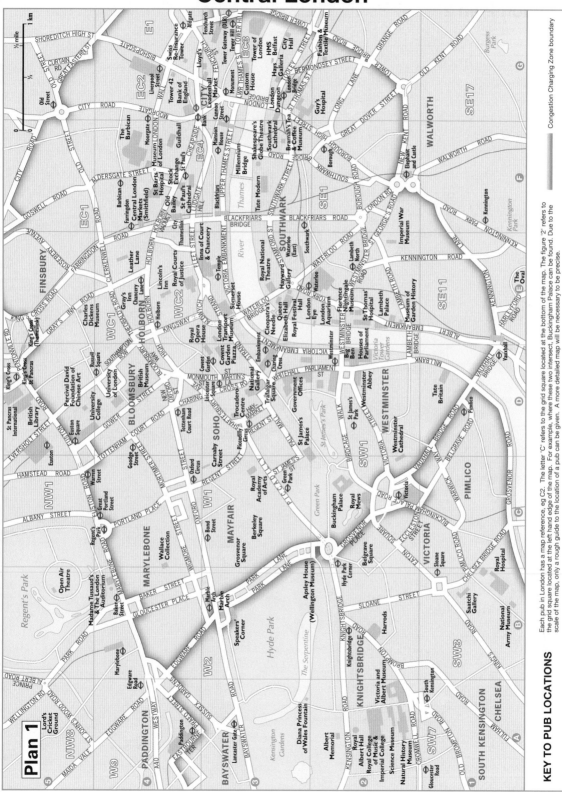

Plan 1

KEY TO PUB LOCATIONS

Each pub in London has a map reference, eg C2. The letter 'C' refers to the grid square located at the bottom of the map. The figure '2' refers to the grid square located at the left hand edge of the map. For example, where these two intersect, Buckingham Palace can be found. Due to the scale of the map, only a rough guide to the location of a pub can be given. A more detailed map will be necessary to be precise.

Congestion Charging Zone boundary

Index

Red entries are Pick of the Pubs

AA Media Limited would like to thank the following photographers and companies for their assistance in the preparation of this book.

Abbreviations for the picture credits are as follows: (t) top; (b) bottom; (l) left; (r) right; (c) centre (AA) AA World Travel Library.

1l Crown Hotel, Wells-Next-The-Sea; 1r The Black Swan, Oldstead; 2 AA/M Moody; 3 Wiveton Bell, Norfolk; 4 Falcon Inn, Denham; 5 AA/C Sawyer; 6 The Queen's Head. Troutbeck; 7t The Horns, Crazies Hill; 7c Alford Arms, Hemel Hempstead; 7b Balmer Lawn Inn, Brockenhurst; 10 Gin Trap Inn, Ringstead; 11 Jack in the Green Inn, Rockbere; 11r The Old Queen's Head, Tylers Green; 12 The Old Bull & Bush; 13tl Adams Picture Library t/a apl./Alamy; 13tr DT Ael/Alamy; 13cr The Old Bull & Bush; 14l AA/N Setchfield; 14tc Holmes Garden Photos/Alamy; 14tr Kevin Britland/Alamy; 14c Travel Scotland – Paul White/Alamy; 15 travelib prime/Alamy; 16 AA/C Sawyer; 17 Rebecca Erol/Alamy; 19 St Austell Brewery Company Ltd; 20l, 20t Hall & Woodhouse; 20bc, 20br AA/C Sawyer; 21l, 22l Everards Brewery; 22l Coniston Brewery; 22r Timothy Taylor & Co Ltd; 25t AA/C Jones; 25b AA/C Sawyer; 26/7 AA/T Mackie; 550/1 AA/D W Robertson; 580/1 Roy Rainford/Robert Harding Picture Library.

Every effort has been made to trace the copyright holders, and we apologise in advance for any accidental errors. We would be happy to apply the corrections in the following edition of this publication.

Readers' Report Form

Please send this form to:–
Editor, The Pub Guide,
Lifestyle Guides,
AA Publishing,
13th Floor, Fanum House,
Basingstoke RG21 4EA

or fax: 01256 491647
or e-mail: lifestyleguides@theAA.com

Please use this form to tell us about any pub or inn you have visited, whether it is in the guide or not currently listed. We are interested in the quality of food, the selection of beers and the overall ambience of the establishment.

Feedback from readers helps us to keep our guide accurate and up to date. However, if you have a complaint to make during a visit, we do recommend that you discuss the matter with the pub management there and then, so that they have a chance to put things right before your visit is spoilt.

Please note that the AA does not undertake to arbitrate between you and the pub management, or to obtain compensation or engage in protracted correspondence.

Date

Your name (BLOCK CAPITALS)

Your address (BLOCK CAPITALS)

Post code

E-mail address

Name of pub

Location

Comments

(please attach a separate sheet if necessary)

Please tick here ☐ if you DO NOT wish to receive details of AA offers or products   PTO

Readers' Report Form *continued*

Have you bought this guide before? ☐ YES ☐ NO

Do you regularly use any other pub, accommodation or food guides? ☐ YES ☐ NO
If YES, which ones?

What do you find most useful about The AA Pub Guide?

Do you read the editorial features in the guide? ☐ YES ☐ NO

Do you use the location atlas? ☐ YES ☐ NO

Is there any other information you would like to see added to this guide?

What are your main reasons for visiting pubs (tick all that apply)
food ☐   business ☐   accommodation ☐
beer ☐   celebrations ☐   entertainment ☐
atmosphere ☐   leisure ☐
other

How often do you visit a pub for a meal?
more than once a week ☐
once a week ☐
once a fortnight ☐
once a month ☐
once in six months ☐